Carol Ambra ✓ P9-CFE-443

SECOND EDITION

A Child's Odyssey
Child and Adolescent Development

SECOND EDITION

A Child's Odyssey
Child and Adolescent Development

PAUL S. KAPLAN
Suffolk Community College

WEST PUBLISHING COMPANY
St. Paul   New York   Los Angeles   San Francisco

♦ TO MY CHILDREN ♦

Stacey, Amy, Jodi, and Laurie

Four of a kind
Each unique

Composition: Parkwood Composition Services, Inc.
Copyediting: Deborah Cady
Cover Art: Claude Monet, *The Artist's Garden at Vetheuil*, 1880; National Gallery of Art, Washington; Ailsa Mellon Bruce Collection.
Cover Design: John Rokusek
Datagraphics: Tom Brucker, Precision Graphics
Illustrations: Rolin Graphics, Cyndie Clark-Huegel, Barbara Hack Barnett
Page Make-up: Diane Beasley

COPYRIGHT ©1986   By WEST PUBLISHING COMPANY
COPYRIGHT ©1991   By WEST PUBLISHING COMPANY
610 Opperman Drive
P.O. Box 64526
St. Paul, MN 55164–0526

All rights reserved

Printed in the United States of America

98 97 96 95 94 93 92   8 7 6 5 4 3 2

Library of Congress Cataloging-in-Publication Data

Kaplan, Paul S.
    A child's odyssey : child and adolescent development / Paul S. Kaplan. — 2nd ed.
        p.   cm.
    Includes bibliographical references and index.
    ISBN 0-314-80198-7 (hard)
    1. Child development.   2. Adolescence.   I. Title.
RJ131.K36   1991
155.4—dc20   90-20092
                                    ∞ CIP

Acknowledgments

Page 20, Fig. 1.1. From Salkind, N. J., *Theories of Human Development*, 1981, p. 37.

Page 25, Table 1.1. From Roche, J. P. Premarital Sex: Attitude and Behavior by Dating Stage in *Adolescence*, 1986.

Page 28, Datagraphic: Reprinted with permissin © American Demographics, January 1990.

Page 56, Dialogue: From Bringuier, J. C. *Conversations with Jean Piaget*. 1980, pp. 24–25.

Page 70, Fig. 2.1: Adapted with permission from *Introduction to Psychology* by D. Coon, p. 235. Copyright © 1986 by West Publishing Company. All rights reserved.

Page 119. Table 3.1: From *The Origin of Personality* by Alexander Thomas, Stella Chess and Herbert G. Birch. Copyright © May 1961 by Scientific American, Inc. All rights reserved.

Page 124, Fig. 3.5: From Scarr, S. and Arnett, J. (1987). Malleability: Lessons from intervention and family studies. In J. J. Gallagher and C. T. Ramey (Eds.), *The Malleability of Children* (p. 82). Copyright © 1987 by Paul H. Brookes Publishing Company. Reprinted by permission.

Page 136, Table 4.1: Reprinted by permission from *Human Intimacy*, by F. Cox. Copyright © 1984 by West Publishing Company. All rights reserved.

Page 152, Fig. 4.1: From Moore, K. L. *Before We Are Born*, 3rd ed., Philadelphia: W. B. Saunders Co., 1988.

Page 157, Fig. 4.2: Reprinted by permission from *Understanding Nutrition* 3rd ed. by E. N. Whitney and E. M. N. Hamilton. Copyright © 1984 by West Publishing Company. All rights reserved.

Page 172, Table 4.3: From *Cultural Perspectives on Child Behavior*. Edited by Daniel A. Wagner and Harold W. Stevenson. Copyright © 1982 by W. H. Freeman and Company. Reprinted with permission.

Page 183, Fig. 5.1: From *The Origin of Form Perception* by Robert L. Fantz. Copyright © May 1961 by Scientific American, Inc.

Page 197, Table 5.1: From *Introduction to Child Development*, 2nd ed., by J. P. Dworetzky. Copyright © 1984 by West Publishing Company. All rights reserved.

Pages 204–205, Fig. 5.3: From *The First Two Years: A Study of Twenty-Five Babies*, by M. M. Shirley. Copyright © 1933, University of Minnesota. Original edition published by University of Minnesota Press, Minneapolis, Minnesota.

(Continued after index.)

Contents in Brief

Contents

PART TWO: *Infancy and Toddlerhood*   177

CHAPTER 6 ♦ Cognitive Development in Infancy and Toddlerhood   226

PART THREE *Early Childhood*   *303*

PART FOUR   Middle Childhood   435

PART FIVE   *Adolescence*   *543*

CHAPTER 13 ♦ Physical and Cognitive Development During Adolescence   544

Preface

♦ WHAT'S NEW?

This is the first question most people ask when they are told that a new edition of a text is being published. An equally important question is *What's Not New?*, that is, what has been preserved from the older edition? To be useful, a new edition must do more than update, add new studies, and rewrite paragraphs. It must reflect the progress in the field, its new directions in thinking, and its present concerns. At the same time, it must be true to the style and general qualities that made it useful in the first place. It is this balance of change and continuity that *A Child's Odyssey*, second edition, presents.

A Child's Odyssey, second edition, retains its chronological approach to child and adolescent development. It retains its scientific outlook, research base, and coverage of important issues. It retains its extensive use of examples, its humor, and its desire to have the reader empathize with children of various ages. *A Child's Odyssey* continues to integrate an appreciation of the child's uniqueness and subjective experience with the scientific study of the principles, theories and research in growth and development.

At the same time, the second edition contains much that is new. The most effective way of demonstrating the integration of what is new with what has been retained is to look at the structure and content of the text.

Pedagogical Features

Each chapter begins with motivational true-false statements. The answers, in this edition, can be found on the following page. There is also a running glossary in the margin of the text and a summary at the end of the chapter. The definitions of all key terms are found in bold print in the margin, and a full glossary is located at the end of the text. The Action/Reaction feature, found at the end of each chapter, presents cases that illustrate various practical situations and problems.

Two new features have been added to the text. The first, called Cross-Cultural Currents describes in detail a research study conducted in a different culture or subculture. Today, there is a new emphasis on cross-cultural understanding. A number of cross cultural examples are presented in the text. However, if students are to understand the need for such research and the difficulties in conducting such studies, they must appreciate the researchers' reasoning and interpretation of the evidence. This requires a fuller presentation of some studies. Among the subjects covered in the Cross-Cultural Current feature are studies of substitute child care in Sweden, schooling in Japan, and child rearing in Kenya.

Another new feature of this edition is the Child in the Year 2000. This feature highlights one issue in each chapter that will be of growing concern as we enter the 21st century. Some of the topics covered include the future of play, gene mapping and sequencing, surrogate parenting, the age at which children should enter school, the future of non-college bound youth, and adolescent risk-taking behavior.

Content

All texts must cover the basic principles and research the field, and the second edition of *A Child's Odyssey* is no exception. As in the first edition, a number of areas which are often of great interest to both professors and students and are often given very short coverage are more extensively covered in this text including day care, child abuse, stepparenting, nutrition and educational experiences at all ages. As in the first text, familial conditions that affect child and adolescent development have been substituted for socioeconomic status. By doing so, the specific factors that affect the child can be identified.

In this edition, many content changes, aside from a general updating of information, can be found. While it is not possible to list all of these changes, the following may give the reader some idea of what is new. In chapter one, the introduction to the field of child and adolescent development, a new section describes the central issues and questions that will appear consistently throughout the text, such as the question of the importance of early experience. A new section on cross-cultural research is also included. In chapter two, perspectives on development, coverage of the information processing viewpoint has been greatly expanded and ethology is now discussed. Chapter three, genetics, includes a discussion of the genetic influence on alcoholism, much new material on Down Syndrome, as well as a new section on modern conceptions of temperament. Chapter four, prenatal development and birth, contains new information on AIDS, the use of cocaine during pregnancy, new material on stress during pregnancy, a new section on technology and birth, and research pertaining to the trend for people to become first-time parents after age thirty.

The chapters covering infancy and toddlerhood contain new information on color vision, the sense of smell, pain, brain development, breast feeding, and an important new section on parenting education progams. An entirely new section on infant emotions is presented and more emphasis is placed on understanding toddler behavior. Issues such as father participation in child care when both parents are employed, infant day care, the employed mother, and family interaction have been extensively rewritten to reflect the latest information available.

Many professors are disappointed that texts do not include any information on language development past age five. In an attempt to rectify this situation, A Child's Odyssey's full-chapter coverage of language development contains material on language development in middle childhood and even adolescence. In addition, new findings on how children learn language and more material on bilingual education are presented.

The chapters covering the period of early childhood include a new section on the changes in kindergarten, as well as new material on the appearance-reality dimension, attention, and schemata and scripts. There is much more coverage of play, specifically dramatic play and rough-and-tumble play. Interest in prosocial behavior, aggressive behavior, and interpersonal relationships during this period has grown, and much new material on these areas is included.

The middle childhood chapters discuss a number of new topics including reading and television, obesity, nutrition, basic academic skills including computer literacy, and creativity. New sections on parental agreement on child rearing, the self-care (latchkey) situation, stepfamilies and stress are presented. The coverage of divorce and single parent families has been updated to present new findings. There is increasing interest in fostering moral development and prosocial behavior and a number of new developments in these areas are described. Throughout the chapters covering early and middle childhood, the influence of television on every area of life is noted. In addition, in the chapters covering both the early and middle childhood years, new approaches to understanding the child's acquisition of gender-role are included.

The chapters covering adolescence include a new section on the health of teenagers today, eating disorders and some very challenging approaches to understanding drug use. They also present evaluations of drug and sex education, suicide prevention, cognition and contraception, and teenagers as parents. The older look at parent-adolescent relationships has been superseded by a new view that sees this period in terms of a renegotiation of relationships, and it is this new view that is presented. The adolescent's school experiences are emphasized in new sections on the junior high school/middle school and high school experience. There is also new material on gender and vocational choice and the experience of children from minority groups.

Organization

The text is organized according to chronological age and stage, with one variation. Many professors prefer to have a separate chapter on language development because the topic raises so many fascinating questions. A full chapter on genetics presents a modern perspective of how genetics affects development throughout childhood and adolescence. A full chapter is also devoted to theories.

Examples and Practical Applications

Examples are liberally used throughout the text. These examples are an integral part of the text, and the applications indicate how the principles of child and adolescent development may be used to understand and predict behavior. I am always looking for new examples which may both illustrate the point and give the reader some understanding of how the child sees and experiences the world.

Issues

Throughout the text, many controversial issues are presented. Some of these issues, such as the effects of the self-care (latchkey) situation on the child's future, infant day care and moral education are frequently discussed in the press or at the dinner table, but often without any relationship to what researchers have discovered. Even when a study is mentioned in the media, it is often presented without the qualifications that are needed to truly understand its findings. In *A Child's Odyssey*, I have attempted to present both sides of many issues, integrate the research available and point out what questions remain to be answered. Where practical conclusions can be offered, they are, indeed, presented and discussed. It is important, though, for students to appreciate child and adolescent development as a constantly evolving psychology, rather than one in which we have all the answers. Throughout the text, the contributions that research and theory make to preventing and solving problems is emphasized.

Tables, Figures and Datagraphics

This text contains a new feature called datagraphics. Instead of merely drawing a graph or presenting data, these special features pictorially represent such data in a more visually appealing manner. As in the first edition, careful attention has been given to tables and figures.

Supplemental Package

An Instructors Manual with a Test Bank written by the author is available. A Study Guide with child observation exercises written by Michael Jaffe of Kean College is also part of the instructional package.

Decisions Concerning Terminology

A word about terminology is in order. As we try to remove older connotations and more accurately describe our terminology, psychologists often update and change their terms. Unfortunately, the changes are not always adopted by everyone and both terms often remain in the literature. Many such changes are reflected in the text. For example, many authorities now use the term gender-differences and gender-roles instead of sex-differences and sex-roles, and the term self-care children is often substituted for the older latchkey children. There is also some difference of opinion as to the use of the term black or African-American. In this text, both are used reflecting the fact that, at this point, there is no agreement. In other areas, the decision has been made to use the older usage. For example, the text uses the terms sex-typing and day care, because alternative forms have yet to garner sufficient acceptance or because they are still used by the overwhelming majority of publications. Such decisions have not been taken lightly, and have been taken with sensitivity in mind.

♦ ACKNOWLEDGEMENTS

I have been fortunate, indeed, that in the planning, writing and publishing of this second edition I have received the help and encouragement of a number of truly excellent professionals at West Publishing Company. I would like to thank Peter Marshall, Laura Mezner Nelson, Jane Bacon, Angela Musey and Beth Kennedy whose expertise, commitment to the project, and contributions I greatly appreciate. I would also like to thank David Quinn and Joyce Malik of the Suffolk Community College Western Campus library for their help in obtaining some difficult to find sources for this text. I am also indebted to the professionals who reviewed this project, and offered constructive criticism. I wish to express my personal gratitude to these members of the academic community:

Nancy Coghill
University of Southwest Louisiana

David Lockwood
Humber College

Jack Demick
Suffolk University

Graham Mathews
Georgia College

Susanne Denham
George Mason University

Phil Mohan
University of Idaho

Shari Ellis
Viriginia Commonwealth University

Ligaya Paguio
University of Georgia

Rick Fabes
University of Arizona

Elizabeth Robertson
University of North Carolina-
Greensboro

Charles LaBounty
Hamline University

Judith Ward
Central Connecticut State University

Deborah Leong
Metropolitan State College of Denver

Richard Willis
Catonsville Community College

This second edition was as much a family affair as the first. I would like to thank my wife Leslie, and my daughters Stacey, Amy, Jodi and Laurie, to whom this text is dedicated, for their patience, understanding and encouragement that made the writing of this text much easier and more pleasant.

PART ONE

◆

Prospects for Personhood

Chemin montant les hautes herbes by Pierre-Auguste Renoir.

CHAPTER ONE

◆

The Study of Development

Breton Girls Dancing, Pont Aven by Paul Gauguin.

Are These Statements True or False?

Turn the page for the correct answers. Each statement is repeated in the margin next to the paragraph in which the information can be found.

1. When asked to remember a long list of toys, young children usually use more memory strategies, such as rehearsal and classification, than their parents do.
2. Children's understanding of friendship remains remarkably stable between early childhood and late adolescence.
3. If we know that a child is negotiating a particular stage of development, psychologists can predict exactly when the child will enter the next stage.
4. Children can learn to walk earlier if they are exposed to a special exercise program.
5. Today, psychologists are more likely than psychologists even ten years ago to take the position that a particular characteristic, such as aggressiveness or sociability, is due almost entirely to environmental factors.
6. Studies show that terrorists's childhood experiences are marked by hopefulness and a surprising lack of anger.
7. Children in countries with high rates of heart disease are likely to have average to low levels of plasma cholesterol in their systems, showing that children's diets have little effect on later physical problems.
8. Observation is a valid tool for conducting research.
9. Questionnaires are especially useful when a researcher wants to obtain a great deal of data in a short period of time.
10. Sweetness is the most important factor in the eating habits of children under the age of four, while familiarity is more important after that age.
11. American mothers are more likely to use their position of power and authority to get their children to do what they want than are Japanese mothers.
12. Most psychological experiments cause no physical or psychological harm to the people who participate in them.

Answers to True-False Statements

1. False. Correct statement. Young children use fewer strategies.
2. False. Correct statement. Children's ideas about friendship change greatly as they negotiate childhood and adolescence.
3. False. Correct statement. Psychologists can predict what behaviors a child may show next, but they cannot predict the exact time the child will show them.
4. True.
5. False. Correct statement. Today, psychologists are more likely than ever before to appreciate the importance of both genetic and environmental factors.
6. False. Correct statement. The childhood experiences of terrorists are filled with hopelessness and rage.
7. False. Correct statement. Children in countries with high rates of heart disease have average to high levels of plasma cholesterol, and there is considerable research linking children's diets to later health problems.
8. True.
9. True.
10. False. Correct statement. Familiarity is most important for children under four, sweetness for children over four.
11. True.
12. True.

Dear Tooth Fairy,
   Please leave ten dollars instead of one, since this tooth really hurt.

Five-year-old child and grandfather
Child: Did God make the world?
Grandfather: Yes, indeed, God made the world.
Child: Grandpa, how old were you when he did it?

A three-year-old has heard "I'll miss you" so often that now whenever anyone leaves, she pipes up with "You're going to miss me."

Scene: Moving day
Characters: Father and four-year-old son
Father: I'll pick up the heavy boxes.
Son: O.K. I'll pick up the not-so-heavy boxes.
Father: Don't say not-so-heavy, say light.
Son: O.K. I'll pick up the light boxes, you pick up the dark ones.

   "What would you do if you had two apples and four people?" I asked my five-year-old daughter, Amy.
   "That's easy, Daddy," she answered. "Just go out and buy two more apples."

A four-year-old, watching the rain pour off a car, asks, "Why is the car sweating?"

◆ CHILD DEVELOPMENT: A LOOK AT THE MYSTERY

Traveling home to New York from visiting with her grandparents in California, my daughter asked, "Daddy, will you get stripes when I get older?" After a moment's reflection, I realized she meant wrinkles. She had just become aware of the aging process.

Childhood is a time of mystery and charm. We have been led to believe that once we are adults the world of the child is permanently closed to us. In one way it is. None of us will ever again experience the first day of school or the joy on our seventh birthday when we received the toy we "always wanted." Still, our status as adults gives us an opportunity to understand that world better.

The process of development is common to all of us, and many aspects of development unfold in a predictable way. Children sit before they walk, and they walk before they run. This predictability permits the scientific study of development.

But within this predictability there is individuality. The "average child" is a myth. Each child experiences different events, and each experiences the same events differently. Some children meet life's challenges enthusiastically; others are more reluctant. Some develop quickly and dramatically; others require more time. Each child is at the same time similar to others and yet unique. It is this combination of predictability and uniqueness that ensures that the scientific study of development will never become dull.

Interest in child development is not new. Societies all over the world throughout history have provided training for their children. Indeed, interest in the moral development of children goes back thousands of years (Borstelmann, 1983). But the scientific study of children is recent, and from it we learn how children develop the skills and understandings they bring to adulthood. It also makes it possible for us to predict the changes and challenges that children face at different periods in their development, which in turn helps us take action that will help children successfully negotiate such hurdles.

Developmental Psychology: The Study of Change

The watchword for all development is change. **Developmental psychology** is the study of how organisms change qualitatively and quantitatively over time. Will scientific understanding and the predictions that it makes possible reduce the charms of childhood? Absolutely not. As researchers have come to understand the reasoning of preschoolers, a new dimension has been added to our appreciation of the child. Everyone who deals with children has favorite stories. The stories become more meaningful when one knows how curiosity and certain behaviors fit into the total pattern

Developmental psychology
The study of how organisms change over time.

Developmental psychologists study how people change qualitatively and quantitatively over time.

of a child's growth and development. On a drive through the countryside one night, my three-year-old daughter looked at the beautiful half-moon and asked seriously, "Who cut the moon in half?" She knew what happened when her mother cut her sandwich in half, so the question made sense to her.

The Nature of Change

To find out how development takes place, we must look at the way a child progressively deals with a problem or concept. For instance, how does a child develop an understanding of money? One team of researchers found that children do this in six stages (Berti & Bombi, 1981).

In the first stage, children are only vaguely aware that money has anything to do with buying and selling. In the second stage, they understand that they must pay for candy and toys, but they think all types of money are the same. To children in this stage a quarter and a dime have the same value. In the third stage, children are aware that there is some difference in money, but they don't really understand the rules for buying and selling. In the fourth stage, they understand that different items cost different amounts, and though they may know that they do not have enough money to buy something they want, they really don't understand why. In the fifth stage, children understand the value of various denominations and the correspondence between money and the price of the item. In the last stage, they understand that the storekeeper should give them back an exact amount of change along with the item.

Here we see the natural development of the concept of money. The changes are predictable in terms of the order in which they will appear. What is not predictable is the exact age at which the child will exhibit a particular stage of understanding. Anna Berti and Anna Bombi found that of sixteen four-year-olds tested, two were in stage one, seven in stage two, five in stage three, and two in stage four. Each child's individuality en-

tered into the equation. Developmental psychologists can demonstrate sequences and make some rough statements about the age distributions surrounding a behavior. For example, the average three-year-old recognizes that money is necessary to buy an item but has no idea of anything else (stage two). Most children do not achieve the last stage until age seven. However, we cannot say that a four-year old is definitely in a certain stage, since children enter and leave these stages of understanding according to their own timetable.

Categories of Change

Developmental psychologists must catalog the ways in which children change. For convenience, change can be divided into two categories— quantitative change and qualitative change (Appelbaum & McCall, 1983). Many changes are both qualitative and quantitative.

QUANTITATIVE CHANGE: HOW MUCH MORE OR LESS? The average eighteen-month old toddler uses up to 20 words, while the average two-year-old uses about 270 words. The average five-year-old understands about 20,000 words. By the age of twelve, this number has jumped to about 50,000 words. The average adolescent entering high school understands about 80,000 words (Polermo & Molfese, 1972). Any changes that involve an increase or decrease in some characteristic are considered **quantitative.** Increases in height and weight fit into this category. In short, anything that can be expressed simply as more or less of some quantity is considered quantitative.

quantitative changes
Changes considered solely in terms of increase or decrease, such as changes in height or weight.

QUALITATIVE CHANGE: A CHANGE IN PROCESS OR FUNCTION A child's understanding of money is a **qualitative** change. Money cannot be understood strictly in terms of more or less. At three, the child understands money differently from the way the child will understand it at six. Such changes are qualitative; that is, they involve a change in process or

qualitative changes
Changes in function or process.

Changes in height are quantitative changes.

function. The nature of the way children understand and use money changes.

Try this experiment. Cut out sixteen pictures from various magazines. Make certain that four pictures show food, four show pieces of furniture, four show toys, and four show items of clothing. Then ask children of various ages to remember as many pictures as they can after being given a minute or two to study them. As you would expect, the older children will remember more of the items than the younger children (Brown, Bransford, Ferrara & Campione, 1983). This is essentially a quantitative change. However, if you had observed them studying the pictures, you would have noticed a fascinating qualitative change in the strategies they used to help them remember the items (Kail & Hagen, 1982). Younger children do not make use of the categories, while older children do (Furth & Milgram, 1973).

In one study, Barbara Moely and colleagues (1969) isolated kindergarten, first-, third-, and fifth-grade students for two minutes to observe the strategies the students would use to remember a series of pictures. A clear developmental pattern emerged. At the kindergarten level, children verbalized the names of the visual stimuli but did little else. By third grade, children were testing themselves, but voluntary grouping or clustering did not begin until grade five. With increasing age, children adopt new and better memory strategies. This shows a change in the quality of their

1. TRUE OR FALSE?

When asked to remember a long list of toys, young children usually use more memory strategies, such as rehearsal and classification, than their parents do.

functioning, not just an increase or decrease in the number of strategies used or words remembered.

Qualitative changes are particularly fascinating. A child's understanding and practice of friendship, for example, change as the child grows (Selman, 1981). Through infancy and toddlerhood, friendship is defined by physical proximity or by a desire to play with the other child's toys. Three- and four-year-olds see friendship in terms of playmates. A friend is someone who plays with you. In the early school years, helping and sharing are important and a definite give-and-take is seen in children's friendships. However, they are motivated by self-interest, not mutuality. Later in elementary school a different perspective develops, and friends are now seen as people with whom children can share good times and problems. They share feelings as well as material needs. However, there is a jealousy and possessiveness here. The final stage, where friendship involves mutuality and trust develops, is seldom obtained before adolescence.

One caution must be noted here. The ages given here and throughout this text are merely reference points. They indicate only the general range during which children may be negotiating a particular stage. The sequence of stages is relatively fixed, but the ages at which children enter and leave each stage varies greatly. Again, this reflects the individuality factor noted earlier. Knowing how a child sees his or her friends, we can now predict the next progression in that child's understanding of friendship, but pinpointing the exact age at which a change to a newer conception of friendship will occur is difficult.

♦ **RECURRING THEMES AND ISSUES IN CHILD AND ADOLESCENT DEVELOPMENT**

As we explore child and adolescent development, certain themes and issues will recur. You will come to recognize these themes and issues in many different contexts throughout the text.

Theme/Issue 1 What Makes Change Occur? Heredity and Environment?

When we watch a baby begin to walk, we are seeing a being impelled toward progress. Time after time, the baby will try, fall, (perhaps cry), get up, and try again. In more subtle ways, the process goes on in a multitude of areas throughout one's life.

What causes these changes? The two mechanisms of genetics and environment are often advanced to account for changes.

MATURATION The unfolding of an individual's unique genetic plan is known as **maturation** (Hottinger, 1980). Maturation largely explains such things as the time a child's teeth erupt, a child's developing the ability to grasp objects and to walk, and the time at which a female first menstruates. The maturational process depends most strongly on the individ-

2. TRUE OR FALSE?

Children's understanding of friendship remains remarkably stable between early childhood and late adolescence.

3. TRUE OR FALSE?

If we know that a child is negotiating a particular stage, psychologists can predict exactly when the child will enter the next stage.

maturation
A term used to describe changes that are due to the unfolding of an individual's genetic plan. These changes are relatively immune to environmental influence.

Skills such as walking depend greatly upon maturation. However, the child also requires an opportunity to practice this skill.

ual's genetic master plan. This master plan, which functions as a time-table of sorts, largely (but not entirely) determines when certain events will occur. The genetic master plan may limit progress as well. For example, before a baby can walk, he or she must have the necessary strength and balance—prerequisites that are determined largely by maturation (Stewart, 1980). The child is ready to walk only when these prerequisites are met. Nutrition is also important, as is experience (Bower, 1977). Infants need the opportunity to practice their skills. Most of the time, these basic experiences are provided without too much difficulty or planning.

There is some evidence that environmental enrichment can optimize development. Infants whose parents actively exercised the child's muscles and walking reflex walked two months earlier than infants who received no training (Zelazo, Zelazo & Kolb, 1972). Yet the rate of maturation is not completely elastic. No one claims that such children can be trained to walk six months earlier.

Evidence also exists that an overwhelmingly poor environment has a disastrous effect on the rate of maturation. Children raised under very poor conditions are often retarded in many areas of development (Bowlby, 1969; Rutter, 1979), but with extra care and attention, the negative effects of a poor environment can be overcome to some degree (Clarke & Clarke, 1976). Milder levels of deprivation do not seem to have any long-lasting effect.

As we shall see in Chapter 3, genetics affects many areas of life, including intelligence, temperament, personality, bodily stature, and physical characteristics.

LEARNING AND EXPERIENCE The maturation process proceeds in much the same way for people in all cultures. Unlike the learning process,

4. TRUE OR FALSE?

Children can learn to walk earlier if they are exposed to a special exercise program.

whose course is largely determined by external events, maturation is determined largely by internal signals. Any relatively permanent changes in behavior caused by interaction with the environment are the result of **learning.** When a child recites the alphabet, imitates a brother's fear of spiders, sings along with daddy, or recognizes mommy, learning has occurred.

A child's understanding of gender roles, morality, language, and problem solving is dependent on learning. Yet we cannot see learning; we can only infer it from behavioral change. The child who solves a mathematics problem that he or she could not solve the week before is said to have learned.

In contrast to maturation, learning is extremely dependent on the environment. Children learn what they see and experience. A child whose parents habitually fight, scream at their children, and encourage their children to take an aggressive stance toward other people will learn to be aggressive. A child whose parents settle disputes calmly and encourage their children to do the same is likely to learn to settle disputes in a peaceful manner. Yet the relationship is not one to one. Peaceful and calm people sometimes emerge from traumatic environments, while a tranquil, supportive environment does not guarantee a well-adjusted child.

Parents are not the only influence on their children. As the child's social world expands, peers, teachers, television, and a host of other environmental factors influence what the child learns. Sometimes there is conflict between outside influences and what is demonstrated at home. Parents can easily control the environment of an infant or toddler, but as the child enters nursery school and elementary school, their control is reduced, and the influence other people have on the child increases. (The processes by which a child learns are discussed in Chapter 2).

THE LINK BETWEEN MATURATION AND LEARNING Learning and maturation cannot be isolated from each other. There are indeed some areas in development, such as growth, that are determined mostly, though not entirely, by one's genetic endowment. Other areas, such as using gestures to make a point, are affected mostly by learning. However, usually both genetic and environmental determinants are important in understanding behavior, and a complete understanding of human behavior must deal with both factors.

Even with such maturationally determined events as walking, some interaction with the environment is necessary, and such external factors as nutrition cannot be ignored. At the same time, to master a skill such as solving crossword puzzles, a certain degree of maturation must be attained. Reading provides a good example of the interaction between maturation and learning. Maturation plays an important role, because children cannot read until they can focus on the task for a reasonable period of time and process the necessary visual information. Learning is essential, because children must be able to recognize the letters and words and pronounce the words correctly. Development is best understood as the result of the interaction of maturation and learning.

It is clear from our discussion of the mechanisms of change that one

learning
Relatively permanent changes in behavior due to interaction with the environment.

Most psychologists would agree that this child's intellectual ability is due to a complex interaction of genetic and environmental factors.

question often asked about a particular characteristic of behavior, be it aggressiveness, sociability, or intellectual ability, is how much of it is due to genetics and how much to environment. Although there is still interest in determining the extent of genetic or environmental causation (Plomin, Loehlin & DeFries, 1985), there is a growing understanding that extreme positions in favor of either one is not in keeping with the facts (Clarke & Clarke, 1986). Most characteristics are influenced by both heredity and environment. As we shall see in Chapter 3, before we can place a numerical value on influence, we must look at the environment as well as the nature of the trait. For example, the ability to hit a baseball reasonably well is probably based upon practice, an environmental influence. However, the truly great hitters in the major leagues have excellent eye-hand coordination and other perceptual motor skills that probably have a genetic basis. Of course, practice is also important, but no amount of practice would make an average twenty-year-old without these innate abilities a great hitter. Although studies of the comparative effects of these two factors certainly will continue, the real challenge is in trying to determine the manner in which environment and genetics interact to create the individual's behavior and influence development (Schaffer, 1986).

Theme/Issue 2 How Important Is the Child's Early Experience?

There is a proverb that says the child is the father of the man. There is some truth to that. Early experience is important. Children who do not receive enough emotional care may show abnormal behavior patterns that limit later social and emotional functioning (Rutter, 1979). Indeed, the psychological makeup of terrorists has been linked to terrorists' experiences in childhood involving hopelessness and rage and a lack of non-violent role models; the only effective role models terrorists had belonged to terrorist groups. In addition, about half the terrorists studied described a life-threatening childhood illness that few in their culture survive. This led them to deny the risk of death in adulthood (Goleman, 1986).

Other studies found that aggression as well as altruism can be traced to childhood influences (Hornstein, 1976). New research also relates early nutrition as important both in later obesity and heart disease. For example, plasma cholesterol is a major factor in heart disease. In countries where the incidence of heart disease is high, children have average to high levels of plasma cholesterol, whereas in countries where the heart disease rate is lower, children have low levels of the substance (DeBruyne & Rolfes, 1989). It seems that all we have to do is look at factors in childhood to explain adult behavior.

But consider these two cases:

Boy, senior year secondary school, has obtained certificate from physician stating that nervous breakdown makes it necessary for him to leave school for six months. Boy not a good all-around student; has no friends—teachers find him a problem—spoke late—father ashamed of son's lack of athletic ability—poor adjustment in school. Boy has odd

5. TRUE OR FALSE?

Today, psychologists are more likely than psychologists even ten years ago to take the position that a particular characteristic, such as aggressiveness or sociability is due almost entirely to environmental factors.

6. TRUE OR FALSE?

Studies show that terrorists' childhood experiences are marked by hopefulness and a surprising lack of anger.

7. TRUE OR FALSE?

Children in countries with high rates of heart disease are likely to have average to low levels of plasma cholesterol in their systems, showing that children's diets have little effect on later physical problems.

mannerisms, makes up own religion, chants hymns to himself—parents regard him as "different."

Girl, age sixteen, orphaned, willed to custody of grandmother, who was separated from alcoholic husband, now deceased. Mother rejected the homely child, who has been proven to lie and steal sweets. Swallowed penny to attract attention at five. Father was fond of child. Child lived in fantasy as the mistress of father's household for years. Four young uncles and aunts in household cannot be managed by the grandmother, who is widowed. Young uncle drinks, has left home without telling the grandmother his destination. Aunt, emotional over love affairs, locks self in room. Grandmother resolves to be more strict with granddaughter since she fears she has failed with own children. Dresses granddaughter oddly. Refused to let her have playmates, put her in braces to keep back straight. Did not send her to grade school. Aunt on paternal side of family crippled; uncle asthmatic (Goertzel & Goertzel, 1962, p. xiii).

These descriptions of the early environments of two children would make it difficult for you to give a positive prognosis for their later adjustments or accomplishments in life. But the first case describes Albert Einstein; the second describes the early life of Eleanor Roosevelt, wife of President Franklin D. Roosevelt and a powerful figure in her own right. So it is apparently not so easy to make sweeping generalizations and predictions based on early childhood data. (In Chapter 12, more will be said about children who, despite experiencing poor environments, still grow up to be fine adults.)

Early experiences are important, but later experiences can compensate at least partially for poor early experiences. Children raised under very poor conditions are often retarded in many areas of development, but with extra care and attention the effects of their environment can to some degree be compensated for (Clarke & Clarke, 1976). A study of children whose early environment was very poor found that the children improved greatly when they were adopted later in childhood (Kadushin, 1976). In another study, children were observed in a mountainous, isolated area of Guatemala (Kagan, 1976; Kagan & Klein, 1973). The researchers described the infants as silent and pathetic and the three-year-olds as passive, quiet, and timid. The eleven-year-olds, however, were active, happy, and intellectually competent. The eleven-year-olds had been restricted in infancy, and adult-child interaction was minimal, but this all changed in the second year of life. When the children began to walk, their social world expanded greatly to include other children, domestic animals, and other adults. In middle childhood, the children were required to do chores and care for younger siblings. When a number of culture-free tests, such as tests involving memory and perception, were administered to the children, the researchers found that by age ten, these Guatemalan children were just as capable as American children. The effects of early experience, then, can be modified to some extent by later experience.

Psychologists often focus on early experience because most children who have a poor start continue to be victims of a poor environment throughout childhood and adolescence, resulting in poor interpersonal

New research shows the relationship between children's nutrition and their future health.

The cases of Albert Einstein and Eleanor Roosevelt demonstrate how difficult it can be to make predictions for people based on early childhood experiences.

relationships in adulthood. If children enter school already behind in certain important skills and nothing is done to help them catch up and achieve, they may fall further behind and never fulfill their potential. This may affect vocational opportunities, the nature of their social world, and their interests in adulthood. In other words, early childhood experience often seems so important because there is no change in the environment in later childhood. Where a positive change does occur, better outcomes are the rule. Of course, prevention is easier and superior to remediation, and it is best to create a good early environment for children instead of trying to reverse the problems caused by poor early experience.

Theme/Issue 3 The Issue of Plasticity

Experience, then, can change the course of development. There seems to be no doubt that the environment affects the progress of development and that positive change can be affected at every age. But just how much can a child be molded by the environment? Are there limits? These questions reflect the issue of **plasticity,** the extent to which an individual can be molded by environmental influence.

The issue of plasticity has some interesting practical implications. Imagine yourself gazing at your first-born child in his or her crib. You would like your child to grow up to be happy, have good interpersonal relationships, and optimize his or her intellectual abilities. To what extent can you help your child develop these particular characteristics? Look at intelligence for an example. You would like to help your child develop his or her cognitive (intellectual) abilities to the maximum, so you embark on a program of stimulating your child, later reading to the child, and perhaps enrolling the child in a preschool that stresses cognitive activities. To

plasticity
The extent to which an individual can be molded by environmental influence.

what extent can this treatment improve your child's intelligence and cognitive abilities? This is an important question in a society that more and more seems to emphasize early cognitive achievement. Walk into any bookstore and you will see many books on the subject of improving a child's intelligence and cognitive abilities. As we shall see in Chapters 7 and 9, although some programs have shown success, especially with children who are at risk for academic difficulties, such programs may have their drawbacks and negative consequences as well.

Are there limits to plasticity? The answer would seem to be yes, although defining such limits is difficult. Perhaps no amount of training could give an average child the intelligence of an Einstein or the musical ability of a Beethoven. On the other hand, we know that environmental stimulation and training can help children improve their intellectual skills. Plasticity is found at all ages, but it appears to decrease with age (Lerner, 1984). This would mean that generally speaking, the earlier we intervene to correct a problem, the easier it will be to correct it.

But what about the child who has not received even the basic care necessary to develop his or her cognitive skills. Can we do anything for that child? This refers to the question of reversibility, or the extent to which a characteristic can be changed once it has already been established (Cairns, 1979). For instance, what of the child who has suffered malnutrition and comes from an unstimulating environment during the early years of life? To what extent can we expect improvement if the environment is changed? As noted in the discussion of early experience, we certainly can improve the situation, but again, to what extent will this improve the child's growth and intellectual skills? Myron Winick and colleagues (1975) followed Korean children suffering from different levels of malnutrition (severe, moderate, and mild) who were adopted by the age of two by middle-class families. Winick found that all developed normal intelligence and grew well, but those who suffered from severe malnutrition were not as intelligent or as tall as those who suffered milder forms of malnutrition. The effects of even severe malnutrition after birth were to some extent reversible, though not entirely.

Plasticity, however, is a double-edged sword (Scarr, 1986). If the environment can influence individuals in a positive direction, it can also retard development. Children with great potential in some field may have an environment that prevents them from developing their talents. Consider a child who enjoys making things with his or her hands but is told by parents and teachers that this ability is inconsequential. Consider a teenage girl who is excellent in mathematics but is told by her friends and perhaps some adults that this ability does not need to be developed.

Just as in the case of early experience, there has been a shift in how we look at the issue of plasticity today. The major questions asked by developmental psychologists is not whether a particular characteristic shows plasticity, but rather, how much plasticity is shown, and at which point in life an individual shows more or less of an ability to be molded (Scarr, 1986). For instance, we know that children develop much of their language abilities during the first five years of life. The question of plasticity would ask how much of a child's language must be developed in

To what extent can this child's development be molded by his or her parents? There is no doubt that behavior is modifiable at all ages, but there may be limits to the degree to which behavior and development can be shaped.

critical (sensitive) period
The period during which an event has its greatest impact.

the early years to be certain that the child's language follows a normal pattern.

To some extent, the question of plasticity and reversibility are intertwined with the concept of **critical period** (or **sensitive period**), the period during which a particular event has its greatest impact on a person. A critical period is also the period during which a person is most susceptible to some influence (Salkind, 1981). Children develop the ability to speak their native language through the early years of childhood. But what if a child cannot hear or is isolated from other people? Will that child learn language as well as other children? Is there a critical period during which a child must learn language and how to read or develop certain cognitive skills? It is a very important concept when looking at development during the prenatal period when we know there are critical periods during which certain particular bodily systems develop. Interference with the development at these times can produce severe injury. (More will be said about this in Chapter 4.) But there may be other critical periods in life. Money and Ehrhardt (1972) found that there was a critical period for learning gender identity (whether one is a girl or a boy). They found that children who, for some reason, perhaps disfigurement or hermaphrodism, were reared as opposite their genetic sex could be switched if the switch occurred during the first eighteen months of life. However, after age three or so, this was almost impossible. There may also be a critical period for attaching oneself to a caregiver. We know, for example, that human beings who do not establish close, loving relationships in early life have difficulty doing so later.

The idea of critical periods is controversial. The concept is not as often used after the prenatal stage. When it is invoked after the birth of the child, it is often used to designate fairly long periods of time, sometimes in terms of years. The critical period for language development is indeed noted in years. The sensitive period for developing attachment for others is looked at in terms of infancy—the first year of life. We know that children who do not receive love and affection during their early years show a number of emotional problems later in life. However, even for these children, a good later environment can help reverse the problems caused by these early deprivations. Plasticity in these cases, however, is reduced with age. It is probably best to see critical periods as the time at which a child is most susceptible to change or some influence rather than some absolute time frame for development.

Theme/Issue 4 The Issue of Stability and Change

Suppose you were given all the information available on a group of infants or preschoolers. Could you predict which children would turn out to be intellectually superior, which would have difficulties in school, or which children would show behavior problems?

In our discussion of early experience, we noted that experience is cumulative, and we looked at the fact that plasticity is a double-edged sword. However, at what age could we predict whether an individual will be an aggressive teenager or adult? On the other side, if an individual was sociable and friendly as a six-year-old, could we make any prediction about the individual at age twelve or fourteen?

These questions reflect the issue of stability and change. If we could say that a particular behavior at age eight is linked to a behavior later on, it gives us the knowledge necessary to try to alter the pattern. Indeed, some constancy has been noted. Children who showed temper tantrums at eight to ten years of age were later judged to be more undercontrolled, irritable, and moody than their even-tempered peers (Caspi, Elder & Bern, 1987). There is evidence that problems in the early caregiver-child relationship in infancy may lead to difficulty in peer relationships later on (Rutter, 1987).

Yet, there is also much evidence of change. Often, the relationship between early and later behavior is positive, though very moderate or even low (Clarke & Clarke, 1986; Rutter, 1987). Many studies seeking stability in intellectual performance and personality have found very low relationships and change more common. In a major study in England, Ken Fogelman (1983) found that although there is certainly a group of children whose problems at early ages continue throughout childhood and adolescence, the general relationship between behavioral ratings at ages seven, eleven, and sixteen was low, with many troubled children at one age moving into the normal category later on. In fact, a majority of children in the extreme group (labeled deviant) had moved out of that category.

The fact is that we can find both continuity and change in development. The findings that change occurs compel us to be careful when making general statements about the future of children at different ages. Changes in environment can, to a considerable extent, change the developmental pattern. In addition, it is a mistake to view the developing child as essentially a passive object on which people operate. The child experiences the environment as an individual, and individual differences in reactions to environmental factors must be taken into account. For instance, one child will react to a stressful situation, such as divorce or family turmoil, differently than another. In addition, the child both affects and is affected by his or her environment.

RECIPROCAL INTERACTION It is far too easy to look at these themes and come to the conclusion that outside influences, parents, teachers, friends, and even psychologists act upon a passive organism, as a potter does on clay. This is not the case, for it ignores the effect the child has on these influences and people. Do you remember a child in school who was always being discourteous to others, whose health habits were poor, who was aggressive, or who did not seem to have the social skills necessary to interact with others successfully? We could look at how the other students in the class treated the child. But more correctly, we should also look at how the child's behaviors affected others. In other words, we must look at both how the child affected and was affected by others (Clarke & Clarke, 1986).

This relatively new perspective is becoming more popular with developmental psychologists. We both affect and are affected by the people around us. Spend some time observing the interactions between a parent and an infant. Perhaps the parent hugs the baby, who responds with a smile. The parent then says something to the baby, who reacts with a

There is a question concerning the stability and change of particular behavior patterns. Will aggressive children become aggressive adults?

vocalization. The baby's vocalization brings a string of verbal praise from the parent. For years, psychologists have looked at the caregiver-child relationship in terms of what the mother or father did to the child, but the effect of the child on the parent was rarely considered. Today, child development specialists look at how each affects the other.

In the preceding example, the actions of both parties served as responses and stimuli, which promoted new actions. The baby's smile stimulated the parent to speak to the child, and this in turn stimulated the baby to vocalize. The interaction proceeded rapidly, with both parties affecting the behavior of the other. We can best understand behavior by looking at the **reciprocal interactions** between the parties. The system is bidirectional, with information flowing from one party to the other and back again (Bell, 1968, 1979).

reciprocal interaction
The process by which an individual constantly affects and is affected by the environment.

This approach is very useful in understanding and perhaps predicting problems. For example, a child may be slow in developing reading skills leading his parents to react with impatience and criticism. These parental behaviors may cause the child to avoid reading or put in only the minimum effort possible. The child's reduction in effort leads to further parental criticism. A knowledgeable teacher may alert parents to the possibility that this scenario could occur and suggest other ways for the parents to react to the child's progress. Any analysis of behavior, then, must consider the effect each party has on the other.

Theme/Issue 5 Continuity and Discontinuity in Development

As noted earlier, developmental psychologists are especially good at predicting what a child who is performing some feat now will accomplish next. Although we can give averages, it is very difficult, if not impossible, to predict exactly when the next development will take place. However, how should we view this progress?

Do children develop in leaps and bounds or gradually? Consider the child who begins to speak. The child has been making other noises, including crying, cooing, and babbling. Would you consider the child's speech as just another gradual and expected improvement in vocalization coming directly from earlier abilities, or a completely different step forward in development, distinct from the vocalizations of the past?

Developmental psychologists have long debated the question of continuity and discontinuity in development. Those who support discontinuity argue that development can be seen in terms of stages, each one qualitatively different from those that came before, much like a ladder with many rungs. Children proceed from stage to stage of development just as they would climb the rungs of a ladder. Psychologists who argue in favor of continuity of development see development in terms of smooth, small steps, explained by looking at past achievements. They see no stages, but rather gradual development. You can see the differences graphically in Figure 1.1. This debate is ongoing, and some of the theorists presented in Chapter 2 will argue for a stagelike discontinuity, while others will argue that development is best seen in terms of continuity.

FIGURE 1.1: Continuous and Discontinuous Change.

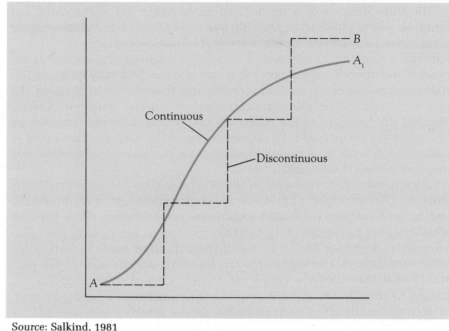

Source: Salkind, 1981

◆ DISCOVERY: RESEARCH IN DEVELOPMENTAL PSYCHOLOGY

Discovering how and why a change occurs—and describing the nature of that change—is exciting. Researchers actively seek such information through well-defined methods of data gathering and experimentation. These methods allow us not only to understand some of the mysteries of childhood but also to answer many practical questions.

One such question came to the forefront years ago when two of the best children's television shows, "Sesame Street" and "The Electric Company," were being developed (Lesser, 1976; Palmer, 1976). The question the developers of the programs asked was, How can we develop a high-quality, high-value show that preschoolers will want to watch? The developers gleaned their answers from their own experiences and from numerous studies on the needs, abilities, habits, likes, and dislikes of preschoolers.

Research in child development offers the best of two worlds: the excitement of journeying into the unknown and the structure of an established scientific discipline. While the excitement keeps researchers motivated, the discipline allows them to contribute to a larger body of knowledge. One of the researcher's goals is to produce a study that can be **replicated,** that is, reproduced by other researchers. To do so, the researcher must clearly define the subjects in the study, the manner in which the study will be carried out, and the statistical analyses used.

replication
The scientific necessity that the description of a study be so detailed that other researchers may reproduce the study.

This allows other researchers to do the study again, checking results and expanding upon the study.

Two factors allow researchers to produce useful studies. The first is access to previous research findings. We build our knowledge brick by brick, research study by research study. The second is the body of information on research methods and data interpretation. This information eliminates the need to reinvent the wheel, for it suggests plans of action that may be useful to the researcher in designing the study.

The Importance of Research Methods

Many students ask why a knowledge of research methods is important. They say, "It's the information that matters. Why worry about how the researcher got it?" But this attitude misses the point. The way a researcher obtains the information—the research methods—largely determines the legitimacy of the study's conclusions. A poorly designed study will produce invalid results.

Knowing about research methods will both allow you to understand the research presented in this text and give you a valuable technique for evaluating information. We live in an information-rich environment. Daily we read of new findings concerning parenting practices or new statistics on teenage pregnancy. Not all the studies that lead to these reports are carefully designed or unbiased. A knowledge of research methods can help you determine which information deserves your attention and which should be ignored. This is important in keeping well informed.

The knowledge gleaned from many research studies has helped make Sesame Street a success.

Choices in Research Design

Researchers have a number of methods from which to choose, and each method has its advantages and disadvantages. Researchers can simply observe the situation, or they can follow one or two children around and collect an extensive amount of data on them. They can elect to interview or survey a group of people, or they can conduct a controlled experiment.

Naturalistic Observation

No matter which method is chosen, observation may enter the picture. There are times, however, when a researcher will simply observe people in their natural environment. At such times, the researcher does not interfere but merely observes. This method is called **naturalistic observation.** For example, what if you wanted to find out how fathers and mothers in Mexico play with their children and compare it to the way American parents interact with their offspring? You might decide to watch such interactions as they occur at home, with the parents' permission. This is exactly what Phyllis Bronstein (1984) did. She arranged for observers to watch and tape record Mexican mothers and fathers interacting with their children. After entering the home, the observer would sit in a corner, taking notes and recording the session. The results? Fathers were found to be more playful with their children than mothers. Mothers were more

naturalistic observation
A method of research in which the researcher observes people in their natural habitat.

nurturant regarding their children's immediate physical needs. In addition, fathers treated sons and daughters differently. They reprimanded sons more than daughters, and they were more intellectually involved with their sons. Mothers tended to treat sons and daughters more equally. Bronstein noted that this pattern is found in many similar studies performed in the United States. Of course, no single study is sufficient to make any generalizations concerning Mexican or American parents, but this study adds to our knowledge of how parents interact with their children.

As valuable as naturalistic observation is, it presents problems. First, observers may disagree as to what they have seen. To counter this possibility, sometimes it helps to videotape the subjects being studied. Second, observers themselves may influence a subject. Would you act the same way if someone was watching you? The very presence of an adult sitting in a classroom or watching parents play with their children may cause subjects to act differently. Research shows that some subjects try to present themselves in their best light, while others may show the opposite reaction (Repp, Nieminen, Olinger, & Brusca, 1988). For this reason, observations must be conducted with an eye to blending into the background as much as possible. Third, although naturalistic observation yields interesting information, it cannot tell us anything about cause and effect. From this experiment, we can make no statement about why fathers treat sons and daughters differently. We cannot say whether some behavior in sons causes fathers to act differently, or whether some personal factor in fathers is the cause of the differential treatment. To improve observations, observers should be well trained. The behaviors they are measuring should be well defined, the subjects should be given a period of adaptation to the observer wherever possible, with the observer being as unobtrusive as possible, and the observations should be systematic and frequent (Repp et al., 1988).

Case Studies

What if you wanted to know how a fourth grader spends an average schoolday? Perhaps you could follow the child around, noting all activities for the day. You might interview parents, teachers, and friends and generally try to obtain as much relevant information as possible. A researcher following the progress of a subject over an extended period of time is conducting a **case study** (Harrison, 1979). The researcher painstakingly records the person's behavior, seeking to identify patterns. In some cases, psychological testing is performed. This approach sounds easy to many people, but after attempting it they often change their minds. Try it yourself. Spend an hour—or a day if you have the time—recording the behaviors of a child (with the parents' permission). You might focus on how the child responds to criticism or praise, or on the child's emotional state when interacting with others. The more activities there are to observe, the more difficult it is to record the behaviors. You will discover that there is a great deal more to observation than you first thought.

8. *TRUE OR FALSE?*

Observation is a valid tool for conducting research.

case study
A method of research in which a person's progress is followed for an extended period of time.

Case studies often yield interesting insights into the functioning of a particular child. For example, Giancotti and Vinci (1986) describe the case of a very depressed five-year-old. They tell about their first contact in a pediatric ward when the child was very agitated, showing jerking movements and telling his parents that "things were going to get him." They describe the background of the child, which was obtained through interviews and medical records, and record their observations and the results of psychological testing. Finally, the play and verbal therapy is described and the child's improvement is noted. In another case, Ransom and colleagues (1979) describe the case of a thirteen-year-old as her family situation changes from a single-parent family (living with her father) through the marriage of her father and the adjustment period following the remarriage.

Although a valuable technique, the case-study approach is of limited use. One can never be quite certain that the child being studied is similar to other children who are the same age or who have a particular condition. Therefore, it is necessary to do many case studies to demonstrate a common behavioral pattern, and by their very nature such observations are time-consuming and expensive. Second, the words that the observer uses in describing the subject of the case study can cause difficulties. The descriptions of the behavior may contain phrases that reflect judgment on the part of the observer. Another researcher might use words with other connotations or may describe a particular scene differently.

Case studies can be useful, though, especially to generate experimental questions which can then be looked at using other means (Wells, 1987). A particularly interesting phenomenon discovered through the use of a case study may form the hypothesis of a study using a methodology that requires the use of many subjects. In addition, case studies give us a unique and valuable look at the individual which is sometimes necessary since other methods of research rely on the group.

The Survey Method

What if you wanted to collect data from a large group of people? The case-study method is too involved for this purpose. If collecting such data is your goal, consider using the **survey,** or interview, method. In a survey or interview, researchers ask a large number of people questions about their own behavior or that of their children, and the answers are tabulated and reported. Most of us are familiar with attitude surveys, such as those conducted by the Gallup organization. Results of such surveys give public officials some idea of how people are thinking and may affect public policy.

Psychologists frequently use such instruments to collect data. The results are sometimes surprising. For example, John Roche (1986) wanted to study the attitudes of college students toward premarital sexual activity. His approach was rather interesting. In part of his study, he asked 280 young people at what point in a dating relationship they thought particular sexual activities were proper. The dating relationship was di-

Surveys are very useful if the questionnaires are constructed carefully and the sample of subjects are representative of the population the psychologist wishes to generalize his or her conclusions to.

survey
A method of study in which data is collected through written questionnaires or oral interviews from a number of people.

vided into five stages, beginning with dating with no particular affection and leading up to stage five—becoming engaged. A portion of the data is found in Table 1.1. Note that in the early stages of dating, many more males than females think that various sexual behaviors are proper. For example, 10 percent of all males believe that in stage one—dating with no particular affection—sexual intercourse is proper, while no females feel the same way. Even in stage three, dating and being in love, 43 percent of the males feel that sexual intercourse is proper, while only 28 percent of the females feel the same way. However, look at the figures for stages four and five—dating one person only and being in love and engaged. The percentages of people considering intercourse proper becomes almost identical. Roche concludes that males expect sexual intimacy earlier in a relationship, females are more likely to tie sexual intimacy to love and commitment, and that men hold more permissive attitudes towards sexuality than females do, but only in the early stages of dating.

There are problems with the survey approach. For instance, in the preceding study, it is difficult to be certain that the group of college students who received questionnaires were representative of other students their age across the nation. The researchers might be able to generalize their findings to their own community, but not any further. Second, some people just refuse to fill out the questionnaire. In this study, only about five percent refused to complete the questionnaire, but in other studies it can be a much higher figure. Those who refuse to participate in a survey may be different in some ways from those who do answer, making interpretation of the data more difficult. Third, you cannot be certain that respondents are telling you truthfully how they feel or act. Finally, it is difficult to construct a fair and unbiased questionnaire. The researcher must be quite careful about how the questions are worded. For example, imagine being asked a number of questions concerning how you discipline or punish your child. If the question is, How often do you spank your child, you might answer one way, but if the question is, How often do you beat your child, you might answer quite differently.

Surveys can be very useful because they allow the researcher to gather a great deal of data in a fairly short amount of time. Still, questionnaires must be constructed with care, the sample carefully chosen, and the interpretations cautiously made.

The Experimental Method

The research methods discussed thus far are very useful in describing a particular behavior or situation. However, they do not normally allow us to make cause-and-effect statements. If, for example, we want to state that under a particular circumstance some action, such as praise, causes some specific outcome, such as a more positive attitude toward chores, we must perform an **experimental study**. The watchword of the experimental approach is control. We must choose two groups (or more) that are equivalent and do something to one group that we do not do to the other(s). In this instance, we must control for every factor possible to make certain that the only difference between the two groups is the amount of praise that children are given.

---

9. *TRUE OR FALSE?*

Questionnaires are especially useful when a researcher wants to obtain a great deal of data in a short period of time.

---

experimental method
A research strategy using controls that allows the researcher to answer a particular question.

TABLE 1.1: Percent Believing Behavior Proper, Percent Reporting Behavior, and Percent Believing What Others Do By Dating Stage and Gender

BEHAVIOR SEX	STAGE 1 DATING WITH NO PARTICULAR AFFECTION			STAGE 2 DATING WITH AFFECTION BUT NOT LOVE			STAGE 3 DATING AND BEING IN LOVE			STAGE 4 DATING ONE PERSON ONLY AND BEING IN LOVE			STAGE 5 ENGAGED		
	Proper	Beh.	Others	Proper	Beh.	Others	Proper	Beh.	Others	Proper	Beh.	Others	Proper	Beh.	Others
Males Light Petting	17%	25%	31%	34%	50%	54%	79%	81%	93%	84%	92%	97%	93%	94%	98%
Females	1%	8%	17%	18%	26%	45%	54%	59%	83%	83%	88%	96%	90%	94%	98%
Males Heavy Petting	11%	18%	23%	23%	33%	44%	64%	68%	82%	76%	81%	94%	83%	88%	95%
Females	0%	6%	9%	9%	19%	31%	39%	42%	75%	71%	82%	94%	84%	93%	96%
Males Intercourse	10%	15%	12%	16%	18%	17%	43%	49%	62%	57%	63%	76%	70%	74%	89%
Females	0%	4%	4%	4%	11%	14%	28%	32%	53%	59%	68%	79%	74%	81%	90%
N Males	84	80	82	84	82	82	84	80	82	84	72	82	84	34	82
N Females	196	188	196	196	191	196	196	176	196	196	169	196	196	69	196

Source: Roche, 1986

The factors of an experiment that are manipulated are called **independent variables**, while the factors that are measured are called **dependent variables**. In our proposed study of the effects of praise on children's attitude toward chores, the independent variable is whether the child receives praise and the dependent variable is a measure of attitude toward chores.

Experimental research typically entails selecting a sample of subjects, randomly assigning these subjects to experimental and control groups, exposing only the experimental group to a treatment that serves as the independent variable while the other group (called the control group) is not exposed to such a treatment, and finally measuring the dependent variable and comparing the groups.

An experiment begins with a question of some interest to the researcher. The question must be worded in such a way that it can be answered experimentally. For example, What do we mean by praise? or What kind of statements can be considered praise? We must also define a way of measuring the dependent variable. All past relevant research must be searched to learn what is already known about the question. This ensures that our research rests on solid ground. It also would allow us to make hypotheses (educated predictions) about what will happen in our experiment.

Now we are ready to choose our sample. We must decide what characteristics we wish our sample to have. Do we want to use children of just one age group? Does it matter if the children live in a house or an apartment? Does it matter if they have siblings or if they are only children? Each decision is important, for if we find that praise causes an improvement in attitude towards chores, we must limit our conclusion

independent variable
The factor in a study that will be manipulated by the researcher.

dependent variable
The factor in a study that will be measured by the researcher.

according to the characteristics of our sample. If we used eight-year-olds, we cannot say that the same thing would necessarily be true of teenagers. Since we want both the experimental group and the control group to be similar, we would try to assign children randomly to either the praised or the nonpraised group. Each child chosen for the experiment has the same opportunity to be placed in the experimental group and receive praise or in the control group and not receive praise. We tell the parents in the praise group to praise their children when they do their chores or to make positive verbal statements about their chores, while we instruct the parents in the nonpraise group not to do so. After a stated amount of time, the researcher evaluates the groups on the dependent variable—attitudes towards their chores. If significant differences exist, we can then make a causal statement that praise caused an improvement in attitude towards household chores. The reasoning is simple. Random assignment allows us to say that both groups were the same at the beginning of the experiment, and because the only difference was the treatment (praise), any differences at the end must be due to the treatment.

Experiments may be designed differently. Some experiments do not use a control group, but rather compare two groups that have been treated differently. For example, a group of children who receives one type of breakfast may be compared to a group who receives a different breakfast on some variable. However, experimental studies all need to control the environment and manipulate particular factors within the environment. To illustrate this, let us take the problem of getting young children to eat their vegetables. Most parents have watched their children subsist on candy and french fries while avoiding anything that contains either vitamins or minerals. In one way, this makes sense. Brussels sprouts and green beans don't compare well to potato chips and ice cream. In addition, these high-calorie, low-nutrition foods are more likely to be advertised on television and to be attractively packaged in the supermarket.

How can parents encourage their children to eat a somewhat balanced diet? Many researchers have observed the food preferences of children. In fact, Leann Lipps Birch (1979) found that familiarity and sweetness were the most important factors in choosing food. Familiarity is most important for children under four, while sweetness becomes the primary factor for children above that age. In another study, Birch (1980) attempted to understand the effects other children might have on the food preferences of preschoolers. First, the food preferences of thirty-nine preschool children were assessed for nine vegetables, including carrots, celery, peas, and cauliflower. For four consecutive days, a child who preferred one vegetable to another was seated with three or four children who preferred a different vegetable. For example, a child who had ranked cauliflower last was seated with children who rated it number one. After a while, the child who did not originally favor the vegetable was greatly influenced by the food preferences of the other children and began to select the nonpreferred vegetable. The child not only chose it but also actually ate it. The results were lasting. Weeks later, children continued to choose and eat their originally nonpreferred food. The food preferences of younger children were more easily modified than those of older chil-

THE CHILD
IN THE YEAR
2000

Looking Ahead

Predicting the future is a national obsession. Every year, books are published predicting some aspect of our future lives. As our world changes at a faster rate, predictions become even more difficult. In less than a decade we enter the twenty-first century. How will life differ for children as we enter the next century? As the chapters of this book unfold, we will try to look into the early part of the next century and predict some of the changes.

Some changes are already becoming apparent. Our new knowledge in genetics and biotechnology will allow greater testing for genetic difficulties. There will be new hope for those who have difficulty conceiving. New ways of predicting the possibilities of birth defects are now being developed, and it may become common for expectant mothers to undergo genetic counseling and various prenatal tests.

After an infant is born, new ways to evaluate the infant will allow psychologists and doctors to better diagnose possible future problems and provide a variety of intervention techniques to help the infant develop normally. In addition, at the present, about half of all mothers with infants are in the labor force. There is reason to believe this trend will continue, making infant day care an important issue.

By the year 2000, some school districts will open their doors to three-year-olds, and a few may even require attendance at that age. An issue now being debated is how early children ought to begin to attend school and what activities children in preschools should participate in.

The schoolage child will find changes, too. Students will find a curriculum somewhat more rigorous than that of the generations that preceded them. Comparisons in achievement will be made not only with their peers within this country but with other children around the world. This will lead to increasing pressure to achieve in school.

Adolescents will also face a world that is changing more quickly, making vocational choices somewhat more difficult. In addition, it is doubtful that the current drug problems and health problems such as AIDS will be conquered, although new approaches may help. Changes in values and attitudes may be altered by these problems. We will also know much more about nutrition than we do now do, and some of our present nutritional ideas will certainly change.

In the area of family life, there may be changes in the way fathers see their role, and the question of just how involved fathers will be in the raising of children will be interesting to watch. The changing family itself is a focus of interest. We used to think of the traditional family in terms of an employed father, a full-time homemaker/mother, and two children. However, the number of so-called nontraditional families that comprise single-parent families, stepfamilies, and two-parent families with employed mothers far exceeds the number of "traditional" families. The child in the year 2000 is far more likely to live in a "nontraditional" family, to need to take care of himself or herself, and to have to deal with more complex family relationships.

Society itself will show some changes. Gender stereotypes may become less profound as roles change, and many more people will be bilingual, a fact that has educational implications.

In "The Child in the Year 2000" features that follow, we will look at the nature of all these changes and try to examine the implications and challenges for children. It is popular to be somewhat pessimistic about changes, but such pessimism is unwarranted. There is no doubt that life for children will be more complex, but it also will bring new opportunities, while research findings will provide an increased knowledge of how to meet the needs of children at every age.

dren. In addition, older children had a greater effect on the food preferences of younger children, perhaps because the older children were bigger and more respected. This study demonstrates that children's food preferences and their actual eating habits can be influenced by exposing the children to peers whose food preferences are different. It offers the hope

10. TRUE OR FALSE?

Sweetness is the most important factor in the eating habits of children under the age of four, while familiarity is more important after that age.

correlation
A term denoting a relationship between two variables.

that exposing a child to others who eat a greater variety of foods may encourage the child to eat a more varied diet.

Experimental studies are often difficult to perform, since a researcher must exercise such great control over the environment. However, the effort is often worth the extra trouble, since only experimental studies can demonstrate cause-and-effect relationships.

Correlations

Often researchers involved in collecting and analyzing the data wish to discover the relationships between two elements in the environment. For example, there is a relationship between scores on intelligence tests and school achievement. Higher intelligence scores are related to higher achievement levels in school. Researchers use the term **correlation** to describe such a relationship. A correlation can be positive, negative, or zero. A positive correlation indicates that relatively large scores on one factor are associated with large scores on another and relatively small scores on one factor are associated with small scores on another. As intelligence increases, so does academic achievement. A perfect positive correlation is written +1.00. A negative correlation indicates that as one factor increases, the other decreases. A perfect negative correlation is written −1.00. For example, we may find a negative correlation between misbehaving in class and grades on a child's report card: the greater the misbehavior, the lower the grades. A zero correlation indicates that there is no relationship between the two factors; for example, there is no relationship between the color of a child's hair and the child's intelligence.

Most correlations are far from perfect. The correlation between scores on an intelligence test and achievement in school as measured by grades hovers between .50 and .60, which is high but not anywhere near perfect (Kubiszyn & Borich, 1987). Other factors besides intelligence, such as

DATAGRAPHIC

More Younger Children; Fewer Older Ones

Source: Reprinted with permission of *American Demographics*, January 1990.

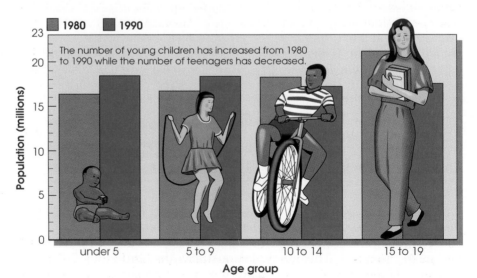

motivation and perserverance, are involved in school success. The important facts to remember about a correlation is that it tells us that a relationship exists, the direction of the relationship (whether it is positive or negative), and the magnitude of that relationship. It does not establish cause and effect.

Cross-sectional and Longitudinal Designs

Developmental research is often concerned with measuring change over time. We may be interested in discovering how children of various ages perceive their parents or how they approach various problems. If you were an investigator interested in the first topic, you could find groups of eight-, ten-, and twelve-year-olds, measure their perceptions of their parents, and compare their perceptions. This is an example of a **cross-sectional** design (see Figure 1.2). On the other hand, you could use a group of eight-year-olds and measure how they perceive their parents today, then wait until they are ten and measure their perception of their parents again, then wait another two years and do it a third time. This is an example of **longitudinal** design (see Figure 1.3). Both methods are popular, and each has advantages and disadvantages.

CROSS-SECTIONAL STUDIES Cross-sectional studies are easier to perform. Groups of different-aged subjects are tested at the same time, and the results are compared. In one study, children ranging from four to eight years of age were told a story about two boys, one of whom can steal some candy from the other (Nunner-Winkler & Sodian, 1988). One of two endings was used. In the first ending, the child is tempted to steal the candy but does not, while in the other, the child does steal the candy. Subjects were asked how the child felt who either stole the candy or resisted the temptation. About three quarters of the four-year-olds and 40 percent of the six-year-olds judged the boy to feel good after stealing the candy, whereas 90 percent of the eight-year-olds thought that the child would experience negative emotions. In the condition in which the child resisted temptation, the results were not as clear-cut, with 59 percent of the four-year-olds, 74 percent of the six-year-olds, and 41 percent of the eight-year-olds believing that the child who resisted temptation would feel negative emotions. The four-year-olds justified the wrongdoer's feelings on the basis of the success of his action (taking the cookie), while the eight-year-olds focused on the moral value of the wrongdoer's action. This study showed a clear developmental change from an outcome-oriented morality (judging the emotions of the wrongdoer according to his or her success) to a morally oriented judgment. Most four-year-olds, though aware that the behavior was wrong, still believe the wrongdoer will experience positive emotions, but few eight-year-olds do.

Cross-sectional studies are useful, but they have their faults. It is difficult to understand the growth and decline of any attribute over an extended period of time, because the same people are not being followed (Nunnally, 1982). In addition, when comparing subjects who differ significantly in age, the effect of growing up in a different generation must

cross sectional study
A research design in which people at different ages are studied to obtain information about changes in some variable.

longitudinal study
A research design in which subjects are followed over an extended period of time to note developmental changes in some variable.

FIGURE 1.2: Cross-sectional Studies
In a cross-sectional study, children of different age groups are tested at the same time
and their scores on some measure compared.

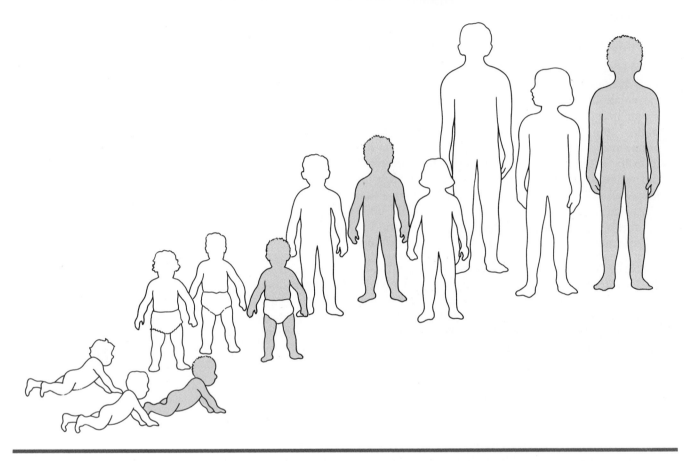

cohort effect
The effect of belonging to a particular generation and of being raised in a historical time.

be taken into account. This is known as the **cohort effect**. Suppose you were noting the differences between fifteen-year-olds and five-year-olds on some measure of attitude. You obtain your data and analyze it. You interpret the differences between them as age related. But it is also possible that the differences are caused by generational or cohort differences (Forman & Sigel, 1979). Certain social, political, or natural events in one generation may not be repeated during the life span of the next. For example, the Great Depression of the 1930s, World War II, the rediscovery of poverty and racism in the 1960s, and the Watergate scandal in the 1970s were events that may have affected one generation and not another. The Vietnam War had a tremendous effect on teenagers growing up in the late 1960s and early 1970s, but it is only history to the younger generation today. It is difficult to screen out such cohort effects.

FIGURE 1.3: Longitudinal Studies
In a longitudinal study, researchers test the same children over a period of time.

LONGITUDINAL STUDIES Longitudinal studies are not as easy to execute as cross-sectional studies. Subjects must be followed over some period of time and retested at stated intervals (Schaie & Hertzog, 1982). Longitudinal studies have been described as the lifeblood of developmental psychology (Appelbaum & McCall, 1983). They allow scientists to identify changes within subjects over age. Such questions as, Do obese children become obese adults? and Do aggressive children remain aggressive into adulthood?, can best be studied using longitudinal research designs.

In one longitudinal study, Nancy Eisenberg-Berg and Karlsson Roth (1980) tested a group of preschoolers from age forty-six months until they were sixty-four months of age to discover changes in how children reasoned about helping others. Subjects were interviewed twice—at the beginning of the experiment and eighteen months later. The researchers found an interesting developmental change. As children aged, they became more concerned with the needs of others and less with the question of whether they would get something in return for their efforts.

Longitudinal studies also have weaknesses. They are more time-consuming, and maintaining contact with subjects over the long term is difficult. Some subjects move away; others simply do not return their questionnaires at various testing periods, leaving the researcher with incomplete data. It is difficult to determine whether those who drop out differ from those who remain throughout the study.

Another problem is the effect of practice and retesting in a longitudinal study (Blanck, Rosenthal & Snodgrass, 1982). Let's say you want to measure the changes in intelligence over the years. If you use the same or a very similar test, the children might become wise to the test and show an improvement simply as a result of practice. On the other hand, using different measures may create problems, because one measure may not be directly comparable to another. As with the cross-sectional approach, the cohort effect should be taken into account. Longitudinal studies performed thirty years ago are interesting, but they may be confounded by specific generational problems, and such studies have to be updated.

Researchers are constantly looking for ways to improve their experiments. Some have suggested mixed models that have both longitudinal and cross-sectional components. For example, one could look at the political opinions of five-year-olds and eight-year-olds and test subjects in both groups every year for four years.

Cross-cultural Research

As you see, no research method is perfect, and each has advantages and disadvantages. We have assumed that the researcher is performing the research in his or her own cultural setting with no language difficulties, though this may not be true. More and more research is being performed in other cultures. Conducting research in different countries presents new problems and opportunities. Even executing research studies in one's own nation on subgroups or minorities whose culture differs can be difficult. Cross-cultural studies are important and valuable if we are to extend our understanding of human development past our own borders (see the Cross-Cultural Current on page 34). Some researchers even argue that unless we look at other cultures it is not possible to make any serious systematic attempt to understand human behavior and development, perhaps because our own cultural biases get in the way (Heron & Kroeger, 1981).

Cross-cultural studies yield many benefits. They help us extend and test theoretical approaches. For instance, a very prominent theorist of intellectual development, Jean Piaget (whose theory we will look at in some detail in the next chapter), believes that the sequences of cognitive development are invariant—that is, children progress from stage one to stage two to stage three in order, without regressing or skipping any stages. Most cross-cultural studies confirm this part of Piaget's theory (see Dasen & Heron, 1981).

Sometimes cross-cultural studies can help us separate one variable from another (Triandis & Brislin, 1984). Let us say we find cancer rates very high in one part of the world and lower in another. We want to know whether this is due to some genetic difference or to some factor in the environment, perhaps diet.

One way to determine this is to follow people from this low-cancer-rate area who move to a higher cancer rate area and see what happens to their cancer rate. If it increases significantly, we can presume that some environmental factor is involved and look for it.

Cross-cultural research also allows researchers to discover how people from other cultures handle their problems and develop. For example, a study of how Japanese and American mothers handle certain daily problems showed an interesting difference (Hess et al., 1986). Japanese mothers were more likely to appeal to feelings—for example, asking children "How do you think I will feel if you don't eat those vegetables?, while American mothers were more likely to use appeals of authority or power, such as, "I told you to eat those vegetables."

Cross-cultural research also widens our perspective and may serve to increase understanding between people and to reduce prejudice. We sometimes think that the way things are in our own country is the way they are throughout the world, but research on competition and cooperation, aggression, fathering, education, and gender differences and stereotypes have shown that this is not true (Adler, 1982).

Last, there is a tendency for people to be so centered on their own culture that they do not recognize the fact that children in other cultures can be ahead or behind on some characteristic, depending upon their environment and culture. It is especially important to look into the context of development to understand why a child develops in a particular manner (Rogoff & Morelli, 1989). We can truly appreciate the importance of environment and culture and reduce our cultural isolation by looking at development in other cultures. Children from Western developed countries are not always ahead. Gustav Jahoda (1983) investigated children's understanding of the concepts of profit in Great Britain and Zimbabwe, a country in southern Africa. Trading for profit is very rare among young children in Great Britain but very common in Zimbabwe. As a result, Zimbabwe children were well ahead of British children on the knowledge of profit and trading. Interestingly, this was true whether or not the Zimbabwe children had engaged in trading. In other words, the society was structured so that the concept was commonly learned very early in life.

Cross-cultural research presents unique problems, however. Accurate translation is one problem. Devising measuring instruments that can be used across cultures is another. The most serious problem, however, is that a concept may have one meaning in one culture and another in a different culture. For example, achievement in Western developed nations like the United States and Canada is an individualistic concept, while in some South Pacific islands it has meaning in a group context, where achievements can be shared for the mutual benefit of everyone in the group (Gallimore, Weiss & Finney, 1974).

Even with these problems, cross-cultural research studies make valu-

11. TRUE OR FALSE?

American mothers are more likely to use their position of power and authority to get their children to do what they want than are Japanese mothers.

Cross-cultural research is becoming more important as its value becomes appreciated.

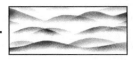

A Case of Misunderstanding

Imagine that you are a nurse or a dietician trying to influence a parent to administer a particular treatment or change a child's diet. Now consider the fact that the parent's roots are in a different culture from yours. How would the parent's cultural background affect the translation of your instructions into action?

The importance of a different cultural background is often misunderstood. Consider the following situation. A Vietnamese mother comes into the doctor's office accompanied by her one-year-old daughter. The physician rises and through an interpreter asks the mother what ails her child. The woman and the doctor both sit down. The doctor takes a relaxed position, sitting with his legs crossed, and smiles at the woman. To put the woman at ease, the doctor compliments her on her beautiful child, then continues asking about the child's symptoms.

It sounds simple and efficient, but the doctor has made so many mistakes and insulted the client so badly that his effectiveness may well be compromised.

Since 1975, more than 750,000 refugees from Southeast Asia have resettled in the United States. As with all new minorities, their culture is misunderstood by many well-meaning professionals who are responsible for providing them with vital services.

The doctor innocently believed he was acting correctly when he asked about symptoms, complimented the child, and sat in a relaxed position. But all three actions can cause problems. First, among Southeast Asians it is considered impolite to ask direct questions immediately. People first make small talk, asking about the entire family and the like, before getting down to business. Second, complimenting a child on her beauty or health may be a problem if the parents come from a rural village in their home country. They may fear that a lurking evil spirit will hear the praise and take the child away. In some villages, children are not named until two years of age because giving the child a beautiful name may draw the jealous attention of the evil spirit. Third, if the patient is Laotian, crossing one's legs and allowing a toe to point toward the patient is considered an insult.

This brings up another problem. We tend to characterize all people who come from Southeast Asia as one group, but this is incorrect. Language, customs, and traditions differ widely among the Vietnamese, Cambodians, Laotians, and Thais. In one incident, a doctor, Marianne Felice, asked a Vietnamese interpreter to talk to a Laotian youth. The Vietnamese interpreter "indignantly" announced that he

---

able contributions to developmental psychology. Although in the past these studies emphasized the differences among cultures, today we are just as interested in discovering similarities among cultures (Heron & Kroeger, 1981).

◆ ETHICAL CONSIDERATIONS IN RESEARCH

Ethical problems arise whenever research is performed. In most universities today, committees review the ethics of each research proposal involving animals or human beings (Cooke, 1982). Many professional organizations, including the American Psychological Association (1973) and the Society for Research in Child Development (1977), have published guidelines for protecting subjects. The federal government has also published such standards (National Commission for the Protection of Human Subjects of Biomedical and Behavioral Research, 1977).

was Vietnamese and "stormed away." Later, Dr. Felice was told that if she had asked the Vietnamese interpreter to translate for a Cambodian patient it would have been worse, because these two countries have been at war for centuries.

Appreciating the differences between these groups is crucial to understanding the behavior of the people who come from the diverse cultures. For example, in Thailand a person who is angry at another does not show anger directly. Instead, the person may turn toward another object or person and scold it or him or her. A doctor must then understand that the words directed toward a dog or a child in his presence may actually be directed at him. Although people from Southeast Asia are likely to forgive Westerners for their bad manners and chalk it up to ignorance, they may still be offended.

Anyone studying child development must also deal with cultural differences. For one thing, we lack good baseline data concerning growth and physical development for Southeast Asian children. No accurate growth curves are available, although work is proceeding on them. Parent-child interactions may also differ. For instance, most American children play pat-a-cake with their parents, but this game is not played in Southeast Asian families. Linguistic differences remain a problem too; for example, asking questions about the color of something can cause problems. In Vietnamese, the word for blue and green is the same, so if you ask what color the sky or a leaf is, the same word will be used to describe both.

Diet and folk medicine raise other problems. Especially in Vietnamese culture, good health is considered to be a perfect equilibrium between hot and cold elements; too much of one or the other is said to cause illness. Diarrhea is attributed to an excess of the cold element, while pustules are related to an excess of the hot element. Drugs and herbs are classified into hot and cold categories, too. Ginger is hot; ginseng is cold. Western medicines are hot; water is cold. Giving water to a patient who is already "cold" is considered poor medicine, and diets are carefully balanced according to this theory of hot and cold.

All this shows that we must take culture and background into account when dealing with people. In addition, assuming that people from Southeast Asia or, for that matter, people who come from Africa or South America are the same is likely to lead to misunderstandings. Even if people come from the same country, the region where they live can make a difference. People who come from cities, agricultural areas, and mountain regions often have different beliefs, practices, and educational backgrounds. If we understand the cultural background of the people we are dealing with or studying, we can develop an appreciation for and a sensitivity to their perceptions of the world, and we can avoid mistakes that contribute to disharmony among people.

Source: M. Felice (1986). Reflections on Caring for Indochinese Children and Youths. *Journal of Developmental and Behavioral Pediatrics* 7, pp. 124–128. K. N. Olness (1986). "Reflections on Caring for Indochinese Children and Youth," *Journal of Developmental and Behavior Pediatrics* 7, pp. 129–130.

Should This Study Be Performed?

Children are continually frustrated in their attempts to reach a toy while a researcher notes their anguished responses. They show a great deal of discomfort. Should experiments that cause such adverse emotional reactions be performed?

A scientist wants to find out whether a particular vaccine will harm an unborn child, in order to determine whether it is safe to give pregnant women. The scientist contacts women who have decided to abort their fetuses and asks permission to inoculate them with the vaccine. After the abortion, the fetuses will be examined for abnormalities. Is such experimentation on the fetus ethical?

A researcher tells a young adult that the purpose of a study is to discover the effects of punishment on learning. One subject will serve as the teacher, first reading a list of word pairs and then testing another subject, who is the student. If the student does not answer correctly, the teachers throws a switch, delivering a painful shock. In reality, no one is receiving any shock at all. The researcher is really seeking to discover whether people will perform potentially damaging actions when encouraged to do so by an authority figure. The subjects have been told a lie, and the researcher is actually studying obedience, not punishment. Is it ethical to lie to a subject? (Milgram, 1963)

Most psychological experiments cause no physical or mental harm. Research studies that contain anything even remotely considered dangerous are rare. However, in the history of psychology some controversial experiments have been performed, and constant vigilance is required. For example, Watson and Raynor (1920) conditioned a nine-month-old baby named Albert to fear rats by presenting a rat followed by a loud noise. After a number of such pairings, Albert feared not only rats but other furry objects as well. Watson did not bother to decondition Albert to the fear, despite a month's advance notice that Albert would be leaving the hospital (Harris, 1979). Was it ethical to condition fear in Albert? Shouldn't Watson have attempted to decondition the baby? The first question could be argued, but Watson definitely was responsible for deconditioning Albert.

In another experiment, Wayne Dennis (1935) sought to discover the effects of environmental deprivation on the development of motor skills. He raised twin girls in an unstimulating environment, where they were given no toys and little attention, and found that they made very slow progress. As a result, Dennis began to appreciate the importance of practice and stimulation on motor development. When the study was over, he gave the girls special attention and training, and they improved, but they still suffered from some problems. Was this experiment really ethical?

Such experiments would probably not pass the muster of ethics committees today. Most researchers are quite concerned about the possibility of harm and seek to minimize or eliminate it. The two most common ethical problems in psychological experimentation today involve the issues of informed consent and deception.

Informed Consent

Ideally, subjects should be told specifically what is expected of them and be encouraged to decide for themselves whether or not they wish to participate in a study. Federal guidelines specify many important features of informed consent (Cooke, 1982). The subjects should be told the purpose of the research, the procedures involved, and the risks and benefits and be presented with a statement noting that they are free to withdraw from the study along with an invitation to ask questions about their participation. Some studies involve small children who naturally cannot give their permission. In such a case, the study is explained to the parents, who then consent to the child's participation. It is assumed that the parents are both capable and responsible for making decisions that are in their child's best interests. If the child is above seven or so, the child's consent should definitely be obtained (see Cooke, 1982). However, the researcher should try to get the permission of children even younger than seven. Often, however, young children have difficulty understanding the

---

12. TRUE OR FALSE?

Most psychological experiments cause no physical or psychological harm to the people who participate in them.

research process, and their limited cognitive abilities do not allow them to understand fully their rights, especially their right to withdraw from the study (Thompson, 1990).

Sometimes the assumption that parents always act in their children's best interest can be questioned. The parents of one severely learning disabled child refused to enroll the child in a special experimental program that might have yielded both valuable research information and great benefits to the child. No injury could have occurred, and the enrichment might have helped the child. But the parents' suspicion and pride led them to refuse to give their consent, and the child was denied a potentially splendid opportunity.

Deception

The most serious ethical problem confronting researchers today is deception. Some researchers argue that they cannot always inform subjects about the true objectives of their study. If they do, the subjects may alter their behavior to match the desires of the researcher. What if the researcher wants to determine whether the gender of the author of a composition would affect students' evaluations of the work. The researcher may tell the subjects that the study is concerned with the content of the story itself and not even mention the name of the author, which appears at the top of the page and clearly reflects the writer's gender. Is this deception warranted? Today, sexism and racism are not fashionable, and if psychologists are to study these areas, subtle deceptions may be necessary. Other psychologists disagree, arguing that deception is morally wrong and harmful to the profession (see Baumrind, 1985).

This difference of opinion among researchers will continue. Those researchers who use deception take on themselves extra responsibilities. After the study, subjects must be informed as to the study's true nature. It is necessary to look into the possible impact on the subject's self-esteem, feelings towards authority figures, and alienation from society, especially for subjects who already perceive themselves to be rejected or alienated from society (Fisher & Tryon, 1988). In addition, during the study, subjects may acquire knowledge that may trouble them, and researchers must provide help for subjects trying to work through what they have learned about themselves (Holmes, 1976a, 1976b).

In a very important article, Ross Thompson (1990) notes that children of different ages are vulnerable to different types of problems. For example, challenges to a child's self-concept are likely to become more stressful with age. If a study purports to find a child's intelligence, the discovery of the score will affect a child of school age more than it will a younger child. On the other hand, a very young child is more likely than an older child to be stressed if separated from an adult. In addition, special risks are taken when we do research on children who are disabled or show some behavioral problem. We must continue to be aware and sensitive to the way children experience the research process. We also need to minimize the stresses for children who participate as part of the field's commitment to establish and maintain standards for the decent treatment of children who are subjects of experiments.

◆ DEVELOPMENTAL PSYCHOLOGY: WHAT'S IN IT FOR ME?

Whenever one approaches a new subject, it is natural to ask about its relevance. "What's in it for me?" is a common question and deserves an answer.

Personal Benefits

Most people marry and raise children. A better understanding of children can lead to a greater appreciation of the problems and potential of children and enable parents to experience more fully the joys of parenting. For example, an understanding of cognitive (intellectual) development may help parents appreciate why their child enjoys a particular game. Very young children enjoy playing peek-a-boo because they are just learning that people still exist even though they can't see them. The child generates an expectation that the parent is still there, which is subsequently validated. When the child sees that the expectation is correct, the child reacts with glee. This reaction means much more to the parent who understands how a child is perceiving the game.

An appreciation of where the child is in the developmental cycle can enable parents to help their children. Knowing what skills are necessary for reading would help a parent understand the best time to begin a particular activity related to learning to read. At the same time, warning signs can be spotted and remedial action taken. In one case, a nine-month-old had stopped babbling. The parents suspected that their child might be suffering from a hearing problem, took the child for a checkup, and discovered that they were correct.

Careers in Working with Children

People who work with children, including teachers, mental health personnel, nurses, nutritionists, child-care workers, nursery school personnel, parent educators, and playground supervisors, need a knowledge of child development. The practical possibilities are endless. For example, teachers could avoid much frustration by understanding that the way they present questions to their students greatly affects how the students answer the questions. Nurses may need to communicate with children in stressful situations, such as undergoing surgery or experiencing a separation due to divorce or the death of a parent, and an understanding of how to explain such occurrences would be helpful. Nutritionists who understand the thinking processes of children are better able to develop strategies to encourage children to eat balanced diets.

Research, Teaching, and Clinical Work

Developmental psychology is a growing field. Many developmental psychologists teach in colleges and universities and perform research. As you read this text, you may begin to form research questions that you may someday be in a position to answer. In addition, there has been a tremendous growth of interest in parenting courses, and developmental psychologists are often called on to design and offer such programs.

Influencing Public Policy

Research can answer practical public-policy questions. The results from scientific investigations can affect public policy toward children (Kiesler, 1979). Developmental psychologists are often called on by government agencies to create and evaluate programs aimed at improving the lives of children (Seitz, 1979). For example, child abuse is a national problem, and developmental psychologists are seeking methods of prevention and treatment. Mental health is a major national problem, and research into the causes and prevention of emotional problems is an ongoing concern (Dusek, 1974). Questions about the effects of television and television advertising on children have been researched, and developmental psychologists are suggesting ways that television can be improved for young children (Huston, Watkins, & Kunkel, 1989). Developmental psychologists' research into the effects of day care on children (discussed later in the text) has made important contributions towards improving the day-care experience for young children (see Garwood, Phillips, Hartman, & Zigler, 1989). By influencing public policy toward children on local, state, and national levels, the nation can carefully nurture its most valuable resource—its children.

◆ THE PLAN OF THIS BOOK

This text uses a chronological approach to child and adolescent development. After initially discussing theories of development, genetics, prenatal growth, and birth, *A Child's Odyssey* covers infancy and toddlerhood, early childhood, middle childhood, and adolescence. The child's physical, social and personality, and cognitive (intellectual) development is discussed under each stage of development. Physical development involves the development of such skills as walking, running, and holding a pencil, as well as changes in stature. Social and personality development includes how children develop their own personality and relate to others. Cognitive development involves how children think, reason, and solve problems. These areas all interact. How a child thinks affects the child's relationship with others. A special chapter on language development is also included.

Each chapter begins with a group of true-false statements; the correct answers are given in a true-false answer box on the page following the statements. In addition, the statements are repeated within the text opposite the paragraph in which their answers can be found. Important terms appear in the text in **boldface,** and a running glossary is provided in the margins. The body of the text contains a number of examples and applications that demonstrate how research may lead to a better understanding of children's behavior as well as practical action aimed at overcoming children's problems. In addition, a number of anecdotes, some humorous, are included. One hope is that you will be able to empathize with the child being described and put yourself into the child's shoes, experiencing the world from the child's perspective.

Three other features of this book deserve mention. Each chapter contains a Cross-Cultural Current feature, which demonstrates how our evolving knowledge of other cultures can make the study of child development richer and more complete. In addition, a feature called The Child in the Year 2000 discusses future trends in the area of child development. Last, at the end of each chapter is a feature called Action/Reaction that presents one or two brief case studies that raise practical issues. This feature offers you the opportunity to apply what you are learning to realistic problems. I must stress that there is no single correct analysis or solution to the situations presented in this feature. Differences of opinion are common, and you the reader, your professor, and your classmates may view the situations from different perspectives and suggest different ways of handling them. If you think you've come up with an especially good solution, please let me know by writing to me through West Publishing Company.

In this introductory chapter, we have examined some of the central themes and issues that surround child and adolescent development and looked at how developmental psychologists perform research to find the answers to particular questions. However, the research questions are often suggested by a theoretical approach, and a knowledge of different approaches is indispensable to understanding child development. It is to these important theoretical approaches that we turn to next.

SUMMARY

1. Developmental psychology is the study of how organisms change qualitatively and quantitatively over time.

2. There are two general categories of change. Quantitative changes involve an increase or decrease in some characteristic, such as the number of words in a child's vocabulary. Qualitative change involves some change in function or process. For example, ten-year-olds use different strategies than five-year-olds when asked to remember a list of words.

3. Most developmental psychologists are interested in how a particular behavior develops over time.

4. One basic issue in developmental psychology surrounds the cause of change. Although some development is probably due more to genetic influence and others to environmental influence, both genetic and environmental influences interact to cause the changes that developmental psychologists seek to investigate. The key to understanding development is to appreciate the various ways in which maturation and learning interact.

5. Changes that are relatively immune to environmental influences and are caused by the unfolding of the individual's unique genetic plan are considered maturational in nature. Learning is usually defined as a relatively permanent change in behavior which can be attributed to interactions with the environment.

6. Early childhood experiences can have a profound influence on later development and behavior. However, the effects of a poor early environment can be remedied, at least to some extent by improving the environment.

7. Human beings are affected or molded by their experiences and environment. However, the extent to which a particular behavior is capable of being molded and the time during which it is most amenable to shaping are controversial questions.

8. Another issue surrounds the question of stability and change. Although there is some evidence for stability throughout childhood and adolescence for some characteristics, there is much evidence for change.

9. When investigating any relationships, developmental psychologists emphasize reciprocal interaction—that is, they look at how children both affect and are affected by their environment.

10. Developmental psychologists dispute whether children develop in a discontinuous manner, that is, in an orderly, sequential set of stages qualitatively different from one another, or in a more continuous manner, with new behaviors directly coming from older behaviors.

11. There are many types of research. In naturalistic observation, the researcher carefully observes and records what occurs in the natural environment. The case-study method involves carefully observing a subject for a substantial period of time and collecting a great deal of information about one or two people. Researchers using the survey method question a number of people, then tabulate and analyze their data. Researchers using the experimental method control the environment, allowing only the desired variables to vary. Such experiments may demonstrate cause and effect. Researchers may also attempt to discover correlations or relation-

ships between variables. These relationships show the extent to which one factor is related to another.

12. In cross-sectional studies, children from various age groups are tested at a particular time. In a longitudinal study, a single group of children is tested at particular intervals. Mixed research designs, which combine features of both, are also being used today.

13. Psychologists are more interested than ever in performing cross-cultural studies. Such studies help us appreciate the many and varied ways culture can affect development.

14. Most psychological experiments cause no physical or psychological harm to their subjects. Today, most universities have committees that examine the ethics of each experiment. Two of the most common ethical problems involve consent and deception.

15. The study of developmental psychology yields great personal benefits, helps people deal better with their children, opens up new vocational possibilities, and suggests ways society may be able to improve the lives of children.

ACTION/REACTION

Scott: On and Off the Timetable

Scott is a playful, exuberant, happy sixteen-month-old, but his physical and mental development is slow. While most children his age are walking and starting to talk, he is just beginning to take some steps and knows very few words.

Scott's parents are concerned. Scott's father wants Scott to take part in rigid exercise and cognitive stimulation programs, both of which he read about in a magazine. Now is the time to begin a program, Scott's father argues, before he falls further behind. Scott's mother doubts the wisdom of such an approach. She wants to leave well enough alone. After all, they've provided a stimulating environment for the boy, and time will take care of the rest.

A special pediatrician examined Scott and informed Scott's parents that nothing was wrong with Scott as far as she could tell. As for the programs advocated by Scott's father, the pediatrician would only say not to overdo it. Scott's father argues that the programs can't do any harm, so why not try? Scott's mother believes that forcing Scott to do things before he is ready could frustrate him and injure his relationship with his parents. The situation is complicated by the presence of a neighbor's child of about the same age who is making great progress and is well ahead of Scott.

1. If you were Scott's parent, what would you do?

To Adopt or Not To Adopt

The Appletons have wanted a child for a long time. They have been told that because of physical problems, they cannot have their own children. So they are looking to adopt.

Although they would like an infant, they find that it is very difficult to adopt a newborn. There are just not as many newborn infants up for adoption as there are couples who wish to adopt. The Appletons have been told that they can adopt a four-year-old child. At first, they were thrilled. However, they are now having some doubts.

They have been told that the preschooler's single parent was not able to take proper care of the child. The child was not fed properly or given the psychological stimulation and personal warmth necessary for optimal development.

The Appletons are wary. The early experience of this child has not been very good, and the couple is afraid that the child may be permanently affected by the poor early environment and may suffer from developmental problems in the social and cognitive spheres. On the other hand, the Appletons have waited a long time for this opportunity and do not know when another will come along.

1. Are the Appletons' fears realistic? If so, why? If not, why not?
2. What would you do if you were in the Appletons' position?

CHAPTER TWO

Perspectives on Development

Bringing in the Maple Sugar by Grandma Moses.

◆ CHAPTER OUTLINE ◆

Predicting Children's Reactions to the Space Shuttle Tragedy
Theoretical Perspectives on Child Development
Piaget's Theory of Cognitive Development
Freud's Psychoanalytic Theory
Erikson's Psychosocial Theory
Nonstage Theories
The Information Processing Approach
Ethology
The Behavioral Approach
Social Learning Theory
The Child in the Year 2000:
Predictability: Power and Caution
How To Use Theories
Cross-Cultural Current:
Explaining Differences in Aggression in Two Communities in Mexico

Are These Statements True or False?

Turn the page for the correct answers. Each statement is repeated in the margin next to the paragraph in which the information can be found.

1. Theories are neither right nor wrong, just useful.
2. Good theories can describe but cannot predict future events.
3. The stage of cognitive development a child is negotiating is accurately determined by considering the child's chronological age.
4. All psychologists agree that children develop in stages.
5. Child development specialists are impressed by the differences between children's thinking and adults' thinking.
6. Most school-age children, ages seven through eleven, have little problem understanding political cartoons.
7. Freud believed that children under the age of ten experience sexual urges comparable to adult sexuality.
8. Freud emphasized the importance of early parent-child interaction to a child's later behavior.
9. It is dangerous for a small and vulnerable toddler to develop a sense of autonomy.
10. In an attempt to understand how we solve problems, psychologists often equate the human mind with the computer.
11. Children who already know something about a topic they are being told about usually find it easier to learn new information than do children who are completely unfamiliar with the topic.
12. For children to learn, they must be reinforced directly.

Answers to True False Statements

1. True.
2. False. Correct statement: Good theories not only can describe development but also can predict it.
3. False. Correct statement: Children enter and leave a particular stage at different times. Ages noted by most theorists are averages and are meant only as rough guides.
4. False. Correct statement: A number of theories attempt to explain children's development without resorting to stages.
5. True.
6. False. Correct statement: Most schoolchildren age seven through eleven cannot understand political cartoons.
7. False. Correct statement: Freud defined sexuality in a broad sense akin to sensuality and did not believe that young children experienced adult sexual feelings.
8. True.
9. False. Correct statement: Developing a sense of autonomy is an important outcome of the toddler stage.
10. False. Correct statement: Scientists using the information-processing approach do not equate human minds with computers. They merely use the computer as an analogy for how processing may occur.
11. True.
12. False. Correct statement: Children may learn by observing others, especially when models are reinforced.

◆ PREDICTING CHILDREN'S REACTIONS TO THE SPACE SHUTTLE TRAGEDY

On the morning of January 28, 1986, millions of people around the country watched on television the long-awaited Challenger space shuttle launch. More children than usual were watching because the shuttle carried a teacher, Christa McAuliffe, who was to give a science lesson in space. In less than a minute and a half into the mission, the space shuttle exploded. Shock and grief spread throughout the country, together with some concern about how the children who had witnessed this tragedy would respond.

Suppose you had been a teacher or a parent watching the Challenger blast off with preschool, schoolage (6 to 12 years), or teenage children. Could you have predicted how each age group would have responded to the incident?

Many developmental psychologists could have and in fact did, because they know how children at various developmental levels reason and deal with information. In fact, the day after the tragedy, Nanci Monaco and Eugene Gaier (1987) conducted a study that, in part, demonstrated just

Millions of people watched the Space Shuttle Challenger explode a minute and a half into its flight. Many children were watching the takeoff and people were especially concerned about its effect on children.

how well psychologists' theories can be used to understand how children at particular age levels will react to an event. After presenting a short, factual review and some background information that included what was known about the tragedy, teachers asked students of various ages for comments and questions. The children's questions and comments could have been predicted by Jean Piaget's theory of cognitive (intellectual) development. In other words, a teacher or parent familiar with Piaget's theory could easily both understand and predict how children of various developmental levels would understand and reason about the tragedy.

♦ THEORETICAL PERSPECTIVES ON CHILD DEVELOPMENT

Many students react to the word *theory* with a groan. A student once told me, "We want the facts, not a bunch of theorizing." It's unfortunate that theory has such a bad reputation, for it is a most useful aspect of psychology.

Why Bother with Theory?

Without a theoretical perspective, data cannot be interpreted. Theory gives facts their meaning (Arndt, 1974). Armed with a knowledge of Piaget's theory, developmental psychologists can accurately predict and explain how children will react to various experiences.

Imagine that you have access to a computerized data base of research findings in child development. You ask for data on intellectual (cognitive) development. The computer spews out thousands of pages of data from study after study. How do you know which studies are germane to your questions? How do you pull the information together to make it intelligible? To give cohesiveness to this voluminous data, you adopt a theory (Thomas, 1979).

A theory can help us relate one fact to another. Asked to determine who has behaved worse—Larry, who broke four dishes while helping to clear off the table, or Howard, who broke two dishes while trying to sneak an extra cookie—most five-year-olds will respond, "Larry." Because young children do not take intent into consideration when judging an action, they see Larry's actions as worse because he broke more dishes (Piaget, 1932). Children who are eight or nine years old begin to factor intent into the equation and say Howard's actions were worse. To understand this developmental progression fully, we need a theory that relates the behavior and thought processes at one age to the behavior and thought processes at another age.

Theory can be of practical help as well. Imagine a mother near the end of her patience. Her five-year-old twins—one with a cup of juice and the other with a glass of juice—are both complaining that the other has more juice. The mother has demonstrated that the cup and the glass contain the same amount of juice, but the twins continue to fight over who has more juice. Later, the twins argue over which piece of clay is bigger—the one shaped like a ball or the one rolled into a wormlike shape—even though the mother has shown the children that both pieces have the same amount of clay. The mother wants to know if this constant bickering over who received more will ever end. By relating earlier behavior to later actions and one behavior to another, theory can help the mother understand why the twins continue to fight and at what point in their development the conflict will end.

Theories also allow us to predict what will happen next. For instance, if a person is negotiating the teenage years, Erik Erikson's psychosocial theory would emphasize the importance of an adolescent's developing a personal identity, with all the complexities that that entails.

Theory is also useful in formulating the right questions for studying and understanding child behavior. Proponents of the various theoretical perspectives ask different questions about the same behavior. Each theorist seeks to understand why children act the way they do, but each approaches the subject differently. A behaviorist, for example, who explains behavior using principles of learning would be interested in discovering the rewards and punishments in a particular child's environment. A social learning theorist might look for the models in the child's life. A psychoanalytic theorist—a follower of Sigmund Freud—might look at the unconscious forces that impel a child's behavior and find them in the child's relationship with his or her parents.

No theory that is presently available explains or predicts all behavior. The power of Piaget's theory was emphasized in the case of the Challenger tragedy. However, there are many areas in which Piaget's theory is not as useful as other theories would be. Developmental psychology does not offer one unified theory. Even within a particular area such as social or cognitive development, a number of theories vie for acceptance.

Good Theory-Bad Theory

How can we tell a good theory from a bad one? Although authorities differ on the number and importance of specific criteria for a good theory, some of the more important are usefulness, testability, predictability, and inclusiveness.

USEFULNESS Theories are neither right nor wrong; they are just useful. The best theory is the one that is the most useful in understanding and making predictions about the phenomenon in which one is interested. No single theory explains every aspect of child development. Some theories explain some areas better than others, and some theories are aimed at particular areas of interest.

For instance, Lawrence Kohlberg spent many years investigating the reasoning behind moral decisions. He asked subjects for their opinions on specific moral dilemmas and constructed an elaborate sequence of stages that describes the development of moral reasoning (see Chapter 12). The more specific a theory, the more limited its application. Thus, while Kohlberg's theory may be useful in looking at the moral decisions an individual makes, it would not be useful in understanding unconscious psychological motives.

The usefulness of a theory is partly determined by the developmental phenomena one is investigating. When a new theory becomes more useful for understanding and predicting phenomena, it should replace an older one. This rarely occurs, however, since a new theory is seldom more useful in every way, and so usually both remain in use.

1. TRUE OR FALSE?

Theories are neither right nor wrong, just useful.

TESTABILITY Ideally, a theory is testable. Researchers should be able to perform experiments that test the theory's hypotheses. This seems simple enough, but this requirement can create quite a problem, since certain theories are harder to test than others. Freud's psychoanalytic theory, for example, is difficult to test experimentally because its main ideas are difficult to define in a way that allows them to be tested empirically (Sarnoff, 1971).

PREDICTABILITY Good theories can be used both to describe and understand present events and to predict future behavior. Think for a moment about the twins' complaining over who had more juice. One of the mother's first questions was, "When would they ever stop fighting?" A good theory would predict the point in the twins' development at which the children would be able to understand that both the cup and the glass could hold the same amount of juice. In the Challenger tragedy, the researchers could have predicted that young children would perceive the tragedy one way and older children in a different way.

2. TRUE OR FALSE?

Good theories can describe but cannot predict future events.

INCLUSIVENESS A theory should be as inclusive as possible. No single theory explains all the concerns of child development, but a theory formulated to help us understand cognitive or social development should answer as many related questions as possible.

OTHER CRITERIA A number of other criteria may be used. For instance, a good theory is economical; that is, it introduces as few new terms and concepts as possible and is clear and concise. Also, good theories tend to spark a great deal of valuable research and give people in the field a new slant on a particular issue.

STAGE AND NONSTAGE THEORIES Theoretical approaches to child development can be divided into two major categories: stage and nonstage theories. Stage theories present development in terms of age-related periods in which people are faced with particular problems and have specific abilities. These theories see development as occurring in a stagelike progression, with movement from stage to stage occurring in an invariant order and with new skills developing from skills acquired in previous stages. Each person progresses through the same stages and cannot skip a stage, but people may enter or leave a particular stage at different ages, so it is incorrect simply to equate ages with stages.

Other psychologists disagree, claiming that it is more useful to understand development in terms of a more continuous process. As noted in Chapter 1, nonstage theorists believe that development is continuous, with new behaviors coming gradually and directly from earlier ones. Stage theorists believe that development is discontinuous, with development best understood in terms of well-defined qualitative "leaps" in a child's abilities.

Three stage theories—Piaget's theory of cognitive development, Freud's psychoanalytic theory, and Erikson's psychosocial theory are described first.

◆ PIAGET'S THEORY OF COGNITIVE DEVELOPMENT

People go to space to find stars and foods for people.
People shouldn't go in the sky.
The rocket died.
Somebody shouldda moved the clouds.
Even my dad said it was sad.
Does this mean we don't get the space lessons?

These are a few of the comments made by five-year-olds the day following the Challenger tragedy. Even a casual look at the comments is enough to convince us that children do not think like adults. In fact, one of Piaget's central ideas is that *children are not little adults.* Perhaps you shrug your shoulders at this rather banal statement, but for years people did not understand that a child's way of thinking and dealing with problems is different from an adult's. People interpreted the differences be-

3. TRUE OR FALSE?

The stage of cognitive development a child is negotiating is accurately determined by considering the child's chronological age.

4. TRUE OR FALSE?

All psychologists agree that children develop in stages.

tween the thinking of children and that of adults as mistakes or as signs of stubbornness against growing up. Jean Piaget devoted his adult life to studying the cognitive (intellectual) development of children. His work is monumental, and his discoveries have a number of important implications.

Piaget used an interesting research method, called the clinical method. He presented subjects with a verbal or physical task, both observing the child tackling the challenge and asking him or her questions about the task. For example, Piaget took two balls of clay and made certain that the child agreed that the balls were equal in mass. He then rolled one ball of clay into a long, thin wormlike shape and asked the child which piece had more clay. Piaget found that most children younger than age seven believed the worm contained more clay because it was longer (Piaget, 1967). Piaget would then question the child to determine why the child believed the worm contained more clay.

Basic Concepts in Piaget's Theory

An appreciation of Piaget's ideas must begin with an explanation of the basic concepts of his theory.

WHAT IS KNOWLEDGE? For most people, knowledge is a set of facts or concepts that an individual has been taught. This rather static view of knowledge allows only for adding more facts to one's storehouse. To Piaget, though, knowledge is equated with action. As Robert Thomas (1979) notes, "To know something means to act on that thing, with the action being either physical, mental or both" (p. 29). The eight-year-old's knowledge of a crystal is based upon the interaction between the child and the object. The relationship between a child and any object is not stable (Piaget, 1970), since it changes as the child matures and becomes more experienced. Knowledge, then, is a process rather than some stable state. Piaget was interested in discovering the different ways children interact with their world to create knowledge. As children mature, their ways of knowing the world change.

FACTORS IN DEVELOPMENT According to Piaget, development involves the continuous alteration and reorganization of the ways in which people deal with their environment (Piaget, 1970). No one seriously believes that the infant, the preschooler, the schoolage child, and the adolescent all see the world in the same manner or interact with objects in the exact same way. Therefore, to understand how a child's interactions change, one must understand the concept of development.

Development is defined by four principal factors: maturation, experience, social transmission, and the process of equilibration. We discussed *maturation*—the gradual unfolding of one's genetic plan for life—in Chapter 1. *Experience* involves the active interaction of the child with his or her environment. *Social transmission* refers to the information and customs that are transmitted from parents and other people in the environment to the child. We can consider this the educational function in

5. TRUE OR FALSE?

Child developmental specialists are impressed by the differences between children's thinking and adults' thinking.

It is a mistake to equate age and stage. These two children are about the same age, yet one may be developmentally ahead of the other.

Jean Piaget conducted research by presenting children of varying ages with problems to solve, noting how they approached them and the nature of their reasoning.

equilibration
In Piagetian theory, the process by which children seek a balance between what they know and what they are experiencing.

the broad sense. Finally, the process of **equilibration** defines development. Children seek a balance between what they know and what they are experiencing. When faced with information that calls for a new and different analysis or activity, children enter a state of disequilibrium. When this occurs, they change their way of dealing with the event or experience, and a new, more stable state of equilibrium is established. In this way, children progress from a very limited ability to deal with new experiences to a more mature, sophisticated level of cognitive functioning. For example, let us say that a child believes that heavy things are big and light things are small. The child is introduced to a styrofoam beam, which looks like wood, but is, of course, much lighter. The child is forced into disequilibrium and is motivated internally to find out more and establish a new equilibrium. This the child does by changing his or her ideas.

To Piaget, children are not simply passive receivers of stimulation. Children actively interact with their environment, and their active experiences impel them to new heights in cognitive functioning and action. Therefore, the child's cognitive development is based not only on information directly and formally transmitted from parents and teachers to the child, but also on the child's personal experiences.

Organization and Adaptation

Two of the most important concepts in Piagetian theory are organization and adaptation. First, people must organize their knowledge in a way that makes the knowledge useful. Second, to survive, every organism must adapt to its environment (Phillips, 1975). Adaptation can be understood in terms of adjustment. As the forces in the environment change, so must the individual's ability to deal with them change.

ORGANIZATION: COGNITIVE STRUCTURES AND SCHEMATA

Watch a three-year-old try to pick up a block. The child easily uses thumb and fingers to grasp the block and then examines the block and places it on top of another block. The child combines the blocks in a primitive way to form a building. It is easy to forget the tortuous steps that led to this behavior. Hand the block to an infant, and the infant places it in his or her mouth. The infant often explores objects by sucking on them.

Sucking is an example of what Piaget calls a schema. The concept of schema is difficult to define (Flavell, 1977) but relatively easy to understand. When an infant places a block in the mouth and sucks on it, the sucking schema is being used. Piaget uses the term **schema** to describe an organized system of actions and thoughts, useful for dealing with the environment, that can be generalized to many situations (Piaget, 1952). These schemata (the plural of schema) are the cognitive structures that underlie patterns of behavior.

Younger children have qualitatively different schemata from those of older children. That is, their way of organizing material and responding to their environment differs as they progress through various stages of development. Other infant schemata besides sucking include looking, listening, grasping, hitting, and pushing (Flavell, 1977).

Schemata are tools for learning about the world. They become more sophisticated as a child matures and as new schemata are developed. For example, an infant presented with a block may first use the sucking schema but later may look at the block and bang it against the side of the crib. Gradually, the child learns to coordinate the schemata, finally being able to pick the block up, examine it, and place it on top of another (a building schema). Preschoolers have developed still other schemata, some involving language.

Schemata can be thought of as actions and strategies that children use to understand and deal with their world and form the bases for later thought. These actions and strategies add structure to the interactions between children and their environment. In infancy, the schemata are all basic and involve types of overt behavior such as sucking and picking things up, while later on they become more symbolic and mental. The eight-year-old given a block can mentally operate on the block. He can imagine placing two blocks together and taking them apart. He does not always have to physically do so. These symbolic schemata that characterize older children are referred to as operations.

An **operation** is an internalized action that is part of the child's cognitive structure. Such actions include plans or rules for solving problems

schema
A method of dealing with the environment that can be generalized to many situations.

operation
An internalized action that is part of the child's cognitive structure.

(Piaget, 1974). For example, Piaget wrote extensively about the operational schema of reversibility, that is, being able to return to one's point of origin. If 3 plus 5 equals 8, then subtracting 5 from 8 will leave 3. You can add something to 3 and then take it away and think your way from one condition to another and then return to the starting point (Phillips, 1975). Schemata and operations form what Piaget calls the cognitive structure of the child. As children develop, their cognitive structures become more and more similar to those of adults. For instance, consider what happens when a magnet is given to children in different stages of development. The infant merely puts the magnet in his or her mouth or perhaps bangs it against the floor. The three-year-old might realize that some objects stick to or want to stay with the magnet. The nine-year-old child realizes that certain objects with certain characteristics are attracted to the magnet and tests out which ones and at which distances. The adolescent forms an abstract theory of magnetism that involves the size and shape of the magnet and distance from the object (Miller, 1989). As children develop, then, their cognitive structures or abilities to deal with the outside world change, and they develop more and more sophisticated strategies for dealing with information.

assimilation
The process by which information is altered to fit into one's already existing cognitive structures.

ADAPTATION The second major concept in Piagetian theory is adaptation, which involves two complementary processes: assimilation and accommodation. **Assimilation** refers to the taking-in process, whether of sensation, nourishment, or experience. It is the process by which new information is filtered or modified to fit already existing structures (Piaget & Inhelder, 1969). When we assimilate something, we alter the form of an incoming stimulus to adapt to our already existing actions or structures (Piaget, 1983). One incorporates things, people, ideas, customs and tastes into one's own activity (Pulaski, 1980). For example, if a child sees an odd-shaped piece of paper and uses it as a paper airplane, the child has assimilated the paper into his or her structure and knowledge of an airplane. You could say that the child has incorporated the paper into his or her already existing idea of an airplane. A baby may bang a rattle against the side of the crib, but when given another toy, perhaps a plastic block, the baby will assimilate it by banging it against the crib as well.

accommodation
The process by which one's existing structures are altered to fit new information.

Accommodation involves modifying existing schemata to meet the requirements of a new experience (Piaget & Inhelder, 1969). When we accommodate, we create new schemata or modify old ones (Brainerd, 1978). For example, a child may be very good at using a one-handed pickup schema, that is, lifting an item with one hand, but when faced with a heavier item, the child has to accommodate, that is, use a two-handed pickup schema.

Assimilation and accommodation work together. Suppose you are riding in a car with a young child and the child points to a large, new Cadillac and says, "Car." "That's right," you remark as you continue driving. The child then spots an old, rusty Volkswagen Beetle and again says,

"Car." You are suitably impressed. After all, even though the Cadillac and the Volkswagen are noticeably different, the child understands that they are both cars—an example of assimilation. As you drive on, the child points to a large truck and says, "Car." You correct her, saying, "No, that is a truck." After a while, the child points out a few more trucks. She has accommodated. Now she has separated her conception of car from that of truck. The child then sees a van, which she may put in either category. Or she may even ask you what it is. In this way, using assimilation and accommodation, the child begins to understand her world.

A nonverbal example of how assimilation and accommodation work together can be seen in an infant's investigating a rattle. The baby may try to assimilate the rattle by using the old sucking schema but must also accommodate the mouth to the size of the rattle. Mary Ann Spencer Pulaski (1980) notes that when an infant begins to understand that there are objects that can go in the mouth and are suckable but not swallowable, the child begins to divide objects into the edible and nonedible. With experience and a timely no from a parent, this schema will be further defined so that the child will not place anything in the mouth that is not food.

The Stages of Cognitive Development

Piaget (1954) argued that children's cognitive development can be viewed as occurring in a sequence of four stages. Each of these stages represents a qualitative advance in a child's ability to solve problems and understand the world. Each stage is described very briefly here, and as each age group is discussed in the text, the appropriate stages will be discussed in greater depth.

THE SENSORIMOTOR STAGE Between birth and about two years of age, infants progress through the **sensorimotor stage.** They investigate their world using the senses (sight, hearing, etc.) and motor activity. They develop **object permanence**—the understanding that objects and people do not disappear merely because they are out of sight. For instance, when a parent leaves the room, an infant is likely to cry. Young infants may believe that the parent has disappeared. Reappearance of the mother or father brings joy and relief. Object permanence is also seen in the child's ability to search for some object (Flavell, 1977). The child's abilities in this stage are limited by an inability to use language or symbols. Children must experience everything directly through their senses and through feedback from motor activities.

sensorimotor stage
The first stage in Piaget's theory of cognitive development, in which the child discovers the world using the senses and motor activity.

object permanence
The knowledge that objects exist even if they are outside one's field of vision.

THE PREOPERATIONAL STAGE From about age two through age seven, children negotiate the lengthy **preoperational stage.** Now the child can use one thing to represent another; for instance, a piece of wood may symbolize a boat. The child's emerging use of symbolism shows itself in expanding language abilities. Language allows children to go beyond direct experience, opening up a new and expanded world. This stage has a number of limitations, though. Children cannot understand conserva-

preoperational stage
The second stage in Piaget's theory of cognitive development, during which children cannot understand logical concepts such as conservation.

tion, that is, the knowledge that quantities remain the same despite change in their appearance. This most famous idea can be easily demonstrated. Fill two glasses equally with water and ask a five-year-old to confirm that each glass has the same amount of water. Then pour the water from one of the glasses into a wider more squat container, perhaps a cup. Now ask the child which container has the greater amount of liquid in it. The child will probably tell you that the glass contains more. The child fails to understand that water is conserved even if it is transferred to another container. The average nine-year-old in a more advanced stage has no trouble with this problem.

Children, especially early in this period, believe that inanimate objects are alive. This animism is responsible for some of the charm of children of this age. Stuffed animals may have a life of their own, and when a stuffed animal is so old that the stuffing has come out, a youngster may insist on a funeral and burial. The child who described the Challenger tragedy with the words "The rocket died" shows this type of thinking.

The preoperational child is also egocentric, believing that each person sees the situation just the way the child does. If a parent is tired or not feeling well, little Kevin may bring the parent a favorite toy. He doesn't understand that daddy or mommy would rather have some peace and quiet and perhaps something to read. Children in this stage believe that everything in the world was created to meet their needs; for example, the sun was created to make the child warm and give the child light. Children in this stage are also artificial, which means that they interpret all phenomena, including natural phenomena, as made by human beings. One child noted that "Somebody shouldda moved the clouds" as an explanation for the shuttle explosion.

concrete operations
The third stage in Piaget's theory of cognitive development, in which the child develops the ability to conserve and becomes less egocentric.

6. TRUE OR FALSE?

Most school-age children, ages seven through eleven, have little problem understanding political cartoons.

formal operations
The fourth and last stage in Piaget's theory of cognitive development, in which the adolescent develops the ability to deal with abstractions and engage in scientific logic.

THE CONCRETE OPERATIONAL STAGE From age seven to about age twelve, children progress through the stage of **concrete operations.** In this stage, many of the preoperational deficiencies are slowly overcome, and children develop the ability to conserve. The child in the stage of concrete operations has difficulty with abstract terms such as freedom or liberty. Things are understood concretely and literally. A saying like "You can lead a horse to water, but you can't make him drink" is often met with a questionable frown, and political cartoons mean nothing to the child in this stage. In short, children in this stage understand the world on a concrete, tangible level. There is much less egocentrism, and these children can see things from other people's points of view. One child in the concrete operational stage noted, "It was sad that Mrs. McAullife's children lost their mother." There is also a sense of fairness shown here, as some said that it's not fair that she died so young.

THE FORMAL OPERATIONAL STAGE During adolescence, children enter the stage of **formal operations.** They develop the ability to test hypotheses in a mature, scientific manner and can understand and communicate their positions on complex ethical issues that demand an ability to use abstractions. They can also think about thinking; that is, they become aware of the process by which they came to hold a particular opinion. These children can consider hypotheses, deal with future orientations, and consider many aspects of a problem. When asked about the Challenger incident, many believed that space exploration must continue, since so much energy and time had already been committed to the endeavor, and they systematically looked and evaluated positions regarding the future of manned space missions. Others looked at the possible lessons learned from the tragedy.

Application and Value

Piaget's basic ideas are very influential in American preschools. His explorations into the way children develop their concepts of time, space, and mathematics, for example, show that children see the world differently from the way adults do. To serve the needs of youngsters better, parents and teachers must understand children's thought processes.

Piaget deemphasized formal learning in his theories, stressing maturation and experience as the foremost factors in cognitive development. This translates into some practical conclusions. For example, Piaget advocates elaborating on concepts that children already know rather than accelerating children's progress. If a child seems to understand addition, the next step is to use the skill in as many ways as possible. Too many people are interested in accelerating cognitive development and ask the question, How fast? rather than than the Piagetian question, How well? Piaget was not very interested in formal teaching strategies, but some educators have applied Piagetian concepts to schools (Furth & Wachs, 1975). For example, Stephen Yelon and Grace Weinstein (1977) note six implications of Piaget's theories for teachers: (1) using Piagetian tasks to determine the intellectual level of students, (2) teaching students with their cognitive level in mind, (3) remembering that children's thought processes are different from those of adults, (4) being careful to sequence instruction carefully, (5) testing children to find the results of teaching, and (6) encouraging social interaction to facilitate learning.

Piaget's emphasis on the active, searching mind of the child has fascinated many. His theory implies that children should be encouraged to discover and to experience, that they are not mere passive receivers of stimulation. Children both initiate action and react to stimuli in their environment. They both are shaped by and actively shape their own environment.

Criticisms and Cautions

Even though we owe a huge debt of gratitude to Piaget for his work, there has been somewhat more criticism directed at Piaget's theory in the past few years. Critics of Piaget's theory argue that Piaget underestimated the influence of learning on intellectual development. In addition, there is evidence both for and against the idea that children progress through a series of stages in cognitive development (Flavell, 1982). For example, there is little doubt that if you test Piagetian stage-related concepts such as conservation exactly the way Piaget did, you get the same results. However, if you change the test situation, you sometimes get different results. For example, when Ina Uzgiris (1968) looked into conservation of substance using a number of different substances, including metal cubes, wire coils, and plastic wire, she found that children could understand the concept when using some substances but not when using others. In other words, it made a significant difference what materials were used. If the same cognitive structures underlie children's thinking, it should not matter. Since it does, this calls into question Piaget's stage-related concepts.

Some specific Piagetian concepts, especially egocentrism, have also come under fire. For example, John Flavell (1975) showed children in the pre-operational stage a number of proposed gifts for their fathers and asked them to choose an appropriate gift. Most of the children chose appropriate gifts, demonstrating that they are able to take the point of view of others when they have had experience in these areas. The nature of the task and the past learning experiences of the child may be more important than Piaget realized.

Piaget's method of research—the presentation of problems to children followed by observation and questioning—is also a source of criticism. This subjective approach is marked by interpretation rather than formal statistical data. Piaget's experiments are not well controlled (Baldwin, 1967). Piaget has, in effect, blazed a trail using his particular method, leaving the research validating his concepts to others. In a series of conversations with Jean-Claude Bringuier (1980), Piaget answered his methodological critics.

Bringuier: But surely, some questions have to be included in order to produce statistics. (Piaget wrinkles his nose.) Just to have a coherent body of information.

Piaget: Exactly. Once the work of clearing away, of groundbreaking, has been done, which consists of discovering new things and finding things that hadn't been anticipated, you can begin to standardize—at least if you like that sort of thing—and to produce accurate statistics. But I find it more interesting to do the work of groundbreaking.

Bringuier: And you're not afraid the individual cases will be too individual?

Piaget: Why, no. What's so remarkable is that the answers show an unbelievable convergence. While you were preparing this interview, I was classifying the new documents that just came. Twenty-five kids I don't know, and they all say the same thing! At the same age!

Bringuier: Because they're from the same social class and the same city?

Piaget: I don't think so.

Bringuier: Because they're at the same level of evolution?

Piaget: Yes.

(Bringuier, 1980, p. 25)

Piaget saw himself as a scientist performing groundbreaking experiments. The extent to which his formulations have been validated by subsequent statistically based research can be debated. Although much research supports Piaget's theory, some does not.

A number of theorists have remained true to Piaget's ideas, his belief in stages and sequences, but emphasize different processes to explain the phenomena described by Piaget. For example, how do children proceed from one stage to another? Piaget argued that equilibration was the mechanism, but many disagree. For example, Robbie Case (1985; 1988) argues that it is not equilibration that is the major mechanism for change in development but rather changes in the child's short-term storage space or working memory capacity. This increases at a regular rate and in an orderly fashion and gives children the opportunity to form new and more complex cognitive structures. Memory capacity and other information processing abilities are discussed later. Other neo-Piagentians argue that cognitive development is more domain specific and affected more by environmental influences.

Piaget's theory is certainly a tremendous step in understanding cognitive development. It has sparked an incredible variety of research. However, it certainly does not answer all the questions about cognitive development. New theoretical approaches, such as the information processing approach discussed later in the chapter, can best be seen as extending and expanding our understanding of the child's intellectual development.

◆ FREUD'S PSYCHOANALYTIC THEORY

Another theorist who formulated a stage theory of human development was Sigmund Freud. Many people have an opinion about Freud's theory. Usually, they are either fascinated by it or reject it out of hand. But if you ask people what Freud said, many do not understand it well at all. Psychoanalytic theory comprises the following major elements.

Levels of Consciousness

Have you ever been unaware of the reasons behind something you've done? Have you ever taken an instant dislike to someone without any apparent reason? Have you ever made a slip of the tongue? If your answer to any of these questions is yes, you may have experienced the unconscious in action.

Sigmund Freud (1900, 1923, 1933) posited three levels of awareness. The **conscious** involves one's immediate awareness and makes up only a small portion of the total mind. The **preconscious** comprises memories that can easily become conscious. For example, you may remember the correct answers to the questions on an exam only after the test is over (Kline, 1972). Finally, some memories are stored in the **unconscious**—the portion of the mind that is beyond normal awareness. Motives may arise from here. The unconscious shows itself in many ways, for instance, through dreams and slips of the tongue.

Freud (1933) believed that behavior could be caused and maintained

conscious
Freudian term for thoughts or memories of which a person is immediately aware.

preconscious
Freudian term for thoughts or memories that although not immediately conscious can easily become so.

unconscious
Freudian term for memories that lie beyond normal awareness.

by early experiences that had apparently been forgotten. These experiences, which are stored in the unconscious, are beyond normal awareness but can still have a profound effect on behavior. For instance, a person may experience sexual difficulties in a marriage because of a traumatic sexual experience in childhood the individual no longer remembers (DiCaprio, 1983).

Freud's insistence that we may not be aware of our true motives and wishes, probably because their gratification is forbidden by society, was criticized by many when Freud suggested it (Eidelberg, 1968). If a child who is angry at his mother kicks a younger sibling—a situation referred to as **displacement**—the child may refuse to admit to feelings of hostility toward his mother. The child is not lying but is probably unaware of those feelings.

The Constructs of the Mind

Freud explained the workings of the mind using three constructs (Freud, 1923, 1940)—the id, the ego, and the superego. The **id** is the source of all wishes and desires. It is unconscious and exists at birth. The id wants what it wants when it wants it and cannot tolerate delay. It functions through the **primary process**, which entails instant gratification for every wish and desire. The infant is, in this sense, complete id.

Within the first year, the **ego** comes into being. Some needs, such as hunger, can be satisfied only by interacting with the real world. The ego, which is partly conscious, operates through the **secondary process**, or **reality principle**. It is responsible for dealing with reality and satisfying the needs and desires of the id in a socially appropriate manner. Whereas the id knows only its subjective reality (I want), the ego must also understand the world outside the mind and the self. As the child grows and matures, the ego becomes stronger, being able to delay gratification and balance the desires of the id with the restraints of the third construct, the superego.

The **superego** is analogous to one's conscience. It contains a set of principles gathered from interacting with others in society and serves as an internal gyroscope. The superego compares your behavior to your **ego ideal**, that is, what you think you should be like. The superego is perfectionistic, seeking to inhibit the id's antisocial desires and causing an individual to experience guilt when transgressing or even considering a misdeed. The ego must mediate between the prohibitions of the superego and the desires of the id. Tension may arise from the pull of the id, the nature of society's prohibitions, and the weight of superego restraint. Life is a compromise, and proper adjustment is a matter of maintaining a delicate balance.

People whose ids are in control and who have not developed a sufficiently strong ego may not be able to delay gratification or restrain their activities. We see this in young children who have little or no ability to wait for attention or food. An individual who has failed to adequately develop a superego may not act in an ethical manner.

displacement
The process by which an emotion is transferred from one object or person to another more acceptable substitute.

id
The portion of the mind in Freudian theory that serves as the depository for wishes and desires.

primary process
The process by which the id seeks to gratify its wishes.

ego
The part of the mind in Freudian theory that mediates between the real world and the desires of the id.

secondary process or **reality principle**
The process by which the ego satisfies the organism's needs in a socially appropriate manner.

superego
The part of the mind in Freudian theory that includes a set of principles, violation of which leads to feelings of guilt.

ego ideal
The individual's positive and desirable standards of conduct.

Defense Mechanisms

The ego has a difficult job. Sometimes it is overwhelmed, and the tension that results is experienced as anxiety. If the anxiety becomes too great, the ego may defend itself by using a large number of protective maneuvers called defense mechanisms. A **defense mechanism** is an automatic and unconscious process that serves to relieve or reduce feelings of anxiety or emotional conflict (Laughlin, 1970). One of the most prominent defense mechanisms is repression (Brenner, 1955). In **repression**, some memory is barred from consciousness and no longer directly bothers us. Henry Laughlin (1970) describes the case of the five-year-old girl who asked to look after her two-year-old sister. She became bored with the assignment and went to play with some friends. The two-year-old walked across the road down to a bay and drowned. The five-year-old experienced tremendous feelings of guilt, but after a while she no longer talked about or even seemed to remember the tragedy, a state of mind encouraged by her family. She had repressed the entire event. There are many other defense mechanisms, described in Table 2.1.

The Psychosexual Stages

One of the most challenging Freudian concepts is that of infantile and childhood sexuality, the idea that infants and children experience sexual feelings (Noam, Higgins & Goethals, 1982). However, Freud did not believe that young children experienced adult sexual feelings. His idea of sexuality resembles what we might consider sensuality and pleasure. Freud saw life as the unfolding of the sexual instinct. This sexual instinct is called **eros**, and the energy emanating from it is known as the **libido**. The libido attaches itself to different portions of the body as the child grows and matures. This is the basis for Freud's **psychosexual stages**. Freud stressed the importance of early experience in the formation of behavior and focused attention on parent-child interactions.

THE ORAL STAGE At birth, an infant's oral cavity (the mouth) is well developed. Infants gain pleasure through sucking and then later biting, which are both oral activities. During the **oral stage,** the child's needs for oral experiences take precedence over all others. However, the child's oral activities are restricted by parents when the child bites someone or spits, and the child encounters authority in the form of the parents' demands (DiCaprio, 1983). If a child is either frustrated or overly stimulated, the child may become fixated; that is, a part of the child remains in a previous stage of psychosexual development, and development is partially arrested (Eidelberg, 1968). This does not mean that a child does not progress to the next step. Rather, the child's personality shows some characteristic of the previous stage of development. According to Freud, fixation at this stage, if it involves sucking, may lead to gullibility (Hall & Lindzey, 1957), dependence and inactivity, and a belief that others will provide the comforts of life for the child (Kline, 1972). Freud also noted an increase in such oral activities as eating and drinking in orally fixated individuals.

defense mechanism
An automatic and unconscious process that reduces or eliminates feelings of anxiety or emotional conflict.

repression
A defense mechanism in which memories are barred from consciousness.

7. TRUE OR FALSE?

Freud believed that children under the age of ten experience sexual urges comparable to adult sexuality.

eros
In Freudian theory, the positive, constructive sex instinct.

libido
In Freudian theory, the energy emanating from the sex instinct.

psychosexual stages
Stages in Freud's developmental theory.

oral stage
The first psychosexual stage, in which sexuality is centered on the oral cavity.

TABLE 2.1: Defense Mechanisms

Defense mechanisms are used to reduce or eliminate unpleasant feelings such as anxiety or emotional conflict. This table shows some of the more prominent mechanisms.

DEFENSE MECHANISM	DESCRIPTION	EXAMPLE
Rationalization	Making up plausible but inaccurate excuses to explain some behavior.	A student who is getting poor grades in school explains it away by telling you, "It's what you learn, not your grades, that are important" or "Schools teach nothing useful anyway."
Denial	A person refuses to believe something has occurred.	A person refuses to believe that someone has died.
Compensation	Making up for a real or imaginary deficiency by putting effort into a similar area (direct compensation) or into a different area (indirect compensation).	An unathletic person who feels physically inferior may buy body-building equipment and work out until he is a first-class weight lifter (direct compensation) or put his efforts into schoolwork to become the best student he can (indirect compensation).
Reaction Formation	An individual experiences feelings that are unacceptable to him or her and so acts in a manner that is contrary to those feelings.	A junior high school girl who likes a boy may act very rude or even hit him to "prove" to her friends that she doesn't really like him.
Projection	Feelings that are unacceptable to oneself are transferred to someone else.	A child who feels angry at his mother for not driving him to the ball game asks her, "Why are you angry at me?" instead of telling her he is angry at her.
Regression	Returning to a time in life that was more comfortable.	A three-year-old girl who is talking and toilet-trained begins to talk baby talk and wet her pants after a baby brother is brought home from the hospital.
Repression	Memories are barred from consciousness so they no longer bother a person.	A person who accidentally struck another with his bat during a baseball game cannot remember the incident.
Displacement	The transfer of feelings from one person or object to another.	A child is angry at his father but yells at his sister.
Rechannelization (Sublimation)	Unacceptable impulses are rechanneled into socially appropriate pursuits.	An aggressive person learns to express himself through sports or music.

8. TRUE OR FALSE?

Freud emphasizes the importance of the parent-child interaction to a child's later behavior.

Fixation at the biting stage may result in a sarcastic or biting personality that is always in conflict with others.

Freud, then, views various childhood experiences as predetermining a number of personality traits. According to him, it is not genetics or even maturation that causes the development of these traits, but rather problems in the early interaction between the child and, at least in the oral stage, the child's parents. Nowhere is this so noticeable as in the next stage, the anal stage.

THE ANAL STAGE At about eighteen months of age, the muscles responsible for elimination mature to the extent where some control is possible. The libido becomes attached to the anal cavity from that age to about three, and this coincides with attempts to toilet train the child. The **anal stage** can be divided into the anal expulsion and the anal retentive substages. In the first substage, the child gains pleasure from expelling the body's waste products. In the second, gratification is obtained from withholding them. If the parents create a situation in which a power struggle rages over bowel and bladder control, an anal retentive character may arise. In that case, the child will gain satisfaction from holding back feces and be likely to have such character traits as miserliness, obstinacy, and incredible orderliness and neatness. If, on the other hand, the child relents and gives feces, especially at inappropriate times, the anal expulsive traits such as cruelty and messiness result. Again, according to Freud's theory, childhood experiences predetermine later personality traits.

THE PHALLIC STAGE At about the age of four, the libido becomes attached to the genital organs: the penis in males and the clitoris in females. There is no difference in the development of males and females in the oral or anal stage (Deutsch, 1945), but beginning in the **phallic stage,** the experience of boys and girls differ greatly.

According to Freud, the young male experiences sexual feelings toward his mother and desires to possess her sexually. His father is a rival for mother's affections, and he desires to rid himself of his father. Freud called this the **Oedipus complex.** The child's sexual attachment to his mother is defined by exclusivity and jealousy (Mullahy, 1948). At the same time, the child realizes that he is at a great disadvantage in competing with his father because of the differences in size, and he fears that his father will discover his desires and castrate him. He experiences castration anxiety. The young boy resolves this dilemma of wanting mother but fearing father's retribution by identifying with father and repressing his feelings toward his mother deep in his unconscious.

In the case of the female, the situation is more complicated, and Freud admitted there was an insufficient amount of knowledge on the subject (Mullahy, 1948). Nevertheless, he did posit a type of Oedipal situation (often called the **Electra complex**) for young girls. The young girl is first attached to her mother, but she turns her affection and attention to her father when she realizes that she does not have a penis. She blames her mother for this situation and desires to take her mother's place in her father's affection. This gives rise to what is called penis envy and to a desire to possess the male organ. Since castration is no threat to the girl, the resolution of the Electra complex is not as important or severe for females as it is for males. Instead of simply repressing her feelings toward her mother, the girl identifies with her mother and continues to build on the relationship she established before the phallic stage (Chodorow, 1981).

Problems in the phallic stage can lead to a variety of personality disturbances. For example, when the resolution of the Oedipal conflict is not positive, a boy may resent his father and generalize this resentment to authority figures later in life (Nye, 1975). A number of sexual problems also date from difficulties in the phallic stage.

Although this is not what Freud had in mind, during the toddler years, toilet training takes center stage. According to Freud, the early interaction between child and parent is very important in determining the course of development.

anal stage
The second psychosexual stage, in which sexuality is centered on the anal cavity.

phallic stage
The third psychosexual stage, in which sexuality is centered on the genital areas.

Oedipus complex
The conflict during the phallic stage in which a boy experiences sexual feelings towards his mother and wishes to do away with his father.

Electra complex
In Freudian theory, the female equivalent to the Oedipus complex, in which the female experiences sexual feelings towards her father and wishes to do away with her mother.

latency stage
The psychosexual phase in which sexuality is dormant.

THE LATENCY STAGE The phallic stage ends with the resolution of the Oedipal situation. The child then enters the **latency stage.** From about six until puberty, the child's sexuality lies dormant. Since a boy has identified with his father, he tends to imitate him at every turn. Some of the antismoking campaigns use this fact in an attempt to encourage fathers to stop smoking. Boys have also repressed their feelings toward their mothers, but since they are so young, their repression generalizes to all females. Thus, eight-year-old boys are likely to stay apart from eight-year-old girls. The sexes appear to segregate, and boys play with boys and girls with girls during this stage.

Realizing that the resolution of the Electra complex is less abrupt in females, we would expect much less of this behavior with girls. Girls do show this aversion to boys, but usually on a much less intense level.

genital stage
The final psychosexual stage, occurring during adolescence, in which adult heterosexual behavior develops.

THE GENITAL STAGE The emergence of puberty, with its hormonal changes and sexual arousal, throws the child out of the latency stage into the **genital stage.** The young adolescent boy turns his attention to a girlfriend, while the young adolescent female seeks a boyfriend. This is the beginning of mature adult sexuality.

Application and Value

Child development specialists differ greatly on the value of psychoanalytic theory to the understanding of children's behavior, but certain aspects of Freud's theory offer useful insights. Freud's emphasis on the importance of the early interaction between parent and child has been largely accepted by psychologists. Freud felt that injuries during the early stages left indelible marks on children, but today we have a more flexible view that allows for subsequent experience to ease the negative effects of poor early experiences. In addition, Freud's theory presented the development of the child in a stage setting that has become very popular. Some of Freud's ideas concerning the unconscious have been of great interest as well, and Freud's description of defense mechanisms has allowed psychologists to obtain new understandings of what were in the past incomprehensible behaviors. Freud's idea that sexuality begins early in life is also challenging. Even though many of Freud's disciples disagreed with the emphasis Freud placed on sexuality, we owe Freud gratitude for raising the issue of childhood sexuality at a time when such ideas were unacceptable. Finally, Freud's theory has served as a focal point for criticism and as a basis for the development of other theories.

Criticisms and Cautions

Psychoanalytic theory was formulated on the basis of Freud's clinical experiences (Cairns, 1983). Freud's patients were troubled, and psychoanalytic theory may have more to say about abnormal development than normal development. It may be a mistake to base our ideas concerning normal development and child rearing on clinical experiences with emotionally troubled people. In addition, Freud's formulations are difficult to test empirically. Some of his concepts, such as instinct and psychic energy, are vaguely or even poorly defined, and none is defined in a manner that would make testing easy (Baldwin, 1967). Finally, Freud's emphasis on sexuality may have grown out of the society in which he lived. Sexuality was frowned on in Vienna at that time, and the idea that sexuality is sinful and unhealthy may have been the cause of many of the problems Freud treated. His ideas may not be as universal as he thought.

◆ ERIKSON'S PSYCHOSOCIAL THEORY

Although accepting some of Freud's concepts, a number of Freud's followers have rejected others. Freud's emphasis on sexuality has troubled many, as has his lack of consideration for the effect cultural differences may have on a child's development. Of all Freud's followers, Erik Erikson has had the greatest influence on the study of child development. Erikson (1963, 1968) argued that human beings develop according to a preset plan called the **epigenetic principle.** This principle consists of two main elements. First, personality develops according to predetermined steps that are maturationally set. Second, society is structured so as to invite and encourage the challenges that arise during these particular stages.

epigenetic principle
The preset developmental plan in Erikson's theory consisting of two elements: that personality develops according to maturationally determined steps and that each society is structured to encourage challenges that arise during these stages.

The Psychosocial Stages

According to Erikson, each individual proceeds through eight stages of development from cradle to grave. Each stage presents the individual with a crisis. If a particular crisis is handled well, a positive outcome ensues. If it is not handled well, the resulting outcome is negative. Few people emerge from a particular stage with an entirely positive or negative outcome. In fact, Erikson argues that a healthy balance must be struck between the two poles. However, the outcome should tend toward the positive side of the scale. Although people can reexperience these crises during a life change, by and large, the crises take place at particular times in life. The resolution of one stage lays the foundation for negotiating the challenges of the next stage.

TRUST VS. MISTRUST: STAGE 1 The positive outcome of the stage of infancy is a sense of **trust.** If children are cared for in a warm, caring manner, they are apt to trust the environment and develop a feeling that they live among friends. If the parents are anxious, angry, or incapable of meeting a child's needs, the child may develop a sense of **mistrust.** Trust is the cornerstone of the child's attitude toward life. For example, children with a sense of trust are inclined to believe that others will come through for them and that people are generally good, while people with a low sense of trust focus on the negative aspects of other people's behavior (Hamachek, 1988).

trust vs. **mistrust**
Erikson's first psychosocial stage, in which the positive outcome is a sense of trust and the negative outcome is a sense of suspicion.

AUTONOMY VS. SHAME OR DOUBT: STAGE 2 Two- and three-year-

9. *TRUE OR FALSE?*
——————

It is dangerous for a small and vulnerable toddler to develop a sense of autonomy.

autonomy vs. **shame** or **doubt**
The second psychosocial stage, in which the positive outcome is a sense of independence and the negative outcome is a sense of doubt about being a separate individual.

Young children have ideas for doing things. If they are told that their ideas are worthwhile and acted upon, they gain a sense of initiative.

olds are no longer completely dependent on adults. Young children practice their new physical skills and develop a positive sense of **autonomy.** They learn that they are someone on their own. If children of this age either are not allowed to do the things they can do or are pushed into doing something for which they are not ready, they may develop a sense of **shame** or **doubt** about their own abilities and fail to develop self-confidence. Parents do not help children acquire a sense of autonomy by allowing them to do everything for themselves. Rather, encouraging children to do what they can do is the key to their developing a sense of autonomy. People with a sense of autonomy have a basic attitude of "I think I can do it" and "I have something of value to offer" (Hamachek, 1988).

INITIATIVE VS. GUILT: STAGE 3 By the time children reach about four years of age, they can begin to formulate a plan of action and carry it through. The positive outcome of this stage is a sense of **initiative,** a sense that one's desires and actions are basically sound. If parents encourage

children of this age to form their own ideas, the children will develop a sense of initiative. If a child is punished for expressing his or her own desires and plans, the child develops a sense of **guilt,** which leads to fear and a lack of assertiveness. Children with a sense of initiative accept new challenges, are self-starters, and have a strong sense of personal adequacy, while those with a sense of guilt show the opposite patterns (Hamachek, 1988).

INDUSTRY VS. INFERIORITY: STAGE 4 During the middle years of childhood, children must learn the academic skills of reading, writing, and mathematics as well as a variety of social skills. At this point, children are required to learn the skills society considers necessary for their future. If a child succeeds in acquiring these new skills and the child's accomplishments are valued by others, the child develops a sense of **industry** and has a positive view of his or her achievements. But children who are constantly compared with others and come up a distinct second may develop a sense of **inferiority.** If a child's cultural, religious, or racial group is considered inferior, a sense of personal inferiority may also develop. Children with a sense of industry enjoy learning about new things and experimenting with new ideas, persevere, and take criticism well (Hamachek, 1988).

IDENTITY VS. ROLE CONFUSION: STAGE 5 During adolescence children must investigate various alternatives concerning their vocational and personal future and develop a sense of who they are and where they belong. The adolescent who develops a solid sense of **identity** formulates a satisfying plan and gains a sense of security. Adolescents who do not develop this sense of identity may develop **role confusion** and a sense of aimlessness and being adrift. Those with a sense of identity are less susceptible to peer pressure, have a higher level of self-acceptance, are optimistic, and believe they are in control of their own destinies, while those with a sense of confusion can be described in the opposite manner (Hamachek, 1988).

STAGES SIX, SEVEN AND EIGHT Erikson's final three stages cover the period of adulthood. Erikson sees the positive outcome of early adulthood as the attainment of **intimacy,** while a person who is fearful or chooses not to enter into close interpersonal relationships may develop a sense of **isolation.** In middle age, people must find a way to remain productive and to help others. This positive outcome Erikson called **generativity,** the negative outcome and danger being a feeling of **stagnation.** Finally, in old age people must develop a positive sense of pride about their accomplishments in life, which Erikson called **ego integrity.** If, on the other hand, all they see is missed opportunities, they may become depressed and bitter, developing a sense of **despair.**

Socialization, Culture, and History

Erikson broadened Freud's conception of growth and development by

initiative vs. **guilt**
The third psychosexual stage, in which the positive outcome is a positive view of one's own desires and actions and the negative outcome is a sense of guilt over one's own actions.

industry vs. **inferiority**
The fourth psychosocial stage, in which the positive outcome is a sense of confidence concerning one's accomplishments and the negative outcome is a sense of inadequacy concerning one's achievements.

identity vs. **role confusion**
The fifth psychosocial stage, in which the positive outcome is a sense of knowing who one is and the negative outcome is a sense of purposelessness.

intimacy vs. **isolation**
The sixth psychosocial stage, occurring during young adulthood, in which the positive outcome is a development of deep interpersonal relationships and the negative outcome is a flight from close relationships.

generativity vs. **stagnation**
The seventh psychosocial stage, occurring during middle adulthood, in which the positive outcome is helping others and the negative outcome is being self-absorbed and stagnated.

integrity vs. **despair**
The eighth, and last, psychosocial stage, occurring during old age, in which the positive outcome is a sense of satisfaction with one's life and the negative outcome is a sense of bitterness concerning lost opportunities.

stressing the importance of socialization, culture, and history. The resolution of each crisis depends on a person's interaction with his or her culture. The search for identity is different for an American than for a South Sea Islander. In our society, industry, the positive outcome of middle childhood, is somewhat dependent on formal school achievement. This is not true in many other cultures. Erikson also noted the importance of the historical period in which people live (Erikson, 1975). Each generation is raised under different social, political, and technological circumstances. Erikson has applied his theories to many great historical personalities, including Martin Luther and Gandhi (Erikson, 1958, 1969).

Application and Value

Erikson's theory, which is clear and easy to understand, serves as an excellent introduction to the general concerns of people at different ages. His emphasis on the importance of culture, socialization, and the historical moment extends our view of the factors that influence children. Erikson sees psychosocial development as continuing throughout life rather than stopping at adolescence. Finally, Erikson's conception of identity has become a cornerstone for understanding adolescence.

Criticisms and Cautions

Criticisms of Erikson's theory follow the criticisms of Freud's theory. Erikson's theory is difficult to test experimentally. Some support for Erikson's concept of identity exists (Hjelle & Ziegler, 1976), but little research has been done on the other stages. In addition, Erikson's theory is rather general and global, and some authorities doubt the existence of all of his stages (Thomas, 1979). Despite these criticisms, Erikson's theory offers a convenient way of viewing development throughout the life span.

◆ NONSTAGE THEORIES

The theories formulated by Piaget, Freud, and Erikson are all stage theories. Although developmental specialists are partial to stage theories, other approaches can be useful. Four such nonstage theories are discussed here. The first—information processing—looks deeply into the cognitive roots of our abilities. The second ethology, emphasizes our biological roots. Two others—the behavioral approach and social learning theory—emphasize the importance of learning.

◆ THE INFORMATION PROCESSING APPROACH

If someone were to announce, "How you ask your question partly determines the answer you receive from another person," you wouldn't see this as a startling breakthrough. After all, ask a child a question in one way, and you might receive a blank stare in return. Perhaps your question was not phrased in a way the child could understand. Were the words too difficult? Did the child understand what you were referring to? Could it be that the child's memory is at fault? I can remember trying to discover who was pilfering cookies from the cookie jar a few years ago. A full box of cookies would be poured into the jar, and less than a day later the jar would be completely empty. Since each child was allowed only two cookies a day and there were only three children, the numbers didn't add up. We asked each daughter separately whether she had taken the cookies and received the suitable wounded look and innocent response. After a number of days in which again the cookie goblin struck, I had an idea. I asked my three-year-old whether she had taken extra cookies and got the same negative response. Then I took two different cookies out of the jar and asked her to point to the type she had been taking from the jar and eating that day. With glee she pointed to the chocolate chip cookie. Since the children had not had their two cookies yet, at least we knew what had happened on that day. (At that point, my wife shook her head and said, "All that psychological education has just impressively succeeded in trapping a three-year-old into a confession.")

Although this was not one of the prouder moments in my career, it does indicate the importance of the way you ask questions and how a child's developmental stage may affect your own strategies as a parent. I don't think this strategy would have worked with my older children.

A Focus on Underlying Processes

Information processing theory emphasizes the way children take in information, process it, and then act on the information. Such factors as attention, perception, memory, the mediating process by which an individual does something to the information, and a response system are important. For instance, my three-year-old's attention was focused on the cookie in both questions. Somehow her program for denying the act was used in the first instance but not in the second. When asked to point out the type of cookie she had taken, the question tripped a different program, which we might call the recognition program.

Information processing specialists often use the computer as an analogy to the workings of the human mind, but this does not mean that they see human beings as computers or robots. The computer analogy helps us understand how children solve problems and use information. What we type into the computer (the input) is roughly analogous to information we gather from the environment through our senses. Some operations are performed on the information according to the program, and the information is encoded and stored in some way that is retrievable. Some processes must occur in our minds that enable us to attend to a particular stimulus, organize it, and remember it so it can be used in the future. The information that is retrieved and used if the proper command is given could be considered output. In the human being, the output could be some motor activity, such as moving the arm to catch a baseball, or it could be verbal, such as coming up with the answer to a math problem. Finally, an individual receives feedback—information noting whether or

information processing theory
An approach to understanding cognition that delves deeply into the way information is taken in, processed, and then acted upon.

10. TRUE OR FALSE?

In an attempt to understand how we solve problems, psychologists often equate the human mind with the computer.

not the movement or answer was effective. Just as the title of a computer program gives some clue as to what the general results of the program will be, human beings may have an upper executive plan, which coordinates the activities described above and guides purposeful behavior.

Information processing theorists are interested in following the information through the system to learn how it is encoded, processed, and retrieved (Sternberg, 1984). Thus, they look at cognition on a very detailed level, investigating the processes of perception, attention, representation, memory, and retrieval.

Patricia Miller (1989) illustrates the information processing viewpoint nicely by describing what happens when a young child first encounters the Dr. Dolittle story with the pushmi-pullyu, a horselike creature with a head at either end and a sharp horn on both heads. The child showers his attention on the picture of the delightful creature, visually encodes the image, and perhaps ignores other items on the page. He processes the visual representation, perhaps by comparing the pushmi-pullyus with his previously stored information about horses and similar creatures, perhaps unicorns. The child is told that you can't sneak up on the creature, because no matter which way you come towards him, he is always facing you, and only one half of him sleeps at a time (Lofting, 1948). The child may notice some implications of the creature and understand why there are no such creatures in zoos. He may be puzzled by how the creature knows whether it is coming or going (Miller, 1989).

Information processors would look at this little scene and ask some very specific questions. For example, how fast did the child process the information? Which details were processed, and which were ignored? How did the child relate the information to already remembered information so that it has meaning? Was the child limited in the amount of information he could process during the time he examined the picture? Did he rehearse the information, and if he did, how? What meaning does he give to the creature? Under what circumstances does he refer to the creature? If we can answer these questions (and others), we can understand the process by which the child has taken in the information about the creature, related it to information already known making the new information meaningful, and finally, decided how and when to use it.

Basic Assumptions and Principles of Information Processing

A number of assumptions and principles of information processing can help us understand the theory (see Bjorklund, 1989). First and simplest is that people process the information; that is, they do something to the information they receive to make it useful. For example, if you did not know how to read, these letters and words and sentences would be unintelligible. You must process them, that is, do something to them in your mind to make sense out of the printed word.

A little less obvious is the notion of limited capacity. We cannot process any and all information; we can deal with only a finite amount at a time. We have only so much mental space in which to operate. For example, most of us have enough capacity to walk and talk at the same time. But if someone asks you to figure out the percentage of people in your class who passed a test, there is a noticeable change in your rate of walking or talking. To solve the problem, you must use some of the capacity that you used before for walking and talking. Some things are so well learned that they become automatic and require little attention, while others require a great deal of attention. For example, a young child learning to read must use a great deal of this processing capacity to sound out words, making it difficult to get much meaning from the words and making reading a chore. As one gets more experienced, the decoding part of reading requires less attention, allowing for more processing of meaning. However, even now, if faced with a very difficult, long word, you will slow down and focus a great deal of your capacity on it.

Another assumption is that information moves through a system. This system, described by Atkinson & Shiffrin (1968), has been very influential in our understanding of information processing (see Figure 2.1). Information first enters the sensory register, in which it remains intact for a very short amount of time. From here, it passes to short-term store, where capacity is smaller but the storage lasts thirty seconds or so. This allows you to hold information long enough to evaluate it and to think about it. It is here that we apply strategies and would solve the arithmetic problem. We live here mentally. If the person does something, such as rehearsal, to the material in short-term memory, a process of transferring the information to long-term store is begun. Psychologists believe that long-term store is laid down in networks where various concepts are related to one another in a meaningful manner. Strong associations are made between closely related concepts, weaker ones between loosely related concepts, and no associations at all between others. For instance, if we are thinking about Columbus, such things as discovering America and being Italian might be strongly related. A bit less strongly related is that Columbus sailed for Spain, and unrelated to Columbus might be that the capital of New York is Albany (Kaplan, 1990). Therefore, long-term storage is a dictionary organized by meaning.

A child's knowledge base plays a very important role in how the child processes information. New memories are not laid down in a vacuum but are related to older ones. The richer the network of memories in a particular area, the easier it is for the child to relate a new incident to an older one. The child looking at the Dr. Dolittle character may be familiar with a number of four-legged animals that look like horses or llamas, making some understanding of the animal possible. We often have a framework on which to hang our memories. For instance, before learning about Columbus, we may have seen a film about explorers or heard or read about what they do. This makes learning about Columbus easier.

Psychologists have recently focused much attention on the importance of what people know—their knowledge base—to what they are trying to know or remember (Chi & Glaser, 1985). Their findings show that the more people know, the easier it is for them to lay down new memories. For example, in one study, students were asked to read a selection on baseball. Those who initially knew more about baseball obtained more

11. TRUE OR FALSE?

Children who already know something about a topic they are being told about usually find it easier to learn new information than do children who are completely unfamiliar with the topic.

FIGURE 2.1: A Model of Human Memory

In the first stage of memory, sensory input registers in the sensory memory. Sensory memories decay very quickly unless they are attended to. Paying attention to sensory memories encodes them into the short-term memory, where they can be held by rehearsal or lost through decay and displacement. To enter the long-term memory, short-term memories must be processed and stored.

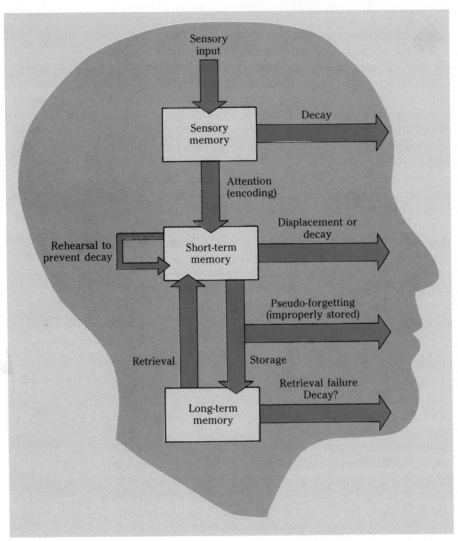

Source: Coon, 1986.

information from the reading (Recht & Leslie, 1988). Thus, an individual's prior experiences will have a significant effect on how new material is processed. The differences in the knowledge base between younger and older children, and generally between children and adults, is partially responsible for some of the differences observed in cognitive functioning.

Last, people use strategies to solve problems and process information in a meaningful manner. People use different strategies as they develop. When given some pictures to study, a young child may simply look at them, the older child will rehearse, while still older children may use different strategies, such as classifying the pictures, to remember them.

The information processing viewpoint is not always seen in a developmental framework, but it can be. Developmental changes in the ability to process information, control one's attention, and use memory strategies develop in a manner allowing one to take a developmental perspective. Throughout this text, the development of attention, memory, and problem-solving strategies is discussed.

Application and Value

The information processing approach allows us to delve more deeply into the same kinds of phenomena that interested Piaget. The Piagetian and information processing viewpoints can complement each other, giving parents and teachers new ways to analyze a child's cognitive growth. The information processing viewpoint shows great promise as a diagnostic aid in dealing with problem-solving concerns. It also opens up new and exciting possibilities in working with children who have hearing, visual, or other sensory handicaps as well as with the mentally retarded. Much research is now under way in an attempt to determine how these children take in information and process it. This may give us some idea of their strengths and weaknesses, allowing us to design better curricula for them.

Criticisms and Cautions

The information processing perspective is so new that it is difficult to analyze it critically at this point. It is hardly a unified field. A number of models have been advanced to account for the numerous subprocesses, such as encoding, memory, and retrieval, involved in processing information. No one yet knows how far the computer analogy can be taken. More importantly, we also do not know whether the mind will yield to the step-by-step analysis of subprocesses vital to the success of the information processing approach. Although the viewpoint is interesting, much work remains before we can truly judge its value for understanding how children develop and process information.

◆ ETHOLOGY

Human beings share a similar biological heritage. While we often concentrate on the differences between human beings, we should be aware of the similarities as well (Tapp, 1981). Scientists who take this approach are known as ethologists. **Ethology** involves the study of organisms in their native habitat. Ethologists emphasize the importance of understanding an organism's biological and evolutionary heritage. They observe and interpret behavior in terms of its functions (Immelmann, 1980) and con-

ethology
The study of animal and human behavior in natural environments.

sider how the behavior is triggered. Ethology also asks the question of what function the behavior may serve in the survival of the organism or the species (Bateson, 1987). The two questions "What is it for?" and "How did it evolve?" often differentiate ethologists from other scientists (Hinde, 1982). Some ethological studies involve animals while others involve human beings sometimes in a cross-cultural setting.

Ethologists often use very detailed observations in their work. For example, they may describe the interaction between a herring gull mother and its chicks and discover the type of behaviors that lead to feeding. Indeed, ethologists have discovered from observation that hungry herring gull chicks peck at a red spot on their mother's yellow beak and that this pecking causes maternal behavior that leads to the chicks' obtaining food. However, what is it about the mother's anatomy that triggers this pecking behavior? Besides observation, ethologists experimentally manipulate variables. For example, using different cardboard models of herring gulls with different colored spots and bills, ethologists have discovered that the color red triggers the pecking and the greater the contrast between the color of the bill and the spot, the greater the amount of pecking (see Immelmann, 1980). The size and shape of the head and its color have no effect. Ethologists, then, use both descriptive and experimental methods in their research.

The ethological approach is a comprehensive one, taking the entire world of the organism into account. Each species has a past evolutionary history which may, in and of itself, be an explanation for a particular behavior. However, perhaps the ethological perspective rather than any of its specific terms or concepts is most helpful in understanding human behavior. Research in the areas of linguistic, emotional, perceptual and physical development show an amazing similarity across cultures, reminding us of our common biological heritage (Tapp, 1981).

The ethological perspective has been utilized in many areas of developmental psychology, most notably the attachment between infant and caregiver (most frequently mother). The formation of a bond with a caregiver is necessary if the infant is to survive. Human infants are born with certain perceptual, sensory and behavioral abilities that promote this attachment. Even the very appearance of an infant may call forth a protective feeling in us (Alley, 1981). A number of infant behaviors may be preprogrammed in such a way that they improve the chances of forming a relationship. John Bowlby (1980) argued that such inborn behaviors as smiling, clinging and crying often elicit maternal behaviors that help form a relationship between caregiver and infant. Some of the infant's sensory abilities may help to promote contact with the caregiver. For example, some authorities claim that the newborns' vision is preprogrammed so that they prefer contours that approximate the human face. Some of the infant's reflexes such as the sucking reflex also serve survival functions. Other behaviors such as smiling and crying help signal the infant's needs and help to form an attachment. The possible functions of other abilities in the newborn which promote caregiving behavior and survival will be discussed in chapter 5.

In another context, some common fears that children have such as fear of the dark and fear of separation may have survival functions. There is also a suggestion that we are biologically programmed to learn some things easier than others. For example, it is relatively easy to learn to avoid certain foods, especially if eating them even once in the past has led to feeling ill. There are other things that are harder to learn and take many more exposures.

Ethologists have found that there are sensitive periods during which a child is ready and willing to profit from an experience. Language learning and some social behaviors may be bounded by specific time periods. In one series of experiments monkeys were systematically deprived of companionship and mothering (Harlow & Harlow, 1966). From birth on, they were isolated from other monkeys, by being reared without any contact with other monkeys. When these monkeys were released between three and six months after their confinement into the company of normal monkeys, they made a recovery becoming socially normal. However, if totally deprived of such contact for six months or longer, they showed no improvement when allowed to interact with other monkeys. Human infants who have been deprived of social contact also show a variety of social and behavioral problems and the longer the deprivation the more difficult it is to reverse it. As discussed in chapter 1, the effects of a negative early environment can be somewhat reversed if an enriched environment is provided later. The concept of sensitive periods where a particular event has its greatest effect is one of the more interesting concepts in ethology.

Years ago, ethologists emphasized rather rigid patterns of behavior. They looked for what they called "species specific behaviors," which were universal, unlearned behaviors within a species. A major component of such behaviors is "fixed action patterns," which refers to an unchanging behavior of all members of a species to certain stimuli in the environment. For example, when the female stickleback fish enters a male's territory during mating season, her presence triggers courtship behaviors involving a dance. His dance signals a particular fixed action pattern in females. The courtship continues in a series of such patterns.

Today, though, a change has occurred in ethology. The term "species typical action patterns" is used, since relatively few patterns, especially with respect to humans, are universal and fixed. Very often they are the result of complex interactions between internal states, past learning and the environment. Ethologists are now interested in the interaction of the biological areas with cognitive processes such as how information is collected, understood and acted upon (Bateson, 1987). Ethologists used to believe that all members of the same species of the same age and gender would behave the same way. The researchers sometimes described a particular behavior of a species in one habitat and argued that it could be generalized to others. However, recent studies have shown ethologists that many of the behaviors of different organisms, even if biologically prewired, vary with the environment. Many species have a number of different modes of behavior which may be selected depending upon the environmental conditions. So, even when looking at a particular species—specific behavior, the environment may determine which of the different inborn modes of behavior is followed.

Application and Value

Ethology reminds us that we are both influenced by and bounded by a biological heritage. It suggests that behaviors commonly found in children all over the world serve specific functions and that to understand the behavior it is necessary to look at the possible functions these behaviors may have in sustaining the child. When we look at some childhood behavior that appears across cultural groups, it is important to ask what function the behavior may serve for the organism. This viewpoint is especially useful when analyzing infant behaviors such as smiling and crying.

Ethological studies using detailed observation have demonstrated that such observations can indeed be objective and scientific. Some of the animal studies conducted by ethologists have suggested models that are useful in understanding human behavior. Some observational studies of animals separated from their mothers have suggested what may happen under certain circumstances to human beings.

Last, ethology takes the entire context of a behavior into consideration. The ethologist does not deny the importance of learning but rather asks us to widen our scope and consider other bases of behavior.

Criticisms and Cautions

The criticisms of the ethological approach for understanding child development center on the extensive use of observations of animal behavior which may not transfer well to human beings. Some doubt that it is a fruitful approach (Kohen-Raz, 1977). Ethological studies of cross-cultural work often suffer from methodological and interpretational difficulties as noted in chapter one. In addition, the consideration of the biological basis for some behaviors should not be used to reduce our appreciation of the plasticity and flexibility of human behavior.

The ethological viewpoint is a valuable one. One major question that is constantly raised is the extent to which our biological heritage underlies our behavior, especially our social behavior. Throughout this text, we will continually see this question asked in one form or another. It remains a controversial question and one that is frequently debated.

◆ THE BEHAVIORAL APPROACH

"Give me a dozen healthy infants, well-formed, and my own specified world to bring them up in and I'll guarantee to take any one at random and train him to become any type of specialist I might select—doctor, lawyer, merchant, chief, and yes, even beggarman and thief, regardless of his talents, penchants, abilities, vocations and the race of his ancestors" (Watson, 1930). This passage was taken from the writings of John Watson, a psychologist who changed the history of psychology. Watson argued that psychologists should study only behavior that is observable. He ruled out directly studying mental processes, such as thinking.

As you can infer from the passage quoted, **behaviorists** argue that the environment determines behavior and that if the environment is altered

behaviorist
A psychologist who explains behavior in terms of the processes of learning such as classical and operant conditioning and emphasizes the importance of the environment in determining behavior.

adequately, behavior change will follow. How does this occur? Behaviorists, such as Watson and, later, B. F. Skinner, explain behavior in terms of the processes of learning, including classical and operant conditioning.

Classical Conditioning

Classical conditioning involves the pairing of a neutral stimulus with a stimulus that elicits a particular response until the stimulus that was originally neutral elicits the response (Reese & Lipsitt, 1970). For instance, suppose every time Kindra is taken to the doctor she experiences some sort of pain—often an injection. After a while, just seeing the doctor will be enough to cause her to cry. The sight of the doctor was probably neutral at first, but when paired with discomfort or pain, it eventually elicited crying. Now whenever Kindra sees the doctor, she may cry.

To understand classical conditioning, some definitions are necessary. An **unconditioned stimulus** is the stimulus that elicits the response prior to the conditioning. In this case, the shot is the unconditioned stimulus, because it caused the crying response before the conditioning took place. The **unconditioned response** is the response to the unconditioned stimulus. The child's crying after receiving a shot is the unconditioned response. The **conditioned stimulus** is the previously neutral stimulus that acquires the ability to elicit a response when it is associated with an unconditioned stimulus. In this case, the doctor is a conditioned stimulus. Only when the doctor's presence was paired with the shot did it cause Kindra to cry. Finally, the **conditioned response** is the learned

classical conditioning
A learning process in which a neutral stimulus is paired with a stimulus that elicits a response until the originally neutral stimulus elicits that response.

unconditioned stimulus
The stimulus that elicits the response prior to conditioning.

unconditioned response
The response to the unconditioned stimulus.

conditioned stimulus
The stimulus that is neutral before conditioning and, after being paired with the unconditioned stimulus, will elicit the desired response by itself.

conditioned response
The learned response to the conditioned stimulus.

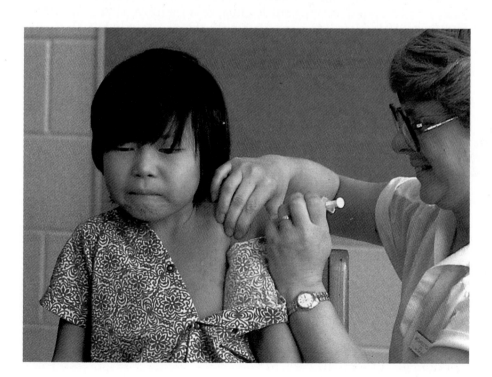

After a couple of times receiving an inoculation, this young child may cry when encountering the doctor.

stimulus generalization
The tendency of an organism that has learned to associate a certain behavior with a particular stimulus to show this behavior when confronted with similar stimuli.

discrimination
The process by which a person learns to differentiate among stimuli.

extinction
The weakening and disappearance of a learned response.

operant conditioning
The learning process in which behavior is governed by its consequences.

reinforcer
Any event that increases the likelihood that the behavior that preceded it will recur.

response that becomes attached to the conditioned stimulus. In this case, it is the child's behavior of crying when she sees the doctor.

Kindra may also exhibit this response with a number of other people who look similar to the doctor. This is called **stimulus generalization.** Experience will teach Kindra to differentiate between the doctor and people of similar appearance. When this occurs, Kindra has learned to **discriminate** between people. She may then cry when she sees the doctor, but not when she sees other people. Will Kindra's fear ever end, or will she always cry in the doctor's office? Perhaps after many experiences in which a visit to the doctor does not mean experiencing pain, the response will be **extinguished**—that is, Kindra will no longer respond to the situation by crying.

Classical conditioning is especially useful for understanding emotional response, such as a child's response to the voice of his or her parents or the experiences of a child in a classroom when faced with a teacher who always criticizes him or her. The teacher was at first neutral but, when paired with constant criticism, may cause the child to feel anxious every time the child hears the teacher's voice or sees the teacher.

Operant Conditioning

In **operant conditioning,** the child's behavior is followed by some event that increases or decreases the frequency of the behavior that preceded it. If the event increases the likelihood that the behavior will recur, the action is said to be **reinforced.** If it decreases the chances of its occurring, it is said to be punished. In operant conditioning, then, behavior is governed by its consequences. Suppose a two-year-old brings you the newspaper. You respond with a smile, a hug, or a thank you. You may then find that this toddler brings you not only the newspaper but also your keys, wallet, handkerchief, and anything else the child can find on the table. The youngster has been reinforced for being helpful.

Reinforcement is a potent force in shaping behavior, but the same reinforcer is not effective in every situation or with every individual. An offer of two more lamb chops to someone who has just finished dinner is not an effective reinforcer, nor would it be effective to someone who hates lamb chops.

Parents are the most important givers of reinforcement during the child's early years. As children grow and their social world expands, reinforcements delivered by peers, teachers, and siblings also become important. In fact, parents and siblings may reinforce children for different behaviors. My three-year-old daughter stuck out her tongue and made a funny face at the dinner table. My wife and I ignored her, but her older sisters thought she was very funny and reinforced her behavior by giving her plenty of attention. She naturally continued to make faces. In fact, she showed stimulus generalization by beginning to make faces in front of her grandparents and aunts when they visited, but she soon learned stimulus discrimination because she received no attention from these people for her behavior. We finally had to tell our other daughters to ignore their sister's behavior and not reinforce it with their attention. It took some time before the three-year-old finally stopped.

As my daughter discovered, the setting is very important. We learn that if we behave in a certain way under some circumstances we will be rewarded, while that same behavior under other circumstances will not be. My daughter learned to make funny faces only in front of her sisters. Generalization and discrimination are important concepts and explain many behaviors. If Pat is reinforced for being aggressive by getting what he wants, he will show this behavior in many contexts. He begins by taking toys away from a younger brother and generalizes this behavior to peers in school. However, he soon learns when this will work and when it will be counterproductive. In other words, Pat must learn to discriminate. Using profanity with friends may be acceptable, but it is inappropriate in front of Grandma. Being aggressive and hostile may be successful in getting his way in early childhood with some peers, but it is ineffective in late adolescence when trying to talk his way out of a speeding ticket.

The behavioral perspective emphasizes the past history of the organism, the setting, and the reinforcers available. No mention is made of what occurs within the mind, of thought processes, or of memory.

Application and Value

The behavioral view is valuable in pinpointing the importance of the environment. Even those who criticize behaviorism usually acknowledge that the environment has a tremendous effect on behavior (May, 1969; Rogers, 1980). The question is whether it has total control or whether internal, cognitive factors, such as thinking and information processing abilities, must also be taken into account to understand the organism better. Another contribution of behaviorism is its emphasis on experimental methodology. Although it may seem stifling at times, experimental methodology does produce high-quality work.

Criticisms and Cautions

The most common criticism of the behavioral view of human development is that it is too mechanical. This approach makes human beings seem too predictable, and the avoidance of such concepts as consciousness, thinking, and subjective experience is a problem. It is doubtful that all human development can be understood on the basis of the principles of learning.

◆ SOCIAL LEARNING THEORY

We do not always have to be reinforced or punished to change our behavior. We can learn by observing and imitating others and by watching the consequences of the behavior of others. If a person touches a hot stove and gets burned, we do not have to do it ourselves.

Learning Through Observation and Imitation

Observation learning and imitation are so common that we may not fully appreciate their importance. Youngsters repeat words they hear and often imitate the gestures they see. One two-year-old girl pointed to her sister as if lecturing and called out with a straight face, "You better do that"— an exact imitation of the way her mother would say it. **Social learning theory** investigates the process of observation and imitation learning (Bandura, 1986).

Sometimes a child's imitation can be embarrassing to parents. One of my friends has a large family spread out over eighteen years. The three-year-old adored his eighteen-year-old brother, who was a senior in high school. Each morning the eighteen-year-old would wake up bleary-eyed and late and walk around the room getting dressed with his eyes only half open. He could never seem to find a pair of socks that matched, and when opening his dresser drawer, he would curse. One day, the mother was opening the drawer to put away the older son's socks. Immediately, the three-year-old ran over and put himself in the mother's way. "Mommy," he said, "You forgot to say &%#!@!"

Imitation is not always exact, however. You may watch your favorite tennis player and try to imitate his or her play, yet you will be limited

social learning theory
The theoretical view emphasizing the process by which people learn through observing others and imitating their behaviors.

Boys and girls who had watched an adult modeling violence were more likely to show violent behavior in that same situation than children who had not witnessed the model's violent behavior.

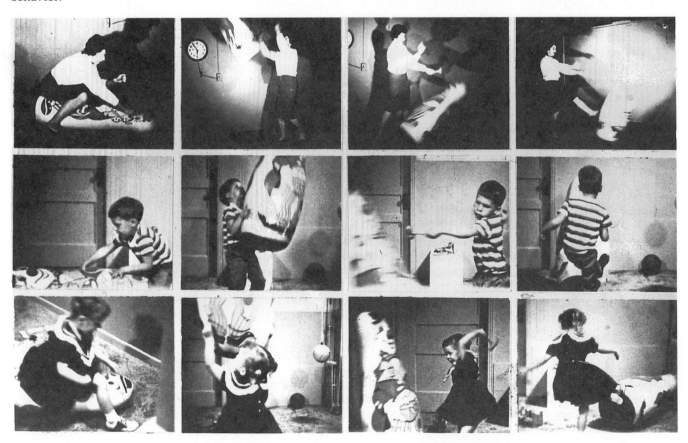

by your own physical ability. We adapt what we see in a creative way that mirrors our own understanding of the situation and our abilities.

Imitation can be seen in many behaviors. For instance, children learn to be aggressive or altruistic through observing respected people engaging in these behaviors (Mussen and Eisenberg-Berg, 1977). People also learn partly through observation how males and females are expected to act within a particular culture (Bandura, 1986).

At times we learn general principles when watching others. Some children watched a model expound on ways to use a cardboard box creatively as a house or a hat. When asked to suggest uses for a tin can, these children showed more creativity but did not use the model's ideas. What they learned was that creativity was acceptable (Navarick, 1979).

Eating and dressing are also influenced by observation, as are fears. For instance, if children see others being afraid of the dark, they may follow suit. One mother was very afraid of spiders but did not want her children to have the same fear. She made a conscious effort to pick up a spider and smile, believing that by modeling this type of behavior her children would be less likely to develop a fear of spiders. This may be beyond the sensitivities of many people who experience a fear, but it has been used in therapeutic situations. When a group of children who were afraid of dogs were exposed to a film showing other children playing with dogs freely and happily, this exposure reduced their fear (Bandura, Grusec & Menlove, 1967).

12. TRUE OR FALSE?

For children to learn, they must be reinforced directly.

The Process of Imitation

We can understand imitation as a four-step process (Bandura 1986, 1977) involving attention, retention, motor reproduction, and motivational processes.

ATTENTION The first step is paying attention to the model. Whether a student pays attention or not depends upon the characteristics of the model, the value of the model's behavior, and the characteristics of the observer. Models who are regular associates or peers, who are personally engaging and prestigious, or who are seen as especially credible gain attention. Models who have high status or are successful, competent, and powerful are also effective. The functional value of the model's behavior is also an important consideration. If the behavior is relevant and understandable, it is likely to garner attention. The characteristics of the learner, including arousal status (is the learner drowsy?), interest, and present and past performance, also influence attention.

RETENTION If the behavior that the child has noticed is to be used, it must first be encoded and stored.

MOTOR REPRODUCTION In this step, the individual selects the behavior and executes it. Motor reproduction is, of course, influenced by the developmental level of the child as well as by the child's history. A child who wants to hit a baseball like his or her favorite ballplayer may not physically be able to. In addition, people learn a number of behaviors through observation that they may never exhibit in their own behavior. Children witness hundreds of murders on television as well as all sorts of other behaviors, including poor behavior in the classroom, but may never perform these acts. The behaviors may be stored, but inhibitions against doing them may prevent a person from acting on the information.

MOTIVATIONAL PROCESSES After a child produces a behavior, some reinforcement must be available to the child. According to Bandura, reinforcement provides children with information about what might happen in the future if they perform the particular behavior. It can also motivate children. Children may remember the consequences of the behavior and later use the information to attain their own ends. They do not have to experience the reinforcement personally.

Three processes function as motivation: direct reinforcement, vicarious reinforcement (seeing others reinforced), and self-reinforcement. Students who anticipate that if they study they will be reinforced are more likely to study. But direct reinforcement is not necessary. Vicarious reinforcement can also affect the probability of performance. If the model is reinforced for doing something, it could encourage such behavior in the observer. Observing others being punished conveys information about which behaviors are and are not tolerated. The third motivator is self-reinforcement, in which an individual reinforces him or herself for performing a particular act.

Social learning theorists believe that to understand how people acquire such complex behaviors as helping and sharing we must appreciate the relationship between the behavior, the environment and personal and cognitive factors. Each factor can influence the other two and, in turn, be influenced by the other two. Albert Bandura (1986) illustrates the reciprocal influence by using the example of a child watching television. Personal preferences certainly influence what the child will watch. However, through their viewing behavior children also influence the environment, in this case, what is televised. If enough children watch a program, it will continue to be broadcast. At the same time, what is televised shapes the children's preferences. Children can only watch what is televised and what children see can shape their preferences.

Consider an elementary schoolchild trying to master reading. As the child does the exercises the teacher suggests and practices his skills, the child's reading improves greatly. This in turn produces changes in the environment, as the teacher may give the child a more positive evaluation and perhaps works harder with the child. At the same time the child can now read different and more interesting books allowing for additional choice. Here we see the behavior (learning to read and practicing) affecting the environment (the teacher's behavior and the physical composition of the room). At the same time, having more choice to read also affects his behavior. Having these additional, more interesting books available he may now read more. Notice that a change in the environment (having more books to read) can lead to a change in the behavior (reading).

Similarly, his success in reading influences his beliefs about reading.

THE CHILD
IN THE YEAR
2000

Predictability: Power and Caution

Consider these two scenarios:

—A child has experienced a very long and difficult birth. There is some concern that the child may have suffered some damage. A psychologist tests the infant's intelligence and cognitive functioning. Based upon this examination, specialists design a program of environmental stimulation and education to improve the child's cognitive abilities.

—A child is born into an abusive family. The father frequently yells and hits the children for just about everything, while the mother is a highly strung individual who punishes the children harshly. The psychologist predicts that because of the unhealthy models available, the child may grow up to abuse his own children. The psychologist designs a program to expose the child to nonviolent models and improve the child's self-concept.

One of the useful features of theory is its ability to predict some future behavior. In the first case, information processing theory has indeed succeeded in finding certain early information processing abilities that predict later cognitive behaviors. In the second case, social learning theory would predict that the child is *at risk* for becoming an adult who abuses his own children. Many modern developmental psychologists are fascinated by the possibility of early intervention, and the search for early behaviors that predict later behavior is an ongoing one.

There is a catch, however. Our ability to predict is far from perfect. Although the correlation between information processing abilities in infancy and later cognitive ability is good, it is far from perfect. And despite what the newspapers and television may say, studies have shown that about one-third of children growing up in abusive homes abuse their own children. This figure is certainly much higher than in the general population, but again is far from 100 percent.

What does this moderate predictability mean for our theories? It certainly does not mean that the theories are not useful. In fact, the evidence supports the theories. However, this moderate predictability indicates that we need to search for even more powerful predictors and that other factors are involved. For example, studies show that most children from violent homes do not violently abuse their own children, and we must find out what the differences are between those who do and those who do not grow up to violently abuse their own children. We also must be careful not to mislabel children early in life.

Our current state of theory and research demonstrates moderate predictive power. In the future, our ability to predict will improve, although it will not become perfect. By the year 2000, though, our predictive abilities will be sorely tested by a society that will emphasize the prevention of problems rather than the remediation of problems. The child in the future will be subjected to more tests and more interventions whose aim is to prevent problems from developing. This in itself is a healthy outlook. It is certainly easier and more cost effective to prevent problems than to remediate them. However, we must balance the benefits of this early testing against the possible problem of overestimating the predictive power of our tests and labeling children prematurely and incorrectly. This balancing act is a difficult challenge but one that psychologists must meet if the dream of preventing serious problems from developing is to become a reality.

He now believes that he can read and this influences his choice of leisure activities. He may now choose to read more. His change in cognition (belief about himself) changed his behavior, while his behavior (learning to read) changed his beliefs about himself. His cognitive change, now believing that he can read, may alter his environment because he may now surround himself with more books in his room as well.

This viewpoint reminds us of the importance of the interaction between the environment, cognitive processes and behavior itself. By looking at this interaction, the complex influences on behavior become more understandable.

Application and Value

Social learning theory reminds us of the importance of observation learning and imitation in determining behavior. It is useful in understanding the genesis of many behaviors—from giving to charity to being aggressive (Bandura & Walters, 1963), from choosing clothing to understanding speech patterns.

Criticisms and Cautions

Social learning theory is not without limitations. In the realm of child development, it completely lacks a developmental framework (Cairns, 1979). The process of imitation is described in terms that give little consideration to maturation or to the differences between the imitative behavior of a toddler and that of an adolescent (Thomas, 1979). As a result, although social learning theory explains some behaviors very well, it has difficulty with age-related developmental changes.

◆ HOW TO USE THEORIES

Each theory in this chapter has its own way of looking at child development (see Table 2.2). The decision to use a particular theory leads a researcher to ask specific questions as demonstrated in the Cross-Cultural Current on page 86. For instance, a researcher who used a behavioral approach might concentrate on what reinforcers were present in a particular environment and look at what behaviors the child had learned throughout childhood. A researcher using a Freudian perspective might ask questions about a child's unconscious motivations and early relationships with his or her caregivers. A researcher who used an information processing approach would consider how a child is interpreting his or her environment and deciding what his or her alternatives are. Each theory adds something to our understanding of child development.

Many child development specialists are aware that there are many ways to look at a particular behavior. This is a strength, not a weakness, since each approach has something different to offer. Some child development specialists are eclectic; that is, they adopt the most useful aspects of various theories rather than work from only one perspective. Such eclecticism is healthy if it allows us to appreciate the many ways a particular behavior can be studied (Rychlak, 1985).

Throughout this book we will be describing behavior from a number of different perspectives. Each perspective may look at the subject from a different point of view, but each has as its purpose a better understanding of the developing child.

TABLE 2.2: Summary of Developmental Theories

THEORY	BASIC PREMISES	VALUES AND STRENGTHS	CRITICISMS AND WEAKNESSES
Piaget's Theory of Cognitive Psychology	1. Children do not think or solve problems in the same manner as adults. 2. Emphasizes the importance of the child's active interaction with the environment. 3. Sees maturation and experience as more important than formal learning in the child's cognitive development. 4. Views cognitive development as occurring in four stages. Each stage shows a qualitative leap forward in the child's ability to solve problems and reason logically. 5. Most complete description of cognitive development from infancy through childhood available.	1. Emphasizes the importance of active experience in child's development. Leads to a view of young children as little scientists sifting through information and actively coping with the world. 2. Descriptions of the way in which children think and approach problems very helpful in understanding children's behavior. 3. Many of the sequences for understanding specific concepts are very challenging.	1. May underestimate the influence of learning on cognitive development and the nature of task on the child's performance. 2. Piaget's style of research has been criticized. Piaget presented children with a problem and sought to discover how they reasoned and tried to solve the problem. His experiments were not controlled.
Freud's Psychoanalytic Theory	1. Behavior is motivated by unconscious thoughts, memories, and feeling. 2. Life is the unfolding of the sex instinct. 3. The child's early experience is crucial to his or her later personality. The manner in which the parents satisfy the child's basic needs is important to later mental health. 4. Children develop through a sequence of stages called psychosexual stages. 5. People protect themselves from anxiety and other negative emotions through unconscious and automatic reactions called defense mechanisms.	1. Encourages developmental specialists to look beyond the obvious visible behavior and seek insights into the unconscious. 2. Emphasizes the importance of the child's early experience and relationships, which in turn focuses our attention on the caregiver-infant relationship. The idea that later problems may be due to disturbed early relationships is challenging. 3. The concept of stages in Freudian theory has become a popular way of viewing the development of children.	1. Since theory is based upon clinical experiences with troubled people, it may have more to say about unhealthy than healthy development. 2. Hypotheses are very difficult to test. 3. Failure to appreciate the importance of culture.

THEORY	BASIC PREMISES	VALUES AND STRENGTHS	CRITICISMS AND WEAKNESSES
Freud's Psychoanalytic Theory (continued)		4. Emphasis on sexuality, while debatable, still alerts us to the existence of sexuality at all ages. 5. Serves as a focal point for other theorists.	
Erik Erikson's Psychosocial Theory	1. Explains development in terms of the epigenetic principle. Personality develops according to predetermined steps that are maturationally set. Society is structured to encourage the challenges that arise at these times in a person's life. 2. Describes development in terms of eight stages from cradle to grave. Each has positive and negative outcomes. 3. Emphasizes the importance of culture and the historical period in which the individual is living.	1. Sees development as continuing over the life span. 2. Importance of culture and historical period adds to our appreciation of factors that affect children's development. 3. Provides a good general overview of crises that occur at each stage of a child's life. Some of these crises, such as identity versus role confusion, have become important in understanding specific periods in a child's life.	1. Difficult to test experimentally. 2. Theory is rather general.
Information Processing	1. Emphasizes the importance of the manner in which children take in information, process it, and then act upon it. 2. Such processes as attention, perception memory, and processing strategies are studied.	1. Yields a detailed look at the processes involved in taking in and processing information. 2. May serve as a diagnostic aid in discovering where people have difficulties in solving problems.	1. It is not a unified approach. A number of models have been advanced. 2. It still awaits adequate testing.
Ethology	1. It is important to consider the evolutionary heritage of a species. 2. Emphasizes the importance of how a particular behavior pattern developed. 3. Emphasizes the function of a particular behavioral pattern to the survival and functioning of the organism and species.	1. Reminds us of the importance of biological heritage. 2. Encourages us to look at the function of behavior. 3. Widens our areas of concern and possible views of causation.	1. Question of how useful animal models and experimentation is to understanding human behavior. 2. Possible problem of overemphasizing inborn patterns of behavior.

THEORY	BASIC PREMISES	VALUES AND STRENGTHS	CRITICISMS AND WEAKNESSES
Ethology (continued)	4. Looks at the importance of the overall environment, what triggers a particular behavior, and the similarities in behavior within a given species. 5. Considers the importance of sensitive periods in the development of the organism. 6. Uses detailed observations in research.		3. Difficult to test the importance of biological bases of behavior in discussing social behaviors.
Radical Behavioral Approach	1. Human behavior may be explained by the processes of learning including classical and operant conditioning. 2. The behavioral approach has been successful in modifying the behavior of people in many situations. 3. The behavioral approach does not deny consciousness and mental processes like thinking, but rather deals with behavior and development in a different manner. 4. Development is seen as continuous with no stages posited to explain progress.	1. Learning theories are clear, precise, and laboratory tested. 2. The emphasis on the environment is important.	1. Some consider it too mechanical. Its avoidance of mental processes such as consciousness and thinking may yield only a partial picture of behavior. 2. Sees little qualitative difference between humans and animals.
Social Learning Theory	1. Human behavior is partially explained through the process of imitation and observation learning. 2. The process of imitation may be explained using a four step process involving attention, encoding and memory, behavioral reproduction, and, finally, reinforcement.	1. Is useful in understanding certain behaviors such as altruism and aggression. 2. Encourages us to look at the models in the person's environment.	1. Lacks a developmental framework. The process of imitation is viewed as the same no matter who is observing. 2. Does not explain age related changes.

Explaining Differences in Aggression in Two Communities in Mexico

Imagine that you are called upon to explain why children in one community are much more aggressive than children who live just a few miles away in another community. Add to this puzzle, the fact that the communities share many similarities. They are both agricultural, speak the same language, have similar local governments, similar diets and are alike in many other ways.

This was the situation faced by Douglas Fry when he investigated two Zapotec Indian communities living in Oaxaca, Mexico. The Zapotec people live in a valley in the center of a mountainous state in southern Mexico. They live in separate communities of about 5,000 people. There are a number of communities in this valley and earlier investigations indicated that these communities differ greatly in their levels of violence. Some are very violent, while others quite peaceful. Why would these communities with so many similarities differ so much in aggression?

If you were faced with this problem, where would you begin? In determining how to investigate this situation, you need to adopt a theoretical viewpoint which would suggest what to look for and how to proceed. In this case, Fry believed that a social learning approach would help explain the differences between the two communities. Perhaps the children in one community are more aggressive because they imitate or in some way learn from observing their parents and other elders in the community. We know that children who witness a great deal of violence, much of it rewarded or accepted, may become aggressive and use aggression in many social situations. The same mechanism may partially explain nonaggressive communities. If elders settle their disputes peacefully and children see few ex-

amples of aggressive behavior, they may adopt these nonviolent behavior patterns.

To investigate the nature of aggression, Fry singled out two communities which, when previously studied, differed greatly in levels of aggression. In a community called La Paz little aggression took place, while in the other called San Andres a much higher level of aggression occurred. (These names are pseudonyms used to protect the identities of the communities.) In San Andres, the more violent community, husbands beat their wives, adults regularly fought at public celebrations and the homicide rate was much higher than in the more peaceful community. Parents in San Andres both advocated and used more severe types of physical punishments. In the peaceful community, these aggressive behaviors were much less common and parents both advocated and used nonphysical means to discipline their children.

Twenty-four children in each community ranging from age three to seven years were observed for more than 70 hours over an eighteen month time span. These children came from different homes and were roughly in the middle economic level of the communities involved. The children from the two communities were similar in a number of demographic variables including age of parents and number of siblings. Informal conversations and interviews were also conducted.

In order to better understand aggression, Fry divided aggression into two categories, serious aggression and play aggression. We know that play aggression involving running, chasing and wrestling differs substantially from true aggression. Such play aggression takes place with a nonthreatening look, sometimes a smile on one's face. In addition, Fry differentiated between aggression involving ac-

SUMMARY

1. Theories give facts their meaning and help us interpret data. Theories allow us to relate one fact to another and predict behavior.
2. A good theory is determined by its usefulness, testability, ability to predict behavior, and inclusiveness.
3. Theories in developmental psychology can be divided into two distinct types. Stage theories emphasize the

idea that children develop in a particular sequence or in stages. The sequence of stages is invariable, progress is always in the forward direction, and no regression occurs. However, children can enter and leave any particular stage at a different age, depending upon individual factors. Nonstage theorists do not agree with the concept of stages, seeing development as a more con-

tual physical contact, threat of aggression without contact, and threat occurring with contact.

Fry found that play fighting and rough and tumble play existed in both cultures, but the children from San Andres engaged in significantly more of it. Play aggression also lasted longer in San Andres. In neither community was serious aggression a very common phenomenon among children, nor did it last very long. However, again, the amount of serious aggression in San Andres was twice as high as in the more peaceful community. Yet the aggressive incidents in the peaceful community lasted much longer. This was explained by the difference in the type of aggression found in these two communities. Most aggression in the La Paz community began with a threat, while very little threat occurred in the San Andres community. This made the entire aggressive incident longer in the La Paz community. Play aggression occurred much more often in both communities than serious aggression with a ratio of 8.8 in San Andres and 9.5 to 1 in La Paz.

Age differences were also found. In San Andres older children engaged in higher rates of most types of serious and play aggression than younger children. On the other hand, older La Paz children engaged in lower rates of most types of serious and play aggression than younger children.

Fry observed that the San Andres children were often rambunctious and mischievous while those from La Paz were usually compliant and well behaved. While the parents in San Andres often stated that they disapproved of fighting they also expressed the belief that a certain amount of aggression and play fighting were normal and the adults did not break up or discourage fights when they saw them. There were even instances where San Andres parents encouraged fighting. They believed that there was little or nothing that parents could do or should do about fighting. Parental attitudes and behavior differed in the peaceful community. In La Paz, fighting was actively discouraged and parents sometimes intervened. Fry concludes that as predicted from social learning theory, Zapotec children from

a peaceful community engaged in less aggression and less play aggression than those from a more violent community. The less frequently occurring aggressive episodes in La Paz were also less severe because much aggression was combined with non-contact threatening. With age, La Paz children become somewhat more restrained while San Andres children become more aggressive. The society in which children live, then, certainly seems to affect their tendency to show aggression.

The observations described in this study support the hypothesis that the differing patterns of aggression in the two communities are passed down from one generation to the next. Children may, indeed, learn aggression from observing their parents and other elders in the society as suggested by social learning theory.

But why should two similar communities show such different patterns? Here, we can only guess at the reasons behind its development. We know that the average person in La Paz owns more land than the average person in San Andres. In fact, some people in San Andres do not own any. There are many more land disputes in San Andres than in La Paz. Perhaps people in San Andres have had to fight more to protect what they see as their land and economic well-being, and this has affected the development of their society. We also know that jealousy is much more common in San Andres, and fights over women, sometimes ending in homicide, are more common. The origin of differences in male jealousy in the communities is unknown but appears to be maintained over the generations.

While such major differences in levels of aggression between these two communities are probably due to many reasons, the use of a social learning explanation certainly makes sense. It explains how children within each community maintain these differences over generations, although the data do not answer the questions about how and why the community differences originally developed.

Source: D.P. Fry, 1988 "Intercommunity Differences in Aggression among Zapotec Children," *Child Development* 59, pp. 1008–1019.

tinuous process, with new behaviors coming directly from older capabilities.
4. Jean Piaget investigated the cognitive, or intellectual, development of the child. He noted that children do not think like adults and described four stages through which children pass between birth and adolescence. Piaget's theory is noteworthy because of his discovery of the sequences of development leading to an adult's understanding of such concepts as mathematics, time,

and space. Piaget also viewed the child as actively involved with the environment and stressed the importance of discovery. His theory has been criticized because it underestimates the importance of formal learning.
5. Psychoanalytic theory emphasizes the importance of the early parent-child relationship. Freud argued that children progress through five psychosexual stages that involve the unfolding of the sexual instinct. Freud's

concepts of stage development, infantile and child sexuality, unconscious motivation, and defense mechanisms are noteworthy. Psychoanalytic theory has been criticized because it is difficult to test, considers sexuality the prime motivation, and emphasizes deviancy.

6. Erik Erikson argued that people proceed through eight stages from the cradle to the grave. Each stage presents people with different tasks. If a task is successfully negotiated, there is a positive outcome; if not, there is a negative outcome. Erikson's theory is noteworthy because it provides a good framework for viewing development, emphasizes the importance of culture and history, and sees life as continuing throughout the life span. It has been criticized because it is overly broad and general and difficult to explore experimentally.

7. Information processing theory focuses on the way people take in information, process it, and finally act on it. Such factors as attention, perception, memory, and response systems are investigated. It is a noteworthy approach because it yields specific information on how a child solves a particular problem. However, it is not

as well developed as other theoretical approaches, and only additional experimentation will determine how useful it will be.

8. Ethology involves the study of organisms in their native habitat. Ethologists are interested in the functions of particular behaviors and how they developed. They emphasize the importance of the organism's biological heritage.

9. Learning theorists or behaviorists do not emphasize the concept of stages but stress the importance of classical conditioning and operant conditioning. It has been criticized for being too mechanical and not adequately taking consciousness and thought processes into consideration.

10. Social learning theorists emphasize the importance of imitation to the understanding of behavior. It has been criticized as lacking a developmental framework.

11. Developmental psychology lacks a unified theory that covers every aspect of development. A researcher will choose the theory that seems most useful in understanding the developmental phenomena of interest.

ACTION/REACTION

Dealing with the Stubborn Child

Lee is an active, engaging two-and-a-half-year-old. He has a mind of his own and a good vocabulary to go along with it. Both his mother, Sharon, and his father, Will, are keenly aware of the importance of providing a stimulating atmosphere for Lee. Both play with him a great deal, but lately Will has been saying that the child is ready for bigger and better things. Will is trying to teach Lee such concepts as in and out and up and down as well as some of the letter sounds. Some number concepts are included in the lessons, as is the concept of grouping things into categories (squares and triangles, for example).

According to Will, however, Lee is stubborn. Lee refuses to work even for a short period of time with his parents. He seems to give the wrong answers on purpose. Will believes that Lee knows the right answers but for some reason just won't try. Sharon has read a few books on child development and thinks things would be better if Lee were left alone to play as he wishes. "Piaget says to let the child alone," she tells her husband.

1. If Will asked your opinion of his teaching strategies and approaches, how would you respond?

2. If you were a psychologist, how would you respond to Sharon's ideas about cognitive development?

The Temper Tantrum

Almost every parent has to handle a child's temper tantrum at one time or another. But what do you do when it's an everyday occurrence?

Carrie is four-years-old and a bright, playful child, but when she doesn't get her way she screams and throws things. She becomes inconsolable. Carrie engages in this behavior with both her parents, but most often with her mother. The mother's response is to give in, try to reason with her, or turn her attention to something else. Carrie's father usually gives in to her before the tantrum begins. When he doesn't, he spanks her. The girl then runs to her mother and screams even more. Since the mother doesn't believe in spanking, she tries to quiet Carrie by playing with her. She has told her husband that the child will become afraid of him when she gets older.

Carrie's mother is at the end of her rope. She can't take the screaming. Carrie's father wants Carrie's mother to ignore it or spank the child, which the mother does not believe to be the best policy. Carrie's mother doesn't know why the tantrums began or why they are getting worse— only that she has to do something.

1. If you were Carrie's parents, how would you handle Carrie's tantrums?
2. If you were Carrie's mother, how would you deal with your husband's behavior toward the child?

◆

CHAPTER THREE

Genetic Influences on Development

Family Tree by Norman Rockwell.

Are These Statements True or False?

Turn the page for the correct answers. Each statement is repeated in the margin next to the paragraph in which the information can be found.

1. All animal species, including human beings, have the same number of chromosomes: forty-six.
2. Fraternal twins are no more genetically alike than any other pair of siblings.
3. If a family has five male children, the chances are quite small that the sixth child will be a boy.
4. The serious genetic disease cystic fibrosis can be cured through massive doses of vitamins.
5. Color blindness is found mostly in males.
6. Left-handedness is largely determined by the environment.
7. At the present time, all that medical science can do for children suffering from genetic diseases is make them more comfortable.
8. Children with the chromosomal disorder of Down syndrome usually require institutionalization by the age of five.
9. Schizophrenia, like cystic fibrosis or Tay-Sachs disease, is transmitted directly from parent to child.
10. There is a genetic basis for being extroverted, that is, having an outgoing personality.
11. Identical twins reared apart are more similar in intelligence than fraternal twins reared together.
12. Genetic counselors have the responsibility to approve or disapprove of their clients' course of action.

Answers to True-False Statements

1. False. Correct statement: Each species has its own number of chromosomes.
2. True.
3. False. Correct statement: The odds stay the same for each conception.
4. False. Correct statement: At the present time there is no cure for cystic fibrosis.
5. True.
6. False. Correct statement: Although there is some environmental input, handedness is largely determined by genetic considerations.
7. False. Correct statement: This is an overly pessimistic view, as the success in treating phenylketonuria shows.
8. False. Correct statement: Most children with Down syndrome are now raised at home.
9. False. Correct statement: What is transmitted is apparently a predisposition to the disorder, not the disorder itself.
10. True.
11. True.
12. False. Correct statement: Genetic counselors offer information that allows their clients to make an informed, personal decision.

◆ THE STRANGE CASE OF TWINS

The "Jim" twins were a fascinating pair. Separated at four weeks of age, they finally met thirty-nine years later. Their similarities, aside from their physical appearance, were incredible. Both had taken law enforcement training and served as deputy sheriffs. Both men owned Chevrolets and vacationed in Florida. Both married and divorced women named Linda and remarried women named Betty. Even their dogs shared the same name—Toy.

Another set of twins separated shortly after birth were named Raymond and Richard. Raymond was adopted into a home of a rich doctor in the same town, while Richard was adopted by a family that was always on the brink of financial disaster. Raymond had every advantage and never experienced poverty. Richard's father never worked, and the family never lived in one place for any length of time. Richard learned to do things for himself. Though the twins came from different backgrounds, their intelligence scores were almost identical, and their character and emotional stability were as alike as if they had been raised together (McBroom, 1980).

Perhaps the most famous and unusual case involved identical twins Oscar Stohr and Jack Yufe, who were separated shortly after birth and did not meet for forty-seven years. Oscar was taken to Germany by his mother and became a Nazi. His brother Jack was raised by his father as a Jew in the Caribbean and spent some time working on a communal farm in Israel. The similarities were obvious from the moment they met. Both sported wire-rimmed glasses and mustaches, and they shared a number of food preferences. But some of the similarities seem to defy explanation. They both always flushed the toilet before using it and read magazines from the back to the front. They showed remarkable similarities in temperament, too. Both had hasty tempers and unusual senses of humor; for example, both enjoyed surprising people by sneezing in elevators (Holden, 1987).

Can these unusual similarities be explained as mere coincidences? This is a matter of dispute. As more twins who have been raised apart are found and tested, such similarities become more difficult to dismiss as statistical accidents. Perhaps genetic endowment plays a larger role in the development of personality and behavior than we thought.

Not all twins reared apart manifest such similarities. In fact, Raymond and Richard differed somewhat in temperament. Richard was more aggressive, probably because he had been protected less and needed to develop a greater sense of self-reliance. So experience is also important in the development of personality and behavior. In addition, while twins reared apart who show striking similarities are constantly hounded by the news media, those who do not are often lost in the shuffle. Not all identical twins show such similarities (other than physical), and the lives of many sets of identical twins differ greatly from each other (Ainslie, 1985). Last, twins separated at birth may actually have more in common than those who have been raised together (Holden, 1980; Farber, 1981). Twins raised together often must assert their individuality from the other. Some twins show a pattern where one is more dominant or outgoing than the other. When they are raised apart, this may not be necessary.

The question of the extent to which genetic endowment affects development and behavior is a controversial one. At the present time, there is no accepted explanation for such similarities. Only one thing is certain. The general public will continue to be fascinated by twins reared apart and reunited, and psychologists will continue to try to unravel the complicated questions that surround such people's similarities and differences.

This chapter looks at the mechanisms of inheritance and the diverse areas in which our genetic endowment has some effect on our lives. In addition, the chapter looks briefly at some of the great advances in genetics and the nature of the choices this new knowledge and technology affords us.

◆ A NEW LOOK AT GENETICS

Historically, the most basic question anyone could ask about genetic influence on development and behavior was what percentage of a particular trait could be attributed to one's genetic endowment. The term **heritability** refers to how much of the variation seen in people in a particular trait, such as intelligence, is due to genetic endowment.

heritability
A term used to describe how much of the variation seen in any particular trait is due to genetic endowment.

Research on heritability is useful. It helps us gain an appreciation of the many aspects of our lives that are affected by our genes, and it has demonstrated that certain traits are more influenced by genetic factors than others. For example, the characteristic of height is under greater genetic influence than is skill at shooting marbles. Yet the results of heritability studies are often incorrectly interpreted, and when this happens the public is misled. Heritability figures are sometimes cited by the media without explanation. The percentage of any particular trait attributed to heredity depends on the specific population studied and the particular environment.

For example, what heritability figure would you place on the ability to play tennis? For most people, the ability to drive that baseline shot past an opponent will depend on the quantity and quality of practice. The heritability index is very low, near zero. However, this may not be the case for a professional tennis player. "An outstanding player must have excellent neuromuscular coordination, and people vary in the limits to which their coordination can be trained" (Sutton, 1980, p. 362). If we exposed every child in North America to an intensive program in tennis, hockey, or any other sport, some would still become more adept at the sport than others. There is some genetic influence on the necessary skills. Yet the genetic influence would be greater in the case of an expert than an occasional Saturday afternoon player.

Musical talent presents us with another illustration. A child's ability to sing passably is due mostly to practice, persistence, training, and motivation, all of which are environmental factors. However, these factors do not account for the vocal qualities of some of the great singers of our time. Almost any child might be able to learn how to sing, but not every child can become a great vocalist, no matter how much training he or she receives. The heritability index would be different for the two groups.

behavior genetics
The study of how genetic endowment influences behavior.

Although the discussion of heritability is useful, it should not be considered the prime question in **behavior genetics,** the study of how genetic endowment affects behavior. As noted in Chapter 1, the crucial question is not **how much** of a particular trait is influenced by our genes, but rather **how** the genetic component and environment interact to produce a particular behavior (Anastasi, 1958; Wachs, 1983). By focusing on the many subtle ways in which the environment interacts with one's genetic endowment, we may someday be able to predict the effect a particular environment might have on a person who has a given set of genes. We could then optimize the development of that person's special talents and abilities.

If scientists find that some behavior is influenced by genetics, does that mean that the behavior is unchangeable, etched in stone? No, it does not. As we shall see, the fact that some genetic influence underlies a particular trait does not mean that it cannot be modified.

Our Human Inheritance and Uniqueness

To understand genetics, we must be aware that experience can be evaluated on two levels. First, each child's experiences are unique and individualistic. No two children experience life in exactly the same manner. Second, there are general rules of development that help us understand why a child acts in certain ways at a particular stage of life. When we look at how our genetic endowment can affect our life, we must investigate both levels. Each of us is biologically unique. The size and functioning of our organs, the volume of hormones produced, even our susceptibility to disease, show marked differences from individual to individual. Indeed, research has tended to stress these differences.

On the other hand, all people have much in common. As human beings, we possess a common biological heritage that is often taken for granted. Every normal child has two eyes, two ears, one stomach, two arms, two legs, a brain, etc. In addition, despite some variations in timing, we develop in a similar fashion. Children sit before they walk, and walk before they run. These maturational sequences are under genetic control (Scarr & McCartney, 1983). We develop spoken language without much formal instruction. Although some differences do exist, children learn language in a remarkably similar fashion whether they are raised in New York City, on a farm in Iowa, or in the Amazon jungle.

◆ HOW WE INHERIT: THE MECHANISMS OF TRANSMISSION

At the moment of conception, when the male's sperm penetrates the female's egg cell, our genetic endowment is set. Genetic individuality is assured by nature itself.

Genes and Chromosomes

The basic unit of heredity is the **gene,** which is composed of deoxyribonucleic acid (DNA). Although no one yet knows for certain, it is thought that human beings have between 50,000 and 100,000 genes (McCusick, 1989). A great international effort to locate each gene and determine its function, called the Genome Project, is now in progress (see The Child in the Year 2000 on page 101). Genes are carried on rod-shaped structures of various sizes called **chromosomes.** Each animal species has its own number of chromosomes. The normal human being has a complement of forty-six chromosomes, or twenty-three pairs. The same forty-six chromosomes are found in every cell of the body except the **gametes,** or sex cells. In a process called **meiosis,** the sex cells divide to form two cells containing twenty-three chromosomes each. This allows human beings to maintain the same complement of forty-six chromosomes from generation to generation. However, these cells do not have to split right down the middle. Their splitting is more random. Which chromosome ends up in which of the split cells is a matter of chance. There are over eight million different possibilities in this process alone.

But this is not the end of the story. During the process of meiosis, some of the genetic material on one chromosome may be exchanged with the material from another. This exchange, called **crossing over,** further com-

gene
The basic unit of heredity.

chromosomes
Rod-shaped structures that carry the genes.

gametes
The scientific term for the sex cells.

meiosis
The process by which sex cells divide to form two cells, each containing twenty-three chromosomes.

1. TRUE OR FALSE?

All animal species, including human beings, have the same number of chromosomes: forty-six.

crossing over
The process occurring during meiosis in which genetic material on one chromosome is exchanged with material from the other.

Genes are carried on chromosomes. Each normal human being has 23 pairs of chromosomes.

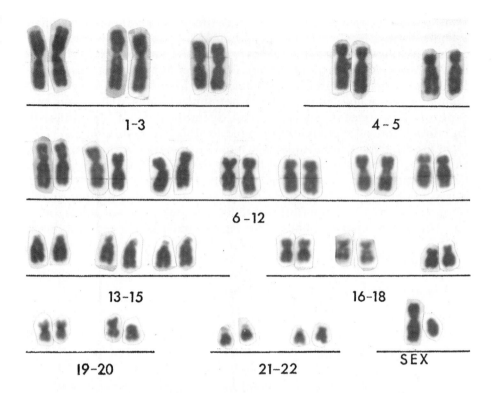

monozygotic or **identical twins**
Twins that develop from one fertilized egg and have an identical genetic structure.

dizygotic or **fraternal twins**
Twins resulting from fertilization of two eggs by two different sperm and whose genetic composition is no more similar than any other pair of siblings.

2. TRUE OR FALSE?

Fraternal twins are no more genetically alike than any other pair of siblings.

sex chromosomes
The twenty-third pair of chromosomes, which determines the gender of the organism.

plicates the situation (Maxson & Daugherty, 1985). When crossing over is taken into consideration, the chances that any two individuals are genetically identical are practically zero. Although human beings share a common species inheritance, each person is also genetically unique. The only exception is identical, or **monozygotic twins,** who result from a single egg and sperm and who share the same genetic composition. Fraternal twins, or **dizygotic twins,** result from two different eggs being fertilized by two different sperm and are no more similar than any other pair of siblings. The randomness of conception is quite impressive. The average man's semen contains between 50 million and 125 million sperm for each cubic centimeter of ejaculate (Rosen & Rosen, 1981). Only one sperm is necessary for conception.

Although sperm are continually being produced in the testicles of the male, females are born with their full complement of egg cells. The average female infant comes into this world carrying approximately two million eggs. About 25,000 are usable when the young girl reaches puberty, though throughout her reproductive life she will probably use only about 350 (Smith & Neisworth, 1975).

The Sex Chromosomes

Twenty-two of the twenty-three pairs of chromosomes look identical. However, the twenty-third pair is different. These chromosomes, called the **sex chromosomes,** are responsible for determining the gender of the

Identical twins share precisely the same genetic makeup while fraternal twins are no more genetically alike than any other pair of siblings.

offspring. There are two types: the X chromosome and the Y chromosome. The genetic composition of a male is XY, while females have two X chromosomes. When meiosis occurs, a male contributes an X chromosome and a Y chromosome, while the female contributes two X chromosomes. If during conception the sperm carrying the X chromosome penetrates the egg's membrane, the offspring will be female. If the sperm carrying the Y chromosome penetrates, the child will be male. Figure 3.1 (page 98) shows that the chances are fifty-fifty that the offspring will be a male.

The chances are the same for each conception. Even if you have seven boys, the chances are still fifty-fifty that the next child will be a girl. Many people fail to understand this basic point, and it is true for all inherited characteristics as well. Some people incorrectly believe that if their first child has a particular genetic problem, the chances of having a normal child are increased or decreased. Reproduction does not work that way. Every conception starts from square one again, and the same odds exist for every pregnancy.

3. TRUE OR FALSE?

If a family consists of five male children, the chances are quite small that their sixth child will be a boy.

FIGURE 3.1: Determination of Sex

The child's mother can contribute only an X chromosome, while the child's father can contribute an X or a Y. Statistically, 50 percent of the conceptions will produce males and 50 percent will produce females. However, other factors, such as conditions in the vagina, influence whether the X- or Y-carrying sperm will reach and penetrate the egg.

FATHER

	X	Y
X	XX	XY
X	XX	XY

MOTHER

Transmitting Dominant and Recessive Traits

Mendelian traits
Traits that follow a rather simple dominant-recessive pattern.

dominant traits
Traits that require the presence of only one gene.

recessive traits
Traits that require the presence of two genes.

How do parents transmit traits to their offspring? With some select characteristics that are inherited because of one gene pair, we can easily determine the possibilities that an offspring will inherit a particular trait. Traits that follow this simple pattern are known as **Mendelian traits,** after the person who discovered and described this method of inheritance. In the last half of the nineteenth century, Gregory Mendel, an Austrian monk with an excellent mathematical background, cross-pollinated tall plants with short plants. The result was many more tall plants. Tallness is a dominant trait, while shortness is recessive. The trait that is expressed when only one gene is present is considered **dominant.** Traits that become visible only when two genes are present are called **recessive.**

A number of genetic disorders follow this pattern, as do characteristics in human beings. For instance, dark is dominant over blond hair, freckles over no freckles, and dimples over no dimples. These characteristics are all due to one gene pair.

Let's look at how dominant traits may show themselves by considering the example of freckles. If the offspring inherits two genes for freckles, the child will show freckles (see Figure 3.2(a), frame 1, page 100). At the same time, if the child inherits two genes for no freckles, the youngster will not have freckles (see Figure 3.2(a), frame 4). But what if one parent passes on to the daughter Susan a gene for freckles, but the gene from the other parent is for no freckles? Since freckles is a dominant trait and no

If this couple chooses to have another child, what are the odds that it will be another boy?

freckles is recessive, Susan will have freckles (see Figure 3.2(a), frames 2 and 3).

Suppose Susan, with one gene for freckles, marries Harry, with no genes for freckles. What are the chances that their children will have freckles? Since Harry does not have freckles, we can assume that both his genes for the trait are no-freckle genes. (Remember, if he had even one gene for freckles, he would show the trait because it is dominant.) Susan has one gene for freckles and one for no freckles. While Harry can contribute only a gene for no freckles, Susan can contribute either a gene for freckles or a gene for no freckles. As you can see in Figure 3.2(b), there is a 50 percent chance that their children will have freckles. Remember that this fifty-fifty chance holds for each child. If Susan's first two children did not show freckles, the same odds hold for her next child. Each conception is new, but the odds always remain the same.

If neither you nor your spouse shows a particular trait, can you still pass it on to your offspring? The answer is yes. To understand this, let us look at the genetic disease known as **cystic fibrosis,** a disorder of the mucus, saliva, and sweat glands. Cystic fibrosis affects many organs, including the lungs, liver, and pancreas (Fischman, 1979). A person with cystic fibrosis has a low resistance to respiratory diseases, suffers digestive problems, and has a tendency to dehydrate because of an excessive amount of salt in the sweat. New antibiotics have increased the life span of individuals with this disease. Between 70 percent and 80 percent of those with the disease survive to at least age twenty if the disease is discovered early and excellent medical treatment is received. Treatment must be continuous, and hospitalization during periods of crisis can be expected. To date there is no cure. Even with excellent care, the disease

cystic fibrosis
A severe genetic disease marked by respiratory problems.

FIGURE 3.2.: Transmission of a Dominant Trait: Freckles

(a) When Both Parents Have One Gene for Freckles
When both parents carry one gene for freckles, there is a 25 percent chance that a child will have two genes for freckles and thus have freckles. There is a 50 percent chance that a child will carry one gene for freckles and, since this is a dominant trait, will have freckles. There is only a 25 percent chance that a child will not have a gene for freckles and so will not have freckles:

(b) When One Parent Has One Gene for Freckles
When one parent has one gene for freckles, there is a 50 percent chance that the child will have freckles.

FATHER

	Freckles	No Freckles
Freckles	1 Freckles Freckles	3 Freckles No Freckles
MOTHER No Freckles	2 No Freckles Freckles	4 No Freckles No Freckles

(a)

FATHER (Harry)

	No Freckles	No Freckles
Freckles	No Freckles Freckles	Freckles No Freckles
MOTHER (Susan) No Freckles	No Freckles No Freckles	No Freckles No Freckles

(b)

4. TRUE OR FALSE?

The serious genetic disease cystic fibrosis can be cured through massive doses of vitamins.

carrier
A person possessing a particular gene or group of genes for a trait who does not show the trait but can pass it on to his or her offspring.

genotype
The genetic configuration of the individual.

often worsens. Cystic fibrosis is responsible for more deaths than any other genetic disease in the United States today (Berdine & Blackhurst, 1985). It is estimated that the disease occurs in one out of every 2000 births. About one person in twenty or thirty is a carrier (Reed, 1975). Today, a test is available which can detect most carriers of the disease (Beaudet, 1990).

Cystic fibrosis is caused by a defective pair of genes on chromosome number 7, and it manifests itself only when both parents transmit the defective gene to their child. A number of genetic diseases as well as some physical characteristics in human beings follow this pattern.

Since cystic fibrosis is caused by two defective genes, the only way a child can be afflicted with it is for both parents to have the defective gene. Neither the mother nor the father need show any symptoms of the disorder, because the disorder is recessive and requires two genes for it to show itself. A person who has one normal gene and one defective gene is called a **carrier**, because the individual will not show the disorder but can pass the defective gene to his or her offspring.

Suppose that two carriers of the disorder marry. What are the odds that their children would suffer from the disorder? To understand the possibilities, two new terms must be introduced: genotype and phenotype. The **genotype** of a person refers to the specific composition of that person's

THE CHILD
IN THE YEAR
2000

Mapping and Sequencing Our Genes

It will cost an estimated three billion dollars and has been compared to the Manhattan Project, the building of the first atomic bomb, and the scientific program to put a human being on the moon. It is the Genome Project: an ambitious ten- to fifteen-year project to map and sequence all the fifty to one hundred thousand human genes. Mapping genes involves finding where the genes for particular characteristics are located on the chromosome, while sequencing genes refers to deciphering the language that tells the gene what to do and when. The project will first map and then sequence the genes (McKusick, 1989). At the present time only 4,550 genes have been identified, and only 1,500 have been located on the chromosomes. Most genes consist of between 10,000 and 150,000 code letters, and only a few genes have been completely deciphered. However, new technology that will allow us

to map and sequence genes more quickly has already been developed and is now being used.

Even at this early point in the project, the knowledge obtained has improved our understanding of many genetic diseases. We know the chromosome on which the defective gene is carried for a number of genetic diseases including Huntington's chorea, Duchenne's muscular dystrophy, and familial Alzheimer's disease (Martin, 1987). Now we are looking for the location of the gene itself. We have found the precise site of the gene responsible for Duchenne's

muscular dystrophy. This new knowledge enables us to discover new ways of determining carrier status and may eventually lead to methods to alter the way the gene shows itself.

What does this mean for the child in the year 2000 and beyond? The new knowledge of the genome—the complete instructions for making a human being (Jaroff, 1989)—will enable scientists to discover the cause of many mysterious inherited disorders and more accurately predict individual's susceptibility to many diseases. It could also open up new ways to treat or prevent them. By the year 2000, genetic counseling may become routine and tests for genetic problems more accurate than ever. In the more distant future, gene therapy, in which scientists alter the genetic instructions to eliminate certain genetic defects, may be available (Jaroff, 1988).

genes. It is a description of the "kinds of genes possessed, regardless of whether they are expressed" (Sutton, 1980, p. 11). Both the mother's and the father's genotypes in Figure 3.3 (page 103) include one gene for cystic fibrosis and one normal gene. The **phenotype** refers to the "observable characteristics of an individual" (Sutton, 1980, p. 11). In this case, because cystic fibrosis is a recessive trait and requires two genes, neither the father nor the mother shows symptoms of the disease and their phenotype is normal. However, they can pass the gene on to their offspring because they are both carriers. Before looking at Figure 3.3 for the answer, try working it out yourself.

In this case, both parents can contribute either a normal gene or a cystic fibrosis gene. If both contribute a normal gene, the child will be normal. This child will be normal in both phenotype and genotype. In other words, the child would not have cystic fibrosis, nor would the composition of the child's genes allow the disease to be passed on to the next generation. There is a 25 percent chance that this would occur.

If one parent contributes a normal gene and one contributes a defective gene, the offspring will not show any trace of the disease. Since normal

phenotype
The observable characteristics of the organism.

functioning is dominant, it masks the defective gene. However, the composition of the child's genes includes an abnormal gene that can be passed on to the next generation. In this case, the phenotype is normal, but the genotype is abnormal. There is a 50 percent chance that this would occur.

Finally, what if both the mother and the father contributed their defective gene? The child would be both genotypically and phenotypically abnormal. The child would have cystic fibrosis and could pass the gene on to the next generation. There is a 25 percent chance of this occurring.

Polygenic Inheritance

If the relationship between genetics and behavior were always so simple, predicting traits would be easy. But genetic transmission is not always so direct. Mendel's success was due partially to luck. Mendel chose very simple characteristics that were determined by a single gene pair. Comparatively few human traits are transmitted in this manner. In addition, most of the characteristics discussed so far are caused exclusively by a person's genotype. The effects of the environment on the expression of one's genetic endowment have scarcely been mentioned. In the real world, the relationship between genotype and phenotype is more complicated (Scarr & Kidd, 1983). Simple models of prediction soon break down as we consider characteristics determined by many gene pairs and that are affected by the environment.

polygenic or multigenic traits
Characteristics that are influenced by more than one pair of genes.

multifactorial traits
Traits that are influenced both by genes and by the environment.

When a characteristic is influenced by more than one pair of genes, the mechanism of inheritance is **polygenic** or **multigenic.** The term **multifactorial** describes a trait that is influenced both by genes and by the environment. However, the terms polygenic, multigenic, and multifactorial are often used interchangeably. Skin color is a polygenic trait. A number of gene pairs are responsible for this trait (Mange & Mange, 1980), but the environment also influences the phenotype. If you have light skin and spend time in the sun, you might get tan. Your genotype has not changed, but your outward appearance, or phenotype, has. Another example is height. Although attainment of adult stature is greatly affected by an individual's genes, the environment also plays a part. Nutrition and health are two prime environmental factors. Japanese teenagers are taller than their parents because their health and nutrition have improved (Curtis, 1975). Even the emotional environment affects growth, since it influences the secretion of growth hormones. Cases of stunted growth occurred in some orphanages where children's psychological needs for love, tenderness, and contact were not addressed even if the children were adequately fed (Gardner, 1972). The environment makes a contribution even in the determination of a trait that is largely influenced by genetic factors.

Sex-linked Traits

If you look at a picture of human chromosomes, the pairs appear identical except for one: the twenty-third pair, which is the sex chromosomes. A female has two X chromosomes, while a male has an X and a Y. The X is three times as large as the Y. It contains many more genes than the Y, and many of the genes found on the X chromosome do not exist at all on the Y. This has profound consequences for males.

Consider what might happen if a female had one defective gene for a recessive trait and one normal gene for normal functioning which is dominant on the twenty-third chromosome. Let us also assume that these genes are found only on the X, not on the Y. The female would not show the effects of the recessive gene, because she possesses a gene for normal functioning to counter it. But what would happen if she had children? She could pass on both her normal gene and the abnormal gene, but unlike our previous cases, the child's gender becomes crucial.

Notice in Figure 3.4 that if the mother contributes a normal X and the father contributes a normal X (as in frame 1), the child will be a female who will show no signs of the disorder and will not pass the disorder on to her offspring. If the mother contributes an abnormal gene on the X chromosome and the father contributes a normal gene for the same trait from the X, the child will be a female who will not show of signs of the disorder but will be a carrier like her mother (frame 2).

But what if the child is male? If the mother contributes a normal gene

FIGURE 3.3: Transmission of a Recessive Trait: Cystic Fibrosis
When Each Parent Carries One Gene
When both the mother and the father carry the gene for cystic fibrosis, the chances are 25 percent that an offspring will have the disease (cystic fibrosis-cystic fibrosis), 50 percent that the child will be a carrier (cystic fibrosis-normal), and 25 percent that the child will not have the disorder or be a carrier.

FATHER

	Normal Gene	Cystic Fibrosis
Normal Gene	Normal Gene Normal Gene	Normal Gene Cystic Fibrosis
MOTHER		
Cystic Fibrosis	Cystic Fibrosis Normal Gene	Cystic Fibrosis Cystic Fibrosis

Note: Some other genetic diseases such as Tay-Sachs disease and phenylketonuria are transmitted in the same way as Cystic Fibrosis.

FIGURE 3.4: Sex-Linked Inheritance
In sex-linked traits, females may carry the defective gene but do not develop the disorder.

FATHER

	X^n	Y^o
X^n	1 $X^n X^n$	3 $X^n Y^o$
MOTHER		
X^d	2 $X^d X^n$	4 $X^d Y^o$

n = normal
d = gene for a disorder—e.g., hemophilia or color blindness.

sex-linked traits
Traits that are inherited through genes found on the sex chromosomes.

and the father contributes his Y (as shown in frame 3), the offspring will be a male who will neither show any signs of the disorder nor be able to pass the disorder on. In this case, because the X is normal there is no need to be concerned. But if the mother transmits the defective X chromosome and the father a Y, the resulting male offspring will show signs of the disorder and may pass it on to the next generation (frame 4). The defective gene on the X has no corresponding normal gene to counter it, so the defective gene on the X is in a position to show itself. **Sex-linked traits** involve female carriers, but it is the male who inherits the trait.

A considerable amount of interest in sex-linked traits exists today. Among the proven sex-linked traits are hemophilia and color blindness. Both hemophilia (a severe blood disorder involving a deficiency in the blood's ability to clot) and color blindness are determined by defective genes found on the X chromosome. Because a female has two X chromosomes, her chances of being a hemophiliac are negligible. She is also far less likely to be color blind. For example, red-green color blindness occurs in about 8 percent of all males but in less than 0.5 percent of females (Restak, 1988). Most of the scientifically documented sex-linked traits are both recessive and pathological (Lips & Colwill, 1978).

Another possible sex-linked characteristic is spatial perception, which involves the ability to "visualize three-dimensional objects on the basis of two-dimensional pictures and do mental rotations and other manipulations on them" (Hyde, 1985, p. 187). Superior spatial ability is correlated with higher mathematical ability (Richmond-Abbott, 1983). The male advantage in this ability may be at least partly explained by sex-linked inheritance, although the evidence is not unanimous in this regard, and environmental factors may also be important (Linn and Petersen, 1985). Spatial perception is not an ability that one either has or does not have. It is present in everyone to varying degrees, and it can be improved through training.

Could some of the other differences between males and females be genetically determined? Perhaps the fact that women normally outlive men can be explained partially by genetic endowment (Kermis, 1984). Psychologists differ sharply on such questions. Except for some genetic diseases and physical traits, the interaction of genes with the environment is crucial to understanding the end product. Still, the possibility of explaining some gender differences using the mechanism of sex-linked genetic transmission is tempting.

Although our genetic endowment is fixed at conception, genetic influences are with us throughout our life. Our genetic endowment affects us in such areas as physical characteristics, disease, development and personality, rate of maturation, and intelligence.

5. TRUE OR FALSE?

———————

Color blindness is found mostly in males.

◆ GENETIC INFLUENCES ON PHYSICAL CHARACTERISTICS

The most striking genetic influence involves physical appearance. Hair and skin color, the shape of the nose, body build, and a thousand other physical characteristics are directly influenced by genes. Even weight may have a genetic basis (see the Cross-Cultural Current on page 106). But if we are genetically unique, why do we still look like some other family members? To answer this question, try the following exercise. The next time you're in class, ask yourself how you recognized the person coming in the door as John, Ted, or Franco. You probably used their body build and facial features as recognition aids. In this regard, some physical features are more important than others. These features are only a very few of the physical characteristics of the individual, but for identification purposes they are crucial.

Another reason for familial similarity involves limitations in our gene pools (the total pool of genes in a population). Consider the number of different nose shapes and eye colors that any individual might inherit. The variety is impressive. However, there may be only a small number of nose shapes or eye colors in a person's gene pool. When we say that two siblings (who are not identical twins) look alike, we are judging them on the basis of a very small number of physical traits whose variety is limited by their gene pool. We ignore their unique genetic endowment, which may be responsible for physical features that are not as useful for recognition purposes.

Most physical features are trivial, biologically speaking. The color of a person's skin or whether one is a little overweight (being grossly overweight is related to increased susceptibility to certain illnesses) makes very little difference from the point of view of biological functioning or intellectual ability. However, these and many other physical characteristics may or may not be valued by the society in which a person lives. Let's look at weight. Today, thin is "in," but that was not always the case. At one time, to be a bit overweight was fashionable and showed you had sufficient food. Today, obese people suffer from discrimination both in the workplace and in social interactions. The same analysis is true of skin color, which is biologically trivial but may be socially important. Any discussion of a physical characteristic, then, must be investigated from both a biological viewpoint (does it lead to some advantage or disadvantage in functioning?) and a social perspective (how is that trait evaluated by the family and society?)

Handedness

Over 90 percent of the general public shows a preference for the right hand. Such preferences are genetically based (Hicks & Kinsbourne, 1976). Usually, children show little preference for either hand until about four months of age, and a few do not develop a preference until well into early childhood. However, the majority show a right-hand preference at a young age.

We live in a right-handed world. Look around in a classroom and note how many desks are left-handed. Probably very few. Demonstrations in class are usually performed by a right-handed teacher for right-handed students, and this makes imitation difficult for left-handed students.

There is evidence of genetic involvement in handedness (Cratty, 1986). If both parents are right-handed, there is a greater possibility that they

Is There a Genetic Basis for Obesity?

When you see obese children walking with their obese parents, do you ever wonder whether their weight problem is due to genetic factors or to environmental factors—or to both? We cannot conclude that just because obese parents tend to have obese children genetics has anything to do with it. Children learn eating habits from their parents. In the past, most psychologists have emphasized the environmental factors that lead to obesity, such as eating habits and lack of exercise. But the possibility remains that there is a genetic basis for obesity. How can this be researched?

One way to discover whether genetic factors are involved in obesity would be to look at adoption studies. Let's say that a child is adopted very early in life. Years later we can compare the child's body mass to that of his or her adoptive parents and biological parents to determine how closely the child resembles each set of parents. If we did this in hundreds of cases, we would have some interesting and valuable information. Unfortunately, however, getting such information about adopted children's biological parents is very difficult in most countries.

But this type of information is available in Denmark from the Danish Adoption Register, which contains the official records of every nonfamilial adoption granted in Denmark. A great deal of information is available, and about 94 percent of the biological mothers and 77 percent of the biological fathers are identified.

Albert Stunkard and his colleagues found information about more than 5,000 adoptees and sent the adoptees a general health questionnaire that included items concerning height and weight. More than 3,500 people returned the questionnaires. The researchers derived a body-mass index from the reported weights and heights of the adoptees by dividing weight in kilograms by the square of the height in meters. These values were then placed into four categories: thin, medium, overweight, and obese. The same information was obtained from biological and adoptive parents.

You may point out that some subjectivity might have entered the picture because heights and weights were self-reported. However, the authors performed two earlier studies in the United States and Denmark in which they compared self-reported weights and heights with actual measured weights and heights and found self-reported features to be quite accurate.

The results showed a "clear relation between adoptee weight class (thin, medium, overweight, and obese) and the body-mass index of the biological parents: there was no apparent relation between adoptee weight class and body-mass index of the adoptive parents" (p. 194). In other words, a clear genetic basis for weight was found. It is just as important that the genetic influences found in this study were not confined to the obese but were present across the whole range of body weights, from very thin to very fat.

The researchers are quick to point out that this does not mean obesity is inherited the same way eye color is. The fact that genetic influences exist tells us nothing about the interactions between the hereditary components and the environmental factors, such as cultural traditions and attitudes toward eating. The genetic predisposition may well be affected by environmental factors. In addition, it is possible that environmental circumstances, such as famine, could prevent the phenotypical expression of this genetic trait. This study in Denmark describes the outcome of gene-environment interactions in an advanced Western society that has an abundance of food.

The problem with a study like this is that people who are obese might misinterpret the results and say, "You see, obesity is genetic," and give up trying to lose weight. This is unfortunate, for the study says nothing about the effectiveness of environmental programs, such as restricting caloric intake or exercising moderately in an effort to control weight. In addition, there is abundant evidence that nongenetic factors are also important determinants of the amount of body fat. The fact remains, however, that if the results of this study are correct, we must appreciate the genetic basis for weight and perhaps, as the authors suggest, target obesity prevention programs at children who are at risk for the problem.

Source: Stunkard, A. J., et al. An Adoption Study of Human Obesity. *New England Journal of Medicine,* January 23, 1986, 314, 193–197.

will have right-handed children than if both parents are left-handed. However, about 50 percent of left-handed parents produce right-handed children. Although genetic factors affect handedness, the way in which they operate is not well understood. There are environmental considerations as well. Some parents strongly encourage their children to be right-handed by placing implements in the right hand or handing them toys in a way that forces them to use their right arm. In some parts of the world, left-handedness is socially unacceptable, and children are forced to be right-handed.

6. TRUE OR FALSE?

Left-handedness is largely determined by the environment.

Many people believe that left-handed children have more difficulty learning particular skills, but any difficulty they have is due to the environment's right-handed bias rather than any inborn deficiency. Generally, children who develop their handedness early do better than those who develop it later or not at all (Williams & Stith, 1980). It makes no difference whether that preference is right or left, just so long as there is some preference.

◆ GENETIC DISORDERS

The March of Dimes Birth Defects Foundation (1987a) has catalogued about 2,000 confirmed or suspected dominant genetic disorders and over 1,000 confirmed or suspected recessive disorders. There are some 250 confirmed or suspected genetic disorders transmitted through the X chromosome. More disorders will undoubtedly be added to the list. Many of these disorders are rare, and some show great variability in the severity of their symptoms. About 3 percent of all newborns have some genetic birth defect, and about 1 newborn in 200 has a chromosomal abnormality (Plomin, DeFries & McClearn, 1990). (The major genetic and chromosomal disorders can be found in Appendix Table 1.)

Why do genetic diseases continue to exist? First, not all genetic diseases are life threatening. Second, the onset of some of these diseases, such as Huntington's chorea, is later in life (Roberts, 1970). In either case, people have children, thereby passing on the genetic disorder.

Huntington's Chorea

Huntington's chorea is a rare, dominant genetic disease that affects the central nervous system. It is caused by a defective gene on the fourth chromosome. The onset is typically in early middle age, after the prime childbearing years. The average age of onset is thirty-five, but variation in age occurs. The individual suffers from progressive mental deterioration and pronounced involuntary muscle movements. The well-known folksinger Woody Guthrie died from this disease.

An individual who possesses the dominant gene and marries someone who is genotypically normal has a 50 percent chance of transmitting the disease gene to his or her offspring. If you had Huntington's chorea in your family background, you would probably want to know whether you carry the gene. Today, a test is available that can determine whether a

Huntington's chorea
A dominant genetic disease affecting the central nervous system.

person has the gene and can therefore help people plan their lives accordingly (Quarrell et al., 1987). This is important. For example, what if someone's father died from the disease and there is no record of the malady in the mother's family? That person would then have a 50 percent chance of possessing the gene. On the more hopeful side, the person would also have a 50 percent chance of being completely free of the disease. Would this knowledge affect the person's decision to have children? The ability to detect the presence of the gene gives affected individuals the information necessary to plan their lives and make decisions based on what is rather than on what might happen.

Tay-Sachs Disease: Hope Through Research

Tay-Sachs disease
A fatal genetic disease most commonly found in Jews who can trace their lineage to Eastern Europe.

Some genetic diseases are more likely to be found in one group of people than another. For example, **Tay-Sachs disease** is most common among Jews whose ancestors came from central and eastern Europe, although members of any other group can inherit the disease.* Tay-Sachs disease is a recessive disorder and is transmitted in the same manner as cystic fibrosis. Infants born with the disease seem normal at birth, but after six months, their progress slows. The disease involves an inborn error in metabolism. The infant's body stores an excessive amount of a material called glycolipid in the cells of the nervous system, causing the cells to swell, rupture, and finally die. As more and more nerve cells die, the baby loses motor abilities and finally become retarded. The disease is incurable. By the age of two or three, the child dies.

A simple test can tell whether one is a carrier of Tay-Sachs. Blood is taken from the fingertip or vein, and the amount of a certain enzyme that breaks down the fatty substances in the nerve cells is measured. People who are carriers will have only half as much of the enzyme as noncarriers, although this is enough for the carrier, and carriers never show any signs of the disease (March of Dimes, 1984). What if both parents are carriers? As in the case of cystic fibrosis, there is a 25 percent chance that each offspring will have the disease. However, the presence of the genetic disease in the fetus can be identified. Current research is attempting to find a way to supply the brain with substitutes that will break down these fatty substances. Researchers are also looking into methods of transplanting genes from normal cells into defective cells to manufacture the chemical (March of Dimes, 1986a).

Phenylketonuria: A Success Story

phenylketonuria (PKU)
A recessive genetic disorder marked by the inability to digest a particular amino acid and leading to mental retardation if not treated.

Studying genetic disorders can be depressing, especially if you consider Huntington's Chorea or Tay-Sachs disease. However, research has made tremendous strides in treating a number of genetic disorders. Perhaps the greatest success story involves the strange case of **phenylketonuria** (PKU).

---

*Many other diseases show a greater incidence in certain ethnic groups. For example, people of Italian ancestry are more likely to suffer from thalassemia (a blood disease), and phenylketonuria (an inability to digest a particular amino acid which, if left untreated, results in mental retardation) is more common among descendants of northern Europeans.

PKU is a rare disorder occurring in approximately one in 8,000 births (March of Dime, 1986b). It involves the inability to digest a particular amino acid called phenylalanine. If left untreated, brain damage leading to retardation results. Not too many years ago, doctors were perplexed by the disorder. Seemingly normal babies rapidly became retarded and developed behavioral disorders. Some 90 percent of these children had to be institutionalized. The normal treatment for children who are not thriving is more nourishment, but in the case of PKU, that is exactly what triggers the problem.

The disease was first recognized in the 1930s, and a urine test for the disorder was developed. About fifteen years later, doctors began treating the disorder with a special diet, low in phenylalanine. Phenylalanine is found in all protein-rich foods, including fish, meats, poultry, eggs, milk, and bread products, so the diet is very restricted (Schild, 1979). Phenylalanine is also found in some soft drinks, many of which are now labeled. Special preparations are required to meet the child's protein needs. This preventive treatment is very successful. Today a blood test to determine whether a newborn baby has PKU is given, usually on the day the baby is scheduled to be discharged from the hospital, and over forty states have PKU screening laws (Plomin et al., 1990).

Three important points about PKU should be kept in mind. First, PKU is an example of a genetic disorder that can be successfully treated. Second, the ravages of the disorder do not occur unless the disorder is triggered by the environment. If every individual in a particular culture were to receive a diet low in the offending protein, the disease would never show itself. PKU illustrates how important the environment can be in the emergence and treatment of genetic disorders. Third, the difficulty of keeping children on the regimen should be noted. Imagine having to keep a child on an extremely strict diet for years. During middle childhood, the diet can usually be relaxed or even abandoned. However, one study assessed children with PKU who abandoned the diet at different ages for both intelligence and achievement. The findings showed that the earlier a child was taken off the diet, the more the child's intellectual abilities were negatively affected. The greatest deficiencies were found in children whose dietary restrictions were ended before age six. The authors of the study suggest that even after the age of eight, children should be kept on a restricted diet (Holtzman, Kronmal, Van Doorninck, Azen, and Koch, 1986).

Imagine you are a child who cannot eat this or that, while all your friends can. Some parents have had difficulty keeping their children on such a diet (Reed, 1975). Prescribing a diet is a great deal easier than following one. In addition, women who have PKU should consult a physician before they become pregnant. If a woman with PKU becomes pregnant while she is not on the diet, her baby is likely to be born retarded because of her abnormal body chemistry. The woman should be placed back on the diet before she becomes pregnant. Unfortunately, some women become pregnant without planning, and the damage may begin before the diet takes effect. In addition, the diet is costly and inconvenient, especially for people who are used to eating whatever they want. Last, some

7. TRUE OR FALSE?

At the present time, all that medical science can do for children suffering from genetic diseases is make them more comfortable.

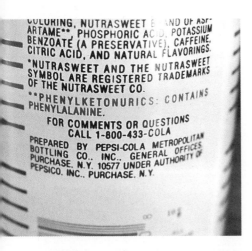

Children with phenylketonuria cannot tolerate anything that contains phenylalanine. Some beverages are labeled for it. For those who do not have this disorder, this amino acid causes no problem at all.

sickle cell anemia
An inherited defect in the structure of red blood cells found mostly in blacks and Latins.

women with PKU may not know that they were ever on a special diet or, if they were, may not know why (March of Dimes, 1986b). Because they were diagnosed and placed on the diet twenty years ago, today these women are leading normal lives and are not retarded. However, their infants may still be affected. The incidence of maternal PKU is increasing today, and this is a relatively new challenge and one that requires attention (Luder & Greene, 1989).

Sickle Cell Anemia: What To Do with Our Knowledge

Sickle cell anemia is an inherited defect in the structure of red blood cells. The sufferer, especially during periods of physical exertion or low oxygen, experiences considerable pain. Although most victims live normal lives, people with severe cases may suffer heart and kidney problems (Fogel, 1984). Periods of crisis requiring hospitalization are not unusual. Resistance to disease is decreased, and the health of the child with sickle cell anemia is usually poor.

Approximately one in ten African Americans is a carrier, and whether one is a carrier can be determined by a simple blood test. We can calculate that on the average, one marriage out of every 100 between black Americans has the potential for producing a child who will suffer from sickle cell anemia. At present, antibiotics and improved medical treatment can help alleviate the symptoms, but some who suffer from severe cases of the disorder die in childhood (March of Dimes, 1986c). With improved treatment, many children with sickle cell anemia will live more normal lives.

Because the detection process is relatively simple and the gene is rather common, some authorities have suggested that mandatory mass genetic screening be instituted. This would make people more aware of their genetic standing so they could make childbearing decisions accordingly. On the surface, this might appear to be reasonable. After all, it would still be an individual decision.

Although no one has any objection to voluntary screening for carrier status, mass involuntary screening raises several important ethical questions (see Shaw, 1976). Some people point out that such screening would be aimed principally at a minority group, and they see something sinister in this. It should be noted that Latin populations are also at risk for the disorder, although the rates for Latins are lower than the rate for blacks in the United States. Aside from the racial issue, how ethical is it to force someone to take a test? Do people have the right not to know whether they are carrying a genetic defect?

One way to sidestep the issue is to recommend the test but not require it. Such a program might not be as effective as one that is mandatory, but it would avoid some difficult ethical issues. On the other hand, recommendations from the government can easily turn into quasi-requirements. Insurance companies and potential employers may learn that an individual is a carrier and increase premiums or refuse that person employment.

No one argues against education, however, and this may be the key. All populations at risk for genetic disorders should be educated about them. In this way, each individual can decide whether he or she wants to submit to a carrier detection test.

Chromosomal Abnormalities

Some inherited disorders are due to chromosomal abnormalities rather than genetic defects. Four of the most important are Down syndrome, Klinefelter's syndrome, Turner's syndrome, and the fragile X syndrome.

DOWN SYNDROME A weekly network television show about a child with a chromosomal disorder? A decade ago, this would have been unthinkable, but the television program "Life Goes On" featuring Corky, a high-school student with Down syndrome, first aired in the late 1980s. The program signified a long-awaited change in our attitude towards the disorder.

Down syndrome (formerly called mongolism) is the most common chromosomal disorder. It occurs approximately once in every 600 births and is caused by the appearance of an extra chromosome on the twenty-first pair (Plomin et al., 1990). The child has forty-seven chromosomes instead of the normal forty-six. The frequency of the disorder increases with the age of the mother. The risk for women under thirty is one in 1,250 births, while those at age thirty-five have a 1-in-365 chance of bearing a child with Down syndrome. At age forty, the chance is one in 110 births, while at age forty-five, the chance increases to one in forty-five births (March of Dimes, 1987b). The disorder is also linked to the father. Problems in cell division in the sperm are estimated to be the cause of the difficulty about 20 percent to 25 percent of the time (Abroms & Bennett, 1980), and there is evidence that the disorder is more common when the father is under twenty or over fifty-five years of age (Arehart-Treichel, 1979). Of course, these data are correlational and do not demonstrate cause and effect, and no single accepted explanation for this correlation has been advanced.

There are three types of Down syndrome. In the most common type, called trisomy, an extra chromosome is found on the twenty-first pair of chromosomes. In the second type, called mosaicism, some of the cells show the extra chromosome while others do not. In the third type, called translocation, all or some part of the extra chromosome on the twenty-first pair becomes attached to another chromosome pair. These last two types of Down syndrome account for only about five percent of the entire number of cases. About 5,000 children a year are born with Down syndrome in the United States (Dullea, 1989).

Most children who suffer from Down syndrome are identified either at birth or shortly after by their physical appearance (Hirsch, 1979). Unusual physical features include folded eyes (which gave the disorder its original name), short digits, flat face, protruding tongue, and harsh voice (Sue, Sue & Sue, 1981). Retardation is associated with the disorder, but the degree of retardation varies greatly. Today, many children with Down

Down syndrome
A disorder caused by the presence of an extra chromosome, leading to a distinct physical appearance and often times mental retardation of varying degree.

8. TRUE OR FALSE?

Children with the chromosomal disorder of Down syndrome usually require institutionalization by the age of five.

Christopher Burke, a teen with Down syndrome, plays Corky on the television series Life Goes On.

syndrome are given special treatment, including special preschool programs, which have improved their cognitive functioning, and many score in the mildly retarded range on intelligence tests (Hallahan & Kauffman, 1988). Children with Down syndrome have a reputation for being lovable, cheerful, and easy to work with, although this is not always so (Bridges & Cicchetti, 1982). When Down syndrome youngsters are compared with other retarded children, they may have a happier disposition, but overgeneralizations should be made with care (Hallahan and Kauffman, 1988). Years ago most children with this disorder were institutionalized immediately after birth, but this is not the case today. Many of these children are now raised at home, which is usually beneficial to the child.

Down syndrome youngsters show the same developmental milestones as normal children, but at a much delayed pace. This includes smiling and laughing, eye contact during play, self-recognition, some attachment behaviors, and symbolic play. Sometimes qualitative differences in development between Down syndrome children and normal youngsters have been noted. In one study, the quality of Down syndrome infants' emotional reaction to being separated from their primary caregivers was compared with that of normal infants. Down syndrome children showed less intense separation distress, they took longer to show it, and they exhibited a diminished range of emotions (Thompson, Cicchetti, Lamb, & Malikin, 1985).

Not too long ago, the life expectancy for Down syndrome children was ten years or less. Congential heart problems are common, and resistance to disease is low. However, medical advances have substantially increased the life span of these children. Approximately 20 percent die during the first two years (Rondal, 1988). However, the majority who survive infancy live well into adulthood (Baird & Sadovnick, 1987). After the age of about forty, people with Down syndrome appear to be more susceptible to diseases that are related to old age. By the time they reach forty or so, many have brain lesions that look like those from Alzheimer's disease, and many show symptoms of senility (Kolata, 1989). The reason may lie in the fact that genes associated with congenital heart defects, brain changes associated with a familial variety of Alzheimer's disease,* and some other disorders are also found on the twenty-first chromosome. Much research today is being conducted into the relationship between various genes on the twenty-first chromosome.

Not only the health and life expectancy of Down syndrome children have improved, but their entire life has changed. This is the first generation who, with the help of early intervention programs, have ventured forth into the normal world of children. Many attend public schools. Although most are in special classes, some attend a few regular classes. They interact with nonretarded children and are tuned into the culture of childhood and adolescence. Many have suffered poor treatment from other children. In fact, two-thirds have faced some harassment, ranging from name calling and teasing to physical aggression (Dullea, 1989). However, despite this negative aspect, most parents would not want a more restrictive atmosphere for their children. Most parents and children rate

*Most cases of Alzheimer's disease are not hereditary (Plomin et al., 1990).

the school experience quite positively, although forming relationships after school is frequently still a problem.

No one knows the extent to which children with Down syndrome, given the opportunities, can function in society. After all, we don't place limitations on other children and we need not place limitations on children with Down syndrome either (Dullea, 1989).

SEX-LINKED CHROMOSOMAL DISORDERS Down syndrome is not the only chromosomal abnormality. Three of the more common chromosomal disorders are caused by problems that occur on the sex chromosomes. In Klinefelter's syndrome, the male receives at least one more X chromosome than he should, thus creating an XXY genotype. This is found in approximately one in 600 male births. Children afflicted with this disorder have small sex organs and are sterile, and many, though not all, are mentally retarded.

Turner's syndrome is caused by lack of an X chromosome. The genotype is expressed as XO. These females are sterile and short and do not mature naturally. They often require estrogen treatments to attain adult stature. Though they often have specific learning problems, they are not usually mentally retarded (Kalat, 1980). They perform poorly on spatial, attention, and short-term memory tasks and show more difficulty accurately discriminating facial expressions. This last deficit may be the basis of some of their frequent problems in social relationships (McCauley, Kay, Ito, & Treder, 1987). Turner's syndrome appears in about one out of every 2,000 female births (Sutton, 1980).

The fragile X syndrome is a recessive sex-linked disorder in which the X chromosome is fragile and breaks easily. It is associated with mental retardation, hyperactivity, and short attention span as well as a number of physical abnormalities (Hagerman & Sobesky, 1989). It occurs in just under one in 1,000 births (Berdine & Blackhurst, 1985).

Predispositions to Disorders

Not all disorders with a genetic base are transmitted directly. Sometimes a predisposition to a disorder, rather than the disorder itself, is passed from parents to children. This is the case with the serious emotional disorder known as schizophrenia as well as with alcoholism.

Schizophrenia

Schizophrenia is a severe mental disorder characterized by hallucinations, delusions, emotional disturbances, apathy, and withdrawal. About 25 percent of the first-time admissions to mental hospitals are diagnosed as schizophrenic, and about 50 percent of the residents of mental hospitals at any one time suffer from the disorder. Schizophrenia is a major international health problem.

A number of twin studies have suggested that a genetic base for schizophrenia exists (McBroom, 1980). If an identical twin is schizophrenic, his or her twin is fifty times as likely to become schizophrenic than any other individual in the general population (Altrocchi, 1980). But identical

schizophrenia
A severe mental disorder marked by hallucinations, delusions, and emotional disturbances.

twins also share a common environment as well as common genotype. To control for environmental differences, a number of studies have compared identical twins (who develop from one sperm and one egg cell) to fraternal twins (who develop from two different sperm and two separate egg cells). Fraternal twins are no more genetically similar than any other pair of siblings. If there is a substantial genetic component, we would expect that if one identical twin became schizophrenic, the other would have an excellent chance of also suffering from the disorder. We would expect that with fraternal twins in which one becomes schizophrenic, the other twin would have a greater chance than the average person on the street of also suffering form the condition, since these twins have about half their genes in common. However, their risk would not be as great as identical twins, who share all their genes in common.

These hypotheses are confirmed by the research in the field. The risk for identical twins in which one becomes schizophrenic is three to six times as great as for fraternal twins in which one shows signs of the disorder (Rosenthal, 1970). The degree of similarity between twins is called the **concordance rate**. It approaches 50 percent for identical twins and 9 percent for fraternal twins when one of the twins has schizophrenia (Gottesman & Shields, 1972). Other studies have been performed on twins separated at birth and raised in different homes. Studies of twenty-eight pairs of such twins show the same 50 percent concordance rate as is commonly found in identical twins raised together (Gottesman, 1978).

There is little doubt that a significant genetic component underlies the disorder (Weisfeld, 1982; Scarr & Kidd, 1983). However, this concordance rate is less than perfect, which means that factors other than genetic considerations are also associated with the development of schizophrenia. The evidence also indicates a strong environmental component. What appears to be transmitted is not the disorder itself but rather a predisposition to acquire the disorder. In other words, all environmental factors being equal, an individual with a family history of schizophrenia is at a greater risk for the disorder than someone with no family history of schizophrenia. At the same time, prenatal, birth, and psychosocial factors are important, too. For example, some prenatal insults leading to brain abnormalities, lack of oxygen to the brain, and birth trauma; some cognitive deficits; and chaotic family situations with communication problems may be implicated (Mirsky & Duncan, 1986). Although genetic factors can make an individual more vulnerable, other factors can be just as important.

Studies indicate that other severe psychological disturbances may have a genetic base. Researchers at the University of London found that genetic factors may contribute to manic depression, usually called bipolar disorder, which is characterized by intense mood shifts between euphoria and profound depression (Hodgkinson et al., 1987). In addition, some research indicates that a genetic factor may be implicated in some cases of Alzheimer's disease, a disease in later life marked by mental deterioration (St. George-Hyslip et al., 1987; Tanzi et al., 1987).

Alcoholism and Genetics

What if you were a member of a family with a history of alcohol-related

concordance rate
The degree of similarity between twins on any particular trait.

9. TRUE OR FALSE?

Schizophrenia, like cystic fibrosis or Tay-Sachs disease, is transmitted directly from parent to child.

problems? One of your parents and a sibling have been treated for alcoholism, and a number of your relatives seem to have drinking problems. Do you think you would be more at risk for alcohol-related problems?

If you said yes, you agree with most experts. Many studies show that alcoholism tends to run in families (Goodwin, 1979). In one study of hospitalized alcoholics, more than 40 percent had a parent who suffered from alcoholism, most often a father. In an analysis of many studies of both alcoholics and nonalcoholics, Cotton (1979) found that alcoholics were more likely than nonalcoholics to have an alcoholic relative. In his analysis, one third of the sample of alcoholics had at least one parent who was alcoholic.

These results, though, do not demonstrate that there is a genetic aspect to alcoholism, for it is possible that the alcoholics learned their drinking behavior by watching their parents. If parents drink excessively, children may learn this pattern. Many studies have attempted to separate the heredity-environment web. Goodwin and colleagues (1973) followed a sample of over 5,000 children in Denmark who were adopted in early childhood. The sons of alcoholics who had been adopted by other families were three times more likely to become alcoholic as adopted sons of nonalcoholics. They were also much more likely to become alcoholic at an early age and to require treatment for their alcoholism. In a famous study in Sweden, Michael Bohman (1978) compared rates of alcohol abuse between adoptees and biological parents. Again, adopted sons whose biological fathers were alcoholic were three times more likely to become alcoholic than adopted sons of nonalcoholic fathers. If the mother was an alcoholic, the sons were twice as likely to become alcoholic. In another study of adoptees of alcoholic and nonalcoholic parents, 22.8 percent of the sons who had alcoholic biological fathers were alcoholics, compared to 14.7 of those who did not have an alcoholic parent, and 28.1 percent of the sons of alcoholic biological mothers were alcohol abusers, compared to 14.7 percent of sons who did not have an alcoholic parent. For women, 10.8 percent of the daughters of alcoholic mothers were alcoholic, compared to 2.8 percent of daughters who did not have an alcoholic biological parent. Having an alcoholic father did not have a significant effect on alcoholism among daughters. There was no relationship between alcoholism in adoptees and their adoptive parents (see U.S. Dept. of HEW, 1985). Studies in both Finland and the United States show a higher concordance rate for alcoholism among identical twins than fraternal twins (Sexias & Youcha, 1985). The conclusion of most studies is that there is a genetic predisposition to alcoholism (Schuckit, 1987). However, there is also considerable evidence for environmental factors being important. Most children of alcoholics do *not* become alcoholic, and this phenomenon has not been adequately studied (Heller, Sher, & Benson, 1982). Some children of alcoholics have made the conscious choice not to drink, and the cognitive factors that lead these people to refrain from alcohol use require more research. In addition, even people with no direct relative being alcoholic can become alcoholic. What is inherited is a predisposition to alcoholism.

Even if we agree that there is a genetic influence in the disease, how might it operate? Studies have shown that enzyme differences in the ability to break alcohol down exist between alcoholics and nonalcoholics. Alcoholics tend to metabolize alcohol differently than nonalcoholics and build up a tolerance easier. Schuckit (1986) compared sons of alcoholic fathers to sons of nonalcoholic fathers. At the time of the study, none of the sons were alcoholics. Even with the same level of alcohol in their systems, the sons of alcoholic fathers reported that they felt less intoxicated than the sons of nonalcoholic fathers. Some metabolic differences may be responsible for this difference. In addition, neurological differences have been found between the two groups (Cloninger, 1987). There are a number of rather complex chemical and neurological differences between the children of alcoholic and nonalcoholic parents.

Predispositions to various types of disturbances, including schizophrenia, bipolar disorders, and alcoholism, are inherited, probably in a rather complex manner. Scientists are now trying to discover chemical or neurological markers that would allow us to discern which people are more at risk than others. We could then give these at-risk individuals information and counseling that would help them to understand their situation and deal with it.

♦ GENETIC INFLUENCES ON DEVELOPMENT AND PERSONALITY

The importance of one's genetic endowment goes beyond physical characteristics and the specific physical disorders caused by genetic and chromosomal abnormalities. One's temperament, behavioral traits, rate of development, and intelligence are also affected by one's genes.

Temperament

At a recent social gathering, two couples (let's call them the Allens and the Johnsons) were discussing their children. Both couples had given birth about the same time, and they all came from similar ethnic, social, and economic backgrounds.

The Allens described their child as happy, eager, regular, and flexible. As Mr. and Mrs. Johnson gripped themselves, the Allens went on to say how easy it was to travel with their child. The child seemed to adapt easily to new situations, and everyone remarked on how well behaved the baby was.

The Johnsons tried to change the subject, but it was too late. Mr. and Mrs. Allen asked the Johnsons about their own child. After all, common courtesy called for them to exchange roles and listen while the Johnson's bragged.

"Well, our child is a bit different," Mr. Johnson began tentatively, wishing he had not accepted the invitation to the gathering in the first place. "A lot different," Mrs. Johnson continued. "He is very intense and stubborn. He cries a great deal and doesn't accept any changes in routine. He's hard to satisfy and doesn't seem to fit any pattern as far as eating and sleeping is concerned."

People with a genetic predisposition to alcoholism become alcoholic more easily, but even people with no family history of alcoholism can become alcoholics.

Parents who have children like the Johnsons' baby are sometimes reluctant to talk about them. At other times, they are desperate to find someone who not only will listen but also will help them deal with these children. It isn't unusual for someone to blame a child's difficulties on some parental action. Indeed, at times, the parents may contribute to the problem. According to a considerable body of evidence, however, the Johnsons might be better off accepting their child as he is and stop blaming themselves. The infant was born with a certain temperament.

Each child is born with a **temperament,** an "individual style of responding to the environment" (Thomas, Chess & Birch, 1970, p. 2). Thomas and his colleagues found nine behavior patterns that a child's temperament comprises (see Table 3.1), including (1) the level and extent of motor activity, (2) the degree of regularity of such functions as eating and sleeping, (3) distractibility when there are changes in the environment, (4) response to new objects or people, (5) adaptability to changes in the environment, (6) persistence, (7) intensity of responses, (8) sensitivity to stimuli, and (9) general disposition. Other scientists interested in temperament argue that a different constellation of behavior patterns define temperament. For example, Buss and Plomin (1984) suggest that three patterns make up temperament: emotionality, activity, and sociability. Emotionality refers to the strength of arousal shown by infants in response to events. Emotional infants show strong fear, anger, or distress even to minimal negative stimuli and are less easily comforted. Activity is the extent to which the child requires movement and expends energy. Sociability is the child's desire for the rewards of being with other people, such as attention.

Thomas and his colleagues found that the majority of children fit into one of three general types. "Easy" children are born that way. Like the child described by the Allens, the easy baby is generally happy, flexible, and regular. Such children get along well with almost everyone and present few problems to their parents or teachers. "Difficult" children, on the

temperament
A group of characteristics reflecting an individual's way of responding to the environment and thought to be genetic.

TABLE 3.1: Measuring Children's Temperament

Alexander Thomas, Stella Chess, and Herbert Birch found the majority of children could be classified as "easy," "slow to warm up," or "difficult" according to how they rate in key categories that are shown in color on a 9-point personality index.

TYPE OF CHILD	ACTIVITY LEVEL	RHYTHMICITY	DISTRACTIBILITY	APPROACH-WITHDRAWAL
	The proportion of active periods to inactive ones	Regularity of hunger, excretion, sleep, and wakefulness	The degree to which extraneous stimuli alter behavior	The response to a new object or person
Easy	Varies	Very regular	Varies	Positive approach
Slow to warm up	Low to moderate	Varies	Varies	Initial withdrawal
Difficult	Varies	Irregular	Varies	Withdrawal

other hand, are intense, demanding, and inflexible and cry a great deal. "Slow to warm up" children do not respond well to changes in their environment, but their reactions are not intense. They exhibit a low activity level and have a tendency to withdraw from new stimuli. Approximately 40 percent of the sample in the study by Thomas and his colleagues could be characterized as easy, about 10 percent as difficult, and another 15 percent as slow to warm up. The remaining 35 percent could not be put into any one of these categories because they showed a mixture of behaviors.

Temperament seems to be relatively stable in infancy. Ratings of infant temperament taken as early as two weeks are related to ratings at two months, and ratings at two-months are related to twelve-month ratings (Worobey & Blajda, 1989). After infancy, there is evidence both for moderate stability and for change. In one study, children's temperament was measured at two months, nine months, six years, and fifteen years. Substantial stability in activity level and sociability factor were found. However, substantial change was found in a factor akin to emotionality (Torgersen, 1989). Perhaps some aspects of temperament change, while others may show stability. However, even if one argues for stability, we should not expect the child to show his or her temperament in the same way. As children mature, the qualities that temperament comprises may manifest themselves differently. For example, at age two months, a child who is easily distractible will stop crying for food if rocked, and at two years, will stop a tantrum if another activity is suggested. The underlying characteristic of distractibility is present, but with age, different behaviors will be shown. Temperament, then, is easiest to see as stable in infancy, and although moderate stability may be found after that, there is also much change that may occur.

Does the temperament of the child affect the parent-child relationship? Theoretically, the possibility that it will affect the parent-child relationship is easy to understand. Children with different temperaments may respond differently to environmental events, and these responses may

TABLE 3.1: Measuring Children's Temperament (continued)

ADAPTABILITY	ATTENTION SPAN AND PERSISTENCE	INTENSITY OF REACTION	THRESHOLD OF RESPONSIVENESS	QUALITY OF MOOD
The ease with which a child adapts to changes in his or her environment	The amount of time devoted to an activity and the effect of distraction on the activity	The energy of response, regardless of its quality or direction	The intensity of stimulation required to evoke a discernible response	The amount of friendly, pleasant, joyful behavior vs. unpleasant, unfriendly behavior
Very adaptable	High or low	Low or mild	High or low	Positive
Slowly adaptable	High or low	Mild	High or low	Slightly negative
Slowly adaptable	High or low	Intense	High or low	Negative

Source: Thomas et al., 1970.

affect their parents' reactions (Mohar, 1988). A child is fortunate if his or her inborn temperament meshes with the parents' abilities and styles. The "difficult" child thrives in a structured, understanding environment but not in an inconsistent, intolerant home. The "slow to warm up" child does best if the parents understand the child's needs for time to adjust to new situations. If the parents do not, they may only intensify the child's natural tendency to withdraw.

Thomas urges parents to work with their child's temperament rather than try to change it. For example, if a child is slow to warm up, parents and teachers should allow the child to warm up to the environment at the child's own pace. Gentle encouragement is best. If the child is difficult, parents are advised to be very consistent and objective in their handling of the child. Teachers should realize that difficult children do poorly in nonstructured, permissive environments and may be easily frustrated by tasks they cannot handle immediately. Firmness and patience are required. Easy children may also face problems related to temperament. Sometimes they are unable to resolve conflicts between their own desires and demands of others.

The research evidence concerning the effect of temperament on parent-child relationships is more complex, though. Temperament may affect how parents see themselves and their roles as parents. Parents who have a child who is rated difficult are more likely to believe that the child's behavior is not under their control, while mothers of easy infants are more likely to believe in their ability to control their child's behavior (Sirignano & Lachman, 1985). Some studies also find that mothers of difficult children are less responsive and mothers of easy babies exhibit more positive maternal behaviors (see Bates, 1987). However, not all research sees temperament as important to parent-child relationships. A study by Daniels and colleagues (1984) found that temperament had little effect on parent-child relations and found no relationship between "difficultness" of temperament and quality of parenting as observed during a series of parent-child interactions.

Even though temperament appears to have a genetic basis (Goldsmith

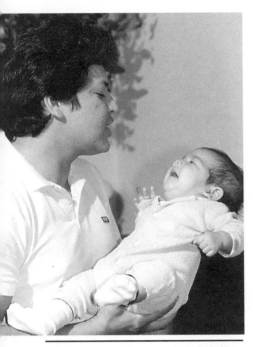

There are temperamental differences in the ease in which a child can be soothed.

& Gottesman, 1981), there is evidence that behavioral orientations may be affected by parenting practices and attitudes. In other words, the child's interactions with the environment may encourage or discourage a specific behavior related to temperament. In a study of infant temperament in three African societies, de Vries and Sameroff (1984) attributed specific differences in temperament to each culture's childrearing practices and parenting orientations. For example, mothers of infants in the Digo culture are not very concerned with time and are more likely to respond to a child's immediate needs. There is little emphasis on how long a child should sleep or the time a child should be fed. Perhaps as a result of this caregiving pattern, Digo infants were rated less regular than infants in the other two African cultures. A child's temperament, then, may also be influenced by environmental factors, including childrearing practices. Even mothers' opinions of temperament can change. When mothers were exposed to a special program to improve mother-infant interaction, not only did their interactions improve but their perceptions of their infants' temperament also greatly improved (Field, Widmayer, Stringer, & Ignatoff, 1980).

Temperament is obviously a complicated and controversial area. In one roundtable discussion with four eminent psychologists, it became obvious that there was agreement on some points and not on others (Goldsmith et al., 1987). Psychologists agree that temperament reflects behavioral tendencies, has biological underpinnings, and is easiest to see directly in infancy but becomes more complex as the child matures. They disagree on just how much of an infant's behavior should be considered as emanating from temperament, on the nature of the specific components that comprise temperament, and on whether the term *difficult child* should be used at all, because of its negative connotation. In addition, there is much disagreement on just how temperament should be defined, and lists of behaviors that temperament comprise differ (Bates, 1987). Despite these differences, the concept of temperament is useful in understanding the factors that underlie a child's tendency to react to certain stimuli in characteristic ways early in life.

Behavioral Traits

"Well, she's got her mother's looks but she took her father's temper" (Wells, 1980, p. 88). How many times have you heard variations of that statement? If your parents are friendly and affectionate, will you be the same? Is extroversion (being outgoing) or introversion (being directed inward) an inherited predisposition? There is evidence that a genetic component underlies this personality dimension (Plomin et al., 1990). Such traits as sociability, emotionality, and activity level also have underlying genetic components (Goldsmith, 1983; Daniels & Plomin, 1985), as to authoritarianism and rigidity (Rose and Ditto, 1983).

The tremendous influence of the environment on personality is obvious, but a genetic basis for various personality traits may also exist. In fact, a review of research involving over 25,000 pairs of twins yielded substantial estimates of heritability for the personality factors of extroversion and neuroticism (the extent to which a person shows negative emotions) (Henderson, 1982). More and more studies have demonstrated the contribution that genetics makes to various personality traits (Holden, 1987; Tellegen, Lykken, & Bouchard, 1988).

Just how would genes affect behavior? Gottesman (1966) notes, "There are no genes for behavior. The genes exert their influence on behavior through their effects at a more molecular level of organization. Enzymes, hormones, and neurons mediate the path between the genes and those psycho-social aspects of behavior termed personality" (p. 199). In other words, genes influence the individual's physiology, which in turn affects behavior.

10. TRUE OR FALSE?

There is a genetic basis for being extroverted, that is, having an outgoing personality.

Rate of Development

It is no secret that children develop at their own rate. The maturation rate reflects each child's unique genetic master plan. Such activities as standing, crawling, walking, and talking are largely, but not exclusively, dependent on the child's genetic endowment (Mischel, 1976).

Statistics show that the "average" child walks or talks at a particular age, but wide variations exist within the range of normal development. When children fall far behind these norms, the situation should be investigated.

It is important to recognize that within the broad "normal" range some children develop faster than others. Serious consequences may result from pushing a child to do something before the child is ready. The concept of **readiness** implies that there is a point in development when a child has the skills necessary to master a particular task. Problems can result when parents and teachers do not understand this. For instance, if a child who does not understand the concept of number is forced by parents to try to add two numbers, the child is destined to fail. The child becomes frustrated. Because an understanding of numbers is essential to success in learning how to add, bitter and unnecessary failure results. Repetition of such experience may lead to a lack of self-confidence. The same argument may hold for any physical or mental challenge.

readiness
The point in development at which a child has the necessary skills to master a new challenge.

◆ GENETICS AND INTELLIGENCE

In the history of psychology, no issue has been more bitterly debated than the influence of genetics on intelligence. Two questions are usually asked: How much of the variable we call intelligence can be attributed to hereditary factors? and How modifiable is intelligence?

The first question involves discovering the heritability of intelligence. The existence of a genetic component in intelligence is well accepted, but someone who offers a numerical percentage figure is likely to be criticized. Some authorities claim that it is impossible to estimate true heritability figures for human traits because we cannot control the environment (Feldman & Lewontin, 1975). After all, people with similar levels of intelligence tend to establish similar environments. Highly intelligent people create more stimulating environments than less intelligent people.

11. TRUE OR FALSE?

Identical twins reared apart are more similar in intelligence than fraternal twins reared together.

Many studies have tried to compare fraternal twins to identical twins. Since identical twins share the same genotype and fraternal twins have only 50 percent of their genes in common, if the identical twins are more similar in intelligence than the fraternal twins, it would indicate genetic involvement.

A number of studies have compared identical to fraternal twins. Nichols (1978) looked at many of these studies, finding that the average correlation for identical twins raised in similar environments was .82 and for fraternal twins was .59. In another twin study, called the Louisville Twin Study (Wilson, 1977, 1983), identical twins, fraternal twins, and nontwin siblings were compared. The intelligence scores of the siblings were similar to fraternal twins, which would be expected, since the two groups share about 50 percent of the genes in common, and again identical twins were more similar than any of the other pairs. In a study of identical twins reared apart, Bouchard (1984) found that the average correlation of identical twins reared in different environments was .76, which is higher than for either fraternal twins or nontwin siblings reared in the same household and closer to the value found for identical twins in the same homes.

The data from adoption studies generally indicate that the intelligence levels of adopted children are more closely related to the children's biological parents than to their adoptive parents (Jencks, 1972; Horn, 1983). In the Texas Adoption Project, 1,230 members of 300 adoptive families were studied when the adopted children were about eight years of age. These adoptive families were well off financially. Although the correlations were low, the intelligence scores of adopted children correlated better with their biological parents than with their adoptive parents (Horn, Loehlin, & Willerman, 1979; Loehlin, Horn, & Willerman, 1989).

Jencks argues that genetic factors are responsible for about half the variation in intelligence we see among people. Others have offered higher and lower figures. Jensen (1969) argues that it approaches 80 percent, while Kamin (1974), who thoroughly criticizes the studies purporting to demonstrate the heritability of intelligence, places the figures at a much lower level. While older studies have ascribed as much as 80 percent of intelligence to genetic factors, newer studies yield values closer to 50 percent (Plomin & DeFries, 1980). This would ascribe approximately half to genetic factors and the other half to the environment.

Any heritability figure should be interpreted cautiously. Problems in defining what we really mean by intelligence and difficulties in research design combine to provide ammunition for both sides (Horn, 1985; Walker & Emory, 1985). Even the same set of data can be interpreted differently, especially if one researcher concentrates on one area of the study while another person favors data from a different portion (McCall, 1981). In addition, most psychologists today accept the fact that an important environmental element underlies intelligence, because none of the correlations in the data noted previously are perfect (Willerman, 1979). No matter which estimate of heritability one uses, both environmental and genetic factors are involved in intelligence (Scarr & Kidd, 1983).

MODIFYING INTELLIGENCE The second question regarding intelligence—that of modifiability—is more important. A number of studies testify to the modifiability of intelligence, but one by Skeels (1966) stands out. In the 1930s, Skeels was working in a bleak orphanage, where the children received little attention and were subjected to a rigid schedule. The children had no toys, and the environment was depressing. Skeels took a special interest in two girls who rocked back and forth and spent most of their time in bed. These two girls were later transferred to a mental institution, where they came under the influence of an older, retarded woman who showered them with attention. Their behavior changed, and they became much more responsive.

Skeels decided to find out more about this phenomenon. A number of children were removed from the sterile setting of the orphanage and allowed to live with older retardates in a better environment. Their intelligence scores improved an average of twenty-nine points, and one child's intelligence score actually rose by more than fifty points. The group that stayed in the depressing environment of the orphanage was found to have even lower intelligence scores than when the study had begun.

The conclusion that a change in environment accounts for the improvement in intelligence has been accepted by most psychologists today, although the methodology has been severely criticized (Longstreth, 1981). Some creative programs have successfully increased the intelligence scores of particular groups. For example, Israel has had considerable success in narrowing, and sometimes even eliminating, the differences in intelligence that were present among many of the diverse groups who settled there. Through an intensive program of enrichment, these differences tended to disappear (Smilansky, 1975).

The genetic influence on intelligence does not limit its malleability (Scarr-Salapatek, 1975). Rather, the genetic factor affects the elasticity of intelligence. Few would argue that any enrichment program could turn a child of below-average intelligence into a genius, but a radical change for the better in the child's environment would probably have a significant effect on the child's intelligence score. A number of programs have attempted to raise the intelligence scores of young children through a variety of educational programs aimed at both children and their parents. Many have been successful in the short term. Much more is said about these programs in Chapter 9.

How can we best picture the effects of genetic and environmental influences on intelligence? We know that both are important. One possible model is shown in Fig. 3.5. If a child is given a normal environment, the intelligence of the child is shown by the solid, dark line at the center of the range of possible intelligence scores. If the child gets an enriched environment, the line goes to the high side; a deprived environment, it goes to the low end. Note that the range is not equally wide at all points. There is a wider space at the lower end between the average environment and the enriched environment than at the upper end (Scarr & Arnett, 1987). This is in keeping with much experimentation showing that intensive early education has a greater positive effect on children from

FIGURE 3.5: Genetic Potential for Intelligence

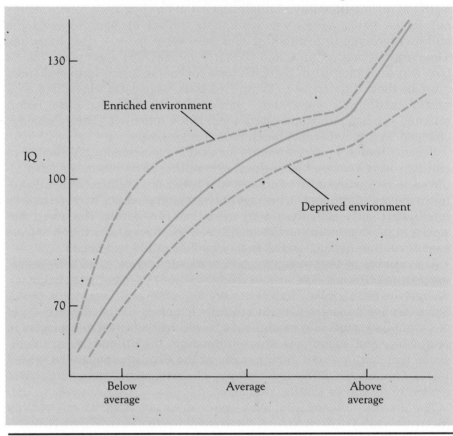

Source: Scarr & Arnett, 1987.

poverty stricken backgrounds than on children from advantaged environments. The environment has an effect on intelligence, but within limits.

◆ GENETIC COUNSELING: FRONTIERS OF KNOWLEDGE

Lisa's brother was mentally retarded and lived away from home. Lisa was never given a reason or a name for her brother's problems. Now Lisa is planning a family of her own and wonders whether she should be concerned.

Ben's father died of a heart attack when he was only 42. Could it happen to Ben? Ben wants to know whether he is at special risk and, if he is, how to protect his own health.

Jennifer is pregnant at age 36 and is concerned about the risk of chromosome problems.

Each of these people sought out genetic counseling for their questions from one of the more than 200 comprehensive genetic counseling centers in the United States.

In many university clinics, professionals trained in genetics are able to help people determine their risks. These genetic counselors help people by (1) diagnosing and describing particular disorders, (2) calculating the probabilities that a disorder will be transmitted to offspring, (3) helping people reach a decision based on genetic information as well as on ethical, religious, and cultural concerns, and (4) describing the treatment and resources available to those seeking such information (Sperber, 1976). On the surface, this seems to present few problems, but appearances can be deceiving. In reality, genetic counseling is fraught with complicated ethical and practical problems that are quite difficult to solve.

For example, will those seeking the information understand and remember it? Sibinga and Friedman (1971) reported that only a small percentage of their sample adequately understood the facts communicated to them about PKU. It was their emotional reaction to what they had been told—not their intelligence level—that interfered with their understanding. In another study, only 35 percent of the sample of people who were told their children carried a dangerous recessive gene but would develop normally because they were carriers appeared for counseling. Many who did appear did not remember the counseling experience three to eight months later, although they remembered being told that their children were normal (Grossman, Holtzman, Charney, & Schwartz, 1985).

There are, therefore, problems in communicating information about particular defects to parents who are emotionally involved (Walzer, Richmond & Gerald, 1976). People often use defenses to deny or reject such information. The realization that something is wrong with their genes and that they might carry a defect can be alarming and can change a person's life. Genetic counselors must be certain their clients understand what they are being told. It is also their duty to help clients deal with emotional reactions to the information.

Most people who seek genetic counseling are faced with some kind of decision. A family with one child who has suffered from a genetic difficulty may have to decide whether to have other children. Others may have to decide whether they should even begin a family. Still others may be forced to decide whether to terminate a pregnancy based on laboratory tests showing that the fetus has some serious genetic defect—certainly a controversial question. Previous generations did not have the information needed to make such decisions, but success with such disorders as PKU have provided an incentive for more screening to take place in the future (Nyhan, 1986). New techniques for screening and diagnosis, some of which will be discussed in Chapter 4, now offer hope of earlier detection of a number of genetic disorders.

Can genetic counselors help people make decisions without allowing their own biases to influence their clients? After all, anyone in the position of a counselor has a great deal of standing and therefore power. A counselor must be careful to explain the facts in terms that will not affect the decision itself. Yet, because helping people deal with their feelings

12. TRUE OR FALSE?

Genetic counselors have the responsibility to approve or disapprove of their clients' course of action.

is one of a counselor's tasks, counselors are in a difficult position. People often ask counselors what they should do—a question genetic counselors cannot answer. Genetic counselors may influence these decisions inadvertently, however, by the way they provide the information. If genetic counseling is used correctly, it can ease people's minds. People can leave genetic counseling knowing they are armed with the information that will allow them to make difficult decisions more rationally.

Concerning the three people who went for genetic counseling. Lisa's brother was reexamined by physicians, leading to a diagnosis of fragile X syndrome, an X-linked disorder responsible for many cases of mental retardation in boys. The disorder was unknown when Lisa's brother was a child. Before getting pregnant, Lisa plans to be tested to see if she is a carrier for the disorder.

Ben's father's high levels of blood cholesterol and early heart attack were caused by familial hypercholesterolemia, an inherited problem that affects one in every 500 Americans. Ben discovered that he had inherited his father's tendency toward high cholesterol (a 50-50 chance). To protect his health, doctors prescribed a low-fat diet, exercise program, and cholesterol-lowering medications.

Jennifer learned that the chance of a chromosomal problem in her pregnancy is about one in 200. After discussing the risks and benefits of prenatal diagnosis with the genetic counselor, she and her husband are deciding whether prenatal testing is the right choice for them (March of Dimes, 1987c, p. 20).

The Environment in Behavior Genetics

"During the 1970s, I found I had to speak gingerly about genetic influence gently suggesting heredity might be important in behavior. Now, however, I more often have to say, 'Yes, genetic influences are significant and substantial, but environmental influences are just as important.'" So says Robert Plomin (1989, p. 110), a recognized authority on behavior genetics. More and more psychologists believe that a genetic basis underlies many characteristics. The change is shown in scientists' attitudes towards the genetic basis of intelligence. In a survey of 1,020 experts in the social sciences, Snyderman and Rothman (1987) found that most believed individual differences in intelligence to be at least partially inherited. We may be in danger of forgetting environmental factors or at least relegating them to a secondary position, one that they do not deserve. Studies demonstrating the genetic contribution to various traits and susceptibilities also clearly show the importance of environmental influences in development. With the exception of some genetic diseases, heritability estimates never even approach a figure that would allow one to argue that the environment was unimportant. It is also a myth that if some aspect of development is genetic, it cannot be changed. Genes do not fix behavior in concrete. Rather, they indicate a range of possible reactions, and it is the environment that determines what phenotype will be developed (Weinberg, 1989). This does not mean that we are completely malleable. There are limits, but environmental influences can be potent.

◆ THE NEW REALITY

There is no doubt that the manner in which modern scientists view the interaction of genetics and the environment is more complicated than it has been in the past. During childhood there are a number of genetically induced paths an individual may take, and it is the environment that determines which path the child follows (McCall, 1981). We are now making some tentative attempts to understand how environment and genetics interact, and such explanations will become very complicated as time goes on.

Some people yearn for the "good old days," when general statements about what was inherited and what wasn't could be made. Things were certainly easier then, even if they were almost always incorrect. The more modern view of the nature-nurture controversy is certainly more complicated and precludes making grandiose statements about heredity causing one thing and the environment causing another. However, it also gives us the opportunity to marvel once again at the complicated process by which a tiny, one-cell fertilized egg develops into a living, lovable infant, and how that infant fulfills its great human promise.

SUMMARY

1. The basic units of heredity are genes, which are carried on chromosomes. Human beings have twenty-three pairs of chromosomes. In the sex cells, however, the chromosome pair splits, so that each sex cell contains twenty-three chromosomes. This split is random, assuring genetic individuality. The twenty-three chromosomes found in both the egg and the sperm cells combine during fertilization to maintain the same forty-six chromosomes found in normal human beings.

2. The first twenty-two pairs of chromosomes appear to be alike, but the twenty-third pair, the sex chromosomes, is different. A female has two X chromosomes, while the male has an X and a Y. The male determines the gender of the offspring, since he can contribute an X or a Y, while the female contributes only an X.

3. A trait that is expressed even if only one gene for it is present is called dominant. The trait that requires two genes to express itself is called recessive.

4. The term genotype describes the genetic composition of the individual, while the term phenotype refers to the person's observable characteristics. An individual's phenotype and genotype may be different.

5. When a particular characteristic is influenced by many genes, we consider the mechanism of transmission to be polygenic, multigenic, or multifactorial. The word multifactorial is sometimes used to denote characteristics influenced by a number of genes as well as by the environment.

6. Since the X chromosome is three times larger than the Y, a number of genes found on the X are not present on the Y. When there is some defect on the X, a male may not be able to counter its effects, since males possess only one X and the gene may not be found at all on the Y. Traits inherited in this manner are called sex-linked traits. Females normally do not show them, because they have two X chromosomes and only one normal gene is necessary to mask the effects of the defective gene. Hemophilia and color blindness are transmitted in this way to males.

7. Our genetic endowment affects our physical characteristics. Since people react to one another on the basis of some of them, these characteristics can become socially important even if they are biologically trivial. Genetic factors are also important in determining handedness and a child's rate of development.

8. A number of genetic disorders have been discovered, including cystic fibrosis, Tay-Sachs disease, phenylketonuria, Huntington's chorea, and sickle cell anemia.

9. If an extra chromosome somehow attaches itself to the twenty-first pair, the infant is born with Down syndrome (formerly called mongolism). Such infants are usually retarded, although the degree of retardation varies, and have a number of distinctive physical attributes.

10. There is a significant genetic component in some major mental disorders, including schizophrenia, as well as

in alcoholism. However, what is transmitted is not the disorder itself, but rather a tendency or a predisposition to suffer from the disorder given a particular environment.

11. Our genetic endowment influences our personality, probably by affecting our biological functioning. Human beings are born with a temperament—an individual way of responding to the environment. In addition, a number of our personality traits, such as introversion and extroversion, sociability, and activity level, appear to have a genetic basis.

12. There appears to be a genetic basis for intelligence, although there is much dispute over the heritability figure. However, no matter what figure is used, an individual's environment greatly affects how these genes will be expressed. Educational programs can raise the intelligence scores of children.

13. Genetic counseling offers couples an opportunity to find out more about their genetic background and the probability that they will have a child with a particular disorder.

14. Heredity and environment interact in many subtle ways. We cannot speak of one in the absence of the other. We must consider both if we are to fully understand how people fulfill their human potential.

ACTION/REACTION

A Secret to Keep?

Kathy and Tom met in their second year of college and became engaged two years later. They agree on most things and are sensitive to each other's feelings. A few nights ago, they watched a television special on cystic fibrosis. The sufferings of a child afflicted with the disorder were depicted graphically, as were the parents' problems in dealing with the child's illness and the parents' own emotions.

Tom stated categorically that he couldn't take that and that "no life was better than that existence." Kathy felt a pang. Her sister had died from the disease five years before she and Tom had met. Kathy had told Tom that her sister had died of pneumonia.

Kathy doesn't know whether she should tell Tom. She knows something about the disease, and since it doesn't run in Tom's family, their children can't be afflicted with it. Why tell Tom something that could upset their marriage plans, when it couldn't have any effect on their children? On the other hand, Kathy recognizes that not being completely honest with Tom is a poor way to start a marriage.

1. If you were Kathy, would you tell Tom? Why or why not?
2. If you were Kathy's parents, would you insist that your child tell Tom?
3. If you were Tom, would you want to know? How would you react to the news?
4. Do people have a moral obligation to inform anyone about their genetic background?

"Aggressive" Genes?

"You're just like your father!" Ina yelled at Jon. "Go on, hit me! Show me what kind of man you are!" All the neighbors know Ina and Jon—the couple is constantly fighting. The entire neighborhood can hear them, and their arguments often erupt into violence, with Jon hitting Ina.

When interviewed, Ina noted that Jon's father had behaved violently toward his own wife, so "it must be in his genes." "His father had a terrible temper," she stated, "just like Jon does." Jon agrees. He states that although he loves Ina, he can't seem to control his temper, just as his father couldn't. Jon had been a very aggressive child and was subject to temper tantrums. When a psychologist suggested that he could change, Jon looked astonished, shook his head, and said, "Once it's in your genes, you can't get rid of it." Both Ina and Jon also told the psychologist that their son was showing the same behavior pattern. They offered this as further proof of their genetics argument.

1. If you were the psychologist, how would you deal with Jon and Ina's attitude?
2. If you were Ina, what would you do?

CHAPTER FOUR

Prenatal Development and Birth

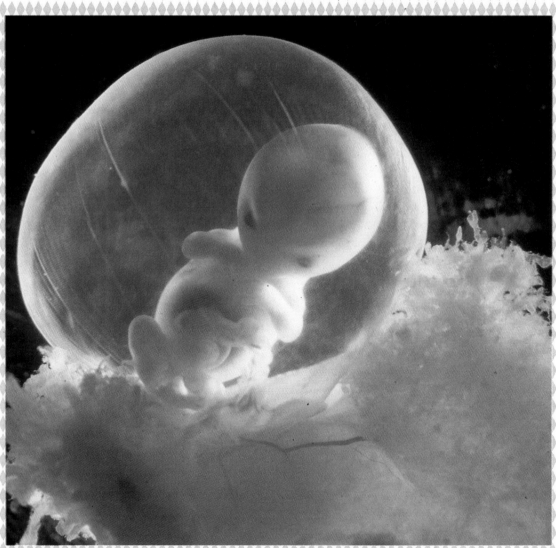

Photo by Lennart Nilsson.

Are These Statements True or False?

Turn the page for the correct answers. Each statement is repeated in the margin next to the paragraph in which the information can be found.

1. The frequency of identical twins is uniform across various cultural and racial groups.
2. The first organ to function is the heart.
3. The infants of women who smoke during pregnancy weigh about half a pound more than the infants of mothers who do not smoke.
4. Infants born to women who used cocaine during pregnancy are more likely to be premature and even to die, but those who survive do not show any behavioral differences when compared to infants whose mothers did not use cocaine.
5. Most children with AIDS received the virus through tainted blood transfusions.
6. Alcohol consumption during pregnancy leads to an Rh problem.
7. Some 70 percent of all birth defects are caused by prenatal insults rather than genetic disorders.
8. Severe malnutrition during pregnancy leads to a condition in which the infant has fewer brain cells.
9. Maternal stress does not affect the fetus, because the systems of the mother and the fetus are separate.
10. Infants born through Cesarean section are more likely to do poorly in school than infants born vaginally.
11. The Lamaze method of birth emphasizes the importance of leaving the mother alone to meditate on her experience.
12. Premature infants today are no more at risk for developmental problems than are normal infants.

Answers to True-False Questions

1. True
2. True.
3. False. Correct statement: The infants of pregnant women who smoke weigh on the average of about a half pound less than the infants of pregnant women who do not smoke.
4. False. Correct statement: Not only is there increased fetal mortality among infants born to women who use cocaine during pregnancy, but such infants also suffer many behavioral deficits, including being less responsive to stimuli.
5. False. Correct statement: Almost all new cases of pediatric AIDS are caused by transmission of the AIDS virus from mother to infant during the prenatal period or birth.
6. False. Correct statement: An Rh disorder is not caused by alcohol consumption.
7. True.
8. True.
9. False. Correct statement: Maternal stress is linked to infants who are irritable as well as to obstetrical problems.
10. False. Correct statement: The evidence shows that children who are delivered by Cesarean section do at least as well in school as children delivered vaginally.
11. False. Correct statement: The Lamaze method encourages the father to participate actively in the birth of the child.
12. False. Correct statement: Despite improvements in medical care, the premature infant is still at a greater risk for developmental problems than the normal infant.

◆ THE DEVELOPING ORGANISM

Margaret and Tim are thrilled at the thought of becoming parents, but their friends and relatives offer all kinds of advice about what Margaret should and shouldn't do during pregnancy, and the newspapers are filled with articles about things that could go wrong during pregnancy and birth. With each report, the concerns of the expectant parents grow. Margaret and Tim have been married for six years and had decided to wait before having children. They are both in their thirties. They've read about new ways to manage birth, and they don't know which way is best. Everyone has a different opinion. Like all expectant parents, they want a happy, healthy baby, but they're afraid something will go wrong. How realistic are their fears?

It is easy to be overwhelmed by the number of environmental, physical, and viral agents that can cause difficulties during pregnancy. Although the threats are real enough, the overwhelming majority of infants will develop normally and emerge from the birth canal ready for life. The birthing choices available today offer an opportunity for parents to become more involved in this important experience. But although these alternative birth methods are often highly touted in the media, research concerning their true value is difficult to find.

This chapter deals with the development of the organism in the womb and the most important odyssey an infant will ever take—birth. Myths and half-truths abound in these areas, and they deserve special attention.

◆ PRENATAL DEVELOPMENT

To understand the importance of the prenatal period, a brief look at the developing organism is necessary.

The Beginning

During ovulation, one egg is allowed to pass into the fallopian tube, where it is exposed to any sperm that are present. Although many sperm may surround the egg cell, only one will penetrate the cell's outer wall. At this moment of conception, the mother's egg cell is fertilized by the father's sperm. When this occurs, there is a rearrangement and an exchange of genetic material, and the genetic endowment of the new being is set for life. This fertilized egg, or **zygote**, continues to travel down the tube into the uterus, or womb.

zygote
A fertilized egg.

In some cases, two eggs may pass into the fallopian tube and be fertilized by two different sperm. The result is dizygotic, or fraternal, twins—two separately developing organisms that are no more genetically similar than any other pair of siblings. The frequency of fraternal twins differs widely among racial groups and occurs more often among African groups than among Caucasians, and more often among Caucasians than among Asians (Bulmer, 1970). The frequency of monozygotic, or identical, twins is uniform across racial groups and cultures at about four pairs in 1,000 pregnancies. Identical twins develop from a single egg and a single sperm. A cell division takes place very early in development, and twins born from a single egg and single sperm have the identical genetic makeup. Those rare cases in which the division into two separate zygotes is incomplete result in twins joined together, or Siamese twins.

1. TRUE OR FALSE?

The frequency of identical twins is uniform across various cultural and racial groups.

From the moment of conception, the developing organism is affected by its genotype and its environment. During the nine months in the womb, its weight will increase one billion times over (Annis, 1978), and an infant will emerge with all biological systems ready for life outside the womb. Table 4.1 on page 136 summarizes prenatal development.

The Germinal Stage

It takes anywhere from a week to ten days or so for the fertilized egg to embed itself in the lining of the uterus. During this period, called the **germinal stage**, the fertilized egg divides again and again and begins the

germinal stage
The earliest stage of prenatal development, lasting from conception to about two weeks.

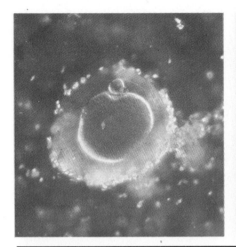

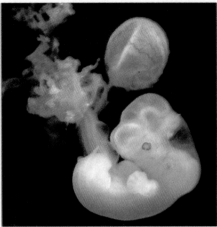

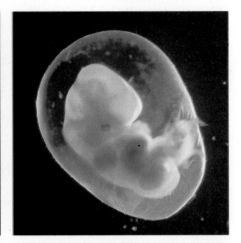

The fertilized ovum has divided for the first time. The chromosomes from the father and mother have united and the genetic composition of the new life is fixed. Cell division starts at once, and the developing cluster of cells moves slowly down the fallopian tube toward the uterus.

Five weeks old and two-fifths of an inch long. The major divisions of the brain can be seen as well as an eye, the hands, the arms, and a long tail. The upper part of the body develops more rapidly than the lower one—development takes place from the top down.

Six weeks old and three-fifths of an inch long. The embryo rests securely in its shock-absorbing amniotic sac. The heart beats rapidly. The brain is growing and the eyes are taking shape. The dark red swelling at the level of the stomach is the liver. The external ears are developing from skin folds.

At eight weeks, 4 cm (1.6 inches), the developing individual is no longer an embryo, but a fetus. Everything that will be found in the fully developed human being has now been established. The fetal stage is a period of growth and perfection of detail. The heart has been beating for a month and the muscles have just begun their first exercises.

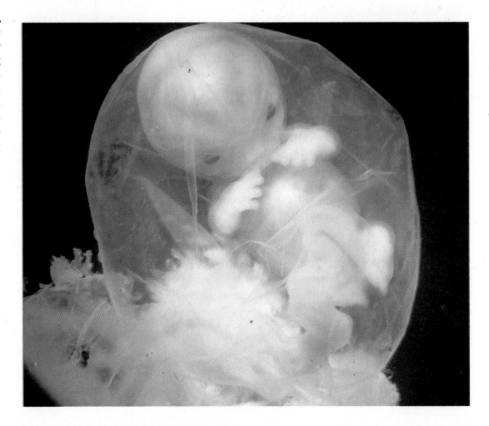

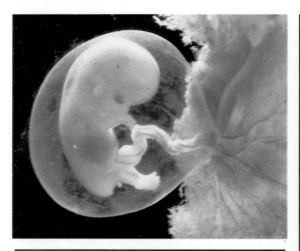

The fetus in the third month. There is never any exchange of blood between mother and fetus. All exchanges of nutrients and oxygen occur by diffusion.

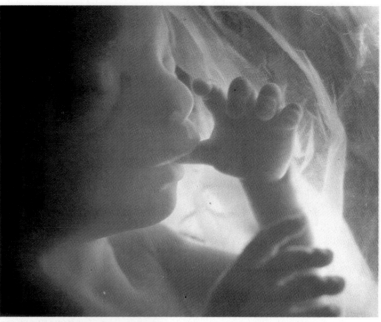

(Above) At four and one-half months, about 18 cm (just over 7 inches). When the thumb comes close to the mouth, the head may turn, and lips and tongue begin their sucking motions—a reflex for survival.

With specially manufactured equipment—a super-wide-angle lens with an ultrashort focal length—the whole fetus is photographed within the amniotic sac. This little girl is just over five months old and roughly 25 cm (10 inches) long.

TABLE 4.1: Summary of Prenatal Development
Prenatal development is orderly and predictable.

TIME ELAPSED	EMBRYONIC OR FETAL CHARACTERISTICS	TIME ELAPSED	EMBRYONIC OR FETAL CHARACTERISTICS
4 weeks 1 month	¼–½ inch long. Head is one-third of embryo. Brain has lobes, and rudimentary nervous system appears as hollow tube. Heart begins to beat. Blood vessels form, and blood flows through them. Simple kidneys, liver, and digestive tract appear. Rudiments of eyes, ears, and nose appear. Small tail.	4 months	4 ounces in weight. Body now growing faster than head. Skin on hands and feet forms individual patterns. Eyebrows and head hair begin to show. Fine, downylike hair (lanugo) covers body. Movements may now be felt.
8 weeks 2 months	2 inches long. 1/30 of an ounce in weight. Human face with eyes, ears, nose, lips, tongue. Arms have pawlike hands. Almost all internal organs begin to develop. Brain coordinates functioning of other organs. Heart beats steadily and blood circulates. Complete cartilage skeleton, beginning to be replaced by bone. Tail beginning to be absorbed. Now called a fetus. Sex organs begin to differentiate.	20 weeks 5 months	10–12 inches long. 8–16 ounces in weight. Skeleton hardens. Nails form on fingers and toes. Skin covered with cheesy wax. Heartbeat now loud enough to be heard with stethoscope. Muscles are stronger. Definite strong kicking and turning. Can be startled by noises.
12 weeks 3 months	3 inches long. 1 ounce in weight. Begins to be active. Number of nerve-muscle connections almost triples. Sucking reflex begins to appear. Can swallow and may even breathe. Eyelids fused shut (will stay shut until the sixth month), but eyes are sensitive to light. Internal organs begin to function.	24 weeks 6 months	12–14 inches long. 1½ pounds in weight. Can open and close eyelids. Grows eyelashes. Much more active, exercising muscles. May suck thumb. May be able to breathe if born prematurely.
16 weeks	6–7 inches long.	28 weeks 7 months	15 inches long. 2½ pounds in weight. Begins to develop fatty tissue. Internal organs (especially respiratory and digestive) still developing. Has fair chance of survival if born now.
		32 weeks 8 months	16½ inches long. 4 pounds in weight. Fatty layer complete.
		38 weeks 9 months	Birth. 19–20 inches long. 6–8 pounds in weight (average). 95 percent of full-term babies born alive in the United States will survive.

Source: Adapted from Cox, 1984.

process of specialization that results in the formation of its organs. On the second day, about thirty hours after fertilization, the cell divides into two new cells (Singer & Hilgard, 1978). At sixty hours, the two cells divide to become four cells (Curtis, 1975). This division continues until, at the end of the first week, over 100 cells are present.

On the fifth day after conception, the cells rearrange to form a cavity. The hollow ball of cells is now called a **blastocyst** (Balinsky, 1970). The majority of cells are found in the outer layer, called a trophoblast, while the rest are found in the inner layer, called the inner cell mass. The outer layer will become structures that enable the embryo to survive, including the yolk sac, the allantois, the amnion, and the chorion. The yolk sac produces blood cells until the developing organism can do so on its own, at which point it disappears. The allantois forms the umbilical cord and the blood vessels in the placenta. The amnion eventually envelopes the organism, holding the amniotic fluid, which protects the organism. The chorion becomes the lining of the placenta. The inner cell mass becomes the embryo.

The survival of the fertilized egg depends on the egg's ability to burrow into the lining of the mother's uterus and obtain nourishment from the mother's system. This process is called **implantation**. It does this by secreting digestive enzymes that allow the blastocyst to embed itself in the maternal tissues. It now develops the ability to feed off its host. It also prevents menstruation by releasing a hormone that maintains the conditions necessary for support.

At about seven or eight days, the inner cell mass has differentiated into two distinct layers: the ectoderm and the endoderm. The ectoderm will develop into the organism's external coverings, including the skin, hair, sense organs, and nervous system. The endoderm becomes the digestive system, the respiratory system, and the glands. At about the sixteenth day, another layer, the mesoderm, appears between the ectoderm and endoderm and develops into the muscles, connective tissues, and the circulatory and excretory systems.

As development continues, the amnion swells and covers the developing organism. The trophoblast develops projections, or villi, that penetrate the uterine wall, allowing the developing organism to receive nutrients more efficiently. The villi on one side organize into the placenta, which is connected to the developing organism by the umbilical cord. The placenta delivers nutrients, removes wastes, and helps combat infection. The germ cell at the end of the first two weeks of life measures about 1/175 inch (Annis, 1978).

The Embryonic Stage

The **embryonic stage** begins at about two weeks and ends at about eight weeks after conception. At two weeks, the tiny mass has just begun to depend on its mother for everything. It is hardly recognizable as a human being. Six weeks later, 95 percent of the body parts will be present (Annis, 1978). During the embryonic period, changes occur at a breathtaking pace.

blastocyst
The stage of prenatal development in which the organism consists of layers of cells around a central cavity forming a hollow sphere.

implantation
The process by which the fertilized egg burrows into the lining of the mother's uterus and obtains nourishment from the mother's system.

embryonic stage
The stage of prenatal development, from about two weeks to about eight weeks, when bone cells begin to replace cartilage.

2. TRUE OR FALSE?

The first organ to function is the heart.

Each system's development follows a particular sequence. At day 31, the shoulders, arms, and hands develop; on day 33, the fingers develop; and on day 34 through day 36, the thumb is completed. The organs form and begin to function in a primitive manner. The first organ to function is the heart, which circulates the blood to the placenta and throughout the developing body. The circulatory system of the embryo is completely separated from the mother's, and no exchange of blood occurs. All exchanges of nutrients and oxygen occur by diffusion. By the end of the first month, the ears, nose, and mouth begin to form, and arms and legs make their appearance as buds. Fingers and toes become defined. Internal organs are now rapidly developing. During this time of extremely rapid growth, the organism is most vulnerable to environmental insult. The embryo is capable of some primitive behavioral reactions. Reflex action occurs as early as the middle of the seventh week. If the mouth is stimulated, the embryo flexes its neck to the opposite side (Richmond & Herzog, 1979).

The Fetal Stage

fetal stage
The stage of prenatal development beginning at about eight weeks and continuing until birth.

During the last seven months of development—the **fetal stage**—the fetus grows and develops at a tremendous rate. At the beginning of the third month, the average fetus is one and one-quarter inches long and weighs less than one-third of an ounce. By the end of third month, it is three inches long and weighs one ounce. Hormonal action during this third month causes the genitals to become defined. If the male hormone testosterone is secreted into the fetal system, it causes the development of male genitalia. In the absence of the male hormone, the fetus will develop female organs. During this third month, the major organs are completed and bones begin to appear and muscles develop. The fetus now moves, kicks its legs, swallows and digests the amniotic fluid, and removes waste products through urination.

During the fourth month, the fetus continues to grow at a fantastic pace. By the end of the month, it is six inches long and weighs six ounces. As it grows, it develops internally. By the fifth month, the fetus sleeps and wakes at regular intervals, and some reflexes, such as hiccupping and swallowing, have developed. The fetus cries and may suck a thumb. At this point, the fetal movements are likely to be felt by the mother, though some mothers experience movement earlier. This is known as quickening.

During the sixth month, the fetus attains a weight of about two pounds and a length of fourteen inches. The facial features are clearly in evidence, and the fetus can make a fist. During the last three prenatal months, the fetus gains a layer of fat that will help keep the infant warm after birth. By the end of the twenty-eighth week, the fetus measures about seventeen inches and weighs about three pounds.

Traditionally, seven months is considered the age of viability, since the fetus has a reasonable chance of survival if born at this time. This is misleading, however, for there is considerable individual variation in weight, health, and developmental readiness. Some seven-month-old fetuses are more ready for an independent existence than others. The availability of excellent perinatal (after-birth) medical care is also an important factor in the survivability of the infant. Many technological innovations are improving the survival chances of these tiny infants.

During the last two prenatal months, the fetus gains about half a pound a week. Its heretofore red, wrinkled appearance disappears somewhat as it puts on weight. The development of the lungs is especially important during these last months. By the end of the normal period of prenatal development, approximately 266 days, the infant is born.

The entire process of fetal development proceeds without any need for conscious maternal intervention. It is directed by genetic forces that we are only just beginning to understand. However, the fetus is also affected by the environment.

Developmental Myths

People used to believe that everything a woman did during pregnancy could have an effect on the unborn infant. Unusual occurrences in a pregnant woman's daily life were thought to influence the personality and physical well-being of the child. Some believed, for instance, that if a rabbit crossed the mother's path the child would be born with a harelip (Annis, 1978). Others believed that if the mother ate or squashed straw-berries, the child would have a strawberry-shaped birthmark. The belief in total environmental control was replaced by the idea that nothing the mother did really mattered. The placenta was viewed as a barrier that did not allow any dangerous elements into the infant's environment and ren-dered various poisons harmless. Today we know that neither viewpoint is correct. The placenta is far from being a total barrier. It allows a number of substances to pass into the system of the fetus. On the other hand, although we no longer believe the superstitions about rabbits and straw-berries, we know that the infant's environment greatly affects the health of the fetus.

◆ THREATS TO THE DEVELOPING ORGANISM

So many things have been linked to birth defects that it is difficult to know just what is safe. This is a great dilemma for Margaret and Tim. They both drink moderately, and Margaret also smokes. Although a num-ber of drugs, illnesses, and chemicals have been linked to birth defects, most infants are born free from defects. Any agent that causes a birth defect is called a **teratogen**, and the number of known or suspected ter-atogens has increased substantially in the past decade or so. The effects of these agents depend upon the type of agent, the dosage, and the genetic characteristics of the fetus. The time at which the fetus is exposed is also important, because some agents are more likely to produce birth defects if they are ingested at a certain time during the pregnancy

Three problems in interpretation of research on teratogens should be noted. First, some research is based on animal experimentation, and al-though the animal model is useful (Vorhees & Mollnow, 1987), any cross-species comparisons should be made with care. Second, much of the data

teratogen
Any agent that causes birth defects.

relating teratogens to human birth defects is correlational because we cannot experimentally expose pregnant women to particular teratogens and conduct controlled experiments. So when a correlation between ingestion of a particular agent and birth defects occurs, it is difficult to isolate the confounding variables such as diet, exercise, anxiety, and the mother's ingestion of other agents. Some pregnant women who take drugs are also undernourished and have not had adequate prenatal care; and some women take a variety of drugs, not just one, and trying to fix responsibility on any one agent is difficult (McGlothlin, Sparks & Arnold, 1970). It is also difficult to determine the exact dosages of drugs used, and this could be an important factor with some teratogens (Richardson, Day & Taylor, 1989). Last, much of the evidence on the effects of specific teratogens deals with gross or very visible deformities or behavioral abnormalities. It is not always easy to discover the more subtle difficulties that may show themselves either later in a child's development or only at specific times, perhaps when the child is stressed. We are only now beginning to research these elements.

Medication

The most famous case of a medication causing birth defects involved the drug thalidomide, which was widely used in Europe as a treatment for morning sickness. A vast number of infants—estimated at over 10,000—were born without limbs or with extremities that were grossly underdeveloped. Relatively few American women had taken the drug because it was never approved by the U.S. Food and Drug Administration.

Other medications have been linked to birth defects, and the research findings on others are contradictory. Tetracycline, a commonly prescribed antibiotic, has been linked to permanent discoloration of the teeth and defective bone growth (March of Dimes, 1983b). While some antibiotics seem safe, our knowledge of most is limited (Knothe & Dette, 1985). The contraceptive pill, if taken right before or during pregnancy, can cause congenital heart disease and other structural abnormalities (U.S. Department of Health and Human Services, 1981a). This is why many doctors recommend that a woman who wants to become pregnant stop taking the pill some months before she plans to get pregnant. Scientists are also concerned about the possible effects that such commonly prescribed prescription drugs as Valium and Librium may have on an unborn child. A large study called the Collaborative Perinatal Project concluded that these "minor tranquilizers" have been linked to the incidence of cleft palate, a birth defect affecting the formation of the roof of the mouth. However, evidence is mixed, and another study did not find this pattern (Rosenberg, Mitchell, Persells, Pashayan, Lovik & Shapiro, 1983). With such contradictory research, it is difficult to sort out which drugs are safe and which are not.

When a thalidomide baby was born, the disability was apparent. It matched the popular stereotype of a birth defect as visible and detected early in life. New parents breathe a sigh of relief at the sight of a healthy, functioning child. It rarely occurs to anyone that something that happened during the prenatal period could haunt a person years later.

Appearances can be deceiving, as with children whose mothers took the synthetic estrogen diethylstilbestrol (DES). From the 1940s through 1971, DES was widely administered to pregnant women (N.Y.S. Department of Health, 1979). It was thought that DES would reduce the incidence of miscarriage, and the drug was prescribed for women who had a history of diabetes. Although some studies doubted the effectiveness of DES, doctors continued to prescribe it. About one million women took the drug (Planned Parenthood, 1979). At first, there seemed to be little cause for concern. As infants, the children born to these women were healthy, but in 1971, Dr. Arthur Herbst discovered a link between prenatal administration of DES and eight cases of a kind of cervical cancer usually found in women over fifty.

The chance of a DES daughter's having the cancerous condition is about one or two in every 1,000 (Orenberg, 1981). However, many DES daughters suffer from genital tract abnormalities. All women whose mothers took the drug should be watched carefully by their doctors. DES sons are also affected by the drug. They sometimes suffer from genital tract abnormalities and benign cysts that require attention from a urologist (N.Y.S. Department of Health, 1979). Evidence also indicates that mothers who took DES run an additional risk of developing breast cancer twenty years after taking the drug (Herbst, 1984). Since, as the DES story demonstrates, the effects of drugs taken during the prenatal stage may not show up for some time, the best advice seems to be to approach all drugs with caution during pregnancy.

People often make blanket statements that no drugs should be taken during pregnancy. Although that is a reasonable dictum, there are times when doctor and patient are forced to decide in favor of administering a potentially dangerous medication to combat a severe condition. For example, certain antibiotics, hormones, anticoagulants, steroids, and antihistamines have been linked to birth defects in animals and human beings. But when there is no other alternative available to treat a particular condition, a **risk-benefit analysis** must be performed, weighing the risks and benefits to the mother and baby of taking or not taking the medication.

risk benefit analysis
A detailed analysis of the risks versus the benefits of a particular choice.

Most drugs taken during pregnancy, though, are not prescribed by doctors. They are available either legally, as in the case of nicotine, caffeine, and alcohol, or illegally, as with narcotics.

NICOTINE About 25 percent of the pregnant women in the United States smoke (March of Dimes, 1990). Nicotine causes a rise in heart rate, blood pressure, and respiration and constricts the flow of blood. The amount of oxygen the fetus receives is reduced (Martin, 1976). Although the effects of nicotine are dose related, smokers are twice as likely as nonsmokers to have low-birthweight babies (Fielding, 1985). The infants of smokers weigh an average of 200 grams (about .5 pound) less than infants of nonsmokers (Vorhees & Mollnow, 1986). In one study, 47 percent of 2,117 women in the sample smoked, and they delivered 64 percent of the in-

3. TRUE OR FALSE?

The infants of women who smoke during pregnancy weigh about half a pound more than the infants of mothers who do not smoke.

Studies show that smoking during pregnancy presents a danger to the unborn child.

fants with low birthweight. In addition, the infants were shorter; had smaller head, chest, arm, and thigh circumferences; and had lower neurological scores than the infants of nonsmokers (Metcoff, Coistiloe, Crosby, Sandstream, & Milne, 1989). The relationship between smoking and small infants seems most significant for women who continue smoking after thirty weeks of pregnancy (Hebel et al., 1988). Other research suggests that the decrease in oxygen from smoking may lead to brain abnormalities and cleft palate (Stechler & Halton, 1982).

Injurious long-term effects from maternal smoking have been noted. A major study found that at seven years of age, children of smokers had lower reading abilities and demonstrated more problems with social adjustment than children of nonsmokers (Davies, Butler & Goldstein, 1972). A positive correlation has been found between smoking during pregnancy and hyperactivity, low achievement, and minimal neurological dysfunction (Landesman-Dwyer & Emanuel, 1979). Maternal smoking during pregnancy has also been linked to poor attention span in the child during the preschool years (Streissguth et al., 1984). Small differences in achievement scores in spelling and reading as well as in attention span were found between a large group of seven-year-old children whose mothers smoked heavily during pregnancy and those children whose mothers had not smoked (Naeye & Peters, 1984).

A major U.S. government report noted that women who smoke during pregnancy increase their chances of spontaneous abortions and miscarriages, fetal death, and birth problems. It concludes that "maternal smoking may adversely affect the child's long-term growth, intellectual development, and behavioral characteristics" (U.S. Department of Health and Human Services, 1981b, p. 238).

One hopeful sign comes from a study that found that mothers who were light smokers or who had stopped smoking before their fourth month of pregnancy reduced their risk of having low-birthweight infants (Butler, Goldstein & Ross, 1972). However, giving up smoking is not easy, and many women either do not try or find it very difficult (Condon & Hilton, 1988). It is clear, though, that the health risks are great and an attempt to quit should be made.

ALCOHOL Most doctors suggest that women abstain from drinking entirely during their pregnancy (Obstetrical and Gynecological Survey, 1988). However, alcohol consumption by pregnant women is fairly common and its consequences are serious. Although estimates of how many women drink vary, one estimate is that 86 percent of women drink at least once during pregnancy, and between 20 percent and 35 percent drink regularly (Rosenthal, 1990). Evidence indicates that alcohol abuse has increased, especially among women in poverty (Little, Snell, Gilstrap, Gant, & Rosenfeld, 1989).

There is no doubt that alcohol consumption can cause birth defects. About 8,000 alcohol-damaged infants are born each year, which is about 2.7 babies for every 1,000 live births (Rosenthal, 1990). One reason it is so difficult to determine the exact number is that only the most obvious cases are detected. Some of the children of alcoholic mothers show a distinct physical appearance and pattern of development. They are shorter and lighter than other children, and their growth and development are slow. They show a number of cranial and facial abnormalities, heart defects, and poor motor development and coordination and tend to be retarded (Furey, 1982; Streissguth, 1977). Their mortality rate is also higher than average. The preceding are characteristics of the **fetal alcohol syndrome.** Damage caused by alcohol appears to be permanent. Even when children of alcoholic mothers are raised in an improved environment, they continue to lag behind, both in physical growth and intellectual development (Hanson, Jones & Smith, 1976).

Since most women are not alcoholics, people generally consider the negative consequences of drinking something that happens to other people. Even the infants of confirmed alcoholics show the full syndrome in only about 35 percent of the cases, again for a variety of reasons, including such factors as individual differences and the time during the pregnancy of drinking (infants may be more or less vulnerable at different times) (Rosenthal, 1990). However, even moderate drinking can affect an unborn child (Streissguth, 1977). In fact, scientists use the phrase **fetal alcohol effect** to describe the less severe spectrum of damage done by alcohol (Vorhees & Mollnow, 1986). Most common among these problems are severe learning and cognitive problems. The fetus is sensitive to alcohol, and the effects of alcohol on it seem to be dose related, with lower doses resulting in some, but not all, of the characteristics of fetal alcohol syndrome (Clarren & Smith, 1978). Although very small amounts of alcohol may not produce birth defects or developmental disabilities, as little as one drink per day increases the risk of miscarriage during the middle months of pregnancy (Harlap & Shiono, 1980). A study of 31,604 pregnant women found that consuming even one drink a day could lead to decreased fetal growth (Mills, Braubard, Harley, Rhoads & Berendes, 1984). Even women who do not drink often can cause serious damage to their infants if they drink in binges. A single binge can raise the alcohol level in an infant's system to the point of causing serious damage to the infant (Mendelson & Mello, 1987).

NARCOTICS Babies of heroin addicts are born addicted to heroin and must go through withdrawal (Brazelton, 1970). They often show disturbances in activity level, attention span, and sleep patterns (Householder, Hatcher, Burns & Chasnoff, 1982). Because these infants are frequently premature and very small, this is sometimes a life-or-death situation. We don't know whether it is the drug itself or the poverty and poor diet that often accompany addiction that lead to this life-threatening situation. Either way, the women and their offspring require extra attention. Comprehensive programs that offer medical help, counseling, and parental education are often successful in improving the lives of these infants (Suffet, Bryce-Buchanon & Brotman, 1981).

COCAINE No drug has received the amount of attention in the media that cocaine has. Although no one knows exactly how many pregnant women use cocaine, it can be assumed that a fairly large number do. In one hospital in an inner city, 10 percent of all newborns tested positive for cocaine (Chasnoff, 1987). In a general survey of physicians subscribing

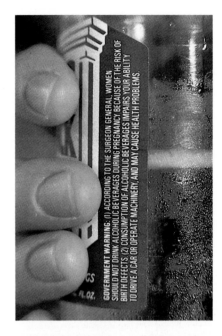

Imbibing alcohol is dangerous to the health of the developing child. Many products contain warnings.

fetal alcohol syndrome
A number of characteristics—including retardation, facial abnormalities, growth defects, and poor coordination—caused by maternal alcohol consumption during pregnancy.

fetal alcohol effect
An umbrella term used to describe damage to a child caused by the mother's imbibing alcohol during pregnancy that is somewhat less pronounced than fetal alcohol syndrome.

to a professional publication, one-fourth of the doctors claimed that as many as five percent of their obstetrical patients used cocaine and one-fourth said one percent of their patients did so (see Chasnoff, 1987). We know that cocaine constricts the blood vessels in the placenta, decreasing blood flow to the fetus, and increases uterine contractions. It is also certain that it takes the fetus much longer than the mother to rid itself of the drug, since the fetal liver is so immature.

4. TRUE OR FALSE?

Infants born to women who used cocaine during pregnancy are more likely to be premature and even to die, but those who do survive do not show any behavioral differences when compared to infants whose mothers did not use cocaine.

Scientists have performed many studies on the effects of cocaine, and their findings are clear. Cocaine taken during pregnancy increases fetal mortality and leads to low birthweight and prematurity (MacGregor, Keith, Bachicha, and Chasnoff, 1989). It also increases the chances of delivery complications (Neerhof, MacGregor, Retzky & Sullivan, 1989). Infants sometimes show cardiac problems (Little, Snell, Klein, & Gillstrup, 1989). Head circumference is often smaller, and these infants are also shorter (Hadeed & Siegel, 1989). Infants' behavior is different from the average newborns; such infants are very irritable and tremulous and are often unable to respond to the human voice or face. They do not interact with others. They are emotionally labile and respond poorly to attempts at comforting them (Chasnoff, 1985, 1987).

The evidence for such problems as poor fetal growth, increased fetal death, prematurity, and behavioral disturbances is so great that it is clear that an effort must be made to educate the public as to the extreme dangers of using cocaine during pregnancy.

MARIJUANA AND LSD Some research shows that marijuana use leads to fetal abnormalities and lack of fetal growth in animals (Annis, 1978). Evidence with human beings is still controversial, and scientists do not understand the full effects of marijuana, angel dust, hashish, or other psychoactive drugs on the human fetus (March of Dimes, 1983b). Marijuana has been linked to poor fetal growth in humans (Zuckerman et al., 1989). Some studies have found behavioral differences for infants of mothers who are regular marijuana users, including lack of response to a light stimulus, tremors, and increased startling (Vorhees & Mollnow, 1986), and differences in the infant's cry as discussed in the Cross-Cultural Current on page 146.

Studies of LSD are difficult to perform since most users also take other drugs. However, some anecdotal evidence shows a relationship between LSD and congenital malformations (Apgar & Beck, 1974). Fetal abnormalities have been found when LSD is given to pregnant mice (Alexander, Miles, Gold & Alexander, 1967). In addition, higher rates of spontaneous abortion and miscarriage as well as neurological defects are found among LSD users (Annis, 1978; Trulson, 1985).

CAFFEINE AND ASPIRIN The status of many commonly taken legal drugs is still controversial. Caffeine, which is found in coffee and tea, is one such drug. There is some evidence that high doses of caffeine increase the frequency of birth defects in animals (March of Dimes, 1983b). Other evidence has failed to reliably link moderate caffeine intake to birth defects (University of California, 1985), but high caffeine intake (four or more cups of coffee a day) should be avoided (March of Dimes, 1985).

Aspirin has been shown to cause damage to the unborn in animal studies (Stechler & Halton, 1982). In human beings, however, the main finding is that aspirin, if taken excessively in the later months of pregnancy, can adversely affect blood clotting in both mother and baby (March of Dimes, 1983b). Even normal doses in the final months of pregnancy can prolong labor and cause maternal heavy bleeding before and after birth (Mendelson & Mello, 1987).

Pollution and Radiation

Pollution and radiation can also adversely affect the unborn child. Mercury has been linked to severe malformations (Stechler & Halton, 1982). In Japan, a number of mothers who had eaten fish laden with mercury gave birth to extremely handicapped children who suffered from cerebal palsy and physical defects (Miller, 1974). PCB, a contaminant sometimes found in water and in fish, can cause immature motor responses as well as other behavioral abnormalities (Jacobson, Jacobson, Fein, Schwartz & Dowler, 1984). Other chemicals can also cause fetal abnormalties, but not enough research exists to label many of them dangerous to the unborn infant.

Radiation has been linked to fetal deaths as well as to a number of structural defects in infants. Studies after the World War II atomic bombings of Hiroshima and Nagasaki found that exposure to radiation increased the rate of spontaneous abortions, miscarriages, and mutations among pregnant women (Annis, 1978). Since there is no safe level of radiation, even lower doses can cause damage. Because radiation accumulates in the body, repeated X-rays can be dangerous. Although there are times when an X-ray is medically required, pregnant women should avoid radiation as much as possible.

Perhaps the most controversial question concerns the effects of computer video display terminals (VDTs) on the outcome of pregnancies. Millions of VDTs are currently in use, and it is estimated that by the year 2000, over one hundred million will be in homes, offices and schools. It is known that VDTs emit several types of radiation. Large-scale, well-controlled studies reporting thus far have found no significant association between VDT use and pregnancy problems (Blackwell & Chang, 1988). In the early 1980s, clusters of miscarriages and birth defects were reported in some areas following VDT use, and a number of studies were performed by the government. The studies investigating the clusters found that the defects were not similar and that the clusters occurred purely by chance. Since many women of childbearing age work on VDTs, in a large population some clusters would be expected.

Others are not so sure and believe that radiation risks—especially microwave radiation and high-intensity electromagnetic fields—cannot be discounted, because we do not know much about them. However, to date the research is encouraging. New studies have been commissioned, and no firm conclusions can yet be made concerning VDT use during pregnancy (March of Dimes, 1989).

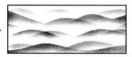

Marijuana and the Newborn: A Study in Jamaica

Sometimes differing practices in other cultures allow scientists to do studies that are very difficult if not impossible to perform in their own countries. For a number of reasons, it is very difficult to conduct studies in this country on the effect of marijuana on the unborn child. Many U.S. women who have used marijuana have also used other drugs, making it difficult to determine the effects of marijuana itself. In addition, since the drug is illegal, observation is difficult and depending upon personal reports of drug use is unreliable. Also, it is difficult to control for prenatal care and other factors. The use of the drug is more accepted however, in Jamaica, and allows a distinct advantage to the researcher seeking to discover the effects of marijuana on the unborn child.

Barry Lester and Melanie Dreher conducted just such a study in Jamaica. This Caribbean country offered some interesting advantages. In this study, the authors controlled for socioeconomic status. They were also able to increase the reliability of reporting on the usage of marijuana not only through self-report measures but also through observations and community informants.

What differences should the investigators look for? Although it is easy to determine major physical and developmental problems in newborns by their appearance and actions, it is more difficult to find the subtle differences that could lead to later problems. The researchers decided to see if there were any differences in the children's cries between users and nonusers of marijuana. They chose this variable because past research has shown the cry to reflect the neurophysiological soundness of the infant and is useful for detection of infants at risk for developmental difficulties. Some differences may actually demonstrate nerve damage and neurological problems.

The sample of pregnant women used was from three rural communities, each of which had a prenatal clinic and a marijuana-using population. Twenty marijuana users were compared with twenty nonusers throughout their pregnancies and birth. Marijuana consumption was determined by formal interview as well as by direct observation during social activities and by informants. The frequency and quantity of marijuana consumption was determined by trimester. (Marijuana in Jamaica is consumed both through smoking marijuana cigars and through drinking marijuana

Disease and Pregnancy

Today's society has been spared the terrible epidemics of the past. We are no longer concerned about smallpox, diphtheria, and polio. Other diseases, however, can affect an unborn child. It is often thought that the more serious a disease is to the mother, the greater the chance it will harm the baby. Although this may generally be true, there are many exceptions.

rubella
A disease responsible for many cases of birth defects.

RUBELLA Commonly called German measles, rubella is a very mild disease. Normally, the sufferer has a rash, feels a bit under the weather for a day or two, and perhaps runs a low-grade fever. Complications are rare. Yet the effects of the rubella virus on a developing embryo can be serious. In the epidemic of 1964–1965, about 50,000 babies were affected. Many died, while many others suffered injuries of varying degrees (Rugh & Shettles, 1971).

Among the damage caused by rubella are congenital cataracts and other eye disorders, congenital heart disease, and damage to the ears and to the central nervous system (Monif, 1969). The effects of disease on the unborn

tea. These cigars contain much more marijuana than the average marijuana cigarette does in the United States.)

The two groups of users and nonusers were similar in income, occupation, and age. All the users smoked the cigars during the first trimester, and fifteen users smoked during all three trimesters of their pregnancy. The frequency ranged from one to twenty cigars per day, and the consumption of marijuana tea from one to eight cups per week. Pregnant women who did not smoke thought that the marijuana was harmful to their infants, but interviewers found that many women who did smoke were also aware of the potential harm.

The results were interesting. The cry was recorded at home on the fourth or fifth day following birth. The differences were significant. The cries of infants whose mothers had smoked marijuana were shorter in duration, had a higher percentage of dysphonation (turbulence or noise), were of higher pitch, showed a wider range, and differed in other ways. The high pitch of the infants' cries was similar to that heard in the cries of the infants of addicts whose infants have to go through withdrawal. The experimenters concluded that marijuana smoking during pregnancy appears to affect the acoustic characteristics of the newborn cry, and these differences may relate to developmental problems later on. Marijuana may have a direct effect on the fetal brain.

In addition, we know that the nature of the cry affects the mother-infant relationship and that certain cries are more aversive to the mother than are others. For instance, we know that the cry of premature or drug-addicted infants creates more tension and stress in the mother. This could cause difficulties in the mother-child relationship. More research is needed on this point.

Despite the fact that these infants were exposed to a higher concentration of marijuana than most American infants, the researchers conclude that their findings provide evidence that any amount of maternal marijuana smoking is a threat to the biological integrity of the infant. It is wrong to think of teratogens only as agents that cause physical malformations or gross developmental difficulties. The effects of some teratogens may be less obvious and may require a look at more subtle indications of later developmental difficulties. Some cause behavioral deficits and growth retardation even without physical malformation. This study demonstrates not only the fact that marijuana is a teratogen but also the necessity of looking at these less obvious yet important factors in determining the effects that certain drugs have on the unborn child.

Source: Lester, B. M., and Dreher, M., Effects of Marijuana Use During Pregnancy on Newborn Cry. *Child Development*, 1989, *60*, 765–772.

fetus are greater during the first eight weeks of pregnancy (Taina, Hanniner & Gronroos, 1985), although infection in the second trimester can result in hearing loss and retarded development (Stevenson, 1973). The disease can persist throughout the prenatal and neonatal periods, and eye damage can continue even after birth. With the advent of a vaccine that prevents rubella, epidemics should become a thing of the past. Unfortunately, not every child is being protected, and isolated cases of rubella-induced defects may still occur.

VENEREAL DISEASE In recent years, increased attention has been paid to the effects that AIDS, herpes, syphilis, gonorrhea, and chlamydia have on the unborn child. Evidence is great that such disorders, which are usually transmitted during sexual intercourse, pose significant dangers to the unborn child (Mascola et al., 1984; Knox, 1984).

AIDS, or acquired immunodeficiency syndrome, is a disorder affecting the immunological system and leading to an inability to fight off disease. It is caused by a virus that can pass through the placenta and infect the infant (Pinching & Jefferies, 1985). Some infants may get the AIDS virus during delivery (March of Dimes, 1988). The chance that an infected mother will transmit the virus is about 30 percent (Blanche et al., 1989; Pizzo, 1989). No one knows why the virus is passed on to some infants and not to others. Not everyone who carries the virus shows immediate symptoms, and in fact, most women who give birth to children with AIDS show no symptoms during their pregnancy (Pizzo, 1989). However, infants infected with the virus are more likely than adults to develop the symptoms (Sande, 1986). Pregnancy itself may increase the risk that a mother who has the virus but has not developed a full case of AIDS will develop AIDS (Pinching & Jefferies, 1985). By July 1989, about 1,600 cases of pediatric AIDS were reported to the government, but it is estimated that in the next few years, between 10,000 and 20,000 cases will be detected (Pizzo, 1989). Almost all new cases of pediatric AIDS are caused by prenatal infection (Pizzo, 1989). The prognosis for these infants is very poor, and the probability of long-term survival is low (Scott et al., 1989).

5. TRUE OR FALSE?

Most children with AIDS received the virus through tainted blood transfusions.

Women who have herpes can transmit it to the baby during the birth process. If the herpes virus reaches the baby's organs or brain, the prognosis is not good, and more than half may die (Corey & Spear, 1986). Antiviral treatment reduces the mortality rate, but impairment is still common (Stagno & Whitley, 1985). To prevent the spread of the virus, doctors often check for lesions in the birth canal and may recommend a Cesarean section.

Syphilis in the expectant mother can cause a number of defects in the infant, including bone and facial deformities, nerve deafness, and fetal death. A number of children of syphilitic mothers will develop syphilis. If the mother-to-be receives treatment before the sixteenth week of pregnancy, the fetus may not be infected (Cave, 1973). After that time, however, certain tissues that protect the infant break down. By the eighteenth week of pregnancy, there is an 80 percent chance that the fetus will be infected if the mother has not been treated (Thompson & Grusec, 1970), but prompt treatment, even after this time, will often prevent damage. Unfortunately, there has been an increase in the incidence of congential syphilis, with 691 cases reported in 1988, up by 54 percent from the previous year (New York Times, 12 December 1989).

Many women who have gonorrhea may be totally unaware of it because they may not show any outward symptoms. Fetuses exposed to gonorrhea are often premature and blind. The standard practice of placing a solution of silver nitrate in an infant's eyes at birth is to protect against blindness in case the mother has gonorrhea. (In many hospitals, erythromycin or tetracycline may be used. Erythromycin combats chlamydia, an infection that also can cause blindness in newborns [Simkin, Whalley & Keppler, 1984].) Antibiotics treat gonorrhea successfully. Before the discovery of such medication, however, about 25 percent of all the children admitted to special schools for the blind could trace their blindness to gonorrhea (Grossman & Drutz, 1974).

Twice as common as gonorrhea is the less publicized sexually transmitted disease known as chlamydia. The infants of mothers with the disease may develop conjunctivitis, pneumonia, and other lung disorders (Schachter, 1989). It can also sometimes cause miscarriage, low birthweight, and infant death (March of Dimes, 1989). Women with chlamydia infections often do not experience symptoms, but relatively new tests have allowed for better screening. Once the infection is found, it is relatively easy to cure. The need for detection and treatment is great, since 155,000 infants are born each year to mothers who have cervical chlamydial infections (Schachter, 1989).

The Mother's Medical Condition

While noting some of the diseases that may affect the fetus, one should not forget the medical condition of the mother. For example, about six percent to eight percent of all pregnant women suffer from hypertension. Maternal hypertension is related to poor fetal growth, increased perinatal death, and many neurological and developmental problems. Diabetes in the mother is also related to many birth defects. These disorders are dangerous to the mother as well. As with so many other maternal medical conditions, competent medical advice and prompt treatment may improve the chances of delivering a healthy child and safeguarding the mother's health.

The Rh Factor

The **Rh factor** consists of a particular red blood cell antibody found in most human beings. Approximately 85 percent of all Caucasians, 93 percent of blacks, and nearly 100 percent of all Asian people, native Americans, and Eskimos have the factor; that is, they are Rh positive (Stevenson, 1973).

In about 13 percent of Caucasian unions, the woman is Rh negative and the man is Rh positive. In such a situation, the baby may be Rh positive and a problem may arise: The mother's body reacts to the Rh positive antibody in the fetus as it would to an invading germ or virus. Since the blood of the fetus does not mix with that of the mother during her pregnancy, the mother is not likely to manufacture antibodies that might injure the fetus. Few fetal blood cells cross the placenta. During the birth, however, especially if it is long and difficult, some cells do cross the placenta, and the mother will manufacture the antibodies. Since the first child of these parents is not likely to be exposed to many of these antibodies, the infant's chances of survival are good.

Once these antibodies are manufactured, however, they tend to remain in the mother's body. The mother also becomes more sensitive to this factor in subsequent pregnancies. During the next pregnancy, the fetus will be exposed to the mother's antibodies, which will cross the placenta and destroy the red blood cells of the fetus (Ortho Diagnostic Systems, 1981). In each successive pregnancy, the risk to the fetus becomes greater and greater, until the chances that a child will be born healthy are quite low. Since 1968, a preventive vaccine for Rh problems has been available. Within seventy-two hours after each birth, miscarriage, or abortion, a shot of the vaccine RhoGAM is administered to block the production of these antibodies. Before this vaccine was available, about 10,000 babies died every year, and 20,000 more were born with severe birth defects from Rh disease (Apgar & Beck, 1974).

Rh factor
An antibody often, but not always, found in human beings.

6. *TRUE OR FALSE?*

Alcohol consumption during pregnancy leads to an Rh problem.

Preventing Birth Defects

Walk into most any clinic or doctor's office and you will see pamphlets advising women what to do and what not to do during pregnancy. The public is constantly exposed to information about drugs, radiation, and diseases that can harm the fetus. Yet pregnant women continue to take drugs and expose their infants to danger. The figures are astounding as well as depressing. Some 82 percent of the pregnant women in one study in Scotland used a prescribed medication (Martin, 1976). Some 65 percent were self-medicated. A study in the United States found that the average number of drugs taken during pregnancy was 10.3. About 15 percent were taking drugs to suppress appetite. About half the pregnant American women drank regularly (Martin, 1976). In a recent study, 11 percent of pregnant women used an illegal drug during their pregnancies (New York Times, 1988).

Chapter 3 looked at some of the major genetic disorders. The chance of bearing a child with a genetic deformity is slight compared with the possibility that a fetus will be injured during the prenatal period. Genetic factors account for only 20 percent of infant defects; chromosomal abnormalities add another 10 percent to the picture. The remaining 70 percent of infant defects are caused by drugs, pollution, disease, and other environmental insults that occur during the prenatal stage (Martin, 1976). As we learn more about which environmental substances are harmful to a fetus, we'll be able to prevent many birth defects.

If we know so much about teratogens, why have we failed to prevent birth defects? The main reason is ignorance. Some women do not have an adequate understanding of the dangers in their environment. The poor and the young are most at risk. The poor have a higher infant mortality rate and a greater number of prenatally caused infant problems. They are often undernourished or malnourished, undereducated, and exposed to a number of teratogens.

Inadequate prenatal care is also a great problem. Many young women do not see a doctor regularly. Hutchins and colleagues (1979) reported on a sample of pregnant teens. They found that 30 percent of pregnant teens under seventeen, 22 percent of the seventeen- to nineteen-year-olds, and 18 percent of the older group (twenty- to thirty-year-olds) failed to see a doctor for prenatal care until the third trimester of their pregnancies. About four percent of the teens received no prenatal care at all (Hutchins, Kendall & Rubino, 1979).

The younger the mother, the more likely it is that she will suffer complications and her infant will show some abnormality (Birch & Gussow, 1970). It is difficult to get the information across to pregnant teens and motivate them to change their health habits.

Another reason for the failure to stem the tide of prenatal insults is that the first three months of pregnancy seem to be the most sensitive to environmental insult. But in the earliest months of pregnancy, a woman may not know she is pregnant and may expose her unborn infant to such an insult. By the time the woman is aware she is pregnant, the critical period may have elapsed and the damage may already have been done.

7. TRUE OR FALSE?

Some 70 percent of all birth defects are caused by prenatal insults rather than genetic disorders.

The systems of the fetus are developing rapidly during these earliest months, and, as a rule, the system that is developing most rapidly at the time of insult is the one that will be affected by a drug or virus (see Figure 4.1).

As noted in Chapter 1, the period during which a particular event has its greatest impact is known as the **critical period.** If an insult occurs at this point, considerable damage may be done. For example, if a mother contracts rubella in the first four weeks of pregnancy, the chance of the baby's being born with one or more defects is about 50 percent. This drops to about 17 percent in the third month and is much lower after the third month (Rhodes, 1961). There are similar critical periods for some drugs, including thalidomide (Lenz, 1966).

critical period
The period during which a particular event has its greatest impact.

In addition, people often choose not to believe facts that run counter to their own day-to-day experiences. Whenever I discuss the dangers inherent in even moderate drinking or smoking, some of my students refuse to believe them. After all, some of their friends were smokers, and their babies turned out healthy. Most drugs or environmental pollutants do not act as radically as thalidomide. They act in tandem with other environmental insults to produce their effects. Thus, the causal linkage is more difficult to discover, and many simply refuse to believe it. Perhaps the best way to view the effects of smoking, some types of pollution, and mild malnutrition on the fetus is to realize that they increase the chances that a problem will develop.

Finally, people have difficulty relating events that occur during pregnancy to their outcome. The time lag involved makes the connection difficult.

◆ FIVE MODERN-DAY ISSUES

As people learn more about the prenatal period, new issues are raised and old issues are perceived differently. Five such issues are especially current: (1) the relationship between the age of the mother and the health

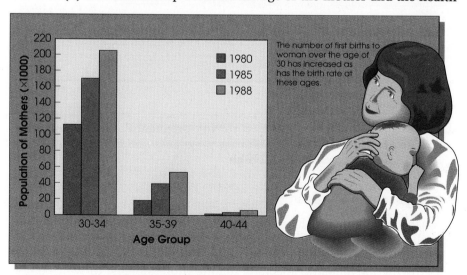

DATAGRAPHIC

Number of First Births by Age of Mothers over 30

Source: National Center for Health Statistics and U.S. Dept. of Health and Human Services, 1990.

FIGURE 4.1: Critical Periods in Prenatal Development

The dark color shows the time during which that particular organ is at greatest risk.

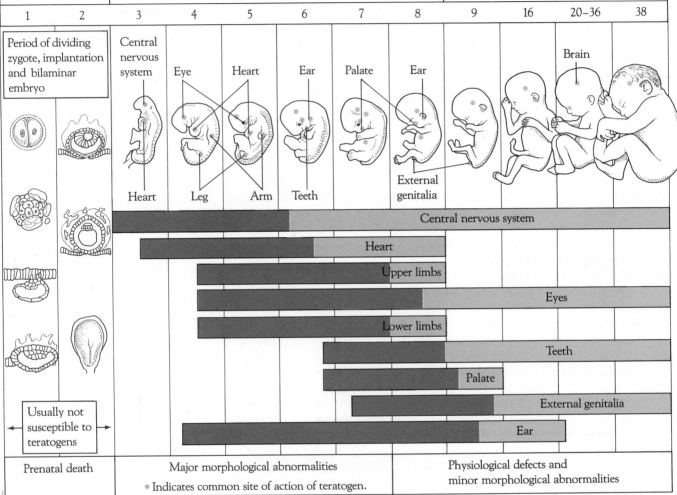

Source: Moore, 1988.

of the fetus, (2) maternal nutrition during pregnancy, (3) stress during pregnancy, (4) the father's role during pregnancy, and (5) the effect of new technology on mother and child.

The Age of the Mother

"It wasn't easy to wait," Margaret confessed. "Everyone was having babies, all my married friends were pregnant, but we decided to wait."

Margaret will be thirty-five when her first child is born, and she is part of a growing movement, especially among professionals, to wait before starting a family. The years between twenty and thirty are physically the safest for childbearing. As a woman ages, the incidence of high blood pressure and delivery complications increases (Fonteyn & Isada, 1988). Later parenting may also present social problems. It may be difficult for parents in their late fifties or sixties to guide adolescents, although very little data is available on this point. And the older parent is at a greater risk for personal injury, incapacitating illness, and death. Still, an increasing number of people choose to start their families in their thirties.

Since the middle 1970s, the birthrate for women above the age of thirty has been growing steadily, increasing over 25 percent. In 1988, mothers over thirty years of age accounted for more than one in four births (National Center for Health Statistics, 1990). A significant increase is found for both the 30- to 34-year-old age group and the 35- to 39-year-old age group. In addition, more and more couples are having their first children in their thirties. In 1970, only one percent of the first-time births were to women age thirty-five and older and only three percent were to women between thirty and thirty-four years of age, while in 1988, 3.5 percent of first births were to women over the age of thirty-five and 12.95 percent were to women between thirty and thirty-four years of age. Some of the increase was probably due to the fact that the generation entering that age group is quite a bit larger than the generation in its early twenties. However, even taking this into consideration, the increase is significant. Many of these couples have postponed having children for economic and career reasons.

Many couples are deciding to wait to have their first child. Although the risks are somewhat greater, with good prenatal care, most women can give birth to healthy children.

There is some evidence that older mothers do very well. They are more likely to have good family support systems and economic stability, and they are more apt to have planned the pregnancy. Certain age-related characteristics that appear important in parenting, such as patience and good judgment, are more likely to be present here, and some studies have found that the age of the mother at birth shows a slight but consistent and positive association with the child's intelligence (Fonteyn & Isada, 1988). The evidence regarding having children in the thirties is easy to interpret. Although the physical risks are greater, the availability of modern diagnostic procedures and better prenatal care reduces the risk somewhat. If there is no evidence of chronic disease, the outlook for the intelligent mother entering the world of parenting in her thirties is quite good (Goldstein, 1980).

The number of births at the other extreme is much more troublesome. The numbers are alarming. In 1988, there were 489,000 births to women under the age of twenty. Of these births, approximately 312,500 were to unmarried women between the ages of 15 and 19, while about 10,000 were to women under the age of fifteen (National Center for Health Statistics, 1990).

More than one million adolescents become pregnant every year, and about 60 percent go on to have their babies. Although more than half are unmarried, 94 percent of these young women who give birth elect to keep their babies. (The formidable social, economic, and familial problems of these young parents are discussed in detail in Chapter 13.)

The pregnant teenager belongs to the highest risk group both for birth complications and for fetal abnormalities (Fogel, 1984). Adolescent mothers suffer the greatest number of prenatal and postnatal problems. This high rate of complications may be explained by the relationship between adolescent pregnancy and such factors as low socioeconomic status, poor education, and poor health care (Stevenson, 1973). Teenage mothers are likely to have repeat pregnancies. Out of fear, ignorance, or the desire to deny the pregnancy, many teens do not seek prenatal care until the last minute. This leads to an increased rate of premature births and fetal deaths.

There is a large difference between teenage mothers and those in their twenties. In a study that compared the two age groups, Rex Culp and colleagues (1988) found that pregnant adolescents were generally less happy about being pregnant and had less social support from both their family and the child's father than were women in their twenties. Adolescent mothers also spoke less to their infants. However, there was a great variation in the feelings among the adolescent group, with some being very unhappy about their situation and others being happy. Therefore, care should be exercised in making generalizations.

The combination of youth, poverty, lack of knowledge, poor nutritional habits, poor health care, and lack of motivation to act on warnings is difficult to combat. Teenage pregnancy is part of a larger social and economic problem that must be approached educationally and medically. This may be nowhere more clear than in the case of maternal nutrition.

Maternal Nutrition

In the past two decades, there has been renewed interest in maternal nutrition during pregnancy. The finding that chronic malnutrition during the prenatal stage leads to an irreversible condition in which the infant has as much as 20 percent fewer brain cells than the normal baby (Winick, 1976) has done much to spur the interest in maternal nutrition. Malnu-

8. TRUE OR FALSE?

Severe malnutrition during pregnancy leads to a condition in which the infant has fewer brain cells.

DATAGRAPHIC

Births to Unmarried Teenage Women, Ages 15–19

Source: U.S. Department of Commerce, 1990

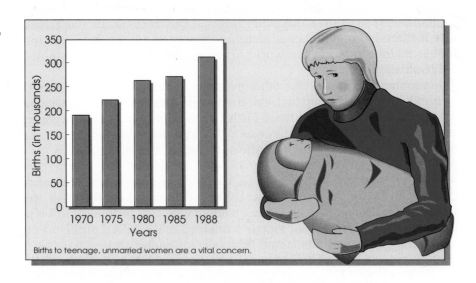

Births to teenage, unmarried women are a vital concern.

trition is related to fetal deformities and impaired physical and intellectual development. Mental retardation, low birthweight, cerebral palsy, and increased susceptibility to disease have been traced to malnourishment during pregnancy (Annis, 1978). Infants who were malnourished during the prenatal stage also show abnormal behavioral patterns, such as withdrawal and irritability (Birch, 1971). The significant correlation between nutritional status and prematurity is especially troublesome because extremely underweight infants are at risk for a variety of developmental problems (Ricciuti, 1980). Studies demonstrate that malnutrition can also lead to increased fetal deaths. During World War II, both in Holland and during the seige of Leningrad where the populations were faced with severe food shortages, the number of stillbirths, premature births, and low-birthweight infants was much higher than average (DeBruyne & Rolfes, 1989).

Although nutrition during pregnancy is crucial to the health of the child, the mother's nutritional history before pregnancy is also important (Sizer & Whitney, 1988). The mother may have suffered from nutritional problems that affect her own physical development and health, reducing her ability to bear a healthy child.

The effects of severe malnutrition on the fetus are well established. But what is the effect of lesser degrees of malnutrition on the fetus? Severe malnutrition is rare in the United States, but some American mothers suffer from some form of malnutrition involving vitamin and mineral deficiencies or even protein deficiencies. Such inadequate diets are often found in young pregnant females (Eichorn, 1979).

Specific nutritional inadequacies in the expectant mother do cause certain fetal problems. Lack of iodine leads to physical deformities and mental retardation. Vitamin deficiencies are related to convulsions and neurological damage (Dakshinamurti & Stephens, 1969). A vitamin D deficiency leads to skeletal malformations (Rector, 1935). Vitamin A deficiencies are linked to spontaneous abortion and miscarriage and visual problems. Inadequate supplies of vitamin C cause skeletal deformities (Annis, 1978). Inadequate folic acid intake is related to anemia (Stevenson, 1973). We do not know how much deficiency is required to cause a particular problem. A small deficiency may cause subclinical problems that may reduce the infant's ability in some area, such as in fighting off infection. In addition, nutritional deficiencies may combine with other factors, such as drugs or disease, to produce a fetal abnormality.

As Figure 4.2 on page 157 demonstrates, the nutritional needs of pregnant women differ from those of nonpregnant women. Each individual pregnant woman should discuss her dietary needs with her physician or with a professional nutritionist. Many doctors will provide women with dietary supplements in the form of vitamins and minerals to be certain that the pregnant woman has adequate nutrition.

Stress During Pregnancy

Consider a pregnant woman whose father dies, whose husband is fired from his job, whose six-year-old is sick, or who experiences any of a multitude of other stresses. Does stress during pregnancy have any effect on the physical or emotional well-being of the baby? So many factors confound the situation that this is a difficult question to answer. For instance, the depressed and anxious pregnant woman may not eat or sleep well. In addition, the stress may continue after the baby's birth, making it difficult to separate prenatal factors from postnatal factors when deciding what may have caused a problem.

Some studies have related continuous stress to the birth of infants who are irritable, squirming, and generally more difficult to care for (Sontag, 1941, 1944; Stechler & Halton, 1982). These babies do not feed as well, and they cry more than infants whose mothers have not been under constant stress (Copans, 1974).

In Finland there is an old belief that stress during pregnancy affects the temperament of the infant. In an interesting study, pregnant women in Helsinki, Finland, were asked about their stress during their regular visits to maternal outpatient clinics, and their ratings of stress were compared to measures of infant temperament when the infants were between six and eight months. The results showed that mothers' subjective analyses of their own stress during the first trimester correlated well with such infant behaviors as slow adaptability, negative mood, easy distractibility, and high intensity. There were no relationships, however, between stress in the second or third trimester and infant temperament (Huttunen, 1989).

The mechanism by which stress leads to such problems is not entirely understood. Stress increases the production of hormones, particularly adrenalin, that may cause such reactions. There is also a relationship between anxiety and physical problems in pregnancy. The more stress a woman is under, the greater the chances of complications during pregnancy and delivery (Gorsuch & Key, 1974).

The Father's Role

After noting the many maternal behaviors that affect the fetus, students often complain that the child's father seems to get away with everything during the prenatal stage. To some extent this is true, since a father's drinking, drug taking, and stressful experiences would not affect the fetus the way that the mother's would. If we look a bit deeper, however, the father's behavior and experiences can affect the pregnancy and the subsequent health of the fetus.

Paternal drug taking prior to pregnancy can affect the father's genes and in turn directly affect the child. In addition, the father's behavior can influence the expectant mother's actions. Women who heed the warnings about drinking, smoking, and avoiding drug intake will increase their chances of giving birth to a healthy child. However, if the father is indulging, the mother may find it more difficult to refrain from such behavior. In addition, the mother's need for emotional support places a responsibility on the father's shoulders. The father can help to reduce the stress and anxiety experienced by the mother. A father's willingness to understand the expectant mother's special needs for support and assistance can help her through this unique time in their lives.

9. TRUE OR FALSE?

Maternal stress does not affect the fetus, because the systems of the mother and the fetus are separate.

FIGURE 4.2: Nutritional Needs of Pregnant and Nonpregnant Women
(over 23 years of age)

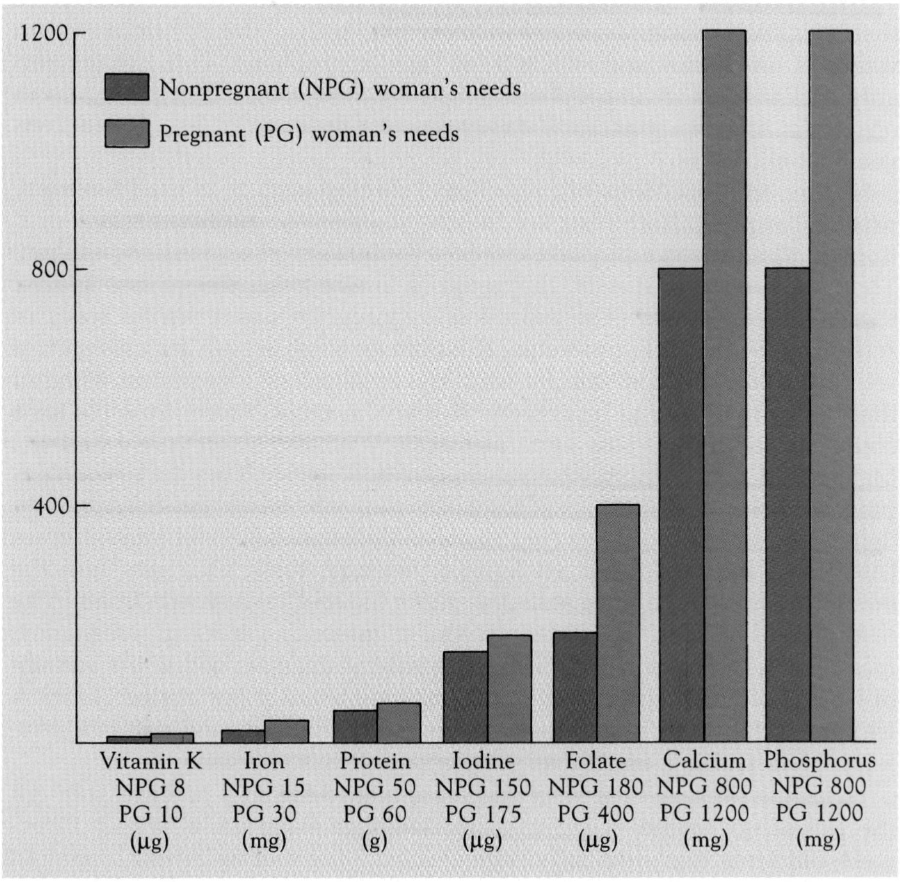

Source: Whitney and Hamilton, 1989.

Technology, Pregnancy, and Birth

Margaret's prenatal care was very different from her mother's. Because Margaret was thirty-five, her doctor had advised her to undergo a test called amniocentesis during her fourteenth week of pregnancy to determine whether the fetus had Down syndrome. In **amniocentesis**, a small amount of amniotic fluid is extracted from the womb. The fluid contains fetal cells that have been discarded as the fetus grows. These cells are cultured and examined for genetic and chromosomal abnormalities.

During this process, the doctor also took a **sonogram**, in which sound waves are used to produce a picture of the fetus (Clark, 1979). Many women undergo sonography to determine the gestational age of the child or to determine whether they are carrying twins. Ultrasound, as it is called, has been used to diagnose a number of rare but important fetal defects and is combined with other techniques to discover cardiac prob-

amniocentesis
A procedure in which fluid is taken from a pregnant woman's uterus to check fetal cells for genetic and chromosomal abnormalities.

sonogram
An image of the developing organism taken through the use of sound waves.

lems in fetuses (Chervenak, Isaacson & Mahoney, 1986).

New procedures that can improve both the diagnosis and treatment of fetal problems are now being used. In one procedure, called **chorionic villus sampling**, cells are obtained from the chorion (an early structure that later becomes the lining of the placenta) during the eighth to twelfth weeks of pregnancy and checked for genetic problems. This is considerably earlier than such problems could have been found through amniocentesis, and the process of analyzing the fluid takes less time (Chervenak et al., 1986).

Neither amniocentesis nor chorionic villus sampling is used for every pregnant woman. Both tests are indicated when the mother is older or if there is some history of problems or a possibility of a prenatal problem. They are intrusive; that is, they require an intrusion into the area near the developing child. The search is ongoing for nonintrusive ways of screening for possible problems. It would be very useful, for example, if we could take a blood sample from the mother and determine whether there is a possibility of a problem. If there is, other, more intrusive tests could be performed. One such screening test is a blood test called the Maternal Serum Alpha-Fetoprotein (MSAFP) test. This test identifies pregnancies that are at higher than average risk for certain serious birth defects and other problems that could affect the fetus. Alpha-fetoprotein (AFP) is a substance that all fetuses produce; some of it gets into the amniotic fluid, and a little actually enters the mother's blood stream. The test, given between the sixteenth and eighteenth weeks of pregnancy, measures the amount of AFP in the pregnant woman's blood. If the amount of AFP is either high or low, other tests are usually performed (Clark & DeVore, 1989; March of Dimes, 1989). Thus the maternal serum alpha-fetoprotein test is a way of screening for possible difficulties.

In some cases when a structural problem is found—perhaps through the use of ultrasound—it can be treated. For example, a twenty three-week-old fetus was surgically removed from his mother's womb, and an operation was performed to correct a blocked urinary tract. The fetus was then returned to the womb (Blackeslee, 1986). In another case, a small valve was implanted in the skull of a fetus that suffered from water on the brain to drain away the fluid, allowing the fetus to develop normally (Volpe, 1984).

When Margaret entered labor, her contractions and the condition of the fetus were constantly monitored with a fetal monitor. This device tells the doctor how the fetus is reacting to maternal contractions and gives an early indication of any fetal distress (Greenlund, Olsen, Rachootin, & Pederson, 1985).

Each of these procedures has limitations and dangers. Some claim that fetal monitoring leads to unnecessary Cesarean sections, because a doctor may know something is not quite right and decide to do a Cesarean section even though the women might be able to deliver vaginally. There is still need for more research on the long-term effect of sonograms. Amniocentesis and chorionic villus sampling are not risk-free procedures, and some complications do occur in a small minority of cases (Rhoads et al., 1989). Alpha-fetoprotein tests have no risk attached, since they are

chorionic villus sampling
A diagnostic procedure in which cells are obtained from the chorion during the eighth to twelfth weeks of pregnancy and checked for genetic abnormalities.

THE CHILD
IN THE YEAR
2000

Reproductive Surrogacy

If a couple were to go to a fertility clinic for artificial insemination—that is, artifically introducing a donor's semen to fertilize a woman's egg—no one would say much. It is a very accepted approach used by thousands of people each year. Hardly a statement criticizing such technology is raised. Will other procedures that would enable couples who cannot conceive to have children receive the same acceptance?

Today, our technology allows us to help such couples in many ways, the most controversial being surrogacy. The term *surrogate mother*, however, is really a poor choice of words, because it glosses over many potential important distinctions. For example, it is now possible to collect ova from almost any woman, fertilize the ova in the laboratory with sperm essentially from any man (called in vitro fertilization), and implant the fertilized ova into almost any woman with a uterus either immediately or after a time during which the fertilized egg is frozen. None of the parties to this technological feat need know each other; on the other hand, they may be intimately related.

In the past ten years or so, many celebrated cases of surrogate mothers have introduced new questions that have never had to be answered before. Many of these cases involve a couple unable to have children and another woman who allows herself to be artificially inseminated with the sperm from the first woman's husband. This other woman is called the surrogate mother. However, suppose the fertilized egg the second woman nourishes was not hers but came from still another woman. Would she still be called a surrogate mother?

Eugene Sandberg (1989) suggests that three different terms for mothers be used. The genetic mother is the producer of or donor of the egg, the gestational mother is the developer of the fetus, and the nurturing mother is the custodian of the child.

Today, the surrogate mother is usually a woman who carries her own fertilized egg for another couple. However, it may not be so in the future. Most women who cannot have children can provide their own eggs but cannot carry the infant adequately. These women can have their egg artifically inseminated and implanted in another womb. If this seems incredible, consider the fact that this has already been done. A mother at age forty-eight delivered triplets for her daughter in South Africa after fertilization of the daughter's egg outside the womb and embryo transfer. This may become more common, especially for women who have difficulty producing healthy infants. A lesser number of women will simply need a genetic surrogate, that is, a donor ovum, but will be able to carry the child themselves. In vitro fertilization and surrogacy may become more common in the future.

The objections that are frequently raised concerning surrogacy involve the legal contracts and monetary issues as well as the potential exploitation of poor women to carry children for the wealthy. The idea that the poor will be used is countered by the argument that the poor tend to be undernourished with poor medical histories, not the type of people who would be chosen as the gestational substitutes.

The importance of the new technology of conception is that in the future couples who have not been able to have children will be able to do so. Will this become acceptable to the public? It is probable that attitude changes will occur. In vitro fertilization, in which the egg is fertilized in the laboratory outside the woman's body and implanted into the mother, elicits much less objection than years ago.

In the year 2000, some forms of surrogacy will probably become acceptable. The technology is already here, and other technological improvements will be available in the future. The expense may also be reduced and the effectiveness of the procedures increased. The question of the increased use of such procedures, though, will depend upon a change in the public's attitude towards each type of surrogacy and medical procedure.

blood tests, but the report of a high or low level of AFP can cause great anxiety to the family even though most times subsequent tests do not show that anything is wrong. Fetal surgery is risky, too, and we do not yet know which fetuses will benefit and which will not. Despite problems, it is clear that technology will continue to offer options that were only dreamed of just a few years ago and that will greatly affect how a woman and her unborn child are treated during the prenatal period and birth.

♦ BIRTH

The process of birth has been shrouded in secrecy. Unlike other societies, young people in the United States have little experience with birth. A century ago, most women gave birth at home, but today the overwhelming majority of births take place in hospitals. It is only recently that films of actual births have been shown on television. A child is likely to develop an attitude of fear rather early from overhearing horror stores about birth complications. Some television programs show labor and birth in the worst light. The dynamics of birth are rarely taught in high school, and young parents may be ignorant of the basic facts surrounding the event.

The Three Stages of the Birth Process

The birth process is divided into three stages. During the **dilation** stage,

dilation
The first stage of labor, in which the uterus contracts and the cervix flattens and dilates to allow the fetus to pass.

When a woman enters labor, her contractions and the condition of the fetus are constantly monitored with a fetal monitor.

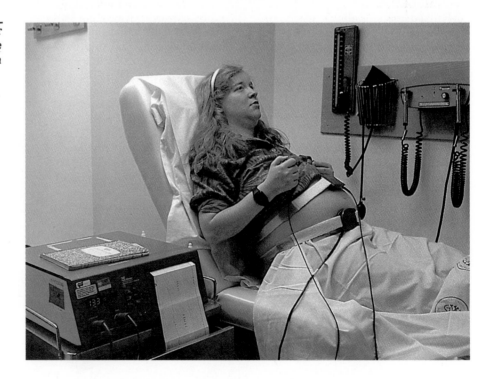

the uterus contracts and the cervix flattens and dilates to allow the fetus to pass through the cervix. The general term **labor** describes this process. This stage can last from about two to sixteen hours, or even longer. It tends to be longer with the first child. When the contractions start, they usually come at approximately fifteen- to twenty-minute intervals and are generally mild. As they continue, they become stronger and more regular. Near the end of this first stage, the nature of the contractions changes. The contractions become more difficult, last longer, and are more frequent. This period, lasting about an hour, is called **transition** and is the most difficult time of labor for many women (Tucker & Ting, 1975). By the end of this stage, the cervix is open about ten centimeters, and contractions are occurring every minute or so.

The second stage of birth involves the actual delivery of the baby. This **expulsion** stage is quite variable and can last anywhere from two to sixty minutes. The baby's head appears, an event referred to as **crowning** (Rugh & Shettles, 1971). The rest of the body soon follows.

The third stage of the birth process involves the **delivery of the placenta,** or afterbirth. During this stage, mild contractions continue for some time. They help reduce the blood flow to the uterus and reduce the uterus to normal size.

Cesarean Birth

If it has been determined that there might be a problem in the birth process, the doctor may advise that the baby be removed surgically through the wall of the abdomen and the uterus. This is major surgery that typically involves a longer hospital stay (often five days, rather than three or fewer for a vaginal delivery). **Cesarean sections,** as this type of birth is called, have become much more common in the past decade. Before 1965, Cesarean sections were performed in about two to five percent of all births. In the early 1970s, the rate rose to six percent, and in 1987 it stood at 24.4 percent (Randal, 1988).

A number of explanations for the dramatic increase in Cesarean sections have been advanced. The safety of the operation has improved markedly both for the mother and for the fetus. The fetal mortality rate from Cesareans is much lower than it was forty years ago, although it is still higher than in vaginal deliveries. Other policies that have led to the increase in Cesarean sections include the practice of repeat Cesarean sections, the increased threat of malpractice suits if anything goes wrong during a difficult vaginal delivery, and an increase in the number of problems that now indicate the need for the procedure (Young, 1982).

The use of a Cesarean section can improve the chances that a fetus in distress will be born healthy and normal. Today obstetricians have a number of technological aids for diagnosing problems. Most women are monitored from the moment they enter the labor room by fetal monitors, which reflect the condition of the fetus (Paul, 1971). For example, babies sometimes have the umbilical cord wrapped around their necks. During labor, the cord is compressed, which can reduce the blood supply to the

labor
A term used to describe the general process of expelling the fetus from the mother's womb.

transition
A period late in labor in which the contractions become more difficult.

expulsion
The second stage of birth, involving actual delivery of the fetus.

crowning
The point in labor at which the baby's head appears.

delivery of the placenta
The third and last stage of birth, in which the placenta is delivered.

Cesarean section
The birth procedure by which the fetus is surgically delivered through the abdominal wall and uterus.

fetus. Doctors can use the fetal monitor to check the baby's heart rate during and after a contraction and diagnose the problem. From that point, the doctor must use his or her knowledge and experience to determine whether a Cesarean is necessary. Doctors faced with evidence of such a problem may decide to practice a conservative, defensive type of medicine rather than risk a difficult vaginal delivery.

This increase in Cesarean sections has become a controversial issue in recent years. One way to reduce the number of Cesareans is to end the standard practice of automatically requiring a woman who has had one Cesarean to deliver her other infants by the same method. Many women who have had Cesarean sections may be able to deliver subsequent babies vaginally (Leary, 1988).

The question often asked is whether there are any long-term consequences of Cesarean birth. The research, although not very extensive, is quite encouraging. Simply stated, there are no negative long-term psychological consequences; in fact, there are even some very interesting positive findings. For example, Entwisle & Alexander (1987) questioned parents and interviewed children in the first and second grades who were delivered either vaginally or by Cesarean section. Among other areas of interest, the data collected included measures of parents' expectations for their children and children's academic achievement. The researchers found no differences on measures of maturity, temperament, or special problems. However, parents of Cesarean children believed that their children had more academic ability, and Cesarean-born children expected to attain higher grades in reading and mathematics, although their standardized academic test scores did not differ from vaginally delivered children. The Cesarean children did receive higher school grades, probably because their parents expected them to and supported superior achievement.

The research describing how mothers and fathers see their infants born by these two different methods is mixed. Some research finds that Cesarean-section parents feed and stimulate their six-month-old infants more than mothers of vaginally delivered infants; other research finds less positive affect; still other research finds no clear difference. A study of forty children born by Cesarean section and forty who were born vaginally found no significant differences in mother-infant interaction, infant behavior, or maternal perception of infant behavior (Kochanevich-Wallace, McCluskey, Fawcett, & Meck, 1988). One finding that appears to be accepted is that fathers of children born by Cesarean are more involved with their infants, for reasons that are not definitely known (Pedersen, Zaslow, Cain & Anderson, 1981). At this time, then, there is no evidence of any long-term problems associated with Cesarean births.

The Effects of Obstetrical Medication

In the United States, obstetrical medication is almost routinely administered to women in labor. About 95 percent of all deliveries utilize drugs to control pain during labor. There is little question concerning the effects of such medication on infants in the first few days of life. Medicated infants are more sluggish than nonmedicated infants (Brackbill, 1979; 1982). In the second day of life, heavily medicated infants sucked at a

10. TRUE OR FALSE?

Infants born through Cesarean section are more likely to do poorly in school than infants born vaginally.

lower rate, sucked for shorter periods of time, and consumed less formula than infants whose mothers received no anesthesia or local anesthesia (Sanders-Phillips, Strauss, & Gutberlet, 1988). Another study found that effects of the drugs on infant behavior were strongest on the first day and were reduced greatly by the fifth day but that there were still differences between the medicated and nonmedicated infants.

By one month there were few differences between the groups, although mothers of unmedicated babies handled their babies more affectionately, and mothers of medicated babies spent more time stimulating their infants to suck. There were no differences in infant behavior, but the mothers perceived their babies differently. Mothers of medicated babies perceived their infants as less adaptable, more intense, and more bothersome. Of course, more difficult deliveries may account for some of these findings, but not for all of them. Perhaps the major effects of medication, at least at one month, are found in the problems mothers have in interacting with infants who were heavily medicated during the first few days. These problems may carry over and be more important in the long term than the effects of the medications themselves (Murray, Dolby, Nation, & Thomas, 1981). Perhaps the early interactions set up expectations and problems that remain to influence the mother's responses.

What of the long term effects of obstetrical medication on the child? At this point, all we can say is that the studies are mixed. Some studies find few differences in infant behavior due to medication (Stechler & Halton, 1982). Others argue that there are long-term behavioral differences (Lester, Heidelise & Brazelton, 1982), especially when faced with challenging tasks.

The effects of obstetrical medication depend on the type of drug, the time of administration, the dosage, and a number of other individual factors not well understood. Some studies that found no effect of drugs on infants' later behavior used samples that were given light doses of medication (Stechler & Halton, 1982). Today, with greater knowledge of the effects of medication on infants and improvements in the anesthesia, babies are perhaps less likely to be heavily medicated. This is not to say that medication is unnecessary or should be avoided in every case. Medication may be needed, but it should be tailored specifically to the patient's needs, keeping the developmental welfare of the infant in mind.

◆ A NEW LOOK AT BIRTH: ALTERNATIVE METHODS

Alternative methods of birth are gaining in popularity. These procedures emphasize the importance of the birth experience for both parents. In the past, both parents were robbed of the birth experience. The mother was medicated, sometimes to the point of oblivion, and was frequently separated from her infant for quite a while after the birth. The father was forced to wait outside the delivery room and could have no part in the birth process. Even visitation hours for the family were restricted.

However, medical and hospital procedures have changed and continue to change. Birth centers are available for those families who wish to give birth outside the high-technology atmosphere of a hospital. These centers may be useful for women who are at lower than average risk for problems in pregnancy (Rooks et al., 1989). There is even a suggestion to locate birth centers inside hospitals so that if emergency treatment is necessary, it is within easy reach of the patient (Lieberman & Ryan, 1989).

In the past twenty-five years, a revolution has occurred in how hospitals manage births, and many patients are now able to choose to participate actively in alternative methods of birth. One method, developed by Fernand Lamaze, concentrates on the experience of the parents during the birth process. Another method, formulated by Frederick Leboyer, emphasizes the importance of the infant's birth experience.

A Personal Experience

Lamaze method
A method of prepared childbirth that requires active participation by both parents.

I had attended the six **Lamaze** (prepared childbirth) sessions with my wife, but I didn't think I would be too affected emotionally by the birth of our baby. After all, I had seen films of births, so it wouldn't be as new to me as it would be to someone with no background in the field.

Every week my wife and I attended the Lamaze class with a group of ten or eleven other couples. During the sessions, the nurse answered all questions and taught the women relaxation methods. We were introduced to the process of birth through a film and were taught a number of exercises that could reduce the discomfort of labor. As a coach, the father-to-be was to be responsible for reminding the woman of the relaxation techniques and breathing methods, supporting the woman, and recognizing changes in the woman's condition during labor. The nurse stated repeatedly that women who successfully complete the program usually require less, and sometimes no, medication during labor, but that if medication was needed, a woman should ask for it. The success of the Lamaze system does not hinge on whether the expectant mother can eliminate the need for medication during childbirth. The nurse emphasized preparing both parents to experience a great moment in their lives and to participate actively in the birth. The atmosphere was relaxed.

Upon arriving at the hospital, my wife was examined and admitted. Instead of saying good-bye to her and waiting in a room for hours, I was welcomed into the labor room. As the contractions became stronger, I helped my wife find a comfortable position and reminded her of the breathing exercises. When my wife was seven centimeters dilated, her contractions became stronger and more difficult to deal with. Nurses checked her progress more frequently, and after some long contractions, the baby's head began to show.

In the delivery room, the doctor told my wife when to push and when to stop. I stood at my wife's head and watched everything, and a mirror was set up for my wife to watch, too. After a short time, the baby emerged and began to cry. There she was, covered with liquid and still attached to her mother through the long, thick, braided umbilical cord. "You have a round little baby girl," the doctor said, showing us the baby, cutting the cord, and delivering the placenta.

The feelings are difficult to describe. They were both joy and relief, a high that will remain with both of us forever.

The Lamaze Method

The most popular alternative birthing method was developed by Fernand Lamaze, who advocated not only the father's presence but also his active participation in the birth process (Lamaze, 1970). Women are taught specific techniques for managing discomfort that reduce the need for pain-killers during labor. Relaxation techniques, breathing methods for the various stages of labor, and a number of other procedures help reduce the discomfort of labor and birth. Finally, the method emphasizes the importance of experiencing the birth and sharing an emotional experience.

Lamaze procedures accomplish their goals. They reduce the amount of medication required, and women giving birth using Lamaze techniques report less discomfort and a more positive attitude toward the process (Cogan, 1980). This does not mean that the women feel no discomfort, although they do report experiencing less pain than women who do not undergo Lamaze training (Melzack, 1984). These women also require fewer painkillers (Charles et al., 1978).

The question of the effect that the father's experience may have on the father-infant relationship is still in doubt. Peterson and colleagues (1979) examined the attitudes of forty-six middle-class Canadian couples planning various delivery methods from the sixth month of pregnancy to six months following the birth. The father's participation was found to be significantly related to the father's attachment to the infant. The researchers advocate better prenatal education for the father and structuring the birth and home environment to encourage active participation by the father.

In a review of the research on father participation in birth, however, Palkovitz (1985) found insufficient evidence to conclude that bonding is

11. TRUE OR FALSE?

The Lamaze method of birth emphasizes the importance of leaving the mother alone to meditate on her experience.

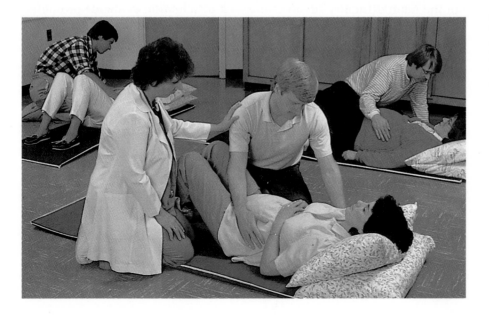

In this prepared childbirth class, both mothers and fathers are getting ready for the experience of the birth of their child, as well as learning how to reduce the discomfort and pain of labor.

encouraged by the father's attendance at the birth. Studies finding positive results for father attendance slightly outnumber studies finding no differences, but these positive studies tend to be less rigorously performed. However, evidence does confirm that the father's attendance at birth and early contact with the infant enhances the marital relationship and the father's feelings of being included, and this can have a positive effect on the family itself (Palkovitz, 1985).

The Leboyer Method

A different tack was taken by Frederick Leboyer (1975), whose method emphasizes the experience of the infant in what has come to be known as the **Leboyer method** of childbirth. Leboyer's book *Birth Without Violence* is not written with the scientific-minded public in mind. It is anything but subtle, and it is not filled with facts, figures, and research studies. Rather, it is an empathic, impassioned plea for treating the infant gently and effecting a smooth transition from life within the womb to life outside.

Leboyer argues that the cries and shrieks of the newborn are not inevitable. They result from a kind of torture, the traumatic removal from a warm, dark, quiet, supporting environment to a cold, bright, noisy one filled with need. Leboyer argues that the baby feels everything and truly experiences the birth process and that what is easiest for the doctor may not be best for the baby. Among other things, Leboyer advocated using dimmed lighting and whispers in the delivery room, placing the infant on the mother's abdomen after birth, waiting minutes before cutting the umbilical cord, providing a bath in which the father plays a leading role, and having both parents massage the infant. He also notes the importance of preparation for childbirth.

Leboyer's theories have not been met with overwhelming medical support. Some disagree with specific procedures, such as dimming the lights, but the main difficulty involves the lack of scientific evidence presented by Leboyer and his supporters to demonstrate the practical value of such procedures. Leboyer's supporters tend to stress the experiential value of the method and construct their cases on the theory that the first moments of life are more important both for parents and for child than was first thought (Berezin, 1980).

Leboyer uses his clinical experiences and theoretical clarity as arguments in favor of his procedures. One study found that babies born by the Leboyer method were physically and behaviorally more advanced than would have been expected (Trotter 1975), but this study has been criticized because it lacked adequate controls.

One excellent study was performed at the McMaster University Medical Centre in Hamilton, Ontario. Women interested in the program were first matched for social class and number of prior pregnancies, then randomly assigned to either a Leboyer group or a non-Leboyer group. Only women who were considered low risk were allowed to participate in the experiment. All Leboyer procedures were carefully followed with this group. For the control group, standard medical practices were used. The lighting was not dimmed, the cord was cut within sixty seconds of delivery, and

Leboyer method
A method of childbirth emphasizing the importance of the birth experience for the child and encouraging such practices as dim lighting, low voices, immediate physical contact with the mother, delay in cutting the umbilical cord, a bath, and a massage.

no bath was given. But in both groups, mothers and fathers actively participated in the birth process, and gentle handling, a norm at this hospital, was given to all infants.

The results showed no significant advantages for the Leboyer method. The researchers stated: "The infants born by the Leboyer method were neither more responsive nor less irritable than the control infants during the neonatal period, nor were there any differences in infant temperament or development at eight months of age" (Nelson et al., 1980, p. 659). Nor did the mothers' perceptions of the two deliveries differ. The only reported difference was that "mothers in the Leboyer group were more likely to attribute differences in the behavior of the infants to the delivery experience" (p. 659). The researchers also reported their fears that there would be greater danger to both infants and mothers were not supported by the study.

While many hypotheses are offered to account for the lack of significant advantages to this method, the most striking one involves the nature of the control group. In the Canadian hospital, even without the use of Leboyer's methods, the delivery and postnatal care were gentle. Hospital procedures encouraged both parental participation and early parent-child interaction. It may well be that the group being compared with the Leboyer sample makes all the difference. Comparing Leboyer babies to a highly medicated, roughly treated, parental-separated sample may be unfair, for hospital procedures are changing in the direction of greater family participation and gentler birth.

On the other hand, the fact that the danger for low-risk mothers and infants appears to be minimal would allow for a greater amount of choice for parents in determining which method of birth to use under normal circumstances. In the last analysis, the details of Leboyer's method may be less important than the humanistic attitudes and approach to birth that Leboyer advocates (Young, 1982).

♦ COMPLICATIONS OF BIRTH

Most pregnancies and deliveries are normal, but sometimes problems do occur. Problems such as anoxia and prematurity may have serious consequences later in childhood.

Anoxia

A deficiency of the oxygen supply reaching the baby, **anoxia,** is the most common cause of brain damage. Such damage may be inflicted either during the birth process or for some time during the prenatal period, when the placenta is detached or infected. Anoxia can lead to a number of birth defects, including cognitive and behavioral problems (Wenar, 1982). Except for the more extreme cases, making predictions about the future development of anoxic children is difficult. Some anoxic children compare well with peers who did not suffer any anoxia. Although anoxia increases the risk for developmental disability in both cognitive and be-

anoxia
A condition in which the infant does not receive a sufficient supply of oxygen.

havioral areas, many anoxic children develop normally and show little difference from their peers when entering school (Wenar, 1982). The quality of care may be most important in staving off possible problems (Sameroff & Chandler, 1975). The better the care, the less likely mildly and moderately anoxic children are to develop these disabilities.

Prematurity: Born at Risk

If you ever see a small, premature infant, you will never forget it. The experience of seeing an infant who is born too early—that is, premature—stays with you. **Prematurity** can be defined in terms of birthweight or the length of the gestation period. Currently, a baby weighing less than 2,500 grams (about five and a half pounds) or one who has been born less than thirty-seven weeks after conception is considered premature. A birthweight below 1,500 grams (about three pounds, five ounces) is designated very low birthweight (March of Dimes, 1986).

Generally, premature infants are categorized into two groups. In the first group are infants born below the weight expected for their gestational age. Some of these babies are born at their normal term; others are born earlier. These infants are called **small-for-date babies.** The other group involves what are called **preterm infants,** those whose birthweights are appropriate for their gestational age but who are born at or before thirty-seven weeks after conception (Kopp & Parmelee, 1979).

The Consequences of Prematurity

Fifteen or twenty years ago, the outlook for premature infants, especially the smaller ones, was very poor. This is no longer the case, however. Even infants who are born very small—between 750 and 1,000 grams (anything less than 2,500 grams is considered low birthweight)—have about a 70 percent chance of surviving if they get good care. Mortality in the smallest infants weighing less than 750 grams is about two-thirds, but even here there is more hope and increased survival compared to years ago. However, for the infants born between 1975 and 1985, 26 percent of those who weighed below 800 grams and survived, 17 percent who weighed between 750 and 1,000 grams and survived, and 11 percent of the survivors with birthweights between 1,000 and 1,500 grams showed major handicaps when observed at one or two years of age (Ehrenhaft, Wagner, & Herdman, 1989). When a group of sixty-five premature infants who weighed less than 1,500 grams at birth and a group of full-term children were compared at nine years of age, the boys who had been premature showed more evidence of emotional problems, including greater amounts of anxiety, depression, social withdrawal, and total behavioral problems. This was not true for females who were born very small, but the researchers argue that boys may simply show their problems at an earlier age (Breslau, Klein, & Allen, 1988). In addition, the types of problems shown by boys and girls may be different. Many of the other infants who do not show major problems will have minor difficulties.

Prematurity is the gravest problem that infants face. Premature infants are at risk for a number of physical and intellectual deficits during childhood (Lawson, 1984). Children who are born premature are more likely

prematurity
Infants weighing less than five and a half pounds or born at or before thirty-seven weeks after conception.

small-for-date infants
Infants born below the weight expected for their gestational age.

preterm infants
Infants born at or before the thirty-seventh week of gestation.

to show intellectual problems and learning difficulties than children who are not premature, and they are more likely later to be placed in classes for the retarded (Caputo & Mandell, 1970). Such children are also at risk for developing a number of social difficulties, since they are especially prone to hyperactivity. Many show neurological problems (Drillien, 1964). In addition, although premature infants comprise only a relatively small percentage of births, they are more likely to die during the first month of life, accounting for about half of all the deaths that occur during this time (Fitzgerald, Strommen & McKinney 1982).

The situation is complicated by the fact that not every premature infant suffers these setbacks. Many premature babies grow up to be superior children and to function well as adults. A variety of outcomes are possible, depending on the size and gestational age of the infant and on subsequent care and upbringing. The lower the birthweight and the shorter the gestation period, the more potentially serious the consequences.

Why are premature infants as a group subject to such risk? First, fetuses that are diseased or have some genetic abnormality are likely to be born early. Second, the premature infant is also likely to be born into a disadvantaged environment (Scarr-Salapatek & Williams, 1973). Although prematurity is found in every socioeconomic group, it is far more common in young women or women living in poverty (Birch, 1968). In fact, white women between twenty and thirty years of age have about a three percent low birthweight rate, whereas economically disadvantaged teenagers have a nine percent rate (Kopp & Kaler, 1989).

The Causes of Prematurity

Sometimes the cause of the prematurity is obvious. For instance, the human uterus is designed to carry one fetus at a time. Twins don't always share the food supply equally, and one twin may weigh much less than the twin sibling (Ross Laboratories, 1977). At other times, an illness or disease in the mother may bring on labor too early. But most often the cause is unknown. A number of factors have been implicated, including the mother's health and nutrition prior to pregnancy; the mother's age, weight, and weight gain during pregnancy; smoking and use of alcohol and other drugs; uterine problems; and lack of prenatal care (Kopp & Parmelee, 1979). Smoking during pregnancy doubles the chance of a woman's having a small-for-date infant (Ounsted, Moar & Scott, 1985). These factors correlate with social class. For instance, the poor are less likely to eat a nutritious diet during pregnancy and are much less likely to avail themselves of prenatal care. Their health prior to pregnancy is also likely to be worse, and the crowded environment in which they tend to live is not ideal, because the woman is probably exposed to more diseases and more stress. In addition, the children of poor women are at a double risk. They are more vulnerable at birth and more likely to be exposed to a poor environment afterward.

Helping the Premature Infant Develop

Our handling of premature infants both from medical and psychological

12. *TRUE OR FALSE?*

Premature infants today are no more at risk for developmental problems than are normal infants.

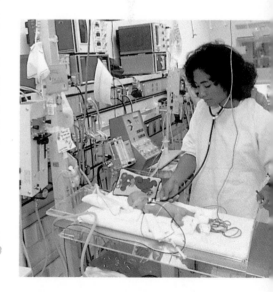

Advances in medical science have helped us save many lives of premature infants.

retinopathy of prematurity
A condition of blindness resulting from an oversupply of oxygen most often administered to premature infants.

standpoints have changed markedly. Years ago, severely premature infants were fed a very weak formula and placed in oxygen-rich environments. However, too rich an oxygen supply led to a condition called **retinopathy of prematurity,** a disorder that causes blindness. Lack of proper nourishment led to developmental problems. Today, we have effective tube-feeding techniques and sophisticated machinery that monitors the infant's vital signs.

On a different level, the effects of the deadening, nonstimulating aspects of hospital care must be reduced. A number of studies have shown that extra rocking and tactile stimulation are highly effective in improving the neurological, motor, and psychological development of premature infants. Premature babies given extra stroking in the hospital by nurses (tactile stimulation) were healthier and gained more weight than a similar group not given such stimulation (Solkoff, Jaffe, Weintraub & Blase, 1969). Parents can be taught to do the same thing. Ruth Rice (1977) trained parents of fifteen premature infants to give their infant a program of tactile stimulation for fifteen minutes four times a day for a month. Another group of premature infants received no such treatment. At four months, each infant was examined by a pediatrician, a psychologist, and a pediatric nurse. None of these professionals had any idea whether the baby had received any tactile stimulation. The results were remarkable. The stimulated infants were superior in mental development, weight gain, and neurological development.

Increased stimulation plays a crucial role in helping premature infants develop more normally. A number of forms of stimulation are used including tactile, visual and kinesthetic (movement). Premature infants are now given visual stimulation through things to look at and auditory stimulation through music and speech, as well as extra handling. Infants given this extra stimulation often show improvements in many areas of development, including increased weight gain, more responsiveness, and a reduction in irritability (Korner, 1986).

Because premature infants require additional care, their parents need more help and support for providing the necessary care for them. Mothers of premature infants make use of grandparents and other sources of community support more often than mothers of full-term infants (Parke & Tinsley, 1986). This support is often necessary as a means of reducing the stress that may overwhelm some parents. Professional help may also be required in such situations.

◆ AFTER THE BIRTH

By the end of the normal period of prenatal development, the average American male infant weighs approximately seven and a half pounds and measures approximately twenty inches. The average female weighs slightly less—about seven pounds—but is more ready for life. She is about four weeks more mature as measured by skeletal age (Annis, 1978) and is more neurologically advanced.

Hospitals have instituted specific procedures to measure the physical functioning and the capacity for independent survival of newborn infants. For example, infants can be evaluated using a rating system called the **Apgar Scoring System** (Apgar, 1953), which measure five physical characteristics: heart rate, respiration, muscle tone, color, and reflex response (see Table 4.2). The neonate (newborn) is given a score of 0, 1, or 2 for each item according to a special criterion. For instance, if the newborn has a heart rate of 100 to 140 beats a minute, the infant receives a score of 2; for 100 beats a minute or below, the infant receives a score of 1: if there is no discernible heartbeat, a 0 is given (Apgar, Holaday, James, Weisbrot & Berien, 1958). The highest possible total score is 10. Some studies suggest that there are differences between infants who have received scores of 7, 8, or 9 and those with a perfect 10. Infants who receive a score of less than 7 need additional watching and care. The Apgar score can alert those responsible for the infant's care to a possible problem.

A more complex assessment for infants is the **Brazelton Neonatal Behavior Scale,** which provides information concerning reflexes and a variety of infant behaviors (Jacobson, Jacobson, Fein, Schwartz & Dowler, 1984). Among the behavioral items are measures of responsiveness to visual stimuli, reactions to a bell and a pinprick, and the quality and duration of the infant's alertness and motor activity (see Table 4.3) (Lester, Heidelise & Brazelton, 1982). The scale is a diagnostic tool but has also been used to research cross-cultural differences among infants.

Apgar Scoring System
A relatively simple system that gives a gross measure of infant survivability.

Brazelton Neonatal Behavior Scale
An involved system for evaluating an infant's reflexes and sensory and behavioral abilities (see Table 4.3).

TABLE 4.2: The Apgar Scoring System
The Apgar Rating System is a relatively simple scale used to rate newborns on survivability. Each child is rated on each of the five behaviors listed below. Each behavior can have a score of 0, 1, or 2. (Highest possible total score is 10.) If the total score is greater than 7, no immediate threat to survival exists. Any score lower than 7 is cause for great concern. If the score is lower than 4, the infant is presently in critical condition.

AREA	SCORE		
	0	1	2
Heart rate	Absent	Slow (<100)	Rapid (>100)
Respiration	Absent	Irregular	Good, infant crying
Muscle tone	Flaccid	Weak	Strong, well flexed
Color	Blue, pale	Body pink, extremities blue	All pink
Reflex response			
Nasal tickle	No response	Grimace	Cough, sneeze
Heel prick	No response	Mild response	Foot withdrawal, cry

Source: Apgar, 1953.

TABLE 4.3: The Brazelton Behavioral Assessment Scale

The Brazelton Scale is used for both diagnostic and research purposes. The examiner rates the child on each of these behaviors while the infant is in a particular state. For example, the child's response to an auditory stimulus (e.g., the examiner's voice), is noted only when the infant is in the quiet alert state. The examiner is interested in discovering what the infant *can* do, not what he or she does.

1. Response decrement to repeated visual stimuli
2. Response decrement to rattle
3. Response decrement to bell
4. Response decrement to pinprick
5. Orienting response to inanimate visual stimuli
6. Orienting response to inanimate auditory stimuli
7. Orienting response to animate visual stimuli—examiner's face
8. Orienting response to animate auditory stimuli—examiner's voice
9. Orienting responses to animate visual and auditory stimuli
10. Quality and duration of alert periods
11. General muscle tone—in resting and in response to being handled, passive and active
12. Motor activity
13. Traction responses as he is pulled to sit
14. Cuddliness—responses to being cuddled by examiner
15. Defensive movements—reactions to a cloth over his face
16. Consolability with intervention by examiner
17. Peak of excitement and his capacity to control himself
18. Rapidity of buildup to crying state
19. Irritability during the examination
20. General assessment of kind and degree of activity
21. Tremulousness
22. Amount of startling
23. Lability of skin color—measuring autonomic lability
24. Lability of states during entire examination
25. Self-quieting activity—attempts to console self and control state
26. Hand-to-mouth activity

Source: B. M. Lester and T. B. Brazelton, 1982.

◆ LOOKING FORWARD

The study of prenatal development and birth is hopeful yet very frustrating. We know so much about preventing birth defects, yet every day we observe pregnant women drinking, smoking, eating improperly, and not availing themselves of proper prenatal care. Despite our knowledge of how to minimize the deficits that seem too often to follow the premature infant through life, relatively few hospitals have excellent postnatal wards where the child's total needs are taken into account. And while teenagers are giving birth at alarming rates, little effort is expended to teach these young parents about the special needs of their infants. Even though we have some of the answers to these problems, it's expensive to disseminate the information we do have and improve the programs that serve the needs of families during this important time of their lives. We pay for our failures in the years to come, since problems that develop at this early stage often lead to psychological, social, and medical problems later in life that we will be forced to deal with.

But what does all this mean to Margaret and Tim, the expectant couple introduced at the beginning of the chapter? Increasing knowledge allows them to make important decisions during pregnancy about what to do and what to avoid. Although there are no guarantees that their baby will be born healthy, they now have the information necessary to improve their chances of having a healthy infant. They can control their smoking and drinking behaviors, and Margaret can follow healthy routines in other areas, such as nutrition. Margaret and Tim are also more aware of alternative methods of birth. For these parents, the new medical knowledge and advances mean that their infant has a better chance of being born free of defects and developing normally in the years to come.

SUMMARY

1. Fertilization occurs when a sperm cell penetrates an egg cell. The germinal stage lasts from conception until about two weeks. During this stage, the fertilized egg travels down the fallopian tube and embeds itself in the womb. The embryonic stage lasts from two to eight weeks. During this time, the heart starts to beat, and 95 percent of the body systems are present. During the fetal stage, from two months until birth, the developing organism continues to develop internally and put on weight.

2. A number of environmental factors can adversely affect fetal development.

3. Thalidomide was once prescribed to relieve the symptoms of morning sickness. It produced many deformities. Diethylstilbestrol (DES) was prescribed for women who had histories of miscarriages. Although the infants were born healthy, some female offspring developed cancer of the cervix and showed structural abnormalities.

4. Smoking has been linked to low-birthweight babies and possibly to learning disabilities, prematurity, and cleft palate. Many children of alcoholic mothers suffer from fetal alcohol syndrome, a condition of retardation and physical defects. Even moderate drinking during pregnancy can cause some fetal abnormality, known as fetal alcohol effect. The combination of smoking and drinking is especially dangerous. The babies of heroin addicts are born addicted and must go through life-theatening withdrawal.

5. Various diseases and disorders, such as rubella, AIDS, herpes, syphilis, gonorrhea, and chlamydia, can cause fetal abnormalities or death.

6. The Rh factor is a particular red blood cell antibody. When the mother is Rh negative and the father is Rh positive, the offspring can be Rh positive, and problems may arise. Antibodies from the mother can pass through the placenta and kill red blood cells in the fetus. Today, women with such problems receive a shot of the vaccine RhoGAM, which blocks the creation of the antibodies.

7. Many women use some kind of drug during their pregnancy. Most birth defects are caused by prenatal insults to the fetus rather than genetic diseases. Many women expose their unborn children to the danger because they do not understand the danger, do not believe the warnings, do not realize they are pregnant at the time, or have difficulty motivating themselves to stop a potentially dangerous activity.

8. A critical period is the time at which an event has its greatest impact. Some teratogens (agents that cause birth defects) are more dangerous at some times than at others.

9. More women over thirty are having children. Although the risk is greater for both mother and baby, good prenatal care can reduce the risk somewhat. Many pregnant teenagers do not get proper prenatal care, are exposed to many teratogens, and may suffer from malnutrition. The risk factor is very high for this group.

10. Serious malnutrition can lead to fewer fetal brain cells. Specific vitamin and mineral deficiencies can lead to fetal deformities. The effects of mild and moderate malnutrition are controversial, but malnutrition may serve to weaken the fetus.

11. Maternal stress has been linked to babies who are irritable as well as to obstetrical problems.

12. Paternal drug taking prior to pregnancy can affect the father's genes. In addition, if the father indulges in drinking and smoking during the mother's pregnancy, the pregnant woman may find it more difficult to refrain from such behavior herself.

13. New technologies now give the doctor and patient more information and choices with regard to fetal examinations. Sonography uses ultrasonic soundwaves to create a picture of the fetus in the womb. Amniocentesis and chorionic villus sampling are used to discover genetic problems. A screening test for alpha feto-protein can alert the physician to a possible problem. Fetal monitoring during labor gives doctors early warnings that something is wrong.

14. During the first stage of birth, the uterus contracts and the cervix dilates. The infant is delivered in the second stage, and the placenta during the third.

15. Cesarean births have increased greatly during the past fifteen years because of improvements in safety, new technological aids allowing doctors to know sooner whether something is wrong, and the tendency for doctors to practice conservative medicine.

16. Babies who are medicated are sluggish and not very alert. The long-term effects of obstetrical medication are controversial at the present time.

17. The Lamaze method of prepared childbirth emphasizes the importance of both parents' participation in the birth process. Relaxation is used to reduce the discomfort of labor and birth and usually less medication is required.

18. The Leboyer method emphasizes the importance of the infant's experience. It involves delivering the child with dimmed lights and quiet voices, placing the infant on the mother's abdomen, waiting minutes before cutting the umbilical cord, and bathing and massaging the infant.

19. A premature infant is one who weighs less than five and a half pounds or who has spent fewer than thirty-seven weeks in the womb. Infants born below the weight expected for their gestational age are small-for-date babies. Preterm infants are those whose birth weights are appropriate for their gestational age but who are born at or before thirty-seven weeks. The cause of most cases of prematurity is unknown. Prematurity is related to infant mortality and intellectual, neurological, and developmental disabilities. Early intervention can help these infants develop more normally. The premature infant has special needs, and parents must learn to cope with these greater demands. Studies show that extra stimulation reduces the possibility that the infant will develop a disability.

20. The average American male infant weighs about seven and a half pounds and measures about twenty inches. Females weigh slightly less than males but are more mature as measured by skeletal age and more neurologically advanced. After birth, the child may be rated on the Apgar Scoring System, which provides caregivers with an idea of the infant's physical condition and chances for survival. A more involved assessment instrument called the Brazelton Neonatal Behavior Scale is both a diagnostic and research tool.

ACTION/REACTION

Under Pressure

When Lisa discovered she was pregnant, everything seemed perfect. Her husband Simon was happy, and both sets of prospective grandparents were thrilled. After reading some articles about childbirth, Lisa mentioned to Simon that she wanted to use the Lamaze method of childbirth to deliver the baby, but Simon was not happy about that. Neither was Lisa's mother, who shook her head and said, "After you feel the first labor pain and get to the hospital, just have them put you out." Simon's mother was just as direct. "They've been delivering babies in the hospital the regular way for generations with no problems. Why try something new?"

Since Simon doesn't want to be in the labor or delivery room, Lisa has asked her best friend, Betty, to be her coach. Simon sees this as an attack on his manhood, and everyone is pressuring Lisa to change her mind. Lisa is terribly upset and can't sleep.

1. If you were Lisa, what would you do? What would you say to Simon and to Lisa's and Simon's mothers?

2. If you were Lisa's friend, how would you advise her?

3. If you were Lisa's doctor and saw how much pressure Lisa was getting from others, would you step in and make suggestions?

What If Something Happens?

Often the actual reason a child is born prematurely remains a mystery. So it was with Sandy and Bob's baby. Cynthia, born after six and a half months, was given only a small chance of surviving. After a few days in the hospital, Sandy went home. She returned to the hospital each day to feed Cynthia and spend time with her, but Bob refused to see the baby at all. He told Sandy that if the baby died it would be worse for him if he had become attached to her. Sandy felt the same way, but she told Bob it was their responsibility to care for Cynthia. What if she, too, refused to see the baby? Bob said he would understand and if she didn't want to see Cynthia until her chances of surviving improved, he could respect that. Sandy was very angry at her husband's attitude and behavior.

Now Cynthia is home and apparently will be all right. Bob now shows a great deal of love, but Sandy is distant with Bob because she is still angry with him. "He gave me no help when the baby was in the hospital," she complains. Her estimation of Bob has been reduced. Bob says that he understands Sandy's feelings but that continuing her cool behavior is pointless.

1. If you were Sandy, how would you have dealt with Bob's behavior at the hospital?
2. If you were Sandy, how would you deal with Bob at home?
3. If you were Bob and felt the same way he did, how would you have dealt with the infant?
4. If you were the pediatrician, would you have intervened?

PART TWO

Infancy and Toddlerhood

The Cradle by Berthe Morisot.

CHAPTER FIVE

Physical Development in Infancy and Toddlerhood

Return of the Cavalier by Richard C. Woodville.

CHAPTER OUTLINE

Are These Statements True or False?

Turn the page for the correct answers. Each statement is repeated in the margin next to the paragraph in which the information can be found.

1. The newborn infant is very nearsighted at birth.
2. Before five months of age, infants do not see color but rather see shades of grey.
3. Infants are born deaf but quickly develop their sense of hearing.
4. Breastfed infants can recognize their mother through their sense of smell.
5. Most of the newborn infant's reflexes become stronger with time.
6. There is a relationship between brain weight and intelligence.
7. The injurious effects of malnutrition can be reduced by a good environment.
8. There has been a significant increase in the percentage of mothers who are electing to breastfeed rather than bottle feed their infants.
9. An infant can be adequately fed using prepared formula rather than breast milk.
10. Females are more mature at birth and continue to develop at a faster rate.
11. Parents see male infants as sturdier than female infants.
12. The earlier parents start to toilet train their child, the shorter the amount of time it takes to do so.

Answers to True False Statements

1. TRUE.
2. FALSE. Correct statement: Some studies suggest that some color vision exists during the first few days of life, but research shows color vision definitely exists by three months.
3. FALSE. Correct statement: Newborns can hear at birth.
4. TRUE.
5. FALSE. Correct statement: Many infant reflexes become weaker and finally terminate.
6. FALSE. Correct statement: Except for very small brains, there is no relationship between brain weight and intelligence
7. TRUE.
8. TRUE.
9. TRUE.
10. TRUE.
11. TRUE.
12. FALSE. Correct statement: The earlier parents start to toilet train their child, the longer it will take to do so.

◆ THE NEWBORN AT A GLANCE

lanugo
The fine hair that covers a newborn infant.

vernix caseosa
A thick liquid that protects the skin of the fetus.

fontanels
The soft spots on the top of a baby's head.

neonate
The scientific term for the baby in the first month of life.

The newborn infant does not resemble the pictures we see on babyfood jars, in soap advertisements, or in the movies. The newborn is covered with fine hair called **lanugo,** which is discarded within a few days. The baby's sensitive skin is protected in the womb by a thick secretion called **vernix caseosa,** which dries and disappears. The head is elongated and measures about one-fourth of the baby's total length. The thin skin appears pale and contains blotches caused by the trip through the birth canal. The head and nose may be out of shape because their soft, pliable nature allows an extra bit of give during birth. They will soon return to normal, but it will be about a year and a half before the bones of the skull will cover the soft spots, or **fontanels.** The legs are tucked in under the baby in a fetal position and will remain that way for quite a while. The newborn wheezes and sneezes and appears anything but ready for an independent existence.

In this chapter, we will examine the physical growth and development of the child from birth through the second year of life. Changes during this time are very noticeable and take place at a breathtaking rate. A few terms require explanation. When the term **neonate** is used, it refers to the baby's first month of life. The term infant refers to the entire first year of life. The toddler period begins at one year and continues until age three (Morrison, 1988).

◆ HOW THE INFANT EXPERIENCES THE WORLD

The newborn cannot survive without care and appears to be ill prepared for entrance into the world. But appearances can be deceiving. Science has recently begun to draw a new and different picture of the capabilities of the newborn. We now know that infants are born well prepared for survival. The neonate is better adapted to the environment and more capable than most people think.

Vision

Adults rely on the sense of vision for much of their information about the world. So do infants. At birth, the visual apparatus of neonate is immature but functional (Aslin, 1987). What can the neonate see?

ACUITY AND ACCOMMODATION You have probably had your visual acuity—your ability to see objects clearly at various distances—examined using a Snellen chart. You stand twenty feet away and are asked to read letters that get progressively smaller until you have difficulty identifying them. Researchers cannot use an eye chart with infants, but an infant's eye movements can be watched to determine whether the baby senses a difference between a figure and its background, for example, stripes. Dayton and his colleagues (1964) varied the width of stripes until the neonates showed no eye movements. These researchers argue that neonates have an acuity of 20/150; that is, they can see at 20 feet what normal

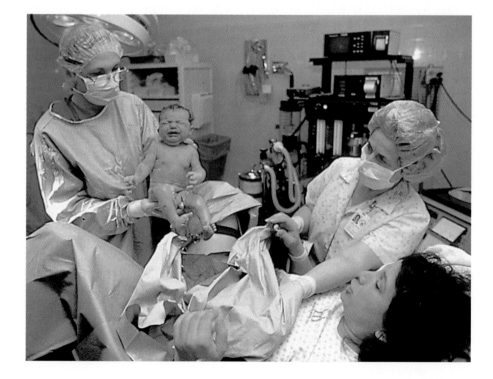

The newborn infant does not look like the infant on the baby food jars but is more ready for life than is generally recognized.

1. *TRUE OR FALSE?*
_____

The newborn infant is very
nearsighted at birth.

adults see at 150 feet. Other estimates are a little worse, approaching between 20/200 and 20/300 (Dobson & Teller, 1978). The newborn is very nearsighted.

The baby also has difficulty focusing. When you look at a chair five feet away and then switch to a blackboard twenty feet away, the curvature of the lens of the eye changes to keep the visual image in focus. Newborns do show some visual accommodation, about a third of the adult level (Bremner, 1988). The best focal distance for the newborn is about 19 centimeters, or 7½ inches (Haynes, White & Held, 1965). Neonates cannot focus well on distant or approaching objects.

As poor as their visual acuity is, though, it serves them well. When a mother holds her newborn, the baby's face is usually a bit less than six inches away, so the baby is able to see her during feeding. Visual abilities improve quickly. Within six months, the infant's visual acuity approaches that of an adult (Cohen, Deloache & Strauss, 1979), and by about two months, the ability to focus approaches adult status (Aslin & Dumais, 1980).

FORM AND PREFERENCE If you were shown two pictures—one of a beautiful mountain scene and the other of a green square on a white background—chances are you would look longer at the first scene. Your interest could be measured by the amount of time you spent looking at the image. This is the same approach used in investigating visual preferences in the newborn.

Consider the fact that you have quite a bit of visual experience and a green square isn't very exciting. Yet what of a newborn, who has had no visual experiences? Would neonates focus on anything in particular or just allow their eyes to wander aimlessly?

Newborns do have visual preferences. They prefer curved lines to straight lines (Fantz & Miranda, 1975), a patterned surface over a plain one (Fantz, 1963), and high-contrast edges and angles (Cohen et al., 1979). The neonate's scanning is not random. It is directed by rules (Haith, 1980) that cause the baby to concentrate on the outline of a figure rather than explore the figure's details (Milewski, 1976). By eight weeks or so, infants develop more adult patterns of scanning and will investigate the interior as well as the contours of a figure (Maurer & Salapatek, 1976). Research shows that infants are sensitive to patterned properties of stimuli from birth (Antell, Caron & Myers, 1985).

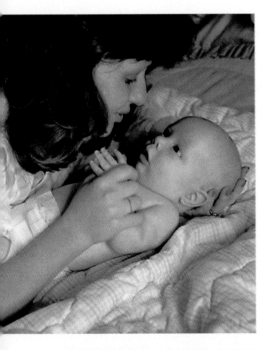

Infants have the visual ability to focus on their caregivers.

A PREFERENCE FOR FACES? How can visual patterns and preferences help the newborn survive? The newborn depends on others for the basic necessities of life, so a visual preference for human faces would be adaptive. In fact, the discovery by Robert Fantz (1961) that this was true greatly excited the scientific world. Fantz showed babies two pictures simultaneously—one off to the infant's right, the other to the left—and measured the time the infant's eyes spent fixated on either one. Fantz found that infants preferred patterns to nonpatterned surfaces and that a picture of a face attracted the most attention (see Figure 5.1). Perhaps the infant comes into the world preprogrammed to recognize faces. Most studies

FIGURE 5.1: Visual Preferences in Infancy

The importance of pattern rather than color or brightness was illustrated by the response of infants to a face, a piece of printed matter, a bulls-eye, and plain red, white, and yellow disks. Even the youngest infants preferred patterns. Color bars show the results for infants from two to three months old; gray bars, for infants older than three months.

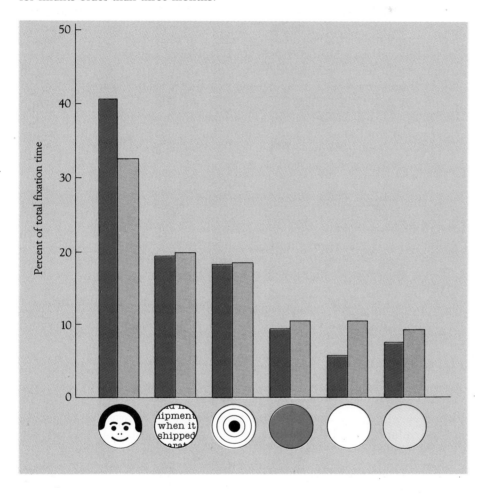

Source: Fantz, 1961.

have indeed shown that by two to four months of age, infants prefer faces to other drawings (Dannemiller & Stephens, 1988), and some studies demonstrate that neonates can even discriminate different facial expressions (Field, Woodson, Greenberg & Cohen, 1982).

Fantz's argument that infants have a natural preference for faces may, however, be premature. Fantz's conclusions have been reinterpreted in terms of the complexity of stimuli, and other researchers have not replicated Fantz's work (Cohen et al., 1979). Others claim that in the absence of experience with faces, neonates do not show a preference for the face

(Small, 1990). At the present time, there is no final answer to this question. Perhaps both sides are correct but are looking at the issue at different levels. On a more detailed level, the infant has a preference for complex stimuli, while on a behavioral level, this translates into an interest in faces, which are common complex stimuli in a newborn's environment.

Can neonates recognize different faces? There is some evidence that infants may recognize particular faces at very early ages. In one fascinating study, two-day-old infants were presented with their own mother's face and a female stranger's face. Neonates gazed longer at their mother's face (Bushnell Sai, and Mullin, 1989). However, in other studies, recognition of mothers was not confirmed until about three months (Kurzweil, 1988). Infants may also prefer certain types of faces. In a series of studies, Judith Langlois (1987; 1990) found that two-month-old, and twelve-month-old infants gazed longer at attractive faces than at unattractive faces. At the present time, there is no agreement on the exact age at which a child can discriminate particular faces, except that such discrimination develops fairly rapidly during early infancy.

COLOR VISION There is recent evidence that neonates can see color. Adams (1989; 1987) discovered that four-day-old neonates were able to discriminate red from green, and neonates as young as three days of age prefer colored over noncolored stimuli. Although very young infants may see red, green, and yellow, it is not until three months of age that they can see blue (Aslin, 1987). It is impossible to say whether neonates see color the same way older people do. For now, we can only make assumptions. However, infants as young as four months do show the same color preferences as adults, gazing more at blue and red than at yellow (Banks & Salapatek, 1983).

SPATIAL AND DEPTH PERCEPTION Do babies live in a two-dimensional or three-dimensional world? Bower and his colleagues (1970) found that infants will move their heads back and place their hands in front of them when viewing a ball coming toward their face. An impressive 70 percent of the infants' hand extensions were in the direction of the ball, and infants made contact with the ball 40 percent of the time (Bower, 1977). When the infants could not contact the ball, they seemed surprised and upset. If this is true, it shows astonishing spatial perception at a very young age. Ball and Tronick (1971) projected a shadow of a ball that was shown as becoming larger and larger, giving the babies the impression that the ball was heading for them. Two-week-old infants drew back and interposed their hands between their face and the shadow.

A number of other researchers have attempted to replicate these studies. Some have noted various aspects of reaching but do not believe they are a coordinated defensive attempt to avoid the oncoming stimulus (DiFranco, Muir & Dodwell, 1978). Neonates ages seven days to fifteen days were placed on a pillow in which their heads were slightly elevated. A ball was suspended from a rod and moved to one of three positions seven to eight centimeters from the babies' eyes, and the babies' movements were photographed (Ruff & Halton, 1978). Only 36 percent of the

2. TRUE OR FALSE?

Before five months of age infants do not see color but rather see shades of grey.

reaches were near contact, and only 7 percent resulted in contact. This is far below Bower's finding. Most of the arm reaching could not be interpreted as directed at the target.

In another study, Claes von Hofsten (1982) used a moving ball to test eye-hand coordination and spatial perception in five-day-old to nine-day-old neonates. As the ball moved back and forth, the infants' movements were videotaped. Hofsten found evidence that eye-hand coordination does occur in the newborn. The infant has the ability to direct both eyes and hands toward an external stimulus. Obviously catching and grasping are not well developed in the infant, and at best, these behaviors can be interpreted only as the very early beginnings of the ability.

To test an infant's depth perception, Gibson and Walk (1960) designed an ingenious experiment. A stand was constructed about four feet above the floor, and an infant was placed on the stand, which contained two glass surfaces. The first was a checkerboard pattern, the other a clear sheet of glass. On the floor beneath the clear glass was another checkerboard pattern, giving the impression of a cliff. This experiment, using what is called the **visual cliff,** showed that children six months or older would not crawl from the "safe" side over the cliff even if their mothers beckoned (see Figure 5.2).

visual cliff
A device used to measure depth perception in infants.

But what about younger children? Testing very young infants on this apparatus is difficult because of their inability to crawl. However, Joseph Campos and his colleagues (1970) placed infants as young as two months on the deep side of the cliff. The heart rate of these infants decelerated, indicating interest not fear. Although young children develop depth perception very early, it is only at six months or later that they develop a fear of the cliff. This contrasts with animals such as dogs, goats, and cats, which show a much earlier avoidance of the cliff.

These experiments show that an early primitive form of depth and spatial perception exists in very young infants. Such infants can locate objects in the visual field and show some minimal eye-hand coordination. The meaning of an infant's responses to visual stimuli, though, is a matter of controversy. Some authorities, like Bower, tend to interpret such responses as an indication of an early, purposeful series of actions, while others disagree sharply. Perhaps the movements Bower observed represent infants visually tracking and orienting themselves to the approaching object that rises on the visual plane. Despite these differences of opinion, it appears that the beginnings of spatial and depth perception are visible in the young infant. Later perceptual capabilities may have their basis in these early responses.

Babies develop depth perception at an early age; in this experiment, a six-month-old infant would not crawl across what looks like a cliff even though its mother beckoned.

VISUAL TRACKING Neonates can track slowly moving objects. Marshall Haith (1966) presented one-day-old to four-day-old neonates with a stationary light and a moving light that traced the outline of a rectangle. The babies reduced their sucking behavior more when presented with the moving light than when they were shown the stationary light. Kremenitzer and her colleagues (1979) found that neonates one to three days old looked in the direction of a moving target, although the skill was not well developed.

FIGURE 5.2: The Visual Cliff Apparatus

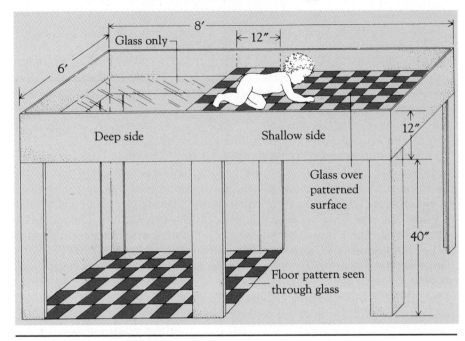

Source: Gibson and Walk, 1960.

VISION RECONSIDERED Taken together, studies of the neonate's visual capabilities show that newborns can indeed see and process information on a very limited basis. Newborns can see forms (Bond, 1972) and track objects, although their visual acuity and ability to focus are poor. Finally, they scan the field according to rules that may be innate, indicating that part of visual processing is indeed inborn.

The perceptual abilities of the infant develop rapidly. During the first weeks, the visual process is directed by prewired programs, but these quickly give way to more adult patterns of scanning, and the infant's visual abilities approach those of adults (Cohen, 1979).

Hearing

Neonates can hear from the moment of birth (Wertheimer, 1961). Muir and Field (1979) found that neonates as young as three days old turned their heads in the direction of a continuous sound. There is some evidence that the auditory threshold (the intensity at which the newborn is capable of hearing) is somewhat higher than in adults (about ten to twenty decibels higher) (Bremner, 1988), but there is no doubt that the newborn can hear.

Some claim that there is evidence for hearing in the womb, although

THE CHILD
IN THE YEAR
2000

Helping Baby Develop

So the little, helpless infant isn't as helpless as he or she seems to be. Even a cursory reading of the research on infant sensory functioning and perception forces one to consider the child's impressive abilities. Why has it taken so long to isolate these abilities? It wasn't so long ago that some people thought that infants were born deaf, could not smell subtle odors, and were basically unable to process much information.

The answer lies in advances in methodology. Working with infants is not easy. Infants may cry, making testing difficult, or worse still, they may fall asleep. Imagine yourself a researcher who has just set up the infant to determine something about his or her abilities only to find when you turn around the infant is asleep. The many different states that infants enter and leave make determination of their abilities difficult. Infants cannot tell us what they see or experience. It takes specialized techniques to discover their capabilities.

Our research has given us a very different look at infancy than we had even thirty years ago. Our progress has been achieved because of advances in research methodology, and these advances have generated some very practical benefits. One very promising technique is the use of **evoked potentials,** a technique for measuring the brain's response to particular stimuli. For example, electrodes can be attached to the scalp of the infant, who is then shown a pattern, such as a checkerboard. As the color of the checks is changed, the waves from the part of the brain that is involved—the occipital cortex—produce a pattern that can then be measured against that produced by other infants. This not only allows us to research what an infant is processing but also has diagnostic value. In this way, amblyopia, a disorder in which the person suffers dim and indistinct vision even though the eye is structurally normal, can be discovered (Patrusky, 1980).

Another type of evoked potential is the auditory brainstem-evoked response (ABR). Electrodes are attached to the scalp, clicks of varying intensities are delivered through an earphone placed over the infant's ear, and brainwave activity is recorded. Estimates of hearing loss can be made by evaluating the brain wave patterns in response to the emitted sounds.

The ABR is also used in the diagnosis of neurological dysfunction (Murray, 1988). Tests enable us to discover particular sensory problems that a child may have that cannot be diagnosed in any other way.

These tests are very involved and probably will not be used for every infant. However, in the next decade, high-risk infants may be tested using these and other high-technology tests as part of a complete battery to determine the sensory functioning of the child. As our methodology improves and research discovers more about the human infant, our knowledge and appreciation of the infant's capabilities increase and old ideas are swept away. The new methodology and research will lead to advances in diagnosing infant problems and will therefore allow us to correct such problems at an early age. For example, if we know that a child suffers from a hearing problem, we may be able to correct it medically, perhaps through surgery. If it cannot be corrected, we might teach the parents to use the senses of vision and touch to stimulate the child. Our interest in infant capabilities will translate into even greater diagnostic possibilities in the future and allow the child in the next century a better chance of developing normally.

this claim is controversial, DeCasper and Fifer (1980) reported that by three days, neonates could discriminate between their mother's voice and that of a stranger as measured by differential sucking on a nipple. Since the newborn has not had extensive experience with the mother's voice, this effect may occur because the baby has heard the mother's voice while developing in the womb. Neonates will suck harder when they hear a familiar voice in a familiar intonation than when they hear the same voice

evoked potentials
A technique of measuring the brain's responses to particular stimuli.

3. TRUE OR FALSE?

Infants are born deaf but quickly develop their sense of hearing.

with an altered intonation (Mehler, Bernoncini, Barriere & Jassik-Gerschenfeld, 1978). In fact, newborns prefer to listen to a tape-recorded passage that their mother had read aloud and prefer melodies that were sung by the mother during pregnancy to those passages and songs not read or sung during pregnancy but introduced after birth (see Aslin, 1987).

The neonate has an auditory capability that is better developed than its visual abilities. Studies have shown that newborns react to pitch, loudness, and even rhythm (Eisenberg, 1970). Newborns coordinate their body movements to other people's speech rhythms (Condon & Sander, 1974).

As with the neonate's visual abilities, the newborn's auditory abilities have survival value since these abilities help the neonate to begin to form a relationship with the caregiver. Human neonates respond to most sounds within the human voice range (Webster, Steinhardt & Senter, 1972) and are more responsive to sounds within the normal human voice range than outside it (Kearsley, 1973). They are also more sensitive to higher pitched sounds (Aslin, Pisoni & Jusczyk, 1983) and can discriminate one sound from another. Infants are also tuned in to language from birth, (Aslin et al., 1983), and as early as one month after birth, they can tell the difference between the sounds of "p" and "b" (Eimes, Siqueland, Juscyzk & Vigorito, 1971). Infants are also partial to music (Walk, 1982). Rhythmic sounds tend to soothe a baby (Salk, 1960).

Smell

The newborn can also use the sense of smell. Neonates move away from a solution with an unpleasant odor (Lipsitt, Engen & Kaye, 1963). Infants as young as seven days old turn preferentially to their mother's breast pad even if offered another woman's breast pad (MacFarlane, 1975), but this ability is not present in two-day-old neonates. Two-week-old breast-fed children could recognize the smell of their mother when presented with gauze pads that had been worn in the mother's underarm area. However, these children could not recognize their father's odors, and non-breastfed children could not recognize either the mother's or the father's odors (Cernoch & Porter, 1985).

4. TRUE OR FALSE?

Breastfed infants can recognize their mother using their sense of smell.

Even bottle-fed neonates can identify the odor of lactating females. When presented with a pad that had been worn on the breast by a nursing mother and a pad that had been worn by a non-nursing mother, two-week-old bottle-fed females turned preferentially toward a pad that had been worn on the breast by nursing mothers (Makin & Porter, 1989). This demonstrates that nursing mothers may produce a general odor that attracts infants as well as very specific odors that allow infants familiar with their mother's odor to distinguish their mother's odor from the scent of other mothers. Such discrimination on the basis of smell is impressive.

Taste

Neonates can taste. They can tell the difference between plain water and a sugar solution (Dessor, Maller, & Turner, 1973). They tend to reject plain water, but if sugar is added, they accept it. Neonates, one to three days old, prefer sucrose to glucose (Engen, Lipsitt & Peck, 1974). They can even tell the difference between sour and bitter substances (Jensen, 1932). They prefer sugar to salt (Pratt, 1954). Some researchers note that the newborn is more sensitive to taste stimuli in early infancy than at any other time (Reese & Lipsitt, 1973). While that is difficult to prove, we can conclude that the sense of taste is functional in the neonate and well developed during infancy and toddlerhood.

Pressure and Pain

Neonates are responsive to tactile stimulation, especially around the mouth. They can feel pain from birth but are not as sensitive to pain for the first day or so. This may reduce some of the infant's discomfort during the birth process. Within a few days, a dramatic increase in this sense occurs (Lipsitt & Levy, 1959), which contributes to the baby's ability to respond to painful stimuli that might be injurious. Unfortunately, this has led to some misunderstanding, with some people concluding incorrectly that neonates do not experience pain or interpret pain as adults do. The neonate does indeed experience pain, and whether the pain is measured using simple motor responses, facial expressions, or a tendency to cry, the infant shows that it is affected by stimuli that cause it pain (Anand & Hickey, 1987). The human neonate's neural pathways as well as the brain centers necessary for pain perception are well developed.

◆ THE SLEEPING-WAKING CYCLE

The neonate is born with a number of sensory abilities that develop rapidly throughout infancy and toddlerhood. The infant actively seeks out variation and new stimuli during attempts to experience and understand the world. This process is facilitated by changes in the sleeping-waking cycle. As infants mature, they spend more time awake and alert, which allows for even more exploration of their environment.

Neonates spend about sixteen or seventeen hours a day sleeping (Parmelee, Winne & Schulz, 1964). The nature of these periods shows some interesting differences between neonates and older children and adults. For example, when both children and adults are awakened from sleep in which they show rapid eye movements (REM), they report vivid dreams. The normal adult spends about 20 percent of sleep time in REM. Normally, the adult begins in non-REM sleep and after about fifty to seventy minutes switches to REM. About 50 percent of an infants' sleep—an astounding one-third of the infant's day—is spent in REM (Roffwarg, Muzio & Dement, 1966). Premature infants show even more REM. An infant born between thirty-five and thirty-eight weeks following conception spends about 58 percent of sleep time in REM. That percentage jumps to 67 percent in infants after thirty-three to thirty-five weeks and to 80 percent for infants born after a gestation period of thirty weeks. In addition, infants typically begin their sleep patterns in REM. By the age of three months, however, the amount of REM sleep is reduced to about 40 percent, and infants are no longer beginning their nights in that state (Minard, Coleman, Williams & Ingeldyne, 1968).

The functions of sleep and REM are probably quite complex in the newborn (Brierly, 1976). Perhaps newborns use the extra REM to provide a self-stimulatory experience, because they sleep so much of the day. The fact that REM sleep decreases as waking time increases provides some evidence in that direction (Roffwarg, Muzio & Dement, 1966). Other psychologists argue that the REM sleep fosters brain organization and development, which is particularly rapid at this stage of life (Berg, 1979).

It is relatively easy to describe waking and sleeping in adults. Not so with infants. While waking and sleeping appear in the newborn, a number of transitional states are present that fit into neither category. As the infant grows, transitional states decrease and the infant's state of waking or sleeping can more easily be measured and classified. Peter Wolff (1966) argues that infants show seven sleeping or waking states:

1. *Regular Sleep.* During this state the infant lies quiet, subdued, with eyes closed and unmoving. The child looks pale, and breathing is regular.
2. *Irregular Sleep.* In this state, the infant does not appear to be still. The infant shows sudden jerks, startles, and a number of facial expressions, including smiling, sneering, and frowning. The eyes, though closed, sometimes show bursts of movement, and breathing is irregular.
3. *Periodic Sleep.* This is an intermediate stage between regular and irregular sleep. The infant shows some periods of rapid breathing and has jerky movements followed by periods of perfect calm.
4. *Drowsiness.* In this state, the infant shows bursts of "writhing" activity. The eyes open and close and have a dull appearance.
5. *Alert Inactivity.* The infant is now relaxed and has a bright, shining appearance but is inactive. The child searches the environment, and breathing is irregular.
6. *Waking Activity.* The infant in this state shows a number of spurts in activity involving the entire body. Respiration is irregular. The intensity and duration of the baby's movements vary with the individual.
7. *Crying.* In this familiar state, the infant cries, and this is often accompanied by significant motor activity. The face may turn red.

It is estimated that 67 percent of the time infants are in sleep, 7 percent in drowsiness, 10 percent in alert inactivity, 11 percent in waking activity, and 5 percent in crying (Berg, Adkinson & Strock, 1973).

The concept of infant waking-sleeping state is important because the response of an infant to a stimulus is a function of the state in which the infant is tested (Parmelee & Sigman, 1983). Some reflexes are stronger and more reliable in one state than the other. The infant's sensory thresholds are also mediated by the baby's state. Before comparing studies, the infant's state must be taken into consideration. The concept of state has practical implications for parents as well (Brazelton, 1980). In the alert inactive state, infants may turn away from strong auditory stimuli toward more gentle voices (see Parmelee & Sigman, 1983). During the transition states, the infant can go either way. If the stimuli awaiting the infant are pleasant, the infant is drawn out into an alert stage and is more responsive. The amount of alertness an infant shows may affect the neonate's opportunities for early stimulation. Parents have more opportunity to interact longer with an infant who shows more alert awake periods (Colombo & Horowitz, 1987).

Infant Crying

A crying infant is totally distressed. At times, the lips quiver and the baby seems to be inconsolable. At that point, if a parent comes, speaks a few soft words, lifts the child from the crib to the shoulder, and pats the baby's back, the baby's world can become whole again. The cry of an infant has survival value. It not only informs others of the baby's condition but also encourages the parents or other caregivers to care for the infant. The cry of an infant can have a physical effect on parents. Wiesenfield and Klorman (1978) found that mothers' heart rates increased as they watched videotape recordings of infants, particularly their own, crying.

The infant emits a number of different cries. There are qualitative differences between babies' cries (Wolff, 1965), and parents are often able to understand the meaning of each cry from environmental cues (Murray, 1979). Besides the birth cry, there is a hunger cry, a pain cry, and a "mad" cry. Each of these can be measured and, perhaps with the exception of the birth cry, recognized by parents. The first cries are probably more reflexive than communicative, although they may soothe the mother by letting her know that the child is alive and all right.

Peter Wolff (1965, 1969) isolated the three types of early cries—the hunger cry, the mad cry, and the pain cry. The hunger cry is heard when the infant is hungry, but it is also heard if there is any environmental disturbance. The cry is rhythmical and follows this pattern:

Cry, Silence, Whistle Sound While Taking in Air, Silence, Cry

The mad cry follows the same general pattern as the hunger cry, except that it is more forceful as more air is pushed past the vocal cords.

The pain cry is different. The first cry is much longer, as is the first rest period. It lasts as long as seven seconds, during which time the infant lies still, holding his or her breath. This is followed by the gasping intake of air and cries of shorter and varying durations. The pain cry is easily recognized. The loud pain cry begins suddenly, and no moaning occurs before it. The initial segments of the pain cry are particularly potent stimuli for both adult males and adult females (Zeskind, Sale, Maio, & Weiseman, 1985).

Both parents and non-parents recognize the differences between these cries. But how do people react to these different cries? Parenting style is more important than the form of crying in eliciting parental reactions. Parents do not respond to the hunger cry in any fixed way. Some always give the bottle or breast when they hear the cry; others check the diaper first. Experienced parents do not come as quickly as do inexperienced parents when they hear this cry. Parental response to the mad cry is less varied than the response to the hunger cry. Parents will go immediately to the crib to check on the baby, but they are not overly concerned. Both

Infant crying is a common state and one which parents must learn to deal with effectively.

parents and nurses recognize the pain cry and rush to attend to the infant. Concern shows both on their faces and in the way they approach their caregiving responsibilities.

Gwen Gustafson and Karen Harris (1990) presented twenty mothers and nonmothers with tapes of an infant crying and told them to care for the infant, which was actually an infant manikin designed for parent training classes. The manikin physically resembled a live infant and could wet and drink. The women's task was to babysit, and the women were told the baby needed a nap. Diapers and bottles were available. Tapes were played of either the hunger cry, which would be ended by feeding the infant, or the pain cry, which would terminate if a diaper pin was pulled out of the infant. How did the subjects react?

Mothers and nonmothers began their response with some combination of picking the child up, putting the infant to the shoulder, talking to the infant, patting or stroking, and rocking. They then checked the diaper or offered a bottle or pacifier. Mothers were somewhat better at guessing the exact cause of the cries and spent more time engaging in activities that might soothe the infant's distress. It seems that the different types of cries represent different distress levels and can be easily interpreted. However, whether they heard cries of a hungry infant or an infant in pain, women used the same set of initial caregiving behaviors. Only when these had failed did they check other possibilities.

In the real world, parents use their knowledge of the situation to determine how to react to the cry. For example, the knowledge that a child just ate would probably rule out hunger. We can conclude, then, that people can differentiate between different types of cries but, in the absence of any previous information, initially attend to cries in the same manner. The differences between mothers and nonmothers in handling the situation demonstrates that experience fine tunes the skill of quieting a baby. People generally know even before they become parents about a number of techniques that are often effective in quieting infants, but experienced people will be better at it than will inexperienced people.

THE EFFECT OF PICKING UP A BABY WHEN THE INFANT CRIES The most effective way to quiet a crying infant is to pick up and hold the baby (Korner & Thoman, 1972). The question that is most often asked is, Will this spoil the child? Not so, say Bell and Ainsworth (1972), who followed twenty-six infant-mother pairs to examine maternal responsiveness to infant crying. Parents tried to reduce crying by giving the babies toys or pacifiers, feeding them, or rocking them. Close physical contact was most often used. Infants whose mothers responded promptly during early infancy cried less frequently in the later months of infancy than those infants whose mothers did not respond as quickly. Picking the baby up did not lead to any more crying later in infancy. Infants who were picked up were more secure and required less contact later in the first year. This strategy fosters mother-infant communication and strengthens the relationship.

On the surface, Bell and Ainsworth's study seems to cast doubt on the behavioral or learning theory approach to infant crying. After all, infant crying, like any other behavior, should be affected by the rewards and punishments available in the environment. Etzel and Gewirtz (1967) found that crying could be reduced if it was ignored, especially if smiling behavior was reinforced at the same time.

Five years after the appearance of Bell and Ainsworth's study, Gewirtz and Boyd (1977) wrote a rejoinder to the study. They pointed out what they saw as technical flaws in the work and noted that Bell and Ainsworth had failed to note the differences between responses to various cries. For instance, behaviorists never advocated ignoring pain cries. Rather, they are interested in reducing crying for attention. In addition, Bell and Ainsworth's conclusions can be explained using a behaviorist perspective. For example, children may have cried less at one year because their mothers responded to precry vocalizations rather than to the cry itself. These vocalizations were reinforced by the children's mothers' behavior. In their reply, Bell and Ainsworth (1977) defended both their methodology and their conclusions.

Whether a child can be spoiled by being picked up remains a controversial question. We know that crying can be shaped through attention or lack of attention, but it is doubtful whether responding to an early infant's cry spoils the child. One factor should be taken into consideration, though. When parents respond to the needs of their child, a bond forms between them that contributes to the development of a sense of trust and security in the infant.

◆ THE NEONATE'S ABILITY TO LEARN

If newborns are to survive, they must learn about their new world. Even noenates can learn through the three processes described in Chapter 2—classical conditioning, operant conditioning, and imitation.

Classical Conditioning

Researchers report some success using classical conditioning with infants (Blass, Ganchrow & Steiner, 1984). For example, Lipsitt and Kaye (1964) succeeded in classically conditioning the sucking reflex by sounding a tone that acts as the conditioned stimulus and following it by inserting a nipple, which acts as the unconditioned stimulus. After pairing the tone and insertion of the nipple, the infants sucked to the tone (the conditioned response). Little (1970) delivered a tone and a puff of air that caused ten-day-old to forty-day-old infants to blink. After a number of pairings, the infants blinked to the sound of the tone. Other studies have also reported success in classically conditioning infants (Rovee-Collier, 1987), but it should be noted that only about half of all the studies report success (Fitzgerald & Brackbill, 1976). Perhaps infants experience difficulty associating the conditioned and unconditioned stimuli (the tone and the air puff in Little's example) because of lack of experience. While acknowledging that the research results are mixed, we can conclude that classical conditioning has been established in the neonate (Sameroff & Cavanaugh, 1979).

Operant Conditioning

No such problem exists with operant conditioning. Einar Siqueland (1968) successfully trained newborns to turn their heads for a chance to suck on a nipple. Most operant conditioning experiments have involved either head-turning or sucking responses. The creativity of researchers working with young infants is shown in a study conducted by Butterfield and Siperstein (1972) concerning the musical preferences of young infants. In this study, infants were allowed to suck on a nipple and were rewarded by being allowed to hear music. The longer they sucked, the more music they heard. Two-day-old infants sucked longer and longer to hear the music but would not do so if sucking led to the music's being turned off. Infants can be conditioned to turn their heads in a particular direction if rewarded with a bit of milk each time they turn in the desired direction (Sameroff & Cavanaugh, 1979).

Imitation

Can neonates imitate? Many, but not all, studies indicate that they can. Andrew Meltzoff and M. Keith Moore (1983) found that newborns from about half an hour old to 71 hours of age imitated an adult's facial gestures

Andrew Meltzoff argues that very young infants can imitate.

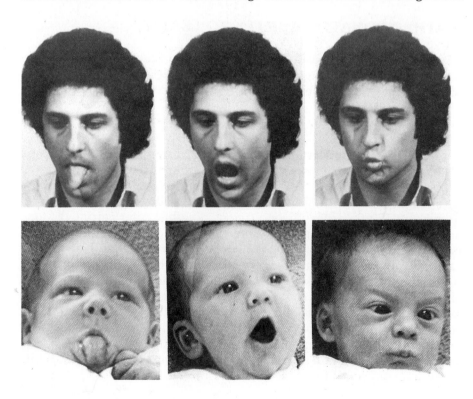

of opening the mouth and sticking out the tongue. Infants less than three days old can imitate head turning (Meltzoff & Moore, 1989). Meltzoff and Moore (1977) found that twelve-day-old to twenty-one-day-old infants imitate facial and manual gestures. Infants opened their mouths and stuck out their tongues when the same behaviors were modeled by an adult. Neonates are more likely to imitate movement than static conditions. In other words, they are more likely to imitate a hand opening and closing if they see the hand open and close than if they merely see an open hand or a closed hand (Vinter, 1986). There is also some evidence that infants can match their own facial expression (happy face or sad face) to a model demonstrating these facial gestures (Field et al., 1983) Newborn infants in Nepal were found to imitate such facial gestures as widened lips, pursed lips, and protruding tongue (Reissland, 1988). Some studies, however, have not succeeded in replicating this imitation of facial gestures (Kaitz, Meschlach-Sarfaty, Auerbach, & Eidelman, 1988).

Habituation

Imagine looking at the same picture hanging over your desk day after day. Eventually you wouldn't even notice it. But what if someone changed the picture while you were out of the room? Would you notice the change? The process by which you spend less and less time attending to a familiar stimulus is known as **habituation** (Brierly, 1976). To respond to the new picture, you must notice that it is different.

habituation
The process by which organisms spend less and less time attending to familiar stimuli.

Psychologists have used the process of habituation to test a number of infant perceptual abilities (Kisilevsky & Muir, 1984). An infant is presented with one stimulus, and the baby's behavior is closely observed. At first the infant shows some interest, but after a time the baby pays less attention to it, perhaps finally ignoring the stimulus altogether. Now you present the infant with another stimulus and observe the behavior. If an increase in attention occurs, the infant has noticed the difference between the two stimuli.

Habituation has been shown in very young infants. One-and-a-half- to three-day old infants habituate to a checkerboard pattern placed on the side of the crib (Friedman & Carpenter, 1971). The three-day-old infants habituated faster to the visual stimuli than younger infants did.

Learning and Development

An infant's ability to profit from his or her experience improves with age. As infants develop, their brains become more capable of processing a greater amount of information at a faster rate. Infants' memory and cognitive abilities allow them to make better judgments about elements in their environment (Parton, 1976). Their improved learning ability is the result of experience with the environment and the infants' developing neurological systems.

Psychologists today have a new respect for the sensory and perceptual abilities of the neonate. The infant comes into this world well prepared to take in and process information as well as to learn.

◆ REFLEXES IN THE NEWBORN

Infants also enter the world preprogrammed with a number of specific responses to their environment in the form of reflexes that enable them to deal efficiently with stimuli in their environment (see Table 5.1). A **reflex** is a simple automatic reaction to a particular stimulus (Kalat, 1981). If you are tapped just below your kneecap, your leg automatically responds by kicking. Infants are born with quite a number of these automatic responses. While the functions of some are obvious, we can only guess at the purposes of others.

Reflexes connected with feeding are well established in the newborn. Place something in an infant's mouth, and the baby will respond with the **sucking reflex.** The infant also shows that **rooting reflex.** If you stroke the neonate's cheek, the baby turns in the direction of the touch. The swallowing reflex is also well developed in the newborn. A number of digestive reflexes—including hiccuping, burping, and regurgitation—are present as well. They allow the child to regulate the intake of food and eliminate gases. Infants are especially likely to demonstrate these reflexes when their parents are in a hurry, such as when the parents are getting ready for an evening out and the infant's schedule is being disrupted.

The functions of other reflexes are either unknown or can only be guessed at. If you slide your finger along the palm of a neonate, the infant's fist will close. This **grasping reflex** is strongest at birth, weaker by two months, and usually disappears by about three months (Illingworth, 1974). In the evolutionary perspective, the grasping reflex might have some survival value. Most primates must hold onto their mothers for protection, and this reflex would facilitate that attachment. The reflex may have once had the same purpose for human infants. Persistence of this response well past the three-month to four-month period may indicate brain damage.

reflex
A relatively simple automatic reaction to a particular stimulus.

sucking reflex
A reflex found in young infants in which an infant automatically sucks when something is placed in the mouth.

rooting reflex
The reflex in young infants in which a stroke on a cheek causes the infant to turn in the direction of the stimulus.

grasping reflex
A reflex in which a stroke on the palm causes the infant to make a fist.

If a baby is held upright and tipped slightly forward with the soles of the infant's feet placed on a hard surface, the infant will step forward as in walking.

The grasping reflex is quite strong in infants

If someone tickled you on the sole of your foot, what would happen to your toes? In adults, the toes curl in, but when the infant's sole is stroked, the toes fan out. This reflex, known as the **Babinski reflex,** normally disappears by the end of the first year.

Of all the reflexes, perhaps the strangest is the **Moro reflex.** This reflex may be elicited in a number of ways. A sudden loud noise or a momentary change in position may cause infants to extend their arms and legs while arching the back, then contract them into a hugging position. The infant also cries. What survival value might this reflex have? T. Berry Brazelton (1981) describes a film of a mother chimpanzee feeding while her baby plays at her side. The mother hears danger and "claps" the chimp on its back. The baby chimp exhibits the Moro reflex, ending with the baby's

Babinski reflex
The reflex in which stroking the soles of a baby's feet results in the baby's toes fanning out.

Moro reflex
A reflex elicited by a sudden loud noise or momentary change in position, causing the back to arch, an extension of the arms and legs, and finally their contraction into a hugging position.

TABLE 5.1: Some Neonatal Reflexes

REFLEX	ELICITING STIMULUS	RESPONSE	DEVELOPMENTAL DURATION
Babinski	Gentle stroke along sole of foot from heel to toe.	Toes fan out; big toe flexes.	Disappears by end of first year.
Babkin	Pressure applied to both palms while baby is lying on its back.	Eyes close and mouth opens; head returns to center position.	Disappears in 3 to 4 months.
Blink	Flash of light or puff of air delivered to eyes.	Both eyelids close.	Permanent.
Diving reflex	Sudden splash of cold water in the face.	Heart rate decelerates; blood shunted to brain and heart.	Becomes progressively weaker with age.
Knee jerk	Tap on patellar tendon.	Knee kicks.	Permanent.
Moro reflex	Sudden loss of support.	Arms extended, then brought toward each other; lower extremities are extended.	Disappears in about 6 months.
Palmar grasp	Rod or finger pressed against infant's palm.	The object is grasped.	Disappears in 3 to 4 months.
Rooting reflex	Object lightly brushes infant's cheek.	Baby turns toward object and attempts to suck.	Disappears in 3 to 4 months.
Sucking reflex	Finger or nipple inserted 2 inches into mouth.	Rhythmic sucking.	Disappears in 3 to 4 months.
Walking reflex	Baby is held upright and soles of feet are placed on hard surface; baby is tipped slightly forward.	Infant steps forward as if walking.	Disappears in 3 to 4 months.*

Source: Dworetzky, 1984.

* Recently, the disappearance of the walking reflex has been questioned. Esther Thelen (Thelen, 1986; Thelen and Fisher, 1982) noted a similarity between the stepping reflex and infants' kicks when lying on their back. As infants mature, they show more kicking, and Thelen argues that these kicks are a forerunner of stepping. The walking reflex disappears because the increase mass of their legs alters the way they can move. The infant's strength is sufficient when the body weight is supported as in the supine position (laying on the back) and its movement is aided by gravity. However, the strength is inadequate to lift the legs or support the weight when the infant is upright. The underlying mechanism, then, has not disappeared, but physical factors such as muscle strength make it impossible for the infant to show it.

hugging himself to the mother's chest, and the mother and baby leave the scene of danger. It is quite an efficient system. Only 20 percent of normal infants in one study showed the Moro reflex at five months of age (Rushworth, 1971), and its presence past six months or so is a sign of possible neurological dysfunction.

Among the most interesting reflexes are those that involve behaviors similar to later walking and swimming. If infants are held upright and pitched a bit forward and the soles of their feet make contact with some hard surface, they will show stepping motions (Cratty, 1979). The stepping reflex cannot be elicited every time (Rushworth, 1971). Some research demonstrates that systematic exercise of the stepping reflex encourages the early development of walking (Zelazo, Zelazo & Kolb, 1972), but this conclusion is still controversial.

You may have seen reports on television of very young infants being "taught" to swim. Basically the "instructors" are capitalizing on the swimming reflex. If infants are placed face down in water they make swimming movements. These babies do not swallow water and can hold their breaths. However, **extreme caution** must be taken because these infants cannot hold their heads above the level of the water and may easily drown. It is best to get both a physician's opinion concerning this activity and an expert's participation, because there is such an obvious danger in this practice. The swimming reflex normally disappears by about the fourth month.

Why Do Some Infant Reflexes Seem to Disappear?

Many other reflexes exist in the newborn. Most of them decrease and terminate with time and are replaced by voluntary behaviors. But why do some infant reflexes disappear with time? One popular theory argues that the infant's cortex is not fully wired in and so nature allows the infant to run on these preprogrammed reflexes. With time, the cortex, which is responsible for more voluntary activities, takes control, actively inhibiting these reflexes. Slowly, voluntary behavior replaces many automatic programs.

Although this theoretical viewpoint has some validity, it seems to fail to answer why some reflexes disappear and not others. In addition, if cortical inhibition is involved, why is it possible to delay the loss of some reflexes through exercise? Indeed, studies show that the stepping reflex can be maintained through exercise (Zelazo, 1976). It is possible that some of these reflexes are important to life within the womb. That is, some reflexes are adaptations to life in the amniotic fluid before birth. In one fetal movement pattern, "the head is flexed backward and turned to one side. This is accompanied by rotation of the trunk and the rest of the body to the same side." In another movement pattern, leg movement occurs almost as if the fetus were pedaling a stationary bicycle, resulting in a somersault as the legs contact the uterine wall (Restak, 1985, p. 121). These patterns can stimulate brain development, especially for those structures involving balance and coordination, as well as stimulate cir-

5. TRUE OR FALSE?

Most of the newborn infant's reflexes become stronger with time.

culation in the skin. These movements also prevent the fetus from adhering to the uterine wall (Restak, 1986). In this theory, the stepping reflex is not the forerunner of walking, but rather allows the fetus to turn around in the womb.

Many of the reflexive activities we see at birth are adaptations to the uterine environment. We know also that many of the movements we see in the womb are reflexive and do not disappear. For example, the fetus shows breathing movements, sighs, yawns, and stretches in the womb. These reflexes stay because they have value not only in the womb but also outside of it. This view sees those fetal reflexes that disappear during the first year of life as purposeful movements in one environment that die out or are replaced because they are no longer appropriate for life after birth (Bremner, 1988). Some reflexes, then, are related to life outside the womb, while others are clearly related to life inside the womb. This explanation is interesting because it forces us to look at the functional value of these reflexes, not only after birth but also before birth. However, it appears better at explaining why some reflexes stay and others do not than explaining how the ones that don't stay disappear.

◆ BRAIN DEVELOPMENT

The change from automatic, preprogrammed, sensory, perceptual, and motor behavior to more voluntary activity is partly due to the development of the infant's central nervous system. At birth, the infant's brain weighs between 325 and 350 grams, while an adult male's brain weighs about 1,400 grams and a female's weighs 1,200 grams. (There is no relationship between brain weight and intelligence, although an adult brain of less than 1,000 grams is usually indicative of intellectual retardation.) The newborn's brain weighs about 25 percent of a mature adult's. It develops rapidly. By six months, it weighs 50 percent of the adult brain's weight, and at two years of age, it weighs three-quarters of an adult's brain (Brierly, 1976). Brain growth allows the infant to develop new skills and capabilities.

Most areas of the brain are not well developed at birth. The brain stem and spinal cord are most advanced (Hutt & Hutt, 1973) because they are involved in critical psychological functions and behavioral responses. Most areas of the upper region of the brain, the cortex, are relatively undeveloped. The sensory and motor areas are functional, but at a primitive level. The neurons that carry instructions from the cortex to the motor nerves lack the insulating cover called a myelin sheath, which is necessary for efficiently conducting impulses (Brierly, 1976). The process of myelinization is faster for the sensory tract than for the motor area. This has survival value because the infant requires the information from the senses to negotiate the environment safely.

Between three and six months, a very important change occurs. The upper portion of the brain, the cortex develops. This switch from control by the lower, more automatic section of the brain to control by the upper, more voluntary centers affects behavior. For instance, many neonatal re-

6. *TRUE OR FALSE?*

There is a relationship between brain weight and intelligence.

flexes disappear within the first half year of life, and many authorities argue that the upper centers of the brain are inhibiting these reflexes (Kalat, 1981).

The development of the brain is swift. Unfortunately, a number of factors can inhibit the development of the brain at this point, leaving the infant with a possible lifelong disability.

The Brain and Experience

The brain does not develop in a vacuum. Rosenzweig and his colleagues (1972), for instance, showed that the brains of rats raised in an enriched or an impoverished environment differ. The brains of the rats from the enriched environment had more spines, which serve as receivers when neurons send messages to each other. Experience makes an imprint on the brain, and lack of basic experience may hinder the brain's development. Although brain development is partly programmed by genes, experience is important. Visual experience speeds up myelinization of nerves in the visual cortex (Morrell & Norton, 1980). Wiesel and Hubel (1965) sewed one eye of a kitten closed for the first four to six weeks of life. After cutting the sutures and allowing the kitten the full use of its eyes, the cells that would normally process visual information for that eye were unable to do so. There is a critical period of four to six weeks in which the cortical cells develop an ability to process information from the eye. After that period, suturing the eye had little or no effect on the kitten.

Experiments like this cannot be performed on human beings, but some evidence suggests that there may be a similar critical period in the development of human sensory abilities. People who are cross-eyed have difficulty focusing both eyes and sometimes undergo operations to reverse the condition. If the operation is performed early in life—up to three years—the condition is corrected, and something like normal vision is restored. This is not true, however, for adults who have the operation; they still show poor focusing even after the operation (Banks, Aslin & Letson, 1975).

To better understand how experience can influence the brain, William Greenough and colleagues (1987) argue that two different types of information and two different types of brain mechanisms should be taken into consideration. Experience-expectant information refers to environmental information that is common to all members of the species, such as being exposed to visual and auditory information. In many sensory areas, the connections between nerve cells are overproduced, and which connections remain depends upon the sensory experience of the individual. This would explain the research (some of it described previously) showing that there is a critical period for the development of many sensory functions. Therefore, early sensory and motor experience is important for the healthy development of sensory abilities and motor skills (Bertenthal & Campos, 1987).

The second type of information is called experience-dependent information and is unique to the individual. It involves learning about one's own environment and requires new connections between neurons to be formed in response to events in the environment.

The development of the brain can help us understand cognitive development. Some authorities argue that there are spurts in the formation of the connections between neurons at particular ages, including two to four months, seven to eight months, twelve to thirteen months, and eighteen to twenty-four months in human infants. Perhaps one additional period in the first four months exists. These spurts are related to leaps in the infant's cognitive abilities (Fischer, 1987). This theory is controversial, and some authorities do not accept it (see McCall, 1987).

Our new knowledge of the development of the brain links the brain's development with various sensory, motor, and cognitive abilities. It also demonstrates that the relationship between experience and brain growth is reciprocal: Brain growth affects the child's abilities, and the experience of the child affects the growth and development of the brain.

♦ GROWTH AND MOTOR DEVELOPMENT

As we have seen, the neonate is born with many impressive perceptual and learning abilities that develop rapidly. However, if you ask parents of infants what their infant is doing, you are most likely to hear about a motor milestone (Thelen, 1987). "She's rolling over." "He's sitting now." "She's crawling around." Parents are always surprised and pleased when their infants master some skill or perform some action for the first time. Nowhere is this rapid development any clearer than in the areas of growth and motor development.

Growth and weight gain during infancy and toddlerhood are shown in the appendix. Heights and weights that fall between the 25th and 75th percentiles are usually considered normal. For instance, a one-year-old male infant may weigh anywhere between 9.49 and 10.91 kilograms and still be within the normal range. Those that fall outside these figures should be examined by a pediatrician but may not indicate any problem.

Gather together pictures of yourself or a sibling from birth to three years of age. The changes in physical appearance tell a story all their own. If your parents kept a record of your growth and weight gain, you will notice a decrease in the rate of growth and weight gain over that period of time. Chapter 4 noted the tremendous increase in both length and weight during the prenatal period. Sometimes the unborn child's weight doubles within a month. Obviously, that rate must slow down. The slowing-down process is evident in the first three years of life. Within six months, the infant has grown more than five inches, and in the next three months, three more inches will be added to the baby's length. In the entire second year, the child grows approximately four inches (Lowrey, 1978).

A self-correcting process also takes place. If a baby's father is tall but the mother is short, the child's growth may be limited in the womb, but the child may catch up during the first six months and return to a normal growth rate (Tanner, 1970). Each child has a preordained path to travel

An infant's motor development gives parents much pleasure.

in physical development (Waddington, 1957). Illnesses, stress, and nutritional inadequacy can deflect the path for a time, but a self-righting tendency called **canalization** takes place. The child's natural growth trajectory can be permanently deflected from its course if environmental deficiencies continue for a long period of time or are very severe.

Factors Affecting Growth

Genetic considerations are most important in determining growth, but environmental elements are important, too. One environmental element is nutrition. Severe malnutrition that occurs early in life and remains untreated can lead to a permanently small stature (Eichenwald & Fry, 1969). Nutrition works both ways. Improvement in nutrition in the United States over the past 100 years has added significantly to the average height of the American population. Improved nutrition in Japan over the past forty years has produced significant increases in the average height of Japan's younger generations.

Disease is another factor that can affect the inborn trajectory. Stress has also been implicated in lack of growth. Lytt Gardner (1972) investigated the growth patterns of children in orphanages where poor treatment and great stress were present. These children were retarded in growth. Such growth retardation due to lack of affection and excessive stress is known as **deprivation dwarfism.**

Principles of Growth and Development

Infants do not develop in a haphazard manner. Their development follows consistent patterns (Shirley, 1931) and is governed by principles that are now well understood. For instance, the head and brain of the infant are better developed at birth than are the feet or hands. The **cephalocaudal principle** explains that development begins at the head and proceeds downward (cephalocaudal means from head to tail). Control of the arms develops ahead of control of the feet. A second rule of development notes that organs nearest to the middle of the organism develops before those farthest away. The **proximodistal principle** explains why the internal organs develop faster than the extremeties. It also correctly predicts that control of the arms occurs before control of the hands, which predates finger control (Whitehurst & Vasta, 1977).

Muscular development follows a path from control of **mass to specific** muscles. First, the individual develops control over the larger muscles responsible for major movements. Then, slowly, control is extended to the fine muscles. This is why younger children use broad, sweeping strokes of the forearm or hand when coloring with a crayon. It is only later that the child gains the dexterity to use finger muscles in a coordinated manner.

Development is also directional. It moves from a state of largely involuntary, incomplete control toward one of voluntary control, from undifferentiation toward subtle differentiation. Under normal circumstances, the movement is forward, with new abilities arising from older ones.

---

canalization
The self-righting process in which the child catches up in growth despite a moderate amount of stress or illness.

deprivation dwarfism
Growth retardation due to emotional factors such as stress and lack of affection.

cephalocaudal principle
The growth principle stating that growth proceeds from the head downward to the trunk and feet.

proximodistal principle
The growth principle stating that development occurs from the inside out—that the internal organs develop faster than the extremities.

mass to specific principle
A principle of muscular development stating that control of the mass or large muscles precedes control of the fine muscles.

Motor Development

Development occurs within a predictable sequence. Nothing demonstrates this as well as the development of such motor skills as crawling, walking, and finally running. The first step a child takes is a milestone for the child and a joyous occasion for the parents. A new world of exploration is now open to the child. Many parents may not be fully aware of the series of accomplishments that lead to walking. Today we can predict what advancements in motor control will occur next, but not necessarily when they will happen. Mary Shirley (1933) made exhaustive observations of a group of children beginning on the day of their birth. These infants all progressed through the same sequence leading to walking. Shirley was interested only in when the baby first performed any of the acts on the chart (see Figure 5.3), such as sitting with support or standing with help, not in how well the baby performed the act. Each of these abilities is perfected with practice.

A word about the ages included in Shirley's chart is in order. Although the sequence of motor development is standard, the ages noted are merely guidelines. If the child's motor development is very late, it should be brought to the attention of a pediatrician, but there are no "average" babies. Each infant will negotiate each stage at his or her own rate. Some will stay longer at one stage than others. The age at which a child develops these abilities is a function of the child's maturation rate as long as the child is well fed and healthy and has an opportunity to practice these skills.

Although Shirley's sequence is well accepted, other researchers have placed different age norms on these accomplishments. The differences are due to a number of factors, including the criteria used to assess success at a task or the timing of the observations. Perhaps you have met parents who tell you how early their children sat up or scooted over to the sofa on their own. Precocious motor development does occur, but it is not related to higher intelligence scores on its own (Illingworth, 1974). However, early emergence of motor abilities allows the child more freedom to explore the environment, to do things on his or her own, and thus to learn. Studies of the gifted show that they walk about a month earlier than average (Kirk & Gallagher, 1979), which is certainly not a significant advantage. Greatly retarded motor development should always be investigated, but even some children who demonstrate delayed development may have normal intelligence.

THE QUESTION OF CULTURAL DIFFERENCES Although individual differences in the rate of motor development are well accepted, the question of cultural differences is more difficult to resolve. More than thirty years ago, Geber & Dean (1957) noted that African infants were more advanced motorically at birth than European infants. A number of other cross-cultural studies followed. Some research supported these findings (Keefer, Dixon, Tronick & Brazelton, 1978), while other research cast doubt on the conclusions (Warren & Parkin, 1974). The question of just how African and European infants differ at birth is still controversial. How-

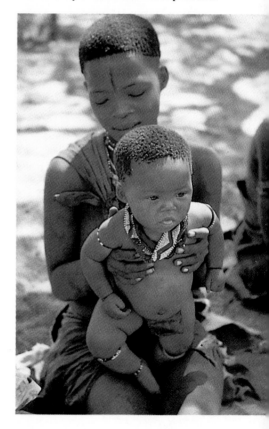

African infants are frequently developmentally ahead of European and American children on motor skills. These are the same skills on which they receive the most practice.

FIGURE 5.3: The Sequence of Motor Development Leading to Walking

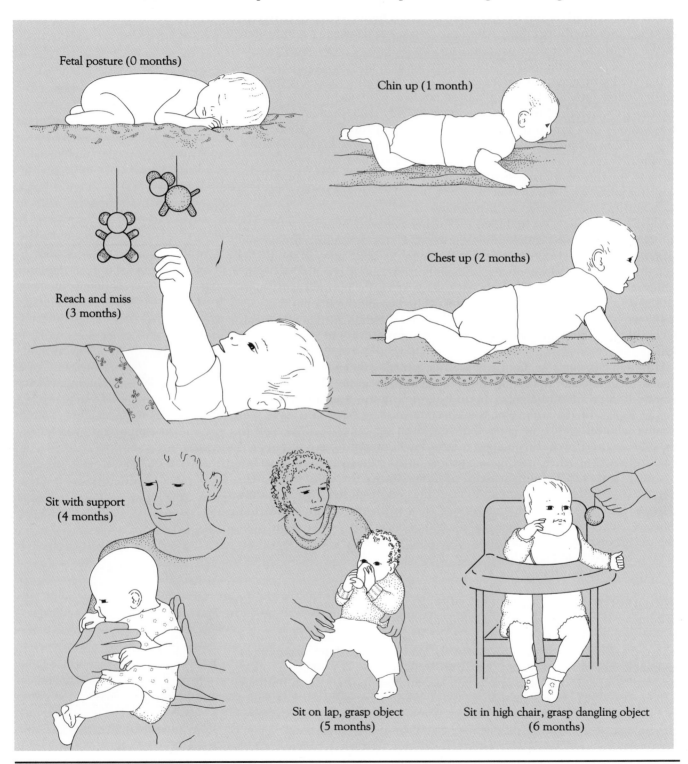

Fetal posture (0 months)

Chin up (1 month)

Chest up (2 months)

Reach and miss (3 months)

Sit with support (4 months)

Sit on lap, grasp object (5 months)

Sit in high chair, grasp dangling object (6 months)

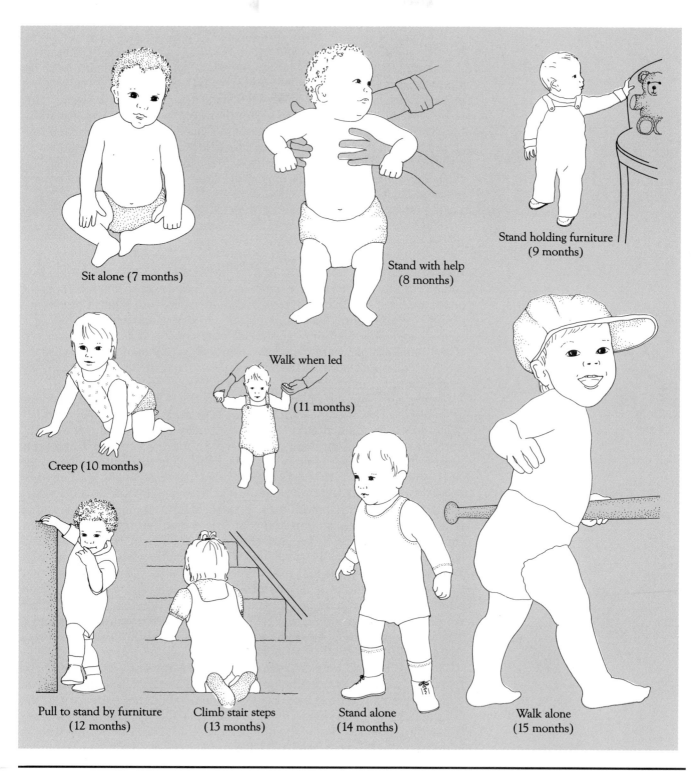

Sit alone (7 months)

Stand with help
(8 months)

Stand holding furniture
(9 months)

Creep (10 months)

Walk when led
(11 months)

Pull to stand by furniture
(12 months)

Climb stair steps
(13 months)

Stand alone
(14 months)

Walk alone
(15 months)

Source: Shirley, 1933.

ever, most researchers agree that African infants reach motor milestones such as sitting and walking before European or American infants do (see Super, 1981).

How can we explain these differences? The most obvious explanation involves a difference in the rate of maturation, which is largely influenced by genetics. While this may be partially true, another explanation is possible. In many African societies, infants are reinforced for their motor behavior, even at very early ages. Parents play games with them using these emerging motor skills. In some tribes, mothers begin walking training very early, and African children are placed in a sitting position and supported much more often than are American babies. Differences in childrearing procedures may partly explain the motor advancement. African infants are precocious on motor skills on which they receive the most practice (Super, 1981).

This raises two questions. First, what is the effect of lack of practice on the development of motor skills? Second, can motor skills be accelerated through a special training program?

THE EFFECTS OF PRACTICE AND STIMULATION No one doubts that some opportunity to practice motor skills is necessary for development of those skills, but there are many roads to mastering them. Dennis and Dennis (1940) found that Hopi Indian children who were reared in a restrictive environment through the use of the cradleboard walked at about at the same age as infants not reared on the cradleboard. These children received excellent stimulation and were allowed off the cradleboard as they matured.

Dennis and Najarian (1957) investigated the development of children growing up in an orphanage in Lebanon. These children showed retarded development in their first year, but by the age of four or six, they were normal. These children were given greater opportunities to explore their environment after age one and this was sufficient to counter their poor early environments. Although Dennis admitted that severe malnutrition results in motor retardation, he does not believe that it caused the retardation in these particular children. Instead, Dennis argued that it was due to environmental restriction and that this deficit could be remedied. If corrected, the effects of a deprived environment can be reduced, and children can motorically catch up. If nothing improves, such children would not develop normal motor abilities. Finally, Dennis argued that Shirley's mean ages at which children achieve motor milestones are met only under favorable environmental conditions (Dennis, 1960). In other words, maturation alone is not sufficient to explain motor development. The environment must be stimulating and provide opportunities for practice as well.

There is, though, one necessary caution in the interpretation of the research on motor development. Generally, when studying motor development, the maturational aspects have been considered primary and the environment given a distinctly secondary place. The documented cases of catchup have also unfortunately been used to place environment as an afterthought. However, Michael Razel (1988) noted that in three studies of isolation and deprivation of infants the results did not show a complete catchup. The idea that a small amount of practice later on is as good as a great deal of practice earlier is simply not true. These infants suffered severe and long-lasting difficulties. Therefore, although later training may help, the idea that the infant does not suffer from the early deprivation or that such deprivation can be completely compensated for is inaccurate. The environment must provide meaningful opportunities for practice.

In most homes, children receive at least minimal stimulation and some opportunity to explore their environment. The question, then, is not one of overcoming stimulus deprivation. Rather, parents are interested in the possibility of hastening motor development. To that purpose, a number of programs aimed at improving motor development have been advanced, and some research has shown them to be effective. Zelazo and his colleagues (1972) found that a specific program of practice capitalizing on the stepping reflex enabled children to walk at an earlier age than expected. This is still a controversial question, however, and evidence for both sides exists (Ridenour, 1978). Parents should be wary of stimulation programs that promise large gains in motor and cognitive development. Our efforts would be better spent on optimizing the environment, allowing each child to take advantage of opportunities to explore and learn when the child is ready.

◆ THREATS TO THE SURVIVAL AND HEALTH OF INFANTS

Most infants born in developed countries survive and thrive. However, the threat to infants in the third world due to poor health practices and malnutrition is great. In the United States, pockets of malnutrition exist, but not in as severe a form as found in underdeveloped countries. Often malnutrition is combined with poor housing, poor health care and poor health practices as well, increasing the danger to the child.

Not all threats are as well understood as malnutrition. Less well understood is Sudden Infant Death Syndrome or (SIDS), which is responsible for many infant deaths in the United States and throughout the world.

Infant Malnutrition

Unfortunately, malnutrition is not rare, It is estimated that 18 percent of the world's children are undernourished and three percent to seven percent are severely malnourished (deMaeyer, 1976). Other figures are higher, and malnutrition in some areas of the world is the norm. Approximately 86 percent of all infants are born in third-world countries, many of them under conditions of extreme poverty (Lozoff, 1989). Laboratory studies of inadequately fed animals indicate that malnutrition leads to deficits in the size and number of brain cells (Dobbing, 1975), and autopsies of severely malnourished infants show that such infants have between 15 percent and 20 percent fewer brain cells than average healthy infants (Winick & Rosso, 1969, Winick, Rosso & Waterloo, 1970).

marasmus
A condition of severe underweight, heart irregularities, and weakened resistance caused by malnutrition.

kwashiorkor
A nutritional problem often found in newly weaned children who are then subjected to a protein-deficient diet.

protein-calorie deficiency
The most common nutritional deficiency in the world, in which neither the number of calories nor the protein consumed is sufficient.

Three of the most commonly asked questions about malnutrition are: How much of the problem of undernourished children is due to malnutrition and how much to family poverty? To what degree are the effects of malnutrition reversible: and What are the effects of various types of nutritional programs on the growth and development of children (Super, Herrera, & Nora, 1990)? We now have some of the answers to these questions.

Infants who are severely undernourished can develop **marasmus,** a condition that involves severe underweight and other physical problems. These children are literally all skin and bones. Their heart is weakened, and their resistance to disease is low. Between the ages of one and three, third-world children can suffer from a common form of malnutrition that involves a protein deficiency called **kwashiorkor,** which comes from the Ghanaian word meaning "the evil spirit that infects the first child when the second child is born" (Hamilton & Whitney, 1982). This occurs in the newly weaned child when the child is subjected to a diet that is very deficient in protein. In this disorder, the child becomes apathetic and inactive, which is probably the body's defense against the malnutrition. Fluid fills the abdomen and legs, and the child is quite weak. Often normal childhood diseases become life threatening. Most of the time, protein and calorie deficiencies are found together (Hamilton & Whitney, 1982). In the third world, this combination, called **protein-calorie deficiency,** is the most common nutritional problem, contributing to the death of literally millions of children each year.

Although such severe cases of malnutrition are rare in Western developed countries, they do sometimes occur in the poorest areas of those nations. However, a number of other deficiencies exist in developed countries. The most common is iron deficiency anemia. In addition, deficiencies in vitamin A, vitamin C, and riboflavin (a B vitamin) are not unusual (Eichorn, 1979). The effects of severe vitamin deficiencies are physically obvious, but the consequences of mild to moderate deficiencies are controversial.

THE LONG-TERM CONSEQUENCES OF MALNUTRITION Malnourished children suffer severe growth problems, and malnutrition may permanently affect their intellectual and emotional development (Eichenwald & Fry, 1969). As noted, many of these children show changes in the brain, including smaller brain size. We know that the behavioral pattern of listlessness and withdrawal, which is instituted automatically to save energy, also reduces exploration and leads to a lack of stimulation that can adversely affect cognitive development (see Lozoff, 1989). Researchers have recently become more cautious in the interpretation of data (Ricciuti, 1980a), for we now know that the relationship between malnutrition and intellectual development is much more complex than first thought.

Malnutrition is found mostly among the poor. It is difficult to evaluate the independent effects of malnutrition on the child (Ricciuti, 1980b). A malnourished child is probably experiencing poor housing, poor sanitation, little or no medical care, increased exposure to disease, poor feeding and child-care practices, and severely limited educational and vocational opportunities (Ricciuti, 1980b). Much of the earlier evidence linking malnutrition to intellectual and emotional deficits may have confused the injurious effects of malnutrition with those of poverty. One study that did control for the poverty factor was performed in Barbados (Galler, 1984) and compared the behavior and development of 129 schoolage children who suffered from severe protein-calorie malnutrition during their first year of life with 129 classmates of similar social background who did not. All the children in this study were born in healthy condition, and the malnutrition ended after the first year because of various nutritional programs. The malnourished children caught up in growth but continued to show deficits in both cognitive abilities and behavior. Their academic performance was poorer, and they averaged twelve points lower in intelligence. Malnourished children suffered from poor memory and attentional problems, and showed frequent tantrums and crying spells. Early malnutrition, then, appears to have serious long-term consequences.

However, the extent of the recovery and the effects of malnutrition are mediated by the environment. As noted in Chapter 1, Korean children suffering from various degrees of malnutrition and adopted before the age of two by middle-class families developed normal intelligence and did well in school (Winick, Meyer, & Harris, 1975). Richardson (1976) discovered that Jamaican children suffering from early severe malnutrition whose families scored fairly high on social background measures had intelligence scores only slightly lower than average. Malnourished children whose families scored low on social background factors scored far below children whose families scored higher. Malnutrition may have a greater impact on children who come from poor environments. The injurious effects of malnutrition may be moderated by improvements in the home environment.

7. TRUE OR FALSE?

The injurious effects of malnutrition can be reduced by a good environment.

Malnutrition is likely to lead to permanent physical and intellectual damage if it is prolonged, if it occurs early in life, and if it is left untreated (Ricciuti, 1980a); Ricciuti, 1980b). Fieldwork in Guatemala among children who suffer from mild to moderate malnutrition demonstates that dietary supplements can somewhat improve intellectual functioning (Townsend et al., 1982). A number of programs have been instituted, and the results are quite interesting and sometimes surprising (see the Cross-Cultural Current on page 210). Some programs that include nutritional education and improved health care have been more successful. The improvement depends somewhat on the age at which the program is begun—the earlier the better (McKay, Sinisterra, McKay, Gomez & Lloreda, 1978). Just providing nutritional supplements, though, may not be sufficient. If these children are to develop normally, their entire environment must be substantially improved as well.

In industrialized countries, especially among the young and poor, some children do not seem to thrive and grow as expected. These children are also developmentally behind their peers. This **failure to thrive syndrome** is often found among children from poor backgrounds whose parents do not meet their children's psychological needs. These children often show medical problems as well. They are frequently malnourished. Such conditions as paternal alcoholism, unemployment, large family size, closely

failure to thrive syndrome
Failure of a child to develop mentally and physically.

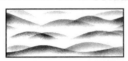

The Effects of Feeding the Hungry . . . After the Feeding Has Stopped

It seems so easy. Simply feed those who are hungry. Yet, it is not as easy as we might think. Providing food has entailed very large costs and many administrative difficulties. In addition, although there have been developmental gains, often such gains have been modest. Some authorities claim that although nutrition is certainly an important step in the right direction, we need family counseling and a change in the environment if we are to expect major gains. On a more technical level, we need fair evaluations of programs, since we have limited resources and must spend our money wisely. Unfortunately, controlled studies in the area of nutritional supplementation and/or family-oriented education programs are not numerous, and the question of the true effects of various programs is often obscured by the confounding influence of family, socioeconomic, and other differences.

It was just this need for controlled studies that made a study performed in Bogota, Columbia, so important. Subjects in the study came from very poor neighborhoods. Two-thirds lived in shacks with limited access to running water and hygienic waste disposal. The remaining third lived in small apartments with communal water and cooking. To be included in the study, the mother had to be pregnant (first or second trimester), the father had to be living with the family, and their young children had to show signs of malnutrition. This certainly made the fetus a candidate for malnutrition and the other problems that come with it. All families were provided with free obstetric and pediatric health care.

The idea of the study was to determine the effects of two interventions carried out from the last trimester of pregnancy through thirty-six months of age. Subjects were randomly assigned to groups that received either nutritional intervention, a home visitation program designed to instruct parents on ways to promote cognitive development, or a combination of the two. A control group that would receive neither would serve as a yardstick against which

to measure the consequences of the intervention. The nutritional intervention consisted of providing the entire family with food supplements, together with demonstrations about hygienic preparation and storage of food. The home visitation program consisted of a trained paraprofessional who helped the parents learn ways of stimulating the child, playing with the child, and improving parent-child interaction. These paraprofessionals also gave parents support in times of need.

Some of the results can be found in Table 1. Notice that food supplementation increased height and weight of the children compared to the control group. Head circumference was also somewhat larger. Home visits themselves had no effect. However, the combination of the two interventions had the greatest positive effect. Food supplementation and, to a lesser extent, home visitation reduced the number of children with stunted growth.

The interventions all stopped when the children were three years old. The children were examined again at age six after three years without any intervention. Here is an important test of the effect of early supplementation. Would the benefits still exist? At this time, some astounding results were found, as shown in Table 2. As you can see, the food-supplemented children retained their advantage over

TABLE 1: Group Statistics at 3 Years of Age

GROUP	WEIGHT	HEIGHT	HEAD CIRCUMFERENCE
	kg	cm	(mm)
A (control)	11.890	85.4	46.7
D (supplemented)..	12.260	87.5	47.1
A1 (home visited)..	11.702	85.3	46.8
D1 (both)..........	12.615	88.5	47.1

spaced children, physical illness in other family members, and social isolation are related to failure to thrive (Lozoff, 1989). Many of the parents of these children are overwhelmed by stresses. It is obvious, then, that there is a need for programs in developed countries as well. Last, nutri-

the control group in both height and weight, although only the advantage in height is statistically significant. However, look at those who were visited at home. Now three years after termination of the intervention, children who had been visited at home were taller and heavier than the control group. Note also that the group that received both interventions was far heavier and taller than those who had received only one or the other intervention. The earlier effect of reducing extreme growth retardation was still present although somewhat weaker at six years of age. Fifty-five percent of the children in the control group showed stunted growth, compared with 17 percent for the group who received both food supplementation and home visitation.

Just how did the home visitation influence growth? There is evidence that the home visitation group's protein intake exceeded that of the control group, even though the visitation curriculm did not include any nutritional information. The causes of this nutritional boost may have come from the changing parent-child interaction. Mothers became more enthusiastic about their children's early development, and fathers became much more involved with their children. They seem to have directed energy and resources towards their children and improved nutrition may have been the result.

The persistent effect of these interventions three years after they had been terminated is important. This is particularly true of the group that received both interventions. This finding gives researchers hope that the gains might continue into adolescence. The fact that the effect of the home visits showed a delayed action effect is also interesting. At three, there was a reduction in the incidence of growth retardation somewhat smaller than for food supplementation, and home visits did not affect typical patterns of growth. Three years later, the effects were visible. The children of the families who had received home visits showed an average growth advantage of about three-quarters of those who had been given food supplements only. Again, the combination was best.

This study is significant for a number of reasons. First, it was methodologically superior to many others, using randomization of subjects. However, this raises an interesting question. Since we know a great deal about the benefits of nutrition, should we supplement the diets of some children in need and not others? This is a difficult question and demonstrates the need to balance our desire for good experimental methodology and our duty to others.

The study's findings that early food supplementation has a significant and long-lasting effect answer an important question. Of particular importance is the large reduction in the number of cases of severe growth retardation. The fact that home visitation showed a delayed action is interesting and surprising and demonstrates the possibility that visitation programs may have a gradual and lasting effect. It would be very interesting to discover the cognitive effect home visitation might have on children. Other studies suggest such an effect can be sizable. The delayed effect of home visitation suggests that focusing family attention on early development can successfully lead to better nutrition and a better family atmosphere.

There are many approaches to reducing the problems caused by malnutrition in the third world. It is clear from this study that giving food supplements, helping the family improve parent-child interactions, and providing good medical care can go a long way towards reducing these problems.

TABLE 2: Group Statistics at 6 Years of Age

GROUP	WEIGHT	HEIGHT	HEAD CIRCUMFERENCE
	kg	cm	(mm)
A (control)	17.124	105.1	49.0
D (supplemented)....	17.649	107.7	49.2
A1 (home visited)....	17.561	107.1	49.0
D1 (both)...........	18.108	109.2	49.4

SOURCE: Super, C. M., Herrera, M. G. and Mora, J. O. Long-Term Effects of Food Supplementation and Psychosocial Intervention on the Physical Growth of Columbian Infants at Risk of Malnutrition. *Child Development*, 1990, 61, 29–49.

tional intervention alone will not solve all the problems. We also need family counseling and social support.

We now have some of the answers to the questions asked at the beginning of this section. Malnutrition affects growth and development, but the effects are mediated by the environment. These effects can be reduced through intervention, although there will probably be some remaining effects. Third, both nutritional programs and some sort of family intervention are probably the best strategy.

Sudden Infant Death Syndrome

sudden infant death syndrome (SIDS)
The diagnosis given to young infants whose cause of death cannot be determined.

A century ago, the survival even of infants born at term in good health could not be assured. So many diseases and hazards existed that the death of infants was not an unusual occurrence. Today, however, with better understanding of the conditions that threaten infants and with better medical care, many more infants survive. One malady that has remained mysterious and that causes thousands of infant deaths a year is **sudden infant death syndrome (SIDS),** commonly called crib death. Perhaps as many as 10,000 infants in the United States die from this mysterious killer every year (DeFrain, Taylor & Ernst, 1982). Victims are most likely to be between two and four months of age. Some 90 percent are younger than six months; 97 percent are younger than one year.

No family, regardless of income and social status, is immune to SIDS. While infants who show low birthweight and whose mothers receive poor prenatal care are at greater risk, three-quarters of all SIDS infants are born into economically advantaged families whose mothers received good prenatal care (Blakeslee, 1989). The child who dies of SIDS is likely to have a young mother and a mother who smokes or a mother who has had many children with short intervals between pregnancies (Guntheroth, 1982). However, many mothers of SIDS victims do not fit this pattern.

The cause of sudden infant death syndrome remains elusive. SIDS is indicated only where no other cause of death can be found. It is strange that a healthy infant would die with no apparent cause. However, research has found that these infants may not be as healthy as they first seem. Between 40 percent and 50 percent of SIDS victims suffer from some respiratory infection right before their death. Some have a history of stress both before and after birth. The Apgar scores of these infants are significantly lower than those of babies who did not suffer from SIDS (Guntheroth, 1982). These babies, then, appear to be members of an at-risk population, although they are essentially normal.

Because many victims of SIDS suffer from mild respiratory infections, research interest has centered on finding a relationship between SIDS and respiration. Many infants stop breathing for brief periods during sleep (a condition known as apnea). However, the SIDS infant does not have any more of these apneic spells than do babies who do not die of SIDS. Perhaps the SIDS victim does not recover from these periods. But why? The SIDS victim may be weaker and possibly does not develop the ability to react to threats to survival. Lewis Lipsitt (1978) argues this theory. In the first month or so, the infant's defensive reactions to respiratory distress are reflexive. However, a learned reaction soon takes its place. Perhaps the victim of SIDS fails to learn to defend against such dangers because of some subtle neurological problem. Some researchers look at the developing brain for the clue. As previously noted, as new brain connections are being formed, myelin sheathing is taking place and old connections are dissolved. Perhaps something goes wrong with these critical switches. Other researchers are looking at subtle defects in the different parts of the brain, including the brain stem, which is responsible for breathing and heart rates during sleep (Blakeslee, 1989).

At times, we can predict which infants will be at risk for the disorder, but again, not all SIDS victims fit any specific pattern. Among those who are most at risk are infants who have suffered an oxygen deficiency, have a high apnea rate, or have almost died once from the disorder. These infants may be monitored in their own home using an apnea monitor, a device that rings an alarm if the infant stops breathing for a specific period of time, allowing parents to respond to the problem. Use of a monitor does not guarantee the infant's survival. Some infants on monitors have died when they could not be revived. In addition, the monitor may cause parents much distress. Parents might feel that they cannot go out or use a noisy appliance because they will not be able to hear the monitor ring (Guntheroth, 1982).

Sudden infant death syndrome is a family tragedy. Parents suffer self-doubt, guilt, and pain. There is a high rate of marital problems and divorce following the experience. When a child is born very prematurely or suffers some lingering disease, parents have time to prepare for the possibility of an impending death, but SIDS does not afford parents that opportunity. The shock is great, the questions are many, and the answers are few.

Parents of SIDS victims can be helped to cope with their grief. Emotional support is available from groups of parents who have suffered similar tragedies. Parents of SIDS victims are given an opportunity in the groups to discuss their feelings and help one another. Professionals may also aid the family by offering parents the facts as we know them today. Sometimes just the knowledge that an autopsy shows no cause of death alleviates some of the guilt.

Sudden infant death syndrome is a mystery. Today, there is hope that with research we may learn more about its causes and eventually be able to prevent this silent killer from striking.

♦ CHOICES IN PARENTING

Most of the choices that affect the child in infancy and toddlerhood are made by the parents. These include feeding, the differences in which children are treated because of their gender, how to deal with the toddler's increasing physical abilities and toilet training.

Breastfeeding or Bottlefeeding

One of the first choices parents must make is whether to breastfeed or bottlefeed their baby. Indeed, a great deal has been written on the subject, some of it misleading. Infants' nutritional needs are different from those of adults (see Figure 5.4), and nutritional decisions throughout infancy

FIGURE 5.4: Nutrient Needs of Three-Month-Olds and Adult Males
(per unit of body weight)
The infant's nutritional needs are vastly different from those of his or her
parents. In the graph, the adult's needs are set at 100 percent.

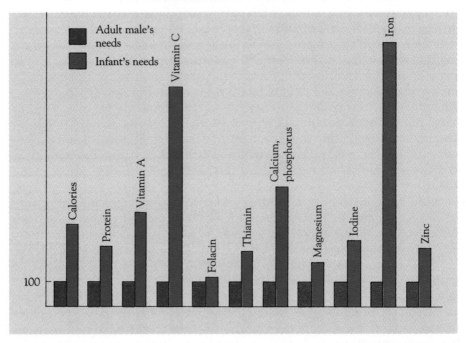

Source: Hamilton et al., 1985.

8. TRUE OR FALSE?

There has been a significant increase in the percentage of mothers who are electing to breastfeed rather than bottlefeed their infants.

and childhood are important to the future health of the child. Although bottlefeeding is very popular in the United States, there has recently been a resurgence of breastfeeding. In 1970, only one-quarter of all new mothers were breastfeeding. In 1989, that figure was about two-thirds (Brody, 1989). In underdeveloped nations, the unfortunate trend away from breastfeeding has been checked, which is an important advance. Without the medical and social checks available in the United States, formula-fed infants may not be getting proper nutrition. Some infant deaths from misuse of prepared infant formulas have been reported. In addition, many parents in underdeveloped countries cannot afford formula. In an attempt to encourage breastfeeding, some countries now severely restrict the importation and use of infant formulas.

There are a number of benefits to breastfeeding. Mother's milk is the natural food for human infants and meets all the requirements for infants, with the possible exception of vitamin D (Woodruff, 1978). Vitamin D deficiency is rarely seen in breastfed infants, though, since that vitamin is synthesized with the help of a normal amount of exposure to sunlight. Mother's milk contains a number of helpful substances not found in prepared formulas. Some antibodies protect the infant against intestinal disorders, and immunities are passed on in breast milk. Although environmental pollutants, such as insecticides, are sometimes found in breast milk, to date, there is no evidence that these chemicals lead to any illnesses in the infant (Rogan, Baniewsha & Damstra, 1980). Mother's milk contains chemicals that promote the absorption of iron. In addition, the incidence of allergies is less in breastfed infants than in infants raised on artificial formulas. Breastfeeding also promotes better tooth and jaw alignment (Hamilton, Whitney & Sizer, 1985). There are significant psychological benefits to the infant who is breastfeeding. The close contact between mother and child encourages the growth and development of the mother-infant bond and satisfies the infant's need for warmth and physical contact.

On the other hand, we now know that some claims made for breastfeeding are incorrect. In the past, it was assumed that breastfed babies consumed only what they needed, whereas bottle-fed infants were encouraged to overconsume. Indeed, breastfed babies consume about 20 percent fewer calories (Brody, 1989). However, we know now that this is because breastfed babies expend less energy when feeding and that when breastfed infants sleep, their metabolic rate is lower than bottle fed infants. Studies of infants both at four months and at four years found no difference with regard to obesity (Brody, 1989).

What about the effects of breastfeeding on the mother? One of the benefits for the mother is that breastfeeding can cut the risk of breast cancer (DeBruyne & Rolfes, 1989). Breastfeeding can also aid in restoring a woman's body to its normal state, since infant sucking stimulates the nerves controlling the muscles of the uterus, causing them to contract and returning the uterus to its normal size. Producing milk also requires energy, which can help mothers lose weight. However, it does not promote easy rapid weight loss. There is some evidence for an increase in bone loss from the spine and hips of women who breastfeed, but the loss seems reversible (Brody, 1989).

Breastfeeding is nutritionally sound. But what about bottlefeeding with prepared formulas? Some advocates of breastfeeding make outlandish, unsubstantiated claims about the benefits of breast milk, and this may make mothers who wish to bottlefeed feel guilty. There is no evidence, however, of long-term differences between breastfed and bottlefed babies (Schmidt, 1979). Nevertheless, whereas the infant's nutritional and psychological needs are normally satisfied naturally during breastfeeding, bottlefeeding may require more thought and concern. The caregiver must be certain to hold the baby close to give the child the physical contact that is so important to infants.

Today, many infant formulas meet the nutritional standards set by the Committee on Nutrition of the American Academy of Pediatrics. Most formulas are based on fortified cow's milk, but the incidence of allergies to cow's milk in infants is estimated to be less than one percent (Woodruff, 1978). A mother may need to bottle feed if she is taking certain medications.

The decision to breastfeed does not have to be a long-term decision. Most women discontinue breastfeeding by four months, which is long

9. TRUE OR FALSE?

An infant can be adequately fed using prepared formula rather than breast milk.

enough to give the infant the immunological and other special advantages (DeBruyne & Rolfes, 1989). In conclusion, although breastfeeding may be preferable, there is no reason that a loving, caring parent should feel guilty about bottlefeeding an infant.

Gender

"It's a boy!" the doctor announced. "A boy," repeated George Ellsworth, with a look of wonder on his face. He began to think of all the things he wanted for his son and the things they would do together—like play ball and work on model airplanes. "How strong he looks," George said to a friend as the looked at the infant through the nursery window.

"It's a girl!" the doctor announced. "A girl," repeated George Ellsworth, with a look of wonder on his face. He began to think of all the things she would do, like play with dolls. "How cute and delicate she looks," George said to a friend as they looked at the infant through the nursery window.

The first announcement made to parents is the baby's gender. In fact, the first question people ask when told a new baby has arrived concerns gender (Intons-Peterson & Reddel, 1984). How important is gender to the way infants are treated? Do any inborn physical differences exist at birth?

GENDER DIFFERENCES AT BIRTH The question of what gender differences are present at birth is difficult to answer. There are contradictions throughout the literature. When differences are demonstrated, they tend to be moderate and unstable (Moss, 1974). Many experimental findings of gender differences have not held up under further investigation (Birns, 1976). Overlap is also common. For instance, if newborn females are more sensitive to certain stimuli, as when a blanket is removed (Bell & Costello, 1964), this does not mean that every female infant will be more sensitive than every male infant. Individual differences must also be taken into account. Still, some differences do appear in the first few days after birth.

One of the most consistent differences is that females are physically more mature at birth and continue to develop at a faster rate than males. Girls are four weeks more advanced in skeletal development at birth (Tanner, 1970), and they reach motor milestones faster than males. The average female child sits up, walks, toilet trains, and talks earlier than the average male child (Kalat, 1980). Another difference is that the average female infant performs more rhythmic behaviors, such as sucking and smiling, than the average male infant (Feldman, Brody & Miller, 1980; Korner, 1973). Still another difference is that males exceed females in large musculature movements, such as kicking. They also show greater muscular strength and can lift their heads higher at birth (Korner, 1973).

HOW PARENTS VIEW SONS AND DAUGHTERS These early differences may affect parental behavior, magnifying the effects of the differences. The more developmentally superior females may be more responsive to parents. Being capable of doing things at an early age may be more rein-

10. TRUE OR FALSE?

Females are physically more mature at birth and continue to develop at a faster rate.

forcing to the parents. Advanced development could then lead to more attention and different types of interaction with the caregivers.

The differences in how parents treat their sons and daughters are more often based upon the different expectations they hold for their children rather than on any real differences between the children. For example, even when male and female infants are the same size, weight, and physical condition, parents see daughters as weaker and more sickly and see males as sturdier and more athletic (Rubin, Provenzano & Luria, 1974). When parents who had not even held their newborns but had merely seen them behind the nursery glass were asked to describe their children, both fathers and mothers described their sons as more alert and stronger and the daughters as more delicate (Rubin et al., 1974). Parents show more concern for the health of daughters than sons (Pedersen & Robson, 1969), even though the male infants are more likely to become seriously ill.

Some indirect evidence indicates that this labeling process continues throughout infancy and toddlerhood. College students were shown videotapes of nine-month-old infants demonstrating negative responses to a loud buzzer (Condry & Condry, 1976). When subjects were told that the infants were male, they described the emotion as anger, but if the infants were described as female, the emotion was labeled fear. In another study, Meyer & Sobieszek (1972) showed videotapes of seventeen-month-old children, describing them as either males and females to male subjects. When the child was labeled male, the men described the child in such stereotyped terms as independent, aggressive, and active. They interpreted those same actions as delicate, passive, and dependent when they were told the toddler was a female. In still another study, thirteen-month-old infants were observed in a play group. Although no gender differences were found in assertive acts or attempts to communicate with adults, the adults attended more to boys' assertive behaviors and less to those of girls. However, adults attended more to girls when they used less intense forms of communication. Eleven months later, gender differences were observed as boys were more assertive but girls talked to the adults who conducted the play groups more (Hagan, Leinbach, & Kronsbert, 1985). From birth on, we perceive and interpret the behaviors of males and females differently. Men are more likely than women to see gender-stereotyped behavior. But does this differential perception lead to differential treatment?

DO PARENTS TREAT SONS AND DAUGHTERS DIFFERENTLY? In their mammoth review of the literature on gender differences, Eleanor Maccoby and Carol Jacklin (1974) were more impressed with the similarities in treatment than with the differences. Although their conclusions have been criticized by some (Block, 1976), we should be wary of claims that a particular difference in treatment leads to some recognizable difference later in life. Most studies are not constructed to allow the jump from early infant treatment to later behavioral differences.

Some studies do find differences in parental treatment, but again, interpretation is difficult. At birth, mothers appear to talk and smile more to

11. TRUE OR FALSE?

Parents see male infants as sturdier than female infants.

girls than to boys (Thoman, Leiderman & Olson, 1972). The qualitative nature of their speech differs as well. They use longer sentences and more repetition than do mothers of boys (Cherry & Lewis, 1976). Male infants receive more physical contact than females, but this changes by three months, when girls receive more contact (Moss, 1967). In later infancy, mothers talk to and play more with daughters than sons. By thirteen months, daughters touch their mothers more than sons (Goldberg & Lewis, 1969).

The opposite pattern is found in fathers' interactions with their infants. In early infancy, fathers spoke more to daughters than to sons (Rubelsky & Hanks, 1971), but this changed at about three months, with fathers verbalizing more to male infants than to female infants. However, the evidence indicates that fathers do not interact much with their infants at this stage. Since most infants spend so much more of their time with their mothers, the verbal interchange between mother and child is perhaps more important in promoting language development than that between father and infant.

As boys and girls develop, other differences in treatment become more noticeable. Smith and Lloyd (1978) noted how a mother's behavior is affected by her perception of gender. Seven toys were placed on a table within reach of a subject who was asked to play with an infant between five and ten months old. Some of the toys were considered stereotyped "male," such as a squeaky hammer and a stuffed rabbit wearing trousers and a bow tie. Some were sterotyped "feminine," such as a doll and a squeaky Bambi. A squeaky pig, a plush ball, and an hourglass-shaped rattle were considered "neutral." The baby's mother presented the infant to the subjects by name. Each baby was dressed in clothing that made the gender seem obvious. Actually, the babies were properly identified to the subject as to gender only sometimes—at other times they were cross-dressed and misrepresented. The subjects presented the doll or the hammer to the baby only when the toy appeared to be gender appropriate.

DATAGRAPHIC

Bringing Up Baby

Source: American Demographic, January 1990, p. 37.

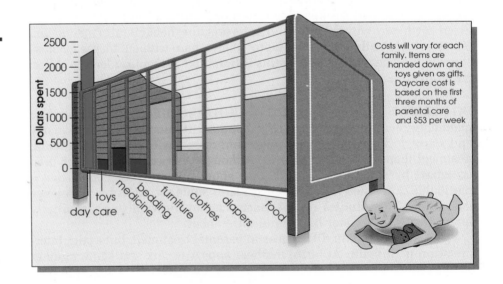

They also reinforced babies perceived as males more often for efforts to crawl, walk, or use their large muscles. Thus, males are reinforced in their attempts to develop their gross motor skills, which involve large-scale physical play.

These differential patterns of reinforcement are also seen with samples of two-year-olds. Beverly Fagot (1978) observed parent-child interactions in twenty-four families, rating forty-six child behaviors and nineteen parental reactions to them. Boys were allowed to play alone more often, and parents were more likely to play with boys than with girls. Girls received more praise and more criticism than boys. Both parents were more likely to stop the play activities of boys. Parents gave more positive feedback to boys when they played with blocks and more negative reaction when they played with dolls. Parents reacted more negatively when girls manipulated objects than when this was done by boys. Girls also received more positive responses when they played with dolls than did boys. Again consistent with other research, fathers seemed more concerned with gender appropriate behavior, giving more negative feedback to boys playing with dolls and other soft toys. Parents criticized girls more often when they attempted to participate in large motor activities such as running, jumping, and climbing. More positive responses were given for their daughters' requests for help.

Parents did not, however, want to restrict their children's playmates to the same gender, nor would they avoid buying what they considered a gender-inappropriate toy if the child wanted it. They showed a willingness to allow the child to follow his or her own pattern of interests as the child grew older, no matter whether they were stereotyped gender-appropriate or not. Some 80 percent planned to encourage an attitude of gender equality in their children as they grew.

In another study, mothers and fathers were videotaped playing with their one-year-old to two-year-old children on two occasions (Eisenberg, Wolchik, Hernandez, & Pasternack, 1985). No differential reinforcement of boys and girls for masculine or neutral play was found, but the gender of the child affected parents' choices of toys to use during the interactions. Parents of boys chose more neutral and masculine toys, and parents of girls chose more neutral toys. Parental toy choice but not parental reinforcement was related to children's play choices. Parents did not actively dissuade or reinforce their young children with regard to playing with toys they chose themselves. However, merely by selecting play items, parents encouraged their children toward some toys and away from others.

In summary, studies show that the child's gender does affect parental treatment. Females receive more verbal feedback and are given more praise for helping and playing with dolls as well as more negative feedback for using gross motor skills. On the other hand, males receive positive encouragement to develop their gross motor skills and are not encouraged to play in a stereotyped "gender-inappropriate" manner.

INTERPRETING EARLY DIFFERENCES While gender is a biological fact of life, people often exaggerate its importance. Three main conclusions stand out quite clearly from the research on gender differences in early

Does the parents' early treatment of their sons and daughters lead to gender differences later in life?

life. First, the initial differences between male and female infants are quite limited at birth (Bee, 1978), confined mostly to the greater number of mouth movements and the faster maturation of females. These may have meaning, because the female infant is more likely to reinforce her parents for social behaviors than the young male.

Second, the treatment of males and females tends to be more similar than different, although the differences may in the end turn out to be important. Parents give both sons and daughters affection and do not generally tolerate aggression from either. However, there is evidence that different patterns of behavior, even in the early years, are reinforced differentially. Males receive greater reinforcement for engaging in physical play, while girls are positively reinforced for asking for help from others and for helping others. Both are reinforced for playing with gender-appropriate toys. Their rooms are even furnished differently. Rheingold and Cook (1975) found that boys' bedrooms not only had more toys but were also gender-related. Athletic equipment was more commonly found in boy's rooms, while the rooms of girls contained more dolls and flowers. The environment itself is shaped at an early age to encourage gender-stereotyped behavior.

Third, although parents often do not vocalize their gender-stereotyped opinions, they may show them in some of their behaviors toward their children. Fathers are stricter in reinforcing these stereotyped gender-appropriate behaviors, especially in their sons, than are mothers. This conclusion is supported by research as well as everyday experience, as a story related by Shirley Weitz (1977) indicates. Weitz was gift shopping for a pregnant friend. She rejected the thought of buying something pink, which would be inappropriate if the baby were male, and looked for something blue, which could be worn by both males and females, or a neutral yellow. She was considering an outfit that had a few ruffles but wasn't frilly or feminine, when the saleswoman said, "I wouldn't buy that if I were you. If the baby's a boy, the father won't want him to wear that" (Weitz, 1977, p. 66). Weitz realized the saleswoman was correct and made another choice. The saleswoman knew it would be the father, not the mother, who would object. Parents are frequently unaware of how they may affect the development of their children and may need consciousness raising if they are to follow their stated aim of allowing children to develop their own abilities.

Dealing with Toddlers

"Infants are easy," said Daphne, running after her two-year-old, who was heading for parts unknown. "You play with them, feed them, change them, and put them in their cribs. . . where they stay." Daphne, as well as most mothers of toddlers, can tell you that dealing with two-year-olds is different. The skills of a two-year-old in walking, muscle control, and communication makes raising one a challenge. Anyone who has ever cared for a two-year-old during the day knows that two-year-olds are active, engaging beings with a mind of their own.

The world is an exciting place to the toddler. There is so much to do

Young toddlers learn by physically doing things. They enjoy repetition.

and explore. Toddlers go until they drop, often becoming very cranky but refusing to take a nap. Sometimes toddlers will just drop and sleep wherever they have been playing. They prefer the wide open spaces and dislike confinement.

There is an exciting quality to their newfound capabilities, and they go from one activity to another with breathtaking speed. No one can mess up a room like a toddler. They have energy that seems unbounded. Yet they can easily get themselves in trouble. They seem to miss the edges of tables by inches, but accidents are common at this age. The toddler is often thrilled by the underside of sinks and cabinets, mainly because these items are at eye level. Toddlers often become interested in things that parents miss on a casual inspection of an area. This is why it is important that caregivers carefully evaluate the child's environment. It is a good idea for parents to get down on their knees to look at the room as a toddler might. One parent who did this found nails sticking out of a piece of paneling that could have injured a child.

Toddlers are no longer completely dependent on other people. This independence is seen in their increasing annoyance when their activities are interrupted or are offered unwanted help. They want to do things in their own way. They have the physical abilities but not necessarily the understanding of what might happen when they do something. For example, that lovely vase within reach of the toddler may well be a thing of the past. It is not that the toddler wants to break it, it is that she may

Toddlers have a great deal of energy and, because they do not always know what is dangerous, must be constantly monitored.

not know that it breaks. Even if you tell her, she may not connect what you are saying with her behavior (Oppenheim, Boegehold, & Brenner, 1984). The toddler is also quite impatient and does not want to wait. There is so much to do and so many things to explore.

As children progress between ages one and three, their verbal abilities improve markedly. They use the word *no* constantly and understand commands even though they may be unable or unwilling to carry them out. By age two, a child may use up to 270 words, can understand many more, and is beginning to put two and three words together. Two-year-olds use their verbal skills to show their independence, saying *"no," "me do it,"* and *"mine"* often. The increased motor behavior, desire for independence, and tendency to get into trouble is why parents often call this age the terrible twos.

But is that label appropriate? Look at the following descriptions of toddlers:

1. Toddlers don't sit still for a minute. They have short attention spans and are highly distractible. They always want their own way and won't share or take turns. Toys always get lost or broken when toddlers play with them.
2. Toddlers are active explorers. They eagerly try new things and use materials in different ways. Toddlers want to be independent and have a strong sense of ownership (Gonzalez-Mena, 1986).

Much of the reason parents believe that their toddlers are so difficult is that they compare them with older children. They also sometimes long for the days when their children's schedules as infants allowed for longer naps.

The second description emphasizes the toddler's natural curiosity and behavior. Simply stated, many people have inappropriate expectations for toddlers and simply do not understand the way toddlers learn. Toddlers learn with their whole bodies (Gonzalez-Mena, 1986). They learn much more through active manipulation than through listening. They are action oriented. If you observe toddlers for a few minutes, this becomes obvious. Toddlers become explorers and absorbed in their world. They do not have a short attention span for their age. When toddlers become interested in something, they can attend to it for a long time. Toddlers enjoy putting things in containers and dumping them out. As toddlers approach about three, they develop simple skills in the area of eye-hand coordination, and some of what seems like random exploration is reduced. The progression from movement that appears to occur just for the sake of movement to more controlled motor activity that seems more oriented towards ends or consequences occurs during toddlerhood (Bullock & Lutkenhaus, 1988).

The choices that parents have in dealing with toddlers are many. It takes special knowledge and skill to understand the toddler, to protect toddlers from what they cannot do or what could injure them, yet not to hover over them, preventing them from learning. Decisions in the area of childproofing are most important. Parents must decide in which areas of the home toys are going to be allowed, where large motor activities that are safe will be encouraged, and how they want to deal with the question of how many items the child can take out to play with at one time.

Toddlers can be very stubborn, and decisions about discipline must be made for the first time. Toddlers will test limits, and power struggles are common. One way to deal with toddlers is to use choices to avoid these struggles (Gonzalez-Mena, 1986). For example, telling a child, "I don't want you walking around while you eat, but you can eat in either the blue chair or the red chair," can resolve a problem. In addition, words may not be sufficient if danger is present, and preventing dangerous behavior by holding an arm before it hits someone or knocks the pot of boiling water off the stove may be necessary. Preventing problems is best, and this often involves understanding that some behaviors, such as wandering about, saying "no," or crying, especially when tired, are to be expected.

Toilet Training

Of all the choices in dealing with very young children, toilet training seems to get the most attention. One of the most common questions is how early to start? McGraw (1940) started to train one twin from each of two pairs as early as two months of age, while their siblings were allowed to wait. The early training did not help. The later trained children trained much more quickly and were soon up to the others. Training started later is faster (Sears, Macoby & Levin, 1957). It is best to train a child when the child is ready.

12. *TRUE OR FALSE?*

The earlier you start to toilet train a child, the shorter the amount of time it takes to do so.

Some parents place a great deal of importance on early toilet training. The expectation that a one-year-old is going to be completely dry day and night not only is unreasonable but also may be harmful, for it can lead to criticism from parents when the child has an accident. Toilet training is a complicated process (Wesley & Sullivan, 1980). The child must learn to pay attention to the signals that the bladder is full, then learn to hold it in until a bathroom is available. Toilet training also requires the maturation of the neurons that govern bowel movements and urination and this varies widely in children. It also requires the child to attend to sensations and perform the necessary actions.

The age at which a child will be ready varies from child to child. Children's bowel control precedes bladder control, and the ability to control elimination during the day precedes the ability to do so at night. Girls are also somewhat ahead of boys. By age three, 84 percent achieve dryness during the day, and 66 percent are dry overnight (Oppel, Harper & Rider, 1968).

Besides the obvious maturational need to control the muscles, there are individual and environmental factors involved in toilet training. Some children do not like being soiled. Others may be aware that friends are not wearing diapers and may train easily and quickly. Still others may require more time and have many accidents. Once a child is maturationally ready, toilet training should not take long, according to Azrin and Foxx (1976), authors of a book on the subject. The authors do not recommend training a child much younger than two years old, and they advocate using reinforcement and imitation. The toddler is carefully taught the mechanics of going to the bathroom, including how to lower and raise his or her pants, and is positively reinforced each step of the way. Then a doll that wets is used to illustrate the elimination process. The child sees the doll placed on a potty and wet. The child is then reinforced for doing the same. Sometimes a candy is used to prompt the child to eliminate. Using this learning technique, the child who is ready can be trained quickly.

The toddler is an active, engaging being who is rapidly gaining the ability to control internal and external aspects of the environment. Control over bladder and bowels gives the child a sense of accomplishment and more freedom from the caregiver. At the same time, developing motor abilities allows toddlers more range to explore their environment.

This chapter has examined the sensory, perceptual, motor, and physical development of the child from birth through toddlerhood. The pattern of increased abilities and skills is impressive. It is clear that the infant is born ready for life, with many abilities that improve rapidly throughout this period. The child makes even more impressive gains in the ability to relate to the world, process information, and communicate. It is to the infant and toddler's developing cognitive abilities that we turn next.

SUMMARY

1. The neonate is born with characteristics and abilities that make survival possible. Newborns can see, hear, smell, and taste. The infant can also experience pain.

2. Neonates spend sixteen to seventeen hours a day sleeping and spend a great deal more time in rapid eye movement sleep than do adults. The infant's sleeping-waking state is related to behavior.

3. A number of cries have been identified in the infant, including the hunger, pain, and mad cries.

4. Classical and operant conditioning have been demonstrated in the infant. Infants can also imitate and habituate.

5. The neonate is born with a number of reflexes, such as the sucking, rooting (turning the head toward a source of stimulation when a cheek is stroked), grasping, stepping, and the swimming reflexes. The functions of other reflexes, such as the Babinski reflex (fanning of the toes when soles of the feet are stroked) and the Moro reflex (extending arms and legs while arching the back, then contracting them in a hugging manner), are not known.

6. The brain grows rapidly in the months following birth, and such factors as nutrition and experience are important in optimizing brain growth.

7. Genetic considerations and nutrition both affect development. Acute illnesses and stress may deflect children from a normal growth projectory, but a self-right-ing process enables children to return to normal when the illness or stress is past. Development occurs in a consistent pattern from the head downward (cephalo-caudal) and from the inside out (proximodistal), and muscular development progresses from mass to specific.

8. Motor development also follows a specific pattern. The rate can be affected by culture, genetic endowment, and the environment. Malnutrition is a major problem in the third world and leads to many developmental problems, including a smaller number of brain cells. The effect of lesser degrees of malnutrition is more controversial. The effects of malnutrition are mediated by the environment.

9. There are nutritional and health advantages to breast-feeding, but there is no evidence of long-term differences between children who were breastfed and those who were bottlefed.

10. Gender differences in infancy are moderate and unstable. Girls are more mature at birth and develop at a faster rate than boys. Females show more oral and facial movements. Males show more large musculature movements, such as kicking, and greater muscular strength.

11. Parents treat their infant sons and daughters differently. Activities requiring gross motor control are more likely to be reinforced in male infants. In toddlerhood,

girls are given more praise and criticism than are boys. Fathers are more rigid with regard to gender-stereotyped behavior than are mothers.

12. Toddlers learn through doing, and they show a desire for independence. During toddlerhood, the child be-gins toilet training. Children who are trained later take less time to train. The toddler's physical abilities often outweigh the child's judgment, making home safety a first priority.

ACTION/REACTION

Doing What Comes Naturally

Penny has a new baby and believes in breastfeeding. She believes it is the natural way to feed an infant and better for both the child and the mother. She has told her younger sister, who is pregnant, that there is no other alternative and that mothers who bottle feed are just plain lazy or ignorant. Penny thinks that the benefits of breastfeeding should be taught in high school, and she approves of the trend away from bottle feeding. She has convinced several of her friends to breastfeed as well.

Last week, Penny and a friend went to a restaurant for lunch. Penny took her baby with herand asked for the last booth. While waiting for her lunch, she began to breastfeed her child. The owner of the restaurant asked her to leave, but Penny refused. She told the owner, "No one has to watch, and what I'm doing is normal and natural. If I had bottle fed the child, no one would care."

1. If you were the owner of the restaurant, what would you have done?
2. If you were Penny's friend, what would you have advised her to do?

Just Let Her Cry?

Margarita and Tomas have two children, Elena (age four years) and Carla (age four months). The only word that describes Elena, according to Elena's parents, is *spoiled*. Elena whines and wants her way with everything, Margarita and Tomas don't want the same thing to happen with Carla.

Tomas believes the problem stems from their early child-rearing practices when they always picked Elena up when she cried. This reinforced Elena for crying. Margarita is not sure about that, but she admits that Elena is now a bit of a problem.

When Carla cries, her parents face a decision. They think they know when she is in pain or has wet diapers, and they always attend to those needs. But when the child is "just crying for attention," what should they do? Should they wait or pick her up? They both find letting the child cry a difficult course of action, but they believe it will be best for all concerned.

Margarita's parents don't agree. They see nothing wrong with Elena and believe it is more important to pick Carla up and comfort her than to "train her."

1. If Margarita asked you how to handle the situation, what advice would you give her?
2. If you were Margarita's parents, would you have offered advice even if you were not asked for it?

CHAPTER SIX

Cognitive Development in Infancy and Toddlerhood

Gabrielle and Jean by Pierre Auguste Renoir.

Intelligence in Infancy
Piaget's Theory of Sensorimotor Development
Information-Processing Skills
Predicting Later Intelligence
Cross-Cultural Current: Raising Infants in Kenya
Parents and the Child's Cognitive Development
Teaching Parents to Parent
The Child in the Year 2000:
Optimizing Infant Cognition: Meeting the Parental Challenge
Conclusions

Are These Statements True or False?

Turn the page for the correct answers. Each statement is repeated in the margin next to the paragraph in which the information can be found.

1. A baby banging a toy against the side of a crib is showing intelligent behavior.
2. The one-month-old infant believes that mother has disappeared when she leaves the room.
3. A five-month-old infant who drops a rattle behind him or her will not turn around and find it.
4. Five-month-old infants show the ability to recognize faces and objects but only for a few minutes, after which they forget them.
5. Infant intelligence tests given to normal infants at six months predict later school achievement fairly well.
6. Parents of competent infants spend many hours teaching their children concepts.
7. Interactions of less than one minute with an infant or a toddler have no effect on the child's cognitive development.
8. Parent-child interactions that are aimed at encouraging cognitive development should be fun for the child.
9. Overstimulation is as great a problem as lack of stimulation.
10. Programs that teach parents how to interact with their children have been largely successful in improving the intellectual functioning of the children.
11. Child development specialists equate fast development with superior development.
12. If children do not receive optimal stimulation by the age of two, they will underachieve throughout their childhood and adolescent years.

Answers to True-False Statements

1. True.
2. True.
3. True.
4. False. Correct statement: Infants of that age show the ability to retain information for days, sometimes even for weeks.
5. False. Correct statement: For normal infants, scores on infant intelligence tests do not predict later intelligence.
6. False. Correct statement: Parents of competent infants do not spend hours teaching their children concepts, but frequently interact with their children and are ready to help their children experience events.
7. False. Correct statement: Interacting briefly with children to share experiences with them is one way to encourage cognitive development.
8. True.
9. False. Correct statement: Lack of stimulation is a more serious problem than overstimulation.
10. True.
11. False. Correct statement: Faster development does not necessarily translate into superior development.
12. False. Correct statement: An excellent later environment can reduce the injurious effects of a poor early environment.

◆ INTELLIGENCE IN INFANCY

A six-year-old reads the word *tiny* from a comic book.

A four-year-old tells his mother that the television show she is watching is "totally awesome."

A three-year-old puts a simple puzzle together.

A two-year-old tells her father that she wants a polar bear for a pet.

An eight-month-old repeatedly bangs a rattle against the side of the crib.

1. TRUE OR FALSE?

A baby banging a toy against the side of a crib is showing intelligent behavior.

If you were asked which of the above events shows intelligence, you would probably say the first four. After all, three of them show verbal abilities and one of them (putting together a puzzle) demonstrates problem-solving skills. Few people, however, would consider the baby's banging the toy against the crib intelligent behavior. But isn't it? If intelligence is considered adaptive behavior, this eight-month-old is learning about causality—that banging the rattle will lead to a predictable noise.

◆ PIAGET'S THEORY OF SENSORIMOTOR DEVELOPMENT

During the first two years of life, children develop a basic understanding of the world around them. They learn to recognize objects and people, to search for objects that are not in their field of vision, to understand cause and effect, and to appreciate the concept of space. The average adult takes this knowledge for granted, but a child's understanding of these concepts takes many months to develop. The manner in which infants develop an understanding of their world was described in detail by Jean Piaget.

Trends and Premises in Infant Cognitive Development

Two important trends underlie Piaget's view of cognitive development in infancy. First, there is a trend from dependence solely on the objective content of the infant's environment toward internal representation. At first, the infant must experience everything. Later, children can create mental images of the world and understand and use language. Second, the infant develops an appreciation that he or she is separate from other objects in the world and that the existence of those objects does not depend on the infant's perception of them (Brainerd, 1978).

Piaget's theory is based on two important premises. First, children are active participants in their own development. Second, development takes place in stages, and each stage acts as a foundation for a succeeding stage (Petersen, 1982). No stage or substage can be skipped, and each must be negotiated in turn.

The Substages of Sensorimotor Development

It is easy to overlook the basic cognitive advances in infancy. The idea that an object exists even when it is out of sight or that by tugging at a string with a toy on the end, the toy will come toward you must be learned. Piaget described the development of such elementary concepts in terms of six substages. He considered the substages of the sensorimotor stage to be invariant: that is, infants go through substage one, then proceed to substage two, then to substage three, and so forth. They never revert to a previous substage, nor do they skip a substage. However, the age at which children negotiate these substages varies from child to child. The ages used here are meant as guideposts and not as absolutes. Children proceed through these substages at their own rate, and the time at which they enter and leave each substage varies.

REFLEXES (0–1 MONTH): SUBSTAGE 1 In substage one, the infant is basically an organism reacting to changes in stimuli. The behavior of infants is rigid and reflexive. Infants are almost entirely dependent on inborn patterns of behavior. Yet they do learn and can be conditioned. During the first month, reflexes are often modified in an infant's everyday experience. For instance, an infant may suck harder on a bottle containing milk than on a toy that is placed in the mouth (Ault, 1977).

PRIMARY CIRCULAR REACTIONS (1–4 MONTHS): SUBSTAGE 2 The most prominent feature of substage two is the emergence of actions that are repeated again and again. These are called **primary circular reactions.** They are primary because they are focused on the infant's body rather than on any outside object (Phillips, 1975). They are circular because they are repeated. The infant tries to recreate some interesting event. For example, the infant may have had a thumb slip into his or her mouth by accident. This is pleasurable, so after the thumb slips out, the infant attempts to find his or her mouth again (Ault, 1977).

primary circular reactions
Actions that are repeated over and over again by infants.

SECONDARY CIRCULAR REACTIONS (4–8 MONTHS): SUBSTAGE 3 An important change occurs in substage three. **Secondary circular reactions** are observed. Infants now focus their interest not on their bodies but on the consequences of some action on their external environment. This is why they are secondary rather than primary reactions. The infant does something that creates some environmental reaction; for instance, an infant shakes a rattle and is surprised to find that the rattle produces a sound. The child may pause, then shake the rattle again, hear the sound, and continue the activity (Flavell, 1985). Piaget (1952) observed that his daughter Lucienne shook her bassinet by moving her legs rapidly, which made some cloth dolls swing from the hood of the bassinet. Lucienne looked at the dolls and smiled and continued the movements.

secondary circular reactions
Repetitive actions that are intended to create some environmental reaction.

COORDINATION OF SECONDARY REACTIONS (8–12 MONTHS): SUB-STAGE 4 In stubstage four, the child coordinates two or more strategies to reach a goal. This shows intention. Means and ends are now separated. The child begins to show perseverance in spite of being blocked. For instance, if you place your hand in front of a toy, the child will brush your hand away. The change can also be seen in terms of play activities. Children enjoy stacking items again and again or banging a pot with a spoon over and over (Willemsen, 1979).

tertiary circular reactions
Repetitive actions with some variations each time.

The infant shaking a rattle is showing secondary circular reactions.

TERTIARY CIRCULAR REACTIONS (12–18 MONTHS): SUBSTAGE 5 We begin to see **tertiary circular reactions** in substage five. Although actions are still repeated and thus circular, they are no longer carbon copies of each other. Children now seek out novelty (Ault, 1977). They are little scientists, experimenting with the world to learn its characteristics and mysteries. The substage-five child picks up objects from the crib and throws them out, listening and watching intently to learn what they sound like and how they look on the floor (Willemsen, 1979). When you put the objects back in the crib, the child may throw them out again.

Ault (1977) describes the difference between the child's employing secondary circular reactions and tertiary circular reactions. Suppose the child is placed in a playpen with lots of toys. The infant in the secondary circular reaction stage drops a block from a particular height again and again. The child does not vary the action. The child in the stage of tertiary circular reactions may drop different items out of the playplen and vary the distance from the ground.

INVENTION OF NEW MEANS THROUGH MENTAL COMBINATION (18–24 MONTHS): SUBSTAGE 6 Substage six marks the beginning of representation (Flavell, 1977). The child can now think of an object independent of its physical existence. The character of play and imitation changes. Children are now capable of **deferred imitation;** that is, they can observe some act and later imitate it. Before going to bed, an eighteen-month-old may make pedaling motions with the feet, just as the child saw older siblings do while riding their bicycles hours before. Children also show some pretend play in this substage (Belsky & Most, 1982). Until now, spoons were something to suck on, eat with, or bang. Now a spoon may stand for another, unrelated object, such as a person or a piece of corn on the cob. The infant has moved from the realm of coordinated actions to that of symbolic representation.

> **deferred imitation**
> The ability to observe an act and imitate it at a later time.

Object Permanence

"Out of sight, out of mind" the saying goes. But for the very young infant, objects that are out of sight quite literally cease to exist. Most students are surprised to discover that infants must tortuously develop an understanding that objects exist outside their perception of them—an understanding known as **object permanence.**

> **object permanence**
> The understanding that an object exists even when it is out of one's visual field.

HOW INFANTS DEVELOP OBJECT PERMANENCE Researchers study the development of object permanence by hiding objects in a variety of ways and observing children's search patterns. Infants develop their ability to understand object permanence in a series of substages (Piaget, 1954).

In substage one (0–1 month), infants look at whatever is in their visual field but will not search for an item or individual that disappears. For instance, the infant looks at mother but doesn't search for her when she leaves the room (Ault, 1977). Instead, the infant looks at something else.

During substage two (1–4 months), the infant looking at some item will continue to look in the direction of the item after it disappears. However, Piaget does not see this as true object permanence, because the search is basically passive (Piaget, 1954).

During substage three (4–8 months), we begin to see some active search for items. Now if an object is partially covered by a handkerchief, the infant tries to lift the cloth to discover the rest of the object (Diamond, 1982). Children who drop something from a high chair look to the ground for it. It is as if they can now anticipate the movement of an item. The child at this stage does not show complete object permanence, however, for the search for the hidden object consists only of a continuation of eye movement—some expectation that something in motion may continue its trajectory. The child will not search for an object that is completely hidden from view.

In substage four (8–12 months), the child will now search for an item that is completely covered by a hankerchief. However, it is here that the child makes an error that has fascinated psychologists for years, called

> *2. TRUE OR FALSE?*
> _____
>
> The one-month-old infant believes that mother has disappeared when she leaves the room.

> *3. TRUE OR FALSE?*
> _____
>
> A five-month-old infant who drops a rattle behind him or her will not turn around and find it.

As infants develop, their search patterns become more sophisticated.

The game of peek-a-boo shows the child's increasing knowledge of object permanence.

the AB error. If the child is allowed to find the item in one place, and the item is then hidden elsewhere while the child watches, the child will still search in the first location (see Figure 6.1) (Wellman, Cross & Bartsch, 1987). Why does this occur? According to Piaget, the child does not really have object permanence and has simply identified the object with a particular location (Diamond, 1982). As we shall see later, other psychologists have very different ideas about this.

In substage five (12–18 months), children can follow the object through its displacements. They no longer search for an item under the first pillow if it is moved to a second one while they are watching (Piaget, 1954). The substage-five child's understanding of object permanence is far from perfect, however. Piaget designed a simple test to demonstrate the child's limitations. His daughter had been playing with a potato and placing it in a box that had no cover. Piaget (1954, p. 266) notes:

> I then take the potato and put it in the box while Jacqueline watches. Then I place the box under the rug and turn it upside down thus leaving the object hidden by the rug without letting the child see my maneuver, and I bring out the empty box. I say to Jacqueline, who has not stopped looking at the rug and who has realized that I was doing something under it: "Give papa the potato." She searches for the object in the box, looks at me, again looks at the box minutely, looks at the rug, etc. but it does not occur to her to raise the rug in order to find the potato underneath.

Note that in this stage the movement from one hiding place to the other must be performed under the child's gaze. The child's search for a hidden object is still based on visual information. No logical inferences are formed, and there is no mental representation of the object.

During the last substage (18–24 months), children become free from the concrete information brought in through their senses. They can now construct a mental representation of the world and locate objects after a series of invisible displacements. They can imagine where an item might be (Diamond, 1982).

OBJECT PERMANENCE AND INFANT BEHAVIOR Piaget's description of the infant's cognitive development explains some common infant behavior. For instance, a child in substage five of the sensorimotor period who is dropping toys out of the playpen despite pleas to stop is not doing this out of any malicious intent. The child is practicing tertiary circular reactions. Or take the example of the old game of peekaboo, in which you cover your face with your hands, then take your hands away. As a child gains more knowledge of object permanence, the child will pull down your hands, exposing your face. The child is validating the expectations that you are still there. Or perhaps a four-month-old begins to cry hysterically after playing alone for a while. You notice that the baby has dropped a toy out of sight. Since children younger than six months do not actively search for hidden objects, you may find that merely picking the toy up and placing it in the baby's field of vision is enough to stop the baby's crying.

FIGURE 6.1: The Stage-Four Search Task.
The experimenter hides the object in the first location (1), whereupon the infant searches successfully (2) But when the experimenter hides the object at the second location (3), the infant searches again at the original location (4).

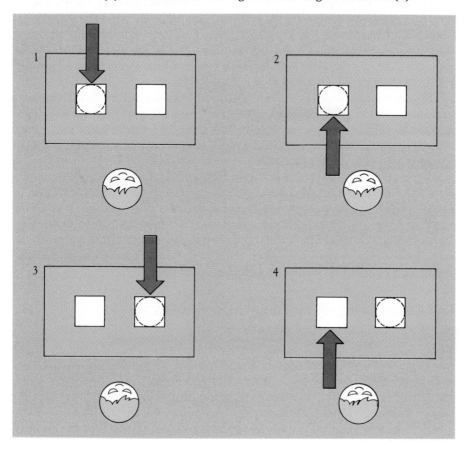

Source: Bremner, 1988.

Piaget's Theory Under Scrutiny

Piaget's description of infant and toddler cognitive development is accepted by many psychologists. Because Piaget's findings are partly based upon his observations of his own children, it is fair to ask whether the account has stood up well to rigorous scientific study. A great deal of research has been performed in an attempt to empirically test Piaget's contentions in this area.

The most popular approach to this problem has been to present tasks that a child in one stage—but not a child in a preceding stage—should be able to do and to note whether the progression holds. Brainerd (1978,

p. 75) puts it this way: "If X is an earlier stage than Y, then children should always pass the X test before they pass the Y test and they should never pass the Y test before the X test."

Experiments have generally supported Piaget's views (Kramer, Hill & Cohen, 1975; Uzgiris, 1973). Studies conducted all over the world have generally supported Piaget's view of the sequence in which children develop cognitive skills (Nyiti, 1982). Piaget's descriptions hold under a variety of environmental conditions, although the development of object permanence and casuality is delayed in some cultures and more advanced in others (Dasen & Heron, 1981).

Although many studies have confirmed Piaget's ideas about the sensorimotor period, some problems remain. First, the way that Piaget presented the tasks to the infants may have affected the infants' reactions. Second, though the concept of substages does serve to focus our attention on particular aspects of a task, why choose six substages? Why not twelve or fifteen (Gratch, 1979)? Third, a fundamental error in logic may have crept into these studies. Just because infants do not successfully complete a particular task does not mean they can't do it. For example, the child may have the ability to perform some task but may not be motivated to do so. Perhaps the infant understands where an object is but cannot perform the necessary physical movements to obtain it. These arguments are too logical to dismiss without further consideration.

The Competency-Performance Argument

The most intriguing argument may be the contention that children may be capable of doing something but for some reason do not do so. Have you ever "known" something but were unable to put it into words? Perhaps you failed as essay test but felt that you knew the information—you just could not perform the required action of putting your knowledge on paper. Perhaps you didn't have the vocabulary or the time. Maybe the pressure was too great. Perhaps the questions were phrased in such a way that the correct response in your memory wasn't tripped.

Whenever an infant does not perform a particular task, Piaget interprets the inability in terms of competency: The child does not have the cognitive sophistication necessary. But some psychologists are not so sure about that. If we change the physical requirements of the task, maybe the results would be different.

Characteristics of the Task and the Infant

There is some evidence to suggest that infants are more capable than Piaget believed. Individual and situational factors influence the infant's performance. For example, when examining object permanence studies, such factors as familiarity with the object and motivation must be taken into account.

The testing procedures may also lead investigators to make the logical error that performance always reflects competency. Even the type of cover used when hiding an object seems to make a difference. Nancy Rader and her colleagues (1979) studied object permanence in infants whose median age was 160 days. They hid plastic keys in a well and covered the keys with either a 12-by-12-inch washcloth or a 7-by-7-inch piece of manila paper covered with blue felt. Infants differed in their success with the task. Some succeeded in uncovering the keys when the paper cover was used but not when the cloth cover was hiding them. The awkwardness of the covers used in an object-permanence test may affect the test's outcome. The infant's physical abilities may also be an important confounding factor in tests of object permanence.

The very nature of the three-dimensional task may affect the infant's search pattern. Young infants have difficulty when an object is placed inside another object. When a rattle is placed in a box, infants are confused because they see the rattle not as being hidden but as having been replaced by the box (Bower, 1979). Bower and Wishart (1972) found that infants who could not find an object that was hidden under a cup could grasp an object dangling in front of them when the lights were turned out in the room. Infants can successfully retrieve objects from behind a two-dimensional barrier, such as a screen, before they can do so from a three-dimensional barrier, such as a box. In addition, their performance on object-permanence tests depends on the spatial characteristics of the barrier. The response demand of the search, such as whether a researcher demands successful retrieval or mere looking, is also a factor (Dunst, Brooks & Doxsey, 1982).

T. G. R. Bower (1971) argues that object permanence develops much sooner than Piaget believed. Infants do not show it, because most studies force children to engage in an active search, which involves eye-hand coordination and motor skills not yet developed.

Interpretations of AB Error

All of these problems can be seen in a most fascinating aspect of sensorimotor development—the AB error. As noted, Piaget found that children between the ages of eight and twelve months (substage four) would often make errors when an object was hidden under pillow A, the child was allowed to search for the object, and in a subsequent trial, the object was placed under pillow B. Even though they had watched the object being placed under pillow B, the children would search for it under pillow A. Piaget explains this in terms of the absence of object permanence. The child has identified the object with an action in a particular place. When the location is changed, the infant searches in the first location because the object is defined by certain actions in location A.

No one doubts that the AB error takes place, but is Piaget's explanation tenable? Some psychologists claim that such factors as memory, spatial knowledge and perceptual processes are more important than Piaget believed they were. Let us first look at memory. Gratch and colleagues (1974) presented infants of about eight or nine months with the standard AB task. The babies were forced to wait different amounts of time before being allowed to search for the item. If the infants were allowed to search immediately, they did not make the mistake of searching in location A first, but if the babies were held back from searching for anywhere from three to fifteen seconds, some of them made the common error of searching in location A. When Adele Diamond (1985) increased the delay between hiding and retrieval, she found that as children aged they were able to tolerate longer delays. This demonstrates the importance of the child's memory in understanding the AB error.

Memory cannot explain the entire problem, though, for infants make the error even when they can actually see the object at point B. Butterworth (1977) obtained errors from many infants when the covers used were transparent rather than opaque, as Piaget used. This presents a problem for those who believe that memory is the main factor. Even when infants can see the object, they search incorrectly.

Familiarity with the covers and distractions may help us to understand this phenomenon. David Yates and J. Gavin Bremner (1988) believe that infants might be distracted by the covers, which would explain why they still make the errors. When infants became familiarized with the transparent covers, they committed many fewer errors.

Other explanations exist as well. Henry Wellman and colleagues (1987) argue that the child in the AB search situation has two pieces of information. One is that the article was at A and the second that the article is now at B. The infant overvalues the first information and infers the object's location on the basis of prior information and experience.

The fact that infants must coordinate what they see with a series of actions may also cause them to make mistakes in the AB situation. They must see the problem, interpret it, and then translate their knowledge into motor movement. What if we could design an experiment to determine understanding of object permanence in which an infant would not have to coordinate any actions at all? Renée Baillargeon and Marcia Graber (1988) showed eight-month-old infants an object that stood on one of two different placemats. Screens were pushed in front of the placemats, hiding the object from view. Next, a human hand, wearing a long silver glove and a bracelet of bells entered the apparatus through an opening in the right wall and "tiptoed" back and forth between the right wall and the right screen. After doing this for 15 seconds, the hand reached behind the right screen and came out with the object and shook it gently.

Sometimes at the beginning of the experiment, the object was located on the right placemat. When later in the trial, the hand located the object behind the right placemat, this would not be surprising. The experimenters called this the "possible event." At other times, the object was initially located on the left placemat, so if the hand found the object behind the right placemat later, this would indeed be surprising. This was called the "impossible event" (see Figure 6.2).

The experimenters reasoned that if the infants remembered the object's location during the 15 seconds in which the hand tiptoed back and forth, they should be surprised at the impossible event (seeing the object retrieved from behind the right screen when they had last seen it occupying the left placemat). Since surprise usually shows itself by attention, infants should look longer at the impossible than the possible event.

Indeed, infants did look much longer when the hand retrieved the object from behind the wrong screen (an impossible event) rather than from behind the correct screen where the object was actually hidden. This suggests that infants remembered the object's location during the entire

FIGURE 6.2: Testing Eight-Month-Olds Location Memory in a Nonsearch AB Task

In the possible event, the object is hidden behind the right screen and, after a delay, is taken from behind the right screen. In the impossible event, the object is hidden behind the left screen but later is taken from behind the right screen. Will eight-month-olds pay more attention to the impossible event therefore showing surprise and a knowledge of where the item should have been retrieved from?

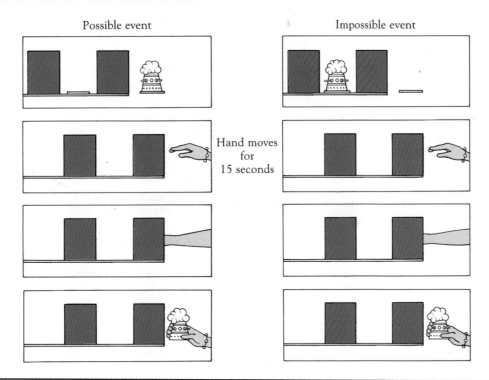

Possible event   Impossible event

Hand moves for 15 seconds

Source: Baillargeon & Graber, 1988.

fifteen-second delay, and their surprise was due to their knowing where the item should be. The researchers suggest that there is a gap between what the infant knows about object permanence and the infant's ability to coordinate this knowledge with action. The infant has difficulty with the AB task because of the inability to coordinate his or her memory and action, and this may be due to the immaturity of the prefrontal cortex of the brain. The infant may know where the object is but may not be able to integrate knowledge and action.

Piaget looked at children's lack of performance and assumed that the children did not have competence, but Piaget did not concern himself with factors that affect performance. Other theorists disagree sharply, believing that the specific tasks that infants were asked to perform by Piaget may hinder infants from showing the ability that Piaget was looking for, just as the need to coordinate memory and action may hide a child's knowledge of object permanence.

When we separated knowledge from coordinated behavior, we find that infants understand object permanence at a considerably earlier age than Piaget believed. A series of experiments by Baillargeon (Baillargeon, 1987; Baillargeon, Spelke & Wasserman, 1985) with infants three and a half, four and a half, and five months old demonstrated that the infants had developed object permanence. Infants were shown a screen moving through a 180–degree arc along a flat surface. The infants habituated to the moving screen. Then a box was placed behind the screen, and infants were shown either a possible or an impossible event. The possible event involved the screen moving's until it reached the box, stopping, and then returning to its initial position. In the impossible event, the screen moved until it reached the box and then kept on going as though the box were not there. It thus completed its full arc before reversing direction.

The researchers argued that if the infants had object permanence and knew that the box continued to exist after it was hidden from view, they would pay more attention to the impossible event than the possible event, since the impossible event should be novel and the possible event was similar to the event to which they had been habituated. Infants beginning at three and a half months paid more attention to the impossible event, demonstrating that they knew the box did not cease to exist.

Baillargeon argues that the results of these experiments show that Piaget's claim that it was not until nine months that infants understood that objects are permanent needs a reevaluation and infants possess this notion long before they can do the coordinated movements necessary to show their knowledge on the standard Piagetian task.

Putting It All Together

Piaget's description of infant cognitive growth is an excellent starting point. His descriptions of how a child progresses in infancy are well accepted. They have focused our attention on this area and encouraged us to form more detailed questions (Gratch, 1979). At the same time, however, the evidence showing that other factors may affect performance should make us wary of making generalizations concerning what an infant or toddler can or cannot do. The specific type of task presented to the infant, the object being hidden, and the nature of the barrier must always be noted. Infants follow Piaget's progression if tested in the standard Piagetian way. However, infants are very sensitive to the demands of the task. An analysis of what skills are necessary for success may yield information concerning why a child fails at a task. When a child must retrieve a hidden object, eye-hand coordination skills, motor skills, three-dimensional perception, and memory abilities are required. Piaget did not detail these skills. That task remained for others. Children who fail a particular task may lack any one (or more) of these skills or abilities. The simple fact is that if you test children the way Piaget did you get Piaget's results. However, by looking more closely at the task—in this case, realizing the importance of coordinating action with what the child knows—we begin to separate what the child knows from the specific ways Piaget used to test these abilities. It may well be that infants are more capable than even Piaget thought they were.

♦ INFORMATION-PROCESSING SKILLS

In earliest infancy, information-processing skills are tied directly to perceptual development. For instance, the development of the senses, such as the ability to focus, would affect the child's ability to process visual information. A number of studies, some of which were described in Chapter 5, deal with the elements of particular patterns that gain an infant's attention. However, do infants have the ability to remember what they experience, and if they do, what is it that they remember?

Memory

Research on early memory focuses on recognition and recall. **Recognition** involves the ability to choose the correct response from a group of answers and is similar to the multiple-choice questions on a test. **Recall** involves producing the correct response on the basis of very limited cues and is similar to the task you face when taking as essay test.

To illustrate the difference, suppose you were presented with a list of one hundred famous people and asked to underline those who were presidents of the United States. You would probably do well on this type of recognition examination. On the other hand, what if you were asked to list all the presidents you can remember? This test of recall is much more difficult. As a rule, our ability to recognize is far better than our ability to recall information (Wingfield & Byrnes, 1981).

recognition
A way of testing retention in which the subject is required to choose the correct answer from a group of choices.

recall
A way of testing retention in which the subject must produce the correct responses given very limited cues.

The Development of Recognition

Testing recognition in infancy is not a difficult task. Very young infants habituate to stimuli. If shown a stimulus, such as a face, an infant will pay attention to it, but if we continually show that face to the infant, the amount of time the baby spends attending to it decreases. Testing recognition involves familiarizing infants of various ages with a stimulus. As they become familiar with the stimulus, the infants pay less and less attention to it. If they then pay more attention to another stimulus presented to them, they have noticed the difference, thus showing recognition.

Using this method, Friedman (1972) showed that one-day-old to three-day-old infants could notice the difference between visual displays. However, only about a third of the original sample demonstrated this, and not all research has been successful in replicating this result (Bjorklund, 1989).

However, by the age of three months, there is no doubt that infants have recognition memory. When three-month-old infants were presented with pictures of their mothers, they were later able to tell the difference between their mother's face and the face of a stranger (Barrera & Maurer, 1981). Some researchers are impressed not only with infants' ability to recognize but also with their retentive abilities. Infants as young as two months were able to recognize a visual pattern and retain it for twenty-four hours (Martin, 1975). Jeffrey Fagen (1973) found that five-month-olds to six-month-old infants familiarized with a face for only two minutes

4. TRUE OR FALSE?

Five-month-old infants show the ability to recognize faces and objects but only for a few minutes, after which they forget them.

were able to recognize it after a delay of two weeks. And this recognition memory is relatively impervious to interference.

One important factor in demonstrating recognition and retention, especially in very young infants, is the amount of time the infant is given to become familiar with the stimulus. The younger the infant, the longer the familiarization periods need to be. In addition, the stimulus needs to be larger for very young infants. Infants are probably born with the ability to recognize visual patterns, but in earliest infancy, they are not awake that much, and their immature visual systems may interfere with recognition when the stimuli are small and the time of exposure fleeting (Olson & Sherman, 1983). As one would expect, recognition improves with age, with older infants showing superior retention on tests of recognition (Rose, 1981).

The recognition memory of infants is impressive, but what are the stimulus characteristics that infants recognize and retain? Infants do not retain everything equally well. For example, three-month-old to four-month-old infants were trained to produce movement in a blue or green mobile. The infants remembered the color of the mobile, but the color was more quickly forgotten than the fact that the mobile would move if kicked (Fagen, 1984). Strauss and Cohen (1978) familiarized five-month-old infants with a three-dimensional styrofoam figure. The figure varied as to shape, color, size, and orientation, and the infant's recognition was measured at various time intervals from ten minutes through twenty-four hours. These infants showed recognition on every dimension when tested immediately, but they recognized only color and form after ten minutes and only form after twenty-four hours. Form is probably the most important element in recognition for infants at this age. Perhaps other experiments will discover a developmental progression in what infants recognize and retain.

The Development of Recall

Studies of recall are not as plentiful as research on recognition. Recognition is a relatively simple type of memory; recall is something entirely different. Piaget (1968) argued that children do not show true recall before one and a half to two years of age. The two-year-old certainly shows recall (Goldberg, Perlmutter, & Myers, 1974), but whether recall has been shown in children much under two years of age is a subject of debate.

Some experiments demonstrate a memory process similar to recall in eight-month-old infants. Brody (1981) first trained infants to touch a lighted face. When the infants did so, they were reinforced by the pleasant sounds of a music box, the sequential illumination of eleven lights around the panel, and a view of a puppet rotating on a turntable for three seconds. After the infants had learned to touch the light for the reward, they were presented with a delay. After the face was lighted, the light was turned off, and a screen covered the face for 250 milliseconds. The screen was then lifted, and the infants were reinforced for touching the face that had been illuminated before the lowering of the screen. After the infants had learned this response, the researcher varied the amount of time in which the screen covered the face by three, six, and nine seconds. Brody found that eight-month-old and twelve-month-old infants could remember the location of the stimulus during the 250 millisecond delay but that only the twelve-month-old infants could tolerate the longer delays.

An increase in recall occurs between eight and twelve months. This period is one of rapid change in an infant's cognitive abilities. Neurological changes that improve memory occur (Kagan, 1979a, 1979b). The infant develops an ability to spontaneously retrieve older information and apply it to current circumstances. This improvement in memory has behavioral implications. For instance, stranger anxiety is rare before seven months, but it increases rapidly between that age and the end of the first year. Separation anxiety occurs when an infant shows anxiety at being left by the parent or caregiver. It emerges between seven and ten months, rises to a peak at thirteen to fifteen months, then declines until, at the age of three, it is rare. Jerome Kagan argues that these events are partly explained by the growth of the infant's memory abilities, which include the ability to retrieve past memories and anticipate future behavior based on past experiences. Suppose the father of a ten-month-old leaves the room. The child remembers the father's former presence and compares it with the current scene in which the father is not there. If the child cannot resolve the differences, distress may occur. In addition, the ten-month-old may cry when mother starts to walk toward the door but does not actually leave the room. Kagan believes that this child can now generate hypotheses about what might happen and is anticipating the mother's exit.

Conditioning and Learning

You may think it amazing that young infants can remember something for minutes, an hour, or a day. However, some of the recent evidence on infants' memory of conditioned responses shows that infants can remember something for days or even weeks. Consider the following possibility. You tie a ribbon to an infant's foot and count the number of times she kicks. Then you attach the other end of the ribbon to a mobile which, if the infant kicks, will move and make a pleasant noise. The three-month-old infant will learn to kick to gain the reinforcement. However, if you then remove the ribbon for a few days or a few weeks and then reattach it, do you suppose the infant will immediately show many more kicking motions than she did before the ribbon was attached to the mobile? Will she "remember" the conditioning? Studies using this technique show that infants as young as three months old showed memory for the conditioning for more than a week and some remembered the conditioning for two weeks (Sullivan, Rovee-Collier, & Tynes, 1979). Another conditioning study found that after one eighteen-minute training session, three-month-old infants displayed memory two weeks later, while two-month-old infants did not (Vander Linde, Morrongiello, & Rovee-Collier, 1985). However, if the training was increased and if it was spread across a number of sessions, long-term retention improved greatly, even for two-month-old infants. Infants can remember events for rather long periods of time, and memory skills improve with age and with longer periods of familiarization with stimuli.

Cognitive Development in Infancy and Toddlerhood

Infants are hardly passive beings just waiting for the world to teach them something (Restak, 1982). They are quite active and develop their abilities quickly. During the first year, the infant becomes a goal-directed being and develops some idea of causality. By one year, the child searches for completely covered objects and has developed some measure of object permanence. The child's memory is also developing, as is the ability to anticipate outcomes. The one-year-old knows the difference between a stranger and a loved one and may be walking and about to talk.

Cognitive development in toddlerhood is impressive. The ability to walk allows children in this age group to explore their environment more fully, and their linguistic abilities improve. By about two years or so, the finer points of object permanence have been mastered, and in the last six months of their second year they can no longer be confused by difficult hiding places. By the end of the second year, the child has developed representational thought—that is, the child can now think without acting (Ault, 1977). Children at this point are no longer sensorimotor in the truest sense of the term—relying solely on the information they have obtained through the senses and motor activity. They can now construct a mental image of the world, and they can defer imitation—seeing an event at one time and imitating it later.

◆ PREDICTING LATER INTELLIGENCE

By this time, you are probably willing to accept the fact that infants show intelligent behavior and are impressed by the development of their cognitive abilities. But do these early infant abilities predict later cognitive abilities? A number of such possible predictors already exist, including infant intelligence tests, information-processing abilities, socioeconomic status, and the characteristics of the home.

Predictions from Tests: The Bayley Scales

Bayley Scales of Infant Development
A test of intelligence administered to children between two months and two and a half years of age.

The most popular way to measure the intellectual abilities of infants and toddlers was devised by Nancy Bayley and her colleagues (Bayley, 1969; Bayley & Oden, 1955). The **Bayley Scales of Infant Development** can be used to assess the abilities of children from two months through two and a half years. The Mental Scale measures such functions as perception, memory, learning, problem solving, and vocalization. The Motor Scale measures such motor abilities as sitting, standing, stair climbing, hand skills, and coordination. The Infant Behavior Record is designed to assess such qualities as attention span, persistence, and emotional and social behavior. The observer is asked to rate the child on responsiveness, co-operativeness, fearfulness, and activity level. While the Bayley scales yield a valid description of the child's intellectual development at the time (Bayley, 1970), can they predict later intellectual development? Can we administer the scales to a child of six months and make any statement concerning that child's intelligence as a second grader at age seven? Do the scales have any predictive validity?

Attempts to predict later intelligence on the basis of infant measures have been disappointing. Most studies have failed to find much predictive validity between scores on the Bayley scales for normal infants and later cognitive abilities (Francis, Self, & Horowitz, 1987). Only after eighteen months does the child's scores on infant intelligence tests have any predictive ability, and then only when added to some measure of socioeconomic status (McCall, 1979). However, the Bayley scales are useful in predicting the intelligence of infants who are neurologically impaired or have some other defect (Rubin & Balow, 1979).

Why don't these scales predict later behavior in normal children? Perhaps the abilities measured by the scales are too unstable to be predictive. Perhaps we are simply measuring the wrong abilities, and other infant capabilities may be predictive.

5. TRUE OR FALSE?

Infant intelligence tests given to normal infants at six months predict later school achievement fairly well.

Information-Processing Skills

Some researchers have recently tried to isolate certain infant information-processing skills that may predict later development (Bornstein & Benasich, 1986). One behavior showing promise in this regard is the speed of habituation during infancy, which is related to measurements on such Piagetian tasks as object permanence during early toddlerhood (Miller et al., 1977) and speaking vocabularies at twelve months (Ruddy & Bornstein, 1982). Another study showed that visual recognition memory at six months predicted scores of tests of cognitive skills from two to six years in preterm infants (Rose & Wallach, 1985). Such information-processing abilities as the ability to encode visual stimuli efficiently and to remember visual or auditory stimuli are related to superior performance on traditional tests of verbal intelligence and language tests during childhood (Bornstein & Sigman, 1986). Although these developments are interesting, this area is quite new, and much more research is needed before its importance can be evaluated.

Socioeconomic Status and Cognitive Development

The socioeconomic status of the child in the first twelve to eighteen months appears to be a good predictor of later intellectual development (McCall, Hogarty, & Hurlbutt, 1972). Socieconomic status is usually analyzed in terms of income, parental education level, and occupational rating (Rubin & Balow, 1979). Low-socioeconomic homes differ greatly from middle and higher socioeconomic homes, especially in the area of verbal behavior (Tulkin & Kagan, 1972). Mothers from low socioeconomic backgrounds talk much less to their infants. Perhaps lack of formal education or the stresses of poverty may prevent these parents from providing the verbal stimulation or the environment necessary for their children to develop adequate cognitive skills.

Yet, there is something unsatisfactory about the entire concept of socioeconomic status. It is far too broad and too general a consideration, and it ignores the wide variations that exist in intelligence within socio-economic levels. It would be better to focus on the differences among families (Ramey, Farran, & Campbell, 1979). General statements noting that a lower socioeconomic status parent does this or that ignore these differences and stigmatize an entire group of people.

Finally, socioeconomic status is not an easy variable to change. Poverty, lack of education, and a low-status job cannot be altered overnight by a child development specialist. Because these factors are so important, professionals may have a societal responsibility to help improve the lot of the poor. However, a more specific approach stressing behaviors and specific environmental variables rather than social class may be more helpful in uncovering clues to intellectual development. These behavioral or environmental factors may be more susceptible to change. For instance, if we find that children of parents who are responsive and who speak to them are intellectually advanced in middle childhood, we can help parents develop these skills and change their pattern of parent-child inter-actions. If we find that the absence of books in the house makes a differ-ence, we can not only provide the books but also teach parents how to use them. We have recently made a start in this direction. We have dis-covered specific types of parent-child interactions and discrete elements of the physical environment surrounding the child that facilitate cogni-tive growth. Studies in other cultures have identified similar factors to be important in determining cognitive abilities (see the Cross-Cultural Current on page 245).

Predictions from the Home Environment

One instrument frequently used to measure various aspects of the home environment is called the **Home Observation for Measurement of the Environment,** or **HOME scale.** This scale provides a measure of the qual-ity and quantity of the emotional and cognitive elements in the home

HOME scale
A scale that provides a measure of the quality and quantity of the emotional and cognitive elements in the home.

DATAGRAPHIC

Children and the Poverty Level, 1987

Source: U.S. Bureau of the Census

Children of minority groups have a much greater chance of living below the poverty level.

Raising Infants in Kenya

Many studies have investigated the effects of the home environment on cognitive development in Western societies. There is no doubt that the nature of the home environment influences the cognitive development of children. But does this same relationship between characteristics of the home environment and the child's cognitive development hold in other societies? As we've noted, psychologists can't take relationships that are found in Western societies and automatically transfer them to non-Western societies.

To determine the effects of the home environment on the cognitive development of children from non-Western societies, studies must be conducted in the particular culture of interest. This was the reasoning behind a study of the home environment and cognitive development among people who lived in the Embu District, about 120 miles from the capital of Kenya, Nairobi. The district is a rural area with no electricity and with running water in only some of the homes. The principal occupation of the people is subsistance farming, with a few cash crops.

The researchers observed more than one hundred toddlers between the ages of fifteen and eighteen months. This age group was chosen because studies in Western societies have shown that although there is a definite relationship between the home environment and cognitive development in the first year, the relationship is much greater beginning in the second year. The children were followed until they were thirty months of age.

Trained local young adults observed both caretaking and protective behaviors as well as interactive behaviors. Some of the behaviors observed involved physical care such as washing, holding/carrying, touching, social interaction, talking to the toddler, and response to the toddler's vocalizations and distress. Since observations were conducted every two months, each toddler was observed between six and eight times.

The assessment tool used was a modified form of the Bayley Mental Scale. This tool was chosen because it measures abilities that develop in all cultures. In addition, the Bayley scales have previously been used successfully in Kenya.

The results paralleled those found in Western societies. The nature of the home environment was associated with the child's development in much the same way it is in the United States and other Western societies. The amount of time the child was talked to and responsiveness to the child's vocalization predicted the child's later cognitive status. Children who were talked to frequently, whose vocalizations were responded to, and who were engaged in sustained social interactions passed more of the items on the Bayley Mental Scale at twenty-four and thirty months than those who did not receive such attention. The amount of time the child was held or carried correlated negatively with the child's development. The researchers suggest that carrying the child extensively after the first year may restrict the child's exploration of his or her environment. Another possibility is that children who are already developing very slowly are more likely to be carried.

Another important finding is the relationship between paternal literacy and cognitive development of toddlers. Perhaps the father's ability to read is related to the economic situation within the home. It may also relate to the intelligence and education of the parents. However, whether or not parents could read, those toddlers who were spoken to and interacted with more were superior in cognitive development to those who did not experience such treatment.

We often think of cross-cultural studies as emphasizing the differences between societies. However, such studies can also emphasize the similarities between different societies. In this case, we can see that for toddlers being raised in a rural area of Kenya as well as for those living in Western societies, particular home factors are associated with improved cognitive development.

Source: Sigman, M., Neumann, C., Carter, E., Cattle, D. J., D'Souza, S., and Bwibo, N. Home Interactions and the Develement of Embu Toddlers in Kenya. *Child Development*, 1988, **59**, 1251–1261.

setting (Elardo, Bradley, & Caldwell, 1977). The inventory measures six factors; the parents' emotional and verbal responsivity, the avoidance of restriction and punishment, the organization of the environment, provision of appropriate play materials, parental involvement with the child, and opportunities for variety in the daily routine. Information is collected

Can you predict the child's later intelligence from his or her socioeconomic status? Although studies find some predictive ability, there are many problems to using it to predict later intelligence.

through interviews and observation. At present, there is a scale for infancy, early childhood, and middle childhood. Table 6.1 (page 248) shows some selected items from the parental responsivity subscales of each of the HOME inventories.

Using the HOME scale, Bradley and Caldwell discovered a "substantial relationship between home environment in the first year of life and IQ at age three" (1980, p. 1145). The HOME score is an effective predictor of IQ and language. Correlations between HOME scores at two, three, and four years of age and later IQ scores are moderate, ranging from .27 to .50 (Bradley, 1989). Evaluations of specific elements of the home are more efficient in predicting future intellectual growth then either infant tests or parental education (Elardo, Bradley, & Caldwell, 1975). For example, the intensity and variety of stimuli are related to intellectual development (Wachs, 1971). Carew and his colleagues (1975) found that positive experiences in verbal and symbolic learning, such as labeling objects; perceptual, spatial, and fine-motor experiences, such as matching and color discriminations; and problem-solving activities were related to IQ scores at three years. In a recent study, the home environments of forty-two, ten- and eleven-year-olds were examined both when the children were infants and again during middle childhood. Significant relationships were found between home environments at between two years and ten years and children's HOME scores at ten years and their achievement test scores and classroom behavior. (Bradley, Caldwell, & Rock, 1988).

At this point, some tentative conclusions can be drawn. Such factors as the responsivity of the caregiver, parental involvement with the child, the variety of stimulation available, the organization of the environment, the caregiver's restrictiveness, and the play materials available at an early age predict later cognitive development. One point should be kept in mind, though. A healthy environment in infancy is usually carried over through childhood. An unhealthy environment in infancy rarely improves greatly in childhood. Some of the relationship between the environment during infancy and later intellectual ability is a reflection of the cumulative effects of the environment throughout childhood and does not solely demonstrate the importance of the earliest environment. Also, some areas of the home environment probably will be more important at different times than other areas.

◆ PARENTS AND THE CHILD'S COGNITIVE DEVELOPMENT

These lessons are easily translated into general prescriptions for child rearing, but caution is necessary. Some parenting books make impossible promises. They imply that if you follow their regimen, your child will become a superior student in school and be ready for an Ivy League college and eternal bliss after adolescence. But there are no magic formulas for producing a genius, and cognitive development is only one aspect of childhood growth and development. In addition, parents may become too involved in technique, ignoring the importance of spontane-

Specific measures from the home environment are fairly accurate in predicting later intelligence.

ity, joy, and play. The cognitive development of their infant boy became an obsession for one professional couple. They smothered their child with stimulation and pressured him to master certain skills. If a child requires stimulation, they reasoned, the more the better. But too much noise and confusion can be harmful to the very activity they want to promote (Wachs, 1976), and there is no reason to believe that higher levels of stimulation are better than moderate levels.

The genetic component in intelligence should also be kept in mind (Scarr & Weinberg, 1978). Even the best environment and care may not produce an Einstein. In addition, environmental variables and genetic factors interact in a highly complex manner. Each child matures according to his or her own genetic blueprint, and particular strategies and environments must be tailored to the child's individual rate of maturation. A child who is developing more quickly may be able to handle a more advanced problem or toy. Children can also influence their own environments. Brighter children may create a better environment for themselves because they are more responsive and reinforcing to their caregivers (Bradely, Caldwell, & Elardo, 1979). Children who are developing more slowly require playthings that are closer to their ability level.

Most factors that affect cognitive development are determined by the child's parents. White (1971) studied the differences between mothers of competent infants and mothers of less competent infants and found three major differences. The mothers of competent children were designers— that is, they constructed an environment in which children were surrounded with interesting objects to see and explore. They were able to understand the meaning that an activity or experience might have for a child and build on it. Second, parents of competent children interacted

6. TRUE OR FALSE?

Parents of competent infants spend many hours teaching their children concepts.

TABLE 6.1: Selected Items from Parental Responsivity Subscales of
the HOME Inventory

Infant/Toddler Version
Parent responds to child's vocalization with a verbal response.
Parent caresses or kisses child at least once during visit.

Early Childhood Version
Parent holds child close ten to fifteen minutes per day.
Parent spontaneously praises child's qualities or behavior twice during
  visit.

Middle Childhood Version
Parent sometimes yields to child's fears and rituals (for example, allows
  night light, accompanies child to new experiences).
Parent responds to child's questions during interview.

Source: Bradley, 1989.

frequently with their children in twenty-second to thirty-second inter-
plays. The children were not smothered with attention, but the parents
were always available and ready to help their children experience events.
The parents often labeled the environment for their children and helped
to share their children's excitement. Third, the parents of these children
were neither overly permissive nor overly punitive. They had firm limits,
but they were not unduly concerned about such minor problems as children making a mess and being a bother.

Parental Activities That Encourage Cognitive Development

The research on cognitive development can be translated into a number
of parental activities that encourage the cognitive growth of children.
Some of these activities are discussed in the following paragraphs.

PROVIDING OPPORTUNITIES FOR EXPLORATION Children are active
learners and need to have all their senses stimulated. Such environmental
stimulants as a mobile above the crib and a few safe, brightly colored toys
are important. A bit later, parents can try to provide experiences for the
infant that involve materials of different colors, textures, and shapes.

LABELING THE ENVIRONMENT It is important to label a child's environment. When the child appears to be communicating in a prelinguistic mode, it is beneficial to say "you want a cracker?" while holding
the cracker up and emphasizing the word.

ENCOURAGING COMMUNICATION As children grow, the number of
verbalizations they utter will increase. A child usually begins to use words
in the second year of life. Parents can encourage communication even in

*Reading to a child is an excellent
way of encouraging cognitive growth
and language learning.*

the prelinguistic stage. When children become older and begin using words, parents can encourage their children to expand their vocabulary. Children need a willing audience and encouragement to develop their linguistic skills.

READING TO THE CHILD Reading to the child can start early, and parents can tailor their technique to the age and ability of the child. For instance, young children can point to various objects in a book, such as a ball. Later, a parent's verbal interactions can expand to questions of color, shape, and so on.

ENSURING BRIEF INTERACTIONS BETWEEN PARENTS AND CHILD Those twenty-second to thirty-second encounters can be valuable. Some people believe that spending every minute of their time with their children is desirable, but this is not the case. As children mature, their attention span will increase, and interactions can become more involved and longer. However, sharing even a brief experience with a child is beneficial.

7. TRUE OR FALSE?

Interactions of less than one minute with an infant or a toddler have no effect on the child's cognitive development.

TAILORING ACTIVITIES TO THE CHILD'S DEVELOPMENTAL LEVEL Most child specialists who write books about parental activities that can optimize cognitive growth note that these activities should be low-key and fun. A problem arises when a child's parents believe they are conducting an academic activity and put pressure on their child to achieve too early (Zinsser, 1981). Parental disappointment, anxieties, and expectations can be communicated to young children quite early and may hinder the very development that parents seek. Infants and toddlers have limited attention spans and may go quickly from activity to activity. Equally important is understanding that enriched environments do not always lead to accelerated or enhanced cognitive or perceptual development. Enhanced environments help when there is a match between the encounter and the child's abilities (Hunt, 1961).

8. TRUE OR FALSE?

Parent-child interactions that are aimed at encouraging cognitive development should be fun for the child.

Overstimulation

If one is good, are three better? Today, there is such an emphasis on early cognitive development that some parents go overboard. After reading that one mobile is beneficial, they place three above the infant's crib.

Parents often make the mistake of believing that if a little is good then a lot is better. This is not the case. Before about six weeks, babies simply turn away from too much stimulation, and overstimulation is not a great problem (White, 1975). However, overstimulation does not produce the desired results (Wachs, Uzgiris & Hunt, 1971). In an overstimulated environment, children may block out stimuli of normal intensity and begin to respond only when stimuli become more and more intense (Wesley & Sullivan, 1980). The difficult question is just how to define overstimulation. What a normal noise level is in one home is deafening for those raised in another. At present, overstimulation remains a vague term.

Overstimulation however, does not seem to be as great a problem as lack of stimulation. Considerably more is known about the tragic effects

Parents sometimes think that more is always better. That is simply not so.

9. TRUE OR FALSE?

Overstimulation is as great a problem as lack of stimulation.

of understimulation and stimulus deprivation, which lead to retardation (Spitz, 1945).

Infants crave and require moderate levels of stimulation, and such stimulation should match their abilities. There is no evidence, however, that the greater the intensity of the stimulation the more beneficial the effects.

♦ TEACHING PARENTS TO PARENT

It seems almost criminal to have information that may improve a child's chances for success in later life and not share it with those who need it most. Parents who read books on the subject and are most interested in creating optimal home environments are often those who need the information least. Children will be more advanced cognitively (or less retarded) if parents do such things as provide them with experiences that will stimulate all their senses, label the environment for them, and provide exploratory experiences. Such information ought to be communicated to parents, and parents should be taught how to help their own children. Indeed, programs have been developed to do precisely this and show considerable success rates.

Programs For Parents

Working with parents is the most efficient approach to improving a child's environment, but ensuring parental involvement in a group is often difficult. Evidence collected over almost three decades shows that children of parents who participate in such programs operate at a more advanced

THE CHILD
IN THE YEAR
2000

Optimizing Infant Cognition: Meeting the Parental Challenge

It is not hard to see the intellectual development in a preschooler or a school-aged child. However, looking at an infant in terms of intelligence and cognitive functioning is more difficult. We owe a debt of gratitude to Piaget for making us aware of the cognitive development that occurs in infancy. As information-processing specialists have looked deeply into infant cognition, we have become more knowledgeable about how infants process information and get to know their world.

However, a fair question to ask is whether people appreciate these advancements in knowledge. Do parents of infants realize what their children can do and are experiencing? Although some parenting magazines have been active in trying to communicate this new knowledge to parents, many parents do not read about these discoveries. Just how much do people know about infant capabilities? What if you gave your friends a test containing questions concerning what infants and young children experience and perceive or at what age they develop certain Piagetian abilities? How do you think they would score? Such tests are available, and they yield interesting results. In one study, mothers were more accurate than a group of college students on their understanding of milestones, such as when a child can do or perceive something, but even mothers were correct only about 66 percent of the time. Pregnant adolescents and teenage mothers tend to underestimate what babies can do, especially with regard to cognitive achievements (see Miller, 1988). Crouchman (1985) found that 61 percent of a sample of mothers did

not expect newborns to see, and other studies reported estimates for the emergence of basic perceptual capacities such as vision and hearing at weeks or even months beyond the correct time. After infancy, people tend to show the opposite pattern and actually overestimate what their children are capable of doing on memory tests and attainment of Piagetian skills (Miller, 1988).

There is no doubt that parents need more accurate information about their children's abilities. The parent in the year 2000 will probably be encouraged to attend more classes aimed at improving parenting skills. Parents of special groups will be targeted. For example, as more parents of infants enter the work force, they may want to know how to optimize their time with their infants. The young parent or the parent of a disabled infant may need special training. In addition, classes will probably do more than just provide information. They will actively involve the parents, perhaps through home visits and discussions with professionals. Of equal importance is the likelihood that parent education programs will be aimed at both mothers and fathers. What does this mean for the child in the year 2000? When parenting skills are improved, the infant becomes

more responsive, and cognitive development is optimized.

There are possible implications for the field of developmental psychology as well. Just as early childhood day care is now considered a specialty, there will be a call for more people to be parenting educators. These educators not only will be involved in teaching parents and making home visits but also will have to develop skills that will allow them to encourage fearful parents to participate in such programs.

This may be the real challenge for the year 2000. Unfortunately, the people who need this training the most are often the least likely to volunteer for parenting programs or to read articles on advances in child development. We may find more calls for such courses in high school, especially since there is some evidence that they may reduce the possibility of child abuse.

There are, then, a number of trends in infant cognitive development that will bear watching. There will be more knowledge about what the infant knows and how the infant develops cognitively, and this information must be delivered to the public. There will be an increase in the need for early parenting courses that will be directed at specific groups of parents (those who must work, those who are young), and there will be the beginning of a need for the training of parenting educators. The real challenge, however, will be to involve the parents who most need this training in a successful program so that infants may develop their early cognitive capabilities to their fullest extent.

10. TRUE OR FALSE?

Programs that teach parents how to interact with their children have been largely successful in improving the intellectual functioning of the children.

cognitive level than children of parents who have not done so (Beller, 1979). When parents are helped to improve the environment of their home, it helps all the children in the home and may carry over to new arrivals. Community support is also enlisted when these strategies work. Finally, friends and relatives who come into contact with these participants obtain at least a smattering of knowledge and may themselves consent to participate at a later time. But what is the most effective and efficient way to teach parents to parent? Is an involved program necessary, or can it be a relatively simple, inexpensive one?

Showing Parents What Their Infants Can Do

The simplest programs simply show parents what their infants can do, and many hospitals have short courses covering a number of areas, such as a child's capabilities, ways of stimulating a child, and answers to "how to" questions. In some of these programs, the capabilities of the newborn are usually demonstrated using the Brazelton Neonatal Assessment Scale as a focal point (See page 172). Some studies have emphasized films, question-and-answer sessions, and demonstrations of what a child is capable of doing. Although these programs show some success, programs that require active involvement by the parents are superior (Parke & Tinsley, 1987).

Barbara Myers (1982) randomly assigned forty-two middle-class families with firstborn infants to one of three groups. In one group, fathers received the training; in another group, mothers received the training; the third group acted as a control receiving no training. The parents in the two experimental groups were taught to perform the Brazelton Scale on their infants while their attention was drawn to the infants' most positive interactive and physical abilities. Data were collected in a number of

Studies show that parents who receive parenting help improve as parents. Parent education programs are often very successful.

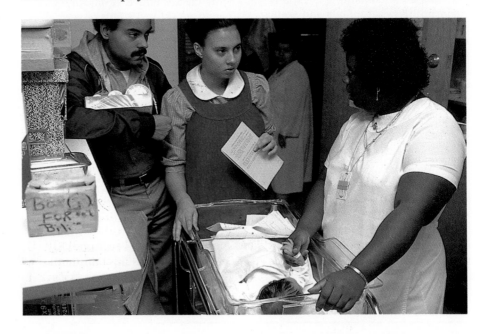

areas, including measures of knowledge of infant behavior, confidence in parenting ability, parents' satisfaction with their infants, and infants' actual behavior.

The parents in both experimental groups scored higher in knowledge about infants, and fathers in the experimental group were more involved in the caregiving of their infants at four weeks than were control fathers. More modest effects were shown for experimental mothers' confidence, and both mothers and fathers in the treatment groups were more satisfied with their parenting. There were no differences in parent-infant interactions during the observation session, perhaps because the treatment does not affect this area or perhaps due to technical reasons that include difficulty interpreting the meaning of particular behaviors. The programs described here are rather short-term efforts that mainly show parents what their infants can do. Although they show some valuable effects, especially if active parental involvement is required, they do not aim at directly teaching parents specific techniques for improving parent-child interaction.

Teaching Parents Specific Parenting Skills

Other programs have concentrated on directly teaching parenting skills through demonstration, information giving, film, discussion, and home visits by professionals. When teenage mothers (sixteen-years-old and younger) were given weekly classes covering such areas as ways to stimulate their infants, nutrition and family planning, and a number of supportive services were offered, significant improvements were found both in the mothers and in the infants (Badger, Burns & Vietze, 1981). The infants showed higher scores on the Bayley tests than a control group, and the mothers were more physically and emotionally responsive to their infants.

In another parent training program, nineteen couples and their four-month-old through twelve-month-old infants were randomly assigned to the training group or the control group. Parents in the training group received lectures, participated in discussions, and watched demonstrations. The material covered emphasized child development, individual variation, knowledge of infant temperament, and methods of responding to different types of infant behavior. The treatment group showed improvements in their interactions with the infants through better anticipation of infant needs and improved response to infant behavior (Dickie & Gerber, 1980). The fact that the infants also showed more responsiveness to their parents demonstrates how parental training can affect the infants themselves in a positive way. The parents in the training groups did not realize that their competency had improved, perhaps because knowledge makes one more aware of one's weaknesses and failings.

One three-year program, called The New Parents as Teachers (NPAT) program, tried to assess the value of high-quality parent education on the skills new parents need to optimize their children's development during the first three years of life (Pfannenstiel & Seltzer, 1989). The program consisted of providing parents with information on child growth and development, periodic developmental and health screenings, monthly home visits by parent educators, and monthly group meetings at neighborhood resource centers. When compared to a control group, children whose parents were in the program scored significantly better on measures of intelligence, auditory comprehension, and language ability. Parents who participated were significantly more knowledgeable. One interesting finding was that the higher the quality of the parental participation and the more active the parent was in the program, the better their children performed. The high-quality parent involvement with the parent educator was the main reason for the effectiveness of this program. Again, as we have seen even with short-term programs, active involvement is the key.

Other home-based programs exist. The most interesting is a verbal interaction program under the directorship of Levenstein (Golden & Burns, 1975; Madden, 1976). This program is beautiful in its simplicity. Beginning in the second year of life, 200 lower income families participating in the study received a visit from a demonstrator who showed parents how to read to their children and use certain toys. The materials were provided by the program. However, a large part of the instruction emphasized verbal interaction between parent and child. For instance, parents were encouraged to label things according to form and color, to elicit responses from children through questions, and to give a considerable amount of positive reinforcement to their children. The children showed dramatic increases in intelligence, and the longer they were involved, the better the results (Beller, 1979). Their reading skills in elementary school were superior as well.

It is clear from this research that programs to train parents to parent are generally successful. Programs that actively involve parents are more successful than more passive programs that merely give information. If these programs are largely successful, why are they not expanded? Money is one limiting factor, as they are costly. In addition, many people believe that the family has the sole responsibility to care for children and that society should take little interest or part in child rearing. Infant programs, day care, and preschool education are considered extras. In addition, people still hold fast to the idea that parenting is a simple skill, something that is instinctual. However, not all parents know how to develop their children's potential. One common question parents ask is, "Just what *can* you do with a baby or a toddler?" Today, when we know what can be done to optimize a child's development, it is unfortunate that such programs are not more widespread.

The Question of Acceleration: The "American Question"

You may have noticed that these programs are trying to improve the environment so that children can develop their own abilities at their own pace. There is no hint of accelerating infants cognitively to make them learn faster. This desire to accelerate is perhaps part of our culture, though.

American educators and parents are often interested in the question of how fast or how early a child can accomplish some academic task. They are impressed with the child who is reading at the age of three or solving algebraic equations at eight. Reflecting this fascination with speed, researchers have raised the question of whether infants can be accelerated through the period of sensorimotor experience. The entire idea really runs counter to Piaget's ideas.

Piaget was reluctant to make any recommendations to teachers or parents concerning how to maximize a child's potential, let alone how to accelerate the child's growth (Vernon, 1976). Remember that Piaget's theory emphasizes the importance of maturation and giving children an opportunity to interact with their environment. It deemphasizes formal instruction. Parents may help their children by designing an environment that is appropriate for the children at their particular point in development and elaborating on that environment, giving children plenty of opportunity to discover things on their own. For instance, when presenting children with objects of different textures, it is beneficial to have a variety of such objects in the environment and to allow the children to explore them at their own rate. This does not mean that the parents remain passive. Indeed, parents should be available, answer questions, interact with the child, and so on, but the emphasis is on discovery, not formal teaching and programming.

Perhaps we should put the question a different way. The purpose of improving interaction with parents and designing a stimulating and appropriate atmosphere for infants is to provide the optimal atmosphere for children to develop their cognitive potential. Particular experiences at certain stages are beneficial, but the goal should not be to see how fast a child can get through Piaget's stages. Instead, the goal should be to provide experiences that will help the child develop according to his or her own rate and abilities. Such an environment is child centered, providing the infant with the opportunities to interact and learn.

There are times when parents and professionals must be more active in designing a program of stimulation, such as when working with premature infants or disabled children. Rose (1980) found significant differences in the recognition memories of full-term and preterm infants, but when preterm infants had received extra stimulation during the early weeks of life, their performance on memory tasks was similar to that of full-term infants. Infants who are not at risk might benefit from a more active program as well, but the power to accelerate development is not unbounded. If cognitive development can be accelerated, an upper limit to this acceleration probably exists. And such acceleration has risks. Parents may place pressure on their infants to perform and hold unreasonable expectations that may interfere with the child's normal development.

The value of trying to accelerate infants through the sensorimotor period is doubtful, especially since correlations between sensorimotor intelligence and later cognitive achievement are so low. Lewis and McGurk (1972) administered the Bayley scales and a scale of object permanence to twenty infants at three, six, nine, twelve, eighteen, and twenty-four months of age. At two years, the children were also given the Peabody Picture Vocabulary Tests, a test of intellectual level. Scores on the Bayley at three months did not predict the scores at six months. In addition, the

11. *TRUE OR FALSE?*

Child development specialists equate fast development with superior development.

Bayley did not predict the child's score on the test of object permanence. Finally, neither test predicted the child's performance on the Peabody. This indicates that the idea of acceleration should be deemphasized. The best course is to design stimulating environments for children and to teach parents how to interact with their infants so that the children can gain the appropriate skills. Rushing a child through this stage of life accomplishes little. Because development is faster does not necessarily make it any better.

♦ CONCLUSIONS

The evidence is clear that such activities as providing a stimulating atmosphere, labeling the environment, interacting in a positive manner with children, and encouraging children to investigate and explore are helpful in promoting cognitive development. Parents can and should be active in these areas, but they must also beware of overdoing it, of pressuring their infants, of believing that somehow faster is always better, of thinking in terms of how fast rather than how well, or becoming school-teachers rather than parents. David Elkind (1973) notes that parents are sometimes made to feel guilty if they do not cover the entire room with mobiles or purchase the newest educational toys. Although mobiles certainly give children something interesting to look at and have value, a homemade mobile made from clothespins is just as good as a fancy one bought from a store. As Elkind (1973), p. 40) notes, "Toys for infants should be chosen on the basis of their safety and their immediate entertainment value, rather than in terms of their long range educational benefit."

12. *TRUE OR FALSE?*

If children do not receive optimal stimulation by the age of two, they will underachieve throughout their childhood and adolescent years.

Finally, there is no magic age at which it is "all over." Cognitive development in infancy is important, but it is possible to improve the lot of a child who has not experienced an optimal early environment if a significant change occurs in the environment later on (Clarke & Clarke, 1977). Although we should not underestimate the importance of such development in infancy, neither should we overestimate it.

We have now seen how the child develops from a newborn infant with few cognitive skills to a two-year-old who has an impressive repertoire of cognitive abilities. Yet the rush of interest in cognitive psychology should not blind us to the importance of the child's personality and social development. After all, we want our children not only to be intellectually advanced but also to develop their personalities and their social abilities. It is to these qualities that we turn next.

SUMMARY

1. According to Jean Piaget, in the first two years of life, children negotiate the sensorimotor stage during which they use their senses and motor skills to learn about the world. They do not have the ability to create mental images or use language or symbols to represent anything.
2. The development of object permanence—the understanding that an object or person exists even when it is out of sight—is an important achievement in infancy.
3. One should not equate competency (knowledge and ability) with performance. Performance depends on motivation, the type of task presented, and other environmental factors. Some recent experimentation demonstrates that infants may be more capable than Piaget believed.

4. Infants have the ability to recognize faces very early, and infants between eight and twelve months of age have some recall abilities.
5. Scores on infant intelligence tests do not predict later intellectual ability very well for normal children.
6. There is a relationship between later cognitive development and the responsiveness of the caregiver, parental involvement with the child, the variety of stimulation the child receives, the organization of the environment, and the play materials available.
7. The best way to optimize the child's intellectual ability is to improve the home environment. Programs aimed at improving the home environment and parent-child interaction have been successful.
8. Allowing children to explore their own world, labeling the environment, encouraging communication, reading to the child, briefly interacting with the child by sharing some experience, and tailoring activities to the child's development level promote cognitive growth.
9. Moderate levels of stimulation are best for the child. The question of how flexible infant cognitive development is has not yet been fully answered.
10. Programs that aim at helping parents develop better parenting skills have been successful. The greater the degree of active parental participation, the more successful the program will be.
11. The so-called American Question asks whether cognitive growth can be accelerated. Such acceleration was discouraged by Piaget, who believed that by designing an appropriate environment and giving children an opportunity to discover the mysteries of life, children can develop their cognitive abilities.

ACTION/REACTION

How Much Is Too Much?

In the past decade, the importance of cognitive stimulation in infancy has been increasingly noted by authorities in the field. One night Lauren and Peter, who are expecting their first child very soon, were invited to Lester and Judy's home for the evening. Lester and Judy have a baby boy, William; naturally, the conversation turned to child behavior and child rearing.

Lester and Judy believe that early intelligence predicts later academic success. "Children need a head start from their parents," they argue. They are determined to work with William as he matures and to help him maximize his cognitive abilities. They both give William plenty of attention, have three mobiles over the crib, and have written the name of each item in the house on strips of paper that are pasted on each piece of furniture. They surround the child with plenty of pictures and are very involved in two exercise and cognitive growth programs. They tell their friends that to do anything less is to reduce William's chances of becoming a top student.

Lauren and Peter were impressed by the way their friends had structured the baby's environment, but they wonder if the environment is too structured, too stimulating, and too confusing for their infant. They must decide just what course to chart for their own new baby.

1. If you were Lauren or Peter, what course would you choose?

Motivating Parents

Mrs. Yamamoto is a high school teacher. A number of her students either are pregnant or have become parents. In fact, a day-care center has been established in her school. During her time in the school, Mrs. Yamamoto has become aware of some parenting difficulties that the students and some people in the community seem to have. Children are frequently left in front of the television set for hours at home, and often the infants, especially after one year of age, do not get sufficient stimulation.

She has decided to do something about it. She is holding seminars with some psychologists and physicians from neighborhood institutions who have donated their time. Mrs. Yamamoto is excited about the program. Unfortunately, attendance in the evening seminars has been poor, and often the people who come already seem to be well acquainted with effective parenting techniques. The question Mrs. Yamamoto is facing is how to motivate parents to come to the seminars. The local school board has asked Mrs. Yamamoto to design a program in conjunction with neighborhood institutions to improve parenting skills, especially among younger and single parents.

1. If you were Mrs. Yamamoto, how would you motivate parents to come to the seminars?
2. If you were Mrs. Yamamoto, what sort of program would you design to help parents improve their parenting skills?

CHAPTER SEVEN

Social and Personality Development in Infancy and Toddlerhood

Kitchen Scene by Utamaro

Setting the Stage
Emotional Development
Attachment
The Caregiver-Child Relationship
The Importance of Early Mother-Child Contact
The Father-Child Relationship
The Employed Mother
Day Care
Cross-Cultural Current: Infant Day Care and Family Policy in Sweden
The Child in the Year 2000: Who's Minding the Children?
Many Roads to Travel

Are These Statements True of False?

Turn the page for the correct answers. Each statement is repeated in the margin next to the paragraph in which the information can be found.

1. By one week, the infant is smiling at the sight of other people.
2. Adults have no difficulty identifying the emotional expressions of infants.
3. Year-old infants' behavior is affected by the emotional expressions of their mothers.
4. Very young infants cry in response to the cries of other infants.
5. Infants show more fear of unfamiliar adults than of unfamiliar children.
6. The quality of infants' attachment to their mothers predicts children's future social maturity but not their cognitive abilities during early childhood.
7. Parents who are very anxious about their new role as parents tend to adapt better than parents who have less anxiety about becoming parents.
8. Older mothers have a more positive attitude toward motherhood than younger mothers do.
9. Early and extended contact immediately after birth is necessary if infants are to develop a healthy attachment to their mothers.
10. Fathers in dual-earner families do more housework and participate more in child care than fathers in single-earner families.
11. In the United States, mothers play with infants and toddlers in a quieter and more verbal manner than fathers.
12. There are no differences in social behavior between children who attend day care and those who are raised at home.

259

Answers to True-False Statements

1. False. Correct statement: Infants do not smile at the sight of others until at least three weeks.
2. True.
3. True.
4. True.
5. True.
6. False. Correct statement: Infants' attachment in infancy is related to both social and cognitive development during the preschool period.
7. False. Correct statement: Parents who are overly anxious do not do as well as parents who are not as anxious.
8. True.
9. False. Correct statement: Although early and extended contact may be desirable, it is not necessary for mothers and infants to form a relationship.
10. True.
11. True.
12. False. Correct statement: There are some differences between day-care-raised children and home-raised children.

♦ SETTING THE STAGE

Like so many American families, Lisa and Tim Walters needed every penny to keep their heads above water. With two children (Beth, age two, and Jon, eight months), a modest home, and two cars, they were just breaking even each month. They had decided that Lisa would stay home and be a full-time homemaker until the youngest child entered elementary school. Then Lisa would return to work. Both agreed that this was the best strategy for them. It combined their belief that the early relationship between mother and child was important with the reality of needing two incomes as the children grew.

But Tim was laid off from his job. Unable to afford a long layoff, he took a lower paying position and returned to school for retraining. Trapped by car payments and a hefty mortgage, Lisa and Tim fell into debt. They finally decided that Lisa should go back to work immediately.

Lisa and Tim are concerned. The two-year-old will have to enter a day-care program, while the baby will either be in a day-care center or be taken daily to Lisa's mother. The parents have a host of questions. How will the experiences affect the children? How will these constant but temporary separations affect their relationship with their youngsters? How will Lisa's working affect the family? Is day care harmful to children?

Many American families are asking the same questions. Over the past thirty years, the number of women in the labor force and the proportion of employed mothers have increased dramatically (see Table 7.1). Some 18.6 percent of married mothers with children under 6 were employed in 1960, 36.8 percent in 1975, and 57.4 percent in 1988. Over 72 percent of all women with children from age six to age thirteen are in the labor force, and 54.8 percent of all women with children under three are employed outside the home (U.S. Department of Commerce, 1989). Half of all women with infants under one year of age are employed. Many people equate the employed mother with the single parent, and indeed most single parents are employed—but more than half of all mothers in two-parent families also are employed.

So the Walters' dilemma is not unusual, and the questions they ask are vital. This chapter investigates the emotional, social, and personality development of infants and toddlers and answers the Walters' questions.

♦ EMOTIONAL DEVELOPMENT

One of the Walters' concerns involves the emotional development of their children. Emotional development in infancy is not an easy area to research. After all, infants cannot verabalize how they feel. Instead, we must study how they feel on the basis of facial gestures, physiological responses, or the sounds they make in response to some stimulus (Eisenberg et al., 1988a). Yet the questions that surround infant emotions are fascinating.

What Emotions Do Infants Show?

As you gaze at a one-week old, the infant seems to be making some movement with his or her mouth that looks like a smile. But is it a smile? What emotions do newborns possess? Infants are born with the musculature capable of forming all the facial movements necessary to show emotion (Ekman & Oster, 1979). However, scientists disagree on what emotions are shown in very early infancy.

There are at least two major theoretical approaches. The first—termed discrete emotion theory—argues that infants possess a very discrete and limited number of emotions (Malatesta, Culver, Tesman, & Shepard, 1989). These specific emotions are innate and include interest, disgust, physical distress, and a precursor of surprise called a startle. Anger, surprise itself, and joy emerge during the next four months, and fear and shyness emerge in the second half of the first year. The social smile emerges sometime between three and six weeks (Izard & Malatesta, 1987). Each of these emotions can be elicited at will. For example, novelty and human faces elicit interest, and bad-tasting foods elicit disgust. The social smile is elicited at three weeks by a high-pitched human voice and at six weeks by the human face. Anger has been found in two-month-old infants in response to pain, and by four months, infants show anger when their arms are restrained.

Emotions emerge mostly because of biological maturation. However, learning also exerts a strong influence. Other emotions such as shame,

The majority of mothers with preschoolers are now in the labor force.

1. *TRUE OR FALSE?*

By one week of age, the infant is smiling at the sight of other people.

TABLE 7.1: Labor Force Participation Rates for Wives, Husband Present, by Age of Own Youngest Child: 1975 to 1988

PRESENCE AND AGE OF CHILD	TOTAL			
	1975	1980	1985	1988
Wives total	44.5	50.2	54.3	56.7
No children under 18.............	44.0	46.0	48.2	49.1
With children under 18...........	44.9	54.3	61.0	65.2
Under 6, total...................	36.8	45.3	53.7	57.4
Under 3	32.6	41.5	50.7	54.8
1 year or under	30.8	39.0	49.4	51.9
2 years	37.1	48.1	54.0	61.7
3 to 5 years...................	42.2	51.7	58.6	61.4
3 years	41.2	51.5	55.1	59.3
4 years	41.2	51.4	59.7	61.4
5 years	44.4	52.4	62.1	63.6
6 to 13 years...................	51.8	62.6	68.1	72.3
14 to 17 years.................	53.8	60.5	67.0	72.9

Source: U.S. Bureau of Labor Statistics, *Monthly Labor Review*, 1986 and 1989.

shyness, guilt and contempt, although not well studied, appear in the first half of the second year of life (Izard & Malatesta, 1987). Early emotional expressions follow a rather predictable timetable. According to discrete emotion theory, emotions and cognitive abilities develop independently at first and interdependence occurs as the child ages.

Discrete emotions are related to specific behaviors in the infant. Six-month-old infants are likely to show facial expressions of joy when they are looking at their mothers, whereas expressions of sadness occur when they are looking away and fussing (Tronick, 1989). When newborns only two hours old were fed solutions that tasted bitter, sweet, sour, or salty, the infants showed different facial responses to each taste except salty. When the sour solution was given to the infants, the infants compressed their cheeks against their gums, tightly squeezed their eyes, lowered their brows, and pursed their lips. The reaction to the bitter solution included a gaping mouth, accompanied by elevation of the tongue in the back of the mouth and other actions that blocked swallowing. The reaction to a sweet substance sometimes involved an initial negative response which passed quickly and was considered a reaction to the syringe used to place the solution into the infant's mouth. It was followed by total facial relaxation. The researchers note that some of the facial actions in response to the nonsweet stimuli are components of adult disgust expressions, but they are not willing at this time to draw any conclusions about the subjective nature of these infant responses (Rosenstein & Oster, 1988). Other psychologists are willing to consider the responses in terms of emotional expression.

Other experts in the area of infant emotions disagree with the argument that infants show discrete emotions from birth, arguing that newborn emotions are actually undifferentiated states of distress or nondistress that only later in infancy differentiate into specific emotions (Sroufe, 1979). They reject the idea of identifiable newborn emotions and claim that such behaviors as responses to pain or distress and the first smiles turn into other identifiable emotions with experience. This does not occur until two or three months. For example, the distress in the first few weeks of life differentiates into rage at three months and anger later on. In this theory, cognition and emotion develop hand in hand.

One of the difficulties in studying the meaning of infant emotions is answering the perplexing question of whether the expression of an emotion (such as disgust) reflects the emotional experience of the infant. It is clear that in adults this is not always the case. You may be bitterly disappointed in a test grade, yet smile anyway to keep up appearances. It is assumed by those, such as Carroll Izard, who argue for the discrete theory that infants' experience matches their expression. Others disagree and argue that emotional experience is meaningful only when such cognitive factors as recognition and appraisal exist. In other words, the infant who is to feel disgust must appraise his or her situation. This requires a degree of cognitive sophistication that is not available in the newborn. As L. Alan Sroufe notes (1979, p. 491), "Only with recognition is there pleasure and disappointment; only with the development of causality, object permanence, intentionality, and meaning are there joy, anger, and fear; only with self-awareness is there shame." As children's cognitive skills develop, children can make finer distinctions in the environment and experience different emotions.

Whether one argues for or against discrete emotions in very early infancy, emotional response can be reliably triggered in infancy by specific environmental stimuli. Hearing mother's voice may bring forth a smile in the infant; later in infancy, seeing the doctor's office may lead to crying. As children develop, both experience and central nervous system development allow them to expand their repertoire of emotions.

Emotional development is also based upon cognitive development. The importance of cognitive processes is shown in a study of four-month-old to eight-month-old infants. The infants watched while someone wearing a scary mask approached them. When the mask was worn by a stranger, the babies cried, but when worn by mothers, the babies laughed (Sroufe & Wunsch, 1972). This demonstrates that the infant is now using cognitive appraisal to "decide" which emotion to show. Between eight and twelve months, infants have the ability to plan and anticipate, and they can therefore show surprise when something unexpected happens.

What Function Do Emotions Serve?

Infant emotions have two major functions or purposes. First, emotions facilitate behavioral reactions to stimuli in the environment (Lamb, 1988). For example, interest is associated with many behaviors, including attention, learning, exploration, and play. Sadness is associated with different

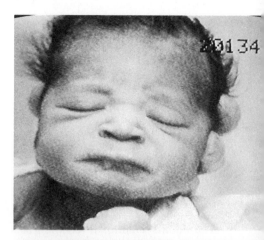

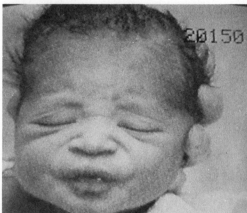

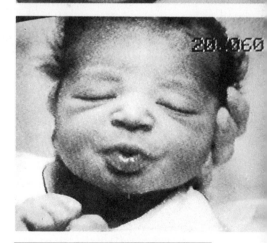

A sweet solution will elicit facial expressions in infants. Initial negative facial actions are followed by relaxation and sucking.

The infants' emotional reactions as demonstrated in their facial expressions and actions affect the caregiver.

2. *TRUE OR FALSE?*
_____

Adults have no difficulty identifying the emotional expression of infants.

behaviors that may include avoidance and a reduction in motor activities (Termine & Izard, 1988). Second, emotional expressions communicate the infant's state to others and encourages the caregiver to help the infant (Lamb, 1988) or interact more with the child. The infant's expressions certainly have an effect on the caregiver. An infant's distress, for example, may cause an adult to search for the root of the problem and do something about it.

Do Parents Understand Their Infant's Emotional Responses?

If part of the function of an infant's emotions is to communicate with caregivers, it is vital for caregivers to read correctly children's expressions. The evidence in this area is overwhelming. We know, for instance, that people from all over the world easily read the facial expressions of other people accurately (Ekam, 1973). The same seems to be true for adults' reading of infant emotions (Emde, Izard, Huebner, Sorce, & Klinnert, 1985). Carroll Izard and colleagues (1980) found that both trained and untrained college students had no difficulty identifying infant emotional responses to a variety of events ranging from happiness and playful interactions to pain from inoculations to the expressions of surprise and sadness.

Can Infants Read the Emotional States of Others?

Infants show emotions, and their emotions are understood and interpreted by adults. But do infants understand the emotions of others? Can an infant interpret the smile on his or her mother's face or the frown on some other adult's face?

Even young infants are aware of their parents' facial expressions. Infants as young as two or three months—and possibly even newborns—can discriminate a variety of facial expressions (Nelson, 1987). Two-month-old infants can discriminate a happy face from a neutral face, and three-month-olds discriminate happy, sad, and surprised faces (Nelson & Horowitz, 1983). Three-month-old infants recognize the difference between smiling and frowning expressions (Barrera & Maurer, 1981). Some studies have even shown that young infants not only can discriminate facial expressions but also can imitate a happy, sad, or surprised expression (Field et al., 1983), although not all studies have been able to replicate this.

Although there is little doubt about an infant's ability to differentiate between some expressions, many researchers claim that in the first few months, infants may not be able to understand the true nature of emotional expression. It is only from about six months on that infants react to different expression, reacting more negatively to a frowning, crying, or sad face than to a happy or neutral face (Kruetzer & Charlesworth, 1973). In the second half of the first year, infants not only can discriminate emotions but also are affected by them, therefore realizing that emotions have meaning.

Social Referencing

How are infants affected by the emotional expressions of others? The phenomenon in which a person uses information received from others to appraise events and regulate behavior is called **social referencing** (Hornik & Gunnar, 1988). There are two types. One involves affective referencing, where people use the emotional expressions of others to determine how to act. The other is instrumental referencing, where infants use the actions of other people as a guide. Instrumental social referencing in infants has not really been examined yet and is sometimes described in terms of observation learning and imitation. Affective referencing, though, has recently been the focus of much interest. Most studies approach it by placing an infant in an ambiguous situation while an adult displays a particular expression. The psychologist then observes how the expression affects the infant's behavior.

Social referencing is reliably found at about a year. What if a year-old child was placed on the safe side of the visual cliff (refer to pages 185–186)? This, as you remember, is a table with a checkerboard pattern on one side and clear glass on the other side. Below the clear side is another checkerboard that makes the clear side look like a cliff. The height of the table can be adjusted in such a way that the infant will neither avoid the cliff because of fear nor find the cliff absolutely safe. The situation is ambiguous, and the infant is uncertain about what to do. The mother stands opposite the infant and is told to either smile, show joy or interest, or show fear or anger. If an infant looks at the mother while she is smiling or showing joy or interest, most infants will cross the deep side. If the mother shows fear or anger, very few infants will cross. If the visual cliff is adjusted so that it is obviously safe, very few infants reference their mothers at all, and those who do and see their mothers showing fear hesitate but cross anyway (Sorce, Emde, Campos, & Klinnert, 1985).

Social referencing is most likely to take place when the situation is ambiguous. Under such circumstances, infants actively search for information (Walden & Ogan, 1988). Although the expressions that most influence infants' behavior are what we consider negative ones, such as fear and sadness (Hornik & Gunnar, 1988), those that we consider positive emotions also affect the behavior of the infant. Saul Feinman and Michael Lewis (1983) investigated ten-month-old infants' reactions to strangers. If the mother spoke to the infant in a positive manner, expressing positive emotion, the infants were friendlier to the stranger than if the mother was neutral. Most studies of infant referencing use mothers, but infants also use social referencing with their fathers (Dickstein & Parke, 1988).

Social referencing is a reasonably new area, and some questions remain to be researched. For example, about a quarter of infants in most studies do not reference at all, and we need to account for these individual differences (Nelson, 1987). In addition, some infants who do reference don't seem to use this information as a guide to their behavior.

There is no doubt that by the end of the first year the infant can distinguish and interpret emotions and is sometimes affected by the emotions of others. Research into infant emotions continues at a rapid rate, and some emotional responses have been researched thoroughly.

social referencing
The phenomenon in which a person uses information received from others to appraise events and regulate behavior.

3. TRUE OR FALSE?
___

Year-old infant's behavior is affected by the emotional expressions of their mothers.

The Smile

When you see an infant smile, it is very hard not to respond with a smile. A smile can communicate information and express an internal emotional experience. An infant's smile also is a potent reinforcer for adults, and a smiling infant encourages interaction with parents.

It is very difficult to determine exactly when an infant begins to smile. Newborns show expressions that look like smiles, but these expressions occur either during sleep or when the infant is drowsy, and they are probably involuntary reactions (Lamb, 1988). Early smiles are probably a release of tension and tied to internal states (Sroufe & Waters, 1976). By three to six weeks, however, infants show voluntary smiling in the waking state. At about three weeks, the smile can be elicited by a human voice (Wolff, 1963). This smile is shown not only to social stimuli, such as voices, but also to nonsocial stimuli, such as bells or a bull's eye. Gradually, smiles become more limited to social stimuli. Infants also smile when they have mastered an action reflecting pleasure or satisfaction.

Smiling is infrequent in the first month or two; then it increases dramatically until four months or so, after which it declines (Gewirtz, 1965; Super, 1981). After four or five months, the frequency of smiling becomes dependent on the infant's culture and family environment. Infant smiling that is reinforced with attention will increase in frequency (Etzel & Gewirtz, 1967). The social nature of the smile continues to develop in infancy. Older infants smile more when they are smiling at someone who is attentive than when the other person is not looking at them (Jones & Raag, 1989).

Every infant in every culture smiles. In fact, smiles are interpreted as positive expressions all around the world, and the development of the smile is basically the same in every society. Blind infants smile in response to social stimuli at about the same time as sighted children, even though they have not seen a smile (Freedman, 1965).

The smile, then, begins as an inborn response, but it soon evolves from an undifferentiated response to internal stimuli to a response that is attached to social stimuli. Its frequency can be increased through reinforcement. If infants are rewarded for smiling by being picked up, talked to, and handled, the frequency of their smiling increases (Brackbill, 1958). The smile contributes to the establishment and maintenance of the infant-caregiver relationship, as most parents take pleasure in interpreting their child's smile as a positive response to their own activity, and their actions are thus reinforced by the child (Eveloff, 1971).

Empathy

When we hear someone crying, it usually has some emotional effect on us. This is true for children as well. In a series of experiments, Simner (1971) exposed newborns to tape-recorded cries of other neonates. These infants responded by beginning to cry. They were more sensitive to the cries of a five-day-old neonate than to either a cry engineered through a computer or the cry of a five-and-a-half-month-old infant. Could such empathy be innate?

When one infant cries, others tend to do so as well. Some authorities argue that young infants experience empathy for others.

Grace Martin and Russell Clark (1982) presented forty infants whose average age was a bit over eighteen hours with tape recordings of their own cry or that of another neonate. These recordings were presented when the infants were both crying and calm. The infants demonstrated a remarkable degree of empathy. Infants who were originally calm tended to cry when they heard the sounds of another neonate crying. Crying infants tended to continue to cry when exposed to the cries of other infants but stopped when they heard recordings of their own cry. Calm infants, hearing their own cries, did not begin to cry.

In a second study, newborns were presented with tapes of a crying chimpanzee, an eleven-month-old child, and another newborn. Newborns exposed to the cry of another newborn tended to cry but didn't cry when exposed to the cry of an eleven-month-old or the chimpanzee. Martin and Clark conclude that neonates as young as eighteen hours can distinguish between their own cries, the cry of another infant or an older child, and that of a chimpanzee and will respond differentially. Neonates seem to have an empathy that is astounding for their age.

According to Martin Hoffman (1979), such reactions are an early rudimentary form of empathy. The further development of empathy, though, requires cognitive advancements. Before about one year, infants are basically empathically aroused without the cognitive abilities that will later be important in experiencing empathy. They do not see themselves as distinct from others. Upon seeing another child get hurt from a fall, a nine-month-old may cry or place her thumb in her mouth and bury her head in her mother's lap. This behavior may be similar to that shown when she, herself, is hurt or feeling badly (Hoffman, 1979).

As children become aware of themselves as distinct from others, they know when another person is in distress and may themselves become very distressed. They may feel compassion, with a desire to help (Hoffman, 1984). However, they assume that the other person is feeling the same way as they are. For example, eighteen-month-old Jeffrey got his mother to comfort his friend Tim who was crying, although Tim's mother was available. Since Jeffrey is used to being comforted by his own mother, he assumed that his friend would also be comforted by Jeffrey's mother, and did not try to get Tim's mother to comfort Tim. Empathy continues to develop as the ability to take another person's point of view increases throughout childhood.

4. TRUE OR FALSE?

Very young infants cry in response to the cries of other infants.

Fear of Strangers

Sometime during the second half of the first year, parents are surpised by the way their infants react to kindly strangers. In the past, the baby has shown curiosity, but now the child may show fear, manifested by crying and agitation. Until about four months of age, infants smile even at strangers, but after that they do so less and less (Bronson, 1968). Most children go through a period in which they react to strangers—and even to relatives they do not see regularly—with fear. The stage usually comes between about seven and ten months and may last through a good portion of the second year (Lewis & Rosenblum, 1975).

fear of strangers
A common phenomenon beginning in the second half of the first year, consisting of a fear response to new people.

5. *TRUE OR FALSE?*
_____

Infants show more fear of unfamiliar adults than of unfamiliar children.

Some studies, though, have questioned whether this **fear of strangers** is inevitable. Harriet Rheingold and Carol Eckerman (1973) allowed an adult female to interact with infants and their mothers for ten minutes before making any attempt to pick up the babies. The mother acted in a friendly manner toward the stranger. The infants were neither fearful nor upset, and they showed positive responses to the stranger.

Infant response to strangers depends on the stranger and the context. Infants show less or no fear of other children, perhaps because they compare the size of these children to themselves (Lewis & Brooks-Gunn, 1982). Female strangers produce less fear than male strangers (Skarin, 1977). If the mother is present and the stranger appears in a familiar place, such as the child's home, less anxiety is generated than when the setting is unfamiliar. In addition, when infants are allowed to investigate the situation on their own, they do not always show stranger anxiety.

It is wrong, then, to conclude that stranger anxiety is inevitable or that the appearance or lack of stranger anxiety indicates any problem (Goleman, 1989). Rather, we can say that stranger anxiety is mediated by a number of factors and depends upon the situation. Because stranger anxiety can be reduced if the meeting takes place in a familiar setting and in the presence of the mother (or perhaps the father) and if the child is allowed time to warm up to the stranger, unfamiliar Auntie Dolores would be better to get acquainted again with mother and father before trying to interact with eight-month-old Hector.

Separation Anxiety

separation anxiety
Fear of being separated from caregivers, beginning at eight or nine months and peaking at between twelve and sixteen months.

Parents are familiar with **separation anxiety**. As the parents are about to go out for the evening, the younger children begin to cry and protest loudly. The memory of that scene may haunt the parents throughout the evening.

Separation anxiety begins at about eight or nine months and peaks at between twelve and sixteen months (Metcalf, 1979). It may continue throughout the second year, but it becomes less intense, if indeed it is found at all, in the third year. Some separations are predictable, as in the case of the mother who every weekday morning takes her child to the day-care center. The child can anticipate predictable separations and knows that mother will return. The environment is familiar, and ideally the child is well acquainted with the substitute caregivers. After a while, children become used to an environment, such as a day-care center, and do not show much, if any, separation anxiety when mother leaves (Maccoby, 1980). Unpredictable separations, such as when a child enters the hospital, are different, however. The child is now presented with an unfamiliar environment, strange people who use ominous looking equipment, and a novel situation.

How a child reacts to any separation depends on the child's age, the familiarity of the situation, and previous experiences. In addition, if the child has familiar toys or a companion such as a sibling or is left with a substitute caregiver with whom an attachment has been formed, separation anxiety can be reduced. Even the possibility that the mother will

Infants often show separation anxiety. They show less anxiety when they are left with familiar people.

leave may be enough to provide some problems, especially in the unpredictable situation. For example, when mother begins to pack for a trip, the child may start to cry and cling to her. The child is anticipating the loss. Any increase in the risk of a separation can trigger some anxiety (Bowlby, 1982).

Separation anxiety can also be a function of temperament. When the brain waves of ten-month-old infants were measured in response to separation from their mothers, infants who cried in response to the separation showed different brain-wave patterns both before and after separations than infants who did not cry (Davidson & Fox, 1989). These differences may be one of the bases for temperament and may demonstrate that reactions to separation are at least partly based upon temperamental differences.

The Infant's Response to Prolonged Separations

The psychological impact of separation depends partly on the length of the separation. Robertson and Bowlby (1952) argue that the child's reaction to prolonged separation goes through three stages: protest, despair, and detachment. In the **protest** stage, children cry and do not allow anyone else to care for them (Schaffer, 1977). The dominant emotion appears to be anger (Shiller, Izard, & Bembree, 1986). In the next stage, **despair**, the child becomes apathetic and may gaze at the ceiling from the crib for hours at a time. Then the final stage, **detachment**, is reached. Now a child "comes to terms with the situation but at a cost of his emotional tie with his mother and his ability to put his trust into any relationship" (Schaffer, 1977, pp. 96–97). If the separation is temporary, upon reunion the child

protest stage
The initial reaction to separation in which the infant cries and refuses to be cared for by substitute caregivers.

despair stage
The second stage in prolonged separation from primary caregivers, in which the child becomes apathetic.

detachment stage
The last stage in prolonged separation from the primary caregivers, in which the child cannot trust anyone else and becomes detached from other people.

may react to the parents with a detached attitude. A bit later, the young-ster may become clingy and refuse to be left alone.

What are the long-term effects of prolonged separation? The early work of John Bowlby showed that these separations could lead to emotional disturbances, but we know that experience is cumulative and that an excellent later environment can mitigate the effects of a poor early en-vironment. A study of children raised in institutions for the first few years and then adopted found no evidence of extensive emotional disturbance. The children also developed good relationships with their adoptive par-ents (Tizard, 1977). In addition, many of the problems Bowlby attributed to separation may have been related to problems that existed before the separation (Rutter, 1979). Finally, the separations Bowlby studied were frequently long and severe, not the type of predictable temporary sepa-rations so common when children are involved in a day-care situation.

♦ ATTACHMENT

Lisa and Tim Walters are aware of the importance psychologists place on the early caregiver-infant bond. They are concerned that the day-care experience will somehow affect this relationship.

The Nature of Attachment

attachment
An emotional tie binding people together over space and time.

Just what is attachment, and how does it develop? Study of the caregiver-infant relationship usually centers on the concept of **attachment**. Ac-cording to Mary Ainsworth (1974, p. 135), "An attachment is an affec-tional tie that one person forms to another specific person, binding them together in space and enduring over time." Attachment is specific, but an infant may be attached to more than one person. Attachment implies an emotional bond that is a positive force in an individual's life. Infants become attached to their primary caregiver, in most instances, the mother. But it is clear that infants also become attached to their fathers, their grandparents, and day-care workers. How this occurs and the functions of this attachment are still a matter of controversy.

One theory of attachment emphasizes its biological roots. Attachment is necessary for the survival and normal development of the infant (Ain-sworth, 1974; Bowlby, 1973). The most famous attachment researcher, John Bowlby (1969), believes that attachment ensures the survival and is a product of evolution. Attachment takes time to form, and it develops along with the child's cognitive abilities. The infant is not born with a natural affinity to the mother. This affinity is learned (Waters & Deane, 1982). So, although attachment has biological roots, learning and cogni-tion also play a part.

Attachment Behavior

Infants begin to recognize the difference between strangers and familiar people in the first four months. Only at about six months do proximity-maintaining behaviors, such as seeking out the caregiver when afraid, occur. Such behaviors as crying when the mother leaves the room or following the mother around begin at about that age (Ainsworth, 1967).

The concept of attachment differs from **attachment behavior**, which involves actions that result in a child's obtaining proximity to another person who is viewed as better able to cope with the world (Bowlby, 1982). In other words, under certain circumstances, such as stress or anxiety, children are motivated to seek out the individual to whom they are attached. Such behaviors are not shown all the time, only when a child's world is threatened in some manner.

As children age, these attachment behaviors change somewhat, and children can accept temporary separations from their mothers. They may feel secure enough to be left with a warm substitute figure without creating too much fuss. Even here, though, acceptance of separation is conditional (Bowlby, 1982). The child must be familiar with the substitute caregiver, not be anxious or ill at the time, and be secure enough to be able to resume contact with the primary caregiver in a short period of time.

Although shown less frequently and less urgently after the third birthday, attachment behavior does not completely disappear at this age. During years four, five, and six, and even through early middle childhood, children may seek out their parents when they have been frightened or have had a difficult day.

Maternal Deprivation

If, as Bowlby believes, attachment is necessary for the emotional growth and development of the infant, we would expect children who have not been able to develop such attachments to suffer greatly.

Indeed, this is the case. Many theorists argue that the early interactions between mother (the primary caregiver) and child are crucial to a child's later development. Sigmund Freud (1935) believed that difficulties in this early relationship were the foundation for emotional disturbance. Children who do not receive adequate care become anxious and are unable to relate to others. Although most research has concentrated on the effects of difficulties in the mother-infant relationship because she is so often the primary caregiver, the evidence can be interpreted in terms of a lack of attachment to a caregiver, whether it is the mother or someone else.

Many early studies found that the consequences of a breakdown in the early mother-child relationship were serious (Rutter, 1979). René Spitz (1945, 1965) compared children who were raised in an orphanage where they received impersonal care from the staff and another group raised by their mothers in what amounted to a prison nursery. The children raised in the prison nursery thrived, while those raised in the orphanage without much attention suffered greatly. Emotional disturbances, failure to gain weight, and retardation were common. The orphanage-raised children also suffered many more physical illnesses. Spitz coined the term **hospitalism** to describe these symptoms.

Some studies of maternal deprivation have been performed on animals. The results offer more evidence about the tragic effects of maternal dep-

attachment behavior
Actions by a child that result in the child's gaining proximity to caregivers.

Infants become attached to a number of people including their grandparents. The nature of the attachment depends upon the relationship between the child and caregiver.

hospitalism
A condition found in children from substandard institutions, marked by emotional disturbances, failure to gain weight, and retardation.

No matter whether the wire or cloth substitute mother fed the infant monkey, the infant ran to the cloth mother when frightened.

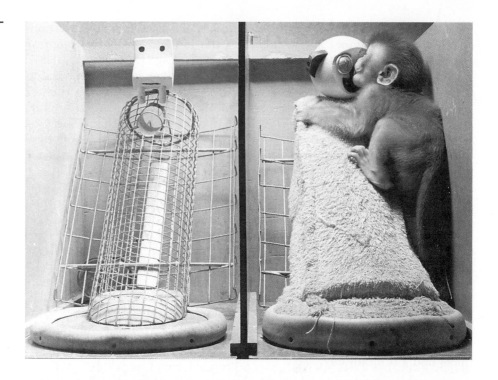

rivation (Harlow, 1959, 1971; Harlow & Suomi, 1971). Harlow raised rhesus monkeys with either a terrycloth monkey or a wire monkey. When frightened, the infant monkeys clung to the terrycloth mothers even if the wire mother had fed them. The infant monkeys were greatly comforted by the softness of the terrycloth mothers. But even though the monkeys raised with the terrycloth mother were more normal than those raised with the wire mother, abnormalities were still present. The monkeys could not play normally, showed rocking movements, bit themselves, were withdrawn, and could not function sexually.

contact comfort
The need for physical touching and fondling.

   Human infants also have this need for **contact comfort.** In other studies, Harlow demonstrated that the injurious consequences of a lack of mothering need not be permanent (Harlow & Harlow, 1962). If infant monkeys were placed with companions before six months of age, the effects of a motherless environment were not as severe and were gradually reversed, but if the situation was not reversed early, problems remained.
   The beneficial effects of an improved environment were demonstrated in a study by Wayne Dennis (1973). Dennis followed children raised in an orphanage in Lebanon. The children received little attention, and their life was one of uninterrupted boredom. When tested after the first year, the children were extremely retarded, but after being adopted, they recovered quickly. Those adopted before the age of two recovered well. At about six years of age, those who were not adopted were transferred to other institutions—one for males, the other for females. The institution serving the females was just as bad as the one from which the girls had come. When tested during middle childhood, the girls were quite retarded. The institution for the males, however, was run differently and

provided a more stimulating environment, filled with toys, educational equipment, and films. The boys had an average IQ of 80, far above the intelligence scores for the girls.

Dennis's observations lead to two conclusions. First, these children had suffered from **stimulus deprivation;** that is, their environment was so unstimulating that it prevented them from developing normally. Second, the consequences of an unfavorable environment, although quite serious, could be remedied to some degree by placing the children in a better, more stimulating environment. The earlier this occurred, the better.

stimulus deprivation
The absence of adequate environmental stimulation.

The Effects of Institutionalization

The work of Bowlby, Spitz, and Dennis has led to great changes in institutional practices. Children's needs for attention, fondling, warmth, and care are now more fully appreciated. Ways to meet their need for a stimulating environment comprised of attentive human beings as well as things to see, hear, and handle have been incorporated into many institutional environments. Caregivers now provide extra stimulation for premature infants, who spend so much of their time isolated from the outside world.

We have learned at least some of our lessons. Institutionalization need not lead to retardation (Saltz, 1973; Wolins, 1970). It is not the institutionalization itself, but rather the quality of the care provided, that determines the outcome. This is further demonstrated by studies showing that some symptoms of maternal deprivation were found in children who are raised in intact homes (Fischoff, Whitten & Pettit, 1971).

Attachment Classifications

Attachment behaviors can be measured using a standardized procedure called the **strange situation** (Ainsworth & Whittig, 1969). This consists of eight standardized episodes in which children are brought to an unfamiliar room where a series of brief separations and reunions with their mothers are observed (Waters & Deane, 1982). Infants are classified as **secure** if they greet their mothers positively, actively attempt to reestablish proximity during the reunions, and show few if any negative behaviors toward their mothers. Secure infants explore the room just before the separation and use their mothers as a base of operations to explore the environment while the mother is still present (Ainsworth, 1979). Infants who actively attempt to regain contact or who interact with the parent following the reunion are classified as secure (Main & Cassidy, 1988).

Two other classifications can be grouped under the heading **anxious attachment.** Infants who are classified as being **anxious/avoidant** ignore their mother's entrance into the room during the reunion and may actively avoid reestablishing contact (Main & Cassidy, 1988). Infants classified as **anxious/ambivalent** show an angry resistance toward the mother upon reunion (Joffe & Vaughn, 1982). They may also show an inability to be comforted by the parent on reunion (Main & Cassidy, 1988). These babies show a great deal of anxiety upon entering the room even before

strange situation
An experimental procedure used to measure attachment behaviors.

secure attachment
A type of attachment behavior in which the infant in the strange situation uses the mother as a secure base of operations.

anxious/avoidant attachment
A type of attachment behavior shown in the "strange situation," in which the child avoids reestablishing contact with the mother as she reenters the room after a brief separation.

anxious/ambivalent attachment
A type of attachment behavior shown during the "strange situation," in which the child both seeks close contact and yet resists it during the mother's reentrance after a brief separation.

the session begins and are quite distressed by the separation. In the reunion, they are ambivalent, seeking close contact and yet resisting it (Ainsworth, 1979). These patterns are relatively stable (Sroufe, 1985), but they can change if there is a major improvement or worsening in the child's environment.

How Attachment Relates to Later Behavior and Personality

The difference in the way children react in the strange situation is interesting in itself. However, its importance is increased by the many studies finding a relationship between type of attachment and later behavior and development. At two years of age, infants who were classified as securely attached at eighteen months were more enthusiastic, more persistent, and less easily frustrated than infants from the other two groups (Matas, Arend & Sroufe, 1978).

Securely attached infants are more socially and cognitively competent as toddlers (Waters, 1978). In one study, twenty-four-month-old infants were tested on the strange situation. When the children were three years old, their parents and preschool teachers were asked about their reading interests and skills. The securely attached children showed more interest in written material. Perhaps children who are securely attached are more likely to show curiosity and a willingness to explore many cognitive areas, including books (Bus & Ijzendoorn, 1988).

Securely attached toddlers are better at negotiating the environment, maneuver more successfully around toys and furniture, and reach more often for objects without stumbling than anxiously attached infants (Cassidy, 1986). The ability of securely attached infants to explore their environment carries over into early childhood (Arend, Gove & Sroufe, 1979).

Infants who were securely attached at twelve months interact faster and more smoothly with a stranger at three years of age than children classified as avoidantly attached (Lutkenhaus, Grossman & Grossman, 1985). The children are also more likely to accept suggestions from their mothers (Matas, Arend & Sroufe, 1978), are more cooperative, and comply more readily with their mothers' instructions (Londerville & Main, 1981). Toddlers who were securely attached at eighteen months received a greater number of positive responses from their peers at three years of age (Jacobson & Wille, 1986). Securely attached children explored their environment more and scored higher on tasks of spatial ability during the preschool years than did anxiously attached children (Hazen & Durrett, 1982).

When children were rated on classification of attachment at eighteen months and their behavior observed at four and a half and five years, securely attached children were superior in social skills (Erickson, Sroufe & Egeland, 1985). The quality of the attachment in infancy is related to better functioning friendships at four years. In still another study, securely attached infants were found to be less likely to protest and show aggression towards mothers and older siblings when mothers played only with the older child. When the mother was not there, secure older siblings were more likely to respond to an infant in distress with caregiving (Teti & Ablard, 1989). The quality of the attachment to mother has implications for all close personal relationships and is related to increased competence in interpersonal relationships (Park & Waters, 1989; Waters, 1979).

The Effect of the Parent-Child Relationship on Attachment

Securely attached infants are superior to anxiously attached children on many measures of behavior and development, a superiority that continues throughout early childhood. Researchers have found some clues as to why some children are securely attached while others are anxiously attached.

The home environments of securely attached and anxiously attached infants differ. Mothers of infants classified as securely attached are more likely to be rated by observers as more sensitive than mothers of infants rated as anxiously attached (Egeland & Farber, 1984). Maternal sensitivity and security of attachment are closely related. Sensitivity involves being aware of infant cues, interpreting the cues correctly, and responding promptly and appropriately (Smith & Peterson, 1988). Mothers of securely attached infants pick their infants up and hug them more often than do parents of anxiously attached infants.

Most of the research was focused on the parents of anxious/avoidant children, because these children's mothers appear to be more rejecting than mothers of securely attached and ambivalently attached infants (Ainsworth, Bee & Slayton, 1971). Whereas parents of anxious/avoidant infants disdain physical contact with their infants (Ainsworth, Blehar & Waters, 1978), they do show affectionate behavior. They tend to kiss their infants but do not encourage other physical contact. These children avoid contact in the strange situation.

Not all modes of showing affection are equal (Tracy & Ainsworth, 1981). When infants are upset, they require physical contact. Perhaps avoidant children desire the contact but realize that they will not receive it from their mothers. The avoidance may be a defensive reaction to past disappointments in this area.

◆ THE CAREGIVER-CHILD RELATIONSHIP

All roads seem to lead back to the basic caregiver-child relationship. But what is it in this relationship that seems to affect infants so greatly?

Trust vs. Mistrust

According to Erik Erikson (1963), our basic attitude toward people develops from the early relationship with our caregivers. If our early needs are met in a warm environment, we develop a sense of **trust,** a feeling that we live among friends and that we can trust others. If, on the other hand, our needs are met with rejection or hostility, we develop a sense of **mistrust,** perceiving the world as a hostile, nonaccepting place and

6. TRUE OR FALSE?

The quality of infants' attachment to their mothers predicts children's future social maturity but not their cognitive abilities during early childhood.

trust
The positive outcome of Erik Erikson's first psychosocial stage, a feeling that one lives among friends.

mistrust
The negative outcome of Erikson's first psychosocial stage, an attitude of suspiciousness.

developing an inability to relate warmly to others. Children's relationships and early experiences form the basis for how the children will see the world later in life.

Autonomy vs. Shame or Doubt

autonomy
The positive outcome of the second stage of Erikson's psychosocial stage, an understanding that the child is someone on his or her own.

Erikson argued that as children negotiate toddlerhood, it is important for them to gain a sense of **autonomy,** an understanding that they are someone on their own and have some control over their own behavior. However, if parents do not allow their children to do what they are able to do and are greatly overprotective, or if they rush their children into doing something for which they are not ready, the children may develop a sense of **shame** or **doubt** concerning their ability to deal with the world around them. Parents do not help children acquire a sense of autonomy by allowing them to do everything for themselves. Rather, encouraging children to do what they are able to do is the key to their developing a sense of autonomy.

shame or doubt
The negative outcome of Erikson's second psychosocial stage, in which the child has a sense of shame or doubt about being a separate individual.

Parent-Child Interaction

Perhaps the most important tenet of attachment theory is that individual differences in infant-caregiver attachment are based on the type of relationship that the infant has with the caregiver (Bridges, Connell, & Belsky, 1988). Some caregivers are more competent than others, and we have some idea of what characteristics competent caregiving comprises. For example, parents who are attentive, meet the infant's needs, provide a relatively anxiety free atmosphere, are skilled in the physical care of the infant, permit increasing freedom with development, show empathy for the infant, and are sensitive to infant cues are competent caregivers. These competent parents express positive affect; provide a safe atmosphere in which the infant can explore; frequently interact with their infants; touch, hold, and smile at their infants a great deal; and provide a stimulating atmosphere for their infants (Jacobson, 1978). Gregory Pettit and John Bates (1989) followed the families of infants from the time the infants were six months of age till the children were four years old. There was a considerable relationship between the frequency of positive interactions, parents showing positive affect to the child, and the absence of problem behavior at four years of age. The use of coercion was related to behavior problems (Pettit & Bates, 1989).

7. TRUE OR FALSE?
─────────────
Parents who are very anxious about their new role as parents tend to adapt better than parents who have less anxiety about becoming parents.

Attitudes and expectations also affect the parent-child relationship. The ability of an individual to visualize him or herself as a parent seems to be an important aspect of parenting (Heinicke, Diskin, Ramsey-Klee & Given 1983). Parents who have positive expectations about parenting adapt well to their new roles, while those who are overly anxious do not (Maccoby & Martin, 1983). Parents who know what to expect of a child at a particular age are less likely to lose their patience. For example, the parent who thinks that a newborn will sleep through the night or that a baby will be quiet during his or her favorite television program is likely to be disappointed.

Attitudes and expectations are somewhat related to age. Many young parents have unrealistic expectations for their infants, thinking of them as toys or dolls (Wise & Grossman, 1980). Reality may come as a shock, and this may affect the young parent's relationship with the child. Older mothers are more likely to have a more positive attitude toward parenthood and to be more responsive to the needs of their children. They also report spending less time away from their children than do younger mothers (Ragozin, Rasham, Crnic, Greenberg & Robinson, 1982). Perhaps older mothers are more secure and more likely to have realistic expectations of parenting.

The parents' background is also important. People generally believe that what they have experienced is the normal way of interacting with others. If children are raised with kindness and love, they will find it easier to give such attention to their own children. Social support is important as well. The social support received from both family and friends is related to maternal sensitivity which, as we've seen, is an important aspect of competence (Crockenberg & McCluskey, 1986). This is most true for parents of irritable infants and shows that mothers require the support of other people, especially when dealing with difficult infants or infants with special needs.

In the past, it was popular to look only at the parents' contribution to the parent-child relationship, but we now know that certain characteristics of the child can also help or hinder the relationship. For example, the responsive, capable infant is more likely to elicit favorable responses than an infant who is unresponsive (Brazelton, Koslowski & Main, 1974). These characteristics affect how children are treated. Infants who are less sociable are less interactive with their mothers, and this may produce anxious attachment relations. Three-month-old children who were less sociable and less people oriented were less likely to focus on and go to their mothers at one year and more likely to be classified as anxious/avoidant (Lewis & Feiring, 1989).

BIDIRECTIONALITY Parent-child relationships are based upon bidirectional influence (Cohn & Tronick, 1988). Parent-child interactions are actually a chain of quick actions and reactions. An action on the part of the child prompts an action on the part of the parent, which may then elicit another action on the part of the child, and so on and so on. The beginning and the end are difficult to define. Infants are small but powerful. "Their power lies in the baby's ability to compel action by its eye-to-eye gaze, smiling, crying, appearing helpless, or thrashing" (Bell, 1979, p. 824). The child's behavior elicits behavior from the parents. For example, many abusive parents report that their children were annoying, showed persistent crying, and were generally abrasive. These behaviors elicited abusive behavior from the children's parents. On the positive side, we find that responsive caregivers lead to improved responsiveness on the part of the infant (Symons & Moran, 1987). Infants who show high levels of responsiveness have mothers who are very responsive during play. The more responsive infant will then influence the caregiver's behaviors in a positive manner.

8. *TRUE OR FALSE?*

Older mothers have a more positive attitude toward motherhood than younger mothers do.

synchrony
The coordination between infant and caregiver in which each can respond to the subtle verbal and nonverbal cues of the other.

Imprinting is a rigid attachment. Here, a number of geese follow Konrad Lorenz who was the first object they saw after hatching.

imprinting
An irreversible, rigid behavior pattern of attachment.

THE SYNCHRONY BETWEEN PARENT AND CHILD Any understanding of the parent-child relationship must look at the second-by-second interactions between the two. This is often summarized under the heading **synchrony**—referring to the basic rhythms that underlie the interaction between parent and child (Schaffer, 1977). Watch a parent feeding his or her baby some mushy cereal, and the meaning of synchrony becomes obvious. The infant's head turns, the baby looks here and there, spits out a little food, blows a bubble, and kicks both feet. At just the right second, as the baby looks up at the parent, the parent has the spoon ready. The timing is amazing. The infant is an active participant, too, looking at the parent at just the right moment, knowing what is coming. The timing is based on an accurate reading of each other's cues. People who do not have regular contact with a particular infant often find it difficult to do things with the child. For instance, they may not be able to read the child's signals and may find themselves trying to shovel cereal into a closed mouth.

Parent and child must cooperate, and each must adapt to the other's behaviors (Osofsky & Conners, 1979). The development of the warm relationship hinges on the development of this synchrony, this understanding of what will happen next. The beginning of this mutual understanding, as well as the basic attachment sequence discussed earlier, starts at birth.

◆ THE IMPORTANCE OF EARLY MOTHER-CHILD CONTACT

In many cases, mothers do not have contact with their infants for some time after birth. Is early contact vital to the development of a healthy mother-child relationship? For many species, separation immediately after birth results in rejection. If a goat is separated from her kid immediately after delivery, she will reject the kid when reunited, but if the separation occurs ten minutes after delivery, no rejection occurs (Klaus & Kennel, 1976). In other species, a critical period for attachment has also appeared. Konrad Lorenz (1937) found that geese follow and attach themselves to the first object they see. When the goslings he was experimenting with opened their eyes and saw him, he became the object of attachment. They followed him everywhere. The geese were capable of forming such a relationship only in the first day and a half. This unlearned, rather rigid, irreversible behavior pattern is called **imprinting.** Could there be such a sensitive period in attachment for human beings? Could the first minutes, hours, or even days after birth be critical for the formation of a bond between mother and child?

Marshall Klaus and John Kennel stirred up controversy by arguing that such a sensitive period in human beings exists (Klaus & Kennel, 1976). The normal procedure in many hospitals is routine separation after birth, with the mother going to the recovery room and the infant going to the nursery. Even days later, contact is often limited. Klaus and Kennel suggested that this lack of early contact is responsible for some later problems in the mother-child relationship.

Such a radical viewpoint was certain to stimulate research, some of which showed that mothers who maintained early contact with their infants demonstrated more maternal behaviors such as soothing, eye-to-eye contact and fondling (Kennel, Voos & Klaus, 1979). Most studies, though, have not found such a linkage, or they have found that any differences disappear within a very short time, about two months (Grossman, Thane & Grossman, 1981; Svejda, Campos & Emde, 1980). Even when separations are long, as in the case of some premature infants, no significant differences in security of attachment have been found between infants separated from their parents at birth and those who were not separated (Rode, Chang, Fisch & Sroufe, 1981).

Klaus and Kennel's claims appear to be exaggerated. Attachment is based on the cumulative effects of mother-child interactions, not on any single brief encounter (Sroufe & Waters, 1977). In fact, Klaus and Kennel (1983), while continuing to argue the benefits of early contact between mother and infant, have modified their position somewhat. They acknowledge that in spite of the lack of early contact, almost all parents become bonded to their babies. Human beings are quite adaptable. Klaus and Kennel still argue that at least thirty to sixty minutes of early contact in privacy should be provided to enhance the process of bonding, and more time should be made available each day. They note that they face a dilemma in how strongly to emphasize the importance of early mother-infant contact. If they emphasize it too strongly, some mothers who miss the early experience may believe that all has been lost for their future relationship with their child. This is completely wrong. Others, however, have interpreted Klaus and Kennel's modified position as either a license to discontinue the practice of early contact or to make it a "rushed charade" (p. 50).

What conclusion can we come to concerning the importance of early mother-child contact. There is some evidence for some short-term positive effects, including more holding and more eye contact (de Chateau, 1987). However, the long-term effects of early mother-infant contact do not appear very strong (Lamb, 1982). Although Klaus and Kennel may have originally overstated their main argument, their work has promoted a needed revolution in the way we look at childbirth and aftercare. Today, women giving birth are less likely to be treated as if they were ill. Babies are not as isolated and fathers and siblings are often encouraged to visit the new babies. In addition, although early contact is not essential, it is probably desirable.

◆ THE FATHER-CHILD RELATIONSHIP

Up to this point, it must have seemed as if children had only one parent—the mother. What about the father? We know a great deal about the mother-child bond, but what about the father-child relationship?

9. TRUE OR FALSE?

Early and extended contact immediately after birth is necessary if infants are to develop a healthy attachment to their mothers.

Where Is Father?

Fathers are not as involved with their infants and toddlers as they are with their older children. Most women have had more experience handling and caring for infants and toddlers than men have. This lack of experience, combined with the cultural prescriptions favoring mothers, causes fathers to be wary of interacting with their babies.

In the United States, mothers greatly exceed fathers in the amount of time spent with their children. Even when the mother is employed outside the home, she is much more likely than the father to take time off to care for the children. Mother is much more likely to be the one to interrupt her career, and even when she continues with employment outside the home, she is usually the person primarily responsible for making child-care arrangements.

Even taking cultural factors into consideration, though, American fathers spend little time with their infants. You might say that this is understandable if father is employed forty hours and mother is a full-time homemaker. But what happens when mother also is employed full time outside the home? Does the father participate more in child care or housework?

There is some controversy here, but it seems that generally fathers help out a little more when mothers work (Pleck, 1985). Maret & Finlay (1984) found that 39 percent of the employed wives had sole responsibility for child care, compared with 56 percent of the nonemployed wives; 42 percent of employed wives were solely responsible for housework, compared with 57 percent of nonemployed wives; and 34 percent of employed wives were solely responsible for washing dishes, compared with 49 percent of the nonemployed wives.

A study by Ann Crouter and colleagues (1987) found that fathers in dual-earner families were significantly more involved in child care than single-earner fathers. There appear to have been some modest increases in the participation of fathers in household tasks and child care when mothers work outside the home (Hoffman, 1989). The effect is more pronounced when mother is employed full time; when there is more than one child in the home; when no teenage children, especially daughters, are at home; and when mother's income is close to father's (Hoffman, 1989). Since this is true even if the father holds rather traditional ideas about what men and women should do, it seems that father is responding to mother's needs and pleas (or threats).

Although most findings show that fathers today do somewhat more, we should not go overboard and believe that there is equality in family life. Every study finds that even when both parents are working, the disparity in time spent is very obvious. In her research for the book *The Second Shift*, which describes dual-earner families, Arlie Hochschild (1989) found that fathers do not do much housework or child care, despite protestations in the mass media to the contrary. She argues that women in dual-earner families work an extra month of twenty-four hour days each year. Women work approximately fifteen hours a week longer than men. Only 20 percent of the men in Hochschild's study share housework equally. Even when couples share the work around the house in an equitable

10. *TRUE OR FALSE?*

Fathers in dual-earner families do more housework and participate more in child care than fathers in single-earner families.

fashion, women do two-thirds of the daily jobs, such as cooking and cleaning up, and most of the daily chores involving the children. Much of what men do involve home and car repairs. Concerning child care, men are likely to take their children on fun outings, while women spend more time on maintenance activities such as bathing and feeding the children.

Father participation is needed to take some of the burden off the mother. However, research has shown other benefits. For both single- and dual-earner families, father involvement predicts higher intelligence scores and academic achievement and greater social maturity for both sons and daughters (Gottfried, Gottfried & Bathurst, 1988).

The father in a single-earner family may become involved in child care because of an intrinsic desire to do so. Since he may voluntarily participate and is the only wage earner, his wife is less likely to demand that he participate. The father in a dual-earner family may become more involved because mother demands it. Perhaps this explains why there is some relationship between father participation in home activities and marital dissatisfaction in dual-earner families but not in single-earner families (Crouter, Perry-Jenkins, Huston, and McHale, 1987).

What do fathers do when they help their employed wives? Most studies find that there is little change in the division of labor. Employed women do twice as much housework as men (Benin & Agostinelli, 1988). Men tend to help out by shopping but don't do much ironing or washing dirty diapers.

In the area of paternal involvement, behavior does not exactly match attitudes. In one poll, 93 percent of the respondents said parents should share the chores equally when both are employed. Yet in 57 percent of the homes where both spouses are employed, women did most of the housework (*Newsday*, June 17, 1986).

Why don't employed women insist on a more equitable distribution of the work? Although some certainly do, many women believe that housework is principally the woman's responsibility, that the woman's demands will adversely affect the marriage, or that their husbands are not competent to do the work (Pleck, 1985).

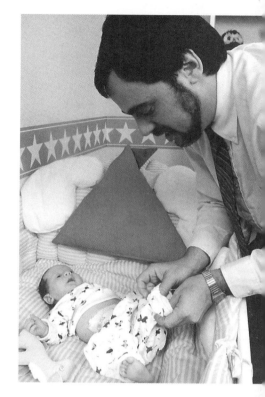

When both parents work, there is some evidence that fathers help out somewhat more, although 50-50 splits are rare.

How Do Fathers Interact with Infants?

The way mothers and fathers interact with infants is different. Mothers and fathers generally do not interact with their infants for the same reasons, nor do they share the caregiving duties equally. Mothers are more likely to provide physical care of the children, especially younger ones, and fathers to play with the children (Atkinson, 1987). In addition, fathers play in more physical and emotionally arousing ways, whereas mothers tend to play in a quieter, more verbal manner, using conventional games like peek-a-boo (Bridges, Connell & Belsky, 1988; Hodapp & Mueller, 1982). Fathers also engage in more unconventional, unpredictable play (Lamb, 1977), but mothers are more responsive to infant cues of interest and attention (Power, 1985). These differences remain fairly constant throughout infancy.

11. TRUE OR FALSE?

In the United States, mothers play with infants and toddlers in a quieter and more verbal manner than fathers.

These differences in interaction explain why children seek out each parent for different reasons (Biller, 1982). Children who seek out their father to play with and their mother when they need care are manifesting not a function of gender but a function of their differential experience with their two parents. The preference is based on the past experience of the child. This interactional difference is culturally determined. Swedish fathers and mothers do not play differently with their infants (Lamb, Frodi & Hwang, 1983), while American fathers and mothers show interactive differences. The qualitative differences between mother-child interactions and father-child interactions decline somewhat in dual-earner families (Stuckey, McGhee, & Bell, 1982).

Why do fathers interact the way they do? The cultural expectation that women will do much of the day-to-day child care is one reason. Another, though, is the idea that men may not know or understand what infants are capable of doing. Fathers who are less involved in child care attribute less competence to infants than those who are more involved and attribute considerably less competence than mothers. The more involved, the less the difference between his own and his wife's ideas about what an infant can do (Ninio & Rinott, 1988). Perhaps one reason, then, that fathers tend to engage less often in verbal and toy play with infants is that men are unfamiliar with what their infants can do. Fathers also tend to see themselves as less skilled. Those who have more skills feel more competent in dealing with their infants (McHale & Huston, 1984). This explains why some research shows that parent education results in greater paternal involvement. Parent training might provide the knowledge and experience necessary to encourage fathers to take a more active interest in their child's development. Such training might start at the high school level (Parke, 1979), and both males and females might benefit. When fathers were given the opportunity to learn and practice caregiving skills in the hospital, they were more involved at three months in the care of their infants and in household tasks (Parke, 1979).

Do Infants Become Attached to Their Fathers?

Many people think of love as a type of pie from which a child can give only a certain amount and that if love is portioned out to too many people, the amount available for any one person is reduced. But this is not true. "Love even in babies has no limits" (Schaffer, 1977, p. 104).

Infants become attached to many people other than their mothers. The quality of a child's attachment depends on the history of the interactions the child has had with the person. Infants do form an attachment to their fathers, even though the interaction between fathers and infants is limited. The attachment between father and infant evolves in much the same manner as it does between mother and child. Infants who are attached to their fathers spend more time looking at their fathers and react emotionally when their fathers enter or leave the room. In addition, "well-fathered" infants are more curious and more likely to explore their environment, are more secure, and are more advanced in motor development (Biller, 1982).

Fathers can be as active in childrearing as they choose.

Fathers and mothers mean different things to children, based on the roles the parents choose to fulfill (Parke, 1981). Infants tend to choose mothers over fathers when they are hungry, wet, or under stress, but in a stress-free environment, they show no preference and may even seek out fathers when they want to play.

When mother, father, and a stranger are present, the child will stay closer to the mother than to the father and closer to the father than to the stranger (Cohen & Campos, 1974). In the strange situation (discussed earlier), children protest the departure of both mothers and fathers, and their play decreases (Kotelchuck, 1972). The attachment to both parents can be quite strong. It is also possible for a child to be securely attached to one parent and insecurely attached to the other.

Fathers as Caregivers

How is father as a caregiver? Equating competence and performance in parenting is a mistake. Fathers may not show as many caregiving behaviors as mothers, but they may be capable of them. Low involvement does not mean low competence (Parke & Sawin, 1976). Experience is important. One man who had to help care for the baby when his wife returned to her job stated, "There is nothing I can't do for that baby. After his first three months, when Nan returned to work after a three-month unpaid maternity leave, he got so used to my feeding him he complained when I left. Now Nan and I split everything: bathing, feeding, changing—it doesn't matter" (Kammerman, 1980, p. 49).

Given the opportunity and enough encouragement, fathers can do a fine job with their children and show many nurturant behaviors. Fathers are just as likely as mothers to hold newborn infants, to rock them, and to talk to them in the hospital (Parke & Sawin, 1976). Fathers are very interested in their children, and they act in a nurturant manner even though they engage in fewer caregiving chores (Parke, 1979). Fathers can accurately recognize the meaning of infant cries and are responsive to the infant's signals, sounds, and mouth movements (Parke, 1981). In fact, research definitely shows that fathers are capable and concerned parents (Easterbrooks & Goldbert, 1984).

The infant's attachment to the mother is not the result of any biological rule of nature. Children attach themselves to many people, depending on the nature of the interactions. The quantity of the interactions is not as important as the quality. When one asks just what the role of the father is in the family, the answer given by Schaffer (1977, p. 104) is "just what he and his wife choose it to be."

◆ THE EMPLOYED MOTHER

Most mothers with young children now are employed outside the home. The question often asked is how the mother's employment affects her children's development. Right at the start, however, you might say that asking such a question is sexist. What about the father? This is a reasonable criticism, but since mothers usually act as the primary caregivers, the question is appropriate. In addition, employment itself may be too broad a variable to be useful. The child's experiences in the day-care arrangement, the amount of time the parents are away, and what happens when the parents come home are crucial mediating concerns (Allnut, 1979). All these factors should be kept in mind when looking at the question of how a mother's employment affects her children's development.

Why Mother Seeks Employment

Women seek employment for a variety of reasons. Most women become wage earners because the family requires their income to maintain a reasonable standard of living. If a woman is a single parent, she is usually forced to seek employment to provide the necessities of life for herself and her children.

This is only part of the picture, however. Most women state a preference to combine marriage and career pursuits (Fitzgerald & Betz, 1983). Women also are more educated than in the past and have prepared for a career that they want to follow. Last, many women feel that a career is an important part of their lives, giving them intellectual and social stimulation and a sense of accomplishment and purpose. Most state that they would remain employed even if they didn't need the money. This dedication to employment is found both in professional and nonprofessional employed women (Hiller & Dyehouse, 1987.) It would be wrong, though, to paint a homogeneous picture. In one poll, 56 percent of the full-time homemakers said they would choose to have a career if they could do it over again, and 21 percent of the employed mothers would happily leave their jobs to stay at home with their children if they could (Groller, 1988).

How does employment affect the mother herself? There are two different findings in this area. First, mothers who are employed generally report being happy and satisfied. They often emphasize the job benefits, including adult contacts, stimulation, and improved morale. When employed and nonemployed mothers are compared on measures of personal satisfaction, employed mothers often report being more satisfied. We must be careful, however, with generalizations. Gove & Zeiss (1987) found that for employed mothers with children at home, happiness depended on whether the mother wanted to be employed or not. The positive relationship between dual roles and happiness for women holds *only* when mothers said they wanted to be employed.

The second finding emphasizes the problem mothers in dual-earner families have in accomplishing everything they want to. It is difficult to be employed full-time, return home to do most of the housework, spend time with the children and one's spouse, and find some time for herself in a twenty-four hour day. Some situations increase the problem. If the mother has little support from the father and other family members, if a child suffers from some disability, or if the mother is a single parent and thus responsible for every aspect of home life, more strain will be evident.

Mother-Child Interaction: Employed vs. Nonemployed Mothers

There are differences of opinion as to whether employed mothers interact differently with their children. Some studies show that employed and nonemployed mothers interact very similarly with their children (Hock 1980) and that child-rearing practices do not differ (Yarrow, 1962). Other studies have found some differences, however. Cohen (1978) found that nonemployed mothers give more positive attention, including affectionate touching, and vocalize more to their infants than mothers who are employed. Another study found that mothers employed more than twenty hours a week spend less time with infants and preschool children than nonemployed mothers, but this difference decreases as the mother's education increases. Often, educated mothers compensate for the lack of time spent with their children during the week by increasing the amount of time they spend with their children on weekends and during off the job hours (Hoffman, 1989). Another difference that is more accepted is that employed mothers emphasize independence training far more than nonemployed mothers (Hoffman, 1989).

The most interesting and controversial finding is that there may be a difference in the way parents in single- and dual-earner families treat their sons and daughters. When mothers are employed, parents interact more positively with their daughters and less positively with their sons, while when mothers are full-time homemakers, parents interact more positively with their sons (Stuckey et al., 1982). When interviewed, employed mothers of preschoolers described their daughters but not their sons in positive terms. Perhaps boys, who tend to be somewhat more active and less compliant, receive harsher words and generally less nurturant treatment.

Some people believe that a mother who works outside the home and who is very committed to her job will have very little time and patience with her children, tending not to communicate well with them. However, this is not the case as long as the mother is also highly committed to parenting. In fact, when there is both a high commitment to work and family, employed mothers use a style of parenting called authoritative, which combines openness to communication with children with the use of firm but flexible rules (Greenberger & Goldberg, 1989).

The attitude parents take towards mother's employment is also important. More problems arise in families where negative attitudes towards maternal employment exist. If parents truly believe it is harmful to the children for the mother to be employed or believe that the children require full-time mothering, more rejection and criticism are directed at the children.

Another important factor in parenting is the mother's satisfaction with her role. The more satisfied the mother is, the more likely she will interact more effectively with her family (Rutter, 1981). As stated previously, the benefits of the mother's employment are most definite only when the mother wants to hold a job. This caveat is often glossed over, though it should not be. Recently, the stereotype of the unhappy homemaker has

D A T A G R A P H I C

Employed Mothers with Children Under the Age of One

Source: U.S. Bureau of the Census.

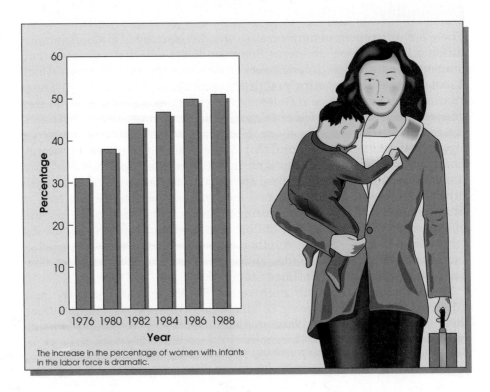

The increase in the percentage of women with infants in the labor force is dramatic.

become common. Depression and boredom are supposedly related to full-time homemaker status. The happy, satisfied employed woman has been held in high esteem. There are definite advantages for the self-esteem of women who are employed (Rutter, 1981). However, the personal benefits are much more likely to be found in mothers who are employed because they want to work outside the home than in those who are employed strictly because of financial necessity (Alvarez, 1985).

The stereotype of the unhappy homemaker is only partly true. Most studies simply compare employed mothers with nonemployed mothers and report the differences so popular in the magazines. However, if you split homemakers into those who want employment and those who don't, a different picture appears (Fiddell & Prather, 1976). The stereotype is accurate only for the woman who finds herself trapped and wants out. The full-time homemaker who is satisfied with her role is just as happy as the employed mother.

Effects of Maternal Employment on Children

Everyone has some opinion about how maternal employment affects the children. Whatever differences have been found—and there have not been many—they depend upon the child's gender and social class. Maternal employment does not have any negative effects on girls and may actually be a positive influence on a girl's development. Daughters of employed mothers tend to be higher achievers, and the mother may serve as an achieving role model (Hoffman, 1979; 1989). Sons of employed mothers do not have the traditional sex stereotypes that children of full-time homemakers frequently have. Children of employed women are more likely to believe that women can be competent, though this finding is stronger for daughters than for sons. Generally, daughters of employed mothers are very well adjusted and do well in school and have higher career aspirations.

Social class is another variable. Males from low socioeconomic backgrounds may view the need for their mothers to be a wage earner as a reflection of their father's failure to earn a living. This could lead to a strain in the father-son relationship. Generally, however, maternal employment does not adversely affect the cognitive development of lower income males, and some studies find higher scores on measures of cognitive development among sons of working-class employed mothers. Studies, though, sometimes show lower cognitive development among sons but not daughters of middle-class employed mothers. A study of middle-class toddlers showed that sons of nonemployed mothers were more cognitively advanced than those of employed mothers. Some studies of middle-class males show that these boys do not do as well on intelligence tests as boys raised by their nonemployed mothers (Hoffman, 1979). Not all studies have shown this superiority in cognitive development. When Ann Crouter and colleagues (1990) compared the school performance and conduct of middle class elementary school children between the ages of 9 and 12, they found no significant differences in grades as reported both by children and their mothers. It should be noted, however, that some studies that have found differences measured achievement tests rather than grades and that this sample was composed of students who were doing well in school.

In addition, when this disadvantage in cognitive development is found, it occurs only when mothers are employed full-time and not when mothers work part-time. (Gottfried, Gottfried & Bathurst, 1988). Why this may occur is open to question. Perhaps the care received by some middle-class children in day care does not match that provided by a mother who is a full-time homemaker. Perhaps some employed mothers are not as involved with their children when they get home from their jobs. The evidence, then, as far as the effect of mother's employment status on the cognitive development of middle class males is mixed, and there is need for additional research in this area.

Of all the areas of concern, none is more controversial than the effects of the mother's employment on both the supervision of the children and the children's socioemotional development. Children of employed mothers take on more responsibilities, and supervision becomes difficult. Indeed, monitoring is especially important for boys in dual earner families. When Ann Crouter and colleagues (1990) compared middle class children from single and dual earner families and factored in gender and parental monitoring, they found that boys from dual earner families who were poorly monitored were reported to show the worst conduct. However, no relationship exists between maternal employment itself and juvenile delinquency or personality disorders (Hoffman, 1974, 1979).

Differences in social behavior between children of employed and nonemployed mothers do appear, but they are minor. Schachter (1981) found that preschool children of employed mothers are more peer oriented and self-sufficient. Children of nonemployed mothers seek out more help and protection and show more jealousy. No differences in emotional adjustment were found. Some long-term studies find that these children are less compliant and more peer oriented, but this depends on the nature of the nonmaterial care they receive (Hoffman, 1989).

In summary, the differences in social behavior are neither great nor negative. The effects of maternal employment can be either negative or positive, depending on many factors. Maternal employment does not lead to massive personal or emotional problems, although there is room for some concern about the cognitive development of middle-class males. This possible problem may be reduced by providing better substitute care and encouraging parents to become more involved in their children's cognitive development.

◆ DAY CARE

Lisa and Tim Walters' concerns center on their children's experience in day care. Many people think of day care only in terms of large urban day-care centers, but most day care does not take place in such centers. A government survey found that about 31 percent of the young children whose mothers are employed outside the home were cared for in the

The effects of infant day care on children's development is a very controversial issue today.

child's home, most likely by a relative (usually a father or a grandparent), while about 37 percent were cared for in someone else's home where the child was somewhat more likely to be cared for by a nonrelative as a relative. About 23 percent were cared for in group care centers, and about 8 percent were cared for by the mother while she is on the job. A very small number (.2 percent) made other arrangements, including allowing the children to care for themselves. About five percent of the people surveyed did not choose to provide any information (U.S. Bureau of the Census, 1988). The overwhelming majority of infants under one year of age whose mothers work are cared for by relatives or the parents themselves (Klein, 1985). Thus, many forms of day care exist, and the day-care centers are the answer right now for a minority of families.

Research on Day Care

To do justice to the research on the effects of day care on a child's development, we must divide the topic into two sections, depending upon the age at which the child enters day care. The research on the effects of the day-care experience on children who enter substitute care before the age of one year is fraught with controversy and misunderstanding. The research on the effects of day care for children who enter after that age is more easily explained and much less controversial.

Day Care and Attachment to Substitute Caregivers

Children in day care form relationships with, and an attachment to, their substitute caregivers (Lewis, 1987). Children show less distress when left with a familiar caregiver than when left with a stranger, and they even show some distress when separated from the substitute caregiver (Ricciuti, 1974). Anderson and colleagues (1981) found that the extent of this attachment depended on the quality of the day-care worker's interaction with the child. Children show high levels of attachment to high-interaction competent caregivers and low levels of attachment to low-interaction caregivers. In the presence of a high-interaction caregiver, the child feels secure enough to explore the environment. Again, the quality, not the quantity, of interaction is most important for the development of positive relationships.

Day Care and Attachment to Mother and Father

With so many young children in day-care settings, there is great interest in the question of how the day-care experience affects a child. When looking at the effects of substitute care on infants, the most common measurement is attachment quality. Earlier in the chapter, the many important connections between secure attachment and later functioning were outlined, so it makes sense to determine the extent, if any, to which attachment is affected by substitute care. The effects of substitute care for infants below the age of one on attachment quality is a matter of sharp debate among psychologists.

Some studies have shown differences between home-reared and day-care children on measures of attachment in the strange situation (Blehar, 1974). Vaughn and colleagues (1985) found some negative effects, mostly for children who received out-of-home care before their first birthday. Secure children who had entered out-of-home care after their first birthday did not show any problems (Vaughn, Deane & Waters, 1985). In another study, infants whose mothers were employed and experienced day care in their own homes by an unrelated person were more likely to show insecure/avoidant attachment patterns in the strange situation than infants whose mothers had remained at home. However, even in this study, 53 percent of those infants whose mothers were employed showed secure attachment, and some as yet unidentified factors must moderate the effects of daily separations for these securely attached infants (Barglow, Vaughn, & Molitor, 1987).

In two studies of middle-class infants, Belsky and Rovine (1988) found that infants exposed to twenty or more hours of substitute care per week were more likely to be classified as anxiously attached than infants of nonemployed mothers or mothers who were employed for fewer than twenty hours per week. In addition, sons whose mothers were employed more than thirty-five hours per week were more likely to be classified as anxiously attached to their fathers. However, these patterns were still not found in a majority of infants in the studies. More than half the infants of employed mothers had secure attachments with their mothers, half showed secure attachments with their fathers and almost two-thirds of the sons showed a secure attachment to at least one parent.

The finding that sons are more vulnerable for insecure attachments to both mothers and fathers was found in another study (Chase-Lansdale &

Owen, 1987). This might possibly be explained by the evidence showing that both mothers and fathers treat boys more negatively than girls in employed families. Employed mothers' one-year-old sons receive less stimulation from both parents than their daughters do or than children of either sex in families in which the mother is not employed (Zaslow, Pederson, Suwalsky, Cain, & Fivel, 1985). Looking at this and other evidence, Belsky (1988) concludes that early substitute care puts a child at risk for insecure attachment and later social and emotional problems.

Before concluding that this is so, however, let's look at the other side of the coin. While some studies may indicate the possibility that infant day care heightens the risk of infants developing insecure/avoidant patterns, the findings still seem to be the exception to the rule (Phillips, McCartney, & Scarr, 1987). Much research around the world shows that such risk is not inevitable (see the Cross-Cultural Current on page 292). After reviewing the studies, some authorities claim that the evidence is substantially weaker than Belsky suggests (Thompson, 1988). The percentage of those infants rated insecure/avoidant is higher but not dramatically so. The difference is not large enough to be a practical problem. Infants whose mothers are employed full time are about seven or eight percent more likely to be classified as anxiously attached. About 36 percent of the infants of mothers with full-time employment and 29 percent of nonemployed or part-time employed mothers have been classified as anxiously attached (Clarke-Stewart, 1988, 1989).

The evidence, then, is just not strong enough to make any conclusions about this important subject. In addition, it is possible that the meaning of anxious attachment patterns may be different for infants reared by different methods. Israeli infants who are raised in kibbutzim (communal, mostly agricultural settlements) differ in attachment patterns from infants who are raised in Israeli cities and attend urban day-care centers (Sagi et al., 1985). The meaning of the attachment categories may not be the same for children not raised at home (Clarke-Stewart, 1989). The strange situation assumes that the infants will be somewhat stressed by the separations and reunions and will therefore show attachment-related behaviors. It is possible that some infants in day care are used to these comings and goings and therefore may not show the same patterns as other children.

Some argue that infant day care is still fairly new and we do not know under what circumstances certain outcomes occur (Richters and Zahn-Waxler, 1988). It would be most unwise to come to a negative conclusion about the effect of infant day care on attachment patterns. Years ago many people believed that institutional rearing of children always led to negative outcomes, but after more research was performed, it became clear that the key issue was one of the qualities of institutional care, not institutional care itself (Chess, 1987). The same may be true for infant day care, which is becoming more prevalent in our society. There may be many factors, including attitude, sensitivity, and responsivity, that are related to infant attachment patterns, and some of these factors may differ between families that place their children in early day care and those

Infant Day Care and Family Policy in Sweden

In most societies, early child care is a controversial issue. In Sweden, about 85 percent of the mothers with children under schoolage work part or full time. Children start school there at seven years. In the United States, the statistic is lower but rising. One major question involves the effects early substitute care may have on the child's subsequent development. Unfortunately, as noted in the chapter, child care includes so many different arrangements that the diversity itself makes it difficult to measure its effects. In addition, it is frequently difficult to compare results from different studies, since the amount of time spent in day care, the age at which the child enters day care, and various home characteristics are often not noted.

Although American studies are divided on the effects of early day care on later development, Swedish research has not generally found many differences between day-care and home-raised children. However, Swedish day care is uniformly excellent, and child care is public and run by municipalities. It can take a number of forms, including day-care centers or family day care (called day mothers or child minders). The centers accept children from their first year of life. The day mothers are hired and licensed by the municipalities and are encouraged to take short training courses. They get sick pay and vacations. In addition, Swedish law

gives parents the right to stay home and take care of their newborn infant for much of infancy without risk of losing their jobs. They are guaranteed 90 percent of their salary through insurance. Presently, a parent can stay home for six or seven months, and so mothers who decide to work during these months are doing so by choice. Fathers can choose to divide the time off with their wives as well.

This certainly differs from the experience of day care in other societies. With this in mind, Bengt Erik Andersson sought to discover the effects of various day-care arrangements on later development and to look at the differences between those who enter day care in their first year and those who do not.

One hundred twenty-eight children from low- and middle-income areas were studied. The families were contacted when children were three or four years old, and contact remained until the children were eight years of age. About a third of the children were placed in day care during the first year of life in a center outside the home. This percentage increased until the fourth year, at which it stabilized at seventy percent. The center is the most common alternative, and as you would expect, the use of day mothers becomes less common as the age of the child increases. Almost all mothers took advantage of staying home for the first six months.

who do not. Remember, the overwhelming majority of infants are cared for in private homes and not in day-care centers. These centers vary significantly in quality, and assessing them is very difficult (Kammerman, 1986).

It is difficult to draw any conclusions on the effects of day care on attachment patterns. Although not all studies have found an increase in anxious attachment patterns, some certainly have. However, most infants in infant day care do show secure attachment, and the extra risk is relatively low. In addition, we do not know the meaning of these attachment patterns among children raised in different ways, and it may also be premature to blame substitute care itself for the problem. It may be that in the future some combination of family characteristics and the characteristics of the substitute care will be responsible for the anxious attachment patterns found in some studies. The findings of increased anxious attachments cannot be ignored, though, and we can only wait for more research clarifying the issue.

A number of measuring instruments were used, including nonverbal and verbal intelligence tests—tests of various cognitive skills, including similarities, classification, vocabulary, and understanding. Teachers were asked to rate school performance as well as social competence, including persistence and independence.

Andersson found that children entering day care at an early age performed significantly better on cognitive tests and received more positive ratings from their teachers in terms of school achievement and social personal attributes than children entering the day care at later ages and were superior to those raised at home. Center-based care was somewhat better for cognitive development than the day mother, but the results were not as clear-cut. Children who entered day care as infants were rated as more persistent and independent and as possessing more verbal ability than other children. They were also less anxious, and their transition to school was less troublesome.

These outcomes are somewhat surprising, given the findings in some American studies. Again, this cross-cultural research helps place research from our culture in perspective. Perhaps the high quality of Swedish day care, the training of personnel, and the ability to use day mothers are some of the reasons for these different findings. However, the ability to stay home for the first months is an unusual advantage. This will be increased to about eighteen months within three years. Most Swedish infants do not enter day care until after their sixth month. After that, good day care and secure employment are the norm. This gives families a type of security not found in the United States.

It may be that the feeling of financial security, combined with the ability to return to the workplace when desired, and the knowledge that good day care is available solve many problems that take up much of the attention of American parents. This study leads to the conclusion that a high-quality day-care facility *combined* with the parents' ability to stay home for the first six months (soon to be even longer) and some financial security seems to lead to positive outcomes.

Andersson suggests that the results of his study raise two interesting and important hypotheses that require testing. First, perhaps day care that begins after the first six months may be more beneficial than day care that begins before that time. Second, the negative effects of early day care may occur primarily when the care is of poor quality.

The results of this study of Swedish day care are interesting, but we cannot then make any general statement about bringing the Swedish model over to this country. However, it does seem to demonstrate that any difficulties found in day care are not inevitable. At the same time, it is impossible to separate the effect of the day care from those of the family policy in Sweden. All we can say is that the Swedish experience is one to look at and evaluate. In the end, it may demonstrate that some approach to a comprehensive family policy along with good-quality day care may be necessary if we are to adapt child care to the future needs of many young couples.

Andersson, B. E., Effects of Public Day-Care: A Longitudinal Study. **Child Development**, 1989, *60*, 857–866.

The Influence of Early Day Care on Behavior and Cognitive Development

Attachment may not be the only area that we are interested in. What about measurements of other variables? Unfortunately, there have been very few attempts to look at later development on the basis of early and extended nonmaternal care. Belsky argues that those experiencing early day care are at risk for heightened aggressiveness, noncompliance, and withdrawal in the preschool and early school years (Belsky, 1988). In other studies, however, benefits of early day care have been noted. In one study, Tiffany Field and colleagues (1988) compared seventy-one preschoolers who entered day care before six months of age with those entering after that age and found that the children with more hours of day-care experience engaged in less inactive watching and solitary play, showed more cooperative play and positive emotions, and had more peer interaction than those with less experience. Margaret Burchinal and colleagues

(1989) reported on a sample of very poor children, comparing children who were randomly assigned to receive extensive university-based intervention group day care, children placed in a regular community day-care center, and children with little or no day care. Both day-care groups began their experiences in early infancy—between six weeks and three months—and continued until kindergarten. Children in both day-care situations showed better intellectual development, with the university program superior. It may be that quality day care is positively related to intellectual development, at least for very poor children.

However, we again see the word *quality*. Infant day care is not always of such high quality. Arminta Jacobson and Susan Owen (1987) noted a great deal of variability among caregivers in the number and nature of their interactions with infants when they studied forty-three female infant caregivers who cared for infants in licensed day-care centers. Although most interactions were positive, the level of stimulation was low and lacked variety. Play with words and toys was infrequent, and there was an absence of any high level of emotion. There is obviously need for more staff training.

Day Care After Age One

It is much, much easier to discuss day care after age one because here the research is fairly consistent. We might assume that if a child from a stimulating environment were to enter a good day-care center, little gain or loss should occur. But if a child comes from a nonstimulating environment and goes into a stimulating environment, some gain should result. If a child comes from a stimulating environment and enters a poor day-care center, one would expect to see negative effects. Indeed, the research supports these notions (Belsky & Steinberg, 1979).

Day care has no injurious effects on the cognitive development of low-risk children (Belsky & Steinberg, 1978). An enriched day-care program may encourage cognitive development in disadvantaged children. In some studies, disadvantaged children reared at home showed a decline in intelligence scores over the first three years or so, while those enrolled in day care did not.

The evidence on the effects of the day-care experience on social development is interesting. Studies show that generally the overall social-emotional adjustment of day-care children is good and compares well with that of home-raised children (Etaugh, 1980; Watkins & Bradbard, 1984). Some differences have been noted, however. Children who experience day care are more outgoing and cooperative but are also more aggressive and boisterous (Clarke-Stewart, 1982). Children enrolled in day care incline toward more aggressiveness, impulsivity, and egocentrism (Belsky & Steinberg, 1978). They also interact more with their peers.

The more time spent in day care, the more time children as young as two years of age spend associating with peers and the less time they spend just looking at others and playing alone (Schindler, Moely & Frank, 1987). However the type of program makes a difference. Children who had been enrolled in a cognitively oriented day-care establishment were more ag-

Studies show that generally the overall social-emotional adjustment of day-care children is good and compares well with that of home-raised children.

gressive in the early years of elementary school than were children who had attended programs that focus on social skills. These children, though, were not considered difficult to manage, and their aggression decreased over time (Haskins, 1985).

When more attention is given to prosocial behaviors in these programs, aggression is reduced and cognitive gains are not affected (Finkelstein, 1982). These results may be due to cultural factors rather than to day care, for studies in other countries do not find these differences. The philosophy of the day-care group may also contribute to these findings. If social skills are stressed, the children will become more socially motivated. In summary, there are differences in the social-emotional area, but there is no evidence that day care causes serious emotional or social problems for children.

12. TRUE OR FALSE?

There are no differences in social behavior between children who attend day care and those who are raised at home.

Day Care and Health

One issue sometimes raised is the health consequences of day care. There is definite evidence that children in day-care facilities are sick more often than children not attending day-care facilities (Bell et al., 1989). In a national study, care in a day-care center or a nursery school increased the number of "sick in bed" days by 1.3 days per year for younger children and .6 day for older preschoolers (Johansen, Leibowitz, & Waite, 1988). This difference does not seem very important, but according to many authorities, it is underestimated by as much as a factor of 4. Because of the high costs of allowing a child to stay home for the day, parents who are employed are more likely to send their child to the center even when the child is marginally ill. However, even considering the factor of 4, that would mean that children are ill 5.2 days more per year if they attend day-care centers.

The strongest indicator for the amount of illness is the number of children in the room (Bell et al., 1989). The more children, the more likely a child is to become ill. There is also some fear that infants who require frequent changing of their diapers may be at risk for intestinal viruses, as some illnesses can be spread through poor hygienic practices. This point again shows the importance of adequate training for day-care workers.

Evaluating Day Care

Much depends on the quality of the day care center. High-quality, stable child care is associated with positive school outcomes (Howes, 1988). All the effects previously described are mediated by the characteristics of the day-care center and the home. Deborah Vandell and colleagues (1988) observed four-year-olds during play at both good and poor-quality day-care centers and again observed these children in play four years later.

FIGURE 7.1: A Day-care Checklist

It's not easy to choose a day-care facility. The following checklist can be used as a basis for comparing day-care centers.

Space and Equipment

Yes No
1. There is adequate space to play.
2. Sufficient storage for material is available.
3. The furniture is child-size and in good condition.
4. The temperature is comfortable (68 to 70 degrees).
5. The lighting is adequate.
6. Materials are available in sufficient numbers so children don't have to wait long to use them.
7. There is enough space outside or inside (a playground or a gym) for children to run or engage in other physical activities.
8. There is adequate space for resting.
9. The eating area is clean and bright.
10. Bathroom facilities are designed for small children.
11. Bathroom facilities are convenient.
12. Electrical outlets are covered when not in use.
13. First-aid supplies are available.
14. All equipment is in good repair (no broken toys or sharp edges).
15. Material (e.g., pots or cages) is available for growing things or taking care of animals.

Space and Equipment

Yes No
16. Books are visible.
17. Puzzles are available.
18. Adequate space is available for dramatic play (raised platforms, rows of wooden crates, etc.)
19. Emergency procedures are clear, and environment allows for safe exit in case of emergency.
20. Smoke detectors and fire extinguishers are evident.

The Program
1. There is an organized daily program.
2. There is variety within the program.
3. Students are encouraged to talk with each other.
4. Children participate in projects.
5. Activities are planned to encourage children to learn by using their senses.
6. Self-expressive activities such as painting and various forms of art are programmed.
7. Children are generally busy, not just sitting around.
8. Children show evidence of learning through discovery and asking questions of the staff.

Source: Adapted from Stines, 1983, and Clarke-Stewart, 1982.

Those from good day-care centers had more friends, showed more friendly interactions with peers, and were rated as more socially competent and happier at age eight than those who had attended poor-quality day-care centers.

How does one evaluate a day-care center? The day-care center checklist in Figure 7.1 may be of some help. In addition, some studies single out certain factors as especially important. One factor is the nature of the program. Although day care should not be thought of as school, such activities as reading to children and playing social games can contribute to intellectual and social growth. Another factor is the caregiver-to-child ratio. If attention and face-to-face interactions are vital to development in early childhood, the better the ratio of caregiver to child, the more likely that day care will be a positive experience (Ruopp, Travers, Glantz & Coelen, 1983). Other factors such as safety, ventilation, security, cleanliness, staff turnover, and cost should also be taken into consideration.

Yes	No	The Program
___	___	9. Small-group activities are encouraged.
___	___	10. Reading and storytelling are part of the program.
___	___	11. Activities that develop the large muscles are evident.
___	___	12. Activities that develop fine-muscle control are evident.
___	___	13. Boys and girls are encouraged to participate in all activities.

Teacher-Child/Teacher-Parent Relationships

Yes	No	
___	___	1. Sufficient staff is available so each child receives individual attention at some point in the day.
___	___	2. A warm relationship with the children is evident.
___	___	3. Staff circulates among all children, does not spend an inordinate amount of time with only one child.
___	___	4. Staff offers suggestions in a positive manner.
___	___	5. Staff trusts and respects children.
___	___	6. Staff encourages children to do things.
___	___	7. Staff does not use threats or punishment.

Teacher-Child/Teacher-Parent Relationships

Yes	No	
___	___	8. Staff does not smoke around the children.
___	___	9. Children understand their responsibilities.
___	___	10. Staff has sufficient training in the field.
___	___	11. Children seem happy.
___	___	12. Children seem to get along with one another.
___	___	13. Staff appears vigilant, knows what is going on at all times.
___	___	14. Staff and administrator encourage parents to visit and become involved.
___	___	15. Communication with parents, such as written notices of special events or changes in program, is adequate.
___	___	16. Checks on who can take child home (dismissal procedures) are adequate.
___	___	17. Staff/teacher conferences are held regularly.

Staff/Child Ratio

Minimum staff-child ratio for day-care centers:

Age	Maximum group size	Staff/child ratio
Birth to 2 years	6 children	1 adult: 3 children
2 to 3 years	12 children	1 adult: 4 children
3 to 6 years	16 children	1 adult: 8 children

THE CHILD
IN THE YEAR
2000

Who's Minding the Children?

Sometimes it is difficult to look a decade or two ahead, but not in the area of infant care. Certain trends that began as early as the 1970s are continuing and show no sign of abating. For example, women will continue to enter the labor force, although it is difficult to predict the exact rate. There will also be more pressure to increase day-care availability. At the same time, there will be more alternative work patterns established that may not require access to full-time day care. The child born around the year 2000 will be likely to spend some time in day care.

Often the debate over day care misses the mark. The question is not whether to provide day care but rather how to provide quality care that is affordable. The need for day care among poor and single mothers of modest means is obvious. How can these women (and sometimes single male parents) make a life for their children and themselves without adequate child-care services? However, the need for day-care services has increased among middle-class women, even in two-parent families for whom finding adequate child care is difficult.

What is the future of day care? As demands increase, government as well as private companies will have to make a greater commitment to daycare. Some companies already provide day-care services, and this will continue to be an important benefit. There may be tax incentives and perhaps local laws mandating day-care facilities for companies employing many workers. Government will be asked to increase its financial support for day-care facilities.

One possible future trend is the direct involvement of school districts in day care. Consider the possibility of elementary schools having a separate wing for day care. The principal has overall responsibility for the school, including the day-care center, but the center is physically separate and run by a director. Although now controversial, please remember that just a few years ago all-day kindergarten was considered radical and nursery school attendance was something that was statistically unusual. Today, of course, all-day kindergarten is found in many communities, and nursery school attendance is common.

It is doubtful, however, that the schools or even employers will be capable of dealing with infant day care. Here, there may be a need for some radical rethinking. Although more centers will open, infant day care by its very nature is more expensive. In addition, many parents may want to stay home with their infants during the child's first months of life. It may be that work schedules will have to be changed to allow mothers and fathers to care for the child. This flexible work time is already permitted in many companies. Mothers and fathers may be allowed paid leave for some months after the birth of the child to care for the child during these early months. This already occurs in Sweden. More part-time job opportunities, shared jobs, and working at home may be the answer for some.

A subtle but important change of attitude may take place in the next ten years or so. Some people still hold the attitude that parents are solely responsible for raising their children without governmental or public support. Others argue, however, that times are changing and we need a more activist approach. The question of whether and how government should help parents raise their children is an important and controversial one. In other words, what should government's family policy be? Should government guarantee day-care availability and encourage alternative work scheduling, allowing mother (or father) to stay home and care for the children without much financial loss, or should the government take a hands-off policy? This debate will continue into the next century and bears watching.

In summary, day care is neither a panacea nor a hell. Some day-care facilities are excellent; others are horrible. The nature of the interactions between the day-care workers and the children will in part determine the quality of a child's experience. Research to date shows that children given high-quality day care do not suffer, and in some cases, children may even benefit from the experience.

FIGURE 7.2: Child Care Arrangements for Children Under 5, 1985
Parents use a wide variety of child care arrangements when mothers are employed.

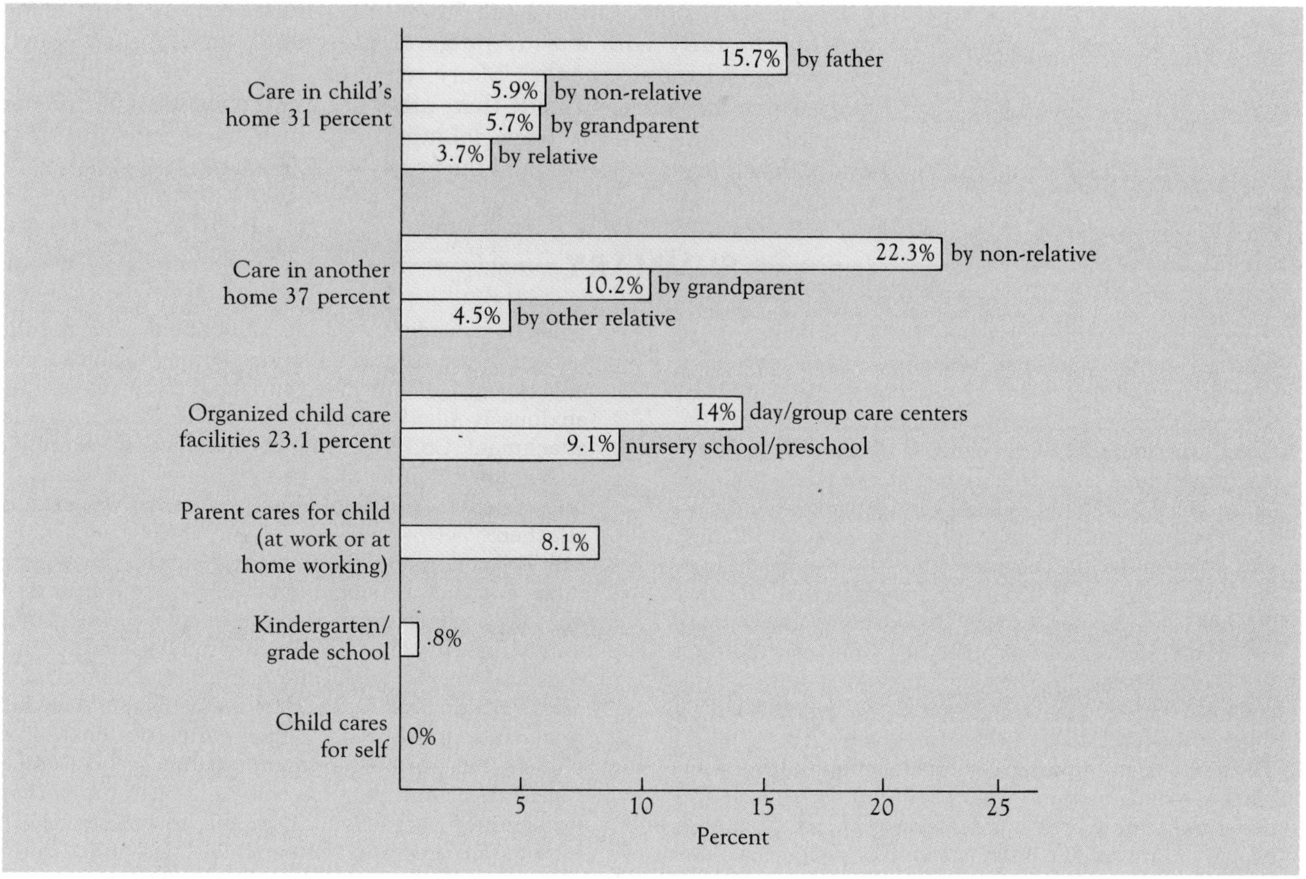

Source: U.S. Department of Commerce, 1990

◆ MANY ROADS TO TRAVEL

To return to our scenario at the beginning of the chapter, Lisa and Tim Walters now have some of the answers concerning their fears that maternal employment and day care might be harmful to their children. They must be certain that the day care provided is of excellent quality. Tim's attitude toward Lisa's working bears scrutiny, as does his ability and willingness to help with the child-care and homemaking chores. Finally, both parents must realize that their responsibilities do not end when they come home from their jobs. They must build into their schedule active involvement with their children. If they choose to leave their children either at a day-care center or with a grandparent, the children will develop some attachment to others but not at the parents' expense.

Much has been said about meeting children's needs, and warm, responsive, understanding adults are required if children are to develop socially and emotionally in a healthy manner. Yet the research shows there is no single way these needs must be met. As Chess and Thomas (1981, p. 221) note, "Just as the child's nutritional requirements can be met successfully with a wide range of individual variation, so can his psychological requirements." Many roads can lead to the same destination. Some are more difficult than others. Parents can provide for their children's needs in many ways, taking into account the personality of the child, the child's own needs, and the family's circumstances (see Figure 7.2).

SUMMARY

1. Discrete emotion theory states that the infant is born with particular emotional responses. Some psychologists argue that this is not so and that children are born with relatively undifferentiated emotions that only become differentiated with cognitive development.

2. Adults are quite competent in recognizing the emotional expressions of infants. Infants can recognize the difference between some facial expressions early in infancy, while the ability to recognize others takes more time to develop. However, it is only after about six months that infants seem to understand the meaning behind the emotional expressions of others. By one year, children use social referencing, in which they look at their caregivers in ambiguous circumstances and are affected by the facial expressions of their caregivers.

3. The smile is an important emotional communicator. Infants as young as three weeks smile to both social and nonsocial stimuli, but as infants develop, social stimuli become more salient. Infants show empathic reactions to other infants, which some psychologists believe is the forerunner of more involved empathic responses that require cognitive sophistication.

4. A child's fear of strangers may begin sometime in the second half of the first year and lasts through most of the second year. The child will show less fear of strangers if the stranger is small or is a female or if the child is allowed to get used to the stranger.

5. Beginning at about eight months of age and peaking somewhere between twelve and sixteen months, children show separation anxiety. Long-term separations from the caregiver may lead to protest, despair, and finally, detachment and serious emotional disturbances.

6. Infants must attach themselves to a caregiver if they are to develop normally. Children who have not had the opportunity to do so often suffer retardation. The tragic consequences of maternal deprivation may be reduced if the child receives excellent care later on.

7. Attachment behaviors can be measured using a stand-ardized procedure of brief separations and reunions known as the strange situation. Three classifications of attachment behavior have surfaced: secure attachment, anxious/avoidant attachment, and anxious/ambivalent attachment. Children who are classified as securely attached are superior in a variety of emotional and cognitive areas to children who are classified as anxiously attached.

8. Erik Erikson argues that the psychosocial crisis during infancy is trust versus mistrust. If the child's needs are met, the child develops a sense of trust. If not, a sense of mistrust may develop. During toddlerhood, the psychosocial crisis is one of autonomy versus doubt. Infants must develop a sense that they are people on their own.

9. Many factors affect the parent-child relationship, including the age of the parent, attitudes and expectations concerning the new role as parent, the parents' background, and sensitivity to the infant's needs. The infant's abilities and temperament also affect the relationship. While the parent's behavior affects the child, the child's behavior also affects the parent.

10. Although early and extended contact between mother and infant is desirable, it is not absolutely necessary to the establishment of a healthy mother-child relationship.

11. Mothers do much more of the housework and childcare than fathers do. When mothers are employed outside the home fathers do somewhat more, but mothers still bear the greater share of the family's work. Infants form attachments to their fathers as well as to their mothers. Mothers and fathers interact differently with their infants—with mothers often performing the daily caregiving chores and fathers playing with the children. Infants often seek out their fathers when they want to play and their mothers when in distress. The involvement of fathers with their infants varies from culture to culture and from family to family.

12. Maternal employment does not have a negative effect on daughters, and employed mothers may serve as an achieving role model. There is some evidence that middle-income males whose mothers are employed are not as cognitively advanced as sons of nonemployed mothers. This may be remedied by providing extra attention to the children when the parents come home. The differences in social behavior between children of employed and nonemployed mothers are minor.

13. Some studies of children placed into day care before their first birthday show that the infants are somewhat more likely to develop anxious attachment patterns. The majority of such infants, though, show secure attachment patterns. The risk, if indeed there is one, is small, and there is great debate over the meaning of these studies.

14. Children who enter day care after their first birthday show few differences compared to children raised at home. Day-care children tend to be more peer oriented and more boisterous. Studies show that in general, day care does not harm the child and in some instances may actually promote development.

15. The day-care experience may be a positive, neutral, or negative one, depending on the quality of the day care, the attitudes of the parents, and the parent-child interactions in the home.

ACTION/REACTION

Angry, Frustrated, But in Love

When Grace was born, Sheila and Jan were ecstatic. Sheila took the first year off work to care for the baby full time, after which she returned to her full-time job. During the day, Sheila's mother takes care of Grace in her own home. After work, Sheila picks up Grace and returns home. Jan gets home about a half hour later. Jan has always been a good husband and gives Sheila emotional support.

Since she has returned to work, Sheila notices that Jan helps out somewhat more. He does the food shopping, will play with the baby, sometimes does some dusting or cleaning, and will take Grace for a trip to the park. However, Sheila still finds herself doing 90 percent of the feeding, diapering, and house cleaning. She feels frustrated and angry, but she is told by her friends that she is lucky, since Jan does help out. If she asks Jan for a specific amount of help, he does it. However, sometimes it takes him so long that she finds it easier to do it herself.

Although she would like more help, she is afraid that any further requests will affect her marriage adversely. There seems to be a definite limit to Jan's willingness and desire to help. In addition, Jan does not volunteer for any of the everyday child care and housework. Although Sheila would like a more equitable arrangement, she does not know if pursuing it is worth a disagreement. She is concerned that although she could obtain some extra help from Jan, it would take a great deal of coaxing and perhaps begin an argument. She wonders if it is worth the cost.

If Sheila asked you, what advice would you give her?

Can Anyone Else Care For My Child?

Because Rita and Todd had not been away without their baby for over a year, they decided to take a trip, and they made arrangements to go on a week-long cruise. Everything seemed set, with Todd's parents ready to babysit.

One night before they were to leave, while Todd's parents were babysitting, Rita noticed a few things that disturbed her. The baby didn't seem to want to eat when Todd's mother tried to feed her. And Rita's mother-in-law didn't seem to have the right approach. Rita told Todd about her doubts, but he dismissed them. When Rita brought up the subject with her mother-in-law, the older woman became indignant and noted that she had been the one who had raised Todd. Things have cooled between Rita and her mother-in-law, and Todd's mother is going through with the babysitting only because the cruise tickets have already been purchased.

1. If you were Rita, what would you do?
2. If you were Todd and witnessed this rift between your wife and your mother, what would you do?
3. If you were the mother-in-law, what would you have said to Rita? What would you do now?

PART THREE

Early Childhood

In the Garden by Camille Pisarro.

CHAPTER EIGHT

The Development of Language and Communication Skills

A Tough Story by John G. Brown.

The Mysteries of Language
The Development of Language
How Words Are Used
How We Learn Language
Cross-Cultural Current: Day Care and Language Development
Encouraging Linguistic Competence: What Parents Can Do
Current Issues in Language and Communication
The Child in the Year 2000: Bilingual Questions
A Wonder Rediscovered

Are These Statements True or False?

Turn the page for the correct answers. Each statement is repeated in the margin next to the paragraph in which the information can be found.

1. American Sign Language, which is used by the hearing-impaired, is recognized as a true language.
2. Infants as young as one month can understand the spoken word.
3. Scientists now understand the meaning of a child's babbling.
4. When infants babble, they utter every sound the human vocal apparatus is capable of producing.
5. After age six, children both produce and comprehend the same number of words, while before that age, children understand more words than they can use.
6. Children's tendency to imitate the speech of their caregivers decreases significantly after age two.
7. Parents use well-formed sentences when speaking to their infants.
8. If a young child does not understand what an adult is saying, the adult usually reduces the number of words used in the next sentence.
9. Middle-class children use more complex sentences and fewer commands than children of working-class parents.
10. Twins are generally not as advanced in linguistic development as their nontwin peers.
11. Black English is a dialect of Standard English.
12. Bilingualism itself leads to cognitive difficulties and academic problems in school.

> ## Answers to True-False Statements
>
> 1. True.
> 2. False. Correct statement: Although young infants can differentiate between sounds, they cannot understand language.
> 3. False. Correct statement: We do not know whether a child's babbling has any meaning attached to it.
> 4. False. Correct statement: Although the range of sounds babbled by infants is impressive, it does not approach every sound humans are capable of producing.
> 5. False. Correct statement: Both children and adults understand many more words than they use in their own speech.
> 6. True.
> 7. True.
> 8. True.
> 9. True.
> 10. True.
> 11. True.
> 12. False. Correct statement: Bilingualism itself does not lead to academic problems in school.

◆ THE MYSTERIES OF LANGUAGE

Most of you have taken a foreign language in high school or college. There you sat, struggling over a text, trying to learn a different grammar and vocabulary. The task is time-consuming and frustrating. Has it ever occurred to you that infants who come into this world with no prior knowledge of any language learn their own language within a few years on the basis of very little formal teaching? Somehow, infants master the basics of their native tongue perfectly, including the difficult sounds and pronunciations that wreak such havoc on students desperately trying to master a second language. How does the child accomplish this feat?

A related mystery involves children's ability to generate sentences they have never heard before. Spend an hour or so listening to preschoolers converse. The creativity involved in generating a new thought will amaze you. While riding through the Mojave Desert from Los Angeles to Las Vegas, my daughter, who at the time was a little over two years of age, was quiet. The night was very dark, and the trip was monotonous. Suddenly, as we approached Las Vegas, she looked at the city and exclaimed "Oo, I see lots of lights." She may have heard each of these words separately before, but not in that exact sequence. She had generated an original thought using words that were easily understood by those around her. The simplicity of her communication should not interfere with our wonder over how a young child creatively uses language.

Some of the aspects of language development defy our attempts to understand them. One of the most puzzling areas of language development is semantics, or how we discover the meaning of words. Children learn to comprehend more than 14,000 new words, or about nine per day, from eighteen months through the preschool years. This is accomplished without any tutoring. This is even more incredible if you realize that often they hear the words only once or twice and the words are always embedded in a sentence often spoken quickly by the speaker (Rice, 1989). Somehow children "fast map" new meanings in a way that remains a mystery.

But why single out language development for special treatment? First, the acquisition of language is perhaps the greatest intellectual feat a person will ever perform. Children are born without knowing language, and within five years or so, they are communicating almost as well as the adults around them. Second, language defines humanity. No other species seems to show the depth and complexity that human beings show in language formation and use. Third, the seemingly simple issue of how children acquire language is really quite complex and requires the kind of full explanation possible only when an entire chapter is devoted to discussing the many facets of language development. Finally, the issues involved in language, such as bilingualism, the importance of the environment, and language and subculture, to name just a few, transcend all ages and stages.

The Nature of Communication

Language and communication are not the same. Language is only one part of communication. **Communication** is the process of sharing information, including facts, desires, and feelings. It entails a sender, a receiver, and a message. **Language** involves arbitrary symbols with agreed-upon meanings (Shatz, 1983). Most of the time it is verbal, but it need not be. American Sign Language (ASL) is a nonverbal language that hearing-impaired people use in the United States. It is a recognized language with a grammar of its own, even though it is not verbal. While communication is a process, language is the means of conveying meaning to someone else. The medium is usually speech, but it doesn't have to be.

For instance, consider the plight of a two-and-a-half-year-old who wants a cracker but can't reach the cracker box. The child wants to send a message to mommy, who is reading a magazine. He can communicate with her in a number of ways. He can verbally interrupt her by saying, "Mommy, gimme cracker," but there are other avenues of communication open. He can cry, make nonlanguage sounds to gain her attention, or physically lead her to the cracker box and point.

As the receiver of the communication, the mother must interpret it—not always an easy task, since children mispronounce words or express their thoughts in individualistic ways. Parents and children often have special words or phrases that stand for particular things. If a child says, "My stomach hurts," it would normally indicate that the child is experiencing gastric distress. However, one of my daughters would use that phrase to indicate that she was either hungry or very full. Because the phrase carried a specific meaning for us, we understood it, but when our

communication
The process of sharing information.

language
The use of symbols to represent meaning in some medium.

1. TRUE OR FALSE?

American Sign Language, which is used by the hearing-impaired, is recognized as a true language.

American sign language is a manual language with a grammar of its own.

phonology
The study of the sounds of language, the rules for combining the sounds to make words, and the stress and intonation patterns of the language.

morphology
The study of the patterns of word formation in a particular language.

morpheme
The smallest unit of meaning in a language.

syntax
The rules for combining words to make sentences.

semantics   *linguistic meaning*
The study of the meaning of words.
                    sentence meaning
grammar
A general term that refers to the total linguistic knowledge of phonology, morphology, syntax, and semantics.

pragmatics
The study of how people use language in various contexts.

daughter visited her grandmother, the phrase was interpreted differently, leading to a nap and no more food (much to my daughter's distress).

Once the mother in the previous scenario interpreted the message, she must communicate an answer. The roles are now reversed: The mother becomes the sender; the child becomes the receiver. Let's say that mother nods her approval. As long as the child understands that this means yes, it is as effective as verbal communication.

The Nature of Language

Just what do children learn when they acquire language? Language has a number of subsystems, including phonology, morphology, syntax, and semantics, as well as rules for social language use, sometimes called pragmatics. **Phonology** studies the sounds of a language, the rules for combining the sounds to make words, and the stress and intonation patterns of the language (Gleason, 1985). For example, the sound "cl," but not the sound "kx," occurs in English. Children must learn how these sounds combine to become words.

The **morpheme** is the smallest unit of meaning in a language. Some morphemes, such as "dog" and "little," can stand by themselves, while others, such as "ed" and "ing" must be added to another word. The rules of **morphology** make certain that some sequences, such as "walked," will occur and that others, such as "walkness," will not.

Every language also has its own rules for combining words to make sentences, called **syntax.** For instance, "John hit Mary" conveys a meaning quite different from "Mary hit John." Children must acquire a vocabulary and understand the meanings behind words. This area is called **semantics.** The general term **grammar** is used to refer to our total linguistic knowledge of phonology, morphology, syntax, and semantics (Best, 1986).

Children must also be able to use language appropriately so that they can express their ideas efficiently and get things done. This ability is called **pragmatics.** For example, children must learn the proper way to ask for something and to use language in social situations. Each language has its own rules, and each culture has its own idea of how language should be used.

◆ THE DEVELOPMENT OF LANGUAGE

Few events bring parents as much joy as their child's first word. It is easy to forget that much has taken place before the child says "dada" or "car." Under normal circumstances, every human child proceeds through similar steps in reaching linguistic competence. The development sequence leading to a mature use of language is impressive.

Prelanguage Communication

Communication between infants and their caregivers does not require language. Smiles, cries, gestures, and eye contact all form a basis for later communication. The nonlanguage interaction between parent and infant approximates a conversation. Although very young infants cannot understand words, they do respond to their caregiver's language (Fernald & Simon, 1984), and some linguistic abilities are present almost from birth (Molfese, Molfese & Carroll, 1982). One-day-old infants respond to speech sounds by moving their bodies in rhythm to them (Condon & Sander, 1974). One-month-old infants are able to discriminate between certain vowels, such as "i-u" from "u-a" and "pa" from "pi" (Trehub, 1973). At two months, infants show the ability to detect phonetic distinctions between syllables differing in consonant or vowel sounds (Bertocini, Bijeljac-Babic, Lusczyk, Kennedy, & Mehler, 1988).

The infant's ability to respond to language and other nonverbal cues leads to a kind of turn taking called proto-conversations (Bateson, 1975). A parent speaks, and the baby responds by smiling or, later, cooing. The parent then says something else, and the pattern continues. The interactions are spontaneous. Let's say mother is feeding the baby. When the infant lets go of the nipple, the mother says, "I don't want any more. I want to burp." These interactions are the beginning of a conversation mode as the infant learns the basis for later communication.

These conversations are not as random as they seem. When speaking to infants younger than six months, mothers use a rising pitch when their infants are not paying attention and the mothers want eye contact (Stern, Spieker & MacKail, 1982). In addition, yes-no questions are spoken with a rising pitch, whereas questions having to do with what and where and various commands are accompanied by a falling pitch.

The infant is also the master of another ability, **cooing.** Cooing involves production of single-syllable sounds, such as "oo." Vowel sounds are often led by a consonant, resulting in a sound like "moo." Infants enjoy

Children use a number of mediums to communicate with their parents including gestures and facial expressions.

2. TRUE OR FALSE?

Infants as young as one month can understand the spoken word.

cooing
Verbal production of single-syllable sounds, such as oo.

babbling
Verbal production of vowel and consonant sounds strung together and often repeated.

3. TRUE OR FALSE?

Scientists now understand the meaning of a child's babbling.

4. TRUE OR FALSE?

When infants babble, they utter every sound the human vocal apparatus is capable of producing.

listening to themselves vocalize, but these early noncrying vocalizations are not meant to be formal communication.

The next step in language development is **babbling,** which involves both vowel and consonant sounds strung together and often repeated. Babbling may begin as early as three months and gradually increases until about nine to twelve months of age. Then it decreases as the child begins to use words. Most infants are babbling by the age of six months (Dale, 1976). Is the babbling infant trying to communicate something?

If infants use babbling as a form of language, we must admit we haven't been able to understand it. Although some parents swear that their child's babbling has some particular meaning, this does not appear to be the case. Scientists have not figured out what meaning any particular babble may have. Some people believe that when children babble they vocalize every possible speech sound the human voice apparatus is capable of producing. This is not the case. Although the variety and range of speech sounds produced are impressive, they do not approximate all the sounds that humans can produce (deVilliers and deVilliers, 1978).

No one really knows why infants begin to babble, but we do know that they do so both when they are alone and when they are in the presence of other people. Perhaps babbling has some self-stimulatory function or is part of a drive to master an emerging ability. Whether it be sitting, standing, or vocalizing, infants have a drive to practice and gain control of their emerging abilities. Even though infants do not need social stimulation to begin to babble, babbling can be increased through social reinforcement (Dodd, 1972). Although babbling begins as a relatively uncoordinated activity, social stimulation does affect the amount of babbling children produce.

The First Word

What exactly constitutes a child's first word? Specialists in language development use two criteria (deVilliers & deVilliers, 1978). The word must approximate some adult word, and it must be used consistently in similar situations. If the baby says "ca" whenever he or she sees a car, it meets both criteria, but if the infant says it only once or says it on other occasions when a car is not present, it may be pure coincidence. Trying to convince a proud parent of this is useless.

Children usually utter their first word anytime between ten and fifteen months, but there is considerable individual variation. Children's first words are not usually those they hear most often. Katherine Nelson (1973) studied the early word acquisition of a number of children and divided the children into two categories. **Expressive children** used words that were involved primarily in social interactions, such as "bye-bye" and "stop it." The early language of **referential children** involved the naming of objects, such as "dog" and "penny." These differing styles followed the linguistic style used by the children's caregivers. The parents of referential children named objects very frequently, while those of expressive children directed their children's activities and emphasized social interactions. The early language of both groups differed. Referential chil-

expressive children
Children who use words involved in social interactions, such as "stop" and "bye-bye."

referential children
Children whose early language is used to name objects, such as "dog" or "bed."

dren used many more different words than expressive children used. Expressive children begin to use language in a social context; referential children use it in cognitive context, such as labeling items when looking at a book (Nelson, 1981).

The first words are, of course, simple. Most contain only one or two syllables. Words are used at first in isolation and are gradually generalized to similar situations. Babbling continues during this one-word stage. For years, psychologists have argued about the meaning of these one-word utterances. Hazel Francis (1975) asks what a child really means when uttering the single word "jam." Does it mean that some jam is on the table or that the child wants jam on a piece of bread? Psychologists call this one-word utterance a **holophrase,** meaning a single word that stands for a complete thought. For instance, a child says "up" and means "pick me up," or the child says "wet" and wants to be changed. Parents must go beyond the word and use the context to interpret the child's ideas. The child saying "wet" may be labeling the condition and may not want to be changed at all. This interpretation casts some doubt on whether the child is really using one-word expressions to indicate entire thoughts. If the child wanders over to the refrigerator and says "jam," mother may say, "So you want some bread and jam." When parents interpret their children's one-word utterances so loosely, establishing what a child really means becomes difficult.

holophrase
One word used to stand for an entire thought.

Toddler's Language

By eighteen months, the child is using up to twenty words. The child names familiar objects and uses gestures easily. Words such as "no," "mine," and "hot" are common, although word usage is inconsistent; that is, a word may be used at one time in the day and not in another. By two years of age, the child is using up to 270 words. Two- to three-word sentences are spoken, and the first pronouns such as "I" appear. Some simple adjectives and adverbs are present. By thirty months, the child is using up to 425 words. The child uses more adjectives and adverbs and often demands repetition from others. The child at this age begins to announce intentions and asks questions (Weiss & Lillywhite, 1976).

The two-word stage is well organized. The child's use of the words is governed by rules that make the meaning of the communication easier to understand. The meaning depends upon specific word orders (Owens, 1990). For example, when expressing ownership, toddlers use a word to stand for the possessor and another for the item possessed, as in "mommy ball" or "baby doll." When something has happened or the child wants something to happen again, the child will use a recurrence word such as "more" or "nuther" and then the object, such as "nuther cracker" (Owens, 1988). There are a number of these rules for toddler language. The important thing to remember is that there is a form and a recognizable logic to the way toddlers' messages are communicated. When about half the child's utterances contain two words, the child begins to use three words. However, the child is still governed by rules for making these short sentences.

Toddlers use particular rules of word order. For example, to show possession, children use the possessor and then the item such as "baby, doll."

telegraphic speech
Sentences in which only the basic words necessary to communicate meaning are used, with helping words such as "a" or "to" left out.

The child's early speech leaves out small words like "a," "to," or "from" and concentrates on the more important words, for example, "Mommy go store" or "baby take toy." This is called **telegraphic speech,** because it is similar to the language found in telegrams where the sender includes only the words absolutely necessary for communication. These important words are commonly stressed by other speakers in the environment, which makes them easier to imitate and learn (Brown, 1973). Parents still must interpret the child's meaning according to the context of the remark, but the thoughts are communicated more precisely at this stage.

Language Development in Early Childhood

By three years of age, the child is using up to 900 words, and his or her sentences are averaging three to four words per sentence. Words such as "when," "time," and "today" show an awareness of time. The child can tell stories that can be understood. Some auxiliary forms appear such as "can," "do," "did," and "be." The child also begins to use the word *because*. By forty-two months, the child is using up to 1,200 words in mostly complete sentences averaging between four and five words per sentence. The rate of speech increases, and asking permission now becomes more common ("Can I?"). In addition, between forty-one and forty-six months, such words as *wasn't* and *couldn't* appear as well as the word *if*, which is used to join two phrases. By four years, the child is using up to 1,500 words, with longer sentences of five to five and a half words. The child now demands a reason for something by asking "why?" or "how?" and questions constantly. The child uses words such as *almost, but,* and *like*. At fifty-four months, the child uses 1,800 words and does less commanding and demanding. The child's sentences are longer, averaging five and a half to six words.

By five years, the child is using up to 2,200 words, and the sentences are again longer, averaging six words. The child now can ask the meaning of a word, and the questions now take on a more adult sound. The child searches for information, asking such questions as, "What is this for?" and "How does this work?" Sentence structure has become more complicated, and the child uses all types of clauses. By sixty-six months, the child is using up to 2,300 words and using sentences averaging six and a half words in length, and some of the grammatical errors described in the next section decrease. By six years, the child is using 2,500 words in sentences thet now average seven words in length (Weiss & Lillywhite, 1976). As the child progresses through the preschool stage, he or she can sustain a conversation for a longer time. The conversations are more focused, and the child's ability to attend to one topic increases.

One of the patterns easily noticed by parents of preschoolers is the increase in the size and complexity of children's utterances. Scientists often measure this development in terms of an increase in the mean length of utterance (MLU), which is found by dividing the total number of morphemes in a sentence by the number of utterances. Between the ages of one and a half and five years, MLU increases approximately 1.2 morphemes a year (Owens, 1988).

Language Development in Middle Childhood

The child's growth in linguistic ability is very obvious before the age of six or so. Certainly, the six-year-old is speaking a language that can be comprehended by others. This does not mean, however, that changes do not take place in middle childhood. In fact, the child improves in every subsystem of language throughout middle childhood. In the area of syntax, the child uses more elaborate phrasing and uses the passive voice, as "got lost" or "was chased." The child now knows that a verb can be made into a noun by adding "er." For example, hunt is a verb, and if you add an "er," the word becomes *hunter*. After seven years, the child understands the adverb "ly," and verb agreement with irregular nouns, such as "The sheep is eating," improves greatly. The child begins to use past participles, such as "eaten," and perfect tenses, such as "has been." Perfect tenses develop slowly, and even though some forms are produced early in this stage, their use may be uneven until later in the period. This gradual development is common during this period. For example, the prepositions "if," "so," and "because" are used much earlier, but their full development does not occur until later in the period. Some forms, such as "although" and "therefore," may not be used until late elementary school or early adolescence.

Naturally, the vocabulary of these children increases as well. Pragmatically, one of the great improvements, as most parents well know, is the schoolage child's ability to use language more subtly. The child's ability to get what he or she wants now improves because, as we shall see in forthcoming chapters, the child in the middle years of childhood can now understand things from other people's points of view. This gives the child the ability to ask for things indirectly, as in "Gee, that cowboy hat looks

Language development is most obvious before early childhood. However, there is much linguistic development in middle childhood.

great." Most parents understand that this is an indirect request. The schoolage child can gain attention in a more socially acceptable manner, ask for things giving a rationalization, and more easily direct the actions of others. The child can now introduce a topic into the conversation, and keep the conversation going for a while, and close the conversation less abruptly than preschoolers can.

Another change is in the way children associate words. If you ask a three-year-old to associate the word *girl*, the child may say "run." However, ask a child who is eight, and you will get "boy" or "woman" (Owens, 1990). The association in early childhood is often syntactic (based upon grammar), while in middle childhood, it is semantic (based upon meaning). This may result from a change in general cognitive processing strategies.

Adolescence

Adolescents use language in more advanced ways. They can use and understand satire, metaphors, and similes. This ability is associated with cognitive advancements such as the ability to use abstractions. For example, young children cannot deal very well with political cartoons, poetry that has abstract meaning, or proverbs. They do not have the cognitive sophistication to do so. Adolescents develop that ability, and their language can show a more philosophical and abstract understanding of the world around them.

Adolescents also show vocabulary gains, especially in some technical areas. In addition, the communication pattern changes. Teenagers are better able to understand the communicative requirements of the situation and appreciate how people's moods and expectations influence their acceptance of communication. The adolescent can more easily bend language to meet the situation. The ability to leave hints and give indirect requests, which began in middle childhood, improves greatly as well.

◆ HOW WORDS ARE USED

If you listen even casually to the speech patterns of young children, you will find some striking differences between their use of language and that of adults. Young children overextend and underextend their use of words and follow grammatical rules with what seems to be blind devotion.

Overextension and Underextension

As they learn language, children make certain kinds of mistakes (Griffiths, 1986). For instance, a young child looking at a magazine might label every picture of a man "daddy" and every four-legged animal "dog." Such a child does know the identity of his or her father and is probably aware of the difference between a cat and a dog.

The type of error in which children apply a term in a broader manner than is correct, called **overextension,** is probably more a problem in pro-

overextension
A type of error in which children apply a term more broadly than it should be.

duction than a problem in comprehension (Whitehurst, 1982). That is, children understand the differences, but they have difficulty producing the correct labels. This was demonstrated well in a study by Katherine Nelson and colleagues (1978), who found that a child who would call all sorts of vehicles, such as an airplane, a truck, or even a helicopter, a car could pick out the correct object when asked to do so. In another study, a child who overextended the word apple to include a number of different foods was able to choose an apple from a group of foods when asked to do so (Thomas & Chapman, 1975).

Children also **underextend** (Anglin, 1977); that is, they use a term to cover a smaller universe than it should. Young children often use the term animal to define only mammals and may deny that people, insects, or birds are animals as well.

Why do children overextend and underextend? Clark (1974; 1978) argues that children learn words and concepts in terms of basic features. This is called **semantic feature theory.** For example, dogs have four legs and fur. If this were so, the child would call all four-legged animals with fur "dogs." Children learn that birds have feathers and fly. Animals fitting that description are placed into the category of bird. However, the categories must be constantly updated, and an ostrich, which has feathers but does not fly, is still a bird. Others argue that rather than learning specific features, the child is actually developing a **prototype**—the most typical instance of a category—and compares other instances to the category. Rosch (1975) found that people formed prototypes for many categories, including colors, birds, and vegetables. When asked to classify whether new items fit into these categories, they compared the new stimuli to the prototype. Some examples are better prototypes than others. For instance, robins are better prototypes of birds than turkeys or penguins. How well a particular example fits a prototype affects how fast we process information. People are faster classifying a robin than a penguin as a bird.

Categorization problems may also arise from the speech directed at children by adults (Anglin, 1977). When a child is young, parents are apt to use such terms as *car* and *dog* rather than *Chevrolet* and *German shepherd.* This is functional, because children need to recognize the difference between a car and truck, but not between a Chevy and a Dodge, but it restricts the child's experience with labels and explains these phenomena. Overextension and underextension may also simply reflect the child's prevailing mental abilities and difficulty in categorizing items.

underextension
The use of a word in a more narrow context than proper.

semantic feature theory
A theory of semantic and concept acquisition that argues that people develop concepts in terms of a concept's basic features.

prototype
The most typical instance of a category.

Overgeneralization of Rules

Once children begin to acquire some of the basic rules of English, they overuse or, as psychologists say, **overgeneralize** them. For example, to make a noun plural, we ordinarily add an "s" to the word, as in "dogs" or "pencils." However, exceptions abound, and the plural of "man" is not "mans" but "men." When creating a past tense, we normally add the suffix "-ed," as in "walked" or "talked." Again, exceptions are plentiful; the past tense of "go" is not "goed" but "went," and the past tense of "see" is not "seed" but "saw." Children will often overuse these rules

overgeneralization
A type of error in which children overuse the basic rules of the language. For instance, once they learn to use plural nouns they may say "mans" instead of "men".

"I drinked the waters". Once children begin to master the rules of grammar, they often overgeneralize them.

and use words like "goed" or "seed." They may have used the word correctly in the past, but now that they know the rule, they apply it to every case, producing such grammatically incorrect forms. With experience, children correct themselves, and most gradually learn the exceptions with little or no formal training.

Comprehension and Production

production
The ability to verbalize language.

comprehension
The understanding of language.

So far we have looked at the **production** of language, but there is another important area—**comprehension.** Psychologists have tended to focus more on production than on comprehension because it is easier to study production. A child produces a word, and parents become aware of the child's linguistic growth. The child's advancement is easy to detect. Studying comprehension is more difficult. A child may understand an order but be physically unable to carry it out. In addition, only action-oriented comprehension, as when a parent shouts "Sally, give me the crayon before you write all over the walls," can be measured. Even in this example, the child may give the parent the crayon but not understand some parts of her parent's command. Mother's menacing tone (intonation) or manual gestures (standing with her hand outstretched) may be enough for Sally to figure out that she had better hand the offending instrument over to her mother immediately.

At every age, children understand more words than they can produce. One fourteen-month-old child could point out his own shoe and his mother's shoe when asked to do so, even though he was unable to speak a word (Huttenlocher, 1974). As children grow into adulthood, they use a greater variety of words in their writing than in their speech. We recognize many more words in print and in someone's else's speech than we ourselves use, and this imbalance remains throughout life.

◆ HOW WE LEARN LANGUAGE

The simplest questions are often the most difficult to answer. This is especially true in the area of language learning. For years, psychologists have been struggling over the question of how a child develops from a being who understands and produces no language to one who can use language with great ease.

Reinforcement and Imitation

At first glance, it appears that children learn language through imitation. This seems true, especially for early vocabulary. Words are symbols that stand for things or ideas. The vocabulary of each language differs. The Spanish word for chair is *silla*, and in Hebrew it is *keesay*. The only way children can learn words is by hearing them and then copying them. Children learn the word *apple* when they have need for the word. They master words in an attempt to communicate with others. When they finally say "chair," they have imitated what they have already heard in their environment.

The effects of imitation on word acquisition is evident. A parent who labels common everyday items is more likely to have a child who has a superior early vocabulary (Nelson, 1973). Children may also pick up unusual words that have shock value. My two-year-old daughter learned the words *horrible, ridiculous,* and *disgusting* very early. She would try some new food, make a face, and say "Disgusting" with all the intonation the word requires. She generalized the use of this word and, after receiving a big kiss from one of her great-aunts, wiped her face and said "Disgusting." The power of the environment is shown by the way children learn words from older siblings and peers, often using them at the wrong time.

There is evidence that the processes of learning can affect both the number and the complexity of verbalizations. Grover Whitehurst and Marta Valdez-Menchaca (1988) exposed American and Mexican two-year-old and three-year-old children to a foreign language. Some children were reinforced if they used the language, while others were not. For example, in the experimental group, if the child used the foreign word for a toy, the toy was immediately handed to the child. Those who were reinforced in this way used many more foreign words. The reinforcement motivated the children to use the words from the new language. Other studies have shown that generally, caregivers who reinforce their children for using complex language have children who indeed use such language. When mothers show approval of their children's verbal behavior, the children's mean length of utterance (MLU) increases. Parents may reward more mature forms of expression by praise or by giving the child what he or she wants, thereby reinforcing particular ways of communicating.

Reinforcement and imitation also have an effect in some areas of prag-

5. *TRUE OR FALSE?*

After age six, children both produce and comprehend the same number of words, while before that age, children understand more words than they can use.

matics. For example, children who are reinforced for saying "please" and "thank you" or who have parents who use such politeness are more likely to use these expressions of courtesy.

B. F. Skinner has attempted to use learning theory to explain the acquisition of syntax and grammar. According to Skinner (1957), operant conditioning, including the processes of reinforcement, generalization, and discrimination, are responsible for language development. Children learn language the same way they learn everything else. They are reinforced for labeling the environment and for asking for things. Through the process of generalization and discrimination children come to reduce their errors and use the appropriate language forms. Of course, imitation also enters the picture, as the child imitates parental speech. Skinner looks at the acquisition of grammar as a matter of generalizing and making inferences. For example, a child may learn the meaning for the phrase "my teddy bear" and then infer that my can be used as in "my cracker," "my television," "my" everything. As we shall see later, this explanation of language development is sharply contested by others.

While imitation and reinforcement are helpful in understanding some areas of vocabulary acquisition and general language usage, they are inadequate to explain language acquisition itself. The overall amount of imitation decreases with age, especially after age two (Owens, 1988). In other words, the usefulness of imitation as a language learning strategy decreases as language becomes more complex. Imitation then, is most important at the single word level.

It is a mistake to think that because the child may learn some early vocabulary and general usage through these processes, all language development can be explained by imitation and reinforcement. There is more to it. To use language correctly, children must acquire rules such as those for changing tense and creating word order. Some of the rules are quite complicated. Try describing the rule by which you would use the phrase "a thing" or "the thing." Most of us use the rule perfectly, but we would be hard-pressed to formulate it.

In addition, it is very difficult to explain how children create original sentences using reinforcement and imitation. All children create original sentences they have not heard before. In addition, how can a child of limited cognitive abilities master the complicated rules of grammar that even adults cannot explain—and do all this without formal training (Bloom, 1975)? Finally, if only the processes of learning are involved, why do children make the same mistakes as they develop their language abilities, and why do they produce such childish speech patterns as telegraphic speech which they do not hear around them? These problems, among others, have led some authorities to argue that some innate biological mechanism must be responsible for language acquisition.

Is Language Acquisition Innate?

Noam Chomsky (1959, 1965, 1972), the leading advocate for the biological or **nativist explanation**, argued that human beings are preprogrammed to learn language. Children require only exposure to the language prevailing

6. TRUE OR FALSE?

Children's tendency to imitate the speech of their caregivers decreases significantly after age two.

nativist explanation
An explanation of language development based on biological or innate factors.

in their own culture. Human beings are born with an innate, biological ability to learn language, called a **language-acquisition device.** Children can acquire the grammar of the particular culture's language because their brain is innately patterned to understand the structure of languages. Children can understand the basic rules of language and form hypotheses about them, which they then test out.

Chomsky's position excited many psychologists and psycholinguists (scientists who study the nature of languages). It explained the interesting similarities that we find in language development around the world. Children in all cultures proceed through the same steps when learning language (Slobin, 1972) and make the same mistakes. These similarities could be explained if the acquisition of language rests on some shared neurological foundation. Language acquisition becomes a maturational activity coinciding with brain development. Some authorities claim that there is a critical period between birth and adolescence for developing language (Lenneberg, 1967). If not developed during that time, the individual's language would be permanently disordered. In addition, Chomsky noted that languages from all around the world share certain similarities, thus establishing a fit between the structure of the mind and human language in general.

Nature v. Nurture—Again

The Chomsky-Skinner debate is a variation of the nature-nurture debate. Current evidence indicates that both nature and nurture are involved in the acquisition of language. Even those who believe in the nativist position admit that the environment is important. As Jean Aitchison (1978, p. 89) states, "Both sides are right: Nature triggers off the behavior, and lays down the framework, but careful nurture is needed for it to reach its full potential." It is equally difficult to take a completely environmental perspective. Human beings are born with an impressive vocal apparatus, allowing them to develop speech (Aitchison, 1978), and all societies seem to use this ability in some way (Bowerman, 1981).

Specific areas of the brain are devoted to language. The cerebral cortex in human beings is divided into two hemispheres, the right and the left. Most people are right-handed, and almost all have their language functions centralized in the left hemisphere. Half the left-handed people also have their language areas localized in the left hemisphere (Gleason, 1985). Scientists found that when specific areas of the brain are injured, certain language-related problems occur. For example, the area responsible for producing speech is called **Broca's area.** Damage here causes a person to have difficulties in speaking, but the person is still able to comprehend language. Damage to another area, called **Wernicke's area,** causes a person to have poor comprehension and speech filled with nonsense words, even though the speech is fluent. The brain also has areas associated with written language (Gleason, 1985).

In addition, a number of factors already noted imply some biological root for language acquisition. Human infants are able to make impressive phonetic distinctions and are attentive to speech quite early in life. Some

language-acquisition device
An assumed biological device used in the acquisition of language.

Broca's area
An area in the brain responsible for producing speech.

Wernicke's area
An area in the brain responsible for comprehension of language.

strategies for processing language may in fact be innate (McNeill, 1970; Slobin, 1973). Finally, particular informational processes, such as memory and attention, may develop according to maturational rules that we are only just beginning to appreciate. Some biological or innate factors are at work in language acquisition, but a complete biological position does not match the facts.

The weaknesses in the nativist position are evident. For example, the existence of a language-acquisition device has not yet been proven. Even if we agree that a neurological basis for language exists, it does not explain the processes involved in language learning. And although the similarities between how children learn language around the world are impressive, recent evidence shows that there are some differences that reflect the nature of the language being learned (Akiyama, 1985). M. Michael Akiyama (1984) tested children on their order of acquiring four types of statements: (1) true affirmatives, such as "You are a child"; (2) false affirmatives, such as "You are a baby"; (3) false negatives, such as "You aren't a child"; and (4) true negatives, such as "You aren't a baby." Three-year-old and four-year-old Japanese-speaking and English-speaking children were asked whether such statements were right or wrong. The English-speaking children found verifying true negatives most difficult, whereas the Japanese-speaking children had the greatest problem with false negatives. The difference in acquisition pattern is due to linguistic differences between English and Japanese. So although some biological foundation for learning language is probable, the nativist position does not fully explain language acquisition either.

The strictly learning theory and nativist positions thus both fail as a complete explanation for language acquisition. One expert, George Miller, put it well: "We had two theories of language learning—one of them, empiricist associationism (learning theory), is impossible ; the other, nativism, is miraculous. The void between the impossible and miraculous remained to be filled" (in Bruner, 1978, p. 33). Two other approaches to language acquisition—emphasizing the importance of cognitive and social factors—are now popular and have begun to fill this void.

Cognitive Theory and Language Development

Language learning involves such cognitive processes as attention, information processing, and retention. The development of these skills affects a child's language abilities. For instance, paying attention to stimuli that are loud or attached to some vital activity (such as feeding), remembering them, making discriminations and judgments about them (such as whether they are the same or different), and classifying according to these judgments are all cognitive processes related to language learning (Peters, 1986). How could children create sentences if they did not have the cognitive ability to remember words? In addition, children must understand something about an object or an idea before using words in a meaningful manner.

Linguistic growth necessarily parallels cognitive growth. The child first uses simple words for things, then proceeds to define classes in terms of

their more abstract qualities, such as color. Language learning and cognitive advancements are intertwined. It is difficult to understand how a child could express a thought such as "all gone" or understand the concept of disappearance unless he or she understood some measure of object permanence (Rice, 1989). Teenagers can use words in a more abstract manner because they have the ability to deal with abstractions. Simple expressions become more exact as a child's cognitive development proceeds. Young children may understand some concept and desire to communicate it, yet not have the proper word in their vocabulary. In fact, if children cannot express a thought using a word that they know, they will invent one (Nelson, 1974).

Even in the area of vocabulary, the cognitive aspects are being recognized as very important. Children first talk about what they know, favorite things, people, and activities (Rice, 1989). Their first words aren't abstract or even words for objects that aren't meaningful to them, such as FAX machine. Rather, children name their bottles or something that has a meaning to them. In addition, in understanding semantic development we now go beyond the idea that children merely hold a picture in their heads of an item and then attach the word symbol to the item. This simple association may be useful for simple words, but the child's understanding of the word and its meaning go beyond this.

As noted previously, semantic feature theory and cognitive theories based on the notion of prototypes have been advanced to account for how children develop their word knowledge. Modern cognitive approaches to linguistic development are searching for identifiable sequences that show the relationships between cognitive advancement and linguistic expression.

Social Interaction and Language Development

Children do not acquire language in a vacuum. They are affected by the linguistic environment that surrounds them, including the home and the day-care center they may attend (see Cross-Cultural Current on page 322). Recent investigations of the nature of a child's early linguistic environment have uncovered information that runs counter to conventional wisdom.

Consider the situation in which infants find themselves. They can hear and discriminate certain sounds, but everyone is talking in a quick, complex, difficult-to-understand manner, and there is little repetition. At first glance, the linguistic environment appears to be confusing and its level much too high for infants. Yet children learn to communicate through language in a relatively short time. It was just such a scenario that appealed to the psychologists who argued in favor of an innate language mechanism. After all, children acquire language on the basis of very fragmented and cognitively advanced input. It all seemed impossible.

This particular argument in favor of the innate mechanism has been laid to rest. Communication aimed at children is neither fragmented nor confusing. Infants receive verbal stimulation from the first days of their lives. This verbal input is well structured and tuned to their level. It begins in the hospital nursery. Certainly new mothers and fathers speak

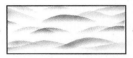

Day Care and Language Development

What happens to the language development of children when they attend a day-care center for long periods of time? That depends on the day-care center, according to Kathleen McCartney (1984), who investigated the language development of 146 preschoolers attending nine day-care centers in Bermuda. Because language skills are so important for later success in school, the effect of the day-care experience on the development of these skills is an issue worth addressing.

The choice of Bermuda as the site for the study is interesting in itself. First, 84 percent of all Bermudan children by age two spend the majority of the work week in some form of nonparental care. When studies of children in American day care are performed, the possibility that these children differ from the child who is not in day care becomes a problem. In Bermuda, the child not in some day-care arrangement is unusual. Another frequent problem in day-care research is that programs differ so much that the results of research using one or two centers may be biased. This study used all the day-care centers in Bermuda that accepted children from infancy through the preschool years. All children three years and older who attended any of these centers for six months or more and their parents were asked to participate.

The children ranged in age from thirty-six months to sixty-eight months. Previous research has demonstrated that the amount and nature of the verbal interchanges between parents and their children are major factors in determining language skill. McCartney hypothesized that the amount and nature of the verbal interchanges between children and their caregivers at the day-care center would also predict language skill.

Many aspects of the day-care environment and the children's intellectual and language development as well as their homes and backgrounds were carefully measured. Verbal interactions with caregivers and peers were divided into four dimensions. Control statements involved commands such as "Stop talking." Expressive comments involved the expression of feelings and attitudes such as "I like your shirt." Representational statements were defined as the giving and receiving of information, as in the statement "The toys are over there." Social comments were aimed at establishing and maintaining social relationships, as in the statement "Let's play with this."

McCartney found that the overall quality of the day-care center was a positive predictor of children's language development, as was the amount of verbal interaction between caregiver and child. The type of caregiver-child interchange was important as well. The proportion of control utterances was a negative predictor of language develop-

7. TRUE OR FALSE?

Parents use well-formed sentences when speaking to their infants.

to their newborn infants from birth. Both male and female hospital workers not only use soothing sounds and baby talk but also speak to newborns as if they actually expect them to understand speech (Rheingold & Adams, 1980). At times, they engage in a dialogue, as the child's movements encourage the adult to say something. Sometimes the hospital staff ask questions and answer their own questions as they think the baby would answer. Infants are treated as individuals from birth and called by their names. In all, this earliest verbal communication is anything but impersonal and random. Infants elicit a great deal of stimulation and from the first are exposed to a linguistic environment.

The old idea that early verbal interchanges are confusing and too difficult for infants is in error. When people talk to infants, they modify their speech. Parents talk to their older infants in shorter sentences, but these sentences are very well formed (Bowerman, 1981; Newport, Gleitman & Gleitman, 1977). The language that parents use to talk to infants is simple and repetitious (Snow, 1977). It contains many questions and

ment. That is, children who received many commands were hampered in their development of important language skills. It is interesting to note that control and representational statements were inversely related to each other. The more control statements (as in commands) given by the caregivers, the fewer the representational statements (giving and receiving information) were communicated to the children. On the other hand, the proportion of representational statements was positively related to language skills. Children benefit when they are given and asked for information.

Another important predictor of linguistic abilities was a child's willingness to initiate a conversation with a caregiver. This was related to the atmosphere created by the caregiver. Children's language skills are optimized when children are encouraged to initiate conversations.

Some specific aspects of the day-care center were particularly important in determining the child's language abilities. Children did better in more structured centers with low noise levels and little time for free play. This does not mean that children should be regimented, nor should we conclude that any one educational theory is superior to any other. It does demonstrate that children benefit when caregivers structure the children's activities to some extent and create an organized environment.

But what about peer exchanges? After all, children do talk to each other in day-care centers. McCartney found that the greater the number of peer conversations, the lower the language scores of the children. Perhaps peer conversations of lesser quality replaced important caregiver talk.

This study demonstrates that a number of factors predict children's language abilities, including the amount and type of caregiver utterances, children's willingness to initiate interactions with their caregivers, and the overall quality of the day-care center, as well as some specific aspects of the center's organization. Good things seem to occur together. It is likely that all these factors exist in the best centers, that is, that superior day-care centers are well organized with structured activities, create an atmosphere in which children talk more with their caregivers, and contain personnel who are more concerned with giving and receiving information than with giving commands.

Studies like this one emphasize the importance of the environment in determining language skills. No matter which theory of language acquisition one subscribes to, the child's linguistic environment is a major predictor of language skill. The challenge is to create a linguistic environment that will help children develop language skills to the fullest. It is clear from this study that day-care centers have a role to play in this area.

Source: McCartney, K. Effect of Quality of Day Care Environment on Children's Language Development, *Developmental Psychology*, 1984, *20*, 244–260.

commands, few past tenses, and few hesitations; is highly pitched; and is spoken with an exaggerated intonation (Garnica, 1977). In short, parents' speech to their linguistically limited children is restrictive and involved with common nouns and comments on what their children are doing (Molfese et al., 1982).

The use of simplistic, redundant sentences is normally referred to as **motherese.** Parents use motherese—with its emphasis on the present tense and simplified, well-formed sentences—to communicate with their youngsters. Infants pay more attention to motherese. Four-month-old infants prefer to listen to motherese over speech directed at adults (Fernald, 1985). Infants are especially sensitive to the pitch. The higher pitch used in communication to an infant elicits the infant's attention (Fernald & Kuhl, 1987).

So young children are likely to be exposed to speech on their own level. All adults and many older children tailor their language to the age and comprehension level of younger children. Even young children use

motherese
The use of simple repetitive sentences with young children.

If a young child does not understand what an adult is saying, the adult usually reduces the number of words used in the next sentence.

Even young children use "motherese", that is short sentences in higher pitch, making it easier for even younger children to understand.

these strategies but do not present their little siblings with much nonverbal information and are not as proficient in the use of these strategies (Tomasello & Mannle, 1985).

The child's reaction to parental speech determines the speaker's choice of words (Bohannon & Marquis, 1977). If a two-year-old shows a lack of comprehension, an adult immediately reduces the number of words in the next sentence. Children are not merely passive receivers of information. Their show of comprehension or noncomprehension serves to control their linguistic environment.

Verbal exchanges between adults and young children do not constitute formal language lessons. The idea that parents somehow sit down and teach their children how to talk is not supported by the facts. However, there is no doubt that parental speech patterns affect the child's linguistic development. One finding that has been popular for many years is that parents do not tend to correct their children for their grammatical errors or reward them for using correct grammar. They are more interested in the correctness of their children's utterances (Brown & Hanlon, 1970). If little Sharon says, "Me girl, " her mother is likely to say, "That's right, you are a girl." On the other hand, if Sharon says, "I am a boy," her mother is likely to correct her immediately.

This finding that parents are more likely to reinforce their children for the truthfulness of what they say than for their grammatical errors has been the subject of some interesting research. Sharon Penner (1987) studied parental responses to grammatically correct and incorrect statements and confirmed the finding that parental approval of what the child says follows both grammatically correct and incorrect utterances to the same degree. However, Penner also found that parents were more likely to expand on their replies when their young children used grammatically incorrect statements than when they used grammatically correct ones. For example, if a child said, "ball fall," the parents said, "Yes, the ball fell," rather then simply, "Go get the ball." This did not occur all the time, but it still happened more than would be expected by chance. Notice that parents first reinforced the child for the correctness of the statement and then expanded on the statement, changing the grammar of the sentence and expanding on the statement's content.

How do parents respond to ungrammatical statements? No one believes for an instant that parents faced with a grammatically incorrect statement say to their children "No, say it this way" or "That is not the correct grammar." Unlike correcting the truthfulness of statements in which this direct correction is likely to occur, perhaps parents provide a correction in a different manner. According to John Bohannon and Laura Stanowicz (1988), that is exactly what happens. The researchers found that parents did not always ignore grammatical or syntactic errors. They analyzed parental responses to many errors, including syntactic mistakes in word order and tense, phonological errors such as "lellow bawoons," and semantic errors such as calling a dog a horse. Semantic errors were relatively infrequent and were found in only about five percent of the speech, but these errors were always corrected by parents, though not by nonparents. If a child, upon seeing a picture of a camel, says, "That is a

When children do not show comprehension of what others are saying, people reduce the complexity of their sentences.

horse," parents will correct the child and tell the child that it is a camel.

The researchers also found that adults responded differently to children's grammatical and ungrammatical sentences. About 34 percent of children's flawed speech received some feedback, including recasts, in which parents kept the meaning but changed the sentence. In other words, if a child said "That are a monkey," the parent would say, "That is a monkey." Parents also responded with expansions in which adults reproduced major parts but added something, and sometimes questions were used to clarify the child's meaning. At the same time, about 35 percent of the time that children showed phonological problems (poor pronunciation), adults in some way followed the statements with expansions or questions. When the speech was well formed, expansions or questions were used only about 14 percent of the time. Adults not only differentially responded to children's speech errors but often provided correct language examples when responding to their children. Parents were more likely than nonparents to do this. The experimenters argue that children do indeed learn from such corrections.

Bohannon and colleagues (1990) suggest that feedback could help children in the following manner. Let us say that the child produces "broke" and "breaked." Whenever the child receives evidence to support the use of "broke," the strength of "broke" increases. Since both "broke" and "breaked" stand for the same thing, they cannot exist at the same time. There is a competition between forms, and one becomes the loser and the other the winner. The world *broke* receives great support, while *breaked* gets hardly any. The child learns from this feedback to use *broke* instead of *breaked*. Not everyone agrees with this analysis. In fact, Peter Gordon

(1990) argues that since corrections occurred in only 34 percent of the ungrammatical utterances, the amount of correction children hear is not sufficient to make a difference. Bohannon and colleagues comment that children can learn from these corrections even though parents only give such feedback about one third of the time. At this point, we can only say that parents correct the child's semantic errors consistently. However, the extent to which correction is given to syntactic errors and the meaning of the corrections are still a matter of controversy.

Language acquisition involves learning a social skill that is useful in the interpersonal context. Language is purely functional. The purpose of speech and language is to communicate thoughts, ideas, and desires to others. Psychologists have become more interested in the nature of this give-and-take on the part of parents and their children. Even before learning language, children begin actively communicating with their parents through gestures and vocalizations (Bruner 1978a and 1978b). These pre-linguistic modes are replaced by standard linguistic modes. Indeed, the child is an active and willing partner. The interactions between mother and child are very much structured in the form of a dialogue and show a progression from the simple to the complex. Even though parents may not be aware of their role as teachers, they do teach their children their native tongue. The infant begins to communicate, and mother responds. The interaction between the two is intense and functional.

Language can be used to direct the actions of others. The child learns that communication involves signaling meaning, sharing experiences, and taking turns. These are prerequisites to learning language. One expert in this area, Jerome Bruner (1978a), sees language development in terms of problem solving. Children must solve the problem of how to communicate their wishes and thoughts to others. They learn language through this interaction with others and by actively using language. Grammar and vocabulary are acquired because they are useful to children in accomplishing their aim of getting across to others what they want and what they are thinking. Notice that in this conception of language development parents tune their linguistic input to the ability level of the child. This theory is sometimes called the **fine-tuning theory.** It explains the finding that children encounter language in a very structured and progressively more difficult and complex manner. Language is learned as an extension of nonlinguistic communication. In fact, Bruner's (1983) theory is a kind of compromise between Skinner's and Chomsky's. Bruner believes that language develops from the interaction between the language and the social environment created by the caregivers and whatever innate language potential children have (see Levine & Mueller, 1988).

Bruner also believes that cognitive development precedes linguistic development. Children know what they want to communicate, and language becomes the necessary vehicle for doing so when they are mature enough to produce it. This view sees language acquisition as arising from need, being based on carefully fine-tuned interactions between mother and child and as an outgrowth of solving the problems of communicating with another individual. When studying a child's linguistic progress, the transactions between mother and child should be investigated. Bruner

fine-tuning theory
A theory noting that parents tune their language to a child's linguistic ability.

(1978a, p. 38) notes that language learning is not a "solo flight in search of rules, but a transaction involving an active language learner and an equally active language teacher."

Systems Reconsidered

We have seen how learning theory, the nativist approach, and cognitive and social factors all contribute to our understanding of how children develop their language abilities. A unified theory of language acquisition is still beyond the state of our knowledge. Human beings appear to be biologically prepared to learn language. However, this, in and of itself, is insufficient without an adequate linguistic environment. Language development arises from the interaction of cognitive abilities and learning strategies and is activated by environmental events, such as the interaction of the child with his or her parents (Warren, 1988). However, language learning is a very complex area, and some of the abilities of children are difficult to explain, such as fast mapping of vocabulary. Perhaps all these factors are involved in some complicated way, or perhaps different facets of language are affected by one factor more than another (Whitehurst & Valdez-Menchaca, 1988).

◆ ENCOURAGING LINGUISTIC COMPETENCE: WHAT PARENTS CAN DO

We have come a long way in appreciating a child's abilities. We now understand the importance of environmental stimulation and cognitive processes in the development of language. We know that children learn language through an active process that involves exposure to a particular linguistic environment. The finding that the nature of this early linguistic interaction determines the child's later language abilities comes as no surprise. Children who are encouraged to verbalize and expand on their language skills develop superior language abilities (Hoff-Ginsberg, 1986). From the earliest age, children interact with people in their environment and learn that they can influence people and events through language.

The development of language is anything but random. The input children receive is also definite and patterned, as demonstrated by motherese (Molfese et al., 1982) and the fine-tuning of the parent-infant interaction (Bruner, 1978b). The repetitive, simplified style of motherese aids the child's comprehension. The parent-child interactions affect the manner in which children produce speech. Children who ask more questions have mothers who do the same (Lord, 1979), but this is not to imply that we are returning to the old imitation theory of language acquisition. Rather, it demonstrates that the linguistic atmosphere surrounding the child is important to the child's language acquisition. Children raised in a linguistically rich environment are superior in their later use of language.

A number of studies have found that language usage differs among middle-class and working-class people. Middle-class youngsters use more expansive language and do better in language activities in school. Chil-

Parents can use many daily activities to help their children develop their language skills.

9. TRUE OR FALSE?

Middle-class children use more complex sentences and fewer commands than children of working-class parents.

10. TRUE OR FALSE?

Twins are generally not as advanced in linguistic development as their nontwin peers.

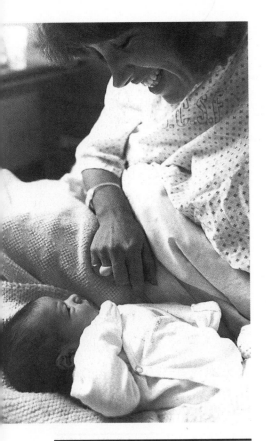

Children are spoken to from earliest infancy.

dren of working-class parents use simpler sentences and more commands (Olim, Hess & Shipman, 1967). The linguistic environment of middle-class children and the interactions between such children and their parents are more expansive (Hess and Shipman, 1965; 1967). We must remember, however, that language is functional and that these children are not deficient in their own native environment. What is somewhat lacking are the specific language abilities required in school. When we look at how well a child knows his or her own dialect, there is no deficiency in rate and amount of linguistic knowledge (Menyuk, 1977).

The importance of the linguistic environment is also shown by a study that compared the language development of twins and nontwins. The twins were not as advanced as single children. The communication pattern between the twin pairs and their mothers was more directive and contained fewer questions or statements that required the children to respond (Tomasello, Mannle, & Kruger, 1986). There is no doubt that the child's linguistic environment affects language development.

Most suggestions for improving linguistic competence are based on the premise that children learn language both by listening and by participating. Parents should not take an artificial attitude toward language development, for the natural flow of parent-child interactions is sufficient for the child to learn the appropriate language. Parents can do more harm than good by trying to force a child to say something the youngster is not ready to say or by providing the child with a language environment that is too complex or inappropriate. Nevertheless, parents can help children in the development of their language by using the following guidelines.

Even at the earliest age, talk to infants. Infants are sensitive to language and learn much about verbalizations and turn taking from early conversations. There are many opportunities to talk to a baby (Honig, 1988). Parents can talk to a child when feeding and changing the child. Toddlers' verbalizations should be greeted with approval. Although it is not always easy to understand what the child means, responding with a positive statement is important. The child's gestures or emotional reactions can also bring a verbal interpretation from the caregiver. For example, if the child seems impatient the caregiver can say, "I know you're hungry. The food is warming up."

Give the child an opportunity to talk. Acquisition of language is an active process. Children need an opportunity to talk and to communicate their thoughts (Cazden, 1981). When children are young, ask "wh--" questions and encourage them to use more than just a yes or a no answer.

Expand on the child's statements. Middle-class parents often expand on their children's statements. For example, if the child says, "Throw ball," a parent might say, "Throw the ball to daddy." Such expansions have a positive effect in broadening the child's language usage in some areas (Hovell, Schumaker & Sherman, 1978).

Label things in the environment. Children benefit from listening to speech that labels the environment. When a baby points at the bottle, it is worthwhile to say, "You want your bottle?"

Read to the child. Reading to a child is beneficial, but there are many ways to do this. When the child is old enough to give some response, try to ask questions that are age appropriate and allow the child to participate in the story. When reading a story, you may ask the youngster to point to the cow or the dog. In time, when children can talk, they can label things themselves and answer such questions as what color it is. Even later, the story may lead to a discussion about farm life and the like.

The importance of such an active reading climate was demonstrated in a study by Grover Whitehurst and colleagues (1988). Parents of toddlers were divided into two groups. Parents in the experimental group were instructed to (1) use open-ended questions that required the children to use more than a yes/no response, (2) encourage the children to tell more, (3) ask the children function/attribute questions (what is the farmer doing?), and (4) offer expansions (repeating statements with some additions, such as if a child said "dog," the parent might say "big dog"). Parents were also told to respond positively to the children's attempts to answer the questions and to reduce the number of questions that the children could answer by pointing. These techniques required the children to talk about the pictured materials. The control group parents were instructed to read in their normal manner. After one month, children in the experimental group scored significantly higher on measures of expressive language ability and showed a higher mean length of utterance, a greater use of phrases, and a lower frequency of single words. Nine months later, the differences were somewhat less but still present. Reading to a child should be an interactive activity.

Use modeling. Children tend to copy the expressions of their parents, so reasonably good linguistic models are important. Finishing sentences, answering questions in an expanded way, using adjectives, and so on, contribute to a rich linguistic environment.

Encourage verbal interaction. Rather than forcing a child to speak and verbalize, using praise and engaging the child in meaningful verbal interactions are worthwhile (Hess & Shipman, 1967).

◆ CURRENT ISSUES IN LANGUAGE AND COMMUNICATION

We have thus far looked at the general sequence of development and at some theoretical viewpoints that explain how children develop language. With this basic knowledge in hand, let's look at some of the fascinating issues in the area of language development.

Black vs. Standard English: Difference or Deficit?

"By the time I get there, he will have gone."

"Time I git dere, he be done gone."

If you were asked which of these sentences would be best received by

Parents label the environment for their children.

Black English
A dialect spoken throughout the
United States by lower-income
blacks but understood by the
overwhelming majority of blacks.

linguistic deficit hypothesis
The belief that a dialect such as
Black English is a hindrance to
learning.

linguistic difference hypothesis
The belief that a dialect such as
Black English is different from
Standard English but not a deficit.

11. *TRUE OR FALSE?*

Black English is a dialect of
Standard English.

an English professor, you would certainly choose the first. While the first sentence illustrates Standard English, the second is Black English. **Black English** is a dialect spoken throughout the United States by lower income blacks and understood by almost all black people (Raspberry, 1970). It contains a consistent, logical, and coherent grammar (Labov, 1970).

At one time it was thought that Black English was simply mispronounced, poorly spoken Standard English, and it was accorded no respect. In fact, since children from ghettos have many language difficulties, it was thought that such problems were caused in part by their initial exposure to and learning of this dialect. This led to what has been called the **linguistic deficit hypothesis.** This dialect was considered to be a deficit—something wrong—not merely different. It was something that a child should give up somewhere along the educational ladder.

Beginning in the late 1960s, however, social scientists began to reconsider this position. After all, if Black English is understood in the child's environment and has a consistent set of rules, why treat it differently from Spanish or French? In some ways, it is even more precise than Standard English. When a teacher asks a black child why his father couldn't make a meeting the night before, the child might answer, "He sick." However, when asked why the father has not attended any of the meetings during the year, the child says, "He be sick" (Raspberry, 1970). Inclusion of the word "be" shows an ongoing chronic status. In Standard English, the answers to both questions might simply be that the father was ill.

Black English is closer to Standard English than French or Spanish, and many argue that Black English is a valid dialect. Black children suffer not from linguistic deficits but from **linguistic differences,** and differences are not necessarily deficits. William Raspberry (1970) presents a nice analogy. He notes that the reason we want children to learn Standard English is that Black English is less negotiable than Standard English, just as trading stamps are less negotiable than cash. What is needed is to help children develop Standard English without forcing them to give up their own dialect, just as a child can learn English as a second language without giving up his or her original language.

Teachers who consider Black English to be inferior to Standard English may reject black children's ideas, essentially turning them off and reducing communication between themselves and their students. Students may also develop feelings of inferiority. Teachers must understand that Black English is a dialect and accept children's ideas without reacting negatively to the dialect. When a teacher misunderstands Black English, it may also lead to frustrating situations for both teacher and pupil. Some black children read the words "I saw it" as "I see it," since both see and saw are pronounced "see" in this dialect (Dale, 1972). Correcting this error is difficult, because black children do not understand that this is an error.

Whether the dialect is called a deficit or a difference, lower-income children from ghettos have difficulty with Standard English. Joan Baratz (1969) asked third graders and fifth graders in Washington, D.C., to repeat thirty sentences. Half the students were white, the other half were black. Fifteen of the sentences were given in Black English, while fifteen were in Standard English. The white children learned the sentences given in

Standard English better than the black children did. The black children learned the sentences given in Black English better than the white children did. This might merely show that children learn verbal material that is more meaningful to them. However, Baratz found that black children translated the Standard English sentences into Black English, and that white children translated the Black English sentences into Standard English. From an information-processing point of view, the problem of black children who are taught to read from kindergarten using Standard English involves the extra time-consuming and inefficient process of not only recognizing the words but also translating them into their own dialect.

Perhaps both the deficit hypothesis and the difference hypothesis miss the mark in one regard. Children must be able to deal with their environment, and therefore Black English has its uses. However, although Black English may be accepted as a dialect, children must learn Standard English if they are to succeed in school and in the world of work. Sandra and Francis Terrell sent six black college women for job interviews. Those who spoke Black English were given shorter interviews and fewer offers. The offers that were made were for lower paying positions. These researchers suggest that children who are encouraged to speak Black English in order to keep their heritage risk being handicapped in the job market (Raloff, 1982b).

Most people who wish to accept Black English as a dialect agree wholeheartedly that black children must learn to speak and write Standard English. Perhaps there has been too much focus on the deficit and difference hypotheses and not enough on how one teaches children a different dialect that they will not hear very much around their homes or neighborhoods. One promising approach is to point out the differences between students' speech and Standard English without criticizing students' speech. Students exposed to these differences show no resentment as long as their speech is not labeled incorrect (Cooper & Stewart, 1987).

Becker and colleagues (1971) developed a very directed and highly structured program designed to upgrade the skills of children from poverty backgrounds. This very behavioral oriented program involved the use of immediate reinforcement, fast-paced instruction, and breaking complex tasks into simpler learning tasks. One of the areas of concern was the learning of Standard English, and some success has been claimed for the program. However, it has been criticized as too structured, and it is not clear whether the results are long lasting. More research is needed on ways of teaching Standard English to children who speak other dialects.

The Bilingual Puzzle

What of the thousands of children in the United States who come from homes in which a foreign language—commonly Spanish—is the primary language? These children, who often come from impoverished backgrounds, face many of the same problems black children do, although their language itself is accepted as a true language. English is the second language for these children, and their success in the United States depends partly on learning Standard English.

What is the best way to educate these children? Some educators propose that a bilingual program be introduced in the school, that subjects such as mathematics and social studies be taught to Spanish-speaking students in Spanish until the children gain sufficient ability in English to function effectively in that language. At the same time, these children would receive instruction in Standard English. Evaluations of these programs have been mixed. Some evidence shows that the programs have helped students achieve scholastically (Crawford, 1987; Willig, 1985). Other researchers disagree, noting that these programs have not been as successful as had been hoped (Baker & de Kanter, 1981). Some note that there is a strong need to emphasize English rather than the child's native language through a process similar to immersion. In such programs, students are taught in English by teachers who know another language but use the other language only to help students who do not understand the materials. Students are encouraged to use English but are also encouraged to ask questions in their native language when necessary (*U.S. News and World Report*, 1986). Other detractors note the difficulty of recruiting effective bilingual teachers and the problems involved when more than one foreign language is used by various children in a class.

The debate over the best way to teach English to these children is ongoing, and more research is needed (August, 1986). Bilingual education is a fact of life in the United States, although it is increasingly under attack. The psychological issues surrounding bilingualism are still with us, and debate over the consequences of bilingualism continues.

At first glance, knowing more than one language seems like a great advantage. However, research in the 1950s indicated that bilingual children did poorly in school and suffered retarded language development in both languages (Segalowitz, 1981). These studies have been criticized for their poor methodology and the questionable testing devices used.

In recent years, however, an about-face on the issue of bilingualism has occurred. In one review of the literature, McLaughlin (1977; 1978) found no clear evidence that bilingualism leads to intellectual or cognitive problems in school. Some of the difficulties encountered by bilingual students are due not to their bilingualism but to poverty, poor housing, lack of intellectual stimulation, and other socioeconomic variables (Diaz, 1985). There is, in fact, evidence that bilingual children are high in verbal and nonverbal intelligence scores and show more cognitive flexibility (Segalowitz, 1981). Some have argued that this is so only in a balanced bilingual situation in which both languages are encouraged and taught. However, often bilingual students are not given any opportunity to continue their native language, which means that they are relatively poor in their primary language (Crawford, 1987).

What conclusions can we make, then, concerning the bilingual child? First, there is nothing inherently inferior about bilingualism, and some evidence indicates that bilingual children have certain advantages over their monolingual peers. Second, poverty and bilingualism are often confused. Many minorities in the United States who speak a language other than English suffer from the degradation of poverty, with all that it entails, including poor self-concept, disillusionment, discrimination, poor opportunity, and so forth. It may be that the clash of cultures, rather than

Should bilingual children be taught subjects other than English in their native language or in English?

THE CHILD
IN THE YEAR
2000

Bilingual Questions

By the year 2000, the number of bilingual children in the United States will have grown, and the growth will probably continue well into the next century. Many people do not seem to understand the differences between the experience immigrants face today and that of immigrants at the beginning of the century. In fact, a number of people point to the success many immigrants have had in learning English and argue that there is no need for any special programs instituted for these children.

This is unfortunate, because times have changed. Although discrimination has always existed, the need for advanced education and training has not. Fifty years ago, an advanced education was not required, and the importance of academic advancement could be minimized. We could afford to wait generations for a family's education and language abilities to develop to the extent that the children could succeed in advanced training or higher education. Most immigrants took low-paying jobs, and their children may have taken a step up, but they still may not have had much advanced training. By the third generation, these families

were routinely sending their children to college.

Today, we do not have this luxury. There are very few jobs that permit a reasonable standard of living that do not require a good education. Today, we see children entering school with poor English skills, and our goal is not just to teach these children basic English. We also want to help them gain the necessary academic skills to succeed throughout school and in the work world. It is only recently that we have asked educators and children to accomplish this feat of language, not in a matter of generations, but in a relatively few years.

How can this be accomplished? There are a number of new approaches being tested in communities across the country. Some teach children the basic subjects in English but allow the child to ask questions in their primary language if they do not

understand the materials. Others offer after-school programs designed to improve language skills. Some people argue that we need a comprehensive course that would expose these children to English, beginning slowly and then progressively becoming more and more advanced. This total immersion concept is often used to teach people a foreign language. It is not yet certain how practical this is at the present time. In the next decade, many more programs will be instituted across the country.

No matter what techniques are used, it is most important to understand that the goals have changed. It is not just a matter of teaching children enough English so that they can get along in society. There is more pressure to teach these children sufficient English so they can succeed in advanced schooling. What we obviously need is a relatively quick way of accomplishing this. Although a practical way of doing this has not yet emerged, we can expect more research activity in this area in the future. It is hoped that the new experimentation in the next decade will bring us closer to a successful answer to this challenge.

bilingualism, actually causes many of the problems noted by teachers in the public schools.

If bilingual programs in the schools are to work, however, they must ensure that all children learn English in a way that allows them to function reasonably well in the outside world. If children leave school knowing mathematics, science, and social studies but functioning poorly in such language-related areas as reading, writing, and speaking, their prospects for educational advancement and employment will be poor. Continuous evaluation of such programs is necessary to be certain that these children are learning and using English.

12. TRUE OR FALSE?

Bilingualism itself leads to cognitive difficulties and academic problems in school.

◆ A WONDER REDISCOVERED

Language development is an area of developmental psychology that is filled with controversy. We have looked at many of the issues surrounding language acquisition, especially the question of how language is acquired. The certainty with which so many psychologists embraced Skinner's and Chomsky's work has long passed. Neither the radical innate posture of Chomsky nor the behavioral learning ideas of Skinner seem sufficient to explain the development of language in children, although both theories explain some aspects of language learning. The more modern approach takes both the laws of learning and the biological basis for language learning into consideration, but it also looks at the nature of the interactions between the developing child and the child's parents. This position views language development as a carefully orchestrated progression of interchanges between an active learner and active teachers, who may not be aware of the role they are playing in the child's language development.

As we begin to tear down the curtain of mystery that surrounds language development, we can appreciate the wonder of it all. The simple sentence of a child is not just an imitation of what the child has heard, nor is it something prewired in. It is the creative expression of an inherently human ability. Looking at it from this standpoint, learning our native tongue is perhaps the greatest intellectual feat that any one of us ever performs.

SUMMARY

1. Communication is the process of sharing information. It may be verbal or nonverbal. Language is a set of agreed upon, arbitrary symbols used in communication. The subsystems of language include phonology, morphology, syntax, semantics, and pragmatics.
2. Infants communicate with the people around them by smiling, crying, and gesturing. They are sensitive to speech sounds from the moment they are born.
3. Babbling, which involves verbalization of vowel and consonant sounds often repeated, begins as early as three months. Children utter their first word anytime between ten and fifteen months of age. Some psychologists argue that children use one word, called a holophrase, to stand for an entire thought. The child's early sentences are called telegraphic, because they contain only those words absolutely necessary for communicating meaning to other people.
4. The length of children's sentences gradually increases, vocabulary increases, and more adult grammar is found as children develop. Although the most dramatic improvements are seen in the first five or six years of life, language development continues throughout middle childhood and adolescence.
5. Young children make predictable errors. They overextend, using words in a wider manner than is proper. They also underextend, using words in a more restrictive sense than is appropriate. Children also overgeneralize rules of language. When they begin to learn the rules of a language, they use them indiscriminately and have difficulty with exceptions to the rules.
6. Behaviorists, such as B. F. Skinner, use the processes of reinforcement and imitation to explain language acquisition. Noam Chomsky argues that a human being is prewired to learn language and merely requires exposure to a language to master it.
7. Cognitive psychologists argue that such factors as attention and memory are involved in language acquisition. In addition, to use a word correctly, a child must know something about an object.
8. Adult speech to young children is well constructed and consists of short, simple sentences with many repetitions. Social interaction is important in language acquisition, because children learn language through interaction with their caregivers, who fine-tune their language to the developmental level of the child.

9. The linguistic environment that surrounds a child is important in the acquisition of language. Middle-class parents tend to use expansive language, while working-class parents tend to use more restricted speech patterns. Parents can help to optimize their children's linguistic process.

10. Black English is a dialect spoken by lower income blacks and understood by most black people in the United States. It has a consistent, logical, and coherent grammar. Many authorities believe that it should be accepted as a valid dialect and that teachers should not reject the ideas of students who use this dialect. However, children who use Black English sometimes have difficulty with Standard English, a knowledge of which is necessary for success in the academic and vocational worlds.

11. Early studies seemed to show that bilingualism was a deficit to learning, but they often confused bilingualism with poverty. Newer studies stress the bilingual child's advantages. It is important for every bilingual child to learn Standard English.

ACTION/REACTION

A Heavy Choice

José is a bright Hispanic seventh grader who came to the United States a year and a half ago. He is trying to learn English, but it isn't easy, because Spanish is spoken both at home and in his neighborhood.

José and his parents face a decision. The school has a new, experimental bilingual program in which José may enroll. Since José is doing fairly well in school, despite his lack of ability in English, he does not have to enter the program, but his parents can request it. In this program, all subjects other than English will be taught in Spanish, allowing José to keep up with his studies in other areas. At this point, his deficiency in English is hampering his progress in mathematics, science, and social studies. José's father believes that the only way to learn English is to live it. He does not want José to enter the program, because he is afraid his son will come out of it with a poor knowledge of English. His mother argues that knowing perfect English won't help if José is far behind in his studies. Teachers in the school are split over the program. José is not sure which path is best either, but he must decide in the next few weeks whether to request entrance into the program.

1. If you were José, would you voluntarily enter the program?

Following the Trends

Risha is a delightful six-year-old child. Her language development has been good, and she speaks well for her age. The only difficulty is that she always uses the immature form "me" or "Risha" instead of "I." For example, she will say, "Me eat an apple," or "Risha eats an apple." This is the only really syntactic error she shows that seems age inappropriate, and it bothers her parents.

Risha is one of four children. Two sisters are older, and she has a two-and-a-half year old brother. Her parents are concerned, because since she is now in school, her poor language usage might make her look childish. Risha's mother feels that they should either correct Risha when she says things in this way or simply not respond to her poor grammar, thereby forcing her to speak correctly. Risha's father believes that this policy of correction will frustrate Risha and perhaps reduce the communication between her and her parents. He is in favor of letting it alone.

1. If Risha's parents asked for your advice, would you agree with Risha's mother or her father? Do you have another solution?

CHAPTER NINE

Physical and Cognitive Development in Early Childhood

Visit from the Doctor—"A Serious Case" by Harry Roseland

Are These Statements True or False?

Turn the page for the correct answers. Each statement is repeated in the margin next to the paragraph in which the information can be found.

1. During early childhood, a child's rate of growth increases.
2. Children grow in spurts during early childhood.
3. By the end of the preschool period, girls are superior at balance and precision and boys at throwing and kicking.
4. The leading cause of death among preschoolers is accidents.
5. Most young preschoolers believe that even inanimate objects are capable of being alive and conscious.
6. The average four-year-old's attention span is four times greater than the average one-year-old child's attention span.
7. Preschool children do not spontaneously use memory strategies such as rehearsal.
8. Preschoolers are more rigid than elementary schoolchildren in their understanding of what should take place and the order in which events should occur.
9. Preschool children cannot tell the difference between television commercials and the programs they accompany.
10. Preschoolers with schoolage brothers and sisters are more likely to watch "Sesame Street" than preschoolers with younger siblings.
11. Children attending Project Head Start classes are less likely than their peers who did not attend the program to be held back in grade or placed in special education classes during their school career.
12. The curriculum of today's kindergarten is more likely to include training in basic academic skills than it was fifteen years ago.

Answers to True-False Statements

1. False. Correct statement: During early childhood the rate of growth decreases.
2. False. Correct statement: If measurements are taken often and carefully, a rather constant rate of growth within a particular period is found.
3. True.
4. True.
5. True.
6. True.
7. True.
8. True.
9. False. Correct statement: Preschoolers do understand the differences between television programming and commercials, although they generally do not understand the motivation behind commercials.
10. False. Correct statement: Preschoolers with younger siblings are more likely to watch "Sesame Street" than children with older siblings.
11. True.
12. True.

◆ THE TIME-LIFE REMOVER

"She (turned) almost full blue. My mother was screaming at me to get away from her. I ignored her. I knew what to do. I said to my mother, 'I saw this on *Benson*' (the television situation comedy). I lifted her up and banged her on her feet. She bended over and she coughed and it plopped out." This is how five-year-old Brent Meldrum describes how he saved the life of six-year-old Tanya Branden, who had something stuck in her throat. Brent is the youngest person ever known to have used the Heimlich maneuver, which he calls "the time-life remover" (*Los Angeles Times*, August 7, 1986).

This incident demonstrates how great the physical and cognitive advances of preschoolers are. Brent showed a surprising ability to learn from television and to translate that learning into action. For Brent to have performed this act, he had to size up the situation correctly, understand what to do, be physically able to perform the maneuver, and finally, ignore the pandemonium that surrounded him as he performed the maneuver.

Anyone who works with preschoolers will be impressed by these children's newfound abilities. Yet we are often surprised when preschoolers treat inanimate objects as if they are real, have difficulty understanding that squat eight-ounce cups and tall eight-ounce glasses hold the same amount of liquid, and have problems solving what seem to be simple problems.

◆ PHYSICAL DEVELOPMENT IN THE PRESCHOOL YEARS

This chapter looks at the physical and cognitive development of preschool children. The expanding motor abilities of preschoolers allow them to attend to what is going on around them rather than having to concentrate just on how they walk and hold things. Preschoolers can now easily take part in many physical activities, satisfying some of their curiosity about the world and learning from their experiences. Their physical skills give them more independence. They now interact more frequently with other children and learn from their social interactions. Eating is no longer a great physical challenge either, for they can handle eating implements with some skill. They can eat by themselves and are affected by the nutritional information around them, especially on television. Finally, many of them attend preschool, in which they use their new physical and sensory abilities as tools to further develop their social and cognitive abilities.

Growth and Development

The rate of growth slows during the early childhood years. About twice as much growth occurs between the first and the third years as between the third and the fifth years (Cratty, 1986). Growth is still readily apparent, however, during this period. The average three-year-old girl stands about 37 inches (94.1 cm) tall and weighs about 29 pounds (13.11 kg). By the age of six, she stands just over 45 inches (114.6 cm) tall and weighs almost 40 pounds (17.8 kg). Boys are a bit taller and heavier throughout this stage and remain so until about the age of eleven. The average three-year-old boy stands just over 37 inches (94.91cm) tall and weighs about 32 pounds (14.62 kg). By the age of six, he stands almost 46 inches (116.1 cm) tall and weighs 45.5 pounds (20.69 kg) (Hamill, 1977). The preschool child grows approximately three inches a year.

These figures can be misleading, however, because variation from the statistical average is to be expected. In addition, simply comparing a child's height or weight to an average does not tell a doctor or a parent whether the child has a growth problem. If the average six-year-old boy weighs 45.5 pounds, what would you say about one weighing 42.5 pounds? Should this alert us to some possible growth problems?

To take such natural variations into account, scientists generally speak of a range of heights and weights that are usual for a child of a certain age in a particular culture. The heights and weights of many children are measured and then divided into percentiles, the fiftieth percentile being the average (see Appendix). Then the height and weight below which 25 percent and above which 75 percent of all boys or girls of a certain age fall are found, and they become the range that is considered normal. For example, the average five-year-old girl weighs about 38.8 pounds (17.66 kg),

Five-year-old Brent Meldrum saved the life of six-year-old Tanya Branden by using the Heimlich maneuver. Brent had seen it on television.

1. TRUE OR FALSE?

During early childhood, a child's rate of growth increases.

Children grow in spurts during early childhood.

but any weight between about 35.8 pounds (16.29 kg) and 42.6 pounds (19.39 kg) is considered normal (Hamill, 1977). Even if a child's height or weight is above the seventy-fifth percentile (larger than 75 percent of his or her age mates) or below the twenty-fifth percentile (smaller than 25 percent of his or her age mates), it may not indicate a problem. Perhaps the parents are very short or very tall. However, it may alert us to a possible problem, and many physicians will look into the situation.

Many people believe that children grow in fits and starts; that is, they grow, then fill out, then grow again. But if measurements are taken carefully, the rate of growth is actually fairly regular (Tanner, 1978).

During the preschool period, body proportions change. At two, the head is about one-fourth the total body size, while by five and a half, it is one-sixth the body size (Cratty, 1970). The preschooler gradually loses that babylike appearance. The amount of fat decreases during this period, with the added weight resulting from the growth and development of muscle tissue. Generally, boys have more muscle tissue, while girls have a bit more fat, but many individual differences can be found. At the beginning of the preschool period, children generally have their full set of baby teeth, and by the end of the period they begin to shed them. Preschoolers look forward to visits from the "tooth fairy," which bring glee and money (as much as a dollar per tooth in some families).

Motor Abilities

By the beginning of the early childhood period, children have mastered the basics of walking and no longer have to pay much attention to standing steadily on two feet. Now they attempt to master their physical environment. They are as likely to run as to walk, their movements are smoother, and they turn corners better. The four-year-old can stand on one foot for two seconds and can negotiate a six-centimeter walking board with a bit of stepping off (Heinicke, 1979). Large muscles are still much better developed than fine muscles, but by age four, the child can hold a pencil in something that resembles an adult's style and can fold a paper in a diagonal manner (Heinicke, 1979).

Children at this stage master many fundamental motor skills, including running, jumping, hopping, skipping, and climbing. The motor development of children in the preschool period is summarized in Table 9.1 on page 342. Children younger than about eighteen months do not usually have the power or balance to leave the ground with both feet in the air, making running and jumping difficult. By the age of three, however, 42 percent can jump, and by four and a half years, 72 percent can (Cratty, 1986). By about three and a half, most children can hop from one to three steps, but they cannot do it with much precision or control. By about five, most can hop for ten seconds or so. Girls are better than boys at this. Skipping is more difficult and is generally not well developed until about five years of age (Corbin, 1980).

Catching a ball is a skill that also develops in early childhood. At about three and a half, the child waits with arms held straight out and elbows fixed. By about four, the hands are at least open to receive the ball, al-

During early childhood, children develop their motor skills, and physical play is important in this regard.

though the elbows are still fixed. By about five, the arms and elbows are held to the sides of the body, allowing them to give when the ball arrives.

The development of such motor skills allows children to explore and physically master the world around them. In the later part of the preschool period, some gender differences become evident, with girls often superior to boys at tasks requiring balance and precision and boys somewhat better at throwing and kicking (Cratty, 1986).

Fine Motor Control

The three-year-old riding a tricycle is the picture many people have when they think of a preschooler. Indeed, the development of gross motor skills, such as running, hopping, and climbing, is readily visible. But the advances in fine motor control are also impressive, although fine motor control lags behind gross muscle development and control. The more subtle development of fine motor control shows itself in the way a child controls a crayon or a pencil.

If you give crayons to children of various ages and watch how they hold and use them, you might be surprised at the progress preschoolers show when compared with younger children. Babies use their entire fists. Toddlers progress to holding the crayon fairly well but use their wrist for drawing, while preschoolers by about age five have improved to the point where they are now holding the crayon better and using the small muscles in the fingers for control. Still, they must concentrate, and their effort lacks the smoothness it will have later. Both maturation and practice are responsible for this improvement in control and coordination (Kellogg, 1970).

Children's Art

Children have a natural affinity for drawing and painting, and their artistic ability can be viewed within a developmental framework, as shown in Table 9.2 on page 344. Give a one-year-old a crayon and a piece of paper, and the scribbling will begin, but the sweeping motion of the arm and the manner in which the crayon is held testify to the immaturity of the child. The scribblings may not remain confined to the paper. There is a kinesthetic enjoyment in scribbling. This lack of voluntary control belongs to the early scribbling stage—the first stage of artistic development (Allen & Herley, 1975). Later, eye-hand coordination and small-muscle control will improve, so that the child can better control a writing instrument. Both maturation and practice are responsible for this improvement in control and coordination. During this advanced scribbling stage, the child can stay within the confines of the paper, and more voluntary control is evident.

At about age three, such basic forms as circles, crosses, and ovals appear in drawings over and over again. The transition between drawing these basic forms and the pictorialism of later childhood art is exhibited in drawings of mandalas, suns, and radials at about age four or five. A mandala is a circle or a square divided by one or more lines inside it (Allen & Herley, 1975). Suns are not necessarily round but may be square or

3. TRUE OR FALSE?

By the end of the preschool period, girls are superior at balance and precision and boys at throwing and kicking.

TABLE 9.1: Development of Locomotor Skills

This table describes the development of locomotor skills in early childhood. Keep in mind that some children will develop these skills earlier than other children.

LOCOMOTOR SKILL	THREE-YEAR-OLD	FOUR-YEAR-OLD	FIVE-YEAR-OLD
Running	Runs with lack of control in stops and starts. Overall pattern more fluid than two-year-old. Runs with flat-foot action. Inability to turn quickly.	Runs with control over starts, stops, and turns. Speed is increasing. Longer stride than three-year-old. Nonsupport period lengthening. Can run 35 yards in 20–29 seconds.	Running well established and used in play activities. Control of run in distance, speed, and direction improving. Speed is increasing. Stride width increasing. Nonsupport period lengthening.
Galloping	Most children cannot gallop. Early attempts are some variation of the run pattern.	43 percent of children are attempting to learn to gallop. During this year, most children learn to gallop. Early gallop pattern somewhat of a run-and-leap step.	78 percent can gallop. Can gallop with a right lead foot. Can gallop with a left lead foot. Can start and stop at will.
Hopping	Can hop ten times consecutively on both feet. Can hop one to three times on one foot. Great difficulty experienced with hop pattern. Attempts characterized by gross overall movements and a lot of arm movement.	33 percent are proficient at hopping. Can hop seven to nine hops on one foot. Hop pattern somewhat stiff and not fluid.	79 percent become proficient during this year. Can hop ten or more hops on one foot. Hop characterized by more springlike action in ankles, knees, and hips. Can hop equally well on either leg.
Climbing	Ascends stairs using mark time foot pattern. During this year, ascending stairs is achieved with alternate foot pattern. Descending stairs mostly with mark time foot pattern. Climbing onto and off of low items continues to improve, with higher heights being conquered.	Ascends stairs using alternate foot pattern. Descends stairs with alternate foot pattern. Can climb a large ladder with alternate foot pattern. Can descend large ladder slowly with alternate foot pattern.	Climbing skill increasing. 70 percent can climb a rope ladder with bottom free. 37 percent can climb a pole. 32 percent can climb a rope with bottom free. 14 percent can climb an overhead ladder with 15-degree incline. Climbing included more challenging objects such as trees, jungle gyms, large beams.
Balance	Balance beam walking pattern characterized by mark time sequences.	Balance beam walking pattern characterized by alternate shuffle step.	Balance beam walking characterized by alternate step pattern.

TABLE 9.1: Development of Locomotor Skills (continued)

LOCOMOTOR SKILL	THREE-YEAR-OLD	FOUR-YEAR-OLD	FIVE-YEAR-OLD
Balance (continued)	Can traverse 25-foot walking path that is one inch wide in 31.5 seconds with eighteen stepoffs.	Can tranverse 25-foot walking path that is one inch wide in 27.7 seconds with six step-offs.	Can tranverse 25-foot walking path that is one inch wide in 24.1 seconds with three step-offs.
	Can walk three-inch-wide beam forward 7.4 feet; backward, 3.9 feet.	Can walk three-inch-wide beam forward 8.8 feet; backward, 5.8 feet.	Can walk three-inch-wide beam forward 11 feet; backward, 8.1 feet.
	44 percent can touch knee down and regain standing position on three-inch-wide beam.	68 percent can touch knee down and regain standing position on three-foot-wide beam.	84 percent can touch knee down and regain standing position on three-foot-wide beam.
Skipping	Skip is characterized by a shuffle step.	14 percent can skip.	72 percent are proficient.
	Can skip on one foot and walk on the other.	One-footed skip still prevalent.	Can skip with alternate foot pattern.
	Actual true skip pattern seldom performed.	Overall movement stiff and undifferentiated.	Overall movements more smooth and fluid.
		Excessive arm action frequently occurring.	More efficient use of arms.
		Skip mostly flat-footed.	Skips mostly on balls of feet.
Jumping	42 percent are proficient.	72 percent are proficient.	81 percent are skillful.
	Jumping pattern lacks differentiation.	Jumping pattern characterized by more preliminary crouch.	Overall jumping pattern more smooth and rhythmical.
	Lands without knee bend to absorb force.	Can do standing broad jump 8–10 inches.	Use of arm thrust at takeoff evident.
	Minimal crouch for takeoff.	Can do running broad jump 23–33 inches.	More proficient landing.
	Arms used ineffectively.	90 percent can hurdle jump five inches.	Can do standing broad jump 15–18 inches.
	Can jump down from 28-inch height.	51 percent can hurdle jump 9½ inches.	Can do running broad jump 28–35 inches, vertical.
	Can hurdle jump 3½ inches (68 percent).		Can jump and reach 2½ inches.
			90 percent can hurdle jump eight inches.
			68 percent can hurdle jump 21½ inches.

Source: Corbin, 1980.

rectangular. After this stage, shapes are combined to form human beings.

Drawing is a valuable childhood activity. It helps children to develop fine motor and eye-hand coordination skills, and it gives children an opportunity to display their creativity. Yet adults often judge children's art by their own standards. Whitener and Kersey (1980) tell about a five-year-old boy who, after seeing a baby hippo at the zoo, became fascinated with the animal. At home, the child began to draw purple hippos with

TABLE 9.2: Emergence of Scribbling, Printing, and Drawing

The child's ability to write and draw develops in the sequence shown below. The sequence is relatively fixed, but the age at which each ability is first shown varies. Children should be encouraged to draw, but it is wise to appreciate just where they are developmentally.

YEAR	SELECTED BEHAVIORS
1	
	Scribbling emerges, repetitive in radial or circular patterns.
2	Multiple and single line crossings.
	Variety of scribbling patterns, various positions on a page.
3	Simple cross may be drawn, using two lines.
	Encloses space; a variety of patterns emerge.
	Figures place in simple combinations using two figures.
	Aggregrates, more than two figures combined.
4	"Suns" drawn with extra lines, sometimes forming faces.
	Human figures emerge, crudely drawn.
	Crude buildings and houses appear.
	Human figures contain more detail; trunks usually absent; "stick" arms, legs, and fingers.
	Boats and cars crudely drawn.
	Circles and squares may be drawn.
5	Animals drawn, trees appear in drawings.
	Refined buildings and houses.
	Better drawings of means of transportation—cars, airplanes, boats, etc.
6	
	Triangles drawn reasonably well.
7	
	Diamonds drawn.
8	
9	
	Three-dimensional geometrical figures drawn.
10	
11	
	Linear perspective seen in drawings.
12	

Source: Cratty, 1979.

pink noses and ears. A knowledgeable first-grade neighbor told the boy that hippos weren't purple, and the boy received similar feedback from other children and well-meaning adults. The boy stopped drawing hippos and later began to draw the standard scene consisting of a house in the middle of the paper near the bottom with a tree on one side, a few flowers on the other side, and a blue sky.

In their travels from school to school, Whitener and Kersey saw many such drawings and wondered why children draw so many of these standard scenes. Their answer: because of the approval the children receive from adults for such drawings. Children learn to conform to their parents' view of the world and keep their creativity within the bounds of adult

The development of fine motor control is shown by how children gain control over crayons during this stage.

acceptance. Certainly children must learn the difference between reality and fantasy, but this need not mean having to draw absolute realism. Rain can be green or pink or purple without injuring a child's sense of reality.

Parents can help their children in this area by providing materials that allow them the freedom to express their creativity. Children require the room, the appropriate clothing (especially for painting), and a variety of materials so they can experiment with color and texture. Adults are wise to avoid interpreting children's art, although this can be difficult. How would you respond if a preschooler asks you what you think a drawing is depicting? Perhaps the best response is to deflect the question so that the child tells you. Most of the time, children are so excited about what they have drawn that this strategy works. One interesting technique is to write a title at the top of the drawing when the child explains it to you. This shows the child that words can be used to describe a work of art.

The nature of a child's drawings will depend on the child's physical and cognitive development as well as on any experiences with art materials. Children enjoy these experiences, but if they get negative feedback or are restricted in their expression, they may begin to draw the ever-present house with the tree and the flowers flanking it, and the value of their activities will be diminished.

Growing Independence and the Need for Supervision

One of the pleasant characteristics of the preschool stage is children's ability to do things on their own. They can dress themselves with some degree of care, eat by themselves, and play by themselves for significant periods of time. Their advances in both gross and fine motor control open new opportunities for private play. Preschoolers no longer need to be

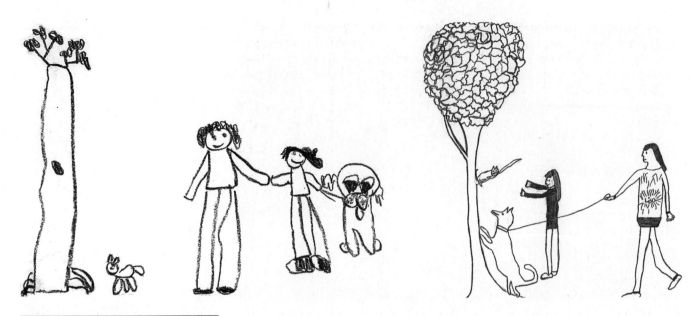

Children's drawings indicate their state of development. These two drawings by Laurie Kaplan, one from age 5 and one from age 10, show her progress.

4. TRUE OR FALSE?

The leading cause of death among preschoolers is accidents.

watched every second, and active, independent preschoolers are engaging beings. They can think of things they want to do and carry them out. Yet their motor skills and desire for independence are greater than their mental ability to understand what is good for them. This can lead to problems in the areas of safety and nutrition.

SAFETY Accidents are the leading cause of death during the preschool years, accounting for more than one-third of all deaths among children (Talbot and Guthrie, 1976). Although the danger of disease has decreased steadily over the past fifty years, the same cannot be said of accidents. Disease, however, still remains a serious problem in developing nations (see Cross-Cultural Current on page 348).

The most common causes of accidental death among children are motor vehicle accidents, fires, drowning, and poisoning. Sometimes, preschoolers run into the street and are struck by cars. Many accidental deaths also result from crashes in which children are passengers in a motor vehicle. The use of secure restraints can prevent many of these tragedies. Some adults believe that holding a baby or a preschooler is sufficient to protect a child from injury during a short stop or an accident, but it is not. One of the themes of parenting in the preschool period is the formation of good safety habits. Buckling up for safety is more than a slogan; it must be an inflexible rule. Since preschoolers observe others in the car, it is essential that the driver and other passengers always fasten their seat belts.

The second leading cause of death among preschool children (third among schoolage children) is fires and burns, which occur most often in the home. Drowning is the next largest cause of accidental deaths and is second among schoolage children. Children can drown in very shallow water. Preschoolers may wander into unfenced swimming pools. Again, supervision is the key.

Poisoning is another prominent cause of accidental death. Children often ingest medicines and household chemicals. One solution is child-proof medicine bottles, but parents do not always properly reseal the containers. Household cleaners should be placed completely out of the reach of preschoolers. In a number of homes, these cleaners are kept in cabinets below the sink, sometimes with special latches. Unfortunately, preschoolers show great ingenuity in opening these latches, and the result can be ingestion of a poisonous substance. A poison control center's telephone number should be available at all times in case of such an accident. Even better, though, is prevention.

Not all accidents can be prevented, because they occur so suddenly. As children grow and their parents relinquish control over their every action, adults are limited in what they can do. However, many accidents are preventable. Using proper restraints in automobiles, placing plastic stoppers in electrical sockets, and locking dangerous chemicals in overhead cabinets can do much to reduce injuries and fatalities among preschoolers.

NUTRITION Infants eat—or don't eat—what you give them. However, preschoolers know what foods are in the house and can tell you what they want. They may want a particular cereal and cry until they get it, refusing anything else. They are old enough to take certain foods, especially snacks, by themselves. Three- and four-year-old children can rank order their food preferences, and these preferences are related to eating habits (Birch, 1979). For example, preschoolers prefer soup that contains more salt, and they prefer salted pretzels to unsalted pretzels (Cowart & Beauchamp, 1986).

The diet of preschoolers tends to be filled with high calorie, low nutrition foods.

Preschoolers prefer more salt in their food than adults do (Beauchamp & Cowart, 1990). Although neonates are neutral in their response to salt, some preference is shown by about four months of age. However, this preference is modifiable, and infants who are fed lower salt diets show less of a preference for salt than infants who are fed a higher salt diet (Harris, Thomas & Booth, 1990). The preference for salt shown by young children is largely based upon their experience with salt. When four-year-olds and five-year-olds were given tastes of either tofu with salt added, tofu with sugar added or plain tofu for nine weeks the differential exposure affected their preference for the food. They began to prefer the food to which they had been exposed, and they showed a decrease in the acceptance of the other two foods (Sullivan & Birch, 1990). In other words, those children who tasted the salty version showed a decrease in their liking of the sweet or neutral tofu. With exposure to a particular taste, children not only prefer that taste but also find the same food with different levels of either salt or sugar less acceptable. This preference for salty, sugared or neutral tofu was not generalized. That is, just because they preferred salty tofu did not mean they preferred everything salty. Food preferences seem more specific. In many homes, though, salting or sugaring foods is a general practice so the child may show a preference for salt and sugar with many foods.

World Health Watch

A five-year-old child around the corner dies of disease, and we are shocked. It is an unusual case. Children's death from disease is very rare in Western countries. Certainly, we have all heard cases of childhood cancer, crib death, and some genetic diseases, but gone are the days when children died by the thousands from measles, tetanus, or whooping cough. This is not the case, however, in most parts of the world. One death in every three in the world is a child under the age of five (Grant, 1988). Each week, more than 250,000 children die from infection and malnutrition in developing countries.

The leading cause of death in young children is diarrhea (see Table 9-A). Most of these children can be saved if they receive a therapy known as oral rehydration therapy, which is a system of actions that begin with parents giving children a special solution that they can make from sugar, salt, and water in the correct proportions. Other steps are taken to prevent dehydration. If the diarrhea persists, the child is given a specially formulated mixture called ORS, or oral rehydration salts. This costs only a few cents and is the standard treatment in most Western hospitals.

Other diseases, such as measles, tetanus, and whooping cough, kill millions each year. Polio is rare in the United States, but 200,000 children are permanently disabled by polio each year throughout the world. These diseases can be eliminated through vaccinations costing about five dollars per child.

Acute respiratory infections also kill many children and can sometimes be prevented or treated using antibiotics that can be administered by community health workers. Still, many parents do not know how to distinguish between a bad cough and a more serious lung infection.

Undernutrition contributes to perhaps as much as one-third of the childhood deaths. Although there is still a lack of food in many areas, in some areas, the problem is the lack of information about how to feed and when to seek professional help. Such information must cover breastfeeding, inoculations, ways to prevent illness, special feeding during and after illness, and when to consult a doctor. Safe water is also a necessity, and information about sanitary waste disposal is important.

The picture, though, should not be one of gloom and doom. Progress has been made. Smallpox has been eradicated, and two-thirds of the children in the Third World are receiving a first dose of DPT vaccine, and half of them complete the full course of vaccinations. Half are being immunized against polio, and 39 percent against measles. Many countries have shown progress.

There is a need for two changes. First, there must be a commitment towards extending inoculations and good medical care to all. This is not expensive, and a great deal of progress has been seen here. Recently, there has been a call by the World Health Organization for increased funding for what is called the "worldwide war on disease" (*New York Times*, May 2, 1990). In addition, during the World Summit for Children which was conducted at the United Nations in New York City in September 1990, the delegates issued a Declaration on Children and a plan to improve the lives of children around the world. The goals include reducing infant and child mortality by one third, reducing severe and moderate malnutrition by half, universal access to safe water, the global eradication of such diseases as polio as well as maintaining a high level of immunization coverage, a reduction of the deaths due to diarrhea in children under five by fifty percent and a reduction of one third in deaths due to respiratory infections. All of this is to be accomplished before the year 2000 (*New York Times*, October 1, 1990). The emergence of low-cost ways of dealing with these major health problems has opened up opportunities for improving the health of the world's children that did not exist twenty years ago.

However, the major challenge may not be getting the money for inoculations and medical care. It may lie in informing parents and changing parental behavior. If parents do not take their children for inoculations, if parents do not know how to deal with diarrhea, if they do not make use of what medical and nutritional programs are available, then any program will fail. The challenge of improving the health of people around the world is a social movement—not just a medical one (Grant, 1988). It will take a variety of professionals in government, education, advertising, voluntary agencies, and business to succeed. Now that the possibility of eliminating these problems is within our grasp, our challenge is to inform people of the possibilities and to motivate people to change their practices and attitudes.

In the United States, there are still some children who have not received their vaccinations. Outbreaks of measles, rubella, and other preventable diseases still occur, but progress is being made on this front. However, the second challenge—that of changing people's attitudes and behaviors—is possibly as great here as it is in other countries. Changes in the way we feed our children, such as a reduction in junk food, helping young pregnant women to abstain from drugs and lead healthy lives, and a number of other health-related changes in attitude and behavior are required. However, there is a difference between the challenges in Western countries and those in underdeveloped countries. In Western countries, access to the information is easier, and spending on health is greater. Any information campaign in a Third World country must be based upon a knowledge of the cultural attitudes and practices in that country.

With a combination of culturally based information programs and the emergence of relatively inexpensive medical treatments to prevent or treat common diseases, the health of children around the world can be improved greatly.

Grant, J. P. The State of the World's Children (New York: Published for UNICEF by Oxford University Press, 1988).

TABLE 9-A: Annual Under-Five Deaths, Developing Countries, 1987*
Of the 14 million child deaths each year approximately 10 million are from only four major causes and all are now susceptible to effective low-cost actions by well-informed and well-supported parents.

DEATHS IN MILLIONS (CUMULATIVE)

14–13–12–11	**Diarrhoeal diseases—5 million** **(also a major cause of malnutrition)**	Of which approximately 3–5 million were caused by dehydration which could have been prevented or treated by low-cost action using ORT.
10		
9	**Malaria 1 million**	Can be drastically reduced by low-cost drugs if parents know signs and can get help.
8	**Measles 1–9 million** **(also a major cause of malnutrition)**	Can be prevented by one vaccination, but it is essential to take the child at the right time—as soon as possible after the age of nine months.
6–5–4	**Acute respiratory infections—2–9 million**	0–6 million whooping cough deaths can be prevented by a full course of DPT vaccine—most of the rest can be prevented by low-cost antibiotics if parents know danger signs and can get help.

DEATHS IN MILLIONS (CUMULATIVE)

3	**Tetanus 0–8 million**	Neonatal tetanus kills 0–8 million. Can be prevented by immunization of mother-to-be.
2–1–0	**Other 2–4 million**	Many of which can be avoided by prenatal care, breast-feeding and nutrition education.

*For the purposes of this chart, one cause of death has been allocated for each child death when, in fact, children die of multiple causes and malnutrition is a contributory cause in approximately one third of all child deaths.

Source: WHO and UNICEF estimates.

In addition, by this age children have received a great deal of information about what foods are appropriate and when. They know that hamburgers are not breakfast foods. They also know when it is considered proper to place extra salt or sugar on foods. Preschoolers' taste preferences for sweet and salty, then, are based upon their experience with these foods and their eating habits are influenced by what they see around them and regard as appropriate.

It is not surprising that the diet of many preschoolers is filled with high-calorie, low-nutrition foods—especially snacks. A desire for sugar is probably innate, and no one would argue that asparagus and cauliflower could beat a bar of chocolate and two cookies in a taste contest. Preschoolers receive much of their nutritional information from watching television. Spend a Saturday morning watching children's television, and you'll find that the commercials are often more colorful and impressive than the programs themselves. The cartoon characters selling sugar-coated cereals are appealing to the preschoolers who watch these commercials, and then demand these foods. Most commercials glorify processed and sweet foods, encouraging poor eating habits. Beyer and Morris (1974) found that 22 percent of the calories ingested by preschoolers came from snacks. Many parents use sweets as rewards, which is another mistake. Learning to eat right is an important skill learned in childhood. An apple or a carrot rather than cookies or candy is a good snack.

Children's appetites are variable. At about twelve months, their appetites usually decrease, probably in accordance with the decrease in the rate of growth (Hamilton & Whitney, 1982). It is not unusual for preschoolers to have periods in which they eat very little. Breakfast is often their best and most important meal, for they are usually hungry in the morning and more likely to be cooperative after a good night's sleep. Unfortunately, many families place little emphasis on breakfast. A good plan to improve children's diets would be to begin with providing youngsters with a nutritious breakfast.

◆ COGNITIVE DEVELOPMENT: THE PREOPERATIONAL STAGE

The advances in motor control and coordination in early childhood enable preschoolers to master their physical environment and learn about their world. Preschoolers actively encounter the physical world and, as we shall see, try to comprehend the phenomena they see around them. In Piagetian theory, children actively learn through their physical and social interactions. It is natural that their expanding physical abilities would allow them to experiment with all sorts of activities and bring them into contact with many novel social situations. Their physical development therefore has an impact on their cognitive development.

preoperational stage
Piaget's second stage of cognitive development, marked by the appearance of language and symbolic function and the child's inability to understand logical concepts such as conservation.

The distinct manner in which preschoolers think was described by Piaget, who argued that the child from age two to age seven progresses through the **preoperational stage.** It is a stage marked by many advances but at the same time by many limitations (see Table 9.3).

TABLE 9.3 The Preoperational Stage

In this stage, children can use symbols and can judge on the basis of appearance. However, they cannot perform mental operations such as reversibility. This stage is a long one, lasting from about two to seven years of age. Children in the later part of the stage are much more advanced than those in the earlier part. Remember, it is incorrect to simply use age to judge cognitive abilities, because children enter and leave a stage at their own individual rates.

CHARACTERISTIC	EXPLANATION	EXAMPLE
Symbolic function	The ability to use one thing to represent another.	A child can use a spoon to represent a hammer. The ability to use words also requires the use of symbols.
Deferred imitation	The ability to observe an act and imitate it at a later time.	A preschooler can see the teacher exercising and can imitate similar actions at a later time without the teacher's presence.
Inability to seriate	The process of placing objects in size order.	Preschoolers cannot place ten blocks of wood in size order. *Can do 5*
Inability to classify	The process of placing objects in different groupings.	Younger preschoolers cannot group plastic objects to varying shapes and colors by shape or color. *4 yr olds can!*
Appearance and reality	The tendency to judge on the basis of appearance.	A child shown a red car will correctly identify the color. If a filter that makes the car look black covers the car, the child will say the car is black. When the filter is removed, the child will again identify the car as red.
Inability to conserve	The inability to understand that quantities remain the same despite changes in their appearance.	If shown two equal-sized lumps of clay, the preschooler will know they are equal. If one is flattened out, the child will believe that the lumps are no longer the same size.
Centering	The tendency to attend to only one dimension at a time.	When comparing the contents of a small thin beaker and a short fat beaker, the preschooler will do so by comparing only one dimension of each, probably height, and will ignore the differences in width.
Irreversible thinking	The inability to begin at the end of an operation and work back to the start.	Preschoolers do not understand that if you add 4 to 2 to make 6, then you can take 2 away from 6 to make 4 again.
Egocentrism	The inability to understand someone else's point of view.	If shown a display and asked how someone standing opposite them is seeing it, preschoolers will not be able to visualize the other person's perspective. Preschoolers believe that the world revolves around them.
Animism	The belief that inanimate objects have a consciousness or are alive.	A preschooler believes that the balloon soared to the ceiling because it did not want to be held.
Artificialism	The belief that natural phenomena are caused by human beings.	A preschooler will see a lake and say it was made by a group of people digging and then filling it up with water from hoses.

Symbolic Function

The child beginning the preoperational stage is able to use one thing to represent or symbolize another (Mandler, 1983). One major illustration of this ability is the acquisition of language. Words represent particular concepts and objects. The ability to use symbolism also manifests itself in nonlinguistic areas. Children may use a spoon to represent a hammer or a toy person to represent the mail carrier. Adults who are attentive to children at play can gain valuable insights into a child's view of the world.

Another manifestation of the ability to use symbolism, first seen at the end of the sensorimotor stage, is deferred imitation. The child can see something occur, store the information, and perform the action at a later date. To do this, the child must preserve a symbolic representation of the behavior during the intervening time. For example, hours after a child sees a brother or sister doing exercises, the child may be found doing a version of the same exercises.

How Preschoolers Reason

To understand a preschooler, one must realize that a preschooler's reasoning is different from that of an adult. Adults reason either inductively or deductively. **Inductive reasoning** proceeds from the specific to the general. For instance, after examining a number of cases of children who do not do their homework, we might conclude that children who do not do their homework do not receive good grades. Adults also use **deductive reasoning,** beginning with a general rule and proceeding to specifics. They may form a rule concerning homework and grades and then apply the rule to specific cases.

TRANSDUCTIVE REASONING AND CAUSALITY Preschool children use **transductive reasoning**—that is, they reason from particular to particular. The simplest example of such reasoning is that if A causes B then, according to the preschooler, B causes A. Piaget found, for example, that his daughter believed that since his shave required hot water, the appearance of hot water meant that daddy would shave (Phillips, 1975). The child's understanding of causality is based on how close one event is to another. As Mary Ann Spencer Pulaski notes, "The road makes the bicycle go; by creating a shadow one can cause the night to come. The thunder makes it rain, and honking the horn makes the car go" (1980, p. 49).

SERIATION AND CLASSIFICATION Parents are often surprised when their preschoolers show a different logic or have difficulty with a particular problem that seems so simple to adults. For instance, ask preschoolers to put a series of sticks in order from largest to smallest, an operation called **seriation** (see Figure 9.1). They simply can't seem to do it. Nor can they **classify** items, at least at the beginning of the preoperational stage (see Figure 9.2). When young children are given a number of plastic shapes, including squares, triangles, and circles of different colors, and are asked to put things that are alike into a pile, most children younger than five do not organize their choices on any particular logical basis. They may

inductive reasoning
Reasoning that proceeds from specific cases to the formation of a general rule.

deductive reasoning
Reasoning that begins with a general rule and is then applied to specific cases.

transductive reasoning
Preoperational reasoning in which young children reason from particular to particular.

seriation
The process of placing objects in size order.

classification
The process of placing objects into different classes.

FIGURE 9.1: Seriation
Young children have difficulty placing things in size order.

FIGURE 9.2: Classification
Young children have difficulty with tasks that require the ability to classify items into various groupings.

put a red triangle and a blue triangle together, but then throw in a red square. No central organizing principle is evident. Some young children do not understand the task at all (Ault, 1977). Late in the preoperational stage, some progress in classification is made. Children can sort items on the basis of one overriding principle—most often form—but they fail to see that multiple classifications are possible.

Preschool children also have difficulty understanding subordinate and superordinate classes (see Figure 9.3). For example, a child may be shown seven green beads and three white beads, all made of wood, and asked whether there are more green beads or more wooden beads. The child will usually say more green beads. Show children a picture of a bouquet containing five roses and three tulips and ask them whether there are more roses or more flowers. They will often say more roses. Preschoolers cannot make comparisons across levels and usually get the problem wrong.

TRANSITIVE INFERENCES Preschoolers also cannot seem to understand **transitive inferences,** an example of which is if Ed is taller than

transitive inferences
Statements of comparison, such as, "If X is taller than Y and Y is taller than Z, then X is taller than Z."

FIGURE 9.3: Subordinate and Superordinate Classification
Are there more green beads or wooden beads? Young children answer more
green beads because they have difficulty making comparisons across levels.

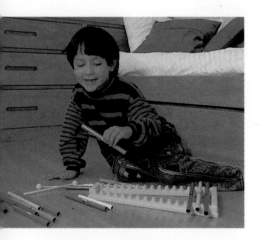

A four year old practices seriation on a xylophone toy. Preschoolers have difficulty in ordering objects from smallest to largest.

conservation
The concept that quantities remain the same despite changes in their appearance.

Sue and Sue is taller than Tim, then Ed is taller than Tim (see Figure 9.4). The preoperational child views comparisons as absolute (Piaget and Inhelder, 1974) and does not understand that an object can be larger than one thing and at the same time smaller than another.

CONSERVATION PROBLEMS Nowhere are the preschooler's differences in perception so obvious than in the child's inability to solve conservation problems (see Figure 9.5). **Conservation** involves the ability to comprehend that quantities remain the same regardless of changes in their appearance. You can test this out yourself in a number of ways. For example, show a preschooler displays of seven pennies in which the coins are either grouped close together or spread apart. The four-year-old is certain that the spread-out display has more pennies than the group of pennies that are close together. Or take two equal lumps of clay and roll each one into a ball. Then, while the child watches, roll one ball into a worm shape and ask the child which form has more clay. The preschooler fails to understand that the forms are still equal in size and believes that one has more clay. Or show a preschooler two identical half-filled beakers of

FIGURE 9.4: Transitive Inferences

If Ed is taller than Sue and Sue is taller than Tim, then Ed is taller than Tim. Young children have difficulty understanding such inferences.

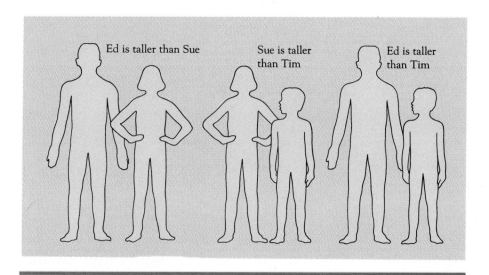

water. The child will tell you the amounts of water are equal. Transfer the water from one beaker to a squat cup and ask the child which container has more water. The answer usually is that the taller beaker contains more liquid.

The preceding examples illustrate the preschooler's failure to understand and successfully perform conservation tasks. The fact that preschoolers cannot correctly judge that pouring a liquid from a tall beaker to a squat beaker does not change the amount of the liquid has fascinated psychologists for years. But why can't preschoolers solve these simple tasks? The answer lies in certain characteristics of a preschooler's thinking.

Characteristics of a Preschooler's Thinking

CENTERING A preschool child can concentrate on only one dimension at a time (Piaget & Inhelder, 1969). This is known as **centering**. For instance, try to explain to a preschooler that a cup and a glass hold the same amount of liquid. Because the containers are shaped differently, the preschooler believes that one container is larger than the other. Preschoolers rely on visual comparison and believe that a tall glass contains more liquid than a fat cup. Preschoolers can attend to only one measure at the same time, and appearances confuse them. In the same way, they have no difficulty knowing that two balls of clay are the same. But when one is rolled into the shape of a worm, they compare the clay shapes on the dimension of length and cannot take both the length and the width into account.

If you present a preschooler with two identical half-filled beakers of water, the child will tell you they are equal. However if you transfer one to a tall, thin beaker, the child will then believe that the tall beaker has more liquid.

centering
The tendency to attend to only one dimension at a time.

FIGURE 9.5: Conservation

When presented with the problems seen below, preschoolers give answers (indicated in the right column) that differ from those of older children. Preschoolers have difficulty with conservation problems.

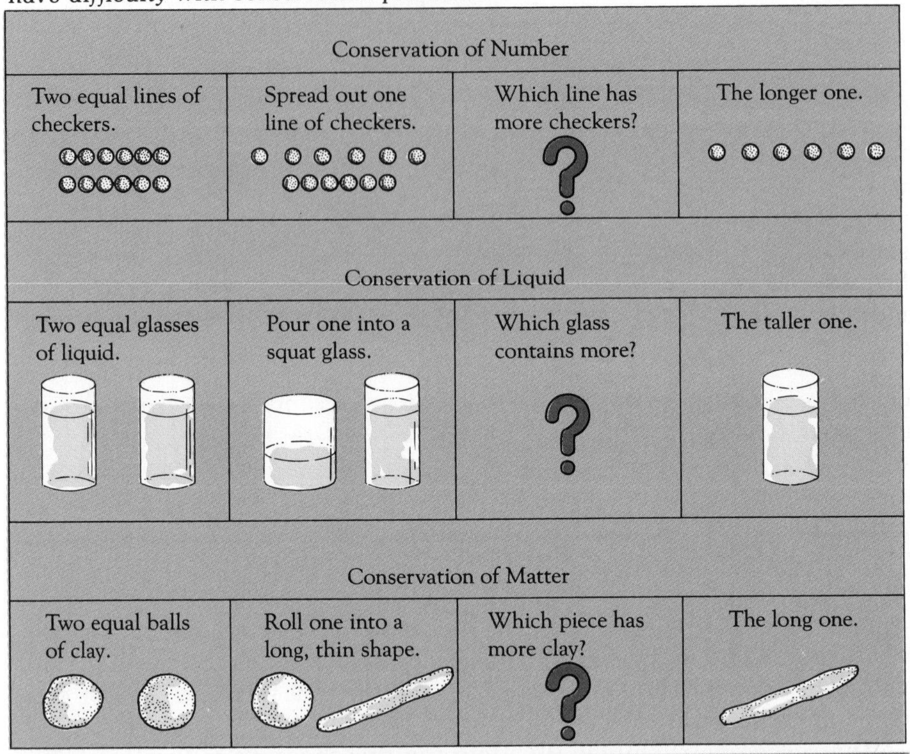

Conservation of Number			
Two equal lines of checkers.	Spread out one line of checkers.	Which line has more checkers?	The longer one.

Conservation of Liquid			
Two equal glasses of liquid.	Pour one into a squat glass.	Which glass contains more?	The taller one.

Conservation of Matter			
Two equal balls of clay.	Roll one into a long, thin shape.	Which piece has more clay?	The long one.

APPEARANCE VERSUS REALITY Generally, preschoolers confuse how things look with what they really are. In other words, preschoolers are confused by the appearance of objects in their environment. For example, show a three-year-old a red toy car and cover the car with a green filter that makes it look black. Now hand the car (without the filter) to the child and then put the car behind the filter again. When you ask the child what color the toy is, the child will say black (Flavell, 1986). Preschoolers are perception bound, basing their judgments simply on how things look to them at the present time, and they have difficulty going behind the information given. The ability to separate reality from appearance increases markedly between three and five years of age (see Gopnik & Astington, 1988).

reversibility
Beginning at the end of an operation and working one's way back to the start.

IRREVERSIBILITY Preschoolers also cannot **reverse** operations. If a clay ball is rolled into a worm shape in front of them, they cannot mentally rearrange the clay back to its original form. Show a child three balls of the same size, each of which is a different color. Place the balls in a cylinder in a certain order (e.g., blue, green, yellow). The preschooler has no difficulty understanding that the balls will come out the bottom of the cylinder in the same order. If, however, you rotate the cylinder 180 degrees, the child will continue to predict the original order and is surprised that the balls leave the cylinder in the opposite order (Piaget, 1967). This inability to reverse an operation affects a preschooler's answers to what seem like simple questions. When a preschooler was asked whether he had a sister, he answered "yes" and gave her name. When asked whether his sister had a brother, he replied "no."

TRANSFORMATIONS When preschoolers notice that change has occurred, they can point to the beginning and the end but do not realize the sequence involved in the change. For example, when young subjects were asked to draw the successive movements of a bar falling from a vertical position, the children did not draw, nor did they later understand, that it went through a series of intermediate positions between the first and last position (Phillips, 1975). In the same way, children faced with a conservation task judge equality on the basis of the beginning and end states. They cannot take intervening states into consideration.

EGOCENTRISM Underlying all the child's reasoning processes is a basic **egocentrism.** The use of this term is unfortunate, because it connotes selfishness. Piaget (1954) argued that children see everything from their own viewpoint and are incapable of taking someone else's view into account. Young children believe that everything has a purpose that is understandable in their own terms and relevant to their own needs. For instance, a boy once asked Piaget why there were two mountains above Geneva. The answer the boy wanted was that one was for adults to climb while the other little one was for children (Pulaski, 1980).

Preschoolers see the entire world as revolving around them. The sun and moon exist to give them light; mothers and fathers exist to give them warmth and to take care of them.

This egocentrism is seen in children's interpretations of their physical world and their social world. Children who know their left hand from their right may not be able to correctly identify the left and right hands of a person standing opposite them. Nursery school teachers are aware of this, and when facing preschoolers they raise the left hand when requesting that the children raise their right (Davis, 1983). Piaget showed a model of three mountains to young children and asked them to consider how the display might look to a doll sitting in different positions around the model (see Figure 9.6). The children could not do this accurately. Preschoolers reason that everyone sees the world as they do.

Egocentrism is found in many social behaviors as well. I can remember coming home on a particularly hard day. It was 98 degrees and the humidity was horrendous. The car had broken down, and a number of other smaller catastrophes had occurred. Seeing me tired and upset, my four-year-old came over and asked me if I wanted her to read a story to me. Since stories make her feel better, she supposed they would do the same for me.

ANIMISM AND ARTIFICIALISM One of the charming aspects of early childhood is the child's belief that everything is capable of being conscious and alive, which is called **animism** (see Figure 9.7). A paper turtle

egocentrism
A thought process in which young children believe everyone is experiencing the environment in the same way they are. Children who are egocentric have difficulty understanding someone else's point of view.

animism
The preschooler's belief that everything, animate or inanimate, is conscious or alive.

FIGURE 9.6: Egocentrism

In Piaget's three-mountains experiment, preschool children had difficuty in visualizing the doll's perspective of the three-mountain display.

5. *TRUE OR FALSE?*

Most young preschoolers believe that even inanimate objects are capable of being alive and conscious.

artificialism
The belief, common among preschoolers, that natural phenomena are caused by human beings.

can be alive; a hammer has a life of its own. This results in unusual behavior. If you step on the turtle, you've just killed something, not just smashed a small toy. A preschooler may bump into a desk, smack it, and say "Bad desk." A book that falls from a shelf didn't want to be with the other books. A balloon that has soared to the ceiling didn't want to be held. Animism is most characteristic of the early part of this stage, and it becomes less evident as children reach the age of four or five (Bullock, 1985).

The young child's reasoning also reflects **artificialism,** the belief that natural phenomena are caused by human beings (Pulaski, 1980). This is a natural outgrowth of what children see around them. Since children view everything as intentional and organized for human use, they explain

FIGURE 9.7: Animism

Young children often ascribe characteristics of living things to inanimate objects.

the world in terms of human causation (Piaget, 1927). Thus, the lake near Geneva was created not by natural forces but by a group of men digging (Pulaski, 1980).

Recent Challenges to Piaget's Views

Preschool children have made great strides since infancy and toddlerhood. They now use language more efficiently and can understand and use symbols with greater ease. However, it is their limitations that are often emphasized. The child is described as lacking communication skills, number and order concepts, and memory skills; having problems in causal relationships; and being egocentric, perception bound, and unable to understand states and transformations (Gelman, 1979; Gelman & Baillargeon, 1983). Preschoolers are described more by what they cannot do (Flavell, 1977), and their charm is due to their ignorance. Of course, preschoolers' reasoning appears reasonable to them. It is only when we take an adult perspective that it seems unusual.

Many of Piaget's ideas concerning the limitations of preschool thought have recently been challenged. These challenges are not based just on the age at which these abilities appear. Psychologists are beginning to realize that preschoolers may not be as limited as first thought. Perhaps preschoolers can classify, are not so egocentric, and can perform transitive inferences—if the situation is structured correctly. These new findings will have a great impact on preschool education.

The observations Piaget made of preschoolers using his standard testing procedures are well founded, and no one seriously doubts the tests' reliability (Gelman & Baillargeon, 1983). If you test a preschooler in the same way Piaget did, you will get the same results. However, the assumption that because preschoolers fail these tests they cannot seriate, classify, or decenter is questionable. Perhaps if the children were tested differently, they might succeed. Indeed, this is exactly what researchers have found.

Preschoolers can arrange things in size order, classify items, and understand inferences if the task is designed in a manner that is ideal for a preschooler's interests and abilities. First, the people who work with preschoolers have to strip away anything that might distract the children, leaving only the most essential elements of the task. Second, the task must be familiar (Brown, Bransford & Ferrara, 1983). Preschoolers are easily sidetracked and do poorly in situations that are strange to them. Their abilities are also easily taxed, so that memory and lack of comprehension can affect performance (Trabasso, 1975).

At times, simple modifications in Piaget's method change the results of the experiment. For example, Inhelder and Piaget (1964) argued that children can seriate if they can place the items in correct order, put additional items into the series, and correct any errors that have been made. So far, this is reasonable. But Piaget used a total of ten sticks in his observations and concluded that true seriation did not occur at this stage. Barbara Koslowski (1980) used a similar approach, but instead of using ten sticks she used four. Using the same criteria as Piaget used, she found that three-quarters of the three-year-olds and four-year-olds tested could put the sticks in size order, about four-fifths could insert two new sticks into the order, and all the children could correct the incorrect insertions. The ability to seriate is present in these children, but ten sticks is simply too many for the preschooler to deal with at one time.

Piaget's concept of egocentrism has also been the focus of much criticism (Ford, 1979). Under specific circumstances, preschoolers are not egocentric; that is, they can understand the viewpoint of others. John Flavell and his colleagues (1981) found that preschoolers understood that an object with different sides, such as a house, looks different from various perspectives but that an object with identical sides, such as a ball, looks the same. In another experiment, children from ages one to three were given a hollow cube with a picture pasted to the bottom of the inside. The children were asked to show the picture to an observer sitting across from them. Almost all the children who were two years or older turned the cube away from them and towards the observer. Thus, they demonstrated some understanding of the other person's perspective (Lempers, Flavell & Flavell, 1977).

Other Piagetian skills have been taught to children at younger ages than thought possible. Rochel Gelman (1969) trained children to conserve by teaching them to respond to the relevant cues and to ignore the apparent visual ones. Ann McCabe and Lina Siegel (1987) succeeded in training kindergarten age children to solve class inclusion reasoning problems. These problems involve presenting a child with a display of two subordinate classes, such as three forks and four spoons, and asking if there are more forks or things to eat with? The child is asked to count the members of each subclass and to count the members of the superordinate class. The child is then asked whether the members of each subclass belong to the superordinate class. After receiving such training, many children were able to solve other class inclusion problems.

Although there are some doubts about the stability of these training studies and the degree to which children transfer their learning to other situations, the studies do demonstrate that young children are more flexible in the development of their reasoning processes than first thought.

Harmonizing the Views

Putting this new information into perspective is difficult. It is only fair to ask for a conclusion concerning the preschooler's mental abilities— can preschoolers draw inferences, decenter, or understand causality in a more or less mature manner? At first glance, the research seems contradictory, but it really is not. Under certain circumstances, preschoolers can do things that Piaget did not think possible.

The key phrase here is "under certain circumstances." Preschool skills are fragile and delicate, and children's abilities in these areas are just developing. Preschoolers can classify and seriate and are not as egocentric if they have experience in a particular skill, if the task is clear and does not tax their memory, and if they can understand the verbal instructions. On the other hand, if the situation is complicated or requires more memory and verbal skills than they have, preschoolers fail at these tasks.

This newfound information is valuable. People working with preschoolers must design an environment in which tasks are simplified and memory requirements are minimized. They must be certain that preschoolers understand what is required of them if they are to bring out these newly developing skills. If this is done, preschoolers can do some very surprising things.

Situational and task factors, than, are of paramount importance. This is also shown in the preschool child's information-processing abilities.

♦ COGNITIVE DEVELOPMENT: INFORMATION-PROCESSING SKILLS

You are a member of a jury who has just heard a case in which a four-year-old was abducted by a stranger, kept for a day, and then released. After some questioning, the child described what happened and identified one of the suspects from a lineup. Although there is some additional evidence presented by the prosecution, the entire case really boils down to whether you believe the testimony of the child. The adult accused of the kidnapping claims innocence. The prosecution argues that the child has the ability to identify the kidnapper and that the child's memory of the incident can be believed. The defense claims that the child is so young and memory so faulty that you cannot believe what the child is saying. In addition, the defense angrily denounces the questioning of the child by the police and social worker, claiming that their questioning led the child to identify the defendant from the lineup.

The study of the preschooler's information-processing skills has a number of important educational and parenting implications. However, as you can see from the case just described, questions about a child's information-processing abilities have legal implications as well. Today, we are more aware of the problems of child abuse than ever before. A child's testimony can be important. In addition, children sometimes witness crimes, and the question of credibility remains. Children are sometimes required to participate in a trial or, at least, to tell their stories of what happened.

Attention

Adults working with preschoolers do not expect young children to maintain their attention for long periods of time, nor do the designers of television programs aimed at young children. Certain aspects of the programs—such as color, movement, surprise, and novelty—are likely to attract and hold attention. Much of the information on the preschooler's attention span comes from studies on how children view television. For instance, puppets and animation usually attract children, probably because of the unusual voices that accompany them (Anderson, Alwitt, Lorch & Levin, 1979). A drum roll, a loud crash or music signals an important event and gains attention (Huston & Wright, 1983). It would be incorrect, however, to view preschoolers merely as beings who are passively manipulated by the environment. Preschoolers attend to messages from television that they understand and that are focused on their interests (Anderson & Field, 1983). Some elements of attention are more important for young children. For instance, children under the age of six focus mostly on color, while children six or older focus on shape and form (Koran & Lehman, 1981). As children mature, their ability to control their attention, to discriminate between what is and is not most important, and to adapt their attention to the demands of a situation improves. Their ability to plan what they are to attend to also shows improvement (Flavell, 1985). These abilities are just developing in the preschooler and develop throughout the elementary school years. This means that even young children can use some limited decision-making power in focusing their attention on television and are not simply manipulated by sights and sounds. This purposeful, planful aspect of attention is commonly accepted in older children and adults.

People enter different situations with ideas about what they should watch for and may voluntarily focus on different aspects of a situation. If you attend a hockey game and are interested in how people play de-

Preschoolers have longer attention spans allowing for more sustained activities.

fense, you may follow a particular player for a few minutes without following the flight of the puck. Psychologists have found that as children mature, their ability to focus their attention voluntarily in a planned, organized, systematic, goal-oriented manner increases (Daehler & Bukatko, 1985). They are also able to maintain their attention for longer periods because they are becoming less easily distracted (Anderson & Lorch, 1983). A fourfold increase in attention span is found between ages one and four (Anderson & Levin, 1976).

The gradual development of voluntary, planned attentional behavior is shown in an often-quoted study by Elaine Vurpillot (Vurpillot, 1968; Vurpillot & Ball, 1979). Children between the ages of four and nine were asked to compare two pictures of houses, each of which contained at least six windows with objects such as flowerpots, hearts, curtains, and socks in the windows. The children's task was to judge whether the houses were identical. As they inspected the houses, their eye movements were tracked. Preschoolers often made their decisions on incomplete information, using only seven of the windows instead of the full twelve or more used by the older children. The best way to accomplish this task is to focus attention on window one of house one and switch attention to window one of house two and so forth. This requires planning. Not one child in the preschool group did this, but almost all of the eight-year-olds and nine-year-olds did.

As we have seen before, however, by changing the task, we can see the fragile beginnings of a particular skill, in this case, attentional strategy. Perhaps if the task can be simplified and the instructions improved, preschoolers might show some attentional strategies. Indeed, research shows that they do. Preschoolers were asked to decide whether two rows of drawings of objects were exactly the same by opening doors that covered the drawings. Four-year-olds but not three-year-olds used the most efficient strategy and could successfully compare the drawings. In addition, in this study, subjects were asked to compare the drawings in the "twin way" for fear that they did not fully understand matching tasks. The researchers conclude that four-year-olds can be strategic if the required judgment is simple (Woody-Ramsey & Miller, 1988). Preschoolers are easily confused when the situation becomes too complex (Miller & Harris, 1988).

Preschoolers, then, are just beginning to control some simple aspects of their attention. There is no doubt that preschool children do not spontaneously restrict their attention to important stimuli unless the stimuli stand out or unless the children receive training (Woody-Ramsey & Miller, 1988). It is necessary to draw children's attention to these more important areas.

These findings on the subject of attention have important implications for people who deal with preschoolers. The fact that a preschooler's attention can be gained and, to some degree, held by using elements of sound, color, novelty, and movement is well known, but the importance of a preschooler's ability to comprehend the material should not be forgotten. Preschoolers will attend more to material they understand. Their lack of sustained attention requires that material be presented in small

6. TRUE OR FALSE?

The average four-year-old's attention span is four times greater than the average one-year-old child's attention span.

segments. The fact that preschoolers may not attend to all the relevant information and will sometimes make decisions based upon partial information, especially if the task is taxing, must be taken into account when working with young children. The task must be simple and the directions given in a way that these young children understand. Specific instructions as to where to place their attention, then, may be of some help (Hochman, 1990). In addition, the fact that these children are easily distracted implies that if attention is required, reducing other competing stimuli is desirable.

Memory Skills

If children are to defer imitation, use symbols effectively, and eventually understand other people's perspectives, they must be able to use their memory effectively. A preschooler's memory skills are far superior to those of a toddler. Between two and four years, the preschooler's already good recognition skills improve (Perlmutter & Myers, 1979). The preschooler's ability to use language allows the child to store memories using words. On the other hand, if you compare a preschooler with a child in the middle years of childhood, the younger child's deficiencies seem overwhelming.

THE CONVENTIONAL VIEW OF PRESCHOOL MEMORY Preschoolers are limited by their inability to spontaneously use memory strategies that many of us take for granted. Suppose you were shown a group of pictures and asked to remember them. You might first group them into categories (foods, buildings, people), then rehearse them. Preschoolers do not use these strategies on their own (Kail & Hagen, 1982). To remember successfully, you had to understand the task, have some idea of the task's difficulty, and then devise an appropriate strategy. You had some idea of what was involved in the memory task. This knowledge of memory processes is called **metamemory** and is discussed more extensively in Chapter 11.

metamemory
People's knowledge of their own memory processes.

If you had been presented with only two items to remember, you probably would have used only a bit of rehearsal. When preschoolers were asked to remember a string of digits, they did not spontaneously use any rehearsal—the simplest strategy—but if they were instructed in the use of rehearsal, their ability to remember the list improved greatly (Flavell & Wellman, 1977). Children can be taught to use rehearsal. However, at a later time, children will not spontaneously use this strategy when confronted with the same task with no instructions on rehearsal (Keeney, Cannizzo & Flavell, 1967). In other words, young children apparently can use this strategy but do not unless they are told to do so.

Children's lack of understanding concerning the demands of the task was demonstrated in another study. Lynne Appel and colleagues (1972) presented pictures to four-, seven-, and eleven-year-old children using one of two different instructions: "Look at the pictures" or "Remember the pictures." If you were told to remember the pictures, you would repeat them to yourself or write them down. If you were told to look at them, you wouldn't do anything special. You understand the problem, however, whereas preschool children do not. They don't seem to know that the problem requires some voluntary, purposeful cognitive activity. Indeed, the four-year-olds did not act any differently when presented with either instruction, but the older children did. Perhaps preschoolers show such poor use of memory strategies because they do not understand what is involved in memory tasks (Flavell & Wellman, 1977).

7. TRUE OR FALSE?

Preschool children do not spontaneously use memory strategies such as rehearsal.

A MORE RECENT LOOK AT MEMORY SKILLS The memory of the preschooler has traditionally been viewed as rather passive, nonstrategic, and nonplanful (Brown et al., 1983), but if we look more deeply, we can see the beginnings of strategy use, and at times children will surprise us with their memories. Again, the characteristics of the task and the test conditions are most important.

Many studies have used artificial situations that require remembering new information for its own sake (Paris and Lindauer, 1982). When the information and situation are more familiar and the goals of remembering are clear, preschoolers show the beginnings of memory strategies, and their ability to recall improves markedly. For instance, Istomina (1975) asked children three to seven years of age to remember a list of five words under two different conditions. Under condition one, children played a game of grocery store and had to recall the items so they could buy them. Under the second condition, children were simply told to remember the items. Children recalled significantly more items under condition one than under condition two. When children were tested on the task of remembering a list, young children did quite well when the words were made up of familiar categories, such as their teachers' names and names of television shows (Lindberg, 1980).

Even the idea that preschoolers are nonstrategic needs rethinking. Preschoolers do use some strategies to remember, such as pointing and looking (Kail & Hagen, 1982). They are competent when asked to use these motor and sensory strategies, but their ability to use verbal strategies, such as rehearsal, is greatly limited.

MEMORY RECONSIDERED This more recent look at the memory skills of the young child matches the newer appreciation of what preschoolers can and cannot do in other cognitive areas. If we watch children in their normal day-to-day life amid familiar situations and tasks whose goals are clear, we find the children can remember more and do begin to use strategies. The abilities of preschoolers, though, are fragile. Young children are easily confounded, and artificial tasks are likely to show their limitations. Taken as a group, the studies in cognition and memory should make us wary about making generalizations about what abilities children do or do not have. Even though preschool children may not show these abilities when tested in a certain way, it does not necessarily mean that they don't have the skills. Rather, it is important to note in what situations children can and cannot successfully perform particular tasks.

The Importance of Prior Knowledge

When we lay down memories, we do not do so in a vacuum. We often have a framework on which to hang our memories. For instance, before hearing about Columbus, we may have seen a film about explorers or been told what an explorer does. This makes learning about Columbus easier. Psychologists have recently focused much attention on the importance of what people know—their knowledge base—to what people are trying to know or remember (Chi & Glaser, 1985). Their findings show that the more people know, the easier it is for them to lay down new memories. This may occur because people who have some prior knowledge have what cognitive psychologists call schemata already formed. The term as used by Piaget was introduced in Chapter 2. Its use by information-processing psychologists is a bit different.

A **schema** is an organized body of knowledge that functions as a framework describing objects and relationships that generally occur. Schemata (the plural of schema) can contain both knowledge about and rules for using knowledge. A schema for a dog may contain ideas about the dog's physical features and activities and different aspects of a dog's behavior as well as ways of treating dogs.

The importance of schemata can best be understood through an example. Consider a preschool teacher talking about hospital procedures and telling children about a nurse taking a patient's blood pressure. It would be easier for children with some prior knowledge of hospitals to understand or visualize this scenario than it would be for children without this knowledge. Such prior knowledge might involve the roles of various people at the hospital, various hospital procedures, and the knowledge of the types of instruments used in hospitals. These schemata underlie our understanding of events and allow us to interpret and clarify what we are experiencing or learning (Chi & Glaser, 1985). The more we know about hospitals and their procedures, the easier it is to understand what is going on in a hospital.

Schemata allow us to encode additional information more meaningfully, since new information can be linked to already encoded information. It also allows us to fill in gaps and to infer. For example, if you tell someone that a cake is baking, the person knows from past knowledge that the cake is baking in an oven. As children mature, their schemata become more complicated and more flexible. A child's background may contain a rich amount of information in one area and a poor amount in another. Because preschoolers generally do not have very rich experiential knowledge, it may come as quite a surprise when these children have difficulty remembering some things while remembering others very well. Some differences in memory between preschoolers and children in middle childhood are due to the more extensive knowledge base of the latter.

A concept similar to schema is script. A **script** is a "structure that describes an appropriate sequence of events in a particular context" (Schank & Abelson, 1977, p. 41). People have numerous scripts, including birthday parties, job interviews, and a schoolday. Adults show a great deal of agreement on these scripts (Bower, Black & Turner, 1979) as do young children on familiar scripts. Nelson (1978) found that four-year-olds de-

schema (information processing)
An organized body of knowledge that functions as a framework describing objects and relationships that generally occur.

script
A structure that describes an appropriate sequence of events in a particular context.

Children develop scripts, that is an understanding of what is supposed to happen in a certain situation and in what order.

scribed daily events at home, in a day-care center, and at a McDonald's restaurant in much the same way as adults would.

Preschoolers are rather rigid in their ideas about what should take place and when (Wimmer, 1980). They will often rebel if people do things that are not in keeping with their idea of the script. Preschoolers may become confused or annoyed if a baby sitter or substitute preschool teacher does things in a manner different from their parents or their regular teacher. Older children also produce more alternative paths in their scripts. For instance, when describing activities such as making a campfire, they offer many more possible paths to accomplishing the task than younger children do. Scripts, then, become more flexible and more complex as children develop.

Scripts form the base for remembering stories and events that are familiar. If you are given information and are familiar with the script, you can fill in missing information. Prior knowledge represented by the script makes the story easier to follow. Young children who are presented with a script that contains an event that is out of order and are asked to recall it either omit the misordered event or put it in the place that is in keeping with their knowledge of how it usually is (Nelson & Gruendek, 1981). Children recognize deviations from the proper script and correct them (Wimmer, 1979). Preschoolers misremember stories if the stories differ from their familiar scripts. For instance, children invent and put appropriate material in stories when they cannot recall what they were told (Mandler & Johnson, 1977).

The knowledge of scripts also affects how children make inferences. Children who are told that Renaldo went to a restaurant and is drinking

8. TRUE OR FALSE?

Preschoolers are more rigid than elementary schoolchildren in their understanding of what should take place and the order in which events should occur.

milk do not need to be told that he probably looked at a menu or had a glass that held his milk. They infer it because they are familiar with the script.

Scripts and schemata show how prior knowledge affects the way new material is processed. One's prior knowledge makes new material meaningful, suggests how one can bridge gaps in what one knows, and helps to organize material (Saloman, 1983).

Recently, there has been much more interest in children's memory for real-world events, since some laboratory studies are somewhat artificial. The findings here relate directly back to the legal case regarding the kidnapping of a four-year-old. Psychologists have found that both context and the child's level of interest are important factors in evaluating a child's memory (Jones, Swift & Johnson, 1988). Children's memories are much better when children participate in some event rather than simply watch or listen. Children also remember more and are generally more accurate in what they remember if they are familiar with an event. The use of scripts helps children increase the general information they recall. However, although there is a general increase in recalled knowledge, children often confuse specific episodes in the past. They may confuse whether something happened during nursery school last Thursday or the Thursday before. On the other hand, very unusual events are well remembered. There was no decrease in the accuracy of children's memory for an unusual kindergarten field trip over a period of six years (Hudson, 1990). In fact, children are more likely to make errors in more familiar events—although they will remember quite a bit about the events—because they confuse one occurrence with another. This means that increased experience with an event leads to greater general knowledge about the event, but it also results in more distortions in recall when compared to memory for novel events (Hudson, 1988).

Young children, though, tend not to tell the entire story. Because they often leave out portions, questioning is necessary if one is to uncover the whole story. Children often report more limited information, but they can be just as accurate as adults (Goodman, 1984). Unfortunately, there is also evidence that preschool children are more suggestible in recall (Ceci, Ross, & Toglia, 1987). These children are more easily led and sensitive to questions.

How does this relate to the jury situation? Obviously, there is no definite answer to the question of whether a four-year-old's memory is good enough to convict an assailant. Adults and older children make mistakes on identifications as well, and there are great individual differences in children at this age. We know that the memories of young children for novel incidents is good and that preschoolers often do not tell the complete story, and so some careful questioning is necessary. On the other hand, preschoolers are more suggestible, and so questioners must be very careful not to lead a child to say something that may not be accurate. To be certain that the questioning does not prejudice the child, it is probably a good idea to record all conversations with the preschooler in a criminal case so that it may be determined that the child has not been led to a conclusion that is counter to the best interests of justice.

◆ THE PRESCHOOLER'S ENVIRONMENT

Jason lives in a home filled with books. His mother reads to him daily, and he watches "Sesame Street" at least once a day. He attended nursery school, where he played with other children, took short trips around the neighborhood, and learned about colors and shapes. Jason's parents encourage him to describe what he saw around him.

Craig's parents put Craig in front of a television set right after breakfast to watch cartoons for hours. They never read to him. Craig mostly played by himself, and his parents spoke to him only to demand something. They never had much time for Craig, and Craig was often cared for by his older brother, who would rather have been doing anything else.

It probably won't surprise you to know that Jason is doing well in elementary school and that Craig is having difficulty. Will Craig catch up? For most children like Craig, the answer is, unfortunately, no. In fact, just the opposite occurs: Such children often fall even more behind. This does not indicate, however, that the game is all over by age five. As has been noted previously, early experience is important, but later experience can compensate for poor earlier experiences. However, if the child's environment is not improved, the child will probably not catch up. In Craig's case, only if Craig's teachers make a concerted and time-consuming effort will Craig close the gap between himself and Jason. It would have been easier to prevent the problem—to structure the environment so that Craig was as ready as Jason for elementary school. Before one can do this, one must understand the features of the preschooler's environment that encourage cognitive growth and school readiness. To begin this investigation, we will look at the main influences on the child: the home, television, and nursery school.

The Home

Children who are more cognitively advanced come from homes in which language is used in an expansive manner. The children are encouraged to express themselves, to label their environment, and to describe their world (Chazan & Cox, 1976). Parents who give information, explain events, and encourage curiosity and exploration help to develop their children's minds so that when the children enter elementary school they are ready for new challenges (Katz, 1980). When Briggs and Elkind (1973) investigated five-year-old readers and nonreaders, they found that early readers came from homes in which the parents' occupational and educational levels were high and the parents read to their children.

Even when not directly involved in a parent-child interaction, children observe those around them. An environment filled with books is not stimulating unless the books are read. If preschoolers see their parents and older siblings enjoying reading, they are more likely to develop a positive attitude toward the activity.

TWO VIEWS OF PARENTS AS TEACHERS Since parental influences are so important, a natural question is, What approach should parents adopt if they want to optimize a preschooler's cognitive development? There are two different models here. The first views parents as environmental engineers who, at the appropriate times, provide materials and opportunities that help their children explore and learn about the world. The parents construct an environment rich in opportunities, allowing their children to discover the world at their own pace and stimulating them to think. Although Piaget never listed recommendations on childrearing (Vernon, 1976), this type of strategy is in line with his thinking. The child learns through discovery, and readiness is taken into consideration. Formal instruction is deemphasized. The day-to-day experiences of the child are educational. A simple walk around the neighborhood becomes a learning experience. There are traffic signs, people working, and a hundred different things to discuss.

The other approach emphasizes the importance of formal instruction. Parents are encouraged to teach their preschooler skills. There is less emphasis on self-discovery and more on planned activities that impart knowledge to the child.

Both extreme methods should be questioned. The parent who merely produces an environment suitable for a child but does not actively interact with the youngster is not maximizing the child's experiences. On the other side, too formal or unnatural a structure may cause a child to resent the parents and reject the instruction. It becomes a "grim business" (Zinsser, 1981). There is no joy, merely pressure. In addition, not all preschool children can be early readers. Many preschoolers do not have the physical abilities, such as the ability to focus on printed words, necessary for success in reading (Moore & Moore, 1973). In such cases, children may feel that they cannot live up to their parents' expectations, and tension could develop, which would interfere with normal development.

Television

A father of a three-and-a-half-year-old boy looked in on his son slightly after dawn expecting to find a sleeping child. Instead, what he found was a wide-awake warrior clutching a plastic sword and chanting "Teenage mutant ninja turtles—heroes in a half shell. Turtle power!" over and over again. Just two weeks earlier, the same child would rise early in the morning, strap on his proton pack, and spend the day patrolling the house busting ghosts. In one afternoon after viewing a videotape, the child had "mutated from ghostbuster to turtle" (*New York Times*, April 25, 1990).

Some 98 percent of all American households have television sets, and 52 percent have more than one—the extra set for the children (Parke & Slaby, 1983). On the average, preschoolers spend 27.8 hours a week watching television (Anderson, Lorch, Field, Collins & Nathan, 1986). If children spend that much time in one activity, the effects of the activity may be substantial.

People are rightfully concerned with the effect of television programming and advertising on children's aggression, prosocial behavior, diet, school achievement, and intelligence. These areas are covered in depth in the discussion of middle childhood in Chapter 11, because much of the research in these areas has been performed on elementary school-children. However, two areas of special concern for the preschooler that have been researched extensively are the influence of commercials on preschool children's behavior and the effectiveness of particular television programs aimed at preschoolers on their social and cognitive development.

ADVERTISING AIMED AT CHILDREN Do children understand the differences between TV commercials and regular television programs? Do they comprehend the purpose behind TV advertising? The average child is exposed to about 20,000 commercials a year, about 5,000 of which are for some type of food (Stoneman & Brody, 1981). By the time a person is twenty years old, he or she has watched one million television commercials.

Television commercials are as carefully produced as the programs they accompany. Children's advertising has three goals: to increase a child's desire for a particular product, to influence the child to ask parents to purchase the item, and to change consumption patterns, that is, to encourage a person to use more of the product (Atkin, 1980).

Advertising is effective in achieving each of these goals. Children do remember what they see on television and ask their parents to purchase the items. Lyle and Hoffman (1972) found that 75 percent of the mothers of preschoolers interviewed noted that their children sang commercial jingles by age three, and 91 percent reported that their children asked for the toys they saw advertised on television. Atkin and Gibson (1980) report that 90 percent of the children exposed to a particular cereal commercial wanted to eat that brand, compared with about 67 percent of a control

Young children watch a great deal of television, especially on Saturday and Sunday mornings.

group. Most advertising aimed at children involves toys, cereals, candy, and fast-food restaurants (Barcus, 1980). As children mature, more personal products take center stage (Liebert, Neale & Davison, 1973).

Children do attempt to influence the purchasing patterns of their parents. Galst and White (1976) followed children ages three through eleven who had been exposed to commercials in a lab setting on a trip to the supermarket. On the average, children tried to influence the purchases of particular foods fifteen times. Children who paid more attention to the advertisements made more requests. The extent to which these attempts are successful varies from parent to parent. Young children make more efforts to influence parental purchases, but older children are more successful. Mothers report yielding more often to older children than to younger children (Ward & Wackman, 1972).

Children exposed to a particular commercial are more likely to increase their use of the product as well (Atkin, 1980). As children watch the programs, they are reminded of the product, and this alters their consumption patterns.

Television advertising aimed at children is controversial. It is too easy to condemn advertising in general. Advertising is a useful process by which people are introduced to a product. However, adults have the ability to recognize and interpret the commercials for what they are—attempts to persuade one to buy. Until recently, it was thought that young children could not even make the distinction between commercials and the television program they were watching, but we now know that children as young as three years old can tell the difference between commercials and regular programs, though the ability increases with age (Levin, Petros & Petrella, 1983). This does not mean that children understand the intent and motives behind commercials. Such understanding is generally not expressed until age seven or eight (Levin et al., 1983). By the sixth grade (age eleven or so), children are downright cynical about commercials (Rubinstein, 1978).

9. *TRUE OR FALSE?*

Preschool children cannot tell the difference between television commercials and the programs they accompany.

DATAGRAPHIC

Televisions Around the World

Source: Field Guide to the Electronic Media, 1986 and Media Commentary Council, 1986.

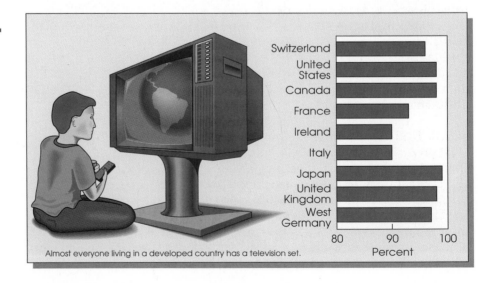

Almost everyone living in a developed country has a television set.

The effectiveness of commercials is increased by the skillful manner in which commercials are produced. Advertisers know how to capture and maintain the attention of children. About 80 percent of the cereal ads use animation in conjunction with nonanimated scenes (Barcus, 1980). Advertisers frequently use unusual sound and visual effects, violent activity, magic, and fantasy to attract attention. Few rational arguments are presented. Cereal ads usually concentrate on taste and texture and give little information about the ingredients except to say that the product is "fortified with essential vitamins" (Barcus, 1980).

What do children learn from commercials? Most ads for cereals, snacks, and gum serve to downgrade the importance of good nutrition and good health habits. When was the last time you saw a children's commercial for candy end with a suggestion that children eat a balanced diet and brush after meals? Toy advertising often deceives children, using photographic techniques to make a doll look larger than it actually is. If there is some statement such as "assembly required," it is presented so fast that children do not understand it.

The combination of efficient and effective psychological techniques of persuasion and an audience incapable of understanding the motives behind commercials may cause us to consider whether television commercials aimed at young children should be permitted at all. Cleaning up children's advertising would seem to be a simple matter, but political and economic forces are at work (Adler, 1980). In addition, censorship and freedom-of-speech issues are often raised (Heinz, 1983), and they should not be taken lightly. Finally, many of the recommendations to improve children's advertising are based on what seems appropriate rather than on solid evidence (Rossiter, 1980). Even so, children do not have the cognitive sophistication to understand the motives behind the commercials and to resist the messages that are presented so well. Children do need some additional protection.

Children's Television

Advertisements are found only on commercial TV stations. Before the late 1960s, children's programs had little focus. Although some were produced by concerned individuals, they were not based on the needs and abilities of young children, as determined by psychological research. That all changed when public television began showing its blockbuster children's programs "Sesame Street" and "Mister Rogers' Neighborhood." Children's television will never be the same.

SESAME STREET Big Bird. Grover. Bert and Ernie. Oscar the Grouch. Most preschoolers know these characters quite well. Since 1969, the face of television has irreversibly changed as bold new experiments in television programming have demonstrated that children's programs can be both entertaining and educational. "Sesame Street" is directed toward teaching inner-city youngsters basic numerical, language, and problem-solving skills (Lesser, 1976). It emphasizes cognitive concerns, although over the years it has covered prosocial behavior, tolerance for others, and attitudinal issues.

The producers of "Sesame Street" knew that to be successful the program had to compete with commercial television (O'Bryan, 1980) and be entertaining as well as educational. The show was fitted to the needs and level of its intended audience. The pace is varied and quick, the now-famous Muppets are present, and animation, splashy color, repetition, and music are used. The show is fun to watch, and children do watch it. "Sesame Street" is the single most popular children's educational program. It accounts for 18.1 percent of the overall viewing for three-year-olds, 12.2 percent for five-year-olds, and 5.5 percent for seven-year-olds (Pinon, Huston, and Wright, 1989). Viewing is highest between ages three and five, peaking at between three and a half and four, when the average child watches about four hours a week of the program. When children reach age six, they begin to see it as babyish, and they have already mastered the most basic and obvious content, including the alphabet and numbers (Huston, et al., 1985). This decline is found for all child-informative programs. Between the age of three and seven, the viewing of child-informative programs decreases, and viewing of comedies and cartoons increases (Huston, Wright, Rice, Kerkman, & St. Peters, 1990). Boys watch more action-adventure programs and cartoons than girls.

The presence of older or younger siblings influences viewing patterns as well. Having younger siblings increases the likelihood of a child's viewing "Sesame Street"; having older siblings decreases it. At one time, middle-class children would watch the program more than children from lower income families, but this is no longer so. Poor and middle-class children watch it about the same amount of time (Pinon et al., 1989).

"Sesame Street" is the most evaluated television program in the history of the medium. Children who watch it regularly learn its central concepts and have an advantage over those who do not watch it. These advantages seem to hold regardless of the socioeconomic level, sex, or ethnicity of the viewer (Ball and Bogatz, 1970, 1972; Bogatz and Ball, 1971). Children gain more from the program if they watch with a parent who can interpret the material and act as a guide (Peters, 1977). Children also imitate the cooperation they see if they are placed in a situation like the one on television, but no generalized effects have been found (Watkins, Huston-Stein & Wright, 1980). Watching "Sesame Street" also has a positive effect on the vocabulary development of children in the age group of three to five years (Rice, Huston, Truglio, and Wright, 1990).

The show is not without critics. The very fast, perhaps frenetic, pace does not leave room or time for rehearsal (Tower, Singer, Singer & Biggs, 1979). "Sesame Street" also shows negative behaviors (Coates, Pusser & Goodman, 1976), such as violence and trickery. Finally, some claim that the positive effects of the show are not as pronounced as some of the research would lead us to believe (Cook et al., 1975).

MISTER ROGERS' NEIGHBORHOOD A show with a completely different format is "Mister Rogers' Neighborhood." This is a slower paced, adult-led show that emphasizes interpersonal skills, imagination, and the understanding of one's emotions (Singer & Singer, 1976; Tower et al., 1979). Research on "Mister Rogers' Neighborhood" shows that the pro-

10. TRUE OR FALSE?

Preschoolers with schoolage brothers and sisters are more likely to watch "Sesame Street" than preschoolers with younger siblings.

Mr. Rogers' Neighborhood is another television show aimed at young children. Its format differs greatly from Sesame Street.

gram is successful in promoting prosocial behaviors, (Friedrich & Stein, 1973). When preschool children were exposed to daily viewing of either "Mister Rogers' Neighborhood," aggressive cartoons, or neutral programs for nine weeks, children who saw "Mister Rogers" improved in task persistence and prosocial behavior, such as cooperation. Watching "Mister Rogers" also led to an increase in fantasy play and imagination (Singer & Singer, 1976; Tower et al., 1979). This increase is noteworthy, since fantasy and pretend play are considered important aspects of a child's development (Rubin, Fein & Vandenberg, 1983). Children who show more imaginative play have better social skills, show greater concentration and more positive affect, are less impulsive, and show more internal control (Tower et al., 1979). The success of "Mister Rogers' Neighborhood" demonstrates that a deliberately slow-paced, repetitive show can be successful in aiding both cognitive and affective development (Singer & Singer, 1983).

fantasy play

"Mister Rogers' Neighborhood" has also been criticized. Its slow pace sometimes makes young children restless (Singer & Singer, 1976), and some parents may have difficulty getting their children to watch the program. But there is a tradeoff in pacing. Kindergarten and first-grade children attend more to fast-paced programs but show greater recall for the material in slow-paced shows (Wright et al., 1984).

Television has a great potential for helping preschoolers develop cognitively and socially. Commercial television has learned something from the success of these shows, and its offerings have improved. However, television has a long way to go to reach its potential in this area.

Nursery School

Thus far, we have looked at the home environment and television as features of a child's environment that encourage cognitive development. However, more children are now attending nursery school, and an increasing number of school systems have opted for all-day kindergartens. The growth in nursery school attendance has been impressive. Nursery school enrollment of three- and four-year-olds more than doubled between 1970 and 1983. In 1970, 14.3 percent of the three- and four-year-olds were attending nursery school, while in 1983 the percentage stood at 33.6 percent. In 1986, about 29 percent of the three-year-olds and 49 percent of the four-year-olds attended nursery school (U.S. Department of Commerce, 1989).

The percentage of children attending a preschool increases with age. Most five-year-olds attend kindergarten. Ninety three percent of the five-year-olds were enrolled in kindergarten in 1983, versus 80 percent in 1970 (Galinsky, 1986). The need for many women to work outside the home and the growth of single-parent families account for part of the increase. In other cases, parents worry that unless their children get a preschool education they will enter elementary school at a disadvantage.

Many authorities no longer differentiate between nursery schools and day-care programs. Today, day-care programs, community preschools, and experimental early education programs are all included under the heading of early childhood education (Clarke-Stewart & Fein, 1983). One additional term needs to be introduced here. **Compensatory education** involves an attempt to compensate for some difference between one group of children and another. Many preschool programs, such as Head Start (discussed later in the chapter), try to help children from economically disadvantaged families develop the attitudes and skills necessary for later success in school.

THE VARIETY OF APPROACHES Suppose you want to send your three-year-old to nursery school. There are two schools in your neighborhood. One focuses on developing cognitive skills; the other emphasizes social skills and developing healthy attitudes toward learning. Which school would you choose?

Nursery schools vary greatly. One may emphasize social and personal growth—getting along with others and gaining a feeling of mastery over the environment. Another may stress the importance of training the senses and developing motor abilities. Still others may emphasize cognitive growth in one of two ways. A cognitively oriented school may follow a Piagetian format by structuring the program to encourage children to discover the world around them and to learn from their own experiences. A second cognitive approach emphasizes the teaching of academic skills and uses a behavioral viewpoint involving repetition and reinforcement. Many preschools claim to have goals in all these areas, so putting one school in a particular category can be difficult. Even so, nursery schools can sometimes be classified according to their goals and programs.

THE TRADITIONAL NURSERY SCHOOL The traditional nursery school emphasizes social and emotional development and may not follow any specific educational theory (McClinton & Meier, 1978). The nursery school program varies considerably from school to school, but it is often characterized by a great deal of freedom, choice, and flexibility. Activities

compensatory education
The use of educational strategies in an attempt to reduce or eliminate some perceived difference between groups of children.

may include story time, listening to music, moving to music, all types of artistic endeavors, trips within the neighborhood (perhaps to the fire department or a donut shop), growing plants, and observing the environment, along with free play. Children are encouraged to cooperate and share. Some Piagetian influence may be in evidence, as teachers often create situations in which children can learn through self-discovery. When used in education, the term *traditional* unfortunately connotes something old-fashioned and out-of-date. This is not the case here. There is nothing wrong with the goals or practices used in the traditional nursery school (Smart & Smart, 1978).

THE MONTESSORI SCHOOL Montessori schools, which use the approach developed by Maria Montessori at the beginning of the twentieth century, have gained popularity all over the world. They stress the importance of educating the senses (Cole, 1955), because Montessori believed there is a close relationship between the senses and the intellect. Training the senses lays the groundwork for reading and writing. As Deasy (1978, p. 82) notes, "Passing fingers across the letters with his eyes shut, listening to the names of the letters and tracing them with his index finger and then a pencil, the Montessori pupil linked the sound of the alphabet with touch, sight and muscular coordination. He had to learn how to write before writing." Every activity in the Montessori school has an educational purpose. For instance, when children color, they do so to improve their ability to hold a writing implement, not to create something beautiful (Cole, 1950).

Many Montessori activities are self-correcting, so that children can proceed at their own rate and no pressure is placed on them. There is no punishment for not finishing an exercise, nor is there much use of reinforcement. In the Montessori classroom, each item has its proper place,

There are many types of nursery schools. In this Montessori school, children learn about shapes by touching them.

and children are expected to keep the room clean and pick up after themselves. Montessori believed that children negotiated sensitive periods during which they showed strong but transient tendencies to learn or develop their abilities. For example, a two-year-old's sensitivity to touch helps the child learn the shapes of letters using sandpaper letters and to exercise the intellect by classifying things by textures and shapes (Northwoods, 1990).

Montessori's system is not without its critics. Play is not emphasized, and this is troubling to those who consider play to be an important part of a child's development (Rubin et al., 1983). Understanding one's emotions is also not a primary goal. Social interaction is present, but it is not really stressed either. Children do not act out plays, nor does the teacher tell stories. There is little use of imagination. These activities are not forbidden, but they are not encouraged. Montessori's methods have been in and out of favor with many educators around the world since their inception. Today, with the emphasis on cognitive growth, they are again in fashion.

THE PIAGETIAN PRESCHOOL If you walked into a traditional preschool, you would see evidences of Piaget's influence. Some ideas from one philosophy or practice are often accepted by others. Montessori's idea of using child-sized furniture is now the norm in preschools. Piaget's ideas of learning through doing are also accepted. In contrast to the Montessori method, Piagetian-based preschools stress play as a learning activity. During play, children are exposed to the viewpoints of others, which challenge their egocentric view of the world. Developing curiosity, independence, and self-confidence, learning to cooperate, and gaining physical control of the environment are definite goals. In the Piagetian preschool, children are not given formal instruction. Instead, teachers act as guides, helping children discover things through active participation. The children are exposed to a wide range of materials that help them gain experience in classification and seriation.

THE BEREITER-ENGLEMANN APPROACH Nowhere is the goal of academic growth addressed as much as in the program developed by Carl Bereiter and Siegfried Englemann known as DISTAR. In this program, children are taught the concepts that are considered necessary by the educational staff. The teacher has an objective and presents the material to small groups of children in a standardized fashion for about twenty minutes or so, with periods of rest, music, or other activities alternating with instructional periods. The exchanges are rapid, and the teacher reinforces the children for giving correct answers. This is a teaching approach, and it is based on the idea that children can be taught the desired concepts if the material is presented clearly and appropriately. For example, children may be taught the concept of equality—that both sides of an equation must be equal. The teacher may present the concept in an appropriate way, ask the children questions, and give much positive reinforcement for correct responses. Englemann and Bereiter argue that disadvantaged children require additional help in cognitive areas, especially language. Their program is an attempt to provide such cognitive training.

DO NURSERY SCHOOLS ACHIEVE THEIR GOALS? Generally speaking, nursery schools accomplish their purposes. Research indicates that children who attend nursery school are generally more advanced than their nonattending peers. This is especially true for children in the lower income groups (Minuchin & Shapiro, 1983). Children who attend preschool programs are more socially competent, outgoing, self-assured, curious, independent, and persistent on a task than those who do not attend. In elementary school, they are better adjusted and more task oriented, goal directed, persistent, cooperative, and friendly (Clarke-Stewart & Fein, 1983). Studies consistently show various benefits for children attending nursery school (Sjolund, 1971). There is no question that nursery school has a positive effect on children from low-income areas and for children at risk for developing later problems in school. The question of the benefits of nursery school for middle-class children and those not in the at-risk category is still controversial. Some evidence now is emerging on this issue. A study of about 200 middle-class elementary schoolchildren found advantages in reading and language skills for boys who had attended a preschool. No effect was found for females (Larsen & Robinson, 1989).

◆ PROJECT HEAD START

The finding that children, especially from poor backgrounds, are likely to benefit from the preschool experience is important (Lazar, Darlington, Murray, Roye & Snipper, 1982). Children from poverty backgrounds who enter school behind their middle-class counterparts are likely to fall further behind as they progress through school. Perhaps if these children could attend a preschool that would help compensate for their different experiences, this cycle could be stopped and they would have a reasonable chance for academic success. This was partially the thinking behind one of the greatest educational and social experiments of the past fifty years: Project Head Start (Cooke, 1979).

Since its inception in 1964, millions of American children have taken part in the great experiment called **Project Head Start** (Zigler & Valentine, 1979), and the federally funded program still continues today. The hope was that a program instituted early enough could give children living in poverty a head start in school and reduce or eliminate the class differences in educational achievement that were so noticeable (Zigler & Berman, 1983).

Project Head Start has both cognitive and noncognitive goals (Washington, 1985). Children learn to work and play independently and to accept help and direction from adults, learn competence and worth, sharpen and widen their language skills, are encouraged to be curious and to grow in ability to channel inner destructive impulses. The program also has health goals.

Hopes were high for Project Head Start, but soon controversy, disappointment, and disillusionment set in. The first evaluations were impressive. Studies showed sizable gains in cognitive abilities and self-esteem (Zigler & Berman, 1983), but it was soon found that the intelligence gains noted did not continue as the children progressed through

A Head Start teacher reads to three and four year olds. Some studies have shown that Head Start children achieve more in reading and mathematics in later years.

Project Head Start
A federally funded compensatory education program aimed at reducing or eliminating the differences in educational achievement between poor and middle-class youngsters.

THE CHILD
IN THE YEAR
2000

Universal Education for Preschool Children

Will the child in the year 2000 attend a preschool completely paid for by the government? Will the child in the year 2000 be compelled to begin school at an early age? These questions are now being asked by many who see the extension of the public school system to the preschool years.

The thinking is easy to understand. If research shows that preschool experiences may enrich a child's cognitive and social growth, why not require all preschoolers to attend school? The movement to open public schools to four-year-olds is gaining strength (Hymes, 1987), for many reasons. The increased number of children whose parents are employed and who must attend day care, the increased popularity of nursery schools, and the fact that special groups of children attending preschool programs gain from such programs have all added to the arguments for beginning public education at a younger age than children do today.

On the surface, this seems reasonable. However, there are problems. For example, the data on middle-class preschool age children are mixed, with some studies showing benefits for middle-class children and other studies showing no differences. The greater benefits are found for lower income children (Kagan, 1985). In addition, any universal public four-year-old school program will be very expensive. Most important, there are possible dangers, especially of pushing children to read and write before they are ready and overselling the public on what can be taught to four-year-olds. These dangers are well brought out in David Elkind's 1987 book *Miseducation*.

No educator or psychologist is opposed to teaching children to read or write when such children are ready. However, "only between 1 and 3 percent of the children are reading with comprehension before entering kindergarten and the majority of children do not show interest in how to read until age five or six" (Elkind, 1987, p. 185). We are miseducating our children if we push them into academic situations for which they are not ready. Too often, educational programs that are designed for schoolage children are being written down to the level of four-year-olds. Elkind believes that we place these young children at a risk for short-term stress and long-term personality damage and that these programs do not serve any useful purpose or have any lasting benefits. Some of these programs communicate inappropriate expectations, and little attention is given to individual differences in development and learning styles. Similar questions are being asked about the kindergarten curricula as well (Egertson, 1987).

The question of universal education for preschool children is controversial. Elkind reminds us that any such program must be developmentally related to the child's needs and abilities, and he encourages us to question the appropriateness of academic training for young children. Others argue that appropriate education can be offered to preschoolers and that the public schools ought to get involved. The controversy is an ongoing one, with no clear answer in sight.

Overall, we can conclude that high-quality, developmentally appropriate preschool experiences do not injure the child or cause later academic problems. As noted, the evidence shows that such experiences may even aid children, especially those from lower socioeconomic backgrounds. Yet, the public should not be oversold on what such programs can accomplish. Such programs also may constitute a danger if too much pressure is placed on young children to develop academic skills before they are ready.

second and third grades (Weinberg, 1979; Westinghouse Learning Corp., 1969). This was often called the fadeout phenomenon (Weinberg, 1979). In other words, the gains in intelligence were temporary, and by the second grade or so, Head Start children did not differ from their classmates in intelligence. This led to a period of intense skepticism on the part of critics and defensiveness on the part of the program's supporters.

The determination of the program's advocates to see the program through its hard times was rewarded, for more recent research demonstrates the beneficial effects of the Head Start experience. The effects are obvious, once you know where to look. The later studies looked at other measures besides intelligence and reported that students who attended a Head Start program were significantly less likely to be retained in grade or to be found in special education classes. The results of studies concerning the reading and mathematics achievement of children who attended a Head Start program are mixed, with some showing Head Start children achieving more in mathematics and reading (Darlington, Roye, Snipper, Murray & Lazar, 1980; Lazar & Darlington, 1982). In fact, a recent study showed that Head Start is superior to other preschool programs (Lee, Brooks-Gunn, & Schnur, 1988). Head Start is also given some of the credit for the improvement in SAT scores among minority youth (Carmody, 1988).

Other advantages have been found, especially for Head Start programs in which parental participation is encouraged and high (Mann, Harrell & Hurt, 1978). The children of parents who were very active in Head Start as board members, volunteers, and so forth performed better on achievement tests (Washington, 1985). Involvement in the program is often the first community involvement for many parents, and most authorities believe even more emphasis should be placed on involving parents (Oyemade, 1985; Sprigle & Schaefer, 1985). Parental involvement helps parents deal with younger siblings as well. Gary and Klaus (1970) found that the younger siblings of children who had attended the program had significantly higher intelligence scores, perhaps because the improved parental interactions carried over to other children. On the whole, Head Start has been successful.

11. *TRUE OR FALSE?*

Children attending Project Head Start classes are less likely than their peers who did not attend the program to be held back in grade or placed in special education classes during their school career.

◆ KINDERGARTEN

Do you remember your experience in kindergarten? Chances are you attended for a half day, you were never tested for anything except perhaps your vision, and you spent the day in playlike activities designed to stimulate your curiosity and social competence. Visit most kindergartens today and you will be very surprised at the changes.

A Change to Full Day

The most obvious change is that today's kindergartners are much more likely to attend a full school day. About half of all kindergartners in the United States attend an extended-day program, and this total is expected to rise (Olsen & Zigler, 1989). Although this is a change from recent practice, it is not a historic change. The kindergarten movement both in America and in Europe started as a full-day program and was reduced to a half day both because it was thought that children needed more contact with their parents and for practical reasons including school overcrowding (Caldwell, 1989).

Why the return to a full-day program? Some claim that we now expect kindergartners to accomplish more in that year, and a full-time program meets these goals. Others argue for a more practical reason: Parents who are employed want their children to attend school full time as soon as possible. In addition, many children have had some preschool experience and are used to being away from the home, making day-long kindergarten more practical. Some, though, question whether the full-day kindergarten is developmentally appropriate.

Screening and Readiness Testing

Another great change is the increasing use of screening and readiness tests at these young ages. Screening to identify children at intellectual risk has become more common both in preschool and in kindergarten. Some tests are used to screen students to discover whether any student has a problem that would prevent him or her from succeeding in school. The student may then be referred for a more rigorous examination or be placed in some special program (Walsh, 1989).

readiness tests
Tests that measure whether a student has attained the skills necessary to master a new skill.

Other tests, called **readiness tests,** are concerned more with the skills that the child has or has not already acquired. They are mostly used to make instructional decisions. Readiness tests are used to assess whether a student has the necessary skills to master a new skill, such as reading. They are given prior to instruction and measure particular skills that are deemed necessary for success in school (DeLawter & Sherman, 1978). Most readiness tests involve reading and mathematics readiness and are administered during kindergarten and sometimes in first grade.

To be useful, a readiness test must measure very detailed and important skills that are necessary for success in school. Many reading readiness tests measure visual discrimination, identification of differences and similarities in written words or figures and in spoken words, auditory discrimination, verbal comprehension, recognition of letters, recognition of words that may have been taught in sample lessons, and skill in drawing or copying (Gronlund, 1976). If a teacher receives information that a student does not have a particular skill, some program might be instituted to help the child develop the skill.

There is some controversy surrounding the use of these tests. Some authorities doubt the predictive validity of such tests (see Graue & Shepard, 1989). In addition, the interpretation of tests with young children must be made with great care. Scoring well on a reading readiness test does not mean that reading success is assured, since readiness tests measure neither attitudes nor attention span. In addition, some children who do not do particularly well on reading readiness tests do learn to read for reasons that are uncertain (DeLawter & Sherman, 1978). Still, readiness tests can yield important information for the teacher.

Whether giving readiness or screening tests, one must be exceptionally careful with interpretation. There is always the chance of misidentification. Children may be incorrectly labeled. In addition, a young child is harder to test than an older child, since the child may or may not be interested in the test. In early childhood, the relationship between motivation and cognition is great. In fact, motivation and cognition form a generalized competence factor (Scarr, 1981). Since motivational and emotional factors influence test results, caution must be used when interpreting test scores.

More Emphasis on Academics

The most profound and controversial change in kindergarten is in curriculum. Over the past two decades, an increasing emphasis has been placed on academic skills. In the past, play was the basis for the kindergarten movement, but this is changing. Programs are now more likely to stress academic skills and group instruction and use commercially prepared materials more often (Nall, 1982). Kindergarten reading programs are now pencil-and-paper oriented, with worksheets, texts, and workbooks (Willert & Kamii, 1985). Some believe that "kindergarten is what first grade used to be" (Walsh, 1989, p. 385). The pressures for this change come from state-mandated standards that require skill mastery, first-grade teachers who want their students to have certain skills before entering first grade, and parents who want kindergarten to place more emphasis on academics than the preschools that their children attended (Walsh, 1989).

Not many studies have evaluated these new changes in the modern kindergarten. Most, though not all, studies that have been performed find that the longer school day and more extended periods of time spent on academics, including language, reading, and mathematics, do increase standardized test scores, especially on some readiness tests (see Olsen & Zigler, 1989). This is especially true for children from at-risk populations. The findings on middle-class children are more mixed, but again mainly positive. Whether these children do better in the long run is still questionable. There is much less evidence to support changes in motivation or general intellectual ability that might lead to significant long-term change (Olsen & Zigler, 1989).

There has been a reaction against this narrowing emphasis on the academic. Kindergarten teachers are frequently caught between their feelings that this may not be the best course for the children and the demands of others. Many teachers are experiencing a philosophy-reality conflict (Hatch & Freeman, 1988). Perhaps the greatest question is whether we are making inappropriate demands on young children, overemphasizing fine motor skills and desk work. Are we rushing children into reading and academic enterprises that they are not ready for? This is a difficult question to answer. Others argue that this narrowing emphasis does not place enough importance on problem solving, motivation, interest in learning, and social competence.

This issue haunts every kindergarten program as well as many nursery school programs. Should the emphasis be on academic skills or more social-motivational ones? One expert, Bettye Caldwell (1989), argues that it is not an either/or situation. The question is not *whether* to educate or care for preschool children. She believes that preschools and kindergarten must provide a blend of education and care, which she labels *educare*. Preschools must offer a "developmentally appropriate mixture of education and care, of stimulation and nurture, of work and play" (Caldwell, 1989, p. 266).

12. *TRUE OR FALSE?*

The curriculum of today's kindergarten is more likely to include training in basic academic skills than it was fifteen years ago.

Over the past two decades, an increasing emphasis has been placed on academic skills in kindergarten.

◆ QUESTIONS FOR THE FUTURE

Cognitive development during the preschool period is impressive. Piaget described the preschooler's abilities and limitations, while new research shows just how sensitive young children are to the type of task and environment surrounding the challenge. Psychologists have gained a genuine respect for the preschool child's abilities.

We now also have a better understanding of how important it is for children to be ready for the formal school experience. As more children experience some type of preschool education, two questions constantly arise. First, how is progress to be measured—on a single factor, such as intelligence or reading achievement, or on a broader measure, which may include personal growth and other factors, along with cognitive measures? Second, should academic demands be made on these young children? Should nursery schools—and especially kindergarten—specialize in helping children gain social skills and develop a positive attitude toward school, or should they try to impart information and skills in some semiformal manner? There is no single answer to these questions, and only further research can give us information on the possibilities and problems involved in adopting a particular course of action.

SUMMARY

1. During the preschool years, a child's rate of growth declines. Preschoolers develop a number of motor skills, including jumping, running, and hopping. The development of the large muscles precedes that of the fine muscles.

2. The leading cause of death among preschoolers is accidents, some of which can be prevented.

3. According to Piagetian theory, children between about two and seven are in the preoperational stage. These children can use symbols and have the capacity to view an action, remember it, and repeat it later.

4. Children in the preoperational stage reason transductively (from specific event to specific event), have difficulty placing things in size order (seriation) and, at least at the beginning of this stage, have problems sorting items into different classes (classification).

5. Preschoolers cannot solve conservation problems (challenges that involve the understanding that quantities remain the same even if their appearance changes). Their tendency to center on one dimension and their inability to reverse operations and to understand transformations are responsible for their problems in this area.

6. Children in the preoperational stage also tend to be egocentric (see everything from their own point of view), believe that everything is capable of being conscious and alive, and believe that natural events are caused by human beings.

7. New evidence shows that many of these abilities are present if preschoolers are tested on tasks that are meaningful to them, simple, and clearly defined. However, these abilities are fragile, and preschoolers will not show these skills all the time.

8. The attention span of preschoolers is superior to that of toddlers, but it is still not as long as it will be in middle childhood. Children are attracted by many aspects of a situation, such as movement, color, and loud noise. As children age, their ability to voluntarily focus their attention in a planned, organized manner increases. This ability is not well developed in preschoolers.

9. Preschoolers do not spontaneously use verbal strategies such as rehearsal as memory aids, but they do show such strategies as looking and pointing. Children do better in familiar situations and with tasks that are meaningful.

10. The child's knowledge base affects memory and performance on a number of tasks. Both children and adults possess a number of scripts or structures describing the sequence of events in a particular situation. These form the basis for understanding events.

11. Parents who label the environment, encourage their children's curiosity, and read to their children tend to maximize their children's cognitive development.

12. Television advertising aimed at children is very effective. Children often ask for the products they see on

television. "Sesame Street" and "Mister Rogers' Neighborhood" are two successful television programs combining entertainment with education.

13. More and more preschoolers are attending early childhood education programs. These programs differ from one another in philosophy and teaching methods. The evidence generally shows that children who attend preschools gain from the experience.

14. Project Head Start is an attempt to provide experiences to help close the gap between children from lower socioeconomic backgrounds and their peers from middle-class backgrounds. While the immediate gains in intelligence are not sustained throughout elemen-

tary school, children who attend these programs are less likely to be left back or to be found in special education classes. Some studies show that they do better in mathematics and reading as well.

15. There have been a number of changes in the kindergarten curriculum. Full-day kindergartens have become more popular, more screening and readiness tests are being administered, and the curriculum has become more academically oriented. All of these changes are very controversial, with some authorities claiming that the emphasis on academics at this age is inappropriate.

ACTION/REACTION

The Nursery School Gambit

Anna and Al decided to send their three-year-old daughter, Lindsay, to nursery school, choosing a school that was close to home and that had an excellent reputation. They believed that Lindsay was very bright, and they wanted the teacher to introduce their daughter to letter sounds and concepts that would lead to early reading and writing.

After three months in the school, Anna and Al saw no visible improvement and went to see the teacher, Ms. Baxter. The teacher explained that the purpose of nursery school was not to teach children to read but to help them develop social skills and a feeling that learning is enjoyable. In the school's program, children learn to cooperate with one another and learn about the world in which they live. They are even "studying" dinosaurs. Ms. Baxter also noted that forcing children to read at an early age is undesirable, because children will learn when they are ready.

But Anna and Al are not satisfied. They believe that Lindsay is ready for more than she is getting. They wonder whether they should switch to another nursery school.

1. If you were Lindsay's parents, what would you do?
2. If you were Lindsay's teacher, would you have explained the school's philosophy any differently?

Why Doesn't Tommy Eat Right?

Like most parents, The Dunns are interested in their preschooler's eating habits. They are both aware of the importance of good nutrition and forming good eating habits. However, their son Tommy doesn't seem to like anything except potato chips, bread and butter, sugared cereals, and snacks. If the Dunns put anything healthy on Tommy's plate, Tommy plays with the food. He sometimes takes a mouthful, but it takes him an eternity to chew and swallow it. The family is finished with the meal by the time Tommy has eaten even a fraction of what is put on his plate.

The situation is complicated by several factors. First, Tommy's best friend, who lives next door, seems to exist on nothing but junk food; and second, Tommy watches a great deal of television and is always asking for the sugared foods that he sees advertised. Tommy's parents are losing patience with Tommy's eating habits and demands for what he sees on television. A few days ago, they yelled at Tommy for asking for candy and not eating his dinner, but they realize this is not the best approach to the problem.

If you were Tommy's parents, what would you do?

CHAPTER TEN

Social and Personality Development in Early Childhood

Children Playing on the Beach by Mary Cassatt.

◆ CHAPTER OUTLINE ◆

Are These Statements True or False?

Turn the page for the correct answers. Each statement is repeated in the margin next to the paragraph in which the information can be found.

1. A preschooler who has a fear of darkness or monsters is unusual and probably in need of therapy.
2. Infants do not recognize their own reflection in a mirror until their second year of life.
3. Most young children's pretend play focuses on common household situations and everyday challenges.
4. Children's rough-and-tumble play always turns into aggressive behavior if it is not stopped by an authority figure.
5. Boys show significantly more rough-and-tumble play than girls.
6. Preschoolers share less and help other children less than children in middle childhood do.
7. Most conflicts between preschoolers are settled through negotiation and compromise.
8. Siblings are more likely to fight than to play with each other.
9. Children of parents who allow their children maximum freedom with few, if any, restrictions are usually self-reliant and show excellent self-control.
10. Unusual as it may seem, parents who physically abuse their children often believe that physical punishment is wrong.
11. The overwhelming majority of abused children grow up to abuse their own children.
12. Research has failed to establish any consistent gender differences in personality or behavior.

Answers to True-False Statements

1. False. Correct statement: Many preschoolers develop fears, but this does not mean that they are necessarily in need of therapy.
2. True.
3. True.
4. False. Correct statement: Rough-and-tumble play does not usually turn into aggression.
5. True.
6. True.
7. False. Correct statement: Most conflicts between preschoolers are settled through insistence, and little negotiation or compromise is used.
8. False. Correct statement: Although antagonistic behavior between siblings is not unusual, the majority of the interactions are positive and play oriented.
9. False. Correct statement: Children of permissive parents do not show much self-reliance or self-control.
10. False. Correct statement: Parents who physically abuse their children believe in physical punishment.
11. False. Correct statement: Since between 25 and 35 percent of all abused children grow up to abuse their own children, it would be incorrect to state that a majority do so.
12. False. Correct statement: Some consistent gender differences have been found.

◆ YOU STAY HOME—I'M GOING FISHING

"You stay home with the mommies and the babies. I'm going fishing," said a four-year-old boy to the little girl he was playing with.

"But I want to come, too," she protested.

"No, you can't, but I'll take you to a Chinese restaurant when I get home."

The little girl was quieted by that promise (Carper, 1978). In this little dialogue, we see a number of areas of social growth in preschoolers. We see imagination and social interaction and some interest in gender roles. The years of early childhood are years of exploration, great advances in social development, and the development of a sense of initiative.

Initiative

initiative
The positive outcome of the psychosocial crisis of the preschool period, involving development of a respect for one's own wishes and desires.

guilt
The negative outcome of the psychosocial crisis of the preschool period, resulting in a sense that the child's acts and desires are bad.

During early childhood, preschoolers enjoy being on the move and taking the initiative (Erikson, 1963). Erikson considers **initiative** the positive outcome of this preschool stage, while the negative outcome is **guilt.** If parents appreciate the importance of encouraging a preschooler's self-guided initiative and curiosity, the child will leave the stage with a sense of initiative. The preschooler is an active experimenter, who tends more to begin than to finish things. He or she has many ideas: Let's bake a cake, go to the movies, eat at McDonalds. If a child's curiosity and activities become a bother to the parents and the parents react with verbal scorn and restrictions, the child is likely to become timid and fearful.

The preschoolers' world is new and very exciting. Unlike the toddler, the preschooler can easily explore his or her environment, and the preschooler's verbal skills allow for more sophisticated interpersonal relationships. The preschoolers' cognitive growth allows for the use of imagination and symbolism. Although infants and toddlers certainly come into contact with other children their age, contacts between preschoolers are noticeably more sustained.

Childhood Fears

The child, though, still shows a strong dependency and is likely to experience fears and anxieties, especially if the child is in an unfamiliar place. Some of the more common fears are of darkness, being alone, storms, ghosts and monsters, animals and insects, and separation. Many children raised in happy, secure environments still develop fears. In fact, almost every child develops some sort of fear during the course of childhood (Poznansky, 1973). Preschoolers often continue to fear separation from parents. Children's increasing awareness of their environment and knowledge of their inability to control events lead to many fears (Verville, 1967). The preschooler's vivid imagination also contributes to fears of darkness, strange creatures, monsters, and goblins. Children at this age magnify and distort events, thinking of the terrible things that could happen (Ross Laboratories, 1979).

At times, a particular experience can make a child quite fearful. A sudden move from a dog or commotion in the street during the night can be the basis for a fear. In addition, some television programs might frighten preschool children, who will sometimes insist that the light be kept on in their room to guard against some imaginary creature. Children usually outgrow their early fears.

Parents should not ridicule children for their fears or shame them before others (Ilg & Ames, 1955). It may also be harmful to force children to face their fears. Children's fears should be respected, and parents are wise to give children time to get used to the environment before helping children adjust to the feared object. If a child is afraid of dogs, parents should allow a child to stay close to them and away from a feared dog for a while.

Children also notice how adults react to particular stimuli, such as insects, dogs, and the dark. If a parent stands on a chair and screams at the sight of a spider, the child learns to fear spiders. Children tend to show many of the same fears their parents have (Bandura & Menlove, 1968). Exposing children to models who cope with a feared stimulus can be effective in reducing fear reactions in children. Albert Bandura and colleagues (1967) exposed forty-eight preschool children with a fear of

1. TRUE OR FALSE?

A preschooler who has a fear of darkness or monsters is unusual and probably in need of therapy.

dogs to a model situation in which a four-year-old child approached a dog in a nonfrightened manner. Some of the children were exposed only to the dog, while a control group simply participated in a play period. The children who had witnessed the preschooler approach the dog without fear showed considerably less tendency to avoid dogs. Thus, a peer model, patience, and understanding appear to help children overcome their fears.

The Emerging Self

A five-year-old girl was playing outside one morning by herself. A neighbor watched the preschooler for a while as the girl played a pretend game. After a while, the adult opened the window and asked the child where her parents were. "Oh, they are inside having breakfast." "Where is your brother?" asked the neighbor. "He is reading in his room," was the girl's reply. "But aren't you lonely?" asked the neighbor. The little girl looked up, smiled, and said, "No, I like me."

Psychologists have for many years been interested in the child's emerging self-concept. The **self-concept** is the picture people have of themselves. You are a student, perhaps very friendly, athletic, proud of the fact that you volunteer at a community shelter, but you consider yourself a poor math student. Notice that your self-concept contains not only your characteristics, roles, and memberships but also some evaluation of these aspects. For example, if you have children, you may think of yourself not only as a parent but also as a good parent.

self-concept
The picture people have of themselves.

Children are not born with a self-concept; a self-concept develops as children mature. We can trace the self-concept's inception to infancy, when children differentiate themselves from the outside world. The knowledge that one is a son or a daughter or a boy or a girl develops during the first years of life, as does the capacity for evaluating these identifications.

Young infants not only have no concept of self but also have no concept of other people. They do not even know that they are separate from others. The beginning of some awareness of self develops in the first year when a child realizes that his or her body is separate from mother's and that the child can make an impact on the environment. When infants are placed in front of mirrors, they sometimes wave their arms and perform other activities, showing that they have some idea of the relationship between what they are doing and what they see in the mirror (Bertenthal & Fischer, 1978). However, infants do not know what they look like, nor do they recognize themselves.

2. TRUE OR FALSE?

Infants do not recognize their own reflection in a mirror until their second year of life.

It is not until the second year of life that children have enough experience to recognize themselves (see Harter, 1988). One way to demonstrate this is to place some rouge on the baby's nose and place the baby in front of a mirror. Only after about fifteen months do children react by touching or pointing to the red nose thus showing some recognition of themselves. Children's growing knowledge of themselves is shown as they become able to use language. By about eighteen months, children can state their name and point out their own picture from a group of toddlers. They learn specific categories—that they are children, not adults—and their gender.

In early childhood, the self-concept is based on external factors such as physical characteristics (Burns, 1979), possessions (Damon & Hart, 1982), and activities, such as "I play baseball." The preschooler describes concrete, observable behaviors and specific examples but tends not to generalize. A girl may like basketball and baseball but does not say she likes sports, or she may like cats and dogs but not say she likes animals. Children's descriptions of self also contain preferences and specific physical characteristics (Harter, 1988). When preschoolers were asked to respond to such statements as "I am a boy/girl who . . . ," more than half of all the responses made references to a particular action (Keller, Ford, & Meacham, 1978). It is not until middle childhood that personality characteristics take center stage and personal comparisons with others (I am taller) become common.

Although these developmental trends are certainly present, we should not automatically conclude that the preschooler lacks any psychological sense of who he or she is (Eder, 1987, 1989). Even young children may have some fairly general concepts that will be the basis for their later, more sophisticated concepts. Preschoolers can produce descriptions of inner states and emotions. They sometimes make statements such as "I don't feel good with grownups" or "I usually play with friends." When asked how they felt when they were scared, children may say that they wanted to run away. These early memories may form the basis for the more general, psychological dispositions shown so commonly in middle childhood.

The self-concept is cumulative; that is, what is formed in early childhood can be reformed later on if there is some major change in the child's life. However, the child's experiences form the basis for later generalizations. The experiences of the preschooler who is told that his or her socially acceptable initiatives are good is likely to evaluate him or herself in such terms. Such early experiences can also directly affect behavior. There is a significant correlation between self-concept and cooperative behavior; that is, preschoolers who have a positive sense of themselves are more likely to show cooperation and other helping behaviors (Cauley and Tyler, 1989).

Young children's self-concept is partially based upon activities such as "I play baseball."

◆ PLAY

Play is such a common experience in early childhood that we tend not to think very much about it. Play is an activity that is performed for sheer enjoyment with no ulterior motive. The focus of play is on the child rather than on what the child is holding, bouncing, or coloring. Play activities are performed for their own sake (Vandenberg, 1978); there is no payoff in candy, attention, or money. Finally, play is enjoyable.

The Development of Play

Try this experiment. Visit a playground and watch the children play. Try to estimate their ages, and then note *how* they are playing. You will probably notice a definite progression (Rubin, Fein & Vandenberg 1983).

A baby is probably uninvolved with the other children. Anything that occurs may be of interest to the infant for only a few seconds. Such **unoccupied behavior** is the first stage of play during which babies may stroke their bodies, play with their hands, or hug a stuffed animal. Later in the first year, children play with simple toys, banging them against something or dropping them. They are basically exploring the properties of the toy and are uninvolved with any other children around them. They may play simple peek-a-boo games with a parent, but the other person is essentially a toy, and no mutuality is evidenced.

Solitary or **independent play** can be seen in young children and remains important in the second and third years of life. However, the transition to a more social type of play can be seen in what Mildred Parten (1932) has called **onlooker play**. During this stage, children watch others with considerable interest and frequently ask questions about what the other children are doing. They are not yet able to join in and thus remain on the outside. This leads to a type of play in which children may seek out the company of others but do not yet interact with them.

After the second year, children are often brought together with their peers. These two-year-olds engage in **parallel play**. They play in the presence of other children but not with them. They do not really interact or cooperate with one another. One gets the feeling that if one child were to leave, the other child could go on alone without any problem. The quality of the sand castle built by either child does not depend on the participation of the other child. Parallel play is found throughout the preschool period, but it decreases with age. It is the primary play behavior in two-year-olds and in some three-year-olds (Smith, 1978).

Active interaction with others emerges during early childhood. Preschoolers actively **associate** with other children and may share, cooperate, have verbal arguments, and play together, but few of these periods are sustained. There is a flightiness to their play and to their interactions with others. Much of the play of preschoolers involves physical practice of skills that have been or are being mastered. Preschoolers' play is active and often physically exhausting.

Beginning in the later part of the preschool period and continuing into middle childhood, children actively **cooperate** with one another. This type of play involves a more or less unified group of children playing a particular game, often in which one or two children lead. Children are able to take specific parts in a game, and they have a more mature understanding of what their role is in the group. There are often distinct rules to the game. If you watch a group of five, six-, or seven-year-olds at the park, you may see this type of behavior. Some children act as leaders and allot roles to the others. Sometimes rebellions break out in the ranks, but children's need for one another is obvious.

Much of what we know about the types of play is due to the work of

unoccupied behavior
A type of play in which children sit and look at others or perform simple movements that are not goal related.

solitary or independent play
Play in which the child shows no interest in the activities of others.

onlooker play
A classification of play in which the child watches others play and shows some interest but is unable to join in.

parallel play
A type of play common in two-year-olds in which children play in the presence of other children but not with them.

associative play
A type of play seen in preschoolers in which they are actively involved with one another but cannot sustain these interactions.

cooperative play
A type of play seen in the later part of the preschool period and continuing into middle childhood, marked by group play, playing specific roles, and active cooperation for sustained periods of time.

Mildren Parten (1932). Nearly forty years later, Keith Barnes (1971) sought to replicate this work. He observed forty-two preschoolers playing in a nursery school similar to the one Parten had described. Two findings are of great interest: The developmental trends found in the progression towards more sophisticated and social types of play for children of different ages was affirmed. However, the preschoolers in 1969 were much less socially oriented in their play than were those in Parten's group nearly forty years earlier. We can only guess at the reasons for this second finding. Barnes's study was not a perfect replication, and the differences between the two studies may be responsible. However, it may also be that certain societal changes are responsible. Perhaps the amount of time spent in front of television, the advent of modern toys that are more conducive to solitary play, or the possibility that children receive more parental reinforcement for playing by themselves is responsible for these changes.

Two-year-olds are often involved in parallel play (left) while preschoolers begin interacting with other children in associative play (middle). In middle childhood, children actively cooperate with one another in play (right).

As children develop, the amount of their social play increases, as does their ability to sustain their attention during play, thus allowing for longer interactions (Huff and Lawson, 1990). Whereas parallel play is common in toddlers, by the time a child is five, the child participates more in associative and cooperative play (Harper & Huie, 1985). This does not mean that once a child is showing one type of play, a previous type is completely eliminated from the child's repertoire. Consider the five-year-old boy who is using his blocks to build a city. The boy may play for hours alone. This does not mean that he is incapable of engaging or unwilling to engage in more social types of play, nor does it indicate immaturity (Roer & Hinde, 1978).

Pretend Play

"Let's play house, You be the mommy and I'll be the daddy.") **Pretend** or **dramatic play** is probably the most interesting type of play. It involves taking the roles of others, which requires the ability to imitate and place oneself in the position of another. As discussed in Chapter 9, the latter ability is primitive in preschoolers and develops slowly as children find themselves in different social situations. Preschoolers are essentially

dramatic play (pretend play)
A type of play in which children take on the roles of others.

egocentric, but you can see some attempts at role taking in their dramatic play.

Usually this type of play takes a standard form. Catherine Garvey (1977) observed a number of preschool children at play. Each child was paired with another and allowed to play undisturbed in a room that contained a variety of play materials. Children as young as two and three years of age engaged in some pretend play, often involving mother and infants. Most of the dramatic play centered on common home situations and everyday challenges. However, some involved participation in fantasy, including protecting others from monsters and putting themselves in fairy tales as specific characters. This dramatic play was spontaneous and flexible. The most common pretend play themes are domestic, television or movie figures, and monsters. The sophistication of such play increases with age.

Pretend play can begin as early as toddlerhood. Since children at age two can use symbols, they can show some pretend play (Piaget, 1962). There is a decline but not a disappearance in dramatic play as children enter middle childhood (Johnson & Yawkey, 1988). As children negotiate the early childhood stage, the amount that they talk during pretend play increases (Fenson, 1984). However, language does not replace gestures; it complements them. Pretend play also has some gender differences, with boys referring to buildings and repairing vehicles and girls preparing a meal or caring for babies (Wall, Pickert, & Bigson, 1989). Gender stereotypes enter play, then, rather early.

As children negotiate the preschool stage, they become better capable of distinguishing between fantasy and reality. It is actually possible for three-year-olds to become frightened by their own pretend play. Consider the following three cases:

> A 3-year-old boy pretended to be a monster in order to scare the adult observers who were present. As he began to walk around the playroom making growling sounds, a look of fear came across his face and he broke into tears that could only be stopped by a good deal of comforting from his mother. He said that he was afraid of the monster, yet no one else in the room had given any suggestions of a monster.
>
> A 4-year-old was playing with an adult who pretended to be a monster. The child became frightened but rather than simply crying or stopping the play, he said "abra-ca-dabra" and waved his hands to turn the adult into something else.
>
> A 5-year-old girl, playing monster became frightened. However, she controlled the fantasy without an external ritual or real life emotional reaction. She simply incorporated into the story the transformation of the monster into one who was kind and ate breakfast with his family (apparently, nobody who would eat breakfast with his family could be dangerous or frightening.) (DiLalla and Watson, 1988, p. 286).

The three-year-old could not control his own fantasy, even though by this age children can differentiate between fantasy and reality on some level. For example, children do not eat the plastic shapes they use to symbolize foods. The four-year-old had some, but not much, control over

3. TRUE OR FALSE?

Most young children's pretend play focuses on common household situations and everyday challenges.

the fantasy, using a ritual to control it. The five-year-old achieved control without any emotional reaction or ritual (DiLalla & Watson, 1988).

As children proceed through the preschool stage, they do not require as many concrete props in their pretend play, and they show better control of their fantasies. Their ability to take the position of someone else develops slowly but adds to the sophistication of their pretend play.

Pretend play is important, for children can use it to cope with their problems, to master situations, and to explore the roles of those around them. Pretend play is, then, a very developmentally important phenomenon.

Rough-and-Tumble Play

One type of play that adults observe often with some displeasure is **rough-and-tumble play.** Such behaviors as play fighting, chasing, wrestling, sneaking up on someone, carrying another child, holding, and pushing can fall into this category (Humphreys & Smith, 1987). This type of play accounts for about 11 percent to 15 percent of children's playground behaviors in both preschoolers and schoolage children (Pellegrini, 1988). It is much more common in boys than in girls. Parents and teachers often discourage it, because they are afraid it will get out of control and escalate into real fighting or because they believe that it will teach antisocial or aggressive behavior (Pellegrini & Perlmutter, 1989). Recently, however, there has been a call for greater tolerance for rough-and-tumble play.

rough-and-tumble play
Physical play such as play fighting, chasing and wrestling.

There is research evidence that boys and girls play differently. Boys engage in much more rough-and-tumble play.

Besides providing the obvious practice of physical skills, some claim that it can lead to engagement in cooperative games. If you ever played tag, you probably remember that it was a game that was governed by rules and involved changing roles from being chased to being the chaser. Rough-and-tumble play is also related to boys' social problem solving and popularity. It requires negotiation skills and constant redefinition of a situation (Humphreys & Smith, 1987). In fact, rough-and-tumble play is related to social competence, while aggression is not (Pellegrini, 1987). Children (mostly boys) who engage in rough-and-tumble play are liked and are good social problem solvers, while the opposite is true of children who engage in aggressive behavior.

Aggressive children appear not to be able to discriminate between rough-and-tumble play and aggression, and people often confuse rough-and-tumble play with aggression, although the two differ greatly. Rough-and-tumble play occurs when no dispute is occurring, while aggressive behavior often occurs in the course of disputes, especially those involving property. In rough-and-tumble play, children rotate roles, whereas this is not the case in aggression. When rough-and-tumble play ends, children do not separate, nor do they have angry feelings towards one another. The opposite pattern is found in aggressive behavior (Humphreys & Smith, 1987).

A person might suggest that rough-and-tumble play certainly has benefits and that it differs from aggression, but does it escalate into aggression? Does a child's play fighting turn into the real thing, forcing adult intervention. Studies show that both popular and unpopular children engage in a similar amount of rough-and-tumble play (Coie & Kupersmidt, 1983). However, when popular children engage in this sort of play, the play does not escalate into aggression, whereas such play by unpopular or rejected children often does (Pellegrini, 1988). Why is this so? Unpopular children may not have the social skills to understand the limits of rough-and-tumble play. In addition, unpopular children who are often aggressive may interpret rough-and-tumble play as a provocation eliciting aggressive responses from them (Dodge & Frame, 1982).

Perhaps we should revise our thinking about rough-and-tumble play. Its physical and cognitive benefits are well established. It does not turn into aggression for popular children who have the social skills and knowledge about limits. It may, however, lead to problems for unpopular, often aggressive, children who lack the social skills or knowledge of limits. There are a number of programs that seek to imbue children with the social skills necessary to join in the fun without resorting to aggression.

Gender Differences in Play

As you watch children play, see if you notice any gender differences. Many studies indicate that boys play much more roughly than girls. The difference is also seen in animal studies performed on chimpanzees. When chimps were allowed contact only with their peers, the males were seen to be more aggressive. Since the chimps had been separated from their parents at birth, they could not have learned these patterns from their

4. TRUE OR FALSE?

Children's rough-and-tumble play always turns into aggressive behavior if it is not stopped by an authority figure.

parents, and it would seem that some biological factor—perhaps hormones—must be responsible (Harlow & Harlow, 1966).

Humans also show these gender differences in play. Males are more aggressive and exhibit more rough-and-tumble play. This difference appears in cultures—whether essentially tribal or technologically advanced—around the world (Whiting & Whiting, 1975). We are not talking about variations in activity levels, for preschool girls are almost as active as preschool boys, although girls seldom act aggressively toward one another or engage in rough-and-tumble play.

Gender differences in play are well documented. Janet DiPietro (1981) brought same-sex groups of four-and-a-half-year-old children three at a time into a mobile home from which the furnishings had been removed. A few toys were present, including a beach ball, a small trampoline, and a Bobo doll, a four-foot tall inflatable punching doll. DiPietro noted that the girls organized themselves and made rules. The girls argued, but they did not resort to physical means of persuasion. The boys, however, played in a rougher fashion, often wrestling. They did not seem angry, nor did they attempt to injure one another. They simply played differently.

While some may argue that males are biologically predisposed to these patterns, other explanations are possible. For example, since various societies may expect males to act more aggressively, males may then simply be complying with society's expectations. The possible presence of some biological predisposition does not negate the importance of learned behaviors.

The Benefits of Play

People tend to overlook the contributions play makes to a child's development. The physical benefits of play are the most obvious. Children tossing a ball around are exercising their muscles and improving their eye-hand coordination. Play often involves muscular activity, which is vital for optimal physical development. As they play, children refine their skills and become more secure and self-assured (Isenberg & Quisenberry, 1988).

In the psychosocial realm, play provides practice in socialization and social skills. Play allows children to handle social situations, such as dominance and leadership, and teaches them to share power, space, and ideas (Rubin & Howe, 1986). Play also allows children to express their feelings and work through conflicts. Children can explore new ways of handling conflicts as they suspend reality, switch roles, and control a situation (Johnson & Yawkey, 1988). Role play encourages children to become less egocentric and gives them practice in role taking (Saltz & Johnson, 1974). It also helps children develop a variety of social and group skills. The frequency with which children engage in social pretend play is positively related to teacher ratings of social competence, peer popularity, and social role-taking ability (Connolly & Doyle, 1988). In social play, children also learn to negotiate and resolve conflict (Rubin et al., 1983). (The developmental benefits of rough-and-tumble play in fostering cooperation and physical skills have already been noted.)

5. *TRUE OR FALSE?*

Boys show significantly more rough-and-tumble play than girls.

THE CHILD
IN THE YEAR
2000

In Defense of Play

It is difficult to choose one aspect of a child's life and focus on how that will change in the year 2000. In doing so, I look at the various areas I have written about and try to choose an area that will show a significant change. This chapter has a number of possibilities, including gender roles and child abuse. However, I think the choice will surprise you. The area I have chosen is one that seems to be the least controversial of them all—play—and the question is one that may sound odd. Do children need someone to defend their right to play?

On the surface, it seems ridiculous to have to defend a child's "right to play." After all, isn't that a good part of what children are supposed to be doing? However, Joan Isenberg and Nancy Quisenberry (1988) have written a fascinating article on the subject, declaring that children's right to play is under attack by a growing segment of society that does not seem to understand the importance of play to development and a society that provides less time for play.

Children's play is denigrated and misunderstood. Despite the fact that it is known to play a crucial role in the child's social, cognitive, and physical development, children's right to play is being challenged by a society that wants more structure, more work, and more adult-directed activity, even from young children. Some play time has been absorbed by incessant television viewing. The calls for more academic work at earlier ages also lead to a further reduction in play time. The attitude that many have taken is echoed in the often heard parental statement, "Oh, he's just playing"—a statement indicating that play is not considered an important activity.

The child in the year 2000 will be subjected to greater pressures towards beginning academic work early and will be asked to submit more and more to adult-led activities. It is doubtful, also, that television time will be reduced. The child thus may have less time to play and less opportunity to direct his or her own play. No one can tell what the consequences of such a reduction, if it occurs, will be. But these trends lead to the conclusion that perhaps children's right to play has to be defended by both parents and teachers. It may be time to question our beliefs about childhood-related activities and better understand the function of these activities.

Although children will certainly be playing in the year 2000 and probably in the year 3000, their right to engage in play must be defended. It is a mistake to place so many demands on children that they do not have adequate opportunity to play and garner the many benefits of play. The demands that children grow up fast and master "work" may, indeed, be a threat to a child's right to play. Perhaps in the busy lives of children, it will be necessary in the year 2000 to actively plan free-play periods for children, even young children, and to increase the general public's understanding of the importance of play in a child's development.

In the cognitive realm, play encourages children to improve their planning and problem-solving abilities. It provides a format that allows young children to integrate their experiences into a coherent structure. Preschoolers must learn about what things happen and when, and during pretend play, children figure out the scripts that occur in various situations. While playing, preschoolers practice their newly acquired skills and, using their imagination, assimilate new information into their cognitive structures (Johnson & Yawkey, 1988). Play also promotes creativity and flexibility because it allows children to experiment without fear of consequences.

Many theorists have argued for the importance of play. For Freud, play provided children with an avenue for wish fulfillment and a way to master traumatic events. As children play, they allow their emotions to show and work out their problems. Erikson (1977), in some ways similar to Freud, emphasized the function play has in allowing children to express some of their anger in a safe situation and to master their problems. Play, then, is an outlet for pent-up frustration and anger. Children act out their problems and thereby reduce their anxieties (Erikson, 1959). One four-year-old girl played house with small doll-like figures. At home, this girl had to share the attention of her parents with her baby sister, who naturally required much care. In her play, daddy would come home and, instead of kissing her and going to see the baby, he would say, "I want to play only with you, not that silly baby. I don't care about her." In her play, she was expressing her true feelings. In fact, some psychologists use play situations as therapy to gain deeper insights into the nature of a child's problems (Axline, 1969).

Piaget (1952) looked at play as an activity that encouraged cognitive development and allowed children to exercise their cognitive abilities and practice their newly learned skills. Play allows the child, through the process of assimilation, to incorporate new ideas, objects, or situations into existing ways of thinking. The child expresses behavior in different ways, using abilities that the child already possesses without fear of failure. For others, play is a self-initiated activity that satisfies a child's innate need to explore and master the environment (Berlyne, 1960). Finally, Jerome Bruner (1972) sees play as a vehicle for learning skills that will be useful later in life. In primates, play serves the purpose of allowing an organism to learn particular skills without fearing the unpleasant consequences of failure. Skills can be mastered in a nonthreatening environment and then used to solve problems later in life. Bruner theorizes that an ape's ability to use tools comes from early play experiences. Perhaps when children play with building blocks, they learn something about mechanics, spatial relationships, and tool use that may be helpful at a later time.

There is no doubt, then, that play is an important developmental activity. Play provides important benefits for children in the cognitive, physical, and interpersonal areas. Many of the preschoolers' interpersonal interactions are negotiated in the context of play; and during the preschool years, the child's interpersonal relationships with peers, siblings, and parents change dramatically.

◆ INTERPERSONAL RELATIONSHIPS

The preschooler plays and interacts with many people, including siblings, peers, and parents. In their play, preschoolers are more socially oriented than toddlers and prefer to play with familiar peers (Rubin et al., 1983). As a child's interpersonal world expands in early childhood, peers gain influence. With increasing age, children spend more time with their peers and less with their parents. While the peer group does not have the power it will have during middle childhood and adolescence, it still influences the preschooler. The growth of preschool programs has exposed many more children very early to the social demands of other children. While toddlers show some ability to participate in social activities, it is in early childhood that these activities become closer to what we might call friendship. More sharing and cooperation occurs, and children's play becomes more social, more dramatic, and more sophisticated. The number of children preschoolers play with at one time also increases. Preschoolers are no longer limited to one-on-one situations. Groups of three and four children are not uncommon.

Children's social interactions are affected and limited by their cognitive abilities. The preschoolers' world is more complicated than the toddler's world, and preschoolers must acquire knowledge that allows them to behave appropriately in different situations. For example, a preschooler may not be required to share toys extensively at home, but sharing may be necessary in the day-care or nursery school setting (Small, 1990). A child can be only as social as his or her level of cognitive functioning will allow (Bjorklund, 1989). A child who cannot take the perspective of another may not voluntarily choose to help another child who requires help, whereas a child who can see things from someone else's perspective may choose to share, use praise, or simply help the other child with a problem. Psychologists are very interested in the relationship between cognitive development and social behavior, which is termed **social cognition**. Some of the areas that are currently of prime interest are interpersonal relationships, aggression, prosocial behavior, turn taking, and moral development.

social cognition
The relationship between cognition and both knowledge about and behavior regarding social situations and relationships.

Relations with Peers

Mothers of toddlers sometimes note that their youngsters have "best friends," but the claim is difficult to evaluate. After all, parents choose which youngsters their toddlers will associate with, and children do not have freedom of choice. This situation changes in early childhood, and research shows that children definitely prefer some children to others. Children play with certain children quite often and with some others only once in a while, and they completely ignore still others (Hartup, 1989). In a study in nursery school, about three-quarters of all the children had at least one child with whom they spent at least 30 percent of their free time (Hinde, Tutmus, Easton, & Tamplin, 1985).

The beginning of friendship becomes apparent as preschoolers react in a more positive manner and are more responsive to their friends than to other children. Of course, preschoolers do play with children whom they do not consider friends, and they often use a temporary friendship status as a means of obtaining entry into a group of children playing, claiming that they will be their friend if they can play. Preschool children, then, form both longer term and temporary friendships. Stable friends play in a more complex and responsive manner, while temporary friendships revolve around a shared interest or activity. The evidence points to both stability and change in preschool friendships. While children maintain some friendships over the years, most children regularly experience making new friends and separating from old ones (Howes, 1988).

Preschool friendships tend to be fragile (Corsaro, 1981), and many, but not all, are fleeting. When four-year-olds were asked why they liked their friend, 47 percent mentioned common activities, 43 percent mentioned play, 28 percent mentioned propinquity (just being there), and 25 percent mentioned possessions (Hayes, 1978). When asked why they did not like some children, 46 percent mentioned aggression, 32 percent deviant behavior, and 28 percent mentioned violation of particular rules.

The main factors in preschool friendships are physical characteristics and transitory play (Selman, 1981). The qualification for friendship is simply being physically present and willing to play (Rubin, 1980). Friendships often form and disintegrate quickly, and friendships are not based upon any real intimacy. The goal of young children's friendship and peer interaction generally is play (Gottman & Mettetal, 1986).

Young children describe a friend as someone who is rewarding to be with, whereas older children describe friends in terms of empathy and understanding (Bigelow & LaGaipa, 1975). Young children describe a friend as someone who participates in shared activities, whereas older children describe a friend as someone who can be intimate and trusted (Berndt, 1978). Young children consider a friend as someone they can share things with, while older children emphasize sharing thoughts and feelings (Youniss & Volpe, 1978). For the preschooler, then, a friend is a playmate. The great concern of friendship is "maximizing the level of enjoyment, entertainment and satisfaction experienced in their play" (Parker & Gottman, 1989, p. 104).

For preschoolers, the qualification for friendship is simply being physically present and willing to play.

A preschooler who is to develop a friendship with another child must be a good playmate, and this depends upon the level of coordination the children can achieve. Coordination can be thought of as the amount of interdependence in the children's play that the children can realize or the extent to which children fit their separate actions together to produce a joint activity or discussion (Parker & Gottman, 1989). If two children are having some conversation while coloring side by side, the level of coordination required is minimal. If they jointly color a picture, though, their level of coordination increases greatly. If, while they are coloring together or drawing lions, they let out a roar together, even more coordination is occurring. The highest level of coordination is required in fantasy play with another child. Fantasy play has the highest potential for reward and enjoyment but also the highest potential for conflict.

Some preschoolers form friendships easily, while others have difficulties. Those children who form friendships easily have superior social skills, including the ability to say something relevant to the interaction and direct it properly to other children as well as respond appropriately (Hazan & Black, 1989). Communication skills are basic to social interaction and influence peer acceptance. Children who do not form friendships use stronger tactics, including aggression, to settle their conflicts than do those who form friendships easily (Gottman, 1983).

One tendency that begins in early childhood and that will become commonplace in middle childhood is having mostly same-sex friends (Lewis & Feiring, 1989). One survey showed that about 36 percent of all best friendships cut across gender among three- and four-year-olds, but this drops to 23 percent for five- and six-year-olds and becomes nonexistent for seven- to eight-year-olds (Rickelman in Gottman, 1986). There are many possible reasons for this change. Perhaps children see same-sex children as more compatible in their play. That is, boys may be aware that other boys will allow them to use rough-and-tumble play. Perhaps same-sex children see each other as more similar, or perhaps adults reinforce children for playing with other children of the same sex. The development of gender role stereotypes may also be a factor (Gottman, 1986). Another possibility is that girls find it difficult to influence boys. As children negotiate early childhood, there is an increase in their attempts to influence one another. Girls make polite suggestions, whereas boys use more direct demands. Boys are becoming less responsive to polite suggestions. Girls' style of influence, then, is more effective with other girls than with boys. Eleanor Maccoby (1990) argues that girls find it troubling to interact with someone who is unresponsive and begin to avoid such partners. Although less is known about boys' avoidance of girls, it appears to become even stronger during this stage. It may be a function of the different types of games and play styles. For whatever reason, as children get older, they play more with children of their own sex and less with children of the opposite sex.

Prosocial Behavior

If you observe preschoolers at play, you will notice that sometimes they share and help while at other times they flatly refuse to do so. Psychologists are interested in behaviors that help others, called **prosocial behaviors.** These behaviors include sharing, helping others in need, and empathizing with others. A specific type of prosocial behavior, called **altruism,** involves actions that help people that are internally motivated and for which no reward is expected. Generally, older children show more prosocial behavior than younger children.

Preschoolers infrequently share, help, and comfort others (Eisenbergberg & Hand, 1979). Preschoolers are much more likely to refuse requests from peers than from adults (Eisenberg, Wolchik, Hernandez, & Pasternack, 1985). When they conform to a request from an adult, they usually cite authority as their justification. In other words, they feel they are obeying an adult. Although peers make more requests for help, compliance with adults is much more common. Altruistic behavior is rare, and more than 80 percent of all helping behaviors are due to compliance or a request for help from someone else. Only about 20 percent of all helping behaviors are self-initiated. Yet nearly two-thirds of all preschoolers perform such self-initiated behavior at some time or another. In other words, preschoolers are indeed capable of self-initiated helping behavior, but they do not do it very often (Stockdale, Hegland, & Chiaromonte, 1989).

Prosocial behavior increases with age, perhaps because older children are more adept at taking the perspective of other children. Older children are much more likely to help or share when there is no reward or adult pressure to do so. When they do, they justify their behavior on altruistic grounds. They are also better able to assist in an appropriate manner.

prosocial behaviors
Voluntary actions that are intended to help or benefit another individual or group.

altruism
A type of prosocial behavior that involves actions that help people, that are internally motivated and for which no reward is expected.

6. TRUE OR FALSE?

Preschoolers share less and help other children less than children in middle childhood do.

Conflict

Most of a preschooler's interactions with others are positive (Hartup, 1970). Fewer arguments occur than one might think. Most preschool conflicts are relatively brief (Shantz, 1987). Preschool conflicts fit neatly into three categories. First, and most common, are those that involve conflicts over possessions (Lauresen & Hartup, 1989). One child wants a toy that the other is playing with at the time (Shantz & Hobart, 1989). The second most common are conflicts over another child's actions or lack of action, as when a child acts the wrong part while playing or refuses to take on a role assigned to him or her. The third category involves factual disputes, which really comprise only about 15 percent or less of these conflicts. By about four and a half to five years of age, disputes in the first two categories are occurring at about equal rates (Shantz, 1987).

The most common way of solving conflicts during this period is insistence (Eisenberg & Garvey, 1981). This strategy tends to keep the conflict going. It is most likely to end when one child surrenders the toy to the other. The second most common strategy is simply to explain why the child should give up the toy. Other strategies, such as suggesting alternatives and compromise, are not used very often, even though they are more likely to end the conflict. Most conflicts are settled without adult interference. In most conflicts, there is one definite winner and one definite loser.

The conflicts between friends and nonfriends are different in some ways but not in others. They do not differ in length or in cause or in the use of aggression. However, conflicts among friends are more likely to

7. TRUE OR FALSE?

Most preschool conflicts are settled through negotiation and compromise.

Many people believe that siblings argue and fight more than they help each other. However, the evidence shows that siblings play together quite a bit and help each other as well.

end through negotiation and disengagement than are conflicts among non-friends. They are less intense and more frequently result in equal or at least partially equal outcomes. Friends are also more likely to continue to socialize following a conflict than are nonfriends (Hartup, Lauresen, Stewart, & Eastenson, 1988). Boys have more conflicts than girls do (Schantz, 1986).

Aggression among small children is always a concern. In about a quarter of the conflicts, verbal and/or physical aggression is used (Hay & Ross, 1982), but this percentage decreases with age. Aggression itself decreases with age. To understand the developmental nature of aggression, Willard Hartup (1974) divided aggressive behaviors into two categories. Instrumental aggression involves struggles over possessions. It is not personal, and its aim is to secure an item. Hostile aggression, on the other hand, is person oriented. This aggression is aimed at injuring the other party. Most young children act aggressively to wrench a toy from another child or to gain space (Hay & Ross, 1982). The finding that aggression decreases with age is probably due to the striking decrease in instrumental aggression. As children mature, verbal alternatives replace physical means of getting something (Parke & Slaby, 1983). Physical aggression, such as hitting, decrease after the third year, whereas verbal aggression increases between ages two and four (Cummings, Iannotti, & Zahn-Waxler, 1989).

However, some preschoolers are clearly more aggressive than others, and aggression itself is a fairly stable characteristic, even in early childhood (Cummings, Iannotti, & Zahn-Waxler, 1989; Olweus, 1979). In other words, aggressive children in early childhood tend to become aggressive children in middle childhood.

Improving Preschool Skills

Concern for preschoolers' social skills is growing. Studies show that peer rejection and aggression in childhood are stable and strongly predict negative outcomes (Parker & Asher, 1987). Good social skills are related to peer acceptance and peaceful interpersonal interactions, and it is clear that distinctions can be drawn in social competence even during the preschool years. Even at this young age, some children are plainly more accepted and popular than others, and these popular children have better social skills. Those preschoolers who do not have good social skills tend to be rejected, and difficulties in social interaction persist into elementary school (Ladd & Price, 1987).

Can anything be done to alter this pattern? Although social skills training is more common in the elementary school years, many preschools emphasize social skills, and some training programs have been advanced. In one program, children with few friends and poor social skills were given training in a number of social skills. This training included the use of puppets to play act different scenarios, with the children later being asked to play act with the puppets and then in play situations with other children. The results showed that these children improved some of their social skills, especially the ability to make positive or neutral suggestions and comments.

A number of general suggestions for improving children's social skills have been made that may be helpful to parents and teachers. They include providing positive feedback when children do perform prosocial behaviors, providing opportunities for children to help one another, and teaching conflict resolution skills, including taking turns, apologizing, compromising, and talking through problems. In addition, reading stories that emphasize helping others may influence children to help people (Morrison, 1988).

Siblings

"My children fight like cats and dogs," a mother of two active boys told me one night. She had come for counseling because she could no longer take the noise, the bickering, the constant fighting. She and her husband had just broken up some "vicious" verbal exchanges, and peace seemed unobtainable.

Do you remember the arguments you had with your siblings? Can you remember the times you depended on them for advice and assistance? The very presence of siblings affects a child's development. Unlike friends, siblings do not leave your home at night. You can limit your contact with them, but you cannot totally avoid them. They compete for parental attention, and their joy and pain affect everyone in the household.

SIBLING SUPPORT More than 80 percent of American children have one or more siblings (Eisenberg & Mussen, 1989), and by the time a child enters kindergarten, he or she has spent twice as much time in the company of siblings as with parents (Bank & Kahn, 1975). In fact, by their first birthday, children have spent almost as much time with their siblings as with their mothers and far more time with siblings than with their fathers (Dunn, 1983). It stands to reason that sibling relationships are important.

Younger children often imitate their older siblings (Pepler, Corter, & Abramovitch, 1982). Sometimes you will see an older child playing with a toy, then leaving it, and a younger sibling imitating the play. The older child is performing what is really a teaching function. The child is a role model for the younger child.

Discussions of siblings usually revolve around sibling rivalry, but psychologists have noted that siblings encourage prosocial actions and fill definite psychological needs. Not only do siblings play together and experience one another's joy and pain firsthand, but they often help one another (Brody, Zolinda, MacKinnon, & MacKinnon, 1985). They can sometimes provide the support and affection that may not be forthcoming from the parents (Dunn & Kendrick, 1982). Preschool children may also act as substitute attachment figures for their younger siblings in the presence of a stranger (Stewart, 1983).

In a series of studies, Rona Abramovitch and colleagues (1979, 1980, 1986) followed siblings as they matured, starting when the younger siblings were one and a half years old and the older siblings were preschoolers to a time when the younger ones were five years old and the older ones were in middle childhood. As the children matured, a common pattern became apparent. The older children initiated more prosocial and combative behaviors, and the young children imitated more. The older siblings clearly dominated the younger ones. Although the distinctions lessened over time, birth order rather than age seemed to be the cause of the domination. And in spite of antagonism, prosocial and play-oriented behaviors constituted a majority of the children's interactions.

Abramovitch asserts that it is incorrect to think of sibling relationships as primarily combative or negative. Positive social interactions increase significantly as children age and siblings can cooperate in game behaviors. In addition, even children as young as three years of age can show distress for their younger siblings (Dunn, 1983). Friendly sibling relationships are associated with the ability to take the perspective of the other person (Howe & Ross, 1990). Sibling relationships are more likely to be pleasant when mothers discuss with an older child how the younger child feels (Howe & Ross, 1990). Preschool children whose mothers discuss the care of a newborn baby and encouraged efforts at such care show more prosocial behavior with their younger siblings (Dunn & Kendrick, 1982). Temperamental differences also seem to affect sibling relationships (Stocker, Dunn, & Plomin, 1989). Children who are highly active and emotionally intense experience more conflict (Brody, Stoneman & Burke, 1987). In addition, more conflict and less friendly relationships are reported in families in which mothers give one child more attention and affection or are more responsive to one child's wishes (Brody, Stoneman, MacKinnon & MacKinnon, 1985). Indeed, many mothers are more affectionate and responsive toward the one child. First-born children get more attention when they are alone with their mothers but are more neglected when the younger sibling is present (Dunn, 1983).

SIBLING ARGUMENTS Siblings bring both joy and pain to one another, and sibling conflict is inevitable. However, arguments disturb the harmony of the house. Should parents intervene in sibling arguments? Let's say a parent stops the older child from picking on the younger. The older child is apt to complain, "You always take his side." On the other hand, if a parent lets it go, the younger one may complain that the parent really doesn't care.

Not all sibling arguments should be lumped together. Sibling quarrels can be classified into three categories (Acus, 1982). Nuisance quarrels start when children are bored or in a bad mood. They are noisy and begin over nothing at all. They end quickly, usually cause no damage, and are forgotten as fast as they start. Parents can't follow them, and trying to get to the bottom of one of these quarrels is next to impossible. A second type, called verbal debate quarrels, can be constructive. This type of quarrel involves rational disagreements that, although loud and strident at times, can serve as training in debating and assertiveness techniques. Each sibling forcefully gives an opinion, although most siblings will not be budged from their opening position. If the two siblings begin viciously attacking each other, however, this type of quarrel can easily turn into the third kind—the destructive quarrel. The destructive quarrel can cause

8. TRUE OR FALSE?

Siblings are more likely to fight than to play with each other.

physical or emotional damage to at least one of the participants. If the quarrel is physical, the smaller child is likely to be hurt. If it is verbal, it often entails picking on the weakest point in a child's armor.

Parents frequently intervene in quarrels between young children, especially when one child is very young. The intervention is also determined partly by the child's gender. In one study of preschoolers with infant siblings, mothers responded more consistently to aggression by a male toddler than aggression by a female toddler. Perhaps mothers have an idea of the level of aggression to accept in their sons but not in their daughters (Kendrick & Dunn, 1983).

As children mature, parents intervene less, and many parents do not know when or whether they should step in. Two considerations should guide parents in this decision. First, if a child might suffer any physical damage, a parent must intervene. One parent was proud that she never intervened in sibling arguments no matter how serious they became. "They have to work out their own problems," she noted. But she changed her tune after the older brother "accidentally" pushed his sister down a flight of steps, breaking the girl's leg. Anyone could see that this was coming. Unable to keep up verbally with his sister, the boy resorted to physical means of persuasion. Children must be taught how to use other means besides physical violence to settle disputes.

The second consideration is more subtle. When siblings argue, they often resort to verbal abuse and name calling. This can become serious if one child picks on some physical or intellectual deficit of the other. For instance, one child who suffered from a learning disability was constantly subjected to abuse that focused on the problem. The child was sensitive about his lagging progress, and his older brother knew he could always upset the younger boy by referring to the problem. The parents took a sound approach. Realizing that this was injuring the child emotionally, they told the offending older brother in absolute terms that he could not resort to such tactics. They used the analogy of a prizefight. There are rules, and one of them is no hitting below the belt. He was free to call his brother names, but he had to steer clear of the problem area.

Some may argue that a child with a learning disability must learn to cope with this kind of taunting. Parents have little control over such statements in the outside world, but in the home they do. Children will receive enough hurt from peers; they need not be confronted with it at home.

Competition or rivalry between children can be intense. It is probably impossible to eliminate sibling jealousy and rivalry, but it can be reduced. Some parents encourage rivalry without knowing it. For instance, they may compare their children. By doing this, they are setting up a contest and increasing sibling rivalry. Parents can also become more sensitive to their children's statements and actions that might demonstrate rivalry and reduce such rivalry by playing up each child's strengths. Encouraging competition between children is undesirable. In one case, a parent promised to give the child with the best report card a moped. Two of the children actively joined in the competition, sometimes disturbing the other on purpose and doing nothing to help each other. The third sibling did not feel able to compete and simply gave up. This child's marks were quite low. The contest caused sibling rivalry to increase greatly.

◆ PARENTS AND PRESCHOOLERS

Peers and siblings are influential to some degree, but parents still have the greatest influence on a child's social and personality development. However, the preschooler's relationship with his or her parents is different from what it was during the toddler stage.

New Competencies

Preschoolers are more verbal and have a greater attention span and a better memory than toddlers. They can engage in simple craft work and participate in storytelling. As preschoolers achieve more independence, their relationship with their parents changes. Parents are now faced with a number of decisions. First, with maturity comes a decrease in dependency and an expanding social world. Second, parents are faced with the questions of discipline and punishment.

Dependency and Increased Independence

Preschoolers engage in less holding on to parents and less tugging and pulling. The preschooler still requires physical contact but does not seek it as often. Nor does the preschooler demand all of mother's attention. Dependent behaviors that are tolerated in a toddler may now be annoying. Parents expect preschoolers to do more on their own and to attain some measure of independence. They also expect their children to develop some control over their actions, especially their aggressive responses (Mills & Rubin, 1990). Children who do not do this may find their behavior rejected by their parents.

The constantly clinging four-year-old may draw criticism from a parent who may have to carry a younger child as well. The more the child wants to be close, the more some parents may reject such behavior. The parent pushes the child away, not wanting to reinforce dependence. But this strategy has the opposite effect and is based on the mistaken notion that dependency in preschoolers is related to dependency in adulthood. It is not. In addition, if children are frustrated in their attempts to obtain nurturance and warmth, their dependent behavior increases as they try to satisfy their needs. On the other hand, children who receive consistent nurturance feel safe and protected. They venture forth, knowing they have a secure base.

Increased Expectations

Some parents expect their children to exhibit more mature behavior at an earlier age than do other parents. Parents approve of the use of more authoritarian means of discipline when they are convinced that the child can understand the rules and act appropriately (Dix, Rible, & Zambarano,

1989). What if a two-year-old breaks a figurine that was sitting on the coffee table? The parent who does not believe that the child understood or is responsible for the behavior will react with disappointment, perhaps even annoyance, yet with understanding. However, the parent who believes the child does or should understand is more likely to yell at or punish the child. Most parents believe that preschoolers can control their actions, at least to some degree, so a sterner type of discipline is seen in these years than in the toddler years.

The Effects of Parenting Style

Parents differ in the way they control their children's behavior. Some exercise a great deal of direct control; others believe that having fewer rules is better. The effects of differing parenting styles were investigated by Diana Baumrind (1967, 1971, 1978, 1980), who isolated three different parenting styles.

Authoritarian parents try to control their children's conduct by establishing rigid rules and regulations. Obedience is greatly valued, and the threat of force is used to correct behavior. Parents' decisions cannot be questioned. The authoritarian parent's word is law. Such parents want to shape, control, and evaluate behaviors in accordance with an absolute standard. Because they value obedience, they favor punitive disciplinary measures. They do not want verbal give-and-take and believe children should accept a parent's word.

authoritarian parenting
A style of parenting in which parents rigidly control their children's behavior by establishing rules and value obedience while discouraging questioning.

Permissive parents make few demands on their children. They are nonpunishing, are open to communication, and do not attempt to shape their children's behavior. Permissive parents are less controlling, and when necessary, they use reason rather than power to control their children. They behave in a nonpunitive, accepting manner towards their children's impulses. They make few demands. They are a resource to be used according to their children's desires, not as active agents involved in their children's behavior. The children regulate their own activities, and the parents avoid exercising control over their children. Such parents do not use overt power.

permissive parenting
A style of parenting marked by open communication and a lack of parental demand for good behavior.

Authoritative parents encourage verbal give-and-take and explain the reasons behind a family policy. Both autonomy and discipline are valued. Limits are set, but the child's individuality is taken into consideration. The parents are warm and do not see themselves as infallible (Baumrind, 1971). Such parents encourage verbal give-and-take and share their reasoning behind their policies. They exercise firm control but allow developmentally appropriate freedom. They demand their children contribute to the family through household tasks. They state their values clearly and expect much. They are responsive, supportive, and respectful of their children's interests.

authoritative parenting
A style of parenting in which parents establish limits but allow open communication and some freedom for children to make their own decisions in certain areas.

As a group, the children of authoritative parents are the most self-reliant, self-controlled, explorative, and contented. The children of permissive parents are least self-reliant, explorative, and self-controlled. The children of authoritarian parents are the most discontented, withdrawn, and distrustful. Authoritative parents combine firm control, encouragement of individuality, and open communication, producing children who

Authoritarian parents tell their children what to do and allow no questioning.

9. TRUE OR FALSE?

Children of parents who allow their children maximum freedom with few, if any, restrictions are usually self-reliant and show excellent self-control.

are independent and competent. They are also warmer and more nurturant than authoritarian parents. Some permissive parents are warm, while others show a coolness and detachment toward their children.

Baumrind (1989) emphasizes the importance of two dimensions of parenting: demandingness and parental responsiveness. Authoritative parents are certainly demanding, but they are also warm, rational, and receptive to the child's communication. This combination of high demandingness and positive encouragement of the child's independent striving is best. Authoritarian parents are very controlling but are less warm and responsive to their children, while permissive parents are noncontrolling and nondemanding but relatively warm. Children raised by permissive parents tend to be immature. Parental control does not interfere with independence as long as children are given an opportunity to develop their own abilities and make their own decisions—within limits. Yet the total parental control that authoritarian parents use produces children who are less competent, less contented, and suspicious. Warmth and discipline are the keys to producing independent, competent children.

◆ CHILD REARING

There is a definite relationship between how parents say they discipline their children and what they really do (Kochanska, Kuczynski, & Radke-Yarrow, 1989). Parents who agree with an authoritarian type of discipline do, indeed, use direct commands, physical punishment, and reprimands. There are, however, cultural differences in how parents discipline their children, as the Cross-Cultural Current on page 412 demonstrates.

Discipline and Punishment

For many families, punishment is synonymous with discipline, but there are important differences. **Discipline** involves the control of others for the purpose of holding undesirable impulses or habits in check and encouraging self-control. It may include reasoning and positive reinforcement for the correct behavior. Discipline also occurs *before* the infringement. **Punishment** is a process by which an undesirable behavior is followed by a negative consequence. It is administered after the damage is done and is always negative. Its purpose is to decrease or completely eliminate a behavior in a particular circumstance. Most behaviors are correct in one instance but not in another. Whereas hitting another child to get a toy is unacceptable, defending oneself when being hit by another child is acceptable. Punishment may teach a child what not to do, but it does not provide any instruction in what the child should do under particular circumstances.

discipline
An attempt to control others in order to hold undesirable impulses in check and to encourage self-control.

punishment
The process by which some aversive consequence is administered to reduce the probability that misbehavior will recur.

Discipline Style

Parents' attempts to control their children's behavior can be placed under two headings. **Power-assertive discipline** involves physical punishment, yelling, shouting, and forceful commands, while **love-oriented discipline** includes praise, affection, reasoning and showing disappointment (Maccoby & Martin, 1983). Authoritarian parents use power-assertive discipline; authoritative parents use both power-assertive and love-oriented discipline. Permissive parents use very little discipline, but when discipline is necessary, they use reasoning—a love-oriented approach.

These discipline styles interact with the emotional tone of the parent-child relationship. When restrictiveness occurs within a context of warmth and acceptance, it can lead to obedience, nonaggressiveness, and other positive outcomes. When it occurs in the presence of hostility, it leads to withdrawal and anxiety (Becker, 1964). When investigating techniques of discipline, both the type of approach (power-assertive or love-oriented) and the emotional tone of the relationship (warm or hostile) must be considered.

Disciplinary style may have a direct influence on children's approaches to resolving conflicts with their peers. Mothers who rely on power-assertive discipline have children who are less accepted by peers. These children believe that aggression and intimidation, such as threatening to hit another child, are likely to lead to successful outcomes (Hart, Ladd, & Burleson, 1990).

power-assertive discipline
A type of discipline relying on the use of power, such as physical punishment or forceful commands.

love-oriented discipline
A type of discipline relying on the use of reasoning or love.

Discipline and Verbal Abilities

Preschoolers can get into more trouble than infants or toddlers because their physical abilities are greater, but their ability to use language gives their parents more options in dealing with their misbehavior. As children mature, they respond to a more rational approach. In a study of one-and-a-half-, two-and-a-half-, and and three-and-a-half-year-olds, toddlers re-

Gaining Compliance from Children in Japan and the United States

Most parents have rules and specific ideas about how they would like their children to behave. Parents want their children to comply with their rules and to begin to regulate their own actions.

Research in the United States has identified a number of child-rearing practices that lead to compliance. These include the use of reasoning and persuasion; establishing and maintaining a warm, supportive, and responsive relationship with the children; and the infrequent use of external rewards, punishments, and unexplained prohibitions. The question asked by Hiroko Kobayashi-Winata and Thomas G. Power is whether these same child-rearing variables lead to child compliance in other cultures—in this case, Japan.

The researchers were interested in whether differences in child compliance result from different child-rearing styles. They reasoned that compliance with parental authority was even more important in Japanese society than in American society. Studies have shown that Japanese parents place a great deal of emphasis on respect for authority and compliance and are taught to include others in their decisions. Japanese mothers use more reasoning and persuasion than American mothers and are less likely to resort to direct appeals to power and authority or to external punishments. They also develop a very supportive and responsive relationship with their children. This pattern is called amae. It connotes interdependence and indulgence, and it encourages a strong sense of dependence on others. The Japanese child strives to know what pleases mother and behaves in that manner.

Although American parents form warm relationships with their children, there is the lingering cultural belief among Americans that children are easily spoiled, and American parents greatly value independence. Studies in the United States show that American children are more likely to resist mothers' demands, and American mothers are more likely to use orders to gain compliance from their children.

This does not mean that American parents do not value compliance. They surely do. However, Americans also value and emphasize independence and personal freedom. In American culture, there is always a balance between individual and group needs, and American parents often believe that children must learn to balance their own needs with the needs of others.

It is difficult to compare parents and children living in vastly different cultures, so the researchers chose twenty Japanese families living temporarily in America and compared them to eighteen American families. The children ranged in age from four through seven years. Mothers and fathers were interviewed in their native language and completed several questionnaires. Parents were asked about the types of child behaviors that they were currently encouraging and discouraging in the areas of self-care skills, household responsibilities, manners and politeness, prosocial behavior, household rules, and other aspects of the child-parent relationship. The children's teachers were also surveyed.

The results demonstrated that child-rearing correlates of compliance were the same for both cultural groups. Reliance on punishment and physical intervention were negatively associated with compliance, while providing opportunities for appropriate behavior was positively related to compliance. The use of reasoning strategies and a warm relationship were related to compliance in each culture.

There were important differences in child-rearing prac-

sponded better to simple commands than to suggestions or questions, whereas preschoolers responded more to suggestions (McLaughlin, 1983). Parents who realize that their preschooler's verbal abilities give them more options are likely to change their discipline strategy and use more complicated verbal techniques instead of mere commands.

Each of the three parenting styles uses discipline in a different way, resulting in different outcomes. Authoritarian parents rely on punish-

tices, though Japanese parents were less likely to report the use of external punishments, such as being sent to one's room, or the use of physical punishment. American parents were more likely to report using praise, and Japanese parents were more likely to report repeating commands and scolding their child. Japanese parents relied mostly on verbal commands, reprimands, and explanations to achieve child compliance, while American parents were more likely to report supplementing these techniques with external punishments and practices. What is most interesting is that the longer the Japanese parents lived in America, the less they reported using verbal techniques to achieve compliance and the greater their use of external punishments.

The researchers argue that these findings reflect broad differences between the cultures. Because of the emphasis on independence and individuality in our culture, American parents may feel it necessary to use powerful, external techniques to ensure compliance because in their child rearing, they may also need to encourage independence and nonconformity. For the Japanese parent, reliance on verbal means is more important because the Japanese hold a different view of individual and group needs. The Japanese see individual needs as achieved through cooperation and dependence on others, and verbal techniques are effective ways of convincing children that compliance is in everyone's best interests.

Both parents and teachers rated American children as more verbally assertive than Japanese children, although teachers viewed the children as equally compliant. As expected, parental correlations for amae were significant only for Japanese families fostering dependent behavior. One of the most interesting findings, though, was that American parents viewed assertiveness and compliance as positively related and believed that both indicated good behavior, while Japanese parents did not. Japanese parents viewed assertiveness as a characteristic of a poorly behaved child. The longer the Japanese parents were in America, the more verbally assertive their children were rated by teachers and the less compliant and emotionally mature they were rated by their fathers. As Japanese children remain in America, they become more assertive and less compliant, and paternal disapproval of this behavior increases.

There is an alternative explanation that should be noted. The use of coercive control techniques was negatively correlated with compliance in both cultures. In other words, the less compliant the child was, the more likely the parents were to use external punishments. It is possible that parents of poorly behaved or difficult children, regardless of culture, are forced to use coercive techniques to control their children. As Japanese children become more assertive and noncompliant, parents may be forced to use more coercive techniques.

The results of this study show that the same types of child-rearing strategies yield compliance in both cultures. However, each culture looks at assertiveness in different ways. American parents and teachers approve of verbal assertiveness and do not see it as misbehavior, whereas Japanese parents view assertiveness as misbehavior. The standards for misbehavior may differ somewhat in different cultures. What we may interpret as good behavior and poor behavior may partially be culturally determined, and child-rearing strategies may be directed at producing what that culture considers a well-behaved child. Last, consider the Japanese parent and child in America surrounded by a culture that values individuality and, sometimes, nonconformity and does not emphasize dependence on others as much. The longer the child remains in the United States, the more likely that some of this individuality and assertiveness will be learned by the child, and this may cause some difficulty with parents who may value a different type of behavior. It remains for other studies to discover how this possible conflict is worked out.

Source: Kobayashi-Winata, H., and Power, T. G., Child Rearing and Compliance: Japanese and American Families in Houston. *Journal of Cross-Cultural Psychology*, 1989, 10, 333–356.

ment, which forces obedience in the short term and rebellion in the long term. Permissive parents rarely use any type of discipline, and this sometimes results in a child without direction. Authoritative parents use both approaches, depending on the situation, but they encourage independence by allowing their children freedom within limits. Perhaps authoritative parents notice the change in a child's verbal and physical abilities and tailor the discipline to the emerging abilities of the child.

Punishment: Uses and Abuses

Psychologists recognize that there is a need for punishment under certain circumstances, but they are concerned about the type of punishment used and the way it is administered. Punishment can be administered in two ways (Karen, 1974). First, a positive reinforcer may be removed. A parent may remove a toy or turn off the television set to punish a misbehaving child. The second procedure involves following the undesirable action with an aversive action. A child who whines may be yelled at or spanked.

While punishment can be effective in decreasing the frequency of an undesirable behavior, it is often administered incorrectly and fails in its purpose. It is overused by some parents, who rarely if ever compliment their children but are always ready with a criticism, and even the strap. To be effective, punishment should be moderate, swift, sure, and combined with rewards for the correct behavior (Altrocchi, 1980). Unfortunately, parents often delay punishment, are inconsistent, use overly severe punishment, and constantly threaten their children—practices that are ineffective over the longer term.

The Effects of Harsh Punishment

Some parents are proud that they are severe disciplinarians and do not spare the rod. They claim success and have difficulty understanding parents who don't use as much punishment. To the casual observer, the harshly disciplined child may seem well behaved, but a deeper look reveals a different picture.

Harsh punishment is effective in temporarily decreasing the undesirable behavior, but over the long term, it is less successful and even damaging (Martin, 1975). Children may correct their behavior temporarily, especially in the presence of the feared parent, but their frustration and anger builds up and eventually explodes. Such children may be sullen and suspicious of authority. Many children who are problems in school are harshly disciplined at home (Martin, 1975). Thus, the stereotype that the problem child in school is rarely disciplined at home may not be accurate.

Child Rearing by the Book

Hundreds of books have been written on how to raise your child, but one wonders how many are based upon psychological research and not on "common sense." Child-rearing advice has been subject to fits, fads, and changes, some of them dramatic. For example, looking at the history of the well-known government publication *Infant Care* we see such changes. In the 1920s, thumb sucking and masturbation were thought so dangerous that as late as 1938, parents were told to use a steel cuff to prevent the baby from bending its arm. By 1942, parents were told that they need not worry and that these activities were harmless (see Christopherson, 1988). There are some practices, though, that research has shown to be more effective and successful than others, and these can be translated into some guidelines.

PREVENTING PROBLEMS Preventing problems is often easier than reacting to them, and studies show that many problems can be prevented. For example, if parents keep their children in conversation or ask them to help them while the parent performs some chore, children show less misbehavior than if the parent waits for misbehavior to occur and then responds (Holden & West, 1989). Preventing such problems requires parents to become aware of the situations in which problems are more likely to occur and do something to prevent them.

EXPLAINING THE REASONS BEHIND A RULE Many parents become upset when a child challenges their rules by asking "Why?" and end the discussion with "Because I said so." This is a counterproductive way of handling the challenge. If parents have a rule, they must have a reason behind it, and explaining the reason is best. Children who understand the rule are more likely to support it and use the reasoning in other similar situations. However, parents should not expect their children to agree with their reasoning.

COMMUNICATING Authoritative parents expect good behavior and provide rules but also are willing to listen to their children and sometimes modify the rules if necessary. A rule concerning bedtime may be modified if the reason is deemed sound. Authoritative parents are also more sensitive to the needs of their children.

ALLOWING CHILDREN TO EXPRESS THEIR EMOTIONS Children can be allowed to express their emotions in a socially acceptable manner. What would be your reply to your five-year-old who said to you, "I hate Aunt Betsy"? Some parents might make the child feel guilty by telling the child how nice Aunt Betsy is. Other parents might become angry at the child's statement and tell the child that he or she has no right to feel that way. The better way is simply to ask the child why he or she feels that way about Aunt Betsy. First, children must learn to express their emotions in a socially appropriate manner. Second, no one needs special permission to feel a particular way.

That does not give the child the right, however, to act in any way he or she deems desirable. The child may discuss the fact that Aunt Betsy pinches his cheeks, and you may want to ask Aunt Betsy to stop doing it. However, this does not give the child the right to kick Aunt Betsy in the shins. While children must be allowed to learn to express themselves in a socially appropriate manner, their freedom of action must be curbed.

AVOIDING INCORRECT PUNISHMENT Parents should be aware of using punishment incorrectly. Punishment may sometimes be necessary. However, the effects of a poorly administered punishment can linger for some time. Parents often rely too heavily on punishment and do not reinforce their children with praise and attention for good behavior. Since the aim of punishment is to decrease or eliminate an undesirable behavior, the child must know which behaviors are acceptable and which are not. The punishment should be just severe enough to be effective but not overly severe, certain, and combined with positive reinforcement for the correct response.

DISCIPLINING THE CHILD'S ACTIONS—NOT THE CHILD Some parents make statements concerning how bad the child is, which focuses on the child rather than on the child's inappropriate behavior. Punishment should be aimed at reducing or eliminating the troublesome behavior, not at injuring the child's self-esteem.

MODELING Parents are models. The type of discipline parents use affects the child's relationships with others, since children model their behavior, to some extent, from what they see.

ALLOWING CHILDREN FREEDOM A child should be allowed as much freedom as developmentally appropriate but be guided by safety and respect for others. Children need the freedom to make mistakes and even to fail. However, a child's freedom should always be guided by both safety considerations and an understanding of how the child's behavior may affect others. For example, the child may want to try to color a picture using one technique and refuse to follow the parents' suggestions. This may be the child's right. However, the child does not have the right to take a crayon that his sister is using without first asking (Christopherson, 1988).

PROVIDING A POSITIVE ATMOSPHERE A positive atmosphere that encourages prosocial development is helpful. Doing things for others and sharing as well as using positive reinforcement should be the norm. Helping children share and giving them age-related responsibilities at an early age also helps.

These certainly do not make up an exhaustive list. However, as you see, the literature does not give much support to a totally hands-off attitude, nor does it support an overbearing "I am the law" attitude. Rather, it advances a middle ground consisting of firmness with reason, flexibility with demandingness, and sensitivity.

◆ CHILD ABUSE

Sometimes punishment goes beyond the point of reason and leads to abuse. In fact, about two-thirds of the incidents of child abuse can be related to parental attempts to discipline or control their children's behavior (Gil, 1970). Most people would like to think of child abuse in terms of mental illness, but although parents who abuse their children suffer from a number of psychological problems (Lystad, 1975), only about five percent show symptoms of serious mental disturbance (Wolfe, 1985). In reality, child-abusing parents cannot be distinguished by appearance or by any psychological tests. Although there are some parental characteristics and attitudes that may tend a parent toward abuse, it is difficult to identify most abusers before the abuse takes place.

What Is Child Abuse?

Child abuse occurs when parents intentionally injure their children. **Neglect** refers to a situation in which the physical care and supervision of the child is inadequate or inappropriate. States vary in their definitions of abuse and neglect, but all states now require such professionals as doctors, nurses, and teachers to report suspected cases of child abuse or neglect. In 1989, more than 2.4 million children were reported to child protective agencies as suspected victims of abuse or neglect, which is a ten percent increase over the previous year's total (Jennings, 1990). More than 1,000 children died from neglect or physical abuse.

The results of child abuse are serious. They include impaired intellectual abilities, language delays, poor self-concept, aggression, and even social and emotional withdrawal (Clapp, 1988).

child abuse
A general term used to denote an injury intentionally perpetrated on a child.

child neglect
A term used to describe a situation in which the care and supervision of a child is insufficient or improper.

Sexual Abuse

One type of abuse—sexual abuse—has recently been the subject of much discussion in the media. Beginning in the mid-1970s and continuing through the 1980s, the public has been swamped with well-publicized cases of sexual abuse (Finkelhor, 1984). Sexual abuse is fraught with a host of definitional and legal problems and carries an even greater stigma than other types of child abuse (Fontana, 1984). It is often a hidden type of abuse that goes unreported. Sexual abuse can involve forcible rape, statutory rape, sodomy, incest, or "indecent liberties," such as genital exhibition and physical advances (Sarafino, 1979). It is the least reported type of child abuse (Schultz & Jones, 1983). In one study of 521 families in the Boston area, nine percent of the parents said that one of their children had been a victim of an attempted or actual incident of sexual abuse (Finkelhor, 1984).

When brought to the attention of the authorities, building a case for sexual abuse may be difficult because the damaging acts are often performed in private with only the child's word to substantiate the charge. The accused adult may question the credibility of a very young victim, charging that the child has been encouraged to make the accusation or is doing it for attention. According to reported incidents, abusers are mostly men, and girls constitute the majority of victims (Canavan, 1981). Sexual abuse is most likely to occur between people who are related, but a child may be victimized by a stranger.

The consequences of sexual abuse can be both physical—such as venereal disease and pregnancy—and emotional. Long-term effects include depression, self-destructive behavior, anxiety, feelings of isolation and stigma, poor self-esteem, difficulty trusting others, substance abuse, sexual maladjustment, and an inability to develop healthy relationships with others (Adams-Tucker, 1982; Browne & Finkelhor, 1986).

Parents often ask what they can do to prevent sexual abuse. Knowing where their children are, what they are doing, and who they are with are obvious precautions, but parents cannot foresee every circumstance. For instance, one six-year-old boy was abused by an older boy when he went to the bathroom in a supermarket while his mother waited in the checkout line (De Vine, 1980).

Parents should remind their children not to accept money or favors from strangers and not to accept a ride or go anywhere with someone they do not know. Children who think they are in danger should be aware that making a scene by running away and screaming for help is acceptable. Since the sexual abuser usually is someone a child knows and trusts, children should be told that they do not have to agree to demands for physical closeness—even from relatives. Finally, children should be encouraged to report any instances of people touching them in intimate places or asking the child to do the same to them (Queens Bench Foundation, 1977).

The increase in publicity surrounding sexual abuse has led to a frank public discussion of the problem. This offers some hope that we can reduce its incidence through prevention and its consequences through early discovery and treatment.

Emotional Abuse or Psychological Maltreatment

Not all child abuse is physical. Consider the parent who constantly screams at and berates his or her children. Imagine a four-year-old who has just spilled some juice hear a parent shout, "You're a stupid, rotten kid. If I had any sense, I'd give you away!" Consider a parent who tells a child who refuses to put his face in the water during a swim class that the child is a coward and that he has made his parents ashamed. Such statements can actually influence children to believe that they are stupid or rotten or cowardly, and as a result, the children begin to act that way—the way they think people expect them to.

DATAGRAPHIC

Number of Children Reported to Public Agencies as Being Abused or Neglected

Source: American Humane Association.

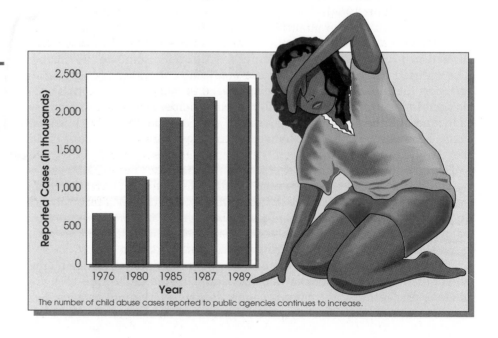

The number of child abuse cases reported to public agencies continues to increase.

Defining **emotional abuse,** sometimes called **psychological maltreatment** (Rosenberg, 1987), is difficult. Certain parental actions can lead to a loss of self-esteem in the child and interfere with the child's emotional development, but it is difficult to define these actions and describe remedial steps. Conceptually, such parental behaviors as rejecting, isolating, terrorizing, ignoring, and corrupting constitute psychological maltreatment (Garbarino, Guthman & Seeley, 1986). These forms of abuse frequently produce emotional and behavioral problems in children (Hart & Brassard, 1987). In the absence of specific guidelines, the courts have taken a hands-off attitude toward everything but the most extreme forms. Perhaps in the future the more obvious cases will be identified, and some help for parents and children will be forthcoming. At this point, however, emotional abuse is a concept in search of a solid definition and some guidelines for action.

emotional or psychological abuse
Psychological damage perpetrated on the child by parental actions that often involve rejecting, isolating, terrorizing, ignoring, or corrupting.

Causes of Child Abuse

To understand the causes of child abuse, the characteristics of the parent and the child involved as well as the nature of the situation must be taken into account.

THE ABUSIVE PARENT What kind of parent abuses a child? Is there a recognizable personality pattern that indicates the potential for abuse? As a group, parents who abuse their children are impulsive, have unmet dependency needs, have a poor self-concept and sense of identity, are defensive, and project their problems onto their children (Green, Gaines & Sandgrund, 1974). They are immature and socially isolated, believe in the value of physical punishment, are afraid of spoiling their children, and have difficulty empathizing with their offspring (Martin, 1978). Although child abuse can be found in every age group and economic level, it is most common among the poor. Child abusers also tend to be young, but this factor may be confounded by socioeconomic status (Kinard & Klerman, 1980). Since young parenthood is related to poverty, poor health care, poor housing, poor family background, and other social factors, abuse may not be related to age itself but rather to the socioeconomic situation and impoverished background that contributes to the abuse.

10. TRUE OR FALSE?

Unusual as it may seem, parents who physically abuse their children often believe that physical punishment is wrong.

These characteristics are general ones. Many parents who are impulsive and isolated do not abuse their children, and this fact has led many professionals to deny that there is any definite "abusive" personality (Green et al., 1974). Although abusive parents differ in some of their reactions to family situations (Frodi & Lamb, 1980), it is difficult to predict abuse simply from a personality profile of a parent.

Some studies have attempted to compare abusive and nonabusive parents' child-rearing practices. Penelope Trickett and Leon Kuczynski (1986) found that abusive parents did not report using physical punishment any more than the control parents did but were more likely to report using more severe forms of punishment, such as striking the face, hitting the child with an object, or pulling the child's hair. Abusive parents can be distinguished more from the quality than from the quantity of their punishment.

Another study compared twenty-eight abusive families with children between the ages of four and eleven and twenty-eight nonabusing families, matched for social class and other variables. Abusive parents were less satisfied with their children, perceived child rearing as more difficult and not very enjoyable, and promoted an isolated lifestyle for both themselves and their children. They also reported much more family conflict (Trickett & Susman, 1988). Abusive families did not encourage autonomous development, were less open to new experiences, and showed less suppression of aggression.

11. TRUE OR FALSE?
━━━━━━━━━━━━━
The overwhelming majority of abused children grow up to abuse their own children.

DO ABUSED CHILDREN GROW UP TO ABUSE THEIR OWN CHILDREN? Between 25 and 35 percent of parents who were abused as children abuse their own children (Kaufman & Zigler, 1987). This means that the general statement that abused children grow up to abuse their own children is greatly overstated (Wisdom, 1989). Although certainly children who are abused are more likely than the general population to do so, most parents who are abused do not abuse their own children.

Why do some abused children grow up to abuse their own children and some do not? Those parents who have broken the cycle of abuse tend to have received emotional support from a nonabusive adult sometime during childhood, participated in therapy at some time in their life, or had a nonabusive, more emotionally stable mate with whom they shared a satisfying relationship. Those who continue the cycle of abuse experience significantly more life stress and more anxiety and are more dependent, immature, and depressed (Egeland, Jacobovitz, & Sroufe, 1988). Therefore, the presence and influence of other supportive and nonabusing adults and/or a helpful counseling relationship are two factors that may reduce the possibility of abuse. Since those who continue the cycle experience more stress, teaching stress reduction and problem-solving skills may help them.

THE ABUSED CHILD Certain characteristics of a child may predispose the child to being a victim of abuse. This statement causes some people to feel uneasy. Any suggestion that the child contributes to the problem is usually met with hostility. The reaction is understandable. It is easier to see a child as a helpless victim of a vicious adult than to look at characteristics of a child that may bring out the worst in a parent. No one is excusing such behavior or blaming an innocent victim. However, a child's personality or physical and intellectual characteristics may combine with an inadequate parent to cause problems (Parke and Collmer, 1975). For instance, children who are premature, who have physical disabilities, or who are mentally retarded are abused more often than children who do not suffer from these conditions (Friedrich & Boriskin, 1976). In addition, children who have difficult temperaments—that is, whose emotional reactions are intense and demanding—are also prone to being abused (Parke & Collmer, 1975). The common characteristic in all these groups is the need for special care. The child whose needs are greater is at risk for abuse.

Abusing parents often hold unreasonable expectations for their children and distorted perceptions of what their children can do (Martin, 1978). Children with physical, emotional, or mental disabilities cannot meet their parents' expectations and are more likely to be abused. Consider the premature baby who requires a great deal of care and attention. The demand may be more than an impulsive, unrealistic parent can handle, and the parent may resort to violence to quiet the child. As the child grows, the pattern is reinforced; physical violence keeps the child in line until the pattern of abuse is well established, and the abuse continues throughout childhood. These abused children often justify the parent's actions on the basis of their own behavior, believing themselves to be generally bad (Dean, Malik, Richards, & Stringer, 1986). The child whose needs are greater, who engenders anger in a parent, or who is difficult to care for is more likely to set in motion abusive parental responses that may become the standard parent-child interaction.

CHARACTERISTICS OF THE SITUATION Any situation that raises the level of tension and stress can promote abuse. For instance, neglect and abuse increase when economic problems within the community increase (Steinberg, Catalano, & Dooley, 1981). Unemployment and underemployment cause stress, and parents may **displace,** that is, transfer their feelings from one person or object to another. Thus, the child may become the object of the parent's anger towards the boss or someone else.

displacement
The process by which an emotion is transferred from one object or person to another, more acceptable substitute.

ACCEPTANCE OF VIOLENCE We live in a society that largely condones violence with respect to children. Ninety percent of families report physically punishing their children at some point in their children's development (Clapp, 1988). In fact, laws covering physical abuse are relatively new. In the nineteenth century, the Society for the Prevention of Cruelty to Animals went to court, arguing that because children were human beings and human beings were animals, children should be protected at least as much as dogs or cats (Lystad, 1975). Shortly after this, some tentative steps toward protection were taken. Physical punishment is often accepted in the United States, even though other methods for discipline are available. The family may, indeed, be one of the most violent of our institutions (Clapp, 1988).

Preventing Child Abuse

It is important to take all three elements—the parent, the child, and the situation—into account when seeking to understand child abuse. We have learned much about the causes of child abuse, and we have also made some progress in preventing and treating both abusers and victims. Some prevention programs involve enrolling parents in educational programs, having professionals visit the homes of parents who have the potential to become abusers, and offering courses on child development in high school. In such courses, teens are taught child-care techniques, given information concerning the nutritional and emotional needs of children, and told where parents can turn for help. The results of such programs are encouraging (Starr, 1979).

Many approaches treat child abusers after the fact. Individual and family therapy, self-help programs such as Parents Anonymous that provide emotional support, and group treatment all claim some success. About half the parents involved in abusive situations can be helped at least to stop physically abusing their children. The victims also need help. Many improve even when there is only a moderate improvement in the home situation (Jones, 1977).

The problem of child abuse is a serious one in many societies. The first steps in improving the situation are admitting that the problem exists and identifying its causes. Today we know that early intervention and a comprehensive treatment program can improve the family situation so that the children will have a chance at a decent and productive life, and the cycle of child abuse can be broken.

◆ GENDER-ROLE ACQUISITION

This chapter has concentrated on the expanding social world of preschoolers, and their changing relationships with peers, parents, and siblings. But the child's social world may also include nursery school, books and the television set. The greater the number of influences on the child, the more difficult it is to focus on the exact cause of a behavioral pattern. Nowhere is this more obvious than in the case of the child's acquisition of his or her gender role.

Gender Differences Under the Microscope

gender differences
The differences between males and females that have been established through scientific investigation.

Is the average male more aggressive than the average female? Is the average female better at verbal tasks than the average male? The term **gender differences** describes differences between the sexes that have been established by scientific research. For example, the average female matures more rapidly than the average male. Eleanor Maccoby and Carol Jacklin (1974) reviewed over 1,600 studies concerning gender differences and concluded that only four differences appeared consistently. Most studies indicated that (1) males are generally more aggressive than females, (2) girls have greater verbal ability, (3) boys excel in visual-spatial ability, and (4) boys excel in mathematical ability. A number of supposed differences were not supported by scientific studies. The hypotheses that girls were more suggestible, had lower self-esteem, had lower motivation, were more social, were better at rote learning, were less analytical, were more affected by heredity, and learned better using their auditory sense than boys were dismissed as not supported by the research. A number of other hypotheses were still in question, including those of male dominance, female compliance, female nurturance, male activity level, female passivity, and male competitiveness.

As valuable as it is, the work of Maccoby and Jacklin is hardly the last word on the subject. A number of criticisms have arisen. For example, Block (1976) noted a number of technical objections to the way the review of the literature had been performed. She objected to the way studies that researched gender differences were placed together, even though they measured the differences in different ways. Others had reviewed much of the same literature and had come to different conclusions. Bardwick (1971) argued that the research demonstrates that females do show more dependency than males. Eagly (1978) suggests that women are more suggestible and more fearful than men. Eaton and Ennis (1986) found that males were more active, and Eagly and Carlike (1981) found that females were more easily influenced. Minton and Schneider (1980) suggest that while males and females do not differ in general ability, they do differ in specific abilities: "Females generally surpass males in verbal fluency, reading comprehension, finger dexterity, and clerical skills, whereas males are superior in mathematical reasoning, visual spatial ability, and speed and coordination of large bodily movements" (p. 319). Minton and Scheider also argue that "females are better at rote memory, especially of verbal and social material" (p. 319).

Four Considerations

The study of gender differences has become frenetic. Some consider any positive finding on gender differences sexist; others seem unable to wait to demonstrate one gender's superiority over the other in some area. Four considerations should be kept in mind whenever anyone announces a positive finding on gender differences.

First, even though a difference between males and females on some characteristic, such as verbal ability, is found, it tells us nothing about its cause. Is the fact that males are generally more aggressive than females due to some environmental factor, such as reinforcement, or to some genetic or hormonal factor? Even the finding that some genetic or hormonal element may underlie the behavior does not mean the behavior itself cannot be modified. Genetic contribution does not imply immutability. Rather, the individual's genotype may influence the range of possible behaviors, but it remains the environment that determines the behavior itself.

Second, most gender differences should not be seen as absolute. The overlap between the genders is tremendous. The average difference between males and females on any particular trait is normally very small, even when it does exist. The differences between individuals within the same gender are far greater than the average differences between males and females. Thus, although males seem to be generally better at advanced mathematics, you will find excellent female math students and males who receive terrible math grades. Stating that males are better in one trait or females are superior in another trait should not blind us to the overlap that exists in these skills or characteristics. Males and females are more similar than they are different.

This leads directly to the third consideration. Just how much of any particular trait can you predict on the basis of an individual's gender alone? As Plomin and Foch (1981, p. 383) ask, "How much do we know about an individual's verbal ability if all we know is the individual's gender?" These researchers note that gender differences provide only about

12. *TRUE OR FALSE?*

Research has failed to establish any consistent gender differences in personality or behavior.

one percent of the variation on verbal ability and only about four percent of the differences in mathematical ability. Janet Shibley Hyde (1984) suggests that only about five percent of difference in aggression between males and females is due to gender. Although these differences do exist, they explain very little about the variation between individuals on any of these traits.

The last consideration is that a gender difference may be found in one circumstance but not in another, making global statements about one trait or another questionable. For example, consider a study of the social interactions of preschoolers. Some of the children have a same-sex partner while others have a cross-sex partner. What if you found that when paired with a boy, girls showed more passive behavior, allowing the boy to play with the toys as they watched. However, when paired with another girl, girls show no evidence for passivity, and intense social interaction is the rule. Could you fairly conclude that girls are more passive? Frequently, gender differences are situational, and making a general statement is often incorrect (Maccoby, 1990).

Gender Identity, Gender Stability, and Gender Consistency

gender identity
One's awareness of being a male or a female.

gender stability
Children's knowledge that they were of a particular gender when younger and will remain so throughout life.

gender consistency (constancy)
Children's knowledge that they will remain boys or girls regardless of how they act, dress or groom.

The term **gender identity** refers to one's awareness of being a male or a female. Evidence indicates that at about age two, children are aware of the labels "boy" and "girl" (Schaffer, 1981), but they do not use them correctly all the time.

Children develop their understanding of gender in a developmental progression described in a study by Slaby and Frey (1975). First, children establish a gender identity. That is, they know whether they are boys or girls. After establishing gender identity, children learn that their gender is **stable.** In other words, children know that they were boys or girls when they were younger and will become men and women when they grow up. Finally, children develop **gender consistency** (also called gender constancy), the understanding that boys remain boys whether or not they have long hair or play female-oriented games.

This progression has been found in many other studies (Eaton & Von Bargen, 1981) and in many different cultures (Munroe, Schimmin & Munroe, 1984). Gender identity is more easily understood by children than gender consistency, with gender stability lying somewhere between. The mean (average) age of attaining these understandings differs widely. For example, although the average age for attaining gender consistency was fifty-five months in Slaby and Frey's study, some children attained it as early as forty-four months, while others did not understand the concept until sixty-seven months of age.

This developmental progression explains some of the unusual behavior we find in young children. If children have not gained an understanding of gender stability or consistency, they may believe that if daddy grows his hair long he will become a female like mommy. A little girl might believe that if her brother wore a dress, he would become a girl like her.

One important aspect of gender consistency involves its ability to direct attention toward appropriate models. Children attend more to same-sex models only when they have acquired gender consistency (Ruble, Balaban & Cooper, 1981; Slaby & Frey, 1975). Older siblings of their gender, parents of the same sex, and television commercials that show peers of the same sex are more likely to influence behavior after children have learned gender consistency. Once children know that gender is permanent and does not change with the situation, they seek out important information from the environment on what is appropriate for their particular gender and what is to be avoided. In seeking to provide preschool children with effective models, it may be important first to understand just where the children are in their development of gender consistency. It is no wonder that toy manufacturers are so careful about how they market their toys and who is seen on television playing with them.

Sex Typing and Gender Roles

"After I cook dinner, I'm going to read the newspaper and play with my children," four-year-old Matthew announced while playing in nursery school. The teacher was astonished and decided to explore this unusual statement with Matthew's mother. "It's simple," Matthew's mother explained. "When my husband comes home from work, he always asks me what's for dinner. I usually reply, 'Anything you cook.' You see, my husband is an excellent cook. He cooks and I clean up." As far as Matthew is concerned, cooking is part of a male's role. However, many children and adults would consider it a female chore.

Sex typing is the process by which an individual acquires the attitudes, values and behaviors viewed as appropriate for one sex or another in a particular culture (Mischel, 1976). Women cook, take care of the children, ask for help, and are rescued (by men) from trying circumstances. Men work full-time jobs, don't ask for help, are action-oriented, and are strong. Sex-typed behavior can be seen in many areas of development. Boys play with trucks; girls play with dolls. Such behavior patterns as methods of aggression, behavior while dissecting a frog, and emotional expressiveness are examples of sex-typed behavior. Girls are taught that crying is acceptable when they are sad; males are taught to hold it in. Boys avoid showing concern for babies; females pay more attention to infants. Studies in laboratory settings show that males of all ages, from preschoolers to young adults, spend less time speaking to and playing with babies than females do (Blakemore, 1981).

When we add up all the behavior patterns and psychological characteristics that seem appropriate for each gender, we are describing the concept of **gender roles**. Gender roles are diffuse and permeate other roles (Maccoby, 1978). Not only are they involved in one's choice of occupation (truck drivers are men, nurses are women), but they also relate to a number of social expectations. For example, consider the social conventions that exist between males and females in the areas of dating and family life. The male picks up the female at her house and drives the car. The male is the breadwinner of the family. Some of these conceptions are changing, but many are still with us today.

sex typing
The process by which an individual acquires the attitudes, values and behaviors viewed as appropriate for one sex or another in a particular culture.

gender roles
Behaviors expected of people in a given society on the basis of whether an individual is male or female.

This young girl exhibits sex-typed behavior in sewing and babysitting.

Just how children acquire the behaviors that are considered "appropriate" for their gender is a matter of great interest and controversy. Let's now look at some theories that seek to explain how children learn their gender roles.

The Biological Approach

Freud once stated that biology was destiny, in other words, that the physiological differences between males and females explained the behavior differences. Few people would go that far today. No single biological explanation successfully explains why males may act one way and females another. Instead, a number of biological factors are suggested that may be taken into account when studying gender roles.

HORMONES Males produce more testosterone, while females produce more estrogen. In laboratory studies, the hormone testosterone is linked to aggressive behavior (Rogers, 1976). However, variations in human behavior cannot be explained merely by citing hormonal differences. Learning is also important. John Money and Anne Erhard (1972) studied children who were born with ambiguous genitals. Some were surgically altered very early in childhood, and these children made successful adjustments to their gender if the surgery took place before the age of two. Those who became female did, however, show a tomboyish nature, including more rough-and-tumble play. This tendency might have been caused by the greater concentrations of testosterone in their systems. Perhaps males are more inclined to be aggressive than females. Despite the inclination, both males and females can be taught to settle disagreements by nonaggressive means.

There is also evidence that hormone levels during sensitive periods in early life may have an organizing effect on the brain, encouraging the development of certain neurons. The brains of animals given doses of hormones show changes, and these may relate to behavioral changes in aggression, parenting styles, and rough-and-tumble play (see Ruble, 1988).

DIFFERENCES IN MATURATION The average female is born more ready for life than the average male. Females are more advanced in central nervous system development and bone formation. Some gender differences may be caused by the interaction of a child's rate of maturation and the child's environment. For example, while gross muscle development in males is superior, females develop fine muscle control more quickly (McGuinness, 1976, 1977). Since children are apt to do both what is easiest and what yields the most positive reinforcement, males may turn their attention to activities in which gross muscle ability and reaction time are vital. Females, on the other hand, having better fine motor control, are apt to concentrate on tasks involving such control.

The argument is that society merely reinforces a difference in abilities that is already present. Boys find baseball easier, succeed at it, and then are reinforced for their efforts. Girls find activities that require fine motor control easier, succeed at them, and are reinforced. The interaction of maturation and the environment may also help explain why boys have so many more reading problems than girls. Females also have a greater attention span, and their eyes are better developed by the time they enter school. Female superiority in language development and reading does not excuse males from learning to read. It only suggests that the average male may find language skills more difficult and may require additional instruction.

GENETIC DIFFERENCES We have already discussed the possibility that genetic differences may affect behavior. The male Y chromosome contains many fewer genes than the female X chromosome, and some characteristics, such as color blindness, are sex-linked. There is evidence that this may also be true of spatial ability, although some studies have cast some doubt on this (Vandenberg & Kuse, 1979).

Even if you are impressed by the biological approach, assignment of unequal roles on the basis of some biological argument cannot be condoned and is not justified by the evidence (Archer, 1976). In the case of gender roles and behavior, biology is not destiny. At this time, the biological contribution to our understanding of how a child acquires a gender role is a large question mark.

Behavior Theories

The most obvious reason that males and females act differently is that they learn different behaviors. These learning experiences can be divided roughly into two compartments. First, boys and girls are treated differently and reinforced for different actions. Second, we might look at the models that surround the child, because children learn by observing others. Both theories emphasize the processes acting on the child from the environment (see Ruble, 1988).

DIFFERENT TREATMENT FOR GIRLS AND BOYS Are boys and girls reinforced for different behaviors? Do parents treat boys and girls differently? Parents do expect different behaviors from their sons and daughters, expecting sons to be stronger and tougher (Richmond-Abbott, 1983). Parents provide their sons with different toys and decorate their rooms in a "gender-appropriate" manner (Rheingold & Cook, 1975). Although parents may not consciously reinforce young children for playing with gender-stereotyped toys (boys with trucks, girls with dolls), they actively channel their children into such standard play (Eisenberg, Wolchik, Hernandez & Pasternack, 1985). The same parents who may say it would not bother them if their son played with dolls are apt to provide only balls, gloves, and trucks for him to play with and encourage him to play with such toys.

Differences in treatment are not difficult to find. Parents encourage sons to be more independent, competitive, and achieving (Block, 1979). They encourage daughters to be more passive and to seek protection (Chafetz, 1974). Girls are viewed as more fragile, and parents play with sons more roughly than they do with daughters (Bee, 1978). Toddlers receive more positive reactions when they engage in what are considered gender-appropriate activities than when they engage in activities deemed appropriate for the other gender (Fagot, 1978). Parents also supervise daughters more, allowing sons more freedom (Block, 1979). Parents demand more independence from boys and are likely to help girls more quickly (Ruble, 1988). Males are punished more, and parents are more likely to be physical with sons than with daughters. Girls tend to receive more praise than boys, but also more criticism (Fagot, 1974). Mothers talk differently to toddler and preschool sons and daughters. Males receive more verbal stimulation, which is thought to encourage cognitive development (Weitzman, Birns, & Friend, 1985).

Fathers are more likely than mothers to treat sons and daughters differently (Bee, 1978). A father is more likely to criticize his son when he sees him playing with dolls than he is to criticize a daughter who is observed beating up a Bobo doll. Mothers are more likely to treat sons and daughters equally.

Boys are more strictly sex-typed than girls. Even though preschool boys and girls both prefer gender-stereotyped toys, boys avoid cross-sexed toys more often than girls do (Williams, Bennett & Best, 1975). Indeed, preschool boys choose sex-typed toys and cling to their choices even if told that the toys not chosen were appropriate for both boys and girls. It is also easier to get girls to switch toy preference than boys. Females show more flexibility in behavior than males. Preschoolers judge female gender-role violations more permissible than male gender-role violations. They were also much less committed to maintaining the female sex-typed behaviors than the male sex-typed behaviors (Smetana, 1986).

These differences, though, do not tell the entire story. Some authorities are more impressed by the similarities in the way males and females are treated by their parents than the differences (Maccoby & Jacklin, 1974). The evidence does not indicate that a simple, straightforward reinforcement approach can answer the question of sex typing. For example, Maccoby and Jacklin (1974) did not find that boys were necessarily reinforced for aggressiveness more than girls. The question is not whether boys and girls are treated differently, but whether these differences are enough to explain later sex-typed behavior patterns. Although some differences in treatment do exist, it is difficult to see how they could be the *sole* determinants of later personality and behavioral differences between the sexes. They are, then, only one part of the puzzle. Another part may be found in an understanding of the role models that surround a child.

ROLE MODELS AND IMITATION Let us return to the case of the little boy who thought nothing of daddy's cooking dinner. Where did the boy get the idea that it was manly to cook dinner for the family? Probably not through direct reinforcement, for little boys hardly get a chance to cook spaghetti dinners for their families. The boy simply observed his father doing so and sees cooking as an activity that is performed by both sexes.

The use of modeling and imitation to explain the acquisition of gender roles is appealing. Indeed, the strength of the imitative response is especially noticeable in young children, who may act like their mothers or

Parents are models for their young children who often identify with them.

fathers or imitate older brothers or sisters to the delight or despair of the parents. Since parents are the most important people in the life of pre-schoolers, the children may model themselves after them (Mischel, 1970). For example, daughters of working mothers have less traditional role concepts and have higher aspirations than girls whose mothers are not employed (Hoffman, 1974). They benefit from observing that their mother as well as their father is valued in the labor market and performs useful functions outside the home.

Parents are not the only models in children's lives. Children are also exposed to models in the outside world—for example, peers, teachers, and characters in children's books and on television. It is often difficult to separate the influence of parents from that of other adults and the media. Although no one doubts the importance of social learning in sex typing, it is sometimes difficult to understand why children exposed to similar environments develop different concepts of gender roles.

Psychoanalytic Theory

No theory is more controversial than Freud's ideas about the development of sex-typed behavior. According to Freud (1924), the development of gender roles arises from events that occur during the **phallic stage.** Until early childhood, both boys and girls have similar psychosexual experiences. However, in the phallic stage, the **Oedipal** situation occurs. The little boy experiences sexual feelings toward his mother and wishes to rid himself of competition from his father. He also fears his father and is afraid that his father will find out about his wishes and castrate him. At the same time, the father is respected as a model of masculinity who is superior to the child. As he matures, the little boy represses his feelings toward his mother and identifies with his father. In this way, he becomes like his father and takes on the appropriate gender role.

The process with females is a bit convoluted. It is sometimes called the **Electra complex.** The little girl is also originally sexually attracted to the mother, but slowly turns her attention to her father when she realizes she does not have a penis (Mullahy, 1948). Blaming her mother for her lack of a penis, she competes with her mother for the father's attention. She does not have to resolve this situation fully, since she doesn't have to worry about castration. She may never fully accept her "appropriate" gender role. Because of this, Freud felt that women were heir to more personality difficulties than men (Freud, 1933; Schaffer, 1981).

One of the most important ideas underlying the psychoanalytic concept of gender roles is **identification.** Children identify with the parent of the same sex and acquire the appropriate gender role. Perhaps the most controversial portion of this theory involves Freud's argument that the girl's discovery that she lacks the male organ is a turning point in her life, which is now dominated by her desire to attain one through her father and later through her husband by having a baby. Freud sees every imaginable character trait of females beginning with what he called penis envy, including inferiority, physical modesty, envy, and psychosexual difficulties. In the end, however, Freud's ideas in this realm have been largely rejected by developmental psychologists, for supporting evidence

phallic stage
Freud's third psychosexual stage, occurring during early childhood, in which the sexual energy is located in the genital area.

Oedipus complex
The conflict in Freudian theory in which the boy experiences sexual feelings towards his mother and wishes to rid himself of his father.

Electra complex
The female equivalent to the Oedipus complex in which the female experiences sexual feelings towards her father and wishes to do away with her mother.

identification
The process by which children take on the characteristics of another person, most often a parent.

is lacking (Sears, Rae & Alpert, 1965). The clinical problems Freud noted can be interpreted in terms of the social roles thrust on women by society (Horney, 1939, 1967). In addition, even though the Oedipal situation has been found in a number of societies (Kline, 1972), it is certainly not universal (Mead, 1974).

The Cognitive-Developmental Theory and Gender Schema Theories

Two theories emphasize the importance of internal rather than external forces: cognitive developmental theory and gender schema theory. Both theories see children as motivated from within to learn gender roles because of a basic desire to master their environment (Kuhn, 1988). Children are motivated to define themselves and seek out information about what they are and how they should act.

Cognitive developmental theory views gender-role development as occurring in two stages. First, the child must develop a sense of gender consistency, that is, that he is a boy or she is a girl forever and that this is not dependent on physical appearance. Once this is attained, the child then actively searches the world for information concerning how a boy or a girl behaves and the ideas that each gender holds (Kohlberg, 1987).

This theoretical approach is noteworthy because it views the child not as a passive receiver of information about gender roles but rather as an active gatherer of information. The child is viewed as searching the environment for information, which is plentiful. The major problem with this approach is its requirement that the child search for information only after he or she has discovered gender consistency. There is evidence both for and against this idea. Certainly, some aspects of sex typing are present before children have developed gender consistency. By four years of age, children indicate a preference for gender-stereotyped toys (Emerich & Shepard, 1984). Gender differentiation in play is found in the early preschool years.

If the theory is correct, after they have developed gender consistency, children should show more attention to same-sex models than they did before they understood the concept. There is some evidence that this is true and some contrary evidence (Ruble, 1988). Of course, one possibility is that before children develop gender consistency, they are not very active in the search, and the gender roles are learned through imitation and reinforcement, while after children develop gender consistency, they are more motivated to actively search for gender information.

Another theory, called gender schema theory, denies the need for gender consistency in determining sex typing. This theory requires only that the child have a sense of gender identity, that is, that he is a boy and she is a girl (Carter & Levy, 1988). The child develops a gender schema, or a body of knowledge, about what boys and girls do that helps children organize and interpret information and influences children's preferences and activities (Bem, 1981). Schemata give children a framework for organizing their perceptions.

Two proponents of this approach, Carol Martin and Charles Halverson (1981), argue that human beings have a natural inclination to categorize. Children have many schemata, including one for gender. They quickly learn society's ideas about being male and female and incorporate them into their category structures. They then use these structures to interpret the world around them. Once they form these schemata, they select only the information that is germane to their own sex and build their own gender role. Part of their concept of their self, then, is the concept of what is appropriate for their sex.

To understand how schemata may function in sex typing, Martin and Halverson (1981) offer the example of a little girl presented with a doll. The girl knows that dolls are for girls and she is a girl; therefore, dolls are for her. The girl will then explore the doll and ask questions and obtain information about it. What if that same girl is offered a toy truck? The girl may think that trucks are for boys, and since she is a girl she will decide that trucks are not for her. The result is avoidance, and no further information will be actively gathered.

How a person interprets experiences involves an interaction between the information in the environment and the child's schema. As children learn society's gender schemata, they learn which characteristics are related to their own sex—and therefore to themselves—and which are not. Sandra Bem (1981) notes that part of the gender schema for boys is strength, while nurturance is part of the schema for girls. The strong-weak dimensión appears to be absent from the female gender schema, and it is very rare for anyone to remark about how strong a girl is. On the other hand, the nurturant dimension is almost absent from the male gender schema, and it is relatively rare for a person to comment on that attribute in males. The child applies this same schematic selectivity to his or her own self and chooses to attend only to the possible dimensions of personality and behavior that are applicable to his or her own sex.

One of the advantages of gender schema theory is that it explains why children maintain their gender stereotypes even in the face of some contrary information. Once a child learns his or her schema, it biases the information processed. Most research shows that gender-consistent information is encoded and remembered better than gender-inconsistent information. When children were shown traditional and nontraditional sex-typed pictures and tested on their memory after one month, children with highly stereotyped gender schemata tended to recall more of the traditional pictures (Signorella & Liben, 1984). Preschoolers viewed films in which there were male and female doctors and nurses and were later asked to identify photographs of what they had seen (Cordura, McGraw, & Drabman, 1979). Children who saw a male doctor and a female nurse were completely accurate. However, most (but not all) of the children who had seen a female doctor and a male nurse reversed the roles and identified the male as the doctor and the female as the nurse. The children's gender schemata acted to maintain the stereotypes. Gender schema theory argues that gender is an organizing principle used to construct a view of the social world and that children are guided by an intrinsic motivation to conform to gender-based cultural standards (Levy & Carter, 1989).

Gender-Role Theories Reconsidered

No single theory can adequately explain how a child acquires a gender role, but each can add greatly to our knowledge. Behavior theory makes us aware of how important the differential treatment of boys and girls by parents and teachers can be. Social learning theory stresses the importance of imitation and the models that surround the child. While few scientists today believe that biological explanations by themselves are sufficient to explain gender roles, maturational, hormonal, and genetic differences add pieces to the puzzle, and despite the problems inherent in the Freudian approach, the significance of identification and the part that both parents may play in the socialization of the child are important to remember. Last, the cognitive developmental approach and gender schema theory emphasize the importance of a child's intrinsic motivation to find out about gender roles and add to our understanding of why it is so difficult to get people to alter rigid ideas about gender roles.

The Limitations of Traditional Stereotypes

Does it really matter whether one has a narrow or a broad definition of what is appropriate for one's sex? The answer is a definite yes. Let's say that little Joey feels like crying but refuses to do so because he thinks it is not manly. He decides that it's best not to express his emotions. Emotional expression remains inconsistent with his definition of gender role. Later in life, Joey may have difficulty expressing his feelings. His definition of being male limits his emotional flexibility. Little Katie, who believes that girls don't get dirty or take leadership positions, has also unnecessarily limited her future activities.

Because the traditional, rigid gender roles seem to be so limiting, Bem (1975) claims that people are better off if they are flexible enough to combine the best characteristics of males and females. Such people are called **androgynous.** Males and females holding to the extreme gender stereotypes are limited by their conception of gender roles. There should be advantages for people who possess the best characteristics of both. Indeed, some research has shown such advantages. Androgynous college students have higher self-esteem (Spence, Helmreich & Stapp, 1975). Fathers who score high in androgyny tend to spend more time with their children (Russell, 1978). There are findings of better adjustment and self-esteem among androgynous individuals as well.

The benefits of androgyny have been questioned, though. Some studies report no differences between androgynous and highly masculine individuals (Ruble, 1988). Other studies have found that masculine males have better overall adjustment and that flexibility and adjustment are more associated with masculinity than with androgyny (Jones, Chernovetz & Hansson, 1978). It seems that the presence of masculine traits rather than adrogyny is related to superior adaptability (Lee & Scheurer, 1983). It may be the masculine aspects of androgyny, including its focus on activity, dominance, and independence, that are responsible for the advantage that androgynous women show over those with more traditional role conceptions (Taylor & Hall, 1982). Another concern is that andro-

androgyny
The state of possessing the best characteristics of masculinity and feminity.

gyny, although an improvement on traditional gender stereotypes, still perpetuates gender-related stereotypic characteristics. It is argued that people ought to go beyond or transcend all traditional stereotypes (Doyle, 1985). Androgyny, then, becomes a transitional concept rather than an ideal alternative to traditional stereotypes.

◆ READY FOR NEW CHALLENGES

Early childhood is a time of great change. The preschooler's social world is expanding rapidly. Parents, peers, nursery school teachers, and siblings all have an effect on children. Preschoolers are active, curious, and playful. If parents and teachers encourage healthful activities, children can gain the sense of initiative that Erikson believes is so important. If parents set limits in a loving atmosphere and allow preschoolers some freedom to choose, the children become competent and independent and develop a positive view of themselves. They are, then, ready for the challenges of middle childhood.

═══ SUMMARY ═══

1. Play is an activity performed for sheer enjoyment with no ulterior motive. It helps develop a child's mental, physical, and social abilities. It serves as an outlet for the child's frustrations and allows the child to experiment with new roles. The complexity of play increases with age. Both pretend play and rough-and-tumble play have important developmental benefits.

2. Preschoolers have more contact with peers than they did when they were toddlers. Although some preschool friendships last throughout the year, most are temporary and lack intimacy. Friendship is defined in the play situation.

3. Preschoolers do show some prosocial behavior but little altruistic behavior. Prosocial behavior increases with age. Most children's conflicts are settled without the aid of adults, most often when one child gives in to another.

4. Siblings may offer support and help as well as serve as sources of discord. Although antagonistic behavior among siblings is not uncommon, most interactions are positive and play oriented.

5. Diana Baumrind identified three types of parenting styles. Authoritarian parents seek to control a child's every action, causing the child to become suspicious and withdrawn. Permissive parents allow almost total freedom and rarely use discipline. The children of such parents do not show much self-control or self-reliance. Authoritative parents give their children freedom within limits. The children of these parents are competent and self-controlled.

6. Discipline involves training in self-control; punishment involves inflicting physical and/or psychological pain or taking away a positive reinforcer for violating a rule. Punishment is most effective when it is moderate, swift, certain, and combined with positive reinforcement for the correct behavior.

7. Child abuse is a major societal problem. To understand abuse, the characteristics of the parents, child, and situation must be taken into account. Sexual abuse is the least reported type of abuse. Psychological or emotional abuse involves actions including rejecting, isolating, terrorizing, ignoring, and corrupting. Many parents who physically abuse their children can be helped to stop abusing them.

8. Research has generally found that males are more aggressive than females, that girls have greater verbal abilities, and that boys excel in visual-spatial tasks and ability in mathematics. Gender differences tell us nothing about the cause of the differences and account for very little of the behavioral differences between individuals. In addition, a great deal of overlap exists between the sexes.

9. Gender roles involve the behavioral patterns and psychological characteristics that are appropriate for each sex. Biological factors—including hormonal, genetic, and maturational—have been advanced as explanations for differences between the genders, but a completely biological explanation is untenable. Children learn their gender roles through operant conditioning and imitation of role models in the environment. Freud

saw gender roles in terms of the resolution of the Oedipal or Electra situation in the phallic stage, when children identify with the parent of the same sex. The cognitive-developmental theory argues that children first learn that they will be a boy or a girl forever and then actively search the environment for information relating to what is appropriate for each gender. Gender schema theory argues that once a child knows his or her sex, the child develops a body of knowledge about what boys and girls do that helps children organize and interpret information and influences children's preferences and activities.

10. People who have the best of both stereotyped male and female characteristics are said to be androgynous and are more flexible in their behavior. However, some authorities argue that we should go beyond gender stereotypes and that the concept of androgyny is a transitional concept.

ACTION/REACTION

But He's a Boy!

The day Greg Perry came home from the hospital, his father bought a football and put it in his crib. Greg's father dreamed of his son being an "All-American." As Greg grew, Mr. Perry continued to give him tennis rackets, baseball gloves, basketballs, and the like. But last week four-year-old Greg asked for a Cabbage Patch doll, and his father hit the ceiling. "My son is not going to be a sissy and play with dolls. No way." Greg's mother sees nothing wrong with Greg's playing with dolls. In fact, she secretly bought him one a few months ago but allows Greg to play with it only when his father is not home so he won't find out.

Greg's nursery school teacher told Mr. Perry that there was nothing wrong with a boy playing with dolls and that he was old-fashioned to think that way. Mr. Perry refused to believe that it wouldn't hurt the child and took offense at the teacher's comments.

1. If you were Greg's mother, how would you handle the situation?
2. How would you rate the teacher's handling of the problem?

A Case of Jealousy

What does it mean to treat children equally? The Smiths must answer that question. They have two sons: Jerry, age six, and Henry, age four. Henry needs more attention than Jerry. He has suffered from continuous health problems, some of which are moderately serious, and tends to be depressed because he can't always play with friends. Henry must be kept still, which sometimes means giving in to his whims and spending a great deal of time with him. Although Jerry knows his brother has not been well, he is jealous of the attention Henry gets and tries to put him down as much as possible. He taunts his brother, and his favorite statement to his parents is "You're not fair."

The Smiths believe that children ought to have responsibilities, and Jerry is required to set the table and run some errands. The Smiths are worried because Henry's problems may continue through middle childhood. Henry may not be able to do his household chores, because he will need extra time to study. The Smiths want to be fair but are not sure that they can be. They try to give Jerry more attention but find that whatever they give is not enough. Jerry continues to complain. They have tried to buy Jerry new toys and to reason with him, but to no avail. Jerry still taunts his brother and complains.

1. If you were Jerry's parents, what would you do to alleviate the problem?

PART FOUR

Middle Childhood

Le Rapas ou les bananes by Paul Gauguin.

CHAPTER ELEVEN

Physical and Cognitive Development in Middle Childhood

Snap the Whip by Winslow Homer.

Are These Statements True or False?

Turn the page for the correct answers. Each statement is repeated in the margin next to the paragraph in which the information can be found.

1. During the elementary school years, a child's growth rate increases.
2. Most children who are obese during middle childhood will remain obese in adulthood.
3. Physical education in elementary school leads to a decrease in academic performance.
4. During middle childhood, boys are superior in running speed, and girls are better at tasks that require agility.
5. Schoolage children can solve abstract hypothetical problems if they are given sufficient time.
6. When elementary schoolchildren claim they understand something, a parent or teacher can be reasonably certain that they do.
7. Japanese elementary schoolchildren are superior to American children in achievement in mathematics.
8. The emphasis in computer literacy courses is on learning how to program computers using different computer languages.
9. The more intelligent an individual is, the greater the chance that he or she will be creative.
10. At present there is no universally accepted definition of intelligence.
11. Intelligence is positively related to school achievement.
12. Children who are intellectually gifted tend to be socially backward.

437

Answers to True-False Questions

1. False. Correct statement: During the elementary school years, the child's rate of growth decreases.
2. True.
3. False. Correct statement: The opposite is true. Physical education tends to improve academic performance in elementary school.
4. True.
5. False. Correct statement: Schoolage children have tremendous difficulties with abstract hypothetical problems, even if they are given plenty of time to solve them.
6. False. Correct statement: The research on metamemory shows that many children do not understand their own level of comprehension.
7. True.
8. False. Correct statement: The emphasis in most computer literacy courses is on computer applications.
9. False. Correct statement: Although average intelligence is probably necessary for creativity, once this criterion is met, there does not seem to be a simple relationship between intelligence and creativity.
10. True.
11. True.
12. False. Correct statement: Most children who are intellectually gifted are socially well adjusted.

◆ THE PHOTO EXERCISE

Collect a group of your childhood photographs. Then guess what age you were when the photographs were taken. Baby pictures are easy. The infant's distinctive look is a giveaway. The changes between ages one and two, two and three, and perhaps three and four are so distinctive that you probably have little difficulty guessing your age. But look at your school photographs. It is difficult to tell whether you were seven or eight, nine or ten. You may make the decision by looking at other cues, such as your hairstyle, or clothing. As children develop during the school years, physical changes occur at a slower rate. Children appear to be marking time, filling in.

◆ PHYSICAL DEVELOPMENT IN MIDDLE CHILDHOOD

Middle childhood is indeed a time of horizontal growth. The gradual changes in height, weight, and appearance can lead us to conclude that little of interest is going on. But this is a mistake. Though the changes may be less spectacular than those that occur in earlier years, they are no less important.

Growth

The rate of growth continues to decline during middle childhood until about age ten, eleven, or twelve (Williams & Stith, 1980). Girls are a bit shorter than boys until adolescence, but because girls experience their adolescent growth spurt about two years earlier than boys, girls are actually taller for a couple of years (see Appendix). By age fourteen or so, boys regain their height advantage (Tanner, 1978).

Chronological and Maturational Age

People often pay lip service to the fact that children mature at their own pace. One child may lose baby teeth at an earlier age or grow faster during childhood than another child. Still, this mental acceptance of individuality often does not coincide with people's feelings. Parents are concerned if their child's development is slower than they expected, although the child's growth may still be within the normal range. We are genetically programmed to reach an optimal height in adulthood. No amount of stretching, health food, exercise, or hormone treatments will make a fairly healthy five-foot-seven-inch male into a six-foot-eight-inch basketball star. Although nutrition, health, and medical care are important in reaching optimal height, each person will reach adult height in his or her own way. But we use chronological age as the marker, and therein lies the problem.

Imagine that three well-nourished, healthy ten-year-old boys are standing next to one another. By coincidence, all were born on the same day in the same year. Would they all be the same height? Probably not, you might answer, because their genetic endowment differs. This is true, but there is another possibility. What if I tell you that Boy 1 is only 8.5 years old in biological or maturational terms, Boy 2 is exactly 10, and Boy 3 is 11.5 years old. Boy 3 is far older than Boy 1 biologically, even though their **chronological ages** as measured in birthdays are the same (Krogman, 1980). This concept of **maturational age** can help us better understand the timing and rate of children's growth. Perhaps we should think of growth from the prenatal period to adulthood as a race that some run faster and some run slower. At any point in the twenty years, some may be ahead, some just on schedule, and some behind. Those that are ahead are maturationally more advanced than those that are behind (Krogman, 1980).

If we think in terms of maturational age, we are forced to consider development as an individual process. In addition, maturational age is a better measure than chronological age of what can be expected of a child (Krogman, 1980). Consider a six-year-old who is maturationally behind yet who may be the same height as another child who is "right on schedule." The child "on schedule" will be more advanced and more ready for school. In fact, studies have shown that many children entering school

1. TRUE OR FALSE?

During the elementary school years, a child's growth rate increases.

chronological age
A person's age according to birthdays.

maturational age
A person's level of maturation relative to his or her peers.

Although people say that children mature at their own rate, often we do not turn this belief into action.

are not physically mature enough to handle the work expected of them and consequently are likely to experience failure in school (Ames, 1986). There is a relationship between body maturation and achievement in first grade (Williams & Stith, 1980).

If maturational age is more important than chronological age, why isn't it used more often? Consider how each is determined. Calculating chronological age is easy. All it entails is a bit of arithmetic, but measuring maturational age is more complex. It involves an examination of X-rays, and this is done only when there is a definite reason for it. For example, a young boy may be lagging behind his peers and have a history of chronic illness, and his doctors and parents may be concerned about his lack of growth. If the doctor believes a problem may exist, an X-ray of the child's wrist might be ordered. The wrist is used for many reasons. First, the amount of radiation that is required is minimal, so X-rays can be repeated at regular intervals. The dosage is about four millirads, about the same amount a child would get spending a week in the mountains (Tanner, 1978). Second, excellent atlases of bone development in the wrist allow us to determine just how advanced a child is on the way to maturity. We may find that the subject is well behind biologically and has a long way to go to reach adult height. In other words, the boy will grow a great deal more. On the other hand, the X-ray may show that the boy's skeletal age is very mature and that the boy is approaching his adult height.

Weight

Although boys are heavier at birth, both sexes are of about equal weight at eight and a half years of age (see Appendix). Girls then become heavier at about nine or ten, and remain so until about fourteen and a half years, when boys equal and surpass girls (Tanner, 1978). The average male at six years of age weighs 45.5 pounds; by eight and a half years, 58.7 pounds (26.66 kg); and by age ten, 69 pounds (31.44 kg). The average six-year-old girl weighs almost 43 pounds (19.52 kg), by eight and a half, 58.5 pounds (26.58 kg), and by ten, 71.6 pounds (32.55 kg). As noted in Chapter 9, however, we should be wary of averages and speak in terms of percentiles. For example, a ten-year-old girl may weigh anywhere between 63 pounds (28.71 kg) and 82.6 pounds (37.53 kg) and still be considered "normal." Substantial deviations from these figures should be investigated. Many deviations may reflect differences in physique or development age, but some may indicate physical problems. Substantial deviations in weight may contribute to psychological problems, as in the case of the overweight or obese child.

Childhood Obesity

Estimates of the extent of obesity among children vary between 5 and 25 percent, depending upon the criterion used. There is no relationship between weight in infancy and later obesity. Overweight infants most often grow into children who are normally weighted. However, beginning in the toddler years and continuing into the preschool period, and throughout the middle years of childhood being overweight is associated with continued obesity. About 80 percent of all obese children will be overweight in adulthood (Rolfes & DeBruyne, 1990). Obese children are more likely to be shunned (Richardson, Goodman & Hastoff, 1961), to have fewer friends (Staffieri, 1967), and to have a poor body image (Mendelson & White, 1985).

Parents often fall victim to the "baby fat" theory, thinking that a fat child is a healthy child. Other parents argue that schoolage children who are obese will grow out of it. Both points of view are wrong. Obese children are not especially healthy, and juvenile obesity is related to adult obesity. The longer a child is obese, the more difficult it is to modify the condition.

Obesity is a complicated disorder that may be caused by a number of factors. Genetic endowment can play a part. Studies performed on the Pima Indian tribe in Arizona, where alarming rates of obesity and diabetes are found, have led some authorities to conclude that there is a relationship between genetics and obesity. Other research, as noted in the Cross-Cultural Current presented in Chapter 3, has also reached that conclusion. Perhaps being able to store fat more efficiently was beneficial when food supplies were very low, but this same efficiency becomes counterproductive if food is plentiful, and obesity is the result (Brody, 1980a).

Obesity seems to run in families. A child has only a 7 percent chance of becoming obese if neither parent is overweight, a 40 percent chance if one parent is overweight, and an 80 percent chance if both parents are overweight (Winick, 1975). But this does not prove that obesity is inherited, because children learn how and what to eat during childhood. Perhaps they are reinforced for eating everything and taking second helpings. Perhaps they witness their parents overeating or consider the evening gluttony the highlight of their day. Some children learn to eat the wrong foods and consume thousands of empty calories from junk food each day. In fact, more than 90 percent of obese children are obese because they consume more calories than they expend (Shonkoff, 1984). Genetic endowment may play some part in obesity, but the child's environment and activity level must be taken into account.

Lack of exercise may be an important consideration. Obese children are less active than their nonobese peers, although they may not always be aware of it (Bullen, Read & Mayer, 1964). Even when they are placed in situations requiring physical activity, such as competitive games, they are far less active than children of normal weight (Winick, 1975). An interesting question arises here. Is the child less active because he or she is obese, or is the child obese because he or she is less active? Perhaps both are correct. Whatever the case, obesity is a major social and physical problem in children that is difficult to correct (Becker & Drash, 1979). Because very heavy dieting can injure children as they develop, it is usually not recommended. One promising approach is to feed children in a nutritious way that will help them maintain a constant weight while they grow. This promotes normal development while restricting the accumulation of body fat (Cataldo & Whitney, 1986).

2. TRUE OR FALSE?

Most children who are obese during middle childhood will remain obese in adulthood.

It has been suggested that children are less active than in the past and that more emphasis should be placed on physical conditioning. Unfortunately, even in preschools, obese children do not participate voluntarily in physically active play (Javernick, 1988). It may be necessary for teachers to encourage these children to participate, and teachers might consider becoming active models in certain physical activities, including dancing and calisthenics. Parents can also help their children by encouraging active play and following doctors' dietary suggestions. Of course, any dietary plan should be executed under a doctor's care.

Physical Fitness and Health

Children who are physically fit are healthier and more resistant to fatigue and stress (Krogman, 1980). Physical fitness may prevent adult heart trouble and increase stamina (Brody, 1980). Physical activity is also needed to support normal growth and development. For example, exercise increases bone width and mineralization (Bailey, 1985). It also has social benefits, since group sports are often important social activities, and being excluded may interfere with a child's social development (Williams & Stith, 1980). Physically fit children have better self-concepts than children low in fitness (Sherrill & Holguin, 1989). Exercise is also a form of entertainment.

Exercise can affect learning. Consider the normal schoolday. The child is expected to stay in his or her seat, is allowed to walk around only when necessary, and leads a fairly inactive life. This is not in keeping with the image of the child as an active being who needs and desires physical activity. Providing regular physical activity improves learning. French doctors and educators were concerned about the heavy intellectual load in French schools that was almost unrelieved by any physical education or recreation. Beginning in 1951, the town of Vanves, a suburb of Paris, inaugurated a program in which the gross amount of time spent in academic activities was reduced, with the time being replaced by physical education, art, music, and other activities. Children did their schoolwork in the mornings. Parents were concerned that their children would fall behind academically or would catch more colds, but just the opposite occurred. Children's academic performance actually improved, and the children were more resistant to stress. The children also appeared happier, were in better health, and showed a more positive attitude toward their work. By 1969, this pattern had spread throughout the rest of France (Bailey, 1975).

We live in a country that appears to be in the middle of a health fitness fad. Health clubs are opening everywhere. Yet, a decade-long study of more than 12,000 children in grades 1 through 12 found a decline in cardiovascular endurance, especially in older children. Children cannot run as fast or as long as they could in 1980. In addition, children over eleven are heavier and fatter, though somewhat stronger. The percentage of children who could satisfactorily complete tests of flexibility, and muscular and cardiovascular endurance declined from 43 percent to 32 per-

3. TRUE OR FALSE?

Physical education in elementary school leads to a decrease in academic performance.

Exercise is important to normal development and maturation.

cent over the past ten years (Brody, 1990). In addition, the activity level of elementary schoolchildren is not high enough to promote physical fitness.

Many students do not engage in any strenuous physical exercise (Parcel et al., 1987), and many children do not receive any physical fitness training at all. Only 36 percent of students in grades 5 through 12 have physical education classes daily, and most elementary schoolchildren have such classes only once or twice a week (Brody, 1990). For those who do receive physical education in the schools, too much of it falls under the heading of competitive sports (Krogman, 1980). Winning may be the most important thing in professional sports, but it may be counterproductive for children in the elementary school years, where the "losers" may be turned off to physical activities. In addition, certain contact activities— so common in football—may lead to physical injuries. Even in baseball, a child who pitches should be watched for elbow and arm problems. The traditional system seems to focus on the athletically gifted or the early maturing child, leaving the vast majority of other students with little interest in physical activity.

Motivating students can also be a problem. If students are to become physically fit and remain fit, they must be motivated to engage in a physically active life. Children in middle school seem to respond well to comments about the short-term benefits of being physically fit, especially in terms of improved physical appearance (Ferguson, Yesalis, Pomrehn, & Kirkpatrick, 1989). However, more research on motivating children to participate in exercise programs and live a life-style that will contribute to physical fitness is needed. Physical education has many potential benefits for children, and a physical education program must address each of the above criticisms.

Nutrition

No one doubts the importance of good nutrition during childhood, but children seem to have little opportunity to develop good eating habits. All around them they see commercials for sugar-coated foods, overindulgence, and an emphasis on tastiness, and they are forced into poor eating habits, such as having to finish everything on their plates.

Relatively few studies have been done on the eating habits of children during their middle childhood years. One major study, the Bogalusa Heart Study, found a consistent pattern of overconsumption of foods high in saturated fat, sugar, and salt, with snack or junk foods high in these elements, accounting for about one-third the children's total caloric intake (Berenson, 1982).

One influence on what children eat is, of course, the family, but the school and television also have major effects. The average child is exposed to thousands of commercials a year. The most common viewing times are after school and on Saturday and Sunday mornings. Most television stations air cartoons, situation comedies, and other children's programs during these times. When John Condry and his colleagues (1988) looked at the content of nonprogram television on weekends and after school, they found an average number of product commercials per hour rose steadily between 1983 and 1987, although the total number of minutes devoted to commercials stayed about the same. The increase was caused by the greater number of short commercials replacing the standard longer ones. The most common commercials were for toys and games, cereals and candy, soda, and other snacks. Children's television viewing is related to children's attempts to influence their parents to buy what the children see; it is also related to the consumption of the foods advertised on television. Howard Taras and colleagues (1989) surveyed mothers of children ages three through eight on their children's television viewing habits, degree of snacking while watching television, and requests for foods advertised on television. The food items were assessed by content of fat, salt, and sugar. The most highly requested foods were high in sugar, followed by those high in fat. Hours spent watching television correlated both with the number of food items requested and with the amount of snacking. Mothers perceived a direct effect of television on their children's diets and physical activity.

Another area of nutritional interest is school lunches. Such lunches are served to about 60 percent of all students, and children receive between a quarter and a third of their daily calories from these meals (Parcel et al., 1987). Many school lunches exceed the national recommendations for total fat and salt. However, even if nutritious lunches are being served, it does not mean that they are being consumed, and there is a great need for nutritional education in the school system.

During the middle childhood years, children accumulate a store of nutrients—especially calcium—that will be drawn on by the body during the upcoming growth spurt. The more dense their bones are before the growth spurt, the better prepared they are for it (Whitney & Hamilton, 1987). Children cannot be counted on to choose a balanced, nutritious diet in a society in which most of the dietary influences are against them. It is the responsibility of parents and schools to educate children and to counter the prevailing influences. Children should be taught as early as possible to eat correctly and slowly, eat moderate amounts, and make mealtimes relaxing occasions during which they can enjoy the company of others who are eating.

Dentition

Besides height and weight gains, a number of other physical changes occur during middle childhood. The forehead becomes flatter, the arms and legs become more slender, the nose grows larger, the shoulders are squarer, the abdomen gets flatter, and the waistline becomes more pronounced (Williams & Stith, 1980). These changes occur gradually. The more noticeable changes are seen in the shedding of the baby teeth and the eruption of the permanent teeth.

The shedding of **deciduous teeth** is perhaps the most obvious physical occurrence during early middle childhood. For children, losing their teeth is a sign that they are growing up. But the gaps left in the mouth can cause temporary cosmetic problems as well as difficulty in pronunciation.

Human beings have a complement of twenty baby teeth and thirty-two permanent teeth. The first permanent tooth is usually the "six-year-molar," which does not replace any baby tooth (Smart & Smart, 1978). This tooth may erupt at any time between four and a half and eight years of age (Krogman, 1980). It is not easily recognizable, and it may become decayed and lost if not properly cared for. Many parents do not put much effort into dental care for their young children, thinking children have "only baby teeth" anyway. This is unfortunate, because premature tooth loss can lead to dental problems, including difficulties with the bite. As a rule, girls lose their baby teeth before boys do.

Again, the importance of nutrition should be noted. First, adequate nutrition, such as ample supplies of calcium, phosphorus, vitamins A, C, and D, and protein, is required for healthy formation of the mouth and teeth. Second, restricting the supply of fermentable carbohydrates is important, as is avoiding sticky sweets. Brushing after meals is necessary to help prevent tooth decay.

Motor Skill Development

The pattern of gradual growth and development that we saw with height, weight, and changes in proportion is also seen in the area of motor skill development. Take a few minutes to watch elementary schoolchildren during recess. Then visit a nursery school and compare the differences between the children's activities at each school. Differences are definitely there but difficult to describe. The elementary schoolchildren run, hop, jump, and throw more easily than the nursery schoolchildren. By the time children enter elementary school, they have developed many motor skills. Besides being able to run, climb, gallop, and hop, they are beginning to master skipping, throwing, catching, and kicking. In addition,

deciduous teeth
The scientific term for baby teeth.

It is not unusual to see teeth missing as children lose their baby teeth and gain their adult teeth.

their balance is reasonably good. During the next six years, their skills are refined and modified (DeOreo & Keogh, 1980).

During middle childhood, running speed and the ability to jump for distance increases (DeOreo & Keogh, 1980). The ability to throw both for accuracy and for distance also improves (Cratty, 1986), as does balance. These improvements are due both to maturation and to practice.

Are boys better than girls at these skills? Boys are superior in running speed and throwing, while girls excel at tasks that require agility, rhythm, and hopping (Cratty, 1986). Boys are also stronger than girls during this period, but girls show more muscular flexibility. Although balance is good in both boys and girls, girls between the ages of seven and nine tend to be superior (Cratty, 1970). Boys can jump higher and farther, girls tend to hop better. Girls also learn to skip sooner (DeOreo & Keogh, 1980).

As with almost all gender differences, the overlap between the sexes is great (Lockhart, 1980), and training and motivation are important factors. Frequently, boys are more motivated to perform on tests of physical ability and are more likely to practice certain skills, such as throwing, that involve the large muscles. In addition, the differences between the average boy and girl on many of these tasks are not very great. If girls are encouraged to develop their skills, they can improve them immensely.

As boys and girls get older, however, differences in their physical abilities become more noticeable (Smoll & Schutz, 1990). Differences in performance before the age of about eleven or twelve are small (Corbin, 1980b), but during adolescence, males continue to improve, while females level off or may even decrease in physical ability (Espenschade, 1960).

To what extent differences in physical performance can be attributed to physiological or environmental factors is a matter of controversy. In a study of more than 31,000 children and adolescents, Thomas and French (1985) found that with the exception of differences in throwing for both distance and speed, they could find no other task with gender differences large enough to be attributed to biological variables. However, in another study of students in grades 3, 7, and 11, Frank Smoll and Robert Schutz (1990) found that the greater amount of fat tissue girls have accounts for much of the differences between boys' and girls' performance on a number of physical tasks, including situps, timed runs, and the standing broad jump. They also found that boys' superior performance increased with age, and the influence of environmental factors became more important with time. In addition, being overweight hindered both boys and girls to the same degree. The degree to which physiological differences between boys and girls affects athletic performance, then, is controversial. However, the importance of the environment and such factors as lack of motivation, lack of reinforcement, fear of physical injury to female internal organs, or fear of appearing too masculine are strong contributors to the progressive gap between male and female scores on physical fitness tests. (Corbin, 1980b).

Certainly society's expectations are different for males and females. Males are expected to participate in rugged sports that require strength. Females are more likely to be encouraged to engage in physical activity

4. TRUE OR FALSE?

During middle childhood, boys are superior in running speed, and girls are better at tasks that require agility.

Children in the middle childhood years develop the intricate movements needed to successfully complete models and more involved projects.

involving agility. Females may not be taught the same physical skills as males. Society's different expectations for the physical abilities and training of males and females are somewhat reduced today from what they were even twenty years ago, but they are still present. This is unfortunate, because the benefits of physical fitness are great for both sexes.

Readiness for School

Think of all the physical, mental, and behavioral skills necessary for academic success. Children must be able to sit in one place, listen to an adult, and attend to lessons (Blank & Klig, 1982). They must be intellectually mature enough to understand what is going on, be emotionally emancipated from their parents so that they can form relationships with others, and have some measure of self-control (Kohen-Raz, 1977). In almost every culture, children begin to attend school sometime between the ages of five and seven. Traditionally, we use the child's chronological age to indicate school readiness, but only a very weak case can be made for this practice. Many children in this age group are simply not ready to master schoolwork (Ames, 1986). For example, many children are not ready to master reading in kindergarten or first grade (Perkins, 1975). A mental age of about six and a half is often considered necessary for acquiring reading skills (Durkin, 1970). This presents a problem, however, because some children may not be mentally, physically, or emotionally mature enough to tackle the challenge. Some children may not have the ability to focus on the reading matter (Moore & Moore, 1976), or they may lack a left-right sequence. They may be too immature to sit in a chair, listen to the teacher, and follow instructions. If children cannot recognize shapes, they cannot begin to learn their letters (Blank & Klig, 1982). Parents may read to their children, provide a home where reading is considered an enjoyable activity, and generally instill in their children a positive attitude toward learning, but even with this excellent background, some children, especially boys, will not be ready for reading instruction by the first grade (Ilg & Ames, 1972).

Since children develop at their own rate, some children will be ready to read before others—a point anxious parents should keep in mind.

◆ THE STAGE OF CONCRETE OPERATIONS

The school experience during the middle years of childhood is so important that these years are often called the school years. As children enter first grade, at about the age of six, the long preoperational stage is drawing to a close, and children are entering the stage of concrete operations. The shift from the preoperational stage to the **concrete operational stage** is gradual. A child does not go to sleep one night in the preoperational stage and wake up the next morning in the concrete stage. The child does not go to sleep egocentric, unable to fully understand classification and conservation, and wake up with fully developed abilities in these areas. These skills develop gradually over the years (see Table 11.1).

concrete operational stage
Piaget's third stage of cognitive development, lasting roughly from seven through eleven years of age, in which children develop the ability to perform logical operations, such as conservation.

TABLE 11.1: The Concrete Operational Stage

In the stage of concrete operations, children can deal with information that is based upon something they can see or imagine. They can mentally operate on objects but cannot deal with abstractions.

CHARACTERISTIC	EXPLANATION	EXAMPLE
Conservation	Children in this stage understand that things remain the same despite changes in appearance.	A child develops the ability to understand that a ball of clay can change shape and still contain the same amount of clay.
Ability to classify	Students can place objects into various categories.	Elementary school students can now group different animals as mammals.
Ability to seriate	Students can place things in size order.	Children can arrange a series of sticks in terms of length or weight.
Ability to reverse operations	Students can follow a process from beginning to end and then back again.	If a teacher rolls a ball of clay into a long wormlike structure, a child in this stage can mentally recreate the ball of clay.
Inability to use abstractions	Students cannot deal with abstract material, such as ideas and statements not tied to something observable or imaginable.	Children may find political cartoons and proverbs puzzling because they cannot understand their abstract meaning.

5. TRUE OR FALSE?

Schoolage children can solve abstract hypothetical problems if they are given sufficient time.

During the concrete operational stage, when considering change, children can deal with concrete objects but not with abstractions (Forman & Kuschner, 1977). They must either see or be able to imagine an object. For example, terms such as democracy, liberty, and justice are just too abstract for these children, although such children can understand democracy in terms of voting and majority rule, and justice in terms of fairness. Students cannot solve purely verbal problems that involve hypotheses. However, if you explain a problem in real, concrete terms, the students will have no difficulty with the challenge (Wadsworth, 1971).

The Decline of Egocentrism

Children in the concrete stage of operations become less egocentric. They understand that other people see the world differently and seek to validate their own view of the world. This is accomplished through social interaction, during which they can share their thoughts and verify their view of the world (Piaget, 1928). In addition, they can now take the perspective of the other person and can imagine what others are thinking of them in a relatively simple way (Harter, 1983). They are capable of being more sensitive to the feelings of others and imagining how others would feel in various situations. Language becomes less egocentric. Preschoolers often use such pronouns as he and she without offering adequate information to the listener concerning the person to whom they are referring. They figure that since they know who they are talking about, so does the listener (Pulaski, 1980). As the child matures, this tendency is greatly reduced.

Reversibility, the Ability to Decenter and Transformations

During middle childhood, the limitations of preoperational thought begin to fade slowly. Children develop the ability to reverse operations—to realize that if they roll a clay ball into a long worm they can reverse the operation and recreate the ball of clay. They develop the ability to decenter,—to take into consideration more than one dimension. Children now realize that the increase in the length of the clay worm compensates for the decrease in its width. They also begin to understand transformations—to understand that as objects change position or shape, they progress through a series of intermediate points. Piaget did not find these abilities in the preschooler.

Conservation

The crowning achievement of the concrete operational stage is the ability to conserve. The simplest example is the famous beaker experiment described in Chapter 9, in which a researcher takes two identical beakers that are tall and narrow and pours equal amounts of liquid into each. Then, in front of the child, the researcher pours the contents of one tall beaker into a squat beaker. The preschool child cannot take both height and width into consideration and cannot reverse the operation of pouring, making conservation impossible (Piaget & Inhelder, 1969). But schoolage children find such problems relatively easy. They may even show surprise when younger children don't get them right.

Conservation of number, substance, weight, and volume occurs at different ages but in a specific order. Piaget (1952) noted this uneven performance within a developmental stage and used the term **horizontal decalage** to describe the phenomenon whereby the child has acquired the underlying principle for solving a problem such as conservation but is not able to apply the principle across the contexts.

CONSERVATION OF NUMBER Show children displays of seven pennies in which the coins either are grouped closely together or are spread out. The four-year-old is certain that the spread-out group has more coins than the other group. The six- or seven-year-old develops a sense of conservation of number and knows that the spacing does not matter.

CONSERVATION OF WEIGHT When one of two equal balls of clay is made into a worm-shaped object and then reformed into a ball, the seven-year-old will probably understand that no clay has been lost in transforming the ball to a worm and back again. However, the child probably will not understand that the two shapes still weigh the same. Conservation of weight comes later, at about age nine or ten (Piaget & Inhelder, 1969).

CONSERVATION OF VOLUME The last conservation problem to be solved correctly is conservation of volume. Make two balls of clay and show

horizontal decalage
A term used to describe the unevenness of development in which a child may be able to solve one type of problem but not another, even though a common principle underlies them all.

Schoolage children show their ability to classify when they start collections of various items.

them to the child. The child should understand that the clay balls are equally large and equally weighted. Then put the clay balls in two identical beakers containing equal amounts of water and show that the balls displace the same volume of liquid because they cause the level of the water to rise the same amount. Then change the shape of one of the balls and ask the child whether the ball would still make the water rise to the previous height (Diamond, 1982). Typically, conservation problems concerning volume are the last to be solved. The ability to solve them appears at about age eleven or twelve (Piaget & Inhelder, 1969).

Seriation and Classification

Schoolage children also further develop the ability to seriate and to classify. They can easily arrange a series of sticks in terms of length and later by weight and finally by volume (Wadsworth, 1971). Their ability to classify also greatly improves. In fact, schoolage children are known for their propensity to collect things (Kegan, 1982). They will collect anything and thereby practice their skills of classification. They begin to realize that an item can be classified in many ways and belongs to a great many classes at one time.

How the Schoolage Child Thinks

The schoolage child's thought processes are certainly a great improvement over those of the preschooler. The preschooler's logic often defies analysis for the parent who is unfamiliar with Piaget's theories. Irreversibility, egocentrism, and the rest are different from what we encounter in adult life. The more logical, less egocentric ways of the elementary schoolchild are more recognizable. These children go beyond what the situation looks like and infer reality from the situation. In the conservation situation, schoolage children are not taken in by the fact that the amount of liquid in one beaker looks greater than the other. They can now decenter and take many more elements of a problem into consideration. This helps them not only in the physical world but also, as we shall see in Chapter 12, in judging events.

In addition, schoolage children develop a quantitative attitude toward tasks and problems. They now understand that problems have precise, quantifiable solutions that can be obtained by logical reasoning and measurement operations. For example, take nine legos and lay them in a perfectly straight line (see Figure 11.1). Then take nine legos and place them end to end but in a jagged fashion. The display of nine legos placed in a straight line looks longer than the display placed in a jagged line. Now tell preschoolers and schoolage children that these legos lines are two roads and ask them who makes the longest trip—the person who drives the car the entire length of the first (straight) road or the driver who drives the entire length of the second (jagged) road. The preschooler is fooled by the appearance of the roads and says the first. The schoolage child answers that they are the same (see Flavell, 1977). The older child is not fooled by how the roads look and recognizes that the total lengths of each road can be divided into subparts and measured.

FIGURE 11.1: Through the Child's Eyes

The first road looks longer than the second road, causing the preschooler to think that it will take the driver of the first car longer than the driver of the second car to get to the end of the road.

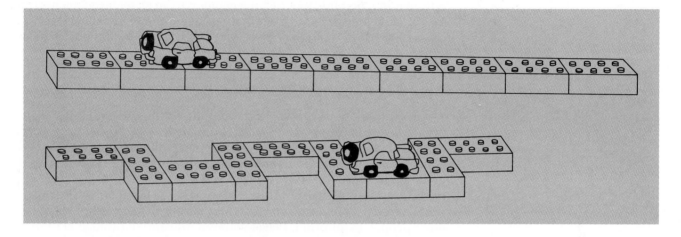

Cultural and Individual Differences

Piaget was well aware that children in other cultures show variability in the age at which they develop concrete operational skills (Bringuier, 1980). Children in the rural areas of Iran showed a two-, three-, and even four-year delay in passing through the same stages, compared with their urbanized peers. The environment becomes more important as a child becomes older. Many studies show that children with no schooling who have little contact with Westerners and who live in poor rural environments do poorer on Piagetian tasks than urbanized youngsters who attend school. Such factors as schooling, urbanization, and the relevance of a particular skill for a particular society affect the onset of concrete operational abilities (Dasen & Heron, 1981).

Limitations of Concrete Operational Thought

While the cognitive abilities of the schoolage child are impressive, these children still have a number of limitations. For instance, ask seven-year-olds to interpret a proverb such as "You can lead a horse to water, but you can't make it drink." You will be very surprised at the answer. These children may say something about not being able to force an animal to drink, or they may show a puzzled expression, or they may attempt a literal interpretation of the saying. They do not understand the more general, abstract meaning of the saying. Political cartoons also require the ability to think in the abstract, and children do not understand them very well. Teachers who are aware of this may attempt to explain difficult concepts such as democracy in more concrete terms that children can understand, perhaps through elections in class, rather than trying to define concepts in abstract, dictionary terms.

Children also have difficulty with hypothetical situations or hypotheses that are contrary to fact. Ask a child, "If all dogs were pink and I had a dog, would it be pink, too?" Children often rebel at such statements (Ault, 1977). They insist that dogs are not pink, and that's that. Children in the concrete stage of operations have great difficulty accepting hypothetical situations.

Applying Piaget to Education

Piaget's ideas about the cognitive abilities of schoolage children have been applied to education. Teachers can provide practice in such skills as classification and seriation. For example, children can learn to classify animals as mammals and nonmammals, vertebrates and invertebrates (Kaplan, 1990). Piagetian teaching encourages the use of social interaction in the learning process. Children who work in groups may learn social skills and help children improve their ability to take the perspective of other people. In addition, Piaget believes in learning through activity and emphasizes the importance of direct experience. Finally, teachers often do not realize that children at this age do not understand abstract or hypothetical explanations. It may be necessary to present concepts in a more concrete manner rather than presenting them in an abstract way.

◆ INFORMATION-PROCESSING SKILLS

Any attempt to understand cognitive functioning during the school years must include a look at information-processing abilities. Success in elementary school requires the ability to place one's attention on the relevant aspects of the lesson as well as the ability to remember what is being taught.

Attention

It is easy to relate a lack of attention to a lack of learning (Berliner, 1987). Children who are easily distracted from the learning task learn less than those who pay attention (Wittrock, 1986). Today, the concept of attention is most often used to describe mental effort that can be applied to a task in varying degrees (Daehler & Bukatko, 1985). It is a cognitive resource that can be used by the individual (Best, 1986). People can choose to place effort on particular information and allocate it as they think best. The preschooler's ability to voluntarily place his or her attention on a relevant area is limited, and the preschooler's attention is often captured by particular characteristics of the stimuli. The preschooler is also easily distracted.

The ability to pay attention despite interference improves with age. Younger children are often more easily distracted by those stimuli around them, and their attention span is shorter (Kaplan, 1990). As children mature, their ability to control their attention, to discriminate between what is and is not most important, and to adapt their attention to the demands of the situation improves (Wittrock, 1987). Their ability to plan what they are to attend to also shows improvement (Flavell, 1985). These abilities are primitive in the preschooler and develop over the elementary school years. When children are not told where to place their attention, older children attend to more relevant information than do younger children (Hale, 1979). When told to focus their attention on something specific, older children find it easier to block out irrelevant information (Small, 1990). Schoolage children are also able to maintain their attention for longer periods because they are becoming less easily distracted.

Recall, Recognition, and Memory Strategies

No matter how it is measured, memory improves as children negotiate middle childhood. Short-term memory improves with age from five to ten years. The typical five-year-old can recall four or five numbers after a single presentation, whereas a ten-year-old can recall six or seven (Williams & Stith, 1980). Recognition memory is generally good at all ages, but it too shows improvement with age (Dirks & Niesser, 1977). Retention is also superior in both recall and recognition during middle childhood.

Just why this improvement occurs is a matter of dispute (Wingfield & Byrnes, 1981). Some maintain that memory capacity improves with age. Others argue that changes in a child's ability to attend to the material and use memory strategies such as rehearsal and classification can explain the improvement (Dempster & Rohwer, 1983). Still others believe that both factors are important (Sternberg & Powell, 1983).

Indeed, children in middle childhood also begin to use verbal memory strategies on their own. John Flavell and colleagues (1966) showed pictures to five-, seven-, and ten-year-olds. The researchers pointed to certain pictures that were to be remembered and measured the rehearsal strategies used by the children. Only 10 percent of the five-year-olds showed any rehearsal, while 60 percent of the seven-year-olds did once, but only 25 percent used the strategy regularly. Some 85 percent of the ten-year-olds verbalized, and 65 percent did so with consistency. As one might expect, recall improved with age. Preschoolers can be trained to use verbal strategies—and these strategies do improve their performance—but when faced with similar problems, they do not use the strategies spontaneously. Perhaps they do not understand the memory process well enough to know that they should. Children in the school years begin to use the strategies more consistently.

As children progress through middle childhood, they also become aware that some strategies are superior to others. Elaine Justice (1985) found that second graders showed no preference for categorization over rehearsal, while sixth graders demonstrated a clear preference for categorization, a more sophisticated strategy. Progress in understanding the relative effectiveness of different strategies continues throughout the elementary school years.

The developmental progression in the use of strategies is quite clear.

Preschoolers may occasionally name an item to be remembered and may point or pay greater attention to it, but they do not yet use any verbal strategy spontaneously. Children in the middle years of childhood use repetition and later demonstrate planning and flexibility in their use of strategies (Brown, Bransford, Ferrara & Campione, 1983).

Metamemory

"After you study the names of the presidents and know them well, come downstairs and I'll test you," said Rachel's mother. With that, nine-year-old Rachel ran upstairs and studied. A little while later, she was ready. Asked whether she knew the presidents, she confidently answered yes. However, it soon became apparent that she knew very few. Rachel's mother got angry, and Rachel ran upstairs in tears.

This scene is repeated in many homes each night. Actually, Rachel and her parents would have an easier time if they understood the concept of **metamemory,** which is defined as knowledge of one's own memory processes. Another term **metacognition,** refers to knowledge of one's own thought processes. Children's knowledge of these processes increases with age. Rachel probably did not know that she didn't understand the work.

A pioneer in this research, John Flavell, suggests that metamemory should be understood in terms of two major categories. The first is sensitivity. If you ask children to remember where they put their shoes, they first must understand what the word *remember* means. The term *remember* is one of the earlier mental verbs used. Children as young as two and a half years of age understand it (Wellman & Johnson, 1979). There is evidence that children as young as four understand the difference between remember and forget, but their understanding is not complete. Young children understand these verbs only in terms of overt behavior (remembering where they hid a shoe). Whether young children really understand what it means to remember something, such as a group of pictures, is open to question and seems to depend partly on the nature of the task (Flavell, 1977). By the time children enter middle childhood, they have an idea of what remembering and forgetting mean and show some sensitivity to various types of instructions.

The second category involves three types of variables or factors that interact to determine how well an individual performs on a memory problem (Flavell, 1985). The first variable involves knowledge of one's own memory abilities. Are you better at remembering faces or names? If your boss orally gave you fifteen things to do, would you understand that you can't remember them all and inform the boss of that fact? Most of us are aware of the circumstances under which our memory tends to fail us, but young children are not.

Flavell and colleagues (1970) showed ten pictures to children of various ages and asked them to estimate the number of pictures they could remember. Most preschoolers and children attending kindergarten thought they could remember all ten pictures, while very few older children thought so. In reality, none could possibly remember them all. Young children overpredict their ability to recall items (Yussen & Levy, 1975). Markman

metamemory
A person's knowledge of his or her own memory process.

metacognition
People's awareness of their own cognitive processes.

(1973) found that second graders and fourth graders were better than kindergartners and first graders in understanding whether they knew items after studying them. Taken together, the evidence is strong that as children mature they become more aware of the limitations and the capacity of their memories and are less likely to overpredict their memory capacity.

The second variable involves the nature of the task. Almost all college students understand that recognition as tested on multiple-choice tests is generally easier than recall as tested on essay exams. When faced with a test on textbook material, one is likely to try to pick out the important facts, the definitions, and the concepts. This ability is not well developed in young children, who often experience difficulty separating the important material from the not-so-important material (Brown & Smiley, 1977). As children mature, their ability to understand the difficulties produced by a particular task increases. Moynahan (1973) found that third graders and fifth graders were more likely than first graders to understand that categorizing items (foods, types of furniture, etc.) made it easier to remember than memorizing a list of unrelated items. Rogoff and colleagues (1974) told six-, eight-, and ten-year-olds that they would be tested on their recognition of forty pictures after a few minutes, a day, or a week. Only the older children studied longer when told they would have to remember the material for a longer period of time.

The third variable is knowledge of strategies. As children mature, they gain the ability not only to use more strategies but also to understand the situations in which one strategy is more useful than another. Would you study differently for a multiple-choice test than for an essay test? When faced with different requirements, eleven-year-olds, but not five-year-olds, adopt different strategies (Horowitz & Horowitz, 1975). As children mature, they gain not only an ability to use more strategies but also the knowledge of which strategies might be more useful under certain conditions.

Implications of Metamemory

With increasing age, children become more aware of their own capacities, can better understand a task, and can match their strategies to the task (Masters, 1981). The study of metamemory has some interesting applications for parents and teachers. For example, if you were teaching children a particular skill and asked them whether they had any questions, they might nod their heads, and you might conclude that they understood what you were teaching. But teachers have found that this is not so, and metamemory research confirms this. Children may not be aware that they do not understand instructions or some concept. They may really believe they do. Markman (1977) tested children of various ages by giving them instructions for a game that had a number of obvious omissions. Young children were not aware of the omissions and failed to seek any clarification of the rules.

Academic progress may be related to children's ability to comprehend their own level of understanding. John Holt, in his influential book *How Children Fail* (1964), noted that part of being a good student is under-

6. *TRUE OR FALSE?*

When elementary schoolchildren claim they understand something, a parent or teacher can be reasonably certain that they do.

standing one's level of comprehension. Good students may be those who often say they do not understand, because they are aware of their level of knowledge. Poor students may not really know whether or not they understand the material. Holt notes, "The problem is not to get students to ask us what they don't know; the problem is to make them aware of the difference between what they know and what they don't" (1964, p. 29).

Children can be taught ways to monitor their own memory strategies. They can be taught strategies that increase their ability to know when they know something and when they don't (Cross & Paris, 1988). One way to do this is to first ask children right before material is taught or read what they think they should know, what they need to know, and what they would like to know and then help them to focus their attention on these areas (Gray, 1987). This is important, because children who are superior on measures of metacognition are better readers (Stewart & Tei, 1983). Good readers can use a variety of strategies—such as rereading, forming an image in their mind, and changing speed—for understanding passages. Asking questions is another skill that appears to separate good readers from poor readers. Again, some of these skills can be taught (Brown, Campione & Barclay, 1979). Children might become better readers if they are helped to develop better metacognitive skills.

Children's Humor

Progress in cognitive development shows itself in many areas of children's lives, including their understanding of humor. Humor serves many purposes. Certainly it enhances human relationships. Laughter can also reduce tension. In fact, young children who experience some frightful situation which turns out to be harmless will laugh at it (Smart & Smart, 1978). Humor helps us deal with our problems and feelings, such as powerlessness. Children in the middle years of childhood often use adults and teachers as the butt of jokes. Humor may also be used to hide embarrassment or uncertainty. A child may trip and then laugh. A sense of humor may also be linked with adjustment. Ann Masten (1986) found that ten- to fourteen-year-old children's appreciation and production of humor were positively related to the child's level of competence. A better sense of humor was associated with academic and social competence. Children who had a good sense of humor were viewed by teachers as more attentive, cooperative, responsive and productive. They were more popular with their peers, who also saw these children as gregarious, happy and as leaders.

But what makes people laugh? A key to understanding humor is incongruity, or the difference between what is expected and what is perceived. Things that do not go together can sometimes be funny. Thomas Shultz (1974) presented children ranging from six to twelve years with a series of riddles each with three answers. The children's appreciation of the humor was evaluated by observing their reactions and asking them to rate the riddle. For example:

Why did the cookie cry?

1. Because its mother had been a wafer so long.
2. Because its mother was a wafer.
3. Because it was left in the oven too long.

Answer one is incongruous, but it is resolved by interpreting wafer as "away for". Answer two is incongruous, but it lacks a resolution, a way of rendering the incongruity understandable within the context of the joke. Answer three eliminates incongruity. Younger children appreciated only the incongruity, while the older children found the resolvable answer the most humorous and the other alternatives less humorous. Young children, then, appreciate humor only in incongruity while older children appreciate humor based upon incongruity and resolution (Shultz & Horibe, 1974).

In addition, the incongruity can be too simple or too complex (Chapman & Sheehy, 1987). A moderate amount of incongruity produces the most humor. Too much incongruity and the joke is difficult to understand, too little and the joke is too simple (McGhee, 1976). The same joke that is moderately incongruous to a younger child and makes the child roll with laughter is too simple and produces little incongruity in the older child. Understanding jokes and riddles requires some mental effort. If the jokes and riddles do not require any mental effort they are too obvious and do not cause us to laugh. If they require too much mental effort they are too difficult and again fail to make us laugh.

Children's understanding of humor develops along with their cognitive abilities and knowledge base. Children can interpret the joke or riddle only in terms of what they know. A joke about a sailor on a ship only makes sense if the child understands what a sailor and a ship are.

The relationship between cognitive abilities and appreciation of humor is easy to demonstrate. Preschoolers do not understand "knock, knock" jokes because these jokes require a knowledge of the double meanings of words which preschoolers simply do not have (Bjorklund, 1989). Paul McGhee tested children in grades one, two, five and also graduate students using jokes that required a knowledge of conservation. For example, "Joey lives near an ice cream store where they give really big scoops of ice cream. One day Joey asked for two scoops, and the man asked if he wanted them in one dish or two. "Oh, just one dish," said Joey, "I could never eat two dishes of ice cream." (1976, p. 422). Other jokes also dependent on a knowledge of conservation were used. About half the first and second graders could conserve on weight tasks while the other half could not. All the fifth graders and college students could conserve. First and second grade children who could conserve found the jokes funny while the non-conserving children did not understand the humor. This demonstrates the importance of cognitive abilities to the understanding of humor. However, although all the fifth graders and adults understood the jokes they did not find them very funny, because as noted previously, the jokes were too simple, and they required too little mental effort. For these young first and second graders who had just developed the ability to conserve, the degree of incongruity and the mental effort required was perfect.

In a second study, McGhee initially discovered which first, second and fifth graders could successfully solve class inclusion problems. He placed ten beads in front of the child and asked the following questions: (1) How many plastic beads are there?, (2) How many brown beads are there?, (3) How many yellow beads are there?, and (4) Are there more brown beads or more plastic beads? Jokes that required a knowledge of class inclusion were then read to the children. For example:

> Johnny, Tom, and Alice all go to kindergarten. One day the teacher asked: "Who has the most different kinds of animals at home?" Johnny said "I've got a dog and a cat." Tom said "I've got three, a dog, a cat and a bird." Finally, Alice stood up and said "I've got you all beat! I've got 81 guppies" (McGhee, 1976, p. 424).

Again the children who had just recently acquired the capacity to understand class inclusion found the jokes more humorous than those children who did not understand class inclusion or who had understood class inclusion for years.

The appreciation of humor shows a developmental perspective. There is some dispute as to when humor is first experienced by a child. Some authorities believe that the ability to understand symbolism is necessary and thus sometime in the late second year of life the child begins to understand humor (McGhee, 1979). Others disagree and believe that even infants as young as four months can understand some forms of humor. They laugh when incongruous events are presented in safe situations (see Chapman & Sheehy, 1987). However, the humorous situation is not verbally presented, nor is any symbolism required to comprehend the humor.

The capacity to understand humor that requires symbols first evolves at between eighteen and twenty-four months, but it is not until after two years that the child begins to understand some verbal jokes (McGhee, 1979). The two-year-old finds it funny when a dog says "meow," and preschoolers find it very funny when someone incorrectly labels something, such as calling a cat "doggie." As children progress through the preschool stage the amount of incongruity needed to produce a laugh becomes greater. Preschoolers may find absurdity very appealing and laugh at a picture of an elephant trying to take a bath in the bathtub. Preschoolers also find rhyming words very funny. Children are also active in producing humor through silliness, teasing, absurdity and using humor to minimize injury to the self-concept, for example, laughing after tripping and falling (Gratch, 1974).

Children in middle childhood have more sophisticated language skills and a greater knowledge base. They are more likely to appreciate humor based upon the double meanings of words and phrases. There is a marked change from early to middle childhood, as surprise and resolution of the joke become as important as incongruity (Shultz, 1974). In early childhood, incongruity may be enough to get the child to laugh. Now, a meaningful resolution is necessary.

As the child progresses through middle childhood, the ability to understand double meanings of words and sentences becomes more pronounced. Most seven-year-olds can represent two meanings of a single word simultaneously. Children's humor develops beyond very simple jokes as their knowledge base and cognitive abilities expand. In addition, as the study by Paul McGhee showed, as children develop conservation and class inclusion skills their ability to understand certain types of jokes improves greatly.

Much humor in the middle years is off-color and deals with taboo subjects such as body functions. Children often use humor to express hostility and make older people, especially authority figures, look foolish. Children in middle childhood enjoy plays on words and puns. For example, a man was locked up in a house with a calendar and a bed. How did he say alive? Answer: He ate dates from the calendar and drank water from the springs on the bed (Williams & Stith, 1980, p. 402). School age children like short jokes with a surprise ending.

At about eleven or twelve, some of the more subtle ambiguities of humor are understood. Adolescents with an ability to understand abstractions may begin to enjoy the humor found in political cartoons.

Children's understanding of humor, then, is associated with developmental changes in their cognitive abilities. The study of children's humor is important in itself, since humor plays a part in interpersonal relations. It also reminds us of the many diverse ways in which cognitive development affects different areas of life.

◆ THE BASIC SKILLS: READING, WRITING, ARITHMETIC, AND COMPUTER LITERACY

The ages between six and twelve are dominated both socially and cognitively by the school experience. Children are faced with a variety of challenges in school, including development of the basic skills of reading, writing, and arithmetic. Not only are these skills necessary for later academic and vocational success, but they affect how a child sees himself or herself. Erik Erikson sees the psychosocial crisis of this stage in terms of industry vs. inferiority. Children who do not measure up to other children in these skills may feel inferior, while children who do well develop a positive sense of achievement. Interest in how children acquire these basic skills has increased, since a number of studies have criticized the achievement of American children in the basic skills.

Reading: The Cognitive Revolution

The most fundamental academic skill is reading. Consider the incredibly complicated process involved in reading. First, the eye must take in a certain amount of information in one brief action lasting between 150 and 300 milliseconds. Then it moves to another position. The information must be recognized as letters and words by comparing the symbols with visual information available in memory storage. Then the entire process of comprehension, whereby words and phrases take on meaning, must take place (Dodd & White, 1980). Reading is a sophisticated cognitive skill that involves perception, attention, memory, and evaluative thinking (Paris & Lindauer, 1982).

These middle childhood years are dominated by the school experience. The evaluation of work in school partially determines the outcome of Erikson's psychosocial crisis of industry versus inferiority.

Modern teaching of reading has been affected by our new understanding of cognitive development. In the cognitive view, learners are involved in an active process whereby they review what they know, link new information to prior information, form and test hypotheses about the meaning of a problem, and assess the strategies necessary to solve the problem (Kaplan, 1990). Learning requires sustained and conscious effort, and researchers have adapted this cognitive view of learning to techniques of reading instruction.

Reading is seen as an active process that goes beyond a literal interpretation of the text material (Athey, 1983; Chall, 1977). In addition, educators now appreciate that many factors affect the reading process (Samuels, 1983). Reading skill is affected by such external factors as the size, style, and legibility of the type, the format and organization of the material, and the style, readability, and difficulty level of the text. Internal factors, such as one's knowledge base and the reader's purpose for reading, also affect one's ability to understand a passage. These external and internal factors interact. The content of the passage is an external factor, but it interacts with the depth of the reader's knowledge about the topic. With some topics, students may indeed show poor comprehension, but for other topics they may demonstrate a reasonably good understanding of the text's message.

We now recognize that different skills are required to understand different types of written material. Not every reading activity is identical with every other. Consider the difference between reading for fun, reading a text for detail, and reading the newspaper for general information. Each may require a different strategy. Poor readers generally do not adjust the strategy to the task. They don't know when to skim and when to read over a paragraph carefully (Forrest & Waller, 1979).

Another change is the emphasis on phonics instruction. The argument over whether phonics or the whole-word approach is better has been going on for 300 years. Lately, there has been a switch to more phonics-based instruction, but the conflict continues.

Modern reading instruction, then, is more likely to use a phonics approach, to stress inferential as well as literal comprehension, and to show an awareness of the need to develop different skills for different reading materials. Cognitive aspects are now considered important, and teachers are more likely to realize the importance of meaning to what children are reading. From a practical viewpoint, cognitive instruction has changed some aspects of reading instruction and has led to the following recommendations. Before teaching reading, teachers should discuss the vocabulary, help students make predictions about what they will be reading based on surveys of the titles and text features, and plan how they will approach the assignment. The idea is for students to actively relate what they are reading to prior knowledge. During reading, students monitor their own comprehension by clarifying information, summarizing text segments, evaluating predictions, and separating important from unimportant information. After reading, the students organize the material through summarizing and categorizing (Jones, 1986).

Reading is fundamental to school achievement, and learning to read at the appropriate time is crucial to academic success. Failure to learn to read by the end of the first grade is associated with later academic failure. The level of reading achievement by the end of sixth grade can predict academic achievement in high school (Bloom, 1976). This does not mean that a poor reader in the second grade cannot be helped, but without special help, children who are behind tend to stay behind. In fact, studies have found that ratings made by kindergarten teachers of a child's general cognitive abilities, classroom skills, and personal and social characteristics as well as measures of the child's early cognitive abilities—including naming letters, memory, perception, and word-matching skills—predicted later achievement (Stevenson, Parke, Wilkinson, Hegion & Fish, 1976). A later study found that kindergarten measures of the ability to name letters and common categories of objects, the ability to associate visual and verbal stimuli, and some other early skills predicted measures of academic performance in high school (Stevenson & Newman, 1986). Without any special help, children who are ahead stay ahead, and those who are behind stay behind.

Since reading is such an important skill, student achievement in this area is constantly monitored. Recent surveys show that basic reading skills continue to gain slightly and that the largest gains are found in children from minority groups. Advanced reading skills showed small but steady declines from the early 1960s to the late 1970s, after which they leveled off and started to climb slightly (The Report of Commission on Reading, 1986).

Because reading is such an important skill, parents sometimes try to force their children to learn to read, but this approach does not work. In

Part 4: Middle Childhood

fact, nonaccelerated children catch up with accelerated readers later on (Wall, 1975). The child's general cognitive level and concrete operational abilities, such as classification, are related to reading achievement (Arlin, 1981; Harrison, 1981). Besides the cognitive factors involved, attitudinal and environmental concerns are important (Bettelheim & Zelan, 1982, Purves, 1977). Parents can do much to encourage a positive attitude in their children toward reading, so that when the children are ready, they will want to read. Children whose parents read to them, ask them questions that go beyond the text, and see reading as a valued activity are motivated to master the skill.

Reading and Television

Both parents and teachers often complain that children do not read enough. Why don't children read more? People often blame television. Some evidence does indicate that there is a negative relationship between television watching and reading and academic achievement (Johnson, Cooper & Chance, 1982). Television, the argument goes, has replaced reading as a leisure activity. Indeed, when fifth graders were asked to rate leisure activities, reading was rated seventh out of nine categories, with television ranked first (Greaney, 1980).

Can restricting television viewing improve a child's reading? Consider what happened when six-year-olds were matched and randomly assigned to either a restricted television viewing group or an unrestricted group. In the restricted group, the children watched half as much television as previously. The results showed that restricting television did improve performance on intelligence tests and that the children did spend more time reading (Gadberry, 1980). Yet it would be a mistake to blame poor reading skills on television watching. The cognitive abilities of the child, the values of the home, and the child's attitude toward reading are also important factors that enter the equation. Some excellent readers watch

DATAGRAPHIC

Weekly TV Viewing by Age

Source: Nielsen Media Research, 1990.

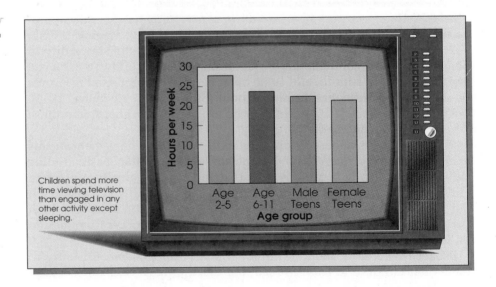

quite a bit of television (Neuman, 1982). Thus, television may be one factor that inhibits reading, but it cannot shoulder the entire blame, which must be shared with the home and the school.

Writing

Interest in student writing increased throughout the 1980s and will continue to grow in the 1990s. Teachers in all areas and at all grade levels are now being encouraged to emphasize writing in their classrooms.

Writing is not simply one unified activity. Students may write for a number of reasons. They may write as a means of communicating personal thoughts or feelings. This type of writing is intrinsically satisfying (Scardamalia & Bereiter, 1986). Writing is also used as a way of demonstrating knowledge and reasoning skills. Here, writing is incidental to some other activity, such as giving a report or taking a test. Last, writing can be used as an exercise in which the purpose of writing is to develop a particular writing skill.

What do we know about how teachers use writing in their classrooms? In a summary of the research on student writing, Susan Florio-Ruane and Saundra Dunn (1987) concluded that students generally write in response to teacher demands and teachers select both the purposes and the format of the writing. In other words, the teacher initiates the writing and makes the decisions about what is to be written and how it is to be written. Most student writing is performed for evaluation purposes, and these evaluations often focus on surface features of language rather than on meaning. In addition, the researchers found that little or no technical support is offered to students while they are writing, that time available is limited, and that any interaction with peers during the writing process is discouraged. Last, they found that little time is spent on revision and that most writing done in schools stays there and is never read by a wider audience. For most written work, then, the teacher gives the assignment, the student follows the teacher's rules, and the teacher evaluates the student's work.

Writing, then, does not seem to be used as a form of practical communication. It is frequently divorced from what is going on inside or outside the classroom. In addition, there is little focus on the process of writing. Revision and rewriting are not emphasized, and the final product is often seen by no one else, nor does it serve as the basis for any further study or discussion. This is unfortunate, for we know that writing instruction is more effective when it is tied to something real, when the process is emphasized, and when students are helped to produce their best work.

How can these ideas be used by the teacher? Consider the following teacher's method of developing writing skills in a class. The teacher informs the students the day before that they will be asked to write something. The next day the teacher writes the topic on the board and reminds the students about the importance of such things as complete sentences and good grammar. The teacher distributes paper and thirty minutes later suggests that the students finish and check their papers for errors. The students then recopy the material and are told that they must submit their compositions the next day. The teacher marks the papers at home, correcting all the errors. After returning the papers to the class, the teacher asks several students who have done well on the assignment to read their papers aloud to the class.

According to Daigon (1982), the teacher's techniques run counter to what we know is important in teaching writing skills. First, the assignment came out of the blue. Writing should come from experience, such as from something that is going on in the classroom. Second, the teacher's reminders about proper form are poorly timed and probably a waste of time. The first task in any assignment is not form and grammar but the formation of a plan to tackle the assignment. It would have been more helpful had the teacher discussed the subject and the objectives of the assignment and helped students to generate ideas. At this stage, students should think and talk about the progress of their writing, collect information, organize their material, and consider what they want to say (U.S. Department of Education, 1987).

Third, the teacher's suggestions that after thirty minutes the students check for errors and make a final draft is also ill timed. It would have been better had the teacher encouraged the students to jot down their ideas freely, uninterrupted by attention to mechanical or grammatical blunders. Maintaining the creative flow of ideas is more important at this stage. Daigon admits that punctuation, capitalization, and grammar are crucial, but these elements are best attended to later.

In addition, the teacher assumed that after thirty minutes the children could merely check their papers. No time was allowed for revision. Most writers consider revision the real task of writing. Revision entails a reorganization and an extensive reevaluation of the product, not merely proofreading. Asking the top students to read their own masterpieces is also a mistake. This only emphasizes the other student's inadequacies. A better idea is to allow the students to draft, revise, and draft again until a good product emerges and then publish all the papers in some form.

For some, these ideas about writing may seem like heresay, but no one is supporting slipshod and ungrammatical writing. What many authorities are now suggesting is that we know that successful writers have a purpose, draft and redraft their writing, and only at the end make the technical corrections that are so important to a good final product.

Arithmetic

The concept of quantity is probably universal (Posner, 1982), but schools are charged with the responsibility of teaching the operations of addition, subtraction, multiplication, and division. Studies show that American students spend less time on mathematics and do more poorly than children in many other societies. First-grade and fifth-grade students in Japan and Taiwan are superior to elementary school students in the United States on basic mathematical skills (Stigler, Shin-Ying, Lucker & Stevenson, 1982; Stigler, Shin-Ying & Stevenson, 1987).

Many young children can count, but this does not mean that they understand the idea of quantity. Children can be taught the names of the

7. TRUE OR FALSE?

Japanese elementary schoolchildren are superior to American children in achievement in mathematics.

numbers—one, two, three, etc. This is seen even in very young children. A two-year-old may produce a smile on her mother's face when she counts from one to ten. This is essentially the rote learning of facts and does not imply an understanding of number. It is common to find young children who can recite the numbers in a rising pitch, as they do on "Sesame Street," but who cannot do it in an even tone (Peterson & Felton-Collins, 1986). Piaget argues that children learn mathematical concepts through a process of discovery (Piaget, 1965; Piaget & Szeminska, 1941). The idea of an infinite series of numbers is not present during early childhood. In fact, Piaget believes that an understanding of numbers and the operations of addition and subtraction, multiplication and division, are normally developed after age seven (Piaget, 1967).

Today, there is more emphasis on the importance of the basic skills.

The concept of number depends upon the student's knowledge of classification and seriation. There is a relationship between performance on such Piagetian tasks as classification and seriation and mathematical achievement (Vaidya & Chansky, 1980). Classification allows one to represent a collection of objects and is necessary if students are to understand the statement that, for example, there are seven pennies and two dimes. This relates to the cardinal property of numbers. Seriation is vital because it relates to the ordinal property (first, second, third). Another important understanding relates to conservation. For instance, it is important to understand that ten pennies are ten pennies regardless of how they are arranged. If we rearrange a particular display of ten pennies, the shape may change, but the number stays the same. Conservation of number occurs at about six or seven years of age. The problems many youngsters in the earliest years of elementary school experience with mathematics can be explained by a child's inability to understand the basic processes that underlie mathematical concepts.

The teacher or parent need not just sit and wait for students to attain a knowledge of classification and seriation. Classification activities can be very helpful. For example, if you have a tray of many different buttons of various sizes and colors, very young children can classify the buttons according to any single attribute you choose. Children who are already in the concrete operational stage can improve their classification skills by categorizing things that are more complex, such as things that are animate or inanimate.

Seriation is more difficult for young children than classification. When classifying, we only have to decide whether an object possesses a particular characteristic (is it round or is it blue?). When placing things in size order, comparisons must be made. To help children with this task, they may be encouraged to arrange rocks on the basis of weight or sticks on the basis of length. Students may discuss the order in which various ingredients for preparing a recipe must be used.

It is important to remember that in the elementary school years, students do best with material that is tied to real-world, concrete ideas. They have difficulty with things that are hypothetical. The early years of mathematics learning involve computation. The picture most people have of learning mathematics is a child sitting at a desk memorizing a multiplication table. Indeed, mathematics does involve learning by rote, but many

Computer literacy starts in the early years of elementary school.

computer literacy
A term used to describe general knowledge about computers that includes some technical knowledge of hardware and software, the ability to use computers to solve problems, and an awareness of how computers affect society.

experts have criticized this aspect of mathematics instruction, emphasizing that thinking and the child's approach to problems are more important than merely obtaining the correct answer (Kamii, 1982). The older method stressed memorization of formulas rather than understanding. The newer method emphasizes the importance of beginning with concrete objects so that students can gain an idea of how mathematics can be used and develop a better understanding of mathematical processes. When this is learned, the children can gradually decrease their dependence on concrete objects (Marjoribanks & Walberg, 1975).

The new look in mathematics does not deny the importance of learning the basic skills, including practice in the multiplication tables. Indeed, practice in the basic skills is critical. However, the new method also takes into consideration the cognitive level of the child, introduces mathematics on a concrete level, and emphasizes thinking and discovery.

Computer Literacy: The New Basic

Recently, the schools have been asked to teach a new basic skill—computer literacy. The number of computers in schoolrooms is increasing greatly (Callison, 1988), and most children will use a computer in their schooling at some time or another. To better understand how the educational process is being affected by computers, we must look at two specific areas of concern. The first area includes the concept of learning about the computer in order to share some basic knowledge of what a computer does. This is sometimes called computer literacy. The second area includes the use of computers for such things as simulations and games, drill and tutorials, and as an instructional aid in the classroom. This is often called computer-aided instruction. The use of the computer as a tool for word processing can be placed under both headings.

What should a student know about the computer to be able to function in society? The computer has obviously affected many areas of life and will continue to do so in the future. Unfortunately, many studies indicate that students know very little about computers. For instance, one report from the National Assessment of Educational Progress (NAEP) investigated three areas: knowledge of computer technology, understanding of computer applications, and understanding computer programming. The results showed a general lack of knowledge about what computers can do and how they work (Bracey, 1988).

The term **computer literacy** means different things to different people. A reasonably good general definition is that computer literacy consists of the skills and knowledge that will allow a person to function successfully in an information-based society (Upchurch & Lochhead, 1987). Computer literacy can be divided into knowledge of and performance with computers. Under the knowledge area, topics that may be taught are familiarity with the components of a computer system (hardware and software) and how they work, information about the history of computing, awareness of the current and projected uses of computers in society, the possible implications of those uses, and knowledge about job opportunities associated with computers. In the performance area, we may want stu-

THE CHILD
IN THE YEAR
2000

Technology and Dependence

I know a family where the parents cannot program their video cassette recorder or use a spread sheet, but their children can. It is not unusual to find children very comfortable with a variety of electronic and technologically sophisticated machines, including computers. As children negotiate elementary school in the next decade, most will become even more familiar with the computer and other new technologies. Some have warned that the increasing emphasis on technology could be detrimental to the child's developing social skills. Of course, there is no reason that computers and sophisticated technology could not be used in a cooperative manner and actually help students with their social skills. In addition, although many schools in the future will depend more on advanced technology, it is doubtful that more than one-third of the day will be spent using such technology.

A more difficult question involves the use of technology which, according to some, may hamper or interfere with the development of academic skills. For example, should a student learning word processing be allowed to use spelling checks and grammar checks? Should a student working

with mathematical computations be allowed to use a calculator? Do such aids interfere with the student's ability to spell, learn grammar, or perform mathematical computations without techno-logical help?

In some schools, the students are not allowed to use spelling checks at all. The use of calculators has recently been the source of considerable dispute. A task force of the National Academy of Sciences urged schools to give all students from kindergarten through grade 12 access to calculators and computers in mathematics class. The task force claims that mathematics education is often nothing more than doing calculations. The newer look in mathematics, which emphasizes reasoning and problem solving, could be enhanced through the use of calculators (Rothman, 1988). Obviously, this is a very

controversial suggestion. The same controversy exists in other fields, as some advocate giving students pocket spellers (West, 1989). Others claim that the use of such instruments in school could lead to a condition in which students will become overly dependent on technology and will not learn how to calculate, spell, or use correct grammar.

These questions and criticisms certainly must be addressed. It is especially important to actively document whether these changes really occur or whether they are merely theoretically possible. This will require additional research.

It is probable, however, that the schoolage child in the next decade will be exposed to and expected to use more sophisticated technology. There is some pressure to develop new educational technologies that will improve achievement in schools. If these advances are demonstrated to be effective, the questions remain of dehumanization and the possible danger of overdependence on technological aids. There is no simple answer to either question. However, these are certainly two questions that will be asked with increasing frequency as we enter the twenty-first century.

dents to be able to use software, write simple programs in one or two languages, and use the computer to solve problems (Brownell, 1987).

The focus of attempts to develop computer literacy has changed within the past decade. Early attempts stressed computer history, terminology, and programming. Although these are still taught to some extent, the focus has changed from learning how a computer works to learning how computers can be used to help solve problems. In other words, applications are stressed. Discussion of how computers are used in our society to solve problems, the computer's possible effect on society, and computer abuse and ethics are now emphasized. This focus on the problem

8. TRUE OR FALSE?

The emphasis in computer literacy courses is on learning how to program computers using different computer languages.

solving and applications is noticeable in the performance area, as many students are now given some experience in using the computer for word processing and are introduced to data bases and spread sheets. Little or no emphasis is placed on programming except for those who may either need the skill because of a scientific interest or feel they will need programming in their future vocation (Trollip & Alessi, 1988).

Computer literacy can be taught in many ways. Some schools offer one-semester courses, others nine-week minicourses. At other times, elements of computer literacy are integrated into the regular academic classroom.

The computer can also be used as a tool for enhancing creativity. Word processing is a good example of this. Consider the student who is writing a composition. The student writes the composition and then realizes that it must be edited. Editing is the most important part of writing, and revision the most difficult. It is this rewriting that forms the drudgery of writing. Word processing allows students to do this more easily. Students who have access to a computer rewrite their work more effectively, especially in the areas of organizing and expanding their ideas (Vockell, 1987).

There are a number of reservations about the use of computers in the educational process. One real concern is the possible lack of social interaction—especially among young children—that could result if computers are used too much (Bork, 1988; Karger, 1988). However, even those schools who use computers extensively appear to be aware of this potential problem and structure interaction into their daily plans (West, 1989).

Another concern is the possible dehumanization of the classroom environment. How will computerization affect the role of both teacher and student? No one can truly answer this at the present time. Still another concern is the overuse of computers for drill and practice (Streibel, 1986). However, computers can be effective in giving students drill and is just one way the computer may be used (Heinich, 1988). Some computer programs go well beyond simple drill and may actually enhance student creativity through use of thought-provoking problem-solving exercises and simulations.

◆ CREATIVITY AND THE SCHOOL

creativity
The production of a novel response that appropriately solves a given problem.

We do not just want our schools to teach the basics. We also want children to be creative. But just what is creativity? We tend to consider creativity in terms of musicians or artists or mental geniuses who seemingly have made quantum leaps in contributing to our ability to understand our world. Yet, this conception of creativity may be too narrow. **Creativity** involves a "person's producing a novel response that solves the problem at hand" (Weisberg, 1986, p. 4). To be creative, the response cannot simply be a repetition of something an individual saw or heard. It must also be appropriate; that is, it must solve the problem it is designed to solve. If a student hopes to solve the problem of increasing the efficiency of a kite, throwing a baseball at the kite may be novel, but it will not solve the problem.

The most popular way of looking at creativity is to consider it to be a type of thinking. Guilford (1967) differentiated between two kinds of thinking: convergent and divergent. **Convergent thinking** involves arriving at an answer when given a particular set of facts and is the type of thinking measured by intelligence tests. **Divergent thinking** involves the ability to see new relationships between things that are still appropriate to a situation.

The most common test of creativity was developed by E. Paul Torrance and is called the Torrance Tests of Creative Thinking (TTCT). The test measures creativity by considering four criteria: (1) fluency, the production of a large number of ideas; (2) flexibility, the ability to produce a variety of ideas; (3) elaboration, the development and embellishment of the ideas; and (4) originality, the production of ideas that aren't obvious (Hennessey & Amabile, 1987). Sometimes, a test measuring just one of these criteria—ideational fluency (the production of a large number of ideas)—is used by itself, because it is highly correlated with other factors, such as originality and flexibility, but is easier to work with (Kogan, 1983).

Not everyone is satisfied with the idea that creativity is solely a type of thinking or is the same as divergent thinking (Mansfield, Busse & Krepelka, 1978). Some consider this a rather narrow definition and point out that evidence shows that divergent thinking in childhood is not highly correlated with creative activities in adulthood (Feldhusen & Clinkenbeard, 1987).

Some see divergent thinking as one—but only one—of the components that creative activity comprises. Daniel Keating (1980) expands the definition of creativity to include, along with divergent thinking, content

convergent thinking
A type of thinking in which people solve problems by integrating information in a logical manner.

divergent thinking
A type of thinking marked by the ability to see new relationships between things that are still appropriate to a situation.

Whenever the term creativity is mentioned, the arts come to mind. However, creativity can occur in every area of life.

knowledge, the ability to communicate, and the ability to critically analyze. Content knowledge is important because it is difficult to think creatively if one does not understand the area in which creativity is taking place. Communication skills are required in the broad sense, since an idea must be communicated to others. The element of critical analysis has rarely been identified with creativity. However, it is an integral part of the process. If an individual has fifteen ideas about what could occur and what should be done to solve a problem, how should that person proceed? A judgment needs to be made so that some avenues can be explored and others left behind. Critical analysis allows one to follow the most promising approach. It is clear, then, that creativity requires a background in the field and other skills that can be encouraged or taught in school.

You may have noticed that intelligence was not included in any of these conceptions of creativity. Some people argue that the higher the person's intelligence, the greater the person's creativity. This is incorrect. Studies show that people with low intelligence scores do indeed show low creativity, but once an average intelligence score is reached, there is little relationship between intelligence and creativity (Hennessey & Amabile, 1986). Creative performance can be found in most people if the atmosphere encourages creativity.

How can creativity be encouraged in the classroom and at home? One way is to use divergent questions, that is, questions that require more thought or analysis rather than simple answers. Providing an opportunity for creative expression is another suggestion. For example, it is possible to encourage students to invent new things (Borton, 1986). This involves giving children an opportunity to do something different while refraining from undue criticism. Creativity requires an atmosphere where different approaches are encouraged. However, creativity does not spring forth without background, and developing thinking skills and providing a base of knowledge are important as well.

◆ FACTORS THAT INFLUENCE ACADEMIC ACHIEVEMENT

Reading, writing, and mathematical achievement do not develop in a vacuum. The general achievement of any student in an elementary school depends on a number of factors, including the nature of the school experience, the child's home, and the student's personal characteristics. It is popular to blame any one of these variables for pupil failure, but educational achievement is affected by all of them.

The School Experience

Each school has its own atmosphere, its own feeling. Some schools are orderly; others have a carnival atmosphere. Some schools are doing a better job than others. Such factors as a safe and orderly environment, an understanding of the goals of the school, administrative leadership, a

9. *TRUE OR FALSE?*

The more intelligent an individual is, the greater the chance that he or she will be creative.

One way of encouraging creativity is to have students actually do something different together.

climate of high expectations, allocation of time to instruction in the basic skills, and frequent monitoring of student progress have been suggested as factors that differentiate schools that are more successful from those that are less successful (Lezotte, 1982). A good relationship between the home and the school is also important. Especially in the early grades, and in school where students require remedial work, smaller classes are an advantage (Rutter, 1983).

Everyone knows that some teachers do a better job than others, but it is difficult to discover just what qualities are common to superior teachers. In fact, no single pattern predominates (Centra & Potter, 1980). One aspect of teaching that is well related to effective learning is the amount of time spent in direct instruction (Kaplan, 1990).

Teachers and the Self-fulfilling Prophecy

One aspect of teacher behavior that has led to a great deal of research—and controversy—is the relationship between teacher expectations and student achievement. Research results indicate that teachers' expectations have an important effect on students' academic achievement (Dusek & Joseph, 1983). But how important are these expectations, and how are they communicated to students?

In 1968, Robert Rosenthal and Lenore Jacobson performed the most famous study on the subject. They chose 20 percent of the children in an elementary school serving a lower income community and told the children's teachers that according to tests, the children were likely to bloom academically during the following year. They planted expectations in the teachers' minds as to the expected academic performance of the children. Their sample included 20 percent from each of three tracks—low, average, and high achievement. Within a year, those labeled late bloomers showed higher academic achievement and greater gains in IQ than those who were not so labeled. They were also rated as having greater potential; being more interested, curious, and happy; and being more intellectually promising. When teachers rated children who were not labeled late bloomers but who nevertheless gained substantially during the year, they did not give those children as much credit or rate them as highly. This was especially true of children in the low track.

At the end of the second year, some differences favoring the group of "late bloomers" still existed, but most of the differences had decreased substantially. The effects were greater in the younger groups than the older groups, but the effects of expectations on the younger students faded much more than the effects on older students. The older children's self-concepts were more resistant to change, but once altered, the change persisted. The results of this study have been explained by invoking the **self-fulfilling prophecy**—the phenomenon that expectations affect the likelihood that a particular event will occur. If you expect students to do well, they are more likely to achieve; if you do not, they are less likely to achieve.

self-fulfilling prophecy
The concept that a person's expectations concerning some event affects the probability that it will occur.

This study's conclusions have, at times, been blindly accepted. However, numerous criticisms and doubts have been raised. The methodology and statistical procedures have been challenged (Elashaff & Snow, 1971), and attempts to replicate the study have yielded mixed results (Cooper, 1979). Some argue that although the self-fulfilling prophecy does exist, it is less widespread than the study would have us believe (Proctor, 1984). Despite these differences, however, the proposition that teacher expectations can and do affect student achievement has been validated by much research. In a four-year study of over 5,000 children, Crano and Mellon (1978) found that teacher expectations based on social characteristics unrelated to academic capabilities had a strong impact on children's achievement. There is no doubt that teacher expectations can influence student academic achievement (Lockheed, 1976).

The real question, then, is not whether the self-fulfilling prophecy exists but rather how important it is. The proposition that severely inaccurate initial expectations substantially alter academic achievement in students is not supported by the research (Cooper & Tom, 1984). Jere Brophy (1983) notes that expectations do not always affect student achievement, but even when they do, the effects make on the average only a five percent to ten percent difference in academic achievement. This of itself is important, but it also means that low student achievement cannot be exclusively explained by or blamed on low teacher expectations.

In addition, not all teacher expectations are based upon irrelevant characteristics. Teacher expectations are largely accurate and based upon valid information, and when differential treatment is found, it is usually due to individualized instruction (Brophy, 1983). When sixth graders were followed, Lee Jussim (1989) found some modest evidence for the self-fulfilling prophecy but much stronger evidence that teacher expectations predicted student performance, not because such expectations cause students to perform in some way but because these expectations are largely accurate.

How are teacher expectations communicated to students? After all, teachers do not say "Peter, you're dumb" or "Jane, you can't pass math." It is most likely that the messages are communicated in more subtle ways, through nonverbal gestures such as a nod or a facial expression.

In summary, teacher expectations do affect student achievement, but not as radically as first thought. Teachers often base their expectations on valid observations, but sometimes other extraneous factors such as race, socioeconomic background, physical appearance, reputation, and sibling performance may influence their expectations (Dusek & Joseph, 1983).

Socioeconomic Status

The fact that children from poor socioeconomic backgrounds do not do as well in school as children from middle-class families is well established (Anderson & Faust, 1973; Coleman, 1966). Why is this so? Children from poor families generally live in crowded conditions, have poorer health care, are not exposed to middle-class experiences such as trips and books, have lower career aspirations, and may not know how to succeed in school (Mandell & Fiscus, 1981). Children from lower socioeconomic backgrounds generally come to school less advanced cognitively. This leads to academic failure, and a vicious cycle ensues. Failure leads to lack of interest and motivation, which leads to more failure. The children's expectations for success are lower as well, although they increase with age (Fulkerson, Furr & Brown, 1983).

Some of these generalizations are now being challenged. The correlations between socioeconomic status and academic achievement are indeed positive, but they range anywhere from a low of +.1 to a high of +.8 (White, 1982). (Remember, a correlation of 1.00 is perfect.) Although socioeconomic status is correlated with achievement, it can explain on the average only five percent of the final results in academic achievement. The traditional indicators of socioeconomic status are occupational level, education, and income, but many studies add to these variables such factors as the size of the family, educational aspirations, ethnicity, and the presence of reading material in the home. These measures of home atmosphere correlate more highly with academic achievement than with any single or combined group of the traditional indicators of socioeconomic status.

Measures of the home environment are better predictors of academic achievement. It would, therefore, be better to concentrate on what home factors affect academic achievement. The parents in many poor families do promote academic achievement in their children. For example, they read to their children, help them with homework, take them to the library, and expand on their language. If we know that these home variables are more predictive of academic achievement, we can then educate parents to change the ways they interact with their children. In addition, by concentrating on home environment rather than socioeconomic status, we turn our attention away from a particular group and toward particular parent-child relationships, home variables, and child-rearing strategies. Focusing on socioeconomic status may mask the truly important home variables that are good predictors of academic achievement.

Some children from the same families attending the same schools do very well in school, while others do not. The reasons involve such individual variables as gender, attitudes, work habits and motivation, cultural differences, and intelligence.

Gender

Do girls or boys do better in elementary school? Even though no gender differences exist in intelligence, girls perform better than boys on measures of reading, spelling, and verbal abilities, while boys, at least in the later elementary school years, do better in mathematics and problems involving spatial analysis (Halpern, 1986). Elementary schoolgirls are generally superior in verbal fluency, reading, and mathematical computation, while boys are superior in mathematics reasoning and spatial relationships (Maccoby & Jacklin, 1974; Marshall & Smith, 1987). A great deal of overlap occurs, with some girls performing better than boys in mathematics and some boys reading better than girls. In addition, many of these gender differences, such as those found in verbal ability, are relatively small (Hyde, 1981), and the differences in mathematics achievement normally show themselves only in the later years of elementary school or at the onset of puberty (Paulsen & Johnson, 1983). In addition, gender differences in cognitive abilities are decreasing, with the sole exception of those differences in the highest level of mathematics performance. Here, males show superior achievement, and the gap has remained constant, at least since 1970 or so (Feingold, 1988). The gap in achievement in other areas has been reduced greatly.

Why should these differences exist? Perhaps girls are physically more ready for school, and this physiological readiness gives them a push toward academic achievement (McGuinnes, 1979). Perhaps the atmosphere of school is considered feminine, with its great percentage of female teachers and its emphasis on obedience and sitting still. Boys and girls experience school in very different ways, and both male and female teachers value the stereotyped feminine traits of obedience and passivity rather than aggressiveness and independence (Etaugh & Hughes, 1975). At least in the early grades, boys may find school achievement more difficult and not in keeping with their view of the "masculine" role model.

Attitudes, Work Habits, and Motivation

Attitudes, work habits, and motivational differences are also factors in achievement. A child's attitudes toward school, the teacher, and the subject itself influence academic achievement. One reason offered for male superiority in mathematics in the later grades is that males expect to do better. These higher expectations are found as early as the first grade, even though boys' grades and abilities are not superior to those of girls (Entwisle & Baker, 1983). Attitudes toward mathematics are particularly important because they are related to mathematical performance in both sexes. Differences in performance are not inevitable, especially when females have positive attitudes toward mathematics (Paulsen & Johnson, 1983). Generally, children in the early years of schooling have a high level of perceived competence, and their perception of their competence diminishes and declines as they go through school and meet with difficulty and sometimes with failure in some area (Frey & Ruble, 1987). This decline in feelings of competence is greater for girls than for boys.

Work habits also affect academic achievement, and this is an area of great concern today. Students are frustrated when they study for a test but do not do well because they either do not know how to study or they have studied the wrong material. Efficient and effective work habits contribute to achievement in school. Finally, motivation is important to success in school (Nicholls, 1979). Motivation may affect attention in class or influence the amount of study time devoted to a particular subject, directly influencing academic achievement.

Cultural Differences

In recent years, there have been a number of disquieting studies concluding that American students do not achieve as much as Japanese and Chinese students. Psychologists have searched for the possible reasons (see Cross-Cultural Current on page 476). Studies find a variety of differences. Chinese and Japanese mothers of elementary school students view academic achievement as a central concern more than American mothers do. Once their children enter school, Chinese and Japanese families devote a great deal more time to assisting their children and providing an environment that encourages achievement. They hold higher standards for their children's achievement. Both Chinese and Japanese mothers stress hard work to a greater degree, and American mothers believe that innate ability is more important than Asian mothers do (Stevenson & Lee, 1990). When asked about their children's activities during the day, Chinese and Japanese mothers mention studying, reading, and playing academically related games, whereas American mothers are more likely to describe social interactions, watching television, and engaging in extracurricular activities such as music and dancing. In a cross-cultural analysis of homework, Chinese children were assigned more homework and spent more time on homework than Japanese children, who in turn were assigned and spent more time on homework than American children (Chen & Stevenson, 1989).

Intelligence

Of all the factors that contribute to academic achievement, none is more controversial than **intelligence.** What does it mean to say that someone is intelligent? How important is intelligence to overall school achievement? Should the term even be used?

intelligence
The ability to profit from experience. A cluster of abilities, such as reasoning and memory. The ability to solve problems or fashion a product valued in one's society.

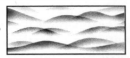

Achievement Differences Among American, Japanese, and Chinese Students: Answering the Question of Why

Time after time, studies have shown that Japanese children perform better than their American peers on a wide range of academic tests. In fact, Asian-American children in American schools generally achieve well above average. The question is, Why? Some authorities claim that the cognitive abilities of Japanese and perhaps also Chinese children simply exceed those of American children. Perhaps the superior cognitive skills of Japanese and Chinese children in the areas of spatial relationships, various types of memory, and vocabulary explain the differences in achievement, especially in the area of reading.

Harold Stevenson and his colleagues decided to test whether this superiority in reading was really due to superior cognitive skills. Specifically, they wanted to know whether children in Japan, Taiwan, and the United States had different scores on particular cognitive tasks. Their second purpose was to discover whether scores on different cognitive tasks could predict reading achievement in the three different cultures.

Some 240 first graders and 240 fifth graders were selected in each of the three cultures. The American children were from Minneapolis, Minnesota; the Japanese children were from the city of Sendai; and the Chinese children came from the city of Taipei on the island of Taiwan. Great care was taken to ensure that the children were representative of all the elementary schoolchildren in those cities.

A variety of cognitive tasks were designed for use in all three cultures. Care was taken to create tasks that were relevant, interesting, comparable in terms of language, and appropriate for all the children. The cognitive tasks measured a wide range of abilities, including spatial relationships, perceptual speed, auditory memory, serial memory for words, serial memory for numbers, verbal memory for brief stories, and vocabulary. Children were also given tests of reading skills that measured comprehension, vocabulary, and the percentage of the test read correctly as well as a test of mathematics skills.

The researchers reasoned that if the children's scores on the various cognitive measures and reading differed significantly, the superiority of achievement might be attributed to differences in cognitive abilities. If, however, the scores of the children in the three cultures on measures of reading achievement differed but no differences in cognitive abilities were evident, then differences in reading achievement are probably due to other factors found in the home and school.

The researchers did find differences in achievement among students in the three cultures. The Chinese children generally scored the highest, followed by Japanese children. In mathematics, the Japanese children performed better than

---

10. TRUE OR FALSE?

At present there is no universally accepted definition of intelligence.

Intelligence has been defined as the ability to profit from one's experiences, a cluster of cognitive abilities, the ability to do well in school, and whatever an intelligence test measures. Howard Gardner, a respected expert in the field defines intelligence as "an ability to solve problems or to fashion a product which is valued in one or more cultural settings (1987, p. 25). Piaget viewed intelligence not as a thing but rather as an ongoing process by which children use qualitatively different ways to adapt to their environment. There is no universally accepted definition for intelligence.

An important question to ask about intelligence is whether it is one quality or is composed of a number of separate and distinct components (Kail & Pellegrino, 1985). If it is one quality, one would expect people who are intelligent to show this quality across a wide variety of tasks. This is referred to as the g factor (general intelligence factor). On the other hand, some psychologists argue that some people perform much better on some tasks than on others and that in addition to having this general

the Chinese children, but both were superior to the American children. There were some exceptions; for example, first-grade American children scored higher on vocabulary than Japanese children. But generally the achievement results indicated that the Japanese and Chinese children had performed better than the American children on tests of these basic skills.

So far, this is in keeping with previous findings. However, what about the children's performance on the cognitive tasks? On a number of cognitive tasks, the American first graders exceeded the scores of both the Chinese and the Japanese children. Generally, the scores of the first-grade Japanese children exceeded those of the Chinese first graders. Although some differences among children in the three cultures did exist in the fifth grade, for the most part, any differences evident in first grade had disappeared by the fifth grade. Children from all three cultures scored similarly on a variety of cognitive measures by the fifth grade.

The results of this study, then, do not support the hypothesis that differences in cognitive abilities are responsible for the superiority of the Japanese and Chinese children in reading and mathematics. Although children in each of these cultures have their own strengths and weaknesses, by the fifth grade they are very similar in level and scores on a variety of cognitive tasks. The same two factors—general cognitive ability and serial memory ability—predicted reading achievement for children in all three cultures.

The importance of environmental differences was evident. For example, the Chinese first graders scored rather low on a number of verbal tasks. In China, a young child is taught to be thoughtful but not talkative. By fifth grade, these children had experienced numerous verbal interactions in school and had caught up. The initial superiority of American first graders on some tasks was explained by their more frequent early exposure to events outside the home, such as outings to museums, movies, sporting events, and the zoo. The Chinese and Japanese children experienced many fewer such outings.

Although the differences in reading achievement are definite, the investigators were impressed by the similarities rather than the differences that characterized cognitive functioning among the Japanese, Chinese, and American youngsters. Based on the results of this study, we might conclude that the answer to the question of why Japanese and Chinese children read better does not lie in the area of differential cognitive abilities. It suggests that we should turn our attention toward a search for more subtle factors in school and the home—some of which are suggested in the text—that may lead to superior achievement. Perhaps such factors as motivation, work habits, parental expectations, or the amount of time spent on developing reading skills in the classroom are the important factors differentiating children in one culture from children in another. Only more research will indicate other elements of the environment that are responsible for the differences.

Source: Stevenson, H. W., Stigler, J. W., Lee, S., Lucker, G. W., Kitamura, S., and Hsu, C., Cognitive Performance and Academic Achievement of Japanese, Chinese, and American Children. *Child Development*, 1985, *56*, 718–734.

factor, people possess specific capabilities (the s factor). Still others deny that any general factor for intelligence exists, insisting that a number of primary abilities are present. For example, Louis Thurstone (1938) argued there are seven primary abilities: verbal comprehension, word fluency, number, spatial abilities, associative memory, perceptual speed, and general reasoning. Today this viewpoint has been expanded in a new approach by Howard Gardner (1983, 1987), who advanced the **theory of multiple intelligences,** that is, the theory that a number of different types of intelligence exist including linguistic, logical-mathematical, musical, spatial, bodily-kinesthetic, interpersonal (social skills), and intrapersonal (the understanding of one's own feelings and using this insight to guide one's behavior) (see Figure 11.2 on page 479). Gardner thinks of the preceding as seven different intelligences that we all possess to some extent, though not on equal levels.

theory of multiple intelligences
A conception of intelligence advanced by Howard Gardner, who argues that there are seven different types of intelligence.

Another new approach is based on an information-processing model. Robert Sternberg (1984, 1985) advanced the **triarchic theory of human**

triarchic theory of human intelligence
A theory of intelligence based on information processing considerations advanced by Robert Sternberg who postulates the following mechanisms of intellectual functioning: metacomponents, which involve the individual's skills used in planning and decision making; performance components which relate to the basic operations involved in actually solving the task; and knowledge acquisition components, which involve processes that are used in acquiring new knowledge.

According to Howard Gardner, there are seven different intelligences. What type of intelligence is being shown here?

intelligence. Sternberg argues that intelligence involves purposeful adaptation to the real-world environment. What is adaptive in one culture may not be in another. An intelligent person in the United States might be quite unable to cope with the requirements of living in a mountainous Asian country. Sternberg also argues that intelligence is shown both with tasks and with situations that are either novel or so "cursory" that performance on them is automatic.

According to Sternberg, intelligence is composed of three components. First, there are metacomponents, or executive skills used in planning and decision making, including recognition of the problem, the various processes involved in selecting a strategy to solve the problem, the allocation of time, and the monitoring of the solution. Second, there are performance components, which are the basic operations involved in actually solving a problem, such as encoding information, inferring relationships between different aspects of the problem, and comparing and constructing different answers. The third component of intelligence is knowledge acquisition. This involves processes useful in acquiring new knowledge, including selective encoding (sifting the relevant from the irrelevant), selective combination (integrating the knowledge in a meaningful way), and selective comparison (rendering the information meaningful by appreciating its relationship to the information).

Sternberg uses his theory to explain both giftedness and mental retardation. He defines giftedness as the ability to think in new and insightful ways. The differences between the gifted and those who are not gifted can be found in the knowledge-acquisition component. Sternberg describes the case of Alexander Fleming, discoverer of penicillin who showed selective encoding when, while gazing at a petri dish containing a moldy culture, he noticed that the bacteria in the area of the mold had been destroyed, presumably by the mold. Fleming encoded the information in a highly selective way, focusing on the part of the field that was relevant to discovery of the drug. On the other hand, Sternberg suggests that the mentally retarded show difficulties mostly in the metacomponents area and differ in the way they use these executive skills. For example, even when mentally retarded people have the knowledge, they don't seem to be able to use it to solve problems.

Clearly, the definition one uses of intelligence affects the way intelligence tests will be constructed. Most intelligence tests are targeted at the schoolage population. Intelligence tests are often given for screening purposes to determine which students are intellectually gifted. At other times, they are used for diagnostic purposes, since there is a high correlation between school achievement and intelligence—about .6 with grades. That is, children who score high on intelligence tests are more likely to do better in school. The correlation between scores on IQ tests and standardized tests of achievement are even higher, falling within the range of .70 to .90 (Kubiszybn & Borich, 1987). Intelligence tests, then, have predictive power in the area of school success, and children who score very low may have difficulty in school. However, notice that the correlation is not perfect, which indicates that other factors, including motivation, background, and work habits, affect how a child performs in school. In

FIGURE 11.2: Gardner's Conception of Intelligence

Linguistic
Language skills include a
sensitivity to the subtle shade
of the meanings of words.

Logical-Mathematical
Both critics and supporters
acknowledge that IQ tests
measure this ability well.

Musical
Like language, music is an
expressive medium—and this
talent flourishes in prodigies.

Spatial
Sculptors and painters are able to accurately
perceive, manipulate, and recreate forms.

Bodily-kinesthetic
At the core of this kind of
intelligence are body control
and skilled handling of objects.

Interpersonal
Skill in reading the moods and
intentions of others is displayed
by politicians, among others.

Intrapersonal
The key is understanding
one's own feelings—and using
that insight to guide behavior.

Source: From "7 Ways to be Bright," *U.S. News and World Report.* Copyright ©
November 23, 1987, U.S. News and World Report.

fact, some psychologists believe that such factors as motivation and adjustment must be assessed if we are to measure the intellectual competence of children (Scarr, 1981).

INTELLIGENCE TESTS In the early 1900s, Alfred Binet was asked to create a test that would identify students who could not benefit from traditional education. Binet used a series of tests that measured a sample of children's abilities at different age levels. At each level, some children performed better than others. Binet simply compared children's performance on these tests to that of others in the age group. If the average

11. TRUE OR FALSE?

Intelligence is positively related to
school achievement.

mental age
The age at which an individual is functioning.

intelligence quotient (IQ)
A method of computing intelligence by dividing the mental age by the chronological age and multiplying by 100.

child had less knowledge than another child of the same age level, that child was less intelligent; if the child knew more, the child's intelligence was higher. Binet used the term **mental age** to describe the age at which the child was functioning. Later, another psychologist, William Stern, proposed the term **intelligence quotient,** or IQ, in which the mental age of a child is divided by the child's chronological age (age since birth) and then multiplied by 100 to remove the decimal. The problem with the IQ is that it assumes a straight-line (linear) relationship between age and intelligence. This is not the case, especially after age sixteen. Today, a more statistically sophisticated way of calculating the intelligence score, called a deviation IQ, is used. The original Binet test has gone through a number of revisions, and today it is called the Stanford-Binet Intelligence Test.

Beginning in the 1930s, David Wechsler began to develop another set of individualized intelligence tests. The Wechsler Intelligence Scale for Children (revised edition) contains a number of subtests that can be divided into two categories: verbal and performance. The five verbal subtests are information, similarities, arithmetic, vocabulary, and comprehension. The five performance subtests include picture completion (pointing out what is missing in a picture), picture arrangement (arranging a group of pictures in sequential order), block design (copying a pattern with blocks), object assembly (putting together puzzle pieces), and coding (a test in which people are asked to translate one set of symbols into another). Two additional subtests, one verbal and one performance, are sometimes used: digit span (a test of immediate recall in which the test taker is asked to repeat random series of digits, sometimes in forward order and sometimes in reverse order) and mazes. A composite or total intelligence score may be obtained.

The correlation between the Stanford-Binet and Wechsler varies, but for the full scale it is .73 (Brown, 1983). This indicates that different tests of intelligence do not tap identical skills but are related. There is also a good relationship between Piagetian tests and scores on the Wechsler Intelligence Scale for Children (Humphreys, Rich & Davey, 1985).

The Stanford-Binet and Weschler Intelligence tests are individual intelligence tests; that is, they are designed to be administered by a psychologist to one child at a time. Some intelligence tests and most tests of academic or cognitive abilities are designed to be given in a group setting. Therefore, they do not require the presence of a psychologist and can be given to many children at the same time.

HOW INTELLIGENCE TESTS CAN BE MISUSED In recent years, much controversy has arisen over the use of intelligence tests. Some criticism has been directed at the possible cultural bias against minorities. In 1971, a group of parents of African-American children who were placed in classes for the retarded sued in federal court, claiming that the placements were discriminatory because they were based on intelligence tests that were culturally biased. Eight years later the court ruled that IQ tests were culturally biased. The famous court case, *Larry P.* v. *Riles*, is well-known. However, about nine months later, in the case of *PASE* v. *Hannon*, after hearing similar testimony and looking over the test one question at a time, a judge decided that intelligence tests, when used with other criteria for determining educational placement, were not discriminatory (Bersoff, 1981). Some psychologists argue that these tests do not show consistent bias against minorities (Cole, 1981). Lack of bias does not make the test socially beneficial, though, and even the appearance of bias—as when students from minority groups are over-represented in classes for the retarded—is undesirable.

In addition, because these tests are highly verbal, they may be inappropriate for children for whom English is not the primary language. Problems with how the tests are used, rather than with the tests' technical fairness, may be at the center of the controversy (Reschly, 1981). In an attempt to free standardized tests of any bias, culture-free tests have been formulated. These depend less on language abilities and speed of responding, and they eliminate items that reflect differential cultural or social experiences. Such tests use matching, picture completion, copying, block designs, analogies, spatial relations, and ability to see relations between patterns (Brown, 1983). But a perfect culture-free test has yet to be invented, and some argue that culture-free tests are impossible (Cahan & Cohen, 1989). Even if one is formulated, it is questionable whether it will predict school performance as well as our present standardized tests do.

Another problem is the interpretation of intelligence as if it were a fixed quality etched in stone. As we have noted many times, it is not. Intelligence can change with one's experience. Finally, although scores on intelligence test correlate with academic achievement, there is a tendency to overrate the test's predictive abilities and to categorize children rigidly (Kaplan, 1977). For example, one of my acquaintances was shocked when her child's fifth-grade teacher told her that her son was doing fine, considering he had an IQ of "only" 105. If intelligence test scores are used in such a manner, the child can truly suffer. Even though such problems exist, intelligence tests will continue to be used, especially in the diagnosis and placement of exceptional children. However, they must be used with care and interpreted correctly if they are to be an aid in the educational process.

◆ CHILDREN WITH EXCEPTIONAL NEEDS

Intelligence tests are often administered to children thought to be in need of special services. Of the 45 million children in public schools today, a little over 10 percent are disabled. These include children who have learning disabilities or communication disorders or are mentally retarded, behaviorally disordered, blind, hearing impaired, or physically disabled. Of these, 85 percent to 90 percent are mildly disabled (Lewis, 1988). About three percent of the school population is considered gifted and are also in need of special services.

The most important law mandating educational services for the disabled is the Education for All Handicapped Children Act, Public Law 94-142. This law does not cover the gifted, although many districts have special programs for gifted children. The law requires all disabled children to receive a free, appropriate education and provides procedures to safeguard the rights of disabled children. The law also requires educational accountability, because educators must develop what is called an individualized education program (IEP), which states the goals of the child's schooling and the methods for attaining them. Parents have the right to participate in all phases of their children's placement and education.

The law also mandates that the child be placed in the least restricted environment. This means that each disabled student must be educated in an environment that is no more restrictive than absolutely necessary. For many years, disabled children were, as standard procedure, routinely separated from their "normal" peers and placed in special classrooms or schools. Today, this is much less common. For most disabled children, this has meant at least partial integration into the regular classroom. About two-thirds of all children with disabilities receive at least part of their education in regular classrooms (Heward & Orlansky, 1988).

Recently, there has been a call for identifying and educating disabled toddlers and preschoolers. A new law—PL99-457—encourages states to begin early intervention with infants and toddlers and requires that services be extended to three to five year olds (Viadero, 1987).

Mainstreaming

mainstreaming
The practice of placing disabled students into regular classrooms.

The practice of placing disabled children in regular classrooms is called **mainstreaming** and is the most controversial part of the law. Public Law 94-142 does not require mainstreaming. It mandates that a child be placed in the least restrictive environment, but it does not require that all children be mainstreamed. Still, for many children, the law has meant integration into regular classrooms.

This integration makes sense. If we want the disabled child to grow up and take his or her place in normal society and if we wish the nondisabled to respect the rights of their disabled peers to live in mainstream society, it makes sense to encourage the two groups to associate with one another as they grow up. Both the disabled and nondisabled benefit from being exposed to and interacting with one another. The disabled child learns to live in the nondisabled world and gains the social skills necessary for independent living. The nondisabled child becomes more accepting of and less prejudiced toward the disabled. A strong case, then, can be made for mainstreaming.

Mainstreaming has brought problems, however. Teachers sometimes walk into classrooms to find they have disabled children to teach but little or no training or information about how to meet the special needs of these children. Little, if any, time is included in the day to work with experts in special education, nor is the exceptional child given much preparation for entering the mainstream.

It is difficult to evaluate mainstreaming. The practice has apparently not led to reduced prejudice or increased acceptance on the part of the nondisabled (Gresham, 1982). In other words, despite being part of the regular class, exceptional children have not been effectively integrated into the social framework of the classroom. This does not mean, however, that maintreaming or the concept of the least restrictive environment is a failure. All it means is that we cannot merely place disabled students into regular classrooms and expect events to take their course. Proximity only gives us an opportunity to help; it does not ensure better acceptance. Strategies aimed at enhancing cooperation between the disabled and non-disabled are required. In addition, exceptional children must be taught appropriate social skills, including conversation and listening skills, so that they can handle social situations (Wanat, 1983). Perhaps all children could use a dose of such training, but it is vital to the success of the exceptional child who may be negotiating a new situation at an initial disadvantage.

The most successful mainstreaming programs have accomplished the following (Salend, 1984):

1. Developed specific criteria deciding who should and should not be mainstreamed and to what extent.
2. Prepared disabled students and their nondisabled peers.
3. Promoted communication among educators.
4. Continually evaluated the progress of exceptional children and provided teacher in-service training to enable teachers to deal better with the challenge of serving students with exceptional needs.

It is impossible to describe, even briefly, every category of exceptional children. We can, however, focus on children from four classifications of exceptionality: students with learning disabilities, students who are hyperactive, children who have been diagnosed as mentally retarded, and students who are gifted.

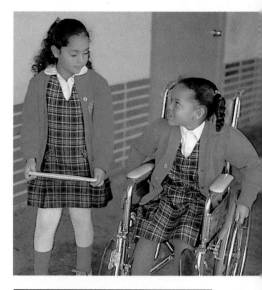

According to law, disabled students are placed in the least restrictive environment, which for about two-thirds of these disabled children has meant some integration in regular classes.

Learning Disabilities

There are children who, despite attending class and having the same teachers as their peers, do not learn well. Some of these children may suffer from **learning disabilities.** Of all the children with exceptional needs, more are placed in the category of learning disabled than in any other category. The term learning disability refers to a group of disorders marked by significant difficulties in acquiring and using listening, speaking, reading, writing, or reasoning skills or mathematics. Children with learning disabilities do not achieve up to their age and ability in some basic skill. To be considered learning disabled, the problem cannot be the result of sensory handicaps such as blindness or of mental retardation, emotional disturbance, or any environmental, cultural, or economic disability (Federal Register, 1977). When diagnosing learning disabilities, three factors stand out: (1) there are academic problems; (2) there is a discrepancy between ability and performance; and (3) the problems are not the result of the exclusions previously noted (Mercer, Hughes & Mercer, 1985).

The child with a learning disability experiences great difficulties in learning to read and developing other academic skills. Learning disability is a global term, however, and there are so many learning disabilities that

learning disability
A group of disorders marked by significant difficulties in acquiring and using listening, speaking, reading, writing, reasoning skills or mathematics.

it is hard to list them all. Learning-disabled children are a heterogeneous group, and no one individual has all the symptoms that might be listed under the heading of learning disabilities. Individuals who have a learning disability might have visual, tactual, or movement and coordination problems. For example, they may have difficulty perceiving the letters and discriminating a *p* from a *b*, or they may not perceive the position of the stimuli correctly, reversing letters or words and reading *saw* for *was*. These problems are common in young children, but they persist in the learning disabled.

Learning-disabled children also can show cognitive disabilities involving disorders of memory and thinking. They do not use memory strategies, such as rehearsal, when appropriate, and they show poor organization skills.

Children with learning disabilities may also experience social problems. They may be rejected because of the way they interact with others (Vaughn, 1985). Learning-disabled children often do not interpret verbal communications properly and often respond in ways that may not be appropriate or sensitive. As the child grows up, such problems as low motivation, distractibility, low self-concept, and organizational problems may remain (Buchanon and Wolf, 1986).

These children are often diagnosed when problems arise in elementary school. They receive help in both the cognitive and the social areas, using special techniques developed for working with learning-disabled students. They can be successful in life. In fact, a major study found that 81 percent of all learning-disabled students are involved in some productive activity, such as working, studying, or raising children, one year after leaving school (Viadero, 1989).

Attention-Deficit-Hyperactivity Disorder

attention-deficit-hyperactivity disorder
A condition used to describe children who are impulsive, overly active, easily distracted and inattentive.

If you spend a few minutes with a child who is easily distracted, hyperactive and impulsive, you will begin to appreciate the patience and skill required for dealing with such children. Children who show these symptoms are classified as having an **Attention-Deficit-Hyperactivity Disorder.** Sometimes people use the terms attentional problems and hyperactivity interchangeably, since the two are related. However, the attentional problems are perhaps even more serious than the hyperactivity and so the disorder is now called attention-deficit-hyperactivity disorder. These children have difficulty in school, and their relationships with their teachers are often strained. They are considered aggressive and annoying and are not accepted by their peers. As these children mature, about 80 percent of them carry some of the symptoms of hyperactivity into adulthood. They do not fidget as much, but they are likely to be impulsive and to have difficulty forming relationships. On the other hand, their impulsivity is not necessarily a problem in the workplace; their employers do not see them as very different from nonhyperactive workers (Sobel, 1979).

Three basic approaches are being used to treat attention-deficit-hyperactivity disorder. Some children with the disorder are often treated with stimulant medications to reduce the symptoms of the disorder. Under such medication, these children become calmer and more attentive (Forness & Kavale, 1988). There is evidence that parents and teachers interact more positively when these children show less disruptive and impulsive behavior (Barkley, Karlsson, Strzelecki, & Murphy, 1984). Some, but not all, evidence indicates that these children's social status improves as the disruptive behavior decreases, but peer appraisals of these children still are not as positive as those of nonhyperactive children (Whalen et al. 1989).

The use of drugs to treat hyperactivity has been widely criticized because the drugs treat only the symptoms, not the underlying cause, and may produce unpleasant side effects. Others have criticized the overuse of the drug. No one claims that drug therapy will improve intelligence or even schoolwork, only that it reduces the symptoms. This does not mean that drug therapy is always the treatment of choice. The very idea of a child's taking medication over a period of years should make us cautious. Some authorities claim that such treatment should be used only as a last resort, and then always in combination with another type of treatment.

One popular nondrug treatment is the Feingold Diet, named after the physician who developed it, Benjamin Feingold. Feingold noted that hyperactivity was related to the consumption of food additives, such as preservatives and artificial colors and flavors. Even some natural chemicals, such as salicylate, might be implicated, and Feingold suggested that children might be genetically predisposed to react to these chemicals. He claimed that if hyperactive children were put on a diet free of these compounds, a significant number would improve (Feingold, 1975).

Although some clinical support for the Feingold Diet has been found, controlled studies have been difficult to conduct, and each has been criticized on methodological grounds. Jean Johnson (1981) suggests that a scarcely significant relationship exists between diet and hyperactivity—especially among young children—and that the success rate with the diet is lower than claimed. The diet may be effective for some children, but not for as many as was first thought.

The third approach to treating the disorder (which may be used in combination with either of the first two) involves manipulating the child's environment and the reinforcements available to the child. For example, providing structure and solid routines and using positive reinforcements are helpful (Walden and Thompson, 1981). Some claim that behavioral intervention is superior to medication (Gadow, 1983). Perhaps in the future we will discover new techniques to give children with an attention-deficit-hyperactivity disorder the opportunity to learn and succeed in school.

Mental Retardation

Years ago, children who were mildly mentally retarded were educated in special classes using special curricula. Today, the situation has changed, and many mentally retarded students are being mainstreamed, not only in art and music but also in science, social studies, and reading. To be considered **mentally retarded,** an individual must meet three criteria.

mental retardation
A condition marked by subnormal intellectual functioning and adjustment difficulties that occurs before a person is 18 years of age.

First the individual must show an intelligence score of below 70 on an individualized intelligence test given in the child's primary language. Second, the retardation must occur before the age of eighteen. Third, a substantial failure in adjustment must be present. Although some objective tests measure adjustment problems, they are of questionable validity, and so this criterion is somewhat subjective. Even so, the adjustment criterion is important because adjustment problems relate to an individual's performance in the areas of social responsibility and self-sufficiency (Grossman, 1973). A child who shows a lack of reasoning or an inability to communicate with others certainly has an adjustment problem.

Most mentally retarded children are classified as mildly retarded and do not look any different from the general population, although both their gross motor skills, such as jumping, and their fine motor skills, such as those involved in finger dexterity, often lag behind normal children (Watson, 1977). These children have difficulty with schoolwork and show many cognitive difficulties (Kirk & Gallagher, 1989). Mildly retarded children are diagnosed in school when it becomes apparent that they are performing on a lower academic level.

Despite problems, if the mildly retarded (55–65 or 69 IQ) receive a good education and proper social and vocational training, many mildly retarded people can learn to lead independent lives (Kaplan, 1990). For many mildly retarded students, vocational training is important. Vocational training includes behavioral and social training as well as learning occupational skills. The mildly retarded can successfully work in unskilled or semiskilled jobs, and research shows them to be effective workers (Brickley & Campbell, 1981).

The moderately retarded (with intelligence levels between about 35 and 50 or 55) will probably not be able to lead an independent existence. The moderately retarded are very slow, especially in language development. Their educational program stresses self-help skills, proper behavior, and limited simple verbal communication. The vast majority of moderately retarded need some care throughout their lives, and special instruction in self-contained classrooms is the norm. Moderately retarded individuals are often employed in sheltered workshops. The workshop environment is noncompetitive and friendly. The jobs may include sorting and packaging. The moderately retarded may live in group homes with other retarded or disabled individuals.

Most severely retarded (25 to 35 or 40 IQ) and profoundly retarded children (below 20 or 25 IQ) are found in institutions and suffer from multiple disabilities, including sensory and motor problems.

Attempts to help the mentally retarded center on educational experiences. Today, the emphasis is on developing the social and personal skills necessary for success in the outside world. There is also a movement toward community-based group homes, where the retarded can live in dignity and with a degree of independence. In this area, the watchword is normalization; that is, the trend is to try to integrate the individual into normal society as much as possible. The degree to which this can be accomplished depends on the severity of the retardation, the education and social training the person receives, and the public acceptance of the retarded as individuals with full rights in the community.

The Gifted and Talented

When the word *gifted* is mentioned, people usually think in terms of people with a high intelligence. Children who score considerably above average on intelligence tests are indeed gifted, but is that all there is to it? What about the child who is artistically gifted? What about the child who is very creative? The federal government defines a gifted child as any child who either has demonstrated or seems to have the potential for high capabilities in general intellectual ability, specific academic aptitude, creative or productive thinking, leadership ability, or the visual and performing arts (Gifted and Talented Children's Act of 1978). The basic educational assumption is that the unique skills and abilities of these children require special curricular alterations (Hershey, 1988).

Stereotypes of the gifted sometimes prevent society from meeting the special needs of such children (Treffinger, 1982). For example, many people believe that the gifted are socially backward, have little or no common sense, and look down on other people (Rickert, 1981). These stereotypes should be laid to rest. The gifted tend to be fast learners and interested in school, but they also tend to be well-adjusted, energetic and physically healthy, intuitive, and perceptive; show superior concentration skills; and be a bit rebellious and original (MacKinnon, 1978; Scott, 1988). They have a positive self-concept and most have good interpersonal relationships (Austin & Draper, 1981). Of course, any picture of the gifted must be drawn with care. The gifted are not a homogeneous population (Juntune, 1982), and though most are well adjusted some are not.

Two general approaches are used in the education of the gifted. Acceleration involves skipping a particular grade or particular unit and being placed in a more challenging situation. It may involve a student's working at his or her own pace and finishing two years of work in one. Advanced placement and extra classes for extra credit are also classified under acceleration (Correll, 1978). Enrichment involves staying at the grade level but being assigned work that goes beyond the usual. Children may either be kept in their normal classroom, be placed in a special room for a few hours a day, or even be placed in a separate classroom. In any case, if they are to fulfill their potential, gifted children require a program that is qualitatively different from the normal school environment.

♦ **THE TOTAL CHILD IN SCHOOL**

The middle years of childhood are dominated by children's school experiences. Schoolage children are expected to learn to read, write, and do mathematics proficiently. When children succeed in school, they develop a positive sense of achievement about their work, which Erik Erikson calls industry. As we have seen, the nature of a child's school experience depends upon many factors.

It is wrong, however, to emphasize school as merely a place of academic learning. The school is also a place to meet friends, to learn to deal with hundreds of social situations, and to begin to develop more personal autonomy and move away from one's parents. Of course, the family re-

12. *TRUE OR FALSE?*

Children who are intellectually gifted tend to be socially backward.

mains the most important influence on the child, but children during the middle years of childhood are deeply affected by an ever widening variety of social experiences, and it is to these experiences that we turn next.

SUMMARY

1. During middle childhood, the rate of growth slows down. Children's motor skills improve and are refined with maturation and experience. Physical changes during this stage are gradual.

2. In almost every society, children begin their education or training at about age six. Still, some children may not be ready to learn to read or to successfully perform school tasks because of physical, cognitive, or behavioral immaturity.

3. According to Piaget, the schoolage child is negotiating the stage of concrete operations. Egocentrism declines, and improvements occur in the ability to solve problems that entail reversibility, the ability to decenter, transformations, seriation, and classification. The crowning achievement is the development of the ability to conserve. The child develops the ability to conserve number, weight, and finally volume.

4. Children in the stage of concrete operations are limited by their inability to understand abstractions and hypothetical problems.

5. During middle childhood, children's ability to voluntarily use their attentional strategies improves greatly, as do their memory abilities. In addition, they begin to use verbal memory strategies, such as rehearsal and classification spontaneously.

6. Metamemory describes an individual's knowledge of the memory process, while metacognition refers to an individual's awareness of his or her own thought processes. Metamemory and metacognitive abilities increase during the school years.

7. As children proceed through elementary school, they are expected to learn how to read, write, and successfully solve mathematical problems. They are also required to develop some knowledge of computers. The advancements in cognitive psychology have greatly influenced the teaching of these basic skills.

8. According to Piaget, true knowledge of mathematical concepts involves an understanding of number conservation, cardinality (1, 2, 3, 4), and ordinality (first, second, third, fourth). Such Piagetian skills as seriation, conservation, and classification are also involved in developing mathematical concepts.

9. A child's academic achievement is affected by the nature of the school and teachers, the pupil's socioeconomic status, the home environment, gender, attitudes, work habits, motivation, cultural differences, and intelligence. The teacher's expectations for a child also can affect academic achievement.

10. Creativity involves divergent thinking and is measured by the number of different solutions to a problem a child may offer (ideational fluency). It also requires knowledge of the basics and the ability to critically analyze. Teachers may encourage or discourage creativity in their classrooms.

11. Intelligence is related to school achievement, but other factors, such as motivation and adjustment, are important.

12. Public Law 94-142 requires education districts to provide an appropriate free education for every child. It also mandates educational accountability through an individualized education program. Finally, it requires that children be placed in the least restrictive educational environment. Mainstreaming is the process by which disabled children are placed in regular classrooms.

13. Children who achieve much below what their intelligence and educational experiences indicate they should be achieving are considered learning disabled. The cause of this discrepancy cannot be cultural differences, socioeconomic level, or sensory disability. Children with attention-deficit-hyperactivity disorder are impulsive and easily distracted. They are treated with medication, changes in diet, and behavior modification.

14. Most mentally retarded children are mildly retarded. Many can be educated to lead productive, independent lives. The moderately retarded can be taught self-care and some skills, but only rarely can they live independent lives. The severely and profoundly retarded require institutional care.

15. Gifted children are children who have superior intellectual, creative, or academic capabilities or manifest talent in leadership or in the performing or visual arts. The gifted are generally well-adjusted.

ACTION/REACTION

The Battle at the Dinner Table

Hope is a bright, cheerful, resourceful nine-year-old. She is also obese. Both her parents are concerned about Hope's weight problem, because it seems to be getting worse. When Hope was an overweight preschooler, her mother believed she would grow out of it, but she didn't. Her father has recently put Hope on a strict diet, but Hope cheats at every opportunity.

Hope's mother asked Hope whether she wants to lose weight, and Hope's answer was, "I guess so." Still, Hope's weight goes up, and Hope's parents are becoming less patient. They watch what Hope eats, but they can't control her eating away from home or even from sneaking snacks at home. They made an appointment for Hope to talk to a friendly neighbor Marge, hoping the child would open up to someone. Hope confided in Marge that she wanted to lose weight but just couldn't. Hope burst into tears. She dislikes her father for harping on her problem.

1. If you were Hope's parents, how would you deal with the situation?

Read, Please Read

Alex Wilson doesn't read. Perhaps that is an overstatement. His reading skills are about a year behind those of the average ten-year-old. Alex is barely passing his courses in school. The problem is that Alex refuses to read at home, either out loud or to himself.

His parents admit that they don't set much of an example. After a hard day's work in which both Mr. and Mrs. Wilson sit in an office and do paperwork, neither feels much like reading at home. Still, they have been told by the child's teacher that Alex needs to do extra reading at home. When Alex comes home from school, he turns on the television set and it stays on. His parents feel like hypocrites turning the television off, since they themselves watch so much of it.

When asked why he doesn't read more, Alex simply says he doesn't like to read. His parents don't understand this, since they have bought many interesting books for him to read.

1. If you were Alex's parents what would you do?
2. Can Alex's teacher do anything to help?

CHAPTER TWELVE

Social and Personality Development in Middle Childhood

Carnation, Lily, Lily, Rose by John Singer Sargent

Are These Statements True or False?

Turn the page for the correct answers. Each statement is repeated in the margin next to the paragraph in which the information can be found.

1. Friendly contacts between boys and girls increase during middle childhood.
2. Parents spend less time with their children during middle childhood than they did when their children were preschoolers.
3. During middle childhood, children raised in an authoritarian setting are better adjusted than those raised in an authoritative household.
4. After a divorce, the custodial parent tends to become stricter and the other parent more permissive.
5. Successful stepfathers immediately assert their authority and spend considerable time concentrating on discipline and then later develop their personal relationships with their stepchildren.
6. Elementary schoolchildren who regularly return home from school to an empty house and call their parents are no more susceptible to peer pressure nor do they have lower self-esteem than children who have a parent present when they get home from school.
7. Aggressive children in middle childhood do not have any friends.
8. As children progress through middle childhood, their conceptions of gender stereotypes become more rigid.
9. As children progress through the elementary school years, they are more likely to judge right and wrong on the basis of the consequences of an action rather than intent.
10. Boys experience more conflict with their peers than girls do.
11. Aggression is one of the most common types of interaction between children.
12. Most aggressive children grow out of this troublesome behavior pattern.

Answers to True-False Statements

1. False. Correct statement: Boys and girls tend to avoid each other during middle childhood.
2. True.
3. False. Correct statement: Children raised in an authoritative manner are better adjusted than children raised in an authoritarian manner.
4. True.
5. False. Correct statement: Effective stepfathers first establish a good relationship with their stepchildren.
6. True.
7. False. Correct statement: Although aggressive children may be rejected by the majority of their classmates, they do have their own group of friends.
8. False. Correct statement: Although children are aware of the gender-role stereotypes, they tend to become more flexible as they progress through this stage.
9. False. Correct statement: One of the important developments in the area of moral reasoning is the child's ability to take the intent and motivation of another person into consideration when judging right and wrong.
10. True.
11. False. Correct statement: Aggression is fairly uncommon in child-child interactions.
12. False. Correct statement: Aggressive children tend to remain aggressive.

♦ THROUGH A CHILD'S EYES

Karen quickly looked around and put the wallet in her pocket. No one had noticed. The wallet had a lot of money in it, and Karen had so many things she wanted to buy. She could return the wallet, since she knew the man who had lost it—a wealthy business executive. Karen's parents would want Karen to return the wallet, but they were busy with their own problems and were in the process of getting a divorce, and Karen was considered the "bad one" anyway. Karen's parents were always saying how dumb Karen was, and Karen's father usually lost his patience when trying to explain something to Karen. In fact, the only adult Karen had any respect for was her aunt, who frequently listened to her, tried to help her, and would give her a kind word.

Then Karen saw her friend, Linda, and got an idea. Linda was very poor, and Karen would enjoy sharing the money with Linda and perhaps with her own small group of friends. She could buy Linda some nice slacks, and they could go to the movies. To Karen's surprise, however,

Linda didn't think they should keep the wallet. "Maybe the man needs it badly and won't be able to buy food for the family," she told Karen. Karen replied that the man who lost it was rich, but Linda just said, "It isn't right to keep it." Karen valued Linda's opinion and realized that if she returned the wallet, she might receive a nice reward. Yet, she still couldn't decide what to do. Now that Linda knew about the wallet, Karen had to make up her mind quickly.

◆ CONCEPTIONS OF MIDDLE CHILDHOOD

During the school years, children's social worlds expand rapidly. Children begin to attend school, and the number and importance of their friendships increase. Their relationships with their parents undergo a definite shift toward greater independence. Children receive feedback from many sources and must develop a sense of their own abilities, strengths, and weaknesses. They are also considered more responsible for their own actions and develop a sense of right and wrong. They are likely to be faced with moral and ethical dilemmas concerning cheating, lying, and stealing, as well as more positive prosocial qualities, including helping and cooperating with others.

Many young children become project-oriented in middle childhood.

Industry, Inferiority, and Measuring Up

Schoolage children become more project oriented and are faced with many academic challenges. If they succeed, they gain what Erik Erikson called a sense of **industry,** the feeling that their work and efforts are valued. Children with a sense of industry enjoy learning about new things and experimenting with new ideas. They show more perserverance and can accept criticism (Hamacheck, 1988). If they do not succeed, they develop a sense of **inferiority,** a belief that they are incompetent and do not measure up to their peers.

During this stage, children take comparisons seriously. If parents compare a child's work unfavorably with that of siblings, the child may stop trying. One of the more difficult parenting tasks is valuing the competencies of each child in the family, especially when one child may be better than the others in a number of areas. Even if parents avoid direct comparisons, implicit comparisons are still present. Such comparisons can cause a special problem for minority children. Children are aware of their racial and religious identifications before middle childhood, but now they become aware of their group's standing compared with that of the majority. These children often learn that their group is not as valued (Spurlock & Lawrence, 1979), and they develop a sense of inferiority.

industry
The positive outcome of the psychosocial crisis in the middle years of childhood, involving a feeling of self-confidence and pride concerning one's achievements.

inferiority
The negative outcome of the psychosocial crisis in the middle years of childhood, involving the child's belief that his or her work and achievements are below par.

The Misunderstood Latency Stage

In Freudian theory, the child has now negotiated the Oedipal situation and enters the **latency stage.** This stage is often misunderstood. A boy resolves his Oedipal problem by identifying with his father ("Me and

latency stage
The psychosexual phase in which sexuality is dormant.

Age segregation is one of the hall-marks of middle childhood.

you, dad") and repressing his feelings toward his mother, and indeed all females. Girls experience less pressure to completely resolve their conflicts in this stage, and many do not fully do so. Sexuality in this stage is hidden or latent, and the segregation of children by gender becomes stronger. Boys play with boys, and girls play with girls. According to Freudians, this segregation occurs because children have repressed their feelings toward the opposite sex to resolve their Oedipal conflicts and contact might reawaken these disturbing emotions. In addition, because girls are developmentally ahead of boys, such grouping allows each sex to explore issues in sexual curiosity and fantasies at its own rate in a more comfortable and less stimulating manner (Solnit, Call & Feinstein, 1979). Sexuality, however, is not absent in this stage, as has often been asserted, but rather is hidden from view.

1. TRUE OR FALSE?

Friendly contacts between boys and girls increase during middle childhood.

♦ THE DEVELOPING SELF-CONCEPT

In the opening vignette, Karen saw herself as the "bad" child in the family. As noted in Chapter 10, psychologists call the picture a person has of himself or herself the self-concept. Another term—**self-esteem**—refers to the value a person may place on various aspects of his or her self. For instance, Karen may think of herself as a good friend to Linda but not so good in other areas.

self-esteem
The value people place on various aspects of their self.

A child's self-concept colors how the child interprets situations as well as the child's behavior and attitudes (Burns, 1979). Consider Karen's situation in school. If she is faced with a difficult arithmetic problem and believes she is a poor student, she will probably give up easily. If she has a positive view of herself as a mathematician, she would most likely approach the problem with the attitude that she can do it. Children with a positive view of their physical self will join in and play sports and games with other children, but those who don't think they are good enough will refuse to play. A vicious cycle ensues, for children who do not practice their motor skills will not develop them to their fullest. They fall further behind their peers until they do not measure up to them. This causes them to refuse to play, leading to a further lack of development.

The child's self-concept and self-esteem also mediate between the child and the child's ability to learn. Children who possess strong self-concepts volunteer their ideas more often in class, while those with a low estimate of themselves are often overwhelmed by school tasks. Positive self-esteem is related to better adjustment in school, more independence, less defensive behavior, and greater acceptance of others. It is also associated with school achievement (Gurney, 1987). Low self-esteem is implicated in the lower academic performance of minority group children (Minuchin & Shapiro, 1983). Children with a positive academic self-concept see themselves as more competent. The relationship between perceived competence and scholastic achievement increases between grades three and six (Entwisle, Alexander, Pallas & Cardigan, 1987).

The self-concept also affects how information is processed. If children believe they are bad, they will believe any such feedback from other people. In this way, the self-concept can cause a self-fulfilling prophecy to develop. Believing that someone will say something negative causes children to anticipate poor evaluations and even to interpret neutral feedback as negative.

Various aspects of the self affect one another. For example, children with a poor physical sense of self who refuse to play ball may place themselves at a social disadvantage because such games form a part of the social scene at this age. These children interact with fewer other children and therefore find it more difficult to develop social skills.

How the Self-concept Develops

The self-concept evolves from a combination of the feedback a child receives from others and the child's evaluation of his or her own subjective experiences. In middle childhood, the child receives feedback from many people, including peers, parents, and teachers. If a parent continually tells a daughter that the daughter "has no brains" and "is stupid", as Karen's parents have done, the girl may believe it.

Children are not just passive recipients of feedback. They also evaluate their own experiences. They experience themselves as being good, bad, aggressive, calm, and honest and compare their experience against a standard set by the society, parents, peers, and finally themselves. Even in the absence of direct feedback, they evaluate these experiences. If a child's experience is not in keeping with that youngster's sense of self, the child may reject his or her subjective experience. For instance, children may believe that they are honest and have difficulty coming to grips with the fact that they copied from a friend during an exam or, as in Karen's case,

In middle childhood, children may believe that they are not good at something and this may affect their participation which causes them not to develop their skills to the fullest possible extent.

kept the wallet when they could have returned it. The experience of dishonesty does not match their conception of themselves as honest.

During middle childhood, a number of factors add to the complexity of the development of a self-concept and self-esteem. First, children are receiving feedback from many more sources. They encounter more children and adults, not all of whom will like them. Some of this feedback is likely to be negative, or at least conflicting. The child who has been the center of attention at home may find that this is not the case in school. Second, children's newly developing cognitive skills affect the development of their self-concept. Children in the concrete operational stage can reason more logically, allowing them to verify the attributes of their self. Children are especially good at developing a self-theory from inductive (specific) experiences. For example, they may come to the conclusion that they are smart because they are good at reading and mathematics or are honest because they return something they found (Harter, 1983).

Children now develop the ability to take another person's point of view, as Linda did when she reasoned that the person who lost the wallet might be sad and in need of the money (Froming, Allen, & Jensen, 1985). They test their self-concepts by making comparisons with others, and because they are no longer as egocentric, they develop the ability to imagine what others are thinking of them. This allows them to anticipate evaluations, correct their behavior, evaluate the action, and react to it emotionally with pride or disappointment.

The Self-concept in Middle Childhood

In early childhood, the self-concept is based on particular characteristics and abilities, such as being a boy or girl and being able to play baseball. In middle childhood, children can now understand the needs and expectations of other people, and their ability to live up to these expectations affects their self-concept (Markus & Nurius, 1984). Children form small groups of friends who expect particular behaviors and attitudes.

In middle childhood, especially after eight years of age, a shift from physical to psychological conceptions of the self takes place (Damon & Hart, 1982). Personality characteristics now take center stage as children separate the external world from their feelings (Damon & Hart, 1982).

Children compare themselves physically with others, and this is reflected in such self-concept statements as "I am taller than Steven." Children are likely to think about themselves in terms of what differentiates them from others. If they are older or younger than their classmates, they will always include their age when asked about themselves (McGuire, McGuire, Child, & Fujioka, 1978).

Social conceptions of belonging, such as being a member of a family, are also common. Children between seven and fourteen years of age often make statements referring to personal attributes, interests and hobbies, beliefs, attitudes, and values. A decrease in statements concerning possessions and appearance occurs (Livesly and Bromley, 1973). The self-concept develops from an external frame of reference to a more internal frame of reference.

Helping to Develop a Positive Self-concept and Building Self-Esteem

What can parents and teachers do to help children build positive self-concepts and improve their self-esteem? Searey (1988) divides attempts to improve self-esteem into four categories: helping children feel more capable, more significant, more powerful, and more worthy. Children will feel more capable if their successful projects or papers are displayed, if they are allowed to teach someone something they are good at, and if they are allowed time and are encouraged to pursue their interests and develop their abilities. Children will feel more significant if they are listened to, are encouraged to participate in groups such as scouting or clubs, are encouraged to volunteer to help others, and if their successes are celebrated. Children will feel more powerful if they are given responsibility and allowed to make certain choices. Children will feel more worthy if they are valued for some quality that makes them special (such as sensitivity to animals or regard for others), if their hobbies are promoted, and if their ideas are discussed openly.

The most powerful forces shaping a child's self-concept are family, peers, and teachers. The child's relationships with others change markedly over the middle childhood years.

◆ THE FAMILY

The family remains the most powerful influence on a child's development and mental health (Bower, 1979). The American family today, however, is a far cry from what it was even thirty years ago. Today, the traditional family consisting of a mother who is a homemaker, a father who works, and two children is less common. In fact, only five percent of the families of children entering school today have an employed father and a homemaker mother (Barney & Koford, 1987).

The number of single-parent families has increased substantially, and one million children each year are affected by divorce. Between 40 percent and 50 percent of all children born in the late 1970s and early 1980s will experience a divorce and spend an average of about five years in a single-parent home before their custodial parent remarries (Glick & Lin, 1986). Three-quarters of all divorced mothers and four-fifths of all divorced fathers remarry. Many of the children of divorce will go through a series of marital transitions from intact family to single-parent family to stepfamily relationships (Hetherington, Stanley-Hagan, & Anderson, 1989). In addition, many elementary schoolchildren experience less parental supervision because both parents have to work, and many return to homes after school in which no parent is present.

On paper, the two-parent family may seem relatively simple—a mother, a father, child one, child two. But appearances are deceiving. Many variables influence the nature and quality of family interactions, including stress, economic problems, the physical environment, and illness. Parent-child relationships are influenced by other relationships within the fam-

If you consider the "traditional" family in terms of a fulltime home-maker mother and an employed father, the number of such families is declining.

ily structure. The family is composed of many small interpersonal systems, each affecting the other. For example, when there are marital problems, fathers tend to give their children less positive reinforcement and are more likely to interrupt them at work and complete a task for them even before their children ask for help (Brody, Pellegrini, & Sigel, 1986). They appear to have less patience. Perhaps some of the difficulties Karen experiences with her father actually arise from the problems her father is having within his marriage.

Changing Relationships

The relationship between parent and child changes in middle childhood. Parents show less physical affection for their children, are not as protective of their children, and generally spend less time with their children (Maccoby, 1980). Children are quite verbal, and parents reason with them more. Children also perceive their parents differently. During the early years of middle parenthood, children strive to please their parents and teachers. They feel great pleasure when they meet the goals these adults set for them and act in a way that their parents want them to. When parent-child relationships in Australia were investigated, certain patterns of similarities and differences between mother-child and father-child relationships were found. Overall, mothers interact more frequently than fathers and much more in the context of caregiving and being responsive to the child's needs. Fathers' contact is greater in the course of play, especially physical play, and fathers are more friendly and verbally playful. Fathers are more likely to respond negatively to dependent behavior, especially in their sons (Russell & Russell, 1987). These findings are similar to those of studies performed in the United States (Bronstein, 1984).

Later in this stage, the child's peers become more important, and fitting

2. *TRUE OR FALSE?*

Parents spend less time with their children during middle childhood than they did when their children were preschoolers.

D A T A G R A P H I C

The Growth of Single Parent Families

Source: U.S. Department of Commerce 1990.

The percentage of families with children headed by a single parent has increased.

in and being accepted in the group take center stage. Children begin to identify less with adults and more with their peers. They may become more argumentative, discourteous, and rebellious and complain of what they perceive as unfairness. They now see parents as human beings who can be—and often are—arbitrary and wrong. Ten-year-olds believe that decisions about who their friends are and other decisions that affect only them are outside their parents' authority (Tisak, 1986). Parents are no longer seen as infallible. Children question more, and parents may get a bit tired of explaining the reasons for certain rules.

Child-rearing Strategies in Middle Childhood

Diana Baumrind's studies of parenting styles were discussed in chapter 10. Baumrind identified three parenting styles. The authoritarian strategy involves the use of demands and power, the placement of strict limits on children's behavior, and no discussion of rules. Authoritarian parents control their children, value obedience and respect, and leave no room for verbal give-and-take. These parents are very demanding but not very responsive to their children's needs and are not very warm (Baumrind, 1988).

Permissive parents, on the other hand, make few demands on their children and are willing to discuss issues. They let their children regulate their own behavior and adopt a very tolerant attitude toward aggressiveness. These parents score low or sometimes medium on scales measuring demandingness and are highly responsive (Baumrind, 1988).

Authoritative parents expect mature behavior, enforce firm rules, encourage independence and communication between themselves and their children, and recognize the rights of both parents and children. Those who fit this pattern are highly demanding and score high or medium in responsiveness (Baumrind, 1988).

The best outcomes are typified by high demandingness and high responsiveness. A factor that complicates any analysis of child-rearing strategies is nurturance. Parental warmth is related to positive outcomes, while coldness and hostility are related to negative outcomes.

Baumrind (1979) based her original study on observations of children in nursery school. She continued her studies, looking at the behavior of these children when they were eight or nine years old. The problems of authoritarian-raised children continued at those ages, especially for boys. Boys showed less interest in achievement and withdrew from social contact. Children who were raised permissively lacked self-confidence and were not achievement oriented. The authoritative-raised children were the most competent and socially responsible. The combination of firm rule enforcement, demands for more mature behavior, better communication, and warmth led to a desirable outcome.

This combination leads to greater self-esteem, as well, as a study by Stanley Coopersmith (1967) shows. Fifth-grade and sixth-grade boys who possessed high self-esteem had parents who set and enforced high stan-

3. TRUE OR FALSE?

During middle childhood, children raised in an authoritarian setting are better adjusted than those raised in an authoritative household.

dards for competence, did not often use coercion, practiced a more democratic style of decision making in which children could question parental judgments, and used punishments that the children deemed fair and just. A warm relationship existed between these children and their parents (Coopersmith, 1967). The child-rearing style in which parents used power and were not open to rational argument was associated with low self-esteem in boys. In another study, Loeb and his colleagues (1980) found that high self-esteem was associated with parents who offered suggestions but left the child some freedom of choice rather than with a directive style, in which parents told the child what to do.

Neither the unbridled use of power nor the permissive style benefits most children. Simply demanding total, unquestioning obedience or nothing at all does not lead to independence or social maturity. Children of authoritarian parents lack social competence with peers, do not take the initiative, lack spontaneity, and have external rather than internal moral orientations to right and wrong. Karen's parents use this style. Children from permissive families are impulsive, aggressive, and lack independence and a sense of responsibility. Children of authoritative parents are independent, take the initiative in the cognitive and social areas of life, are responsible, control their aggressive urges, have self-confidence, and are high in self-esteem (Maccoby & Martin, 1983). Baumrind (1988) concludes that generally, parents who are both demanding and responsive produce children who are most socially responsible.

Taken as a whole, the research on parenting in middle childhood yields no surprises. Children benefit when their parents show warmth and acceptance, set appropriate rules and enforce them, show some flexibility in that they listen to their children and are responsive to them, and give their children some room for personal choice, responsibility, and freedom.

Do Parents Agree on How to Raise Their Children?

One last issue should be raised. Parents do not always agree on their child-rearing strategies. We have all know families in which one parent is more authoritarian than another and wondered whether this would make much of a difference. Minor disagreements in child rearing probably occur in every family. Generally, high agreement between parents indicates more adaptive functioning than low agreement, which often is related to conflict and familial disorganization (Simons, McCluskey, & Mullett, 1985). When parents have major disagreements over parenting, less effective parenting is often the result (Minuchin, 1985).

This is only half the story, however, for we find that parents using more effective child-rearing strategies tend to agree with each other, while parents using less effective strategies not only disagree with these effective parents but also disagree with other less effective parents! When James Deal and his colleagues (1989) investigated the issue of parental agreement on child rearing, they found that parents who agreed with each other were characterized by positive interactions both between spouses and between parents and children, could confront problems in a positive way, had good communication, and used rational discipline techniques.

Parents who agree with each other tend to be more effective parents and use more effective parenting techniques. The high-agreeing parents were all in agreement on variables indicative of being effective parents. In addition, besides agreeing with their spouses, they had much in common with other effective parents.

The story was different, however, with parents who disagreed with each other on child-rearing strategies. These parents were often using poor strategies, and they disagreed both with their spouses and with the other parents in the study. There was no consensus at all. It seems that the great Russian novelist Tolstoy understood this when he claimed that all happy families resemble one another; every unhappy family is unhappy in its own way (see Deal, Halverson, & Wampler, 1989).

The Experience of Divorce

Not only is divorce an event, it is an experience that affects the entire family forever. Five and ten years after a divorce, the divorce remains the central event of the childhood years and casts "a long shadow" over those years (Wallerstein, 1983, p. 233). Divorce itself brings many changes. Not only is the child's world torn asunder, but the child's entire lifestyle may be disrupted. Financial problems may force the family to move to a new neighborhood, and the daily routine may be altered. Most children do not see these changes in a positive light even years after the divorce (Wallerstein, Corbin, & Lewis, 1988).

IMMEDIATE REACTIONS TO DIVORCE Almost all children find divorce a painful experience. The early symptoms may differ, but they include anger, depression, and guilt (Hetherington, 1979). Children often show such behavioral changes as regression, sleep disturbances, and fear (Wallerstein, 1983). Children may grieve for the absent parent and may respond with aggression or noncompliance (Hetherington, Stanley-Hagan & Anderson, 1989). Parent-child relationships may also change. The custodial parent, usually the mother, becomes stricter and more controlling, while the other parent becomes permissive and understanding though less accessible. Both parents make fewer demands for children to mature, become less consistent in their discipline, and have more difficulty communicating with the children (Hetherington, Cox & Cox, 1978). Parents' discipline practices become poorer (Forgatch, Patterson, & Skinner, 1988), and conduct problems are not uncommon (Brody & Forehand, 1988).

After the initial period, some children show a remarkable ability to recover, while others do not. Some adapt well in the early stages and some show delayed effects. How quickly a child recovers from the initial shock depends on whether there is a stable environment after the divorce and on the social supports available to the child (Kurdek, 1981). Often those supports are not present. Parents are confused, and must rearrange their own lives. Grandparents, aunts, and uncles are often judgmental, and their relationships with both the parents and the children may change. Peer relationships may suffer, as some children feel guilty about what is happening. Family friends may be forced to take sides and maintain con-

4. *TRUE OR FALSE?*

After a divorce, the custodial parent tends to become stricter and the other parent more permissive.

tact with only one parent. The main social supports are weakened at a time when increased support is required.

LONG-TERM EFFECTS OF DIVORCE Many of these initial reactions either become less severe or disappear by the end of the first year (Hetherington, 1979), but the long-term effects of divorce on children can be severe. In one study of children whose parents divorced during their middle childhood years, the functioning of half had improved, while about one-quarter of the subjects had become significantly worse (Kelly & Wallerstein, 1976). Children from one-parent families do not differ in academic ability or intelligence, but they are absent from school more often, are more disruptive, have lower grades, and are viewed by teachers as less motivated (Minuchin & Shapiro, 1983).

Parent-child relationships may also worsen. Children in divorced families often perceive their relationships with their parents, most often their father, more negatively than children from intact families (Fine, Moreland, & Schwebel, 1983). A majority of children whose parents were divorced when they were in middle childhood expressed feelings of sadness and an increased sense of vulnerability (Wallerstein, 1987). Even though it had been over ten years since the divorce, the children spoke sadly of their loss of the intact family and especially of the lack of contact with their noncustodial parent. They expressed a great concern of being betrayed in relationships, and anxieties about personal commitments were high. Half the boys and one-fourth of the girls were considered poorly adjusted and at high risk at this ten-year followup.

The long-term effects, though, are dependent on a number of factors. For instance, if parents continue to quarrel whenever they meet after the divorce, children will suffer (Wallerstein, 1983). Children recover best when both parents are involved and there is a minimum of conflict (Abarbanel, 1979). Unfortunately, conflict does not end with the divorce. About

DATAGRAPHIC

Divorces

Source: National Center for Health Statistics and U.S. Department of Health and Human Services, 1989.

The first year in which 1 million divorces were registered was 1970. The highest number was recorded in 1981.

two-thirds of the exchanges between ex-spouses two months after the divorce are marked by conflict (Hetherington et al., 1978). On the other hand, the child benefits if both parents remain concerned and active in the child's life and if they have a warm relationship with the child. Adjustment problems will be less severe if financial problems and parental conflict are minimized and if social supports exist (Kurdek, 1981). However, the parents' difficulties involving finances, loneliness, fear, anxiety about the future, and loss of social supports reduce the parents' ability to give their children what they need to soften the blow.

DIVORCE AND THE AGE OF THE CHILD Children faced with a divorce at various ages must negotiate different problems. For instance, younger children experience fears of abandonment and a lack of warmth. Preschoolers are quite vulnerable, although most do recover from the initial shock after a year or so (Allison & Furstenberg, 1989; Wallerstein & Kelly, 1979). Continued deterioration after one year is linked to continuing family disorder. Preschoolers do not understand what is going on, and parents don't explain much to preschoolers (Wallerstein & Kelly, 1979). In addition, preschool boys negotiating the Oedipal situation may experience guilt when the father leaves the home. They are not as able to understand the divorce and may blame themselves and fear abandonment by their parents (Wallerstein, Corbin & Lewis, 1988). Preschoolers are often very distressed and show regressive behavior and separation anxiety.

Schoolage children experience loyalty problems, including feelings that they have to choose between their parents. Children in elementary school feel powerless and frightened and frequently are angry at one or both parents and may support one parent. About one-half show severe drops in achievement during the year (Wallerstein et al., 1988). Older children have a difficult time coping with anger. Adolescents often show acute depression, acting-out behavior, emotional and social withdrawal, and anxiety about their future (Wallerstein et al, 1988).

DOES DIVORCE AFFECT BOYS AND GIRLS DIFFERENTLY? One generally accepted, but not unanimous, research finding is that the long-term effects of divorce are greater for boys than for girls (Kurdek, 1981; Hetherington, 1979). Boys are much more likely to suffer psychological, social, and academic problems. Boys are also more likely to show acting-out behaviors than are girls (Hetherington et al., 1989). We can only guess at the reasons for this. In the majority of cases, mothers gain custody, and perhaps the absence of the male authority figure may have an especially injurious effect on boys (Huston, 1983).

On the other hand, perhaps girls are affected as much, although they react differently. Psychologists now appreciate the influence fathers have on their daughters' development. Girls raised in one-parent families have more difficulty relating to men later on. Mavis Hetherington (1972) found that girls from divorced families were more flirtatious, sexually precocious, and seductive, while girls raised in widowed families were more withdrawn (Hetherington, 1972). Therefore, paternal absence affects daughters as well as sons.

Family Discord and Behavior Problems

It is not difficult to find studies that compare children from divorced families and children from intact families and find that children in divorced families have significantly more problems. Paul Allison and Frank Furstenberg (1989) found that five years after the divorce, children whose parents had divorced were significantly worse off on measures of problem behavior, academic performance, and psychological distress as measured by reports from parents, teachers, and the children themselves. The differences may not be due to divorce itself, however, but to family problems that existed long before the divorce took place.

Sometimes the divorce itself is blamed for the children's problems, but family turmoil—whether it ends in divorce or not—creates problems for children (Emery, 1982). The more open and intense the hostility, the more serious the children's problems. Marital turmoil is also related to underachievement in school. In one interesting longitudinal study, the personalities of children from intact families were assessed. A number of these families later experienced divorce. The behavior of the boys prior to divorce was affected negatively by the stress in the family. Such problems as uncontrolled impulsiveness and aggressiveness were common. Again, the behavior of girls was found to be less affected than that of boys. The researchers conclude that some of the problems considered to be consequences of divorce may be present prior to the divorce (Block, & Gjerde, 1986).

Prescriptions for Divorcing Parents

The extent to which a divorce has long-term effects depends on the quality of the family life after the divorce as well as on how well the children can work through their own problems. Children must accept the divorce, work through their feelings, reestablish routines, and reformulate relationships with both parents (Wallerstein, 1983). They must disengage from the conflict and resume their normal activites. If parents make an effort to maintain good relationships with the children, reestablish stable and healthy living patterns, agree on child-rearing issues, and understand what the children are going through, the negative effects of divorce can be minimized. Children do their best when both parents are involved, when there is minimum conflict, and when parents agree on child-rearing techniques (Abarbanel, 1979).

Stepparenting: Myths and Facts

Most parents who divorce will remarry. When their parents remarry, children being raised in one-parent families have to adjust to still another change. The problems of stepparenting are now becoming more noticeable as more children find themselves sharing a home in which one parent is not a biological parent.

Stepparenting and stepfamilies are surrounded by myths (Visher & Visher, 1979). Often people see stepfamilies as identical to nuclear families, but they are very different. Not only are children living with a new parent, but each individual comes to the new family after having experienced a loss. The child must adjust to a new set of rules, and the parents must learn to share the child with a biological parent who lives in another home. The problems of readjustment can be difficult. In addition, each parent may have his or her own children as well, so two or more children may be living with one biological parent and one stepparent.

In such fairy tales as "Cinderella" and "Sleeping Beauty," the step-mother is wicked and the father is good but weak. This stereotype has come down to us, and many people regard the state of being a stepmother as the epitome of wickedness. Although our estimation of the stepfather's role is not as bad, it is hardly healthy. In reality, stepparents are neither as bad as Cinderella's nor as good as what was portrayed on the "Brady Bunch."

The last myth is that of instant love—that the nuclear family once torn asunder by divorce is now back together and living happily ever after. This conflicts with the wicked stepparent myth, but is just as false. Step-parents may not instantly fall in love with their stepchildren, and step-children may resent or merely tolerate the presence of the stepparents.

Stepparenting presents unique problems, especially in the area of discipline. Imagine marrying into a family with a parent and two children. They have been a one-parent family for some time and have established certain patterns. You, the new parent must learn how to discipline the children, which patterns can change, and which must be left alone. It is a difficult job, and one for which little training is available.

In the period following a remarriage, children must accept the remarriage and resign themselves to the fact that their biological parents will not get back together again. The child may resent the stepparent's attempts to discipline and may feel that the entrance of the new parent threatens the relationship they have with their biological parents (Hetherington et al., 1989).

Directly following the remarriage, the children may show more problem behaviors. Most younger children eventually form a reasonably good relationship with a competent stepparent, but adolescents may have more difficulty. They may more actively challenge the new family. There is some evidence that girls have more difficulty than boys adjusting to a remarriage of the biological mother who has custody (Brand, Clingempeel, & Bowen-Woodward, 1988). In fact, over time, preadolescent boys in families with stepfathers are more likely than girls to show improvements in their adjustment (Hetherington, Cox & Cox, 1985). Perhaps girls have developed a very strong relationship to their mother during the time when their mothers were unmarried and the entrance of the new male stepparent is seen as threatening to the relationship. Perhaps the presence of a male increases the tension in the family more for a daughter than for a son. Whatever the reason, girls may have more difficulty adjusting to the new family structure.

There is always a period of adjustment in any remarriage, and some time is needed for readjustment (Bray, 1988). Improvement takes place with time. Successful stepfathers initially spend more time establishing good relationships with their stepchildren and are warm and involved

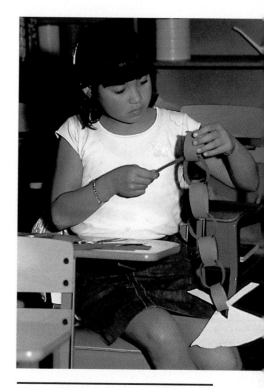

Many children in stepfamilies may have to make two gifts, one for their biological mother or father and one for their stepmother or stepfather.

5. TRUE OR FALSE?

Successful stepfathers immediately assert their authority and spend considerable time concentrating on discipline and then later develop their personal relationships with their stepchildren.

latchkey or self-care children
Elementary schoolchildren who must care for themselves after school hours. (Some include junior high school students in the definition.)

but do not initially assert too much parental authority (Hetherington et al., 1989). While acceptance of the stepfather by stepsons is related to the behavior of the stepfather toward the stepson, this is not the case with stepfather-stepdaughter relationships where there is no correlation between the two, and acceptance is much more difficult to obtain (Hetherington et al., 1989). Stepmothers are more active and involved in discipline than stepfathers. When positive relationships exist between stepparents and stepchildren, the children are less aggressive and show higher levels of self-esteem (Clingempeel & Segal, 1986).

It is commonly believed that children do not thrive in stepfamilies because the adjustments are so difficult. However, the most common finding of studies comparing stepfamilies with nuclear families on adjustment or cognitive functioning is that there is little or no difference (Clingempeel & Segal, 1986). In fact, when you compare stepfamilies with single-parent families, the presence of a stepfather reduces some of the negative effects of divorce for boys, and males score higher both on measures of cognitive development and on measures of adjustment (Oshman & Manosevitz, 1976; Santrock, 1972).

There is no doubt that stepfamilies are faced with many adjustments. However, research in this area shows that living in a stepfamily can be a positive experience, depending upon the quality of the relationship between parents and children.

Latchkey or Self-Care Children

When Karen comes home from school, neither one of her parents is home. Both her parents work, and she spends about two and a half hours after school alone. Karen is one of the growing number of **latchkey** or **self-care children**. No one really knows how many such children exist in the United States. Estimates of the number of elementary schoolchildren who are home alone after school range from two million to ten million, and it is estimated that about 15 percent of the children from ages six to nine and about 45 percent of the children from nine to eleven fall into the category (Goleman, 1988). The public is greatly concerned about the safety and development of these children (Campbell & Flake, 1985). A nationwide poll found that teachers look to the lack of supervision at home after school as a major reason for lack of achievement (Flax, 1987). Many parents agree.

Are these opinions substantiated by research? When Deborah Vandell and Mary Corasaniti (1988) investigated third-grade children from a middle-class, suburban neighborhood who returned home to their mothers, attended day-care centers, stayed with sitters, or returned home alone or to their siblings, they found no differences between latchkey and mother-cared-for children in academic achievement, popularity, or competence. However, there were significant differences between children who attended day-care centers, with these day-care raised children being less popular and achieving lower grades and lower scores on standardized achievement tests. The children who stayed at home with sitters also received more negative peer nominations than latchkey and mother-care children. The researchers suggest that the parents in this study may have provided rules and emotional support. But why did the children in day care do more poorly? First, the day-care setting was not of good quality, and as noted in Chapter 7, day-care quality is of prime importance. Second, perhaps these parents placed their children in the day-care situation because the children already had difficulties and needed the extra care.

This pattern of few, if any, differences has been found in many studies. Hyman Rodman and colleagues (1985) compared forty-eight self-care children with forty-eight matched children with adult care on such variables as self-esteem, locus of control, social adjustment, and interpersonal relationships and found no significant differences. Laurence Steinberg (1986) criticized this research, however, since Rodman used only children who usually went directly home after school. Steinberg also argued that the public was more concerned about the possibility that these unsupervised children might get into trouble, especially since other studies have shown that a lack of parental monitoring is related to delinquent activity. Instead, Steinberg measured susceptibility to peer pressures in children grades five through nine, finding that children and adolescents who report home after school were not significantly different from other children but that children who were removed from adult supervision were more susceptible to peer pressure to engage in antisocial activity. Adolescents whose parents knew their children's whereabouts were less susceptible, even if the supervision was somewhat lax. Unfortunately, nearly half of the self-care youngsters seem not to go directly home (Steinberg, 1988). Steinberg concludes that parental monitoring is most important and that even long-distance monitoring, as when children call their parents at work to tell them that they're home, can be useful.

When John Diamond and colleagues (1989) compared fifth and sixth graders who were alone or with younger siblings for at least two hours each day after school for a year with nonself-care children, they found few differences, but the ones they found may be important. Latchkey boys had more behavior problems, as described by both parents and the children themselves, and the researchers found a trend towards lower academic achievement. However, the interpretation of this and other studies comparing latchkey to non-latchkey children is complicated by the fact that the status of being a latchkey child may depend upon poverty and living in a one-parent family. It may be these other factors rather than the self-care experience that are responsible for some of the findings. The researchers suggest that the problems that their study uncovered may be due to the stresses of a one-parent family living in poverty rather than the latchkey situation. Children who come from lower income families or those who experience a great deal of anxiety may have more difficulties in the self-care situation. It may be important, then, to find out why a child is in self-care.

With the number of self-care children increasing, some organizations have begun to institute survival courses for these children and their parents. These courses encourage parents to evaluate the maturity level of their children and the ability of their children to be alone. They also teach children safety and survival skills, such as how to talk to strangers

Many elementary schoolchildren return home from school to an empty house. New research has discovered the importance of parents knowing where their children are and communicating with them on a regular basis.

6. *TRUE OR FALSE?*

Elementary schoolchildren who regularly return home from school to an empty house and call their parents are no more susceptible to peer pressure nor do they have lower self-esteem than children who have a parent present when they get home from school.

on the phone, discriminating between emergencies and nonemergencies, and caring for younger siblings. A study of 1,000 children found that after such courses, children feel more confident about handling both emergencies and everyday situations. However, the children strongly wished that a parent were home with them or would call them. They experienced a sense of independence and accomplishment, but they also felt frightened, lonely, and bored (Gray & Coolsen, 1987).

It is difficult to interpret all the work on latchkey children because there are so many important variables. The definitions used sometimes differ, and the nature of the family situation that forces the child into the self-care situation may be important. The child whose parents are in a desperate situation may already have a great deal of stress to deal with and may leave their child in the self-care situation for many more hours per day. It is then possible that instead of blaming the latchkey situation for whatever problems (if any) are found, it may be other family variables that are at fault. Last, there is an important difference between those children who come directly home and whose parents use some sort of supervision and those who do not, and parents should be encouraged to provide long-range supervision for their children.

◆ STRESS

A change in family structure is stressful. However, even children in intact families are exposed to many different stressors. Such children must adapt to stressful situations in school and in their relationships with peers. In the middle years of childhood, children develop the cognitive ability to understand their parents' and teachers' expectations and feel the pressure of these expectations. Because they are no longer as egocentric, they are more sensitive to insults or unfavorable comparisons.

Children often can cope with a single stressor well (Rutter, 1980). But when children are exposed to multiple stressors, the effect is not just additive but multiplicative. When a child must deal with some stress, such as the death of a loved one or failure, it is then best to try to maintain stability in other areas of life. This is why divorce, which brings about multiple changes in a child's life, can have such negative consequences. If possible, the number of changes that are introduced into a child's life following divorce should be as few as possible so that the child has the opportunity to adjust to the divorce.

There is adequate research relating stress to a number of problems. Earlier we noted how changing family circumstances sometimes lead to poor adjustment and emotional difficulties. There are positive correlations between children's stress and anxiety, depression, behavior problems, delinquency, physical illness, and accident proneness (Clapp, 1988). Stress also adversely affects intellectual functioning.

It is estimated that as many as 35 percent of all American children suffer from stress-related health problems (*U.S. News and World Report*, 1986). Yet many children who are exposed to a great deal of stress do not develop such problems. Consider the case of Michael. Born to teenage parents, he was a premature infant who spent his first three weeks in the hospital. Immediately after his birth, his father went to Southeast Asia for two years with the U.S. Army. By the time Michael was eight, he had three younger siblings and his parents were divorced. His mother left the area and had no further contact with the children. By age 18, though, Michael had high self-esteem and good values, was liked by his peers, and was successful in school (Werner, 1984).

Children like Michael used to be called invulnerable, since they were not very affected in the long term by great amounts of stress. Today we know that this term is not correct. Since no child is invulnerable to stress, the more modern term is **stress-resistant** or **resilient** (Rutter, 1985). Some children seem to bounce back and can cope with pressures that seem at times to be too much for any child. These children are not uncommon, and in the past decade or so, psychologists have searched for factors that differentiate stress-resistant children from others. These factors can be grouped under the headings of protective factors within the child, within the family, and outside the family.

Resilient children show a strong social orientation as well as autonomy, even during the preschool period (Werner, 1984). They seem to lack fear and are self-reliant. Sociability and independence are characteristics that mark these children and make them more resistant to problems (Anthony, 1974). The child's temperament is another factor, as the more flexible, adaptable, and easygoing child is more likely to cope better with stress than the more difficult child (Wertlieb, Weigel, Springer, & Feldstein, 1987). The more adaptable child also receives more positive responses from others, which reduce the stress (Rutter, 1985). Stress-resistant children often find hobbies and outside interests a refuge from the problems of the family. They also tend to be active in after-school activities, which allow them to be away from the poor home environment. These children also tend to use better problem-solving strategies and are less likely to catastrophize, that is, make a mountain out of a molehill. They do not focus on the negative aspects of a situation (Brown, O'Keeffe, Sanders, & Baker, 1986).

The relationship with parents is the greatest buffer or protective device in childhood. Consider a child in the middle of the bombing of Britain in 1940 during World War II. Many children were evacuated from London and other cities to safe areas outside these cities. Between a quarter and a half of all children evacuated developed symptoms of high anxiety. Those who were the worst adjusted had previous conflicts with parents, while those with warm, supportive relationships handled the stress the best. The group that developed the least amount of neurotic symptoms were those who stayed in the cities with their parents where they could retain the warm relationship they had with them (see Clapp, 1988). The relationship seemed to have a protective effect on the child.

Children who have a good relationship with at least one parent tend to do better than those who do not. But the positive relationship with an adult does not have to be with a parent. Sometimes an older sibling, a grandparent, or another adult—perhaps a teacher—can serve as a role model and confidant. In fact, stress-resistant children seem to be very

stress-resistant (resilient) children Children who do not appear to be negatively affected by stress and are able to cope with it and turn out healthy in the long run.

active in finding these adults (Werner, 1984). When third and fifth graders were rated on problem-solving skills, social support, amount of stress, and behavior problems, children who were competent problem solvers had higher levels of social support and showed fewer behavioral problems (Dubow & Tisak, 1989). Social support moderates the effects of stress (Wertlieb, Weigel, & Feldstein, 1989). In Karen's case, her relationship with her parents is very poor, but she has a good relationship with her aunt, and this may help her adjust to the stresses in her family.

Children who are resilient are frequently involved in taking care of others, most commonly, younger siblings. This concept is called required helpfulness. When children living in terrible family circumstances were observed, Werner and Smith (1982) found that many of the stress-resistant children had assumed the responsibility for their younger siblings. Helping others may increase their coping skills and morale and generally give them a sense of purpose.

This emphasis on stress-resistant children is refreshing. Instead of looking at the factors that cause behavioral problems, we are looking at why some children are able to transcend or cope with these stressors while others are not. We can begin to use this knowledge to help children who find themselves under a great deal of stress. First, we know that once the child is exposed to a particular stressor, he or she requires time to adjust before going on to cope with the next stressor. Therefore, buffering the child from multiple stressors is a good idea. We also know that children who have warm relationships with their parents, a single parent, or adults outside the nuclear family do best, so building relationships is important. In addition, since resilient children have hobbies and interests outside the home, encouraging participation in extracurricular activities is desirable. Such participation allows the child to focus attention elsewhere and obtain a sense of self-esteem from such activities. Resilient children also have a sense of responsibility, and caring for others and encouraging these children to become involved in meaningful helping activities can bring self-respect and a sense of purpose. Resilient children also tend to be sociable and independent, and helping children develop friendships with others is another possibility.

◆ PEER RELATIONSHIPS IN MIDDLE CHILDHOOD

One of the important features of middle childhood is the growing influence of other people outside the family, including other children and teachers.

Spending More Time with Other Children

As children mature, they spend more time with their peers. At age two, about 10 percent of a child's social interactions involve other children, while by age eleven, the percentage increases to 50 percent (Barker and Wright, 1955). Peer interactions are very different from adult-child interactions. Child-child interactions involve companionship and amusement;

adult-child interactions involve protection, care, and instruction (Damon, 1983). Children turn to parents for affection and reliable aid, but they turn to their friends when they want companionship (Furman & Buhrmester, 1985). They have more power with friends as well. Children understand this difference. They see adults and older children as more helpful, but they look to age-mates for play. Their behavior reflects these perceptions. They show more submission and appeal when interacting with adults and more social behavior and domination when interacting with peers (Edwards & Lewis, 1979).

Children in middle childhood see the peer group as most influential in the areas of activities and social behavior. Older adolescents see peer influence as more global and far-reaching and involving appearance, attitudes, and values (O'Brien & Bierman, 1988). As children progress through school, they less often see parents as the most important providers of companionship, and children of the same sex become more important in this area (Buhrmester & Furman, 1987).

The years between about eight and ten see another interesting shift. An influential theorist, Harry Stack Sullivan (1953), emphasized the importance of the preadolescent intimate relationships with children of the same sex, which he called chumship. At this age, intimacy involves knowledge and understanding of a friend's feelings, honesty, loyalty, and the ability to share. Intimacy is relatively low at age eight, but it increases as the child progresses through preadolescence (Jones & Dembo, 1989).

Children in middle childhood normally have more than one "best friend". In fact, friends are often found in small groups of children (Berndt, 1989). Social contacts increase dramatically in class, and small, informal groups often arise. These children are aware of the standards of the group, and much of the communication in these friendship groups is in the form of gossip (Parker & Gottman, 1989). This gossip concentrates on an exploration of the similarities of each group member, reveals attitudes and beliefs that the members share, and often involves criticizing other children. As the children gossip, they are affirming their norms and the values of the group. For example, they may criticize another child because he or she is bossy or aggressive, tells lies, or is a tattletale.

During middle childhood, much children's communication with their friends is in the form of gossip.

Popularity and Unpopularity

Some children have a great many friends, while others do not. In fact, 5 percent to 10 percent of all elementary schoolchildren are named by no one in their class as a friend (Asher & Renshaw, 1981), and about 12 percent are named by only one person as a friend (Gronlund, 1959). Such a lack of popularity can have many undesirable consequences for a child.

Children who are not popular are more likely to be low achievers and dropouts (Putallaz & Gottman, 1981) and to suffer from emotional difficulties (Newman, 1982). Teachers can identify children who are popular as well as those who have difficulty relating to other children (Vosk, Forehand, Parker, & Richard, 1982). Popularity and rejection are also fairly stable patterns across time (Bukowski & Newcomb, 1984).

Children who are popular are physically attractive, share interests with other children, are friendly, outgoing, and enthusiastic, know how to give positive reinforcement, and have good interpersonal skills (Dion, 1983; Hartup, 1970). Late in middle childhood, such traits as loyalty and empathy become important. Deviant and negative reactions to others are related to rejection (Hartup, 1983). Children who are unpopular are likely to have deficits in social skills. They do not interact well with other children, criticize others, and are aggressive. It is not that aggressive and unpopular children do not have friends. They do. They usually play with other aggressive or unpopular children (Cairns, Cairns, Neckerman, Gest, & Gariepy, 1988). Aggressive children are members of very solid peer clusters throughout elementary school. These children may be generally rejected by the majority of children, but they do find other children with whom they can share a relationship, and their relationships are no less meaningful to them.

One way to help unpopular children is to teach them the social skills they lack. Such a program can work if it is combined with structured peer involvement. In other words, children who learn social skills need to be included in programs that allow them to show and practice their new skills (Bierman and Furman, 1984).

Friendship: A Developmental Perspective

Karen was willing to share her money with her friend Linda. Karen values Linda's friendship, and their friendship has a stable quality that we associate with such relationships. It has previously been noted that in the preschool years, friendships do occur, but they are often fleeting and transitory. They form and disintegrate very quickly, despite the fact that some do continue for an entire year in nursery school. There is little intimacy involved.

In the early school years, a gradual change takes place. Wyndol Furman and Karen Linn Bierman (1983) investigated the change in children's perceptions of friendship between four and seven years of age. Common activities, affection, support, and being near were all found to be important, but expectations concerning affection and support increased with age, while references to physical characteristics decreased. Older children saw support, helping, sharing, and affection as more important than common activities. Children in the early grades of elementary school are likely to form friendships on the basis of sharing and helping (Bigelow, 1977). By the second grade, they are aware of the differences between friends and mere acquaintances (Furman & Bierman, 1984). Friendships become more stable as children progress from grade one to grade four (Berndt & Hoyle, 1985). As children mature, they begin to look at psychological compatibility (Rubin, 1980) and see friends as people with whom they can share good times and problems. Friendships are based on deeper values, such as intimacy, trust, loyalty, and faithfulness (Berndt, 1981).

Selman's Developmental Model of Friendship

A useful model describing the development of friendship, devised by Robert Selman (1981), is summarized in Table 12.1. Selman sees children

7. TRUE OR FALSE?

Aggressive children in middle childhood do not have any friends.

TABLE 12.1: How Children Perceive Friendship

Children's understanding of friendship changes as children mature and affects how they will behave towards their companions.

STAGES OF REFLECTIVE UNDERSTANDING OF CLOSE DYADIC FRIENDSHIPS

Stage 0: Momentary physicalistic playmates. Conceptions of friendship relations are based on thinking that focuses upon propinquity and proximity (i.e., physicalistic parameters) to the exclusion of others. A close friend is someone who lives close by and with whom the self happens to be playing at the moment. Friendship is more accurately playmateship. Issues such as jealousy or the intrusion of a third party into a play situation are constructed by the child at Stage 0 as specific fights over specific toys or space rather than as conflicts that involve personal feelings or interpersonal affection.

Stage 1: One-way assistance. Friendship conceptions are one-way in the sense that a friend is seen as important because he or she performs specific activities that the self wants accomplished. In other words, one person's attitude is unreflectively set up as a standard, and the "friend's" actions must match the standard thus formulated. A close friend is someone with more than Stage 0 demographic credentials; a close friend is someone who is known better than other persons. "Knowing" means accurate knowledge of others' likes and dislikes.

Stage 2: Fair-weather cooperation. The advance of Stage 2 friendships over the previous stages is based on the new awareness of interpersonal perspectives as reciprocal. The two-way nature of friendships is exemplified by concerns for coordinating and approximating, through adjustment by both self and other, the specific likes and dislikes of self and other, rather than matching one person's actions to the other's fixed standard of expectation. The limitation of this stage is the discontinuity of these reciprocal expectations. Friendship at Stage 2 is fair weather—specific arguments are seen as severing the relationship, although both parties may still have affection for one another inside. The coordination of attitudes at the moment defines the relation. No underlying continuity is seen to exist that can maintain the relation during the period of conflict or adjustment.

Stage 3: Intimate and mutually shared relationships. At Stage 3, there is the awareness of both a continuity of relation and affective bonding between close friends. The importance of friendship does not rest only upon the fact that the self is bored or lonely; at Stage 3, friendships are seen as a basic means of developing mutual intimacy and mutual support; friends share personal problems. The occurrence of conflicts between friends does not mean the suspension of the relationship, because the underlying continuity between partners is seen as a means of transcending foul-weather incidents. The limitations of Stage 3 conceptions derive from the overemphasis of the two-person clique and the possessiveness that arises out of the realization that close relations are difficult to form and to maintain.

Stage 4: Autonomous interdependent friendships. The interdependence that characterizes Stage 4 is the sense that a friendship can continue to grow and be transformed through each partner's ability to synthesize feelings of independence and dependence. Independence means that each person accepts the other's need to establish relations with others and to grow through such experiences. Dependence reflects the awareness that friends must rely on each other for psychological support, to draw strength from each other, and to gain a sense of self-identification through identification with the other as a significant person whose relation to the self is distinct from those with whom one has less meaningful relations.

Source: S. R. Asher and J. M. Gottman, eds., 1981.

as developing their conceptions of friendships in stages. In Stage 0, friendship is based on proximity. Stage 1 (called one-way assistance) involves a rather selfish view in which friends are seen as important if they satisfy the child's own needs. Our friend knows what we like and don't like. When children enter Stage 2—fair-weather cooperation—they see friendship as a two-way street. However, these reciprocal relationships are tenuous, and simple arguments often wreck the relationship. In Stage 3—intimate and mutually shared relationships—some understanding of continuity, affection, mutual support, and the sharing of personal problems exists. On the negative side, possessiveness is apparent in this type of close relationship. Finally, Stage 4—autonomous interdependent friendships—involves both independence and dependence, accepting each other's needs to have separate friendships outside the relationship.

As children develop, their definition of friendship changes from one involving concrete behaviors to more abstract terms (Shantz, 1983). It changes from the self-centered orientation of perceiving friends as satisfying one's own needs to perceiving friendship as mutually satisfying, and from an emphasis on the momentary or transient positive interactions between individuals to a relationship that endures over time and conflict. For these changes to occur, advances in cognitive functioning are necessary. Children cannot develop mutuality unless they can take a friend's point of view into consideration, an ability that develops in middle childhood.

Friendship Patterns and Gender

Same-sex friendships are the rule during middle childhood. Boys and girls do talk with each other, but their relationships lack intimacy and involvement. Active rejection of the opposite sex is rare; avoidance is the usual course of action (Hartup, 1983). Whatever cross-sex friendships do develop are less stable than same-sex relationships (Tuma & Hallinan, 1979). This segregation reaches its peak during the late elementary school or early junior high school years (Schofield, 1981). Of course, individual differences do exist, and some fast-developing seventh graders may be ready to develop cross-sex friendships.

Why do boys stay with boys and girls associate with girls during this period? Freud explained it in terms of the resolution of the Oedipal situation, as described earlier in this chapter. Other interpretations for gender segregation have been advanced. They include lack of compatibility in play, encouragement from parents to form friendships with children of the same sex, and the formation of gender-role stereotypes (Hartup, 1983). For example, boys do not expect girls to want to join in their games (Schofield, 1981). They perceive girls as having different interests and participating in different activities. They may also be aware of the relationships between the genders that await them during adolescence, including dating, romance, and sex. Peer pressure may also be a factor. A sixth-grade boy interested in forming a relationship with a girl may find himself under peer pressure not to do so. The young girl may also be the butt of rumors and jokes and find it easier to avoid a boy than to risk her friends' criticism. Whatever the reason, the growth of same-sex friendships during this period helps the child develop the ideals of friendship and intimacy that prove so important when the child begins to form cross-sex relationships in adolescence.

Gender Stereotypes: Alive and Well in the 1990s

A few years ago, a TV commercial was aired in which a mother stated her approval of her daughter's attempt to emulate her older brother. The picture showed a girl in pigtails sliding safely into third base. Because the purpose of a commercial is to sell a product, this must mean that being a tomboy—having what we might call male-stereotyped interests— is acceptable for elementary schoolchildren. The opposite would probably never be shown, however. Can you imagine a commercial showing a boy playing with dolls with a girl and the mother saying, "When my little boy wants to keep up with his sister, I let him"? Girls are allowed to take on some of the characteristics usually assigned to males during the elementary school years, but boys are not encouraged to take on stereotyped competencies of females. In middle childhood, parents continue to treat sons and daughters differently, and parents allow their sons more freedom.

Young elementary schoolchildren know what activities are associated with males and females and are rather inflexible in their assignment of "gender-appropriate" activities (Williams & Stith, 1980). They have already acquired their initial stereotypes (Emmerich & Shepard, 1982). Kindergartners and second and fourth graders were presented with a story and a list of adjectives that adults had previously evaluated as applying more to males or females. Subjects were asked to indicate whether a boy or a girl was involved. Almost all the kindergarten children associated aggression with males. Although second graders knew more about gender stereotypes than kindergarten children, the differences between second and fourth graders were small. Awareness of masculine stereotyped behaviors, such as aggression, was acquired earlier than awareness of stereotyped female characteristics, reflected by such adjectives as emotional and appreciative (Williams, Bennett & Best, 1975).

As children mature, they become less rigid in their stereotypes (Huston, 1983). After about age seven, children no longer accept such stereotypes as absolute and are willing to make exceptions (Carter & Patterson, 1982). This tendency should not be overemphasized. Children have limits in what they will accept, and the resistance of boys to change is likely to be greater than that of girls. Whereas boys show an increased preference for male-stereotpyed activities, girls do not show the same growing preference for stereotyped female activities (Carter & Patterson, 1982). Boys have much stricter ideas about gender-role preferences than girls do, and boys greatly value their own stereotyped competencies.

Schools contribute to gender-role stereotyping in a number of ways. Teacher-student interactions, unequal access to programs, and sexist treatment of people in school materials all contribute to gender-role stereotyping. Finally, the role models available to children in schools are often limiting (Minuchin & Shapiro, 1983).

Differences exist in the way teachers interact with boys and girls. Although elementary schoolteachers interact more with boys than with girls, much of this interaction is critical. Teachers are more likely to reprimand boys (Serbin, O'Leary, Kent & Tonick, 1973). Boys are more likely to be

It is acceptable for girls to take on some of the "stereotyped" competencies of males. Do you think boys are as free to adopt such "female stereotyped competencies" as being gentle or playing with dolls?

8. TRUE OR FALSE?

As children progress through middle childhood, their conceptions of gender stereotypes become more rigid.

seen as causing trouble, and girls do not receive as much harsh discipline in school as boys. When teachers attend to task-oriented activities in class, boys still receive more attention than girls (Fagot, 1977). In addition, when children demand attention, teachers respond to boys with instructions and to girls with nurturance. Girls are also given more attention when physically close to teachers, while boys are given more attention when they are far away. Perhaps teachers expect good behavior from girls but feel that boys require encouragement. Male and female teachers are not very different in their views of student behavior. Perhaps these interactions reinforce physical proximity and conformity in girls and more task oriented behavior in boys (Kaplan, 1990).

Think about the behaviors and traits that are valued in elementary school. Children are expected to sit still and be neat, very polite, and quiet. Elementary school is perceived by most children as a feminizing experience (Minuchin & Shapiro, 1983). Girls are more likely to have these characteristics. They adjust more easily to school, show superior achievement, and express less criticism of the school (Minuchin & Shapiro, 1983).

Teachers have very well defined concepts of gender roles and both expect and desire the orderly, dependent behavior that is in conflict with the traditional stereotyped gender roles of males (Lee & Gropper, 1974). They also tend to concentrate on different areas when evaluating boys and girls. When the amount of time teachers spent on different subjects with second-grade boys and girls was investigated, it was found that teachers were more likely to spend time with boys on mathematics and with girls on reading. By the end of the year, the girls were ahead of boys on reading (Leinhardt, Seewald & Engel, 1979).

Teachers are also likely to attribute failure to different causes. Boys' failures are often perceived by teachers as being due to lack of motivation, while girls' failures are attributed to lack of ability (Dweck, Davidson, Nelson & Enna, 1978; Dweck & Bush, 1976). This may lead to a condition in females called learned helplessness—the state in which a girl believes that she can do nothing to change her situation. If a girl believes that she lacks ability, she simply won't try very hard. These differences in teacher-student interactions may contribute to gender stereotyping.

Many school materials communicate the message that females are less important than males. Some elementary school texts do not portray women in positive roles, nor do they show women holding major positions or performing important tasks (Shepherd-Look, 1982). Although texts are now showing less restrictive gender roles, women's contributions in many fields are still undervalued.

Unequal access to various programs is seen mostly on the high school level, where students are differentially encouraged to take various subjects. However, even in the elementary school, girls may be told that physical education is not as important for them or are told not to worry as much about science and mathematics. Finally, role models in the schools are quite stereotyped. The overwhelming majority of elementary school-teachers are women, while most of the school principals are men. Almost all the school secretaries are female, and almost all the custodians are male. This reinforces the male view that school is a female-oriented experience.

It is clear that boys and girls experience school differently. Teachers admire and reinforce feminine-stereotyped behavior in elementary school. Traditionally, this feminizing experience has been seen as affecting boys far more than girls, because the latter's adjustment and achievement in elementary school are superior (Busch-Rossnagel & Vance, 1983). The various problems males develop in elementary school are sobering. Twice as many boys as girls show articulation errors, three times as many boys are stutterers, the incidence of reading problems is three to five times as common in boys, mental retardation is higher in males, the ratio of boys to girls who are referred for emotional and/or behavior problems is two to one, and boys have a higher rate of schizophrenia, delinquency, academic underachievement, hyperactivity, enuresis (bed wetting), and autism (Shepherd-Look, 1982). Two-thirds of all students left back are male (Davis, 1983). These differences are large and disturbing. Males are far more vulnerable than females. Perhaps they have more difficulty adjusting to the school environment, are not as ready physically or mentally, or find school a stifling experience not consistent with their idea of what a male should be doing.

Authorities, however, have recently reevaluated their analysis of the differential experiences of males and females in school (Busch-Rossnagel & Vance, 1982). Despite the figures, most males seem to recover in secondary school to compete successfully with females. In fact, the long-term negative effect may be greater for girls, since the stereotyped behaviors, which include dependency, submission, obedience, and conformity, are negatively correlated with later academic success. Despite their impressive success in elementary school, girls may suffer later. Perhaps the soundest conclusion is that sex-typing behavior affects boys and girls differently but probably injures both in the long run.

Kohlberg's theory stresses the importance of the reasoning behind an act—Why this child would do ___ , not whether he (she) did or did not do it.

◆ THE DEVELOPMENT OF MORALITY

Whether children are male or female, we are interested in their moral development—their sense of right and wrong. The second Karen picked up the wallet, she was faced with a moral question. Children are faced with moral decisions every day. Cheating, lying, and stealing are daily temptations in school. Decisions about when to obey and when to disobey, when to fight back and when to turn away, and whether to return some lost article are fairly common. Three distinct approaches to the study of morality have been advanced. The first studies children's **moral reasoning**—their ideas about justice and about right and wrong—and is typified by the theories of Jean Piaget and Lawrence Kohlberg. The second is the psychoanalytic viewpoint, which stresses the development of a child's conscience. The third is the diverse social learning and behavioral tradition, which emphasizes how such behaviors as honesty and altruism are learned. Each approach looks at moral development in a different way and taps different elements of morality.

moral reasoning
An approach to the study of moral development stressing the importance of the child's ideas and reasoning about justice and right and wrong.

Piaget on Moral Reasoning

If you have access to five-, eight-, and twelve-year-old children, try this experiment. Present the children with the following problem: "Janet broke one dish trying to sneak into the refrigerator to get some jam. Jennifer broke five dishes trying to help her mother. Who was naughtier?" Piaget (1932) investigated a child's sense of right and wrong through a series of interviews in which he presented children of various ages with such problems as this. The reasoning of young children was in sharp contrast to that of older children. Young children simply stated that the girl who broke five dishes was naughtier than the girl who broke one. They had difficulty taking intent into consideration when evaluating moral questions. Older children had less difficulty understanding intent and answered, as adults would, that Janet's behavior was worse than Jennifer's.

Piaget looked at morality in terms of how a child develops a sense of justice and a respect for the social order (Maccoby, 1980). He argued that children's understanding of rules follows a general sequence.

Preschoolers and children in the early school years consider rules sacred and untouchable and created by an all-powerful authority figure. In this stage of **moral realism,** rules are inflexible, and justice is whatever authority or law commands. The letter, not the spirit, of the law is important (Mussen & Eisenberg-Berg, 1977), and children will become upset if people try to change the rules. Children believe in the absoluteness of values—things are either right or wrong. It is during these years that children evaluate acts on the basis of their consequences, not on the basis of an individual's intent or motivation.

At about age seven or eight, the intermediate stage is reached. Children now interact with peers and develop some type of reciprocal give-and-take understanding. What is fair is more important than the position of authority. Punishments may or may not be fair, depending on the crime committed.

The stage called **moral relativism** emerges at about age eleven or twelve. Children can now take extenuating circumstances into account and weigh them in their moral judgments. Children become more flexible, and rules are changeable. Children in the stage of moral relativism take intent into account when assessing moral questions.

Children gain a better understanding of morality through social interaction and cognitive growth (Piaget, 1932). For instance, as children progress through the concrete stage of cognitive development, they become less egocentric and are able to understand another person's intentions and motivations. They can also take more than one element into consideration at a time when evaluating a complex dilemma. But just because children are able to do so does not necessarily mean they will take intent into account in every situation. Even adults don't. For example, some parents may become very angry at their children for making a mess in the kitchen, even though the children were just trying to help.

Age-related differences in children's understanding of consequences and intent are well established. Children younger than seven years of age rely primarily on consequences when evaluating another person's ac-

moral realism
The Piagetian stage of moral reasoning during which rules are viewed as sacred, and justice is whatever the authority figure says.

moral relativism
The Piagetian stage of moral reasoning in which children weigh the intentions of others before judging their actions right or wrong.

9. *TRUE OR FALSE?*

As children progress through the elementary school years, they are more likely to judge right and wrong on the basis of the consequences of an action rather than intent.

Children below the age of seven or so often follow rules with blind devotion believing that they cannot be changed.

tions. Children older than ten or so rely on intentions. Between about seven and ten, children rely on either one of these (Ferguson & Rule, 1982).

Piaget's ideas have been criticized on a number of grounds. First, making judgments such as who is naughtier is a very special type of moral judgment. Piaget does not deal with questions about what a child should do in a particular situation (Rest, 1983). Second, a number of studies have varied such factors as the amount of damage and the degree of intentionality and found that under certain circumstances, even small children understand that deliberate damage is "naughtier." When children are asked to evaluate stories one at a time, many studies have found both intent and damage had significant effects across age groups from four-year-olds to college students (Leon, 1982). Children as young as four can sometimes understand the moral intention of others if the language and cognitive demands are reduced (Keasey, 1978).

From Piaget's work we can conclude that children acquire an appreciation of the rules and a concept of justice in an orderly sequence. However, Piaget's formulations in this area are rather narrow. To truly understand moral reasoning, we must look at the theoretical approach developed by Lawrence Kohlberg.

Kohlberg's Theory of Moral Reasoning

Heinz's wife has cancer. There is a drug that might cure her, but the only dose is owned by a pharmacist who wants a great deal of money for it. Heinz doesn't have the money. Should he steal it? Lawrence Kohlberg (1969, 1976) presented dilemmas like this one to many subjects and after

Part 4: Middle Childhood

careful study proposed a model that describes the development of moral reasoning. Kohlberg sees moral reasoning as developing in a three-level, six-stage sequence, which is summarized in Table 12.2. The stages are sequential and universal; that is, they are applicable to every culture, and no stages are ever skipped. Each stage requires more sophisticated skills than the one that preceded it.

How would you have answered the dilemma described above? Most students state immediately that Heinz should steal it. However, Kohlberg is not interested in the answer itself. It is the reasoning behind the choice that is of interest and that determines what stage of moral reasoning a person is in.

As Kohlberg's three levels and six stages are reviewed below, keep in mind that it is the moral reasoning, not the answer itself, that determines one's stage of moral development.

preconventional level
Kohlberg's first level of moral reasoning, in which satisfaction of one's own needs and reward and punishment serve as the basis for moral decision making.

LEVEL I: PRECONVENTIONAL MORALITY At the **preconventional level,** people make decisions on the basis of reward and punishment and the satisfaction of their own needs. If Karen reasoned at this level, she might keep the wallet because it satisfies her immediate desires. On the other hand, she might not, because she is afraid of getting caught and being punished. Morality is defined strictly by the physical consequences of the act.

Stage one: punishment and obedience orientation.

An individual in Stage 1 avoids breaking rules because it might lead to punishment. This person shows complete deference to rules. The interests of others are not considered.

Stage two: instrumental relativist orientation.

In Stage 2, the right actions are those that satisfy one's own needs and only sometimes the needs of others. However, the only reason for helping others is that they will then owe you something—a debt to be collected at a later time. There is a sense of fairness in this stage, and a deal is acceptable.

conventional level
Kohlberg's second level of moral reasoning, in which conformity to the expectations of others and society in general serves as the basis for moral decision making.

LEVEL II: CONVENTIONAL MORALITY At the **conventional level,** conformity is the most important factor. The individual conforms to the expectations of others, including the general social order. Karen might keep the wallet if she reasons that anyone would keep it—and it's just too bad for the owner. On the other hand, she might not keep it if she reasons that it is against the rules and she would not be doing the "right" thing or being a good girl.

Stage three: interpersonal concordance, or "good boy/nice girl" orientation.

Living up to the expectations of others and being good are the important considerations for a person in Stage 3. The emphasis is on gaining approval from others by being nice.

Stage four: "law-and-order" orientation.

TABLE 12.2: Summary of Kohlberg's Stages of Moral Reasoning

Lawrence Kohlberg views the development of morality in terms of moral reasoning. The stage of moral reasoning at which people can be placed depends upon the reasoning behind their decisions, not the decisions themselves.

I. PRECONVENTIONAL LEVEL

The child is responsive to cultural rules and labels of good and bad, right or wrong, but interprets these either in terms of the physical or hedonistic consequences of action (punishment, reward, exchange of favors) or in terms of the physical power of those who enunciate the rules. The level is divided into two stages:

Stage 1: Punishment and obedience orientation. The physical consequences of action determine its goodness or badness regardless of the meaning or value of these consequences. Avoidance of punishment and unquestioning deference to power are valued in their own right, not in terms of respect for an underlying moral order (the latter being Stage 4).

Stage 2: Instrumental relativist orientation. Right action is that which instrumentally satisfies one's own needs and occasionally the needs of others. Human relations are viewed in terms of the marketplace. Fairness, reciprocity, and equal sharing are present but are always interpreted in a physical, pragmatic way. Reciprocity is a matter of "you scratch my back and I'll scratch yours," not of loyalty, gratitude, or justice.

II. CONVENTIONAL LEVEL

Maintaining the expectations of the individual's family, group, or nation is perceived as valuable in its own right, regardless of consequences. The attitude is not only one of *conformity* to personal expectations and social order but also of loyalty to it, of actively *maintaining*, supporting and justifying it, of identifying with the persons or group involved in it. This level has two stages:

Stage 3: Interpersonal concordance, or "good boy/nice girl" orientation. Good behavior is that which pleases or helps others and is approved by them. There is much conformity to stereotypical images of what is majority or "natural" behavior. Behavior is frequently judged by intention—"he means well" becomes important for the first time. One earns approval by being "nice."

Stage 4: "Law and order" orientation. Orientation is toward authority, fixed rules, and the maintenance of the social order. Right behavior consists of doing one's duty, showing respect for authority, maintaining the social order for its own sake.

III. POSTCONVENTIONAL, AUTONOMOUS, OR PRINCIPLED LEVEL

The person makes a clear effort to define moral values and principles that have validity and application apart from the authority of the groups or persons holding these principles, and apart from the individual's own identification with these groups. This level has two stages:

Stage 5: Social-contract, legalistic orientation. Generally with utilitarian overtones. Right action is defined in terms of general individual rights and standards that have been critically examined and agreed upon by society. The person is clearly aware of the relativism of values and opinions and so emphasizes procedural rules for reaching consensus. Aside from what is constitutionally and democratically agreed upon, right is a matter of personal "values" and "opinion"; emphasis is thus on the "legal point of view," but with the possibility of changing law in terms of rational considerations of social utility rather than freezing in terms of Stage 4. Outside the legal realm, free agreement and contract is the binding element. This is the "official" morality of the U.S. government and Constitution.

Stage 6: Universal ethical principle orientation. Right is defined by the decision of conscience in accord with self-chosen *ethical principles* appealing to logical comprehensiveness, universality, and consistency. These principles are abstract and ethical (the Golden Rule, the categorical imperative); they are not concrete moral rules like the Ten Commandments. At heart, these are universal principles of *justice of the reciprocity and equality of human rights,* and of respect for the dignity of human feelings as individual persons.

Source: Kohlberg, 1971.

A person in Stage 4 is oriented toward authority and toward maintaining the social order. The emphasis is on doing one's duty and showing respect for authority. Sometimes people in this stage reason, "If everyone did it, then. . . ."

postconventional level
Kohlberg's third level of moral reasoning in which moral decisions are made on the basis of individual values that have been internalized.

LEVEL III: POSTCONVENTIONAL MORALITY People in the **postconventional level** have evolved moral values that have been internalized. These values are individualized and not dependent on one's membership in any particular group. Since such moral reasoning usually does not occur until adolescence at the earliest, we would not expect Karen to show such reasoning. However, if this dilemma occurred at a later age, Karen might return the wallet because she herself values honesty and integrity, even if it means she has to do without something. In Karen's case, the reasoning for keeping the wallet is admittedly strained. Karen, however, might reason, that the wealthy person who lost the wallet does not need the money as much as she and Linda need it and that even if she were caught she would be helping another human being in need—her friend. Karen's values of friendship, loyalty, and giving to others would become most important here.

Stage five: social-contract, legalistic orientation.

In Stage 5, correct behavior is defined in terms of individual rights and the consensus of society. Right is a matter of personal values and opinions, but the emphasis here is on the legal point of view.

Stage six: universal ethical principle orientation.

In the highest stage, Stage 6, the correct behavior is defined as a decision of conscience in accordance with self-chosen ethical principles that are logical, universal, and consistent. This involves being able to weigh the ethics of various viewpoints and reasoning, and creating abstract guidelines to direct one's behavior. (see Kohlberg and Kramer, 1969).

People rarely reason solely in one stage. More often, they may be predominantly in one stage but also partly in the stages before and after. A person may be 40 percent in Stage 3, 30 percent in Stage 2, and 30 percent in Stage 4. Change involves a gradual shift in the percentage of reasoning from one stage to the next rather than a wholesale switch from one stage to the next higher stage (Carroll & Rest, 1982).

Kohlberg's theory has been applied successfully to many cultures (Snarey, Reimer & Kohlberg, 1985). When Nisan and Kohlberg (1982) studied rural and city subjects ages ten through twenty-eight in Turkey, they found evidence for the universality of the stage sequence. City subjects were well ahead of villagers in development. People's experiences influence their level of moral reasoning. Perhaps the constant interpersonal contacts and possibility for experiencing more sophisticated moral dilemmas lead to higher moral reasoning in urban dwellers.

There is also evidence that the stages are indeed sequential (Kohlberg, Colby, Gibbs, Speicher-Dubin & Powers, 1978; Walker, 1982). People do not skip stages, although they enter and leave them at varying times. Sequential development in non-Western cultures has been shown at least through Stage 4 (Carroll & Rest, 1982). Cross-cultural studies have not been clear, though, in finding level III (postconventional) moral reasoning in all non-Western cultures.

MORAL REASONING AND GENDER If you look at the descriptions of Kohlberg's stages, you will notice that the emphasis in the higher stages of moral reasoning is on justice and on individual rights and the rights of others. Higher moral reasoning seems to have little to do with interpersonal relationships. According to Carol Gilligan (1982), women have a different orientation to moral questions. They see moral questions more in terms of how these issues affect interpersonal relationships rather than in strictly individualistic terms. Male emphasis in moral reasoning is on individual rights and self-fulfillment.

The differences in moral reasoning are rooted in the varying experiences boys and girls have in childhood. For example, boys learn to be independent, assertive, achievement oriented, and individualistic and to attach great importance to the rule of law. This is similar to the Stage 4 perspective. On the other hand, women are raised to be more concerned with the rights and needs of others and to be interested in interpersonal relationships (Hotelling & Forrest, 1985). They are more oriented toward interpersonal connectedness, care, sensitivity, and responsibility to other people rather than toward abstract principles of justice (Muuss, 1988). They tend to see moral difficulties as conflicts between what they themselves want and the needs and wants of others, and they may base their decisions on how relationships with others will be affected. Harmony rather than justice may be the guiding principle. Sensitivity to the needs of others, instead of strict individual rights, becomes the criterion to apply in such dilemmas. This seems more like the Stage 3 perspective. However, Gilligan notes that neither reasoning is superior—the stages are just different, and these differences should be understood and respected.

Kohlberg's theory fails to take these differences into account. Karen may look at how her actions might affect her relationships with others rather than simply look at some abstract rules of justice. Some interesting evidence in favor of this point of view comes from studies showing that five-and seven-year-old boys and girls settle their disputes differently. Boys are more likely to use threats and physical force and to pursue their own goals, while girls try to reduce conflict, and their goal is to improve harmony (Miller, Danaher, & Forbes, 1986). Boys also experience more conflict with peers than girls do.

Gilligan's ideas are controversial, with some studies failing to find consistent gender differences (Walker, 1984; 1989). The argument continues, though. All we can say at the present time is that gender differences in moral reasoning may exist, and we should be careful in stating that a particular type of reasoning is higher or lower—it may simply be different. Even if consistent gender differences are subsequently not supported by research, Gilligan's contribution lies in broadening our view of moral reasoning to include the idea that the moral person may integrate concepts of abstract justice and the concern for others (Muuss, 1988).

IS MORAL REASONING RELATED TO MORAL BEHAVIOR? Would a person reasoning at a Stage 5 level act differently from a person reasoning at a stage 1 level? As the individual progresses toward Stage 6, we would

---

10. TRUE OR FALSE?

Boys experience more conflict with their peers than girls do.

think that moral behavior such as honesty and resisting temptation would increase. Although nothing in Kohlberg's theory necessitates a link between moral reasoning and moral behavior, it is an important question (Blasi, 1980).

Most studies find a relationship between moral reasoning and moral action (Blasi, 1980; Kohlberg, 1987), but the strength of the relationship varies from area to area. Some support is found for the idea that people at higher moral stages are more honest, but there is little support for the idea that people at the postconventional level resist social pressure to conform in their actual moral actions. Only relatively weak associations are found between progressing to higher levels of moral reasoning and whether a child will cheat, yield to temptation, or behave altruistically if there is a personal cost attached to it (Maccoby, 1980). For example, college students were found to cheat less as their level of their moral reasoning increased. However, although subjects low in moral judgment cheated more, those high in moral judgment also cheated when the temptation became strong (Malinowski & Smith, 1985). Therefore, although a relationship between moral reasoning and moral behavior exists, other factors help determine whether a person will perform an act.

EVALUATING KOHLBERG'S THEORY Although Kohlberg's theory gives us a valuable framework for understanding moral development, it has been criticized. One problem is the discrepancy between reasoning and action. For whatever reason, people sometimes proceed in ways they think are theoretically best, and sometimes they do not (Chandler & Boyes, 1982). In addition, it is possible to reason at any level and still find a reason to cheat, lie, or steal. More predictability is needed. In addition, Kohlberg's theory assumes that each stage is definite and that a person should reason fairly consistently in different situations. Although there is not much research in this area, the few studies that do look at this issue do not support this consistency (Hoffman, 1988). But perhaps the greatest problem with Kohlberg's theory is that moral reasoning may be only a part of the overall process people use to convert environmental information into an action sequence.

According to James Rest (1983), there are four stages to this sequence. First, a person must be sensitive enough to notice and evaluate a situation in terms of moral questions. Then the person attempts to reason the problem out. (This is where Kohlberg's moral reasoning theory fits in.) In the third stage, environmental influences are taken into consideration. (How much will the decision personally cost the person? How important is getting a good grade when cheating may be easy?) Finally, there may be practical difficulties in implementing the plan of action. You may want to help someone who has just suffered a heart attack but not know how to do cardiopulmonary resuscitation.

Reasoning About Different Types of Transgressions

Another problem with both Kohlberg's and Piaget's theories is that they do not draw any real distinctions between different types of moral dilemmas. Elliot Turiel (1983) (Turiel, Nucci, & Smetana, 1988) argues that children easily distinguish between moral rules and conventional rules. A moral rule is one that pertains to preventing people from doing harm to one another, such as stealing, while social conventional rules pertain to rules that facilitate and regulate social interactions, such as forms of greeting and dress (Weston & Turiel, 1980). Children view conventional rules as changeable and as determined by the group or society, while moral rules are independent of consensus. When preschool children were asked, "If there were no rules in school about . . . . , would it be all right to do it?," over 80 percent of the preschoolers considered social conventional transgressions wrong only if a rule against them existed in school, whereas moral transgressions were considered wrong even if no rule existed (Nucci & Turiel, 1978).

Donna Weston and Elliot Turiel (1980) presented children between the ages of five and eleven with four hypothetical situations: (1) a child takes all his clothes off in the playground at school after getting too warm from playing; (2) a child hits and pushes another child out of a swing after discovering all the swings are taken; (3) a child goes outside to play and leaves some toys on the floor after playing with them; and (4) a child refuses to share his or her snack with a visitor who asks for some. Weston and Turiel found that children discriminate between the different types of rules. Children at all ages considered the rule concerning hitting someone fundamentally different from the rules involving leaving toys on the floor, refusing to share, or even nakedness. The prohibition against hitting others was treated as unalterable while the other three could be changed. This difference is also found in other cultures (see the Cross-Cultural Current on page 526). Children react differently to violations of these rules as well. Turiel (1978) found that very young children resisted any attempts to convince them that it was all right to hit someone, even if there was no rule against it.

When looking at the violation of some rule, then, it is important to take the type of rule into account. Even young children realize that not all rules are the same and can differentially interpret and respond to moral and social transgressions. This ability is even more pronounced in middle childhood.

The Psychoanalytic Conception of Morality

When children are considering an action, do they hear a "small critical voice" exhorting them to improve their behavior? Do they experience guilt if they perform some forbidden act? Psychologists who follow Freud believe so. Morality is viewed as involving the development of the **superego**. Children between the ages of about four and six years resolve their sexual fantasies toward their parents, called the Oedipal situation, by identifying with the parent of the same sex. The superego arises out of this identification.

The superego consists of two parts: the **ego ideal** and the **conscience**. The ego ideal consists of the individual's standards of perfect conduct, which are formed when the child identifies and internalizes the ideals

superego
The portion of the mind in psychoanalytic theory in which the conscience is found as well as standards of conduct internalized from parental teachings.

ego ideal
Part of the superego that consists of the individual's standards of perfect conduct.

conscience
Part of the superego that causes an individual to experience guilt when transgressing.

But Is It Also Wrong in Korea?

When some finding of interest is made by a psychologist in a Western culture, it is natural to try to discover whether it is also found in other cultures and to what degree. A number of Western studies have indicated that children see moral issues as different from social conventions. Moral issues are viewed as universal and not dependent on authority figures. They include not stealing or hitting others. On the other hand, social conventional issues are not seen as universal and are under the control of authority figures or the society itself. In our own society, whether one should use one's hands or eat with a fork and spoon would be an example of such social conventional rules. Children reason about moral issues in terms of justice and the welfare of people, whereas they often see social conventional issues in terms of maintaining the social order and regulating interpersonal relationships. American children differentiate between the two in early childhood.

Myung-Ja Song, Judith Smetana, and Sang Yoon Kim wanted to know whether Korean children also saw these distinctions. Korean social norms are guided by traditional Confucian ethics, which include respect for elders, obedience to parents, courtesy in relationships, and duty to community over individual rights. Korean society is more traditional and conforming than American society. The justification for obeying rules commonly involves conformity to authority or duty.

Usually, when cross-cultural work in Asian settings is conducted, it takes place in an isolated rural village. However, since the 1960s, Korea has been rapidly undergoing urbanization. The investigators believed that this tendency

to research Asian rural cultures and then compare them to more urban and suburban Western cultures confounds culture itself with living in urban or rural areas. Since Korean society is more urbanized, it is better to compare urban Koreans to Western urban dwellers. Despite Western influence in the cities, Korean education is controlled by a state agency, and Korean culture and history are taught and valued.

Middle-class and upper middle class children attending kindergarten, third and sixth grade, and junior and senior high school in the second largest Korean city, Busan, were presented with short vignettes describing moral and conventional acts. In each vignette, the main character was described as being the same age and sex of the subject. The moral vignettes included hitting, stealing, not paying back borrowed money, and giving up a seat to an older man on a bus. For example, "Hawaja wanted to have a doll, but she has no money to buy it. Yesterday she stole a doll at the department store."

The social conventional items included eating food with one's fingers, not greeting elders cordially, not putting shoes in the shoe rack before entering the classroom, and a girl's wearing earrings and using nail polish. For example, "Jyungsoo, does not greet her elders cordially. Yesterday, she came across an old man who was her neighbor on the road, and she passed him without greeting him." In Korean society not greeting elders cordially is considered a serious social transgression. Children are taught correct table manners and courtesy, and this etiquette is strictly enforced. Placing one's shoes in a shoe rack before entering the classroom is a school rule across Korea, and wearing earrings and using nail polish are not acceptable.

and values of the adults around. The second part of the superego is the child's conscience, which causes the child to experience guilt when misbehaving (Eidelberg, 1968; Freud, 1933). Before the superego is formed, all resistance to temptation exists outside the individual (Solnit, Call & Feinstein, 1979). The child is afraid that he or she will lose the parents' love or that the parents will punish the child. After the formation of the superego, the regulation is internalized. Even if the parents are not present, the child acts in ways that would make the parents proud and experiences guilt when acting badly. The attitude that "I" shall be as my

Each subject was interviewed separately. The interviewer presented the subject with a description of the moral and conventional acts and asked a number of questions that sought to discover whether the children thought these acts were wrong, why, whether they would be wrong in another society, or whether it would be wrong in Korea even if there were no rules against it.

The results showed that Korean children of all ages viewed moral transgressions as more generally wrong and worse than social conventional rule transgressions. The large majority of Korean children viewed social conventional rule transgressions as wrong, although more of the younger children thought so than the older children. However, children of all ages clearly understood the differences between violating a social convention and violating a moral rule.

Younger subjects were likely to view all transgressions as less permissible than older subjects. The social conventional transgression that bothered the subjects the most was not greeting one's elders, which was seen as more generally wrong and worse than the other social transgressions. As expected, the need for moral rules was seen in terms of promoting the general welfare and fairness, while conventional items were justified in terms of social conformity, tradition, and coordinating interpersonal relationships. Although not greeting elders was seen as more serious than violating the other social norms, it was still justified in conventional terms.

The results of this study show that Korean children of all ages distinguish between moral and social convention and justify rules covering both domains differently. These findings are very similar to those reported in studies of American children.

Some age-related trends are interesting. Younger children believed that it was wrong to violate moral transgressions because it would hurt others, while older children emphasized the importance of obligation to others. Younger children justified their feelings about transgression social conventional rules on the basis of some external sanctions, whereas older children saw the need for these practices in terms of tradition. There were some age differences in how these children viewed the social transgressions. Younger children evaluated wearing earrings and using nail polish as more wrong than did older children.

One cross-cultural difference was found. Korean children seemed to expect to be rewarded with praise for conforming to the social conventional rules, whereas American children often cite fear of punishment as their justification for conforming to these rules. As expected, Korean children who are schooled on courtesy and status saw these factors as more important than American children.

The authors note that this group of Koreans with some contact with Western culture still holds traditional Korean values. Contact with the West has not led to complete assimilation of Western values.

It is clear that both Korean and American children differentiate between transgressions of moral and social conventional rules. As one would expect, American and Korean children who are raised in different societies will certainly rate some transgressions, even within these domains, as less permissible than others.

It is sometimes easy to characterize a society like Korea as traditional and uniform, but this and other studies have shown that this is not so. Like Western children, Korean children do not have a uniform orientation to all transgressions and see two different types of rules—with one more universal and important than the other.

Source: Song, M-J., Smetana, J. G., and Kim, S. Y., Korean Children's Conceptions of Moral and Conventional Transgressions. *Developmental Psychology*, 1987, 23, 557–582.

parents would like me to be if they were here" (Solnit et al., 1979, p. 186) guides behavior.

Research on the psychoanalytic conception of morality is mixed. Children do identify with older people, including their parents (Kline, 1972), but their moral values are hardly carbon copies of their parents' values. Although some similarity exists, the idea that children totally copy their parents is unacceptable (Damon, 1983). In addition, if identification is so important, various aspects of moral behavior, such as honesty and generosity, should show a strong correlation because they are formed through the same process of identification. However, only a moderate correlation between these behaviors is found, and the inconsistency in moral actions is difficult to explain using only the process of identification. Thus, identification may be one factor, but it certainly is not by itself sufficient to explain moral development.

The Learning Approach to Morality: Studying Behavior

Some psychologists approach moral development by studying the behavior itself—including sharing, helping, and giving as well as lying, stealing, and being aggressive—instead of looking at the moral reasoning of the individual. They explain moral behavior in terms of the situation, the child's background, the models available to the child, and the reinforcements that are present in the environment.

Learning theorists argue that moral behavior is learned like any other behavior. Operant conditioning explains some of it. Children who are reinforced with praise and attention for giving and sharing are more likely to give and share. Social learning theorists add imitation to the picture. Much of a child's behavior is influenced by watching how others—both adults and peers—deal with life's challenges (Bandura, 1986). If we observe people we respect helping others or giving to charity, we are more likely to do so ourselves. Of course, this may not always be the case. We do not imitate everything we see. Such factors as the characteristics of the model, the consequences of the behavior, and our own characteristics affect imitation (Bandura, 1977).

Cognitive factors, such as how we perceive a situation and process the information are also important. For instance, aggressive children are more likely than nonaggressive children to believe that aggression will get them what they want and find it easier to be aggressive (Perry, Perry, & Rasmussen, 1986). Another factor is competence to deal with a particular situation. A person who feels competent may act one way; the same person, when feeling bewildered, may act in a totally different manner.

How to Foster Moral Development

How can we foster moral development? In an attempt to formalize moral and ethical educational experiences, a number of school-related programs have been advanced.

Values clarification courses emphasize the importance of a child's experiencing the process of valuing rather than treating values as objects (Raths, Harmin, & Simon, 1966). In values clarification courses, students are challenged to discover their own values. The teacher does not try to inculcate a set of values into the students. The teacher offers a number of anecdotes, simulations, and other activities that aim at getting students to freely adopt and clarify their own values. For example, students are asked to make choices and identify their priorities or preferences in an exercise called rank ordering. In values voting, the teacher asks students, "How many of you . . . ?" Students respond with hand signals showing whether they are in favor or against the idea and to what extent (Read, Simon & Goodman, 1977).

Lately, there has been a reaction against values clarification. There seems to be an overemphasis on the process and little stress on the results or the end product (Ryan, 1981). Nor is information given to the students relating to what our culture has discovered about moral and ethical questions (Ryan, 1986). There is no right and no wrong (Bauer, 1987). The neutrality required by the teacher is also troublesome. At times, teachers may experience problems when they must remain neutral in the face of questionable decisions on the part of the students. Last, many authorities argue that fostering democratic values such as tolerance and understanding cannot be left to self-discovery and that students cannot be allowed to find their own values without input from adults.

A similar, but not identical, approach uses Kohlberg's dilemmas (such as the case of Heinz) in an attempt to improve moral reasoning. Students are encouraged to play the role of different characters within the dilemmas. A dilemma is offered to the class in the form of a story, and the students determine how the dilemma should be resolved, giving reasons for their solutions which are then shared in group discussion. Specially written dilemmas can be used with young children (Kohlberg & Likona, 1987). The teacher probes, explains, and suggests. Although there is a preferred type of reasoning, there is not necessarily a preferred answer. Kohlberg is not morally neutral and argues that there are universal moral principles that ought to be held that include respect for the individual and tolerance. These principles arise not from lecture but from rational argument and thoughtful decisions about values that may be in conflict with other values (Power & Kohlberg, 1987).

Kohlberg's approach is not entirely verbal and cognitively oriented, for he understood that moral reasoning and morality itself is based upon experience. Thus, Kohlberg argued for transforming schools into just communities. This involves establishing democratic structures and student participation in making and enforcing rules and policies. In some schools that have adopted some participatory democratic practices, students are given a real voice and have decided to mandate restitution for victims of theft, to voluntarily switch classes to achieve greater racial integration, and to enforce no cutting rules by accepting responsibility to help other students get to class (Kohlberg & Lickona, 1987). Teachers are encouraged to be democratic and especially to explain the reasons behind rules. Of course, there are limits to student participation, but students need to feel that they have some power to submit grievances and get things done—a feeling that few students have in today's schools.

Criticism of Kohlberg's attempts at moral education through dilemmas centers around the highly verbal nature of Kohlberg's dilemma-based approach. It is also not clear whether such a verbal program will lead to better moral behavior (Ryan, 1986).

A third approach that focuses more on product than on process is the character building or teaching approach (Bauer, 1987). The basis of this approach is that teachers and parents need to actively plan to transmit societal values to children.

Teaching Morality in the Future

All around us we see questionable moral decisions. Reports of cheating, poor conduct, vandalism, and selfishness are constantly in the newspapers, only occasionally interrupted by a report of self-sacrifice, which seems to be the exception rather than the rule. More serious evidence of social disintegration involving arrests and criminality are splashed all over the news, while we are told that students do not seem to understand or treasure democratic values. We seem very much to be a society in crisis. We also see the problems that result from intolerance and bigotry and wonder if anything can be done to improve the situation.

The schools have a part to play in this crisis of morality. They have been asked to instill particular values, such as tolerance, into students, even if they are not taught at home. The child in the year 2000 will probably face many of the same moral dilemmas, and if present trends continue, the schools will be asked increasingly to engage in programs that will enhance moral development.

But just how can the school system deal with such societal and moral problems? The values clarification approach described in the chapter has met with resistance. Allowing students to "choose their own values" has slipped out of favor. The moral dilemma program, it is noted, is also quite verbal and may not be tied to action. The teaching approach has become more popular, but the problems of preaching to students what they should do or having students simply mouth the sentiments that their teachers want to hear haunt this approach. Certainly, verbal

methods can contribute to reducing prejudice and forming values. However, if any program is to succeed, it must also have an activity component in which ideas are put into action.

In the future, programs to foster tolerance or encourage the formation of values will contain solid action components. Students will be encouraged to participate in an array of specially designed programs that will require them to put their moral beliefs into action. This can take many forms. For example, some schools have programs in which children help other children through a structure called peer tutoring. Children who are having difficulty may be paired with older children who can help them. These older children are given special training in how to tutor, and they do not have to be the best students in the class. Their responsibility is simply to help these younger children achieve. There are many other forms of peer tutoring.

Other action-oriented programs are also possible. Some programs encourage students to "adopt" an elderly person, others to help the homeless. Still other programs aim at cleaning the neighborhood or helping the physically challenged. At present, about eight percent of the schools around the country

offer credit for such programs. That percentage may increase in the future.

The desire to foster tolerance and integration also must contain an action-oriented program. Certainly, investigating one's attitudes is important, but demanding some action in this realm is just as important. We noted in the last chapter that just placing children together does not seem to encourage tolerance. When many schools were integrated, it was assumed that physical proximity would encourage interaction, dispel prejudice, and reduce intergroup problems. However, the results have not been particularly promising (Weyant, 1986). We have not seen the expected precipitous drop in racial prejudice or the increases in interaction between blacks and whites. The same sort of findings occurs when the research on mainstreaming of disabled children is examined.

The lack of progress should have been predicted. Gordon Allport (1954) argued that to succeed in reducing prejudice, contact needs to be planned to fulfill three characteristics. First, the groups must have equal status. Second, they should share a common goal. Third, they must engage in activities that are supported by authority figures. Unfortunately, these three components often have been lacking. Status differences are often maintained, and many classrooms do not encourage cooperation. Active cooperation can be increased by using cooperative learning strategies in which two or more students work together to reach some academic goals. By engaging in activities in which students share the same goal, prejudices are overcome.

There are no easy solutions for the moral problems and transgressions we see around us. Although the school may preach tolerance and respect, the conflicting messages from parents or from society itself may counter the school's influence. The school cannot alter parental prejudice. However, if a child's experiences are enriched, the school may help to reduce prejudice in children.

The child in the year 2000 will face a society with substantially the same social and economic problems exhibited today. The need for tolerance and understanding between groups will be as great as it is today. In the future, activity-based programs will supplement those aimed at attitude change so that students will be encouraged to live their ideals and practice what they preach. In this way, the school will confront the social and moral problems that so plague our society.

The teaching approach is conducted through what Kevin Ryan (1986) calls the five E's. The first is example. Teachers and parents are role models and must act in accordance with that responsibility. In addition, the literature of our culture and historical figures can teach by example (Rothman, 1988). For instance, the biographies of Martin Luther King and Helen Keller may help to broaden a student's horizons.

The second E is explanation. If rules are to be established and enforced, students deserve to know the reasons behind them.

The third E is exhortation. There are times when teachers and parents must encourage and exhort students to persevere or, in some cases, to change. Ryan notes that a student who may be flirting with racism may need to realize that his views are undesirable, and heart-to-heart talks may be necessary.

The fourth E is environment. The teacher must create a moral environment, which may not always be easy. This includes a balance between competition and cooperation and individual and community responsibility, along with the discussion of what ought to be.

The last E is experience, an area that is being increasingly emphasized. Students require experiences that allow them to put their values into action. Community and school-based programs that emphasize helping others and improving the environment can serve as excellent vehicles for that purpose. Through such volunteer work, students can experience the values of responsibility and helping others.

The teaching approach is becoming more popular but has been roundly criticized (Rodman, 1987). At times, society has merely paid lip service to its values, and students see hypocrisy in teaching values that may not be echoed in their neighborhoods, their families, or the classroom. Students may rightly realize that these values are not practiced in our society. While it is true that sometimes the approaches based upon moral reasoning are too verbal, the teaching approach may also suffer from the same fate unless a concerted effort is made to structure in situations in which students can put their values into practice.

◆ PROSOCIAL AND ANTISOCIAL BEHAVIOR IN MIDDLE CHILDHOOD

It is tempting to divide the world into those who are honest and helpful and those who are not, those who give and share and those who are selfish. In our everyday conversations, we are likely to do this—for example, labeling one child as honest and another as selfish. This traitlike approach has not worked well. In their landmark studies, Hugh Hartshorne and Mark May (1928) tested thousands of children on a number of tasks. They concluded that children's behavior varied with the situation. A child could be honest in one situation and not in another. One who cheated on an athletics test might or might not cheat on an arithmetic test (Cairns, 1979). This situational view of honesty prevailed for some time, but later research using statistical techniques not available to Hartshorne and May discovered a carryover of honesty from one situation to the next, although it was not very strong (Burton, 1963). It seems that although some people are more honest than others, we cannot say that a person will be honest in every situation.

Prosocial Behavior

Everyone likes to see children share, help each other, settle disputes in a peaceful manner, and give to others who are less fortunate. These and other prosocial behaviors form the basis for good interpersonal relationships. But what makes one child more likely to share or to comfort another in a time of trouble and another child to ignore the situation.

Social scientists have identified a number of factors that affect prosocial behavior. One of them is culture. We pride ourselves on being a prosocial society, and indeed, Americans donate a good deal of money to charity. Yet American children are not as willing to share or to give as children in other societies. Children from India, Kenya, Okinawa, Mexico, the Philippine Islands, and the United States were observed in a variety of social interactions. Every one of the Kenyans and 73 percent of the Mexican children showed prosocial behavior in amounts that exceeded the median of all children in the study, while only 8 percent of the American children exceeded this median. Differences were found between the three societies that showed the most prosocial behavior—Kenya, Mexico, and the Philippines—and the other three. Such behaviors were encouraged in cultures where children lived in extended families and had greater responsibilities and where the social structure was simpler.

There are also differences between rural and urban individuals within the same country. Schoolchildren in Mexican villages and small towns are less competitive and more likely to avoid conflict than are urban middle-class Mexicans or Mexican-Americans (Eisenberg & Mussen, 1989). Changes occur when rural people move to urban areas. Canadian Indian children are more cooperative than urban Canadians. However, when Indians attended an integrated school, they were more competitive than Indians who had maintained traditional contacts. Still, the urban Canadians were affected, as they took on some of their Indian peers' cooper-

Placing one's values into action has become more popular as schools try to encourage prosocial behavior.

ative orientations (Eisenberg & Mussen, 1989). In a rural setting, children must often cooperate and work with others to survive, while middle-class urban parents often regard some competitiveness as necessary for success in society. Children learn the social norms within their society.

Another variable is child rearing, which is related to culture. A relationship exists between certain child-rearing practices and prosocial attitudes and behavior. Parents who use reasoning techniques combined with affection outside the discipline situation raise children who practice prosocial behavior (Hoffman, 1979). This is especially true if parents make an effort to point out to children the effect of their behavior on the other person. Parents also serve as models for their children. If children observe their parents helping and sharing, they are more likely to do the same.

Even within particular cultures there are wide individual differences in prosocial acts. One individual variable is age. Although young children show some prosocial behavior, such behavior increases somewhat with age (Peterson, 1983), although the degree to which this is true depends upon the type of prosocial behavior examined. One reason for this increase can be found in cognitive development, especially the abilities to take someone else's viewpoint and improvements in moral reasoning (Eisenberg, Shell, Lennon, Bellover, & Mathy, 1987). This leads to an increase in empathy, which is related to higher levels of prosocial reasoning. In fact, there is a good relationship between the ability to feel empathy and sympathy, and cooperation, socially competent behavior, and inhibition of aggression (Eisenberg, 1989).

Personality variables also play a part. Children who are free to express their own emotions are more likely than children who are constricted in this area to assist others. Sociability is another personality characteristic associated with prosocial behavior.

Last, the situation is important. A child will be more likely to help another if the personal cost is low than if it is high. Asking a five-year-old to share green beans is likely to be greeted with joy, but ask the same child to share a piece of cake and you get a different reaction. In addition, if children feel competent to help, they are more likely to do so.

Television and Prosocial Behavior

Children's prosocial behavior is also affected by what they watch on television. When groups of preschoolers were exposed to aggressive cartoons, "Mr. Rogers' Neighborhood," or neutral films, the children exposed to the prosocial programs displayed more prosocial behavior than children in the other groups (Friedrich & Stein, 1975). Other studies report similar findings. When Ahammer and Murray (1979) presented some preschoolers with portions of commercial television programs that contained prosocial content, such as "The Brady Bunch" and "Lassie," while other preschoolers were shown programs in which such scenes had been removed, those who saw the prosocial content showed more cooperative behaviors.

Elementary schoolchildren are similarly affected. Elementary schoolchildren were shown a "Lassie" program in which a boy risked his life to save his dog. Other children were shown either a "Lassie" program without such prosocial behavior or a situation comedy. Later, each child had an opportunity to help puppies in distress, but to do so they would have had to forfeit an opportunity to win a valuable prize. The children who had witnessed the prosocial program were more likely to help (Sprafkin, Liebert, & Poulos, 1975). So watching prosocial programs can have a positive effect on a child's behavior.

Another area of considerable interest is the issue of racial, gender, or age stereotypes. Children's attitudes may be adversely influenced if women or members of minority groups are constantly portrayed in a stereotyped manner. Some evidence shows that children who see programs that are less stereotyped tend to have fewer stereotypes (Liebert & Sprafkin, 1988). There is some evidence for change here, as a study of American and Canadian television found that women are more likely today than in the past to be shown on television in nontraditional roles and occupations (Rosenwasser, Lingenfelter & Harrington, 1989).

There is no doubt, then, that exposure to prosocial television may help foster prosocial development. However, television is only one influence among many.

Aggression and Antisocial Behavior

A casual look at the newspapers may lead one to believe that aggressive behavior in childhood is common, but it is not. A study of highly aggressive boys found that only two to three aggressive actions occur per

1,000 social interactions (Patterson & Cobb, 1971). Yet the behavior is common enough. Almost all parents have to handle aggression in their young children (Sear, Maccoby & Levin, 1957). Aggression in the classroom is a serious problem, and the aggressive-disruptive behavior pattern is one of the most common problems presented in mental health facilities (Cullinan & Epstein, 1982). Children are also the recipients of much aggression. Between 84 percent and 97 percent of all parents use physical punishment on a child at some point (Parke & Slaby, 1983).

The social consequences of aggression are great. Aggressive children are generally unpopular (Clarizio & McCoy, 1983) and are more likely to be targets of aggression (Dodge & Frame, 1982). Aggressive children are also likely to be male. Between three and six times as many boys as girls are referred to mental health agencies for aggressive behavior (Cullinan & Epstein, 1982). Boys are also more likely to be the targets of aggression (Cairns, 1979). The gender differences are rather constant across age and culture. Some argue that hormones predispose males toward aggression (Maccoby & Jacklin, 1980), and the evidence for this hormonal theory in animals is strong. The question is whether it holds for human beings. Some argue that the evidence does not indicate such a link (Tieger, 1980), while others note that the research, although inconclusive, does lean toward such a conclusion (Maccoby & Jacklin, 1980). The argument will continue for many years, but both sides readily acknowledge that social factors are involved in aggressive behavior.

Some people believe that the aggressive child will outgrow the aggressive behavior, but this is just wishful thinking (Cullinan & Epstein, 1982). Aggression is rather stable over long periods of time for both boys and girls (Olweus, 1977, 1979, 1982). When more than 600 children were followed from the time they were eight years of age to the time that they were thirty years old, the more aggressive eight-year-olds developed into the more aggressive thirty-year-olds (Huesman, Eron, Lefkowitz & Walder, 1984). As noted in Chapter 10, the nature of aggression changes in middle childhood as instrumental aggression—struggles over possessions—declines. In other words, although overall aggression decreases in middle childhood, very aggressive children tend to remain aggressive.

Factors Affecting Aggressiveness

The same factors that we noted were responsible for prosocial behavior—namely, culture, personality, family relationships, and outside influences such as television—operate to influence aggression in children as well.

Certain cultures encourage, or at least tolerate, aggressiveness. If aggressiveness is modeled in society, it is thought to be the proper way to deal with problems. Our own society seems to have a love/hate relationship with violence. On one hand, violence is condemned and punished (albeit violently). On the other hand, our heroes use violence freely, sometimes without regard for the law, and children see violence all around them, some of which is rewarded.

Family variables are also important. Consider the children who watch their parents ague violently, are hit hard and often, and discover that they

11. TRUE OR FALSE?

Aggression is one of the most common types of interactions between children.

12. TRUE OR FALSE?

Most aggressive children grow out of this troublesome behavior pattern.

get what they want by being aggressive toward others. We could predict that these children would be aggressive, and research confirms our hypothesis (Parke and Slaby, 1983).

Certain child-rearing strategies are related to aggression in children, according to a study performed by Robert Sears and his colleagues (1957). They include permissiveness and punitiveness. Parents who were very permissive tended to raise aggressive children. In addition, the more punishing the parents, the more aggressive their children. The combination of permissiveness and punitiveness led to the most aggressive children. If parents allow their children to vent their aggressive impulses, children think it is acceptable. They are then harshly punished for it, which causes frustration and anger, which in turn leads to further aggression. This aggressiveness does not remain confined to the home. In a sample of third graders, parental use of physical punishment was related to the child's aggressiveness at school (Eron, Walder & Lefkowitz, 1971).

Aggressive behavior can also be learned through modeling. A child who sees authority figures being aggressive may act aggressively, too. In a series of studies, children were exposed to live or filmed models acting aggressively against a Bobo doll. They were then given the opportunity to play with the doll. Usually, the children imitated whatever they saw. If exposed to aggressive actions, they acted aggressively; if shown constructive actions, they imitated those actions (Bandura, 1986; Bandura, Ross & Ross, 1961). Violence is often used to solve interpersonal disputes at home, and children learn to use it to get their own way. In families where husbands and wives use verbal or physical aggression to resolve disputes, parents also use such aggression against their children, and children use it against their siblings (Parke & Slaby, 1983). Violence between siblings is a common type of home violence.

Peer groups also influence aggressive behavior (Parke and Slaby, 1983). This may occur in three ways. Children may model themselves after a violent individual, especially if the model gains something of value through violence. Second, the peer group may reinforce the violent deeds. Although aggressive individuals are often rejected by the majority of children, they may find a group in which this behavior is acceptable. This leads us to the third point—the social norms of the peer group. Some groups reject violence more than others.

Violence on Television

Another influence on aggressive behavior is television. By the time a child graduates from high school, he or she has seen 13,000 violent deaths on television (Gerbner & Gross, 1980). More than 85 percent of all programs, 95 percent of the cartoons, and 70 percent of the programs shown in prime time contain violence (Gerbner, 1986). Two-thirds of all television programming aimed at children is violent. Since children may learn to be aggressive by viewing violent behavior, the question of television violence and children's aggression is an important one.

If every child exposed to violence on television imitated such violence, there would be a great public outcry, and parents would exercise considerable care in what their children watch. But this is not the case. The decision to be aggressive is not a simple one, and it is difficult to factor out what causes a violent action (Cairns, 1979). The evidence indicates, however, that viewing television increases the probability of violent action (Liebert & Sprafkin, 1988).

Although some people seem to be more susceptible than others to violent suggestion, children of both sexes and of all ages, social classes, ethnic groups, and personality characteristics may be affected (Huesmann, Lagerspetz & Eron, 1984; Lefkowitz & Huesmann, 1980). Both males and females may be equally influenced, with people who are more aggressive within each gender being more affected than others. Although children at every age are susceptible, a particularly sensitive period during late middle childhood, around eight or nine years of age, has been found (Eron, Huesmann, Brice, Fischer & Mermelstein, 1983). Exposure to violence peaks at about the third grade, but the correlation between aggressiveness and viewing violence increases until ages ten to eleven, suggesting a cumulative effect beyond this sensitive period. In addition, seeing violence that appears justified and realistic has a greater aggressive meaning than seeing violence that appears unjustified or brings negative consequences to the aggressor. Although television violence can have an effect even if the viewer is not emotionally aroused, its effect is greater if the viewer is initially angry or frustrated.

How does television influence violence? Two experts in the field, Robert Liebert and Joyce Sprafkin (1988), suggest three ways. First, some children may directly imitate. It is possible that children will directly copy what they see on television. Obviously, though, there are other factors involved, as most children do not directly imitate. Aggressive children, though, may learn different ways to be aggressive by watching television. Second, televised violence disinhibits aggression. People have certain inhibitions against violence, and witnessing aggression may reduce these inhibitions. Third, television violence may lead to antisocial attitudes and encourage children to accept violence as a way of dealing with problems. We get used to violence on television and come to accept it as a normal part of life (Drabman & Thomas, 1975). We become desensitized to violence and no longer take it seriously (Thomas, Horton, Lippincott & Drabman, 1977). This desensitization may explain the difficulty we have arousing the public to take action to stop violent crime; it may also be part of the reason that people are not willing to help a victim of crime.

There appears, then, to be a relationship between aggression and television violence. However, a relationship does not demonstrate cause and effect. Perhaps aggressive children simply watch more violent television. There is some truth to this. In an analysis of two very large long-term studies, Leonard Eron (1982) concluded that television violence is indeed one cause of aggressive behavior. However, aggressive children also prefer to watch more and more violent behavior, establishing a circular pattern. Eron reasons that aggressive children are unpopular and spend more time watching television. The violence that they see reassures them that their behavior is appropriate and teaches them new ways to act aggressively.

This makes them even more unpopular and sends them back to the television for another dose of violence. Whatever the reasons, the link between aggression and viewing violence on television is well established.

Television violence, then, is a real factor in increasing the likelihood that people will act aggressively. However, not all people who watch violent television programs become aggressive. So television is only a part of the total picture.

A Guide to Television Viewing

Television viewing has become an integral part of our culture. Children spend more time watching the television than anything else except sleeping. In the last four chapters, we've looked at the influence of television on cognitive and social development and noted some of its effects. Parents and teachers have some responsibility in helping children to deal with what they see on television. Several curricula exist that are aimed at young elementary school students and attempt to do just this. One developed by Aimee Dorr and colleagues (1980) is designed to (1) decrease the degree to which children perceive the programs as real, (2) increase children's tendencies and ability to compare television content with information from other sources, (3) diminish the credibility children ascribe to television by teaching children about the economic goals of television, and (4) teach children to apply the information from the first three areas to the valuation of television content. The developers found that kindergartners and second graders exposed to a six-hour curriculum learned much about television and applied what they learned to the content of what they saw.

Parents should also become involved in regulating their children's television viewing, and the following suggestions may help parents in this regard.

KNOW WHEN CHILDREN ARE WATCHING Today, many American families have more than one television set, the second one being used almost exclusively by the children and sometimes found in the children's rooms or in the basement. Thus, parents don't always know how much time their children are spending in front of the television set. Parents might want to ask their children to keep a log noting the time they start and stop watching television. Parents may then keep closer track of how many hours per day their children spend watching television.

KNOW WHAT CHILDREN ARE WATCHING Not all television programs are suitable for youngsters. In addition, some programs may contain material that requires parental explanation. It is a good idea to check on the type of programs children are watching.

CHOICE OR CHANCE When children sit down to watch television, do they have a specific program in mind? Do they enjoy a particular program, or do they watch television merely to pass the time? If children are merely passing time, there may be more profitable activities available to them.

Parents can encourage children to question and discuss the values being portrayed on the television screen.

FAMILY VIEWING Television viewing is often a passive experience. However, it need not be. As you watch television as a family, encourage children to question the values being portrayed on the screen. Spend time discussing these values, being certain to listen to your children's opinions. Don't be afraid to point out the consequences of an action on television or criticize behaviors that aren't proper. Many television shows raise moral, ethical, and behavioral questions, which can lead to profitable family discussions.

NO TELEVISION WHEN . . . Since television often provides an easy escape for children, it is important to set limits on when children can watch programs. For example, watching television during meals is usually not a good idea. Tranquil discussion is better. In addition, when children's friends are around, an afternoon of play is in order, not a full afternoon of television viewing.

BEWARE OF USING THE TELEVISION AS A BABYSITTER Parents of very young children frequently leave their children in front of the television set for hours while they do their housework. The television set is no substitute for active interaction.

BE AWARE OF GROWTH OPPORTUNITIES Sometimes new words or concepts are presented on a television program. Television viewing can offer surprising ways of increasing children's knowledge.

LOOK FOR PROGRAMS THAT ARE ENTERTAINING AND VALUABLE Some programs have successfully combined entertainment and education. Some of these programs are especially produced with young people in mind. Others, such as some nature programs, appeal to a broader audience. Be on the lookout for such programs.

TELEVISION TIED TO READING Some successful television specials and series have been taken from books. Children should be encouraged to read the original. In addition, seeing a program on the Old West, for example, may interest a youngster enough to go to the library and read a book on the subject. A television program may excite interest that can be carried over into reading.

BE FLEXIBLE In an attempt to limit television time, some parents become inflexible. Limiting television watching on school nights is a reasonable policy, but at times, a special program may be shown that children may wish to watch. Rules should not be inflexibly administered.

Television has an influence on many areas of life. Taken in moderation and with some attention to understanding the nature of programming and advertising, it can serve as a source of entertainment and education. If children are going to watch so much television, it stands to reason that they must be helped to develop the skills necessary to evaluate what they are seeing and place it in proper perspective.

♦ MIDDLE CHILDHOOD IN PERSPECTIVE

The schoolage period is often considered one of horizontal growth. Middle childhood is often seen as the calm before the storm of change that occurs in adolescence. Unfortunately, this has led to the mistaken notion that middle childhood is a stagnant period, which is untrue. Unlike the early years, when cognitive, physical, and social growth are obvious, changes during middle childhood are more gradual. We must look harder to find them. However, as we have seen, significant changes are taking place. The child's social world is expanding as friends and teachers become more important. Children are given more freedom and responsibility at home. Because parents will not be with them all the time, children must develop their own sense of right and wrong and decide how they will handle their interpersonal relationships.

These trends are seen in Karen's dilemma. There are no parents or even adult figures present to tell Karen what to do. Karen must reason and act on her own and decide whether to give the wallet back or keep it. Her background, her relationships with her parents, her self-concept, and numerous other factors will influence her reasoning and final behavior.

It comes as no surprise, then, that psychologists have found that children who emerge from middle childhood with a positive self-concept, good working relationships with their parents, a healthy relationship with friends, and a good feeling about their own academic and social capabilities are ready to tackle the challenges that await them during adolescence.

SUMMARY

1. According to Erik Erikson, the positive outcome of middle childhood is the development of a sense of industry, while the negative outcome is viewed in terms of inferiority.

2. Freud noted that children resolving the Oedipal situation next enter a latency stage, when sexuality is hidden. Boys' and girls' groups are segregated.

3. During middle childhood, children get feedback from many different people. Their self-concept develops from a combination of this feedback and their own evaluation of their subjective experiences.

4. Children's relationship to their parents changes during middle childhood. Children become more independent and later in the stage are greatly influenced by peers. They also become more argumentative and question parental judgment more often.

5. Children's immediate reaction to divorce involves anger, depression, and guilt. Normally, children recover from the initial shock after a year or so, but the long-term effects of divorce can be serious if parents continue to argue, if serious financial problems exist, and if social supports are unavailable.

6. The stepfamily situation requires adjustments on everyone's part. Stepfathers who attempt to build a good relationship with the children before trying to discipline them do better than if they do not first attend to the personal relationships.

7. Anywhere between two and ten million children take care of themselves after school. These children are called latchkey or self-care children. Evidence indicates that if the child comes right home after school and parents monitor the child even from a distance, the experience does not yield negative results. However, many children do not go home straight after school and are not monitored. Some schools and social agencies offer training for self-care children.

8. Children often cope well with a single stressor but when exposed to multiple stressors they develop stress related problems. Some children are stress-resistant or resilient. These resilient children show a strong social orientation, are flexible and more adaptable. They tend to be active in after-school activities and use better problem-solving strategies than other children. A good parent-child relationship can be a buffer against the negative consequences of stress. Children who take care of others are more resilient as well.

9. Children who are popular tend to be friendly, have good social skills, share interests with their peers, and be physically appealing. Children's conceptions of friendship change over time as they become more cognitively sophisticated.

10. In middle childhood, boys show an increased preference for stereotyped male activities, while girls do not show such a preference for stereotyped female activities. Parents continue to treat sons and daughters differently. Sex typing in schools is also well documented.

11. Piaget and Kohlberg both advanced theories of moral reasoning. Piaget noted that young children do not take intent into consideration when judging actions and see rules as unchangeable. Older children are more flexible and take intent into consideration.

12. Lawrence Kohlberg explained the development of moral reasoning in terms of three levels, each of which contains two stages. It is the reasoning behind the moral decision, not the decision itself, that determines the level of moral reasoning.

13. Freud viewed morality in terms of the development of the superego. This occurs through identification.

14. Behaviorists are more interested in studying moral behaviors, such as cheating and altruism, than in the reasoning behind the behavior. The environment as well as the situation itself affects moral behavior.

15. Prosocial behavior is encouraged when parents use rational methods of discipline and point out how the child's behavior helps others. The models children observe around them as well as the reinforcements they experience or witness are also important. Children who watch prosocial behavior on television are influenced by it.

16. Children who observe a great deal of aggression at home, are harshly disciplined, or are taught that aggression is an acceptable method of gaining what they want tend to be violent. Aggressive behavior can also be imitated.

17. Most studies indicate that observing violent behavior on television increases the likelihood that the child will act aggressively. It also desensitizes children to violence.

ACTION/REACTION

That Seven-Letter Word—Divorce

The fighting was unbearable. The only practical solution was divorce, as far as Stanley and Christina were concerned. However, their feelings were not matched by their children's. Emil, age eleven, and Rose, age nine, both blamed their mother for "throwing their father out." In truth, Christina did ask Stanley to leave after a particularly bad argument, and they both agreed to seek a divorce.

During the legal proceedings, relationships between the parents worsened. Stanley would complain that Christina's lawyer was trying to get all his money. Christina became angry, believing that Stanley was turning the children against her.

Now that the divorce is final, things haven't changed much. Whenever Christina and Stanley talk to each other, they argue. The children still blame Christina and want to live with their father. Christina has had to be stricter with the children but finds it difficult. She hopes that someday they will appreciate her efforts to be certain they do their homework and act respectfully, but she doubts it. She must work to supplement her income and comes home tired and depressed.

Recently, Christina was called to school because Emil had been caught lying about his homework and forging his mother's signature on notes. Stanley blames it on Christina and her "active" social life. Christina quips back that if Stanley would give her more financial support and stopped undercutting her authority, things would be better.

1. If you were Christina or Stanley, what would you do?

Friends

Every day that her third-grade class goes outside for recess, Mrs. Kimbel knows what she will see. The other children break into loose groups and play while Kelly sits by herself or seeks out the company of much younger children who may be in the school yard. At times, Kelly tries to enter one of the groups of children, only to be rejected or, more commonly, ignored.

Kelly is not aggressive, does not bully anyone, and certainly has never teased a classmate. She just does not seem to know how to enter the groups and does not sustain conversations well. She is one of the youngest students in the class and is somewhat shy. She does not appear to be interested in what her other classmates are concerned with and is what you might call an unpopular child.

Kelly is an average to somewhat below average student in school. She tends to be slow to learn new things, but her intelligence is within the normal range.

In a conference with Kelly's father, Mrs. Kimbel learned that Kelly was the third of four children, and although there is some sibling fighting, it does not seem any worse than any other family. Kelly does not get that much attention from her parents, because they both must work. Although Kelly's father did admit that Kelly's grades were not as good as those of his other children, he does not seem very distressed over them and claims that no overt comparisons are ever made, at least, by the parents.

Kelly's parents are aware of Kelly's unpopularity and her tendency to play with younger children. They are concerned about this. At home, she plays mostly by herself, although a few children her age will come over and play. Still, they are concerned about her interpersonal relationships.

1. If you were Kelly's teacher or parent what, if anything, would you do?

PART FIVE

◆

Adolescence

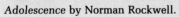
Adolescence by Norman Rockwell.

CHAPTER THIRTEEN

Physical and Cognitive Development During Adolescence

Handball by Ben Shahn (1939).

Are These Statements True or False?

Turn the page for the correct answers. Each statement is repeated in the margin next to the paragraph in which the information can be found.

1. The sequence of developmental changes in adolescence is still largely a mystery.
2. Menstruation is one of the earliest signs of puberty in females.
3. Early maturing males have a social advantage during adolescence.
4. Teenagers whose health and family history put them in a high-risk group for later developing cardiovascular disease alter their behavior to reduce their risk.
5. Most sufferers from anorexia nervosa, a condition marked by self-starvation, come from poor, uneducated, lower income families.
6. Antismoking campaigns have been more successful at preventing teens from beginning to smoke than at motivating older people to stop smoking.
7. Drug abuse prevention programs have generally not been very effective.
8. People who talk about committing suicide rarely make a suicide attempt.
9. The ability to interpret proverbs and political cartoons develops during adolescence.
10. Most early adolescents believe that everyone will be looking at them when they walk into a restaurant, store, or classroom.
11. The birthrate among teenagers in the United States today is higher than any time in the twentieth century.
12. About 20 percent of all parents refuse to let their children participate in sex education programs in school.

Answers to True False Statements

1. False. Correct statement: The general sequence is quite predictable, although the age at which any particular change occurs varies from person to person.
2. False. Correct statement: Menstruation is actually one of the later changes in puberty.
3. True.
4. False. Correct statement: Unfortunately, teenagers who are at risk for cardiovascular disease in the future do not alter their behavior to reduce such risks.
5. False. Correct statement: Most sufferers of anorexia nervosa come from affluent, well-educated, middle-class families.
6. False. Correct statement: Antismoking campaigns have been more successful at motivating people to stop smoking than at preventing adolescents from starting to smoke.
7. True.
8. False. Correct statement: People who talk about committing suicide are more likely to attempt it.
9. True.
10. True.
11. False. Correct statement: The birthrate among teenagers in the 1950s was actually higher than it is today. However, most teenagers giving birth in the 1950s were married, whereas most teenagers giving birth today are not.
12. False. Correct statement: Only about three percent of all parents refuse to allow their children to participate in sex education courses.

◆ PHYSICAL CHANGE IN ADOLESCENCE

Ask anyone to state the ways adolescents differ from elementary schoolchildren and you will probably get a long list of the physical differences. These changes are well-known and quite obvious. Much less obvious and rarely listed are the cognitive changes that take place during this period. This chapter looks at the meaning of these physical and cognitive changes for adolescents as well as for those around them.

Most adolescents are acutely aware of their physical selves. Early adolescence is a time of tremendous physical change that affects the adolescent's self-concept and behavior. Although the sequence of this physical change is predictable, the timing of the change varies considerably from person to person. For example, the average age for the first menstrual flow among American teens is approximately 12.8 years (Tanner, 1970), but a girl may begin menstruating anytime between ten and sixteen and a half years and still be within the normal range.

1. TRUE OR FALSE?

The sequence of developmental changes in adolescence is still largely a mystery.

◆ PUBERTY AND ADOLESCENCE

Some people use the terms *puberty* and *adolescence* synonymously. Actually, **puberty** refers to the physiological changes involved in the sexual maturation of the individual as well as other body changes that occur during this period (Sommer, 1978). Body changes directly related to sexual reproduction are called **primary sex characteristics.** They include maturation of the testes in males and of the ovaries in females. Changes that are not directly related to reproduction but that distinguish males from females are called **secondary sex characteristics** (Forisha-Kovach, 1984). Secondary sex characteristics include beard growth in males and breast development in females. When the term *puberty* is used to mark an event in someone's life, it refers to the time at which the reproductive system becomes mature and sexual reproduction is possible (Chumlea, 1982). In females, puberty is marked by the onset of menstruation. In males, it is not as easily determined and relates to the ability to ejaculate mobile sperm. Puberty, then, is a "biological ripening." Adolescence, on the other hand, is a behavioral-cultural ripening (Krogman, 1980). **Adolescence** refers to the stage from puberty to adulthood and covers the entire psychological experience of a young person during that period.

puberty
Physiological changes involved in sexual maturation, as well as other body changes that occur during the teen years.

primary sex characteristics
Body changes directly associated with sexual reproduction.

secondary sex characteristics
Physical changes that distinguish males from females but are not associated with sexual reproduction.

adolescence
The psychological experience of a young person from puberty to adulthood.

The Female Adolescent Develops

Many people believe that menstruation is the first sign of puberty. Actually, menarche, the first menstrual flow, is a late occurrence that takes place after a number of other changes have occurred (see Table 13.1). Shortly after the growth spurt begins, girls develop breast buds, and the

---

TABLE 13.1: Maturation in Girls
Although there may be normal variations in the sequence of physical and sexual maturation in girls, the following sequence is typical:

1. Adolescent growth spurt begins.
2. Downy (nonpigmented) pubic hair makes its initial appearance.
3. Elevation of the breast (the so-called bud stage of development) and rounding of the hips begin, accompanied by the beginning of downy axillary (body) hair.
4. The uterus, vagina, labia, and clitoris increase in size.
5. Pubic hair is growing rapidly and becoming slightly pigmented.
6. Breasts develop further; nipple pigmentation begins; areola increases in size. Axillary hair is becoming slightly pigmented.
7. Growth spurt reaches peak rate and then declines.
8. Menarche, or onset of menstruation, occurs (almost always *after* the peak rate of growth in height has occurred).
9. Pubic hair development is completed, followed by mature breast development and completion of axillary hair development.
10. Period of "adolescent sterility" ends, and girl becomes capable of conception (up to a year or so after menarche).

Source: Conger and Petersen, 1984.

breadth of their hips increases. Then, when the growth spurt is at its maximum, changes in the genital organs take place. They include maturation of the uterus, vagina, labia, and clitoris as well as the breasts. When growth slows considerably, menarche takes place. At this point, a number of other changes in fat and muscle composition are also occurring. Following menarche, most of the changes are nonsexual, including further changes in body shape and voice (Krogman, 1980).

Even though all normal females progress through these physical changes, each adolescent girl experiences them as novel and challenging. Each pubescent female develops within her own environment, specific culture, and subculture and is exposed to a different set of peers and parents. The importance of her subjective experience should not be lost in any biological discussion of general physical development or norms.

THE GROWTH SPURT The growth spurt is one of the earliest and most recognizable body changes. Because this spurt begins about two years earlier in girls than in boys, twelve-year-old girls are generally taller and heavier and have larger muscles than twelve-year-old boys (see Appendix) (Tanner, 1970). The growth rates during this period are exceeded only by those during the prenatal stage and the first year of life (Morgan, 1984). Although all structures grow at this time, they do not enlarge at the same rate. The hands and feet reach adult size first, causing many adolescents to complain about having hands or feet that are too big. Parents can alleviate some of this distress by simply telling their children that when they are fully grown their proportions will be correct.

If girls of twelve or thirteen are physically more advanced than boys the same age, why do early adolescent boys outshine girls in sports? Although the answer may involve differences in physiology, different interests and training—both of which are environmental factors—are probably the keys. In our society, males are encouraged to develop their bodies through athletic competition, while females are not. With the growth in popularity of such sports as tennis, gymnastics, swimming, and jogging, as well as new federal government requirements for colleges that mandate more emphasis on female athletics, some changes are taking place. We might also expect that because of different rates of maturation, female athletes may be capable of developing their potential at an earlier age than men. Indeed, women champions in gymnastics and tennis are often much younger than their male counterparts. The earlier growth spurt and maturation, combined with excellent training, allow them to develop their full potential at an earlier age than males.

MENSTRUATION Of all the body changes that occur in adolescence, menstruation is the most dramatic (Logan, 1980). It is also the most ritualized. Various societal laws and customs prescribe what may and may not be done during the time of the menstrual flow. For example, one tribe in Borneo confines girls going through menarche in dark cells suspended by poles for long periods of time. When they conclude menarche, they are again introduced to the sun, flowers, earth, and so forth. One South African cattle-rearing tribe believes that the cattle would die instantly if they walked over ground on which even a drop of menstrual blood had

2. TRUE OR FALSE?
_____

Menstruation is one of the earliest signs of puberty in females.

Women champions in tennis, such as Jennifer Capriati, are often younger than their male counterparts, partly because of their earlier maturation.

fallen. To prevent this, special paths are available for women to use so that they will not have contact with the ground cattle may frequent (Williams, 1977).

Even in our own society, taboos are plentiful. In some homes, women are considered too unclean to touch food or utensils during their period, and daughters are often taught to be ashamed of menstruation. This contrasts with the experience of male adolescents, who are taught to focus on their body changes as symbols of sexual strength (Breit & Ferrandino, 1979). The reproductive function of the menstrual cycle is underscored, while female sexuality is denied. A number of cultural "don'ts" appear, such as swimming, going barefoot, and participating in sports during the menstrual period, and girls are told that no one should know that they are having their period.

Some teens know little about this important change, but some educational progress has been made in this area. Today, most female adolescents at least have been given some biological information about what is happening (or about to happen) to them. They are subjected to fewer restrictions, and discussion today is more likely to be more honest.

How do teenage girls evaluate the experience? Most American women consider it a negative or, at best, neutral experience. Many feel insufficiently prepared and experience surprise, embarrassment, or fright (Logan, 1980). At the same time, they often feel pride (Whisnant & Zegans, 1975). When girls in late elementary school, junior high, and high school were asked for their reactions to their first menstrual period, the reactions were decidedly mixed. Most reported some physical distress and an immediate desire for secrecy. Girls who were less prepared or who began menstruating early were most likely to evaluate the experience negatively. The researchers conclude that although the experience produces some confusion and ambivalence, especially in those who are very young or who are not well prepared, it is not as traumatic as once thought (Brooks-Gunn & Ruble, 1982; Ruble & Brooks-Gunn, 1982). The initial reaction to the first menstrual period may be anxiety, but this decreases rapidly as the months pass (Rierdan & Koff, 1980).

The Male Adolescent Develops

The first signs of puberty in males are the growth of the testes and scrotum along with the appearance of pubic hair (see Table 13.2). This is followed about a year later by a spurt in height and growth of the penis. The prepubertal growth spurt in males occurs approximately two years after the average female has experienced her growth spurt. Again, the sequence of events is predictable, but the time at which they occur varies from person to person. The trunk and legs elongate. Leg length reaches its adult proportions before body breadth does. The last growth change to occur is a widening of the shoulders (Stolz & Stolz, 1951). This progression demonstrates why an adolescent boy grows out of his trousers a year before growing out of his jackets (Tanner, 1970). Muscles develop, in part because of the secretion of testosterone, and the heart and lungs increase dramatically, as does the number of red blood cells.

TABLE 13.2: Maturation in Boys

Although there may be some individual variations in the sequence of events leading to physical and sexual maturity in boys, the following sequence is typical:

1. Testes and scrotum begin to increase in size.
2. Pubic hair begins to appear.
3. Adolescent growth spurt starts; the penis begins to enlarge.
4. Voice deepens as the larynx grows.
5. Hair begins to appear under the arms and on the upper lip.
6. Sperm production increases, and nocturnal emission (ejaculation of semen during sleep) may occur.
7. Growth spurt reaches peak rate; pubic hair becomes pigmented.
8. Prostate gland enlarges.
9. Sperm production becomes sufficient for fertility; growth rate decreases.
10. Physical strength reaches a peak.

Source: Conger and Petersen, 1984.

The Secular Trend: Taller, Earlier, and Heavier

secular trend
The trend toward earlier maturation today compared with past generations.

In the past 100 years or so, each new generation has been taller and heavier than the preceding one. In addition, each new generation has entered puberty at a slightly earlier age. These developmental tendencies, known collectively as the **secular trend,** have been the focus of much research. The trend is unmistakable. Since 1900, children have been growing taller at the rate of approximately one centimeter and heavier by half a kilogram (1.1 pounds) each decade (Katchadourian, 1977).

Menstruation is also occurring at an earlier age. In Norway in the 1840s, the average age was seventeen; in 1950 it was thirteen years, four months. In Germany in 1860, it was sixteen years, six months; in 1935, it was thirteen years, five months. Generally, among European populations, the age of menarche has decreased over the past century from a range of fifteen to seventeen years to twelve to fourteen years today (Roche, 1979).

Not everyone agrees with the conclusion that women are menstruating at a much earlier age than previous generations. After a review of very early records, Vern Bullough (1981) concluded that adolescent women from ancient times through the Middle Ages experienced their first period between the ages of twelve and fifteen. The situation is complicated by the fact that even within the same country there may be substantial differences in the age at which people reach their adult height or girls menstruate. For example, in Romania, the average age of menarche is 13.5 years in larger towns and cities and 14.6 years in smaller villages (Tanner, 1970).

The secular trend is thought to be due to improvements in health and nutrition, a decline in growth-retarding illnesses during the first five years of life, and better medical care (Krogman, 1980). Whether the decrease has been substantial or minimal, the secular trend is definitely leveling off in the United States and Western Europe (Steinberg, 1985). This leveling off may indicate that there are limits to how much these factors can affect the onset of puberty and influence the course of the physical changes that occur during this stage of life.

What Causes Puberty?

Although we do not yet understand exactly what triggers puberty, three structures are thought to be primarily responsible. They are the hypothalamus (a part of the brain), the pituitary gland, and the gonads, or sex organs—the testes in males and the ovaries in females (Sommer, 1978). The hypothalamus produces chemicals known as releasing factors, which are carried in the bloodstream to the pituitary gland, stimulating it to produce substances called gonadotropins, which stimulate the gonads. The gonads then produce the sex hormones that cause changes in the body (see Figure 13.1) (Sommer, 1978).

The level of hormones in the body is kept in balance. During childhood, the level of gonadotropins is quite low, but for some reason, the secretion of these hormones increases in later childhood. The gonads grow and produce more sex hormones. The hypothalamus is sensitive to sex hormones circulating in the body. As the amount of sex hormones increases, the output of the hypothalamus' releasing factors decreases, thereby reducing the pituitary's output of gonadotropins and regulating the amount of sex hormones in the body.

Just why these changes are triggered by the hypothalamus remains a question. Scientists believe that during childhood the hypothalamus is extremely sensitive to the amount of sex hormones secreted. As puberty approaches, however, the central nervous system matures and becomes less sensitive to the hormone levels, causing the hormones to appear in greater concentrations (Chumlea, 1982).

The changes that take place during adolescence are largely determined by hormones. One such group of hormones is the sex hormones. Scientists use the term **androgens** to refer to the group of male hormones that include testosterone and **estrogens** to denote a group of female hormones that include estradiol (Kalat, 1980). Although both males and females produce both sets of hormones, females produce more estrogens and males produce more androgens. During adolescence, the sex hormones are secreted into the bloodstream in great quantity. The androgens cause secondary sex characteristics, such as lower voice, beard growth, and growth of hair on the chest, underarms, and pubic area. Estrogens encourage breast development and broadening of the hips (Kalat, 1980).

androgens
A group of male hormones, including testosterone.

estrogens
A group of female hormones, including estradiol.

♦ EARLY AND LATE MATURATION

Can you imagine what it would be like to see all your friends physically maturing while you seem to remain childlike? Because the age at which any individual enters or leaves puberty varies greatly from one person to another, some teens will mature early, while others must wait for nature

FIGURE 13.1: Observable Effects of Sex Hormones
The sequence and amount of effect vary from individual to individual.

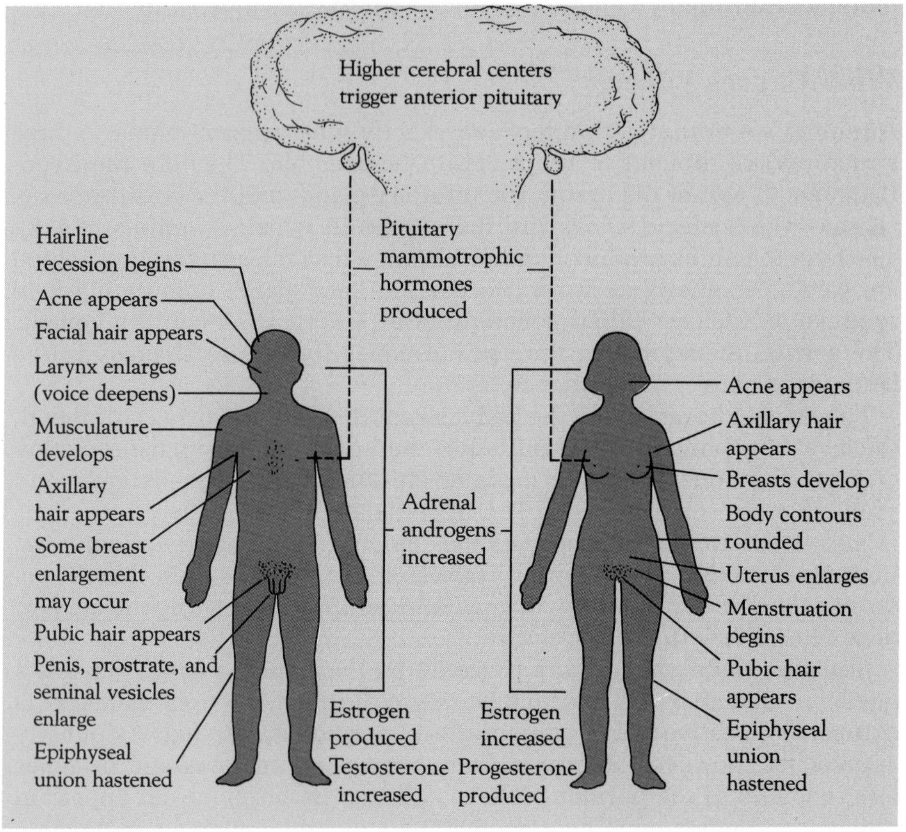

Source: Jensen, 1985.

to take its course. Does the timing of puberty affect the personality and self-concept of adolescents?

Most people are neither very early in maturing nor very late. They fall somewhere in between. There is some evidence, however, that teens who mature either very early or very late may be affected by this experience. Early maturing males seem to have a substantial social advantage during adolescence over late maturers. Early maturing boys are considered more masculine, more attractive, and better groomed. Late maturers are considered tense and childish and are seen as always seeking attention. Peers see them as bossy, restless, and less attractive and as having less leadership ability (Jones & Bayley, 1950). Late maturers are also viewed as more rebellious and dependent (Mussen & Jones, 1957). The fact that they are seen as both more rebellious and more dependent demonstrates a basic conflict in their personalities. Late maturers of college age have not

3. TRUE OR FALSE?

Early maturing males have a social advantage during adolescence.

yet resolved their basic conflicts from childhood, tend to seek both attention and affection, and do not gain positions of dominance or leadership (Weatherley, 1964). The late maturer separates himself psychologically from both his parents and his peers. Weatherley also found that early and average maturing boys were very similar in personality structure, meaning that early maturation itself may not be the benefit it has been thought to be. It may be that what has actually been measured in previous studies is the lack of late maturation.

Late maturers continue to have problems into their thirties (Jones, 1957). The late maturers are still less settled, less self-controlled, and more rebellious, and they have a lower self-concept. Not all the findings are negative, however, as late maturers also are more assertive and insightful. In addition, in their forties, the differences diminish greatly, and some personality advantages in favor of later maturers are found. The early maturers become more conforming and rigid, whereas the late maturers become more flexible and, again, more insightful (Jones, 1965).

Other studies have also hinted at some advantages for the late maturer. Peskin (1967, 1973) found that early maturers became less active, more submissive, and less curious as they matured. Whereas the early maturing boy may have a social advantage, the later maturer was superior in some intellectual areas. Ames (1957) found that early maturers had more personal and social success but were not as happy in their marriages as later maturers. The problems that seemed to arise in early maturers in middle-age—namely, inflexibility and being very conforming—were present even during adolescence. Early maturing boys, then, seem to have a social advantage during adolescence and early adulthood, but their personalities are more rigid and prevent personal growth in the middle years. Later maturers, although experiencing some difficulties in adolescence, show some advantages beginning in middle age.

Early and Late Maturation in Females

The effects of early and late maturation in adolescent girls is less clear. Some studies find that early maturing girls are better adjusted in young adulthood as measured at the age of thirty years (Peskin, 1973) and that late maturing girls are more likely to suffer from anxiety (Weatherley, 1964). However, other studies do not find any advantages for early maturing females (Jones, 1949; Jones & Mussen, 1958). Some evidence even indicates disadvantages for the early maturer. Robert Staffieri (1972) found that early maturing girls are not considered attractive, because they were fatter, whereas later maturers were thinner and judged more conventionally attractive. Perhaps whether the changes take place in elementary or junior high school makes a difference (Faust, 1960). Early developing girls in elementary school receive fewer positive comments, but the situation is reversed in junior high school, where the early developing female receives more positive feedback. The evidence, then, is mixed regarding the effects of early and late maturation in females. The differences that do exist seem to be less important and more transient than those found in males.

The timing of puberty may affect how parents deal with their teenage children. Whether the child experiences early or late puberty seems more important to the perceptions of parents than to how the adolescents look at themselves. Parents perceive they have less conflict with early maturing sons than with moderate or late maturing sons. On the other hand, early maturing daughters are perceived to be a source of more stress and anxiety for their parents than late and on-time maturing daughters (Savin-Williams & Small, 1986). The adolescents, on the other hand, generally did not see the timing of puberty as affecting their relationship with their parents, except that early maturing girls reported a bit more conflict with their parents.

The Effect of Puberty on Parent-Child Relationships

Pubertal status itself—that is, how developed the child is—seems to have an effect on parent-child relationships. In other words, irrespective of whether it is early or late, the physical development of the child may affect the child's relationship with his or her parents. As children begin to develop, they become more aloof and dissatisfied, and more conflict occurs. When Laurence Steinberg (1988) examined adolescents between the ages of eleven and sixteen and their parents twice over a one-year period, he found that puberty increased adolescent autonomy, and reports of closeness between parents and children decreased. Pubertal maturation, itself, then, causes some changes that are beyond those that can be attributed to the chronological age of the adolescent (Steinberg, 1987).

Body Image

Just about every television situation comedy has a scene in which the entire family is waiting for the teenager to leave the bathroom after having just broken the "total time spent in the bathroom" record. Yet behind this comedy lies something deeper. Teenagers' bodies are changing very quickly. These bodily changes require adjustments both in thoughts and in feelings (Richards, Boxer, Petersen, & Albrecht, 1990). Although some teens cope very well with these changes, many are not completely at home in their new bodies. Many want to change aspects of their physical selves, mostly their height, weight, and complexion (Burns, 1979). For example, in one sample of teenage girls, although 81 percent of the subjects were assessed to be within the ideal weight range or even underweight, 78 percent wanted to weigh less, and only 14 percent were satisfied with their current weight (Eisele, Hertsgaard, & Light, 1986). Girls are much more likely to suffer from poor body image than boys and are generally less satisfied with their bodies.

In adolescence, a good part of one's self-esteem is determined by body image. There is a link between physical attractiveness and high self-esteem, and between dissatisfaction with one's body and low self-esteem (Grant & Fodor, 1986). There is also a relationship between negative body image, depression, and compulsive eating (Attie & Brooks-Gunn, 1989; Brooks-Gunn and Warren, 1989). The combination of peer pressure and media

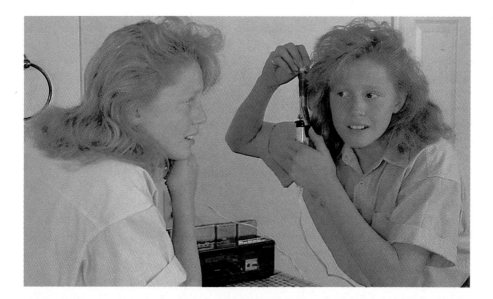

During adolescence, one's appearance becomes a central focus of attention.

advertising encourages teens to try to change what can be changed to meet some stereotyped, socially approved image. It takes time for teens to become comfortable with their bodies and accept those elements, such as height, that cannot be changed. As the child matures, a compromise in physical appearance is often struck between the stereotype and the reality, and a positive body image may be attained.

◆ THE HEALTH OF TEENAGERS TODAY

Traditionally, adolescence has been seen as a time at which health is excellent. To some extent, this is true today. The mortality rate of adolescents is lower than any other group, with the exception of young children (Millstein, 1989). Adolescents are rarely hospitalized and have low rates of both disability and chronic disease. If we look at death by disease, adolescents do seem healthy.

But there is another view. According to a commission formed by the National Association of State Boards of Education and the American Medical Association, this is the first generation that is less healthy, less cared for, and less prepared for life than their parents were at the same age (National Association of State Boards of Education, 1990).

The health problems of adolescents are mainly, but not exclusively, found in the behavioral areas. The commission noted the problems caused by excessive drinking, drug use, sex, and violence. One million teenage girls—almost one in ten—become pregnant, and 2.5 million adolescents contract a sexually transmitted disease. It is estimated that one in four high school students will contract such a disease before graduating from high school (Millstein, 1990). The suicide rate for teenagers has doubled since 1968, and violence is an epidemic even in the schools. One hundred thirty thousand students bring guns to school every day, and homicide is the leading cause of death among 15 to 19-year-old blacks. More than half of all high school seniors become drunk at least once a month, and accidents relating to alcohol are the leading cause of death among teenagers. In the 1950s, less than 5 percent of those entering the sophomore year of high school had experimented with drugs compared to over 30 percent in 1987 (Leary, 1990; National Association of State Boards of Education, 1990). In 1987, 92 percent of high school seniors had used alcohol, 50.2 percent had used marijuana, and 15.2 percent had used cocaine at least once (Johnston, 1988). As noted in Chapter 11, there is also a question about the physical fitness of today's youth and decreasing activity levels both in the United States and in Canada (see Shaw & Kemeny, 1989).

Television viewing is also a source of concern, especially among those teens who are heavy viewers. In one survey of fifteen-year-olds, 19.2 percent reported watching television for less than two hours a day, 62.6 percent reported they watched two to four hours a day, and another 18.2 percent spent more than four hours a day watching television. Light viewers were more physically fit, emotionally stable, sensitive, imaginative, physically active, self-confident, and were less troubled than heavy viewers (Tucker, 1987). Stress is also a health-related concern, with ten percent of high school students in one survey stating that they did not handle stress very well (Armacost, 1989). These problems become more pronounced as children progress through the adolescent years (Millstein, 1990).

The relationship between these behaviors and health is obvious in some cases, such as drinking and traffic accidents. In other cases, it may not show up for many years. Smoking, lack of activity, and poor eating patterns may take their toll later in life. Even when teenagers are in a high-risk group, they do not change their behavior. When Matthew Adeyanju (1990) followed teenagers who were determined to be at risk for later cardiovascular disease by measuring their blood pressure and weight and taking a family history, he found that these at-risk teens were still eating saturated fats, were taking in a great deal of salt, were not exercising, and were drinking. Many were smoking and generally engaged in other unhealthy behaviors as if they had nothing to worry about. Adeyanju notes that it is important to identify potentially high-risk adolescents and institute preventive measures.

While teenagers may appear healthy, there are real doubts about the true state of their health. The problems of disease may have faded somewhat (with the exception of venereal disease), but many adolescent behaviors place teenagers in a high-risk group for future health problems.

4. TRUE OR FALSE?

Teenagers whose health and family histories put them in a high-risk group for later developing cardiovascular disease alter their behavior to reduce their risk.

♦ **NUTRITION AND EATING PROBLEMS IN ADOLESCENCE**

Since teens are so concerned with body image, it stands to reason that eating would be a major concern. During the teenage years, the recommended daily allowances for most vitamins and minerals increase (Rolfes & DeBruyne, 1990). Eating patterns in adolescence are variable, and no one pattern has been found. Some teenagers have good diets, while the diets of others are deficient (Whitney & Hamilton, 1984). In one survey, a little less than half the college students skipped breakfast more than half of the time, and 81 percent noted that they snacked one to three times a day, with 4 percent admitting snacking four or more times each day (Hertzler & Frary, 1989). The diets of female adolescents are a special concern. Girls are more likely than boys to overestimate their weight (see Fowler, 1989). Some become overly preoccupied with their self-image and this may decrease the quality of their diet (Newell, Hamming, Jurich, & Johnson, 1990). Severe dieting is a common but often ineffective way to lose weight.

Eating disorders are not uncommon. Obesity is the most talked about problem. However, other eating disorders, including anorexia nervosa and bulimia, are also serious concerns.

Obesity

Between 10 and 15 percent of all teenagers are obese (Whitney & Hamilton, 1984). Obesity increases risks for hypertension and coronary disease, and it leads to a negative body image and poor self-concept. Obese teenagers also have more difficulty developing a coherent identity (Shestowsky, 1983). Obesity creates a social problem for the teen. Because our society's view of beauty and attractiveness is equated with being thin, the obese person is out of step with current fashion. The obese person also faces discrimination by peers (Fowler, 1989).

Obese children become obese teens, and obese teens become obese adults. Obese teens with a history of overweight have a 28-to-1 chance of becoming and remaining obese adults. (Zakus, Chin, Yeown, Herbert & Held, 1979). But people can become obese at any age. Parental supervision of eating habits during the teen years usually wanes as the adolescent gains personal freedom. Social and academic pressure during adolescence may lead to increased caloric intake (Hubbler, Wilder & Kennedy, 1969). Many students use food to quiet their anxiety, and the less physically active life many older teens lead runs counter to the active life some led in childhood.

There is no easy cure for obesity. Certainly nutritional information is needed, because teens eat an enormous amount of junk food and their diet is often rich in starch but deficient in basic nutrients (Miller, 1980). However, not everyone appreciates or accepts such information. Schafer (1979) found a relationship between self-concept, choice of diet, and acceptance of nutritional information. Women with positive self-concepts both chose better diets and were more influenced by nutritional information than women with poor self-concepts. It is often difficult to get obese people, who generally have poor self-concepts, to accept nutritional information and to change their eating patterns. In addition, many teens use crash diets, semistarvation, or fad diets in a desperate attempt to lose weight or maintain their weight. This can cause physical damage, especially to the kidneys, and these approaches are not effective in the long run. They may also rob the body of nutrients necessary for healthy development.

Perhaps a combination of increased physical activity under a doctor's care, nutritional information, reduction in the consumption of junk food, and psychological support provided by the peer group and family members can help the obese teen lose weight and keep it off. It is often easier to prevent obesity than to cure it. But some modest success in weight reduction has been reported for a program that included nutritional information, the identification of behaviors contributing to obesity, and the alteration of these behaviors as well as an increase in physical activity (Brandt, Maschoff, & Chandler, 1980). However, long-term weight loss is difficult, and the battle against fat is a lifelong process.

Anorexia Nervosa

When Karen Carpenter, the well-known singer, lost her twelve-year battle to anorexia nervosa in 1983, many people had never heard of the unusual and sometimes fatal disorder. Today, most people know about it because the media has given it so much attention, but few truly understand it.

Although **anorexia nervosa** literally means loss of appetite (Wear, 1982), the name is misleading. It is a disorder marked by self-imposed starvation and involves an abnormal fear of becoming obese, a disturbance of body image, significant weight loss, and a refusal to maintain even a minimal normal body weight (American Psychiatric Association, 1980). Anorexics have an appetite, but they are proud of being able to control their hunger.

Anorexia nervosa is one of the few psychological problems that can be fatal, claiming between 15 percent and 21 percent of those afflicted (Halmi, 1978). The overwhelming number of anorexia sufferers—about 96 percent—are female (Halmi, 1978), and the onset of the condition is typically between the ages of twelve to eighteen. No one knows for sure why so many sufferers are female. It may have to do with the differences between how females and males perceive their bodies. Females tend to see their bodies as effective only if they are attractive, which means thin, while males prize dominance, which translates into large proportions and physical strength (Grant & Fodor, 1986).

Anorexics usually show little overt rebellion toward their parents, but they suffer deep conflict on the dependent-independent dimension. They are often raised in educated, success-oriented, middle-class families that are quite weight conscious. They are also perfectionistic and are described by their parents as model children (Smart, Beaumont, & George, 1976). The disorder is not rare. About one in 250 female adolescents suffers from this condition.

Anorexics are obsessed with food, weight loss, and compulsive dieting and are quite active physically (Grant & Fodor, 1986). Once they achieve significant weight loss, anorexics do not stop but continue until they are too slim to be physically healthy. Losing weight becomes an obsession,

anorexia nervosa
A condition of self-imposed starvation found most often among adolescent females.

5. *TRUE OR FALSE?*

Most sufferers from anorexia nervosa, a condition marked by self-starvation, come from poor, uneducated, lower income families.

and they fear they will lose control if they eat a normal diet. Controlling their weight becomes the passion of life. Changes in their physiology, thinking, and personality occur. They misperceive their weight, believing they are fat or about to become so. Their condition becomes serious as their bodies begin to waste away. Menstruation ceases, they become ill and anemic, they cannot sleep, they suffer from low blood pressure, and their metabolism rate decreases (Bruch, 1978).

The cause of anorexia is still a mystery. One theory emphasizes the effect that society's view of the glamorous female as very thin and the popularity of books on dieting have on teens. Yet females receive double messages, because women's magazines are likely to offer suggestions on how to make rich desserts, and at social functions women find themselves surrounded by calorie-rich foods. Unable to integrate these messages, the anorexic develops a fear of losing control, of eating too much, and of gaining weight. Freudian theory asserts that anorexia is a defense against sexuality and an attempt to regress back to a preteen stage, especially since the anorexic stops menstruating. Those emphasizing a family approach note that anorexics come from rigid, overprotective families where conflicts are avoided and people are overinvolved with each other. This interferes with the formation of a personal identity. Still others believe that there is some basis in biology or that a neurological dysfuntion exists (Muuss, 1985).

The treatment of anorexia is varied. In severe cases, intravenous feeding is necessary. Family therapy that focuses on the relationships among family members and behavior modification to reinforce the anorexic to eat properly may be required (Muuss, 1985). This combination of therapies is often successful.

Bulimia

Imagine someone eating a gallon of ice cream and ten brownies and doughnuts and then purging the system of the food by forcing oneself to vomit. Such a dangerous pattern of behavior is characteristic of another eating disorder, known as bulimia. **Bulimia** involves episodic binge eating often followed by induced vomiting (Voget, 1985). Sufferers of this condition are aware that their behavior is abnormal but are afraid of losing control over their eating. Depression and extreme self-criticism are common after the binge. Often the food is sweet, easy to chew, highly caloric and can be eaten very quickly. The binge eating may be brought on by some emotional difficulty, such as stress, loneliness, depression, rejection, or rage (Muuss, 1986). It may also be preceded by a diet (Whitney & Hamilton, 1984).

Bulimics binge secretly. They stop their eating when they experience stomach pain, require sleep, are interrupted by someone, or induce their vomiting. Just as those with anorexia, these teens have an obsession with their body image. The fluctuations in weight, however, are rarely extreme enough to be as life-threatening as they are with anorexia, and these teens—unlike the anorexic—often appear physically normal.

Estimates of the prevalence of bulimia differ widely. About 5 percent

bulimia
An eating disorder marked by episodic binging and purging.

of college students show occasional binging, but other estimates run as high as 15 or 20 percent (Muuss, 1986). Only 5 to 10 percent of all bulimics are males. Bulimics are perfectionistic, are high achievers, and fear losing control. They often believe that others are watching them, and they are constantly worried about how others are perceiving them. Female bulimics are very concerned about pleasing men and being attractive. They often jump from one eating fad to another. They make lists of forbidden foods and begin by denying themselves these foods. Later, they break down and binge. They have unreasonably high goals and may believe that if they gain any weight at all they will be fat or that if they can't stick to a diet they are failures (Muuss, 1986).

The treatment for bulimia involves group therapy in which bulimics have the support of others to help them overcome their problems. They often need to be taught how to handle stress and—for females—to define femininity in a broader context (Rosenhan & Seligman, 1984).

◆ DRUG USE

One of the greatest health problems among teenagers is drug use. Studies show that students are using drugs (including alcohol) at an earlier age, making elementary and junior high school students prime targets for drug education (Minix, 1987). Any high school teacher will confront a student body in which one in four of his or her students smoke pot and two out of three use alcohol (Tower, 1987a). Although adolescent drug use is common, estimates such as the ones previously noted vary. Drug use is affected by the models and reinforcements in the home as well as the peer environment. In every drug related category, school dropouts have higher rates of drug use than students who graduate (Rosenberg & Berberian, 1975).

DATAGRAPHIC

Drug Use Among High School Students

Source: National Institute on Drug Abuse, 1988

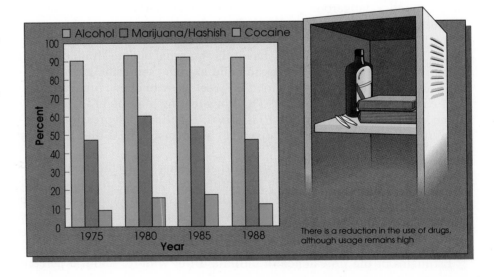

Alcohol

When I served as a counselor in a junior high school, one teacher reported a student who constantly reeked of alcohol. The student's mother was called to the school. When I told her that her son had a drinking problem, she sighed with relief and said, "Gee, and I thought he was on drugs."

Just like this parent, many adults think it is natural for teens to get drunk once in a while or to have a drink or two. Males look at getting drunk as a rite of passage, a sign of maturity. Although females drink less, their rate of alcohol consumption has risen (Lowney, Winslow, & Winslow, 1981). The figures on adolescent alcohol use show that it is by far the most popular drug used by youths between the ages of twelve and seventeen (Nathan, 1983).

The overwhelming majority of adolescents have used alcohol at some time in their lives, but frequently this is in the presence of their parents— one interesting difference between the use of this drug and the use of other drugs. Alcohol is the drug of choice because it is readily available and in many circles socially acceptable. Its use is often modeled by parents. Parental use of alcohol is related to adolescent use (Blum, 1970). Parental attitudes are also important. Adolescents who think their parents have permissive views about drug taking in general are more likely to drink (McDermitt, 1984). However, peer pressure is also a factor, as peer attitudes and use are important influences on the adolescent.

Many adolescents drink only occasionally, but some students use alcohol on a daily basis. Although people tend not to take alcohol use very seriously, the facts prove otherwise. More than half of the jailed inmates convicted of violent crimes were drinking before they committed the offense, and more than half the highway deaths are alcohol related (New York State Council on Alcoholism, 1986). The carnage on our highways has caused an outcry, with the legal age for drinking being raised to twenty-one in many states.

Smoking

Despite all the evidence linking smoking with such diseases as cancer and heart disease, smoking is still a national health problem. Most adolescent smokers say they will quit in a few years, but this does not happen. About one third of adolescents smoke, and about 19 percent smoke on a daily basis. A greater proportion of female than male adolescents report smoking daily, and the only group to show an increase in smoking is white females ages 18–24 (Adeyanju, 1989).

The increase in female smokers has been especially great. One reason for this increase may involve general rebellion and the movement toward throwing off the shackles of conventionalism. For instance, girls who smoke are more socially outgoing but much more rebellious. They report getting drunk more often, have lower grades, dislike school more, and are more likely to have sexual relations and use marijuana than their nonsmoking peers (Jarvik, Cullen, Gritz, Vogt, & West, 1977).

Smokers generally score higher on extroversion but lower on other personality measures, such as agreeableness and strength of character (Smith, 1969). Cigarette ads for men show the macho image; the ads directed toward females show the independent, sexy, outgoing, having-fun, rebellious attitude that often is attractive to females seeking an identity in a world that now gives them more choices. Smoking follows the same peer-parent use pattern as alcohol consumption. Both peer and parental factors predict future smoking. Those who have friends and parents who smoke, who experience lower levels of parental support, and whose friends have lower expectations for general and academic success are more likely to smoke (Chassin, Presson, Sherman, Montello, & McGrew, 1986).

6. TRUE OR FALSE?

Antismoking campaigns have been more successful at preventing teens from beginning to smoke than at motivating older people to stop smoking.

Antismoking campaigns have been directed at various segments of the population—pregnant women, fathers who have young children who may imitate, teenage girls who are trying to maintain an image, and so on. These campaigns have been more successful in motivating adults to quit smoking than in encouraging teens not to start.

Studies suggest that adolescents perceive smoking as having social benefits (Leventhal & Cleary, 1980). Whether or not an adolescent smokes may depend on the teen's view of the social image of the smoker. If it is close to the teenager's view of the ideal person, he or she is likely to smoke.

Sixth and eighth graders have mixed views of smokers (Barton, Chassin, Presson, & Sherman, 1982). They rated smokers as less healthy, less wise, less obedient, and less likely to act their age. The sixth graders also perceived smokers as less likely to achieve in school and less desirable as friends. However, they rated smokers as tougher and more interested in the opposite sex, and saw them as more peer group oriented than nonsmokers. These are powerful positive attributes in early and mid-adolescence. Students in both grades believed that smokers were more likely to drink—a negative for sixth graders but not for eighth graders. Findings for males and females were similar.

According to Barton and his colleagues, children in the younger grades are most affected by the negative image of the smoker. The more negative the image, the less likely the sixth graders were to smoke. But in the eighth grade, smoking is related to the positive qualities of the smoker. Perhaps antismoking campaigns can use this difference and emphasize the negative image of the smoker to the younger children, while campaigns directed at the mid-adolescent must improve the image of the nonsmoker. Only time will tell whether such a strategy will be effective.

Illicit Drugs

Although the incidence of marijuana use has leveled off, it is still high (Brook, Gordon, Brook, & Brook, 1989). Perhaps more than any other drug, marijuana symbolizes adolescent rebellion. In fact, its use is correlated with feelings of rebellion against parental rules and tolerance for deviant behavior (Brook, Lukoff, & Whiteman, 1978). Whereas marijuana use tends to decline as people age, alcohol and cigarette use continues to expand. About 47.2 percent of all high school seniors have used marijuana at some time and about 3.3 percent use marijuana daily (Johnston, 1988). There has been a decrease in marijuana use among high school students.

Most marijuana use takes place only occasionally and for recreational purposes, and users are not much different from nonusers. Differences have been noted, though—for example, nonusers have more affectionate relationships with their fathers (Brook, Whiteman, & Gordon, 1981), and users are more defensive and rebellious (Mayer & Ligman, 1989)—but many differences are found at the extreme (Archer & Lopata, 1979). Regular heavy users are much more rebellious and angry, show a lack of responsibility, and score high on measures of sensation seeking (Brook, Whiteman, & Gordon, 1981). They see themselves as inadequate, have friends who smoke marijuana heavily, often come from turbulent homes filled with discord, and show an inability to conform to rules. For these heavy users, marijuana use is an act of defiance. It modifies such disturbing emotions as anger, reinforces fantasies of effortless and grandiose success, and enables the adolescent to withdraw from conflicts, especially those having to do with competition and achievement (Hendin, Pollinger, Ulman, & Carr, 1981). Regular marijuana use is associated with the amotivational syndrome, a pattern of loss of energy and diminished school performance. The amotivational syndrome is found more often in high school than in college students, suggesting that younger students are more susceptible (Brook, Gordon, Brook, & Brook, 1989).

Although an adolescent's first drink is usually in the family setting, peer pressure is more important in determining the initial use of marijuana. However, peer pressure is not necessarily the only or most critical factor in initiation of such drug use, although it may contribute to it (Noren-Hebeisen & Hendin, 1984). In one challenging study, most adolescents surveyed said that although they had been offered marijuana at parties they had never felt pressured to use it. Those who had experienced peer pressure in this area stated they had felt the pressure only once or twice.

Sheppard and colleagues (1985) argue that although some young people are exposed to pressure, it is not the predominant reason for drug use. They suggest that one reason users spend time with other users is that drug taking is often a group activity. In addition, drug users may actively seek out others who use the drug and who are likely to share similarities in personality and social desires. Males use marijuana more than females, and this is particularly true at the heavy use range.

Of all the illicit drugs, cocaine has recently been the subject of more media attention than any other substance. Cocaine is a stimulant, affecting the central nervous system and producing feelings of euphoria. Physiological changes include extreme changes in blood pressure, increases in heart and respiration rates, insomnia, nausea, tremors, and convulsions. Cocaine use can lead to paranoid behavior, and potent forms such as crack are especially addictive (New York State Division of Substance Abuse Services, 1986).

Use of cocaine has increased markedly over the past few decades. Its use among high school seniors seems to have declined slightly of late, but 15 percent of all high school seniors report that they have used cocaine, and 5.6 percent report using crack, a more potent form of cocaine, sometime in their lives (Johnston, 1988). The message about the dangers of cocaine and crack has been accepted at least verbally by many students, with 87 percent of all high school seniors disapproving of even trying the drug once (Johnston, 1988). The personality patterns of crack and cocaine users differ somewhat, although most crack users have used cocaine first. Crack users have poorer grades, are more depressed, and are more alienated from their families (Ringwalt & Palmer, 1989). Cocaine users are also more likely to believe that use of cocaine can lead to health problems. Crack users are less likely to admit to the health hazards of crack.

New and Controversial Views of Drug Usage

Imagine being able to predict drug use as early as the preschool stage. If we could do so, we might be able to intervene early in the child's development and prevent drug abuse. Jack Block, Jeanne Block, and Susan Keyes (1988) reported the results of a longitudinal study of children beginning when they were three or four years old. When these children were fourteen years of age, drug usage could be predicted on the basis of a type of personality profile known as ego undercontrol. Ego undercontrol involves being unable to delay gratification, reacting quickly, being very emotionally expressive, showing rapidly shifting moods, overreacting to minor frustrations, and being easily irritated. A lack of ego resilience—which involves an inability to initiate activities; to be vital, energetic, or self-reliant; to trust one's own judgment; and to recover after a stressful experience—was also important for girls. Children showing these patterns appear to be susceptible to drug use later on. If adolescence is a time of experimentation and testing limits, it makes sense that adolescents would be most likely to use drugs. Unlike previous studies that concentrated on peer status and peer associations, this study shows that certain personality characteristics that can be seen early in life can predispose an individual to drug taking. Peer groups may be important at the moment of choice regarding drug use, but research must look at how adolescents come to belong to groups that use or do not use drugs. The possibility of predicting drug use from early personality patterns is very controversial today, and more research is needed in this area.

Using portions of the same sample of adolescents when they were eighteen years of age, Jonathan Shedler and Jack Block (1990) announced some interesting and controversial findings. Respondents were questioned about their drug use and placed into one of three categories. Subjects who had never tried marijuana or another illicit drug were called abstainers. Subjects who had used marijuana once or twice, a few times, or once a month and who had tried no more than one other drug were called experimenters. Those who reported using marijuana once a week or more and who had tried at least one drug other than marijuana were called frequent users.

To no one's surprise, frequent users relative to experimenters were found to be not as responsible or productive, unpredictable, unable to delay gratification, very rebellious, prone to push limits, self-indulgent, critical, not very well liked or accepted, and to have difficulties showing warmth. Generally, the picture described is of a troubled adolescent, interpersonally alienated, emotionally withdrawn, unhappy, and maladjusted. As early as age seven, frequent users were unable to form good relationships with others, were insecure, were uncooperative, and showed emotional distress. Mothers of these children were relatively cold, unresponsive, and underprotective, giving their children little encouragement.

The surprise and controversy springs from the study's findings concerning the experimenters and absolute abstainers. The researchers found that the experimenters, as a group, were psychologically healthy. The total abstainers were described as fastidious, proud of being "objective," moralistic, and somewhat overcontrolled. In childhood, these children were overcontrolled, timid, fearful, anxious, not very warm or responsive, and not very cheerful. Their mothers were perceived as relatively cold and unresponsive but were overly interested in performance. Their interactions seem not very enjoyable.

The researchers explain their results in a number of ways. First, two-thirds of their sample had tried marijuana at least once, and this experimentation with marijuana was not, therefore, statistically deviant. In addition, the extensive period of adolescence is a time of transition, and some experimentation may be expected. Since the experimenters seemed to be a relatively average set of teens, it is not unusual to find that some experimenters are psychologically healthy, sociable, and responsible. These experimenters did not use marijuana as an outlet for emotional distress or a way of escaping from poor interpersonal relationships or family problems. It is important to note that the researchers are *not* saying that the use of drugs shows psychological health, because this is certainly untrue. In fact, a study conducted by Albert Marston and colleagues (1988) found that abstaining high school students reported better physical and mental health than other students who used drugs. The frequent drug abusers show a form of maladjustment, while the profiles of total abstainers show patterns that are basically a private matter for the individual and will not attract social attention or cause society any problems.

The researchers conclude that the peer-oriented explanation of drug use is inadequate, and personality characteristics may be more important than previously thought. As noted in both studies, drug use has particular developmental and personality patterns. Current policy assumes that peer influence leads to experimentation and this leads to abuse. The "just say no" track is designed to reduce experimentation. But peer influence alone is not an adequate explanation for drug use, and especially not for drug abuse. It might also be time to look at the underlying psychological syndrome that supports drug abuse. Treating children who show alienation, impulsivity, low ego resilience, and low ego control and encouraging more empathic parenting patterns may in the long term be more effective than present efforts aimed simply at reducing experimentation with drugs.

Finally, the researchers understand the possibility that the controversial findings can be misinterpreted. They also know that the results will "sit badly" with drug counselors who know from their own experience that there is no safe level of drug use and it is dangerous to suggest otherwise. Total abstinence is the only policy, drug counselors suggest. The authors believe that there is no contradiction with these therapists' ideas, and they agree with the total abstinence policy.

Shedler and Block's study only shows that in a nonselected, average sample, occasional experimentation with marijuana is not permanently destructive and that many adolescents have experimented with marijuana and have not become drug abusers. The seeming contradiction between this study and the experience of drug counselors is explained by the different nature of the groups seen by the researchers and by drug abuse professionals. Those people seen by drug counselors tend to be a highly selected subpopulation in which drug use is highly destructive, differing greatly from the more average teenage population that was examined in the research study. Shedler and Block conclude their study with a plea not to be misinterpreted. Their findings do not suggest that drug use improves adolescent psychological health, and they do not wish to encourage any such interpretation.

Drug Education

Everyone is in favor of drug education, and most people believe it should start early. In fact, in a survey of elementary school principals, 89 percent said drug education should begin by the third grade, and 65 percent would favor starting it in kindergarten (Viadero, 1987a). In the area of drug education, there is little question concerning the need to teach or even what should be taught. The key question is the effectiveness of drug education.

Drug abuse prevention programs have generally not been very successful (Goodstadt, 1987; Tobler, 1986). One reason is that these programs cannot remove the social problems that may lead to drug abuse. A student may use drugs for immediate pleasure, as a means of experimentation, to show rebelliousness, and because of peer pressure to use drugs. These reasons are easy to understand. However, drugs may also be used as an escape from the harsh realities of life, such as failure, rejection, and family problems (Tower, 1987). Personality characteristics consistently related to drug abuse are low self-esteem and feelings of not being competent or wanted (Heron, 1988). Of course, some students with these characteristics will not become drug abusers.

To be effective, drug education programs must deal with the issue of how to help adolescents find alternative ways of dealing with their problems. More research is needed on why some teens with such problems become attracted to drug use and become drug users or abusers and why some adolescents do not. However, these complicated family, societal,

7. TRUE OR FALSE?

Drug abuse prevention programs have generally not been very effective.

and personal problems cannot be addressed very well with only the resources available in the schools, and society must address the social problems that lead to drug abuse (Forbes, 1987).

Another problem is the assumption that just giving teens the information about the dangers of drug abuse is sufficient to reduce drug use. It isn't. Information is important, and teaching adolescents the facts about drugs is necessary, but it is not sufficient in itself to reduce drug use. Information is frequently accompanied by the use of scare tactics, which are ineffective (Minix, 1987; Sagor, 1987). Programs that use recovering addicts or police or narcotics agents who try to scare students with lurid stories just don't work, perhaps because the recovering addicts often reinforce students' belief that tough people like themselves can use drugs and not become addicted.

With the preceding in mind, many drug prevention programs have changed their emphasis from giving information to teaching personal decision-making strategies and focusing on personal goals (Minix, 1987). Many modern programs, then, besides giving the facts, emphasize the social aspects of life and focus on social skills training and decision-making skills. Some programs advocate targeting students at high risk for abusing drugs, including those who show poor relationships with their parents, a history of some drug use, low self-esteem, delinquency, low academic motivation, tolerance for risk taking, family or peer use of drugs, early nicotine use, and psychological problems (Brenna, 1983).

Everyone seems to believe that drug taking is a major problem. However, drug prevention programs have not been very successful.

♦ SUICIDE

Suicide is the second leading cause of death among people between the ages of fifteen and twenty-one (accidents are first). Nationally, suicide increased by more than 200 percent between 1960 and 1980, although the suicide rate has leveled off in recent years (Frederick, 1985; Viadero, 1987b). It is the eighth leading cause of death among children between the ages of five and fourteen (Bernhardt & Praeger, 1985). It is estimated that 11 percent of all youths in the 15- to 19-year-old age group have attempted suicide, with more than 5,000 succeeding in taking their own lives during 1985 (Frederick, 1985; Hobart, 1986).

The most common cause of suicide, according to most experts is depression (Gispert, Wheeler, Marsh, & Davis, 1985). A sense of hopelessness seems to pervade suicide victims (Farberow, 1985; Schneidman, 1970). Those who attempt suicide often have a family history of breakdown, divorce, and suicide, have few friends, and suffer from rejection (Wenar, 1982). Most experienced a large number of stressful events in childhood, with a marked increase in stress in the year preceding the attempt. Other predisposing factors include early death of a parent, rejection in love, academic pressure to achieve, and failure (Hendin, 1985).

Whenever a suicide occurs in a community, people start looking for answers and clues. Indeed, in a majority of cases, clues are found. About

8. *TRUE OR FALSE?*
_____

People who talk about committing
suicide rarely make a suicide
attempt.

80 percent of the adolescents communicate their feelings and intentions
to other people before attempting suicide (Shafii, 1985). Research has
provided us with some clues to predict the possibility of suicide, but
unfortunately we do not always pay attention to them. For instance, many
people believe that people who talk about suicide never actually do it.
This is not so. People who talk about suicide are actually more likely to
attempt it. Other warning signs include giving things away and talking
about "ending it." A previous attempt at suicide is also a warning that a
future attempt might be made if the predisposing factors are not controlled or adequately dealt with (Colt, 1983). Situations that cause extreme anxiety, depression, and hopelessness should put a person on guard
that suicide may be contemplated (Schneidman, 1970). Familial determinants include divorce, poor communication, conflict, unavailable parents, high parental expectations, mental illness, job loss, suicide of a
family member, and alcoholism (Allen, 1987). Sometimes parents have a
"do your own thing" or an "I come first" attitude that affects children.
The loss or lack of a confidant is another problem when these potential
victims lose the one person in whom they could confide.

Some school districts offer classes in which students are taught how
to recognize the warning signs and help their troubled friends. Such classes
also introduce students to available community resources. California has
a program that is a four-hour curriculum. Evaluations of the program
show a significant gain in the understanding of suicide prevention techniques, and school staff and parents completing suicide awareness seminars appreciate the practical advice. Over 40 percent of the California
program students say they liked learning how to help themselves and
others who have feelings of depression. The California program has had
a positive impact on the knowledge and attitudes of the students, who
have thus become better able to recognize the signs and symptoms of
potential suicide (Nelson, 1987).

One interesting outcome of the evaluation of the New Jersey curriculum
is that most of the teens questioned reported that because of the program
they were more likely to use a hotline to help themselves or their family
deal with problems (Viadero, 1987c). In many communities, suicide prevention centers have hotlines for emergency help. Although these hotlines are quite effective (Farberow, 1985), long-term help is usually necessary. The evaluation of the New Jersey program also indicated that most
students already held what were considered "desirable" attitudes about
suicide, such as taking seriously a friend's stated intention to commit
suicide.

Not all students see these programs as desirable, and some describe
them as upsetting and boring. Disagreement exists on the total effect that
school programs and films on suicide may have on already troubled students. Could they cause a troubled student to consider suicide? The studies on this are difficult to interpret. Some question the repetition of the
suicide theme, while others claim that the conclusion that programs or
films on the subject may encourage suicide in troubled students is premature (Viadero, 1987d). More research is certainly needed on the subject.

◆ COGNITIVE ADVANCES IN ADOLESCENCE

During our discussion of the physical changes that occur in adolescence, as well as of eating disorders, some patterns appear repeatedly. Adolescents are capable of perceiving the world as other people do and evaluating themselves as they think others will. Their self-consciousness seems to stem from their ability to consider how other people might be evaluating them and then to act to influence this assessment.

The attitude that "people will think I am......." is especially powerful in early and middle adolescence. At the same time, other cognitive changes that relate directly to behavior are taking place, although they are less obvious. These changes allow teens to think differently from elementary schoolchildren and begin to develop their own values.

◆ THE STAGE OF FORMAL OPERATIONS

Between the ages of about eleven or twelve and fifteen, children enter the **formal operations stage** and develop some important capabilities (Inhelder & Piaget, 1958; Piaget, 1972). As with all other Piagetian abilities, these develop over time, and an adolescent may show one skill but not another at a particular point in development.

formal operations stage
The last Piagetian stage of cognitive development, in which a person develops the ability to deal with abstractions and reasons in a scientific manner.

Combinational Logic

Give elementary schoolchildren a problem in which they must find all the possible alternatives. You may be surprised to find that they do not approach the task in a scientific manner. For example, Inhelder and Piaget (1958) presented subjects of varying ages with five jars of a colorless liquid and told them that some combination of these chemicals would yield a yellow liquid. Preschoolers, who are in the preoperational stage, simply poured one into another, making a mess. Children in the concrete stage of operations combined the liquids, but did not approach the task with a systematic strategy. Adolescents formed a strategy for combining the liquids and finally solved the problem.

This finding can be extended to other situations. Adolescents can give all the possible solutions to a particular problem. If asked why something might happen, they understand that there are many different motives behind behavior. If you ask adolescents to answer the question "Why didn't Justin do his homework?", you'll get a number of answers, some possible and many improbable. This demonstrates another similar skill—the ability to divorce oneself from what is real.

Separating the Real from the Possible

"What if human beings were green?" Ask a child this question, and the youngster may insist that human beings are not green. But adolescents can accept a proposition and separate themselves from the real world (Ault, 1977). They can form hypotheses and test them out, which entails separating themselves from the real and considering the possible. Adolescents can reflect on a verbal hypothesis, and the elements of the hypothesis do not have to exist in real life.

The ability to do this affects behavior. Parents may have difficulty with adolescents who can and do suggest alternatives that may not be feasible or that parents simply do not like. The separation of what is from what can or could be allows the adolescent to begin to think about a better world. Their "why" questions are based on possibilities divorced from reality, and they are capable of suggesting other alternatives. But their lack of experience in the real world limits their ability to consider some of these possibilities in practical terms.

Using Abstractions

9. TRUE OR FALSE?

The ability to interpret proverbs and political cartoons develops during adolescence.

The ability adolescents have to separate themselves from the trappings of what is real stems partly from their newfound ability to create and use abstractions. Children in the stage of concrete operations have difficulty understanding political cartoons and adages such as "You can lead a horse to water, but you can't make him drink." They are still reality bound and have difficulty with abstract thought. They may actually picture a horse being led to water. But adolescents develop an ability to interpret abstractions, allowing them to develop internal systems of overriding principles. They can now talk in terms of ideals and values. Such concepts as freedom, liberty, and justice take on additional significance when they are separated from their situational meaning. As we shall see in another section, adolescents can now form their own values based on these overriding principles.

Hypothetical-Deductive Reasoning

These emerging abilities allow the adolescent to engage in what Piaget called hypothetical-deductive reasoning. Basically, this is the ability to form a hypothesis, which then leads to certain logical deductions. Some of these hypotheses may be untestable, such as "What if all human beings were green?" while others may be capable of being investigated scientifically. This type of reasoning is necessary for scientific progress. No one has ever seen an atom, but the developments in atomic theory have greatly affected our lives (Pulaski, 1980).

Thinking About Thinking

Adolescents also develop the ability to think about thinking (Ault, 1977). Teens often think back on their own thought processes and consider one thought the object of another. This ability allows them to consider the development of their own concepts and ideas.

The abilities to (1) use combinational logic, (2) separate the real from the possible, (3) interpret abstractions, and (4) engage in hypothetical-deductive logic combine to allow adolescents to reason out problems on a higher level than they could during childhood. Adolescents are capable of accepting assumptions in the absence of physical evidence, developing hypotheses involving if-then thinking, testing out these hypotheses, and reevaluating them (Salkind, 1981). The thinking of adolescents, as summarized in Table 13.3, is also more flexible because adolescents can consider a number of alternatives, weigh them, and then discard those that do not fit the situation. This ability to attack problems logically has great value in mathematics and science, and in life generally. The development of formal operational reasoning is related to doing well in school, although, as the Cross-Cultural Current on page 572 demonstrates, other factors are also important. With these newfound abilities, it is natural for adolescents to question, to consider what may be rather than what is, to look at their own system of beliefs, and to be concerned with abstract questions involving overriding principles.

Functioning at the Formal Operational Level

These abilities sound quite impressive, and they are. But not all adolescents, or even all adults, reason on this level (Neimark, 1975, 1982). Although older adolescents tend to be further along in using formal oper-

TABLE 13.3: The Formal Operational Stage
In the stage of formal operations, adolescents develop the ability to deal with abstract information and theoretical propositions. They can formulate and test hypotheses in a scientific manner.

CHARACTERISTIC	EXPLANATION	EXAMPLE
Combinational logic	The ability to find all the possible alternatives	When asked what the president could have done in a certain situation, a teenager will produce a great many alternatives, some real, some impractical. If given five jars of colorless liquid and told that some combination will yield a yellow liquid, an adolescent will use an efficient and effective strategy that will produce all possible alternatives.
Separating the real from the possible	The ability to accept propositions that are contrary to reality and to separate oneself from the real world.	A teenager can discuss propositions such as, "What if all human beings were green?"
Using abstractions	The ability to deal with material that is not observable.	An adolescent understands higher level concepts such as democracy and liberty as well as the abstract meaning in proverbs.
Hypothetical-deductive reasoning	The ability to form hypotheses and use scientific logic.	A teenager uses deductive logic in science to test a hypothesis.

The Missing Ingredient

Why do bright teenagers fail? We know that formal operational abilities are related to achievement in secondary school. That is, students who possess the ability to abstract and can use hypothetical-deductive logic tend to do better in school than those who do not. Yet, it has been a mystery why some adolescents from certain minorities, such as dialect-speaking Hawaiian adolescents, Eskimos from the North Slope of Alaska, and certain Native American children, do not achieve in school, despite developing these abilities. This is especially true for those who come from poverty backgrounds.

Carol Feldman, Addison Stone, and Bobbi Renderer reasoned that many of these students do have formal operational reasoning abilities but do not use them in school. They hypothesized that this may be because of a lack of the ability to use these skills to solve problems. Psychologists use the term *transfer* to refer to the ability to use a skill learned in one situation to solve a problem in another situation. Perhaps high achievers show this transfer, whereas low achievers do not.

Feldman, Stone, and Renderer went one step further by asking why some students would show transfer and others would not. The simplest possibility is that children who do not show transfer do not see how such reasoning can be applied to a new situation, probably because they are not able to describe the new problem or situation in a way that allows them to use the skills they have.

Consider what happens when someone is faced with a problem and must decide how to deal with it. The person must describe the problem in a way that allows him or her to know whether he or she should use strategy one or strategy two. The person performs a sort of internal dialogue concerning the problem. This requires linguistic abilities, and here is where the difficulty may be found. Language enables us to convert a problem into different forms. In other words, for transfer to take place, the new problem has to be verbally described and interpreted in a way that encourages the transfer of some ability the person already has. Anyone who has mastered language should be able to do this.

Remember, however, that the Hawaiian students described in the first paragraph speak a different dialect in school than at home or with their friends. They speak a dialect called Hawaiian Creole English at home but speak only Standard American English in school. There is no overlap, and the Hawaiian children see their dialect as inappropriate for use in academic settings. These children not only are bidialectical but also are members of a society that ascribes completely different functions to the two dialects. Therefore, if these students are to do well in school, they will have to have great proficiency in Standard English, a dialect they do not use very often outside of school.

The answer seems obvious—just give them practice in Standard English. Encourage them to speak it as much as possible. There is a major problem here, however. These adolescents understand Standard English well but often refuse to speak in class. They are frequently embarrassed by their Standard English, refuse to use their own dialect

ational thinking, they do not use it on every problem where it would be appropriate (Roberge & Flexer, 1979). It is estimated that only about half the adult population attains the final stage of formal operations (see Muuss, 1982).

Why doesn't everyone show formal operational reasoning? Some claim that people may be competent enough to succeed at a task but for one reason or another do not perform it successfully (Flavell & Wohlwill, 1969). They fail because of fatigue, the way the problem is structured, or lack of experience with problems requiring such abilities. There is some evidence that people can be taught to use formal operational reasoning when appropriate (Danner & Day, 1977; Kuhn, 1979).

Others suggest that not all people require the use of formal operations

in academic settings, and therefore remain quiet in class. These children simply do not talk in school. They are silent, and this pattern of silence is found among several Native American groups and Alaskan Eskimos as well. This is interesting, because these children are talkative outside of class. It would not be surprising, then, if the Hawaiian children do not verbally encode the problems very well, because they have less experience doing so. To summarize, we have a group of bright children who speak two dialects—one at home and another at school. Many of these children have the formal operational skills necessary for success but do not seem to use them, perhaps because they lack the ability to set the problems up in a way that would allow them to use their advanced reasoning process.

To find out if this is the case, the researchers tested sixty-seven high school students from a rural, agricultural community at the southern end of the island of Hawaii. All students spoke Hawaiian Creole with their friends and at home but spoke only Standard English at school. Achievement tests—tests to assess language proficiency in Standard American English and a test that measured both formal operational ability and the ability to transfer—were administered to these students.

The results affirmed the importance of transfer. The ability to transfer was a powerful predictor of school achievement. Transfer makes an important contribution to school achievement. In the words of the researchers, "We found a strong relation between transfer and school achievement in formal operational, dialect-speaking adolescents, a relation that gets stronger as the transfer task gets harder, more distant, or abstract. Ability to transfer procedures across contexts is evidently itself an important skill, one that is necessary for school achievement" (Feldman, Stone, & Renderer, 1990, pp. 482–483). In addition, the ability to use Standard English was found to be related to the ability to transfer.

The results show the importance of language ability to transfer and the importance of transfer to academic achievement. The Hawaiian children need active encouragement to become more verbal in class. But this is not easy to do. One possibility is accepting their dialect and encouraging it in school, since they are certainly verbally skilled in it. However, even if the dialect were accepted in school, the students would not see it as appropriate. Their culture separates the use of the dialect from the use of Standard English. When these adolescents do talk in school, they try to produce their best approximation of Standard English. Some way must be found to encourage these adolescents to verbally participate in school lessons. This study was conducted on Hawaiian students, and it would be interesting to see whether the same relationships hold for other children, such as Eskimos or Native American children who are also described as very quiet in class.

This research gives us a better understanding of why some bright children do not do well in school. Some of the problem may stem from an inability to transfer which stems from the children's linguistic problems. This better understanding of the dynamics of the problem brings us to consider a very practical educational question. How can we encourage these students to use their verbal abilities in school? A way must be found to overcome these students' embarrassment and unwillingness to speak, for only in that way can they develop their linguistic skills and use their intellectual abilities to the fullest extent.

Source: Feldman, C.F., Stone, A., and Renderer, B., Stage, Transfer, and Academic Achievement in Dialect-Speaking Hawaiian Adolescents. *Child Development*, 1990, 61, 472–484.

in their daily lives. Consider the cross-cultural differences that have been discovered. Studies of formal operations in non-Western cultures show that people in these cultures generally perform more poorly when presented with Piagetian tasks that require formal operational reasoning (Dasen & Heron, 1981). It may be that Piaget's stage of formal operations is basically applicable only to adolescents in Western technological societies who are exposed to a great deal of formal education. Indeed, schooling does seem to be an important variable in determining whether people reach the formal operational stage. Schooled non-Western adolescents do better on these tests than unschooled non-Western adolescents (Rogoff, 1981).

Such evidence led Piaget (1972) to reevaluate this area of his theory.

He recognized that education, vocational interests, and one's society and culture determine performance on tests of formal operations. Perhaps the environments necessary to progress from sensorimotor to preoperational to concrete operational thinking are basic and exist in the overwhelming majority of societies, but formal operational reasoning may require a more technological, structured environment. It requires a particular type of stimulation found most often at the upper levels of schooling. The nature of the environment may be more important in performing at this level than it is at earlier levels. In addition, this type of abstract reasoning may not be necessary for effective functioning in many societies. Piaget viewed it as the ultimate achievement, but that may be so only in Western cultures. We have little idea what may constitute the ideal last stage of cognitive growth in other societies.

Finally, even within the same age groups in Western societies, some people perform better than others on tasks requiring formal operations. People mature at different rates and are exposed to different challenges. Individual differences in attaining formal operations skills should be expected, and indeed are found.

◆ COGNITIVE GROWTH AND BEHAVIOR IN ADOLESCENCE

The formal operational abilities just described can help us understand how teenagers come to be concerned with societal problems and develop their own morals and values. They also help us understand much of the social behavior that is common during the adolescent years.

Adolescent Egocentrism

When teaching at a junior high school some years ago, I received a strange note from a mother. All it said was to please call her that morning concerning her daughter Jennifer's absence from school the day before. Jennifer appeared to be well, but she was acting a bit shy. When I called her mother, I was surprised to learn that Jennifer had played hookey from school for the first time in her life. The reason? Jennifer had gone to the hairdresser and was not pleased with her new look. She refused to be seen, even though her mother said she looked fine. Her mother made certain Jennifer attended school the next day. Jennifer's evaluation of her new look was anything but positive, and Jennifer had imagined that every student in the class would be staring at her and evaluating her the same way she evaluated herself.

The concern of adolescents with their appearance is a hallmark of the teenage years, as is their tendency to imagine that everyone is looking at them and evaluating their actions when they walk into a room. In fact, early adolescent eighth graders in one study were found to be significantly more self-conscious than both younger children and older adolescents (Elkind & Bowen, 1979). Adolescents often look at themselves in the mirror and imagine what others will think about them. Adolescents can now think about thoughts—both their own and those of others. However, a logical error occurs. Teenagers can understand the thoughts of others, but they fail to differentiate between the objects toward which the thoughts of others are directed and those that are the focus of their own thoughts (Peel, 1969). Because teens are concerned primarily with themselves, they believe that everyone else is focusing on them too and that others are as obsessed with their behavior and appearance as they are (Buss & Thompson, 1989). The inability to differentiate between what one is thinking and what others are thinking constitutes what David Elkind (1967) calls **adolescent egocentrism.** This leads to two interesting phenomena: the imaginary audience and the personal fable.

THE IMAGINARY AUDIENCE The phenomenon of the imaginary audience is illustrated by Jennifer's feelings about her appearance which caused Jennifer to miss school. Jennifer anticipated the reactions of her classmates, but her anticipation was biased because she was convinced that her classmates would see her the way she saw herself. Adolescents often believe that when they walk into a room everyone focuses their attention on them. They anticipate people's reactions. Adolescents are always onstage in front of others (Elkind, 1985). They create an **imaginary audience,** believing that everyone is looking at and evaluating them. Other people constitute the audience, but the audience is imaginary because most of the time the adolescent is not really the focus of attention.

The imaginary audience phenomenon leads to self-consciousness and the adolescent's mania for privacy. The self-consciousness stems from the conviction that others are seeing and evaluating them in the same way that they see themselves. The mania for privacy may come either from what Elkind calls a "reluctance to reveal oneself" or from a reaction to

adolescent egocentrism
The adolescent failure to differentiate between what one is thinking and what others are thinking.

imaginary audience
A term used to describe adolescents' belief that they are the focus of attention and being evaluated by everyone.

Many teenagers invoke an imaginary audience, believing that everyone will notice them. These teens may be more involved in how they are being seen by the other person than in actually seeing and interacting with the other person.

10. *TRUE OR FALSE?*
—————
Most early adolescents believe that everyone will be looking at them when they walk into a restaurant, store, or classroom.

being constantly scrutinized by others. **Privacy becomes a vacation from evaluation.**

Adolescents, then, are deeply involved with how others will evaluate them. As they dress, act, and groom, they imagine how others will see them. Elkind notes that when the boy who combed his hair for hours and the girl who carefully applied makeup meet, **both are more concerned with being observed than with being the observer.**

The imaginary audience slowly disappears during later adolescence to a considerable extent. Teens begin to realize that people may not react to them the way they think. They also come to accept the fact that people are not as interested in them as they thought. **However, another phenomenon caused by adolescent egocentrism—that of the personal fable—lasts much longer.**

personal fable
The adolescents' belief that their experiences are unique and original.

THE PERSONAL FABLE "You can't know how it feels to be in love with someone who doesn't know you exist," said one adolescent to his parents. He was convinced that only he could suffer such feelings of unrequited love, of loneliness, of despair. As adolescents reflect on their own thoughts and experiences, they come to believe that what they are thinking and experiencing is absolutely unique in the annals of human history. The belief that what they are experiencing and thinking is original, new, and special is known as the **personal fable.** Evidence of the personal fable is found in the diaries of adolescents. As we will see a bit later, the **personal fable may be responsible for a great many adolescent risk-taking behaviors.**

The personal fable declines somewhat as the adolescent enters young adulthood, but it may never be completely extinguished.

◆ MORALS AND VALUES IN ADOLESCENCE

Look at any mass demonstration for a cause and you will usually see young people in the thick of it. Whether the cause is nuclear disarmament, free speech, or a cleaner environment, the **idealism and values of adolescents often show themselves in a visible activism.** Adolescents who do not join groups and demonstrate also develop their own values and personal philosophy. Their **newfound abilities to understand abstract and overriding principles and values—such as freedom, liberty, and justice— and to separate the real from what is possible allow them to formulate their own personal principles and ideas about right and wrong.**

Cognitive Development and Moral Reasoning

Lawrence Kohlberg, whose theory of moral reasoning was discussed in Chapter 12, argued that moral reasoning is related to cognitive growth and development. The higher stages of moral reasoning require more sophisticated cognitive abilities. If this is true, adolescents progressing from concrete to formal operations should show an increased ability to reason at higher levels. Indeed, research has demonstrated a correlation between cognitive level and moral reasoning (Kohlberg, 1987).

Adolescents operating at the formal operations stage have the ability to reason at Kohlberg's higher stages. Harris and colleagues (1976) found the intelligence and level of moral reasoning for thirty-three fifth-grade boys. The boys' peers were asked about their moral conduct, and a test of honesty was administered. The results? Not only were cognitive ability and level of moral reasoning related, but higher reasoners also demonstrated more resistance to temptation and were seen by their peers as more caring about the welfare of others. The higher stages of moral reasoning require at least the beginnings of formal operations (Weiss, 1982).

The Higher Stages of Moral Reasoning

Just what is the nature of these higher stages of moral reasoning? Kohlberg's Stage 4 involves reasoning that is oriented toward doing one's duty and maintaining the social order for its own sake. Stage 5 involves a contractual legalistic orientation that empasizes not violating the rights of others and having respect for the welfare and majority will of others. Stage 6 is a more individualistic orientation in which decisions are made involving individual conscience and one's own principles. Adolescents who are developing formal operational skills are better able to reason at these higher levels of moral reasoning. But even if they have this ability, many adolescents do not function at this level. In fact, most people do not develop beyond Stage 4 (Shaver & Strong, 1976).

The personal fable, the teenager's belief that he or she is unique and invulnerable is one of the explanations for teenagers' risk-taking behavior.

Why Doesn't Everyone Reason at Stage 6?

Why do some people use Stage 6 reasoning while others do not? Perhaps the best way to understand this is to invoke the competency-performance argument. Cognitive advancement makes more sophisticated moral reasoning a possiblity but does not assure it. Other factors may enter the picture. The content of the problem is one variable (Fischer, 1980), as are the consequences of the moral decision. When people are faced with a dilemma in which the personal consequences are great, they are likely to demonstrate lower level moral thinking (Sobesky, 1983). Generally, when people are confronted with a problem, their cognitive skills form the upper limit of their abilities to reason, but the situation itself will affect the actual behavior.

The adolescent's moral reasoning cannot be neatly placed into one stage (Kohlberg, 1969). At times, adolescents operate on a higher level; at other times, they operate on a lower one (Holstein, 1976). Thus, moral reasoning may be inconsistently applied to various problems. Indeed, we see this inconsistency often, and parents may have difficulty understanding their child's highly moral stand on one issue and lower-level reasoning on another.

The development of formal operations gives the adolescent the tools with which to solve a problem at the higher levels of moral reasoning. It does not mean that these tools will be used. All we can say is that formal operations are necessary but not sufficient for the development of higher moral reasoning processes. Many other factors, including personal qual-

THE CHILD
IN THE YEAR
2000

Adolescent Risk Taking

When sixteen-year-old Nadine found out she was pregnant, she didn't know what to do. She tried to hide it but couldn't. Her mother cried, and her father yelled at her and only wanted the name of the boy. Although a number of her friends were engaging in sexual relations, Nadine told them, "I just got caught." She had thought of the possibility that she would get pregnant but dismissed it. The subject had never come up in the conversations between Nadine and her boyfriend, Brian. Nadine is now faced with a number of problems, as is eighteen-year-old Brian. They can marry or not. She can bear the child, turn it over for adoption, or make some agreement with her parents about raising her child. She can have an abortion. Nadine is confused, and since she is now in her fourth month of pregnancy, she has a time limit. She is feeling overwhelmed.

We are often confused by the seemingly illogical behavior of teenagers in taking incredible risks. After hearing about cases of drug overdoses, drunken and dangerous driving, and teenagers engaging in sexual intercourse without any contraceptive protection, we wonder what is going on. How can a teenager believe that he or she won't get into an accident and get hurt? How can teenagers have sex and not think about the possible

consequences? Just about all the teenage health problems in developed countries are caused directly by teenage risk-taking behaviors. Although there is no such thing as complete safety, the chances that many teenagers take are illogical unless one understands the personal fable.

Teenagers are told that they are at the height of their physical and mental powers, that their future is bright and unlimited, and that they are unique individuals. They tend to believe that they are invincible and that nothing can happen to them. They take risks like not wearing seatbelts, speeding, and taking drugs, believing that the laws of physics and biology somehow do not apply to them. It becomes easy to take risks when a person believes that "it really can't happen to me."

In the year 2000, we will still be faced with the problems of teenage pregnancy, drug abuse, and the AIDS epidemic. We know that scare tactics do not work, nor is information sufficient to reach

teenagers. A positive development stems from the new research which demonstrates that comprehensive programs emphasizing early intervention, prevention, and reasoning skills may help. We also know that when adolescents have goals and high aspirations and are optimistic about their future, they are less likely to engage in these behaviors. Yet the fundamental problem of risk taking remains. We must find some way to counter the personal fable and the tendency to take risks. We must find some way to help adolescents understand that they are not exceptions to the rules and that although they are each experiencing their world for the first time, they are not invincible.

It will be a challenge for psychologists to do more research into this tendency to take risks in adolescence. It may be here where we can discover important ways of dealing with behaviors that are self defeating in the long run but yield immediate gratification. This does not negate the other approaches to dealing with the problems, but argues that this is a missing ingredient that must be dealt with if we are to be successful in dealing with these problems. Eventually we will find effective methods of countering the personal fable and risk-taking behaviors. It is, at this point, a frontier of research.

ities, family background, and the characteristics of the situation, determine whether these abilities will be used.

Moral Reasoning and Prosocial Behavior

Are high levels of moral reasoning related to more prosocial behavior? Kohlberg says yes (Kohlberg & Turiel, 1971), while others are skeptical (Wonderly & Kupfersmid, 1980). You may recall Stanley Milgram's (1968) famous study in which he asked subjects to obey a researcher and deliver what they thought were painful shocks to an innocent subject whose only crime was answering a question incorrectly on a learning-memory test. No shocks were really delivered, but the "teachers" did not know this. The study was really one of obedience. Kohlberg and Turiel (1971) reported that 75 percent of the Stage 6 subjects tested on Milgram's obedience tests did not comply, while only 13 percent of the subjects reasoning at the other moral stages refused to deliver the shocks. This sounds impressive, but notice that 25 percent of the Stage 6 sample delivered the shocks. In addition, some studies have failed to find differences between the behavior of children reasoning in the upper stages and that of those in the lower stages (Wonderly & Kupfersmid, 1980). All we can say at this point is that there is a positive relationship between level of moral reasoning and behavior, but it has not been found in all studies, and even where it has been found, it is far from perfect.

Values and Attitudes

The development of formal operations is related to certain cognitive abilities that allow adolescents to develop their own values. But what values do most adolescents hold, and have these changed over the years?

Values are constructs that serve as internal guides for behavior (McKinney & Moore, 1982). They are beliefs that certain patterns of conduct or end states are better than others (Rokeach, 1973). To some extent, values are culturally determined. For example, many hunter and gathering societies require teamwork to survive, and the values of cooperation and sharing are crucial. Obedience was a value greatly admired by the Pilgrims and the Puritans.

values
Constructs that serve as internal guides for behavior.

A poll of 17,000 high school students found that more than 75 percent of the students stated that their goal was a good marriage and a happy family life. Over two-thirds thought that having strong friendships was important and only 4 percent of noncollege-bound youth and 10 percent of college freshmen thought that being a community leader was important (Bachman & Johnston, 1979). These students' lack of desire for community involvement is something of a disappointment. However their parents probably agree with these values.

Some values and attitudes have changed significantly over the past twenty years. Each year since 1966, the attitudes and values of 280,000 college freshmen have been surveyed at about 550 two-year and four-year colleges and universities nationwide. Alexander Astin and his colleagues (1989) took data from nearly six million first-year college students and analyzed them for trends. In the United States, the 1960s were a time of social upheaval, involving civil rights and great changes in sexual attitudes.

When adolescent values in the 1960s, 1970s and 1980s are compared, some interesting trends appear. In the late 1960s, students were more interested in social interpersonal morality. Values relating to one's relationship with society were most important. By 1975, however, the climate had changed, and students were more interested in personal achievement and less involved with society. For example, while only 44 percent of the 1967 sample believed it was essential to be well off financially, 75.4 percent of the freshmen believed so in 1989. While 14 percent of the 1966 freshmen planned to major in business, 24.5 percent of the 1989 group did (Astin, Korn & Berz, 1989). The changes in freshmen's views of social roles are startling. In 1967, some 57 percent of the freshmen believed that activities of married women are best confined to the home and family, while only 25.9 percent of the 1989 group believed the same. Figure 13.2 depicts some of these changes.

Political Philosophy

Values and attitudes affect one's view of politics. Adolescents see law and politics differently from the way younger children see them. When adolescents and younger children were asked "What is the purpose of laws?" Joseph Adelson (1972) found striking differences between the answers of adolescents and those of preadolescents. Younger children answered that laws were necessary so that people didn't get hurt or so that people wouldn't kill or steal. Adolescents of about fifteen or sixteen years of age viewed law in more abstract and principled terms—laws ensure safety, enforce government policy, and act as guidelines for determining right and wrong.

Subjects younger than age eleven focus on the consequences of law and order for themselves, while older adolescents go beyond this and see the legal system from the point of view of the community as a whole (Adelson & O'Neil, 1966). Preadolescents look at law and government in terms that are concrete, absolute, and authoritarian and evaluate them on the basis of how they affect particular individuals; for example, seatbelts are necessary to protect the driver and passengers. Adolescents are less authoritarian and more sensitive to individual rights and personal freedom. They may see the conflict between requiring seatbelts for the good of everyone and the loss of personal freedom that comes with regulation— a conflict that younger children do not see. When Gallatin and Adelson (1971) asked what these younger children thought of a law requiring men to have a yearly medical checkup, they noted the good the law might do and frequently were willing to accept the idea. Older subjects saw that the good must be weighed against individual freedom. Preadolescents see government in personal terms, personifying it in terms of the president, mayor, or police officer, while older adolescents see it in terms of abstract properties (Sprintall and Collins, 1984). Children see government as powerful and good, but by about the eighth grade, they are more skeptical (Merelman, 1971).

The political attitudes of today's freshmen are different from what they were just two decades ago. In 1970, some 34 percent thought of themselves as liberal, while in 1989 only 21.7 percent did. Whereas 45 percent saw themselves as middle of the road in 1970, some 53.6 percent now do. The percentage of freshmen considering themselves politically conservative increased from 17 percent in 1970 to 21.3 percent in 1989.

FIGURE 13.2: Changes in Freshmen's Attitudes

Alexander Astin, and his colleagues surveyed nearly six million first-year college students. Some of their results are graphically represented in the following frames.

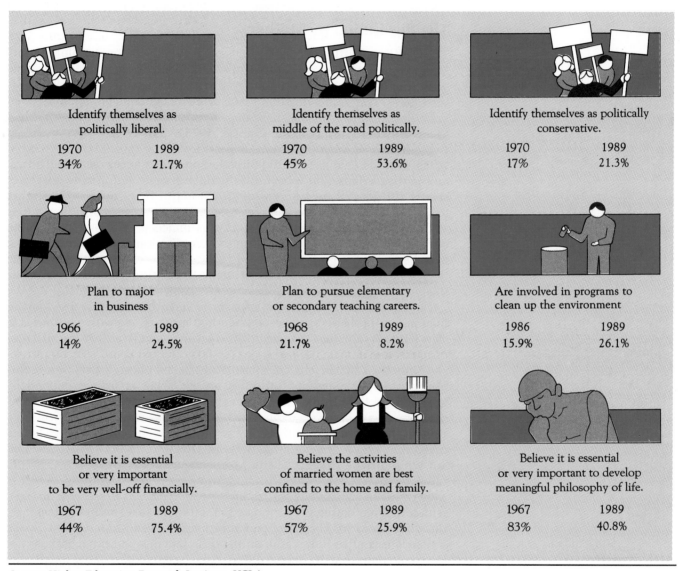

Source: Higher Education Research Institute, UCLA.

◆ ADOLESCENT SEXUALITY

The physical and cognitive changes that we have been looking at thus far affect many areas of functioning, but one area that is currently the center of attention is sexuality. Sexuality is a basic concern of adolescence. Ac-

genital stage
The final psychosexual stage, occurring during adolescence, in which adult heterosexual behavior develops.

cording to Freud, adolescents enter the **genital stage,** during which the libido—hidden during the latency phase—reappears. Physical drives are strong and cannot easily be repressed, and as a result, adolescents turn their attention to heterosexual relationships (Freud, 1925, 1953).

The Revolution in Attitudes

The traditional attitude concerning sexuality reflects the double standard. Males were permitted sexual freedom, while females were denied it. Males were encouraged to experiment, yet sanctions against female sexuality were great. The sexual needs of males were recognized, but females' needs were denied, even during marriage. The double standard has, at least to some degree, been reduced (Shope, 1975). Attitudinal differences between males and females have narrowed.

The attitude change is in the direction of greater acceptance and a live-and-let-live orientation to sex. In a widely quoted nationwide survey of sexual attitudes, Robert Sorenson (1973) found that adolescents did not believe that premarital sex, in and of itself, was right or wrong. As long as both partners were willing (force was unacceptable) and it occurred within an affectionate relationship, no negative sanctions were attached to it. Sexual behavior is considered more a matter of personal choice than the business of society (Chilman, 1983). The attitudes of adolescents are likely to be much more permissive than those of their parents.

The revolution in attitudes appears to have been greater for females than males, probably because women had more conservative attitudes to start with. Yet the idea that sex itself is taken casually or that the attitudes of males and females are identical is false. Females are still more conservative than males and are more likely to see sex as a part of a loving relationship. Adolescents' attitudes toward what is proper depend on how serious they think the relationship is. Both males and females become more permissive as the relationship gets more serious. And both believe that more sexual intimacy is proper when one is in love or engaged than when one is dating without affection, or even with affection but without love (Roche, 1986). However, males and females show differences in what they believe is appropriate at the beginning stages of dating, with males being more permissive than females. In the later stages—which include dating only one person, being in love, and engagement—the differences for the most part disappear. Males, then, expect sexual intimacy earlier in the relationship, while females tie sexual intimacy to love and commitment (Roche, 1986). Adolescents today show less fearful and more matter-of-fact attitudes than teens in the previous generations and less moral conflict or guilt about sex. However, sexual affairs are still not viewed by the majority as casual encounters.

Adolescents' attitudes are generally more liberal than their actual behavior. While adolescents are tolerant of other people's sexuality, their personal standards are somewhat stricter (Chilman, 1983). Oftentimes, teenagers will say that they agree with a particular practice, but when asked whether they engage in it, they say no (Hass, 1979).

Four conclusions are indicated by these data. First, adolescent sexual attitudes are quite tolerant and more liberal than in the past. Second, the attitudes of male adolescents are still more liberal than female attitudes, especially concerning sex in the early part of a relationship. Third, sex is not seen as a casual act. And fourth, adolescents seem to be somewhat more conservative in their behavior than in their attitudes.

Sexual Behavior

If attitudes towards sex have changed quite a bit, what about actual sexual behavior? The most common type of sexual experience for adolescents is masturbation, but when people speak of the sexual revolution, they are usually referring to what they see as the tremendous increase in the rate of sexual intercourse. Has there been a revolution in sexual behavior?

After reviewing a number of studies on the subject, Philip Dreyer (1982) notes that between 1925 and 1973 the percentage of high school girls reporting premarital sex tripled from 10 percent to 35 percent, and the rate for college females rose from 25 percent to 65 percent. Studies show that approximately 44 percent of the high school females and 74 percent of the college women reported engaging in premarital sex. For males, the rates have risen, but since the initial rates were higher, the rise is not as dramatic. In 1925, about 25 percent of the high school males and 55 percent of the college men reported having premarital sex. Today, about 56 percent of the high school men and 74 percent of the college men report experiencing sex. Studies indicate that high school males are more likely to be sexually active than high school females but that the virginity rates among college men and women are almost the same (Dreyer, 1982). In the National Longitudinal Survey of Youth, 60 percent of the white male teens had intercourse by age eighteen, and 60 percent of the white female teens by age nineteen. Sixty percent of the black male teens had intercourse by age sixteen, and 60 percent of the black teenage girls by age eighteen (Hofferth, 1987).

The increase in premarital sexuality is now accepted by most researchers. However, whether one wants to call this a revolution or an evolution depends on one's personal point of view. Certainly, the change in attitudes has been more radical than the change in behavior (Lerner & Spanier, 1980).

Some explain increasing rates of sexual intercourse in terms of its more open coverage by the media, the reduction of sanctions against premarital sex, the movement toward women's equality, the increase in availability of birth control and abortion, earlier maturation, and the faster pace of our society. Society in general is more accepting of premarital sex, and adolescents are exposed to much more sexual stimulation through the media. Perhaps there has been some increase in group pressure as well (Hechtman, 1989).

It is difficult to predict future trends. When a questionnaire regarding sexual philosophy, behavior, and relationships with the most recent partner was given in 1974, 1979, and 1986 at a small New England college, the trends were interesting. Sexual behavior increased dramatically between 1974 and 1979, but the 1986 results were very similar to the 1974

TABLE 13.4: Incidence of Sexual Experience (in percent) Among
Three Samples

	PERCENT			TOTAL NUMBER OF PARTICIPANTS		
Year	Men	Women		Men N	Women N	Total
1974	82.6	74.8		184	163	347
1979	91.0	88.4		111	155	266
1986	78.4	74.8		125	170	295

TABLE 13.5: Age at First Coitus (in percent) of
Sexually Experienced Students

	WOMEN			MEN		
Age	1974 N = 121	1979 N = 137	1986 N = 128	1974 N = 152	1979 N = 101	1986 N = 98
≤15	6.6	40.9	8.0	24.3	46.5	13.7
16	6.6	25.6	12.8	17.8	23.8	29.5
17	26.4	10.2	24.8	16.4	11.9	30.5
18	32.2	10.9	26.4	29.6	11.9	11.6
≤19	28.1	12.4	28.0	11.8	5.9	14.8

Source (both tables): Murstein, Chalpin, Heard, & Vyse, 1989.

pattern (Murstein, Chalpin, Heard, & Vyse, 1989). Some of these findings
are summarized in Table 13.4 and Table 13.5. The exact percentages are
less important than the trend. What we see here is a movement to more
conservatism but certainly not a return to sexual attitudes and behavior
patterns of thirty or forty years ago. This demonstrates the importance of
recognizing that sexual behavior and attitudes change with the times and
that it is difficult to predict future trends.

Contraceptive Use

If the incidence of premarital sex has increased substantially and sexual
attitudes have become more liberal, what about contraceptive use? The
statistics are depressing. Between one-third and two-thirds use no contraception during their first sexual intercourse (Morrison, 1985). Many
teens run the risk of becoming pregnant either because they use no contraception or because they use an ineffective method. The majority of
teens do not look for any contraceptive assistance until they have been
sexually active for about a year. This is especially distressing because
one-half of all first pregnancies occur in the first six months after teens

begin engaging in intercourse (Zabin, Kantner, & Zelnik, 1979). Most sexually active teens have had intercourse at least once without using any form of birth control (Dreyer, 1982). Contraceptive use increases with age, and the use of oral contraceptives increases in steady relationships and in marriage. Although some increase in contraceptive use during the late 1970s and the 1980s may have occurred, these increases are not significant. Many teens are experimenting with sex and not protecting themselves against pregnancy. Why?

Cognition and Contraception

Many teens simply do not consider the possibility that they will get pregnant, and if they do think about it, it is only a passing thought. As many as 40 percent of the females in Sorenson's (1973) study stated that sometimes they do not really care whether they get pregnant or not. Asked, "Do you ever worry about the possibility that you might become pregnant?", 16 percent of the nonvirgin girls said "never," 12 percent said "hardly ever," 41 percent said "sometimes," and 29 percent said "often." Some 25 percent of the males also stated that they always trusted to luck that the girl would not become pregnant.

We often think that the sexually active teen is a well-informed person and knowledgeable about the facts of conception, but that is not what the research shows (Morrison, 1985). Between 10 percent and 25 percent of teens questioned did not believe they could become pregnant the first time they had intercourse. When adolescents were asked to identify the time during the menstrual cycle when the greatest risk of pregnancy existed, less than half answered correctly. Less than half the teens sampled knew that sperm could live for three days, with one-third believing they live less than one day. About one-third of Sorenson's respondents believed they couldn't get pregnant if they didn't want to, even if they had sex without using some contraceptive method, while one quarter of another sample believed that a woman must have an orgasm to become pregnant.

Adolescents know something about the different methods of contraception, with older teens knowing more than younger teens. Their attitudes toward contraception, however, are negative or neutral at best. Many do not believe that even reliable forms of contraception really work.

Adolescents do not use contraception regularly because of erroneous beliefs about fertility, indifference to becoming pregnant, lack of knowledge regarding where to get contraceptives, and negative attitudes toward contraceptive devices themselves (Morrison, 1985). Some teenagers do not visit a family planning clinic because they are under the erroneous impression that they need their parents' consent (Brooks-Gunn & Furstenberg, 1989). Some teens are afraid of using an oral contraceptive or note that they are not in a continuous sexual relationship. The fact that contraception must be planned and that planned sex seems to lose its romantic quality and spontaneity may also be a reason for the sporadic use of contraceptives (Reichelt, 1976). Many teens also deny that they are sexually active and may not be mature enough to accept the fact that they are engaging in intercourse (Dreyer, 1982). The first encounter is rationalized as an accident—a moment of passion or a chance event. Most methods of birth control demand that the person acknowledge that he or she is sexually active and view sexual encounters realistically (Pestrak & Martin, 1985).

Many adolescents do not have the cognitive ability to cope with these facts. For example, the personal fable enables adolescents to believe that they are immune to the danger and cannot get pregnant. Some are restricted to here-and-now thinking, and younger teens find the entire subject of conception difficult to understand.

Teenage Pregnancy

One in five fourteen-year-old girls today will become pregnant before reaching the age of eighteen, and more than one million teenagers become pregnant each year. Of these, 600,000 give birth (Perlez, 1986). Some 95 percent of these young mothers keep their infants. The odds are quite high that a second pregnancy will occur within the next three years. In fact, over half the pregnant teens in one study became pregnant again within three years (Furstenberg, 1979).

The United States leads all Western developed countries in its rate of adolescent pregnancy, abortion, and childbearing even though the age of initiation and rates of sexual activity are comparable. The difference is most striking among the youngest teenagers—those under fifteen—who are more than five times as likely to give birth as girls in other developed countries (Hayes, 1987). Women who are poor or very young are most likely to become pregnant again. Although the rates of pregnancy are about half as great in Canada, and about one-third opt for abortion, still only four percent give their infants up to adoption. Of those who keep their infants, less than half are married (Hechtman, 1989).

Teenage pregnancy and parenthood are greater problems today than they were in the past. Although the teenage birthrate was higher in the 1950s than it is today, unlike then, the majority of teenage births today occur out of wedlock. For example, in 1950, less than 15 percent of births to teenagers were out of wedlock, while today the figure easily exceeds 50 percent (Davis, 1989).

The Consequences

The consequences of adolescent pregnancies are serious for the entire family. If the pregnant teen decides to get married, the odds against a successful marriage are great. The rates of separation and divorce are much greater among couples where the woman was pregnant at the time of the marriage than among couples where she was not pregnant (Hofferth, 1987; Kelly, 1982). Teenage marriages are generally less stable, and if the extra stress of pregnancy is added, the potential for discord increases. Whether there is a marriage or not, an adolescent pregnancy affects the future of everyone concerned—baby, mother, father, and grandparents.

11. TRUE OR FALSE?

The birthrate among teenagers in the United States today is higher than any time in the twentieth century.

THE INFANT Infants born to teenage mothers have more health problems than the average infant. They have a 30 percent greater risk of dying before their first birthday than babies of mothers between the ages of twenty and twenty-four years (Foster & Miller, 1980). Babies born to teenagers have lower birthweights, are more often premature, and have a greater chance of having a birth defect (Strobino, 1987). These problems are caused by poor nutrition, drugs, and lack of prenatal care. Although there may be some problems due simply to the immaturity of the childbearing system in some very young females, many of these problems are not inevitable. But ignorance, denial, and other psychological factors combine to prevent the pregnant adolescent from seeking out the best care for herself and her infant during the crucial prenatal period. The rates of child abuse are higher in young families, as is the chance that living circumstances will be inadequate and at the poverty level.

Teenage pregnancy is a national problem. More than one million teenagers become pregnant each year.

THE MOTHER Pregnancy is the most common reason that female students drop out of school. Somewhere between 50 percent and 66 percent of female dropouts claim pregnancy as the reason for failure to finish school. Most pregnant teenagers do not finish high school at all (Gordon & Dickman, 1980). The younger a woman is when she bears her first child, the fewer the years of education she will receive (Moore & Waite, 1977). Mothers who have babies in their teens have lower incomes and hold lower prestige jobs than their classmates. They also express less satisfaction with their jobs in their twenties. They often suffer from depression and experience a conflict between independence from and submission to their parents who helped them through the trying time (Zougher, 1977). In fact, family support is vital to these young mothers and their babies. Those who receive family support adapt better to these challenges than those who do not receive such social, psychological, and financial help (Furstenberg, 1981).

It would be wrong to believe that all teenage pregnancies are the result of accidents or ignorance. One pregnant sixteen-year-old told a reporter, "I figured this would be something that could be mine—nobody could take it, and it would have a little piece of me left that would give me a reason for living." Some girls become pregnant as a way to get attention or to get a boy to marry them (Perlez, 1986).

There is a wide variety of reactions to the news of pregnancy. In one survey of teenage mothers, 45 percent reported that they felt happy or very happy when first learning they were pregnant, while 25 percent felt upset or very upset (Martin and Baenen, 1987). Most mothers want the baby's father to be involved in the raising of the child. With time, most come to accept their pregnancy and parenthood. It is only after they give birth that the financial problems, the rigors of parenthood with its loss of freedom, and either a poor marriage or lack of any support from the father force these young women to regret their decision.

THE YOUNG MOTHER AS PARENT The young mother does not seem to be ready for her role. Most of the children of teenage mothers will spend their time in homes where the father is not present and are very likely to live in poverty. In fact, of all the families with children younger than six headed by mothers who gave birth as teenagers, two-thirds live below the poverty level (American Home Economics Association, 1986). Adolescent mothers tend to be impatient, insensitive, and prone to punish their children. Their behavior is characterized as highly physical and less verbal than that of more adult mothers (see Garcia-Coll, Hoffman, & Oh, 1987). When fifty teenage mothers were interviewed, the HOME inventory was completed, and videotapes of two-hour observations were made, adolescent mothers were found to call more frequently on others, especially other adolescents, for help with their child. They received less help from the father and more from their own mothers than did nonadolescent mothers. They were not only less verbal but also less responsive and involved, and showed less positive emotion towards their child. Their HOME scores were also much lower. These findings are common across a number of ethnic and socioeconomic groups (Garcia-Coll, Hoffman, & Oh, 1987).

The adolescent mother's style of parenting is not conducive to the child's optimal development. Children born to adolescent mothers lag behind their peers in cognitive, social, and school performance, and are at greater risk than their peers for maladjustment (Dubow & Luster, 1990). These teenage parents often reach out for help and require it. If they are to successfully raise their children, they must be provided with the type of parenting education discussed in Chapter 6.

THE FATHER Little information about the adolescent father is available. Society is usually most interested in identifying the father and forcing him to accept his legal responsibilities, not in finding out more about him. The stereotype of the adolescent father as uncaring, uninterested, and immature may not always be accurate. It is true that a substantial minority of fathers do not admit parenthood, perhaps out of ignorance, disbelief, or refusal to accept the obligations of fatherhood (Furstenberg, Brooks-Gunn, & Chase-Lansdale, 1989). As a group, though, these fathers are more similar to adolescents who have not fathered a child than they are different (Earls & Siegel, 1980). However, the profiles of the unwed father that do exist show that he is frightened, withdrawn, and confused and often feels guilty about his girlfriend (Barret & Robinson, 1981). He may not come forward out of fear, and many cannot deal with the pregnancy at all (Freedman, 1986).

The consequences of early parenthood can be severe for the father, too. Because both mothers and fathers are educationally retarded, it is an uphill climb to succeed in the world of work (Card & Wise, 1978). Often, teenage fathers find themselves in dead-end jobs, and, faced with the difficulty of supporting a family, many of them "slide into unemployment" (Freedman, 1986, p. 5). They may also not have the maturity necessary to handle the situation, whether they get married or not. In addition, they often face a dilemma. If they live with their parents, conflict often results, and if they try to live by themselves, they may not be ready for the responsibilities (Parke & Neville, 1987).

Many teenage fathers express concerns about supporting new families and finishing school, and they are concerned about the welfare of the child, the mother, and their relationships with their in-laws. Their feelings of alienation are great (Elster & Panzarine, 1983). In many cases, there is some contact with their offspring even if marriage does not take place, but it is not extensive and declines with time (Lorenzi, Klerman & Jekel, 1977). There are many variations, though, with some marrying and having extensive contact, some cohabiting, and others with little or no contact. As a group, they are not ready for fatherhood (Parke & Neville, 1987).

THE EXTENDED FAMILY Most parents are shocked to learn that their unmarried daughter is pregnant (Furstenberg, 1976). Teens who seek abortions do not normally consult their parents, but those who carry their pregnancies to term almost always do (Fox, 1981). When the decision is made to bear the child, a definite progression is seen. First, the parents are angry and disappointed. This is followed by a stage of gradual acceptance and a growing closeness between mother and daughter.

The quality of the relationship between the pregnant teen and her parents during the pregnancy determines what will happen after the birth. If the bond is close, marriage is much less likely to occur, and young mothers frequently stay with their parents (Furstenberg, 1981). Most young mothers will stay if their parents indicate a desire to help them. Those who are helped by their parents, especially until the child is attending school, are in a better economic position than those who leave to be on their own. Grandmothers provide much of the care in these situations (Forbush, 1981). Many young mothers who return to school are better off years later, although problems do exist, and the benefits should not be overstated. As the child matures, a deterioration in family relationships may take place. Mother remains in a subordinate position because she is dependent on her family.

Even considering these problems, though, it is clear that the young parents need help. Whether they live at home or marry, or whether the new mother tries to make it on her own, the young parent needs counseling and support from the time the pregnancy begins through the prenatal period and delivery and into the early years of parenthood. Since subsequent pregnancies are common, sex education is also required.

Sex Education Today

I wish my parents had canned the stork story and fairy tale explanations and told me the truth.

I wish my parents had sat me down and told me about sex instead of just saying, "Don't let no one in your pants."

I wish my parents had been more open about sex and not treated it as a big dark secret to be discovered and experienced after marriage.

I wish my parents spoke to me about birth control and let me know that in trouble I could turn to them.

There are just a few of the responses from a questionnaire given to 450 Syracuse University undergraduates. About 90 percent indicated that sex

The majority of parents favor sex education in the schools, and programs are becoming more common. However, it is estimated that less than 15 percent of American children receive comprehensive sex education.

12. TRUE OR FALSE?

About 20 percent of all parents refuse to let their children participate in sex education programs in school.

was not honestly discussed in their homes (Gordon, 1981). In fact, only about ten percent of the students were satisfied with their parents' efforts at sex education.

The majority of teens have no formal sex education from either teachers or parents; they learn about sex from their peers. Parents favor sex education in the schools by a wide margin. Some surveys show that as many as 80 percent of all Americans are in favor of sex education in the schools (Barron, 1987). When sex education is offered in school, less than three percent of all parents refuse to let their children participate (Scales, 1978). Although some parents may be opposed to sex education, most favor it, and only a very few will forbid their children to take part in it. The truly controversial question is, What should be taught?

Most parents want their own values taught, and there is a great difference of opinion as to what should be included in the sex education curriculum. Once we get past the standard biological content, questions concerning contraception and values arise. Although some parents do not want contraception taught or birth control devices made available to students, most do (Rinck, Rudolph, & Simkins, 1983). Other parents are afraid that the teacher will encourage sexuality or teach values that differ from those "taught" at home.

Sex education programs are becoming more common, but it is estimated that less than 15 percent of American children receive comprehensive sex education—now often called family life education—that covers such diverse areas as reproduction, getting along with others, understanding one's emotions and development, knowing what to do about sexual abuse, and AIDS education.

Everyone agrees that the family is the basic transmitter of education about sexuality. Indeed, sex education programs in the schools can be seen as a way to supplement the family's efforts and not as an attempt to take over what is, and continues to be, a parental responsibility. However, the statistics show that parents are NOT talking to their children about sex in an honest and open manner. A recent poll conducted by Planned Parenthood found that although teens cite their parents as the most important source of information on sex, pregnancy, and contraception, only a third had discussed contraception with their parents. Those who had discussed contraception were about twice as likely as those who hadn't to use contraceptives if they were sexually active (Wattleton, 1987). Of course, even if parents do speak to their children, there is no guarantee that it will have the desired effect. In addition, the research is difficult to interpret, because often parental communication occurs only after the teen has already begun to engage in sexual intercourse.

Only about a third of the teens in the Planned Parenthood survey had taken school sex education courses, and again, sexually active teens who had had comprehensive sex education were more likely to use contraceptives than were those who hadn't.

Those who harbor the most misconceptions and myths about sex are those who have not had comprehensive sex education. Adolescents whose parents talk to them about sex tend to be less sexually active. When a great deal of communication occurs, teens are more likely to share the sexual values of their parents (Fischer, 1986). Although the evidence is clear that sex education conducted by parents can be effective in transmitting values and encouraging the use of contraception if the teenager becomes sexually active, the evidence indicates that most parents do not provide comprehensive sex education for their children.

The need for sex education, then, is great but what are its purposes? Some see sex education as a way of reducing the teenage pregnancy problem, while others simply believe students should be given correct information about sex. Still another group argues that sex education should stress personal responsibility. It is the nature of the objectives that should determine the type of program offered. If all we wish to do is to offer students correct information, a biologically based program is sufficient. However, studies have demonstrated that such programs will not lead to a reduction in teen pregnancy, because they ignore moral and values issues.

The High School and Beyond Survey, which examined the attitudes of 10,000 high school females, found a relationship between personal and parental attitudes and sexual behavior. Teens who have high educational expectations and who believe they have control over their lives are much less likely to have a child out of wedlock. Teenage girls whose parents show concern for where they are, their grades, and their future are also less likely to bear children.

While the High School and Beyond Survey did not find a relationship between having had sex education classes and bearing children, an earlier study by Zelnik and Kim (1982) found that sexually active young women who have been exposed to sex education courses are less likely to become pregnant. No support at all was found for the oft-made statement that having had sex education or birth control information increases sexual activity (Goldberg, 1987b). While opponents of sex education have used this study to show that sex education courses don't work, advocates stress that knowledge of contraception is necessary but not sufficient, that decision-making abilities and values must be discussed.

Most students want more than biological information in sex education courses; they want to discuss values. Parents also want values discussed, especially those related to abstinence. School programs are better off admitting to parents from the beginning that there is no such thing as a value-free program and discussing the values that will be stressed. This honest approach is best and is more likely to gain public support (Scales, 1982).

In an attempt to reduce teenage pregnancy, some communities, realizing that more than frank information is required, have made counselors and clinics available in the schools and have discussed with students where to go for contraceptive counseling (Zabin, Kantner, & Zelnik, 1986). The more ambitious the objectives, the more comprehensive the programs must be. A short program covering nothing but a bit of biology cannot be compared with a program that includes discussion of values and offers information concerning contraception and where contraceptive counseling is available. Studies generally show that those students who have taken a comprehensive sex education course have more factual knowledge about sex (Kirby, Alter & Scales, 1979).

There is no evidence that sex education alters personal values in any way that increases sexual behavior (Zelnik & Kim, 1982). Studies show that comprehensive sex education leads neither to higher levels of teen pregnancy nor to greater sexual activity, and some (but not all) studies find it increases the likelihood that teens will use birth control (Wattleton, 1987). One study showed not only that 15- and 16-year-olds who had taken a course in sex education were less likely to experiment at that young age but also that parental roles are not undermined by sex education programs (Furstenberg, 1985).

Finally, one interesting experimental program was conducted in Baltimore in which junior and senior high school students not only received sex education but also were presented with information in their homerooms by social workers that dealt with the services offered at a local clinic. For several hours each day, staff members assigned to each school made themselves available for individual counseling. After school, a special clinic across the street or a few blocks away offered open group discussion and individual and group counseling that emphasized personal responsibility, goal setting, parental communication, and health care, including contraception.

The results of the experiment showed better contraception and sex knowledge (something other studies have shown), as well as a delay in the age of first intercourse. Students attended the clinic sooner after initiating sexual activity, and there was an increased use of contraception among those who were sexually active. This behavior was especially noticeable among the younger teens, who usually show less responsible sexual behavior. The program altered behavior partially because access to high-quality free services, including professional counseling, was assured (Zabin, Kantner, & Zelnik, 1986).

AIDS Education

No disease in the past 100 years has had the shocking effect that AIDS (acquired immune deficiency syndrome) has had on the American public over the past several years. As of June 1989, The Center for Disease Control had received reports of 98,255 cases of AIDS in the United States (MDPH, 1989). It is projected that by 1991, the total will be close to 270,000. AIDS cripples the body's natural defenses, leaving the body vulnerable to opportunistic diseases that healthy bodies fight easily (Schram, 1986). AIDS is caused by a virus that some call the lymphadenopathy virus (LAV) and others call the HTLV-111 virus (the human t-cell lymphotropic virus) (Gong, 1985). But not everyone who comes in contact with the virus will immediately develop AIDS. An estimated 1.5 million Americans now carry the virus but display no symptoms, and no one knows for certain what percentage of these people will eventually exhibit symptoms of AIDS. However, even if these people are not presently showing symptoms, they can pass the virus on to others.

Relatively few teens today have the virus, but teen sexual and drug-taking behavior make adolescents a group at risk for coming into contact with the virus. The two most common means of transmission are through sexual contact and the use of infected drug syringes. Decisions in the areas of sex and drugs initiate patterns of behavior that affect the student for years to come (Drotman & Viadero, 1987; Flax, 1987). A third method of transmission is prenatal, which was discussed in Chapter 4.

How much do teens know about AIDS? Early studies in the 1980s showed relatively poor knowledge of AIDS, but more recent studies find that adolescents do know something about AIDS, although their knowledge is uneven. One-fifth of adolescents in one survey did not know that AIDS could be transmitted through semen (Di Clemente, Zorn, & Temoshok, 1986). Generally, teens appear now to have a moderate knowledge of AIDS, although some specifics appear to be missing.

Even when students know the facts, however, their behavior does not alter very much, and whatever changes they make are ineffective. In one survey, only 40 percent of adolescents said that they were more selective in sex partners and engaged in sexual relations less often (Carroll, 1988). When juniors and seniors in college were surveyed, they had good knowledge of AIDS, but only about one-third noted that they had made some changes in their sexual behavior, mostly in the area of becoming more selective (Roscoe and Kruger, 1990).

Studies of AIDS education programs in the schools have not been many, but the federal report "How Effective Is AIDS Education?" found that few students have changed their behavior, and those who modified their conduct did not make effective changes. This may be the "It won't happen to me" syndrome. So again, just teaching the facts may not be enough. Unfortunately, many who are "more selective" report looking for signs such as blisters or other physical manifestations, believing it is safe if they see nothing unusual about the person. Others believe that if the person is nice, he or she won't have AIDS (Strunin & Hingson, 1987). Of course, the lack of change may also indicate that some of these teens are already engaging in safer sexual practices. The goals of many AIDS programs include convincing students to delay sexual intercourse, reduce the number of sexual partners, and use birth control techniques such as condoms.

AIDS education is now mandated in most states, and the Surgeon General advocates that it begin by nine or ten years of age (Flax, 1987). One question, though, is how explicit should it be. For example, many people advocate emphasizing abstinence (Viadero, 1987b), while others believe the schools should teach about the use of condoms, which provide some protection. Should the emphasis be placed on explicit teaching of the sexual techniques that are most and least likely to cause contact with the AIDS virus? Or should it simply be placed on abstinence as the only "certain" way to prevent the spread of AIDS?

AIDS education programs must offer students the facts and discuss prevention, including sexual abstinence and fidelity, as well as the use of condoms and careful selection of sex partners, and the dangers of using needles and syringes. It must deal with knowledge, attitudes, and behavior. Taking responsibility for one's own health and the health of others are values that must be addressed (Yarber, 1988). AIDS education is a necessary part of the curriculum, but more research is needed to discover the most effective approach to changing attitudes and behavior in this area.

◆ ADAPTING TO CHANGE

It is easy to recite the list of physical changes that occur in adolescence, but more important than any list is an understanding of the subjective experiences of each adolescent in coping with these changes. Although it is more difficult to cite the cognitive changes that take place during adolescence, these changes are just as important, and their contribution to adolescent behavior should be appreciated.

When these changes are applied to an issue such as sexuality, adolescent behavior becomes more understandable. But how can parents and teachers help adolescents deal with the issues surrounding sexuality? The answer seems to lie in helping adolescents use their developing cognitive abilities to make sound personal decisions. Adolescents need information, but they also need help in developing their decision-making skills (Scales, 1983). These skills require the ability to communicate, the development of personal and spiritual values, and the ability to see the problems and consequences of any decision. These abilities can be taught and developed, but they come through dialogue, not lectures (Tangri & Moles, 1987).

Adolescents must make decisions in other areas besides sexuality— decisions about identity and vocational choice as well as decisions about interpersonal relationships. It is to these areas of social and personality development that we turn next.

SUMMARY

1. Puberty refers to the physiological changes leading to sexual maturity, while adolescence refers to the individual's psychological experiences during this period of life. The sequence of physical development during adolescence is predictable, although the age at which each change occurs varies from person to person.

2. Females normally experience their growth spurt before males do. After the growth spurt, the genital organs and breasts develop. Menstruation then occurs. In males, pubic, body, and facial hair appear after the growth spurt. At about the same time, the sexual organs mature. Deepening of the voice and widening of the shoulders occur later.

3. The fact that each new generation for the past hundred years or so has been taller and heavier and menstruated earlier than the previous one is known as the secular trend. It is leveling off or even stopping in the United States.

4. Early maturation in males is a social advantage during adolescence and early adulthood. In middle adulthood, however, early maturers tend to be less flexible and less insightful. The effects of early and late maturation in females are unclear.

5. Teenagers' health is usually considered excellent. Today, however, there are grave doubts about the health of teenagers, based upon teenagers' tendency to engage in behaviors that have negative health consequences both for the near and the long term.

6. Nutrition and eating disorders are not uncommon in adolescents. Obesity is a major medical and social problem. Anorexia nervosa, a disorder involving self-imposed starvation, can be fatal. Bulimia involves binging and purging of the system.

7. Adolescent drug use is common. Alcohol is the most abused drug, and its acceptability makes combatting excessive use difficult. Cigarette smoking has increased among females. Despite the health hazards of smoking, many teens see the social image of the smoker as a positive one. More than any other drug, marijuana symbolizes adolescent rebellion. Although some differences have been found, users and nonusers are for the most part more similar than different. Heavy users, however, are quite different. They are more angry, show a lack of responsibility, have difficulty conforming to rules, and are defiant. They use marijuana to reinforce fantasies of effortless success and to withdraw from conflicts. The use of cocaine and crack is a serious problem among adolescents as well. Drug prevention strategies have not been very successful, but some new approaches hold out more hope.

8. Suicide is the second leading cause of death among people between the ages of fifteen and twenty-one, with accidents leading the list. Most suicide victims are depressed and have a pervading sense of hopelessness. Many give clues, such as talking about suicide or giving treasured items away, or have a history of a previous suicide attempt or a suicide in their family. Suicide prevention centers are effective in giving help in emergencies.

9. During the stage of formal operations, adolescents develop the ability to find possible alternatives to problems, to separate the real from the possible, to form hypotheses and test them out, to interpret abstractions, and to think about their own thoughts.

10. Adolescents often have difficulty differentiating between their own thoughts and those of others, leading to egocentric thinking. Out of this egocentrism comes the imaginary audience, in which adolescents often believe everyone else is looking at them, and the personal fable, in which they believe their experiences and thoughts are absolutely unique in the annals of human history.

11. According to Kohlberg, adolescents' more sophisticated cognitive abilities allow them to function at higher levels of moral reasoning. However, most people do not develop past Kohlberg's Stage 4. In adolescents, there is a positive relationship between the level of moral reasoning and prosocial behavior.

12. Adolescents value marriage, family life, and friendships, and their values are apt to be similar to those of their parents. During the past twenty years, values relating to personal achievement have become more prominent than those having to do with one's relationships with society.

13. Adolescent attitudes toward sexuality are more liberal than in the past. Females are still more conservative than males, although the gap is narrowing. Males expect intimacy sooner in a relationship than females do. There has been an increase in premarital sex over the past fifty years, but adolescent sexual behavior tends to be more conservative than adolescents' attitudes would indicate.

14. Many sexually active teens do not use contraception regularly. Use increases with age. Many teens do not use any contraceptive device because they deny their sexuality, do not believe they can become pregnant, believe that contraception diminishes the romantic nature of the experience, or are ignorant of the biological facts of life.

15. Teen pregnancy is a widespread problem for everyone

concerned. Infants born to teenage mothers have more health problems, and teen mothers are more likely to drop out of school. Teenage mothers do not tend to engage in behaviors that would optimize the child's development. Teenage fathers are often found in dead-end jobs.

16. Most parents favor sex education in school but want their own values taught. Sexually active young women who are exposed to sex education are less likely to become pregnant. Sex education should aim at giving young people the skills, knowledge, and attitudes that will allow them to make intelligent choices. Sex education courses do not relieve the home of its responsibility in this area.

17. Studies show that teenagers have a moderate knowledge of AIDS but do not change their behavior in ways that would effectively reduce the likelihood that they will contract the AIDS virus.

ACTION/REACTION

But I Know It All Anyway

Parents often find telling their children about the facts of life difficult. Mr. and Mrs. Adams found it impossible. Every time they tried to talk about sex to their fifteen-year-old son, Ray, he looked bored and said, "I know all that." But Ray's parents aren't so sure.

The Adamses became very concerned when one of Ray's friends became pregnant. They held their breath, hoping Ray wasn't the father, and thankfully he wasn't. But they are not certain Ray knows as much as he thinks he does. This suspicion was heightened when Ray's older sister told them that Ray had made a few comments about male and female anatomy that were factually incorrect.

One problem Mr. and Mrs. Adams have is finding a way to tell Ray about the facts of life. They find the subject difficult to talk about. Their parents didn't tell them much, and they learned about sex from "the street." They think things are different now and that they should do their best to give their son some sex education. But how?

1. If you were Ray's parents, how would you proceed.

Mirror, Mirror on The Wall

Lisa's parents understand what early and middle adolescence is like. They know that their daughter wants to be accepted into the crowd and is very concerned about her physical image. They were prepared for her spending quite a bit of time fixing her hair and makeup and talking for hours on the telephone with her friends. They were not prepared, however, for some of her other behaviors.

Lisa is of about average weight but still considers herself overweight. She sometimes diets stringently, refusing to eat, and then breaks the diet and overeats. She refuses to shop with her mother, insisting that she go with her friend and buy her own clothing. Lisa's mother allows her to do it, but she is genuinely unhappy with the clothing that her daughter buys. She does not think that her daughter is wearing the clothing that makes her look her best or, for that matter, is wearing her hair and makeup in a way that is flattering.

Lisa seems to take what Lisa's mother considers to be minor events, such as being invited to a party, as most important, and Lisa's mother is especially concerned because Lisa's grades are not as good as they could be. All Lisa says is that her parents do not understand and have never felt rejected. Lisa talks back more, which is causing a strain on the whole family.

Lisa's parents understand the importance of the peer group and the problems involved in early adolescence, but they do not know how they should react. You are a good friend of the family, and they ask you the following questions.

1. How should they react to Lisa's clothing and fashion?
2. How should they deal with her talking back?
3. How should they deal with their daughter's dependence on her friends?

CHAPTER FOURTEEN

Social and Personality Development During The Adolescent Years

Nanny and Rose by Scott Prior.

Are These Statements True or False?

Turn the page for the correct answers. Each statement is repeated in the margin next to the paragraph in which the information can be found.

1. It is more difficult for a person to achieve an identity today than it was a century ago.
2. Periods of confusion in adolescence usually signal the probability of mental illness.
3. Once an individual forms an identity, the identity is immune to change despite disruptions in life.
4. Males can achieve intimacy before they find their identity, whereas females must find their identity before they can achieve true intimacy.
5. Peer influence usually peaks during the late junior high school and early high school years.
6. When parents communicate with their adolescent children, they tend to explain their views rather than try to understand their teens' opinions and attitudes.
7. Parents become more comfortable with their role as their children proceed through the years of adolescence.
8. Friends try to control the adolescent's behavior more than parents do.
9. Most parents think the generation gap is greater than it actually is.
10. College students today are less likely than they were fifteen years ago to believe that an occupation is appropriate only for either males or females.
11. Within the past decade, high school course work has become more rigorous.
12. Most high school dropouts have intelligence scores within the normal range.

599

Answers to True False Statements

1. True.
2. False. Correct statement: Periods of confusion are not unusual in adolescence and do not necessarily signal mental illness.
3. False. Correct statement: Although identity achievement is the most stable of all the statuses, a person's identity can change if the individual's life situation alters substantially.
4. False. Correct statement: For both males and females, identity achievers are generally better able to form intimate relationships. When a gender difference is found, females can sometimes achieve intimacy before identity, but very few men can.
5. True.
6. True.
7. False. Correct statement: Parents are actually more comfortable with their role when their children are eleven than when they are seventeen years of age.
8. False. Correct statement: Parents usually try to control the adolescent's behavior more than friends do.
9. False. Correct statement: Most parents minimize the differences in attitudes between them and their children.
10. True.
11. True.
12. True.

◆ WILL THE REAL ADOLESCENT PLEASE STAND UP?

What words would you use to describe a teenager? Do such adjectives as rebellious, conforming, searching, peer-oriented, sensitive, insensitive, confused, irreverent, independent, stressful, alienated, private, ambivalent, moody, insecure, and tense come to mind? Some of these terms seem contradictory. The well-known striving for independence is matched by the need for security and dependence. The hopefulness and future orientation accompany feelings of hopelessness and confusion.

The period of adolescence is usually perceived as a time of confusion, stress, and rebellion. In one of the first major modern works on adolescence, G. Stanley Hall (1904) described the period as one of "storm and stress." This has remained the popular conception of adolescence, especially in Hollywood films, which often portray adolescents as confused, alienated, and isolated and buffeted between the old and useless standards and beliefs of the older generation and the more modern but dangerous examples of their peers. Relationships with parents are viewed as argumentative, and slavish devotion to peers is shown as the norm. With the possible exception of old age, no stage in life is subjected to more stereotyping than adolescence. The stereotypes and misconceptions are responsible for the dislike and distrust that many people hold for adolescents (Varenhorst, 1984).

Yet such simplistic notions of adolescents often meet with murmurs of disagreement, especially among adolescents themselves. Many adolescents have good relationships with their parents and are not totally conforming to their peers. They make their own decisions and do not seem very confused. Which of these two views of adolescence comes closer to describing what really occurs during the teen years?

◆ THE SEARCH FOR A PERSONAL IDENTITY

Adolescents are negotiating a transitional stage between the simpler elementary school years and the commitments of early adulthood. They must somehow integrate the lessons of the past with the realities of the present and the possibilities of the future. They must evaluate and develop their unique abilities and choose a lifestyle, vocation, and personal definition. In other words, the adolescent must search for and form a personal identity.

Identity vs. Role Confusion

Who am I?
Where do I belong?
Where am I going?

These three questions typify the adolescent's search for a personal identity (Ruittenbeck, 1964). Erik Erikson (1959) saw the positive outcome of adolescence as the formation of a solid, personal **identity,** while the negative outcome of adolescence is an aimlessness known as **role confusion** or **role diffusion** (the state of now knowing who one really is). Adolescents are walking a tightrope. Their task is to surrender the older dependent ties and childhood identifications with their parents and develop a separate identity while continuing a healthy relationship with their elders (Siegel, 1982). If they are to function as adults, they must be able to make their own decisions. They cannot simply be carbon copies of their parents. On the other hand, the attitudes and values gained from parents during childhood serve as anchors, providing security in a sea of change. If adolescents totally abandon these attitudes and values, they may become bewildered and utterly confused. In addition, surrendering older ideals assumes all such ideals to be dysfunctional, a conclusion that is difficult to support. Adolescents have a difficult course to chart. But is it more difficult today than it was years ago?

identity
The sense of knowing who you are.

role confusion (role diffusion)
In psychosocial theory, the negative outcome of adolescence, which involves feelings of aimlessness and a failure to develop a personal identity.

Is Finding an Identity More Difficult Today?

Developing an identity involves choosing from various alternatives. Knowing what alternatives are available and having some freedom to choose are important considerations. Imagine yourself a farmer in the plains of the old American West in the early 1800s. Your life is mapped out for you. You will marry the boy or girl a few farms down the road, buy a farm in the same area, and have as many children as possible so that the land can be worked efficiently. News travels slowly. Your knowledge of the alternatives available is minimal, and your freedom to act is even less.

Now let's look at the situation in that same Western environment today. Television, the print media, and the movies have brought almost instant information to the community from all over the world. Schooling is universal, and farming has become so technological that it requires higher education. Along with this information explosion, different values and many new choices surround teenagers. No longer is the young teenage girl expected to bear as many children as possible. No longer is farming the only vocation available. No longer are people so isolated that other possibilities are unknown. People now have many more choices and a greater degree of freedom to choose their own course. And with choice come doubt and anxiety.

These factors—more choices and a greater degree of freedom to choose—combine to make forming an identity more difficult today than it was a century ago. One other factor is important. Society is changing at a faster rate than ever before. The skills necessary to prosper in the years ahead are likely to change along with the rest of society. Not long ago, a high school education was considered relatively unnecessary, computers were the toys of science fiction writers, and manufacturing jobs were considered secure. The lack of stability in society means that teens must predict what vocations and skills will be needed in a changing world if they are to prepare adequately for it.

The Four Identity Statuses

Achieving an identity depends on two variables: **crisis** and **commitment** (Marcia, 1967). In a **crisis,** one actively faces and questions aspects of one's personal identity. For instance, a student may have to choose a major and be faced with this decision when approaching the junior year. In the personal sphere, the student may be dating someone for a while and may have to decide whether to get more deeply involved. The second aspect, **commitment,** involves making a firm decision concerning some question and following a plan of action that reflects this decision. A person who investigates many vocational choices and decides on a business career follows the appropriate course of study. The decision to end a relationship or to become engaged leads to different behavioral paths.

Adolescents differ in the extent to which they have experienced crises or made commitments. A prominent researcher in this field, James Marcia (1967, 1980), grouped adolescents into four categories according to their experiences with crises and commitments (Table 14.1). One group of adolescents, termed **identity diffused** consisted of adolescents who may or may not have experienced a crisis but have not made any commitments. The **identity foreclosure** group consisted of teens who had not experienced a crisis but had made commitments anyway. The **identity mora-**

---

1. *TRUE OR FALSE?*

It is more difficult for a person to achieve an identity today than it was a century ago.

crisis
In psychosocial theory, a time in which a person actively faces and questions aspects of his or her own identity.

commitment
In psychosocial theory, making a decision concerning some question involved in identity formation and following a plan of action reflecting the decision.

identity diffusion
An identity status resulting in confusion, aimlessness, and a sense of emptiness.

identity foreclosure
An identity status marked by a premature identity decision.

identity moratorium
An identity status in which a person is actively searching for an identity.

torium group contained adolescents who were presently experiencing a crisis but had not yet made any commitments. The **identity achievers** were adolescents who had already experienced crises and had made their commitments. It is worth taking a more detailed look at each of these statuses.

IDENTITY DIFFUSION An individual in the identity-diffused state has not made any commitments and is not presently in the process of forming any. Even if there has been a crisis, it has not resulted in any decisions (Waterman, 1982). Identity-diffused people may actively seek noncommitment, actually avoiding demanding situations. They may also appear aimless, aloof, drifting, and empty (Orlofsky, Marcia, & Lesser, 1973). Although they may experience periods of confusion, they are not mentally ill, and their psychological profiles appear normal (Oshman & Manosevitz, 1974). These people's self-esteem, however, is not very high. Some students become alarmed at this description because they have experienced periods in which the description very closely fits them or someone close to them.

Identity diffusion is negative only when an individual leaves adolescence and the early part of young adulthood without making commitments. A period of confusion often precedes the establishment of a firm identity. Adolescents face decisions in many areas of identity formation at the same time, including sexual intimacy, occupational choice, and psychosocial self-definition, and periods of bewilderment are not uncommon (Erikson, 1959). Overprotected adolescents may find themselves challenged in college when they are exposed to many different people espousing different attitudes and moral standards. They have to evaluate

identity achievement
An identity status in which a person has developed a solid personal identity.

2. TRUE OR FALSE?

Periods of confusion in adolescence usually signal the probability of mental illness.

TABLE 14.1: James Marcia's Four Identity Statuses

IDENTITY STATUS	DEFINITION
Identity Achievement	An identity achiever has experienced doubt (crisis) in personal goals and values, has considered alternatives, and is committed at least tentatively to some expressed value positions and career plans.
Identity Foreclosure	A foreclosure displays a commitment similar to that of the identity achiever but has not appraised alternatives to personal goals and values; choices often express parental preferences.
Identity Moratorium	A moratorium has questioned goals and values and considered alternatives but is still doubtful and uncommitted; predominating is an active effort to become informed and to make suitable choices.
Identity Diffusion	An identity diffuser might or might not have experienced doubt over goals and values; he or she does not evidence a serious or realistic inclination to examine concerns about goals and values; he or she expresses no commitments to an ideology or to career plans.

SOURCE: Hummel and Roselli, 1983.

these people and their attitudes in the light of past learning and experiences. At the same time, they may be faced with vocational and political considerations, such as which groups to join or which positions of leadership to vie for. We might expect a period of diffusion to occur, and indeed it often does.

IDENTITY FORECLOSURE Do you know people who always seem to have it "all together," who knew what they wanted at a very early age, and who appear very confident and secure? These seemingly lucky people have formed a commitment, but it may not be their own. It may be one handed down to them by their parents. They identify very well—perhaps too well—with their parents. For example, a boy may have known since childhood that he was destined to enter his father's business. He doesn't consider anything else, and he refuses to develop any talents that lie in another direction. In another situation, a young woman may have chosen her mate very early in life and not explored other possible choices or alternatives to marriage.

Identity foreclosure is a secure status. The people in this group appear to function well and do not suffer through periods of crisis. They show little anxiety (Marcia & Friedman, 1970). Identity-foreclosed people are often envied by their peers. After all, they have a direction in life and are following a definite path. But this security is purchased at a price. Their path is not one they have chosen themselves, and foreclosed individuals may later find themselves mired in an unhappy lifestyle. As Petitpas (1978, p. 558) notes, "This outward appearance might only be a temporary veneer that could age and crack in time leaving the individuals with a crisis of being locked into an occupation or marriage in which they can no longer function." We can only wonder how many adults are unhappy because they failed to discover what they really wanted in life and instead merely followed a path laid out for them by someone else.

There is another side to identity foreclosure. Some adolescents may be foreclosed because they do not have the opportunity to search or the knowledge of what is available. Many poor and minority youths simply do not believe they have many choices. Some must enter the labor force as soon as possible to support themselves and their families. Others may not have the basic academic skills necessary for more advanced study that would open up better vocational opportunities. For these teens, foreclosure is forced on them by circumstances, by lack of knowledge about their choices, or by their belief that they do not have any power to control their own destinies. (More about identity formation and minority youth is presented in the Cross-Cultural Current on page 606.)

IDENTITY MORATORIUM Adolescents who are presently experiencing a crisis but whose commitments are vague are considered to be in the identity moratorium status. This is a period of delay in which a person is not yet ready to make a definite commitment (Erikson, 1968). Many possibilities are being explored, some of them radical, but final commitments tend to be more conservative. Many who were radicals during the 1960s are now living conservative lives and are members of the political

There is nothing wrong with people entering the "family business" as long as it is their own choice and is not forced upon them.

establishment. They often have made professional commitments that involve human services (Nassi, 1981).

The moratorium state is not a happy one. The adolescent may be dissatisfied with everything and everyone. The campus reformer may indeed be searching for something. This reformer sees everything that is wrong but is less successful in suggesting what realistic steps can be taken to alleviate the problems. People in this status are active and troubled. Quick to debate and frequently in opposition to their parents, they are often hostile toward their peers as well. They are engaged in what seem like perpetual struggles with authority figures (Donovan, 1975).

Identity moratorium is the least stable of all the statuses (Waterman, 1982), but it may be a necessary status, for when a person makes a commitment, it is that individuals' own, made after a period of searching for one's own answers. Studies show that about three-quarters of college students who were in this status when they began college could later be said to have achieved an independent identity by graduation (Waterman & Waterman, 1971).

IDENTITY ACHIEVEMENT Identity achievers have made it. They have experienced their crises, solved them, and made their commitments. Their goals are realistic, and they can cope with shifts in the environment (Orlofsky, Marcia, & Lesser, 1973). Their independent personal identities are not carbon copies of their parents' identities, nor are they totally the opposite of their parents'. Their identity includes some of the parents' values and attitudes, while omitting others. They are well adjusted (Bernard, 1981) and have good relationships both with peers and with authority figures (Donovan, 1975).

Predictions from Identity Status

If you know someone's identity status, can you predict anything about the person's behavior or standing in the community? The answer is yes, but we must keep in mind that people can move from one group to another as they experience a crisis or make a new commitment. Although the identity achiever status is relatively stable, it can change (Douvan & Adelson, 1966). An unusual experience might lead one back to a moratorium. For example, after spending a number of years preparing to become a newspaper reporter, one young woman found she could not find a job and had to search all over again for an occupational identity. Or consider the divorced person who may have to search anew for a personal or social identity because the original one is no longer viable.

Research shows that there is a relationship between one's present status and specific behaviors. For example, identity achievers have the highest grade-point averages of any of the other statuses (Cross & Allen, 1970) and have better study habits (Waterman & Waterman, 1971). Identity achievers also perform better under stress (Muuss, 1982). If we compare people in all four statuses, identity achievers show the least self-consciousness, while identity-diffused individuals exhibit the most self-consciousness—perhaps because identity achievers have a higher accep-

3. TRUE OR FALSE?

Once an individual forms an identity, the identity is immune to change despite disruptions in life.

Identity and Minority Status

Consider the adolescent trying to answer the many questions that surround vocational, spiritual, and personal identity. Minority youth have an additional task, as they must also develop some ethnic identity. But how does this take place?

Jean Phinney (1989) suggests that Erikson's and Marcia's work can be helpful in understanding the development of ethnic identity. Many minority youth begin by internalizing the views held by the majority group of their own group. This is similar to identity foreclosure in that people may without question take on the values to which they have been exposed. However, this does not always have to be negative. It is possible for these people, if they are exposed to positive ideas, to be proud. It is also possible that some minority youth have not been faced with issues of ethnicity and therefore give little thought to them. These young people may not consider ethnicity very important and do not think about it. This might be considered diffusion, but little research has been conducted in this area. Phinney sees these two statuses as constituting a general first stage in identity formation.

A period of exploration then ensues. It is not always clear what stimulates this exploration. This period of exploration, or moratorium, involves experimentation and inquiry. There is an attempt to clarify personal implications of eth-

nicity. About one-third of all black eighth graders in an integrated school were engaged in some form of exploration involving such activities as talking with their families about such issues and reading books on the subject (Phinney & Tarver, 1988). This is hypothesized as the second stage of the process.

Last, there is identity achievement. These people have resolved questions and made commitments. They feel better about who they are and are confident. This entails an acceptance of themselves as members of a minority group.

Jean Phinney (1989) used both interviews and questionnaires to determine whether the proposed stages of ethnic identity development can be applied to adolescents of different ethnic backgrounds. Ninety-one American-born tenth graders from two high schools in the Los Angeles area were given measures of ego identity and adjustment. They included fourteen Asian Americans, twenty-five African Americans, twenty-five Hispanics, and twenty-seven white students of European ancestry.

More than half of all subjects in all three minority groups were diffused or foreclosed. A little less than one quarter were in the moratorium stage (one-quarter of all Hispanics), and again just less than a quarter were in the identity-achieved stage. The percentages were remarkably similar across ethnic groups. The white subjects could not be placed into a status because, with the exception of a few subjects

intimacy vs. isolation
The sixth psychosocial stage, occurring during young adulthood, in which the positive outcome is a development of deep interpersonal relationships and the negative outcome is a flight from close relationships.

tance of self and a more stable self-definition (Adams, Abraham, & Markstrom, 1987). Identity-foreclosed people score much higher on measures of authoritarianism and are more conservative, obedient, and loyal to conventional values than people in the other statuses (Muuss, 1982). In early adolescence, they also show a tendency to underachieve in school (Streitmatter, 1989). Moratorium subjects are the most anxious.

Probably the most important finding is that identity achievement is linked to the depth of intimacy developed in early adulthood. The ego crisis of young adulthood can be expressed as **intimacy vs. isolation** (Erikson, 1968). Intimacy involves the development of very close personal relationships, while isolation involves a lack of commitment. Intimacy requires that two people share their identities, not that there be a complete merging of selves. Problems may occur for people who choose marriage or parenthood as a way out of an identity dilemma. These people really have not resolved the identity issue—it is still on the back burner,

who noted their European ancestry, ethnicity was not an identity issue, and they could not think of anything besides American.

Scores for ego identity showed a consistent increase from the first stage (diffusion/foreclosure) to the third stage (achievement of ethnic identity). The three ethnic groups showed no significant differences as to stage or adjustment. The three groups saw different issues as important in the resolution of ethnic identity, though. For Asian Americans, pressures to achieve academically and concerns about college admissions quotas were important issues. Asian Americans also felt the need to distinguish themselves from recent immigrants. Many black females were struggling with white standards of beauty that did not apply to them, while black males seemed more concerned with possible job discrimination and the need to distinguish themselves from a negative image of black adolescents. Hispanics saw prejudice as a recurrent theme, and some subjects noted conflicting values between their own and the majority culture.

This study showed that the three stages of ethnic identity development hold for a number of ethnic groups. Regardless of the specific group, minority youth face a need to deal with their membership in an ethnic group. More than half of all the subjects were in the initial stage, characterized by lack of exploration. About one-quarter of the subjects showed evidence of involvement in an ethnic identity search, although this stage was initiated not by some dramatic encounter but rather by an increasing awareness of the importance of the issue and the need to understand it. The other one-quarter of the subjects were identity achievers. It is possible that with increasing age, high school students will show greater evidence of ethnic identity search.

Only one-fifth of all the subjects, including some from each stage, had negative attitudes towards their own group, including a desire to change their ethnicity if they could.

The study also demonstrated the parallel between ethnic and ego identity. The ethnic identity stages were significantly related to an independent general measure of ego identity. There is a link between ethnic identity and ego identity, but more research is needed in this area.

The process of ethnic identity development has implications for overall adjustment. Minority group membership itself did not affect adjustment, as scores did not differ among the three minority groups or between the minority groups' scores and the scores of their white peers. However, those minority adolescents who had explored and were clear about the meaning of their ethnicity showed higher scores on self-evaluation, sense of mastery, social and peer interactions, and family relations than the diffused and foreclosed adolescents. Ethnic identity, not membership, is the key to understanding self-esteem and adjustment.

This model gives us an understanding of the development of ethnic identity. It seems that it is important for minority youth to come to understand, accept, and value their heritage and that this is a part of their ego identity as a whole.

Source: Phinney, J. S., Stages of Ethnic Identity Development in Minority Group Adolescents. *Journal of Early Adolescence*, 1989, 9, 34–49.

waiting for an opportunity to show itself. Resolution of identity issues can be delayed, but not always shelved forever.

People in the moratorium and achievement statuses experience deeper levels of intimacy than people in the other two statuses (Fitch & Adams, 1983). In a landmark study, Orlofsky and colleagues (1973) determined the identity status of fifty-three male juniors and seniors at a university in New York. The researchers also rated the subjects on the presence or absence of close interpersonal relationships and the degree of openness, closeness, and commitment in these relationships. Data on personality and social relationships were also collected.

Identity achievers scored very high on measures of intimacy, while the identity-diffused and identity-foreclosed subjects scored poorly. The foreclosed and diffused subjects were the most isolated. The moratorium subjects were somewhere in the middle. Identity-foreclosed subjects had the greatest need for social approval, were least autonomous, and had not modified their family ties. Autonomy and intimacy were related, and identity achievers were found to have successful, mature, intimate relationships; moratorium subjects were similar to achievement subjects, but a bit behind. Most moratorium subjects had intimate relationships with close friends but had not formed enduring heterosexual relationships. Foreclosed and diffused subjects were involved in some relationships, but the relationships lacked the depth and genuine closeness of the achievement group. The results of this study confirm that progress toward achieving a mature identity is related to the ability to achieve intimacy.

Although the basic relationship between identity and intimacy is correct, some authorities now claim that the relationship may be slightly different for males and females. In one study, a number of women, but only one man, were found to be high in intimacy but low in identity. It may be that some women deal successfully with intimacy issues prior to identity issues (Schiedel & Marcia, 1985). This surprising finding may have to do with the difference between the search for identity that males and females conduct.

The Process of Identity Formation

How does a person form an identity? A healthy identity must be fused from past, present, and future considerations. Taking everything from one's past may lead to identity foreclosure, yet taking nothing may lead to identity diffusion. Most people who progress through a moratorium do develop a solid identity (La Voie, 1976), and periods of role diffusion do not necessarily indicate any lasting personality problems.

The years between eighteen and twenty-one seem especially crucial for development of an identity. Before this time, the overwhelming number of young people are either foreclosed or diffused (Archer, 1982; Meilman, 1979), and only very limited changes occur before or during the high school years (Waterman, 1982). The experience of schooling, especially college, seems to encourage people to question.

If forced to describe the activities that seem to be most important, they would have to be personal searching and role experimentation. Finding an identity requires questioning and reconsidering older identifications and values (Newman & Newman, 1988). This may take effort and cause much anxiety.

It is not unusual for students to envy people who seem to have already made up their minds, but shortcuts to identity formation can be dangerous. Sometimes people try to take a shortcut by accepting the values and aspirations of other people. This reduces the anxiety but is a type of foreclosure. Others suspend their search for identity by adopting an all-embracing ideology or cause. This may involve a cult and a slavish devotion to an ideology. The cult's ideas are always fixed and are not to be debated but are to be totally accepted. The adoption of this ideology gives the adolescent a ready answer to all questions, but just as in the case of an individual who completely accepts the values of other people, it is purchased at a price. There is no further searching or personal growth.

4. *TRUE OR FALSE?*

Males can achieve intimacy before they find their identity, whereas females must find their identity before they can achieve true intimacy.

Do Males and Females Take Different Paths to Identity?

Males and females may approach identity formation from different perspectives. Their searches and their abilities to explore alternatives may differ. For one thing, their parents' attitudes towards lifestyles and the models available to males and females are not the same. In addition, males tend to focus on intrapersonal factors, such as vocational identity and personal identity, while women are more likely to tie their identities to interpersonal relationships (Schiedel & Marcia, 1985).

I sometimes ask students in my classes whether they think about the impact their future vocation will have on their family life. The responses of males and females differ. Males are more likely to focus solely on economic issues while females, who are interested in economic issues too, also focus on how their vocational pursuits will combine with future family and caregiving responsibilities. Jobs and vocational identities, which are now considered by females to be part of their lives, are not necessarily seen as vital factors in self-actualization but rather are sometimes viewed as something they can fall back on, allowing some measure of independence (Hyde, 1985). The future family remains the focus of their quest (Greenglass & Devins, 1982).

Like any generalization, this is not true in every case. Some men do consider their family roles, and some women do not define achievement in interpersonal terms. However, the differences do seem to exist. The extent to which this may change in the future is open to question. Neither males nor females now see a woman's place as exclusively in the home (Astin, Korn & Berz, 1989). This may mean that women are accurately perceiving their new role as both worker and primary family caregiver. Men may not yet see their dual responsibility in these balanced terms.

There may be consequences to the fact that men still do not see their role in balanced terms. As discussed in Chapter 7, women often find themselves with two full-time jobs, one at their place of employment and another at home, while men do not. There may be conflicts between what Arlie Hochschild described as "faster-changing women and slower-changing men" (1989, p. 11). Women may expect a more equal sharing of the homemaking and child-rearing chores, while men, who do not see their role or identity as changing that much, may not. The differing expectations may form a basis for dissatisfaction and interpersonal problems. It remains to be seen how different couples will deal with these differing expectations within a marriage.

◆ RELATIONSHIPS WITH PARENTS AND PEERS

"I wish my parents would get off my back. They're always criticizing everything I do. They must have been saints when they were in their teens. If they would just let me alone, I'd be okay."

"My parents and I get along pretty well. They listen to me and I listen to them—although we don't agree on everything. I have a good set of friends, and my parents like them."

"The one problem I have with my parents is that they don't seem to trust me. They think I'm still eleven years old. They don't want to discuss rules, they just want to lay down the law. They repeat everything four hundred times, especially the warnings."

These are some of the responses from fourteen- and fifteen-year-olds when I asked about their relationships with their parents. During adolescence, the relationship between parents and children changes. One task of adolescence is to establish a firm and independent identity, and this necessitates some separation between parent and child and involves attaining some degree of independence and autonomy. Parents are often put in the position of criticizing the same behavior they themselves indulged in when they were adolescents and that they fully expect from their teens (Petersen & Offer, 1979). The stereotype of the adolescent-parent-peer triangle is often one of tremendous conflict between parent and child and the almost total replacement of parental influence by peers. This stereotype, so popular in the movies and on television, has largely been discarded by psychologists as not in keeping with the facts.

Parental vs. Peer Influences

Fitting into the crowd is very important, especially to younger teens.

It is no secret that peer influence increases during middle childhood and into adolescence. The amount of time spent with parents declines, and the sheer quantity of time spent with friends increases. The peer group serves a number of functions in adolescence. It often provides support for adolescents who are striving for independence, because peers are facing the same challenges. Peers help adolescents develop social skills and an identity (Coleman, 1981). The peer group serves as a reference group and gives teens another evaluation of their actions. In early adolescence, dependence on parents decreases and dependence on peers increases. Adolescents become more emotionally autonomous from their parents; they idealize their parents less and relinquish some of their childhood dependence on them. This is accompanied by increased susceptibility to peer influences (Steinberg & Silverberg, 1986). Yet the picture of slavish devotion to peers does not fit the facts.

Adolescents in late junior high and early high school (eighth and ninth grade) seem to be most influenced by peers. Thomas Berndt (1979) presented 251 children from third, sixth, ninth, and eleventh or twelfth grades with hypothetical situations in which a child was encouraged by peers to perform antisocial acts (such as stealing or cheating), neutral acts (such as choosing hobbies, entertainment, and eating places), or prosocial acts (such as performing charitable deeds). In third grade, conformity to parents was greater than conformity to peer expectations. Berndt found evidence of conflict, but third graders usually decided in the direction of their parents. Peer influences became more pronounced between the third grade and the sixth grade, yet Berndt found no increase in parent-peer conflict.

In this period, children can isolate the peer world from the familial environment. Many early adolescents use language with their peers that they do not use at home. When I taught junior high school, I found that many girls who were not allowed by their parents to wear jeans or makeup at school would change into a pair of jeans or apply makeup they had hidden in their lockers. At the end of the school day, they would change back and scrub their faces clean. While some had argued with their parents over these issues, many simply decided to live in two worlds. Early adolescents seem to be able to separate their worlds—not discussing with their parents what they do with their peers, and vice versa.

By ninth grade, peer conformity is at its peak, and conflict between parents and adolescents is common. Berndt believes that two factors are involved in this increasing conflict. First, antisocial conformity is at its peak here, and parents who may be able to look the other way concerning hairstyles and taste in music (more neutral stimuli) cannot disguise their concern about antisocial acts. Second, the push toward independence is particularly strong at this age. Berndt cites studies showing that adolescents at this point often report the greatest number of disagreements with their parents. By the junior and senior years of high school, some conflict remains, but peer influence seems to decline somewhat, and conventional behavior increases. This pattern continues into young adulthood. The children's responses to these situations showed that conformity to peers for antisocial acts peaked at the ninth grade level and declined thereafter (Berndt, 1979).

Males are generally more willing than females to follow their peers in antisocial behavior, but in other facets of conformity, this is not the case (Brown, Clasen, & Eicher, 1986). Traditionally, females have been considered less autonomous and more conforming. However, any gender gap that may have existed in autonomy and conformity is narrowing and even disappearing (Steinberg & Silverberg, 1986).

5. TRUE OR FALSE?

Peer influence usually peaks during the late junior high school and early high school years.

Areas of Influence

If teenagers have questions concerning the latest styles or musical trends, whom would they consult—parents or peers? If they have questions concerning their future occupation, would they ask peers or seek out some older person? Once we rid ourselves of the idea that parents are unimportant and that the peer group means everything, things become much clearer. We can give the peer group its due and reserve for authority figures other areas.

The influence of either generation depends on the situation (Brittain, 1969). Adolescents perceive peers and parents as competent guides in different areas (Brittain, 1963). The peer group is viewed as more knowledgeable in surface and social areas, such as styles and feelings about school, but in deeper values, adolescents report being closer to their parents. Hans Sebald (1989) asked high school students in 1963, 1976, and 1982, "if you had to decide between your friends' and your parents' opinion and feelings in the following situations, whose opinions would you consider more important?" As expected, the answer depended on the

Studies show that the peer group has its greatest impact on such areas as dress, music and style.

situation. Family, educational, and financial concerns were more parent oriented, while almost all social activities were peer oriented. Sebald also found an increase in general peer orientation between 1963 and 1976 and then a reduction from 1976 to 1982, but not quite back to the 1963 levels.

This division of influence meshes well with common experience. Adolescents are influenced by the opinions of people who they believe have superior knowledge in a particular area. For instance, I have found students eager for vocational information from perceived sources of expertise, often older adults. This does not mean that they do not discuss career options with their friends, just that in this area they seem to realize that some older people know more.

It is a mistake to see adolescents as completely buffeted between parents and peers without minds of their own. Decisions adolescents make are often based on a reasoned sense of independence. Adolescents are able to sort alternatives into levels, assigning priority to various questions (Larson, 1972). In other words, in less important areas, such as whether to go to a party, adolescents will accept the opinions of parents or peers, but in more important issues, such as whether to tell the principal who broke the door, they are likely to make an independent decision (Larson, 1972). Even so, the influence of the peer group is impressive.

Communication with Parents and Peers

Communication with peers differs greatly from communication with parents during adolescence. Parents are more directive, sharing their wisdom, whereas communication with peers often shows greater mutuality

It is important to listen to teenagers. Unfortunately, adults are frequently more interested in explaining their points of view to teens than in listening to them.

and sharing of similar experiences (Hunter, 1984). Parents may not like to listen to their adolescents who are in the process of formulating their own values and opinions, especially if their children are taking positions that are different from theirs. On the other hand, parents may counter these unwanted views with a long lecture, which is usually an ineffective method of communication. Parents tend to concentrate more on explaining their own viewpoints than on trying to understand their child's views (Hunter, 1985). In short, parents are more directive with their adolescents, while peers tend to share more and appear to be more open with their peers. In addition, much parental communication comes as criticism. This is unfortunate because positive and supportive communication enables children to explore their identity in greater depth. Generally, parents who support their children by creating an atmosphere that fosters respect for the opinions of others, mutuality, and tolerance make it possible for their children to explore identity alternatives (Grotevant & Cooper, 1986). Adolescents who have the support of their families actually feel freer to explore identity issues (Cooper, Grotevant, & Condon, 1982).

Parenting style also continues to have an effect on adolescents. Children whose parents use an authoritative style of parenting earn higher grades than their peers who describe their parents as using either a permissive or an authoritarian style (Dornbusch, Ritter, Liederman, Roberts, & Fraleigh, 1987). This is consistent across ethnic, socioeconomic, and various family structures. In a longitudinal study, Laurence Steinberg and his colleagues (1989) found that adolescents who described their parents as treating them in a warm, democratic, but firm manner were likely to develop positive attitudes and beliefs about their achievement and work and, again, do well in school.

6. TRUE OR FALSE?

When parents communicate with their adolescent children, they tend to explain their own views rather than try to understand their teens' opinions and attitudes.

Renegotiating Relationships with Parents

Communication problems sometimes make it difficult for adolescents to renegotiate their relationships with their parents. Adolescents must redefine their relationships with their parents and their roles within the family in preparation for leaving the family and leading independent lives (Feldman & Gehring, 1988). This redefinition is explained by two popular models (Grotevant & Cooper, 1985). The first sees the adolescent severing his or her ties with parents, often leading to a new dependency on peers. The other sees parent-child relationships basically as stable throughout adolescence and downplays the idea that meaningful conflict arises.

If we look at early adolescence, we see some evidence for the first theory, and if one looks at late adolescence, some evidence for the second can be deduced. However, the newer perspective of adolescence as a whole sees the relationship between adolescents and their parents as moving toward a new symmetry and equality as the years of adolescence roll by. This view sees autonomy and remaining connected with one's family as complementary, not opposite, processes. Adolescents who consider themselves most autonomous rate their relationships with their parents as close, perceive their parents as role models, and often turn to their parents for advice (Kandel & Lesser, 1969).

Adolescence is not a time of complete break or total stability. Rather, a gradual renegotiation between parents and adolescents takes place as the relationship changes from the more authoritarian, superior-subordinate relationship to one that involves greater mutuality (Grotevant & Cooper, 1986). The growth of independence and autonomy does not require severing ties with parents and refusing to use them as pillars of emotional support. In fact, it is very likely that parents continue to be called upon to support the adolescent's growth and development in many areas, including identity formation and independence (Ryan & Lynch, 1989). Earlier evidence tended to overemphasize the separateness of adolescents from their families and underestimated the continuing family connectedness that continues to exist (Feldman & Gehring, 1988). Most adolescents report closeness and positive feelings between family members (Barnes & Olson, 1985).

Successful parenting requires some change in parenting practices, and some conflict between parents and adolescents does occur. Parents expect their children at age seventeen to make some decisions on their own. They realize some renegotiation of power is necessary. This is reflected in parental behavior, as parents are more autocratic and interact in a more rule based manner with their eleven-year-olds than with their seventeen-year-olds. At the same time, although their relationships become less rule bound as their children progress through adolescence, these parents become more uncomfortable with their role as parents (Newman, 1989). This change towards greater mutuality and sharing power is not an easy one for parents to undertake.

The difficulties parents and adolescents have in renegotiating power are reflected in the changes in family cohesiveness that are perceived by adolescents. As adolescents progress from the sixth to the twelfth grade,

There are two models of parent-adolescent relationships. One emphasizes conflict while the other does not. The conflict theory seems much more applicable to early rather than later adolescence.

7. TRUE OR FALSE?

Parents become more comfortable with their role as their children proceed through the years of adolescence.

they see a decrease in family cohesiveness and more equivalence in power, although parental power still is seen as greater than the power of children. The ideal family is portrayed by both parents and adolescents as both high in cohesion and with moderate power differences between parents and their children and with equality of power between parents (Feldman & Gehring, 1988).

The decrease in cohesion coincides with the decreasing amount of time spent with parents and the increase in peer involvement and autonomy. Although it is common to find adolescents feeling somewhat more distant from their parents, this decrease in family cohesion is not seen as desirable, and adolescents often express a desire for more family closeness. Adolescents, then, see family cohesion as compatible with autonomy. Adolescents frequently see this reduction in parental power, especially with their fathers, as the teen years progress, but they still see a difference and do not believe exact equality of power to be desirable.

Dissatisfaction with power and cohesiveness is related to age. Sixth graders are dissatisfied with their power but not with family cohesion, while twelfth graders are more dissatisfied with cohesion than power. Satisfaction with cohesion, then, decreases as satisfaction with power increases. This is true for both male and female adolescents (Feldman & Gehring, 1988). These changes, including the renegotiation of power, take place gradually over the adolescent years.

Just how does this renegotiation take place? Fumiyo Tao Hunter and James Youniss (1982) looked at changes in three functions of interpersonal relationships in students from the fourth, seventh, and tenth grades and in college. The control function involved being told what to do and disagreeing. The intimacy function described self-disclosure and empathy, among other aspects of the relationship. The nurture function referred to giving and helping acts.

The control function was found to be greater in the parent-adolescent relationship across all age groups. In other words, at every age, parents try to control the behavior of adolescents much more than friends do. The attempts at control, though, lessen as the adolescent enters college. The intimacy function showed a change as the adolescent matured. It was greater for parents at fourth grade but was surpassed by peers by tenth grade. By mid-adolescence to late adolescence (seventh to tenth grade), friendship patterns become more intimate, and there is a decrease in this function for parents, after which there is a characteristic increase.

Again we see the pattern in which mid-adolescence seems to be the most trying period for parent-child relationships, with improvement occurring later on. There is an increase in parent-child conflict and disagreement between early and mid-adolescence (Montemayor, 1983). Even though friendships continue to become more intimate in later adolescence, the increase in parental intimacy demonstrates that the growing intimacy with age-mates need not interfere with that portion of the relationship with parents. The nurturance factor remains very high throughout adolescence for the parent-child relationship. Although there is an increase in this helping function for friends, it never surpasses the level of helpfulness in parent-child interactions.

8. TRUE OR FALSE?

Friends try to control the adolescent's behavior more than parents do.

The most interesting change is in intimacy. Ruth Sharabany and her colleagues (1981) investigated changes in this area in fifth, seventh, ninth, and eleventh graders. Intimacy involves frankness and spontaneity, sensitivity and knowing, attachment, exclusiveness, imposing and taking, trust and loyalty. Male relationships generally show a lower degree of intimacy than those formed by females. Females are more expressive and report more giving and sharing than males. Females also develop intimacy with the opposite sex faster than males do. In the fifth grade, boys and girls relate to the opposite sex with little intimacy. By the seventh grade, girls report far more intimacy toward boys than boys report towards girls. This discrepancy is maintained through the eleventh grade. Intimacy with same-sex friends remains strong, but with maturity, a reduction in attachment and exclusiveness takes place. By the eleventh grade, the differences in intimacy between same-sex and opposite-sex friends are reduced. It appears that girls in mid-adolescence are more ready to commit themselves to intimate friendships than boys. Perhaps the socialization of males away from expressiveness partly explains this finding. Since boys may not be as ready to form relationships at this age, it may be wise for a girl to understand that she may be more ready to share than the average male of her age group.

These studies show that the relationships with parents and with peers are dynamic, changing with maturity and experience. Peers and parents provide different social worlds for adolescents (Montemayor, 1982). Adolescents interact with their parents in such activities as shopping, eating, and doing chores but spend more time with peers playing games and talking. Most of the free time spent with parents involves watching television, for which many adolescents do not show much enthusiasm. Perhaps parents would do better if they reduced the amount of time they spend watching television with their adolescents and directed their efforts to more active social activities.

Still, there is good news in this for parents. The restructuring of relationships during early and middle adolescence may be difficult, but it does not put parents out in the cold. In addition, by late adolescence, an improvement in the parent-child relationship occurs, and there is less conflict. We now know that the relationship in adolescence with its increase in autonomy does not mean complete emotional disengagement from parents. The autonomy occurs in the atmosphere of connectedness within the family (Hill, 1987). This increase in autonomy occurs gradually over a period of time, usually without tremendous amounts of storm and stress. It involves increasing self-management as rules change and develops within a family context (Alessandri & Wozniak, 1989).

The abandonment of the conflict model of adolescence does not, of course, mean that the period is conflict free. The period of early adolescence when both parents and children are adjusting to rapid changes is often seen by family members as one of disruption and conflict. Families with younger adolescents often perceive more stress and less organization than do families with older adolescents. However, adolescents do not see it this way. Younger adolescents do not perceive this increase in disorganization and stress, perhaps because they are so centered on their own

development. More interestingly, older adolescents do not see the reduction in conflict, and they tend to perceive more conflict than their parents do. They may even be somewhat motivated to perceive more conflict than really exists, since they are nearing the point of leaving the home, and conflict may make it psychologically easier for the adolescent to leave home.

The Generation Gap Revisited

For adolescents and adults to interact effectively, they must have some idea of how each views the other as well as some ability to communicate. Just how accurately do adolescents and their parents see each other and understand each other's point of view? Lerner and his colleagues (1975) asked undergraduate students and their parents to note their feelings on a number of issues—such as racism, war, sex, and drug use. Subjects checked the alternatives from 1, meaning "strongly agree," to 7, indicating "strongly disagree." They were asked to rate not only statements that reflected their own attitudes but also statements mirroring the beliefs of their parents and peers. Parents were asked to rate their own stands on issues as well as to predict where their children and other teens stood on those issues.

The results? Most actual differences were in the direction of intensity. In other words, the differences between the generations are a matter of degree, with one generation agreeing or disagreeing more strongly with a position than the other. The popular term **generation gap** is often used to denote what is seen as the ever-widening gap between the standards, values, and opinions of generations. Most studies find that the generation gap is more apparent than real (Lerner, Karson, Meisels & Knapp, 1975) and that the differences are more a matter of degree or intensity than anything else. In the area of sex and drugs, though, qualitative differences do exist (Chand, Crider & Willets, 1975).

generation gap
The differences in attitudes among various generations.

Although the generation gap may not be as great on most issues as first thought, the perceptions each group has of the attitudes of the other group are mistaken. Adolescents overestimate the gap between their parents and themselves, while parents consistently underestimate it. Each group views the other as more conservative than it actually is.

9. TRUE OR FALSE?

Most parents think the generation gap is greater than it actually is.

Why should this perceived gap be so much greater than the actual gap? Perhaps parents want to see themselves as closer to their children, while adolescents are motivated to separate themselves more from their parents. This could also reflect poor communication between the generations.

Often, teenagers are more liberal than their parents or grandparents regarding when it is proper to do something. They are more likely to approve of age norm violations than older people (Roscoe and Peterson, 1989). In other words, if they see an older person doing something normally reserved for younger people, they are much more likely to accept it than their parents or grandparents are.

Adolescents also believe that they should be able to do certain things at a younger age than their parents do. They hold a different timetable for independence, and this causes some conflict. It is not that parents refuse to accept their children's growing independence and competen-

cies, they just see specific privileges and behaviors as appropriate at a later time. When 200 sixth graders (average age 11.9 years) were asked to decide the age at which they expected to engage in certain behaviors, their estimations were always somewhat earlier than those of their parents (see Table 14.2). The researchers surveyed only the parents of boys but suggest that since the parents of girls are usually even more conservative, they would expect the differential to be somewhat greater. When these behaviors are ranked in terms of the ages at which both parents and peers think something should be allowed, the order is very similar (Feldman & Quatman, 1988). In this survey, Asian Americans were also compared to Anglo-Americans and believed they would engage in particular behaviors at a later age than their Anglo-American peers. The later esti-

TABLE 14.2: When Should Children Be Allowed to Participate in Specific Activities?
Average age at which teenagers and parents believe activities should begin or when children should be allowed to:

| | GENERATION | |
	Child $N = 200$	Parent $N = 170$
Overall Timetable	15.6	16.6
Composite Scores	15.0	15.6
Oppositional Autonomy		
Autonomy	15.7	16.6
Social	15.3	16.2
Leisure	14.7	16.4
Items		
1. Choose hairstyle even if your parents don't like it.	14.8	14.1
2. Choose what books, magazines to read.	13.2	14.3
3. Go to boy-girl parties at night with friends.	14.8	13.9
4. Not have to tell parents where you are going.	17.2	18.9
5. Decide how much time to spend on homework.	13.0	15.0
6. Drink coffee.	16.0	17.5
7. Choose alone what clothes to buy.	13.7	14.7
8. Watch as much TV as you want.	14.3	17.2
9. Go out on dates.	15.4	16.1
10. Smoke cigarettes.	20.3	20.5
11. Take a regular part-time job.	16.2	16.6
12. Make own doctor and dentist appointments.	17.4	17.9
13. Go away with friends without any adults.	15.8	18.5
14. Be able to come home at night as late as you want.	17.7	19.4
15. Decide what clothes to wear even if your parents disapprove.	15.8	16.0
16. Go to rock concerts with friends.	16.1	17.3
17. Stay home alone rather than go out with your family.	14.5	15.0
18. Drink beer.	18.9	19.3
19. Be able to watch any TV, movie, or video show you want.	15.3	17.4
20. Spend money (wages or allowance) however you want.	13.4	14.1
21. Stay home alone if you are sick.	13.4	14.2

Source: Feldman and Quotman, 1988.

mation of these Asian-American children demonstrates the importance of culture. In many Asian-American families, there is an intense emphasis on family and a greater identification with parents and tradition.

◆ CAREER CHOICE

"If only I knew what I wanted to be, I'd be able to do better in school." This is one of the more common complaints of adolescents. Erik Erikson (1968) acknowledged the importance of a vocational identity. Its importance is nicely shown by the fact that college students who chose occupations that mirrored their measured abilities and interests showed more successful resolutions of Erikson's first six stages, including identity formation in adolescence (Munley, 1975, 1977). The process of vocational development starts in childhood as children observe the occupations around them and imagine themselves working in them (Super, 1953). But it is in high school that students begin to realize that they are facing a career decision. This decision is a vital part of forming an identity in adolescence.

The Importance of Career Choice

For many, choosing a vocation is difficult. A vocation determines not only how much money you will make but also your lifestyle (McIlroy, 1979). The average male will spend approximately 80,000 hours, or about 30 percent, of his total life at work (Miller, 1964). Because women are entering the full-time job market at an increasing rate, this figure has meaning for them, too. In adolescence, career choice also complements newfound mental abilities, as students can now deal with such hypotheses as what if they do this or that, and they can plan for their future more constructively.

The two most important factors in career choice are knowledge of oneself and knowledge of the job market. Knowing oneself includes understanding what one wants in a job or career and having a realistic appraisal of one's abilities and personal resources. Knowing the job market involves understanding the vocational alternatives and the requirements for entry-level positions.

Factors in Making a Career Choice

What causes someone to decide to become a teacher or an auto mechanic? Personal characteristics enter into the decision. Intellectual ability and achievement in high school also have an effect on vocational choice. The student who cannot pass chemistry would probably not go into chemical engineering, nor would someone with two left feet decide to be a dancer. On the other hand, a relatively large span of intelligence levels is found in most careers. Cronbach (1970) found that although accountants are generally more intelligent than miners, some miners are brighter than some accountants. Although general relationships hold, the relationship between intelligence and vocational choice should not be overemphasized.

Personal experiences are also factors. Suppose your father truly dislikes his job and comes home every night disheartened and consumed by this aversion. It might affect your feelings about your father's occupation. The same would be true if your parents loved their work. Your personal needs, many of which may have been based on experiences during childhood, may cause you to enter one field of study rather than another (Roe, 1957, 1964). In addition, personality and problem-solving orientation can affect career choice. Holland (1973) identified six different personality types and found them related to different careers. For example, people who are task oriented or who prefer to work independently tend to enter scientific vocations. There is some evidence that when people enter fields congruent with these characteristics they are more satisfied. However, there are many other factors involved, and simple relationships are not always found (Gati, 1989). Other factors might be practical ones, such as a desire to enter the work force early. Knowing that it takes eight years to earn a doctorate in a particular field might deflate one's enthusiasm if early earning power is a factor. Other practical factors might involve being able to pay for training and to meet entrance requirements. Finally, gender and socioeconomic status are factors in career selection, and will be discussed shortly.

Sometimes career choice is due to chance. A person may merely be at the right spot at the right time. Baumgardner (1975) surveyed college alumni and found that 72 percent had entered their occupations on the basis of circumstantial factors or some combination of circumstances and planning. Only 28 percent felt that career planning had led directly to their job. Baumgardner's work reminds us that chance, once-in-a-lifetime opportunities, and nonplanned factors enter into career choice. Another interesting finding is that adolescents are more certain of what they do not want to be than what they do want to be (Housely, 1973). Career planning, then, may be seen as a process of elimination.

Gender, Socioeconomic Status, and Career Choice

Ideally, people take their abilities, interests, and goals into consideration when they choose a vocation. Chance factors enter the equation too. But vocational choice involves a person's considering what he or she wants to do and following some program of study or training to achieve it. Not everyone makes such a conscious decision. Conscious career choice is viable only for people who believe they have the opportunity and the resources to succeed and who live in an environment that makes it possible for them to carry out their plans (Harmon & Farmer, 1983). For some women and members of many ethnic and racial minority groups, this is not always the case.

Women and Careers

Years ago, one could say with certainty that a girl would grow up, get married, and lead a rather conventional existence. Women who did work outside the home often chose nonprofessional jobs. This is not so today

FIGURE 14.1: Women and Careers
There is no doubt that women have been entering professional
fields at an increasing rate.

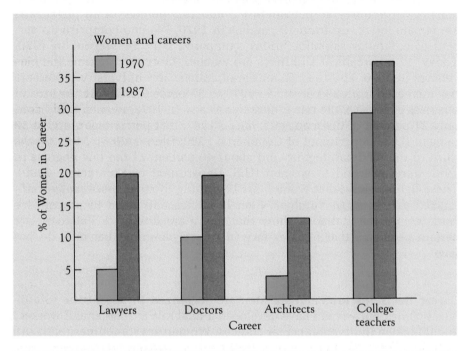

Source: U.S. Department of Commerce, 1990.

(Figure 14.1). In this decade, nine of every ten women can expect to work
outside the home sometime in their lives. In fact, most women today state
that they prefer to combine marriage and career pursuits (Fitgerald & Betz,
1983). In addition, although women are still overrepresented in certain
fields, such as clerical and service positions, more women are entering
what might be called nontraditional fields. A nontraditional field is one
in which the overwhelming majority—more than two-thirds—are workers of one sex (Hayes, 1985).

Nontraditional Careers for Women: Two Views The trend for women to
enter nontraditional fields can be analyzed in two ways. The first is pessimistic. For example, 74 percent of all schoolteachers are female, as are
69 percent of retail sales workers. Women comprise 86 percent of librarians, 95 percent of nurses, and 99 percent of secretaries. They comprise
only 2 percent of the firefighters, 2 percent of construction workers, 3.4
percent of mechanics, 11 percent of police officers, and just 7 percent of
engineers. Although 45 percent of all workers are women, only 38 percent
of executives or managers are women. (Bloom, 1986; U.S. Department of
Commerce, 1989). Most women are still opting to enter traditional fields,
even if these fields are professional, such as teaching. There is some

change in the number of women who want to enter nontraditional fields, such as the sciences, but it has been a relatively small change overall.

The other evaluation is more optimistic, seeing women as making substantial though uneven progress. In 1970, only 5 percent of lawyers were female, while today 20 percent are. Some 19.5 percent of all physicians are female today, up from 10 percent in 1970. Women comprise 32 percent of computer scientists today, compared with 14 percent in 1970. Today, 12.6 percent of architects are women, more than double the percentage in 1970, and the percentage of college and university professors has increased from 29 percent in 1970 to 37 percent today. In the area of business executive, the rise is also significant. In 1972, women comprised only 27 percent of the managers, but in 1987, that percentage stood at 37 percent (U.S. Department of Commerce 1989; Bloom 1986). More than a third of the medical degrees and about 40 percent of the law degrees in 1987 were awarded to women (U.S. Department of Commerce, 1990). These figures show that women are beginning to enter these male-dominated fields in large numbers. Female adolescents need to prepare for careers, and the statistics show that many are doing so. Yet there are certain problems that females face in career planning that men do not face.

Career Decisions for Females Men are socialized to accept the role of breadwinner, but women have developed a dual role as mother and worker, and this often limits their career choices. Women are sometimes reluctant to enter careers in the sciences because they see problems combining family life and a career in this area (McLure & Piel, 1978). Women today are, however, entering some nontraditional careers. The female doctor or lawyer is becoming common, but the woman entering chemistry, physics, and engineering is still a rarity. In addition, we know that even women with very high grades do not necessarily look toward higher level posi-

DATAGRAPHIC

Engineering Women

Source: National Science Foundation

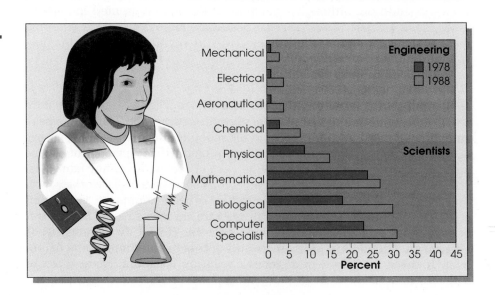

tions (Church, 1983). Perhaps women's grades show women their ability but are not used to determine future plans, as women are more influenced by other social and familial factors than men are. Why?

We all know stories about women who have been discouraged by some remark from a professional or even a peer concerning the inappropriateness of achieving in some area. The media demonstrates such sexism, too. Television and movies rarely show women in scientific fields, and when they do, the women seem to be incapable of having normal family lives and a career too. The occupational literature can also be biased (Heshusius-Gilsdorf & Gilsdorf, 1975). Parents sometimes propagate sexist attitudes by discouraging their daughters from achieving in certain fields. School counselors are also blamed for discouraging females from developing their potential, but the students often are the ones who already have a sexist view of career choices. In many instances, counselors of both sexes are less stereotyped in their views of work and gender roles than the females they are counseling (Hawley, 1982).

Some careers are also stereotyped, causing either men or women to consider them inappropriate. Children ranging in ages from five to thirteen years are strongly gender typed with respect to job choices, with girls less rigid than boys (Henderson, Hesketh, & Tuffin, 1988). The evidence of the existence of gender stereotyping for careers by college students has been popularly accepted for some time (Albrecht, Bahr, & Chadwick, 1977). However, more recent studies show some interesting changes, including a general decline in the degree to which college students stereotype occupations by gender. This does not mean that typically male-dominated occupations such as engineer and architect are no longer stereotyped. They are, but to a much lesser degree than in the past. The reduction in stereotyping is much greater for male-dominated occupations than for female-dominated occupations. Some stereotypes for female-dominated occupations, such as registered nurse, have declined somewhat, while others, such as flight attendant, dietitian, and elementary schoolteacher have changed just a little (White, Kruczek, & Brown, 1989). These stereotypes are found for both men and women. There has been, then, some general reduction in occupational stereotypes, mostly in the direction of male-dominated occupations no longer being seen as exclusively male. While some female-dominated jobs have declined in stereotyping, this is less the case.

There is also considerable evidence that women now expect employment at higher levels than in the past. Although women are still more committed to homemaking and family than men are (Farmer, 1983), they are moving towards higher occupational choices (Brizzi, 1986).

WOMEN WHO ENTER NONTRADITIONAL CAREERS Women who enter nontraditional careers differ from those who do not (Auster and Auster, 1981). Women who achieve in male-dominated professions have mothers who were employed and acted as role models for them. The higher the social status of the position held by the mother, the less traditional the choice made by the daughter (Treiman and Terrell, 1975). The father also influences this decision. Daughters choosing nontraditional careers often have close relationships with their fathers and model themselves after the male parent as well. Both parents also support their

10. TRUE OR FALSE?

College students today are less likely than they were fifteen years ago to believe that an occupation is appropriate only for either males or females.

There are now more career opportunities open to women than ever before.

daughter's decision to enter a nontraditional field. Socioeconomic status is important, too. A positive relationship exists between higher socioeconomic status and a nontraditional career choice. Women choosing nontraditional careers also tend to be oldest or only children and come from relatively small families. Peers may exert a positive or negative influence on the choice of a nontraditional career. Other studies have found a correlation between androgyny in females (those whose personalities comprise both masculine and feminine traits) and choice of nontraditional careers (Clarey & Sanford, 1982). Other people besides parents can be important, including mentors and husbands (Wilson, Weikel, & Rose, 1982). Women choosing nontraditional careers also have beliefs in a more equitable division of labor in marriage and have less conventional attitudes generally (O'Donnell & Andersen, 1978), including less traditional gender-role attitudes (Keith, 1981).

Today, though, the background differences between women making traditional and nontraditional choices are narrowing (Fitzpatrick & Silverman, 1989). More recent research is showing that the characteristics once ascribed to women making nontraditional choices can now be ascribed to high-achieving women, whether or not they choose a nontraditional career. In addition, we are finding that the differences between those who choose nontraditional careers and those who do not remain strong only for those choosing careers in which very few women are employed (Fitzpatrick & Silverman, 1989).

We can conclude that more females will be employed in the future and that many more will be entering male-dominated occupations. However, this will not mean that occupations will no longer be gender stereotyped or that an equal number of males and females will be found in each field. Gender stereotypes still exist, and although both men and women will enter many nontraditional fields, those fields will continue to remain dominated by a single sex (Gerstein, Lichtman, & Barokas, 1988).

Career Decisions for Males

Because men are expected to make career choices and become the main breadwinner in the family, fewer changes in the career histories of men should be expected. Even so, some are appearing. Many of the stereotypes that surround vocational choice for men can be seen as operating in men's favor (Skovholt & Morgan, 1981). For example, personal characteristics such as strength and determination are rated positively. So are men's job choices, such as engineer and electrician. In addition, the rewards that include power, money, and status are positively evaluated by society. For men, occupational success often means high self-esteem. Success in life is often measured by success in vocational pursuits.

We can look at this in two ways. First, these advantages explain why men are less willing than women to explore nontraditional life and career patterns (Hawley & Even, 1982). Because they choose high-status positions, men experience less urgency to question their lifestyles.

Two negative factors are becoming evident, however. First not all men are going to succeed, and vocational failure often leads to self-esteem problems in men. Other problems, including violence in the family, deterioration in health, family trauma, and stress, follow this narrow focus in life. Second, even if males succeed, their lives may become narrow (Kaplan & Stein, 1984). In many cases, they have not developed the relationships with their families that they would have liked. In addition, for many men, nontraditional lifestyles and careers would seem appropriate, but they hesitate to enter female-dominated occupations and perhaps therefore do not develop their true potential.

If men are given an advantage by their status, it is a two-edged sword. Consciousness raising will be necessary if men are to go beyond their narrow base and balance their affiliative and leisure activities with their jobs. In addition, female-dominated occupations must be opened to men who have the talents to succeed in them. This again entails a change in attitude and values on the part of society.

Gender stereotyping of occupations traditionally populated by men has decreased dramatically, but gender typing of female-dominated fields has decreased less so. When men decide to enter a nontraditional field, they may have even more difficulties, since most of these fields do not have the status that male-dominated fields do. Men may choose not to enter female-dominated fields because of the lower earnings in many of those fields, a fact that is known in early adolescence. In addition, there is a prestige and status problem. Women are given higher prestige ratings than men in traditional female occupations (Hayes, 1986). There are also societal and parental pressures against men entering these fields, and males have a more restricted idea of gender-appropriate behavior than females do. In addition, schools tend to discourage men form entering these fields, and the problem of discrimination against men in these fields exists. Sometimes men entering some of these fields may not be seen as having the "sex-appropriate" attitudes, often involving nurturance, necessary for the position. Indeed, sex discrimination has been found in the job application stage when men inquire about female-dominated occupations (see Hayes, 1986). Just as in the case of women entering nontraditional fields, men entering female-dominated fields may face discrimination from their co-workers.

Men, though, may decide to enter these fields because of personal abilities, the desire for self-fulfillment, and what sometimes are seen as advantages of being the male minority. Men in some vocations, such as elementary schoolteachers and librarians, have been successful in reaching executive positions (Hayes, 1986).

Although there has been progress in reducing stereotyping, the progress should not be overemphasized. Males still choose male-dominated occupations and are not likely to choose nontraditional jobs. Females today are somewhat more likely to choose nontraditional careers, but they often see the need to work out the relationship between the career and their future family responsibilities. Women from high socioeconomic backgrounds are more likely to chose nontraditional careers than women from low socioeconomic backgrounds (Hannah & Kahn, 1989). If vocational choice is to be a reality, occupational stereotyping must be reduced and information and counseling given to allow students to make decisions based upon fact and aptitude, not on the "gender appropriateness" of an occupation.

Socioeconomic Status and Career Choice

Career choice is a misnomer for the poor, many of whom are members of minority groups. Many poor people do not have any choices, or at least do not see any, and adolescents from poverty backgrounds are less likely than middle-class teens to have high vocational aspirations (Bachman, 1978). For many African American males from poverty backgrounds, there is no real career exploration period. Such young men may take a job in their teens, but after that first job, they may work at a succession of unrelated jobs for fifty years. No career ladder is present.

Occupational choice may be limited by lack of economic resources and racial discrimination. The lack of high-achieving role models complicates the situation. Most middle- and upper-income youngsters believe that they can influence their own futures; that is, they have an **internal locus of control**. But this is not the case with poorer children, who have an **external locus of control** and believe that they are at the mercy of the system, the outside world, or luck. They are more fatalistic in their view (Farmer, 1978). If they do not believe they have the power to change things, why plan?

All in all, the poor face barriers of discrimination and a history of lack of success with the system. This does not mean that they lack motivation to succeed, only that to succeed they must have some belief in the effectiveness of their own efforts, called **self-efficacy**. For example, let's say you want to become a chemist but don't believe that even if you study hard you can make it. You might not even know what is necessary. The first problem is one of changing a view toward life, while the second requires adequate vocational information and counseling. The economically disadvantaged are also hindered by their poorer educational background and academic skills.

The failure in this area is reflected in the tremendous unemployment rate among minority teenagers. Any programs that aim at promoting reasonable vocational choices must deal with the lack of information concerning vocations and the problems associated with poverty. They must also change basic attitudes, which often run counter to the planning necessary to succeed in obtaining upper-level jobs.

There is both good and bad news concerning career choices for minorities. For example, in 1970, about a half million black men and women were attending college, while in 1985 that figure stood at about 755,000. The proportion of blacks in white-collar jobs has increased greatly over the past twenty-five years, and the percentage of blacks in professional and technical areas has increased somewhat. In 1970, blacks constituted 2 percent of the doctors, 1 percent of the lawyers and judges, and 2.9 percent of the teachers. In 1987, 3.7 percent of the doctors, 3.4 percent of the lawyers and judges, and 9.4 percent of the teachers were black (U.S. Department of Commerce, 1989). While this shows some progress, the progress has been slow. In addition, the unemployment rate is greater for minority youth than for whites. This higher unemployment rate probably reflects both the lack of skills and the high percentage of school dropouts found among minority youths.

internal locus of control
The belief that one is in control of one's own fate.

external locus of control
The belief that one is at the mercy of other people or of fate.

self-efficacy
A term describing people's beliefs about what they can and cannot accomplish.

Teenagers and Work

Many high school students work, and traditionally, we have respected this. A number of commissions have advanced the notion that when teenagers work it gives them a greater understanding of the job market, engenders greater responsibility, and may develop both self-esteem and a work ethic (see Meyer, 1987). Teenagers who work often do so to earn money that they can spend on personal items. In fact, parents tend to agree that teenagers have the right to spend the money on whatever they please, since they earned it. Therefore, there is some measure of independence involved in earning money.

Teenagers from low socioeconomic backgrounds are less likely to be employed, but those who are employed work many more hours than adolescents from high socioeconmic backgrounds (Schill, McCartin, & Meyer, 1985). In other words, teenagers from higher socioeconomic backgrounds are likely to work at part-time jobs, which offer fewer hours. As teenagers proceed through the adolescent years, they tend to work more hours (Meyer, 1987).

More recently, though, there have been some doubts about the benefits of work, especially for those who work many hours. For one thing, most of the jobs that are open to adolescents do not provide much training in useful skills and provide little opportunity for growth or challenge (Greenberger & Steinberg, 1986). So there is some doubt that there is really much benefit aside from remuneration. More challenging is the suggestion that teenagers who work have lower grades than nonworkers (Steinberg, Greenberger, Garduque, & McAuliffe, 1982). This is the case, however, only if teenagers work many hours. Many youth who expect to go on to college see less gain from working many hours, since this reduces their study time and involvement in after-school activities, and therefore are less committed to work (Meyer, 1987). Those with lower grades are more committed to work and see work differently. This may be a vicious cycle. Young people, especially those from lower socioeconomic backgrounds or who are less successful in school, are likely to be working the most hours. This overwhelming work schedule contributes to lower grades, since these students lack time to study. Students who do well in school and have plans to further their education are more likely to work a moderate number of hours so as not to injure their academic standing; this in turn increases their chances to study (Meyer, 1987). It is now suggested that teenagers should not work more than fifteen hours per week (Greenberger & Steinberg, 1986).

◆ THE SECONDARY SCHOOL TODAY

The daily life of most adolescents is focused around the school. It is in the school where most adolescents meet their friends and must deal with the more complex interpersonal relationships found in adolescence. It is in the school where the more advanced academic skills necessary for the world of work are partially developed. It is in the school where information about jobs, college, and future careers is most available to students. The secondary school is a different place today than it was even twenty years ago.

The Junior High/Middle School Experience

Junior high schools (grades seven to nine) have a short history. They began in the early part of this century. You may have grandparents who still remember (sometimes with fondness) the kindergarten through eighth-grade grammar school. The junior high school was originally designed to bridge the gap between the relatively easy curriculm of the elementary school and the more demanding work of high school (Smith, 1987). It was seen as a way of preparing students for the increasing challenge of academic work. It was also advocated on a developmental basis. Early adolescence is certainly a period of rapid physical, cognitive, and social changes. It is a transitional period in which children have different needs that may be best met in a school environment fundamentally different from the elementary school (Walker, Kozma, & Green, 1989). These are critical years, and the potential for increased risk taking in many areas—delinquency, sex, and drugs—calls for a special environment dedicated to the needs of students of this age (Manning & Allen, 1987).

Recently, there has been a shift in the organization of schools for young adolescents. Children are entering puberty earlier, and some believe that ninth graders belong in high school. Therefore, the middle school concept containing grades six, seven, and eight, or sometimes five, six, seven, and eight was born (Smith, 1987). Again, the central idea of giving students a transitional experience is present.

Junior high schools and middle schools differ from elementary schools in a number of ways. Students have more than one teacher, and they travel from class to class. They may have a special science teacher, another for math, and the like. The school's organization is less like an elementary school, and each teacher may have different requirements.

There has been some question as to how young adolescents adapt to this change from elementary to junior high school. Some adolescents feel a sense of anonymity, which impacts negatively on their self-concept (Thornburg & Glider, 1984). They feel less attached to the school. Other evidence notes a decline in the self-esteem of girls (but not for boys) the year following transition to junior high school (Blyth, Simmons, & Carlton-Ford, 1983). When these girls went on to high school, the year following this transition also saw a decline in self-esteem. Boys who made the transition from elementary to junior high and girls who stayed in elementary school through the eighth grade showed no decline. Why did some girls but not boys show the decline in self-esteem? The reason may be found in the multiple stresses girls experience at this time. For many girls, the transition to junior high school coincides with many other developmental changes, especially physical ones, whereas this is not the case for males (Simmons, Blyth, Van Cleave, & Bush, 1979). It is much more likely that girls will be in the midst of significant physical changes between sixth and seventh grade than boys will.

Not everyone has found the same problems in the transition from elementary to junior high school, but where problems do occur, females seem more vulnerable. When Barton Hirsch and Bruce Rapkin (1987) examined the transition to junior high school, they found self-esteem unchanged from the end of the sixth through the middle of seventh grade and then actually an increase in seventh grade. Girls, though, were more likely to report depressive symptoms and hostility than boys.

The fact that the transition *can be* a problem for some students, though, has been accepted. A majority of students, however, adjust well. Editha Nottelmann (1987) studied young adolescents in grades five and six who either changed to a new school or did not. She found that self-esteem was actually higher in the transition than in the nontransition group. Most junior high school students liked going to the new school because that is where they met their friends, and they liked the bigger schools, access to more than one teacher, more opportunities for a wider range of instruction, and just the idea of being treated more grown up. Some children were, however, uneasy about leaving elementary school and found the adjustment difficult. About one-third of the sample were not fully adjusted to the new school after a year but said they were "somewhat" used to it. We can conclude that although a majority of children will make the transition well, a minority of students will not, and girls may especially be at risk for some problems if the transition coincides with significant changes in their physical development.

One negative change that is often seen for both boys and girls is a decline in perceived quality of school life. Students do not believe their teachers are as warm and caring, and they perceive the school as more impersonal (Barton & Rapkin, 1987). Students often feel somewhat insignificant in a larger school, and feelings of anonymity are not uncommon. Teachers can do much to reduce these problems. Since junior high school students sometimes feel anonymous, it is important that teachers learn the names of their students and try to show interest in their individual abilities and talents. Teachers need to be more supportive, as students in junior high often do not see them that way.

The importance of teacher support was demonstrated in a study of the attitudes that 1,301 students had for mathematics before and after transition to junior high school. When students went from elementary school-teachers who they perceived to be low in support to junior high school-teachers who they perceived to be high in support, the value of math was enhanced. When students moved from teachers they perceived to be high in support to teachers they perceived to be low in support, they experienced a sharp decline in both the intrinsic value and the perceived usefulness of math and these attitudes are related to achievement in mathematics (Midgley, Feldlaufer, & Eccles, 1989). Teacher support involves the teacher acting in a friendly and encouraging manner. Unfortunately, students often find their junior high school teachers to be less supportive than their teachers in elementary school were (Feldlaufer, Midgley, & Eccles, 1988).

The period of early adolescence is also a period of great change in autonomy and social interaction. There is a need for exploration, so more choice in learning activities may be needed. In addition, because students may be overwhelmed by having to satisfy many teachers, they must be taught organizational skills. Furthermore, since these are years of physical, cognitive, and social change, more health-related discussions with a special emphasis on these changes may be required. The school also must allow students time for peer interactions within the framework of extracurricular activities and minicourses that may allow students to follow their interests. Encouraging students to study together and offering cooperative learning techniques can also serve to improve social skills (Manning & Allen, 1987).

In 1989, the Carnegie Corporation issued an important report entitled *Turning Points: Preparing American Youth for the 21st Century*. The report noted the importance of the early adolescent period, young adolescents' tendency towards experimentation, and the "unprecedented choices and pressures" that they experience. Middle grade schools are potentially the most powerful force to help young people during these years. Yet, the middle schools have not been meeting the needs of young people in a changing world. The report suggests a number of changes including dividing large middle grade schools into smaller communities for learning, teaching a core academic program, the elimination of tracking by achievement level, more teacher involvement in decision making, fostering health and fitness, connecting the school with the community through service opportunities, and establishing partnerships with other community organizations. These suggestions are certainly welcome, but we must go even further and create a specialty in early adolescence. There has been little commitment to the work of the junior high school, and there appears to be no adequate framework from which to understand early adolescent development (Thornburg, 1986). Most teachers do not receive much training in working with junior high schoolage students. The junior high school and middle school ages are formative ones, but not enough is said about them in many teacher-training programs. Teaching in this area must be considered a speciality, and it needs greater public exposure and support.

The High School

The overwhelming majority of adolescents today attend high school, a change from earlier in the century when the high school graduate was a rarity. The most important change in the past decade or so is the tendency for high school course work to be more rigorous. This is found in the junior high/middle school to some extent as well. This increase in rigor is a reaction to two types of studies. First, a number of studies have compared curriculum and achievement levels of students in Japan and other nations to those in the United States and concluded that we need more rigor in the curriculm at all levels, including high school. A survey of learning in twenty countries found that American eighth graders were slightly above international average in math computation but well below average in problem solving (IAEEA, 1987). A study of science achieve-

11. *TRUE OR FALSE?*
_____

Within the past decade, high school course work has become more rigorous.

ment in seventeen countries show that American students ranked fourteenth, below all major industrialized nations (IAEEA, 1988).

Second, some studies have investigated the knowledge base of secondary school students and found it wanting in general. In a study of 8,000 high school juniors conducted by the National Endowment for the Humanities National Assessment of Educational Progress, one in three did not know when Columbus discovered America. The students were not asked to identify the exact year; their answers had to be within fifty years of the correct date. About one in three could not recognize the two countries that were the United States' principal enemies in World War II, and more than a third did not know what checks and balances are. About 90 percent could not identify "To be or not to be" as a quotation from *Hamlet* (Finn & Ravitch, 1987). Another study of high school students conducted by the Joint Council on Economic Education found that most students don't understand basic economic terms, and another study found that 20 percent of Americans in their twenties could not read at an eighth-grade level (*Newsday*, Jan. 27, 1989).

The report that had the greatest impact, however, was entitled *A Nation At Risk*, which publicized the results of eighteen months of study by a panel called the National Commission on Excellence in Education (1981). The commission documented many problems in the educational system and recommended, among other things, stricter requirements for graduation, especially in English, mathematics, science, foreign language, and social studies; a lengthening of the school year; and curricula reform. The trend towards greater rigor in the secondary school, especially high school, will continue into the near future.

Another major change is the movement toward minimum competency testing in high school. Minimum competency tests are intended to ensure that each graduate has certain basic skills. These tests are an outgrowth of the movement to improve educational accountability and be certain that a high school diploma certifies some basic knowledge. The great majority of states now require some form of minimum competency test, although the tests vary in what they measure and in the cutoff for success.

Minimum competency tests have explicitly standards for passing and are the ultimate in pass/fail tests, since the consequences of passing or failing are so important. Students who fail minimum competency tests are usually given extra help. As the test continues to be given to graduating class after graduating class, the percentage of students who fail decreases dramatically, probably because teachers now have an understanding of what will be covered on the test and teach accordingly (Kaplan, 1990).

Another trend is the desire to teach thinking and reasoning skills in the curriculm (Kaplan, 1990). It is not enough to teach the facts and basic concepts. We also want our students to be able to use advanced thinking skills, such as analysis and inference, and to be able to evaluate material.

There has also been a call for high schools to focus on health, moral, and family issues. For example, there is a clamor for more drug and sex education programs and for courses covering family living, which includes basic information on child development, relationships, and the like.

The Future and Non-college Bound Youth

High schools proudly announce the academic scholarships and the names of the colleges to which their graduates have been accepted. Counselors guide students carefully through their possible college choices and "College Nights," where sometimes hundreds of colleges are represented, are common. But what of the non-college bound student?

Many high schools emphasize college so much that those students who will not go on to college are frequently given less attention. The majority of American students who go on to college from high school seem to find their way into the job market. The same cannot be said, however, for those who will go right into the job market from high school. Many will end up in jobs that offer little advancement.

Things are different in some other countries. In Germany, Sweden, and Denmark, after finishing their compulsory schooling, students can enroll in a two- to four-year program paid for by the government which trains them for entry into a wide variety of occupations. Since there is close cooperation between school and industry, workers graduating from this training program are valued and can obtain employment.

A report entitled *America's*

Choice: High Skills or Low Wages? from the National Center for Education and the Economy (1990) suggests some significant changes for students who will not be going on to college. These include a certificate of initial mastery, which would demonstrate that the student had mastered basic skills. Perhaps it would be required on a national basis. Although all students would be required to obtain such a certificate it would be especially important for those entering the job market immediately after high school.

The report also calls for the introduction of youth centers for students who have difficulty achieving in the normal high school environment. Although work experience would be part of the mission of these youth centers, the centers would also specialize in alternative educational methods of teaching and learning.

Last, the report advocates more aid to technical and professional education so as to give students a chance to learn a job-related skill. Many of the jobs that are the fastest growing require advanced training but not necessarily college. The report actually calls for all students to receive four years of education beyond the certificate of initial mastery at some time in their lives.

Although the recommendations of this report are expensive and probably will not be totally accepted, the report has highlighted an important and often underpublicized concern. In the next century, the need for people with technical skills will increase. Better vocational information services will be necessary for the non-college bound student. As more research is conducted on non-college bound youth, we will see a movement towards providing these adolescents with adequate services and training so that they can earn a living in a more complicated society. This will mean some significant changes in attitudes towards these students as well as some provision for alternatives after graduation. At this point, few services and opportunities are open to these students after they graduate. This may change as we begin to adopt some of the proposals suggested in this report.

Last and probably the most recent, is a call for better counseling and preparation for those who are not going on to college (which is discussed in this chapter's Child in the Year 2000 feature.)

The Changing High School

As you can plainly see, today's high school is changing. One of the difficulties with secondary education generally is the multitude of goals that has been established for it. No consensus exists on the goals and objectives of secondary schools in the United States (Smith, 1987). The relative importance of social, health, and academic goals has changed over the years as different social and academic movements have influenced education. In addition, the schools are increasingly being called upon to do more than teach the basics. Despite increased emphasis on academics, the schools have also been asked to deal with societal problems, ranging from drug use to teenage pregnancy to moral standards and delinquency concerns. As the high school curriculum becomes more challenging and the number of elective courses decreases, will enough time be left to accomplish these social tasks?

A more fundamental question is whether the schools are equipped to deal adequately with the social challenges they face. Last, although many welcome the new academic rigor, there is a question of whether we are forgetting social objectives and the interpersonal needs of the student.

Gender and Achievement in High School

Adolescent girls and boys do not achieve identically in secondary school, even though there are no significant differences in intelligence. In elementary school, girls do at least as well as boys, and perhaps better, but in high school, their achievement slips. Even among very bright women, the number who get the training necessary to reach top levels of professional fields are fewer than one would expect, given their high school attainments.

The gap between males and females closes rapidly in high school, with males finally surpassing females in achievement, especially in science and mathematics. In elementary school, girls do better and are perceived as better students than males (Bernard, 1981). Elementary schoolteachers value female competencies, and boys receive more punishment, but a drastic change occurs in secondary school. Males begin to value school achievement more, and teachers value the gender-role competencies of males more highly (Bernard, 1981). In other words, in elementary school, females may be more comfortable and find that their noncompetitive, highly social, more obedient behavior brings them praise and is greatly valued by teachers, but in secondary school, males become more aware of their future and take school more seriously. Teachers begin to value the aggressiveness and competitiveness of males more, while the opposite is true for females.

Reasons for Differences in Achievement

The fact that males catch up and females decline in academic achievement does not tell us anything about why this happens. There are many theories but few real facts. Women have an achievement orientation equal to that of men. They are also as persistent, and their general self-esteem is just as high (Richmond-Abbott, 1983). However, men and women sometimes value achievement in different areas. Women tend to see their achievement in terms of interpersonal competencies and skills, while men look for achievement in the more objective, academic-oriented areas.

Women do not expect to do as well as men in math and science, even though they may have done well previously (Richmond-Abbott, 1983).

Women's achievement motivation is different, not less. This may be a function of socialization practices. Competition and achievement in the world of work are deemphasized for females, as women are encouraged to take marriage and their future family into consideration. In addition, males do not like to compete with females, and women who do compete are often less popular (Williams, 1977).

It is obvious that expectations are different for men and women in high school. Women may be discouraged from taking higher-level courses, such as physics or calculus, while males are expected to do so (Schaffer, 1981). We are all probably aware of the scene in which someone tells a bright adolescent female that she should not bother taking an advanced math course because it's a waste of time. After all, what is she going to do with it, anyway? This type of blatant sexism has been held up to public scrutiny and criticized, as it should be. But such statements are probably less common than the subtle communication of expectations. In many schools and homes today, females are not actively restricted from these areas; they are simply not encouraged to take such courses. Female career choices may be restricted by a number of factors, including the lack of available role models in the sciences, socialization practices that tend to run counter to achievement, and the encouragement of interpersonal competence over academic competence. Females do not have to be actively dissuaded from achieving. Lack of encouragement produces the same result.

In high school, attitudes toward specific subjects also change. Until about eighth grade, the types of mathematics courses taken by males and females are just about the same. By eleventh grade, however, males take

Why are there so few female students in advanced science and math classes? The answer may lie in society's expectations and the lack of encouragement many receive from friends, family and the schools.

more advanced courses. Some claim that this mathematical superiority in adolescence can be attributed to better spatial perception. This factor, however, even if important to some degree, could not account for the large differences in achievement in the sciences found in research studies. In one study, Julia Sherman (1980) found that although boys' ability in this area increased slightly more than girls', the difference was not significant. However, male and female attitudes toward math were very different. Females considered math a province of males, and their attitudes were less positive toward it than those of their male peers. These differing expectations and attitudes contribute to the lack of female achievement in the sciences.

This restriction shows itself in the things males and females take into account when making a career choice in the early years of college. As noted previously, males and females take different things into account when making a career choice. Women consider their future family responsibilities and the possibility that they would not have the time to devote to careers that required either great time commitment or commuting long distances. Men usually do not take such things into consideration when choosing their careers. Perhaps this understanding that women's life plans differ from those of males is present even in high school when considering various vocational possibilities and deciding to follow some course of study.

One last point is in order. In adolescence, boys do not suddenly become great scholars while females become failures. Rather, males as a group begin to surpass females, especially in the more technical subjects, and the number of underacheiving females increases during adolescence (Schaffer, 1981).

Minorities in High School

Fewer minority teenagers graduate from high school, and the achievement of minority students in high school is a continuing concern. Historically, minority youth, especially from lower income backgrounds, have not performed well (Reed, 1988). Over the past few years, measures of academic achievement in reading writing and mathematics for both black and Hispanic youth have improved but remain below comparable white students (see Jackson & Hornbeck, 1989).

This lack of achievement in school will be the center of even more concern in the future. It is not only a matter of concern for groups of adolescents whose futures are compromised by poor achievement but also a simple matter of demographic changes. It is estimated that over the period of 1982 to 2020, the number of Hispanic children will more than triple, from 5.9 million to 18.6 million. The population of black youth under eighteen will rise by 22 percent, from 9.3 million to 11.9 million. A 69 percent increase in the population of other ethnic groups, especially Asian, will take place (Natriello, McDill, & Pallas, 1987). In 1982, about 73 percent of the schoolage population was white, while in the year 2020, it will be 54.5 percent. There is no doubt that if our country is to prosper, ways must be found to improve the achievement of these young people.

One of the major problems is grouping these young people from different cultural groups together under the heading of minority youth. These young people come from different cultural, environmental, and social backgrounds and may have different difficulties. For example, Hispanic Americans as well as some young people belonging to other minorities have difficulties in their verbal skills and require specific help in this area (refer to Chapter 8). In addition, many Hispanic Americans come from a background that emphasizes cooperation more than individual achievement, which does not mesh with the more individualized achievement orientation of American schools. For Native American children, there is also less of an emphasis on individual achievement and much more on group-oriented achievement, and this can lead to difficulties in school (LaFromboise & Low, 1989). The family values of interdependence with others and sharing may not be reflected in school. In addition, there may be a reluctance to talk in school, as noted in Chapter 13's Cross-Cultural Current, and communication patterns may be different.

Black youth face a combination of social and environmental problems. A disproportionate number of black children live in poverty, poor housing, and crime-ridden areas, and many black children are born into and raised in single-parent families (Edelman, 1985). These children born into single-parent families are especially vulnerable to school failure, since they are more likely to live in poverty, their health is poorer, and their mothers are less likely to promote optimal development and are under more stress (Comer, 1985). Programs that aim at overcoming these problems can help, especially if they emphasize parental involvement (Comer, 1985). There are also a number of specific teaching strategies that work (Brophy, 1982). Many schools in primarily black neighborhoods are starved for funds and are lacking in a safe and orderly environment.

Asian Americans have always been thought to do well, and indeed they have achieved. However, the stereotypes of the bright, conscientious Chinese and Japanese are very limiting and may give teachers unreason-

DATAGRAPHIC

College Participation Rates of Black and White Students*

*Students surveyed are 18- to 24-year-old high school graduates and living at home or dependent primary family members.

Source: U.S. Department of Commerce, Bureau of Census.

The percentage of White high school graduates enrolled in college has increased while the percentage of Black high school graduates has decreased since the mid 1970s.

able expectations based only upon ethnic identity. These students frequently have limited skills in English (Huang and Yu, 1989). They may also have difficulties negotiating a culture whose values differ greatly from those at home (Nogata, 1989).

One common thread that unites most minority youth is poverty. Often students from poverty backgrounds have a poor history with the schools, have been labeled unintelligent, and are channeled into less challenging programs. Their attitudes toward school and motivation may be poor, and they often see little relationship between what they learn in school and their real world. They may have no safe and quiet place to study, and the level of family support may be low. They suffer higher suspension and dropout rates (Reed, 1988). Poor academic achievement is more often a consequence of cultural, social, and environmental factors than of lack of ability (Gibbs & Huang, 1989).

There is no single answer to the problem of underachievement among our youth. We must rid ourselves of the idea that all students learn or can be taught in the same way and use whatever strategies will work. One of the suggestions for teachers who will teach minority youth is to become more knowledgeable about their cultural and family backgrounds and to observe teachers of these children who are very effective in their methods (Kaplan, 1990).

Dropping Out of School

One of our most serious academic problems is our dropout rate. High school dropouts are more likely to live on or near the poverty level, to experience unemployment, and to depend on government for support (Steinberg, 1985). Although the majority of students finish high school, a large minority do not. The high school graduation rate declined from 71.7 percent in 1985 to 71.1 percent in 1988 (*New York Times*, 1990). However, the national average naturally does not reflect fairly large variations across districts. Minority students, who are usually raised in poverty-stricken circumstances, have a higher dropout rate than middle-class students. In some urban areas, the rate can range from 40 percent to 60 percent (Reed, 1988), and in some schools, the rate is even higher (Cairns, Cairns, & Neckerman, 1989).

The dropout rate is distressing because it represents a waste of human resources. Although some studies have found that the average dropout has a lower intelligence score, most more recent studies show that this is true only for those who drop out before high school. The average high school dropout has an average intelligence score (Sprintall & Collins, 1984). Many students who do not finish high school have not developed their potential. In addition, the financial differences between graduates and nongraduates are great, especially as these young people move through adulthood. Dropouts do not usually find jobs that have solid futures, because their skills are poor. Third, many dropouts will face unemployment or underemployment throughout life, which will affect their self-concepts and family relationships.

School holds little promise for dropouts. As a group, dropouts are poor

12. TRUE OR FALSE?

Most high school dropouts have intelligence scores within the normal range.

readers. As many as 80 percent of the dropouts are one year behind their peers in reading, and 50 percent are at least two years behind (Grinder, 1973). Dropouts have poor grades, experience failure, and show little or no interest in school. Many of these students have been left back a grade. They often come from backgrounds of poverty, large families, or families in which discord and divorce are common (Bachman, Green, & Wirtanen, 1972). Their homes generally do not offer much intellectual stimulation. Dropouts also show a history of school-related problems, including high rates of delinquency and school suspension (Sprintall & Collins, 1984). Their personality profiles show that they are hostile and resentful, have low self-esteem, and are less likely to have definite values and goals than high school graduates (Conger & Petersen, 1984). When Robert Cairns and his colleagues followed a sample of 475 children beginning in seventh grade through high school, they found that 14 percent of their sample had dropped out before completing grade eleven. Eighty two percent of the males and 47 percent of the females who had dropped out showed higher levels of aggressiveness and low levels of academic achievement. As early as the seventh grade, subjects who subsequently dropped out became friends with other youths who were also at risk for dropping out (Cairns, Neckerman, Ferguson & Gariepy, 1989). Early school dropout was reasonably predictable and could be identified by the seventh grade.

Most factors that differentiate graduates from dropouts are present before these teens drop out (Bachman, O'Malley, & Johnston, 1978). Because the low self-esteem, high rates of delinquency, and high rates of drug abuse are found before the students stop attending school, they are not the consequences of dropping out. Dropping out is not an event as much as it is the result of a long process of failure, poor adjustment, low aspirations, low intellectual stimulation, and poverty. It can be predicted.

Many school districts recognize that the dropout problem is a serious one that requires bold new approaches. Some have instituted programs in which potential dropouts attend alternative schools or work-study programs and receive more attention and tutoring in basic academic skills. All these approaches show promise, but because the problem is such a complicated one, the solution may require a variety of programs and approaches.

Delinquency

Adolescents who have difficulty in school and are potential dropouts are frequently involved in delinquent activities. Concern about youth crime or delinquency is certainly not new, and statistics show that it is a serious ongoing problem. In 1988, some 29 percent of the arrests for the FBI crime index offenses of murder, forcible rape, robbery, assault, burglary, larceny-theft, motor vehicle theft, and arson were under the age of eighteen, and 44 percent were under the age of twenty-one (FBI, 1989). Males comprise 80 percent of all arrests and 89 percent of the arrests for violent crimes. Of course, most delinquent actions are not as serious as murder and rape. The most frequent complaints against boys involve joyriding, drunken driving, burglary, malicious mischief, auto theft, and illegal drug use. Girls are most likely to be reported for running away and for illicit sexual behavior (U.S. Department of Commerce, 1986). More than 1,600,000 people under the age of eighteen were arrested in 1988 (FBI, 1989).

Most people think of delinquents as coming from broken homes and poverty-stricken backgrounds. Indeed, delinquency flourishes where family discord and abuse are prevalent, where gangs reinforce criminal acts, and where discipline is either very severe and punitive or very lax (Fox, 1985). Delinquency has been thought of as a problem emanating from lower income youth, and there is some evidence for this, but the relationship between delinquency and socioeconomic status is found only in large cities and not in smaller cities and towns (Clarizio & McCoy, 1983). Others deny that there is such a relationship at all. The way socioeconomic status and delinquency are measured influences the relationship between them. Whatever relationship there is tends to be weak (Siegel & Senna, 1988).

Some 80 percent of all young people admit doing something delinquent at one time or another, and the fastest rate of increase in delinquent behavior is among suburban teens (Steinberg, 1985). This might be expected, since abuse, family discord, antisocial peer groups, and inconsistent discipline exist in the suburbs as well as in urban areas. Perhaps the statistics that show greater prevalence of delinquent acts in poor areas are skewed because the justice system is more likely to try to imprison the poor than the more affluent (Jensen, 1985).

Delinquents, as a group, are impulsive, resentful, socially assertive,

The public is very concerned about crime. Psychologists understand much more about the causes of such conduct.

defiant, and suspicious and lack self-control. They often feel inadequate and see themselves as lazy or bad (Conger & Petersen, 1984). When Ronald Slaby and Nancy Guerra (1988) compared the cognitive patterns of antisocial aggressive juvenile offenders with those of high-aggressive and low-aggressive high school students, they found that the offenders see social problems in hostile ways, are impulsive, seek little explanation, generate fewer solutions, anticipate few consequences for aggression, and believe in aggression as a legitimate way to solve problems (Slaby & Guerra, 1988). Aggressive adolescents generally were more likely to show these cognitive patterns than nonaggressive high school students.

Children who are delinquent usually have poor relationships with their parents. In many of the homes that yield delinquents, there is a lack of family routine; inconsistent discipline in which parents yell, threaten, and nag but do not follow through; and an inability to deal with family problems (Wilson & Herrnstein, 1985). The family relations of delinquents are characterized by rigidity, lack of cohesion, and little positive communication, and delinquents' peer relations are often are characterized by high levels of aggression (Blaske, Borduin, Henggeler, & Mann, 1989). Parent-child interactions lack warmth and intimacy and are characterized instead by rejection and indifference.

Lack of supervision is also a problem, especially in single-parent families. In one study, the mothers in single-parent families were found to have more difficulty controlling their teenagers. Adolescents in these mother-only households were more likely to make decisions without direct parental input, to lack parental supervision, and to exhibit deviant behavior when compared with two-parent or extended families controlled for socioeconomic status (Dornbusch et al., 1985). Youths who believe that their parents know what they are doing and whom they are with are less likely to engage in criminal acts than are unsupervised youths. Many parents of children considered beyond control are inconsistent rule setters, not very likely to praise, are less likely to show interest in their children and show high levels of hostile detachment (Siegel & Senna, 1988).

The importance of peer influence, especially during the early and middle years of adolescence when peer pressure is at its strongest, should also be considered.

Delinquency is not necessarily a permanent condition. Although adult criminals have a history of juvenile delinquency, most adolescents who have delinquency problems do not go on to lives of crime (Moffitt, 1990).

There is no simple answer to delinquency. Although some programs have attempted to prevent delinquency, many have not been effective. In one well-publicized program, budding delinquents were taken to Rahway State Prison in New Jersey, where they got a glimpse of their future. Inmates spent hours talking to the young people about prison life. Unfortunately, followup studies showed that this program was not effective in preventing delinquency (Finckenauer, 1979).

Some community-based programs have been successful, especially those that provide recreational activities, work directly both with gangs and with individuals, and include campaigns for community improvement (Clarizio & McCoy, 1983). Community involvement seems to be one key. In the educational realm, alternative schools offer some hope. Finally, some have advocated family interventions. For instance, delinquents usually have negative interpersonal relationships with others, including family members, often because of their social behavior and the reactions others have to it.

Some programs hope to reduce these negative interactions by teaching the parties better ways to interact (Henggeler et al., 1986). Others have looked at the possibility of altering some of the cognitive and social skills of these troubled youth. A twelve-session program using an eight-step sequence of social problem solving that involves identifying the problem, stopping and thinking, answering the questions why is there a conflict and what do I want, thinking of solutions, looking at the consequences, doing something, and evaluating the consequences, was found to increase skills in solving social problems, reduce the youths' endorsement of beliefs in aggression as a way of solving problems, and reduce aggressive behavior. However, these changes did not endure over time, possibly because the environment to which these youths returned did not support the changes (Guerra & Slaby, 1990). It may be possible to change the cognitions that mediate aggressive behavior, but we must find a way to encourage youths to continue using what they have learned.

♦ EXPLODING THE MYTHS

As we've seen, the caricature of the adolescent as giving up dependence on parents and forming a total dependence on peers is incorrect. The commonly held belief that parents' relationships with their adolescents are uniformly poor must also be reevaluated in view of recent research. This chapter has exposed and, one would hope, exploded, a number of myths.

The period of adolescence is one in which people are faced with important decisions in every area of life. A great deal has been recently written about moral education and the nature of personal choices. As we have seen, parents need not abdicate their special relationships with their children during this stage of their children's development. Supervision and guidance are part of a parent's responsibilities, but so is preparation for independent adulthood. Constant criticism, harsh punishment, and strict warnings are often ineffective, especially if they occur in a cold, hostile environment. Adolescents will be affected most by what they see and experience—and communication is most important. As Haim Ginott (1969, p. 243) said, "Character traits cannot be taught directly: no one can teach loyalty by lectures, courage by correspondence, or manhood by mail. Character education requires presence that demonstrates and contact that communicates. A teenager learns what he lives and becomes what he experiences. To him, our mood is the message, the style is the substance, the process is the product."

SUMMARY

1. Erik Erikson viewed the formation of a personal identity as the positive outcome of adolescence. Role confusion or role diffusion—the failure to answer the fundamental questions of identity—is the negative outcome of the stage.

2. James Marcia extended Erikson's conception of identity to include four identity statuses. Identity diffusion is a status in which a person has not begun to make any commitments. This status is considered negative only when an individual leaves adolescence without making reasonable progress toward finding an identity. Identity foreclosure is a status in which a person has made commitments prematurely. Identity moratorium is a temporary status in which an individual is not ready to make commitments but may be exploring possibilities. Identity achievers have gone through their crises and made their commitments. People who are identity achievers are generally more ready to form intimate relationships.

3. Forming a personal identity involves searching, and this effort may create anxiety in many people. Some try shortcuts, such as totally accepting others' values, fervently taking on a cause, or joining a group that is very strict and does not allow questioning, such as a cult.

4. Males and females may take different paths to identity formation. Males focus on intrapersonal factors, while women tend to tie their identities to interpersonal relationships. Some changes are taking place in this area, however, as many women now seek to balance a career with family responsibilities.

5. The popular picture of adolescence as a period of continuous conflict between parents and children and the replacement of parental influence by peers is not in keeping with findings of studies in this area. Although peer influence is significant, it does not replace that of parents. Most adolescents have good relationships with their parents. The period of adolescence is best seen as a time when children renegotiate their relationship with parents.

6. Peer influence peaks in the late junior high or early high school years. Traditionally, females have been considered less autonomous and more conforming, but these differences are narrowing and even disappearing. Peer influence is greater in the areas of social interaction, styles, and attitudes toward school than in the realm of deeper values.

7. Parents are more likely to be directive, to want to share their wisdom, and to explain their views than to listen to the opinions of their teens. Peer communication shows more give-and-take.

8. The generation gap is not as wide as first thought. Differences in the way the generations see the world are often a matter of degree, but each misperceives the opinions of the other.

9. The choice of a vocation affects one's entire lifestyle. For many female and minority youths, vocational choice is limited. However, women have made progress entering male-dominated occupations. The choice of a nontraditional career requires family support and adequate models. There has been some progress for minority youths entering the professions, but many minority adolescents do not have high vocational aspirations, lack adequate role models, and find that their choices are limited by lack of academic skills, economic resources, or racial discrimination. In addition, these young people are less likely to believe that they have the power to influence their own futures.

10. The junior high school and middle school were established to ease the transition to high school and to provide for the rapidly changing needs of young adolescents. Although most children adapt well to the transition to the intermediate school, the transition may be a problem, especially for females who may also be in the midst of many important physical changes. Many junior high school students, though, do not perceive their teachers as warm and encouraging and see the junior high school environment as somewhat impersonal.

11. High schools are changing in many ways. The course work is becoming more rigorous, minimum competency tests are now being given, thinking skills are emphasized, and family/health issues are being covered. There is a special, evolving concern for students who do not go on to college.

12. Most high school dropouts have average intelligence scores but lack academic skills, have little interest in school, and show a history of school-related problems. They are more likely to come from poor, large families or families where there is discord and divorce. Dropouts are more likely than graduates to find themselves in dead-end jobs.

13. Twenty-nine percent of all arrests for serious crimes in 1988 were of adolescents under the age of eighteen. Delinquents are most likely to come from homes filled with discord, where there is no supervision and where discipline is inconsistent and either very lax or very stringent.

ACTION/REACTION

What Am I To Be?

Kim had wanted to be a writer as long as her parents could remember. She excelled in writing all through her elementary, junior high, and high school years. Now in college, she finds herself with a problem. She did well in her early writing courses, but she notes that the other students in her more advanced classes are superior to her. After looking into the employment opportunities available in journalism, she has decided to seek a new major.

Kim has also lost interest in school. She goes to classes but is not doing well. She has a good relationship with her parents. She told them that without a goal there seems little reason to go to school. "Everyone needs a purpose." She is confused and unhappy.

This is complicated by the pressures of her boyfriend, Mark, who wants to get married as soon as possible. Mark is in graduate school, and they both will have to work for some time to survive financially. Before this semester, Kim told Mark that she wasn't ready. Now she is wavering.

Kim's parents have nothing against Mark. In fact, they like him. But they are afraid that once Kim goes to work she'll never go back to school. In addition, they're concerned that this radical change in Kim's marriage plans is associated with her change of major. When they confronted Kim with this, Kim admitted that could be so. However, she was quick to add that she and Mark would be getting married in a few years anyway.

1. If you were Kim, what would you do?
2. If you were Kim's parents, what would you do?
3. If you were Mark, what would you suggest to Kim?

Freedom for One, Slavery for the Other

Pamela is on strike. As far as she's concerned, she is a second-class citizen in her home, and she is tired of it. She's sixteen now, and according to Pam, her parents treat her like a nine-year-old. Pam has a strict curfew of eleven o'clock on weekends and must always tell her parents where she is and what she will be doing. When she get's home, what she calls "the inquisition" begins.

What bothers Pamela most is that her seventeen-year-old brother can come and go when he pleases and is not subject to "the inquisition." This is especially frustrating, because Pam thinks she is more mature than her brother. Another source of contention is the daily chores. Again, Pam's brother seems to get away with murder, while Pam has chores that take a lot of time.

Pam's parents had once seen a counselor, and they agreed to see the counselor again with Pam in hopes of straightening the situation out. They told the counselor that they were strict with Pamela but not overly so. They give Pam privacy, but they feel a responsibility to know where she is and what she's doing. If Pam is at a friend's house, she can stay out later, but Pam's parents don't want Pam "hanging out" anywhere. The family lives in a tough neighborhood, and Pam's parents are afraid something will happen to Pam.

As for allowing the brother more freedom, the parents note that the boy works part-time and he "can't get pregnant or raped." When it was suggested that he could get a girl pregnant, the parents shook their heads. "He's too smart for that." Pam's parents also claim that both children have chores. Pam's brother mows the lawn and takes out the garbage. Pam helps her mother cook and clean. Both children are responsible for their own rooms and laundering their own clothes.

1. If you were the counselor, what would you suggest?
2. If you were Pam's parents, what changes, if any, would you agree to?
3. If you were Pam, what would you do?

Glossary

accommodation The process by which one's existing structures are altered to fit new information.

adolescence The psychological experience of a young person from puberty to adulthood.

adolescent egocentrism The adolescent failure to differentiate between what one is thinking and what others are thinking.

altruism A type of prosocial behavior that involves actions that help people that are internally motivated and for which no reward is expected.

amniocentesis A procedure in which fluid is taken from a pregnant woman's uterus to check fetal cells for genetic and chromosomal abnormalities.

anal stage The second psychosexual stage, in which sexuality is centered on the anal cavity.

androgens A group of male hormones, including testosterone.

animism The preschooler's belief that everything, animate or inanimate, is conscious or alive.

anorexia nervosa A condition of self-imposed starvation found most often among adolescent females.

anoxia A condition in which the infant does not receive a sufficient supply of oxygen.

anxious attachment A general classification of insecure attachment shown in the "strange situation" consisting of either avoidant behavior or ambivalent attachment behavior.

anxious/ambivalent attachment A type of attachment behavior shown during the "strange situation," in which the child both seeks close contact and yet resists it during the mother's reentrance after a brief separation.

anxious/avoidant attachment A type of attachment behavior shown in the "strange situation," in which the child avoids reestablishing contact with the mother as she reenters the room after a brief separation.

Apgar Scoring System A relatively simple system that gives a gross measure of infant survivability.

artificialism The belief, common among preschoolers, that natural phenomena are caused by human beings.

assimilation The process by which information is altered to fit into one's already existing cognitive structures.

associative play A type of play seen in preschoolers in which they are actively involved with one another but cannot sustain these interactions.

attachment An emotional tie binding people together over space and time.

attachment behavior Actions by a child that result in the child's gaining proximity to caregivers.

attention deficit hyperactivity disorder A condition used to describe children who are impulsive, overly active, easily distracted and inattentive.

authoritarian parenting A style of parenting in which parents rigidly control their children's behavior by establishing rules and value obedience while discouraging questioning.

authoritative parenting A style of parenting in which parents establish limits but allow open communication and some freedom for children to make their own decisions in certain areas.

autonomy The positive outcome of the second stage of Erikson's psychosocial stage, an understanding that the child is someone on his or her own.

autonomy vs. shame or doubt The second psychosocial stage, in which the positive outcome is a sense of independence and the negative outcome is a sense of doubt about being a separate individual.

babbling Verbal production of vowel and consonant sounds strung together and often repeated.

Babinski reflex The reflex in which stroking the soles of a baby's feet results in the baby's toes fanning out.

Bayley Scales of Infant Development A test of intelligence administered to children between two months and two and a half years of age.

behavior genetics The study of how genetic endowment influences behavior.

Black English A dialect spoken throughout the United States by lower-income blacks but understood by the overwhelming majority of blacks.

behaviorists Psychologists who explain behavior in terms of the processes of learning such as classical and operant conditioning and emphasize the importance of the environment in determining behavior.

bilingual A term describing people who can function in more than one language.

blastocyst The stage of prenatal development in which the organism consists of layers of cells around a central cavity forming a hollow sphere.

Brazelton Neonatal Behavior Scale An involved system for evaluating an infant's reflexes and sensory and behavioral abilities.

Broca's area An area in the brain responsible for producing speech.

bulimia An eating disorder marked by episodic binging and purging.

canalization The self-righting process in which the child catches up in growth despite a moderate amount of stress or illness.

carrier A person possessing a particular gene or group of genes for a trait who does not show the trait but can pass it on to his or her offspring.

case study A method of research in which one person's progress is followed for an extended period of time.

centering The tendency to attend to only one dimension at a time.

cephalocaudal principle The growth principle stating that growth preceeds from the head downward to the trunk and feet.

Cesarean section The birth procedures by

which the fetus is surgically delivered through the abdominal wall and uterus.

child abuse A general term used to denote an injury intentionally perpetrated on a child.

child neglect A term used to describe a situation in which the care and supervision of a child is insufficient or improper.

chorionic villus sampling A diagnostic procedure in which cells are obtained from the chorion during the eighth to twelfth weeks of pregnancy and checked for genetic abnormalities.

chromosomes Rod-shaped structures that carry the genes.

chronological age A person's age according to birthdays.

classical conditioning A learning process in which a neutral stimulus is paired with a stimulus that elicits a response until the originally neutral stimulus elicits that response.

classification The process of placing objects into different classes.

cohort effect The effect of belonging to a particular generation and of being raised in a historical time.

commitment In psychosocial theory, making a decision concerning some question involved in identity formation and following a plan of action reflecting the decision.

communication The processing of sharing information

compensatory education The use of educational strategies in an attempt to reduce or eliminate some perceived difference between groups of children.

comprehension The understanding of language.

computer literacy A term used to describe general knowledge about computers that includes some technical knowledge of hardware and software, the ability to use computers to solve problems, and an awareness of how computers affect society.

concordance rate The degree of similarity between twins on any particular trait.

concrete operational stage Piaget's third stage of cognitive development, lasting roughly from seven through eleven years of age, in which children develop the ability to perform logical operations, such as conservation.

conditioned response The learned re-

sponse to the conditioned stimulus.

conditioned stimulus The stimulus that is neutral before conditioning and, after being paired with the unconditioned stimulus, will elicit the desired response by itself.

conscience Part of the superego that causes an individual to experience guilt when transgressing.

conscious Freudian term for thoughts or memories of which a person is immediately aware.

conservation The concept that quantities remain the same despite changes in their appearance.

contact comfort The need for physical touching and fondling.

conventional level Kohlberg's second level of moral reasoning, in which conformity to the expectations of others and society in general serves as the basis for moral decision making.

convergent thinking A type of thinking in which people solve problems by integrating information in a logical manner.

cooing Verbal production of single-syllable sounds, such as oo.

cooperative play A type of play seen in the later part of the preschool period and continuing into middle childhood, marked by group play, playing specific roles, and active cooperation for sustained periods of time.

correlation A term denoting a relationship between two variables.

creativity The production of a novel response that appropriately solves a given problem.

crisis In psychosocial theory, a time in which a person actively faces and questions aspects of his or her own identity.

critical (sensitive) period The period during which an event has its greatest impact.

crossing over The process occurring during meiosis in which genetic material on one chromosome is exchanged with material from the other.

cross sectional study A research design in which children of different ages are studied to obtain information about changes in some variable.

crowning The point in labor at which the baby's head appears.

cystic fibrosis A severe genetic disease marked by respiratory problems.

deciduous teeth The scientific term for baby teeth.

deductive reasoning Reasoning that begins with a general rule and is then applied to specific cases.

defense mechanism An automatic and unconscious process that reduces or eliminates feelings of anxiety or emotional conflict.

deferred imitation The ability to observe an act and imitate it at a later time.

delivery of the placenta The third and last stage of birth, in which the placenta is delivered.

dependent variable The factor in a study that will be measured by the researcher.

deprivation dwarfism Growth retardation due to emotional factors such as stress and lack of affection.

despair stage The second stage in prolonged separation from primary caregivers, in which the child becomes apathetic.

detachment stage The last stage in prolonged separation from the primary caregivers, in which the child cannot trust anyone else and becomes detached from other people.

developmental psychology The study of how organisms change over time.

dilation The first stage of labor, in which the uterus contracts and the cervix flattens and dilates to allow the fetus to pass.

discipline An attempt to control others in order to hold undesirable impulses in check and to encourage self-control.

discrimination The process by which a person learns to differentiate among stimuli.

displacement The process by which an emotion is transferred from one object or person to another, more acceptable substitute.

divergent thinking A type of thinking marked by the ability to see new relationships between things that are still appropriate to a situation.

dizygotic or fraternal twins Twins resulting from fertilization of two eggs by two different sperm and whose genetic composition is no more similar than any other pair of siblings.

dominant traits Traits that require the presence of only one gene.

Down syndrome A disorder caused by the presence of an extra chromosome, leading to a distinct physical appearance and often times mental retardation of varying degree.

dramatic play (pretend play) A type of play in which children take on the roles of others.

ego The part of the mind in Freudian theory that mediates between the real world and the desires of the id.

ego ideal The individual's positive and desirable standards of conduct.

egocentrism A thought process in which young children believe everyone is experiencing the environment in the same way they are. Children who are egocentric have difficulty understanding someone else's point of view.

Electra complex The female equivalent to the Oedipus complex in which the female experiences sexual feelings towards her father and wishes to do away with her mother.

embryonic stage The stage of prenatal development, from about two weeks to about eight weeks, when bone cells begin to replace cartilage.

emotional or psychological abuse Psychological damage perpetrated on the child by parental actions that often involve rejecting, isolating, terrorizing, ignoring, or corrupting.

epigenetic principle The preset development plan in Erikson's theory consisting of two elements: that personality develops according to maturationally determined steps and that each society is structured to encourage challenges that arise during these stages.

equilibration In Piagetian theory, the process by which children seek a balance between what they know and what they are experiencing.

eros In Freudian theory, the positive, constructive sex instinct.

estrogens A group of female hormones, including estradiol.

ethology The study of animal and human behavior in natural environments.

evoked potentials A technique of measuring the brain's responses to particular stimuli.

experimental method A research strategy using controls that allows the researcher to answer a particular question.

expressive children Children who use

words involved in social interactions, such as "stop" and "bye-bye."

expulsion The second stage of birth, involving actual delivery of the fetus.

external locus of control The belief that one is at the mercy of other people or of fate.

extinction The weakening and disappearance of a learned response.

failure to thrive syndrome Failure of a child to develop mentally and physically.

fear of strangers A common phenomenon beginning in the second half of the first year, consisting of a fear response to new people.

fetal alcohol effect An umbrella term used to describe damage to a child caused by the mother's imbibing alcohol during pregnancy that is somewhat less pronounced than fetal alcohol syndrome.

fetal alcohol syndrome A number of characteristics—including retardation, facial abnormalities, growth defects, and poor coordination—caused by maternal alcohol consumption during pregnancy.

fetal stage The stage of prenatal development beginning at about eight weeks and continuing until birth.

fine-tuning theory A theory noting that parents tune their language to a child's linguistic ability.

fontanels The soft spots on the top of a baby's head.

formal operations stage The last Piagetian stage of cognitive development, in which a person develops the ability to deal with abstractions and reasons in a scientific manner.

gametes The scientific term for the sex cells.

gender differences The differences between males and females that have been established through scientific investigation.

gender roles Behaviors expected of people in a given society on the basis of whether an individual is male or female.

gene The basic unit of heredity.

generation gap The differences in attitudes among various generations.

generativity vs. stagnation The seventh psychosocial stage, occurring during middle adulthood, in which the positive outcome is helping others and the nega-

tive outcome is being self-absorbed and stagnated.

genital stage The final psychosexual stage, occurring during adolescence, in which adult heterosexual behavior develops.

genotype The genetic configuration of the individual.

germinal stage The earliest stage of prenatal development, lasting from conception to about two weeks.

grammar A general term that refers to the total linguistic knowledge of phonology, morphology, syntax, and semantics.

grasping reflex A reflex in which a stroke on the palm causes the infant to make a fist.

guilt The negative outcome of the psychosocial crisis of the preschool period, resulting in a sense that the child's acts and desires are bad.

habituation The process by which organisms spend less and less time attending to familiar stimuli.

heritability A term used to describe how much of the variation seen in any particular trait is due to genetic endowment.

holophrase One word used to stand for an entire thought.

HOME scale A scale that provides a measure of the quality and quantity of the emotional and cognitive elements in the home.

horizontal decalage A term used to describe the unevenness of development in which a child may be able to solve one type of problem but not another, even though a common principle underlies them all.

hospitalism A condition found in children from substandard institutions, marked by emotional disturbances, failure to gain weight, and retardation.

hostile aggression Aggression that is aimed at injuring another person.

Huntington's chorea A dominant genetic disease affecting the central nervous system.

id The portion of the mind in Freudian theory that serves as the depository for wishes and desires.

identification The process by which children take on the characteristics of another person, most often a parent.

identity   The sense of knowing who you are.

identity achievement   An identity status in which a person has developed a solid personal identity.

identity diffusion   An identity status resulting in confusion, aimlessness, and a sense of emptiness.

identity foreclosure   An identity status marked by a premature identity decision.

identity moratorium   An identity status in which a person is actively searching for an identity.

identity vs. role confusion   The fifth psychosocial stage, in which the positive outcome is a sense of knowing who one is and the negative outcome is a sense of purposelessness.

imaginary audience   A term used to describe adolescents' belief that they are the focus of attention and being evaluated by everyone.

implantation   The process by which the fertilized egg burrows into the lining of the mother's uterus and obtains nourishment from the mother's system.

imprinting   An irreversible, rigid behavior pattern of attachment.

independent variable   The factor in a study that will be manipulated by the researcher.

inductive reasoning   Reasoning that proceeds from specific cases to the formation of a general rule.

industry   The positive outcome of the psychosocial crisis in the middle years of childhood, involving a feeling of self-confidence and pride concerning one's achievements.

industry vs. inferiority   The fourth psychosocial stage, in which the positive outcome is a sense of confidence concerning one's accomplishments and the negative outcome is a sense of inadequacy concerning one's achievements.

inferiority   The negative outcome of the psychosocial crisis in the middle years of childhood, involving the child's belief that his or her work and achievements are below par.

information process theory   An approach to understanding cognition that delves deeply into the way information is taken in, processed, and then acted upon.

initiative   The positive outcome of the psychosocial crisis of the preschool period, involving development of a respect for one's own wishes and desires

initiative vs. guilt   The third psychosexual stage, in which the positive outcome is a positive view of one's own desires and actions and the negative outcome is a sense of guilt over one's own actions.

instrumental aggression   Aggression that involves struggles over possessions.

integrity vs. despair   The eighth, and last, psychosocial stage, occurring during old age, in which the positive outcome is a sense of satisfaction with one's life and the negative outcome is a sense of bitterness concerning lost opportunities.

intelligence   The ability to profit from experience. A cluster of abilities, such as reasoning and memory. The ability to solve problems or fashion a product valued in one's society.

intelligence quotient (IQ)   A method of computing intelligence by dividing the mental age by the chronological age and multiplying by 100.

internal locus of control   The belief that one is in control of one's own fate.

intimacy vs. isolation   The sixth psychosocial stage, occurring during young adulthood, in which the positive outcome is a development of deep interpersonal relationships and the negative outcome is a flight from close relationships.

kwashiorkor   A nutritional problem often found in newly weaned children who are then subjected to a protein-deficient diet.

labor   A term used to describe the general process of expelling the fetus from the mother's womb.

Lamaze method   A method of prepared childbirth that requires active participation by both parents.

language   The use of symbols to represent meaning in some medium.

language-acquisition device   An assumed biological device used in the acquisition of language.

lanugo   The fine hair that covers a newborn infant.

latchkey or self-care children   Elementary schoolchildren who must care for themselves after school hours. (Some include junior high school students in the definition.)

latency stage   The psychosexual phase in which sexuality is dormant.

learning   Relatively permanent changes in behavior due to interaction with the environment.

learning disability   A group of disorders marked by significant difficulties in acquiring and using listening, speaking, reading, writing, reasoning skills or mathematics.

Leboyer method   A method of childbirth emphasizing the importance of the birth experience for the child and encouraging such practices as dim light, low voices, immediate physical contact with the mother, delay in cutting the umbilical cord, a bath, and a massage.

libido   In Freudian theory, the energy emanating from the sex instinct.

linguistic deficit hypothesis   The belief that a dialect such as Black English is a hindrance to learning.

linguistic difference hypothesis   The belief that a dialect such as Black English is different from Standard English but not a deficit.

longitudinal design   A research design in which the same subjects are followed over an extended period of time to note developmental changes in some variable.

love-oriented discipline   A type of discipline relying on the use of reasoning or love.

mainstreaming   The practice of placing disabled students into regular classrooms.

marasmus   A condition of severe underweight, heart irregularities, and weakened resistance caused by malnutrition.

mass to specific principle   A principle of muscular development stating that control of the mass or large muscles precedes control of the fine muscles.

maturation   A term used to describe changes that are due to the unfolding of an individual's genetic plan. These changes are relatively immune to environmental influence.

maturational age   A person's level of maturation relative to his or her peers.

meiosis   The process by which sex cells divide to form two cells, each containing twenty-three chromosomes.

Mendelian traits   Traits that follow a rather simple dominant-recessive pattern.

mental age   The age at which an individual is functioning.

mental retardation A condition marked by subnormal intellectual functioning and adjustment difficulties that occurs before a person is 18 years of age.

metacognition People's awareness of their own cognitive processes.

metamemory People's knowledge of their own memory processes.

mistrust The negative outcome of Erikson's first psychosocial stage, an attitude of suspiciousness.

monozygotic or identical twins Twins who develop from one fertilized egg and have an identical genetic structure.

moral realism The Piagetian stage of moral reasoning during which rules are viewed as sacred, and justice is whatever the authority figure says.

moral reasoning An approach to the study of moral development stressing the importance of the child's ideas and reasoning about justice and right and wrong.

moral relativism The Piagetian stage of moral reasoning in which children weigh the intentions of others before judging their actions right or wrong.

Moro reflex A reflex elicited by a sudden loud noise or momentary change in position, causing the back to arch, an extension of the arms and legs, and finally their contraction into a hugging position.

morpheme The smallest unit of meaning in a language.

morphology The study of the patterns of word formation in a particular language.

motherese The use of simple repetitive sentences with young children.

multifactorial traits Traits that are influenced both by genes and by the environment.

nativist explanation An explanation of language development based on biological or innate factors.

naturalistic observation A method of research in which the researcher observes organisms in their natural habitat.

neonate The scientific term for the baby in the first month of life.

object permanence The understanding that an object exists even when it is out of one's visual field.

Oedipus complex The conflict during the phallic stage in which a boy experiences sexual feelings towards his mother and wishes to do away with his father.

onlooker play A classification of play in which a child watches others play and shows some interest but is unable to join in.

operant conditioning The learning process in which behavior is governed by its consequences.

operation An internalized action that is part of the child's cognitive structure.

oral stage The first psychosexual stage, in which sexuality is centered on the oral cavity.

overextension A type of error in which children apply a term more broadly than it should be.

overgeneralization A type of error in which children overuse the basic rules of the language. For instance, once they learn to use plural nouns they may say "mans" instead of "men".

parallel play A type of play common in two-year-olds in which children play in the presence of other children but not with them.

permissive parenting A style of parenting marked by open communication and a lack of parental demand for good behavior.

personal fable The adolescents' belief that their experiences are unique and original.

phallic stage Freud's third psychosexual stage, occurring during early childhood, in which the sexual energy is located in the genital area.

phenotype The observable characteristics of the organism.

phenylketonuria (PKU) A recessive genetic disorder marked by the inability to digest a particular amino acid and leading to mental retardation if not treated.

phonology The study of the sounds of language, the rules for combining the sounds to make words, and the stress and intonation patterns of the language.

plasticity The extent to which an individual can be molded by environmental influence.

play An activity dominated by the child and performed with a positive feeling.

polygenic or multigenic traits Characteristics that are influenced by more than one pair of genes.

postconventional level Kohlberg's third level of moral reasoning in which moral decisions are made on the basis of individual values that have been internalized.

power-assertive discipline A type of discipline relying on the use of power, such as physical punishment or forceful commands.

pragmatics The study of how people use language in various contexts.

preconscious Freudian term for thoughts or memories that although not immediately conscious can easily become so.

preconventional level Kohlberg's first level of moral reasoning, in which satisfaction of one's own needs and reward and punishment serve as the bases for moral decision making.

prematurity Infants weighing less than five and a half pounds or born at or before thirty-seven weeks after conception.

preoperational stage The second stage in Piaget's theory of cognitive development, during which children cannot understand logical concepts such as conservation.

preterm infants Infants born at or before the thirty-seventh week of gestation.

primary circular reactions Actions that are repeated over and over again by infants.

primary process The process by which the id seeks to gratify its wishes.

primary sex characteristics Body changes directly associated with sexual reproduction.

production The ability to verbalize language.

Project Head Start A federally funded compensatory education program aimed at reducing or eliminating the differences in educational achievement between poor and middle-class youngsters.

prosocial behaviors Voluntary actions that are intended to help or benefit another individual or group.

protein-calorie deficiency The most common nutritional deficiency in the world, in which neither the number of calories nor the protein consumed is sufficient.

protest stage The initial reaction to separation in which the infant cries and refuses to be cared for by substitute caregivers.

prototype The most typical instance of a category.

proximodistal principle The growth principle stating that development occurs from the inside out—that the internal organs develop faster than the extremities.

psychosexual stages Stages in Freud's developmental theory.

puberty Physiological changes involved in sexual maturation, as well as other body changes that occur during the teen years.

punishment The process by which some negative consequence is administered to reduce the probability that misbehavior will recur.

qualitative changes Changes in function or process.

quantitative changes Changes considered solely in terms of increase or decrease, such as changes in height or weight.

readiness The point in development at which a child has the necessary skills to master a new challenge.

readiness tests Tests that measure whether a student has attained the skills necessary to master a new skill.

recall A way of testing retention in which the subject must produce the correct responses given very limited cues.

recessive traits Traits that require the presence of two genes.

reciprocal interaction The process by which an individual constantly affects and is affected by the environment.

recognition A way of testing retention in which the subject is required to choose the correct answer from a group of choices.

referential children Children whose early language is used to name objects, such as "dog" or "bed."

reflex A relatively simple automatic reaction to a particular stimulus.

reinforcer Any event that increases the likelihood that the behavior that preceded it will recur.

repression A defense mechanism in which memories are barred from consciousness.

retinopathy of prematurity A condition of blindness resulting from an oversupply of oxygen most often administered to premature infants.

reversibility Beginning at the end of an operation and working one's way back to the start.

Rh factor An antibody often, but not always, found in human beings.

risk benefit analysis A detailed analysis of the risks versus the benefits of a particular choice

role confusion (role diffusion) In psychosocial theory, the negative outcome of adolescence, which involves feelings of aimlessness and a failure to develop a personal identity.

rooting reflex The reflex in young infants in which a stroke on a cheek causes the infant to turn in the direction of the stimulus.

rubella A disease responsible for many cases of birth defects.

schema (information processing) An organized body of knowledge that functions as a framework describing objects and relationships that generally occur.

schema (Piagetian Theory) A method of dealing with the environment that can be generalized to many situations.

schizophrenia A severe mental disorder marked by hallucinations, delusions, and emotional disturbances.

script A structure that describes an appropriate sequence of events in a particular context.

secondary circular reactions Repetitive actions that are intended to create some environmental reaction.

secondary process or reality principle The process by which the ego satisfies the organism's need in a socially appropriate manner.

secondary sex characteristics Physical changes that distinguish males from females but are not associated with sexual reproduction.

secular trend The trend toward earlier maturation today compared with past generations.

secure attachment A type of attachment behavior in which the infant in the strange situation uses the mother as a secure base of operations.

self-concept The picture people have of themselves.

self-efficacy A term describing people's beliefs about what they can and cannot accomplish.

self-esteem The value people place on various aspects of their self.

self-fulfilling prophecy The concept that a person's expectations concerning some event affects the probability that it will occur.

semantic feature theory A theory of semantic and concept acquisition that argues that people develop concepts in terms of a concept's basic features.

semantics The study of the meaning of words.

sensorimotor stage The first stage in Piaget's theory of cognitive development, in which the child discovers the world using the senses and motor activity.

separation anxiety Fear of being separated from caregivers, beginning at eight or nine months and peaking at between twelve and sixteen months.

seriation The process of placing objects in size order.

sex chromosomes The twenty-third pair of chromosomes, which determines the gender of the organism.

sex-linked traits Traits that are inherited through genes found on the sex chromosomes.

sex typing The process by which an individual acquires the attitudes, values and behaviors viewed as appropriate for one sex or another in a particular culture.

shame or doubt The negative outcome of Erikson's second psychosocial stage, in which the child has a sense of shame or doubt about being a separate individual.

sickle cell anemia An inherited defect in the structure of red blood cells found mostly in blacks and latins.

small-for-date infants Infants born below the weight expected for their gestational age.

social cognition The relationship between cognition and both knowledge about and behavior regarding social situations and relationships.

social learning theory The theoretical view emphasizing the process by which people learn through observing others and imitating their behaviors.

social referencing The phenomenon in which a person uses information received from others to appraise events and regulate behavior.

solitary or independent play Play in which the child shows no interest in the activities of others.

sonogram An image of the developing organism taken through the use of sound waves.

stimulus deprivation The absence of adequate environmental stimulation.

stimulus discrimination The process by which a person learns to differentiate among stimuli.

stimulus generalization The tendency of an organism that has learned to associate a certain behavior with a particular stimulus to show this behavior when confronted with similar stimuli.

strange situation An experimental procedure used to measure attachment behaviors.

stress-resistant (resilient) children Children who do not appear to be negatively affected by stress and are able to cope with it and turn out healthy in the long run.

sucking reflex A reflex found in young infants in which an infant automatically sucks when something is placed in the mouth.

sudden infant death syndrome (SIDS) The diagnosis given to young infants whose cause of death cannot be determined.

superego The portion of the mind in psychoanalytic theory in which the conscience is found as well as standards of conduct internalized from parental teachings.

survey A method of study in which data are collected through written questionnaires or oral interviews from a number of people.

symbol Anything that can represent something else, such as words symbolizing an object.

synchrony The coordination between infant and caregiver in which each can respond to the subtle verbal and nonverbal cues of the other.

syntax The rules for combining words to make sentences.

Tay-Sachs disease A fatal genetic disease most commonly found in Jews who can trace their lineage to Eastern Europe.

telegraphic speech Sentences in which only the basic words necessary to communicate meaning are used, with helping words such as "a" or "to" left out.

temperament A group of characteristics reflecting an individual's way of responding to the environment and thought to be genetic.

teratogen Any agent that causes birth defects.

tertiary circular reactions Repetitive actions with some variations each time.

theory of multiple intelligences A conception of intelligence advanced by Howard Gardner, who argues that there are seven different types of intelligence.

transductive reasoning Preoperational reasoning in which young children reason from particular to particular.

transition A period late in labor in which the contractions become more difficult.

transitive inferences Statements of comparison, such as, "If X is taller than Y and Y is taller than Z, then X is taller than Z."

triarchic theory of human intelligence A theory of intelligence based on information processing considerations advanced by Robert Sternberg.

trust The positive outcome of Erik Erikson's first psychosocial stage, a feeling that one lives among friends.

trust vs. mistrust Erikson's first psychosocial stage, in which the positive outcome is a sense of trust and the negative outcome is a sense of suspicion.

unconditioned response The response to the unconditioned stimulus.

unconditioned stimulus The stimulus that elicits the response prior to conditioning.

unconscious Freudian term for memories that lie beyond normal awareness.

underextension The use of a word in a more narrow context than proper.

unoccupied play A type of play in which children sit and look at others or perform simple movements that are not goal related.

values Constructs that serve as internal guides for behavior.

vernix caseosa A thick liquid that protects the skin of the fetus.

visual cliff A device used to measure depth perception in infants.

Wernicke's area An area in the brain responsible for comprehension of language.

zygote A fertilized egg.

Appendix Tables

TABLE 1: Major Genetic and Chromosomal Disorders

DISORDER	DESCRIPTION/ IDENTIFICATION	INCIDENCE	CAUSE
Cleft Palate and Cleft Lip	Two sides of upper lip or palate fail to close	One in 700 births or about 5,000 per year	Multifactorial; multiple causes including genetic, prenatal insults, malnutrition, and drugs
Club Foot	Ankle and foot deformities; foot twisted in and down	One in 400 births or about 9,000 cases per year; twice as frequent in boys	Multifactorial
Congenital Heart Defects	Heart defects of varying degrees of severity	20,000 cases per year or one in 175 births	Multifactorial; often cause is unknown
Cystic Fibrosis	Thick mucus affecting lungs and secretions from organs	One in 25 Caucasians are carriers and 1 in 2,000 births have the disease. 30,000 people afflicted	Defective Cl^- transport that blocks the ion's release and the release of water from cells. Gene located on chromosome 7.
Diabetes I (Juvenile-onset)	Pancreatic problem brought on by lack of insulin	Ten percent of all cases; one child in 2,500	Multifactorial; 20 to 50 percent concordance in monozygotic twins; associated with certain virus and infections
Diabetes II (Adult-onset)	Pancreatic problem brought on by lack of insulin receptors or defective insulin	About 90 percent of all cases; five million Americans with disease	Multifactorial; nearly 100 percent concordance in monozygotic twins; associated with diet and obesity
Down Syndrome	Distinctive physical appearance allows for early identification	One in 600 births increasing with age of parents, especially mother; one in 30 for women in early 40s	Chromosomal abnormality; extra chromosome 21
Fragile X Syndrome	Mental retardation in males and females	One in every 2,000 males and in some females that are carriers	X chromosome breakage
Hemophilia	Lack of blood clotting	One in 10,000 births	Sex linked disorder (X-chromosome)
Huntington's Chorea	Deterioration of central nervous system and body during middle age	Extremely rare	Dominant trait; Gene on chromosome 4
Hydroencephalus	Excess fluid buildup in brain	One in 500 births	Multifactorial
Kleinfelter's Syndrome	Abnormal sexual development, sterility, absence of secondary sex characteristics: about half are mentally retarded: Identification in adolescence	One in every 600 male births	Chromosomal abnormality: XXY; cells have an extra X-chromosome

TABLE 1: Major Genetic and Chromosomal Disorders (continued)

PROBLEMS	TREATMENT	PRENATAL DETECTION	CARRIER DETECTION
Speech and cosmetic problems	Surgery	No	No
Walking difficulties	Casts and/or surgery	No	Possible
Depends upon severity of disorder; can be fatal	Surgery	Sometimes through ultrasound	No
Unable to breathe because of thick mucus, increase rate of lung infections. Blockage of pancreas, most die in their teens	Antibiotics and drugs to check infections and promote decongestion	Yes, 70% can be detected	Yes
Depending upon severity, diabetes may lead to serious medical problems, blindness, and death	Administration of insulin, dietary restrictions	No	No
Depending upon severity, diabetes may lead to serious medical problems, blindness, and death	Administration of insulin, dietary restrictions	No	No
Moderate to severe retardation and physical problems especially involving circulatory and respiratory systems	Good medical care and surgery to correct structural heart problems; special education and help for parents to enable them to care for child at home	Yes	Possible in 5 percent of cases.**
Mental retardation, long faces, large testicles, 10–15% of autistic males have a break in their X.	None	Yes	Yes, 20% of fragile X males do not show signs of the syndrome
Potential life threatening crises whenever injured	Blood transfusions and administration of "clotting factor"	Yes*†	Yes*
Disorder is fatal	None	Yes*	Yes*
Brain damage; can be fatal	Surgery	Sometimes	No
Mental retardation, emotional problems, sperm usually not produced, some breast development	Administration of testosterone	Yes	No

TABLE 1: Major Genetic and Chromosomal Disorders

DISORDER	DESCRIPTION/ IDENTIFICATION	INCIDENCE	CAUSE
Muscular Dystrophy (Duchenne)	Progressive muscular deterioration; there are many diseases which fall under this title; the most common form, called Duchenne, begins in childhood	One in 4,000 males have Duchenne	Duchenne is a recessive X-linked (almost always boys are affected); other forms follow other patterns
Neurofibromatosis Type-1	Benign tumors of Schwann cells surrounding peripheral nerves (Elephant man syndrome)	One in 3,500 births or about 1,000 per year. (70,000 people afflicted in U.S.)	Caused by problem with tumor suppressor gene located on Chromosome 7
Phenylketonuria (PKU)	Inability to process phenylalanine prevents brain development; blood test can identify disorder two days after birth	One in 10,000 births; more often found among North Europeans	Recessive trait; abnormal gene
Pyloric Stenosis	Digestive difficulties caused by an overgrowth of muscle in the lower stomach; identification early in infancy since infants cannot keep food down and do not gain weight	One in every 200 boys and one in every 1,000 girls	Multifactorial
Rh Disease	Blood disorder	7,000 babies per year	If mother is Rh negative and baby is Rh positive some of mother's antibodies may kill baby's red blood cells
Sickle Cell Anemia	Blood disorder causes damage to vital organs; diagnosed through blood test	One in every 400–600 Blacks; one in every 1,000–1,500 Hispanics	Recessive trait; abnormal gene
Spina Bifida	Spine fails to close; noticeable at birth	One in 1,000 births	Multifactorial
Tay Sachs Disease	Enzyme deficiency causes buildup of fat in nerve cells; leads to retardation, blindness, and convulsions; identification through exaggerated startle response and psychomotor retardation in infancy	One in every 25 American Jews is a carrier	Recessive trait; abnormal gene
Thalasemia (Cooley's Anemia)	Severe anemia and listlessness; identified through blood test	3 to 10 percent of Greeks and Italians are carriers; about 1,000 cases per year	Partially recessive trait; abnormal gene on an autosome

TABLE 1: Major Genetic and Chromosomal Disorders (continued)

PROBLEMS	TREATMENT	PRENATAL DETECTION	CARRIER DETECTION
Weakening and wasting away of muscles leads to physical incapabilities and death	Physical therapy and surgery	Yes*	Yes*
Tumors around nerves, learning disabilities, increased incidence of malignant cancers	Surgery	In some cases but in most cases, No	No
If left untreated condition leads to mental retardation, restlessness, and irritability	Low phenylalanine diet; no cow's milk	Yes*	Yes*
Can be fatal if not corrected	Surgery	No	No
Blood problems, multiple medical difficulties: can be fatal	Transfusions; prevention possible if mother receives shot of Rh immune globulin after birth, miscarriage, or after prenatal diagnosis	Yes	Yes
Problems vary depending upon severity of disorder; can be fatal	Medical care to reduce pain and severity of disorder	Yes*	Yes*
May lead to paralysis and problems in bladder and bowel control	Surgery, physical therapy, and training in personal hygiene	Yes	No
Disease is fatal in all cases; death occurs usually between the ages of three to five years	Not available	Yes	Yes
Severe anemia causes many physical problems	Blood transfusions and bone marrow transplants	Yes*	Yes*

TABLE 1: Major Genetic and Chromosomal Disorders

DISORDER	DESCRIPTION/ IDENTIFICATION	INCIDENCE	CAUSE
Turner's Syndrome	Females with short stature, delayed sexual development, infantile genitalia, swelling of feet, hands, and neck, heart abnormalities	One in every 2,000–3,000 live births	Chromosomal problems: Forty-five chromosomes, cells are missing a sex (Y or X) chromosome. They are symbolized OX.

*A new method that requires only routine amniocentesis uses sophisticated chemical techniques to study variations in DNA called polymorphisms. The polymorphisms are compared with those signifying a particular genetic disorder thus allowing for detection of the abnormal gene signifying the disorder. This method has been used in the detection of hemophilia, cystic fibrosis, muscular dystrophy, phenylketonuria, sickle cell anemia, and thalasemia among others. Carrier detection is found through testing tissue from adults. Both prenatal and carrier detection require the genetic evaluation of close relatives as well.

**About five percent of Down's Syndrome incidence is due to an unbalanced translocation (chromosomal rearrangement). Such cases are independent of maternal age. If one of the parents is known to "carry" this chromosome rearrangement (translocation) in a balanced fashion, then all pregnancies should be monitored by prenatal diagnosis. Carriers of chromosomal translocations are identified by performing a chromosomal analysis of their blood.

TABLE 2: Growth in Infancy and Toddlerhood
All data is presented in centimeters. To convert to inches multiply by .39.

| SEX AND AGE | PERCENTILE | | | | | | |
	5th	10th	25th	50th	75th	90th	95th
Male	Recumbent length in centimeters						
Birth	46.4	47.5	49.0	50.5	51.8	53.5	54.4
1 month	50.4	51.3	53.0	54.6	56.2	57.7	58.6
3 months	56.7	57.7	59.4	61.1	63.0	64.5	65.4
6 months	63.4	64.4	66.1	67.8	69.7	71.3	72.3
9 months	68.0	69.1	70.6	72.3	74.0	75.9	77.1
12 months	71.7	72.8	74.3	76.1	77.7	79.8	81.2
18 months	77.5	78.7	80.5	82.4	84.3	86.6	88.1
24 months	82.3	83.5	85.6	87.6	89.9	92.2	93.8
30 months	87.0	88.2	90.1	92.3	94.6	97.0	98.7
36 months	91.2	92.4	94.2	96.5	98.9	101.4	103.1
Female							
Birth	45.4	46.5	48.2	49.9	51.0	52.0	52.9
1 month	49.2	50.2	51.9	53.5	54.9	56.1	56.9
3 months	55.4	56.2	57.8	59.5	61.2	62.7	63.4
6 months	61.8	62.6	64.2	65.9	67.8	69.4	70.2
9 months	66.1	67.0	68.7	70.4	72.4	74.0	75.0
12 months	69.8	70.8	72.4	74.3	76.3	78.0	79.1
18 months	76.0	77.2	78.8	80.9	83.0	85.0	86.1
24 months	81.3	82.5	84.2	86.5	88.7	90.8	92.0
30 months	86.0	87.0	88.9	91.3	93.7	95.6	96.9
36 months	90.0	91.0	93.1	95.6	98.1	100.0	101.5

Source: P. V. V. Hamill et al., 1977.

TABLE 1: Major Genetic and Chromosomal Disorders (continued)

PROBLEMS	TREATMENT	PRENATAL DETECTION	CARRIER DETECTION
Child has normal intelligence although perceptual deficits are common; physical stature and sexual problems may lead to social problems	Hormone therapy, counseling	Yes	No

†Fetal blood may be sampled by a process called fetoscopy. This has a risk of miscarriage of 3 to 5 percent as compared to the ½ of 1 percent risk associated with amniocentesis.

Sources: L. F. Annis, 1978; V. Apgar and J. Beck, 1973; D. Bergsma, 1979; R. M. Goodman and R. J. Gorlin, 1983; N. J. Karagan, 1979; A. P. Mange and E. J. Mange, 1980; March of Dimes, FACTS, 1984; S. Sassower, 1985; D. W. Smith, 1982; R. Thompson and A. P. Thompson, 1980; Cahill, 1987; J. S. Colome, 1990; J. Stone, 1987.

TABLE 3: Weight Gain in Infancy and Toddlerhood
All data is given in kilograms. To convert to pounds multiply by 2.2.

SEX AND AGE	PERCENTILE						
	5th	10th	25th	50th	75th	90th	95th
Male	Weight in kilograms						
Birth	2.54	2.78	3.00	3.27	3.64	3.82	4.15
1 month	3.16	3.43	3.82	4.29	4.75	5.14	5.28
3 months	4.43	4.78	5.32	5.98	6.56	7.14	7.37
6 months	6.20	6.61	7.20	7.85	8.49	9.10	9.46
9 months	7.52	7.95	8.56	9.18	9.88	10.49	10.93
12 months	8.43	8.84	9.49	10.15	10.91	11.54	11.99
18 months	9.59	9.92	10.67	11.47	12.31	13.05	13.44
24 months	10.54	10.85	11.65	12.59	13.44	14.29	14.70
30 months	11.44	11.80	12.63	13.67	14.51	15.47	15.97
36 months	12.26	12.69	13.58	14.69	15.59	16.66	17.28
Female							
Birth	2.36	2.58	2.93	3.23	3.52	3.64	3.81
1 month	2.97	3.22	3.59	3.98	4.36	4.65	4.92
3 months	4.18	4.47	4.88	5.40	5.90	6.39	6.74
6 months	5.79	6.12	6.60	7.21	7.83	8.38	8.73
9 months	7.00	7.34	7.89	8.56	9.24	9.83	10.17
12 months	7.84	8.19	8.81	9.53	10.23	10.87	11.24
18 months	8.92	9.30	10.04	10.82	11.55	12.30	12.76
24 months	9.87	10.26	11.10	11.90	12.74	13.57	14.08
30 months	10.78	11.21	12.11	12.93	13.93	14.81	15.35
36 months	11.60	12.07	12.99	13.93	15.03	15.97	16.54

Source: P. V. V. Hamill et al., 1977.

TABLE 4: Growth in Early Childhood

The slowing rate of growth during early childhood is shown in this table. The data are given in centimeters. To convert to inches, multiply by .39.

| SEX AND AGE | PERCENTILE | | | | | | |
	5th	10th	25th	50th	75th	90th	95th
Male	Stature in centimeters						
3.0 years	89.0	90.3	92.6	94.9	97.5	100.1	102.0
3.5 years	92.5	93.9	96.4	99.1	101.7	104.3	106.1
4.0 years	95.8	97.3	100.0	102.9	105.7	108.2	109.9
4.5 years	98.9	100.6	103.4	106.6	109.4	111.9	113.5
5.0 years	102.0	103.7	106.5	109.9	112.8	115.4	117.0
5.5 years	104.9	106.7	109.6	113.1	116.1	118.7	120.3
6.0 years	107.7	109.6	112.5	116.1	119.2	121.9	123.5
Female							
3.0 years	88.3	89.3	91.4	94.1	96.6	99.0	100.6
3.5 years	91.7	93.0	95.2	97.9	100.5	102.8	104.5
4.0 years	95.0	96.4	98.8	101.6	104.3	106.6	108.3
4.5 years	98.1	99.7	102.2	105.0	107.9	110.2	112.0
5.0 years	101.1	102.7	105.4	108.4	111.4	113.8	115.6
5.5 years	103.9	105.6	108.4	111.6	114.8	117.4	119.2
6.0 years	106.6	108.4	111.3	114.6	118.1	120.8	122.7

Source: P. V. V. Hamill et al., 1977.

TABLE 5: Weight Gain in Early Childhood

The data are given in kilograms. To convert to pounds, multiply by 2.2.

| SEX AND AGE | PERCENTILE | | | | | | |
	5th	10th	25th	50th	75th	90th	95th
Male	Weight in kilograms						
3.0 years	12.05	12.58	13.52	14.62	15.78	16.95	17.77
3.5 years	12.84	13.41	14.46	15.68	16.90	18.15	18.98
4.0 years	13.64	14.24	15.39	16.69	17.99	19.32	20.27
4.5 years	14.45	15.10	16.30	17.69	19.06	20.50	21.63
5.0 years	15.27	15.96	17.22	18.67	20.14	21.70	23.09
5.5 yeas	16.09	16.83	18.14	19.67	21.25	22.96	24.66
6.0 years	16.93	17.72	19.07	20.69	27.40	24.31	26.34
Female							
3.0 years	11.61	12.26	13.11	14.10	15.50	16.54	17.22
3.5 years	12.37	13.08	14.00	15.07	16.59	17.77	18.59
4.0 years	13.11	13.84	14.80	15.96	17.56	18.93	19.91
4.5 years	13.83	14.56	15.55	16.81	18.48	20.06	21.24
5.0 years	14.55	15.26	16.29	17.66	19.39	21.23	22.62
5.5 years	15.29	15.97	17.05	18.56	20.36	22.48	24.11
6.0 years	16.05	16.72	17.86	19.52	21.44	23.89	25.75

Source: P. V. V. Hamill et al., 1977.

TABLE 6: Growth in Middle Childhood
Stature is noted in centimeters. To convert to inches, multiply by .39.

| SEX AND AGE | PERCENTILE | | | | | | |
	5th	10th	25th	50th	75th	90th	95th
Male			Stature in centimeters				
6.0 years	107.7	109.6	112.5	116.1	119.2	121.9	123.5
6.5 years	110.4	112.3	115.3	119.0	122.2	124.9	126.6
7.0 years	113.0	115.0	118.0	121.7	125.0	127.9	129.7
7.5 years	115.6	117.6	120.6	124.4	127.8	130.8	132.7
8.0 years	118.1	120.2	123.2	127.0	130.5	133.6	135.7
8.5 years	120.5	122.7	125.7	129.6	133.2	136.5	138.8
9.0 years	122.9	125.2	128.2	132.2	136.0	139.4	141.8
9.5 years	125.3	127.6	130.8	134.8	138.8	142.4	144.9
10.0 years	127.7	130.1	133.4	137.5	141.6	145.5	148.1
10.5 years	130.1	132.6	136.0	140.3	144.6	148.7	151.5
11.0 years	132.6	135.1	138.7	143.3	147.8	152.1	154.9
11.5 years	135.0	137.7	141.5	146.4	151.1	155.6	158.5
12.0 years	137.6	140.3	144.4	149.7	154.6	159.4	162.3
Female							
6.0 years	106.6	108.4	111.3	114.6	118.1	120.8	122.7
6.5 years	109.2	111.0	114.1	117.6	121.3	124.2	126.1
7.0 years	111.8	113.6	116.8	120.6	124.4	127.6	129.5
7.5 years	114.4	116.2	119.5	123.5	127.5	130.9	132.9
8.0 years	116.9	118.7	122.2	126.4	130.6	134.2	136.2
8.5 years	119.5	121.3	124.9	129.3	133.6	137.4	139.6
9.0 years	122.1	123.9	127.7	132.2	136.7	140.7	142.9
9.5 years	124.8	126.6	130.6	135.2	139.8	143.9	146.2
10.0 years	127.5	129.5	133.6	138.3	142.9	147.2	149.5
10.5 years	130.4	132.5	136.7	141.5	146.1	150.4	152.8
11.0 years	133.5	135.6	140.0	144.8	149.3	153.7	156.2
11.5 years	136.6	139.0	143.5	148.2	152.6	156.9	159.5
12.0 years	139.8	142.3	147.0	151.5	155.8	160.0	162.7

Source: P. V. V. Hamill et al., 1977.

TABLE 7: Weight Gain in Middle Childhood
All data are given in kilograms. To convert to pounds, multiply by 2.2.

SEX AND AGE	PERCENTILE						
	5th	10th	25th	50th	75th	90th	95th
Male	Weight in kilograms						
6.0 years	16.93	17.72	19.07	20.69	22.40	24.31	26.34
6.5 years	17.78	18.62	20.02	21.74	23.62	25.76	28.16
7.0 years	18.64	19.53	21.00	22.85	24.94	27.36	30.12
7.5 years	19.52	20.45	22.02	24.03	26.36	29.11	32.73
8.0 years	20.40	21.39	23.09	25.30	27.91	31.06	34.51
8.5 years	21.31	22.34	24.21	26.66	29.61	33.22	36.96
9.0 years	22.25	23.33	25.40	28.13	31.46	35.57	39.58
9.5 years	23.25	24.38	26.68	29.73	33.46	38.11	42.35
10.0 years	24.33	25.52	28.07	31.44	35.61	40.80	45.27
10.5 years	25.51	26.78	29.59	33.30	37.92	43.63	48.31
11.0 years	26.80	28.17	31.25	35.30	40.38	46.57	51.47
11.5 years	28.24	29.72	33.08	37.46	43.00	49.61	54.73
12.0 years	29.85	31.46	35.09	39.78	45.77	52.73	58.09
Female							
6.0 years	16.05	16.72	17.86	19.52	21.44	23.89	25.75
6.5 years	16.85	17.51	18.76	20.61	22.68	25.50	27.59
7.0 years	17.71	18.39	19.78	21.84	24.16	27.39	29.68
7.5 years	18.62	19.37	20.95	23.26	25.90	29.57	32.07
8.0 years	19.62	20.45	22.26	24.84	27.88	32.04	34.71
8.5 years	20.68	21.64	23.70	26.58	30.08	34.73	37.58
9.0 years	21.82	22.92	25.27	28.46	32.44	37.60	40.64
9.5 years	23.05	24.29	26.94	30.45	34.94	40.61	43.85
10.0 years	24.36	25.76	28.71	32.55	37.53	43.70	47.17
10.5 years	25.75	27.32	30.57	34.72	40.17	46.84	50.57
11.0 years	27.24	28.97	32.49	36.95	42.84	49.96	54.00
11.5 years	28.83	30.71	34.48	39.23	45.48	53.03	57.42
12.0 years	30.52	32.53	36.52	41.53	48.07	55.99	60.81

Source: P. V. V. Hamill et al., 1977.

TABLE 8: Growth in Adolescence
Stature is given in centimeters. To convert to inches, multiply by .39.

SEX AND AGE	PERCENTILE						
	5th	10th	25th	50th	75th	90th	95th
Male	Stature in centimeters						
12.0 years	137.6	140.3	144.4	149.7	154.6	159.4	162.3
12.5 years	140.2	143.0	147.4	153.0	158.2	163.2	166.1
13.0 years	142.9	145.8	150.5	156.5	161.8	167.0	169.8
13.5 years	145.7	148.7	153.6	159.9	165.3	170.5	173.4
14.0 years	148.8	151.8	156.9	163.1	168.5	173.8	176.7
14.5 years	152.0	155.0	160.1	166.2	171.5	176.6	179.5
15.0 years	155.2	158.2	163.3	169.0	174.1	178.9	181.9
15.5 years	158.3	161.2	166.2	171.5	176.3	180.8	183.9
16.0 years	161.1	163.9	168.7	173.5	178.1	182.4	185.4
16.5 years	163.4	166.1	170.6	175.2	179.5	183.6	186.6
17.0 years	164.9	167.7	171.9	176.2	180.5	184.4	187.3
17.5 years	165.6	168.5	172.4	176.7	181.0	185.0	187.6
18.0 years	165.7	168.7	172.3	176.8	181.2	185.3	187.6
Female							
12.0 years	139.8	142.3	147.0	151.5	155.8	160.0	162.7
12.5 years	142.7	145.4	150.1	154.6	158.8	162.9	165.6
13.0 years	145.2	148.0	152.8	157.1	161.3	165.3	168.1
13.5 years	147.2	150.0	154.7	159.0	163.2	167.3	170.0
14.0 years	148.7	151.5	155.9	160.4	164.6	168.7	171.3
14.5 years	149.7	152.5	156.8	161.2	165.6	169.8	172.2
15.0 years	150.5	153.2	157.2	161.8	166.3	170.5	172.8
15.5 years	151.1	153.6	157.5	162.1	166.7	170.9	173.1
16.0 years	151.6	154.1	157.8	162.4	166.9	171.1	173.3
16.5 years	152.2	154.6	158.2	162.7	167.1	171.2	173.4
17.0 years	152.7	155.1	158.7	163.1	167.3	171.2	173.5
17.5 years	153.2	155.6	159.1	163.4	167.5	171.1	173.5
18.0 years	153.6	156.0	159.6	163.7	167.6	171.0	173.6

Source: P. V. V. Hamill et al., 1977.

TABLE 9: Weight Gain in Adolescence
All data are given in kilograms. To convert to pounds, multiply by 2.2.

SEX AND AGE	PERCENTILE						
	5th	10th	25th	50th	75th	90th	95th
Male	Weight in kilograms						
12.0 years	29.85	31.46	35.09	39.78	45.77	52.73	58.09
12.5 years	31.64	33.41	37.31	42.27	48.70	55.91	61.52
13.0 years	33.64	35.60	39.74	44.95	51.79	59.12	65.02
13.5 years	35.85	38.03	42.40	47.81	55.02	62.35	68.51
14.0 years	38.22	40.64	45.21	50.77	58.31	65.57	72.13
14.5 years	40.66	43.34	48.08	53.76	61.58	68.76	75.66
15.0 years	43.11	46.06	50.92	56.71	64.72	71.91	79.12
15.5 years	45.50	48.69	53.64	59.51	67.64	74.98	82.45
16.0 years	47.74	51.16	56.16	62.10	70.26	77.97	85.62
16.5 years	49.76	53.39	58.38	64.39	72.46	80.84	88.59
17.0 years	51.50	55.28	60.22	66.31	74.17	83.58	91.31
17.5 years	52.89	56.78	61.61	67.78	75.32	86.14	93.73
18.0 years	53.97	57.89	62.61	68.88	76.04	88.41	95.76
Female							
12.0 years	30.52	32.53	36.42	41.53	48.07	55.99	60.81
12.5 years	32.30	34.42	38.59	43.84	50.56	58.81	64.12
13.0 years	34.14	36.35	40.65	46.10	42.91	61.45	67.30
13.5 years	35.98	38.26	42.65	48.26	55.11	63.87	70.30
14.0 years	37.76	40.11	44.54	50.28	57.09	66.04	73.08
14.5 years	39.45	41.83	46.28	52.10	58.84	67.95	75.59
15.0 years	40.99	43.38	47.82	53.68	60.32	69.54	77.78
15.5 years	42.32	44.72	49.10	54.96	61.48	70.79	79.59
16.0 years	43.41	45.78	50.09	55.89	62.29	71.68	80.99
16.5 years	44.20	46.54	50.75	56.44	62.75	72.18	81.93
17.0 years	44.74	47.04	51.14	56.69	62.91	72.38	82.46
17.5 years	45.08	47.33	51.33	56.71	62.89	72.37	82.82
18.0 years	45.26	47.47	51.39	56.62	62.78	72.25	82.47

Source: P. V. V. Hamill et al., 1977.

References

Abarbanel, A. (1979). Shared parenting after separation and divorce: A study of joint custody. *American Journal of Orthopsychiatry, 49,* 320–329.

Acus, L. K. (1982, January 24) Quarreling Kids? How to Handle Them. Long Island, *Newsday,* 16 ff.

Abramovitch, R., Corter, C., & Lando, B. (1979). Sibling interaction in the home. *Child Development, 50,* 997–1003.

Abramovitch, R., Corter, C., & Pepler, D. (1980). Observations of mixed-sex sibling dyads. *Child Development, 51,* 1268–1271.

Abramovitch, R., Corter, C., Pepler, D. J., & Stanhope, L. (1986). Sibling and peer interaction: A final follow-up and a comparison. *Child Development, 57,* 217–229.

Adams, G. R., Abraham, K. G., & Markstrom, C. A. (1987). The relations among identity development, self-consciousness and self-focusing during middle and late adolescence. *Development Psychology, 23,* 292–298.

Adams, R. J. (1987). An evaluation of color preference in early infancy. *Infant Behavior and Development, 10,* 143–150.

Adams, R. J. (1989). Newborns' discrimination among mid-and long-wavelength stimuli. *Journal of Experimental Child Psychology, 47,* 130–141.

Adams-Tucker, C. (1982). Proximate effects of sexual abuse in childhood: A report on 28 children. *American Journal of Psychiatry, 139,* 1252–1256.

Adelson, J. (1982). The Political imagination of the young adolescent. In J. Kagan & R. Coles (Ed.), *Twelve to sixteen: Early adolescence,* New York: Norton.

Adelson, J., & O'Neil, R. P. (1966). Growth of political ideas in adolescence: The sense of community. *Journal of Personality and Social Psychology, 4,* 295–306.

Adeyanju, M. (1990). Adolescent health status, behaviors and cardiovascular disease. *Adolescence, 25,* 155–169.

Adler, L. L. (1982). Cross-cultural research and theory. In B. B. Wolman (Ed.), *Handbook of developmental psychology* (pp. 76–88). Englewood Cliffs, NJ: Prentice-Hall.

Adler, R., & Faber, R. (1980). Background: Children's television viewing patterns. In R. P. Adler, G. S. Lesser, L. K. Meringoff, T. S. Robertson, J. R. Rossiter, & F. Ward. (Eds.), *The effects of television advertising on children: Review and recommendations* (pp. 13–28). Lexington, MA: Lexington Books.

Adler, R. P. (1980). Children's television advertising: History of the issue. In *Children and the faces of television: Teaching, violence, spelling* (pp. 237–251). New York: Academic Press.

Ahammer, I. M., & Murray, J. P. (1979). Kindness in the kindergarten: The relative influence of role playing and prosocial television in facilitating altruism. *International Journal. of Behavioral Development, 2,* 133–157.

Ainslee, R. C. (1985). *The psychology of twinship.* Lincoln, NB: University of Nebraska Press.

Ainsworth, M.D.S. (1967). Infancy in Uganda: Infant care and growth of attachment. Baltimore: Johns Hopkins University Press.

Ainsworth, M.D.S. (1974). The development of infant-mother attachment. In B. Caldwell & H. Riciutti (Eds.), *Review of child development* (Vol. 3). Chicago: University of Chicago Press.

Ainsworth M.D.S. (1979). Infant-mother attachment. *American Psychologist, 34,* 932–938.

Ainsworth M.D.S., & Bell, S. M. (1977). Infant crying and maternal responsiveness: A rejoinder to Gewirtz and Boyd. *Child Development, 48,* 1208–1216.

Ainsworth, M.D.S., Bell, S. M., & Slayton, D. J. (1971). Individual differences in the strange situation behavior of one-year-olds. In H. R. Schaffer (Ed.), *The origins of human social relations.* London: Academic Press.

Ainsworth, M.D.S., Blehar, M. C., Waters, E., & Wall, S. (1978). *Patterns of attachment.* Hillsdale, NJ: Erlbaum.

Ainsworth, M.D.S., & Wittig, B.A. (1969) Attachment and the exploratory behavior of one-year-olds in a strange situation. In B.M. Foss (ed.) *Determinants of Infant Behavior.* Vol. 4, (pp. 113–136). London: Methuen.

Aitchison, J. (1978). *The articulate mammal: An introduction to psycholinguistics.* New York: Universe Books.

Akiyama, M. M. (1984), Are language-acquisition strategies universal? *Developmental Psychology, 20,* 219–229.

Akiyama, M. M. (1985). Denials in young children from a cross-linguistic perspective. *Child Development, 56,* 95–102.

Albrecht, S. L., Bahr, H. M., & Chadwick, B. A., (1977). Public stereotyping of roles, personality characteristics, and occupations. *Sociology and Social Research, 61,* 223–240.

Alexander, G. J., Miles, B. E., Gold, G. M., & Alexander, R. B. (1967). LSD: Injection in early pregnancy produces abnormalities in off-spring of rats. *Science, 157,* 459–460.

Allen, A. W., & Harley, D. (1975). *Art through your child's eyes.* New York: Allen and Herley.

Allen, B. P. (1987), Youth suicide. *Adolescence, 22,* 271–288.

Alessandri, S. M., & Wozniak, R. H. (1989). Perception of the family environment and intrafamilial agreement in belief concerning the adolescent. *Journal of Early Adolescence, 9,* 67–81.

Alley, T. R. (1981) Headshape and the Perception of Cuteness. *Developmental Psychology, 17,* 650–655.

Allison, P. D., & Furstenberg Jr., F. F. (1989). How marital dissolution affects children: Variations by age and sex. *Developmental Psychology, 25,* 540–550.

Allnut, B. L. (1979). The motherless child. In J. D. Call, J. D. Nosphitz, R. L. Cohen, & I. N. Berlin (Eds.), *Basic handbook of child psychiatry.* New York: Basic Books. (pp. 373–378).

Allport, G. W. (1954). *The nature of prejudice.* Reading, MA: Addison-Wesley.

Altrocchi, J. (1980). *Abnormal psychology*. New York: Harcourt Brace Jovanovich.

Alvartez, W.–F. (1985) The meaning of maternal employment for mothers and their perceptions of their three-year old children. *Child Development, 56*, 350–361.

American Home Economics Association (1986). Preventing adolescent pregnancy: Promising new approaches. *Journal of Home Economics, 78*, 42–47.

American Psychiatric Association. (1980). *Diagnostic and statistical manual of mental disorders* (3rd. ed.). Washington, DC.: American Psychiatric Association.

American Psychological Association (APA) (1973). *Ethical principles in the conduct of research with human beings*. Washington, DC.: American Psychological Association.

American Psychological Association (APA) (1975). *Careers in psychology*. Washington, DC.: American Psychological Association.

Ames, L. B. (1986, Summer) Ready or not. *American Educator, 10*, 30–34.

Ames, R. (1957). Physical maturing among boys as related to adult social behavior: A longitudinal study. *California Journal of Educational Research, 8*, 69–75.

Anand, K. J. S. & Hickey, R. R. (1987) Pain and Its Effects in the Human Neonate and Fetus. *New England Journal of Medicine, 317*, 1321–1329.

Anastasi, A. (1958). Heredity, environment, and the question of "How?" *Psychological Review, 65*, 197–208.

Anastasi, A. (1988). *Psychological testing* (6th ed.). New York: Macmillan.

Anderson, C. W., Nagle, R. J., Roberts, W. A., & Smith, J. W. (1981). Attachment to substitute caregivers as a function of center quality and caregiver involvement. *Child Development, 52*, 53–61.

Anderson, D. R., Alwitt, L. J., Lorch, E. P., & Levin, S. R. (1979) Watching children watch television, in G. Hale & M. Lewis (eds). *Attention and Cognitive Development*. New York: Plenum.

Anderson, D. R., & Field, D. E. (1983) Children's attention to television: implications for production in M. Meyer (ed.) *Children and the Formal Features of Television*. New York: Sauer.

Anderson, D. R. & Levin, S. R. (1976) Young children's attention to Sesame Street. *Child Development, 47*, 806–811.

Anderson, D. R., & Lorch, E. P. (1983). Looking at television: Action or reaction? In J. Bryant and D. R. Anderson (Eds.), *Children's understanding of television* (pp. 1–30). New York: Academic Press.

Anderson, D. R., Lorch, E. P., Field, D. E., Collins, P. A. & Nathan, J. G. (1986) Television viewing at home: age trends in visual attention and time with TV. *Child Development, 57*, 1024–1033.

Anglin, J. M. (1977). *Word, object, and conceptual development*. New York: W. W. Norton.

Annis, L. F. (1978). *The child before birth*. Ithaca, NY: Cornel University Press.

Antell, S. E., Caron, A. J. & Myers, R. S. (1985) Perception of relational invariants in newborns. *Developmental Psychology, 21*, 942–948.

Anthony, E. J. (1974). The syndrome of the psychologically invulnerable child. In E. J. Anthony & C. Koupernik (Eds.), *The child and his family 3: Children at psychiatric risk*. New York: Wiley.

Apgar, V. (1953). A proposal for a new method of evaluation of the newborn infant. *Current Researchers in Anesthesia and Analgesia, 32*, 260–267.

Apgar, V. & Beck, J. (1974) *Is My Baby All Right?* New York: Pocket Books.

Apgar, V., Holaday, D. A., James, L. S., Weisbrot, I. M., and Berien, C. (1958). Evaluation of the newborn infant: Second report. *Journal of the American Psychological Association, 168*, 1985–1988.

Appel, L. F., Copper, R. G., McCarrell, N., Sims-Knight, J., Yussen, S. R., & Flavell, J. H. (1972). The development of the distinction between perceiving and memorizing. *Child Development, 43*, 1365–1481.

Applebaum, M. I., & McCall, R. B. (1983). Design and analysis in developmental psychology. In P. H. Mussen (Ed.), *Handbook of child psychology* (4th ed.) (Vol. 1, pp. 415–477). New York: Wiley.

Archer, J. (1976). Biological explanations of psychological sex differences in B. B. Lloyd & J. Archer (eds). *Exploring Sex Differences*. London: Academic Press.

Archer, J., & Lopata, A. (1979). Marijuana revisited. *American Personnel and Guidance Journal, 57*, 244–252.

Archer, S. L. (1982). The lower boundaries of identity development. *Child Development, 53*, 1555–1556.

Arehart-Treichel, J. (1979, December 1). Down's syndrome: The father's role. *Science News*, pp. 381–382.

Arend, R. A., Grove, F. L., & Sroufe, L. A. (1979). Continuity of early adaptation: From attachment in infancy to ego-resiliency and curiosity at age 5. *Child Development, 50*, 950–959.

Arndt, W. B., Jr. (1974). *Theories of personality*. New York: Macmillan.

Asher, S. R., & Renshaw, P. D. (1981). Children without friends: Social knowledge and social skill training. In S. R. Asher & J. M. Gottman (Eds.), *The development of children's friendships* (pp. 273–297).

Aslin, R. N. (1987). Visual and auditory development in infancy. In J. D. Osofsky (Ed). *Handbook of infant development* (pp. 5–98). New York: Wiley.

Aslin, R. N. & Dumais, S. T. (1980) Binocular vision in infants: a review and a theoretical framework in L. Lipsitt & H. reese (eds). *Advances in Child Development and Behavior*. New York: Academic Press.

Aslin, R. N., Pisoni, D. B., & Jusczyk, P. W. (1983). Auditory development and speech perception in infancy. In P. H. Mussen (Ed.), *Handbook of child development* (4th ed.) (Vol. 2 pp. 573–589). New York: Wiley.

Astin, A. W. (19856). *The American freshman: Twenty year trends, 1966–1985*. Los Angeles: Higher Education Research Institute, U.C.L.A.

Athey, I. (1983) Language development factors related to reading development. *Journal of Educational Research, 76*, 197–203.

Atkin, C. K. (1980). Effects of television advertising on children. In E. L. Palmer & A. Dorr (Eds.), *Children and the faces of television: Teaching, violence, selling* (pp. 287–307). New York: Academic Press.

Atkin, C. K., & Gibson, W. (1980). Children's nutrition learning from Television advertising. Cited in C. K. Atkin, Effects of television advertising on children. In E. L. Palmer & A. Dorr (Eds.), *Children and the faces of television: Teaching, violence, selling* (pp. 287–307). New York: Academic Press.

Atkinson, A. M. (1987). Fathers' participation and evaluation of family day care. *Family Relations, 36*, 146–151.

Atkinson, R. C., & Shiffrin, R. M. (1968). Human memory: A proposed system and its control processes. In W. K. Spence & J. T. Spence (Eds.) *The psychology of learning and motivation: Advances in research and theory* (pp. 89–105). New York: Academic Press.

Attie, I., & Brooks-Gunn, J. (1989). Development of eating problems in adolescent girls. *Developmental Psychology, 25,* 70–79.

August, D. L. (1986, May). *Bilingual Education Act, Title 2 of the Education Amendments of 1984.* Washington Report. Washington Liaison Office of the Society for Research in Child Development.

Ault, R. (1977). *Children's cognitive development.* New York: Oxford University Press.

Auster, C. J., & Auster, D. (1981). Factors influencing women's choice of nontraditional careers: The role of family, peers, and counselors. *Vocational Guidance Quarterly, 29,* 253–265.

Austin, A. B. & Draper, D. C. (1981) Peer relationships of the academically gifted: a review. *Gifted Child Quarterly, 25,* 129–133.

Axline, V. M. (1969). *Play therapy* (rev. ed.) New York: Ballantine Books.

Azrin, N. H., & Foxx, R. (1976). *Toilet training in less than a day.* New York: Pocket Books.

Bachman, J., Green, S., & Wirtanen, I. (1972). *Youth in transition, Vol. 3, Dropping out–Problem or symptom?* Ann Arbor: Institute for Social Research, University of Michigan.

Bachman, J. G., & Johnston, L. D. (1979, September). The freshmen. *Psychology Today,* pp. 78–87.

Bachman, J. G., O'Malley, P. M., & Johnston, J. (1978). *Adolescence to adulthood: Change and stability in the lives of young men.* Vol. 6 of *Youth in transition.* Ann Arbor: University of Michigan Institute for Social Research.

Bachrach, A. J., Erwin, W., & Mohr, J. P. (1965). The Control of Eating Behavior in an Anorexic by Operant Conditioning Techniques, in L. P. Ullman and L. Krasner (eds.) *Case Studies in Behavior Modification.* New York: Holt, Rinehart and Winston.

Badger, E., Burns, D., & Vietze, P. (1981). Maternal risk factors as predictors of developmental outcome in early childhood. *Infant Mental Health Journal, 2,* 33–43.

Bailey, D. A. (1975) The growing child and the need for physical activity in M. S. Smart & R. C. Smart (eds.), 1978, School-Age Children: Development and Relationships (pp. 50–61). New York MacMillan.

Baillargeon, R. (1987). Object performance in 3½-and 4½ month infants. *Developmental Psychology, 23,* 655–665.

Baillargeon, R., & Graber, M. (1988). Evidence of location memory in 8-month-old infants in a nonsearch ab task. *Developmental Psychology, 24,* 502–512.

Baillargeon, R., Spelke, E. S., & Wasserman, S. (1985). Object permanence in five-month-old infants. *Cognition, 20,* 191–208.

Baird, P. A., & Sadovnick, A. D. (1987). Life expectancy in Down syndrome. *Journal of Pediatrics, 849,* 110.

Baker, K. A., & deKanter, A. A. (1981). *Effectiveness of bilingual education: A review of the literature.* Washington, DC: U.S. Department of Education, Office of Planning, Budget, and Evaluation.

Baldwin, A. L. (1967) *Theories of child development.* New York: Wiley.

Balinsky, B. I. (1970). *An introduction to embryology* (3rd ed.). Philadelphia: Saunders.

Ball, S., & Bogatz, G. (1970). *The first year of "Sesame Street": An evaluation.* Princeton: Educational Testing Service.

Ball, W., & Tronick, E. (1971). Infant responses to impending collision: Optical and real. *Science, 171,* 818–820.

Bandura, A. (1986) *Social Foundations of Thought And Action: A Social Cognitive Theory.* Englewood Cliffs, N.J.: Prentice Hall.

Bandura, A. (1977). *Social learning theory.* Englewood Cliffs, NJ: Prentice-Hall.

Bandura, A. & Menlove, F. L. (1968). Factor determining vicarious extension of avoidance behavior. *Journal of Personality and Social Psychology, 8,* 99–108.

Bandura, A., Grusek, J. E., & Menlove, F. L. (1967). Vicarious extinction of avoidance behavior. *Journal of Personality and Social Psychology, 5,* 516–523.

Bandura, A., Ross, D., & Ross, S. A. (1961). Transmission of aggression through imitation of aggressive models. *Journal of Abnormal and Social Psychology, 63,* 575–582.

Bandura, A., & Walters, R. H. (1963). *Social learning and personality development.* New York: Holt, Rinehart and Winston.

Bank, S., & Kahn, M. D. (1975). Sisterhood-brotherhood is powerful: Sibling subsystems and family therapy. *Family Process, 14,* 311–337.

Banks, M. S., Aslin, R. N., & Letson, R. D. (1975). Sensitive period for the development of human binocular vision. *Science, 190,* 675–677.

Banks, M. S., & Salapatek, P. (1983). Infant visual perception. In P. H. Mussen (Ed.), *Handbook of child development* (4th ed.) (Vol. 2, pp. 435–573). New York: Wiley.

Barcus, F. E. (1980). The nature of television advertising to children. In E. L. Palmer & A. Dorr (Eds.), *Children and the faces of television: Teaching, violence, selling* (pp. 273–284). New York: Academic Press.

Barglow, P., Vaughn, B. E., & N. Molitor (1987). Effects of maternal absence due to employment on the quality of infant-mother attachment in a low-risk sample. *Child Development, 58,* 945–955.

Barker, R. G., & Wright, H. F. (1955). *The Midwest and its children.* New York: Harper & Row.

Barkley, R. A., Karlsson, J., Strzelecki, E., & Murphy, J. V. (1984). Effects of age and Ritalin dosage on the mother-child interactions of hyperactive children. *Journal of Consulting and Clinical Psychology, 52,* 750–758.

Barnes, H. L., & Olson, D. H. (1985). Parent-adolescent communication and the circumplex model. *Child Development, 56,* 438–447.

Barnes, K. E. (1971). Preschool play norms: A replication. *Developmental Psychology, 5,* 99–103.

Barney, J., & Koford, J. (1987, October). Schools and single parents. *The Education Digest,* pp. 40–43.

Barrera, M. E. & Maurer, D. (1981) Recognition of mother's photographed face by the three-month-old infant. *Child Development, 52,* 715–716.

Barret, R. L., & Robinson, B. E. (1981). Teenage fathers: A profile. *Personnel and Guidance Journal, 60,* 226–228.

Barron, J., (1987, November 8). Sex education programs that work in public schools. *New York Times,* Section 12, pp. 16–19.

Barton, J., Chassin, L., Presson, C. C., &

Sherman, T. J. (1982). Social image factors as motivators of smoking initiation in early and middle adolescence. *Child Development, 53*, 1499–11511.

Bates, J. E. (1987). Temperament in infancy in J. Osofsky (Ed.), *Handbook of infant development* (2nd ed.) (pp. 1101–1150). New York: Wiley.

Bateson, P. P. G. (1987) Ethology in R. L. Gregory (ed). *The Oxford Companion to the Mind* (pp. 228–230). Oxford University Press.

Bauer, G. (1987, March). Teaching morality in the classroom. *Education Digest*, 2–5.

Baumrind, (1967). Child care practices anteceding 3 patterns of pre-school behavior. *Genetic Psychology Monographs, 75*, 43–88.

Baumrind, D. (1971). Current patterns of parental authority. *Developmental Psychology Monograph, 4*, (1, Part 2).

Baumrind, D. (1978, March). Parental disciplinary patterns and social competence in children. *Youth and Society*, pp. 239–276.

Baumrind, D. (1980). New directions in socialization research. *American Psychologist, 35*, 639–652.

Baumrind, D. (1985). Research using intentional deception: Ethical issues revisited. *American Psychologist, 40*, 165–175.

Bayley, N. (1970) The development of mental abilities in P. H. Mussen (ed.) *Carmichael's Manual of Child Psychology.* New York: Wiley.

Bayley, N. (1969) *The Bayley Scales of Infant Development.* New York: Psychological Corporation.

Beaudet, A. L. (1990). Cystic fibrosis. *New England Journal of Medicine.*

Beauchamp, G. K. & Cowart, B. J. (1990). Preference for high salt concentrations among children. *Developmental Psychology, 26*, 539–546.

Beauchamp, G. K., Cowart, B. J., & Moran, M. (1986). Developmental changes in salt acceptability in human infants. *Developmental Psychology, 29*, 17–25.

Becker, D. J. & Drash, A. L. (1979) Endocrinology in J. D. Noshpitz (ed.). Basic Handbook of Child Psychiatry, Vol. 1 (pp. 601–621). New York: Basic Books.

Becker, W. C. (1964). Consequences of different kinds of parental discipline. In M. L. Hoffman & H. W. Hoffman (Eds.), *Review of child development research*

(Vol. 1). New York: Russell Sage Foundation.

Becker, W. C., Engelmann, S., & Thomas, D. R. (1971). *Teaching: A course in applied psychology.* Chicago: Science Research Associates.

Bee, H. (1978). *Social issues in developmental psychology* (2nd ed.). New York: Harper & Row.

Bell, D. M., et al. (1989). Illness associated with child day care: A study of incidence and cost. *American Journal of Public health, 79*, 479–484.

Bell, R. Q. (1968). A reinterpretation of the direction of effects in socialization. *Psychological Review, 75*, 81–95.

Bell, R. Q. (1979). Parent, child, and reciprocal influences. *American Psychologist, 34*, 821–827.

Bell, S. M., & Ainsworth, M. D. (1972). Infant crying and maternal responsiveness. *Child Development, 43*, 1171–1190.

Beller, E. K. (1979) Early intervention programs, in J. Osofsky (ed.). *Handbook of Infant Development* (pp. 852–897). New York: Wiley.

Belsky, J. (1978). The Effects of daycare: A critical review. *Child Development, 49*, 929–949.

Belsky, J. (1978a). Three theoretical models of child abuse. *Child Abuse and Neglect, 2*, 37–49.

Belsky, J. (1980). Child maltreatment: An ecological integration. *American Psychologist, 35*, 320–335.

Belsky, J. (1988). The "effects" of infant day care reconsidered. *Early Childhood Research Quarterly, 3*, 235–273.

Belsky, J. & Most, R. K. (1982). Infant exploration and play in J. Belsky (ed). *In The Beginning* (pp. 109–121). New York: Columbia University Press.

Belsky, J., & Rovine, M. J. (1988). Nonmaternal care in the first year of life and the security of infant-parent attachment. *Child Development, 59*, 157–168.

Belsky, J., & Steinberg, L. D. (1979, July-August). What does research teach us about day care? *Children Today*, pp. 21–26.

Bem. S. L. (1981). Gender schema theory: A cognitive account of sex typing. *Psychological Review, 88*, 354–364.

Benin, M., & Agostinelli, J. (1988). Husbands' and wives' satisfaction with the division of labor. *Journal of Marriage and the Family, 47*, 975–984.

Berdine, W. H., & Blackhurst, A. E. (1985).

An introduction to special education (2nd ed.). Boston: Little, Brown.

Berenson, G., Frank, G., Hunter, S., Srinivasan, S., Voors, A. & Webber, L. (1982) Cardiovascular risk factors in children: should they concern the pediatrician. *American Journal of Diseases of Children, 136*, 855–862.

Berezin, N. (1980). *The gentle birth book.* New York: Simon and Schuster.

Berg, W. K., and Berg, K. M. (1979). Psychophysiological Development in Infancy: State, Sensory Functioning and Attention, in J. Osofsky (ed.), *Handbook of Infant Development* (p. 283). New York: Wiley.

Berg, W. K., Adkinson, C. D., & Strock, B. D. (1973). Duration and frequency of periods of alertness in the newborn. *Developmental Psychology, 9*, 434.

Berliner, D. C. (1987). But do they understand. In V. Richardson-Koehler (Ed.), *Educators' handbook* (pp. 259–295). New York: Longman.

Berlyne, D. E. (1960). *Conflict, arousal, and curiosity.* New York: McGraw-Hill.

Bernard, H. S. (1981). Identity formation during late adolescence: A review of some empirical findings. *Adolescence, 16.*

Berndt, T. J. (1979). Developmental changes in conformity to peers and parents. *Developmental Psychology, 15*, 608–617.

Berndt, T. J. (1981a). Relations between social cognition, nonsocial cognition and social behavior: The case of friendship. In J. H. Flavell & L. Ross (Eds.), *Social cognitive development.* Cambridge: Cambridge University Press.

Berndt, T. J. (1981b). Effects of friendships on prosocial intentions and behavior. *Child Development, 52*, 636–643.

Berndt, T. J. (1989). Friendships in childhood and adolescence. In W. Damon (Ed.). *Child development: Today and tomorrow* (pp. 332–349). San Francisco: Jossey Bass.

Berndt, T. J. & Hoyle, S. G. (1985) Stability and change in childhood and adolescent friendship. *Developmental Psychology, 21*, 1007–1015.

Bernhardt, G. R. & Praeger, S. G., (1985) Preventing child suicide: the elementary school death education puppet show. *Journal of Counseling and Development, 63*, 311–312.

Bersoff, D. N. (1981) Test bias: the judicial report card. *New York University Edu-*

cational Quarterly, 13, 2–9.

Bernstein, A. C., and Cowan, P. A. Children's Conception of How People Get Babies. Child Development, 1975, 46, 77–91.

Bertenthal, B. I., & Campos, J. J. (1987). Commentary—New directions in the study of early experience. Child Development, 58, 560–568.

Bertenthal, B. I., & Fischer, K. W. (1978). Development of self-recognition in the infant. Developmental Psychology, 14, 44–50.

Berti, A. E., & Bombi, A. S. (1981). The development of the concept of money and its value: A longitudinal study. Child Development, 52, 1179–1183.

Bertoncini, J., Bijeljac-Babic, R., Lusczyk, P. W., Kennedy, L. J., & Mehler, J. (1988). An investigation of young infants' perceptual representations of speech sound. Merrill Palmer Quarterly, 18, 34–52.

Best, J. B. (1986). Cognitive development. St. Paul: West.

Bettelheim, B. & Zelan, K. (1982, March). Why children don't like to read. Education Digest, 2–6.

Beyer, N. R., & Morris, P. M. (1974). Food attitudes and snacking patterns of young children. Journal of Nutrition Education, 6, 131–134.

Bierman, K. L., & Furman, W. (1984). The effects of social skills training and peer involvement on the social adjustment of preadolescents. Child Development, 55, 151–162.

Bigelow, B. J. (1977). Children's friendship expectations: A cognitive-developmental study. Child Development, 48, 246–253.

Bigelow, B. J., & La Gaipa, J. J. (1975). Children's written descriptions of friendship: A multidimensional analysis. Developmental Psychology, 11, 857–858.

Biller, H. B. (1982). Fatherhood: Implications for child and adult development. In B. B. Wolman (Ed.), Handbook of development psychology (pp. 702–720). Englewood Cliffs, NJ: Prentice-Hall.

Birch, H. G. (1971, March). Functional effects of fetal malnutrition. Hospital Practice, pp. 134–148.

Birch, H. G. (1976). Health and the education of socially disadvantaged children. In H. Bee (Ed.), Social issues in developmental psychology (pp. 269–291). New York: Harper & Row.

Birch, H. G., & Gussow, J. D. (1970). Disadvantaged children. New York: Harcourt, Brace and World.

Birch, L. L. (1979) Preschool childrens' preferences and consumption patterns. Journal of Nutritional Education, 11, 189–192.

Birch, L. L. (1980). Effects of peer models' food choices and eating behaviors on preschoolers' food preferences. Child Development, 51, 489–496.

Birns, B. (1976). The emergence and socialization of sex differences in the earliest years. Merrill-Palmer Quarterly, 22, 229–257.

Birren, J. E., Kinney, D. K., Schaie, K. W., & Woodruff, D. S. (1981). Developmental psychology: A life-span approach. Boston: Houghton Mifflin.

Bjorklund, D. F. (1989). Children's thinking: Developmental function and individual differences. Belmont, CA: Wadsworth.

Blackeslee, S. (1989, February 14). Crib death: Suspicion turns to the brain. New York Times, pp. C1, C3.

Blackeslee, S. (1986, October 7). Fetus returned to womb following surgery. New York Times, C1.

Blackwell, R., & Chang, A. (1988). Video display terminals and pregnancy: A review. Obstetrical and Gyneological Survey, 44, 128–129.

Blakemore, J.E.O. (1981). Age and sex differences in interaction with a human infant. Child Development, 52, 386–388.

Blanche, S., et al. (1989). A prospective study of infants born to women seropositive for human immunodeficiency virus type 1. New England Journal of Medicine, 320, 1643–1647.

Blanck, P. D., Rosenthal, R., Snodgrass, S. E., DePaulo, B. M., Zuckerman, M. (1982). Longitudinal and cross-sectional age effects in nonverbal decoding skill and style. Developmental Psychology, 19, 491–498.

Blank, M. & Klig, S. (1982) The child and the school experience in C. B. Kopp & J. B. Krakow (eds.) The Child: Development in a Social Context, (pp. 456–508). Reading, Mass.: Addison-Wesley.

Blasi, A. (1980). Bridging moral cognition and moral action: A critical review of the literature. Psychological Bulletin, 88, 1–45.

Blaske, D. M., Borduin, C. M., Henggeler, S. W. and Mann, B. J. (1989). Individual, family, and peer characteristics of adolescent sex offenders and assaultive offenders. Developmental Psychology, 25, 846–855.

Blass, E. M., Ganchrow, J. R., & Steiner, J. E. (1984). Classical conditioning in newborn humans 2–48 hours of age. Infant Behavior and Development, 7, 223–235.

Blatt, M., and Kohlberg, L. The Effects of Classroom Moral Discussion upon Children's Level of Moral Judgment. Journal of Moral Education, 1975, 4, 129–161.

Blehar, M. C. (1974). Anxious attachment and defensive reactions associated with day care. Child Development, 44, 683–592.

Block, J. H. (1976). Issues, problems, and pitfalls in assessing sex differences: A critique of the psychology of sex differences. Merrill-Palmer Quarterly, 22, 283–308.

Block, J. H. (1979) Socialization influences on personality development in males and females. American Psychological Association's Master Lecture Series. Washington, DC: American Psychological Association.

Block, J. H., Block, J., & Gjerde, P. F. (1986) The personality of children prior to divorce: A prospective study. Child Development, 57, 827–840.

Block, J., Block, J. H., Keyes, S. (1988) Longitudinally Foretelling Drug Usage in Adolescence: Early Childhood Personality and Environmental Precursors. Child Development, 59, 336–355.

Bloom, B. S. (1976) Human Characteristics and School Learning. New York: McGraw-Hill.

Bloom, D. E. (1986, September). Women and work. American Demographics, pp. 25–30.

Bloom, L. M. (1975). Language development. In F. D. Horowitz (Ed.), Review of child development research (Vol. 4). Chicago: University of Chicago Press.

Blum, R. H. et al. (1970). Society and Drugs, Vol. 1. San Francisco: Jossey-Bass.

Bogatz, G., & Ball, S. (1971). The second year of "Sesame Street": A continuing evaluation. Princeton: Educational Testing Service.

Bohannon, J. N., MacWhinney, B., & C. Snow (1990). No negative evidence revisited: Beyond learnability—or who has to prove what to whom. Developmental Psychology, 26, 221–227.

Bohannon, J. N., & Marquis, A. L. (1977). Children's control of Adult Speech. *Child Development, 48,* 1002–1008.

Bohannon, J. N., & Stanowicz, L. (1988). The issue of negative evidence: Adult responses to children's language errors. *Developmental Psychology, 24,* 684–689.

Bohman, M. (1978). Some genetic aspects of alcoholism and criminality: A population of adoptees. *Archives of General Psychiatry, 335,* 269–276.

Bond, E. (1972). Form perception in the infant. *Psychological Bulletin, 77,* 225–245.

Bork, A. (1989) Ethical Issues Associated with the Use of Interactive Technology in Learning Environments. *Journal of Research on Computing in Education, 21,* 121–128.

Bornstein, M. H. (1989) Information Processing (Habituation) in Infancy and Stability in Cognitive Development. *Human Development, 32,* 129–136.

Bornstein, M. H. & Benasich, A. (1986) Infant habituation: assessments of individual differences and short-term reliability at five months. *Child Development, 57,* 251–274.

Bornstein, M. H. & Sigman, M. D. (1986) Continuity in mental development from infancy. *Child Development, 57,* 251–274.

Borstelmann, L. J. (1983). Children before psychology: Ideas about children from antiquity to the late 1800s. In P. H. Mussen (Ed.), *Handbook of child psychology* (4th ed.) (Vol. 1, pp. 1–41). New York: Wiley.

Borton, T. (1986). 8 ways to encourage inventive thinking. *Learning, 15,* 94–96.

Bottoms, S. F., Rosen, M. G., & Sokol, R. J. (1980, March 6). The increase in caesarean birth rate. *New England Journal of Medicine,* pp. 559–563.

Bouchard, T. J. (1984). Twins reared together and apart: What they tell us about human diversity. In S. W. Fox (Ed.), *Individuality and determinism.* New York: Plenum.

Bower, E. M. (1979). School-age issues of prevention. In J. D. Noshpitz (Ed.), *Basic handbook of child psychiatry* (Vol. 4, pp. 139–149). New York: Basic Books.

Bower, G. H., Black, J. B. & Turner, T. J. (1979) Scripts in memory for text. *Cognitive Psychology, 11,* 177–220.

Bower, T.G.R., Broughton, J. M., & Moore, M. K. (1970). Infant response to approaching objects: An indication of response to distal variation. *Perception and Psychophysics, 9,* 193–196.

Bower, T.G.R. (1971) The object in the world of the infant. *Scientific American, 225,* 30–38, Offprint no. 539.

Bower, T.G.R. (1977). *A primer of infant development.* San Francisco: Freeman.

Bower, T.G.R. & Wishart, J. G. (1972). The effects of motor skill on object permanence. *Cognition, 1,* 165–172.

Bowerman, M. (1981). Language development. In H. C. Triandis & A. Heron (Eds.), *Handbook of cross-cultural psychology* (Vol. 4, pp. 93–187). Boston: Allyn and Bacon.

Bowlby, J. Attachment and Loss, vol. 3: Sadness and Depression. New York: Basic Books, 1980.

Bowlby, J. (1951). *Maternal care and mental health.* New York: Columbia University Press.

Bowlby, J. (1969). *Attachment.* New York: Basic Books.

Bowlby, J. (1973). *Attachment and loss, Vol. 2, Separation: Anxiety and anger.* New York: Basic Books.

Bowlby, J. (1982) Attachment and loss: retrospect and prospect. *American Journal of Orthopsychiatry, 52,* 664–678.

Boyer, E. L. (1983). *High school: A report on secondary education in America.* New York: Harper & Row.

Bracey, G. W. (1988, October). Computers and learning: The research jury is still out. *Electronic Learning,* pp. 8, 28+.

Brackbill, Y. (1958). Extinction of the smile: Responses in infants as a function of reinforcement schedule. *Child Development, 29,* 115–124.

Brackbill, Y. (1982). Lasting effects of obstetrical medication on children. In J. Belsky (Ed.), *In the beginning* (pp. 50–55). New York: Columbia University Press.

Bradley, R. H. (1989). Home measurement of maternal responsiveness. In M. H. Bornstein (Ed.), *Maternal responsiveness: Characteristics and consequences* (pp. 63–75). San Francisco: Jossey Bass.

Bradley, R. H., Caldwell, B. M. & Elardo, R. (1979) Home environment and cognitive development in the first two years: a cross-lagged analysis. *Developmental Psychology, 15,* 246–250.

Bradley, R. H. & Caldwell, B. M. (1980) The relation of home environment, cognitive competence and IQ among males and females. *Child Development, 51,* 1140–1148.

Bradley, R. H., Caldwell, B. M., & Rock, S. L. (1988). Home environment and school performance: A ten-year follow-up and examination of three models and environmental action. *Child development, 59,* 852–868.

Brainerd, C. J. (1978). *Piaget's theory of intelligence.* Englewood Cliffs, NJ: Prentice-Hall.

Brand, E., Clingempeel, W. E., & Bowen-Woodward, K. (1988). Family relationships and children's psychological adjustment in stepmother and stepfather families: Findings and conclusions from the Philadelphia Stepfamily Research Project. In E. M. Hetherington & J. D. Arasteh (Eds.), *Impact of divorce, single parenting and stepparenting on children* (pp. 299–324). Hillsdale, NJ: Erlbaum.

Brandt, G., Maschoff, T., & Chandler, N. S. (1980). A residential camp experience as an approach to adolescent weight management. *Adolescence, 60,* 807–822.

Bray, J. H. (1988). Children's development during early remarriage. In E. M. Hetherington & J. D. Arasteh (Eds.), *Impact of divorce, single parenting and stepparenting on children.* (pp. 279–298). Hillsdale, NJ: Erlbaum.

Brazelton, T. B. (1970). Effects of prenatal drugs on the behavior of the neonate. *American Journal of Psychiatry, 126,* 95–100.

Brazelton, T. B. (1981). *On becoming a family: The growth of attachment.* New York: Delacorte Press.

Brazelton, T. B., Koslowski, B., & Main, H. (1974). The origins of reciprocity: The early infant-mother interaction. In M. Lewis & L. A. Rosenblum (Eds.), *The effect of the infant on its caretaker* (pp. 49–76). New York: Wiley.

Breit, E. B., & Ferrandino, M. M. (1979). Social dimensions of the menstrual taboo and the effects on female sexuality. In J. H. Williams (Ed.), *Psychology of women: Selected readings* (pp. 228–241). New York: W. W. Norton.

Bremner, J. G. (1988). *Infancy.* New York: Basil Blackwell.

Brenna, H. B. (1983) Empirical foundations of family based approaches to adolescent substance abuse in T. J. Glynn et al. (eds.) *Preventing Adolescent Drug Abuse: Intervention Strategies.* Washington, DC.: NIDA U.S. Government Printing Office.

Brenner, C. (1955). *An elementary text-*

book of psychoanalysis. Garden City, NY: Doubleday/Anchor.

Breslau, N., Klein, N., & Allen L. (1988). Very low birthweight: Behavioral sequelae at nine years of age. Journal of the American Academy of Child and Adolescent Psychiatry, 27, 605–612.

Brickey, M. & Campbell, K. (1981) Fast food employment for moderately and mildly retarded adults. Mental Retardation, 19, 113–116.

Bridges, F. A., & Cicchetti, D. (1982). Mothers' ratings of the temperament characteristics of Down's syndrome infants. Developmental Psychology, 18, 238–244.

Bridges, L. J., Connell, J. P., & Belsky, J. (1988). Similarities and differences in infant-mother and infant-father interaction in the strange situation: A component process analysis. Developmental Psychology, 24, 92–101.

Brierly, J. (1976). The growing brain. Windsor, Eng.: NFER Publishing Co.

Briggs, C., & Elkind, D. (1973). Cognitive development and early reading. Developmental Psychology, 9, 279–280.

Bringuier, J. C. (1980). Conversations with Jean Piaget. Chicago: University of Chicago Press.

Brittain, C. V. (1963). Adolescent choices and parent-peer cross-pressures. American Sociological Review, 28, 385–391.

Brittain, C. V. (1969). A comparison of rural and urban adolescents with respect to peer vs. parent compliance. Adolescence, 13, 59–68.

Brizzi, J. S. (1986). The socialization of women's vocational realism. Vocational Guidance Quarterly, 34, 225–233.

Brody, G. H., & Forehand, R. (1988). Multiple determinants of parenting: Research findings and implications of the divorce process. In E. M. Hetherington & J. D. Arasteh (Eds.), Impact of divorce, single parenting, and stepparenting on children (pp. 135–155). Hillsdale, NJ: Erlbaum.

Brody, G. H., Pellegrini, A. D., & Sigel, I. E. (1986). Marital quality and mother-child and father-child interactions with school-aged children. Developmental Psychology, 22, 291–296.

Brody, G. H., Zolinda, S., MacKinnon, C. E., & MacKinnon, R. (1985). Role relationships and behavior between preschool-aged and school-aged siblings. Developmental Psychology, 21, 124–129.

Brody, J. E., (1989a, July 13). Changing times and medical advances make later pregnancies more common and much less risky. New York Times, p. B5.

Brody, J. E., (1989b, August 10). Breast feeding. New York Times, p. B10.

Brody, J. E. (1990, May 24). Preventing children from joining yet another unfit generation. New York Times, p. B14.

Brody, J. E. (1988, August 30). Widespread Abuse of Drugs By Pregnant Women is Found. New York Times, p1+.

Brody, J. E. (1980) Tending to obesity, inbred tribe aids diabetes study. New York Times, C1, C5.

Brody, R. (1981) Visual short-term memory in infancy. Child Development, 52, 242–250.

Bronson, G. (1968). The development of fear. Child Development, 39, 409–432.

Bronstein, P. (1984). Differences in mothers' and fathers' behaviors towards children: A cross-cultural comparison. Developmental Psychology, 20, 995–1003.

Brook, J. S., Gordon, A. S., Brook, A., & Brook D. W. (1989). The consequences of marijuana use on intrapersonal and interpersonal functioning in black and white adolescents. Genetic, Social and General Psychology Monographs, pp. 351–369.

Brook, J. S., Lukoff, I. F., & Whiteman, M. (1978) Family socialization and adolescent personality and their association with adolescent use of marijuana. Journal of Genetic Psychology, 133, 261–271.

Brook, J. S., Whiteman, M., Gordon, A. S., & Brook, D. W. (1984). Identification with Parental Attributes and Its Relationship to the Son's Personality and Drug use. Developmental Psychology, 20, 1111–1119.

Brook, J. S., Whiteman, M., & Gordon, A. S. (1983). Stages of drug use in adolescence: personality, peer, and family correlates. Developmental Psychology, 19, 269–277.

Brooks-Gunn, J. (1989) Pubertal processes and the early adolescent transition in W. Damon (ed.) Child Development today and Tomorrow, (pp. 155–176). San Francisco: Jossey-Bass.

Brooks-Gunn, J., & Furstenberg, F. F. (1989). Adolescent sexual behavior. American Psychologist, 44, 249–157.

Brooks-Gunn, J., & Ruble, D. N. (1982). The development of menstrual-related beliefs and behavior during adolescence. Child Development, 53, 1567–1577.

Brooks-Gunn, J., & Warren, M. (1989). Biological and social contributions to negative affect in young adolescent girls. Child Development, 60, 40–55.

Brooks-Gunn, J. & Warren, M. P. (1988) The psychological significance of secondary sexual characteristics in nine-to-eleven year-old girls. Child Development, 59, 1061–1069.

Brooks-Gunn, J., Rock, D. & Warren, M. P. (1989) Comparability of constructs across the adolescent years. Developmental Psychology, 25, 51–60.

Brophy, J. (1982, April). Successful teaching strategies for the inner-city child. Phi Delta Kappan, pp. 527–530.

Brophy, J. E. (1983). Research on the self-fulfilling prophecy and teacher expectations. Journal of Educational Psychology, 75, 631–661.

Brown, A. L., Bransford, J. D., Ferrara, R. A., & Campione, J. C. (1983). Learning, remembering and understanding. In P. H. Mussen (Ed.), Handbook of child psychology (4th ed.) (Vol. 3). New York: Wiley.

Brown, A. L., Campione, J. C., & Barclay, C. R. (1979). Training self-checking routines for estimating test readiness: Generalization from list learning to prose recall. Child Development, 50, 501–512.

Brown, A. L., & Smiley, S. S. (1977). Rating the importance of structural units of prose passages: A problem of metcognitive development. Child Development, 48, 1–8.

Brown, B. B., Clasen, D. R., & Eicher, S. A. (1986). Perceptions of peer pressure, peer conformity, dispositions, and self-reported behavior among adolescents. Developmental Psychology, 22, 521–530.

Brown, F. G. (1983). Principles of educational and psychological testing. New York: Holt, Rinehart and Winston.

Brown, J. M., O'Keeffe, J., Sanders, S. H., & Baker, B. (1986). Developmental changes in children's cognition to stressful and painful situations. Journal of Pediatric Psychology, 11, 343–357.

Brown, R. (1973). Development of the first language in the human species. American Psychologist, 28, 97–106.

Brown, R., & Hanlon, C. (1970). Derivational complexity and the order of acquisition in child speech. In R. Brown (Ed.), Psycholinguistics (pp. 155–207). New York: Free Press.

Browne, A. & Finkelhor, D. (1986) Impact of child sexual abuse: a review of the research. *Psychological Bulletin, 99*, 66–77.

Brownell, G. (1987). *Computers and teaching*, St. Paul: West.

Bruch, H. (1978). *The golden cage: The enigma of anorexia nervosa*. Cambridge, MA: Harvard University Press.

Bruner, J. (1972). The nature and uses of immaturity. *American Psychologist, 27*, 687–708.

Bruner, J. (1978a, September). Learning the mother tongue. *Human Nature*, pp. 11–19.

Bruner, J. (1978b). Learning how to do things with words. In J. S. Brunerand & A. Garton (Eds.), *Human growth and development: Wolfson College lectures.* (pp. 62–85). Oxford: Clarendon Press.

Bruner, J. S. (1983). The acquisition of pragmatics commitments. In R. M. Golinkoff (Ed.), *The transition from prelinguistic to linguistic communication* (pp. 27–42). Hillsdale, NJ: Erlbaum.

Buchanan, M., & Wolf, J. (1986). Comprehensive study of learning disabled adults. *Journal of Learning Disabilities, 19*, 34–38.

Buhrmester, D., & Furman, W. (1987). The development of companionship and intimacy. *Child Development, 58*, 1101–1114.

Buis, J. M., & Thompson, D. N. (1989). Imaginary audience and personal fable: A brief review. *Adolescence, 24*, 773–781.

Bukowski, W. M., & Newcomb, A. F. (1984). Stability and determinants of sociometric status and friendship choice: A longitudinal perspective. *Developmental Psychology, 20*, 941–953.

Bullen, B. A., Read, R. B., & Mayer, J. (1964). Physical activity of obese and non-obese adolescent girls appraised by motion picture sampling. *American Journal of Clinical Nutrition*, pp. 211–215.

Bullock, M. (1985). Animism in childhood thinking: A new look at an old question. *Developmental Psychology, 21*, 217–226.

Bullock, M., & Lutkenhaus, P. (1988). The development of volitional behavior in the toddler years. *Child Development, 59*, 664–675.

Bullough, V. (1981). Age at menarche: A misunderstanding. *Science, 213*, 365–366.

Bulmer, M. G. (1970). *The biology of twinning in man.* London: Oxford University Press.

Burns, R. B. (1979). *The self-concept: Theory, measurement, development and behaviour.* London: Longman.

Burton, R. V. (1963). Generality of honesty reconsidered. *Psychological Review, 70*, 481–499.

Bus, A. G., & Ijzendoorn, M. H. Van (1988). Attachment and early reading: A longitudinal study. *Journal of Genetic Psychology, 149*, 199–210.

Busch-Rossnagel, N. A., & Vance, A. K. (1982). The impact of the school on social and emotional development. In B. B. Wolman (Ed.), *Handbook of developmental psychology* (pp. 452–471). Englewood-Cliffs, NJ: Prentice-Hall.

Bushnell, I.W.R., Sai. F., & Mullin, J. T. (1989). Neonatal recognition of the mother's face. *British Journal of Developmental Psychology, 7*, 3–15.

Buss, A. H., & Plomin, R. (1984). *Temperament: Early developing personality traits.* Hillsdale, NJ: Erlbaum.

Butler, N., Goldstein, H., & Ross, K. (1972). Smoking in pregnancy and subsequent child development. *British Journal of Medicine, 4*, 573–575.

Butterfield, E. C., & Siperstein, G. N. (1972). Influence of contingent auditory stimulation upon non-nutritional suckle. In J. F. Bosma (Ed.), *Third symposium on oral sensation and perception: The mouth of the infant.* Springfield, IL: Thomas.

Butterworth, B. (1977). Object disappearance and error in Piaget's stage IV task. *Journal of Experimental Child Psychology, 23*, 391–401.

Cahan, S., & Cohen, N. (1989). Age versus schooling effects of intelligence development. *Child Development, 60*, 1239–1249.

Cairns, R. B. (1979). *Social development: The origins and plasticity of interchanges.* San Francisco: Freeman.

Cairns, R. B. (1983). The emergence of developmental psychology. In P. H. Mussen (Ed.), *Handbook of child development* (4th ed.) (Vol. 1, pp. 41–103). New York: Wiley.

Cairns, R. B., Cairns, R. D., & Neckerman, H. J. (1989). Early school dropout: Configurations and determinants. *Child Development, 60*, 1437–1452.

Cairns, R. B., Cairns, B. D., Neckerman, H. J., Gest, S. D., & Gariepy, J. L. (1988). Social networks and aggressive behavior: Peer support or peer rejection? *Develop-*

mental Psychology, 24, 815–823.

Cairns, R. B., Cairns, B. D., Neckerman, H. J., Ferguson, L. L. & Gariepy, J. L. (1989) Growth and aggression:1. childhood to early adolescence. *Developmental Psychology, 25*, 171–184.

Caldwell, B. M. (1989). All-day kindergarten—assumptions, precautions, and overgeneralizations. *Early Childhood Research Quarterly, 4*, 261–267.

Callison, W. (1988, February/March). Future of computers in classrooms. *Thrust*, 36–37.

Campbell, L. P., & Flake, A. E. (1985). Latchkey children—What is the answer? *The Clearing House, 58*, 381–383.

Campos, J., Langer, A., & Krowitz, A. (1970). Cardiac responses on the visual cliff in prelocomotor human infants. *Science, 170*, 196–197.

Canavan, J. W. (1981). Sexual child abuse. In N. S. Ellerstein (Ed.), *Child abuse and neglect: A medical reference* (pp. 233–253). New York: Wiley.

Caputo, D. V., & Mandell, W. (1970). Consequences of low birth weight. *Developmental Psychology, 3*, 363–383.

Caratz, J. C. (1969). A bi-dialectical task for determining language proficiency in economically disadvantaged Negro children. *Child Development, 40*, 889–901.

Card, J. J., & Wise, L. L. (1978). Teenage mothers and teenage fathers: The impact of early childbearing on the parents' personal and professional lives. *Family Planning Perspectives, 10*, 199–205.

Carew, J. V., Chan, I. & Halfar, C. (1975) Observed intellectual competence and tested intelligence: their roots in the young child's transactions and his environment in S. Cohen & T. J. Comiskey (eds) (1977). *Child Development: Contemporary Perspectives* (pp. 29–44). Itasca, Ill.: Peacock.

Carmody, D. (1988, September 21). Head Start gets credit for rise in scores. *New York Times*, p. B9.

Carnegie Corporation (1989). *Turning points: Preparing youths for the 21st century.* New York: Carnegie Corporation.

Carper, L. (1978, April). Sex roles in the nursery, *Harper's*, pp. 35–42.

Carroll, J. L., & Rest, J. R. (1982). Moral development. In B. Wolman (Ed.), *Handbook of human development* (pp. 434–452). Englewood Cliffs, NJ: Prentice-Hall.

Carter, D. B., & Levy, G. D. (1988). Cognitive aspects of children's early sex-role development: The influence of gender schemas on preschoolers' memories and preferences for sex-typed toys and activities. *Child Development, 59,* 782–793.

Carter, D. B., & Patterson, C. J. (1982). Sex roles as social conventions: The development of children's conceptions of sex-role stereotypes. *Developmental Psychology, 18,* 812–825.

Case, R. (1985). *Intellectual development: Birth to adulthood.* Orlando, FL: Academic Press.

Case, R., Hayward, S., Lewis, M. & Hurst, P. (1988) Toward a Neo-Piagetian theory of cognitive and emotional development. *Developmental Review, 8,* 1–51.

Caspi, A., Elder, G. H., & Bem, D. J. (1987). Moving against the world: Life-course patterns of explosive children. *Developmental Psychology, 23,* 308–313.

Cassidy, J. (1986). The ability to negotiate the environment: An aspect of infant competence as related to quality of attachment. *Child Development, 57,* 331–337.

Cataldo, C. B., & Whitney, E. H. (1986). *Nutrition and diet therapy: Principles and practices.* St. Paul: West.

Cauley, K., & Tyler, B. (1989). The relationship of self-concept to prosocial behavior in children. *Early Childhood Research Quarterly, 4,* 51–61.

Cave, V. G. (1973). The role of immunoglobulins in the early diagnosis of congenital syphilis. In L. Nicholas (Ed.), *Sexually transmitted diseases.* Springfield, IL: Thomas.

Cazden, C. B. (1981). Language development and the preschool environment. In C. B. Cazden (Ed.), *Language in early childhood education.* Washington, DC: National Association for the Education of Young Children.

Ceci, S. J., Ross, D. F., & Toglia, M. P. (1987). Age differences in suggestibility: Psychological implications. *Journal of Experimental Psychology: General, 116,* 38–49.

Centra, J. A. & Potter, D. A. (1980) School and teacher effects: an interrelational model. *Review of Educational Research, 50,* 273–290.

Cernoch, J. M., & Porter, R. H. (1985). Recognition of auxiliary odors by infants. *Child Development, 56,* 1593–1598.

Chafetz, J. S. (1977). The bringing-up of Dick and Jane. In S. Cohen & T. J. Comisky

(Eds.), *Child development: Contemporary perspectives* (pp. 196–201). Itasca, IL: Peacock.

Chall, J. (1977). *Reading 1967–1977: A decade of change and promise.* Bloomington, IN: Phi Delta Kappan Educational Foundation.

Chand, I. P., Crider, D. M., & Willets, F. K. (1975). Parent-youth disagreement as perceived by youth: A longitudinal study. *Youth and Society, 6,* 365–375.

Chandler, M., & Boyes, M. (1982). Social-cognitive development. In B. B. Wolman (Ed.), *Handbook of developmental psychology* (pp. 387–400). Englewood Cliffs, NJ: Prentice-Hall.

Charles, A. G., Norr, K. L., Block, C. R., et al. (1978). Obstetric and psychological effects of psychoprophylactic preparation for childbirth. *American Journal of Obstetrics and Gynecology, 44,* 131.

Chasnoff, I. J. (1987). Perinatal effects of cocaine. *Contemporary Ob/Gyn, 26* (March of Dimes reprint) Entire issue.

Chasnoff, I. J., Burns, W. J., Schnoll, S. H., & Burns, K. (1985). Cocaine use in pregnancy. *New England Journal of Medicine, 315,* 305–307.

Chassin, L., Presson, C. C., Sherman, S. J., Montello, D., & McGrew, J. (1986). Changes in peer and parent influence during adolescence. Longitudinal versus cross-sectional perspectives on smoking initiation. *Developmental Psychology, 22,* 327–334.

Chazan, M., & Cox, T. (1976). Language programmes for disadvantaged children. In V. P. Varma & P. Williams (Eds.), *Piaget: Psychology and education* (pp. 182–299). Itasca, IL: Peacock.

Chen, C., & Stevenson, H. W. (1989). Homework: A cross-cultural examination. *Child Development, 60,* 551–562.

Cherry, L., & Lewis, M. (1976) The preschool teacher-child dyad: Sex differences in verbal interaction. *Child Development, 46,* 532–535.

Chervanak, F. A., Isaacson, G. & Mahoney, M. J. (1986, July 31) Advances in the diagnosis of fetal defects. *New England Journal of Medicine, 315,* 305–307.

Chess, S. (1987). Comments: "Infant day care: A cause for concern." *Zero to Three, 7,* 24–25.

Chess, S., & Thomas, A. (1981) Infant bonding: mystique and reality. *American Journal of Orthopsychiatry, 52,* 213–222.

Chi, M.T.H., & Glaser, R. (1985). Problem solving ability. In R. J. Sternberg (Ed.), *Human abilities: An information processing approach.* New York: Freeman.

Chilman, C. S. (1983) *Adolescent Sexuality in a Changing American Society* (2nd edition). New York: Wiley.

Chodorow, N. (1981). Oedipal asymmetries and heterosexual knots. In S. Cox (Ed.), *Female Psychology: The emerging self* (pp. 228–248). New York: St. Martin's Press.

Chomsky, N. (1959). A review of B. F. Skinner's verbal behavior. *Language, 35,* 26–58.

Chomsky, N. (1965). *Aspects of the theory of syntax.* Cambridge, MA: M.I.T. Press.

Chomsky, N. (1972) *Language and Mind* (enlarged edition). New York: Harcourt, Brace, Jovanovich.

Christopherson, V. A. (1988). The family as a socialization context. In T. D. Yawken & J. E. Johnson (Eds.), *Integrative processes and socialization* (pp. 123–139). Hillsdale, NJ: Erlbaum.

Chumlea, W. C. (1982). Physical growth in adolescence. In W. W. Wolman (Ed.), *Handbook of developmental psychology* (pp. 471–486). Englewood-Cliffs, NJ: Prentice-Hall.

Church, A. G. (1983). Academic achievement, level of occupational plans, delay of gratification, personal control, and self-concepts for males and females in introductory anthropology. *Psychology: A Quarterly Journal of Human Behavior, 20,* 121–130.

Clapp, G. (1988). Television: Today's most important socializer? In G. Clapp (Ed.), *Child study research,* (pp. 57–85). Lexington, MA: Lexington Books.

Clarey, J. H., & Sanford, A. (1982). Female career preference and androgyny. *Vocational Guidance Quarterly, 20,* 258–265.

Clarizio, H. F., & McCoy, G. F. (1983). *Behavior disorders in children* (3rd ed.). New York: Harper & Row.

Clark, A. L. (1979) Applications of physiological perspectives in A. L. Clark & D. D. Affonso with T. R. Harris (eds). *Childbearing: A Nursing Perspective* (2nd Edition) (pp. 277–322). Philadelphia: Davis.

Clark, E. (1974), Some aspects of the conceptual basis for first language acquisition. In R. Schiefelbusch & L. Lloyd (Eds.), *Language perspectives—Acquisition, re-*

tardation and intervention. Baltimore: University Park Press.

Clark, E. V. (1978). Strategies for communicating. *Child Development, 49,* 953–959.

Clark, S. L., & DeVore, G. R. (1989). Prenatal diagnosis for couples who would not consider abortion. *Obstetrics and Gynecology, 73,* 1035–1037.

Clarke, A. M., & Clarke, A.D.B. (1976). *Early experience: Myth and evidence.* New York: The Free Press.

Clarke, A. M., & Clarke, A.D.B. (1986). Thirty years of child psychology: A selective review. *Journal of Child Psychology and Psychiatry and Allied Disciplines, 27,* 719–759.

Clarke-Steward, A. (1982, September). The day-care child. *Parents.*

Clarke-Stewart, K. A. (1988). The "effects" of infant day care reconsidered" *Reconsidered, 3,* 293–319.

Clarke-Stewart, K. A. (1989). Infant day care: Maligned or malignant? *American Psychologist, 44,* 266–274.

Clarke-Stewart, K. A., & Fein, G. G. (1983). Early childhood programs. In M. M. Haith & J. J. Campos (Eds.), *Handbook of Child psychology* (Vol. 2, pp. 917–1001). New York: Wiley.

Clarren, S. K., & Smith, D. W. (1978). The fetal alcohol syndrome. *New England Journal of Medicine, 298,* 1063–1067.

Clingempeel, W. G., & Segal, S. (1986). Stepparent-stepchild relationships and the psychological adjustment of children in stepmother and stepfather families. *Child Development, 59,* 474–484.

Cloninger, C. R. (1987). Neurogenetic adaptive mechanisms in alcoholism. *Science, 236,* 410–416.

Coates, B., Pusser, H., & Goodman, I. (1976). The influence of "Sesame Street" and "Mister Rogers' Neighborhood" on children's social behavior in the preschool. *Child Development, 47,* 138–144.

Cogan, R. (1980). Effects of childbirth preparation. *Clinical Obstetrics and Gynecology, 23,* 1–14.

Cohen, L., & Campos, J. (1974). Father, mother and stranger as elicitors of attachment behavior in infancy. *Developmental Psychology, 10,* 146–154.

Cohen, L. B. (1979). Our developing knowledge of infant perception and cognition. *American Psychologist, 34,* 894–899.

Cohen, L. B., Deloache, J. S., & Strauss, M. S. (1979). Infant visual perception. In J. Osofsky (Ed.), *Handbook of infant development* (pp. 393–439). New York: Wiley.

Cohen, S. E. (1978). Maternal employment and mother-child interaction. *Merrill-Palmer Quarterly, 24,* 189–197.

Cohn, J. F., & Tronick, E. Z. (1988). Mother-infant face-to-face interaction: Influence in bidirectional and unrelated to periodic cycles in either partner's behavior. *Developmental Psychology, 24,* 386–393.

Coie, J. D., & Kupersmidt, J. B. (1983). A behavioral analysis of emerging social status in boy's groups. *Child Development, 54,* 1400–1416.

Cole, L. (1974). Basic ideas of the Montessori method. In S. Coopersmith & R. Feldman (Eds.), *The formative years: Principles of early childhood education* (pp. 114–122). San Francisco: Albion.

Cole, N. S. (1981). Bias in testing. *American Psychologist, 36,* 1067–1078.

Coleman, E. (1981). Counseling adolescent males. *American Personnel and Guidance Journal, 60,* 215–219.

Coleman, J. S., et al. (1966). *Equality of educational opportunity survey.* Washington, DC: U.S. Government Printing Office.

Colombo, J., & Horowitz, F. D. (1987). Behavioral state as a lead variable in neonatal research. *Merrill-Palmer Quarterly, 33,* 23–437.

Colt, G. H. (1983, September-October) Suicide. *Harvard Magazine, 46–53, 63–66.*

Comer, J. P. (1985). Empowering black children's educational environment. In H. P. McAdoo & J. L. McAdoo (Eds.), *Black children* (pp. 123–139). Beverly Hills: Sage.

Condon, J. T., & Hilton, C. A. (1988). A comparison of smoking and drinking behaviors in pregnant women: Who abstains and why? *Obstetrics and Gynecology Survey, 44,* 51–53.

Condon, W. S., & Sander, L. W. (1974). Synchrony demonstrated between movements of the neonate and adult speech. *Child Development, 65,* 456–462.

Condry, J., Bence, P., & Scheibe, C. (1988). Nonprogram content of children's television. *Journal of Broadcasting and Electronic Media, 32,* 255–269.

Condry, J. G., & Condry, S. (1976). Sex differences: A study of the eye of the beholder. *Child Development, 47,* 812–819.

Conger, J. J., & Petersen, A. C. (1984). *Adolescence and youth* (3rd ed.). New York: Harper & Row.

Cook, T. D., Appleton, H., Conner, R. F., Shaffer, A., Tomkin, G., & Weber, S. J. (1975). *"Sesame Street" revisited.* New York: Russell Sage Foundation.

Cooke, R. A. (1982). The ethics and regulation of research involving children. In B. B. Wolman (Ed.), *Handbook of developmental psychology* (pp. 149–175). Englewood Cliffs, NJ: Prentice-Hall.

Cooke, R. E. (1979). Introduction in E. Zigler & J. Valentine (Eds.), *Project Head Start: A legacy of the war on poverty.* New York: The Free Press.

Cooper, C. R., Grotevant, H. D., & Condon, S. M. (1982). Methodological challenges of selectivity in family interaction: Assessing temporal patterns of individuation. *Journal of Marriage and the Family, 44,* 749–754.

Cooper, H. M. (1979). Pygmalion grows UP: A model for teacher expectation communication and performance influence. *Review of Educational Research, 49,* 389–410.

Cooper, H. M. & Tom, D.Y.H. (1984) Teacher expectation research: a review with implications for classroom instruction. *Elementary School Journal, 85,* 77–89.

Cooper, P., & Stewart, L. (1987). *Language skills in the classroom.* Washington, DC: National Education Association.

Coopersmith, S. (1967). *The antecedents of self esteem.* San Francisco: Freeman.

Copans, S. A. (1974). Human prenatal effects: Methodological problems and some suggested solutions. *Merrill-Palmer Quarterly, 20,* 43–52.

Corbin, C. B. (1980a). Childhood obesity. In C. B. Corbin (Ed.), *A textbook of motor development* (pp. 121–128). Dubuque, IA: W. C. Brown.

Corbin, C. B. (1980b). The physical fitness of children: A discussion and point of view. In C. B. Corbin (Ed.), *A textbook of motor development* (pp. 100–107). Dubuque, IA: W. C. Brown.

Cordua, G. D., McGraw, K. O., & Drabman, R. S. (1979). Doctor or nurse: Children's perceptions of sex typed occupations. *Child Development, 50,* 590–593.

Corey, L., & Spear, P. G. (1986). Infections with herpes simplex viruses. *New England Journal of Medicine, 314,* 749–754.

Correll, M. M. (1978). *Teaching the gifted*

and talented. Bloomington, IN: Phi Delta Kappan.

Corsaro, W. A. (1981) Friendship in the nursery school: social organization in a peer environment in S. R. Asher & J. M. Gottman (eds). *The Development of Children's Friendships* (pp. 207–242). Cambridge, Mass: Cambridge University Press.

Cotton, N. S. (1979). The familial incidence of alcoholism. *Journal of Studies on Alcohol, 40,* 89–116.

Cowart, B. J., & Beauchamp, G. K. (1986). *The importance of sensory context in young children's acceptance of salty tastes. Child Development, 57,* 1034–1039.

Crano, W., & Mellon, P. (1978). Causal influences of teachers' expectations on children's academic performance: A cross-lagged panel analysis. *Journal of Educational Psychology, 79,* 39–49.

Cratty, B. J. (1970) *Perceptual and motor development in infants and children.* New York: Macmillan.

Cratty, B. J. (1979) *Perceptual and motor development in infancy and childhood* (2nd ed.). New York: Macmillan.

Cratty, B. J. (1986). *Perceptual and motor development in infants and children* (3rd ed.). Englewood Cliffs, NJ: Prentice-Hall.

Crawford, J. (1987, March 25). Bilingual education works, study finds. *Education Week,* p. 16.

Crockenberg, S., & McCluskey, K. (1986). Change in maternal behavior during the baby's first year of life. *Child Development, 57,* 746–754.

Cronbach, L. J. (1970). *Essentials of psychological testing* (3rd ed.). New York: Harper & Row.

Cross, D. R., & Paris, S. G. (1988). Developmental and instructional analyses of children's metacognition and reading comprehension. *Journal of Educational Psychology, 80,* 131–142.

Cross, H. J., & Allen, J. G. (1970). Ego identity status, adjustment, and academic achievement. *Journal of Consulting and Clinical Psychology, 34,* 288.

Crouter, A. C., MacDermid, S. M., McHale, S. M. & Perry-Jenkins, M. (1990) Parental monitoring and perceptions of children's school performance and conduct in dual-and single-earner families. *Developmental Psychology, 26* 649–657.

Crouter, A. C., Perry-Jenkins, M., Huston, T. L., & McHale, S. M. (1987). Processes underlying father involvement in dual-earner and single-earner families. *Developmental Psychology, 23,* 431–441.

Cullinan, D. & Epstein, M H. (1982) Behavior disorders in N. G. Haring (ed). *Exceptional Children and Youth,* 3rd ed. (pp. 207–239). Columbus, Ohio: Merrill.

Culp, R. E., Appelbaum, M. I., Osofsky, J. D., & Levy, J. A. (1988). Adolescent and older mothers: Comparison between prenatal maternal variables and newborn interaction measures., *Infant Behavior and Development, 11,* 353–362.

Cummings, E. M. (1987) Coping with background anger in early childhood. *Child Development, 58,* 976–985.

Cummings, E. M., Iannotti, R. J., & Zahn-Waxler, C. (1989). Aggression between peers in early childhood: Individual continuity and developmental change. *Child Development, 60,* 887–896.

Curtis, H. (1975). *Biology* (2nd ed.), New York: worth.

Daehler, M. W., & Bukatko, D. (1985). *Cognitive development,* New York: Knopf.

Daigon, A. (1982, December). Toward righting writing. *Phi Delta Kappan,* pp. 242–246.

Dakshinamurti, K. & Stephens, M. (1969). Pyridoxine deficit in neonatal rats. *Journal of Clinical Neurology, 16,* 1515–1522.

Dale, P. S. (1976). *Language development: Structure and function* (2nd ed.). Hinsdale, IL: Dryden Press.

Damon, W. (1983). *Social and personality development.* New York: W. W. Norton.

Damon, W., & Hart, D. (1982). The development of self-understanding from infancy through adolescence. *Child Development, 53,* 841 –864.

Daniels, D., & Plomin, R. (1985). Origins of individual differences in infant shyness. *Developmental Psychology, 21,* 118–122.

Daniels, D., Plomin R., & Greenhalgh, J. (1984). Correlates of difficult temperament in infancy. *Child Development, 55,* 1184–1194.

Danner, F. W., & Day, M. C. (1977). Eliciting formal operations. *Child Development, 48,* 1600–1606.

Darlington, R. B., Royce, J. M., Snipper, A. S., Murray, H. W., & Lazar, I. (1980). Preschool programs and the later school competence of children from low-income families. *Science, 208,* 202–204.

Dasen, P., & Heron, A. (1981). Cross-cultural test of Piaget's theory. In H. C., Triandis & A. Heron (Eds.), *Handbook of cross-cultural psychology* (Vol. 4, pp. 295–343). Boston: Allynn and Bacon.

Davidson, R. J., & Fox, N. A. (1989). Frontal brain asymmetry predicts infants' response to maternal separation. *Journal of Abnormal Psychology, 98,* 127–131.

Davies, R., Butler, N. & Goldstein, H. (1972). *From Birth to Seven.* London: Clowes.

Davis, G. A. (1983). *Educational psychology: Theory and practice.* Reading, MA: Addison-Wesley.

Davis, R. A. (1989). Teenage pregnancy: A theoretical analysis of a social problem. *Adolescence, 24,* 19–27.

Dayton, G., Jones, M., Aiu, P., Rawson, R., Steele, B., & Rose, M. (1964). Developmental study of coordinated eye movements in the human infant, 1: Visual acuity in the newborn human: A study based on induced optokinetic nystagmus recorded by electro-oculography. *Archives of Ophthalmology, 71,* 865–870.

Deal, J. E., Halverson, C. F., & Wampler, K. S. (1989). Parental agreement on child-rearing orientations: Relations to parental, marital, family, and child characteristics. *Child Development, 60,* 1025–1035.

Dean, A. L., Malik, M. M., Richards, W., & Stringer, S. A. (1986). Effects of parental maltreatment on children's conceptions of interpersonal relationships. *Developmental Psychology, 22,* 617–626.

Deasey, D. (1978). *Education under six.* New York: St. Martin's Press.

DeBruyne, L. K., & Rolfes, S. R. (1989). *Life cycle nutrition: Conception through adolescence.* St. Paul: West.

DeCasper, A. J., & Fifer, W. P. (1980). Of human bonding: Newborns prefer their mothers' voices. *Science, 208,* 1174–1176.

de Chateau, P. (1987). Parent-infant socialization in several Western European countries. In J. D. Osofsky (Ed.), *Handbook of infant development* (pp. 642–669). New York: Wiley.

DeFrain, J., Taylor, J., & Ernst, L. (1982). *Coping with sudden infant death.* Lexington, MA: D. C. Heath.

Dempster, F. N., & Rohwer, W. D. (1983). Age differences and modality effects in immediate and final free recall. *Child Development, 54,* 30–41.

Dennis, W. (1935). The effect of restricted

practice upon the reaching, sitting and standing of two infants. *Journal of Genetic Psychology, 47,* 17–32.

Dennis, W., & Dennis, M. G. (1940). Cradles and cradling customs of the Pueblo Indians. *American Anthropologist, 42,* 107–115.

Dennis, W. & Jajarian, P. (1957) How reversible are the effects? in S. J. Hutt & C. Hull (eds.) (1973). *Early Human Development* (pp. 274–288). London: Oxford University Press.

Dent, H. E. (1987). The San Francisco public schools experience with alternatives to I.Q. testing: A model for non-biased assessment. *Negro Education Review, 38,* 146–162.

DeVries, M. W., & Sameroff, A. J. (1984). Culture and temperament: Influences on infant temperament in three East African societies. *American Journal of Orthopsychiatry, 54,* 83–96.

Desor, J. A., Maller, O., & Turner, R. E. (1973). Taste in acceptance of sugars by human infants. *Journal of Comparative and Physiological Psychology, 84,* 496–501.

Deutsch, H. (1973). *The psychology of women* (Vols. 1 and 2). New York: Bantam Books (first published 1945).

deVilliers, J. G., & deVilliers, P. A. (1978). *Language acquisition.* Cambridge, MA: Harvard University Press.

DeVine, R. A. (1980, November). Sexual abuse of children: An overview of the problem. In *Sexual Abuse of Children: Selected Readings.* Washington, DC: U.S. Department of Health and Human Services, DHHS Pub No78-30161, pp. 3–7.

DeVries, M. W., & Sameroff, A. J. (1984). Culture and temperament: Influences on infant temperament in three East African societies. *American Journal of Orthopsychiatry, 54,* 83–96.

Diamond, A. (1985). Development of the ability to use recall to guide action, as indicated by infants' performance on AB. *Child Development, 56,* 868–884.

Diamond, J. M., Kataria, S., & Messer, S. C. (1989). Latchkey children: A pilot study investigating behavior and academic achievement. *Child and Youth Care Quarterly, 18,* 131–140.

Diamond, N. (1982). Cognitive theory. In B. B. Wolman (Ed.), *Handbook of developmental psychology* (pp. 3–23). Englewood Cliffs, NJ: Prentice-Hall.

Diaz, R. M. (1985). Bilingual cognitive development: Addressing three gaps in current research. *Child Development, 56,* 1376–1388.

DiCaprio, N. S. (1983). *Personality theories: A guide to human nature* (2nd ed.). New York: Holt, Rinehart and Winston.

Dickie, J. R., & Gerber, S. C. (1980). Training in social competence: The effect on mothers, fathers, and infants. *Child Development, 51,* 1248–1251.

DiFranco, D., Muir, D., & Dodwell, P. (1978). Researching in very young infants. *Perception, 7,* 385–392.

DiLalla, L. F., & Watson, M. W. (1988). Differentiation of fantasy and reality: Preschoolers' reactions to interruptions in their play. *Developmental Psychology, 24,* 286–292.

Dion, K. K. (1973). Your children's stereotyping of facial attractiveness. *Developmental Psychology, 9,* 183–188.

DiPietro, J. (1981). Rough and tumble play: A function of gender. *Developmental Psychology, 17,* 50–58.

Dirks, J., & Neisser, U. (1977). Memory for objects in real scenes: The development of recognition and recall. *Journal of Experimental Child Psychology, 23,* 315–328.

Dix, T., Ruble, D. N., & Zambarano, R. J. (1989). Mother's implicit theories of discipline: Child effects, parental effects and the attribution process. *Child Development, 60,* 1373–1392.

Dobbing, J. (1977). Human brain development and its vulnerability. In R. L. Smart & M. S. Smart (Eds.), *Readings in child development and relationships* (2nd ed.) (pp. 49–61). New York: Macmillan.

Dobson, V., & Teller, D. Y. (1978). Visual acuity in human infants: A review and comparison of behavioral and electrophysiological stimulation. *Vision Research, 18,* 1469–1484.

Dodd, B. J. (1972). Effects of social and vocal stimulation on infant babbling. *Developmental Psychology, 7,* 80–83.

Dodd, D. H., & White, R. M. (1980). *Cognition: Mental structures and processes.* Boston: Allyn and Bacon.

Dodge, K. A., & Frame, C. L. (1982). Social cognitive biases and deficits in aggressive boys. *Child Development, 53,* 620–635.

Donovan, J. M. (1975). Identity status and interpersonal style. *Journal of Youth and Adolescence, 4,* 37–55.

Dornbusch, S., Ritter, P., Liederman, P., Roberts, D., & Fraleigh, M. (1987). The relation of parenting style to adolescent school performance. *Child Development, 58,* 1244–1257.

Dornbusch, S. M., Carlsmith, J. M., Bushwall, S. J., Ritter, P. L., Leiderman, H., Hastof, A. H., & Gross, R. T. (1985). Single parents, extended households and the control of adolescence. *Child Development, 56,* 326–341.

Door, A., Graves, S. B., & Phelps, E. (1980). Television literacy for young children. *Journal of Communication, 71*–83.

Douvan, E., & Adelson, J. (1966). *The adolescent experience.* New York: Wiley.

Doyle, J. A. (1985). *Sex and gender.* Dubuque, IA: Brown.

Drabman, R. S., & Thomas, M. H. (1975). Does TV violence breed indifference? *Journal of Communication, 25,* 86–89.

Dreyer, P. H. (1982). Sexuality during adolescence. In B. B. Wolman (Ed.), Handbook of developmental psychology (pp. 559–602). Englewood Cliffs, NJ: Prentice-Hall.

Drillien, C. M. (1964). *The Growth and development of the prematurely born infant.* Edinburgh: Livingstone.

Drotman, P. & Viadero, D. (1987, September 30). Expert's answers to frequently asked questions about AIDS. *Education Week,* 6.

Dubow, E. F., & Luster, T. (1990). Adjustment of children born to teenage mothers: The contribution of risk and protective factors. *Journal of Marriage and the Family, 52,* 393–404.

Dubow, E. F., & Tisak, J. (1989). The relation between stressful life events and adjustment in elementary school children: The role of social support and social problem-solving skills. *Child Development, 60,* 1412–1424.

Dullea, A. (1989, October 12). Opening the world to a generation. *New York Times,* pp. C1, C6.

Dunn, J. (1983). Sibling relationships in early childhood. *Child Development, 54,* 787–812.

Dunn, J., & Kendrick, C. (1982). *Siblings: Love, envy and understanding.* Cambridge, MA: Harvard University Press.

Dunst, C. J., Brooks, P. H. L. & Doxsey, P. A. (1982). Characteristics of hiding places and the transition to stage 4 performance in object permanence tests. *Developmental Psychology, 18,* 671–681.

Durkin, D. (1974). Confusion and misconceptions in the controversy about kindergarten reading. In S. Coopersmith & R. Feldman (Eds.), *The formative years: Principles of early childhood education* (pp. 228–235). San Francisco: Albion.

Dusek, J. B. (1974). Implications of developmental theory for child mental health. *American Psychologist, 29,* 19–25.

Dusek, J. B., & Joseph, G. (1983). The bases of teacher expectancies: A meta-analysis. *Journal of Educational Psychology, 75,* 327–346.

Dweck, C. S., & Bush, E. S. (1976). Sex differences in learned helplessness, 1: Differential debilitation with peer and adult evaluators. *Developmental Psychology, 12,* 147–156.

Dweck, C. S., Davidson, W., Nelson, S., & Enna, B. (1978). Sex differences in learned helplessness, 2: The contingencies of evaluative feedback in the classroom, and 3: An experimental analysis. *Developmental Psychology, 14,* 268–276.

Dworetzky, J. P. (1984). *Introduction to child development.* St. Paul: West.

Eagly, A. H., & Carlike, L. L. (1981). Sex of Researchers and sex typed communications as determinants of sex differences in influenceability: A meta-analysis of social influence studies. *Psychological Bulletin, 90,* 1–20.

Eagly, A. H. (1978). Sex differences in influenceability. *Psychological Bulletin, 85,* 86–116.

Earls, F., & Siegel, B. (1980). Precocious fathers. *American Journal of Orthopsychiatry, 50,* 469–480.

Eaton, W. O., & Ennis, L. R. (1986). Sex differences in human motor activity level. *Psychological Bulletin, 100,* 19–28.

Eaton, W. O., & Von Bargen, D. (1981). Asynchronous development of gender understanding in preschool children. *Child Development, 52,* 1020–1027.

Edelman, M. W. (1985). The sea is so wide and my boat is so small: Problems facing black children today. In H. P. McAdoo & J. L. McAdoo (Eds.), *Black children* (pp. 72–85). Beverly Hills: Sage.

Eder, R. A. (1989). The emergent personalogist: The structure and content of 3½, 5½, and 7½-year-olds' concepts of themselves and other persons. *Child Development, 60,* 1218–1229.

Education Week (1989, August 2). Report on National Health Objectives, 11.

Edwards, C. P., & Lewis, M. (1979). Young children's concepts of social relations: Social functions and social objects. In M. Lewis & L. A. Rosenblum (Eds.), *The child and its family: Genesis of behavior* (Vol. 2). New York: Plenum.

Egeland B., & Farber, E. (1984). Infant-mother attachment: Factors related to its development and changes over time. *Child Development, 55,* 753–771.

Egeland, B., Jacobovitz, D., & Sroufe, L. A. (1988). Breaking the cycle of abuse. *Child Development, 59,* 1080–1089.

Egertson, H. A. (1987, May 20). Recapturing kindergarten for 5-year-olds. *Education Week,* 28–29.

Ehrenhaft, P. M., Wagner, J. L., & Herdman, R. C. (1989). Changing prognosis for very low birth weight infants. *Obstetrics and Gynecology, 74,* 528–535.

Eichenwald, H. F., & Fry, P. G. (1969). Nutrition and learning. *Science, 163,* 644–658.

Eichorn, D. H. (1979). Physical development: current foci of research, in J. Osofsky (ed.), *Handbook of Infant Development* (pp. 253–283). New York: Wiley.

Eidelberg, L. (Ed.) (1968). *Encyclopedia of psychoanalysis.* New York: The Free Press.

Eimas, P. D., Siqueland, E. R., Jusczyk, P., & Vigorito, J. (1971). Speech perception in infants. *Science, 171,* 303–306.

Eisele, J., Hertsgaard, D., & Light, H. K. (1986). Factors related to eating disorders in young adolescent girls. *Adolescence, 21,* 283–290.

Eisenberg, N. (1989). The development of prosocial and aggressive behavior. In M. H. Bornstein & M. E. Lamb (Eds.), *Social, emotional and personality development* (pp. 461–486). Hillsdale, NJ: Erlbaum.

Eisenberg, N. (1988b). The development of prosocial and aggressive behavior in M. H. Bornstein and M. E. Lamb (eds.). *Social, Emotional and Personality Development* (2nd ed.) (pp. 461–486). Hillsdale, N.J.: Erlbaum.

Eisenberg, N., & Garvey, C. (1981). Children's use of verbal strategies in resolving conflicts. *Discourse Processes, 4,* 149–170.

Eisenberg-Berg, N., & Hand, M. (1979). The relationship of preschoolers' reasoning about prosocial moral conflicts to prosocial behavior. *Child Development, 50,* 356–363.

Eisenberg, N., & Mussen, P. H. (1989). *The roots of prosocial behavior in children.* New York: Cambridge University Press.

Eisenberg, N., Shell, R., Lennon, R., Bellover, R., & Mathy, R. M. (1987). Prosocial development in middle childhood: A longitudinal study. *Developmental Psychology, 23,* 712–718.

Eisenberg, N., Wolchik, S. A., Hernandez, R., & Pasternack, J. F. (1985). Parental socialization of young children's play: A short-term longitudinal study. *Child Development, 56,* 1506–1514.

Eisenberg, N. A. et al., (1988b). Differentiation of vicariously induced emotional reactions in children. *Developmental Psychology, 24,* 237–247.

Eisenberg, R. B. (1970). The organization of auditory behavior. *Journal of Speech and Hearing Research, 13,* 461–464.

Eisenberg-Berg, N., & Roth, K. (1980). The development of children's prosocial moral judgment: A longitudinal follow-up. *Development Psychology, 16,* 375–376.

Elardo, R., Bradley, R., & Caldwell, M.B.A. (1975). The relation of infants' home environments to mental test performance from six to thirty-six months: a longitudinal analysis. *Child Development, 46,* 71–76.

Elardo, R., Bradley, R., & Caldwell, M.B.A. (1977). Longitudinal study of the relation of infants' home environments to language development at age three. *Child Development, 48,* 595–603.

Elkind, D. (1967). Egocentrism in adolescence. *Child Development, 38,* 1025–1034.

Elkind, D. (1973). Infant intelligence in D. Elkind & D. C. Hetzel (eds.) (1977). *Readings in Human Development: Contemporary Issues in Developmental Psychology* (2nd ed.) (pp. 30–40). New York: Harper and Row.

Elkind, D. (1985). Egocentrism redux. *Developmental Review, 5,* 218–226.

Elkind, D. (1987). *Miseducation,* New York: Knopf.

Elkind, D., & Bowen, R. (1979). Imaginary audience behavior in children and adolescence. *Developmental Psychology, 15,* 38–44.

Elster, A. B., & Panzarine, S. (1983). Teen-age fathers: Stresses during gestation and early parenthood. *Clinical Pediatrics, 22,* 700–703.

Emde, R. N., Izard, C., Huebner, R., Sorce, J. F., & Klinnert, M. (1985). Adult judgments of infant emotions: Replication studies within and across laboratories. *Infant Behavior and Development, 8,* 79–88.

Emerich, W., & Shepard, K. (1984). Cognitive factors in the development of sex-typed perferences. *Sex Roles, 11,* 997–1007.

Emery, R. E. (1982). Interparental conflict and the children of discord and divorce. *Psychological Bulletin, 92,* 310–330.

Engen, T., Lipsitt, L. P. & Peck, M. B. (1974) Ability of newborn infants to discriminate sapid substances. *Developmental Psychology, 10,* 741–744.

Entwisle, D. R., & Alexander, K. L. (1987). Long-term effects of cesarean delivery on parents' beliefs and children's schooling. *Developmental Psychology, 23,* 676–682.

Entwisle, D. R., Alexander, K. L., Pallas, A. M. & Cadigan, D. (1987). The emergent academic self-image of first graders: its response to social structure. *Child Development, 58,* 1190–1206.

Entwisle, D. R., & Baker, D. P. (1983). Gender and young children's expectations for performance in arithmetic. *Developmental Psychology, 19,* 100–209.

Erikson, E. (1958). *Young man Luther: A study in psychoanalysis and history.* New York: W. W. Norton.

Erikson, E. H. (1959). The problem of ego identity. In *Identity and The Life Cycle.* New York: Norton, 1980.

Erikson, E. (1963). *Childhood and society.* New York: W. W. Norton.

Erikson, E. (1968). *Identity: Youth and crisis.* New York: W. W. Norton.

Erikson, E. (1969). *Gandhi's truth.* New York: W. W. Norton.

Erikson, E. H. (1981). The problem of ego identity. In L. D. Steinberg (Ed.), *The life cycle: Readings in human development* (pp. 189–198). New York: Columbia University Press.

Erikson, M. F., Sourfe, L. A. & Egeland, B. (1985). The relationship between quality of attachment and behavior problems in preschool in a high-risk sample in I. Bretherton & E. Waters (eds.) Growing Points of Attachment Theory and Research, *Monographs of the Society for Research in Child Development, 50,* nos. 1–2, Serial no. 209, 147–167.

Eron, L. D. (1982). Parent-child interaction, television violence, and aggression of children. *American Psychologist, 37,* 197–212.

Eron, L. D., Huesmann, L. R., Brice, P., Fischer, P., & Mermelstein, R. (1983). Age trends in the development of aggression, sex typing, and related television habits. *Developmental Psychology, 19,* 71–78.

Eron, L. D., Walder, L. O., & Lefkowitz, M. M. (1971). *Learning of aggression in children.* Boston: Little, Brown.

Espenschade, A. S. 91960). Science and medicine of exercise and sport. In W. R. Johnson, *Motor Development* (pp. 419–439). New York: Harper and Row.

Etaugh, C. (1980). Effects of nonmaternal care on children: Research evidence and popular views. *American Psychologist, 35,* 309–319.

Etaugh, C., & Hughes, V. (1975). Teachers' evaluations of sex-typed behaviors in children: The role of teacher sex and school setting. *Developmental Psychology, 11,* 394–395.

Etzel, B. C., & Gewirtz, J. L. (1967). Experimentation model of caretaker-maintained heart-rate operant crying in a six and a twenty week old infant: Extinction of crying with reinforcement of eye contact and smiling. *Journal of Experimental Child Psychology, 5,* 303–317.

Evaloff, H. H. (1971). Some cognitive and affective aspects of early language development. *Child Development, 42,* 1895–1907.

Fagen, J. F. (1973). Infants' delayed recognition memory and forgetting. *Journal of Experimental Child Psychology, 16,* 424–450.

Fagen, J. F. (1984). Infants' long term memory for stimulus color. *Developmental Psychology, 20,* 435–441.

Fagot, B. (1974). Sex differences in toddler's behavior and parental reactions. *Developmental Psychology, 10,* 554–558.

Fagot, B. I. (1977). Influence of teacher behavior in the preschool. *Developmental Psychology, 9,* 198–206.

Fagot, B. I. (1978). The influence of sex of child on parental reactions to toddler children. *Child Development, 49,* 459–465.

Fagot, B. I., Hagan, R., Leinbach, M. D., & Kronsberg, S. (1985). Differential reactions to assertive and communicative acts of toddler boys and girls. *Child Development, 56,* 1499–1505.

Fantz, R. L. (1961, May). The origin of form perception. *Scientific American,* pp. 16–21.

Fantz, R. L. (1963). Pattern vision in newborn infants. *Science, 140,* 296–297.

Fantz, R. L., & Miranda, S. B. (1975). Newborn infant's attention to form of contour. *Child Development, 46,* 224–228.

Farber, S. (1981, January). Telltale behavior of twins. *Psychology Today,* pp. 58–62, 79–80.

Farberow, N. L. (1985). Youth suicide: a summary. In L. L. Peck, N. L. Farberow & R. E. Litman (eds). Youth Suicide, (pp. 191–205). New York: Springer.

Farmer, H. S. (1978). Career counseling implications for the lower social class and women. *Personnel and Guidance Journal, 56,* 467–472.

Farmer, H. S. (1983). Career and home-making plans for high school youth. *Journal of Counseling Psychology, 30,* 40–45.

Faust, M. S. (1960). Developmental maturation as a determinant in prestige of adolescent girls. *Child Development, 31,* 173–184.

Federal Bureau of Investigation (FBI) (1986, July). Uniform Crime Reports, 1985, Washington, DC: U.S. Department of Justice.

Federal Register, (1977). Education of handicapped children. U.S. Office of Education. *Federal Register, 42,* 65082–65085.

Feingold, A. (1988). Cognitive gender differences are disappearing. *American Psychologist, 43,* 95–104.

Feingold, B. F. (1975). Hyperkinesis and learning disabilities linked to artificial food flavors and colors. *American Journal of Nursing, 75,* 797–803.

Feinman, S., & Lewis, M. (1983). Social referencing at ten months: A second-order effect in infants' responses to strangers. *Child Development, 54,* 878–888.

Feldhusen, J. F., & Clinkenbeard, P. A. (1987). Creativity instructional materials: A review of research. *Journal of Creative Behavior, 20,* 1153–1182.

Feldlaufer, H., Midgley, C., & Eccles, J. S. (1988). Student, teacher, and observer perceptions of the classroom environment before and after the transition to junior high school. *Journal of Early Adolescence, 8,* 133–156.

Feldman, C. F., Stone, A., & Renderer, B. (1990). Stage, transfer, and academic achievement in dialect-speaking Hawaiian adolescents. *Child Development,* 472–484.

Feldman, J. F., Brody, N., & Miller, S. A. (1980). Sex differences in non-elicited neonatal behaviors. *Merrill-Palmer Quarterly, 26,* 63–73.

Feldman, M. W., & Lewontin, R. C. (1975). The heritability hang-up. *Science, 190,* 1163–1168.

Feldman, S. S., & Gehring, T. M. (1988). Changing perceptions of family cohesion and power across adolescence. *Child Development, 59,* 1034–1045.

Feldman, S. S., & Quantman, T. (1988). Factors influencing age expectations for adolescent autonomy: A study of early adolescents and parents. *Journal of Early Adolescence, 8,* 325–343.

Fenson, L. (1984). Developmental trends for action and speech in pretend play. In I. Bretherton (Ed.), *Symbolic play: The development of social understanding* (pp. 249–264). New York: Academic Press.

Ferguson, K. J., Yesalis, C. E., Pomrehn, P. R., & Kirkpatrick M. B. (1989). Attitudes, knowledge, and beliefs as predictors of exercise intent and behavior in schoolchildren. *Journal of School Health, 59,* 112–115.

Ferguson, T. J., & Rule, B. G. (1982). Influence of inferential set, outcome intent, and outcome severity on children's moral judgments. *Developmental Psychology, 18,* 843–851.

Fernald, A. (1985). Four-month-old infants prefer to listen to mothers. *Infant Behavior and Development, 8,* 181–195.

Fernald, A., & Kuhl, P. (1987). Acoustic determinants of infant preference for mothers speech. *Infant Behavior and Development, 10,* 279–293.

Field, T., Masi, W., Goldstein, S., Perry S., & Parl, S. (1988). Infant day care facilitates preschool social behavior. *Early Childhood Research Quarterly, 3,* 341–361.

Field, T. M., Widmayer, S. M., Stringer, S., & Ignatoff, E. (1980). Teenage, lower class, black mothers and their preterm infants: An intervention and developmental follow-up. *Child Development, 51,* 426–436.

Field, T. M., Woodson, R. W., Cohen, D., Greenberg, R., Garcia, R., & Collins, R. (1983). Discrimination and imitation of facial expressions by term and preterm neonates. *Infant Behavior and Development, 6,* 485–489.

Fielding, J. E. (1985). Smoking: Health effects and control. *New England Journal of Medicine, 313,* 491–498.

Finckenauer, J. (1979). Scared straight. *Psychology Today, 13,* 6–11.

Fine, M. A., Moreland, J. R., & Schwebel, A. I. (1983). Long-term effects of divorce on parent-child relationships. *Developmental Psychology, 5,* 703–714.

Finkelhor, D. (1984, July-August). How widespread is child sexual abuse? *Children Today,* pp. 18–20.

Finkelstein, N. W. (1982). Aggression: is it stimulated by day care? *Young Children, 37,* 3–9.

Finn. C. E., & Ravitch, D. (1987, October). What our 17-year-olds don't know. *American School Board Journal,* pp. 31–33.

Fischer, K. W. (1980). A theory of cognitive development: The control and construction of hierarchies of skills. *Psychological Review, 87,* 477–531.

Fischer, K. W. (1987). Commentary-relations between brain and cognitive development. *Child Development, 58,* 623–633.

Fischman, S. E. (1979). Psychological issues in the genetic counseling of cystic fibrosis. In S. Kessler (Ed.), *Genetic counseling: Psychological dimensions* (pp. 153–165). New York: Academic Press.

Fischoff, J., Whitten, C. F., & Pettit, M. (1971). A psychiatric study of mothers of infants with growth problems due to maternal deprivation. *Journal of Pediatrics, 72,* 209.

Fisher, C. B., & Tryon, W. W. (1988). Ethical issues in the research and practice of applied developmental psychology. *Journal of Applied Developmental Psychology, 9,* 27–39.

Fitch, S. A., & Adams, G. R. (1983). Ego identity and intimacy: Replication and extension. *Developmental Psychology, 19,* 839–845.

Fitzgerald, H. E. & Brackbill, Y. (1976). Classical conditioning in infancy: development and constraints. *Psychological Bulletin, 83,* 353–376.

Fitzgerald, H. E., Strommen, E. A., &

McKinney, J. P. (1982). *Developmental psychology: The infant and young child* (rev. ed.). Homeword, IL: Dorsey Press.

Fitzgerald, L. F., & Betz, N. E. (1983). Issues in the vocational psychology of women. In W. B. Walsh & S. H. Opipow (Eds.), *Handbook of vocational psychology* (pp. 83–161). Hillsdale, NJ: Erlbaum.

Fitzpatrick, J. L., & Silverman, T. (1989). Women's selection of careers in engineering: Do traditional-nontraditional differences skill exist? *Journal of Vocational Behavior, 34,* 266–278.

Flavell, J. H. (1975). *Development of role-taking and communication skills in children.* Huntington, NY: Krieger.

Flavell, J. (1977). *Cognitive Development.* Englewood Cliffs, New Jersey: Prentice-Hall.

Flavell, J. H. (1982). On cognitive development. *Child Development, 53,* 1–10.

Flavell, J. H. (1985). *Cognitive Development* (2nd ed.). Englewood Cliffs, NJ: Prentice-Hall.

Flavell, J. (1986). The development of children's knowledge about the appearance-reality distinction. *American Psychologist, 41,* 418–426.

Flavell, J. H., Beach, D. H., & Chinsky, J. M. (1966). Spontaneous verbal rehearsal in memory tasks as a function of age. *Child Development, 37,* 283–299.

Flavell, J. H., Flavell, E. R., Green, F. L., & Wilcox, S. A. (1981). The development of three spatial perspective-taking rules. *Child Development, 52,* 356–368.

Flavell, J. H., Friedrichs, A. G., & Hoyt, J. D. (1970). Developmental changes in memorization processes. *Cognitive Psychology, 1,* 324–340.

Flavell, J. H., & Wellman, H. M. (1977). Metamemory. In R. V. Kail & J. W. Hagen (Eds.), *Perspectives on the development of memory and cognition.* Hillsdale, NJ: Erlbaum.

Flavell, J. H., & Wohlwill, J. F. (1969). Formal and functional aspects of cognitive development. In D. Elkind & J. H. Flavell (Eds.), *Studies in Cognitive Development* (pp. 67–120). New York: Oxford University Press.

Flax, E. (1987a, June 24). Koop warns of an explosion of AIDS among teen-agers. *Education Week,* p. 7.

Flax, E. (1987b, September 9). Teachers cite latchkey situations as cause of learning distress. *Education News,* p. 17.

Florio-Ruane, S., & Dunn, S. (1987). Teaching writing: Some perennial questions and some possible answers. In V. Richardson-Koehler (Ed.), *Educators' handbook: A research perspective* (pp. 50–84). New York: Longman.

Fogel, A. (1984). *Infancy: Infant, family and society.* St. Paul: West.

Fogelman, K. (Ed.) (1983). *Growing up in Great Britain.* London: Macmilllan.

Fontana, V. J. (1984, July-August). When systems fail: Protecting the victim of child sexual abuse. *Children Today,* pp. 14–18.

Fonteyn, V. J., & Isada, N. B. (1988). Non-genetic implications of childbearing after age thirty-five. *Obstetrical and Gynecological Survey, 43,* 709–719.

Forbes, D. (1987). Saying no to Ron and Nancy: school-based drug abuse prevention program in the 1980s. *Journal of Education, 169,* 80–90.

Ford, M. E. (1979). The construct validity of egocentrism. *Psychological Bulletin, 86,* 1169–1188.

Forbush, J. B. (1981). Adolescent parent programs and family involvement. In T. Ooms (Ed.), *Teenage Pregnancy in a Family Context: Implications for Policy* (pp. 254–277). Philadelphia: Temple University Press.

Forgatch, M. S., Patterson, G. R. and Skinner, M. L. (1988). A mediational model for the effect of divorce on antisocial behavior in boys. In E. M. Hetherington & J. D. Arasteh (Eds.), *Impact of divorce, single parenting, and stepparenting on children* (pp. 135–155). Hillsdale, NJ: Erlbaum.

Forman, G. E., & Kuschner, D. S. (1977). *The child's construction of knowledge: Piaget for teaching children.* Monterey, CA: Brooks/Cole.

Forman, G. E. & Sigel, I. E. (1979). *Cognitive Development: A Life-Span View.* Belmont, California: Wadsworth Publishing Company.

Forness, S. R., & Kavale, K. A. (1988). Psychopharmacological treatment: A note on classroom effects. *Journal of Learning Disabilities, 21,* 144–147.

Forrest, D. L., & Waller, T. G. (1982). Cognitive and metacognitive aspects of reading. Cited in S. G. Paris and B. K. Lindauer. The development of cognitive skills during childhood. In B. B. Wolman (Ed.), *Handbook of developmental psychology* (pp. 333–349). Englewood Cliffs, NJ: Prentice-Hall.

Fosburgh, L. (1977, August 7). The make-believe world of teen-age pregnancy. *New York Times magazine,* 14.

Foster, C. D., & Miller, G. M. (1980). Adolescent pregnancy: A challenge for counselors. *Personnel and Guidance Journal, 59,* 236–241.

Fowler, B. A. (1989). The relationship of body image perception and weight status to recent change in weight status of the adolescent female. *Adolescence, 24,* 557–567.

Fox, V. (1985). *Introduction to criminology.* (2nd ed.) Englewood Cliffs, NJ: Prentice Hall.

Francis, H. (1975). *Language in Childhood: Form and Function in Language Development.* New York: St. Martin's Press.

Francis, P. L., Self, P. A., & Horowitz, F. D. (1987). The behavioral assessment of the neonate: An overview. In J. D. Osofsky (Ed.), *Handbook of infant development* (pp. 723–780). New York: Wiley.

Frederick, C. J. (1985). An introduction and review of youth suicide. In M. L. Peck, N. L. Farberow, & R. E. Litman (Eds.), *Youth Suicide* (pp 1–19). New York: Springer.

Freedman, S. G. (1986, December 2). New focus placed on young unwed fathers. *New York Times,* 1.

Freud, S. (1962, originally published 1923). *The Ego and the Id.* New York: W. W. Norton.

Freud, S. (1925/1953) *Three Essays on the Theory of Sexuality.* London: Hogarth.

Freud, S. (1957, originally published 1900). *The Interpretation of Dreams.* In J. Strachey (ed.), *The Standard Edition of the Complete Psychological Works of Sigmund Freud.* Vol. 4. London: Hogarth Press.

Freud, S. (1962, originally published 1923). *The Ego and the Id.* New York: W. W. Norton.

Freud, S. (1961). *New introductory lectures on psychoanalysis.* New York: W. W. Norton (originally published 1933).

Frey, K. S., & Ruble, D. N. (1987). What children say about classroom performance: Sex and grade differences in perceived competence. *Child Development, 58,* 1066–1078.

Friedman, S., & Carpenter, G. C. (1971) Visual response decrement as a function of age of human newborn. *Child Development, 42,* 1967–1973.

Friedrich, L. K., & Stein, A. H. (1975). Prosocial television and young children: The effects of verbal labeling and role playing on learning and behavior. *Child Development, 46,* 27–38.

Friedrich, W. N., & Boriskin, J. A. (1976). The role of the child in abuse: A review of the literature. *American Journal of Orthopsychiatry, 46,* 580–591.

Frodi, A. M., & Lamb, M. E. (1980). Child abusers' responses to infant smiles and cries. *Child Development, 51,* 238–241.

Froming, W. J., Allen L., & Jensen, R. (1985). Role-taking and self-awareness: The acquisition of norms governing altruistic behavior. *Child Development, 56,* 1223–1228.

Fulkerson, K. F., Furr, S., & Brown, D. (1983). Expectations and achievement among third-, sixth-, and ninth-grade black and white males and females. *Developmental Psychology, 19,* 231–236.

Furey, E. M. (1982, September). The effects of alcohol on the fetus. *Exceptional Children, 49,* 30–34.

Furman, W., & Bierman, K. L. (1983). Developmental changes in young children's conception of friendship. *Child Development, 54,* 549–556.

Furman, W., & Bierman, K. L. (1984). Children's conceptions of friendship: A multimethod study of developmental changes. *Developmental Psychology, 20,* 925–932.

Furman, W. & Buhrmester D. (1985). Children's perceptions of the personal relationships in their social networks. *Developmental Psychology, 21,* 1016–1024.

Furstenberg, F. F. (1979). Premarital pregnancy and marital instability. In G. Levinger & O. Moles (Eds.), *Divorce and separation: Context, causes and consequences.* New York: Basic Books.

Furstenberg, F. F. (1981). Implicating the family: Teenage parenthood and kinship involvements. In T. Ooms (Ed.), *Teenage pregnancy in a family context: Implications for policy* (pp. 131–165). Philadelphia: Temple University Press.

Furstenberg, F., Jr. (1976). The social consequences of teenage parenthood. *Family Planning Perspectives, 8,* 148–164.

Furstenberg, F. F., Brooks-Gunn, J., & Chase-Lansdale, L. (1989). Teenaged pregnancy and childbearing. *American Psychologist, 44,* 313–320.

Furth, H. G., & Milgram, N. A. (1973). Labeling and grouping effects in the recall of pictures by children. *Child Development, 44,* 511–518.

Furth, H. G., & Wachs, H. (1975). *Thinking goes to school.* New York: Oxford University Press.

Gadberry, S. (1980). Effects of restricting first graders' TV-viewing on leisure time use, IQ change, and cognitive style. *Journal of Applied Developmental Psychology,* pp. 45–47.

Gadow, K. D. (1983). Effect of stimulant drugs on academic hyperactive and learning disabled children. *Journal of Learning Disabilities, 16,* 290–299.

Galinsky, E. (1986). *Investing in Quality Child Care: A Report for A.T. & T.* New York: Bank Street College.

Gallatin, J., & Adelson, J. (1971). Legal guarantees of individual freedom: A cross-national study of the development of political thought. *Journal of Social Issues, 27,* 93–108.

Galler, J. R. (1984). The behavioral consequences of malnutrition in early life. In J. R. Galler (ed.) *Human Nutrition: A comprehensive Treatise* Vol. 5 (pp. 63–111). Nutrition and Behavior. New York: Plenum.

Gallimore, R., Weiss, L., & Finney, R. (1974). Cultural differences in delay of gratification: A problem of behavior classification. *Journal of Personality and Social Psychology, 30,* 72–80.

Galst, J., & White, M. A. (1976). The unhealthy persuader: The reinforcing value of television and children's purchase-influencing attempts at the supermarket. *Child Development, 47,* 1089–1096.

Garbarino, J., Guttman, E., & Seeley, J. (1986). *The Psychologically Battered Child: Strategies for Identification, Assessment, and Intervention.* San Francisco: Jossey-Bass.

Garcia-Coll, C., Hoffman, J., & Oh, W. (1987). The social ecology of early parenting of caucasian adolescent mothers. *Child Development, 58,* 955–964.

Gardner, H. (1983) *Frames of Mind,* New York: Basic Books.

Gardner, H. (1987). Beyond the IQ: Education and human development. *Harvard Educational Review, 57,* 187–193.

Gardner, L. I. (1972, July). Deprivation dwarfism. *Scientific American,* pp. 76–82.

Garnica, O. K. (1977). Some prosodic and paralinguistic features of speech directed to young children. In C. E. Snow & C. A. Ferguson (Eds.), *Talking to children: Language input and acquisition.* Cambridge: Cambridge University Press.

Garvey, C. (1977). *Play.* Cambridge, MA: Harvard University Press.

Garwood, S. G., Phillips, D., Hartman, A., & Zigler, E. F. (1989). As the pendulum swings: Federal agency programs for children. *American Psychologist, 44,* 434–441.

Gati, I. (1989). Person-environment fit research: Problems and prospects. *Journal of Vocational Behavior, 35,* 181–193.

Geber, M., & Dean, R.F.A. (1957). The state of development of newborn African children. *The Lancet, 272,* 1216–1219.

Gelman, R. (1969). Conservation acquisition: A problem of learning to attend to relevant attributes. *Journal of Experimental Child Psychology, 7,* 167–187.

Gelman, R. (1979). Preschool thought. *American Psychologist, 34,* 900–905.

Gelman, R., & Baillargeon, R. A. (1983). A review of some Piagetian concepts. In P. H. Mussen (Ed.), *Handbook of Child Psychology* (4th ed.) (Vol. 3, pp. 167–231). New York: Wiley.

Gerbner, G., & Gross, L. (1980). The violent face of television and its lessons. In E. L. Palmer & A. Dorr (Eds.), *Children and the faces of television: Teaching, violence, selling* (pp. 149–162). New York: Academic Press.

Gerbner, G., Gross, L., Signorielli, N. & Morgan, M. (1986). Television's mean world: violence profile No. 14–15. Cited in R. M. Liebert & J. Sprafkin (1988). *The Early Window.* New York: Pergamon Press.

Gerstein, M., Lichtman, M., & Barokas, J. U. (1988). Occupational plans of adolescent women compared to men: A cross-sectional examination. *Career Development Quarterly, 36,* 222–230.

Gewirtz, J. (1975) The course of infant smiling in four child-rearing environments in Israel. In B. M. Moss (Ed.), *Determinants of infant behavior* (pp. 205–261). New York: Wiley.

Gewirtz, J., & Boyd, E. F. (1977). Does maternal responding imply reduced crying: A critique of the 1972 Bell and Ainsworth report. *Child Development, 48,* 1200–1207.

Gibbs, J. T., & Huang, L. N. (1989). *A conceptual framework for assessing and treating minority youth in children of color: Psychological interventions with minority youth* (pp 1–30). San Francisco: Jossey-Bass.

Gibson, E. J., & Walk, R. D. (1960, April). The "visual cliff." *Scientific American,* pp. 64–71.

Gifted and Talented Children's Act of 1978, P. L. 96–561, Section 902.

Gil, D. G. (1970). *Violence against children: Physical child abuse in the United States.* Cambridge, MA: Harvard University Press.

Gilligan, C. (1982). *In a different voice.* Cambridge, MA: Harvard University Press.

Ginott, H. G. (1969). *Between parent and teenager.* New York: Macmillan.

Gispert, M., Wheeler, K., Marsh, L., & Davis, M. S. (1985). Suicidal Adolescents: Factors in evaluations. *Adolescence, 20,* 753–762.

Gleason, J. B. (1985). *The development of language.* Columbus, OH: Merrill.

Glick, P. C., & Lin, S. (1986). Recent changes in divorce and remarriage. *Journal of Marriage and the Family, 48,* 737–747.

Goertzel, V., & Goertzel, M. G. (1962). *Cradles of eminence.* Boston: Little, Brown.

Goldberg, K. (1987, January 21). Values said to be key factor in teenage pregnancy. *Education Week,* 5.

Goldberg, S., & Lewis, M. (1969). Play behavior in the year-old infant: Early sex differences. *Child Development, 40,* 21–31.

Goldberg, S., Perlmutter, M. & Myers, N. (1974). Recall of related and unrelated lists by 2-year-olds. *Journal of Experimental Child Psychology, 18,* 1–8.

Golden, M. & Birns, B. (1975). Social class and cognitive development. *Merrill-Palmer Quarterly, 21,* 1783–195.

Goldsmith, H. H., & Gottesman, I. I. (1981). Origins of variation in behavioral style. A longitudinal study of temperament in young twins. *Child Development, 52,* 92–103.

Goldsmith, H. H. (1983). Genetic influences on personality from infancy to adulthood. *Child Development, 54,* 331–355.

Goldsmith, H. H., et al., (1987). What is temperament? Four approaches. *Child Development, 58,* 505–530.

Goldstein, M. (1980, November). Parenthood after 30. *Long Island*, p. 2.

Goleman, D. (1988, September 22). Studies play down dangers to latchkey children. *New York Times*, p. 12.

Goleman, D. (1989, June 6). New research overturns a milestone of infancy. *New York Times*, pp. C1+.

Goleman, D. G. (1986, September 2). The roots of terrorism are found in brutality of shattered childhood. *New York Times*, pp. C1, C8.

Gong, V. (1985). *AIDS—Defining the syndrome*. New Brunswick, NJ: Rutgers University Press.

Gonzalez-Mena, J. (1986). Toddlers: What to expect. *Young Children, 42*, 85–90.

Goodstadt, M. S. (1987, February). School-based drug education: What is wrong? *Education Digest*, pp. 44–47.

Goodwin, D. W., Schulsinger, F., Hermansen, L., Guze, S. B., & Winokur, G. (1973). Alcohol problems in adoptees raised apart from alcoholic biological parents. *Archives of General Psychiatry, 28*, 238–243.

Goodwin, D. W. (1979). Alcoholism and heredity. *Archives of General Psychiatry, 36*, 57–61.

Gopnik, A., & Astington, J. W. (1988). Children's understanding of representational change and its relation to the understanding of false belief and the appearance-reality distinction. *Child Development, 59*, 26–38.

Gordon, P. (1990). Learability and feedback. *Developmental Psychology, 26*, 217–221.

Gordon, S. (1981). Preteens are not latent, adolescence is not a disease. In L. Brown (Ed.), *Sex education* (pp. 82–101). New York: Plenum.

Gordon, S., & Dickman, I. R. (1980). Sex education promotes responsible sexual behavior. In B. Leone & M. T. O'Neill (Eds.), *Sexual values: Opposing viewpoints* (pp. 50–53). St. Paul: Greenhaven Press.

Gorsuch, R. L. & Key, M. A. (1974). Abnormalities of pregnancy as a function of anxiety and life stress. *Psychosomatic Medicine, 36*, 352–362.

Gottesman, I. I. (1966). Genetics and personality. In J. J. Hutt & C. Hutt (eds.) (1973). *Early Human Development* (pp. 17–25). London: Oxford, University Press.

Gottesman, I. I. (1978). Schizophrenia and genetics: Where are we? Are you sure?

In L. C. Wynne (Ed.), *The nature of schizophrenia*. New York: Wiley.

Gottesman, I. I., & Shields, J. (1972). *Schizophrenia and genetics: A twin study vantage point*. New York: Academic Press.

Gottfried, A. E., Gottfried, A. W., & Bathurst, K. (1988). Maternal employment, family environment, and children's development: Infancy through the school year. In A. E. Gottfried & A. W. Gottfried (Eds.), *Maternal Employment and Children's Development: Longitudinal Research* (pp. 11–58), New York: Plenum.

Gottman, J. (1983). How children become friends. *Monographs of the Society for Research in Child Development, 48* (Serial No. 201).

Gottman, J., & Mettetal, G. (1986). Speculations about social and affective development: Friendship and acquaintanceship through adolescence. In J. M. Gottman & J. G. Parker (Eds.), *Conversations of friends* (pp. 192–241). Cambridge, England: Cambridge University Press.

Gove, W. R., & Zeiss, C. (1987). Multiple roles and happiness. In F. J. Crosby (Ed.), *Spouse, parent, worker* (pp. 125–137). New Haven, CT: Yale University Press.

Grant, C. L., & Fodor, I. G. (1986). Adolescent attitudes toward body image and anorexic behavior. *Adolescence, 21*, 269–281.

Grant, J. P. (1988). *The state of the world's children 1988*. New York: Oxford University Press for UNICEF.

Gratch, G. (1979). The development of thought and language in infancy. In J. Osofsky (ed.). *Handbook of Infant Development* (pp. 439–461). New York: Wiley.

Gratch, G., Appel, K. J., Evans, W. F., LeCompte, G. K. & Wright, N. K. (1974) Piaget's stage 4 object concept error: evidence of forgetting or object conception? *Child Development, 45*, 71–77.

Graue, M. E., & Shepard, L. A. (1989). Predictive validity of the Gesell school readiness tests. *Early Childhood Research Quarterly, 4*, 303–317.

Gray, E., & Coolsen, P. (1987, July/August). How do kids really feel about being home alone? *Children Today*, pp. 30–32.

Gray, S. W., & Klaus, R. A. (1970). The early training project—A seventh year report. *Child Development, 51*, 908–924.

Greaney, V. (1980). Factors related to amount and type of leisure time reading. *Reading Research Quarterly, 15*, 337–357.

Green, A. H., Gaines, R. W., & Sandgrund, A. (1974). Child abuse: Pathological syndrome of family reaction. *American Journal of Psychiatry, 131*, 882–886.

Greenberger, E., & Goldberg, W. A. (1989). Work, parenting, and the socialization of children. *Developmental Psychology, 25*, 22–36.

Greenberger, E., & Steinberg, L. D. (1986). *When teenagers work*. New York: Basic Books.

Greene, E. (1986, November 5). Shifts in students' attitudes seen as threat to liberal arts. *The Chronicles of Higher Education*, pp. 32–35.

Greenglass, E. R., & Devins, R. (1982). Factors related to marriage and career plans in unmarried women. *Sex Roles, 8*, 57–72.

Greenlund, S., Olsen, J., Rachootin, P., & Pedersen, G. T. (1985). Effects of electronic monitoring on rates of early neonatal death, low Apgar score, and cesarean section. *Acta Obstet. Gyncol Scand, 64*, 75.

Greenough, W. T., Black. J. E., & Wallace, C. S. (1987). Experience and brain development, *Child Development, 58*, 539–560.

Gresham, F. M. (1982). Misguided mainstreaming: the case for social skills training with handicapped children. *Exceptional Children, 48*, 422–430.

Griffiths, P. (1986). Early vocabulary. In P. Fletcher & M. Garman (Eds.), *Language acquisition* (2nd ed.) (pp. 297–307). London: Cambridge University Press.

Grinder, R. L. (1973). *Adolescence*. New York: Wiley.

Gronlund, N. E. (1959). *Sociometry in the classroom*. New York: Harper.

Grossman, H. J. (ed.). (1973 and 1977). *Manual on Terminology and Classification in Mental Retardation*. Washington, DC.: American Association on Mental Deficiency.

Grossman, K., Thane, E., & Grossman, K. E. (1981). Maternal tactual contact of the newborn after postpartum conditions of mother-infant contact. *Developmental Psychology, 17*, 158–169.

Grossman, L. K., Holtzman, N. A., Charney, E., & Schwartz, A. D. (1985). Neonatal screening and genetic counseling for sickle cell trait. *American Journal of*

Disabled Children, 139, 241.

Grossman, M., & Durtz, D. J. (1974). Venereal diseases in children. *Advances in Pediatrics, 21*, 97–137.

Grotevant, H. D., & Cooper, C. R. (1985). Patterns of interaction in family relationships and the development of identity exploration in adolescence. *Child Development, 56*, 415–428.

Grotevant, H. D., & Cooper, C. R. (1986). Individuation in family relationships. *Human development, 29*, 82–100.

Guerra, N. G., & Slaby, R. (1990). Cognitive mediators of aggression in adolescent offenders: 2. Intervention. *Developmental Psychology, 26*, 269–277.

Guilford, J. P. (1967). *The nature of human intelligence.* New York: McGraw-Hill.

Guntheroth, W. G. (1982). *Crib death: Sudden infant death syndrom.* Mount Kisco, NY: Futura Publishing Company.

Gurney, P. (1987). Self-esteem enhancement in children: A review of research findings. *Educational Research, 29*, 130–135.

Gustafson, G. E., & Harris, K. L. (1990). Women's responses to young infants' cries. *Developmental Psychology, 26*, 144–152.

Hadeed, A., & Siegel, S. R. (1989). Maternal cocaine use during pregnancy: Effect on the newborn infant. *Pediatrics, 84*, 205–210.

Hagerman, R. J., & Sobesky, W. E. (1989). Psychopathology in fragile X syndrome. *American Journal of orthopsychiatry, 59*, 142–149.

Haith, M. M. (1966). The response of the human newborn to visual movement. *Journal of Experimental Child Psychology, 3*, 237–243.

Haith, M. M. (1980). *Rules babies look by: The organization of newborn visual activity.* Hillsdale, NJ: Erlbaum.

Hale, G. A. (1979). Development of children's attention to stimulus components. In G. A. Hale & M. Lewis (Eds.), *Attention and cognitive development* (pp. 43–64). New York: Plenum.

Hall, C. S., & Lindzeym, G. (1957). *Theories of personality.* New York: Wiley.

Hall. G. S. (1904). *Adolescence: Its psychology and its relations to physiology, anthropology, sociology, sex, crime, religion and education.* New York: Appleton.

Hallahan, D. P., & Kauffman, J. M. (1988). *Exceptional children: Introduction to special education* (4th ed.). Englewood Cliffs, NJ: Prentice-Hall.

Halmi, K. A. (1978). Anorexia nervosa: Recent investigations. *Annual Review of Medicine, 29*, 37–149.

Halpern, D. F. (1986). *Sex differences in cognitive abilities.* Hillsdale, NJ: Elbaum.

Hamachek, D. E. (1988). Evaluating self-concept and ego development within Erikson's psychosocial framework: A formulation. *Journal of Counseling and Development*, pp. 354–360.

Hamachek, D. E. (1969). Characteristics of good teachers and implications for teacher education. *Phi Delta Kappan, 50*, 341–345.

Hamill, D. D., Leigh, J. E., McNutt, G. & Larsen, S. C. (1981). A new definition of learning disabilities. *Learning Disability Quarterly, 4*, 372–382.

Hamill, P.V.V. (1977). NCHS Growth curves for children. *Vital Health Statistics: Series 11, data from the National Health Survey, No. 165.* Washington DC: U.S. Government Printing Office (DHEW no. 78-1650).

Hamilton, E.M.N., & Whitney, E. N. (1982). *Nutrition: Concepts and controversies* (2nd ed.). St. Paul: West.

Hamilton, E.M.N., Whitney, E. N. & Sizer, F. S. (1985). *Nutrition: Concepts and controversies* (3rd ed.). St. Paul: West.

Hannah, J. S. (1989). The relationship of socioeconomic status and gender to the occupational choices of grade 12 students. *Journal of Vocational Behavior, 34*, 161–189.

Hanson, J. W., Jones, K. L., & Smith, D. W. (1976). Fetal alcohol syndrome: Experience with 41 patients. *Journal of the American Medical Association, 235*, 1458–1466.

Harlap, S., & Shiono, P. (1980, July 26). Alcohol, and incidence of spontaneous abortions in the first and second trimester. *The Lancet*, pp. 173–176.

Harlow, H. F. (1959, July). Love in infant monkeys. *Scientific American*, pp. 68–74.

Harlow, H. F. (1971) *Learning to love.* San Francisco: Albion.

Harlow, H. F., & Harlow, M. K. (1962). Social deprivation in monkeys. *Scientific American, 207*, 136–146.

Harlow, H. F., & Suomi, S. J. (1971). Social recovery by isolation-reared monkeys.

Proceedings of the National Academy of Science, 68, 1534–1538.

Harlow. H. F., & Harlow, M. K. (1966). Affection in primates. *Discovery, 27*, 11–17.

Harmon, L. W. & Farmer, H. S. (1983). Current theoretical issues in vocational psychology. In W. B. Walsh & S. H. Osipow (eds.) *Handbook of Vocational Psychology*, vol 1. Foundations, (pp. 39–83). Hillsdale, N.J.: Erlbaum.

Harper, L., & Huie, K. (1985). The effects of prior group experience, age, and familiarity on the quality of organization of preschoolers' social relations. *Child Development, 56*, 704–717.

Harris, N. S. (1979). Whatever happened to little Albert. *American Psychologist, 34*, 151–160.

Harris, S., Mussen, P., & Rutherford, E. (1976). Some cognitive, behavioral, and personality correlates of maturity of moral judgement. *Journal of Genetic Psychology, 128*, 123–135.

Harrison, N. S. (1979). *Understanding behavioral research.* Belmont, CA: Wadsworth.

Harrison, P. L. (1981) Mercer's adaptive behavior inventory, the McCarthy scales, and dental development as predictors of first-grade achievement. *Journal of Educational Psychology, 73*, 78–82.

Hart, C. H., Ladd, G. W., & Burleson, B. R. (1990). Children's expectations of the outcomes of social strategies: Relations with sociometric status and maternal disciplinary styles. *Child Development, 61*, 127–138.

Hart, S. N. & Brassard, M. R. (1987). A major threat to children's mental health: Psychological maltreatment. *American Psychologist, 42*, 160–166.

Harter, S. (1983). Developmental perspectives on the self-system. In E. M. Hetherington (Ed.), *Handbook of child psychology* (pp. 103–197). New York: Wiley.

Harter, S. (1988). Developmental processes in the construction of self. In T. D. Yawkey & J. E. Johnson (Eds.), Hillsdale, NJ: Erlbaum.

Hartshorne, H., & May, M. A. (1928) *Studies in the nature of character.* (Vol. 1). New York: Macmillan.

Hartup, W. W. (1970). Peer interaction and social organization. In P. H. Mussen (Ed.), *Carmichael's manual of child development* (3rd ed.). New York: Wiley.

Hartup, W. W. (1974). Aggression in childhood: Developmental perspectives. *American Psychologist, 29,* 336–341.

Hartup, W. W. (1983). Peer relations. In P. H. Mussen (Ed.), *Handbook of child psychology: Socialization, personality, and social development* (4th ed.) (Vol. 4, pp. 103–197). New York: Wiley.

Hartup, W. W., Lauresen, B., Stewart, M. I., & Eastenson, A. (1988). Conflict and the friendship relations of young children. *Child Development, 59,* 1590–1601.

Haskins, R. (1985). Public school aggression among children with varying daycare experience. *Child Development, 56,* 689–703.

Hass, A. (1979). *Teenage sexuality: A survey of teenage sexual behavior.* New York: Macmillan.

Hatch, J. A., & Freeman, E. B. (1988). Kindergarten philosophies and practices: Perspectives of teachers, principals, and supervisors. *Early Childhood Research Quarterly, 3,* 151–166.

Hawley, P. (1982). The state of the art of counseling high school girls. Ford Foundation Faculty Fellowship for Research on Women's Role in Society, Project No. 0675P, June 1975. Cited in P. Hawley, B. Even. Work and sex-role attitudes in relation to education and other characteristics. *Vocational Guidance Quarterly, 31,* 101–109.

Hawley, P., & Even, B. (1982). Work and sex-role attitudes in relation to education and other characteristics. *Vocational Guidance Quarterly, 31,* 101–109.

Hay, D. F., & Ross, H. S. (1982). The social nature of early conflict. *Child Development, 53,* 105–113.

Hay, D. F. and Ross, H. S. (1982) The Social Nature of Early Conflict. Child Development, 53, 105–113.

Hayes, C. D. (1987). Adolescent pregnancy and childbearing: An emerging research focus. *Risking the Future* (Vol. 2). Washington, DC: National Academy Press.

Hayes, D. (1978). Cognitive bases for liking and disliking among pre-school children. *Child Development, 49,* 906–909.

Hayes, R. (1986). Men's decisions to enter or avoid nontraditional occupations. *Career Development Quarterly, 34,* 89–101.

Haynes, H., White, B. L., & Held, R. (1965). Visual accommodation in human infants. *Science, 148,* 528–530.

Hazen, N. L., & Black, B. (1989). Preschool peer communication skills: The role of social status and interaction context.

Child Development, 60, 867–877.

Hazen, N. L., & Durrett, M. E. (1982). Relationship of security of attachment to exploration and cognitive mapping abilities in 2-year-olds. *Developmental Psychology, 18,* 751–759.

Hechtman, L. (1989). Teenage mothers and their children: Risks and problems: A review. *Canadian Journal of Psychiatry, 34,* 569–575.

Heinich, R. (1988). The use of computers in education: a response to Streibel. *Educational Communication and Technology, 36,* 143–145.

Heinicke, C. M. (1979). Development from two and one-half to four years. In J. D. Noshpitz (Ed.), *Basic handbook of child psychiatry* (Vol. 1, pp. 167–178). New York: Basic Books.

Heinicke, C. M., Diskin, S. D., Ramsey-Klee, D. M., & Given, K. (1983). Pre-birth parent characteristics and family development in the first year of life. *Child Development, 54,* 194–208.

Heinz, J. (1983). National leadership for children's television. *American Psychologist, 38,* 817–820.

Heller, K., Sher, K. J., & Benson, C. S. (1982). Problems associated with risk of overprediction in studies of offspring of alcoholics: Implications for prevention. *Clinical Psychology Review 2,* 183–200.

Henderson, N. D. (1982). Human behavior genetics. *Annual Review of Psychology, 33,* 403–440.

Henderson, S., Hesketh, B., & Tuffin, K. (1988). A test of Gottfreson's circumscription. *Journal of Vocational Behavior, 32,* 37–48.

Hendin, H. (1985). Suicide among the youth: psychodynamics and demography. In M. L. Peck, N. L. Farberow, & R. E. Litman (eds). *Youth Suicide* (pp. 19–39). New York: Springer.

Hedin, H., Pollinger, A., Ulman, R. & Carr, A. C. (1981). Adolescent Marijuana abusers and their families. *NIDA Research Monograph 40,* Washington, DC: Department of Health and Human Services.

Henggeler, S. W., Rodick, J. D., Borduin, C. M., Hanson, C. L., Watson, S. M., Urey, J. R. (1986). Multisystemic treatment of juvenile offenders: Effects on adolescent behavior and family interaction. *Developmental Psychology, 22,* 132–141.

Hennessey, B. A., & Amabile, T. M. (1987). *Creativity and learning.* Washington, DC: National Education Association.

Herbst, A. L. (1984, November). Diethylstilbestrol exposure: 1984. *New England Journal of Medicine, 311,* 1433–1435.

Heron, A., & Kroeger, E. (1981). Introduction to developmental psychology. In H. C. Triandis & A. Heron (Eds.), *Handbook of cross-cultural psychology* (Vol. 4, pp. 1–17). Boston: Allyn and Bacon.

Heron, B. (1988). Eliminating drug abuse among students. *The Clearing House, 61,* 215–216.

Hershey, M. (1988, February). Gifted child education. *The Clearing House,* pp. 280–282.

Hertzler, A. A., & Frary, R. B. (1989). Food behavior of college students. *Adolescence, 24,* 349–355.

Heshusius-Gilsdorf, L. T., & Gilsdorf, D. L. (1975). Girls are Females, Boys Are Males: A Content Analysis of Career Materials. American Personnel and Guidance Journal, 54, 206–212.

Hess, R., & Shipman, V. (1967). Parents as teachers: How lower and middle class mothers teach. In C. S. Lavatelli & F. Stendler (Eds). (1972) *Readings in child behavior and development* (3rd ed.) (pp. 436–446). New York: Harcourt Brace Jovanovich.

Hess, R. D., and Camara, K. A. Post-Divorce Family Relationships as Mediating Variables in the Consequences of Divorce for Children. Journal of Social Issues, 1979, 35, 4.

Hess, R. D., Hiroshi, A., & Kashiwagi, K., et al. (1986). Family influences on school readiness and achievement in Japan and the United States: An overview of longitudinal study. In H. Stevenson, H. Azuma, & K. Makuta (Eds.), *Child development and education in Japan* (pp. 147–166). New York: Freeman.

Hetherington, E. M. (1972). Effects of father absence on personality: Development in adolescent daughters. *Developmental Psychology, 7,* 313–321.

Hetherington, E. M. (1979). Divorce: A child's perspective. *American Psychologist, 34,* 851–859.

Hetherington, E. M., Stanley-Hagan, M., & Anderson, E. R. (1989). Marital transitions. *American Psychologist, 44,* 303–312.

Heward, W. L., & Orlansky, M. D. (1988). *Exceptional children* (3rd ed.). Columbus, OH: Merrill.

Hicks, R. E., & Kinsbourne, M. (1976, May 28). Human handedness: A partial cross-fostering study. *Science*, pp. 908–910.

Hill, J. P. (1987). Research on adolescents and their families: Past and prospect. In C. E. Irwin (Ed.) *Adolescent social behavior and health* (pp. 15–32). San Francisco: Jossey-Bass.

Hiller, D. V., & Dyehouse, J. (1987). A case for banishing "dual career marriages" from the research literature. *Journal of Marriage and the Family, 49,* 787–795.

Hinde, R. A. Tutmus, G., Eston, D., & Tamplin, A. (1985). Incidence of "friendship" and behavior with strong associates versus nonassociatives in preschoolers. *Child Development, 56,* 234–245.

Hirsch, B. J., & Rapkin, B. D. (1987). The transition to junior high school: a longitudinal study of self-esteem, psychological symptomatology, school life, and social support. *Child Development, 58,* 1235–1244.

Hirsch, J. G. (1979). Helping the family whose child has a birth defect. In J. D. Noshpitz (Ed.), *Basic handbook of child psychiatry* (pp. 121–128). New York: Basic Books.

Hjelle, L. A., & Zeigler, D. J. (1976). *Personality.* New York: McGraw-Hill.

Hobart, T. Y. (1986, October 13). Helping the young defeat the scourges of drugs, alcohol and suicide. *New York Teacher,* p. 10.

Hochman, D. (1990). Chairperson, early childhood education program. Suffolk Community College, Selden, New York. Personal communication.

Hochschild, A. (1989). *The second shift.* New York: Viking.

Hock, E. (1980). Working and nonworking mothers and their infants: A comparative study of maternal caregiving characteristics and infant social behavior. *Merrill-Palmer Quarterly, 26,* 79–101.

Hodapp, R. M., & Mueller, E. (1982). Early social development. In B. B. Wolman (Ed.), *Handbook of Developmental Psychology* (pp. 284–298). Englewood Cliffs, NJ: Prentice-Hall.

Hodgkinson, S., et al. (1987). Molecular genetic evidence for heterogeneity in manic depression. *Nature, 325,* 805–806.

Hoff-Ginsberg, E. (1986). Function and structure in maternal speech: Their relation to the child's development of syntax. *Developmental Psychology, 22,* 155–163.

Hofferth, S. L. (1987). *Social and eco-nomic consequences of teenage childbearing in risking the future* (Vol. 2, pp. 123–145). Washington, DC: National Academy Press.

Hoffman, L. (1974a). Effects of maternal employment on the child: A review of the research. *Developmental Psychology, 10,* 204–228.

Hoffman, L. W. (1974b). Fear of success in males and females, 1965 and 1971. *Journal of Consulting and Clinical Psychology, 42,* 353–358.

Hoffman, L. W. (1979). Maternal employment. *American Psychologist, 34,* 859–865.

Hoffman, L. W. (1984). Work, family, and the socialization of the child. In R. D. Parke (Ed.), *Review of child development research* (The Family) (Vol. 7, pp. 223–282).

Hoffman, L. W. (1989). Effects of maternal employment in the two-parent family. *American Psychologist, 44,* 283–293.

Hoffman, M. L. (1979). Development of moral thought, feeling, and behavior. *American Psychologist, 34,* 958–966.

Hoffman, M. L. (1988). Moral development. In M. H. Bornstein & M. E. Lamb (Eds.), *Social, emotional and personality development* (pp. 497–548). Hillsdale, NJ: Erlbaum.

Hofsten, C. von (1982). Eye hand coordination in the newborn. *Developmental Psychology, 18,* 450–462.

Holden, C. (1980, November). Twins reunited: More than the faces are familiar. *Science,* pp. 55–59.

Holden, C. (1987). The genetics of personality. *Science, 237,* 598–600.

Holden, G. W., & West, M. J. (1989). Proximate regulation by mothers: A demonstration of how differing styles affect young children's behavior. *Child Development, 60,* 64–70.

Holland, J. (1973). *Making vocational choices.* Englewood Cliffs, NJ: Prentice-Hall.

Holmes, D. S. (1976a). Debriefing after psychological experiments, I: Effectiveness of post-deception dehoaxing. *American Psychologist, 31,* 858–868.

Holmes, D. S. (1976b). Debriefing after psychological experiments, II: Effectiveness of post-experimental desensitization. *American Psychologist, 31,* 868–876.

Holstein, C. B. (1976). Irreversible, stepwise sequence in the development of moral judgment: a longitudinal study of males and females. *Child Development, 47,* 51–61.

Holt, J. (1964). *How children fail.* New York: Pitman.

Holtzman, N. A., Kronmal, R. A., Van Doorninck, W., Azen, C., & Koch, R. (1986). Effect of age at loss of dietary control on intellectual performance and behavior of children with phenylketonuria. *New England Journal of Medicine, 314,* 593–597.

Honig, A. S. (1988).The art of talking to a baby. *Baby, 3,* 12–14, 16–17.

Horn, J. M. (1985). Bias? Indeed! *Child Development, 56,* 779–781.

Horn, J. M., Loehlin, J. C., & Willerman, L. (1979). Intellectual resemblance among adoptive and biological relatives: The Texas adoption project. *Behavior Genetics, 9,* 177–207.

Horney, K. (1939). *New ways in psychoanalysis.* New York: W. W. Norton.

Horney, K. (1967). *Feminine psychology.* New York: W. W. Norton.

Hornik, R., & Gunnar, M. R. (1988). A descriptive analysis of infant social referencing. *Child Development, 59,* 626–635.

Hornstein, H. (1976). *Cruelty and kindness: A new look at aggression and altruism.* Englewood Cliffs, NJ: Prentice-Hall.

Horowitz, A. B., & Horowitz, V. A. (1983). The effects of task-specific instructions on the encoding activities of children in recall and recognition tasks. Cited in R. S. Siegler, Information processing approaches to development. In P. H. Mussen (Ed.), *Handbook of Child Psychology* (4th ed.) (Vol 1, pp. 129–213). New York: Wiley.

Hotelling, K., & Forrest, L. (1985, November). Gilligan's theory of sex-role development: A perspective for counseling. *Journal of Counseling and development,* pp. 183–186.

Hottinger, W. (1980). Early motor development: Discussion and summary, In. B. Corbin (Ed.), *A textbook of motor development* (2nd ed.) (pp. 31–41). Dubuque, IA: Wm. C. Brown.

Householder, J., Hatcher, R., Burns, W. & Chasnoff, I. (1982). Infants born to narcotic-addicted mothers. *Psychological Bulletin, 2,* 453–468.

Housely, W. F. (1973). Vocational decision making: A function of rejecting attitudes. *Vocational Guidance Quarterly, 21,* 288–293.

Hovell, M. F., Schumaker, J. B., & Sherman, J. A. (1978). A comparison of parents' models and expansions in promoting children's acquisition of adjectives. *Journal of Experimental Child Psychology*, 25, 41–57.

Howe, N., & Ross, H. S. (1990). Socialization, perspective-taking, and the sibling relationship. *Developmental Psychology*, 26, 160–165.

Howes, C. (1988b). Same- and cross-sex friends: Implications for interaction and social skills. *Early Childhood Research Quarterly*, 3, 21–37.

Howes, C. (1988a). Peer Interaction of Young Children. Monographs of the Society for Research in Child Development. Serial No. 217, Vol. 53, No. 1.

Huang, L. N., & Yu, W. Y. (1989). Chinese American children and adolescence. In J. T. Gibbs & L. N. Huang (Eds.), *Children of color* (pp. 30–67). San Francisco: Jossey Bass.

Hubble, J., Wilder, R., & Kennedy, C. E. (1969). The student as physical being. *Personnel and Guidance Journal*, 48, 229–233.

Hudson, J. A. (1990). Constructive processing in children's event memory. *Developmental Psychology*, pp. 180–188.

Huesmann, L. R., Lagerspetz, K., & Eron, L. D. (1984). Intervening variables in TV violence—Aggression relation: Evidence from two countries. *Developmental Psychology*, 20, 746–776.

Humphreys, A. P., & Smith, P. K. (1987). Rough and tumble friendship and dominance in school children: Evidence for continuity and change with age in middle childhood. *Child Development*, 58, 201–212.

Hunt, J. McV. (1961). *Intelligence and Experience*. New York: Ronald Press.

Hunter, F. T. (1984). Socializing procedures in parent-child and friendship relations during adolescence. *Developmental Psychology*, 20, 1092–1100.

Hunter, F. T., & Youniss, J. (1982). Changes in functions of three relations during adolescence. *Developmental Psychology*, 18, 806–812.

Huston, A. C. (1983). Sex-typing. In E. M. Hetherington (Ed.), *Handbook of child psychology* (4th ed.) (Vol. 4, pp. 387–469). New York: Wiley.

Huston, A. C., Wright, J. C., Rice, M. L., Kerkman, D., & St. Peters, M. (1990). Development of television viewing patterns in early childhood: A longitudinal investigation. *Developmental Psychology*, 26, 409–421.

Huston, A. C., Watkins, B. A., & Kunkel, D. (1989). Public policy and children's television. *American Psychologist*, 44, 424–434.

Huston, A. C., Wright, J. C., Eakins, D., Kerkman, D., Pinon, M., Rosenkoetter, L., & Truglio, R. (1985). Age changes in Sesame Street viewing: A report to children's television workshop. Lawrence Kansas; University of Kansas, Center for Research on the Influence of Television on Children.

Hutchins, F. L., Kendall, N., & Rubino, J. (1979, July). Experience with teenage pregnancy. *Obstetrics and Gynecology*, pp. 1–6.

Hutt, S. J., & Hutt, C. R. (1973). *Early human development*. London: Oxford University Press.

Huttenlocher, J. (1974). The origins of language comprehension. In R. L. Solso (Ed.), *Theories in cognitive psychology*. Potomac, MD: Erlbaum.

Huttunen, M. O. (1989). Maternal stress during pregnancy and the behavior of the offspring. In S. Dopxiadis (Ed.), *Early influences shaping the individual* (pp. 175–182). New York: Plenum.

Hyde, J. S. (1981). How large are cognitive gender differences? *American Psychologist*, 36, 892–901.

Hyde, J. S. (1984). How large are gender differences in aggression: A developmental meta-analysis. *Developmental Psychology*, 20, 722–736.

Hyde, J. S. (1985). *Half the human experience: The psychology of women* (3rd ed.). Lexington, MA: D.C. Health.

Hymes, J. L. (1987). Public school for four-year-olds. *Young Children*, 62, 51–52.

Ilg, F. L., & Ames, L. B. (1955). *Child behavior*. New York: Harper & Row.

Ilg, F. L., & Ames, L. B. (1972). *School readiness*. New York: Harper & Row.

Illingworth, R. S. (1974). *The development of the infant and young child: Normal and abnormal*. Edinburgh: Livingstone.

Immelmann, K. (1980). *Introduction to Ethology*. New York: Plenum.

Inhelder, B., & Piaget, J. (1958). *The growth of logical thinking*. New York: Basic Books.

International Association for the Evaluation of Educational Achievement (1987). *The underachieving curriculum: Assessing U.S. school mathematics from an international perspective* (a national report on the second international mathematics).

Intons-Peterson, M. J., & Reddel, M. (1984). What do people ask about a neonate? *Developmental Psychology*, 20, 358–360.

Isenberg, J., & Quisenberry, N. L. (1988, February). Play: A necessity for all children. *Childhood Education*, pp. 138–145.

Istomina, Z. M. (1982). The development of voluntary memory in pre-school-age children. Cited in S. G. Paris & B. K. Lindauer, The development of cognitive skills during childhood. In B. B. Wolman (Ed.), *Handbook of developmental psychology* (pp. 333–349). Englewood Cliffs, NJ: Prentice-Hall.

Izard, C. E., & Malatesta, C. Z. (1987). Perspectives on emotional development 1: Differential emotions theory of early emotional development. In J. D. Osofsky (Ed.), *Handbook of infant development* (pp. 494–555). New York: Wiley.

Jackson, A. W., & Hornbeck, D. W. (1989). Educating young adolescents. *American Psychologist*, 44, 831–836.

Jacobson, A., & Owen, S. S. (1987). Infant-caregiver interactions in day care. *Child Study Journal*, 17, 197–209.

Jacobson, A. L. (1978, July). Infant day care: Toward a more human environment. *Young Children*.

Jacobson, J. L., Fein, G. G., Jacobson, S. W., & Schwartz, P. M. (1984). Factors and clusters for the Brazelton scale: An investigation of the dimensions of neonatal behavior. *Developmental Psychology*, 20, 339–354.

Jacobson, J. L., Jacobson, S. W., Fein, G., Schwartz, P. M., & Dowler, J. K. (1984). Prenatal exposure to an environmental toxin: A test of the multiple effects model. *Developmental Psychology*, 20, 523–533.

Jacobson, J. L., & Wille, D. E. (1986). The influence of attachment pattern on developmental changes in peer interaction from the toddler to the preschool period. *Child Development*, 57, 338–347.

Jahoda, G. (1983). European "lag" in the development of an economic concept: A study in Zimbabwe. *British Journal of Developmental Psychology*, 1, 113–120.

Jaroff, L. (1989, March 20). The gene hunt. *Time*, pp. 62 +.

Jarvik, M. E., Cullen, J. W., Gritz, E. R., Vogt, T. M., & West, L. J. (Eds.) (1977). *Research on smoking behavior.* U.S. Department of Health, Education and Welfare, NIDA Research Monograph 17. Washington, DC: U.S. Government Printing Office.

Javernick, E. (1988, January). Johnny's not Jumping: Can we help obese children? *Young Children*, pp. 18–23.

Jencks, C. (1972). *Inequality: A reassessment of the effects of family and schooling in America.* New York: Basic Books.

Jennings, L. (1990, April 11). Child-abuse reports in 1989 up 10% over '88, state-by-state survey finds. *Education Week*, p. 8.

Jensen, A. R. (1969). How much can we boost I.Q. and Scholastic Achievement? *Harvard Educational Review, 39,* 1–123.

Jensen, K. (1932). Differential reaction to taste and temperature stimuli in newborn infants. *Genetic Psychology Monographs, 12,* 363–479.

Jensen, L. C. (1985). *Adolescence: Theories, research, application.* St. Paul: West.

Joffe, L. S., & Vaughn, B. E. (1982). Infant-mother attachment: Theory, assessment, and implications for development. In B. B. Wolman (Ed.), *Handbook of developmental psychology* (pp. 190–204). Englewood Cliffs, NJ: Prentice-Hall.

Johansen, A. S., Leibowitz, A., & Waite, L. J. (1988). Child care and children's illness. *American Journal of Public Health, 78,* 1175–1177.

Johnson, J. A. (1981). The etiology of hyperactivity. *Exceptional Children, 47,* 348–354.

Johnson, J. E., & Yawkey, T. D. (1988). Play and integration. In T. D. Yawkey & J. E. Johnson (Eds.), *Integrative processes and socialization* (pp. 97–119). Hillsdale, NJ: Erlbaum.

Johnson, R. R., Cooper, H., & Chance, J. (1982). The relation of children's television viewing to school achievement and I.Q. *Journal of Educational Research, 76,* 294–297.

Johnston, L. D. (1988). *Summary of 1987 drug study results.* Ann Arbor, MI, University of Michigan, News and Information Services.

Jones, B. (1986, April). Quality and equality through cognitive instruction. *Edu-cational Leadership*, pp. 4–11.

Jones, C. O. (1977). Development of children from abusive families. In A. W. Franklin (ed.). *Child Abuse* (pp. 61–71). Edinburgh, Churchill-Livingston.

Jones, D. C., Swift, D. J., & Johnson, M. A. (1988). Nondeliberate memory for a novel event among preschoolers. *Developmental Psychology, 24,* 641–646.

Jones, G. P., & Dembo, M. H. (1989). Age and sex role differences in intimate friendships during childhood and adolescence. *Merrill-Palmer Quarterly, 35,* 445–462.

Jones, K. L., Smith, D. W., Streissguth, A. P., and Myrianthopoulus, N. (1974). Outcomes in offspring of chronic alcoholic women. *The Lancet, 1,* 1076–1078.

Jones, M. C. (1957). The later careers of boys who are early and late maturers. *Child Development, 28,* 113–128.

Jones, M. C. (1965). Psychological correlates of somatic development. *Child Development, 36,* 899–911.

Jones, M. C., & Bayley, N. (1950). Physical maturing among boys as related to behavior. *Journal of Educational Psychology, 41,* 129–148.

Jones, M. C., & Mussen, P. H. (1958). Self conceptions, motivations and interpersonal attitudes of early- and late-maturing girls. *Child Development, 29,* 491–501.

Jones, S. S., & Raag, T. (1989). Smile production in older infants: The importance of a social recipient for the facial signal. *Child Development, 60,* 811–819.

Jones, W. H., Chernovetz, M. E., & Hansson, R. O. (1978). The enigma of androgyny: Differential implications for males and females? *Journal of Consulting and Clinical Psychology, 46,* 298–313.

Juntune, J. (1982). Myth: the gifted constitutes a single homogeneous group! *Gifted Child Quarterly, 26,* 9–10.

Jussim, L. (1989). Teacher expectations: Self-fulfilling prophecies, perceptual biases, and accuracy. *Journal of Personality and Social Psychology, 57,* 469–480.

Justice, E. (1985). Categorization as a preferred memory strategy. *Developmental Psychology, 21,* 1105–1110.

Kadushin, A. (1976). Adopting older children: Summary and implications. In A. M. Clarke & A. D. B. Clarke (Eds.), *Early experience: Myth and evidence* (pp. 187–213). New York: Free Press.

Kagan, D. M., & Squires, R. L. (1984). Eating disorders among adolescents: Patterns and prevalence. *Adolescence, 73,* 15–31.

Kagan, J. (1965). Reflectivity-impulsivity and reading ability in primary grade children. *Child Development, 36,* 609–628.

Kagan, J. (1976a). Resilience and continuity in psychological development. In A. M. Clarke & A. D. B. Clarke (Eds.), *Early experience: Myth and evidence* (pp. 97–122). New York: Freeman.

Kagan, J. (1976b). Emergent themes in human development. *American Scientist, 64,* 186–196.

Kagan, J. (1979a). Overview: perspectives on human infancy. In J. Osofsky (ed.). *Handbook of Infant Development* (pp. 1–29). New York: Wiley.

Kagan, J. (1979b). The form of early development. In P. H. Mussen, J. J. Conger, & J. Kagan (1980). *Readings in Child and Adolescent Psychology: Contemporary Perspectives* (pp. 18–22). New York: Harper and Row.

Kagan, S. I. 1 (1985, December 11). Four-year-olds in the public schools. *Education Week,* 24.

Kail, R., & Hagen, J. W. (1982). Memory in childhood. In B. B. Wolman (Ed.), *Handbook of developmental psychology* (pp. 350–367). Englewood Cliffs, NJ: Prentice-Hall.

Kail, R., & Pellegrino, J. W. (1985). *Human intelligence: Perspectives and prospects.* New York: Freeman.

Kaitz, M., Meschlach-Sarfaty, O., Auerbach, J., & Eidelman, A. (1988). A reexamination of newborns' ability to imitate facial expressions. *Developmental Psychology, 24,* 3–8.

Kalat, J. W. (1981). *Biological psychology.* Belmont, CA: Wadsworth.

Kamii, C. (1985). Leading primary education toward excellence. *Young Children, 40,* 3–9.

Kamin, L. J. (1974). *The Science and Politics of I.Q.* Hillsdale, J. J.: Erlbaum.

Kammerman, S. B. (1980). *Parenting in an unresponsive society: Managing work and family life.* New York: The Free Press.

Kammerman, S. (1986). Infant care usage in the United States. Cited in Belsky, J. Infant day care: a cause for concern. *Zero to Three, 7,* 1–7.

Kandel, D. & Lesser, G. S. (1969). Parent-adolescent relationships and adolescent independence in the United States and Denmark. *Journal of Marriage and The Family, 31,* 348–358.

Kaplan, P. S. (1977, March 13). It's the I.Q. tests that flunk. *New York Times,* p. 26.

Kaplan, P. S. (1990). *Educational psychology for tomorrow's teacher.* St. Paul: West.

Kaplan, P. S., & Stein, J. (1984). *Psychology of adjustment.* Belmont, CA: Wadsworth.

Karen, R. L. (1974). *An Introduction to Behavior Therapy and Its Application.* New York: Harper and Row.

Karger, H. J. (1988, December). Children and microcomputers: A critical analysis. *Educational Technology,* pp. 7–11.

Katchadourian, H. (1977). *The biology of adolescence.* San Francisco: Freeman.

Katz, L. G. (1980, August). Should you be your child's parents? *Parents,* pp. 88–90.

Kaufman, J., & Zigler, E. (1987). Do abused children become abusive parents. *American Journal of Orthopsychiatry, 57,* 186–192.

Kearsley, R. B. (1973). The newborn's response to auditory stimuli: A demonstration of orientation and defensive behavior. *Child Development, 44,* 582–590.

Keasey, C. B. (1978). Children's developing awareness and usage of intentionality and motivation. In C. B. Keasey (Ed.), *Nebraska symposium on motivation* (Vol. 25). Lincoln, NB: University of Nebraska Press.

Keating, D. P. (1980). Four faces of creativity: The continuing plight of the intellectually underserved. *Gifted Child Quarterly, 24,* 56–61.

Keefer, C. S., Dixon, E., and Tronick, L. B., and Brazelton T. B. (1982). Gusii infants' neuromotor behavior: Use of the neonatal behavioral assessment scale in cross-cultural studies. Cited in B. M. Lester & T. B. Brazelton, Cross-cultural assessment of neonatal behavior. In D. A. Wagner & H. W. Stevenson (Eds). *Cultural perspectives on child development* (pp. 22–54) San Francisco: Freeman.

Keeney, T. J., Cannizzo, S. R., & Flavell, J. H. (1967). Spontaneous and induced verbal rehearsal in a recall task. *Child Development, 38,* 953–966.

Kegan, R. (1982). *The evolving self: Problem and process in human development.* Cambridge, MA: Harvard University Press.

Keith, P. M. (1981). Sex-role attitudes, family plans, and career orientation: implications for counseling. *Vocational Guidance Quarterly, 29,* 244–253.

Keller, A., Ford, L. M. & Meacham, J. A. (1978). Dimensions of self-concept in preschool children. *Developmental Psychology, 14,* 483–489.

Kellogg, R. (1970). *Analyzing children's art.* Palo Alto, CA: Mayfield.

Kelly, J. B. (1982). Divorce: The adult perspective. In B. B. Wolman (Ed.), *Handbook of developmental psychology* (pp. 734–750). Englewood Cliffs, NJ: Prentice-Hall.

Kelly, J. B., & Wallerstein, J. S. (1976). The effects of parental divorce: Experiences of the child in early latency. *American Journal of Orthopsychiatry, 46,* 20–33.

Kendrick, C. & Dunn, J. (1983). Sibling quarrels and maternal responses. *Developmental Psychology, 19,* 62–71.

Kermis, M. D. (1984). *The Psychology of Human Aging.* Boston: Allyn and Bacon.

Kiesler, S. B. (1979). Federal policies for research on children. *American Psychologist, 34,* 1009–1017.

Kinard, E. M., & Klerman, L. V. (1980). Teenage parenting and child abuse: Are they related? *American Journal of Orthopsychiatry, 50,* 481–488.

Kirk, S. A. & Gallagher, J. J. (1989). *Educating Exceptional children* (6th ed.). Boston: Houghton Mifflin.

Kisilevsky, B. S., & Muir, D. W. (1984). Neonatal habituation and dishabituation to tactile stimulation during sleep. *Developmental Psychology, 20,* 367–374.

Klaus, M., & Kennell, J. H. (1976). *Maternal-infant bonding.* St. Louis: C. V. Mosby.

Klaus, M. H., & Kennell, J. H. (1983). *Bonding: The beginning of parent-infant attachment.* New York: New American Library.

Klein, R. P. (1985). Caregiving arrangements by employed women with children under 1 year of age. *Developmental Psychology, 21,* 403–406.

Kline, & Susser, J., Shrout, P., Stern, Z., Warburton, D. (1980, July 26). Drinking during pregnancy and spontaneous abortion. *The Lancet,* pp. 176–180.

Kline, P. (1972). *Fact and fancy in Freudian theory.* London: Methuen.

Knothe, H. & Dette, G. A. (1985). Antibiotics and pregnancy: toxicity and teratogenicity. *Infection, 49,* 13.

Knox, D. (1984). *Human Sexuality: The Search for Understanding.* St. Paul, Minnesota: West.

Kobayashi-Winata, H., & Power, T. G. (1989). Child rearing and compliance. *Journal of Cross-Cultural Psychology, 20,* 333–356.

Kochanevich-Wallace, P. M., McCluskey-Fawcett, K. A., & Meck, N. E. (1988). Method of delivery and parent-newborn interaction. *Journal of Pediatric Psychology, 13,* 213–221.

Kochanska, G., Kuczynski, L., & Radke-Yarrow, M. (1989). Correspondence between mothers' self-reported and observed child rearing practices. *Child Development, 60,* 56–64.

Kogan, N. (1983). Stylistic variation in childhood and adolescence: creativity, metaphor and cognitive style. In P.H. Mussen (ed.) *Handbook of Child Psychology* (4th edition). New York: Wiley.

Kohen-Raz, R. (1977). *Psychophysiological aspects of cognitive growth.* New York: Academic Press.

Kohlberg, L. (1969). Stage and sequence: The cognitive-developmental approach to socialization. In D. A. Goslin (Ed.), *Handbook of socialization theory and research.* Chicago: Rand-McNally.

Kohlberg, L. (1976). Moral stages and moralization: The cognitive-developmental approach. In T. Lickona (Ed.), *Moral development and behavior.* New York: Holt, Rinehart and Winston.

Kohlberg, L. (1987). The young child as a philosopher. In L. Kohlberg (Ed.), *Child psychology and childhood education* (pp. 13–43). New York: Longman.

Kohlberg, L., Colby, A., Gibbs, J., Speicher-Dubin, B., & Powers, C. (1978). *Assessing moral development stages: A manual.* Cambridge, MA: Center for Moral Education.

Kohlberg, L., & Kramer, R. (1969). Continuities and discontinuities in childhood and adult moral development. *Human Development, 12,* 93–120.

Kohlberg, L., & Lickona, T. (1987). Moral discussion and the class meeting. In R. DeVries with L. Kohlberg, *Programs of early education* (pp. 142–188). New York: Longman.

Kohlberg, L., & Turiel, E. (1971). Moral development and moral education. In G. Lesser (Ed.), *Moral development and moral education.* Chicago: Scott, Foresman.

Kolata, G. (1989, December 5). Understanding Down syndrome: A chromosome holds the key. *New York Times*, p. C3.

Kopp, C. B., & Kaler, S. R. (1989). Risk in infancy. *American Psychologist, 44*, 224–231.

Kopp, C. B., & Parmelee, A. H. (1979). Prenatal and perinatal influences on infant behavior. In J. D. Osofsky (Ed.), *Handbook of infant development* (pp. 29–75). New York: Wiley.

Koran, J. J., & Lehman, J. R. (1981, January). Teaching children science concepts: The role of attention. *Science and Children*.

Korner, A. F. (1973). Sex differences in newborns with special reference to differences in the organization of oral behavior. *Journal of Child Psychology and Psychiatry, 14*, 17–29.

Korner, A. & Thoman, E. (1972). The relative efficacy of contact and vestibular proprioceptive stimuli in soothing neonates. *Child Development, 43*, 443–454.

Koslowski, B. (1980). Quantitative and qualitative changes in the development of seriation. *Merrill-Palmer Quarterly, 26*, 391–405.

Kotelchuck, M. (1976). The nature of the child's tie to his father. Cited in M. Kotelchuck, The infant's relationship to the father: Experimental evidence. In M. Lamb (Ed.), *The role of the father in child development* (pp. 329–344). New York: Wiley.

Kramer, J., Hill, K. & Cohen, L. (1975). Infants' development of object permanence: a refined methodology of new evidence for piaget's hypothesized ordinality. *Child Development, 46*, 149–155.

Kremenitzer, J. P., Vaughn, H. G., Kurtzberg, D., & Dowling, K. (1979). Smooth-pursuit eye movements in the newborn infant. *Child Development, 50*, 442–448.

Kreutzer, M. A., & Charlesworth, W. R. (1973). Infants' reactions to different expressions of emotion. In C. A. Nelson, The recognition of facial expressions in the first two years of life: Mechanisms of development. *Child Development, 58*, 889–909.

Krogman, W. M. (1980). *Child growth*. Ann Arbor: University of Michigan Press.

Kubiszyn, T., & Borich, G. (1987). *Educational testing and measurement* (2nd ed.). Glenview, IL: Scott, Foresman and Company.

Kuhn, D., Ho, V. & Adams, C. (1979). Formal reasoning among pre and late adolescents. *Child Development, 50*, 1149–1152.

Kurdek, L. A. (1981). An integrative perspective on children's divorce adjustment. *American Psychologist, 36*, 856–866.

Kurzweill, S. R. (1988). Recognition of mother from multisensory interactions in early infancy. *Infant Behavior and Development, 11*, 235–243.

Labov, W. (1977). The study of nonstandard english. In V. P. Clark, P. A. Eschholz, & A. F. Rosa (Eds.), *Language* (2nd ed.) (pp. 439–450). New York: St. Martin's Press.

Ladd, G. W., & Price, J. M. (1987). Predicting children's social and school adjustment following the transition from preschool to kindergarten. *Child Development, 58*, 1168–1189.

La Fromboise, T. D., & Low, K. G. (1989). *American Indian children and adolescents in children of color: Psychological interventions with minority youth* (pp. 114–148). San Francisco: Jossey-Bass.

Lamaze, F. (1970). *Painless Childbirth*. Chicago: Regnery.

Lamb, M. E. (1988). Social and emotional development in infancy. In M. H. Bornstein & M. E. Lamb (Eds.), *Social, emotional and personality development* (pp. 359–411). Hillsdale, NJ: Erlbaum.

Lamb, M. E., Frodi, M., Hwang, C. P., & Frodi, A. M. (1983). Effects of paternal involvement on infant preferences for mothers and fathers. *Child Development, 54*, 450–458.

Landesman-Dwyer, S. and Emanuel, I. (1979). Smoking during pregnancy. In J. Belsky (ed.). *In The Beginning* (pp. 37–45). New York: Columbia University Press.

Langlois, J. H., Roggman, L. A., Casey, R. J., Ritter, J. M., Riser-Danner, L. A., & Jenkins, V. Y. (1987). Infant preferences for attractive faces: Rudiments of a stereotype? *Developmental Psychology, 23*, 363–370.

Langlois, J. H., Roggman, L. A., & Riser-Danner, L. A. (1990). Infants' differential social responses to attractive and unattractive faces. *Developmental Psychology, 26*, 153–160.

Larsen, J. M., & Robinson, C. C. (1989). Later

effects of preschool on low-risk children. *Early Childhood Research Quarterly, 4*, 133–144.

Larson, L. E. (1972). The influence of parents and peers during adolescence: The situation hypothesis revisited. *Journal of Marriage and the Family, 34*, 67–74.

Laughlin, H. P. (1970). *The ego and its defenses*. New York: Appleton-Century-Crofts.

Lauresen, B., & Hartup, W. W. (1989). The dynamics of preschool children's conflicts. *Merrill-Palmer Quarterly, 35*, 281–297.

La Voie, J. C. (1976). Ego identity formation in middle adolescence. *Journal of Youth and Adolescence, 4*, 371–385.

Lazar, I., Darlington, R, Murray, H., Royce, J., & Snipper, A. (1982). Lasting effects of early education: A report from the consortium for longitudinal studies. *Monographs of the Society for Research in Child Development, 47*, 2–3, serial number 195

Leary, W. E. (1988, October 27). Birth experts caution on repeated caesareans. *New York Times*, Oct. 27, 1988, p. B16.

Leary, W. E. (1990, June 9). Gloomy report on the health of teen-agers. *New York Times*, p. 24.

Leboyer, F. (1975). *Birth without violence*. New York: Knopf.

Lee, A. L., & Scheurer, V. L. (1983). Psychological androgyny and aspects of self-image in women and men. *Sex Roles, 9*, 289–306.

Lee, P. C., & Gropper, N. B. (1974). Sex-role culture and educational practice. *Harvard Educational Review, 42*, (no. 3), 369–410.

Lee, V. L., Brooks-Gunn, J. L., & Schnur, E. (1988). Does Head Start work? A 1-year follow-up comparison of disadvantaged children attending Head Start, no preschool, and other preschool programs. *Developmental Psychology, 24*, 210–223.

Lempers, J. D., Flavell, E. R., & Flavell, J. H. (1977). The development in very young children of tacit knowledge concerning visual perceptions. *Genetic Psychology Monographs, 95*, 3–53.

Lenneberg, E. H. (1967). *Biological foundations of language*. New York: Wiley.

Lenz, W. (1966). Malformations caused by drugs in pregnancy. *American Journal of Diseases of Children, 112*, 99–106.

Leon, M. (1962). Rules in children's moral judgments: Integration of intent, damage and rationale information. *Developmental Psychology, 18*, 835–842.

Lerner, R. M. (1984). *On the nature of human plasticity*. New York: Cambridge University Press.

Lerner, R. M. Karson, M., Meisels, M., & Knapp, J. R. (1975). Actual and perceived attitudes of late adolescents and their parents: The phenomenon of the generation gaps. *Journal of Genetic Psychology, 126*, 195–207.

Lerner, R. M., & Spanier, G. B. (1980). *Adolescent development: A life-span perspective*. New York: McGraw-Hill.

Lesser, G. S. (1976). Applications of psychology to television programming: Formulation of program objectives. *American Psychologist, 31*, 135–137.

Lester, B. M., Heidelise, A., & Brazelton, T. B. (1982). Regional obstetric anesthesia and newborn behavior: A reanalysis towards synergistic effects. *Child Development, 53*, 687–692.

Levanthal, H., & Cleary, P. (1980). The smoking problem: A review of the research and theory in behavioral risk modification. *Psychological Bulletin, 88*, 370–405.

Levine, K. & Mueller, E. (1988). In T. D. Yawkey & J. E. Johnson (Eds.), *Integrative processes and socialization: Early to middle childhood.* (pp. 207–225). Hillsdale, NJ: Erlbaum.

Levy, G. D., & Carter, D. B. (1989). Gender schema, gender constancy, and gender-role knowledge: The roles of cognitive factors in preschooler's gender-role stereotype attributions. *Developmental Psychology, 25*, 444–450.

Lewis, M. (1987). Social development in infancy and early childhood. In J. D. Osofsky (Ed.), *Handbook of infant development* (pp. 419–494). New York: Wiley.

Lewis, M. & Brooks-Gunn, J. (1972). The relations of infants to people. In J. Belsky (Ed.). *In The Beginning* pp. 166–172). New York: Columbia University Press.

Lewis, M., & Feiring, C. (1989a). Early predictors of childhood friendship. In T. J. Berndt & G. W. Ladd (Eds.), *Peer Relationships in Child Development* (pp. 246–274). New York: Wiley.

Lewis, M., & Feiring, C. (1989b). Infant, mother, and mother-infant interaction behavior and subsequent attachment. *Child Development, 60*, 831–838.

Lewis, M. & McGurk, H. (1972). Evaluation of infant intelligence. *Science, 178*, 1174–1177.

Lewis, M. & Rosenblum, L. A. (1975). *Friendship and Peer Relations*. New York: Wiley.

Lewis, P. H. (1988, November 6). A great equalizer for the disabled. "Education Life." *New York Times*. Section 4A, pp. 61–67.

Lezotte, L. W. (1982, November). Characteristics of effective schools and programs for realizing them. *Education Digest, 27*–29.

Liebert, R. M., Neale, J. M., & Davison, E. S. (1973). *The early window: Effects of television on children and youth*. New York: Pergamon Press.

Liebert, R. M., & Sprafkin, J. (1988). *The early window: Effects of television on children and youth* (3rd ed.). New York: Pergamon Press.

Lindberg, M. (1980). The role of knowledge structures in the ontogeny of learning. *Journal of Experimental Child Psychology, 30*, 401–410.

Linn, M. C., & Petersen, A. C. (1985). Emergence and characterization of sex differences in spatial ability: A meta-analysis. *Child Development, 56*, 1479–1498.

Lips, H. M., & Colwill, N. L. (1978). *The psychology of sex differences*. Englewood Cliffs, NJ: Prentice-Hall.

Lipsitt, L. (1982). Perinatal indicators and psychophysiological precursors of crib death. In J. Belsky (Ed.), *In the beginning: Readings on infancy* (p. 74). New York: Columbia University Press.

Lipsitt, L. P., Engen, T., & Kaye H. (1963). Developmental changes in the olfactory threshold of the neonate. *Child Development, 34*, 37–46.

Lipsitt, L. P., & Kaye, H. (1964). Conditioned sucking in the newborn. *Psychonomic Science, 1*, 29–30.

Lipsitt, L. P., & Levy, N. (1959). Electrotactual threshold in the neonate. *Child Development, 30*, 547–554.

Little, B. B., Snell, L. M., Gilstrap, L. C., Gant, N. F., & Rosenfeld, C. R. (1989). Alcohol abuse during pregnancy: Changes in frequency in a large urban hospital. *Obstetrics and Gynecology, 74*, 547–550.

Little, B. B., Snell, L. M., Klein, V. R., & Gilstrap, L. C. (1989). Cocaine abuse during pregnancy: Maternal and fetal

implications. *Obstetrics and Gynecology, 73*, 157–160.

Livesley, W. J., & Bromley, D. C. (1973). *Person perception in childhood and adolescence*. London: Wiley.

Lockhart, A. S. (1980). Motor learning and motor development during infancy and childhood. In C. B. Corbin (Ed.). *A Textbook of Motor Development* (Second Edition) (pp. 246–253). Dubuque, Iowa: Brown.

Lockheed, M. (1976). Some determinants and consequences of teacher expectations concerning pupil performance. In *Beginning Teacher Evaluation Study: Phase 2.* Princeton, N.J.: Educational Testing Service.

Loeb, R. C., Horst, L., & Horton, P. J. (1980). Family interaction patterns associated with self-esteem in preadolescent girls and boys. *Merrill-Palmer Quarterly, 26*, 203–217.

Loehlin, J. C., Horn, J. M., & Willerman, L. (1989). Modeling IQ change: Evidence from the Texas Adoption Project. *Child Development, 60*, 993–1005.

Lofting, H. (1948). *The story of Doctor Dolittle*. Philadelphia: Lippincott.

Logan, D. D. (1980). The menarche experience in twenty-three foreign countries. *Adolescence, 58*, 247–257.

Londerville, S., & Main, M. (1981). Security, compliance and maternal training methods in the second year of life. *Developmental Psychology, 17*, 289–299.

Longstreth, L. E., (1981). Revisiting Skeel's final study: A critique. *Developmental Psychology, 17*, 620–625.

Lorenz, K. (1937). The companion in the bird's world. *AUK, 54*, 245–273.

Lorenzi, M. E., Klerman, L. V. & Jekel, J. F. (1977). School-age parents: How permanent a relationship? *Adolescence, 45*, 13–22.

Los Angeles Times. Hero, 5, can do it but can't say it. *Los Angeles Times*, August 7, 1986, p. 2.

Lowney, J., Winslow, R. W., & Winslow, V. (1981). *Deviant reality: Alternative world views* (2nd ed.). Boston: Allyn and Bacon.

Lowrey, G. (1978). *Growth and development of children* (7th ed.). Chicago: Year Book Medical Publishers.

Lozoff, B. (1989). Nutrition and behavior. *American Psychologist, 44*, 231–237.

Luder, A. S., & Greene, C. L. (1989). Maternal phenylketonuria and hyperphenylalaninemia: Implications for medical practice in the United States. *American Journal of Obstetrics and Gynecology, 161*, 1102–1105.

Lueptow, L. B. (1981). Sex-typing and change in the occupational choices of high school seniors, 1964–1975. *Sociology of Education, 54*, 16–24.

Lutkenhaus, P., Grossman, K. E., & Grossman, K. (1985). Infant-mother attachment at twelve months and style of interaction with a stranger at the age of three years. *Developmental Psychology, 56*, 1538–1542.

Lyle, J., & Hoffman, H. R. (1972). Explorations in patterns of television viewing by preschool-age children. In E. A. Rubinstein, G. A. Comstock, & J. P. Murray (Eds.), *Television and social behavior 4: Television in day to day life: Patterns of use.* Washington, DC: U.S. Government Printing Office.

Lystad, M. H. (1975). Violence at home: A review of the literature. *American Journal of Orthopsychiatry, 46*, 328–345.

Maccoby, E. E. (1980). *Social development: Psychological growth and the parent-child relationship.* New York: Harcourt Brace Jovanovich.

Maccoby, E. E., (1990). Gender and relationships: A developmental account. *American Psychologist, 45*, 513–521.

Maccoby, E. E., & Jacklin, C. N. (1974). *The psychology of sex differences.* Stanford, CA: Stanford University Press.

Maccoby, E. E., & Jacklin, C. N. (1980). Sex differences in aggression: A rejoinder and reprise. *Child Development, 51*, 964–980.

Maccoby, E. E., & Martin, J. A. (1983). Socialization in the context of the family: Parent-child interaction. In P. H. Mussen (Ed.), *Handbook of child development* (4th ed.) (Vol. 4, pp. 1–103). New York: Wiley.

MacFarlane, A. (1975). Olfaction in the development of social preferences in the human neonate. Cited in Brazelton, T. B. (1981). *On Becoming a Family: The Growth of Attachment.* New York: Delacorte Press.

MacGregor, S. N., Keith, L. G., Bachicha, J. A., & Chasnoff, I. J. (1989). Cocaine abuse during pregnancy: Correlation between prenatal care and perinatal outcome. *Obstetrics and Gynecology, 74*, 882–885.

MacKinnon, D. (1978). *In Search of Human Effectiveness.* Buffalo, N.Y.: Creative Education Foundation.

Main, M., & Cassidy, J. (1988). Categories of response to reunion with the parent at age 6: Predictable from infant attachment classifications and stable over a 1-month period. *Developmental Psychology, 24*, 415–427.

Makin, J. W., & Porter, R. H. (1989). Attractiveness of lactating females' breast odors to neonates. *Child Development, 60*, 803–811.

Malatesta, C. Z., Culver, C., Tesman, J. R., & Shepard, B. (1989). The development of emotion expression during the first two years of life. Monographs of the Society for Research in Child Development, 54, Nos. 1–2, Serial No. 219.

Malinowski, C. I., & Smith, C. P. (1985). Moral reasoning and moral conduct: An investigation prompted by Kohlberg's theory. *Journal of Personality and Social Psychology, 49*, 1016–1027.

Mandell, C. J. & Fiscus, E. (1981). *Understanding Exceptional People.* St. Paul, Minnesota: West.

Mandler, J. M. (1983). Representation. In P. H. Mussen (Ed.), *Handbook of child psychology* (4th ed.) (Vol. 3) (pp. 420–495) New York: Wiley.

Mandler, J. & Johnson, N. (1977). Remembrance of things passed: Story structure and recall. *Child Development, 9*, 111–151.

Mange, A. P., & Mange, E. J. (1980). *Genetics: Human aspects.* Philadelphia: Saunders.

Mann, M. J., Harrell, A., & Hurt, M. A. (1978). *A review of Head Start research since 1969 and an annotated bibliography.* Washington, DC: U.S. Government Printing Office, No. 017-092-00037-5.

Manning, M. L., & Allen, M. G. (1987). Social development in early adolescence. *Childhood Education, 18*, 172–176.

Mansfield, R. S., Busse, T. V. & Krepelka, E. J. (1978). The effectiveness of creativity training. *Review of Educational Research, 48*, 517–536.

March of Dimes. (1983). *Be good to your baby before it is born.* White Plains, NY: March of Dimes.

March of Dimes. (1985). Robert Matousek, statistician. Personal correspondence concerning estimates of number of preg-

nant women who smoke.

March of Dimes. (1986a).*Tay-Sachs.* Public Health Education Information Series.

March of Dimes. (1986b). *PKU.* Public Health Education Information Series.

March of Dimes. (1986c). *Sickle cell anemia.* Public Health Education Information Sheet: Genetic Series.

March of Dimes. (1987a). *Down syndrome.* Public Health Education Information Sheet: Genetic Series.

March of Dimes. (1987b). *Congenital AIDS.* Public Health Education Information Sheet.

March of Dimes. (1989). *VDT facts.* Public Health Education Information Sheet.

Marcia, J. (1967). Ego identity status: Relationship to change in self-esteem, "general maladjustment," and authoritarianism. *Journal of Personality, 35*, 118–133.

Marcia, J. (1980). Identity in adolescence. In J. Adelson (Ed.), *Handbook of adolescent psychology.* New York: Wiley.

Marcia, J. E., & Friedman, M. L. (1970). Ego identity status in college women. *Journal of Personality, 38*, 249–263.

Maret, E., & Finlay, B. (1984). The distribution of household labor among women in dual-earner marriages. *Journal of Marriage and the Family, 46*, 357–364.

Marjoribanks, K., & Walberg, H. J. (1975). Ordinal position, family environment and mental abilities. *Journal of Social Psychology, 95*, 77–84.

Markman, E. M. (1973). Facilitation of part-whole comparisons by use of the collective noun "family." *Child Development, 44*, 837–840.

Markman, E. M. (1977). Realizing that you don't understand: A preliminary investigation. *Child Development, 46*, 986–992.

Markus, H. J., & Nurius, P. S. (1984). Self-understanding and self-regulation in middle childhood. In W. A. Collins (Ed)., *Development during middle childhood,* pp. 147–184. Washington, DC: National Academy Press.

Marshall, S. P., & Smith, J. D. (1987). Sex differences in learning mathematics: A longitudinal study with item and error analysis. *Journal of Educational Psychology, 79*, 372–381.

Marston, A. R., Jacobs, D. F., Singer, R. D., Widaman, K. F., & Little, T. D. (1988). Adolescents who apparently are invulnerable to drug, alcohol, and nicotine use.

Adolescence, 91, 593–597.

Martin, A., & Baenen, N. R. (1987). School-age mothers' attitudes toward parenthood and father involvement. *Family Therapy, 14,* 147–159.

Martin, B. (1975). Parent-child relationships. In F. D. Horowitz (Ed.), *Review of Child Development Research* (vol. 4, pp. 463–540). Chicago: University of Chicago Press.

Martin, C. L., & Halverson, C. F. (1981). A schematic processing model of sex-typing and stereotyping in children. *Child Development, 52,* 1119–1132.

Martin, G. B., & Clark, R. D. (1982). Distress crying in neonates: Species and peer specificity. *Developmental Psychology, 18,* 3–9.

Martin, H. (1978). A child-oriented approach to prevention of abuse. In A. W. Franklin (Ed.), *Child abuse: Prediction, prevention and follow-up* (pp. 9–20). London: Churchill-Livingston.

Martin, J. C. (1976, Winter). Drugs of abuse during pregnancy: Effects upon off-spring structure and function. *Journal of Women in Culture and Society (Signs) 2,* 357–368.

Mascola, L., Pelosi, R., Blount, J. H., Binkin, N. J., Harris, C. M., Jarman, B., Landon, G. P., & McNeil, B. J. (1984, October 5). Congenital syphilis. *Journal of the American Medical Association, 252,* (1981) 1719–1723.

Masters, J. C. (1981) Developmental Psychology. In M. R. Rosenzweig & L. W. Porter (Eds.), *Annual Review of Psychology, 32,* 117–153.

Matas, L., Arend, R., & Sroufe, L. A. (1978). Continuity of adaptation in the second year: The relationship between quality of attachment and later competence. *Child Development, 49,* 547–556.

Matheny, A. P., Riese, M. L. & Wilson, R. S. (1985). Rudiments of infant temperament: Newborn to 9 months. *Developmental Psychology, 21,* 486–495.

Maurer, D., & Salapatek, P. (1976). Developmental changes in the scanning of faces by young infants. *Child Development, 47,* 523–527.

Maxson, L. R., & Daugherty, C. H. (1985). *Genetics: A human perspective.* Dubuque, IA: Wm. C. Brown.

Mayer, J. E., & Ligman, J. D. (1989). Personality characteristics of adolescent marijuana users. *Adolescence, 24,* 965–975.

Mayer, R. E. (1977). Thinking and Problem Solving: An Introduction to Human Cognition and Learning. Glenview, Ill.: Scott, Foresman.

McBride, S. and Belsky, J. (1988) Characteristics, Determinants, and Consequences of Maternal Separation Anxiety. *Developmental Psychology, 24,* 407–414.

McBroom, P. (1980). Behavioral genetics. *National Institute of Mental Health Science Monograph.* Washington, DC: Department of Health Education and Welfare.

McCall, R. B. (1979). The Development of intellectual functioning in infancy and the prediction of later I.Q. In J. Osofsky (Ed). *Handbook of Infant Development* (pp. 707–742). New York: Wiley.

McCall, R. B. (1981). Nature-nurture and the two realms of development: A proposed integration with respect to mental development. *Child Development, 52,* 1–12.

McCall, R. B. (1987a). Developmental function, individual differences, and the plasticity of intelligence. In J. J. Gallagher & C. T. Ramey (Eds.), *The malleability of children* (pp. 15–25). Baltimore, MD: Paul Brookes.

McCall, R. B. (1987b). The media, society, and child development research. In J. D. Osofsky (Ed.), *Handbook of infant development* (2nd ed.) (pp. 1199–1256). New York: Wiley.

McCartney, K. (1984). Effect of quality of day care environment on children's language development. *Developmental Psychology, 20,* 244–261.

McCauley, E., Kay, T., Ito, J., & Treder, R. (1987). The Turner syndrome: Cognitive deficits, affective discrimination, and behavior problems. *Child Development, 58,* 464–474.

McClinton, B. S., & Meier, B. G. (1978). *Beginnings: The Psychology of early childhood.* St. Louis: C. V. Mosby.

McClure, G. T. & Piel, E. (1978). College bound girls and science careers. Perception of barriers and facilitating factors. *Journal of Vocational Behvior, 12,* 172–183.

McCusick, V. A. (1989, April 6). Mapping and sequencing the human genome. *New England Journal of Medicine,* pp. 910–915.

McDermitt, D. (1984). The relationship of parental drug use and parents' attitude concerning adolescent drug use to adolescent drug use. *Adolescence, 73,* 89–97.

McGlothlin, W. H., Sparkes, R. S., & Arnold, D. O. (1970). Effects of LSD on human pregnancy. *Journal of the American Medical Association, 212,* 1483–1487.

McGraw, M. B. (1940). Neural maturation as exemplified in achievement of bladder control. *Journal of Pediatrics, 16,* 580–589.

McGuinnes, D. (1979). How schools discriminate against boys. In S. Hochman & P. Kaplan (Eds.), *Readings in psychology: A Soft approach* (rev. ed.) (pp. 74–79). Lexington, MA: Ginn.

McGuinness, D. (1976). Sex differences in the organization of perception and cognition. In B. Lloyd & J. Archer (Eds.), *Exploring sex differences,* (pp. 123–157). London: Academic Press.

McGuire, W. J., McGuire, C. V., Child, P., & Fujioka, T. (1978). Effect of ethnicity in the spontaneous self-concept as a function of one's ethnic distinctiveness in the social environment. *Journal of Personality and Social Psychology, 36,* 511–520.

McHale, S. M., & Huston, T. L. (1984). Men and women as parents: Sex role orientations, employment, and parental roles with infants. *Child Development, 55,* 1349–1361.

McIlroy, J. H. (1979). Career as life-style: An existential view. *American Personnel and Guidance Journal, 57,* 351–356.

McKay, H., Sinisterra, L., McKay, H. G., Gomez, H., & Lloreda, P. (1978). Improving cognitive ability in chronically deprived children. *Science, 200,* 270–278.

McKinney, J. P., & Moore, (1982). Attitudes and values during adolescence. In B. B. Wolman (Ed.), *Handbook of human development* (pp. 549–559). Englewood Cliffs, NJ: Prentice-Hall.

McLaughlin, B. (1977). Second-language learning in children. *Psychological bulletin, 84,* 438–459.

McLaughlin, B. (1978). *Second language acquisition in childhood.* Hillsdale, NJ: Erlbaum.

McLaughlin, B. (1983). Child compliance to parental control techniques. *Developmental Psychology, 19,* 667–674.

McNeill, D. (1970). The development of language. In P. H. Mussen (Ed.), *Carmichael's manual of child psychology* (3rd ed.). New York: Wiley.

Mead, M. (1974). On Freud's view of female psychology. In J. Strouse (Ed.), *Women and analysis.* New York:

Grossman.

Mehler, J., Bertoncini, J., Barriere, M. & Jassik-Gerschenfeld, D. (1978). Infant recognition of mother's voice. *Perception, 7*, 491–497.

Meilman, P. W. (1979). Cross-sectional age changes in ego identity status during adolescence. *Developmental Psychology, 15*, 230–231.

Meltzoff, A. N. (1977). Imitation of facial and manual gestures by human neonates. *Science, 198*, 75–78.

Meltzoff, A. N., & Moore, M. K. (1983). Newborn infants imitate adult facial gestures. *Child Development, 54*, 702–709.

Meltzoff, A. N., & Moore, M. K. (1989). Imitation in newborn infants: Exploring the range of gestures imitated and the underlying mechanisms. *Developmental Psychology, 25*, 954–963.

Melzack, R. (1984). The myth of painless childbirth. *Pain, 19*, 321.

Mendelson, B. K., & White, D. R. (1985). Development of self-body in overweight youngsters. *Developmental Psychology, 21*, 90–97.

Menyuk, P. (1977). *Language and maturation.* Cambridge, MA: M.I.T. Press.

Mercer, C. D., Hughes, C., & Mercer, A. R. (1985). Learning disabilities definitions used by state education departments. *Learning Disability Quarterly, 8*, 45–55.

Merelman, R. M. (1971). The development of policy thinking in adolescence. *American Political Science Review, 65*, 1033–1047.

Metcalf, R. D. (1979). Organizers of the psyche and EEG development: Birth through adolescence. In R. L. Noshpitz (Ed.), *Basic handbook of child psychiatry* (Vol. 1, pp. 63–72). New York: Basic Books.

Metcoff, J., Coistiloe, P., Crosby, W. M., Sandstread, H. H., & Milne, D. (1989). Smoking in pregnancy: Relation of birth weight to maternal plasma carotene and cholesterol levels. *Obstetrics and Gynecology, 64*, 302–308.

Meyer, J., & Sobieszek, (1972). Effect of a child's sex on adult interpretations of its behavior. *Developmental Psychology, 6*, 42–48.

Meyer, K. A. (1987). The work commitment of adolescents: Progressive attachment to the work force. *Career Development Quarterly, 36*, 140–147.

Midgley, C., Feldlaufer, H., & Eccles, J. S. (1989). Student/teacher relations and attitudes toward mathematics before and after the transition to junior high school. *Child Development, 60*, 981–992.

Milewski, A. E. (1976). Infants' discrimination of internal and external pattern elements. *Journal of Experimental Child Psychology, 22*, 229–246.

Milgram, S. (1963). Behavioral study of obedience. *Journal of Abnormal and Social Psychology, 67*, 371–378.

Milgram, S. (1973). Some conditions of obedience to authority. In R. Flacks (Ed.), *Conformity resistance and self-determination: The individual and authority* (pp. 225–239). Boston: Little, Brown.

Miller, D. C. (1964). Industry and the worker. In H. Borow (Ed.), *Man in a world at work.* Boston: Houghton Mifflin.

Miller, D. J., Ryan, E. B., Short, E. J., Rikes, P. G., McGuire, M. D., & Culler, M. P. (1977). Relationships between early habituation and later cognitive performance in infancy. *Child Development, 48*, 658–661.

Miller, M. J. (1980). Cantaloupes, carrots and counseling: Implications of dietary interventions for counselors. *Personnel and Guidance Journal, 58*, 421–425.

Miller, P. H. (1989). *Theories of developmental psychology,* New York: Freeman.

Miller, P. H., & Harris, Y. R. (1988). Preschoolers' strategies of attention on a same-different task. *Developmental Psychology, 24*, 628–634.

Miller, P. M., Danaher, D. L., & Forbes, D. (1986). Sex-related strategies for coping with interpersonal conflict in children aged five and seven. *Developmental Psychology, 22*, 543–548.

Miller, R. W. (1974). Susceptibility of the fetus and child to chemical pollutants. *Science, 184*, 812–813.

Miller, S. A. (1988). Parents' beliefs about children's cognitive development. *Child Development, 59*, 259–286.

Mills, J. L., Braubard, B. I., Harley, E. E., Rhoads, G. G., & Berendes, H. W. (1984, October 12). Maternal alcohol consumption and birth weight: How much drinking during pregnancy is safe? *Journal of the American Medical Association, 252*, 1875–1879.

Mills, R. S. L., & Rubin, K. H. (1990). Parental beliefs about problematic social behaviors in early childhood. *Child Development, 61*, 138–152.

Millstein, S. G. (1989). Adolescent health: Challenges for behavioral scientists. *American Psychologist, 44*, 837–843.

Minard, J., Coleman, D., Williams, G., & Ingledyne, E. (1968). Cumulative REM of three to five day olds: Effect of normal external noise and maturation. *Psychophysiology, 5*, 232.

Minix, N. A. (1987). Drug and alcohol prevention education: A developmental social skills approach. *The Clearing House, 61*, 162–165.

Minton, H. L., & Schneider, F. W. (1980). *Differential psychology.* Monterey, CA: Brooks/Cole.

Minuchin, P. (1985). Families and individual development: Provocations from the field of family therapy. *Child Development, 56*, 289–302.

Minuchin, P. P., & Shapiro, E. K. (1983). The school as a context for social development. In E. M. Hetherington (Ed.), *Handbook of child psychology: Socialization, personality and social development* (Vol. 4, pp. 197–275). New York: Wiley.

Mirsky, A. F., & Duncan, C. C. (1986). Etiology and expression of schizophrenia: Neurobiological and psychosocial factors. *Annual Review of Psychology, 37*, 291–321.

Mischel, W. (1970). Sex-typing and socialization. In P. H. Mussen (Ed.). *Carmichael's Manual of Child Psychology,* (Third Edition). New York: Wiley.

Mischel, W. (1976). *Introduction to personality* (2nd ed.). New York: Holt, Rinehart and Winston.

Moely, O. H., Olson, F. A., Halwes, T. G., & Flavell, J. H. (1969). Production deficiency in young children's clustered recall. *Developmental Psychology, 1*, 26–34.

Moffitt, T. E. (1990). Juvenile delinquency and attention deficit disorder: Boys' developmental trajectories from age 13 to age 15. *Child Development, 61*, 893–910.

Mohar, C. J. (1988). Applying the concept of temperament to child care. *Child and Youth Care Quarterly, 17*, 221–238.

Molfese, D. L., Molfese, V. J., & P. L. Carroll. (1982). Early language development. In B. B. Wolman (Ed.), *Handbook of developmental psychology* (pp. 301–323). Englewood Cliffs, NJ: Prentice-Hall.

Monaco, N. M., & Gaier, E. L. (1987). Developmental level and children's responses to the explosion of the space shuttle Challenger. *Early Childhood Research Quarterly, 2*, 83–95.

Money, J., & Ehrhardt, A. (1972). *Man and woman, boy and girl*. Baltimore: Johns Hopkins University Press.

Monif, G. R. (1969). *Viral Infections of the Human Fetus*. London: Macmillan.

Montemayor, R. (1983). Parents and adolescents in conflict: All families some of the time and some families most of the time. *Journal of Early Adolescence, 3*, 88–103.

Moore, K. A., & Waite, L. F. (1977). Early childbearing and educational attainment. *Family Planning Perspectives, 9*, 220–225.

Moore, R. S., & Moore, D. R. (1973, October). How early should they go to school? *Childhood Education*.

Moore, R. S., & Moore, D. R. (1976, June). How early should they go to school? *Childhood Education*, pp. 13–18.

Morgan, B. L. (1984). Nutritional needs of the female adolescent. *Women's Health, 9*, 15.

Morrell, P., & Norton, W. T. (1980). Myelin. *Scientific American, 242*, 88–119.

Morrison, D. M. (1985). Adolescent contraceptive behavior: A review. *Psychological Bulletin, 98*, 538–568.

Morrison, G. S. (1988). *Early childhood education today* (4th ed.). Columbus, OH: Merrill.

Moss, H. (1967). Sex, age and state as determinants of mother-infant interaction. *Merrill-Palmer Quarterly, 13*, 19–37.

Moss, H. (1974). Early sex differences and mother-infant interaction. In R. C. Friedman, R. M. Richart, & R. L. Van de Weile (Eds.), *Sex differences in behavior*, New York: Wiley.

Moya, F. & Thorndike, V. (1962). Passage of drugs across the placenta. *American Journal of Obstetrics and Gynecology, 84*, 1778–1798.

Moynahan, E. D. (1973). The development of knowledge concerning the effect of categorization upon free recall. *Child, Development, 44*, 238–246.

Muir, D. & Field, J. (1979). Newborn infants orient to sounds. *Child Development, 50*, 431–436.

Mullahy, P. (1948). *Oedipus: Myth and complex*. New York: Hermitage Press.

Munley, P. H. (1977). Erikson's theory of psychosocial development and career development. *Journal of Vocational Behavior, 10*, 261–269.

Munroe, R. H. , Shimmin, H. S., & Munroe, R. L. (1984). Gender understanding and sex-role preference in four cultures. *Developmental Psychology, 20*, 673–683.

Murray, A. D. (1979). Infant crying as an elicitor of parental behavior: An examination of two models. *Psychological Bulletin, 86*, 191–215.

Murray, A. D. (1988). Newborn auditory brainstem evoked responses (ABR's): Prenatal and contemporary correlates. *Child Development, 59*, 571–588.

Murray, S. F., Dolby, R. M., Nation, R. L., & Thomas, D. B. (1981). Effects of epidural anesthesia on newborns and their mothers. *Child Development, 52*, 71–82.

Murstein, B. I., Chalpin, M. J., Heard, K. V., & Vyse, S. A. (1989). Sexual behavior, drugs, and relationship patterns on a college campus over thirteen years. *Adolescence, 24*, 125–139.

Mussen, P. H., & Eisenberg-Berg, N. (1977). *Roots of caring, sharing and helping*. San Francisco: Freeman.

Mussen, P. H., & Jones, M. C. (1957). Some conceptions, motivations and interpersonal attitudes of late- and early-maturing boys. *Child Development, 28*, 242–256.

Muuss, R. E. (1982). *Theories of adolescence* (4th edition). New York: Random House.

Muuss, R. E. (1985). Adolescent eating disorder: Anorexia nervosa, *Adolescence, 20*, 525–536.

Muuss, R. E. (1986). Adolescent eating disorder: Bulimia. *Adolescence, 21*, 257–267.

Muuss, R. E. (1988). Carol Gilligan's theory of sex differences in the development of moral reasoning during adolescence. *Adolescence, 23*, 235–243.

Myers, B. J. (1982). Early intervention using Brazelton training with middle-class mothers and fathers of newborns. *Child Development, 53*. 462–472.

Nall, S. W. (1982). Bridging the gap: Preschool to kindergarten. *Childhood Education, 59*, 107–110.

Nassi, A. J. (1981). Survivors of the sixties: Comparative psychosocial and political development of former Berkeley student activists. *American Psychologist, 36*, 753–762.

Nathan, P. E. (1983). Failures in prevention: Why we can't prevent the devastating effects of alcoholism and drug abuse. *American Psychologist, 38*, 459–468.

National Association of State Boards of Education (1989). *Code blue: Uniting for healthier youth*. Alexandria, VA: National Association of State Boards of Education.

National Association of State Boards of Education (1990). *Code blue: uniting for healthier youth*. Alexandria, Va.: National Association of State Boards of Education.

National Center for Clinical Infant Programs (1986). *Infants Can't Wait: The Numbers*. Washington, DC.: National Center for Clinical Infant Programs.

National Center for Education and the Economy (1990). *America's choice: High skills or low wages?* Rochester, NY: National Center for Education and the Economy.

National Commission on Excellence in Education (1981). *A nation at risk*. Washington, DC: U.S. Department of Education.

National Commission for the Protection of Human Subjects of Biomedical and Behavioral Research (Eds.) (1977). *Report and recommendations: Research involving children*. Washington, DC: U.S. Government Printing Office.

National Institute on Drug Abuse. *Drugs and American High School Students 1975–1983*. Washington, DC: National Institute on Drug Abuse.

Natriello, G., McDill, E. L., & Pallas, A. M. (1989). In our lifetime: Schooling and the disadvantaged. Unpublished manuscript cited in A. W. Jackson & D. W. Hornbeck. Educating young adolescents. *American Psychologist, 44*, 831–836.

Navarick, D. J. (1979). *Principles of Learning: From Laboratory To Field*. Reading, MA: Addison-Wesley.

Neerhof, M. G., MacGregor, S. N., Retzky, S. S., & Sullivan, T. P. (1989). Cocaine abuse during pregnancy: Peripartum prevalence and perinatal outcome. *American Journal of Obstetrics and Gynecology, 161*, 633–638.

Neimark, E. D. (1982). Adolescent thought: Transition to formal operations. In B. B. Wolman (Ed.), *Handbook of human development* (pp. 486–503). Englewood Cliffs, NJ: Prentice-Hall.

Nelson, C. A. (1987). The recognition of facial expressions in the first two years of life: Mechanisms of development, *Child Development, 58*, 889–910.

Nelson, C. A., & Horowitz, F. D. (1983). The perception of facial expressions and stimulus motion by two- and five-month-old infants using holographic stimuli. *Child Development, 54,* 868–878.

Nelson, F. L. (1987). Evaluation of a youth suicide school program. *Adolescence, 22,* 813–825.

Nelson, K. (1973). Structure and strategy in learning to talk. Monograph of the Society for Research in Child Development, *38* (1-2, serial no. 149).

Nelson, K. (1974). Concept, word, and sentence. *Psychological Review, 81,* 267–285.

Nelson, K. (1978). How children represent knowledge of their world in and out of language: a preliminary report. In R. S. Siegler (ed.) *Children's Thinking: What Develops.* Hillsdale, N.J.: Erlbaum.

Nelson, K. (1981). Individual differences in language development: Implications for development and language. *Developmental Psychology, 17,* 170–188.

Nelson, K. & Gruendel, J. (1981). Generalized event representations: basic building blocks of cognitive development. in M. E. Lamb & A. L. Brown (Eds.) *Advances in Developmental Psychology,* Vol. 1. Hillsdale, N.J.: Erlbaum.

Nelson, N. M., Murray, W. E., Saroj, S., Bennett, K. J., Milner, R., & Sackett, D. L., (1980, March 10). A randomized clinical trial of the Leboyer approach to childbirth. *New England Journal of Medicine, 302,* 655–660.

Neuman, S. B. (1982). Television viewing and leisure reading: A qualitative analysis. *Journal of Educational Research, 75,* 299–304.

New England Regional Genetics Group Prenatal Collaborative Study of Down Syndrome Screening (1989, March). Combining maternal serum alpha-fetoprotein measurements and age to screen for Down Syndrome in pregnant women under age 35. *American Journal of Obstetrics and Gynecology, 160,* 575–577.

New York State Department of Health. (1979). *DES: The wonder drug women should wonder about.* New York: New York State Department of Health.

New York State Division of Alcohol and Alcohol Abuse (1986). *Alcohol Abuse,* New York State Division of Alcohol and Alcohol Abuse.

New York State Division of Substance Abuse Services (1986). *Crack Down on Crack: What You Should Know.* New York State Division of Substance Abuse Services.

New York Times (1990, May 3). Students' learning and graduation rates slip. New York Times, p. B12.

New York Times (1989, December 12). Reports of congenital syphilis rise. *New York Times,* p. C12.

New York Times (1990, April 25). High-tech toddler. *New York Times,* p. 28.

Newell, G. K., Hammig, C. L., Jurich, A. P., & Johnson, D. E. (1990). Self-concept as a factor in the quality of diets of adolescent girls. *Adolescence, 25,* 117–127.

Newman, B. M. (1989). The changing nature of the parent-adolescent relationship from early to late adolescence. *Adolescence, 96,* 915–923.

Newman, P. R. (1982). The peer group. In B. B. Wolman (Ed.), *Handbook of developmental psychology* (pp. 526–536). Englewood Cliffs, NJ: Prentice-Hall.

Newman, P. R., & Newman, B. M. (1988). Differences between childhood and adulthood: The identity watershed. *Adolescence, 92,* 551–557.

Newport, E. L., Gleitman, H., & Gleitman, L. R. (1977). Mother, I'd rather do it myself: Some effects and non-effects of maternal speech style. In C. E. Snow & C. A. Ferguson (Eds.), *Talking to children: Language input and acquisition.* Cambridge: Cambridge University Press.

Newsday (1986, June 17). Polls apart on doing chores. *Newsday* p. 4.

Newsday (1989, January 27). U.S. math education just doesn't add up. . . . and, in other bad news. *Newsday,* pp. 5, 15.

Nichols, R. C. (1978). Twin studies of ability, personality, and interests, *Homo, 29,* 158–173.

Nicholls, J. G. (1979). Quality and equality in intellectual development: The role of motivation in education. *American Psychology, 34,* 1071–1084.

Ninio, A., & Rinott, N. (1988). Fathers' involvement in the care of their infants and their attributions of cognitive competence to infants. *Child Development, 59,* 652–664.

Nisan, M., & Kohlberg, L. (1982). Universality and variation in moral judgment: A longitudinal and cross-sectional study in Turkey. *Child Development, 53,* 865–876.

Noam, G. G., Higgins, R. O., & Goethals, G. W. (1982). Psychoanalytic approaches to developmental psychology. In B. B. Wolman (Ed.), *Handbook of developmental psychology.* Englewood

Cliffs, NJ: Prentice-Hall.

Nogata, D. K. (1989). Japanese American children and adolescence. In J. T. Gibbs & L. N. Huang (Eds.), *Children of color* (pp. 67–114). San Francisco: Jossey-Bass.

Norem-Hebeisen, A. & Hedin, D. (1984). Influences on adolescent problem behavior: causes, connections, and contexts. In *Adolescent Peer Pressure* (pp. 21–47). Washington, DC: U.S. Department of Health and Human Services.

Northwoods Montessori School (1990). Northwoods Montessori Center. School publication.

Nottelman, E. D. (1987). Competence and self-esteem during transition from childhood to adolescence. *Developmental Psychology, 23,* 441–451.

Nucci, L. P., & Turiel, E. (1978). Social interactions and the development of social concepts in preschool children. *Child Development, 49,* 400–407.

Nunnally, J. C. (1982). The study of change: measurement, research strategies and methods of analysis. In B. B. Wolman (Ed.), *Handbook of Developmental Psychology* (pp. 133–149). Englewood Cliffs, N.J.: Prentice-Hall.

Nunner-Winkler, G., & Sodian, B. (1988). Children's understanding of moral emotions. *Child Development, 59,* 1323–1339.

Nye, R. D. (1975). *Three views of man.* Monterrey, California: Brooks/Cole.

Nyhan, W. L. (1986). Neonatal screening for inherited disease. *New England Journal of Medicine, 313,* 43–44.

Nyiti, R. M. (1982). The validity of "Cultural Differences Explanations" for cross-cultural variation in the rate of Piagetian cognitive development. In D. A. Wagner and H. W. Stevenson (Eds.). *Cultural Perspectives on Child Development* (pp. 144–166). San Francisco: Freeman.

O'Brien, S. F., & Bierman, K. L. (1988). Conceptions and perceived influence of peer groups: Interviews with preadolescent and adolescents. *Child Development, 59,* 1360–1365.

O'Bryan, K. G. (1980). The teaching face: A historical perspective. In E. L. Palmer & A. Dorr (Eds.), *Children and the faces of television: Teaching, violence, selling* (pp. 5–16). New York: Academic Press.

Obstetrical and Gynecological Survey (1988). Comments on rubella susceptibility and the continuing risk of infection in pregnancy. *Obstetrical and Gynecological Survey, 43,* 38–19.

O'Donnell, J. A., & Andersen, D. G. (1978). Factors influencing choice of major and career of capable women. *Vocational Guidance Journal, 26,* 214–222.

Olim, E. G., Hess, R. D., & Shipman, V. C. (1967). Role of mothers' language styles in mediating their preschool children's development. *School Review, 78,* 414–424.

Olsen, D., & Zigler, E. (1989). An assessment of the all-day kindergarten movement. *Early Childhood Research Quarterly, 4,* 167–187.

Olson, G. M., & Sherman, T. (1983). Attention, learning, and memory in infants. In P. H. Mussen (Ed.), *Handbook of Child Psychology* (Vol. 2, pp. 1001–1081). New York: Wiley.

Olweus, D. (1977). Aggression and peer acceptance in adolescent boys: Two short-term longitudinal studies of ratings. *Child Development, 48,* 1301–1313.

Olweus, D. (1979). Stability and aggressive reaction patterns in males: A review. *Psychological Bulletin, 86,* 852–875.

Olweus, D. (1982). Development of stable aggressive reaction patterns in males. In R. Blanchard & C. Blanchard (Eds.), *Advances in the Study of Aggression* (Vol. 1). New York: Academic Press.

Oppel, W. C., Harper, P. A., & Rider. R. V. (1968). The age of attaining bladder control. *Pediatrics, 42,* 614–626.

Oppenheim, J., Boegehold, B., & Brenner, B. (1984). *Raising a confident child.* New York: Viking.

Orenberg, C. L. (1981). *DES: The complete story.* New York: St. Martin's Press.

Orlofsky, J. L., Marcia, J. E., & Lesser, I. M. (1973). Ego identity status and the intimacy versus isolation crisis of young adulthood. *Journal of Personality and Social Psychology, 27,* 211–219.

Ortho Diagnostic Systems (1981). *What Every Rh Negative Woman Should Know About Rho GAM.* Raritan, N.J.: Ortho Diagnostic Systems.

Oshman, H., & Manosevitz, M. (1974). The impact of the identity crisis on the adjustment of late adolescent males. *Journal of Youth and Adolescence, 3,* 207–216.

Oshman, H. P. & Manosevitz, M. (1976). Father absence: Effects of stepfathers upon psychosocial development in males. *Developmental Psychology, 12,* 479–480.

Osofsky, J. D., & Connors, K. (1979). Mother-infant interaction: An integrative view of a complex system. In J. Osofsky (Ed.), *Handbook of Infant Development* (pp. 519–549). New York: Wiley.

Ounsted, M., Moar, V. A. & Scott, A. A. (1985). Risk factors associated with small-for-dates infants. *British Journal of Obstetrics and Gynecology, 92,* 226.

Owens, R. E. (1988). *Language development.* Columbus, OH: Merrill.

Owens, R. E. (1990). Development of communication, language, and speech. In G. H. Shames & E. W. Wiig (Eds.). *Human communication disorders* (pp. 30–74). Columbus, OH: Merrill.

Oyemade, U. J. (1985). The rationale for Head Start as a vehicle for the upward mobility of minority families: A minority perspective. *American Journal of Orthopsychiatry, 55,* 591–602.

Palkovitz, R. (1985). Father's birth attendance, early contact, and extended contact with their newborns: A critical review. *Child Development, 56,* 392–407.

Palmer, E. L. (1976). Application of psychology to television programming: Program execution. *American Psychologist, 31,* 137–139.

Parcel, G. S., Simons-Morton, B. G., O'Hara, N. M., Baranowski, T., Kolbe, L. J., & Bee, D. E. (1987). School promotion of healthful diet and exercise behavior: An integration of organizational change and social learning theory interventions. *Journal of School Health, 57,* 150–156.

Paris, S. G., & Lindauer, B. K. (1982). The development of cognitive skills during childhood. In B. B. Wolman (Ed.), *Handbook of developmental psychology* (pp. 333–350). Englewood Cliffs, NJ: Prentice-Hall.

Park, K. A., & Waters, E. (1989). Security of attachment and preschool friendships. *Child Development, 60,* 1076–1082.

Parke, R. D. (1979). Perspectives on father-infant interaction. In J. D. Osofsky (Ed.), *Handbook of Infant Development* (pp. 549–591). New York: Wiley.

Parke, R. D. (1981). *Fathers.* Cambridge, MA: Harvard University Press.

Parke, R. D., & Collmer, C. W. (1975). Child abuse: An interdisciplinary analysis. In E. M. Hetherington (Ed.), *Review of child development research* (Vol. 5). Chicago: University of Chicago Press.

Parke, R. D., & Neville, B. (1987). *Teenage fatherhood in risking the future* (Vol. 2, 145–174). Washington, DC: National Academy Press.

Parke, R. D., & Sawin, D. B. (1976). The father's role in infancy: A reevaluation. *The Family Coordinator, 25,* 365–371.

Parke, R. D., & Slaby, R. G. (1983). The development of aggression. In E. M. Hetherington (Ed.), *Handbook of child psychology: Socialization, personality and social development* (4th ed.) (Vol. 4, pp. 547–643). New York: Wiley.

Parke, R. D., & Tinsley, B. J. (1987). Family interaction in infancy. In J. D. Osofsky (Ed.), *Handbook of infant development* (pp. 579–642). New York: Wiley.

Parker, J. G., & Asher, S. R. (1987). Peer relations and later adjustment: Are low-accepted children "at risk"? *Psychological Bulletin, 102,* 357–389.

Parker, J. G., & Gottman, J. M. (1989). Social and emotional development in a relational context. In T. J. Berndt & G. W. Ladd (Eds.), *Peer relationships in child development* (pp. 95–133). New York: Wiley.

Parmelee, A. H., & Sigman, M. D. (1983). Perinatal brain development and behavior. In P. H. Mussen (Ed.), *Handbook of child development* (3rd ed.) (Vol. 2, pp. 95–157). New York: Wiley.

Parmelee, A. H., Wenne, W. H., & Schulz, H. R. (1964). Infant sleep patterns from birth to sixteen weeks of age. *Journal of Pediatrics, 65,* 576–582.

Parten, M. (1932). Social participation among preschool children. *Journal of Abnormal and Social Psychology, 27,* 243–269.

Parton, D. A. (1976). Learning to imitate in infancy. *Developmental Psychology, 47,* 14–31.

Patrusky, B. (1980, July). Diagnosing newborns. *Science,* pp. 26–39.

Patterson, G. R., & Cobb, J. A. (1971). A dyadic analysis of "aggressive" behaviors. In J. P. Hill (Ed.), *Minnesota symposium on child psychology* (Vol. 5). Minneapolis: University of Minnesota Press.

Paul, R. H. (1971). *Fetal Intensive Care: Intrapartum Monitoring Case Examples.* Los Angeles: University of Southern California USC Medical Center.

Paulsen, K. & Johnson, M. (1983). Sex role attitudes and mathematical ability in 4th-, 8th-, and 11th-grade students from a high socioeconomic area. *Developmental Psychology, 19*, 210–214.

Pedersen, F. A., & Robson, K. S. (1969). Father participation in infancy. *American Journal of Orthopsychiatry, 39*, 466–472.

Peel, E. A. (1969). Intellectual growth during adolescence. In R. E. Grinder (Ed.). *Studies in Adolescence*, 2nd edition (pp. 486–497). New York: Macmillan.

Pellegrini, A. D. (1987). Rough-and-tumble play: Developmental and educational significance. *Educational Psychologist, 22*, 23–43.

Pellegrini, A. D. (1988). Elementary-school children's rough-and-tumble play and social competence. *Developmental Psychology, 24*, 802–807.

Pellegrini, A. D., & Perlmutter, J. C. (1989). Classroom contextual effects on children's play. *Developmental Psychology, 25*, 289–297.

Penner. S. G. (1987). Parental responses to grammatical and ungrammatical child utterances. *Child Development, 58*, 376–384.

Pepler, D., Corter, C., & Abramovitch, R. (1982). Social relations among children: Comparison of siblings and peer interaction. In K. Rubin & H. S. Ross (Eds.), *Peer relationships and social skills in childhood* (pp. 209–227). New York: Springer-Verlag.

Perkins, H. V. (1975). *Human development*. Belmont, CA: Wadsworth.

Perlez, J. (1986, December 1). Children with children: Coping with a crisis. *New York Times*, p. 1.

Perlmutter, M., & Myers, N. A. (1979). Recognition memory development in two- to four-year-olds. *Developmental Psychology, 15*, 73–83.

Perry, D. G., Perry, L. C., & Rasmussen, P. (1986). Cognitive social learning mediators of aggression. *Child Development, 57*, 700–711.

Peskin, H. (1973). Influences of the development schedule on learning and ego functioning. *Journal of Youth and Adolescence, 2*, 273–290.

Pestrak, V. A., & Martin, D. (1985). Cognitive development and aspects of adolescent sexuality. *Adolescence, 20*, 981–987.

Peters, A. M. (1986). Early syntax. In P. Fletcher & M. Garman (Eds.), *Language acquisition* (2nd ed.) (pp. 307–326). London: Cambridge University Press.

Peters, D. L. (1977). Early childhood education: An overview and evaluation. In H. L. Hom & P. A. Robinson (Eds.), *Psychological processes in early education* (pp. 1–23). New York: Academic Press.

Petersen, G. A. (1982). Cognitive development in infancy. In B. B. Wolman (Ed.), *Handbook of Developmental Psychology* (pp. 323–333). Englewood Cliffs, NJ: Prentice-Hall.

Peterson, A. C., & Offer, D. (1979). Adolescent development: Sixteen to nineteen years. In J. D. Noshpitz (Ed.), *Basic handbook of child psychiatry* (Vol. 1, pp. 213–233). New York: Basic Books.

Peterson, G. H., Mehl, L. E., & Leiderman, P. T. (1979). The role of some birth-related variables in father attachment. *American Journal of Orthopsychiatry, 49*, 330–339.

Peterson, L. (1983). Influence of age, task competence, and responsibility focus on children's altruism. *Developmental Psychology, 19*, 141–148.

Peterson, P. E., Jeffrey, D. B., Bridgwater, C. A., & Dawson, B. (1984). How pronutrition television programming affects children's dietary habits. *Developmental Psychology, 20*, 55–64.

Peterson, R., & Felton-Collins, V. (1986). *The Piaget handbook for teachers and parents*. New York: Teacher's College Press.

Petitpas, A. (1978). Identity foreclosure: A unique challenge. *American Personnel and Guidance Journal, 56*, 558–562.

Pettit, G. S., & Bates, J. E. (1989). Family interaction patterns and children's behavior problems from infancy to 4 years. *Developmental Psychology, 25*, 413–421.

Pfannenstiel, J. C., & Seltzer, D. A. (1989). New parents as teachers: Evaluation of early parent education programs. *Early Childhood Research Quarterly, 4*, 1–18.

Phillips, D., McCartney, K., & Scarr, S. (1987). Child-care quality and children's social development. *Developmental Psychology, 23*, 537–543.

Phillips, J. L. (1975). *The origins of intellect: Piaget's theory* (2nd ed.). San Francisco: Freeman.

Phinney, J. S. (1989). Stages of ethnic identity development in minority group youth. *Journal of Early Adolescence, 9*, 34–49.

Phinney, J., & Tarver, S. (1988). Ethnic identity search and commitment in black and white eighth graders. *Journal of Early Adolescence, 8*, 265–277.

Piaget, J. (1928). *Judgment and reasoning in the young child*. New York: Harcourt, Brace and World.

Piaget, J. (1932). *The moral judgment of the child*. London: Routledge and Kegan Paul.

Piaget, J. (1952). *The child's conception of number*. New York: Humanities Press.

Piaget, J. (1954). *The construction of reality in the child*. New York: Basic Books.

Piaget, J. (1960). *The child's conception of physical causality*. Totawa, NJ: Littlefield (originally published 1927).

Piaget, J. (1962). *Play, dreams, and imitations*. New York: Norton.

Piaget, J. (1965). *The child's conception of the world*. Totowa, NJ: Littlefield.

Piaget, J. (1967) *Six psychological studies*. New York: Vintage.

Piaget, J. (1968). *On the development of memory and identity*. Worcester, MA: Clark University Press.

Piaget, J. (1970). *Genetic epistemology*. New York: Columbia University Press.

Piaget, J. (1972). Intellectual evolution from adolescence to adulthood. *Human Development, 15*, 1–12.

Piaget, J. (1974). *Understanding causality*. New York: W. W. Norton.

Piaget, J. (1983). Piaget's theory. In P. H. Mussen (Ed.), *Handbook of child psychology* (Vol. 1, pp. 103–129). New York: Wiley (originally published 1970).

Piaget, J., & Inhelder, B. (1969). *The psychology of the child*. New York: Basic Books.

Piaget, J., & Inhelder, B. (1974). *The child's construction of quantities: Conservation and atomism*. London: Routledge and Kegan Paul (originally published 1942).

Piaget, J., & Szeminska, A. (1952). *The child's conception of number*. New York: Humanities Press (originally published 1941).

Pinching, A. J., & Jeffries, D. (1985). AIDS and HTLV–111/LAV infection: Consequences for obstetrics and perinatal medicine. *British Journal of Obstetrics and Gynecology, 92*, 1211.

Pinon, M. F., Huston, A. C., & Wright, J. C. (1989). Family ecology and child characteristics that predict young children's educational television viewing. *Child Development, 60*, 846–857.

Planned Parenthood (1979). *Daughters of DES mothers*. New York: Planned Parenthood Federation of America.

Pleck, J. H. (1985). *Working wives/working husbands*. Beverly Hills, CA: Sage.

Plomin, R. (1989). Environment and genes: Determinants of behavior. *American Psychologist, 44*, 105–112.

Plomin, R., & DeFries, J. C. (1980). Genetics and intelligence: Recent data. *Intelligence, 4*, 15–24.

Plomin, R., DeFries, J. C., & McClearn, G. E. (1990). *Behavioral genetics: A primer* (2nd ed.). New York: Freeman.

Plomin, R., & Foch, T. T. (1981). Sex differences and individual differences. *Child Development, 52*, 383–385.

Plomin, R., Loehlin, J. C., & DeFries, J. C. (1985). Genetic and environmental components of "environmental" influences. *Developmental Psychology, 21*, 391–402.

Polermo, D. S., & Molfese, D. L. (1972). Language acquisition from age five onward. *Psychological Bulletin, 78*, 409–428.

Posner, J. K. (1982). The development of mathematical knowledge in two West African societies. *Child Development, 53*, 200–208.

Power, C., & Kohlberg, L. (1987, May). Using a hidden curriculum for moral education. *Education Digest*, pp. 10–13.

Power, T. (1985). Mother- and father-infant play: A developmental analysis. *Child Development, 56*, 1514–1525.

Poznansky, E. O. (1973). Children with excessive fears. *American Journal of Orthopsychiatry, 43*, 428–438.

Pratt, K. C. (1954). The neonate. In L. Carmichael (Ed.), *Manual of child psychology* (2nd ed.). New York: Wiley.

Proctor, C. P. (1984, March). Teacher expectations: A model for school improvement. *Elementary School Journal*, 469–481.

Pulaski, M.A.S. (1980). *Understanding Piaget*. New York: Harper & Row.

Purves, A. C. (1977). What is being achieved in reading and writing? *New York University Educational Quarterly, 9*, 8–14.

Puttallaz, M., & Gottman, J. M. (1981). Social skills and group acceptance. In S. R. Asher & J. M. Gottman (Eds.), *The development of children's friendships* (pp. 116–149). Cambridge: Cambridge University Press.

Quarrell, O. W. Q., Tyler, A., Upadhyaya, M., Meredith, A. L., Youngman, S., & Harper, P.S. (1987). Exclusion testing for huntington's disease in pregnancy with a closely linked DNA marker. *Lancet, 1*, 1281.

Queens Bench Foundation. (1980, November). Sexual abuse of children: A guide for parents. In *Sexual abuse of children: Selected readings*. Washington, DC: U.S. Department of Health and Human Services, DHHS Pub. No. (OHDS) 78-30161, pp. 173–181.

Rachlin, H. (1976). *Introduction to modern behaviorism*. San Francisco: Freeman.

Rader, N., Spiro, D. J. & Firestone, P. B. (1979). Performance on a Stage 4 object-permanence task with standard and nonstandard covers. *Child Development, 50*, 905–910.

Ragozin, A. S., Basham, R. B., Crnic, K. A., Greenberg, M. T., & Robinson, N. M. (1982). Effects of maternal age on parenting role. *Developmental Psychology, 18*, 627–635.

Raloff, J. (1982). Reports from the 1982 meeting of the American Speech Language Hearing Association's Meeting in Toronto, Canada. *Science News, 122*, 360.

Ramey, C. T., Farran, D. C. & Campbell, F. A. (1979). Predicting I.Q. from mother-infant interaction. *Child Development, 50*, 804–814.

Randal, J. E. (1988, December 6). Risks of caesarean sections. *Newsday*, p. 11.

Raspberry, W. (1970, April). Should ghettoese be accepted? *Today's Education*, pp. 30–31, 34–41.

Raths, L. E., Harmin, M., & Simon, S. B. (1966). *Values and teaching*. Columbus, OH: Charles E. Merrill.

Razel, M. (1988). Call for a follow-up study of experiments on long-term deprivation of human infants. *Perceptual and Motor Skills, 67*, 147–158.

Read, D. A., Simon, S. B., & Goodman, J. B. (1977). *Health education: The search for values*. Englewood Cliffs, NJ: Prentice-Hall.

Recht, D. R., & Leslie, L. (1988). Effect of prior knowledge on good and poor readers' memory of text. *Journal of Educational Psychology, 80*, 16–20.

Rector, J. M. (1935). Prenatal influences in rickets. *Journal of Pediatrics, 6*, 16.

Reed, E. (1975). Genetic anomolies in development. In E. M. Hetherington, S. Scarr-Salapatek, & G. M. Siegel (Eds.), *Review of child development research* (Vol. 4). Chicago: University of Chicago Press.

Reed, R. (1988). Education and achievement of young black males. In J. T. Gibbs

(Ed.), *Young, black, and male in America: An endangered species*. Dover, MA: Auburn House.

Reese, H. W., & Lipsitt, L. P. (1970). *Experimental child psychology*. New York: Academic Press.

Reichelt, P. (1982). Cited in P. H. Dreyer, Sexuality during adolescence. In B. B. Wolman (Ed.), *Handbook of developmental psychology* (pp. 559–601). Englewood Cliffs, NJ: Prentice-Hall.

Reissland, N. (1988). Neonatal imitation in the first hour of life: Observations in rural Nepal. *Development Psychology, 24*, 464–470.

Report of the Commission on Reading: What We Know About Learning to Read. (1986, Winter). *American Educator, 9*, 24–30.

Repp, A. C., Nieminen, G. S., Olinger, E., & Brusca, R. (1988). Direct observation: Factors affecting the accuracy of observers. *Exceptional Children, 55*, 29–36.

Reschly, D. J. (1981). Psychological testing in educational classification and placement. *American Psychologist, 36*, 1094–1103.

Rest, J. R. (1983). Morality. In P. H. Mussen (Ed.), *Handbook of Child Psychology: Cognitive Development* (4th ed.) (Vol. 3, pp. 556–630). New York: Wiley.

Restak, R. M. (1982). Newborn knowledge. *Science*, 58–65.

Restak, R. M. (1986). *The infant mild*. New York: Doubleday.

Restak, R. M. (1988). *The mind*. New York: Bantam.

Rheingold, H. L., & Adams, J. L. (1980). The significance of speech to newborns. *Developmental Psychology, 16*, 397–403.

Rheingold, H., & Cook, (1975). The contents of boys' and girls' rooms as an index of parents' behavior. *Child Development, 46*, 459–463.

Rheingold, H. L., & Eckerman, C. O. (1973). Fear of the stranger: a critical examination. In H. W. Reese (Ed.), *Advances in child development and behavior* (Vol. 8). New York: Academic Press.

Rhoads, G. G., et al. (1989, March 9). The safety and efficacy of chorionic villus sampling for early prenatal diagnosis of cytogenetic abnormalities. *New England Journal of Medicine, 320*, (no. 10), 609–617.

Rhodes, A. J. (1961). Virus infections and congenital malformations. Papers delivered at the First Conference on Congenital Malformations (pp. 106–116). Philadelphia: Lippincott.

Ricciuti, H. (1974). Fear and development of social attachments in the first year of life. In M. Lewis & L. A. Rosenblum (Eds.), *The origins of human behavior: Fear.* New York: Wiley.

Ricciuti, H. N. (1980a) Adverse environmental and nutritional influences on mental development: A perspective. Paper delivered at the American Dietetic Association, Atlanta.

Ricciuti, H. N. (1980b). Developmental consequences of malnutrition in early childhood. In E. M. Hetherington & R. D. Parke (Eds.), (1980b). *Contemporary readings in child psychology* (2nd ed.) New York: McGraw-Hill.

Rice, M. L. (1989). Children's language acquisition. *American Psychologist, 44,* 149–157.

Rice, M. L., Huston, A. C., Truglio, R., & Wright, J. (1990). Words from "Sesame Street": Learning vocabulary while viewing. *Developmental Psychology, 26,* 421–429.

Rice, R. D. (1977). Neurophysiological development in premature infants following stimulation. *Developmental Psychology, 13,* 69–76.

Richards, M. H., Boxer, A. M., Petersen, A. C., & Albrecht, R. (1990). Relation of weight to body image in pubertal girls and boys from two communities. *Developmental Psychology, 26,* 313–321.

Richardson, S. A. (1981). The relation of severe malnutrition in infancy of school children with differing life histories. Cited in S. A. Ricciuti, Developmental consequences of malnutrition. In E. M. Hetherington & R. D. Parke (Eds.), *Contemporary readings in child psychology* (2nd ed.) (pp. 21–25). New York: McGraw-Hill.

Richardson, S. A., Goodman, U., Hastorf, A. H., & Dornbusch, S. A. (1961). Cultural uniformity in reaction to physical disabilities. *American Sociological Review, 26,* 241–247.

Richmond-Abbott, M. (1983). *Masculine and feminine.* Reading, MA: Addison-Wesley.

Richters, J. E., & Zahn-Waxler, C. (1988). The infant day care controversy: Current status and future directions. *Early Childhood Research Quarterly, 3,* 319–337.

Rickert, E. S. (1981). Media mirrors of the gifted: E. Susanne Richert's review of the film "Simon." *Gifted Child Quarterly, 25,* 3–4.

Ridenour, M. V. (1978). Contemporary issues in motor development. In *Motor development: Issues and applications* (pp. 39–63). Princeton: Princeton Book Company.

Rierdan, J., & Koff, E. (1980). The psychological impact of menarche: Integrative versus disruptive changes. *Journal of Youth and Adolescence, 9,* 49–58.

Rinck, C., Rudolph, J. A., & Simkins, L. (1983). A survey of attitudes concerning contraception and the resolution of teenage pregnancy. *Adolescence, 72,* 923–929.

Ringwalt, C. L., & Palmer, J. H. (1989). Cocaine and crack users compared. *Adolescence, 24,* 851–859.

Roberge, J. R., & Flexer, B. K. (1979). Further examination of formal operational reasoning abilities. *Child Development, 50,* 478–484.

Roberts, J. A. F. (1970). *An introduction to medical genetics* (5th ed.). London: Oxford University Press.

Robertson, J., & Bowlby, J. (1952). Responses of young children to separation from their mothers. *Courrier Centre Internationale Enfance, 2,* 131–142.

Roche, A. F. (1979). Secular trends in stature, weight and maturation. In A. F. Roche (Ed.), Secular trends in growth, maturation and development of children. *Monographs of the Society for Research in Child Development, 44,* 3–27.

Roche, J. P. (1986). Premarital sex: Attitudes and behavior by dating stage. *Adolescence, 81,* 107–121.

Roe, A. (1964). Personality structure and occupational behavior. In H. Borow (ed). *Man in a World At Work.* (196–215). Boston: Houghton Mifflin.

Rode, S. S., Chang, P. N., Fisch, R. O., & Sroufe, L. A. (1981). Attachment patterns of infants separated at birth. *Developmental Psychology, 17,* 188–191.

Rodman, B. (1987, May 27). Diverse group urges instruction in democratic values. *Education Week,* p. 5.

Rodman, H., Pratto, D. J., & Nelson, R. S. (1985). Child care arrangements and children's functioning: A comparison of self-care and adult-care children. *Developmental Psychology, 21,* 413–418.

Roffwarg, H. P., Muzio, J. N., & Dement, W. C. (1966). Ontogenic development of the human sleep-dream cycle. *Science, 152,* 604–619.

Rogan, W., Bagniewska, A. & Damstra, J. (1980). Pollutants in breast milk. *New*

England Journal of Medicine, 26, 1450–1453.

Rogers, C. R. (1980). *A Way of Being.* Boston: Houghton Mifflin.

Rogers, L. (1976). Male hormones and behavior. In B. B. Lloyd & J. Archer (Eds.), *Exploring sex differences* (pp. 185–213). London: Academic Press.

Rogoff, B. (1981). Schooling and the development of cognitive skills. In H. C. Triandis & A. Heron, *Handbook of cross-cultural psychology* (vol. 4, pp. 233–295). *Developmental psychology.* Boston: Allyn and Bacon.

Rogoff, B., & Morelli, G. (1989). Culture and American children: Section introduction. *American Psychologist, 44,* 341–343.

Rogoff, B., Newcombe, N., & Kagan, J. (1974). Planfulness and recognition memory. *Child Development, 45,* 972–977.

Rokeach, M. (1973). *The nature of human values.* New York: The Free Press.

Rolfes, S. R., & DeBruyne, L. K. (1990). *Life span nutrition.* St. Paul: West.

Rondal, J. A. (1988). Language development in Down's syndrome: a life-span perspective. *International Journal of Behavioral Development, 11,* 21–36.

Rooks, J. P., Weatherby, N. L., Eunice, K. M., Stapleton, S., Rosen, D., & Rosenfield, A. (1989). Outcomes of care in birth centers. *New England Journal of Medicine, 321,* 1804–1810.

Rosch, E. (1975). Cognitive representations of semantic categories. *Journal of Experimental Psychology: General, 104,* 192–223.

Roscoe, B., & Kruger, T. L. (1990). AIDS: Late adolescents' knowledge and its influence on sexual behavior. *Adolescence, 25,* 39–46.

Roscoe, B., & Peterson, K. L. (1989), Age-appropriate Behaviors: A comparison of three generations of females. *Adolescence, 93,* 167–177.

Rose, R. J., & Ditto, W. B. (1983). A developmental-genetic analysis of common fears from early adolescence to early adulthood. *Child Development, 54,* 361–368.

Rose, S. A. (1981). Developmental changes in infants' retention of visual stimuli. *Child Development, 52,* 227–233.

Rose, S. A. & Wallace, I. F. (1985). Visual recognition memory: a predictor of later cognitive functioning. *Child Development, 56,* 853;–861.

Rosen, R., & Rosen, L. R. (1981). *Human sexuality*. New York: Knopf.

Rosenberg, J. S. & Berberian, R. M. (1975). A report on the dropout study, Yale University School of Medicine. In G. A. Austin & M. L. Predergast (1984). *Drug Use and Abuse: a Guide to Research Findings*, Vol. 2, (pp. 560–562). Santa Barbara, Calif.: ABC-Clio Information Services.

Rosenberg, L., Mitchell, A. A., Parsells, J., Pashayan, H., Lovik, C., & Shaprio, S. (1983, November 24). Lack of relation of oral clefts to diazepan use during pregnancy. *New England Journal of Medicine*, pp. 1185–1188.

Rosenberg, M. S. (1987). New dimensions for research on the psychological maltreatment of children. *American Psychologist, 42*, 166–172.

Rosenhan, D. L., & Seligman, M. E. P. (1984). *Abnormal psychology*. New York: W.W. Norton.

Rosenstein, D. & Oster, H. (1988). Differential facial responses to four basic tastes. *Child Development, 59*, 1555–1569.

Rosenthal, D. (1970). *Genetic Theory and Abnormal Behavior*. New York: McGraw-Hill.

Rosenthal, E. (1990, February 4). When a pregnant woman drinks. *New York Times Magazine*, pp. 30–32 +.

Rosenthal, R., & Jacobson, L. (1968). *Pygmalion in the classroom: Teacher expectations and pupils' intellectual development*. New York: Holt, Reinhart and Winston.

Rosenwasser, S. M., Lingenfelter, M., & Harrington, A. F. (1989). Nontraditional gender role portrayals on television and children's gender role perceptions. *Journal of Applied Developmental Psychology, 10*, 97–105.

Rosenzweig, M. R., Bennett, E. L., & Diamond, M. C. (1972, February). Brain changes in response to experience. *Scientific American*, pp. 22–29.

Ross Laboratories (1977). *Your child's fears*. Columbus, OH: Ross Laboratories.

Rossiter, J. R. (1980). Children and television advertising: Policy issues, perspectives, and the status of research. In E. L. Palmer & A. Dorr (Eds.), *Children and the faces of television: Teaching, violence, spelling* (pp. 251–271). New York: Academic Press.

Rothman, R. (1988a, April 20). Computers,

calculators in math urged. *Education Week*, p. 9.

Rothman, R. (1988b, March 16). Schools must teach values, says A.S.C.D. *Education Week*, p. 7.

Rovee-Collier, C. (1987). Learning and memory in infancy. In J. D. Osofsky (ed.), *Handbook of infant development* (pp. 98–149). New York: Wiley.

Rubelsky, F., & Hanks, C. (1971). Fathers' verbal interactions with infants in the first three months of life. *Child Development, 5*, pp. 42–48.

Rubin, K. H., & Howe, N. (1986). Social play and perspective taking. In G. Fein & M. Rivkin (Eds.), *The young child at play: Reviews of research* (Vol 4, pp. 113–125). Washington, DC: National Association for the Education of Young Children.

Rubin, J. Z., Provenzano, F. J., & Luria, Z. (1974). The eye of the beholder: Parent's view on sex of newborns. *American Journal of Orthopsychiatry, 43*, 720–731.

Rubin, K. H., Fein, G. G., & Vandenberg, B. (1983). Play. In E. Hetherington (Ed.), *Handbook of child development* (4th ed.) (pp. 693–775). New York: Wiley.

Rubin, R. A. & Balow, B. (1979). Measures of infant development and socioeconomic status as predictors of later intelligence and school achievement. *Developmental Psychology, 15*, 225–227.

Rubin, Z. (1980). *Children's friendships*. Cambridge, MA: Harvard University Press.

Rubinstein, E. A. (1978, November/December). Television and the young viewer. *American Scientist*.

Ruble, D. N. (1988). Sex role development. In M. H. Bornstein and M. E. Lamb (Eds.), *Social, emotional and personality development* (2nd ed.) (pp. 411–451). Hillsdale, NJ: Erlbaum.

Ruble, D. N., Balaban, T., & Cooper, J. (1981). Gender constancy and the effect of sex-typed televised commercials. *Child Development, 52*, 667–673.

Ruble, D. N., & Brooks-Gunn, J. (1982). The experience of menarche. *Child Development, 53*, 1557–1566.

Ruddy, M. G. & Bornstein, M.H. (1982). Cognitive correlates of infant attention and maternal stimulation over the first year of life. *Child Development, 53*, 183–188.

Ruff, H. A., & Halton, A. (1978). Is there directed reaching in the human neonate.

Developmental psychology, 14, 425–426.

Ruff, H.A., & Lawson, K. R. (1990). Development of sustained, focused attention in young children during free play. *Developmental Psychology, 26*, 85–94.

Rugh, R., & Shettles, L. B. (1971). *From contraception to birth: The drama of life's beginnings*. New York: Harper & Row.

Ruittenbeck, H. M. (1964). *The individual and the crowd: A study of identity in America*. New York: New American Library.

Ruopp, R., Travers, J., Glantz, F., & Coelen, C. (1983). Children at the center (final report of the National Day Care Study). Cited in E. Zigler & S. Muenchow, Infant day care and infant-care leaves: A policy vacuum. *American Psychologist, 38*, 91–95.

Rushworth, G. (1971). On postural and righting reflexes. In C. B. Kopp (Ed.), *Readings in early development: For occupational and physical therapy students*. (pp. 6–21). Springfield, IL: Thomas.

Russell, G. (1978). The father's role and its relation to masculinity, femininity, and androgyny. *Child Development, 49*, 1174–1181.

Russell, G., & Russell, A. (1987). Mother-child and father-child relationships in middle childhood. *Child development, 58*, 1573–1585.

Rutter, M. (1979), Maternal deprivation, 1972–1978: New findings, new concepts, new approaches. *Child Development, 50*, 283–305.

Rutter, M. (1980). School influences on children's behavior and development: The 1979 Kenneth Blackfan lecture, Children's Hospital Medical Center, Boston, *Pediatrics, 65*, 208–220.

Rutter, M. (1981a). Social-emotional consequences of day care for pre-school children. *American journal of Orthopsychiatry, 51*, 4–29.

Rutter, M. (1981b). The city and the child. *American Journal of Orthopsychiatry, 51*, 610–625.

Rutter, M. (1983). School effects on pupil progress: Research findings and policy implications. *Child Development, 54*, 1–29.

Rutter, M. (1985). Resilience in the face of adversity: Protective factors and resistance to psychiatric disorder. *British Journal of Psychiatry, 147*, 598–611.

Rutter, M. (1987). Continuities and discontinuities from infancy. In J. D. Osofsky (Ed.), *Handbook of infant development* (2nd ed.) (pp. 1256–1296). New York: Wiley.

Ryan, K. (1981). *Questions and answers on moral education,* Bloomington, IN: Phi Delta Kappa Educational Foundation.

Ryan, K. (1986, November). The new moral education. *Phi Delta Kappan,* pp. 228–233.

Ryan, R. M., & Lynch, J. H. (1989). Emotional autonomy versus detachment: Revising the vicissitudes of adolescence and young adulthood. *Child Development, 60,* 340–356.

Rychlak, J. F. (1985). Eclecticism in psychological theorizing: Good and bad. *Journal of Counseling and Development, 63,* 351–354.

Sagi, A., Lamb, M. E., Lewkowicz, K. S., Shoham, R., Dvir, R., & Estes, D. (1985). Security of infant-mother, father, and metapelet attachments among kibbutz-reared Israeli children. In I. Bretherton & E. Waters (Eds.), *Growing points of attachment Theory and Research Monographs of the Society for Research in Child Development,* Vol. 50, No. 1–2, 257–276.

Sagor, R. (1987). Looking for peace in the war on drugs. *NAASP Bulletin, 71,* 84–87.

Salend, S. J. (1984). Factors contributing to the development of a successful mainstreaming program. *Exceptional children, 50,* 409–416.

Salk, L. (1960). The effects of the normal heartbeat sound on the behavior of newborn infants: Implications for mental health. *World Mental Health, 12,* 168–175.

Salkind, N. J. (1981). *Theories of human development.* New York: D. Van Nostrand.

Salomon, G. (1983). Television watching and mental effort: a social-psychological view. In J. Bryant and D. R. Anderson (eds.) *Children's Understanding of Television* (pp. 181.–196) New York: Academic Press.

Saltz, E., & Johnson, J. (1974). Training for thematic-fantasy play in culturally disadvantaged children. *Journal of Educational Psychology, 66,* 523–630.

Saltz, R. (1973). Effects of part-time "mothering" on IQ and SQ of young institutionalized children. *Child Development, 44,* 166–170.

Sameroff, A. J., & Cavanaugh, P. J. (1979). Learning in infancy: A developmental perspective. In J. Osofsky (Ed.), *Handbook of infant development* (pp. 344–393). New York: Wiley.

Sameroff, A. J., & Chandler, M. J. (1975). Reproductive risk and the continuum of caretaker causality. In F. D. Horowitz (Ed.), *Review of child development research* (vol 4). Chicago: University of Chicago Press.

Samuels, S. J. (1983). A cognitive approach to factors influencing reading comprehension. *Journal of Educational Research, 76,* 261–265.

Sandberg, E. C. (1989). Only an attitude away: The potential for reproductive surrogacy. *American Journal of Obstetrics and Gynecology, 160,* 1441–1446.

Sande, M. A. (1986). Transmission of AIDS: The case against casual contagion. *New England Journal of Medicine, 314,* 380–382.

Sanders-Phillips, K., Strauss, M. E., & Gutberlet, R. L. (1988). The effect of obstetric medication on newborn infant feeding behavior. *Infant Behavior and Development, 11,* 251–263.

Santrock, J. W. (1972) Relation of type and onset of father absence to cognitive development. *Child Development, 43,* 455–469.

Sarafino, E. P. (1979, February). An estimate of nationwide incidence of sexual offenses against children. *Child Welfare,* pp. 127–135.

Sarason, I. G., & Sarason, B. R. (1980). *Abnormal psychology* (3rd ed.). Englewood Cliffs, NJ: Prentice-Hall.

Sarnoff, I. (1971). *Testing Freudian concepts: An experimental social approach.* New York: Springer.

Savin-Williams, R. C., & Small, S. A. (1986). The timing of puberty and its relationship to adolescent and parent perceptions of family interactions. *Developmental Psychology, 22,* 342–348.

Scales, P. (1978). Sex education policies and the primary prevention of teenage pregnancy. Cited in E. R. Allgeier & A. R. Allgeier (1984) *Sexual Interactions.* Lexington, Mass.: D. C. Heath.

Scales, P. (1981). Sex education and the prevention of teenage pregnancy: An overview of policies and programs in the United States. In T. Ooms (Ed.), Teenage pregnancy in family context: Implica-

tions for policy pp. 213–254. Philadelphia, Temple University Press.

Scales, P. (1982). Offset outrage: let parents help land your sex education program. *American School Board Journal, 7,* 32–33.

Scardamalia, M. & Bereiter, C. (1986). Research on written composition. In M. C. Wittrock (Ed.), *Handbook of research on teaching* (3rd ed.) (pp. 778–804). New York: Macmillan.

Scarr, S. (1981). Testing for children: Assessment and the many determinants of intellectual competence. *American Psychologist, 36,* 1159–1167.

Scarr, S. (1986). How plastic are we? *Contemporary Psychology, 31,* 565–567.

Scarr, S., & Arnett, J. (1987). Malleability: Lessons from intervention and family studies. In J. J. Gallagher & C. T. Ramey (Eds.), *The malleability of children.* (pp. 71–85). Baltimore: Paul Brookes.

Scarr, S., & Kidd, K. K. (1983). Developmental behavior genetics, In P. H. Mussen (Ed.), *Handbook of child psychology* (4th ed.) (Vol. 2, pp. 345–433). New York: Wiley.

Scarr, S., & McCartney, K. (1983). How people make their own environments: A theory of genotype-environment effects. *Child development, 54,* 424–435.

Scarr, S. & Weinberg, R. A. (1978). The influence of "family background" on intellectual attainment. *American Sociological Review, 43,* 674–692.

Scarr-Salapatek, S. (1975). Genetics and the development of intelligence. In E. M. Hetherington, S. Scarr-Salapatek, & G. M. Siegel (Eds.), *Review of child development research* (Vol. 4, pp. 1–58). Chicago: University of Chicago Press.

Scarr-Salapatek, S., & Williams, M. L. (1973). The effects of early stimulation on low birth weight infants. *Child Development, 44,* 94–101.

Schachter, F. F. (1981). Toddlers with employed mothers. *Child Development, 52,* 958–964.

Schachter, J. (1989). Why we need a program for the control of chlamydia trachomatis. *New England Journal of Medicine, 320,* 802–803.

Schafer, R. (1979). The self-concept as a factor in diet selection and quality. *Journal of Nutrition Education, 11,* 37–39.

Schaffer, H. R. (1986). Child psychology: The future. *Journal of Psychology and*

Psychiatry and Allied Discipline, 27, 761–779.

Schaffer, K. F. (1981). *Sex roles and human behavior.* Cambridge, MA: Winthrop.

Schaffer, R. (1977). *Mothering.* Cambridge, MA: Harvard University Press.

Schaie, K. W., & Hertzog, C. (1982). Longitudinal methods. In B. B. Wolman (Ed.), *Handbook of developmental psychology* (pp. 91–116). Englewood Cliffs, NJ: Prentice-Hall.

Schank, R. C., & Abelson, R. P. (1977). *Scripts, plans, goals and understanding.* Hillsdale, NJ: Erlbaum.

Schiedel, D. G., & Marcia, J. E. (1985). Ego identity, intimacy, sex role orientation and gender. *Developmental Psychology, 21,* 149–160.

Schild, S. (1979). Psychological issues in genetic counseling of phenylketonuria. In S. Kessler (Ed.), *Genetic counseling: Psychological dimensions* (pp. 135–151). New York: Academic Press.

Schill, W. J., McCartin, R., & Meyer, K. A. (1985). Youth employment: Its relationship to academic and family variables. *Journal of Vocational Behavior, 26,* 155–163.

Schindler, P. J., Moely, B. E., & Frank, A. L. (1987). Time in day care and social participation of young children. *Developmental Psychology, 23,* 255–262.

Schmitt, M. H., (1970, July). Superiority of Breast-Feeding: Fact or Fancy. *American Journal of Nursing,* 1488–1493.

Schofield, J. W. (1981). Complementary and conflicting identities: Images and interaction in an interracial school. In S. R. Asher & J. M. Gottman (Eds.), *The development of children's friendships* (pp. 53–91). Cambridge: Cambridge University Press.

Schramm, N. R. (1986, August 10). AIDS: 1991. *Los Angeles Times,* pp. 10–16.

Schuckit, M. A. (1986). Genetic and clinical implications of alcoholism and affective disorder. *American Journal of Psychiatry, 143,* 140–153.

Schuckit, M. A. (1987). Biological vulnerability to alcoholism. *Journal of Consulting and Clinical Psychology, 55,* 301–309.

Scott, G. B., et al. (1989). Survival in children with perinatally acquired human immunodeficiency virus type 1 infection. *The New England Journal of Medicine, 321,* 1791–1796.

Scott, M. E. (1988, Spring). Learning strategies can help. *Teaching Exceptional Children.* pp. 30–34.

Searey, S. (1988). Developing self-esteem. *Academic Therapy, 23,* 453–460.

Sears, R. R., Maccoby, E. E., & Levin, H. (1957). *Patterns of child rearing.* New York: Harper & Row.

Sears, R. R., Rae, L., & Alpert, R. (1965). *Identification and child rearing.* Stanford, CA: Stanford University Press.

Sebald, H. (1989). Adolescents' peer orientation: Changes in the support system during the past three decades. *Adolescence, 96,* 937–945.

Segalowitz, N. S. (1981). Issues in the cross-cultural study of bilingual development. In H. C. Triandis & A. Heron (Eds.), *Handbook of cross-cultural psychology* (Vol. 4, pp. 55–93). Boston: Allyn and Bacon.

Seitz, V. (1979). Psychology and social policy for children: Introduction. *American Psychologist, 10,* 1007–1009.

Self, P. A., and Horowitz, F. D. (1979). The Behavioral Assessment of the Neonate: An Overview in J. Osofsky (Ed.), *Handbook of Infant Development.* New York: Wiley, 126–165.

Selman, R. L. (1981). The child as a friendship philosopher. In S. R. Asher & J. M. Gottman (Eds.), *The development of children's friendships* (pp. 242–273). Cambridge, MA: Cambridge University Press.

Serbin, L. A., O'Leary, K. D., Kent, R. N., & Tonick, I. J. (1973). A comparison of teacher response to the preacademic and problem behavior of boys and girls. *Child Development, 44,* 796–804.

Sexias, J. S., & Youcha, G. (1985). *Children of alcoholism.* New York: Crown.

Shafii, M., Carrigan, S., Whittinghill, J. R. & Derrick. (1985). A psychological autopsy of completed suicide in children and adolescents. *American Journal of Psychiatry, 142,* 1061–1064.

Shantz, C. U. (1983). Social cognition. In J. H. Flavell & E. M. Markman (Eds.), *Handbook of child psychology* (4th ed.) (Vol. 3, pp. 495–556).

Shantz, C. U. (1986). Conflict, aggression, and peer status: an observational study. *Child Development, 57,* 1322–1332.

Schantz, C. U. (1987). Conflicts between children. *Child Development, 58,* 293–306.

Shantz, C. U., & Hobart, C. J.. (1989). Social conflict and development: Peers and siblings. In T. J. Berndt & G. W. Ladd (Eds.), (pp. 71–95). *Peer relationships in child development,* New York: Wiley.

Sharabany, R., Gershoni, R., & Hofman, J. E. (1981). Girlfriend, boyfriend: Age and sex differences in intimate friendship. *Developmental Psychology, 17,* 800–809.

Shatz, M. (1983). Communication. In P. H. Mussen (Ed.), *Handbook of child psychology* (4th ed.) (pp. 841–891). New York: Wiley.

Shaver, J. P., & Strong, W. (1976). *Facing value decisions: Rationale-building for teachers.* Belmont, CA: Wadsworth.

Shaw, M. W., (1976). Legal issues in medical genetics. In M. A. Sperber & L. F. Jarvik (Eds.), *Psychiatry and genetics.* New York: Basic Books.

Shedler, J., & Block, J. (1990). Adolescent drug use and psychological health. *American Psychologist, 45,* 612–631.

Shepherd-Look, D. L. (1982). Sex differentiation and the development of sex roles. In B. B. Wolman (Ed.), *Handbook of developmental psychology.* (pp. 403–434). Englewood Cliffs, NJ: Prentice-Hall.

Sheppard, M. A., Wright, D. & Goodstadt, M. S. (1985). Peer pressure and drug use: Exploding the myth. *Adolescence, 20,* 949–958.

Sherman, J. (1980). Mathematics, spacial visualization, and related factors: Changes in girls and boys, grades 8–11. *Journal of Educational Psychology, 72,* 476–482.

Shestowsky, B. (1983). Ego Identity development and obesity in adolescent girls. *Adolescence, 71,* 550–559.

Shiller, V. M., Izard, C. E., & Bembree, E. A. (1986). Patterns of emotion expression during separation in the strange-situation procedure. *Developmental Psychology, 22,* 378–382.

Shirley, M. M. (1931). *The first two years: A study of twenty-five babies* (Vol. 1), *Postural and locomotor development.* Minneapolis: University of Minnesota Press.

Shirley, M. M. (1933). *The first two years: A study of twenty-five babies* (Vol. 2), *Intellectual development.* Minneapolis: University of Minnesota Press.

Shneidman, E. S. , Barberow, N. L. & Litman, R. E. (1970). *The Psychology of Suicide.* New York: Science House.

Shonkoff, J. P. (1984). The biological substrate and physical health in middle childhood. In W. A. Collins (Ed.), *Development during middle childhood* (pp. 24–70). Washington, DC: National Academy Press.

Shope, D. F. (1975). *Interpersonal Sexuality*. Philadelphia: Saunders.

Sibinga, M. S., & Friedman, C. J. (1971). Complexities of parental understanding of phenylketonuria. *Pediatrics, 48,* 216–224.

Siegel, L. J., & Senna, J. J. (1988). *Juvenile delinquency* (3rd ed.). St. Paul: West.

Siegel, O. (1982). Personality development in adolescence. In B. B. Wolman (Ed.), *Handbook of developmental psychology* (pp. 537–549). Englewood Cliffs, NJ: Prentice-Hall.

Simkin, P., Whalley, J. & Keppler, A. (1984). *Pregnancy, Childbirth, and the Newborn*. Deephaven, Minn.: Meadowbrook Books.

Simmons, R. G., Blyth, D. A., Van Cleave, E. F., & Bush, D. M. (1979). Entry into early adolescence: The impact of school structure, puberty, and early dating on self-esteem. *American Sociological Review, 38,* 553–568.

Simons, C., McCluskey, K., & Mullett, M. (1985). Interparental ratings of temperament for high and low risk infants. *Child Psychiatry and Human Development, 15,* 1678–1679.

Simner, M. L. (1971). Newborn's response to the cry of another infant. *Developmental Psychology, 5,* 136–150.

Singer, D. G., & Singer, J. L. (1976). Family television viewing habits and the spontaneous play of preschool children. *American Journal of Orthopsychiatry, 46,* 496–502.

Singer, J. L., & Singer, D. G. (1983). Psychologists look at television: Cognitive, developmental, personality, and social policy implications. *American Psychologist, 38,* 826–835.

Singer, S., & Hilgard, H. R. (1978). *The biology of people*. San Francisco: Freeman.

Siqueland, E. R. (1968). Response patterns and extinction in human newborns. *Journal of Experimental Child Psychology, 6,* 431–442.

Sirignano, S. W., & Lachman, M. E. (1985). Personality change during the transition to parenthood: The role of perceived infant temperament. *Developmental Psychology, 21,* 558–567.

Sjolund, A. (1981). The effect of day care institutions on children's development: An analysis of international research. Cited in K. A. Clarke-Stewart & G. G. Fein, Early child programs. In P. H. Mussen (Ed.), *The handbook of child psychology* (pp. 917–1001). New York: Wiley.

Sharin, K. (1977). Cognitive and contextual determinants of stranger fear in six- and eleven-month-old infants. *Child Development, 48,* 537–544.

Skeels, H. M. (1966). Adult status of children with contrasting early life experiences: A follow-up study. *Monographs of the Society for Research in Child Development, 31,* no. 3.

Skinner, B. F. (1957). *Verbal behavior*. New York: Appleton-Century-Croft.

Skovholt, T. M., & Morgan, J. I. (1981). Career development: An outline of issues for men. *Personal and Guidance Journal, 60,* 231–237.

Slaby, R. G., & Frey, K. S. (1975). Development of gender constancy and selective attention to same-sex models. *Child Development, 46,* 849–856.

Slaby, R. G., & Guerra, N. G. (1988). Cognitive mediators of aggression in adolescent offenders: 1. Assessment. *Developmental Psychology, 24,* 580–588.

Slobin, D. I. (1972, July). Children and language: They learn the same way all around the world. *Psychology Today,* pp. 18+.

Slobin, D. I. (1973). Cognitive prerequisites for the development of grammar. In C. A. Ferguson & D. I. Slovin (Eds.), *Studies of Child Language Development*. New York: Holt, Rinehart and Winston.

Small, M. Y. (1990). *Cognitive development*. San Diego, CA: Harcourt Brace Jovanovich.

Smart, D. E., Beaumont, P. J., & George, G. C. (1976). Some personality characteristics of patients with anorexia nervosa. *British Journal of Psychiatry, 128,* 57–60.

Smart, M. S., & Smart, R. C. (1978a). *Preschool children: Development and relationships* (2nd ed.). New York: Macmillan.

Smart, M. S., & Smart, R. C. (1978b). *School-age children: Development and relationships* (2nd ed.). New York: Macmillan.

Smetana, J. G. (1986). Preschool children's conceptions of sex-role transgressions. *Child Development, 57,* 862–871.

Smith, C., & Lloyd, B. (1978). Maternal behavior and perceived sex of infant: Revisited. *Child Development, 49,* 1263–1265.

Smith, E. A., & Caldwell, L. L. (1989). The perceived quality of leisure experiences among smoking and nonsmoking adolescents. *Journal of Early Adolescence, 9,* 153–162.

Smith, G. M. (1969). Relations between personality and smoking behavior in preadult subjects. *Journal of Consulting and Clinical Psychology, 33,* 710–715.

Smith, P. B., & Pederson, D. R. (1988). Maternal sensitivity and patterns of infant-mother attachment. *Child Development, 59,* 1097–1102.

Smith, P. K. (1978). A longitudinal study of social participation in pre-school children: Solitary and parallel play reexamined. *Developmental Psychology, 14,* 517–523.

Smith, R. M., & Neisworth, J. T. (1975). *The exceptional child: A functional approach*. New York: McGraw-Hill.

Smith, T.E.C. (1987). *Introduction to education*. St. Paul: West.

Smoll, F. L. & Schutz, R. W. (1990). Quantifying gender differences in physical performance: A developmental perspective. *Developmental Psychology, 26,* 360–370.

Snarey, J. R., Reimer, J., & Kohlberg, L. (1985). Development of social-moral reasoning among kibbutz adolescents: A longitudinal cross-cultural study. *Developmental Psychology, 21,* 3–18.

Snow, C. E. (1977). The development of conversation between mothers and babies. *Journal of Child Language, 4,* 1–22.

Snyderman, M., & Rothman, S. (1987). Survey of expert opinion on intelligence and aptitude testing. *American Psychologist, 42,* 137–144.

Sobel, D. (1979, December 4). Hyperactive children suffer as adults. *New York Times,* C1.

Sobesky, W. E. (1983). The effects of situational factors on moral judgments. *Child Development, 54,* 575–584.

Society for Research in Child Development (Development Interest Group) (1977). *Ethical standards for research with children* (p. 39). Chicago: Society for Research in Child Development.

Solkoff, N., Jaffe, S., Weintraub, D., & Blase, B. (1969). Effects of handling on the subsequent development of premature babies. *Developmental Psychology, 1,* 765–768.

Solnit, A. J., Call, J. D., & Feinstein, C. B. (1979). Psychosexual development: Five to ten years. In J. D. Noshpitz (Ed.), *Basic handbook of child psychiatry* (pp. 184–190). New York: Basic Books.

Sommer, B. B. (1978). *Puberty and adolescence.* New York: Oxford University Press.

Song, Myung-Ja, Smetana, J. G. & Kim, S. Y. (1987). Korean children's conceptions of moral and conventional transgressions. *Developmental Psychology, 23,* 577–582.

Sontag, L. W. (1941). The significance of fetal environmental differences. *American Journal of Obstetrics and Gynecology, 42,* 996–1003.

Sontag, L. W. (1944). War and the fetal-maternal relationship. *Marriage and Family Living, 6,* 3–4.

Sorce, J. F., Emde, R. N., Campos, J., & Klinnert, M. D. (1985). Maternal emotional signaling: Its effect on the visual cliff behavior of 1-year-olds. *Developmental Psychology, 21,* 195–200.

Sorenson, R. C. (1973). *The Sorenson Report: Adolescent sexuality in contemporary America.* New York: World.

Spence, J. H., Helmreich, R., & Stapp, J. (1975). Ratings of self and peers on sex-role attribution and their relationship to self-esteem and concept of masculinity and feminity. *Journal of Personality and Social Psychology, 32,* 29–39.

Sperber, M. A. (1976). Psychiatry and metacommunication in genetic counseling. In M. A. Sperber & L. F. Jarvik (Eds.), *Psychiatry and genetics: Psychosocial, ethical and legal considerations.* New York:

Spitz, R. (1945). Hospitalism: An inquiry into the genesis of psychiatric conditions in early childhood. *Psychoanalytic Study of the Child, 1,* 53.

Spitz, R. (1965). *The first year of life: A psychoanalytic study of normal and deviant development of object relations.* New York: International Universities Press.

Sprafkin, J. N., Liebert, R. M., & Poulos, R. W. (1975). Effects of a prosocial televised example on children's helping. *Journal of Experimental Child Psychology, 20,* 119–126.

Sprigle, J. E., & Schaefer, L. (1985). Longitudinal evaluation of the effects of two compensatory preschool programs on fourth- through sixth-grade students. *Developmental Psychology, 17,* 835–858.

Sprintall, N. A., & Collins, W. A. (1984). *Adolescent psychology: A developmental view.* New York: Random House.

Spurlock, J., & Lawrence, L. E. (1979). The black child. In J. D. Noshpitz (Ed.), *Basic handbook of child psychiatry* (Vol. 1, pp. 248–256). New York: Basic Books.

Sroufe, L. A. (1979a). Socioemotional development. In J. D. Osofsky (Ed.), *Handbook of infant development* (pp. 462–519). New York: Wiley.

Sroufe, L. A. (1979b). The coherence of individual development: Early care, attachment and subsequent developmental issues. *American Psychologist, 34,* 834–842.

Sroufe, L. A. (1985). Attachment classification from the perspective of infant-caregiver relationships and infant temperament. *Child Development, 56,* 1–14.

Sroufe, A., & Waters, E. (1977). Attachment as an organizational construct. *Child Development, 48,* 1184–1189.

Sroufe, L. A., & Wunsch, J. (1972). The development of laughter in the first year of life. *Child Development, 43,* 1326–1344.

St. George-Hyslip, P. H., et al. (1987). The genetic defect causing familial Alzheimer's disease maps on chromosome 21. *Science, 235,* 855–886.

Staffieri, R. J. (1967). A study of social stereotype of body image in children. *Journal of Personality and Social Psychology, 7,* 101–104.

Staffieri, R. J. (1972). Body build and behavioral expectancies in young females. *Developmental Psychology, 6,* 125–127.

Stagno, S., & Whitley, R. J. (1985). Herpes simplex virus and varicella-zoster virus infections. *New England Journal of Medicine, 313,* 1327–1329.

Starr, R. Y. (1979). Child abuse. *American Psychologist, 34,* 872–878.

Stechler, G., & Halton, A. (1982). Prenatal influences on human development. In B. B. Wolman (Ed.), *Handbook of developmental psychology* (pp. 175–189). Englewood Cliffs, NJ: Prentice-Hall.

Steinberg, L. (1985a). *Adolescence.* New York: Random House.

Steinberg, L. (1985b). Early temperament antecedents of adult Type-A behavior. *Developmental Psychology, 21,* 1171–1180.

Steinberg, L. (1986). Latchkey children and susceptibility to peer pressure: An ecological analysis. *Developmental Psychology, 24,* 295–296.

Steinberg, L. (1987). Impact of puberty on family relations: Effects of pubertal status and pubertal timing. *Developmental Psychology, 23,* 451–460.

Steinberg, L. (1988). Reciprocal relation between parent-child distance and pubertal maturation. *Developmental Psychology, 24,* 122–128.

Steinberg, L., Catalano, R., & Dooley, D. (1981). Economic antecedent of child abuse. *Child Development, 52,* 975–985.

Steinberg, L., Elmen, J. D., & Mounts, N. S. (1989). Authoritative parenting, psychosocial maturity, and academic success among adolescents. *Child Development, 60,* 1424–1436.

Steinberg, L., & Silverberg, S. B. (1986). The vicissitudes of autonomy in early adolescence. *Child Development, 57,* 841–851.

Steinberg, L., Greenberger, E., Garduque, L., & McAuliffe, S. (1982). Students in the labor force: Some costs and benefits to schooling and learning. *Evaluation and Policy Analysis, 4,* 363–372.

Stern, D. N., Spieker, S., & MacKain, K. (1982). Intonation contours as signals in maternal speech to prelinguistic infants. *Developmental Psychology, 18,* 727–736.

Sternberg, R. J. (1985). General intellectual ability. In R. J. Sternberg, (Ed.), *Mechanisms of cognitive development* (pp.163–187). New York: Freeman.

Sternberg, R. J., & Powell, J. S. (1983). The development of intelligence. In P. H. Mussen (Ed.), *Handbook of child psychology* (Vol. 3, pp. 341–420). New York: Wiley.

Stevenson, H. W., et al. (1985). Cognitive performance and academic achievement of Japanese, Chinese, and American children. *Child Development, 56,* 718–734.

Stevenson, H. W. & Lee, S. Y. (1990). Contexts of achievement. *Monographs of the Society for Research in Child Development* (Vol. 55, no. 1–2). (Serial No. 221).

Stevenson, H. W. & Newman, R. (1986). Long-term prediction of achievement and attitudes in mathematics and reading. *Child Development, 57,* 649–6559.

Stevenson, H. W., Parke, T., Wilkinson, A., Hegion, A., & Fish, E. (1976). Longitudinal study of individual differences in cognitive development and scholastic achievement. *Journal of Educational Psychology, 68,* 377–400.

Stevenson, R. E. (1973). *The fetus and newly born infant: Influences of the prenatal environment.* St. Louis: C. V. Mosby.

Stewart, M. J. (1980). Fundamental locomotor skills. In C. J. Corbin (Ed.), *A textbook of motor development* (pp. 44–52). Dubuque, IA: Wm. C. Brown.

Stewart, O., & Tei, E. (1983). Some implications of metacognition for reading instruction. *Journal of Reading, 26,* 36–42.

Stewart, R. B. (1983). Sibling attachment relationships: Child-infant interactions in infancy. *Developmental Psychology, 19,* 192–200.

Stigler, A. E., Shin-Ying, L., Lucker, G. W., & Stevenson, H. W. (1982). Curriculum and achievement in mathematics: A study of elementary school children in Japan, Taiwan, and the United States. *Journal of Educational Psychology, 73,* 315–322.

Stockdale, D. F., Hegland, S. M., & Chiaromonte, T. (1989). Helping behaviors: An observational study of preschool children. *Early Childhood Research Quarterly, 4,* 533–544.

Stocker, C., Dunn, J., & Plomin, R. (1989). Sibling relationships: Links with child temperament, Maternal behavior, and family structure. *Child Development, 60,* 715–728.

Stolz, H. R., & Stolz, L. M., (1951). *Somatic development of adolescent boys.* New York: Macmillan.

Stoneman, Z., & Brody, G. H. (1981). Peers as mediators of television food advertisements aimed at children. *Developmental Psychology, 17,* 853–858.

Streibel, M. J. (1986). A critical analysis of the use of computers in education. *Education Communication and Technology, 34,* 137–161.

Streissguth, A. P. (1982). Maternal alcoholism and the outcome of pregnancy. In J. Belsky (Ed.), *In the beginning* (pp. 45–50). New York: Columbia University Press.

Streissguth, A. P., Martin, D. C., Barr, H. M., Sandman, B. M., Kirchner, G. L., & Darby, B. L. (1984). Intrauterine alcohol and nicotine exposure: Attention and reaction time in four-year-old children. *Developmental Psychology, 20,* 533–542.

Streitmatter, J. L. (1989). Identity development and academic achievement in early adolescence. *Journal of Early Adolescence, 9,* 99–116.

Strobino, D. M. (1987). *The health and medical consequences of adolescent sexuality and pregnancy: A review of the literature in risking the future* (Vol. 2, pp. 93–123). Washington, DC: National Academy Press.

Stuckey, M. R., McGhee, P. E., & Bell, N. J. (1982). Parent-child interaction: The influence of maternal employment. *Developmental Psychology, 18,* 635–644.

Stunkard, A. J. et al. (1986). An adoption study of human obesity. *New England Journal of Medicine, 314,* 193–197.

Sue, D., Sue, D. W., & Sue, S. (1981). *Understanding abnormal behavior.* Boston: Houghton-Mifflin.

Suffet, F., Bryce-Buchanon, C., & Brotman, R. (1981). Pregnant addicts in a comprehensive care program: Results of a follow-up survey. *American Journal of Orthopsychiatry, 51,* 297–307.

Sullivan, H. S. (1953). *The Interpersonal theory of psychiatry.* New York: Norton.

Sullivan, M. W., Rovee-Collier, C. K., & Tynes, P. M. (1979). A conditioning analysis of infant long-term memory. *Child Development, 50,* 152–162.

Super, C. M. (1981). Cross-cultural research on infancy. In H. C. Triandis & A. Heron (Eds.), *Handbook of cross-cultural psychology* (Vol. 4, pp. 17–55). Boston: Allyn and Bacon.

Super, C. M., Herrera, M. G., & Mora, J. O. (1990). Long-term effects of food supplementation and psychosocial intervention on the physical growth of Columbian infants at risk of malnutrition. *Child Development, 61,* 29–50.

Super, D. (1953). A theory of vocational development. *American Psychologist, 8,* 185–190.

Sutton, H. E. (1980). *An introduction to human genetics* (3rd ed.). Philadelphia: Saunders.

Svejda, M. J., Campos, J. J., & Emde, R. N. (1980). Mother-infant "bonding": Failure to generalize. *Child Development, 51,* 775–779.

Symons, D. K., & Moran, G. (1987). The behavioral dynamics of mutual responsiveness in early face-to-face mother-infant interactions. *Child Development, 58,* 1488–1496.

Taina, E., Hanninen, P., & Gronrros, M. (1985). Viral infections in pregnancy. *ACTA Obstet. Scand, 64,* 167.

Talbot, N. B., & Guthrie, A. (1976). Health care needs of American children. In N. B. Talbot (Ed.), *Raising children in modern America: Problems and prospective solutions.* Boston: Little, Brown.

Tangri, S. & Moles, O. (1987). Parents and community. In V. Richardson-Koehler (Ed.). *Educators' Handbook* (pp. 519–555). New York: Longman.

Tanner, J. M. (1970). Physical growth. In P. H. Mussen (Ed.), *Carmichael's manual of child development* (3rd ed.) (pp. 77–155). New York: Wiley.

Tanner, J. M. (1978). *Foetus into man: Physical growth from conception to maturity.* Cambridge, MA: Harvard University Press.

Tanzi, R. E., et al. (1987). Amyloid beta protein gene: cDNA, mRNA distribution and genetic linkage near the Alzheimer locus. *Science, 235,* 880–884.

Taras, H. L., Sallis, J. F., Patterson, T. L., Nader, P. R., & Nelson, J. A. (1989). Television's influence on children's diet and physical activity. *Developmental and Behavioral Pediatrics, 10,* 176–180.

Tellegen, A., Lykken, D. T., & Bouchard, T. (1988). Personality similarity in twins reared apart and together. *Journal of Personality and Social Psychology, 54,* 1031–1039.

Termine, N. T., & Izard, C. E. (1988). Infants' responses to their mothers' expressions of joy and sadness. *Developmental Psychology, 24,* 223–230.

Teti, D. M., & Ablard, K. E. (1989). Security of attachment and infant-sibling relationships: A laboratory study. *Child Development, 60,* 1519–1529.

Thelen, E. (1987). The role of motor development in developmental psychology: A view of the past and an agenda for the future. In N. Eisenberg (Ed.), *Contemporary topics in developmental psychology* (pp. 3–34). New York: Wiley.

Thoman, E. B., Leiderman, P. H., & Olson, J. P. (1972). Neonate-mother interaction during breast feeding. *Developmental Psychology, 6,* 110–118.

Thomas, A. Chess, S., & Birch, H. G. (1970, August). The origins of personality. *Scientific American,* pp. 102–109.

Thomas, J. R., & French, K. E. (1985). Gender differences across age in motor performance: A meta-analysis. *Psychological Bulletin, 98,* 260–282.

Thomas, M. H., Horton, R. W., Lippincott, E. C., & Drabman, R. S. (1977). Desensitization to portrayals of real-life aggression as a function of exposure to television violence. *Journal of Personality and Social Psychology, 35,* 450–458.

Thomas, R. M. (1979). *Comparing theories*

of child development. Belmont, CA: Wadsworth.

Thompson, A. P. (1976). Client Misconceptions in Vocational Counseling. *American Personnel and Guidance Journal, 55,* 30–34.

Thompson, R. A. (1988). The effects of infant day care through the prism of attachment theory: A critical appraisal. *Early Childhood Research Quarterly, 3,* 273–283.

Thompson, R. A. (1990). Vulnerability in research: A developmental perspective on research risk. *Child Development, 61,* 1–17.

Thompson, R. A., Cicchetti, D., Lamb, M. E., & Malikin, C. (1985). Emotional responses of Down's syndrome and normal infants in the strange situation: The organization of affective behavior in infants. *Developmental Psychology, 21,* 828–842.

Thompson, W. R., & Grusek, J. A. (1970). Studies of early experience. In P. H. Mussen (Ed.), *Carmichael's manual of child development.* New York: Wiley.

Thornburg, H. D. (1986, January). Is the beginning of identity the end of innocence? *The Clearing House,* 217–219.

Thornburg, H. D., & Glider, P. (1984). Dimensions of early adolescent social perceptions and preferences. *Journal of Early Adolescence, 4,* 387–406.

Thurstone, L. L. (1938). *Primary mental abilities.* Psychometric Monographs, No. 1.

Tieger, T. (1980). On the biological basis of sex differences in aggression. *Child Development, 51,* 943–963.

Time Magazine, If Slang Is Not a Sin. *Time,* November 8, 1982, 91.

Tisak, M. S. (1986). Children's conception of parental authority. *Child Development, 57,* 166–176.

Tobler, N. S. (1986). Meta-analysis of 143 adolescent drug prevention programs: Quantitative outcome results of program participants compared to a control or comparison group. *Journal of Drug Issues, 16,* 537–568.

Tomasello, M., & Mannle, S. (1985). Pragmatics of sibling speech to one-year-olds. *Child Development, 56,* 911–917.

Tomasello, M., Mannle, S. & Kruger, A. (1986). The linguistic environment of one to two year old twins. *Developmental Psychology, 22,* 169–176.

Torgersen, A. M. (1989). Genetic and environmental influences on temperamental development: Longitudinal study of twins from infancy to adolescence. In S. Doxiadis (Ed.), *Early influences shaping the individual* (pp. 269–283). New York: Plenum.

Tower, R. B., Singer, D. G., Singer, J. L., & Biggs, A. (1979). Differential effects of television programming on preschoolers' cognition, imagination, and social play. *American Journal of Orthopsychiatry, 49,* 265–281.

Tower, R. L. (1987) *How schools can help combat student drug and alcohol abuse.* Washington, DC: NEA Professional Library.

Townsend, J. W., Klein, R. E., Irwin, M. H., Wens, W., Yarbrough, C. & Engle, P. L. (1982). Nutrition and preschool mental development. In D. A. Wagner & H. W. Stevenson (Eds.). *Cultural Perspectives on Child Development* (pp. 124–146). San Francisco: Freeman.

Trabasso, T. (1975). Representation, memory, and reasoning: How do we make transitive inferences? In A. D. Pick (Ed.), *Minnesota symposia on child psychology* (Vol. 9). Minneapolis: University of Minnesota Press.

Tracy, R. L., & Ainsworth, M.D.S. (1981). Maternal affectionate behavior and infant-mother attachment patterns. *Child Development, 52,* 1341–1343.

Treffinger, D. J. (1982). Demythologizing gifted education. An editorial essay. *Gifted Child Quarterly, 26,* 3–8.

Trehub, S. (1973). Infants' sensitivity to vowel and tonal contrasts. *Developmental Psychology, 9,* 81–96.

Treiman, D., & Terrell, K. (1975). Sex and the process of status attainment: A comparison of working women and men. *American Sociological Review, 40,* 174–200.

Triandis, H. C., & Brislin, R. W. (1984). Cross-cultural psychology. *American Psychologist, 39,* 1006–1017.

Trickett, P. K., & Kuczynski, L. (1986). Children's misbehaviors and parental discipline strategies in abusive and nonabusive families. *Developmental Psychology, 22,* 115–123.

Trickett, P. K., & Susman, E. J. (1988). Parental perceptions of child-rearing practices in physically abusive and nonabusive families. *Developmental Psychology, 24,* 270–277.

Trollip, S. R., & Alessi, S. M. (1988). Incorporating computers effectively into classrooms. *Journal of Research on Computing in Education, 22,* 70–81.

Tronick, R. (1989). Emotions and emotional communication in infants. *American Psychologist, 44,* 112–120.

Trotter, R. J. (1975, September 15). The new face of birth. *Science News,* pp. 106–108.

Trulson, M. E. (1985) LSD: *Visions or nightmares.* New York: Chelsea House.

Tucker, L. A. (1987). Television, teenagers, and health. *Journal of Youth and Adolescence, 16,* 415–425.

Tucker, T., & Bing, E. (1975). *Prepared Childbirth,* New Canaan, CT: Tobey.

Tulkin, S. R., & Kagan, J. (1972). Mother-child interaction in the first year of life. *Child Development, 43,* 31–41.

Tuma, N., & Hallinan, M. T. (1979). The effects of sex, race and achievement in school children's friendships. *Social Forces, 57,* 1265–1285.

Turiel, E. (1978). Distinct conceptual and developmental domains: Social-convention and morality. In C. B. Keasey (Ed.), *Nebraska symposium on motivation* (vol. 25). Lincoln, NE: University of Nebraska Press.

Turiel, E. (1983). *The development of social knowledge: Morality and convention.* Cambridge, England: Cambridge University Press.

Turiel, E., Nucci, L. P., & Smetana, J. G. (1988). A cross-cultural comparison about what? A critique of Nisan's (1987) study of morality and convention. *Developmental Psychology, 24,* 140–143.

U.S. Department of Commerce. (1989). Statistical Abstract of the United States. 109th Edition. Washington, DC: U.S. Department of Commerce.

U.S. Department of Education (1987). *What works: Research about teaching and learning* (2nd ed.). Washington, DC: U.S. Department of Education.

U.S. Department of Health and Human Services (1981a). *The health consequences of smoking for women: A report to the Surgeon General.* Washington, DC: U.S. Department of Health and Human Services.

U.S. Department of Health and Human Services (1983). *Prenatal care.* Rockville, MD: U.S. Department of Health and Human Services, Public Health Services, DHHSA pub. no. 83–5070.

U.S. News and World Report (1986, October 27). Children under stress. *U.S. News and World Report.*

University of California (1985). *Berkeley Wellness Letter* (Vol. 1, issue 5), Caffeine.

Upchurch, R. L., & Lochhead, J. (1987). Computers and higher-order thinking skills. In V. Richardson Koehler (Ed.), *Educators' handbook* (pp. 139–165). New York: Longman.

Uzgiris, I. C. (1968). Situational generality of conservation. In I. E. Sigel & F. H. Hooper (Eds.), *Logical thinking in children: Research based on Piaget's theory.* New York: Holt.

Uzgiris, I. C. (1973). Patterns of cognitive development in infancy. *Merrill-Palmer Quarterly, 19,* 181–204.

Vaidya, S., & Chansky, N. (1980). Cognitive development and cognitive style as factors in mathematics achievement. *Journal of Educational Psychology, 73,* 326–330.

Vandell, D. L., & Corasaniti, M. A. (1988). The relation between third graders' after-school care and social, academic, and emotional functioning. *Child Development, 59,* 868–876.

Vandell, D. L., Henderson, V. K., & Wilson, K. S. (1988). A longitudinal study of children with day-care experiences of varying quality. *Child Development, 59,* 1286–1293.

Vandenberg, B. (1978). Play and development from an ethological perspective. *American Psychologist, 33,* 724–739.

Vandenberg, S. G., & Kuse, A. R. (1979). Spacial ability: A critical review of the sex-linked major-gene hypothesis. In M. Whittig & A. Petersen (Eds.), *Determinants of sex related differences in cognitive functioning.* New York: Academic Press.

Vander Linde, E., Moorongiello, B. A., & Rovee-Collier, C. (1985). Determinants of retention in 8-week-old infants. *Developmental Psychology, 21,* 601–614.

Varenhorst, B. (1984). The adolescent society. In *Adolescent peer pressure,* 1–21. Washington, DC: U.S. Department of Health and Human Services.

Vaughn, B. E., Deane, K. E., & Waters, E. (1985). The impact of out-of-home care on child-mother attachment quality: Another look at some enduring questions. In I. Bretherton & E. Waters (Eds.)., *Growing points of attachment theory and research. Monographs of the Society for Research in Child Development, 50,* nos. 1–2, serial no. 209, pp. 110–136.

Vaughn, S. (1985). Why teach social skills to learning disabled students? *Journal of Learning Disabilities, 18,* 588–591.

Vernon, P. E. (1976). Environment and intelligence. In V. P. Varma, & P. Williams (Eds.), *Piaget, psychology and education* (pp. 31–42). Itasca, IL: Peacock.

Verville, E. (1967). *Behavior problems of children.* Philadelphia: Saunders.

Viadero, D. (1987a, April 1). Principals say drug education should begin early. *Education Week,* p. 6.

Viadero, D. (1987b, June 15). Youth actions seen unchanged by AIDS scare. *Education Week,* p. 16.

Viadero, C. (1987c, October 28). Studies shed new light on teenage suicides. *Education Week,* p. 7.

Viadero, C. (1987d, January 28). Panel to develop model suicide-prevention program for schools. *Education Week,* p. 5.

Vinter, A. (1986). The role of movement in eliciting early imitations. *Child Development, 57,* 66–71.

Visher, J. S., & Visher, E. B. (1979). Stepfamilies and stepchildren. In J. D. Noshpitz (Ed.), *Handbook of child psychiatry* (pp. 347–354). New York: Basic Books.

Vockell, E. L. (1987). The computer and academic learning time. *The Clearing House, 61,* 72–75.

Voget, F. X. (1985). Bulimia. *Adolescence, 20,* 46–50.

Volpe, E. P. (1984). *Patient in the womb.* Macon, GA: Mercer University Press.

Vorhees, C. V., & Mollnow, E. (1987). Behavioral teratogenesis: Long-term influences on behavior from early exposure to environmental agents. In J. D. Osofsky (Ed.), *Handbook of infant development* (pp. 913–972). New York: Wiley.

Vosk, B., Forehand, R., Parker, J. B., & Rickard, K. (1982). A multimethod comparison of popular and unpopular children. *Developmental Psychology, 18,* 571–575.

Vurpillot, E. (1968). The development of scanning strategies and their relation to visual differentiation. *Journal of Experimental Child Psychology, 6,* 632–650.

Vurpillot, E., & Ball, W. A. (1979). The concept of identity and children's selective attention. In G. Hale & M. Lewis (Eds.), *Attention and cognitive development.* New York: Plenum.

Wachs, T. D. (1976). Utilization of a Piagetian approach in the investigation of early experience effects: Research strategy and some illustrative data. *Merrill-Palmer Quarterly, 22,* 11–30.

Wachs, T. D. (1983). The use and abuse of environment in behavior-genetic research. *Child Development, 54,* 396–407.

Wachs, T. D., Uzgiris, I. C., & Hunt, J. M. (1971). Cognitive development in infants of different age levels and from different environmental backgrounds: An explanatory investigation. *Merrill-Palmer Quarterly, 17,* 283–317.

Waddington, C. H. (1957). *The strategy of the genes.* London: Allen and Unwin.

Wadsworth, B. (1971). *Piaget's theory of cognitive development.* New York: David McKay.

Walden, E. L., & Thompson, S. A. (1981). A review of some alternative approaches to drug management of hyperactivity in children. *Journal of Learning Disabilities, 4,* 213–217.

Walden, T. A., & Ogan, T. A. (1988). The development of social referencing. *Child Development, 59,* 1230–1241.

Walk, R. d. (1981). *Perceptual development.* Monterey, CA: Brooks-Cole.

Walker, E., & Emory, E. (1985). Commentary: Interpretive bias and behavioral genetic research. *Child Development, 56,* 775–779.

Walker, J. H., Kozma, E. J., & Green, R. P. (1989). *American education: Foundations and policy.* St. Paul: West.

Walker, L. J. (1982). The sequentiality of Kohlberg's stages of moral development. *Child Development, 53,* 1330–1336.

Walker, L. J. (1984). Sex differences in the development of moral reasoning: A critical review. *Child Development, 57,* 667–691.

Walker, L. J. (1989). A longitudinal study of moral reasoning. *Child Development, 60,* 157–166.

Wall, S. M., Pickert, S. M., & Bigson, W. B. Fantasy play in 5- and 6-year-old children. *Journal of Psychology, 123,* 245–256.

Wall, W. D. (1975). *Constructive education for children.* London: Harrap and Co.

Wallerstein, J. S. (1983). Children of divorce: The psychological tasks of the child. *American Journal of Orthopsychiatry, 53,* 230–243.

Wallerstein, J. S. (1987). Children of divorce: Report of a ten-year follow-up of early latency-age children. *American Journal of Orthopsychiatry, 57,* 199–211.

Wallerstein, J. S., Corbin, S. B., & Lewis, J. M. (1988). Children of divorce: A 10-year study. In E. M. Hetherington & J. D. Arasteh (Eds.), *Impact of divorce, single parenting, and stepparenting on children* (pp. 197–215). Hillsdale, NJ: Erlbaum.

Wallerstein, J. S., & Kelly, J. (1979). Divorce and children. In J. D. Noshpitz (Ed.), *Basic handbook of child psychiatry* (Vol. 4, pp. 339–347). New York: Basic Books.

Walsh, D. J. (1989). Changes in kindergarten: Why here? Why now? *Early Childhood Research Quarterly, 4,* 377–393.

Walzer, S., Richmond, J. B., & Gerald P. S. (1976). The implications of sharing genetic information. In M. A. Sperber & L. F. Jarvik (Eds.), *Psychiatry and genetics: Psychosocial, ethical and legal considerations* (pp. 147–162). New York: Basic Books.

Wanat, P. E. (1983). Social skills: an awareness program with learning disabled adolescents. *Journal of Learning Disabilities, 16,* 35–38.

Ward, S., & Wackman, D. (1972). Television advertising and intrafamily influence: Children's purchase influence attempts and parental yielding. In E. A. Rubinstein, G. A. Comstock, & J. P. Murray (Eds.), *Television and social behavior 4: Television in day-to-day life: Patterns of use* (pp. 516–525). Washington, DC: U.S. Government Printing Office.

Warren, S. F. (1988). A behavioral approach to language generalization. *Language, Speech and Hearing Services in the Schools, 19,* 292–303.

Washington, V. (1985). Head Start: How appropriate for minority families in the 1980s. *American Journal of Orthopsychiatry, 55,* 577–590.

Waterman, A. S. (1982). Identity development from adolescence to adulthood: An extension of theory and a review of the literature. *Developmental Psychology, 18,* 341–359.

Waterman, A. S., & Waterman, C. K. (1971). A longitudinal study of changes in ego identity status during the freshman year at college. *Developmental Psychology, 5,* 167–173.

Waters, E. (1978). The reliability and stability of individual differences in infant-mother attachment. *Child Development, 49,* 483–494.

Waters, E., & Deane, K. E. (1982). Theories, models, recent data and some tasks for comparative developmental analysis. in L. Hoffman, R. Gandelman, & R. Schiffman (Eds.), *Parenting: Its causes and consequences* (pp. 19–54). Hillsdale, NJ: Erlbaum.

Watkins, B. A., Huston-Stein, A., & Wright, J. C. (1980). Effects of planned television programming. In E. L. Palmer & A. Dorr (Eds.), *Children and the faces of television: Teaching, violence, selling* (pp. 49–71). New York: Academic Press.

Watkins, H. D., & Bradbard, M. R. (1984, Fall). The social development of young children in day care: What practitioners should know. *Child Care Quarterly,* pp. 169–187.

Watson, J. B. (1930). *Behaviorism* (rev. ed.) Chicago: University of Chicago Press.

Watson, J. B. & Rayner, R. (1920). Conditioned emotional responses. *Journal of Experimental Psychology, 3,* 1–14.

Wattleton, F. (1987). American teens: Sexually active, sexually illiterate. *Journal of School Health, 57,* 379–380.

Weatherley, D. (1964). Self-perceived rate of physical maturation and personality in late adolescence. *Child Development, 35,* 1197–1210.

Webster, R. L., Steinhardt, M. H. & Senter, M. G. (1972). Changes in infants' vocalizations as a function of differential acoustic stimulation. *Developmental Psychology, 7,* 39–43.

Wehrabian, A. (1970). Measures of vocabulary and grammatical skills for children up to age six. *Developmental Psychology, 2,* 439–446.

Weinberg, R. A. (1979). Early childhood education and intervention: Establishing an American tradition. *American Psychologist, 34,* 912–916.

Weinberg, R. A. (1989). Intelligence and IQ: Landmark issues and great debates. *American Psychologist, 44,* 98–105.

Weisberg, R. W. (1986). *Creativity, genius and other myths.* New York: Freeman.

Weisfeld, G. E. (1982). The nature-nurture issue and the integrating concept of function. In B. B. Wolman (Ed.), *Handbook of developmental psychology* (pp. 208–23). Englewood Cliffs, NJ: Prentice-Hall.

Weiss, C. D., & Lillywhite, H. S. (1976). *Communication disorders: A handbook for prevention and early intervention.* St. Louis, MO: C. V. Mosby.

Weiss, R. J. (1982). Understanding moral thought: Effects on moral reasoning and decision making. *Developmental Psychology, 18,* 852–861.

Weitz, S. (1977). *Sex roles: Biological, psychological and social foundations.* New York: Oxford University Press.

Weitzman, N., Birns, B., & Friend, R. (1985). Traditional and nontraditional mothers' communication with their daughters and sons. *Developmental Psychology, 56,* 894–898.

Wellman, H. M., Cross, D., & Bartsch, K. (1987). Infant search and object permanence: A meta-analysis of the A-not-B error. Washington, DC: *Monographs of the Society for Research in Child Development* (Vol. 51, No. 3), Serial No. 214.

Wells, B. W. P. (1980). *Personality and heredity: An introduction to psychogenetics.* London: Longman.

Wells, K. (1987). Scientific issues in the conduct of case studies. *Journal of Child Psychology and Psychiatry and Allied Disciplines, 28,* 783–790.

Wenar, C. (1982). *Psychopathology from infancy through adolescence.* New York: Random House.

Werner, E. E. (1984, November). Resilient children. *Young Children,* pp. 686–692.

Werner, E. E., & Smith, R. S. (1982). *Vulnerable but invincible: A study of resilient children.* New York: McGraw-Hill.

Wertheimer, M. (1961). Psycho-motor coordination of auditory-visual space at birth. *Science, 134,* 1962.

Wertlieb, D., Weigel, C., & Feldstein, M. (1989). Stressful experiences, temperament, and social support: Impact on children's behavior symptoms. *Journal of Applied Developmental Psychology, 10,* 487–505.

Wertlieb, D., Weigel, C., Springer, T., & Feldstein, M. (1987). Temperament as a moderator of children's stressful experiences. *American Journal of Orthopsychiatry, 57,* 234–245.

Wesley, F., & Sullivan, E. (1980). *Human growth and development: A psychological approach.* New York: Human Sciences Press.

Westinghouse Learning Corporation (1969, June). *The impact of Head Start: An evaluation of effects of Head Start on children's cognitive and affective development.* Executive Summary, Ohio University. Report to the Office of Economic Opportunity. Washington, DC. Clearinghouse for Federal Scientific and Technical Information (EDO93497).

Weston, R., & Turiel, E. (1980). Act-rule relations: Children's concepts of social rules. *Developmental Psychology, 16*, 417–425.

Weyant, J. M. (1986). *Applied social psychology,* New York: Oxford University Press.

Whalen, H., Henker, B., Buhurmester, D., Hinshaw, S. P., Huber, A., & Laski, K. (1989). Does stimulant medication improve the peer status of hyperactive children? *Journal of Consulting and Clinical Psychology, 57*, 545–549.

Whisnant, L., & Zegans, L. (1975). A study of attitudes towards menarche in white middle-class American adolescent girls. *American Journal of Psychiatry, 132*, 809–814.

White, B. L. (1971). *Human infants: Experience and psychological development.* Englewood Cliffs, NJ: Prentice-Hall.

White, B. L. (1975). *The first three years of life.* Englewood Cliffs, NJ: Prentice-Hall.

White, C. B. (1975). Moral development in Bahamian school children: A cross-cultural examination of Kohlberg's stages of moral reasoning. *Developmental Psychology, 11*, 535–536.

White, K. R. (1982). The relation between socioeconomic status and academic achievement. *Psychological Bulletin, 91*, 461–481.

White, M. J., Kruczek, T. A., & Brown, M. T. (1989). Occupational sex stereotypes among college students. *Journal of Vocational Behavior, 34*, 289–298.

Whitehurst, G. J. (1982). Language development. In B. B. Wolman (Ed.), *Handbook of developmental psychology* (pp. 367–384). Englewood Cliffs, NJ: Prentice-Hall.

Whitehurst, G. J., Falco, F. L., Lonigan, C. J., Fischel, J. E., DeBaryshe, B. D., Valdez-Menchaca, M. C., & M. Caulfield. (1988). Accelerating language development through picture book reading. *Developmental Psychology, 24*, 552–560.

Whitehurst, G. J., & Valdez-Menchaca, M. C. (1988). What is the role of reinforcement in early language acquisition? *Child Development, 49*, 430–441.

Whitehurst, G. J. & Vasta, R. (1977). *Child Behavior.* Boston: Houghton Mifflin.

Whitener, C. B., & Kersey, K. (1980, November/December). A purple hippopotamus? Why Not? *Childhood Education,* pp. 18–20.

Whiting, B. B., & Whiting, J. W. M. (1975). *Children of six cultures.* Cambridge, MA: Harvard University Press.

Whitney, E.N.W., & Hamilton, E.M.N. (1984). *Understanding Nutrition* (3rd ed.). St. Paul. MN: West.

Whitney, E. N. & Hamilton, E.M.N. (1987). *Understanding Nutrition,* (Fourth Edition). St. Paul, MN: West.

Wiesel, T. N. & Hubel, D. H. (1965). Extent of recovery from the effects of visual deprivation in kittens. *Journal of Neurophysiology, 28*, 1060–1072.

Willemsen, E. (1979). *Understanding infancy.* San Francisco: Freeman.

Willerman, L. (1979a). *The psychology of individual and group differences.* San Francisco: Freeman.

Willerman, L. (1979b). Effects of families on intellectual development. *American Psychologist, 34*, 923–929.

Williams, J. E., Bennett, S. M., & Best, D. L. (1975). Awareness and Expression of sex stereotypes in young children. *Developmental Psychology, 11*, 635–642.

Williams, J. H. (1977). *Psychology of women: Behavior in a biosocial context.* New York: W. W. Norton.

Williams, J. W., & Stith, M. (1980). *Middle childhood: Behavior and development* (2nd ed.). New York: Macmillan.

Willig, A. E. (1985). A meta-analysis of selected studies on the effectiveness of bilingual education. *Review of Educational Research, 55*, 269–317.

Wilson, J., Weikel, W. J., & Rose, H. (1982). A comparison of nontraditional and traditional career women. *Vocational Guidance Quarterly, 31*, 109–117.

Wilson, J. Q., & Herrnstein, R. J. (1985). *Crime and human nature.* New York: Simon and Schuster.

Wilson, L. M. K. & Waterhouse, J. A. H. (1984). Obstetric ultrasound and childhood malignancies. *The Lancet, 997, 2.*

Wilson, R. S. (1977). Mental development in twins. In A. Oliverio (Ed.), *Genetics, environment, and intelligence.* Amsterdam: Elsevier.

Wilson, R. S. (1983). The Louisville twin study: Developmental synchronies in behavior. *Child Development, 54*, 298–316.

Wimmer, H. (1979). Processing of script deviations by young children. *Discourse Processes, 2*, 301–310.

Wimmer, H. (1980). Children's under-standing of stories: Assimilation by a general schema for actions or coordination of temporal relations? In F. Wilkening, J. Becker, & T. Trabasso (Eds.), *Information integration by children.* Hillsdale, NJ: Erlbaum.

Wingfield, A., & Byrnes, D. L. (1981). *The psychology of human memory.* New York: Academic Press.

Winick, M. (1975). *Childhood obesity.* New York: Wiley.

Winick, M. (1976). *Malnutrition and brain damage.* New York: Oxford University Press.

Winick, M., Meyer, K. K., & Harris, R. C. (1975). Malnutrition and environmental enrichment by early adoption: Development of adopted Korean children differing greatly in early nutritional status is examined. *Science, 190*, 1173–1175.

Winick, M. & Rosso, P. (1969). Head circumference and cellular growth of the brain in normal and marasmic children. *Journal of Pediatrics, 74*, 774–778.

Wisdom, C. S. (1989). Does violence beget violence? A critical examination of the literature. *Psychological Bulletin, 106*, 3–28.

Wise, S., & Grossman, F. K. (1980). Adolescent mothers and their infants: Psychological factors in early attachment and interaction. *American Journal of Orthopsychiatry, 50*, 454–468.

Wittrock, M. C. (1986). Students' thought processes. In M. C. Wittrock (Ed.), *Handbook of research on teaching* (3rd ed.) (pp. 247–315). New York: MacMillan.

Wolfe, D. A. (1985). Child-abusive parents: An empirical review and analysis. *Psychological Bulletin, 97*, 462–482.

Wolff, P. H. (1963). Observations on the early development of smiling. In B. M. Foss (Ed.), *Determinants of infant behavior* (vol. 2). London: Methuen.

Wolff, P. H. (1969). The natural history of crying and other vocalizations in early infancy. In B. M. Foss (ed.) *Determinants of Infant Behaviour, 4*, 81–111.

Wolins, M. (1970). Young children in institutions. *Developmental Psychology, 2*, 99–109.

Wonderly, D. M., & Kupfersmid, J. H. (1980). Promoting postconventional morality: The adequacy of Kohlberg's aim. *Adolescence, 15*, 609–631.

Woodruff, C. W. (1978). The science of infant nutrition and the art of infant feeding. *Journal of the American Medical As-*

sociation, 240, 657–661.

Woody-Ramsey, J., & Miller, P. H. (1988). The facilitation of selective attention in preschoolers. *Child Development, 59,* 1504–1514.

Worobey, J., & Blajda, V. M. (1989). Temperament ratings at 2 weeks, 2 months, and 1 year: Differential stability of activity and emotionality. *Developmental Psychology, 25,* 257–264.

Wright, J. C., Huston, A. C., Ross, R. P., Calvert, S. L., Rolandelli, D., Weeks, L. A. Raeisse, P., & Potts, R. (1984). Pace and continuity of television programs: Effects on children's attention and comprehension. *Developmental Psychology, 20,* 653–667.

Yarrow, M. R., Scott, P., de Leeuw, L. D. & Heinig, C. (1962). Child rearing in families of working and non-working mothers. In H. Bee (ed.), Social Issues in Developmental Psychology 2nd ed. (112–129). New York: Harper and Row.

Yates, D. J., & Bremner, G. (1988). Conditions for Piagetian stage 4 search errors in a task using transparent occluders. *Infant Behavior and Development, 11,* 411–417.

Yelon, S. L., & Weinstein, G. W. (1977). A *teacher's world: Psychology in the classroom.* New York: McGraw-Hill.

Young, D. (1982). *Changing childbirth: Family birth in the hospital.* Rochester, NY: Childbirth Graphics.

Youniss, J, & Volpe, J. (1978). A relational analysis of children's friendship. In W. Damon (Ed.), *Social cognition: New directions for child development* (pp. 1–22). San Francisco: Jossey-Bass.

Yussen, S. R., & Levy, V. M. (1975). Developmental changes in predicting one's own span of short-term memory. *Journal of Experimental Child Psychology, 19,* 502–508.

Zabin, L. S., Kantner, J. L., & Zelnik, M. (1979). The risk of adolescent pregnancy in the first months of intercourse. *Family Planning Perspectives, 4,* 215–222.

Zakus, G., Chin, M. L. Keown, M., Herbert, F., & Held, M. (1979). A group behavior modification approach to adolescent obesity. *Adolescence, 55,* 481–491.

Zaslow, M. J., Pederson, F. A., Suwalsky, J. T. D., Cain, R. L., & Fivel, M. (1985). The early resumption of employment by mothers: Implications for parent-infant interaction. *Journal of Applied Developmental Psychology, 6,* 1–16.

Zelazo, P. R. (1976). From reflexive to instrumental behavior. In L. P. Lipsitt (Ed.), *Developmental Psychobiology: The significance of infancy.* Hillsdale, NJ: Erlbaum.

Zelazo, P. R., Zelazo, N. A., & Kolb, S. (1972). Walking in the newborn. *Science, 176,* 314–315.

Zelnik, M., & Kim, Y. J. (1982, May-June). Sex education and its association with teenage sexual activity, pregnancy and contraceptive use. *Family Planning Perspectives, 14,* 117–126.

Zeskind, P. S., Sale, J., Maio, L. W., & Weiseman, J. R. (1985). Adult perceptions of pain and hunger cries: A synchrony of arousal, *Child Development, 56,* 549–554.

Zigler, E. & Anderson, K. (1979). An idea whose time had come: The intellectual and political climate. In E. Zigler & J. Valentine (Eds.), *Project Head Start—A legacy of the war on poverty* (pp. 3–21). New York: The Free Press.

Zigler, E., & Berman, W. (1983). Discerning the future of early childhood intervention. *American Psychologist, 38,* 894–907.

Zigler, E., & Valentine, J. (1979). *Project Head Start—A legacy of the war on poverty.* New York: The Free Press.

Zinsser, C. (1981, October). The preschool pressure cooker. *Working mother,* pp. 61–64.

Zougher, C. E. (1977). The self-concept of adolescent girls. *Adolescence, 12,* 477–488.

Zuckerman, B., et al. (1989). Effects of maternal marijuana and cocaine use on fetal growth. *New England Journal of Medicine, 320,* 762–768.

Name Index

Subject Index

Photo Credits

6 (left) Mary Kate Denny/PhotoEdit; 6 (right) Deborah Cady; 7 (left) Elizabeth Crews; 7 (middle) Mary Kate Denny/PhotoEdit; 7 (right) L. Druskis/Stock, Boston; 8 Lawrence Migdale/Photo Researchers, Inc.; 10 Tony Freeman/ PhotoEdit; 11 Blair Seitz/ Photo Researchers, Inc.; 13 Mary Kate Denny/PhotoEdit; 14 (left) Goro/Black Star; 14 (right) Bill Walker/UPI Bettman Newsphotos; 16 Stephen McBrady/PhotoEdit; 18 Suzanne Szasz/Photo Researchers, Inc.; 21 Dick Davis/ Photo Researchers, Inc.; 23 Norman Prince; 33 Norman Prince; 45 Glenn Hudson/ Black Star; 49 Michael Hayman/Black Star; 50 Bill Anderson/Monkmeyer; 61 Ray Ellis/Photo Researchers, Inc.; 64 Suzanne Szasz/ Photo Researchers, Inc.; 75 © Guy Gillette/Science Source/Photo Researchers, Inc.; 78 Courtesy of Albert Bandura, Stanford University; 97 Myrleen Ferguson/PhotoEdit; 99 Mary Kate Denny/ PhotoEdit; 110 Richard Anderson; 112 ABC Photography Dept./ AP Wide World Photos; 117 Richard Hutchings/InfoEdit; 120 Tony Freeman/PhotoEdit; 130–135 All photos © Lennart Nilsson. All photos originally appeared in A Child is Born by Lennart Nilsson (New York: Dell Publishing Company) and Behold Man by Lennart Nilsson (Boston: Little, Brown and Company). 142 Felicia Martinez/PhotoEdit; 143 Richard Anderson; 153 Frank Siteman/Stock, Boston; 160 Robert Brenner/ PhotoEdit; 165 Joseph Nettis/Stock, Boston; 169 Peter Menzel/Stock, Boston; 181 M. Richards/PhotoEdit; 182 Myrleen Ferguson/PhotoEdit; 185 William Vandivert, Scientific American, April 1960; 191 Elizabeth Crews; 194 From A. N. Meltzoff and M. K. Moore in Science, 1979, 198, 75–78. Copyright © 1977 by the AAAS; 196 (left) Elizabeth Crews; 196 (right) Elizabeth Crews; 201 Elizabeth Crews; 203 Irven DeVore/Anthro Photo File; 219 Roy Kirby/ Stock, Boston; 221 Patricia Agre/Photo Researchers, Inc.; 222 Suzanne Szasz/Photo Researchers, Inc.; 230 Robert Brenner/ PhotoEdit; 232 (upper) Elizabeth Crews; 232 (lower) Elizabeth Crews; 246 Roswell Angier/Stock, Boston; 247 Robert Brenner/PhotoEdit; 248 Robert Brenner/PhotoEdit; 250 Elizabeth Crews; 252 A Glauberman/Photo Researchers, Inc.; 261 Robert Brenner/PhotoEdit; 263 Rosenstein, D. and Oster, H. (1988) Child Development; 264 Richard Hutchings/Photo Researchers, Inc.; 266 Ulrike Welsch/Photo Researchers, Inc.; 269 Elizabeth Crews; 271 Bruno Maso/PhotoEdit; 272 Courtesy of the University of Wisconsin Primate Laboratory; 278 Thomas McAvoy, Life Magazine © Time Inc.; 281 Spencer Grant/Photo Researchers, Inc.; 283 Comstock; 289 Joseph Schuyler/Stock, Boston; 295 Elizabeth Crews; 308 Stephen McBrady/PhotoEdit; 309 Elizabeth Crews; 312 Susan Woog Wagner/Photo Researchers, Inc.; 313 Elizabeth Crews; 316 Rick Smolan/Stock, Boston; 324 Ray Ellis/ Photo Researchers, Inc.; 325 Elizabeth Crews; 327 Elizabeth Crews; 328 Elizabeth Crews; 329 Elizabeth Crews; 332 Elizabeth Crews; 339 AP/Wide World Photos; 340 Elizabeth Crews; 345 Alan Oddie/PhotoEdit; 347 Robert Brenner/ PhotoEdit; 354 Elizabeth Crews; 355 Elizabeth Crews; 362 Elizabeth Crews; 367 Gabor Demjen/Stock, Boston; 371 Elizabeth Crews; 375 Lynn Johnson/Black Star; 377 Deborah Cady; 379 Elizabeth Crews; 383 Lawrence Migdale/Stock, Boston; 391 Larry Mulvehill/Photo Researchers, Inc.; 393 (left) Elizabeth Crews; 393 (middle) Elizabeth Crews; 393 (right) Stephen McBrady/PhotoEdit; 395 Elizabeth Zuckerman/PhotoEdit; 401 Deborah Cady; 403 Tony Freeman/PhotoEdit; 410 Robert Brenner/PhotoEdit; 426 Susan Johns/Photo Researchers, Inc.; 428 Elizabeth Crews; 440 Mary Kate Denny/PhotoEdit; 443 Tony Freeman/PhotoEdit; 445 Suzanne Szasz/Photo Researchers, Inc.; 446 Larry Mulvehill/Photo Researchers, Inc.; 450 Bob Daemmrich/Stock, Boston; 460 Suzanne Szasz/Photo Researchers, Inc.; 465 Tony Freeman/PhotoEdit; 466 Myrleen Ferguson/PhotoEdit; 469 Mary Kate Denny/PhotoEdit; 471 Elizabeth Crews; 478 Lawrence Migdale/Photo Researchers, Inc.; 483 Stephen McBrady/PhotoEdit; 493 Lawrence Migdale/Photo Researchers, Inc.; 494 Mary Kate Denny/PhotoEdit; 495 Myrleen Ferguson/ PhotoEdit; 497 Billy E. Barnes/Stock, Boston; 505 Mary Kate Denny/PhotoEdit; 507 Robert Brenner/PhotoEdit; 511 Myrleen Ferguson/PhotoEdit; 515 Ray Ellis/Photo Researchers, Inc.; 517 Tony Freeman/PhotoEdit; 519 Gregory K. Scott/Photo Researchers, Inc.; 533 Myrleen Ferguson/PhotoEdit; 539 Spencer Grant/Stock, Boston; 548 Jean-Paul Pelissier/Reuters/Bettman Newsphotos; 555 Myrleen Ferguson/PhotoEdit; 567 Arthur Tress/ Photo Researchers, Inc.; 575 Jeffry W. Myers/Stock, Boston; 577 Rafael Macia/Photo Researchers, Inc.; 587 Richard Hutchings/ Photo Researchers, Inc.; 590 David R. Frazier/Photo Researchers, Inc.; 604 Tony Freeman/PhotoEdit; 610 Mary Kate Denny/ PhotoEdit; 612 Elizabeth Zuckerman/PhotoEdit; 613 Rhoda Sidney/PhotoEdit; 614 Richard Hutchings/InfoEdit; 624 Norman Prince; 634 Elizabeth Crews; 639 Steve Starr/Picture Group.

Credits for Part- and Chapter-Opening Fine Art

1 Pierre-Auguste Renoir: "Road climbing through high grass"; Musee d' Orsay, Paris. Scala/Art Resource, NY.

2 Paul Gauguin: "Breton Girls Dancing, Pont Aven"; National Gallery of Art, Washington; Collection of Mr. and Mrs. Paul Mellon.

42 Grandma Moses (1860–1961): "Bringing in the Maple Sugar"; Copyright © 1989, Grandma Moses Properties Co., New York. Anna Mary Robertson Moses began painting in old age and became internationally known as "Grandma Moses."

90 Norman Rockwell: "Family Tree"; Reprinted with permission from "The Saturday Evening Post" and The Curtis Publishing Company. Printed by permission of the estate of Norman Rockwell. © 1959 by the estate of Norman Rockwell.

177 Berthe Morisot: "The Cradle"; Musee d' Orsay, Paris. Scala/ Art Resource, NY.

178 Richard Caton Woodville: "The Cavalier's Return"; The New York Historical Society, New York City.

226 Pierre-Auguste Renoir: "Gabrielle and Jean"; Grenoble Museum. Scala/Art Resource, NY.

258 Utamaro Hitsu: "Kitchen Scene" (detail); Spaulding Collection of Japanese Prints, Museum of Fine Arts, Boston.

303 Camille Pisarro: "In the Garden"; Narodni Gallery, Prague. Giraudon/Art Resource, NY.

304 John G. Brown: "A Tough Story" (1886); North Carolina Museum of Art, Raleigh. Purchased with funds from the State of North Carolina.

336 Harry Roseland: "Visit from the Doctor—A Serious Case"; Courtesy of Demosthenes D. Dasco, M.D.

386 Mary Cassatt: "Children Playing on the Beach"; National Gallery of Art, Washington; Ailsa Mellon Bruce Collection.

435 Paul Gauguin: "Le Rapas ou les bananes"; Musee' d' Orsay, Paris. Giraudon/Art Resource, NY.

436 Winslow Homer: "Snap the Whip"; The Metropolitan Museum of Art, Gift of Christian A. Zabriskie, 1950. (50.41)

490 John Singer Sargent: "Carnation, Lily, Lily, Rose"; Tate Gallery, London. Art Resource, NY.

543 Norman Rockwell: "Adolescence"; Reprinted with permission from "The Saturday Evening Post" and The Curtis Publishing Company. Printed by permission of the estate of Norman Rockwell. © 1949 by the estate of Norman Rockwell.

544 Ben Shahn: "Handball" (1939). Tempera on paper over composition board, 22¾ × 31¼ inches. Collection, The Museum of Modern Art, New York, Abby Aldrich Rockefeller Fund.

598 Scott Prior: "Nanny and Rose". Gift of Stephen and Sybil Stone Foundation. Museum of Fine Arts, Boston.

Acknowledgments—Continued

Pages 210–211, Tables 1 and 2: From Super C. M., Herrera, M. G. and Mora, J. O. Long-Term Effects of Food Supplementation and Psychosocial Intervention on the Physical Growth of Columbian Infants at Risk of Malnutrition. *Child Development*, 1990, 61, 29–49. © The Society for Research in Child Development, Inc.

Page 214, Fig. 5.4: Reprinted by permission from *Nutrition: Concepts and Controversies*, 3rd ed., by E. M. N. Hamilton, E. N. Whitney, and F. S. Sizer. Copyright © 1985 by West Publishing Company. All rights reserved.

Page 218, Datagraphic: Reprinted with permission © *American Demographics*, January 1990.

Page 233, Fig. 6.1: From Bremner, J. G. The Stage IV Search Task from *Infancy*, 1988, p. 111.

Page 237, Fig. 6.2: From Baillargeon, R. and Graber, M. Developmental Psychology, July 1988, p. 505. © American Psychological Association.

Page 248, Table 6.1: Adapted from Bradley, R. H. "Home Measurement Responsiveness" in M. H. Bornstein (ed.), Maternal Responsiveness: Characteristics and Consequences. New Directions for Child Development, no. 43, San Francisco: Jossey-Bass, 1989, p. 65. Used with permission of publisher.

Pages 296–297, Fig. 7.1: Adapted from "A Day-Care Checklist, by Joyce P. Stines, 1983. Used by permission of J. P. Stines.

Pages 342–343, Table 9.1: From Charles B. Corbin, *A Textbook of Motor Development*, 2nd ed. Copyright © 1980 Wm. C. Brown Publishers. Dubuque, Iowa. All rights reserved. Reprinted by permission.

Page 344, Table 9.2: From Perceptual and Motor Development in Infants and Children, by J. B. Cratty. Copyright © 1979. Reprinted by permission of Prentice-Hall, Inc., Englewood Cliffs, New Jersey.

Page 349, Table 9.A: Grant, J. P. *The State of the World's Children* (New York: Published for UNICEF by Oxford University Press, 1988).

Page 372, Datagraphic: From the *1986 Field Guide to the Electronic Media*. Media Commentary Council, 1986.

Page 418, Datagraphic: American Humane Association, Denver, Colorado. National Study on Child Neglect and Abuse Reporting. Annual and National Committee for Prevention of Child Abuse.

Page 462, Datagraphic: Data based on November 1989 source Nielsen Media Research.

Page 479, Figure 11.2: From "7 Ways to be Bright," *U.S. News and World Report*. Copyright © November 23, 1987, *U.S. News and World Report*.

Page 513, Table 12.1: From "The Child as Friendship Philosopher," by R. L. Selman. In *The Development of Children's Friendships*, S. R. Asher and J. M. Gottman, eds. Copyright © 1981. Reprinted by permission of Cambridge University Press.

Page 521, Table 12.2: From Kohlberg, L. *Cognitive Development and Epistemology*, T. Mischel, ed., 1971, pp. 164–165.

Pages 547 and 550, Tables 13.1 and 13.2: Charts from *Adolescence and Youth*, 3/ed. by John Janeway Conger and Anne C. Petersen. Reprinted by permission of Harper Collins Publishers.

Page 552, Fig. 13.1: Reprinted by permission from *Adolescence: Theories, Research and Applications* by L. C. Jensen. Copyright © 1985 by West Publishing Company. All rights reserved.

Page 581, Fig. 13.2: From the Higher Education Research Institute, UCLA.

Pages 584, Tables 13.4 and 13.5: Murstein, B. I., Chalpin, M. J., Heard, K. V., and Vyse, S. A. Tables 2 and 3 from "Sexual Behavior, Drugs, and Relationship Patterns on a College Campus Over Thirteen Years" in *Adolescence*, 1989, p. 129.

Page 603, Table 14.1: From "Identity Status and Academic Achievement in Female Adolescents," by R. Hummel and L. L. Roselli. In *Adolescence*, 1983, Vol. 18. Reprinted by permission. Copyright © 1983.

Page 618, Table 14.2: From Feldman, S. S. and Quotman, T., *Journal of Early Adolescence*, 1988, p. 333. © 1988 by Sage Publications, Inc. Reprinted by permission of Sage Publications, Inc.

Page 636, Datagraphic: From U.S. Department of Commerce, Bureau of Census, Current Population Surveys—Special Analysis by ACE's Division of Policy Analysis and Research.

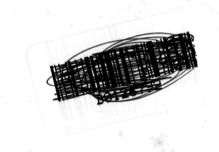